BRITANNICA.

LONDON:

PRINTED BY AND FOR JOHN NICHOLS.

M DCC LXXX.—M DCC XC.

KRAUS REPRINT CO.   AMS PRESS, INC.
New York
1968

Printed in U.S.A.

ADVERTISEMENT.

THE Publisher of the BIBLIOTHECA TOPOGRAPHICA BRITAN-
NICA cannot dismiss the concluding Number without expressing his grateful acknowledgements for the candour with
which these Volumes have been uniformly received.

The original plan of the Work, formed in the year 1780
without any ostentatious promises *, was, to preserve, either from
MSS. or by the republication of scarce Tracts, some valuable
articles of BRITISH TOPOGRAPHY; to be printed in occasional
Numbers, neither confined to stated periods of time, to the
same price, nor to any given quantity of sheets: nor were
they always to be adorned with cuts; but to be paged in
such a manner that the general articles, or those belonging
to the several Counties, might form a separate succession to bind
in suitable classes.

With satisfaction he looks back on the ten years which have
been employed in compiling and printing, when he reflects how
much his undertaking has been facilitated by the communications
of ANTIQUARIES whose assistance would confer honour on any
publication; and who need not here be particularized, as in
general the name of the author is prefixed to the several articles of communication.

One Friend, however, it would be unpardonable not to mention;
and on the subject of TOPOGRAPHY it is a name of peculiar

* See the Advertisement and the Queries prefixed to the " History of Tunstall."

a 2   eminence.

eminence. Not only the original fuggeftion of the plan was from Mr. Gough; but the moft unremitting and difinterefted affiftance has been received through the whole progrefs of this extenfive undertaking. To him are the heartieft acknowledgements moft gratefully offered. To him is the Reader indebted if any thing agreeable or ufeful be found in thefe Eight Quarto Volumes.

Having been hitherto, as has been faid, confined neither to time nor price, it is proper that fome paufe fhould be made in a Work of fuch magnitude. To obviate all difficulties on this head, and that the Numbers already publifhed may be claffed into regular Volumes, the BIBLIOTHECA is now clofed, with the Publifher's beft thanks to the Purchafers for their indulgence; and not without a hope of again addreffing them in a future Work on the fubject of BRITISH ANTIQUITIES, which may be printed in uniformity with the prefent, but under a Title that fhall make it entirely diftinct.

June 4, 1790.   J. NICHOLS.

ISBN 978-1-5277-7472-8
PIBN 10891530

GENERAL CONTENTS

OF THE

FIRST VOLUME.

* Two of thefe, Plates VII. and VIII. are now fiıft added in N° LII.

TOPOGRAPHICA

BRITANNICA.

N° I.

CONTAINING

1. QUERIES for the better Illuftrating the Antiquities and Natural Hiftory of Great Britain and Ireland.

2. The Hiftory and Antiquities of TUNSTALL in Kent. By the late Mr. Edward Rowe Mores.

———————

LONDON,
PRINTED FOR J. NICHOLS,
PRINTER TO THE SOCIETY OF ANTIQUARIES:
SOLD BY T. PAYNE AND SON, CASTLE STREET, ST. MARTIN'S;
H. PAYNE, IN PALL-MALL; C. DILLY, IN THE POULTRY;
J. WALTER, CHARING-CROSS; N. CONANT, FLEET-STREET;
AND E. BROOKE, BELL-YARD, TEMPLE-BAR.
MDCCLXXX.

AMONG the various Labours of Literary Men, there have always been certain Fragments whofe Size could not fecure them a general Exemption from the Wreck of Time, which their intrinfic Merit entitled them to furvive ; but, having been gathered up by the Curious, or thrown into Mifcellaneous Colleations by Bookfellers, they have been recalled into Exiftence, and by uniting together have defended themfelves from Oblivion. Original Pieces have been called in to their Aid, and formed a Phalanx that might withftand every Attack from the Critic to the Cheefemonger, and contributed to the Ornament as well as Value of Libraries.

With a fimilar View it is here intended to prefent the Publick with fome valuable Articles of BRITISH TOPOGRAPHY, from printed Books and MSS. One Part of this Colleation will confift of Republications of fcarce and curious Traas ; another of fuch MS. Papers as the Editors are already poffeffed of, or may receive from their Friends.

It is therefore propofed to publifh a Number occafionally, not confined to the fame Price or Quantity of Sheets, nor always adorned with Cuts ; but paged in fuch a Manner, that the general Articles, or thofe belonging to the refpeaive Counties, may form a feparate Succeffion, if there fhould be enough publifhed, to bind in fuitable Claffes ; and each Traa will be completed in a fingle Number.

Into this Colleation all Communications confiftent with the Plan will be received with Thanks. And as no Correfpondent will be denied the Privilege of controverting the Opinions of another, fo none will be denied Admittance without a fair and impartial Reafon.

Q U E R I E S

PROPOSED TO

The Nobility, Gentlemen, Clergy, and others, of *Great Britain* and *Ireland*,

With a view of obtaining,

From their Anfwers refpecting the Places of their Refidence,

The moft perfect Account of the ANTIQUITIES and
NATURAL HISTORY of thofe Kingdoms.

ADVERTISEMENT.

AS there is no fcience which is not capable of being facilitated by general rules, that of Antiquity fo far as it relates to the illuftration of our national Topography and Hiftory, however ably purfued by thofe great names who have written our beft County Hiftories, may ftill be forwarded, by fuggefting even to the moft incurious obferver fubjects worthy his notice, and the communication of which to others may yield the double benefit of inftruction, both to the antiquary and the citizen.

A kind. of analyfis of ecclefiaftical, civil, and natural hiftory has been held out in different forms by feveral gentlemen, who have employed themfelves in collecting county hiftories in the prefent century.

The firft idea feems to have been fuggefted by the celebrated Edward Lhuyd, who printed a folio fheet undated, intituled, " Parochial Queries in order to a Geographical Dictionary, a Na- " tural Hiftory, &c. of Wales. By the Undertaker. E. L."

Francis Peck purfued it for England in QUERIES which· he circulated for the natural hiftory and antiquities of Leicefter and Rutland fhires, in a fingle folio fheet, 1729; many of which are too trivial to deferve notice.

Anthony Hammond, efq. publifhed a very fhort " Inquifitio Parochialis," 1731, in the " Republic of Letters," vol. VII. p. 228.

Thefe were followed on a more enlarged plan by Mr. Blomfield, in Queries circulated for a hiftory of Norfolk, 1736; Mr. Hutchins for Dorfet, 1739; the prefent dean of Exeter, for Devon, foon after; Mr. Walwyn circulated fome very brief ones for Herefordfhire, 1749. Dr. Rawlinfon (in what year does not appear) circulated queries for a defcription of Oxfordfhire, but obtained accounts only of two parifhes.

The

The Dublin Society prefixed a fet, principally in natural hiftory, to their hiftory of the county of Down, 1744, 8vo. Thefe were taken up by Dr. Burton, 1758, who accompanied them with an excellent fcheme and propofals for illuftrating the county of York, a fet of additional queries for civil and ecclefiaftical hiftory, and the hiftory of the parifh of Hemingborough;—a proper fpecimen for the Northern part of the kingdom. Mr. Mores circulated a fet of Queries through Berkfhire, 1759, in order to facilitate his perambulation previous to his defign of writing a hiftory of that county.

One would have thought fuch a plan fhould have originated from the Society of Antiquaries, did we not know, however extraordinary the avowal, that fuch a plan has no place in their fyftem, nor, if held out by any individual, has any fupport from their patronage as a body, however liberally affifted by particular members. It will not therefore feem furprizing if this Society, or rather the induftrious Mr. Theobald in their name, did not put out fuch queries till after fo many collectors for county hiftories had fet the example. Still lefs fhall one wonder that their enquiries met with fo imperfect a return, or that the inquifitive and public fpirited compiler Mr. Edward Cave caught hold of their Queries, and gave them more general circulation in his Magazine for April 1755. In anfwer to them he obtained fhort defcriptions of five or fix parifhes, which if not fo full as might have been wifhed, yet fhewed how fuch returns might be made; while Mr. Theobald obtained only a defcription of one place in Berkfhire, if he did not draw it up himfelf.

Mr. Pennant, in 1771, applied the Society's Queries to the illuftration of Scotland, where his laudable enquiry met with fuitable returns, and he has certainly kindled a fpirit of enquiry among the natives, which it were to be wifhed might be faid of the fifter kingdom, after what the Phyfico-Hifto-

rical

rical Society at Dublin have attempted there, who to 4000 fets of Queries obtained but forty anfwers. The laft propofer of Queries for England was Mr. George Allan, of Darlington, in his " Addrefs and Queries for the Palatinate of Durham, 1774." 4to. An unfortunate member of the Society of Antiquaries attempted the fame year to intereft that learned body in the refult of their own Queries, which he reprinted in 12mo fize; but the extravagance of his ideas on this fubject was fufficient to fink his défign.

It were as abfurd as ungenerous in any man to claim an exclufive right in meafures calculated for the extenfion of knowledge, efpecially when intended for individuals to avail themfelves of the returns for the moft univerfal ufe, not to confine themfelves to particular effays, fet off in all the elegance of language for a work which rejects enlarged defcriptions of places, or hiftorical narratives, becaufe perhaps incapable of being firft read in public, or of affording entertainment to a mifcellaneous and polite audience. To this miftaken policy we might afcribe it that fo many curious communications have been fmothered; and we may venture to augur the refufal of more which will obtrude themfelves upon the public eye in fome other channel. Truth of every kind will find its way in this inquifitive age; and though refpectable focieties, with all the caution of ftatefmen, or the prudence of -antient virgins anxious for their chaftity, declare they are not anfwerable for the errors or abfurdities of their members in the very moment of publifhing them, thefe errors and abfurdities will be detected and expofed without referve, and with greater warmth, by obfcurer perfons envious of ill-acquired fame, injured by the lofs of priority in difcovery, or concerned to facrifice hypothefis, prejudice, or falfe philofophy, on the altars of experiment, truth, and common fenfe.

The

The following Queries are intended to comprehend all that have before been circulated, fomewhat differently modified and enlarged. But after all his care the republifher is fenfible they want the recommendation of novelty, and earneftly wifhes to fee the plan enlarged as well as anfwered. He anticipates too the difappointment of their former editors ; fome by receiving no anfwer at all ; fome by being overloaded with minute particulars ; yet he cannot help flattering himfelf, that as he has made ufe of all the lights that have been held out before him, the fubject is now fet in fo full a point of view, that fome gentlemen of leifure may be ftill affifted in their enquiries, by having their path fo minutely marked out. Thofe to whom the firft part of thefe Queries may feem uninterefting will, it is hoped, make a proper ufe of the fecond, to improve our commerce and manufactures from the fources which nature has placed among ourfelves, and within every man's reach. But if at laft the editor fhould find himfelf difappointed in every expectation, he will acquiefce in the mortification which fo many greater names have experienced before him ; confcious of the purity and difintereftednefs of his own intentions, and the fallibility of the fondeft human wifhes.

It is obvious that the Anfwers to many Queries in the fecond part muft depend on long practice and obfervation ; and it is to be prefumed perfons will be candid enough, as well as fufficiently attentive to their own reputation, not to obtrude hafty or ill-founded obfervations on the public, for whofe fole benefit this defign is propofed.

May 4, 1780.

QUERIES *propofed to the* NOBILITY, GENTLEMEN, CLERGY, *and others, of* GREAT BRITAIN *and* IRELAND ;
With a view of obtaining, from their Anfwers refpecting the Places of their Refidence, a more perfect Account of the Antiquities and Natural Hiftory of thofe Kingdoms than has yet appeared.

The Anfwers to be addreffed to the Editor of the BIBLIOTHECA TOPOGRAPHICA BRITANNICA, *to the Care of* J. Nichols, *Printer,* Red-Lion-Paffage, Fleet-Street, POST PAID.

1. WHAT is the antient and modern name of the parifh, and its etymology ?

2. What is its diftance from the hundred town, county town, or next market town ?

3. By what parifhes is it bounded, E. W. N. and S.? and what are its length and breadth ?

4. What diftance is it from London and the chief towns round, and what is the price of carriage per hundred weight ?

5. What is the extent of the parifh ?

6. What number of hamlets, villages, townfhips, chapelries, inn-fhips, diftricts, wards, are in it? their names and fituation? and to what divifion, hundred, liberty, or conftabulary belonging ?

7. What are the number of its houfes and inhabitants of every kind, and of its teams? Lift of freeholds and copyholds, and their holders ?

8. What number of perfons have been married, chriftened, and buried, for the fpace of 20 years laft paft, compared with the firft 20 years of the regifter? When did the regifter begin? Are any curious remarks made therein?

9. What manors are or were in it, and who are or were lords thereof ?

10. What are the names and qualities, arms and defcent, of their proprietors ?

b   11. Are

11. Are there any particular cuſtoms or privileges, or remarkable tenures, in any of the manors in the pariſh ? What courts, and
their cuſtoms ? What exempt juriſdictions civil or eccleſiaſtical ?

12. What caſtle, fort, ancient manor or manſion houſe, ſeat,
villa, or other remarkable buildings, are or have been in the pariſh ?
and the dimenſions of their largeſt apartments or galleries ?

13. What coats of arms, inſcriptions, dates, or other ornaments and figures, are or were carved or painted in and about
any of their buildings ?

15. In what manor, dioceſe, deanry, and hundred, does the
CHURCH ſtand?

16. Is it dedicated to any ſaint ? When and by whom was it
built, of what materials, and has it a tower or ſpire?

18. What are its dimenſions, number of ailes, chapels, and
bells?

19. Are there any ancient or modern monuments, grave-
ſtones, or braſs plates ? and what inſcriptions and arms in the
church, chancel, or ſteeple, or on the bells, plate, cheſts, pews,
ſcreens, &c. or, in the church-yard ? Are the font, altar-piece, or
plate, remarkable? Or, are there any other remains of antiquity ?

20. Are there any painted figures, arms, or inſcriptions, in
the windows ?

21. Are there any tables of benefactions, or other inſcriptions
which are worthy notice, painted or carved in or about the
church, within or without? or any parochial library in the
church or parſonage ?

22. What chantries, altars, ſhrines, lights, images, gilds, or
roods, appear to have been in the church ; or what privileges
and indulgencies annext to it ? What reliques, miracles, and
legends ?

23. Are there any vaults or burial-places peculiar to any ancient or other families ? and what extraordinary interments or
preſervation of bodies ?

24. Is

24. Is the living a rectory, vicarage, donative, or finecure?

25. Are the computed worth of the living and its rate in the King's books rightly ftated in Ecton's Thefaurus?

26. Who are, or have been, patrons?

27. Who are, or have been, incumbents as far back as you can trace? and were any of them remarkable for their writings, fufferings, or other particulars? of what univerfity or college, what their degrees and preferments, and where buried?

28. Are there any lands belonging to the glebe or vicarage, or any copy of the endowment, or any terrier? Has it been augmented by queen Anne's bounty? What are the firft-fruits, tenths, fynodals, procurations and penfions paid out of the profits?

29. Who is poffeffed of the great tithes? what may their reputed value be? and is any modus paid thereout, and to whom?

30. Is there any chapel of eafe in the parifh? how is it fupported? and who are, or have been, incumbents? and of what value may the cure be fuppofed?

31. What charities or benefactions belong to the parifh? when and by whom given? how improved, or how loft?

32. Are there any Diffenting or other meeting-houfes, or Popifh chapels? and what number of each perfuafion may be in the parifh?

33. Are there any colleges, alms-houfes, free or other fchool, or hofpital; by whom and when founded, for how many objects, and whether abufed or loft; or the prefent ftate?

34. Have there been any abbies, priories, friaries, nunneries, hermitages, fanctuaries, or other religious houfes; or are there any remains or ruins of them? by whom founded, and to whom granted? what charters, cartularies, ledger-books, rentals, ftatutes, deeds, wills, obituaries, bede-rolls, or other writings, feals, habits, fhrines, or other fragments, belonging to any church, monaftery, chantry, gild, hofpital, fchool, or other charity?

35. Are there any croffes or obelifks, infcribed or carved ftones, circles of rude ftones, fingle ftones on hillocks, or other-

wife,

wife, hollows wrought into rocks, fingle ftones placed horizontally or over one another, or any beacons, in the parifh ?

36. Are there any barrows or tumuli, or extraordinary mounts ? have any been opened, and what has been found therein ?

37. Are there any *Roman*, *Saxon*, or *Danifh* caftles, forts, camps, roads, ditches, banks, pits, or other extraordinary earth-works, or pieces of antiquity remaining in your parifh; and what traditions or hiftorical accounts are there of them ?

38. Have there been any vaults, pavements, urns, pieces of pottery, lamps, weapons, armour, feals, rings, buckles, odd pieces of metal, ftatues, bufts, carvings, altars, images, coins, or other pieces of antiquity, *Roman*, *Saxon*, *Danifh*, or other, or bones of extraordinary fize, dug up in your parifh; when and by whom; and in whofe cuftody are or were they ?

39. Have there been any remarkable battles fought, on what fpot, by whom, when, and what traditions are there relating thereto ? or what the fufferings or adventures of the clergy or gentry in the civil wars ?

40. Have any councils, fynods, parliaments, or other meetings, civil or religious, been held in it ?

41. Have you any wake, Whitfun ale, doles, or other fuch cuftoms, ufed in the parifh; or any annual or other proceffions or perambulations ?

42. What markets or fairs are kept in the parifh; what commodities are chiefly brought for fale; are they the manu-factures or produce of the country, live cattle, or other things; what toll is paid, and to whom ?

43. Is there any ftatute fair for hiring of fervants, and how long has it been eftablifhed ? What are the ufual wages for men and maid fervants, &c. for each branch of hufbandry?

44. Are there any manufactures carried on in the parifh, and what number of hands are employed ? What rare pieces of art have been invented or made by any of the parifhioners ?

45. What

45. What is generally a day's wages for labourers in hufbandry and other work; and what for carpenters, bricklayers, mafons, or other mechanics, &c.?

46. What are, or have been, the prices of provifions, beef, veal, mutton, lamb, pork, pigs, geefe, ducks, chicken, rabbits, butter, cheefe, &c.?

47. What is the annual rent or value of the lands or houfes in the parifh, or townfhip? what is the poor's rate in the pound *communibus annis*? and how much land-tax is paid at 4s. in the pound?

48. What common, or quantity of wafte land, may be in the parifh?

49. Are there any forefts, chaces, parks, or warrens; of what extent, number of deer, &c.? any heronries, decoys, or fifheries?

50. What is the ufual fuel? is it coal, wood, heath, furze, turf, or peat? and the prices paid on the fpot?

51. Is there any great road leading through the parifh, and from noted places?

52. Do any rivers, or brooks, or navigable canals, rife in or run through the parifh? when and on what terms were the acts for making them navigable obtained? what fort of boats are ufed on them, and what is the price of carriage per hundred or ton to your parifh?

53. What bridges, when, and by whom built, of what materials, what number of piers or arches, the length and breadth of the bridge, and width of the arches? are they fupported by private or public coft?

54. Has the parifh given birth or burial to any man eminent for learning, or other remarkable or valuable qualifications?

55. What particular games, fports, cuftoms, proverbs, or peculiar words or phrafes, or names of places, perfons, animals, vegetables, or things, are ufed; and what notions or traditions obtain among the common people?

56. Are

56. Are there, in any of the gentlemen's or other houses, any pictures which give infight into any hiftorical facts, or any portraits of men eminent in art, fcience, or literature ; any ftatues, buftos, or other memorial, which will give any light to paft tranfactions ? or what manufcripts in any language, books of arms, pedigrees, lives, fignatures, patents, diplomas, perambulations, furveys, plans, pictures or drawings of any perfons, buildings or views relating to the parifh, in the poffeffion of any perfon in the parifh, or their acquaintance ?

To thefe Queries if applied to *Cities, Market,* or *Corporate Towns,* may be added others refpecting their hiftory, foundations, ftreets, buildings, walls, gates, churches, wards, parifhes, charters, privileges, immunities, corporations, companies, gilds, government, and lift of mayors, fheriffs, recorders, reprefentatives, electors, bifhops, deans, and other cathedral members; rates, taxes, trade, manufactures, fieges, accidents by fire, or otherwife.

QUERIES *relating to the* NATURAL HISTORY *of the* PARISH.

1. WHAT is the appearance of the country in the parifh; is it flat or hilly, rocky, or mountainous, open or inclofed; and the terms and mode of modern inclofing ?

2. Do the lands confift of woods, arable, pafture, meadow, heath, or what ?

3. Are they fenny or moorifh, boggy or firm, fertile or barren ?

4. Is there fand, clay, chalk, ftone, gravel, loam, or what is the nature of the foil ?

5. Have you any marble, moorftone, lime-ftone, free-ftone, ftone for building, coal, flate, pipe-clay, brick-clay ? how is it got out, and how worked ?

6. What minerals, falts, ochres, chalks, clays, marles, molds, earths, fands, gravels, flints, pebbles, &c. does the foil contain ?

7. Is

7. Is there any marl, fullers earth, potters earth, or loam, or any other remarkable foils?

8. Are there any bitumen, naphtha, alum, calamine, black-lead, bifmuth, mercury, antimony, or other fubftances of that nature, found in the earth?

9. What ftrata of foil do they meet with on digging wells or other openings, and at what depth?

10. What petrifactions or foffils, either ftone or wood, are found in the parifh, and in what ftrata? Are there any figured ftones, fuch as echinitæ, belemnitæ, &c.; any having the impreffion of plants or fifh, or any foffil marine bodies, fuch as fhells, corals, &c. or any petrified parts of animals; any tranfparent pebbles, cryftallizations, or any fubftances otherwife remarkable; or foffil-trees, nuts, &c.?

11. Are there any mines? to whom do they belong, and what do they produce; their courfe and depth, the manner of working, and what obfervations have been made on them, or accidents by damps or otherwife? and what are the laws and cuftoms of thefe feveral mines?

12. How low do the fprings lye, and what fort of water do you meet with in the feveral parts of the parifh?

13. Are there any periodical fprings, which rife and fall, ebb and flow, and at what feafons, or bury themfelves under ground, or petrify and incruft, or produce any other extraordinary effects?

14. Are there any mineral fprings, frequented or not; at what feafons of the year reckoned beft, and what diftempers are they frequented for? What are their qualities, virtues, weight, and analyfis; and what cures attefted or wrought by them?

15. Are there any hot waters or wells for bathing, and for what diftempers frequented? any wells or ftreams formerly accounted holy?

16. Are there any lakes, meers, pools, or water-falls; what their depth and height; where do they rife, and whither do they run?

17. Are

17. Are there any fubterraneous rivers, which appear in one place, then fink into the earth, and rife again?

18. Are there any mills on the rivers, and to what ufes are they employed?

19. What is the proportion of arable, and meadow or pafture?

20. What are the chief produce of the lands, and in what proportion?

21. What is the general price paid for lands, arable, meadow, pafture, &c.

22. What fort of manure is chiefly ufed for the land, and what is the price of it on the fpot?

23. What are the methods of tillage; what forts of ploughs, and other inftruments of hufbandry are ufed; or have any new methods of cultivation been introduced?

24. What experiments have been made in agriculture, gardening, or the management of orchards, vineyards, hop-grounds, woods, or underwoods, cattle, poultry, bees, or fifh-ponds?

25. Does the parifh produce any quantities of timber, of what fort; and what are the prices on the fpot per load or ton?

26. What trees thrive beft, or are moft common?

27. What plants, fhrubs, grains, moffes, graffes, trees, fruits, flowers, are peculiar or moft common? what ufes are they applied to, and what their virtues?

28. Are there any and what quantities of faffron, woad, teazels, or other vegetables of that fort, growing in the parifh; and what prices do they fell for on the fpot?

29. Are there any hop or cherry gardens, or vineyards? and what is the price of their produce on the fpot?

30. Are there any apple or pear orchards in the parifh; what kind of cyder or perry is made, and at what fold for per hogfhead on the fpot?

31. Is the parifh remarkable for breeding any cattle of remarkable qualities, colour, fize, value, or number, and how fold; with other general obfervations?

32. Are

32. Are any quantities of sheep raised or fed in the parish; and on what do they chiefly feed?

33. What is the nature of the air; is it moist or dry, clear or foggy; healthy, or subject to produce agues, fevers, or other diforders; and at what time is it reckoned most fo, and by what probable caufe?

34. A register of weather and general state of the air for one year at least, kept by different persons, with incidental remarks, on the plan of " The Naturalists Journal," by the Hon. Daines Barrington.

35. What are the kinds of birds, insects, or reptiles, common or rare?

36. What forts of fish do the rivers produce, what quantities, what are their prices on the spot, and in what seasons are they best?

37. What is the height of the mountains or hills, and what observations have been made on them?

38. Are there any remarkable caves or grottos, or other openings in the earth, natural or artificial?

39. Are the people of the country remarkable for make, fize, strength, complexion, longevity, or any bodily or natural qualities? or have there been any exceptions to the general rules in their feveral cases?

40. What strange accidents, wonderful events, or extraordinary difeafes and cures, have happened; or uncommon deaths, discoveries of murder, apparitions; what legends and traditions obtain about them, or what their atteftation?

41. Is any part of the parish subject to inundations or land floods, or to be overwhelmed by torrents of fand, and their effects?

42. Hath there been any remarkable mifchief done by thunder and lightning, storms, whirlwinds, or earthquakes?

43. Are there any remarkable echoes?

44. Have any remarkable phænomena or meteors been obferved in the air?

c

If the Parish is on the SEA COAST.

45. Is the shore flat, sandy, high, or rocky, and the encroachment or returns of the sea on it?

46. What are the courses of the tides on the shore, or out at sea, the currents at a mile's distance, and other things worthy remark?

47. What kind of fish are caught there, in what quantity, at what prices sold, when most in season, how taken, and to what market sent?

48. What number of fishing vessels, of what sort, how navigated, and what number of hands are there in the parish?

49. How many ships, and of what burthen, belong to the parish?

50. What are the names of the creeks, bays, harbours, headlands, sands, rocks, or islands, near the coast?

51. What sea animals, plants, sponges, corals, shells, &c. are found on or near the coast?

52. Are any remarkable sea weeds used for manure, or curious on any other account?

53. Are there any remains of piers, camps, batteries, blockhouses, or other works, on the cliffs or shore; or any extraordinary caverns under them?

54. Have there been any remarkable battles or sea fights near the coast, any remarkable wrecks or accidents, which can give light to any historical facts?

55. What light-houses, or beacons?

THE

HISTORY AND ANTIQUITIES

OF

TUNSTALL

IN KENT.

BY THE LATE

EDWARD ROWE MORES, F.A.S.

FAITHFULLY PRINTED FROM THE AUTHOR'S MS.

TO WHICH ARE PREFIXED, BY THE EDITOR,

MEMOIRS of Mr. MORES.

PEDIGREE OF EDWARD-ROWE MORES.

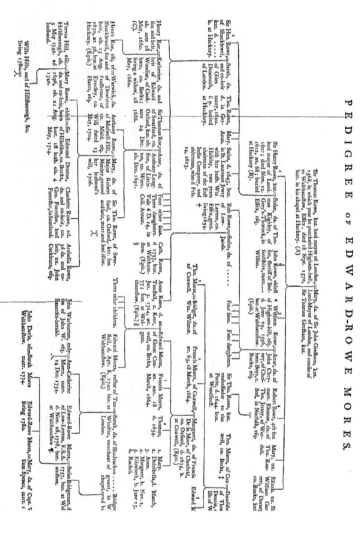

*** See a curious pedigree of the Rowe family, I. 9—58, and the pedigree of Sir William Rowe, knt. lord-mayor of London, C. 14—486, 6 D. 14—441. all in Coll. Armor.

Trevor Hill, visc...=Mary Rowe, eldest=Sir Edmund Denton, 2d.   Charlotte Rowe, 2d.   Arabella Rowe,
Hillsborough, ob.   da. and co-heir, born   of Hillsdden, co. Bucks,   da. and co-heir, un-   3d and co-heir, un-
5 May, 1742.   ad   1696, ob. 21 Aug.   barr. 1st husb. ob. 4   der Geo. Forrester, lord   der, un. John
husband.   1742.   May, 1714.   Forrester, in Scotland.   Cockburn, esq.

Wills Hills, earl of Hillsborough,
living 1760.

John Warburton, only=Ann-Catherine   Edward-Rowe Mores,=Susan Bridgeman, died
fon of John W.   esq. Mores, marr.   of Low-Leyton, E.S.A.   1757, bur. at Walth-
Somerfet-herald.   14 Dec. 1754.   d. Nov. 28, 1778, bur.   amstow.
   at Walthamstow ¶.

John Davis, of=Sarah Mores   Edward-Rowe Mores,=Mary, da. of Capt. Wil-
Walthamstow.   marr. 1774.   living 1780.   liam Spence, marr. 1779.

₊ See a curious pedigree of the Rowe family, I. 9—38, and the pedigree of Sir William Rowe, knt. lord-mayor of London, C. 24—486, 6 D. 14—241. all in Coll. Armor.

* Arg. on a chevron B. between 3 trefoils party per pale G. and B. 3 bezants. Crest, a flag's head couped G. Rowe.

† C. 21—133. in Coll. Arm.

‡ C. 12—64. in Coll. Arm.

§ A quatrefoil in a lozenge.

‖ In a lozenge, baron, A. on a fefs coupé G. between 3 heath-cocks, S. a gethe O. Mores, imp. A. a quaterfoil O. Rowe.

¶ Arms on his archievement in Walthamstow church, baron, Mores, quartering the two coats of Rowe the quatrefoil, and trefoils as above ; femme S. 10 places, on a chief A. a lion paffant S. gutte A. Bridgeman.

(A) A monument with a knight in armour and his lady kneeling, for the most part hid by a gallery ;
stands against the south wall of the south side of Hackney church.

Under the knight this inscription in capitals:

   Sir Thomas Rowe lieth buried heart,
    Of London knight and alderman,
   Who has as martyr and rule did beare
    To right the caufe of every man.
    A merchante venturer was hee,
     Of Merchante Tailors companie ;
    A citizen by birth alfo,
    And eke his wife dame Mary Rowe.

Under her:
    In wedlocke one and thirtie yeare
    They [did continue man and] wife ;
    All [even children the did beare,]
    [But foure of them have left then lyfe,]
    And three of them do yet remaine ;]
    Fower [of them fonnes and 3 daughters twaine
    Her foule [we hope with God in] blieff,
    And do[th remaine in Abraham's] breft.

The words in books being hid by a pillar of the gallery are fupplied from Strype. The coat was Sable, a chevron.
charged with three befants between as many cinquefoils.

(B) In a chapel at the east end of the fouth side of Hackney church againft the fouth wall, is a large handsome
monument to Sir Henry Rowe, who built this chapel. His figure in armour, mantle and ruff, bareheaded, kneels
under an arch, as does his lady in a ruff, a mantle with commous furred fleeves, and a gold chain, under another.
Under him kneel three fons in gowns and ruffs ; the middle one bearded : under her three daughters in ruffs. Be-

Under him this inscription in Roman capitals:
   Here (under fine of Adam's firft defection)
    Refts in the hope of happie refurrection,
    Sir Henry Rowe [fonne of Sir Thomas Rowe,
    And of dame Mary, his deer yoak followe]
    Knight and right worthy (as his father late)
    Lord Maior of London, with his vertuous mate,
  Under her:
    Dame Sufanne (his twice fifteen years and feaven
     Their iffue five (furviving of eleaven)
    Fower named here in their fower names foot paft,
    The fift is found if eccho found the laft.
    Sad orphans all but each their brcie moft eldeze,
    Who built them 1611, the Novembris 12, Ætatis 68.

Quam pic obiit, anno falutis 1612, die Novembris 12, Ætatis 68.
   Over him, in the fpandrile of the arch the arms of London, and the Mercers Company; over her thofe of the
Merchant Taylors. Over him above : Gules, a quatrefoil O. Rowe imp. Arg. a fefs Sable, Kighley. Over her
above a wolf fhield impaled. Between them above quarterly, 1. Rowe. 2. A chevron Az. between three trefoils
per pale Gules and Az. Rowe. 3. Az. a chief Or. over all a lion rampant A. bâtone S. Goldwell. 4. Per fefs
G. and Az. 3 fleurs de lis, G. 3 faulter hands couped Or. Haute. 5. G. 3 faulter hands couped A. Malmains. 6. Or.
on a crofs ingrailed G. a crefcent Or. Haute. 7. G. a lion flatant guardant Or. crowned A. 8. A. a bend
G. between two cottifes nebule S. Surrender. 9. Or a fleur de lis S. Palmer. 10. G. 3 faulter hands coupe
ermine . . . 11. Or. 3 bars . . . 12. G. with a chief Or . . . . 13. Gules within a border Az. 3 lions rampant Or. Croft a flag's
head couped G. with which her children . . . . The fhields over the children are fo much defaced that one can only
make jut the chevrons on the baron and femme fide alternately. From the inscription it fhould feen the names of
the children were once over their heads.

(C) An alter tomb at the eaft end of the chapel has the following inscription in capitals:
   " In memoriam Henrici Rowe de Shacklewell in co. Middlefex, armig. qui dunt in uxorem Warwick Se-
   verten unum e filiis Deodati Staverton de Eversley in comitat. Southampton, armig. obiit 15 die Augufti, anno
   " Dom. 1670, & ætat. fuæ 56. Pofuit hoc illi moeftiffimus conjux."
   This chapel is now the property of Wills Hills, earl of Hillsborough, in right of his mother Mary thief daughter
and co-heir of Anthony Rowe, of Motwell-hill, co. Middlefex, and of North-Afton, co. Oxford, efq. whofe elder
brother fold the manor of Shacklewell to Mr. Tyfon, the perfent lord, but referred to his own family this burial
place, in which he was depofited not many years ago, having been fupported by the contribution of his friends.

MEMOIRS of the AUTHOR.

EDWARD-ROWE MORES, M.A. F.S.A. defcended from an antient family, which had been feated from the beginning of the fixteenth century at Great Coxwell [*], in the county of Berks, and allied by his grand-mother to that of Rowe, which had been fettled at Higham-Benfted in Walthamftow, in the county of Effex, ever fince the middle of the fame century [†], was born January

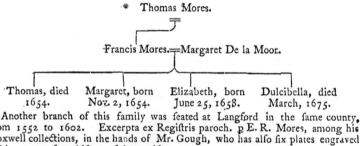

Another branch of this family was feated at Langford in the fame county, from 1552 to 1602. Excerpta ex Regiftris paroch. p E. R. Mores, among his Coxwell collections, in the hands of Mr. Gough, who has alfo fix plates engraved at his expence for a hiftory of this parifh.

† Higham-Benfted manor, in Walthamftow parifh, was the feat of the Rowe's from 1568, when it was purchafed by Sir Thomas Rowe, lord mayor of London that year, who died 1570 [a], and was buried in Hackney church in a chapel built by him, as was alfo his fon Sir Henry, lord major of London 1607, who died 1612, and his grandfon Henry, all fucceffively lords of the manor of Shaklewell. Sufan daughter of the laft Henry married William Haliday, alderman of London and chairman of the Eaft India company, who died 1623, and was buried in St. Lawrence Jewry with his wife (who died 1645) and two daughters. (Strype's Survey of London, I. b. 3. p. 57.) Their four monuments, and a view of Higham hall, were engraved at the expence of Mr. Mores, whofe grandmother was of this family.

In

[a] Morant's Effex, I. 35. He married Mary daughter of Sir John, and coufin to Sir Thomas Grefham; Robert his younger fon was father to Sir Thomas Rowe ambaffador from James I. to the Mogul and the Porte, who died 1644, and is buried at Woodford.

January 13, 1730, at Tunſtall in Kent, where his father was

In the north aile of Walthamſtow church is a family vault of the Mores and Rowes, over which are theſe inſcriptions on flat ſtones :

Here lyeth the body of Mrs.
Catherine Rowe ſiſter to Mrs.
Ann Mores mentioned on the
adjacent monument; who departed
this life Nov. 10th 1737.
She by her laſt will & teſtament
ordered to be buried near to the
grave of her ſaid dear ſiſter, and to
have inſcribed on her tomb ſtone
the prayer of the humble Publican
Luke xviii. 13.
God be merciful to me a ſinner.
On the top of the ſtone a quatrefoil in a lozenge. *Rowe.*

On an oval marble monument againſt the ſouth ſide of the north aile is this inſcription :

Near this place
lyeth interred the body
of Miſtreſs Anne Mores daughter of Robert Rowe Eſq. the eldeſt
ſurviving ſon of Sir William Rowe of
Higham Hill in this pariſh Knight. She
was married to Edward Mores of Great
Coxwell in the county of Berks, Gent, by
whome ſhe had four children, but of them
only remains her entirely devoted & af-
feſtionate ſon Edward Reſtor of Tunſtall in
Kent, who in memory of her, the moſt tender
and indulgent yet prudent and beſt of Mothers
exemplary for all the duties of a truly humble
devout & zealous chriſtian, hath ereſted.
this monument.
She died at the parſonage of Tunſtall
aforeſaid, Jan. the fifth A. D. MDCCXXIV. aged
LXXVII years & XI days.

Pſalm xxxv. 14. *I went heavily as one
that mourneth for his mother.*

rector

rector for near 30 years*.   He was educated at Merchant Tay-

Here alfo lyes the body of the above named Edward
Mores who died on the 8ᵗʰ day of April 1740 in Grace
Church ftreet London & whofe efpecial defire
it was to be buried in the fame grave with his
faid deareft mother.
In a lozenge, *Mores* impaling *Rowe*.

On a brafs plate fet in ftone againft the wall of the Monox chapel at Walthamftow
is this infcription, with the arms of Rowe:

" Gulielmus Rowe de Higham hill in comitatu Effex, generofus, Thomæ Rowe
militis filius natu tertius, Oxonii in Collegio Merton optimarum artium ftudiis præ-
clare inftitutus cum fumma laude, non folum domi magiftri in artibus adeptus eft dig-
nitatem, fed etiam foris in Germania & Gallia ob fummam eruditionem et pietatem,
viris eruditis, præcipue autem Immanueli Tremellio & Theodoro Bezæ longe cha-
riffimus fuit.   In matrimonium duxit Annam Cheyney de Chefham Boys in comitatu
Buckingham armigeri filiam.   Beneficus erat in pauperes, et in omnes pro facultatibus
fuis hofpitalis.   Pacem et coluit ipfe & aliis ut eam mutuis officiis confirmaret
auctor fuit.   Quum pecunia ad ufus publicos exigeretur, ne major quam pro rata
portione vicinis fuis imperaretur diligenter curavit, et imperatæ ne tenuiores exhauriti
fequeretur bonam partem ipfe diffolvit: denique et fuis et alienis veræ pietatis & virtutis exemplar propofuit.   Demum vitæ honeftæ et pie tranfactæ parem for-
titus exitum, ipfi jucundum, amicis et vicinis luctuofum, Junii 29° die obiit 1596.

Thoma patre fatus, Gulielmus Roüs eodem
Qui Londinenfi Prætor in urbe fuit,
Notus homo patriis, externis notus in oris,
Tanta doctrina cognitione fuit.
Pacis amans, Pietatis amans, populoque benignus,
Cui loculus nullo tempore claufus erat.
Natis quinque Pater, natabus quatuor: ifto
Commifit moriens offa tegenda folo.

* See an account of him, p. 58. He married the fifter of Mr. Windfor, an
eminent undertaker, in Union Court, Broad Street.   His father was Edward
Mores of Great Coxwell, in the county of Berks, where his grandfather Francis
died, and is buried in the chancel, on the fouth wall of which the following epitaph
is erected to his and his wife's memory:

Here lieth the body of	Francis Moore of Clanfield in the
Margret the loveing	county of Oxford, efq. and of
wife of Francis Mores of	Mary his wife. she deceafed
Great Coxwell Gentleman.	This life in hope of a better
Shee wafe the mother of ten	The eleventh day of Septem
children, viz. four fonns,	ber in the yeare of our
fix daughters, and the	Lord God 1675.
two and twenty child of	

or's

lor's School*; and admitted a commoner of Queen's College, Oxford, June 24, 1746. While he refided at Oxford, 1746, he affifted in correcting an edition of Calafio's Concordance†, intended by Jacob Ilive ‡, a crazy printer, who afterwards affociated with the Rev. William Romaine, and publifhed this Concordance in 4 volumes folio, 1747. Before he was twenty, Mr. Mores publifhed at Oxford in 4to. 1748, " Nomina & Infignia gentilitia No-" bilium Equitumque fub Edvardo primo rege militantium ;" the oldeft treafure, as he ftyles it, of our nobility after Domefday and the Black Book of the Exchequer. He had alfo printed, except notes and preface, a new edition in 8vo. of Dionyfius Halicarnaffenfis " de claris Rhetoribus," with vignettes engraved by Green, the few copies of which were fold after his death. In 1752 he printed in half a 4to. fheet, fome corrections made by Junius in his own copy of his edition of Cædmon's Saxon paraphrafe of Genefis, and other parts of the Old Teftament, Amftelod. 1655 ; and in 1754 he engraved 15 of the drawings from the MS. in the Bodleian library. The title of thefe plates is " Figuræ quædam; " antiquæ ex Cædmonis monachi paraphrafeos in Genefim exem-" plari pervetufto in bibliotheca Bodleiana adfervato delineatæ ; " ad Anglo-Saxonum mores, ritus, atque aedificia feculi, præcipue " decimi, illuftranda in lucem editæ. Anno Domini MDCCLIV." Thefe plates are now in the poffeffion of Mr. Gough.

In 1752 he was elected a member of the Society of Antiquaries, and two years after was one of a committee for examining

---

* Mr. Mores had made a few collections for a hiftory of this fchool, and lifts of perfons educated there. A view of it was engraved by Mynde, in 1756, for Maitland's edition of " Stowe's Survey," 1756, infcribed " Scholæ Mercatorum Scifforum. " Lond. facies orientalis. Negatam à Patronis D; Scholaris, *Edv. Rowe Mores*, arm. " A. M. S. A. S."

† See his " Differtation on Founders," p. 64.
‡ Of whom, fee more in the Anecdotes of Mr. Bowyer, 4to. p. 130.

the

the Minute-books of that fociety, with a view to felecting from thence papers proper for publication *.

Being intended for orders by his father, he took the degrees of B. A. May 12, 1750, and M. A. Jan. 15, 1753; before which time he had formed confiderable collections relative to the Antiquities, &c. of Oxford, and particularly to thofe of his own college, whofe archives he arranged, and made large extracts from, with a view to its hiftory. He had engraved three plates of the Black Prince's apartments there, fince pulled down, drawn and engraved by that very ingenious artift B. Green. Twenty-eight drawings at his expence, by the fame hand, of antient gates, halls, &c. fince ruined or taken down, are now in the poffeffion of Mr. Gough, as alfo fome collections for a Hiftory of Godftow nunnery, by Mr. Mores, for which a plate of its ruins was engraved, and another of Iffley church†. His MSS. relative to his own College, with his collections about All Souls College, fell after his death into the hands of Mr. Aftle, who has prefented the former to Mr. Price of the Bodleian Library.

Mr. Mores appears to have affifted Mr. Bilfon in his burlefque on the latter fociety, publifhed in a folio fheet, intituled, " Propofals for printing by fubfcription, the hiftory of the Mallardians," treating them as a fet of ftupid *bon vivans*; at leaft he may be prefumed to have contributed the prints of a cat faid to have been

---

* A more numerous committee were appointed for the fame purpofe 1762. But ftill the publication lingered till 1770, when the firft volume of the Archæologia appeared. Many valuable Differtations and Communications ftill remain unfelected from the early Minute-books.

† Other plates engraved at Mr. Mores' expence were four of antique feals, two filver coins of Richard and John, found in digging the foundation of the new town-hall at Oxford. Thefe coins are infcribed IOHAES ----- Rev. --- ONETA MER- IIARI --- ICI --- Rev. MONETA MERTVN; and are now in the hands of Mr. Burrell. A feal found near Canterbury in the poffeffion of Edward Jacob, mayor of Feverfham, 1750; another of Dunfcroft, cell to Roche abbey in the county of York, in the hands of Mr. Warburton; another of William Bate, mafter of St. John Baptift's hofpital, near the old caftle at Carlifle, in thofe of Dr. Ducarel.

ftarved.

ſtarved in their library, and of two antient grotefque buſts caived on the ſouth wall of the college, the plates of which were in his poſſeſſion.

When Mr. Mores left the univerſity he went abroad, and is reported to have taken orders; but whether this tradition has any better foundation than his affectation of wearing his academical habit, and calling it that of a Dominican friar, we do not pretend to vouch. It has been ſaid that he entered into deacon's orders in the church of England, to exempt himſelf from ſerving civil offices. Thus much however is certain, that in the letters of adminiſtration granted to his ſon, on his dying inteſtate, he is ſtyled " the " *Rev.* Edward-Rowe Mores, *D. D.*" but from what biſhop he received ordination we have not yet diſcovered. On his return to London, he reſided ſome years in the Heralds' College, intending to have become a member of that Society, for which he was extremely well qualified by his great knowledge and ſkill in heraldic matters; but altering his plan, he retired about 1760 to Low- Leyton, in which village he had reſided ſome time before, and while he was churchwarden there confiderably improved the church. Here, on an eſtate left him by his father, he built a whimſical houſe on a plan, it is ſaid, of one in France.

In 1759 he circulated queries for a parochial Hiſtory of Berkſhire, but made no confiderable progreſs. His collections on that ſubject are now in the poſſeſſion of Mr. Gough.

The Equitable Society for affurance on lives and ſurvivorſhip by annuities of 100l. increaſing to the ſurvivors, in ſix claſſes of ages from 1 to 10—10 to 20—20 to 30 — 30 to 40—40 to 50—50 to the extremity of life, owes its exiſtence to Mr. Mores. It had been firſt ſuggeſted and recommended in lectures in 1756, by Mr. James Dodſon, mathematical maſter at Chriſt's hoſpital, and author of the " Mathematical Repoſitory," who had been refuſed admiſſion into the Amicable Society on account of his age; but he dying November 23, 1757, before his deſign was

3   completed,

completed, except the plan of reimburfement to him and his 54 affociates, Mr. Mores undertook to apply for a charter in 1761, but failing of fuccefs, he, with 16 more of the original fubfcribers, refolved to perfevere in eftablifhing their fociety by deed. It was hereby provided that Mr. Mores fhould be perpetual director, with an annuity of 100l. He drew up and publifhed in 1765, " A fhort account of the Society," in 8vo. (of which a feventh edition with additions was printed in 1767), " The Plan " and Subftance of the Deed of Settlement," " The Statutes," " Precedents of fundry Inftruments relating to the Conftitu- " tion and Practice of the Society, London, 1766," 8vo. The " deed of fettlement, and the declaration of truft, 1768," " A lift of the policies and other inftruments of the fociety, as " well general as fpecial," 8vo; but fome difputes arifing between Mr. Mores and the original members of this fociety, he feparated from them that year. There were printed, " Papers re- " lating to the difputes with the charter fund proprietors in the " Equitable Society, by order of a general court held the 3d day " of November, 1767, for the ufe of thofe affured on the lives " of others, who fhall apply for the fame, 1769," 8vo. This fociety ftill fubfifts, and their office is in Bride-ftreet, near Black-Friars bridge, to which it was removed from Nicholas lane, Lombard ftreet, 1775*. All Mr. Mores's papers on this fubject are now in the hands of Mr. Aftle.

---

* It affures any fums or reverfionary annuities on any lives, for any number of years, as well as for the whole continuance of the lives, at rates fettled by particular calculations, and in any manner that may be beft adapted to the views of the perfons affured: that is, either by making the affured fums payable certainly at the failure of any given number of lives, or on condition of furvivorfhip, and alfo by taking the price of the affurance in one prefent payment, or in annual payments, during any fingle or joint lives, or any terms lefs than the whole continuance of the lives. The plan of this fociety is fo extenfive and important, that, if due care is taken, it may prove a very great public benefit. Price on Reverfionary Payments, 1771, p. 123, who propofes fome improvements on this plan.

In the latter part of life, Mr. Mores (who had long turned his thoughts to the fubject of early Printing) began to correct the ufeful publication of Mr. Ames *. On the death of Mr. John James of Bartholomew Clofe (the laft of the old race of letter-founders) in June, 1772, Mr. Mores purchafed all the curious parts of that immenfe collection of punches, matrices, and types, which had been accumulating from the days of Wynkyn de Worde to thofe of Mr. James. From thefe a large fund of entertainment would probably have been given to the curious, if the life of Mr. Mores had been prolonged. His intentions may be judged of from his valuable " Diſſertation on Typographical " Founders and Founderies." As no more than 80 copies of it were printed, it will at leaft be confidered as a typographical curiofity. Mr. Nichols, who purchafed the whole impreſſion, has fubjoined a fmall Appendix to it.

Mr. Mores was a moft indefatigable collector, and poſſeſſed great application in the early part of his life, but in the latter part gave himfelf up to habits of negligence and diſſipation, which brought him to his end by a mortification in the 49th year of his age, at his houfe at Low Leyton, Nov. 28, 1778. His large collection of curious MSS. and valuable library of books were fold by auction by Mr. Paterfon in Auguft following. Of the former his " Hiftory and Antiquities of Tunftall in " Kent†," the only papers that were completed for the prefs, and for which he had engraved a fet of plates out of the many drawings taken at his expence, was purchafed at the fale by Mr. Nichols, who has now given it to the publick as a fpecimen of parochial antiquities, which will fhew the ideas of this induftrious Antiquary, and his endeavour to

---

* Mr. Nichols has a tranfcript of his few corrections on that book.
† Several Vifitations of Kent, with large additions by Mr. Mores, were purchafed by Mr. Lafted.

make

make even the minuteſt record ſubſervient to the great plan of national hiſtory. Several books of Engliſh antiquities with his MS. notes, and the moſt valuable part of ſuch of the MSS.* and ſcarce tracts as relate to our local antiquities, were purchaſed by Mr. Gough. Mr. Aſtle purchaſed his epitome of the Regiſters of the See of Canterbury, preſerved in the Archiepiſcopal Library at Lambeth, beginning with the firſt Regiſter called Peckham, A. D. 1279, and ending with that of Archbiſhop Teniſon in 1710; and his "Excerpta ex Regiſtris Cur. Prærog. Cantuar." 3 vols. 8vo; vol. I. containing extracts from wills in the Prerogative-office, from 1385 to 1533; vol. II. extracts from 1533 to 1561; vol. III. extracts from 1592 to 1660. To the firſt volume is prefixed a learned and curious diſſertation concerning the authority of the Prerogative Court†, with the names of the ſeveral Regiſters. Mr. Aſtle has alſo his catalogue of the Rolls preſerved in the Lambeth library, made in the year 1758; his collections for the Hiſtory and Antiquities of the City of Saliſbury, containing ſeveral curious particulars and tranſcripts of records, &c. with ſome ſhort Annals of the Univerſity of Oxford, from 1066 to 1310; and a MS. in Latin intitled "De Ælfrico Archiepiſcopo Dorovernenſi Commentarius. Auc- "tore Edwardo-Rowe Mores, A. M. Soc. Antiq. Lond. Soc." This laſt MS. is in the hand-writing of Mr. Mores, and ſeems to have been intended for publication. It contains ten chapters; the firſt ſeven relate to Archbiſhop Ælfric; Cap. 8. is intitled " De Ælfrico Bata;" Cap. 9. " De Ælfrico Abbate Meildunenſi;"

---

* Among theſe laſt were imperfect alphabetical liſts of incumbents in Canterbury and Rocheſter dioceſes, ſome corporation rentals for Saliſbury, ſome other collections for which place, and ſeveral rolls of ancient deeds, were bought by Mr. Topham: the originals of Batteley's " Antiquitates Rutupinæ," Ballard's " Memoirs " of illuſtrious Ladies," &c. Among the former, Browne Willis's " Mitred Abbies," and Dr. Tanner's " Notitia Monaſtica."

† By his intimacy with the late Mr. St. Eloy, one of the regiſters of the prerogative court, he got acceſs to that office, and had thereby an opportunity of drawing up the above learned account.

 Cap. 10.

Cap. 10. "De allis Ælfricis." An Appendix is fubjoined, containing tranfcripts of Saxon charters and extracts from hiftorians concerning Archbifhop Ælfric.

Mr. Mores married Sufannah daughter of Mr. Bridgman, an eminent grocer in Whitechapel, who was before his father-in-law by having married the widow of his father. By this lady, who died in 1767, and lies buried in the church yard at Walthamftow with the infcription given below *, he had a daughter, Sarah, married in 1774 to Mr. John Davis, houfe painter at Walthamftow, who died before her father; and a fon, Edward-Rowe, married in 1779 to Mifs Spence. Mr. Mores' only fifter was married in 1756 to Mr. John Warburton, (fon of the late antiquary and Somerfet herald John Warburton, efq.) who has refided at Dublin many years, and is now purfuivant of the court of exchequer in Ireland.

* Sufannæ Mores,
Annorum triginta feptem liberorum binorum matri
amantiffimæ, fideliffimæ, dilectiffimæ.
Conjugi
fupremum mariti donum
Mitem placide reddidit animam
Derelictum
Luctu
Fide folum leniendo obruens
Octavo die Jan. Incarnat. Anno
MDCCLXVII.

Mr. Mores was buried by her, and his atchievement in Walthamftow church has Quarterly 1. 4. Mores. 2 G. a Quatre foil O. 3. *Rowe.* Impaling Sab. 10 plates, on a chief A. a lion paffant Sa. gutte *A. Bridgeman.*

P R E F A C E.

TWO reasons have induced the Editors to open their work with the following fragment of our topographical antiquities: its intrinsic merit as to the manner in which it is executed, which may make it serve as a plan for parochial descriptions, and the motive which led its compiler to draw it up. It was Mr. Mores's birth-place; his father had been rector many years, and the parish registers were drawn up on a plan conformable to the ideas of our industrious antiquary, and consistent with his endeavours to make even the minutest record subservient to the great plan of national history. In this view he published his " Nomina & Infignia gentilitia no- " bilium equitumq; sub EDVARDO primo rege militantium," the oldest treasure, as he styles it, of our nobility after Domesday and the Black book of the Exchequer, comprehending both their titles and their arms, neither of which were classed in any other registers till the institution of the Heralds College under Richard III.

From the utility of such a record, the transition is obvious to every subordinate aid, from funeral monuments, parish registers, arms interspersed on or about buildings, &c. The second of these were first instituted by Thomas lord Cromwell, who, after the transports of reformation were a little subsided, could not but recollect the use of monastic registers and obituaries. It will admit of a doubt, whether these were so extensively useful as the register of the meanest parish at present:

a but

but that the moſt copious pariſh regiſter is capable of improvement we need only confult Mr. Bigland's excellent tract
on the ſubject, where the plan of ſuch improvement is ſo
largely diſcuſſed.   What effect penalties have had to make the
entries in theſe regiſters exact, let the ſeveral acts of parliament
from 1538 to 6 and 7 William III ſpeak *.

Modern epitaphs are much more genealogical than antient
ones, and in innumerable inſtances deſcents ſupply the place of
eulogies.   Theſe might be entered in regiſters, and whatever
particulars of the parties buried, or of parochial hiſtory, an induſtrious incumbent or his repreſentative could pick up.   Great
confuſion of names might be prevented by attending to diſ-
tinctions in baptiſmal and marriage entries.

Theſe particulars Mr. Mores had the ſatisfaction to find in
ſome degree attended to in TUNSTALL regiſters, of which he
gave the following extract in the dedication to his book before
cited, p. xxvii.

    " Præfata feṛe omnia (ſays he) in regiſtro de *Tunſtall* in com.
" Canc. aliquatinus obſervata vides: quæ licet ſit villa tantum,
" & nunc propter illicitam rectoris per decem annos abſentiam
" vix digna ſacerdotali videtur incola, fuit ampliſſimarum olim
" familiarum habitaculum, prout monumenta plurima, plurima
" in feneſtris depicta inſignia adhuc ibidem viſenda, pluri-
" morum etiam ſacrilegè direptorum reliquiæ palam common-
" ſtrabunt.

    " Exemplar regiſtri ex mente mea componendi hoc eſto; è
" Tunſtallenſi decerptum & meis additamentis auctum.

1538 Mr Symon Jenninges parſon of Tunſtall was buried 27 Nov. [he has left
    behind him this memorial on the walls of the columbary † belonging to
    the parſonage:

        * Naſh's Worc. I. 207.   † Which probably he built.

                                                        1538.

PREFACE.

1538.

S. Jenyns: pries pour luy.]

1539 Sir William Crowmer kt died 20 Jul. and was buried 21: die ♉. [he was son of Sir James Cr. kt, & was Sheriff of Kent in the years 1503 & 1509.]

1545 Will. Rowe [son of Sir Tho. Rowe kt and Mary da. of Sir John Gresham kt] was borne uppon St Thomas eaven being the xxii day of Dec. anr. 1545 his Godfathers Sir William Tucker & Mr. William Harding, & Lady Anne Pargiter his godmother. [ex MSto penes me.]

1556 James Longe, a good howseholder, aged 71, and worthy of perpetual memory, was buried 18 Oct.

1561 Walter Crowmer esq; [son of Sr William Cr. kt.] & Eliz. daughter of Sr John Guildeford kt were married at Boughton Mallarde 1 Oct.

1562 James son of William [& Eliz.] Crowmer was born, baptised and buried 25 Maij.

1568 John Longe [son of Will. L. of Piltock in this parish,] and Phyllis Bull [of Milton] were married 10 Jan.

1569 James son of William [& Eliz.] Crowmer was born 24 Dec.

1584 Christopherus Webbes S. T. B. filius Joh. W. de Gillingham in com. Cant. armigeri, in Coll. Scti Joh. Cantabr. (ut opinor) educatus,] rector ecclesiæ Tunstallensis, [huc admissus per mortem Petri Pott rectoris ultimi qui 10 C . 15 4 obiit, inductus ci menf. ann. ab collatus die menf. an ..] legit articulos illi ad legendum injunctos 21 Febr. hora precum matutinarum, audientibus omnibus parochis ann. R. R. Eliz. 27. coram his testibus subscriptis;

    Will. Crowmer.

    Walt. Harlakenden.

    Will. Tonge.

    Sam. Ton e.

    & other.

1597 Frances [daugh. of John Somers, esq; and] wife of James Crowmer, esq; died [in childbed] 27 Apr.

1598 William Crowmer, esq; justice of the peace & quorum, died 12 Maij, aged 67, and was buried 18th.

1601 Hen. son of Walter & Suf. Harlakenden [of Ufton in this parish] was buried 18 Oct. being slaine 15 of the same month towards evenin_ _aged 27.*]

* See Noy's Reports, p. 48.

1613 𝕾𝔦𝔯 𝕵𝔞𝔪𝔢𝔰 𝕮𝔯𝔬𝔴𝔪𝔢𝔯 [𝕶𝔱. 𝔰𝔬𝔫 𝔬𝔣 𝕾𝔯 𝕸𝔦𝔩𝔩𝔦𝔞𝔪 𝔞𝔫𝔡 𝕮𝔥𝔯. 𝕮𝔯. 𝔷 𝔥𝔦𝔤𝔥 𝔰𝔥𝔢𝔯𝔦𝔣𝔣 𝔬𝔣 𝔱𝔥𝔦𝔰 𝔠𝔬𝔲𝔫𝔱𝔶 𝔦𝔫 𝔱𝔥𝔢 2𝔡 𝔶𝔢𝔞𝔯 𝔬𝔣 𝔱𝔥𝔢 𝔯𝔢𝔦𝔤𝔫 𝔬𝔣 𝔥𝔦𝔰 𝔭𝔯𝔢𝔰𝔢𝔫𝔱 𝔪𝔞𝔧.] 𝔡𝔦𝔢𝔡 27 𝔐𝔞𝔯𝔱. [𝔞𝔤𝔢𝔡 44] 𝔞𝔫𝔡 𝔴𝔞𝔰 𝔟𝔲𝔯𝔦𝔢𝔡 8 𝔄𝔭𝔯. [𝔲𝔫𝔡𝔢𝔯 𝔞 𝔫𝔬𝔟𝔩𝔢 𝔪𝔬𝔫𝔲𝔪𝔢𝔫𝔱, 𝔦𝔫 𝔱𝔥𝔢 𝔠𝔥𝔞𝔭𝔢𝔩 𝔬𝔫 𝔱𝔥𝔢 𝕾. 𝔰𝔦𝔡𝔢 𝔬𝔣 𝔱𝔥𝔢 𝔠𝔥𝔞𝔫𝔠𝔢𝔩, 𝔯𝔢𝔭𝔯𝔢𝔰𝔢𝔫𝔱𝔦𝔫𝔤 𝔱𝔥𝔢 𝔰𝔱𝔞𝔱𝔲𝔢𝔰 𝔬𝔣 𝔥𝔦𝔪𝔰𝔢𝔩𝔣 𝔞𝔫𝔡 𝔇𝔞𝔪𝔢 𝔐𝔞𝔯𝔱𝔥𝔞 𝔥𝔦𝔰 𝔰𝔢𝔠𝔬𝔫𝔡 𝔩𝔞𝔡𝔶 𝔭𝔯𝔞𝔶𝔦𝔫𝔤 𝔟𝔢𝔣𝔬𝔯𝔢 𝔞𝔫 𝔞𝔩𝔱𝔞𝔯: 𝔦𝔫 𝔱𝔥𝔢 𝔰𝔞𝔪𝔢 𝔞𝔱𝔱𝔦𝔱𝔲𝔡𝔢 𝔞𝔯𝔢 𝔯𝔢𝔭𝔯𝔢𝔰𝔢𝔫𝔱𝔢𝔡, 𝔲𝔫𝔡𝔢𝔯 𝕾𝔯 𝕵𝔞𝔪𝔢𝔰, 𝕱𝔯𝔞𝔫𝔠𝔢𝔰 𝔥𝔦𝔰 𝔢𝔩𝔡𝔢𝔰𝔱 𝔡𝔞𝔲𝔤𝔥𝔱𝔢𝔯 𝔟𝔶 𝔞 𝔣𝔬𝔯𝔪𝔢𝔯 𝔴𝔦𝔣𝔢; 𝔲𝔫𝔡𝔢𝔯 𝔩𝔞𝔡𝔶 𝔐𝔞𝔯𝔱𝔥𝔞, 𝕰𝔩𝔦𝔷𝔞𝔟𝔢𝔱𝔥, 𝔐𝔞𝔯𝔱𝔥𝔞 𝔷 𝕮𝔥𝔯𝔦𝔰𝔱𝔦𝔞𝔫 𝔱𝔥𝔢𝔦𝔯 𝔬𝔱𝔥𝔢𝔯 𝔡𝔞𝔲𝔤𝔥𝔱𝔢𝔯𝔰: 𝔴𝔦𝔱𝔥 𝔱𝔥𝔢𝔰𝔢 𝔦𝔫𝔰𝔠𝔯𝔦𝔭𝔱𝔦𝔬𝔫𝔰 *."

Mr. Mores the fame time gives due praife to two vicars who had inferted a feries of their predeceffors in their regifters with memoirs of their lives: Mr. Johnfon, vicar of Cranbrook, and Dr. Saunders, vicar of Blockley in Worcefter diocefe; to whom we may add Dr. Oakes, rector of Long Melford, Suffolk, who caufed the names of all the preceding rectors he could collect from 1309 to himfelf to be infcribed on two marble tablets fixed up on each fide of the chancel above the reach of injury.

So much may fuffice for the original defign of this little hif‑ tory. In its execution Mr. Mores may be fairly prefumed to have exerted all that the *dulcedo natalis joli* calls forth. He pro‑ feffes to have drawn his materials chiefly from printed books. Had the compiler of the general hiftory of that county, of which Tunftall makes fo fmall a part, confined himfelf only to thofe fources, how much would he have improved that long‑ expected and voluminous work! But had he penetrated more intimately (for, notwithftanding the profeffion of the preface, fcaice any fuch appear among his authorities) into the κειμήλια of records, inquifitions, chartularies, regifters, and that fund of materials which are open to every diligent inveftigator, what a hiftory of KENT, that county of Britain to which her firft invader pays fuch a compliment, would have arifen under the pen of Mr. HASTED!

---

* As inferted in p. 80, 81.

HISTORY AND ANTIQUITIES

O F

T U N S T A L L.

C H A P. I.

Of the Village of Tunſtall, *its Situation and Extent.*

THE village of Tunſtall lies about the middle of the north ſide of Kent, agreeably and healthfully ſituated upon a riſing ſpot of ground, and over ſundry towns, villages, rivers, and the iſle of Shepey lying beneath, it has a delightful proſpect of the ocean, diſtant about 10 miles.

According to the civil diviſion of this county, Tunſtall is placed in the bailiwic and hundred of Milton, lathe of Scray, eaſt diviſion of the county, and upper diviſion of juſtices in that lathe (*a*); and, according to the eccleſiaſtical diviſion of the county, is in the deanry of Sittingbourne, and dioceſe of Canterbury (*b*).

Tunſtall is ſurrounded by the pariſhes of Sittingbourne, Milſtead, Bredgar, Borden, and Milton, (from the market-town of which name it is diſtant two miles to the ſouth) is in compaſs about five miles, and contains near 856 acres of land; it is rated to the land-tax at   *l. per ann.* and by a twelve-penny rate raiſes for the relief of the poor the ſum of 28*l.* 14*s.*

(*a*) Kilburne, p. 278.   (*b*) Ibid.

B   The

The total amount of rents in the parifh of Tunftall, 30 Maij, 1757, was computed at 594*l. per ann.* but this computation was made in fome meafure favourable to the occupiers; from thence, however, and from the known rents of certain of their lands a proportion being formed, the true yearly amount may be fuppofed to be 725*l.* 4*s.* 8*d.* nearly.

It has been before obferved, that Tunftall is fituated upon an afcent; and little doubt is to be made that this eminence of fituation gave name to the place, the very name being fufficiently expreffive of that eminence; for Dunftall (an appellation which ftill prevails among the vulgar), being tranflated from the language of our anceftors, points out to us *the high place,* or, *the place upon the hill* (*c*).

If we look into the antient ftate of this place, and carry ourfelves back to the time of the general furvey, the moft diftant period we can arrive at with any profpect of fuccefs, we fhall find that Tunftall in the time of king Henry I. was little more than a private manor, not yet diftinguifhed with the name and privileges of a parifh, without a church (if fo much may be concluded from the filence of Domefday book upon this head), fubject to its temporal lord, and inhabited by nine villans (*d*), each of whom (a fkilful antiquary (*e*) informs us) had a farm, and performed the works of hufbandry for their lord.

The time when Tunftall was erected into a parifh appears not; but whenever that was accomplifhed, it is fufficiently plain that a fpirit of devotion, rather than the number of inhabitants, occafioned a church to be founded here; for fo lately as the year 1557, the number of families refiding here was no more than 16, and the number of parifhioners threefcore (*f*); fince that time indeed thefe numbers have been augmented, and upon an exact account taken by myfelf June 2, 1757, the ftate of the place was this :

(*c*) From the Saxon ðun and ꝼꞇeal. (*d*) Lib. de Domefday. (*e*) Chauncy's Hertf. p. 12. (*f*) Archdeacon Harpsfield's Vifitat. inter MSS. *Tann.*

Houfes

Houfes (whereof one empty)　　**17**
Families,　　-　　-　　-　　**20**
Parifhioners,　　-　　-　　115

whereof 53 are children, fo that in the fpace of 200 years Tunftall has nearly doubled the number of its inhabitants. Five teams are kept in this parifh.

C H A P. II.

Of the capital Lords of Tunftall.

THE moft early period which affords us information of a place fo obfcure as this, whereof I treat, is the reign of king Edward the Confeffor; at which time we read that Tunftall was held by OSWARD, a Saxon of rank and dignity, who had large poffeffions in the county of Kent, of which he was fheriff in the reign of that king.

Ofward, therefore, we are to look upon as the moft antient owner and capital lord of this place; an appellation which, according to the fenfe in which I fpeak, is not indeed ftrictly applicable to the times preceding the ingrefs of the Normans; but as he held Tunftall immediately of the crown, I chufe to mention him under this denomination.

The acceffion of William I. to the crown of England brought with it an almoft entire change in the government, cuftoms, and ufages of this kingdom. But of all the alterations which were then introduced, none were more great or more fenfibly felt by our Saxon anceftors than the change of property which enfued thereon, and the new kind of tenure which was then impofed upon the eftates of this realm. For the Norman king, defirous of fecuring by policy what he had obtained by force

or

or fraud, difpoffeffed the Englifh of their poffeffions, and diftributed them amongft his Norman followers, at the fame time
fubjecting their lands to a military tenure, and creating thofe
feodal duties, conditions, and fervices, with which the nation
was afterwards burthened for the fpace of 600 years.

Of thofe who attended the expedition of the duke of Normandy into England, no perfon was more eminently ferviceable
to him therein than ODO the bifhop of Baieux, his half brother,
a man formed by nature for a warfare very different from that
to which he was engaged by his profeffion. For his fignal fervices he was created by his brother earl of Kent, and enriched
with a prodigious quantity of thofe lands which were then
taken from their antient owners.

Tunftall was part of them; and at the time of the general
furvey, was held of the bifhop of Baieux, by HUGO DE PORTE,
being thus recorded in Domefday book:

" Hugo de Port ten de epo *TYNESTELLE* . p . III . folins

" . . . . . . 7 dim fe defd . Tra . ē . IIII . car . In dño funt . II . car.

" 7 IX . uilli cũ . I . car . 7 IX . ferui . Silua . x . porc . 7 falina de . XII.

" denar . T.R.E . 7 poft . ualeb . VII . lib . Modo . VIII . lib.

" Ofuuard tenuit de rege . E."

Hugo de Port tenuit de epifcopo *Tuneftelle* pro III folinis . . . . . & dim'
fe defendebat. Terra eft IIII car'. In dominico funt II car' & IX villani
cum I car' & IX fervi. Silva x porc' & falina de XII denar'. Tempore
Regis Edwardi & poftea valebat VII lib'. modo VIII lib'. Ofuuard tenuit
de Rege Edwardo.

But in the next reign Odo falling from his allegiance, and
promoting a confpiracy againft king William II. in behalf of
Robert Curthofe, then duke of Normandy, whom he wanted
to advance to the throne of England, loft all his honours and vaft
power, and for ever abjured the kingdom: whereupon his lands,
as I fuppofe, efcheated to the crown; by which means the in-
termediate

termediate dependence between the king and de Port being then extinguifhed, the latter and his pofterity became the capital lords of this place, which they held of the crown in the fame manner as Odo before had held it.

Hugo de Port was poffeffed of 67 lordfhips in the county of Southampton(*g*); and making Bafing the head of his barony, Tunftall became dependent upon that manor, being held as parcel thereof, and apparently tenant thereto. To him fucceeded HENRY de Port his fon and heir, whofe fon and heir

JOHN de Port 12 Henry II. 1163 (*h*), upon the affeffment of the aid for marrying the king's daughter, certified the knights fees he then held to be in number 55 de vet. feoff. & 2 de novo. To him fucceeded

ADAM de Port his eldeft fon, conftituted governor of the caftle of Southampton, 15 John ; but being afterwards accufed for the death of king Henry II. he was thereupon adjudged to forfeit all his lands. His fon

WILLIAM, rejecting the name of de Port, affumed the furname of S. JOHN, writing himfelf *Willielmus de S'co Johanne fil. et h. Adæ de Port*, and 15 John gave 500 marks to the king for livery of all the lands of Adam de Port his father ; and moreover covenanted to provide, at his own proper cofts, ten foldiers well fitted with horfes and arms to ferve the king for one whole year in Poictou.

ROBERT de S. John his fon and heir fucceeded ; who dying about the 5th year of Henry III. 1263,

JOHN de S. John his fon and heir had livery of his lands, who 10 Edward I. 1282, being in the expedition then made into Wales, had fcutage of all his tenants in the counties of Hereford, Southampton, Kent, Suffex, Berkfhire, and Warwickfhire, who

---

(*g*) Dugd. Bar. I. 463.　　　　(*h*) See the Red-book.

held

held of him by military fervice (*i*). He died 30 Edward I. 1302, leaving iffue

JOHN de S. John his fon and heir, who the next year doing his homage, had livery of the lords of his inheritance. He died the 14th of May, 12 Edward II. 1319, feifed as capital lord of this place, which was held of him, as parcel of his manor of Bafing, by *Stephen de Cobham* the younger, by the fervice incident to one knight's fee, and was then valued at the income of   per annum. He left iffue

HUGO de S. John his fon and heir, aged 19 years at his father's death, who in the very next year died likewife, feifed of the capital lordfhip in 'like manner of this place, which was then reckoned at   per annum, leaving iffue

EDMUND de S. John his fon and heir, aged 4, who dying in his minority, and in ward to the king, 21 Edward III. 1348, his fifters MARGARET and ISABELL became his heirs. The former being the wife of John de S. Philibert, the latter of Henry de Burgherfh, betwixt whom partition of the lands of their inheritance being made, the manor of Bafing fell to

John de S. Philibert and the aforefaid Margaret, who dying the 19th of October, 35 Edward III. 1362, and her fon and heir John in lefs than a month afterwards, the whole inheritance vefted in Ifabell her fifter, then the wife of Lucas de Poynings, Henry de Burgherfh her former hufband being before dead; whereupon the faid

LUCAS DE POYNINGS having iffue by the faid Ifabell, and doing his homage, had livery of all thofe lands fo defcended to her. This Ifabell, furviving both her hufbands, died the 16th of October, 17 Richard II. 1394, feifed in like manner of this place, which was held of her as one knight's fee by Sir Robert Knoles, knt. and was valued then at no more than   , leaving

(*i*) Qu. Rot. de fcutag. Wall.

Sir

Sir THOMAS DE POYNINGS, knt. lord afterwards Thomas lord St.
John her fon and heir, who died the 7th of March, 7 Henry VI.
1428, feifed as capital lord of this place, which was holden of
him as parcel of his manor of Bafing by William Crowmer, and
was then valued at   , leaving *Conftance* the wife of John
Paulet, *Alice* the wife of John Orrell, and *John Bonevile* his heirs,
of whom Conftance and Alice were the daughters of *Hugh* de
Poynings his fon, who died in the life-time of his father, and
John Boneville the fon of *Joanna* the third daughter of the faid
Hugh: Conftance aged 20, Alice 19, and John Boneville 16, who
had livery of the land of their inheritance 8 Henry VI.

PEDIGREE of PORT.

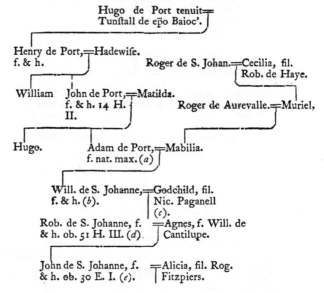

(a) R·t P·p. 18 Joh.   (b) Fin. 15 Joh. m 9 for livery of all his father's lands.
(c) Pat 1 H III m 2 grant of all his lands to Joh Marefchel (d) Rot. Vafc. 38 H. III. m, 18. cart. lib. War.
(e) Clauf 51. 51 H. III, m. 5. livery. Scutag. Wall. 10 E. I. m. 4. Efc. 30 E. I. n. 36.

John

John de S. Johan. f. & h.═Iſabella, fil.
æt. 28, 30 E. I. ob. 14 │ Hug. de Courtney.
Maij 12 E. II. (*f*).

Hugo de S. Johanne,═Mirabell.
f. &. h. æt. 26. 3 Ed.
III. ob. 2 E. III. ſei-
fit. de 16 feod. in com.
Kantie (*g*).

Margar. ux. Joh. Edm. de S. Johanne,═Elizabeth. Iſabell. ux. Hen.
de S. Philiberto. ob. infr. æt. 21 Ed. III. de Burgherſh,
ob. 19 Oct. 35 (*i*).   poſtea Lucæ de
Ed. III. (*h*).   Poynings (*k*).

Lucas de Poynings.═Iſabella, vid. Hen.
(*l*).   de Burgherſh, ob.
        16 Oct. 17 R. II. (*m*)

Sir Tho. de Poynings,═Matilda (*n*).
f. & h. æt. 36. 17 R.
II. ob. 7 H. VI. (*o*).

Hugo de Poynings,═Iſabella.
ob. in vita patris.

Conſtantia, ux. (*p*) Alicia, ux. Johanna, ux. ═
Joh. Paulet. (*q*). Joh. Orrell. Joh. Bonevile.

            John Bonevile.

Joh. Paulet.═Eleanor, f. & coh.
      Rob. Ros de Gedney,
      co. Linc. arm.

Joh. Paulet, mil.═Elizabeth.

Gul. Paulet, d. S. Joh. ob. 10 Mart. 1571.

(*f*) *Fin.* 30 E. I. m 4 livery. *Eſc.* 3 E III. n 67. (*g*) *Eſc* 11 E III n. 49. (*h*) *Eſc.* 35 E. III. n. 49.
(*i*) *Clauſ.* 21 E III p. 2. m 16. Partition of his lands, *Clauſ* 21 E III. m. 10.
(*k*) *Clauſ* 23 E. III. p. 1. m 17 *Clauſ* 29 E III dorſ. m. 21 *Fin.* 23 E III. p 1 m. 24.
(*l*) *Pat.* 31 E. III p. 3. m 5 (*m*) *Eſc.* 17 R. II. n 45. (*n*) *Fin.* 17 R. II. m. 14.
(*o*) *Eſc.* 7 H VI c. 69. *Clauſ.* 8 H. VI. m. 19. aſſign dot. *Eſc* 31 H. VI, n. 28.
(*p*) *Eſc.* 21 H. VI. 22.   (*q*) *Fin.* 8 H. VI. m. 18. lib.

C H A P. III.

Of the mesne lords of Tunstall.

IN the preceding chapter I have briefly touched upon the changes introduced by the Normans, so far as was necessary for the perfect understanding of what I was then about to deliver: the same method I shall observe in this chapter likewise, wherein I propose to treat of the mesne lords of this place, or, to use a term more universally understood, the lords of the manor of Tunstall.

Though there are but few persons who have not a due notion of what is meant by a manor, yet every one is not acquainted with the nature and original of its constitution; points very necessary to be known by those who shall peruse, as well these, as other memoirs of the like nature.

To convey to them this piece of knowledge in as few words as may be, let it be remembered, that the Conqueror was exceedingly liberal to his Norman friends, insomuch that the whole kingdom was divided amongst a number of persons, each of whom, upon an equal partition, must at a moderate computation have possessed a quantity of land much too great to have been under the immediate inspection of any single person. Those, therefore, who had been thus enriched, partly because of the extent and distance of their possessions, and partly in alleviation of the services they were obliged to perform for them, made a further division of their respective lands, granting certain quantities to certain inferior tenants upon certain conditions and services to be performed therefore. These inferior tenants fixed their abode upon the lands which they thus held; but nevertheless made a further division of them: part they reserved to themselves for the use of their families by the name

C of

of demefn lands, the remaining part they parcelled out amongft tenants ftill inferior to themfelves, and holding of them by fuch rents and fervices as they thought meet to impofe.

This laft fub-divifion is what we are now talking of, and what at this day we are to underftand by the term *manor*, fo named from the refidence of the lord thereon ; who then, and in fome meafure now likewife, maintains a jurifdiction over thofe within his diftrict.

So that the mefne lords of Tunftall, though their title implies a fubjection, and to a lefs intelligent reader may convey an idea of inferiority, are neverthelefs perfons of confiderable confequence : and to fuch as defire an acquaintance with the hiftory of this place, the account of them is of greater importance than that of any other perfons whatfoever ; inafmuch as they were moft intimately connected therewith, and were immediately interefted in whatever could affect or concern the fame.

But in refpect to the mefne lords of this place, record has not been altogether fo favourable to us as we found it in the preceding chapter.

The next family that had any intereft here (as far as I have hitherto difcovered) was the ARSICS ; and of them MANASSER Arfic is the firft whom I can with any certainty mention. He held of John de Port one knight's fee of the old feofment 12 Henry II (*k*).

His fon ALEXANDER Arfic, 8 Richard I. 1197, was difcharged of his fcutage upon the expedition then lately made into Normandy for his knights fees in this county (*l*).

To him fucceeded JOHN Arfic his fon and heir, who married Margaret daughter of Richard de Vernon ; but he dying iffuelefs about the 7th year of king John's reign, 1206, ROBERT de Arfic his brother and heir gave one hundred pounds for his relief and

(*k*) Lib. Nig. Scacc. p. 73, ed. Hearne.   (*l*) Rot. Pip. 8 Ric. I. Kent.

livery

livery of thofe lands which defcended to him by the death of his faid brother without iffue; and had the king's precept to the fheriffs of Oxford and Kent accordingly (*m*).

PEDIGREE OF MANASSER ARSIC.

Arms : A chief indented Gules or Sable. Rot. antiq. p. 589.

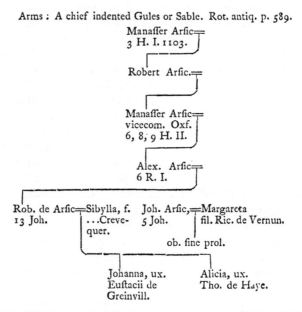

Manaffer Arfic⸺
3 H. I. 1103.

Robert Arfic.⸺

Manaffer Arfic⸺
vicecom. Oxf.
6, 8, 9 H. II.

Alex. Arfic⸺
6 R. I.

Rob. de Arfic⹀Sibylla, f.   Joh. Arfic,⹀Margareta
13 Joh.   ...Creve-   5 Joh.   fil. Ric. de Vernun.
     quer.

ob. fine prol.

Johanna, ux.   Alicia, ux.
Euftacii de   Tho. de Haye.
Greinvill.

Of this Robert de Arfic (*n*) was the manor of Tunftall pur-chafed by that moft eminent perfon and unfortunate favourite
HUBERT

(*m*) Clauf. 6 Joh. m. 7.

(*n*) This Robert de Arfic married Sibylla daughter of ⸺ Crevequer, and dying left iffue by her two co-heireffes, Johanna afterwards married to Euftace de Greinvill, and Alicia the wife of Thomas de Haye, who 29 Henry III. 1245, paffed away all their intereft in whatfoever de-fcended to them from Robert de Arfic then father, unto Walter de Gray, archbifhop of York. Dugd. Bar. I. 539.

Of

HUBERT DE BURGO, who obtained the king's confirmation thereof to himſelf and Margaret his fourth wiſe, the daughter of William king of Scotland, and their lawfully begotten heirs, September 14, 1227 (*o*).

Ann. 1232. At this time the pope's uſurpations by exactions, proviſions, diſpoſing churches to aliens, and other innovations, became ſo intolerably oppreſſive to the people of England, that a general commotion and oppoſition againſt him and his agents was ſtirred up throughout the kingdom : letters of complaint were every where diſperſed againſt them ; the fermours were prohibited from accounting with the Romans for their rents ; and the biſhops were deterred by incendiary threatenings from interpoſing their authority in their behalf. In conſequence hereof, divers barns of the Romans were broke open, and their corn was either ſold at an eaſy rate, or given to the poor (*p*).

The news of theſe proceedings being carried to Rome, the king, in compliance with the pope's peremptory mandate, iſſued forth writs to the ſheriff of each county, commanding them to enquire diligently after thoſe who had ſeized on the goods, and threſhed out the corn, of the Romans (*q*).

And it appearing that Hubert de Burgo had been an abettor of theſe violences, the king directed his precept to the ſheriffs, requiring them to make livery of the eſtates of Hubert unto

---

Of the poſſeſſions thus granted, the manor of Tunſtall ſhould ſeem to have been part, which, as a certain French record informs us, was in the ſame year, amongſt other things, given by the archbiſhop to his nephew Walter de Gray, ſire de Rotherfeld. Regiſt. Honor. de Richm. p. 60. Upon what authority this aſſertion is grounded, I know not. Certain it is, that Hubert de Burgo had the king's confirmation of this manor previous to this gift of the archbiſhop, and yet equally certain it is, that the ſame king by his charter, dated at Weſtminſter, 12th of June, 29th of his reign, did grant to Walter de Gray, the ſon of Robert de Gray, and nephew of Walter archbiſhop of York, all the right which he then had, or at any time might have, in the manors of Tunſtall and Shepeye. Cart. 29 Henry III. m. 1. a difficulty which I have never yet been enabled to reconcile.

(*o*) Cart. 11 Henry III. p. 2. m. 3.

(*p*) Mat. Par. p. 255. See a fuller account of this matter in Fox's Martyrol. vol. I. p. 311.

(*q*) Clauſ. 18 Henry III. m. 11.

I   Robert

Robert Paſſelewe of Paſſelewe (r), to the end that out of the rents and iſſues thereof, thoſe who had thus ſuffered might have ſatisfaction equal to their reſpective loſſes (s). And purſuant thereto, poſſeſſion of thoſe lands which he had lately purchaſed in Tunſtall was delivered to Paſſelewe for the ſaid purpoſe (t).

The before-mentioned worthy perſon and faithful ſervant to the king, Hubert de Burgo, after variety of ſufferings, ended his days at Banſtede in Surry, 4 id. May, 1243, 27 Henry III. and his corps was honourably interred within the church of the Black-Friers, then ſituated in Holborn, on the back-ſide of Lincoln's-inn ; to which convent he had been a large benefactor, having, amongſt other things, beſtowed on them his palace at Weſtminſter, afterwards purchaſed by the archbiſhop of York, and now called White-hall (u).

JOHN de Burgo, the eldeſt ſon of earl Hubert, doing his homage 27 Henry III. (which was the year wherein his father died) had livery of the lands of his inheritance (x) ; but I believe that Tunſtall was part of the dowry of Margaret his mother, who dying 44 Henry III. this John was found to be her next heir, and of full age upon the 29th of July (y) ; in which year he obtained a charter of free-warren for his manors of Newington and Tunſtall (z).

The ſaid John married Hawiſia, daughter and heir of William de Lanvaley (a). When he died I know not : but he left iſſue

JOHN de Burgo his ſon and heir ; whoſe daughter Margaret marrying Sir STEPHEN DE PENSHERST (b) or PENCHESTER, the famous lord-warden of the cinque-ports, the inheritance of

(r) See Weever, 644. (s) Clauſ. 18 Henry III. m 13. (t) Prynne's Pap. Uſurp. vol II. p 448.
(u) Dugd. bar vol. I p. 699. (x) Rot. Vaſc. 27 Henry III. m. 5.
(y) Eſc. 44 Henry III. n. 14. (z) Cart. 44 Henry III. m. 4.
(a) Dugd. Bar. vol I. p 700.
(b) Dodſw. Collecten. vol. LXI fol. 78, b. ex 10t. eſc. poſt mort. Marg. 2 Edward II.

Tunſtall went with her to him, who, 7 Edward I. 1279, claimed all the uſual privileges for this manor (c), ſo that this Stephen de Pencheſter was the ſon in law, and not father in law, as Mr. Harris from the Dering MSS. aſſerts, p. 284. But Q. whether this Margaret was daughter to the firſt or ſecond John?

PEDIGREE of HUBERT DE BURGO.

Arms: Gules three lozenges Vaire.

Holinſhed's Chron. II, 1072.

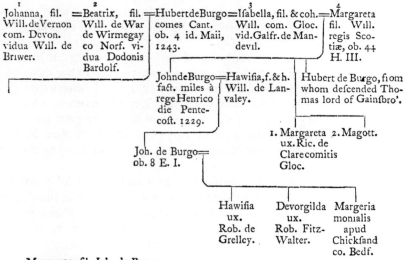

Johanna, fil. = Beatrix, fil. = Hubert de Burgo = Iſabella, fil. & coh. = Margareta
Will. de Vernon   Will. de War   comes Cant.   Will. com. Gloc.   fil. Will.
com. Devon.   de Wirmegay   ob. 4 id. Maii,   vid. Galfr. de Man-   regis Sco-
vidua Will. de   co Norf. vi-   1243.   devil.   tiæ, ob. 44
Briwer.   dua Dodonis   H. III.
      Bardolf.

John de Burgo = Hawiſia, f. & h.   Hubert de Burgo, from
fact. miles à   Will. de Lan-   whom deſcended Tho-
rege Henrico   valey.   mas lord of Gainſbro'.
die Pente-
coſt. 1229.

1. Margareta 2. Magott.
ux. Ric. de
Clare comitis
Gloc.

Joh. de Burgo =
ob. 8 E. I.

Hawiſia   Devorgilda   Margeria
ux.   ux.   monialis
Rob. de   Rob. Fitz-   apud
Grelley.   Walter.   Chickſand
      co. Bedf.

Margareta, fil. Joh. de Burgo maritos habuit primum Steph. de Pencheſter, ſecundum Rob. de Orreby. Eſc. poſt mort. Margar. 2 E. II. ex Dodſw. collectan. vol. LXI. fol. 78,b.

(c) Philip. ut ſupr.

Of

Of this Sir Stephen de Penchefter I have to add, that he
was high fheriff of the county of Kent 53 Henry III.; and that 9
Edward I. he and Margaret his wife had licence from the crown
to embattle their manfion-houfe at Alington in this county (d);
that Penchefter-tower in Dover-caftle was named from him (e);
and that he dying between the 24th and 34th years of king
Edward I. 1301, was buried in the church at Penfhurft, under
a marble monument, whereon the portraiture of a knight compleatly armed is, or was, to be feen.

Upon the death of Sir Stephen de Penchefter, MARGARET his
widow fucceeded to the poffeffion of this place, in which fhe
had an intereft for life by virtue of a demife from Anthony Bek
bifhop of Durham ; who had therein enfeoffed the faid Stephen
and Margaret, to hold to the faid Stephen and Margaret, and the
heirs of the faid Stephen for ever.   But this life eftate deter-
mining upon the death of the lady Penchefter, which happened
2 Edward II. 1309, by an inquifition taken at Tunftall, in craft.
Epiph. Domini 2 Edward II. *Johanna* the wife of Henry de Cobbeham of Rundale and *Alice* the wife of John de Columbariis were
found to be the daughters and next heirs of the faid Stephen, of
whom the former was aged 40 and upwards (f), the latter 30 and
upwards. This inquifition having been executed at this very place,
and with more precifion and greater exactnefs than any which I
have met with relating thereto, I have thought fit to give a copy of
it in the appendix ; the rather, for that I have feen many extracts
from it in the collections of antiquaries, and moft of them
erroneous ; and for this further reafon, that, if my memory fails
me not, the original is much worn, and in fome danger of becoming illegible.

In the 34th year of the reign of king Edward I. a fine was
levied between the faid ALICE late the wife of John de Colum-

---

(d) Quod Stephen de Penchefter et Margareta ux. ejus poffint kernellare domum fua de Alington in com. Kent. Pat. 9 Edward I.

(e) Hift. p. 3/3.   (f) Efc. 2 Ed ard II. n. 66.

bers, querent, and the aforefaid bifhop of Durham, def. of
one moiety of the manor of Tunftall (except 50 acres of land,
1 acre of wood, and xviiid. rent) which Margaret late the wife
of Stephen de Penchefter then held for term of her life, to
remain after her deceafe to the faid Alice and her heirs, by
the fervices thereunto appertaining (*g*). And

The next year another fine was levied between Henry Cobeham and JOHANNA his wife, querents, and the faid bifhop, def.
of the other moiety of this manor (except as is aforementioned),
which Margaret late the wife of Stephen de Penchefter then
held for term of her life, to remain after her deceafe to the faid
Henry and Joan, and the heirs of the faid Joan, under the
fervices thereto belonging (*b*).

The faid Alice died about 7 Edward III; for, 16 cal. June,
1334, Philip de Columbers, knt. and Stephen de Columbers, cl.
the fons and executors of the laft will of the faid Alice, being
perfonally prefent before archbifhop Stratford, in his manor of
Otford, renounced the probate of the will of the faid Alice,
made before the bifhop of Rochefter, as done coram non judice,
the faid Alice having been poffeffed of bona notabilia in different
diocefes; whereupon the archbifhop pronounced the faid will
to be good, and granted Edmund de Polle, an executor named
in the faid will, renouncing the adminiftration to the faid Philip
and Stephen, referving to himfelf a power of doing the like to
Robert de Shipton, the other executor, whenever he fhould think
proper to make requeft for the fame (*i*).

But Alice de Columbers before her death had, as I conceive,
parted with her mediety to her fifter Johanna, and her hufband
Sir Henry de Cobham.

This Henry de Cobham, 12 Edward I. was in the expedition
then made into Wales, on the behalf of the abbot of St. Au-

(*g*) Fin. 34 Edward I.   (*b*) Fin. 35 Edward I.   (*i*) Regift. Alb. in Aichiv. Lamethan. fol. 32. b.

guftin

guftin Cant. and there performed the fervice of one knight, for which he had 20 pounds from the abbot. 14 Edward I. with Joan his wife, he obtained the king's charter for a market every week upon the Thurfday at Groombrigge in Kent; and a fair yearly on the eve-day and morrow after the feaft of St. John ad Port. Lat. 22 Edward I. being then a knight, he was con- ftituted governor of the ifles of Gernefey and Jerefey; and 34 Edward I. made conftable of Dover caftle, and warden of the cinque-ports; and 3 Edward II. had livery of the lands of the inheritance of Joan his wife(*k*); which I therefore fuppofe de- fcended unto her upon the death of Margaret her mother. By his wife Johanna he had iffue

STEPHEN DE COBHAM, who, 34 Edward I. when prince Ed- ward was knighted with bathing and other facred ceremonies, received the like honour with him and many others(*l*). Upon the death of Joan his mother, 18 Edward II. 1325, performing his fealty, he fhared in the lands of her inheritance(*m*); and Tunftall, whether by means of a gift from Alicia his aunt of the mediety which was hers, or otherwife, came undivided to him; and upon an inquifion taken at Alnodynton, the 15th of May, 3 Edward III. 1329, after the death of John de St. John, it was found that this Stephen de Cobham, by the name of Stephen de Cobham, junior, held the manor of Tunftall, with the appurtenances, by the fervices incident to one knight's fee(*n*). He was fummoned to parliament amongft the barons of this realm from 20 Edward II. to 6 Edward III. in which year he died, leaving John his fon and heir, 13 years of age(*o*).

But this family deferting the inheritance, Tunftall became part of the eftate of THOMAS DE BROTHERTON(*p*), earl of Norfolk and marefcal of England; and with MARGARET one of his daughters

(*k*) Dugd. Bar. II. 66. (*l*) Dugd. Bar. II. 71. (*m*) Ibid. (*n*) Efc. 3 Ed. III. p. 1. n. 67.
(*o*) Dugd. ut fupr.   (*p*) Dugd. Bar. II. 64.

and

and coheireſſes went by marriage firſt to JOHN DE SEGRAVE (*q*), and afterwards to Sir WALTER DE MANNY (*r*).

This Walter de Meduana, Maney, or Manny, deſcended from Walter de Meduana (*s*), who in king Henry the third's time held twenty knights fees in this county, was ſummoned as a baron to ſit in parliament from 21 to 44 Edward III (*t*). was with king Edward III. at the ſiege of Calais (*u*), near which place, ſo great truſt did that king repoſe in him, that he and his ſon Edward the black prince fought under his colours in a private habit againſt Monſieur de Charmy, as Daniel tells us in his chronicle.

Sir William Dugdale ſays (*w*), that Sir Walter de Maney held Dunſtaple in Kent, which is certainly a miſtake for Tunſtall, but not in right of his wife.

In the liſt of thoſe of this county who paid aid for making the Black Prince knight, 20 Edw. III, I find " de dnō Waltero " de Menny pro 1 feodo quod Margeria de Penceſtre tenuit in " Tunſtall de Johanne de ſcō Johanne xls. (*x*)"

(*q*) John de Segrave died 27 Ed. III. His widow married Sir W. Manny, 32 Ed. III. She died 22 Rich. II. and was buried at the Grey friars, London. Stowe.

(*r*) Phil. ut ſupr.   (*s*) See Weever, p. 438.

(*t*) Prynne's Abridgm.   (*u*) Militant. ſub Edv. 1° & 3°, p. 93.   (*w*) Baronage, II. p. 150.

(*x*) Dodeſw. vol. 65. fol. 86, a. MS. Warb. p. 19. Manet comput. in ſcac, tranſcript. ejuſd. in MS. Warburton.

PEDIGREE of WALTER DE MEDUANA.

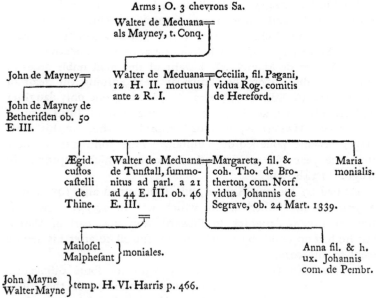

Arms ; O. 3 chevrons Sa.

Walter de Meduana꓿
als Mayney, t. Conq.

John de Mayney꓿

John de Mayney de
Betherifden ob. 50
E. III.

Walter de Meduana꓿Cecilia, fil. Pagani,
12 H. II. mortuus │ vidua Rog. comitis
ante 2 R. I. │ de Hereford.

Ægid.   Walter de Meduana꓿Margareta, fil. &   Maria
cuftos   de Tunftall, fummo-│coh. Tho. de Bro-   monialis.
caftelli   nitus ad parl. a 21 │therton, com. Norf.
de   ad 44 E. III. ob. 46 │vidua Johannis de
Thine.   E. III.   │Segrave, ob. 24 Mart. 1339.
           ꓿

Mailofel ⎫
Malphefant⎬moniales.

John Mayne ⎫
Walter Mayne⎬temp. H. VI. Harris p. 466.

Anna fil. & h.
ux. Johannis
com. de Pembr.

See Weever, p. 432, 433.

The

The next mention I find of Tunftall, is in an obfcure note which I met with in a folio volume of collections made by Nicholas Charles, Lancafter herald, in the library of Queen's college, Oxford. Archiv. F. 18. fol. 186, a.

" Gilb. Champneys and Elizabeth his wife *where* the manor " of Tunftall and 1000 acres of marfh in Elmley, which Sir " Water Manny held for term of his life, &c. dat. 44 Edward " III." the meaning of which I do not at prefent underftand.

Sir Walter de Manny (*x*), knight of the moft noble order of the garter, died upon the Thurfday next enfuing the feaft of St. Hillary, 46 Edward III, 1372 (*y*), leaving one only daughter and heirefs ANN, aged 17, and then the wife of JOHN, fon of LAURENCE HASTINGS, earl of Pembroke, who, by this marriage, became poffeffed of Tunftall. This John was no more than one year old at his father's death, which happened in Auguft, 1348 (*z*).

He had by his lady Ann(*a*), one fon, named alfo JOHN, aged 3 years at his father's death, which was in 1375. His wife was PHILIPPA, daughter to Edward Mortimer, earl of March, but he had no child, by which means the eftate after his demife went to his cozen

Sir EDWARD HASTINGS, knight, who for fome difpleafure taken againft him by the king, was committed to the Fleet, where he died childlefs, and king Richard feized on his eftate, though afterwards REGINALD DE GREY laid claim to it. The title he had to it appears to be this : Reginald de Grey, who was created baron of Ruthin by king Edward I. wedded Elizabeth, daughter of John lord Haftings of Bergavenny (*b*), fifter to

(*x*) The arms of Manny are in one of the church windows. Of the family of Haftings and Grey. Vid. Dugd. Waiw. p. 1024, &c.

(*y*) Dugd. Bar. II. 150..

(*z*) Rot. Efc. 22 E. III. n. 47. See Dodfw. Collectan. vol. V. f. 4. b. and Vincent, p. 419, whofe accounts differ.

(*a*) Qrære why Tunftall fhould come to the daughter of Manny rather than to the daughter fo Segrave, for they each had a daughter by Mary.

(*b*) See Bridges's Northamptonfhire, I. p. 274.

John

John de Haftings, great grandfather to the laft earl Haftings (c); by which means the pofterity of Grey became heirs to the laft John de Haftings, earl of Pembroke; and this Reginald lord Grey of Ruthyn being lineally defcended from the faid Elizabeth was by fome inquifitions found to be his coufin and next heir of the whole blood (d).

The faid Reginald de Grey, together with RICHARD TALBOT, 15 Rich. II. 1392, brought a pleading againft JOHN LE SCROPE, who pretended fome title to the eftate of the fore-mentioned John de Haftings (e), though upon what grounds I know not.

Thefe two, however, refcued Tunftall from collateral claim; and about the beginning of the reign of king Henry IV conveyed it to Sir ROBERT KNOLLYS, knight (f), who with feveral other valiant gentlemen had been knighted about the year 1381, for his fervice in affifting William Walworth, mayor of London againft the rebel Wat Tyler, and enfranchifed alfo a citizen of London (g). He it was who built the bridge at Rochefter over the Medway.

But the intereft of Sir Robert Knolles in Tunftall feems to be of a more early date; for the monks of the Charter houfe, which was founded by Sir Walter de Manny, whom we have already mentioned, exchanged the manor of Pancras with Robert Knolles, for the yearly rent of xl pounds iffuing out of the manor of Dunftall, 4 Rich. II. 1381. I have my intelligence from the laft edition of the Notitia Monaftica, p. 322, col. b. where the author quotes his authority for this, Pat. 4 R. II. p. 1. m. 15. (b)

(c) Dodfw. vol. V. f. 4. b.   (d) Dugd. Bar. I. 578.   (e) Phil. ut fupr.
(f) See Weever, p. 436.   (g) Stowe, p. 87. ed. 1633.
(b) Pat. 4 R. II. m.   Quod Rob. de Knolles mil. & Conftantia ux. ejufd. poffint amortizare priori Carthuf. juxt. Lond. xl¹. annuatim exeunt. de m. fuo de Dunftall in excamb. pro manerio de St. Pancras, in com. Midd.
The purport of this patent follows; "R. concedit quod m. de Pancras cum p'tin. quod Rob de Knolles mil. & Conft. ux. tenent ad term. vit. & quod poft mort. eorum legi debent remanere, remaneant priori & conv. Carth. & fucc. apud Weftm. 18 Oct." Pat. 4 R. II. p. 1. m. 15.

From

From Sir Robert Knolles Tunſtall went by purchaſe to the CROWMERS, and in this knightly family continued for ſeveral generations. As they were ſo long reſident here, even till their name became extinct, and were the greateſt ornaments we can boaſt, I ſhall be more explicit in my account of them.

PEDIGREE of JOHN CROWMER.

Arms: Arg. a chevron engrailed between 3 corniſh choughs proper.

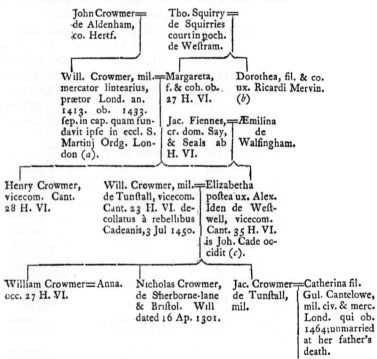

John Crowmer de Aldenham, co. Hertf. = Tho. Squirry de Squirries court in poch. de Weſtram.

Will. Crowmer, mil. mercator lintearius, prætor Lond. an. 1413. ob. 1433. ſep. in cap. quam fundavit ipſe in eccl. S. Martinj Ordg. London (a). = Margareta, f. & coh. ob. 27 H. VI.

Dorothea, fil. & co. ux. Ricardi Mervin. (b)

Jac. Fiennes, cr. dom. Say, & Seals ab H. VI. = Æmilina de Walſingham.

Henry Crowmer, vicecom. Cant. 28 H. VI.

Will. Crowmer, mil. de Tunſtall, vicecom. Cant. 23 H. VI. decollatus à rebellibus Cadeanis, 3 Jul 1450. = Elizabetha poſtea ux. Alex. Iden de Weſt- well, vicecom. Cant. 35 H. VI. is Joh. Cade oc- cidit (c).

William Crowmer = Anna. occ. 27 H. VI.

Nicholas Crowmer, de Sherborne-lane & Briſtol. Will dated 16 Ap. 1301.

Jac. Crowmer de Tunſtall, mil. = Catherina fil. Gul. Cantelowe, mil. civ. & merc. Lond. qui ob. 1464; unmarried at her father's death.

(a) Vid. Dugd. hiſt. of Imbanking, &c. p. 62.   (b) Harr. p. 148.   (c) See extracts from the Prerog. Office, p. 45.

Geo.

Geo. Crowmer,
ep. Armachan.
ob. 16 Mart.
1542-3.

Will. Crowmer=Alicia, fil. unica
de Tunftall, mil. | Will. Haute de
vicecom. Cant. | Hautefborne,mil.
19 H.VII.& 1 H. | qui floruit 13 E.
VIII. ob. 20 Jul. | IV. 1473.
1539, & fep. in
eccl.de Tunftall.

Margareta, ux.
Joh. Rycils de
Æflingham in
Trendefbury,
ob.2 Dec.1596.
& fep. in eccl.
de Tunftall.

Anna, ux.
Will. Whetnall. arm.
de Hextall-court in
E. Peckham, vice-
com. Canc. 18 Hen.
VIII.

Elizabetha 1mo
ux. Ric. Lovelace
de Sittingbourne,
mil. 2do Willielmi
Finch, Cantuarien-
fis, mil. & bar. (d)

Joh. Crowmer, =Johanna, fil.
fepult. apud Sit- | . . . Ifake.
tingbourne 1539.

Bennetta, ux.
Tho. Afhbornham.

Elizabetha, ux.
Hen. Bourn de
Sharfted, re-
núpta Chriftof.
Tucker.

Gracia, ux.
Steph. Ellis.
poftea Nic.
Finch.

Jac. Crowmer=Anna, fil.
de Tunftall, | Edv. Wotton,
arm. ob. 30 | mil.
Maij 1541.

Eliz. ux.
Edv. Tirrell
de Beeches
in Rawreth
co. Eff. arm.

Cath. ux.
Onuphr.
Evias.

Cicilia, ux.
Hen. Iftley,
mil.

Jana, ux.
Rob. Engham.

Sir

Wood's MSS. C. 10. f. 81. b.—In the houfe of Mr. Tho. Whetnell, of E. Peckham, amongft other arms were extant thofe of Crowmer and Whetnall, 1677.

Whetnall's arms were Vert, a bend ermine.

In Sittingbourne church, 1603, were quarterly Crowmer & Squirry impaling quarterly 1 & 4 a faltire cantoning 4 gryphons heads erafed 2 & 3 . . . a chief, over
all a bend engrailed.

Crowmer impaling . . . . on a chevron G. 3 efcocheons Or.

From a MS. in Mr. New's poffeffion, the writer of which fays thefe are the arms
of John Crowmer, of Fulfton, efq. and his two wives Guildeford and Grove.

(d) See their defcendants in Queen's coll. archives, F. 15. pt. 2. f. 22.

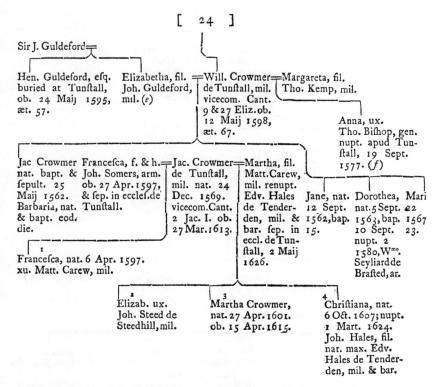

Sir J. Guldeford⹀

Hen. Guldeford, efq. | Elizabetha, fil. ⹀Will. Crowmer⹀Margareta, fil.
buried at Tunftall, | Joh. Guldeford, | de Tunftall, mil. | Tho. Kemp, mil.
ob. 24 Maij 1595, | mil. (*e*) | vicecom. Cant.
æt. 57. | | 9 & 27 Eliz. ob.
| | 12 Maij 1598,
| | æt. 67.

Anna, ux.
Tho. Bifhop, gen.
nupt. apud Tun-
ftall, 19 Sept.
1577. (*f*)

Jac Crowmer Francefca, f. & h.⹀Jac. Crowmer⹀Martha, fil.
nat. bapt. & Joh. Somers, arm. | de Tunftall, | Matt. Carew,
fepult. 25 ob. 27 Apr. 1597, | mil. nat. 24 | mil. renupt.
Maij 1562. & fep. in ecclef. de | Dec. 1569. | Edv. Hales
Barbaria, nat. Tunftall. | vicecom. Cant. | de Tender-
& bapt. eod. | 2 Jac. I. ob. | den, mil. &
die. | 27 Mar. 1613. | bar. fep. in
| | eccl. de Tun-
| | ftall, 2 Maij
| | 1626.

Jane, nat. | Dorothea, | Mari
12 Sept. | nat. 5 Sept. | æ2
1562, bap. | 1563, bap. | 1567
15. | 10 Sept. | 23.
| nupt. 2
| 1580, Wᵐᵒ.
| Seyliard de
| Brafted, ar.

1
Francefca, nat. 6 Apr. 1597.
xu. Matt. Carew, mil.

2
Elizab. ux.
Joh. Steed de
Steedhill, mil.

3
Martha Crowmer,
nat. 27 Apr. 1601.
ob. 15 Apr. 1615.

4
Chriftiana, nat.
6 Oct. 1607; nupt.
1 Mart. 1624.
Joh. Hales, fil.
nat. max. Edv.
Hales de Tender-
den, mil. & bar.

Rob. Crowmer, induct. ad rect. de Vang dioc. Lond. 1496. Newc. II. 613.
Ric. Cromer, ord. Auguftini frat. fact. S. T. P. Oxon. 17 Jun. 1523.
Geo. Cromer, induct. ad rect. Stanford le Hope 19 Julii 1511. Newc. II. 548.
Walt. Cromer, M. D. fuit à med. Hen. VIII. uxor ejus fuit Alicia . . . de quibus vide Newc. I. 727.
. . . . Cromer, fact. D. D. Cantab. 1525. Filiam habuerunt Elizam uxorem Tho. Loveden, de Lamburn, co. Berk.
Dr. . . . . . Cromer, Cantabrigienfis, in carcerem religionis caufa detrufus temp. Mariæ reginæ. Faft. I. 36.
Walter Grime als. Cromer, monk, afterwards prebend of Norwich. Willis Mit. Abb. I. 281.

(*e*) Some account of this family in Weever, p. 235. See Baronetage, vol. IV.   (*f*) See Baronetage, I. 417.

The original of this family is to be fearched for in Hertfordſhire (*i*). At Yardley in that county is a manor called Cromer, which in all probability borrowed its name from its poffeffors before the time of king Henry III. (*k*)

But the firſt of the name whom I have any knowledge of was JOHN CROWMER of Aldenham in Hertfordſhire (*l*), the father of

Sir WILLIAM CROWMER (*m*), knight, citizen and draper of London, ſheriff of the ſaid city, an. 1405, and lord-mayor in the years 1413 and 1423: he was ſworn to execute the office of mayor and likewiſe the office of eſcheater for the city of London, 30 Oct. 2 Henry VI, at the preſentation of William Weldern, mayor, Henry Barton, Robert Taterſhale, and other citizens (*n*). This gentleman purchaſed the manor of Tunſtall of Sir Robert Knolles.

He married Margaret, daughter and heireſs of Thomas Squirry, of Squirries-court in the pariſh of Weſtram in this county (*o*); and dying in the year 1433, was buried under an ancient tomb on the ſouth ſide of the church of St. Martin Ordgar in London, in a chapel of his own foundation (*p*).

Sir William Crowmer by his will, in 1421, gave to the pariſh of St. Martin Ordgar, his houſe or tenement in Sweeting's-lane, and likewiſe his houſes and gardens in Crutched-Friers, for the repairs and ornaments of the ſaid church, and for the uſe of the poor (*q*). He left by his will, which was proved in the prerogative court of Canterbury by Margaret his wife, to the fabric of Tunſtall church xl. to the poor of the pariſh xl. and for amending the bad roads at Tunſtall xxl.

(*ı*) Man. de Cromer, co. Hertf. Vid. Monaſt. vol. I. p. 931, b. Camden's Remains, 1614. p. 113.
(*k*) Chauncey, p. 54.   (*l*) Fuller's Worth. in Hertf. p. 31.
(*m*) See Pat. 1 H. V. at the end of Bale's Proceſs againſt lord Cobham, p. 150. 152.
(*n*) Mich. Preſentat. 2 H. VI. Rot. 1. 6.   (*o*) Viſit. Kent, 1574, p. 136..
(*p*) Stowe, p. 238.   (*q*) Newc. I. 417.

She

She married afterwards Robert lord Poynings, whom she likewise survived, and made her will 18 August, 26 Hen. VI, by the title of Margaret lady Poyning, and directed her body to be buried in the church of St. Martin's Orgar, in the sepulchre where her good husband Crowmer laid: and ordered that a priest should pray for her there for the space of seven years. She made her own son William Crowmer her executor, to whom she gave the residue of all her goods, after bequeathing, amongst other legacies, to William Crowmer, her grandson, one hundred pounds: to her daughter Alianor Poynings ten pounds, and to Thomas Seynt John ten pounds. She died in the year 1448, her will being proved 27th of November in that year (r).

His son and heir WILLIAM Crowmer of Tunstall, esq; succeeded him. He was high sheriff of Kent, 23 Henry VI, 1445, and was beheaded at Mile-End, 3 July, 1450, by Jack Cade and his infamous adherents, because he had married Elizabeth, the only daughter of Sir James Fiennes, lord Say and Sele, whom they had also barbarously massacred in Cheapside. Being thus suddenly deprived of life, Mr. Crowmer died intestate, and the administration of his effects was committed to Sir William Fynes, knight, his brother in law, and Thomas Wynflowe, citizen and draper of London, 18 July, 1450 (s).

Not satisfied with this piece of cruelty, Cade ordered the body of lord Say to be drawn naked through the town into Southwark, and there to be quartered. Whether Sir William was treated in the same manner I do not find : but their heads were both stuck upon poles and carried before Cade through the streets of London; and, out of mockery, were made to kiss each

(r) Reg. Staff. archiep. Cant. fol. 167. a. 172. b.
(s) Reg. Staff. arch. Cant. f. 190. a.

3

other

other at every corner, till they were at laſt fixed upon London bridge (*t*).

Sir William Dugdale ſays (*u*), lord Say's untimely death happened the 4th of July, Sir William Say, knight, his ſon and heir, by Emeline his wife, daughter of . . . . . Cromer, being about that time 24 years of age. For this he quotes Eſc. 29 Hen. VI. n. 29. and H. 12. in Off. Arm. b. 4. a. But of all the accounts which I have hitherto ſeen, this is the only one that ſays lord Say married a daughter of Crowmer. Other pedigrees, and particularly one in Mr. Dodſworth's Collections, vol. LXXXI. f. 23. call his wife Æmelina de Walſingham.

I have ſeen a copy of the will of this lord Say, dated 12 April, 28 Henry VI; in it are mentioned Emelye his wife, Sir William Fenys, his ſon, and Elizabeth, Emelye, and Jane, his daughters; ſo that Sir William Crowmer's lady was the eldeſt, but not the only daughter of Sir James Fiennes (*w*).

He was ſucceeded by his ſon Sir JAMES Crowmer, knight, who by Catherine, daughter of Sir William Cauntelo, knight, citizen and mercer of London, whom I find to have been patron of the church of Murſton, 1472 (*x*): left iſſue Sir William Crowmer his eldeſt ſon (*y*).

Of this lady Crowmer, or ſome other of the family of Cauntelo, there ſeems to be a memorial in the eaſt window of the chancel; I think there are two lines of an inſcription remaining, but when I was laſt at Tunſtall in 1750, I could make nothing ſatisfactory out of it. The arms of Cauntelo, by miſtake, impaling Crowmer, quartering Squirry, are in the eaſt win-

(*t*) Weever, p. 279. (*u*) Bar. vol. II. p. 246. (*w*) MSS. Aſhm. 831. 18.
(*x*) Regiſt. Bourchier arch. Cant. f. 106. b.
(*y*) Viſit. ut ſupr. Reg. Milles in Off. Prerog. Cant. f. 214. a.

dow

dow of the north ifle, from which we conclude, that Sir James Crowmer, or his lady, or both, had fepulture here.

Whether Henry Crowmer, of Tunftall, as Fuller puts him down, who was fheriff of this county 21 Henry VI, were a younger brother to this Sir James, as according to the order of time one may not unreafonably fuppofe, or in what other degree of relationfhip he ftood with thefe whom we are now treating of, I have not yet difcovered.

Sir WILLIAM Crowmer, knight, eldeft fon of Sir James Crowmer, bore the office of high fheriff for this county, 19 Henry VII, and 1 Henry VIII, 1504 and 1509; and dying 20th of July, 1539, was buried in the parifh church of Tunftall, where his arms are ftill to be feen in the painted windows (z).

His wife was Alicia the only daughter of Sir William Haut, of Hautefborne, knight, of whom I can fay no more at prefent than that her arms, impaled with her hufband's, are to be feen in the church windows; and that if fhe was buried here, as I fuppofe fhe was, her death happened before her hufband's; for the parifh regifter, which is a very exact one, takes no notice of it.

Sir William Crowmer laft mentioned had two brothers, George Crowmer, rector of Murfton in this county, a living formerly in the patronage of the family: this he refigned in the year 1513 (a), and was afterwards confecrated bifhop of Armach in April 1522 (b), and John Crowmer, who with Johanna Ifake, his wife, was buried in Sittingbourne church, 1539 (c).

He had alfo three fifters, of whom Margaret was wife of John Rycils, and was buried here in the chancel: fhe dying Dec.

(z) Pronus eccl. de Murfton 1528. Wafh. 396, a.
(a) Philipot, p. 343. Vifitat. ut fupr. Ware, p. 25, in which laft author fee more of him.
(b) Reg. Waltham, f. 348, b.   (c) Weever, p. 279.

I

1496, as an infcription on brafs, copied by Weever but imperfectly, informs me.

JAMES Crowmer of Tunftall, efq. only fon of Sir William Crowmer, married Anne, daughter of Edward Wotton. He dyed 30 Maij, 1541, and was buried amongft his anceftors, leaving one only child (then of the age of 10 years) Sir William Crowmer of Tunftall, knight, high fheriff of Kent 9 and 27 Elizabeth (d). He was a party in the infurrection raifed in this county by Sir Thomas Wyatt againft the intended marriage of queen Mary with the king of Spain; and 11th February, 1554, was upon that account, together with certain others, committed prifoner to the Tower (e); and by means of his attainder, the manor of Tunftall and all other his poffeffions were forfeited to the crown (f). He was in the commiffion for the peace 17th February, 1596 (g). This Sir William was twice married; 1ft to Margaret, daughter of Sir Thomas Kemp, knight, afterwards at Bocton Malherbe to Elizabeth, daughter of Sir John Guildford, knight, October 1, 1561 (h). He died 12th Maij, anno Domini 1598, ætat 67. By his firft venter he had only one daughter, married 19 Sept. 1577, to Thomas Bifhop, gent. but by his fecond he was father of his only furviving fon

Sir JAMES Crowmer of Tunftall, knight, born 24th December, 1569, high-fheriff of this county, 2 Jac. I, 1604, and diftinguifhed in the regifter of archbifhop Abbot, by the appellation of *ftrenuus nuper dominus Jac. Crowmer, mil.* (i). He married two wives, Frances, daughter and heir of John Somers, efq. who died in childbed 27th April, 1597; by her he had one

(d) Pron. eccl. de Mufton, 1561. Parker, I, 350, b.
(e) Stowe's Annals, p. 622. (f) ; p. 01. 1 and 2 Ph and M. 10t. 19.
(g) Lambard's Peramb. p. 33. (h) Reg. de Tunft. (i) Tom. I. fol. 411. a.

daughter

daughter named Frances, born 6th April, 1597, afterwards the wife of Sir Matthew Carew, knight.

His second lady was Martha, daughter of Sir Matthew Carew, knight, who being left a widow was remarried to Sir EDWARD HALES of Tenterden, knight, and was here buried 11th Maij, 1626. By her he had three more daughters, Elizabeth, wife to Sir John Steed, of Steed-Hill, knight, whose son I suppose was Crowmer Steed, esq. whom being in his minority, and in the wardship of the crown, king Charles the First presented to the church of Murston, 19th February, 1630(*k*): Martha, born 27th April, 1601, and Christian born 6th October, 1697.

Thus ended this noble family, Sir James dying 27th Martij, 1613, two hundred years from their first settlement here; and in him, I used to think, that the name of Crowmer had been extinguished; but I read that George Cromer of London, who had issue male, died 20th June, 1631, aged 79, and was buried at Oakham in Surry(*l*).

As for the two daughters of Sir James Crowmer, Martha and Christian; the former dyed unmarried 14th April, 1615, and is complimented in the parish register with the title of Πότνα γυναικῶν. Christian was married 1 Mart. 1624, to JOHN, eldest son of Sir Edward Hales, then of Tenterden in this county, knight and baronet, (which said Sir Edward married the widow of Sir James Crowmer) by Deborah only daughter and heiress of Walter Harlakenden, of Woodchurch, esq. and by this match was Tunstall added to the possessions of the Hales's.

In a chapel on the south side of the chancel is a sumptuous monument of Sir James Crowmer, and, which is something remarkable, the only one of this family to be seen in the church except a small plate of brass which I have before taken notice

(*k*) Reg Abbott, 3. b. 193, a.   (*l*) Aubrey vol. III, p. 244.

of.

of. Indeed there are three large ftones which have been fhamefully robbed of their brafs plates; and thefe might belong to the Crowmers though I cannot affirm that they did. The monument I am fpeaking of exhibits the ftatues of Sir James and lady Martha Crowmer praying before an altar, and of the four daughters in the fame attitude; the infcriptions are pretty long, and as they are to be met with elfewhere I fhall here omit them.

The manfion houfe of the Crowmers is not now in being; it was fituated about a quarter of a mile from the church fouthwards, a little beyond a large meadow named the Shooters Meadow. I am told that it was begun to be rebuilt by Sir James Crowmer juft before his death; that after his death the materials were purchafed by Sir Robert Vyner, and carried to London; and that his dwelling-houfe in Lombard-ftreet, now the general poft-office, was built with them.

The ancient habitation of the Crowmers was at Grove-end: Sir James removed it to the place here mentioned as a better fituation; but his magnificent feat was never finifhed. The ruinated houfe at the bottom of the ftreet was built for Sir Edward Hales about 1655, by Mr. John Grove, his fteward. This is the houfe which Philipot, p. 343, calls a fabric of that ftupendous magnificence that it at once obliges the eye to admiration and delight. This houfe, however, muft have been built fooner than 1655. Sir Edward Hales died 1654. Philipot, I think, fays it was building when he wrote, which was about the year 1635; he was making collections in the year 1633: but after all it may be queftioned whether this is really the houfe which Philipot meant; it certainly does not deferve the character he gives of it.

The fcite of the manfion-houfe is to this day called The Ruins. The foundations which may eafily be traced, fhew the building to have been of a large extent: befides the bare foundations

dations there is nothing remaining but a capacious vaulted cellar, not long fince a receptacle for beggars and other diforderly perfons who reforted here to the great annoyance of the neighbours, and committed fome robberies hereabouts.

Amongft thefe was one Peter . . . . . . a bricklayer's labourer, a tall raw-boned Irifhman, who, not long before the fact I am going to mention, had been employed in fome work at my father's houfe. This man affaulted a perfon of one of the neighbouring villages as he was returning home by night, and took from him feveral little matters, which though of no great value, yet being found upon him ferved to give us fome light into the occafion of his death.

The day after the robbery, while he was in the adjacent barn called the Ruins Barn, waiting for a bundle of ftraw which James Speer (a Scotchman born at Merrymore in the fhire of Air) the thrafher was making up for him, the conftable of the hundred, with his attendants, arrived at the cellar in order to difperfe the vagrants who had fettled there, which he feeing, and, as was fuppofed, imagining their bufinefs was with him upon account of the robbery, retired in great hafte to the then uninhabited feat of Sir John Hales, where a few days after he was difcovered by one Thomas Love, a young lad of this parifh, hanging upon a ftaple of one of the chamber doors, in fuch manner that great part of his body lay upon the floor. His knife and fhoes were found in the window at the further end of the room. The jury bringing in their verdict felf-murder, he was buried in the road before the faid houfe under the hedge on the right hand as we go towards the tenement now the widow Love's.

I mention this affair that if in after-times this fellow's bones fhall chance to be difcovered, the inhabitants may account for it without the affiftance of a murder or fome other wonderful tale, which upon fuch occafions the common people are fo apt to feign.

At

At a little diftance from The Ruins is a fmall coppice, or as we call it a fhave, where, in January, 1738, feveral hundred broad pieces of gold were dug up. The boy before-mentioned, Thomas Love, led the way to this difcovery; for, turning afide as he was going on an errand, he perceived four or five of thefe pieces lying upon the ground, which he took away with him; but not knowing what they were, and carelefsly playing with them at Daniel Wood's, a farmer at Highftall foreftall, Wood got knowledge of the place where they were found; and going thither made himfelf mafter of a very handfome treafure; but not being able to keep the fecret he refunded 624 of the broad pieces for the ufe of the crown, though Sir John Hales claimed the whole, it being thought that his anceftor had concealed them there during the civil wars.

Mrs. Tyfoe, mother-in-law to the rev. Mr. Tyfoe, vicar of Bredgar, was vifiting at Sir Edward's houfe, when they were concealed, and very well remembered the hiding of them; it was immediately after the defeat at Maidftone. She faid alfo that a large parcel of jewels were depofited in the fame fhave, then called the Gafcoyne walk; I fuppofe from cherry-trees of that name which might grow there. Upon the credit of Mrs. Tyfoe's account thefe jewels have been often fearched for, but hitherto without fuccefs.

I come now to fpeak of the Hales, prefent lords of Tunftall, a family of great antiquity; but as their intereft here is not of fo long ftanding, I fhall go no higher that the laft century, beginning with

F

Sir

Sir EDWARD HALES, knight, who was advanced to the dignity of a baronet 1611; he ferved in feveral parliaments, and took part with thofe that raifed the rebellion againſt king Charles I. He died October 6th, 1634, aged 78 (*m*). This is he for whom the noble monument in Tunſtall church was erected with his effigies in full proportion cut in marble. His wives were *Deborah*, daughter and heir of Martin Harlackenden of Woodchurch, efq. and *Martha* the relict of Sir James Crowmer.

JOHN, the eldeſt fon of Sir Edward, by Deborah his firſt lady, married Chriſtian, the youngeſt of the daughters and coheirs of Sir James Crowmer aforefaid; and by this marriage was Tunſtall brought into the family of Hales. This John died in the life-time of his father, and left iſſue

Sir EDWARD Hales, baronet, a zealous royaliſt, who in his younger years rifqued his perfon and fortune in the caufe, infomuch that he was forced to abfcond and live beyond the feas on account of the great debts he had contracted for the king's fervice. He died in France fome years after the Reſtoration, and left iſſue by his lady *Anne* one of the daughters and coheirs of Thomas lord Wotton of Bocton Malherbe

Sir EDWARD Hales, baronet, his fon and heir, who was a great favourite with king James II, and was by him created earl of Tenterden. He died in France, and was buried in the church of St. Sulpice in Paris, 1695. He married *Frances* daughter of Sir Francis Windibank of Oxfordſhire, knight, and had iſſue five fons and feven daughters. Of thefe

---

(*m*) See the ep. ded. to Powell's Tom of all Trades. Lond. 1631. 4to.

Sir

Sir JOHN Hales, baronet, married two wives, by the former, *Hellen* daughter of Sir Richard Bealing of the kingdom of Ireland, fecretary to the queen-dowager of king Charles II, he had iffue

EDWARD Hales, efq. who never enjoyed either the title or eftate, but died in prifon during the life-time of his father (*n*). He married the relict of Capt. Bulftrode, and left iffue only one fon

Sir EDWARD Hales, bart. born at Sutton-Barn in Borden parifh, but educated in France, where he refided till he fucceeded to the title and eftate of his grand-father; who as he had lived fo he died in an unaccountable manner (nobody knows when), and was buried amongft his anceftors at Tunftall 20th January, 1744.

(*n*) Purfuant to an order of the high court of chancery, the creditors of Edward Hales, late of St. Stephen's, near Canterbury, efquire, deceafed, mentioned in a report of James Lightbourn, efq. deceafed, late one of the mafters of the faid court, dated the 7th of September, 1734, or their reprefentatives, are peremptorily to come in and claim their debts before Edmund Sawyer, efq. one of the mafters of the faid court, at his chambers in Lincoln's-Inn, London, on or before the 11th day of July next. Further information may be had of Meff. Anthony and Thomas Benn, attoinies, in Pudding-lane. Daily Advertifer, May 31, 1753.

PEDI-

PEDIGREE of EDWARD HALES.

Arms; G. 3 arrows paleways Argent headed Or.

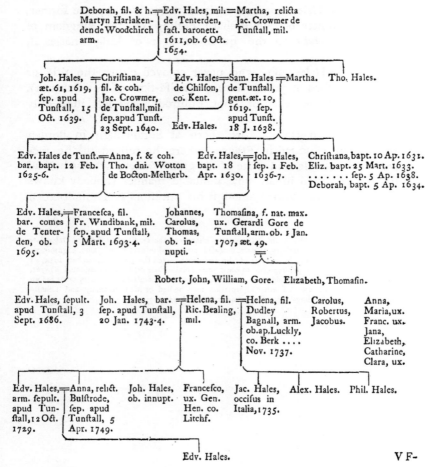

Deborah, fil. & h.=Edv. Hales, mil.=Martha, relicta
Martyn Harlaken- | de Tenterden, | Jac. Crowmer de
den de Woodchirch | fact. baronett. | Tunstall, mil.
arm. | 1611, ob. 6 Oct.
| 1654.

Joh. Hales, =Christiana,   Edv. Hales=Sam. Hales =Martha.   Tho. Hales.
æt. 61, 1619, | fil. & coh.   de Chilson, | de Tunstall,
sep. apud | Jac. Crowmer,   co. Kent. | gent. æt. 10,
Tunstall, 15 | de Tunstall, mil. | 1619. sep.
Oct. 1639. | sep. apud Tunst.   Edv. Hales. | apud Tunst.
| 23 Sept. 1640. | 18 J. 1638.

Edv. Hales de Tunst.=Anna, f. & coh.   Edv. Hales,=Joh. Hales,   Christiana, bapt. 10 Ap. 1631.
bar. bapt. 12 Feb. | Tho. dni. Wotton   bapt. 18 | sep. 1 Feb.   Eliz. bapt. 25 Mart. 1633.
1625-6. | de Bocton-Melherb.   Apr. 1630. | 1636-7.   . . . . sep. 5 Ap. 1638.
                                       Deborah, bapt. 5 Ap. 1634.

Edv. Hales,=Francesca, fil.   Johannes,   Thomasina, f. nat. max.
bar. comes | Fr. Windibank, mil.   Carolus,   ux. Gerardi Gore de
de Tenter- | sep. apud Tunstall,   Thomas,   Tunstall, arm. ob. 1 Jan.
den, ob. | 5 Mart. 1693-4.   ob. in-   1707, æt. 49.
1695.   nupti.

Robert, John, William, Gore.   Elizabeth, Thomasin.

Edv. Hales, sepult.   Joh. Hales, bar. =Helena, fil. =Helena, fil.   Carolus,   Anna,
apud Tunstall, 3   sep. apud Tunstall, | Ric. Bealing, | Dudley   Robertus,   Maria, ux.
Sept. 1686.   20 Jan. 1743-4. | mil. | Bagnall, arm.   Jacobus.   Franc. ux.
                                          ob. ap. Luckly,   Jana,
                                           co. Berk . . . .   Elizabeth,
                                           Nov. 1737.   Catharine,
                                                         Clara, ux.

Edv. Hales,=Anna, relict.   Joh. Hales,   Francesco,   Jac. Hales,   Alex. Hales.   Phil. Hales.
arm. sepult. | Bulstrode,   ob. innupt.   ux. Gen.   occisus in
apud Tun- | sep. apud   Hen. co.   Italia, 1735.
stall, 12 Oct. | Tunstall, 5   Litchf.
1729.   Apr. 1749.

Edv. Hales.

V F-

V F T O N

Is a place of repute feated in this parifh, and was once part of the SHURLANDS, with whom it continued till by an heir general of that name, ALICIA only daughter of Sir Robert de Shurland, who was made a knight banneret by king Edward I. at the fiege of Carlaverock; it was carried in marriage to Sir WILLIAM DE CHEYNEY, whofe father alfo had been knighted at Carlaverock.

WILLIAM de Cafineto or Cheney, eldeft fon of William before-mentioned, died poffeffed of Vfton 8 Edward III, and was fucceeded in the poffeffion by ROBERT Cheyney his brother and heir, then of the age of 30 years. This Robert died 36 Edw. III, leaving his fon RICHARD Cheyney 10 years old; which Richard marrying afterwards MARGARET the daughter and coheirefs of Robert Crall had iffue by her *William* and *Simon* Cheyney. Of thefe two SIMON Cheyney, as I take it, poffeffed Vfton. His fon and heir JOHN Cheyney of Sittingbourne, efq. had one only daughter named FRANCES, the wife of John Aftley, efq. In this eminent family it remained for many defcents, till at length Frances the daughter and heirefs of John Cheyney of Sittingbourne, efq. added it to the eftate of her hufband John Aftley, of Hill-Morton and Melton-Conftable, efq. where it ftayed but a very fhort time; for their daughter BRIDGET wedding Walter, fon of Thomas Harlakenden of Woodchurch, efq. it went with her to him. She was buried in Tunftall church 28th June, 1569.

William Maries, who was fheriff of this county 21 Henry VI. held his fhrievalty here (o).

(o) Harr. p. 428. See Weever, p. 280.

PEDI-

PEDIGREE OF WILLIAM DE CHEYNEY.

Arms; Az. fix lions rampant, Argent a canton Erm. Fuller. Thefe were the arms of *Shurland* and without the canton of *Leybourne*.

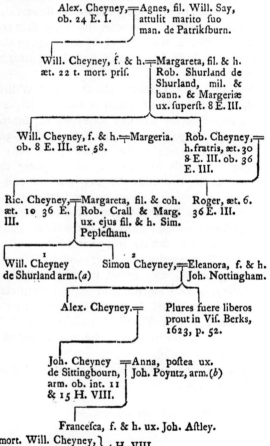

Alex. Cheyney,＝Agnes, fil. Will. Say,
ob. 24 E. I. | attulit marito fuo
man. de Patrikfburn.

Will. Cheyney, f. & h.＝Margareta, fil. & h.
æt. 22 t. mort. prif. | Rob. Shurland de
Shurland, mil. &
bann. & Margeriæ
ux. fuperft. 8 E. III.

Will. Cheyney, f. & h.＝Margeria.   Rob. Cheyney,＝
ob. 8 E. III. æt. 58.   h. fratris, æt. 30
8 E. III. ob. 36
E. III.

Ric. Cheyney,＝Margareta, fil. & coh.   Roger, æt. 6.
æt. 10 36 E. | Rob. Crall & Marg.   36 E. III.
III. | ux. ejus fil. & h. Sim.
Peplefham.

    1   2
Will. Cheyney   Simon Cheyney,＝Eleanora, f. & h.
de Shurland arm. (a)   Joh. Nottingham.

Alex. Cheyney.＝   Plures fuere liberos
prout in Vif. Berks,
1623, p. 52.

Joh. Cheyney ＝Anna, poftea ux.
de Sittingbourn, | Joh. Poyntz, arm. (b)
arm. ob. int. 11
& 15 H. VIII.

Francefca, f. & h. ux. Joh. Aftley.

Inq. poft mort. Will. Cheyney, } 4 H. VIII.
Inq. poft mort. Rog. Cheyney, }

(a) Hence the Cheyneys of Woodhey co. Berk. & lord Cheyney.   (b) Vid. lib. Intrat. f. 232. b. edit 1546.

PEDIGREE of WALTER HARLAKENDEN.

Arms; Az. a fefs Erm. between 3 lions heads erafed Or.

Bridgida, f. & h. ═Walt. Harlakenden═Sufanna,
Joh. Aftley de   de Vfton, arm.   ob. 26
Melton Conftable,   Maij,
fep. apud Tunft.   1587.
28 Jun. 1569.

Henr. bapt.   Eliz. bapt. 7   Walt. Herlakenden,   Joh. Harlakenden,
19 Mart.   Dec. 1578,   bapt. 21 Apr. 1577.   nat. 12 Sept. 1583.
1574-5, fep.   nupt. 22 Feb.
18 Oct. 1601.   1602, Thomæ
          Awdley.

Zach. Harlakenden,═Margareta,   Jonath. Harlakenden,   Sarah, bapt.
nat. 3 Mart. 1565,   ob. 3 Oct.   nat. 29 Maij, 1568.   28 Maij,
ob. 26 Sept. 1603.   1603.   1580.

Walt. Harlakenden,   Dorothea,   Mich. bapt.   Anna, nat.
bapt. 26 Sept. 1602.   nat. 3 Maij,   17 Jun. 1581.   2 Dec. 1581,
                  1567, ob.   fep. 3 Dec.   fep. 13 Aug.
                  in cunis.   1590.   1603.

Walt. Harlakenden.═Jana, fil. Tho. Prude   Sufanna, nat.
                  de Waltham, co. Kent.   2 Dec. 1586.
                                    ob. in cunis.

Silvefter Harlakenden═Elizabetha,
de Vfton, ob. 19 Mart.   fil. Tho. . . .
1659, æt. 54.

Will. Harlakenden,   Sil. Harlakenden,═Elizab.   John bapt.   Rebecca, bapt.
bapt. 19 Aug. 1640.   bapt. 30 Dec. 1641.   Dec. . . .   24 Maij, 1646.
ob. infans.   ob. 22 Jan. 1678.   1647.   Maria bapt. 9 Nov. 1649,
                                     James bapt.   ob. 22 Maij, 1659.
                                     10 Feb.   Martha, bapt. 3 Dec.
                                     1652-3.   1650, ob. inf.
                                     ob. inf.   Sara. bapt. 26 Oct. 1654,
                                             ob. inf.

Thomas, fep.   Sil. Harlakenden,   Joel Harlakenden, bapt.
10 Dec. 1674.   bapt. 13 Jun. 1676.   10 Feb. 1678-9, ob. inf.

Jane Burftone, daughter to Mrs. Harlakenden, buried at   Sar. Harlakenden, buried 14 Jan. 1633.
Tunft. 24 Jan. 1599.   A child of Rog Harlakenden buried 21 Sept. 1639.
Tho. Harlakenden, bapt. 4 Maij, 1606.

PEDIGREE of HENRY CLIFFORD.

Henry Clifford,=Jana Harlakenden.
arm. nupt. 2ɔ
Dec. 1587.

Walt. Clifford,	Joh. Clifford,	Ursula, nat. 26 Nov.
nat. 19 Sept.	fepult. 22	1588, fepult. 21
1590, ob. inf.	Sept. 1603.	Sept. 1603.

G O R E - C O U R T.

This was anciently the feat of a family whofe name was
at-Gore, and in old court rolls frequently *de la Gore*. *John* atte-
Gore, as I judge, owned this place 2 Edward II, and *Henry* at-
Gore died poffeffed of it 31 Edward III, as Mr. Philipot informs
us; but I have not feen any record which countenances fuch
affertion It ftaid in this name for feveral generations; but
at laft *James* Gore fold it to *Thomas Royden* of Eaft Peckham;
and his fon parted with it the fame way to Mr. *Chriftopher Wood*,
and his grandfon was the poffeffor of it in Philipot's time.

So far the Kentifh writers.

PEDIGREE of GERARD GORE.

Gerard Gore =Thomafina, f. nat. max.
de Tunft. arm. | Edv. Hales, ob. Jan.
1707, æt. 49.

Rob. Gore.	Joh. Gore.	Will. Gore.	Elizabeth, buried here 12 Apr. 1717.
			Thomafina, buried here 19 Dec. 1746.

Will. de la Gore, 44 H. III. Prynne, III, 116.

Will. atte Gore, official. archiep. Cant. 45 H. III. Ib. 119. b.

Mr. Will. de la Gore, prebend. in eccl. de Nonington, 25 E. I. Prynne, III, 716.

Tho. atte Gore. Efc. 30 E. I. n. 19. Monaft. I. 289. b.

Hen. de Gore, 31 E. 3. Harr. p. 145.

Walt. Gore, 12 H. VI. Fuller.

Will. Gore buried at Tunftall, 27 Apr. 1558. Reg.

Reginald panetarius & fratres fui petunt verfus Alured de la Gore & Sibyllam ux.
ejus dim. carucat. terre cum ptin. in Sevenoch. Plac. 2 Joh. de diverf. terminis, rot. 9.

5

Indeed

Indeed I am apt to fufpect that Mr. Philipot may be miftaken here, who feeing in an index at the Tower a reference to an inquifition of this date, took it for granted that the fame was an inquifition taken upon the death of Henry atte Gore, and concluded that he muft have died fo feifed; but in truth the record referred to is no more than a return to a writ of inquifition *ad quod dam.* wherein the jury certify, that it is not to the damage of the king or any other perfon if licence be granted for this Henry atte Gore to enfeoff Henry Willy, chaplain, in 28 acres of land lying in Sydingbourne, and held of the king in capite, and for the faid Henry Willy after plenary feifin thereof obtained to refeoff the faid Henry atte Gore and Alice his wife in the faid lands to hold to them and to the heirs of the faid Henry for ever. This return further fets forth, that the faid land was held of the king in capite by the fervice of a 66th part of one knight's fee: that its true value was ix' iiij^d at iiij the acre; that the faid Henry atte Gore had befides one meffuage and fourfcore acres of land in Sydingbourne which were held of queen Philippa as of her manor of Milton, in gavelkind by the fervice of 30^s per aanum, that the true yearly value of this meffuage was 3^s 4^d and of the fourfcore acres of land xl^s at 6^d the acre.

This inquifition was taken at Milton the Thurfday after the feaft of S. Barnabas, 31 Edward I. (*p*).

Robert atte Gore of Tunftall, by deed(*q*) dated at Sydingbourne, ult. May 5, Richard II, 1382, conveys to Thomas atte Sherche

(*p*) Bund. Efcaet. 31 E. III. p. 2. n. 8.

(*q*) Chart. Mifcellan vol. X. nu. 122. in biblioth. Lamethana.

Sciant prefentes & fut. quod ego Rob. atte Gore de Tunftalle dedi, conceffi & hac prefenti carta m̃ confirmavi Tho. atte Sherche & Johæ ux. de Sydingbourne 7 acr. terr. ad ' in. fuis jac. in poch. de Sydingbourne in campo voc. Fogeeleftonesfelde inter terr. n Huffy verfus fouth weft & north & regiam fhatam vocat. Chiltoneftret verfus eaft. hend. & tenend. p̃dc̃as 7 acr. terr. cum fepib & ōib. alijs ptin. fuis p̃dc̃is Tho. atte Shche & Johæ. ux. ej h. & aff. ipĩus Tho. jure ħeditar. in ppet. de capitalib. d̃nis ipi feodi p fervicia inde d̃c. p ann. debita & de jure confueta. & ego p̃dc̃us Rob. & h. mei warantizabimus p̃dc̃as 7 acr. terr. cum fepib. & ōib. alijs ptin. fuis p̃dc̃is Tho. atte

G   S.

Sherche of Sydingbourne and Joan his wife, and the heirs and
affigns of the faid Thomas, 7 acres of land lying in Sydingbourne, in a field called Fogheleftonesfeld, between the land of
Henry Huffy towards the fouth weft and north, and abutting
upon the king's ftreet called Chiltone-ftreet towards the eaft.

21 Dec. 1674. Chriftopher Wood, of Canterbury, fon of
Matthew Wood, transferred the property of this manor to *Charles
Segar* of Tunftall, who dying in June or July, 1679, left iffue
three fons and one daughter. Of thefe Henry died; and *Wil-
liam* parting with his fhare to the elder fon *Charles* Segar of
Borden, this manor of Gore with all its rights, members, and
appurtenances, was by him and his fifter Jane Netherfole of
Barham in this county, widow, conveyed to the rev. *Edward
Mores*, clerk, rector of this parifh 11th October, 1723, and his
fon *Edward Rowe* Mores is the prefent owner.

P I S T O C K.

A fmall manor placed by the Kentifh writers in Rodmerfham
parifh, though it is in this parifh was anciently part of the revenues of the nunnery of Minfter in the ifle of Shepey; who
gave it them I know not. It was 29 Henry VIII. granted to Sir
Thomas Cheyney; but his extravagant fon *Henry* lord Cheyney,
alienated it 13 Elizabeth to *Richard Thornhill*, efq. who, on his
deceafe, gave it to his fecond fon Sir *John* Thornhill, and his
defcendant and heir *Charles* Thornhill, efq. was the poffeffor in
Philipot's time.

S. & Joh. vx. ej. h. aff. ipi. Tho. contra ões gentes in ppet. In cuj. rei teft. pfenti
cartæ fig. meum appofui. Dat. apud Sydingbourne ult. die menf. Maij anno regni
regis Rici fecdi poft conq. His teft.

> Hen. Huffy,
> Ric. atte Gore,
> Hug. de Merftone,
> Simon Mahew,
> Ric. Bakere,
> Laur. de Dene,
> Joh. atte Lee,
> Joh. Toghe, & alijs.

THE

The South West Prospect of the Parish Church of Tunstall in the County of Kent.

THE CHURCH

is built of flint, and, as the generality of churches in this county are, is a neat building; it confifts of a body, two fide iffes,
and a chancel; there is alfo a chapel on the fouth fide of the
chancel, at the weft end is a tower, and therein a pretty ring of
bells, five in number, the oldeft of which was caft in 1573. It
is in the deanry of Sittingbourne and diocefe of Canterbury, and
is dedicated to St. John the Baptift.

Of its antiquity I can fay nothing with certainty. Honorius,
archbifhop of this fee, firft ordained parifhes; and as we may
fuppofe he was particularly careful of his own diocefe, fo we
may perhaps, with fome fmall appearance of truth imagine,
that Tunftall had a church fo early as in his time, though the
prefent building is by no means to be thought of this antiquity,
or indeed any older than the well-known remarkable period of
church-building in England.

The patrons of the church were formerly the lords of the
manor, who alfo were frequently the founders of our parochial
churches; one of thefe, Hubert de Burgo, gave the patronage of
Tunftall to the archbifhop of Canterbury, Richard Wetherfide,
and his fucceffors for ever *(r)*. This donation was confirmed by
king

(r) Ex cartular' archiepi Cant' in Bibl. Bodl. int' MSS. Tann. n° 223, fol. 86, b.
" Oïb' sce mris ecclie filijs ad quos pfens carta pvenerit Hubertus de Bergo com'
Kanc' falm in Dño. Noverit univerfitas vra nos dediffe, conceffiffe, & hac pfenti carta
nra confirmaffe venabili patri dño Ric' Dej gra Canc' archiepo in libam, pura, & ppet'
eleemofynam advocacoe ecclie de Tunftall cu ptin' hend' & tenend eid dno archiepo
& fucc' fuis archiep' Cant' libe, quiete, & integre cu oïb' ad dcam advocacoem ptin'
et nos et hedes nri advocacom illa cu ptin' pdco dno archiep' & fucc' fuis archiep'
Cant' warantizabimus in ppet' & ut hec nra donaco rata & ftabilis in ppet' pfevet'
pfens fcriptu figilli nri munimine duxim' roborand: Hijs teft', dñis

J. Lin-

king Henry III. by charter dated at Weſtminſter, Oct. 9, anno
1229, regn. 13ᵐᵒ; a copy of· both theſe writings is here inſerted
from the cartulary of the archbiſhop of Canterbury, amongſt
biſhop Tanner's MSS. in the Bodleian library *(s)*.

In the taxation of ecclefiaſtical benefices made by the order of
Pope Nicholas VI, 20 Edward I, *(t)* Tunſtall is thus rated :

Eccleſia de Tunſtall, xxxv marc.

At the time of archdeacon Harpsfield's viſitation 1557 *(u)*,
the ſtate of Tunſtall was as follows :.

J. Lincoln.		Steph. de Segrave ⎱ mil..
H. Bathon..		Bertr. de Crioll ⎰
R. Ciceſtr.	epis.	Ranulph Butone.
A. Cov. & Lich.		Gilſo Butone & mult' alijs."
H. Roff.		
R. Lond,		

N. B. In the original charter, which is in the library of MSS. at Lambeth in
Cart. Miſcellan. vol. II. Nº 50, the two firſt witneſſes were, J. Bathon, H. Linc.
the two laſt, Ranulf Britone, Guil. Britone. In cæteris concordat cum nͬo tranſ-
cripto Nov. 13, 1754. The ſeal, which was of green wax, is loſt from the original ;
but a cord of red ſilk to which it was appendant yet remains. On the back of the
original, in an old hand, this number in a later hand, " in the parchment book,
fol. 5, & fol. 45."

(s) Ex cartular' archiep̄i Cant. int' MSS. Tann. f. 79, a.
" Hen. Dei gͬa rex Angl' dn̄s Hib' dux Norman' & Aquit' com' Andeg', archieꝑis, eꝑīs,
abb', priorib', com', baron', juſtic', foreſtarijs, vicec', ꝑpoſitis, miniſtris, ballivis, & oīb'
fidelib' ſuis ſalͫm. Sciatis nos conceſſiſſe & ꝑ'enti cart' n̄ra firmaſſe veɳabilɪ io Xꝑopatri
Ricͦ ead' gͬa Cantuar' archiep̄o ecclɪa de Tunſtall cū oīb' ad eam ecclɪa ptɪn' q̄ɪ ɧet ex
dono dileꞓi & fidelis n̄ri Hub' de Burgo com' Canc' ſicut carta ejuſd' Hub' racͦnabi-
liter teſtatur; quare volumus & firmiter ꝑcɪpim' q̄d ꝑdͨus archiep' & ſuccᷓ ſui aɪchieꝑi
Cant' ɧeant & teneant ꝑdͨa ecclɪa cū oīb' ptɪn ſuɪs libere, quiete, & integre cū oībᷓ
ad eccl' ɪllɑ ptinent' in lɪb' pur' & ꝑpet' elɪmoſ' : Hɪjs teſt'

	Bertramo de Crioll ⎱	Ranul. Britone.
	Steph. de Segrave ⎰	Will. Biiton & mult' alijs.
dn̄is J. Bathon.		
H. Linc.		dat' aꝑd Weſt' ꝑ manū ven'
A. Cov. & Litch		patris R. Ciceſtr' eꝑi cancellarij
H. Roff.		n̄ri ix die Oꞓ. ann' reg' n̄ri 13mº."ᷓ
R. Lond.		

(t) MS. in Hyperoo Bodl. nu. 129.
(u) See archbp. Winchelſea's decɪee in Dugd. Warw. p. 649.

Tunſtall.

Tunſtall. Rector, Dr. William Bunker.

    Rectoria ex patronatu d'ni archiep'i valet li. 14.

    Parochiani 60.

    Familiæ 16.

In Ecton's Liber valorum it ſtands thus:

Tunſtall, a rectory dedicated to St. John Baptiſt; patron the archbiſhop of Canterbury, certified val. 14*l.* 8*s.* 4*d.* yearly, tenths 1*l.* 8*s.* 10*d.* proxies 5 ſol.

In a taxation made 1384, 8 Richard II, the half-tenth of Tunſtall is rated at 13*s.* 4*d.* ſo that the living was then valued at 13*l.* 6*s.* 8*d.* or 20 marks (*x*).

In a liſt of the benefices in the collation of the archbiſhop of Canterbury about 1400, entered in the regiſter of archbiſhop Arundell, part I. f. 258. b. it ſtands thus :

Decanat. de } Eccl. de Tunſtall, xxv^marc.
Sydyngborne

In purſuance of the act of parliament made 26 Henry VIII, the true value of the rectory of Tunſtall was thus returned to the commiſſioners :

    " Decanat. de Sydyngborn.

Tunſtall.

    The certificat of Sir Symons Jenys pſon there made by
    Svmon Spacherſt his farmer.

Firſt, the ſame Symon Spacherſt paieth to the ſaid pſon yerly, viij^h.
Item, paid to the preſt for his wages, vj^h xiij^s iiij^d.

    Summa, xiiij^h xiij^s iiij^d.

Whereof deducted for proxies yerly, v^s.

    Summa de claro, xiiij^h viij^s iiij^d.

    X^ma inde, xxviij^s x^d.

(*x*) Stevens's Suppl. vol. I. p. 43. Thorne, col. 2173.

The

The old parfonage houfe was begun to be pulled down July 10, 1712. The foundation of the cellar for the new one begun July 22.

I proceed now to the account of thofe incumbents of this church whofe names I have recovered, and fuch particulars of their lives as I am at prefent acquainted with; which as it contains but an imperfect feries I fhall firft premife that this is not owing to any negligence of mine, but to want of opportunity for fearching at thofe places where the proper materials for compleating it are repofited. The fame muft be alledged in excufe for any other defects which may be found in the preceding pages; for I have never yet applied myfelf *ex profeffo* to treat of the antiquities of this place, or had recourfe to any of the public offices neceffary to be confulted on this occafion, though I hope fhortly fo to do. Moft of what I have faid occurred to me in the courfe of my fearches for a very large work which I am engaged in ; and as my additions to the former hiftories of this place are chiefly fetched from printed volumes of our antiquities, they ferve in a remarkable manner to fhew how capable of improvement the prefent hiftories of this county are, and what unpardonable indolence the lateft writer on this fubject is guilty of.

R E C T O R E S.

LAMBERTUS DE MONNETO is the firft I have hitherto met with; by birth an Italian as his name fhould intimate, and one particularly favoured by John Peckham, archbifhop of Canterbury; for in the year 1281, when the profits of this his benefice were upon the point of fequeftration by reafon of the dilapidated condition of his church, the archbifhop by his mandate iffued from S. Malling Jan. 10, 1281-2, fuperfeded

feded the fequeftration, and undertook, when the defects of reparation fhould be fignified unto him, to fee himfelf to the fufficient amendment of the fame(*y*). Monneto, who was not in full orders, prefuming upon this favour of the arch-bifhop, ventured to abfent himfelf from an ordination fome time after holden at Croyden, at which he was particularly cited to appear, which occafioned the archbifhop to direct a fequeftration of his benefice till he fhould have taken thofe orders which the quality of his preferment did require(*z*), to which end he was cited to appear before the archbifhop on the Friday next following, the Sunday on which is fung the fervice beginning with " Mifericordia Domini," in the fifth year of archbifhop Peckham's confecration 1283, with which citation I fuppofe he did comply.

Befides the rectory of Tunftall he had alfo the benefice of Subchirche and a canonry in the collegiate church of South Mallyng in the year 1283. He moved a fuit againft the ex-ecutors of John the Roman of Olford; a commiffion for hear-ing of which was directed to the Dean of the Arches from Mortlake April 25 in this year (*a*); and in the year 1284, he was proxy for the archbifhop in a certain caufe moved againft him by the archbifhop and convent of Fifcamp in Norman-dy(*b*). After which I meet with nothing more of him till I read of his death which happened in the beginning of May, 1287; whereupon the rectory of Tunftall, agreeable to the confti-tution of the council of Lyons, was, by the archbifhop, com-mitted to the care of Richard de Feryng archdeacon of Can-terbury, 3 non. Maij, 1287 (*c*).

JOHN DE HELPRINGHAM, prefbyter, fucceeded Monneto in the rectory of Tunftall, being inftituted thereto 3 id. Jun. 1287 (*d*).

(*y*) Peckham, 59. b.   (*z*) Ib. 61. a.   (*a*) Ib. f. 146. a. fee f. 182. b. 186. b.
(*b*) Ib. f. 172. a.   (*c*) Ib. f. 31. b.   (*d*) Ib.

He

He was at this time vicar of Wengham in this county; which vicarage he refigned upon his collation to this rectory, but had licence from the archbifhop to hold it together with Tunftall, till Michaelmas 1287 ; what became of him afterwards I know not; but 12 cal. Aug. 1310(*e*), I find archbifhop Winchelfey conferring this rectory then vacant (though by what means appears not) upon

ANDREW DE BREEG, clerk, who declined the offer, and intimated his refufal of it by M. de Bereham, the archbifhop's chancellor, 14 cal. Sept. following (*f*), whereupon

SIMON DE MEPHAM, prefbyter, was collated to this rectory 4 non. Nov. 1310(*g*), and had letters of induction of the fame date directed to the archdeacon's official on that behalf. He was born at Mepham in this county (*h*), from whence alfo he derived his name: he was educated in Merton college, Oxon, where he commenced doctor in divinity, and was efteemed very learned in the profeffion of theology for thofe times : he was prebend of the church of Chichefter, and 6 cal Jun. 1295, was collated to a canonry in the cathedral church of Landaff (*i*); 10 cal. Jun. 1314, he had licence from archbifhop Reynolds to be abfent one whole year from his parifh of Tunftall, for the fake of profecuting his ftudies (*k*), as I fuppofe, at the univerfity of Oxford; for I find him this very year amongft the regents in divinity who examined and condemned certain theological errors which were publicly maintained in the fchools by the Dominicans and other friars(*l*) : at length being freely elected by the convent of Chrift Church in the month of Dec. 1327; he was confecrated archbifhop of Canterbury non. Jul. 1328 (*m*): he died at his palace of Maghfelde 1323, and

(*e*) Reg. Winchelf. f. 47. b.   (*f*) Ib.   (*g*) Ib. f. 48. b.
(*h*) Lambard's Peramb. ed. 1596, p. 490.   (*i*) Tann. Biblioth. p. 522.
(*k*) Reg. Reynolds, f. 10. a.   (*l*) Antiq. Oxon. p. 153.   (*m*) Tann. ut fupr.

was

was buried in his own cathedral where he lies under a tomb of black marble on the north fide of St. Anfelm's chapel. Who fucceeded in the rectory of Tunftall upon his promotion to the fee of Canterbury I have not found; but about 30 years afterwards

WILLIAM DE IOCELYN, alias ISLEP, who was crofs-bearer to archbifhop Iflep, and very probably related to him alfo, quitted this rectory for the rectory of Clyve(n); to which latter he was inftituted 11 Mart. 1558(o). Upon this exchange

WILLIAM IN THE HERNE(p) was inftituted to the rectory of Tunftall 9 cal. Maij, 1358, and had letters for induction thereinto directed to the archdeacon's official and to Sir Simon rector of Wicheling(q). He continued not long here, but refigned his benefice 5 cal. Sept. following(r); which refignation being certified to the archbifhop under the feal of the abbat of Thorney,

WILLIAM DE ISLEP having refigned his rectory of Clyve 6 Nov. preceding(s) was again inftituted hereto 17 cal. Jan. 1338(t), and had letters of induction in like manner directed to the official of the archdeacon and to Sir Simon, rector of Wicheling before-mentioned: fhortly after this his fecond inftitution he made a fecond exchange of this rectory with a namefake

JOHN DE ISLEP, rector of Foxley in the diocefe of Norwich, who was inftituted to the rectory of Tunftall 18th Feb. 1360, and had letters of induction thereto dated 4 cal. Mart. following (u). He died not long after, and was fucceeded by

WILLIAM DE TUNSTALL, br. who was inftituted hereto 4 id. Oct. 1361 (x). He had been rector of the church of Hamme,

---

(n) Reg. Iflep, f 280. a.   (o) Ib. f. 279. b.
(p) One Will. de Herne of Reculver, oid deacon 1316. extie Reg. p. 49.
(q) Reg. Iflep, f. 280. a.   (r) Ib. f. 280. b.   (s) Ib. f. 281. a.   (t) Ib.
(u) Ib. f. 286. b.   (x) Ib. f. 291. a.

H   which

which he refigned in the year 1358 (*y*), and was at this time
rector of Woodchirch, which he refigned upon his inftitution
to this benefice (*z*).

ALANUS DE SLEDDALE, clerk, was collated upon the death of
Tunftall 3 id. Jun. 1363 (*a*), having then received only the
firft tonfure. On Sunday 9 cal. Jan. following, being the
eve of the nativity of our Saviour, he was ordained acolyte in
the archbifhop's chapel at Charyng by William bifhop of
Rochefter (*b*); and 15 cal. Jun. 1364, he was ordained prieft
in the parifh church of Wye ad titulum eccl. fuæ, by the
fame prelate, by virtue of a commiffion from the archbifhop
of Canterbury (*c*) in the year 1365. He refigned his rectory of Tunftall for that of Saltwood (*d*); and in the year
1638, being then rector of Hethe, was conftituted an executor of the will of Simon Breedon, M. D. canon of Cicefter;
by whom was bequeathed to him as a legacy, a filver cup
with a foot and cover; in the bottom of which cup ftood the
image of a man (*e*). 1 July 1876, being then rector of Saltwood, he had licence from archbifhop Sudbury to be abfent
from his benefice for the fpace of one year (*f*), after which
time I find him no more. One Alanus de Sleddale, canon
of the collegiate church of Gnoufhale in the diocefe of Litchfield, was ordained an acolyte by letters dimiffory in the church
of St. Mary-le-Bow 2 Mart. 1386, ad tit. preb. fuæ (*g*), but
he muft have been a different perfon from our rector.

(*y*) Reg. Iflep. f. 281. a.   (*z*) Ib. f. 291. a.   (*a*) Ib. f 301. b.   (*b*) Ib. f. 324. b.
(*c*) Ib. f. 225. a.   (*d*) Ib. f. 307. a.
(*e*) Reg. Wytles, f. 122. a.—Simon Breedon, M. D. of whom we have an account in Leland,
was eminent for his fkill and accurate obfervations in aftionomy, as well as famous for his library
which he collected with great care and affiduity : he was firft of Baliol then of Merton and as fome
fay of Queen's college likewife in the univerfity of Oxon ; to which laft mentioned college he be-
queaths in his will here mentioned Bartolomeus de naturis rerum. He was canon of Cicefter,
rector of Biddenden, and warden of Maidfton hofpital; and died 14 cal. Maij, 1372, on which day
his will was proved. Ant. Wood's M. C. Mert.
(*f*) Reg. Sudb. f. 3. b.   (*g*) Reg. Courtney, f. 308. b.

JOHN

JOHN MARCYL or MARCELLY, clerk, rector of Saltwood, was collated to this rectory 13 cal. October, 1365, upon the exchange made between him and Sleddale *(h)*. He likewise at his coming hither was no more than a *primo tonsurate*; and 15 cal. March following, being Quadragesima Sunday, was ordained an acolyte at Maghfelde, at an altar erected in the archbishop's chamber *(i)*. 2 cal. March following he was ordained sub-deacon in a private oratory near the chamber of the archbishop, within the said manor of Maghfelde *(k)*; and lastly, upon Easter day in the same year, viz. 2 non. April, 1366, he was ordained a priest in the archbishop's chapel at Maghfelde aforesaid *(l)*. He exchanged this rectory, for the neighbouring one of Ivychurch, with

THOMAS PRESTON, who was instituted hereto 3 cal. Sept. 1368 *(m)*, and within a few days exchanged it for the rectory of Hadlegh, with

JOHN BASSETT, instituted hereunto non. Sept. 1368 *(n)*, who in a few weeks after (Preston having in the mean time exchanged his rectory of Hadelegh with William Palmer, for the rectory of Chelsea, in the diocese of London) made another exchange of Tunstall for Chelsea with

THOMAS PRESTON before-mentioned, who was a second time instituted hereto 14 cal. Nov. 1368 *(o)*, and had letters of induction, bearing equal date, directed to the official of the archdeacon of Canterbury. What became of this church-merchant afterwards I know not, for I cannot think with Mr. Newcourt, that this is the same person who was rector of St. Mary, Lothbury; but as he thought meet to return hither again, it is to be hoped he ended his days here; if so, he was probably succeeded by

(h) Reg. Islep, f. 307. a.　　*(i)* Ib. f. 326. b.　　*(k)* Ib.　　*(l)* Ib.
(m) Reg. Langh. f. 105. a.　　*(n)* Ib. f. 105. b.　　*(o)* Ib. f. 107. a.

JOHN

JOHN WAYTE, whom I meet with as rector of this place in the year 1383 *(p)*, when he exchanged it for the rectory of St. Andrews, Holborn, in the diocefe of London, with

RICHARD HOLME, who received inftitution 15 April, 1383 *(q)*, in the perfon of Walter Lokyngtond, his proctor, who in the name of his principal making the profeffion of canonical obedience to the fee of Canterbury, letters of induction were granted to him, directed to Walter Cheltenham, the commif-fary-general *(r)*; but by fome means or other this living was again vacant not long after; for

THOMAS BUTILLER, chaplain, was admitted hereto 20 Oct. 1385, at the prefentation of the crown by reafon that the tempora-lities of the archbifhopric were then vacant *(s)* and in the king's hands (though by what means I have not learned); and having received inftitution and made his profeffion of cano-nical obedience, letters for his induction were directed to the dean of Sittingbourne *(t)*.

JOHN CATTELYN, prefbyter, was collated to this rectory 24 Maij, 1386, and had letters of induction directed to the dean of Sittingbourne. The next month he exchanged for Green-ford-magna in the diocefe of London, with

JOHN LYNTON. This exchange was compleated 15 June 1386 *u)*, when Lynton received inftitution to the rectory of Tunftall, and had letters directed to John Lejer, alias Leyer, parifh prieft of Frenfted, and John George, clerk, jointly and feparately for his induction *(x)*. This John Lynton was re-giftrar of the court of Canterbury, and keeper of the regifters of that court, having his habitation in the parifh of St. Faith, London, whereupon the 5th Dec. 1391, in the prefence of John Perch, clerk, notary public, he refigned his church of

---

(p) Reg. Courtn. f. 249. b.   *(q)* Ibid.   *(r)* Ibid.   *(s)* Ibid. f. 258. a.
(t) Ibid.   *(u)* Ibid. f. 262. a.   *(x)* Ibid. f. 262. b.

Tunftall in expectation of obtaining that of Eynesford in the deanry of Schorſham, at the ſame time making proteſtation that he did not thereby intend, in any meaſure, to recede from, or give up, his right in the former, unleſs he ſhould obtain plenary and peaceable poſſeſſion of the latter (*y*), to which he was accordingly admitted within ten days then next follow-ing (*z*). 7th Oct. 1399, he was collated to the rectory of St. Dunſtan in the Eaſt, London (*a*), where he died in the be-ginning of July, 1401 (*b*).

NICHOLAS SALWY, chaplain, was collated to this rectory upon the removal of Lynton to that of Eynesford before-mentioned, and inſtituted herein 18 Dec. 1391 (*c*), whether by means of an exchange with Lynton or otherwiſe, I am uncertain : chopping and changing of benefices was a kind of trade amongſt the clergy of this age; and was now exerciſed in ſo ſcandalous a manner, that many were defrauded by an un-equal exchange, and ſome wholly deprived of their prefer-ment by the knavery of theſe eccleſiaſtical traffickers. To put a ſtop to theſe ſimoniacal dealings, whereby it frequently happened, that a perſon unfit for one curacy ſwept to himſelf the profits of many ; a mandatory letter iſſued from arch-biſhop Courtney, 5th Mart. 1391-2, putting the biſhops in mind of their duty, and requiring them, upon their canonical obedience, to execute their powers againſt theſe iniquitous practices, and to put in force thoſe canons and laws which were ſubſiſting againſt them (*d*).

WILLIAM BAKER, chaplain, 31ſt Oct. 1416, was collated to this rectory, then vacant by the death of the laſt incumbent (*e*); as was alſo

(*y*) Reg. Mort. Dene. Bourgch. Courtn. f. 201. a.   (*z*) Ibid. f. 201. b.
(*a*) Reg. Arund. part I. f. 262.   (*b*) Ibid. f. 278.
(*c*) Reg. Mort. Dene, Bourgch. Courtn f. 201. b.   (*d*) Spelm. Concil. vol. II. p. 641.
(*e*) Reg. Chich. I. f. 78 a.

JOHN

JOHN BOSEHAM, chaplain, 1ſt Jan. 1416-7, upon the deceaſe of the ſaid William Baker (ƒ).

THOMAS GLOUCESTRE, deacon, was collated to this living by archbiſhop Chicheley, 8th Sept. 1419 (*g*), but by what means it was then vacant is not ſaid.

WILLIAM CLERK, chaplain, was collated hereto by the ſame archbiſhop, 5th Maij, 1428 (*h*), but whether he immediately ſucceeded Glouceſtre I know not. After him I meet with

RICHARD CAUNTON (*i*), rector of this church, upon whoſe reſignation ſucceeded

ROBERT PYKE, who was inſtituted hereto in the perſon of William Coke, his proctor, 8th Sept. 1446 (*k*), and reſigning the living in Nov. following,

THOMAS BRAG, chaplain, was inſtituted hereto 3 Dec. 1446 (*l*), as was

ROBERT TOFT, A. M. 23 Maij, 1450 (*m*).

THOMAS KYNGE is the next I have hitherto met with. Upon his reſignation

THOMAS BALYS, chaplain, was collated to this rectory by archbiſhop Bourgchier 4 Maij, 1473 (*n*). How long he continued here, what became of him, or who ſucceeded him, I know not, but

ALEXANDER CROWMER, A. M. was collated to this rectory then vacant by the death of the laſt incumbent, 1ſt Mart. 1490-1 (*o*). A relation he was doubtleſs to Sir James Crowmer, knight, at this time lord of Tunſtall, but in what degree I have not yet diſcovered.

ROBERT WHETELEY, A. M. ſucceeded upon the death of Crowmer, being inſtituted hereto 6th Jul. 1492 (*p*), at the

(ƒ) Reg. Chich. I. f. 82. a.   (*g*) Ibid. f. 101. a.   (*h*) Ibid. f. 172. a.
(*i*) Reg. Staff. f. 90. a.   (*k*) Ibid. f. 90. a.   (*l*) Ibid f. 91. b.   (*m*) Ibid. f. 104. b.
(*n*) Reg. Bourgch. f. 107. b.   (*o*) Reg. Mort. II. 148. a.   (*p*) Ibid. f. 151. b.

collation

collation of archbiſhop Morton. His ſucceſſor in all probability was

RICHARD SYMONS, preſbyter, upon whom archbiſhop Morton confiding in his circumſpection, induſtry, and fitneſs for the charge, and moved by the evident neceſſity or utility of the church, conferred this rectory 5th Dec. 1499, to be held in commendam for the ſpace of ſix months from the date of this collation, according to the conſtitution of Gregory X. but he continued longer here than ſix months; for

THOMAS SMYTH, A. M. was collated to this rectory, then vacant by the death of the ſaid Symons, 4th Dec. 1502. He remained here till September 1513; at which time he reſigned this benefice.

RADULPH WULF, chaplain, was collated thereto 9th Sept. 1513. He died 20th Jun. 1525, and was buried in the chancel of his church, where his effigy in braſs is ſtill to be ſeen in the habit of a prieſt at high maſs.

SYMON JENYNS, as I conceive ſucceeded him; and might be the laſt Roman Catholic miniſter of this pariſh. He was buried here 27th Nov. 1538. He has left an *orate* upon the walls of the dove-houſe belonging to the parſonage, which I therefore ſuppoſe he built.

WILLIAM BOUŃKER was his immediate ſucceſſor; but the date of his inſtitution I have not ſeen; or any more of him than that he was rector at the time of archdeacon Harpsfield's viſitation, and that he was buried here 15th Jun. 1560.

THOMAS THACKER; he was buried here 29th Sept. 1572, and probably came immediately after Bounker.

JOHN COLDWELL ſeems to be the next. I meet with him in the pariſh regiſter under the year 1577, where he is called Mr. Dr. Coldwell. Shortly after this

PETER

PETER POTT, A. M. (*q*) became rector of Tunftall (*r*). He firft occurs in 1581. He died 10th Oct. 1584, and had for his fucceffor

CHRISTOPHER WEBBES, theol. bac. born at Gillingham in this county, educated in St. John's college, Cambridge, of which he became prefident. He was the father of a numerous off-fpring (*s*). He died 7th Jan. 1610, in the 63d year of his age, and was interred in the chancel, where, on a brafs plate, is fome account of him.

ROBERT CHEKE, D. D. by his great age feems to have imme-diately fucceeded Mr. Webbes. He was the younger fon of an ancient family in Suffolk, and, like his predeceffor, had been, I fuppofe, brought up at Cambridge, for I do not find his name in the lifts of our graduates. He was ordained prieft 8th Feb. 1600, prefented to the 4th ftall in Rochefter cathedral, 2d Sept. 1616; to the vicarage of Hoo 17th Jul. 1622, which laft he refigned in 1625; being a quiet peace-able man, he had a ftipend of 20*l.* per ann. affigned him, referved out of the church eftate on the diffolution of deans and chapters by the rump gentry in 1646. He died 5th Jul. 1647, æt. 78. There is an handfome monument erected to his memory by Mary, his widow, againft the north wall of the chancel.

ROBERT DIXON, A. M. by education a Cambridge man alfo, fuc-ceeded Dr. Cheke. He was of St. John's college in that uni-verfity: he was ordained 21ft Sept. 1639. He lived in the times of anarchy and confufion, and was a great fufferer in the royal caufe, being in the year 1644, taken prifoner as he

(*q*) Adn.. ad lect. log. Ariftot. 18 Nov. 1569, determ. xlm. feq. adm. ad incip. 3 Jul. 1573.

(*r*) One Peter Pott was prefented by queen Elizabeth to the rectory of St. Clement's in the fuburbs of Oxon, 17 Mart. 1574-5. Park. II. 58. b. Admitted to the vicarage of Milton juxta Sittingbourne, 15 Feb. 1577-8. Giind. 178, b.

(*s*) 1ft Feb. 1584-5, Chriftopher Webbe, cl. fac. th. prof. adm. concionator. un. in eccl. cath. Cant. vac. per mort. Joh. Ingulden, fac. th. bac. Reg. Whitgift, tom. I. f. 459. a.

4

paffed

paſſed throngh the Crown yard in Rocheſter, in his return from preaching a funeral ſermon at Graveſend, and carried to Knoll-houſe near Seven Oak in this county, then made a priſon for malignants as the loyal party were called.

As this happened before Mr. Dixon was poſſeſſed of the living of Tunſtall, he muſt either have had other preferment in this county, or the author of this account of his ſufferings be miſtaken in his chronology.

From Knoll he was removed to Leeds caſtle in Kent, then another priſon alſo; where he was cloſely kept priſoner for about fourteen months, under great hardſhips and ill-uſage by one Franklyn, the pretended governor of that caſtle. The crimes laid to his charge were his loyalty to king Charles I, and his refuſing to take the oath called the Solemn League and Covenant; which he never took.

Afterwards he was ſequeſtered from this living; where a parliament party came for him at midnight, ſwearing they would cut him as ſmall as herbs for the pot; but a ſervant of Sir Edward Hales, bart. (who was juſt before in the ſame night taken out of his bed from his lady and carried away priſoner), having given private notice of their approach, Mr. Dixon eſcaped into Oak-wood, not far from his houſe, where, for about a week, he lay night and day for fear of his life, and was there ſupplied with ſmall matters privately ſent him, until in a lay habit he fled and ſo eſcaped that ſtorm. But his houſe was rifled and plundered, and by degrees he and his family quite undone and baniſhed the county. Great ſums of money were exacted out of him while he had any thing by ſequeſtrators, committee-men, and ſuch like; and he was told by one Sir Charles Sidley, that not one of his coat ſhould be left to piſs againſt the wall before he had done with them; but the ſame Sir Charles (by what motive was never known to Mr. Dixon) did after that become ſo much his friend as

I   that

that he brought him off from fome other trouble before the committee as I think they were called.

When king Charles II was reftored, Mr. Dixon, by the recommendation of the aforefaid Sir Edward Hales, was inftituted prebend of the third ftall in the cathedral of Rochefter, Auguft 9, 1660, and refigning his living of Tunftall to a fon of both his names, was collated to the vicarage of St. Nicholas, Rochefter, Auguft 22, 1660, and commenced D. D. at Cambridge. He died in May 1688. He has written the " Nature of the two Teftaments. Lond. 1674." fol. and the " Degree of Confanguinity and Affinity defcribed. Lond. 1676." 8vo.

This account is taken from Walker's Sufferings of the Clergy, part II, p. 231, to whom it was communicated by Mr. James Dixon, fon to Mr. Robert Dixon. This James was born at Tunftall in January, 1648, and was baptized the 27th of the fame month : he was living here in 1680, when he ftiled himfelf an efquire; refided afterwards at Town-Sutton, was coroner of the county and at length dying was buried here July 26, 1716. He married Elizabeth Cayfar of Hollingbourn, by whom he had iffue two fons and one daughter; one of whom Robert Dixon, practifed the law at Town-Sutton aforefaid, and was buried at Tunftall Auguft 14, 1742.

ROBERT DIXON, A. M. fon of the preceding Robert Dixon, D. D. a fecond of thofe names is the next I have yet feen: he was rector in 1678. Whether he be the fame with Robert Dixon, A. M. who was curate here in 1669 I know not. He was buried here March 25, 1711, and was fucceeded by

EDWARD MORES, clerk, collated to this parfonage May 7, 1711. He built the parfonage-houfe on the glebe entirely at his own expence, 1712. He gave, at the defire of his pious mother, (who had given the filver falver in her life-time) the filver flaggon for the communion, and added thereto a filver plate for the offering, 1731. He refided conftantly with his people

ple

ple till the time of his death, which, after a long and painful illnefs, happening at London April 8, 1740, he was interred at Walthamſtow according to his exprefs defire; and was ſucceeded in his living by one who has not been feen there fince his induction (t).

On the north fide of the chancel at Tunſtall is an handfome cenotaph, with a buſto of Mr. Mores and an infcription too long to be inferted here.

This gentleman, defcended from an antient and genteel family at Great Coxwell in the county of Berks, was admitted to the order of a deacon in the cathedral church of S. Paul, London, Dec. 4, 1704, and received the order of prieſthood in the pariſh church of S. Anne, Weſtminſter, Jan. 6, 1705-6, being then aged 24 years. He was collated to this rectory May 7, 1711, and inducted into the real and actual poffeffion of the fame by Robert Elwick, vicar of Bredgar 15th of the fame month, by virtue of a commiffion from Thomas Bouchier, LL. D. official of the archdeacon of Canterbury.

Mr. Mores wrote " Funeral Entertainment; or a practical difcourfe clearly ſhewing the incomparable excellency of Balaam's wiſh. Lond. 1702 and 1704." 12mo. A treatife compofed by the author when he was very young, in purfuance of an hint given by Mancheſter al Mondo in his book *De Contemplatione Mortis*; " that it would be much more fuitable and expedient, " inſtead of rings and gloves, to difpofe of pious books at func- " rals; for they would inſtruct to a good ufe of thofe objects." " The Pious Example. Lond. 1725." 8vo. A difcourfe occafioned by the death of Mrs. Anne Mores, late of Tunſtall in Kent, who departed this life Jan. 5, 1724-5.

(t) We have the following remaikable account from a village in Kent, about 16 miles diftant from Cante.bury, viz. the place having been upwaids of 12 yeais deftitute of a minifter, the pariſhioners, willing to turn their want of a rector to the beſt advantage, have app epproved the parionage-houſe to the ufe of the pariſh pooi, and have fold the chuich. Lond. Evening, Fi 18, 1752.

From

From the account already given of the preceding rector it is easy to guess under what circumstances this living must of necessity have come to his successor; and agreeably thereto the next thing we meet with is a licence from the archbishop of Canterbury, dated July 8, 1712, impowering Mr. Mores wholly to take down the old parsonage house of Tunstall, which could stand no longer (*u*), and to build a new commodious and fit house for the said rectory, at his own expence, in its stead: accordingly the old parsonage house was begun to be pulled down July 10, 1712, and the foundation of the new one begun 22d of the same month.

Mr. Mores having by this means at his own charge provided for the future residence of a minister upon the spot, and being, exclusive of his profession, a gentleman by birth, character, and fortune, it may reasonably be supposed that at least an ordinary respect was shewn to him by those for whose advantages he had been so remarkably solicitous; but neither these nor more weighty considerations are a sufficient safeguard against the assaults of mischievous and malicious men; and for the encouragement of those who may be hereafter minded to go and do likewise, be it known, that the only recompense he met with from his parishioners was a continued series of abuses, insults, and oppression.

The first acknowledgement received for his benefaction was an advance of his parsonage in 1717, in the assessment to the land-tax from £.54 to £.100 per ann. but as the tythes of his living were let for no more than £.95 per ann. which sum included the tenths, procurations, and other deductions, by a proper application the same was reduced to £.90 per ann. which was £.36 per ann. more than the living was rated at when Mr. Mores first received it.

(*n*) Mr. Mores found only a few broken walls and rooms some sinking and others open to the sky; the chimnies down, and the floors destroyed or spoiled.

4

Pl. II. p.60.

The Parsonage House of Tunstall, in the County of Kent, built in the Y. 1722. at ý expence of the Rev.ᵈ Edward Mores then Rector.

a. Remains of the old parsonage house which stood farther from the road. b. The cowhouse built by Simon Lowre, sac. th. bac. rector of Tunstall who died 1558.

About this time one Thomas Banifter came from Sitting-bourne to fettle here, and being defirous of a leafe of the par-fonage in the year 1719, applied to the rector for that purpofe, offering a confiderable increafe of rent if Mr. Mores would turn the then prefent tenant out of it; but thefe difhoneft endeavours to fupplant another perfon meeting with a different reception from what Banifter hoped for or expected, he took the firft opportu-nity of expreffing his refentment. And in the year 1720, be-ing then affeffor, took upon him to raife the parfonage again to £.95; and to prevent a redrefs of this injury gave the rector notice by letter, that the place appointed by the commiffioners for hearing of appeals was at one place, when in fact it was at another at confiderable diftance; by which means the rector loft the opportunity of relief, and was conftrained to pay the money, though as it afterwards appeared no more was paid into the hands of the receiver-general that year than had been paid the former year; fo that the overplus ceded to the ufes of Mr. Ba-nifter.

The next year Jacob Banifter, brother to this Thomas, being then affeffor (with one Thomas Hunt, whom he excluded from having any fhare in making the affeffment) went ftill further, and from £.90 and £.95 advanced the parfonage to £.110; making the affeffment from a copy written by Thomas Wilkins, and according to his pofitive order how every body fhould be taxed.

This Wilkins was a gentleman then lately come into t' parifh: I fay a gentleman, though fuch a one he was that it is to be hoped neither this nor any other parifh will be fpeedily troubled with his like again; but of him more hereafter.

This affeffment (in which I fhould have faid the two affeffors were each abated £.10 per ann.) the rector appeared againft, and the matter being heard before the commiffioners June 6, 1721, the parfonage was by them directed to be affeffed at £.90.

Banifter

Banifter was feverely reprimanded, and very narrowly efcaped a fine upon the occafion.

Thus ended the bufinefs of the land-tax: but that was not the only grievance which Mr. Mores had fubjected himfelf to by having been a benefactor to the parifh. Upon the 24th of July, 1720, at a veftry publicly appointed and holden for the parifh, a certain rate was granted to Thomas Banifter, then overfeer of the poor, for the relief of the poor and payment of parifh debts. This rate Banifter accordingly prepared, dated July 31, but did not produce it till Auguft 7, at another veftry, when he defired the inhabitants then affembled to fign it; but fome of them objecting becaufe the day was Sunday, and others becaufe Mr. Wilkins was not there, it was deferred till the next day; at which time the parifhioners being again affembled in the chancel (the place where the parifh meetings are ufually held) Wilkins contended that the parfonage houfe fhould be rated diftinctly from the parfonage; though that was rated to the full and higher than any eftate in the place; which the rector objecting to, and pleading againft, was told by Mr. Wilkins that he had no bufinefs there, and with much abufive language was directed to go out of the church. The rector feveral times perfuaded him to peace, but he ftill continued his railing, clamour, and oaths, and the inhabitants departed without figning the rate.

Auguft 12th, the rector and the church-warden attended Mr. Juftice Kenrick, and gave him an account of thefe matters in compliance with his own requeft and direction; for he, by repeated complaints, being well acquainted with the riotous proceedings and fcandalous deportment of Wilkins, had directed that in cafe of any further abufes on his part he might have notice of them; the refult of this conference was, that the juftice faid he would bind Wilkins to his good behaviour; and as to the rate, it muft be figned by as many as they could get; that Sunday was as fit a day as any for that purpofe, and that it fhould be afterwards

wards confirmed by the juftices at their fitting: the rector accordingly the Sunday following fent for Banifter, and having
perufed the rate, told him his intentions of having it figned in
veftry that very day, which he was affured was no improper
day, and the rather to be chofen by them as they were then
moft likely to be free from the difturbances of Wilkins, who
was very feldom feen in the church upon a Sunday ; to all
which Banifter affented, and the parifhioners being affembled
after the evening fervice, the rector, the church-warden, and
every other perfon prefent, figned the rate, except Banifter the
overfeer, who perfifted in a refufal, becaufe as he faid, though
he was willing to oblige the rector, yet he was unwilling to dif-
oblige Mr. Wilkins, who had fworn, that he would pay no taxes
unlefs the parfonage houfe was rated according to his direction.

A few days before the fitting of the juftices, the rate was fent
by Banifter to Mr. John Hawker, clerk to the juftices, with a
letter, defiring him to produce it at the fitting, whither the rector
and the church-warden went in expectation of it, and to have
it confirmed. When Mr. Hawker declared to the fitting, that
the rate had been indeed left with him, but that word was afterwards fent to his houfe that he fhould not carry the rate to
the fitting: this trifling and underhand management gave fo
much offence, and very juftly too, that a warrant iffued againft
Banifter, requiring him to come and fhew caufe why the rate
was not brought according to his promife made to Thomas
Hunt, the churchwarden, who was fummoned as an evidence in
the caufe.

The 6th of Sept. Hunt informed the rector, that he had been
warned by the borfholder to meet Banifter before the juftice the
next day, between 10 and 11 in the forenoon; at which time
the rector and Hunt attended, but Banifter came not at all; however the day after Banifter called at the parfonage, and told the
rector he was then going to the juftice with the rate; the rector
having

having remonftrated againft the trouble and difappointment he
had occafioned the pieceding day, defired him to defer the bufinefs to another day, when Hunt and himfelf might go likewife; but Banifter pretending a fear of the juftice's difpleafure,
fet forth immediately and waited at the juftice's near four hours,
in a feeming expectation of the rector and Hunt; the confequence of which was, a letter from Mr. Kenrick, couched in the
following terms, which as a fpecimen of the jufticiary ftyle and
manner of writing, I infert literatim:

" Thomas Hunt.

" Mr. Banifter, the Overfeer of the poor for your parifh, was
" heer yefterday, attending moft part of the Day for Mr. Mores,
" according to his promife (I ftand amaz'd at the contradictions)
" Banifter fayes, he did not promife, to come laft Wednefday.
" you may have all your juft payments, and Accounts allow'd
" you, no occafion for the Seffions Bufines—All the Difpute and
" difference lieth heer, whither the parfon fhall be Seffed for his
" houfe—Take the Words of the Act—And alfo to raife
" Weekly, or otherwife (by taxation of every inhabitant, parfon,
" Vicar, and other—much more I could fay to you—

" Give no farther particular trouble (for Ile' hear none)
" To your Friend,
" Faverfham   . . . . Kenrick."
" Sep. 10, 1720.
" Your Bufines has given me more
" Trouble, then the Whole Divifion."

The rector heard no more either of the rate or of Banifter till
the 22d of November, when Banifter called at the parfonage and
demanded the poor's rate for the parfonage houfe, rated diftinct
from the parfonage at £.15 per annum; upon the fight of the
book the rector perceived that it was the fame rate which had
been figned by himfelf in veftry the 14th of Auguft; but that
the parfonage houfe had been inferted fince by the addition of
another line which was not there before; and that the date of
the

the rate had been altered from July 31 to July 30. This falfe and deceitful management, together with fo manifeft a forgery, determined the rector not to pay the money demanded, and he accordingly refufed the payment of it, and gave Banifter the proper notice that he fhould appeal to the quarter feffions for relief; which Banifter feemed at firft. to difregard, faying, that the rate was figned by the juftices (though whether before or after the alteration appeared not), and ufing feveral threats and menacing expreffions, adding afterwards, much entreaty and perfuafion to induce the rector to pay the money; but he perfifting in his refufal, Banifter went his way, and the rector expected and intended to appeal agreeably to the notice which he had given for that purpofe.

It is fomething wonderful, that any gentleman in commiffion for the peace fhould countenance fo notorious an act of injuftice as this moft certainly was, by fubfcribing his name in confirmation of this rate; and more fo, that a magiftrate fhould promife to any party in a caufe what was promifed to Banifter in this; who, as he himfelf openly declared, was affured by letter, that nothing more fhould be heard which the rector particularly fhould fay, or have to fay, concerning the rate, and the grievance which he complained of thereby. But whatever Mr. Juftice Kenrick's fentiments of this affair might be, other perfons as capable of judging between right and wrong were of a very different opinion; and what their opinion was the following letter, felected out of many others of the fame import, will declare, the reverend perfon who was the writer of it is too well known to need any commendation here.

"Reverend Sir,

"I will take the firft opportunity that offers itfelf to talk "with Mr. Sole about the affair you mention. I am forry to

K   "hear

" hear your uneafinefs encreafes by the injurious treatment you
" receive from fome perfons in your parifh, which I would have
" you bear with patience ; not doubting but by a timely appli-
" cation to the cant-juftices, your grievances will be redreffed.
" Your cafe is really very hard, and I am entirely perfuaded, that
" the refolution of the juftices will be given in favour of you ;
" otherwife incumbents will have little encouragement to be
" benefactors to their cures ; fince, inftead of having their
" names gilded with characters of gold, they muft expect no-
" thing but frowns and impofitions if your cafe is made a pre-
" cedent. Founders and benefactors are in all places that I
" have been in defervedly held in the greateft efteem ; and I
" cannot but be furprized at the injuftice and ingratitude of thofe
" who would have you rated for the money you have laid out
" upon your manfion-houfe. I blefs God, and

　　　　　" I am, Reverend Sir,
　　　　　　　" Your friend and fervant,
　　　　　　　　　　" John Barman."

Notwithftanding the notice of appeal given upon the 21ft of
December following, the rector being then from home, came
Banifter to the parfonage-houfe, bringing with him two other
perfons, and alfo Mr. Cooke of Tonge, who was then conftable,
and by virtue of a warrant from fome juftices as he faid (though
who they were nobody knows) feized and forcibly carried away
a large quantity of pewter and other utenfils from the parfonage-
houfe, behaving in the rudeft and moft indecent manner, although Mr. Cooke (who during the whole tranfaction behaved
with the greateft civility) perfuaded him to proceed refpectfully
and quietly, and not to take away a quantity of goods, in value
fo much exceeding what the affeffment amounted to.

December the 24th, the rector received a letter from Banifter,
offering, that upon payment of the rate, and a fmall prefent to
　　　　　　　　　　　　　　　　　　　　　　　the

the men who had accompanied him, he would reftore the goods which he had taken away; to which the rector fent for an-fwer only, that this was an improper feafon for fuch difturbances; and December the 26th, in a letter, repeated to him the notice he had before given of his intended appeal, at the fame time appointing him to appear at the feffions, and to bring with him the book in which the affeffment was written.

The 6th of January the appeal was heard at Canterbury, when it appearing evidently that the rate had been unduly made, and the parfonage-houfe inferted after the making of it, the affeff-ment upon the parfonage-houfe was in all points quafhed, and the rector's goods were ordered to be reftored.

A few days afterwards a perfon was fent to demand the goods of Banifter, who refufed to reftore them, faying, that he had them not, but had fold them according to law. The rector waited fome days to fee whether he would alter his mind, and comply with the order of the court; but he ftill continuing obftinate in his refufal, was very fhortly afterwards arrefted.

Beginning now to be fenfible of his fituation, the rector was moved by Jacob Banifter and fome others, that the matter might be accommodated, and his brother releafed; but whether the terms were fuch as could not be complied with, or for what other reafon appears not; the caufe went on to iffue, and was to have been tried at the enfuing affizes, at which time the rector and his witneffes attending at Maidftone, July 25, 1721, received a meffage from Banifter, requefting an interview, which being granted, Banifter defired that the affair might drop, and propofed to throw all the expences, as well the rector's as his own, into the parifh accounts, and that the whole fhould be difcharged out of the poor's rate, and declared himfelf very confident, that by his own influence, and that of his brother and Jacob, Wilkins and fome others, he could perform that feat;

but

but the rector refusing to be reimburfed by the oppreffion of fuch as were innocent, rejected his ridiculous and unjuft propofal; however, the matter being refumed the next day by the interceffion of friends, and the ftrongeft affurances that all mifunderftandings and refentment fhould be for ever laid afide and forgotten, and that fuch conceffion fhould be looked upon as a perpetual obligation and a proof of the rector's kindnefs, and a manifeftation of his known averfion to litigation and quarrels, an arbitration was concluded upon, and the bufinefs referred to Robert Elwick of Bredgar, clerk, and Nicholas Jackfon of Linftead, gentleman; the rector's compliance wherein was much blamed by his acquaintance and friends, and he himfelf had reafon afterwards to wifh he had been lefs condefcending.

The bond of arbitration being figned, the fincerity of Banifter's affeverations appeared immediately, by the fteps which were taken to prevent the arbitration taking place, and the vifible endeavours of himfelf and his abettors to put off the rector with fair words till the time limited for the determination of the affair fhould expire. However, September 19, the arbitrators met, and notwithftanding the falfe affidavits procured by the villainy of Baker the attorney, the matter appeared fo plain, that Mr. Jackfon could not but admit that the treatment of the rector had been above meafure fcandalous; but yet he was unwilling to award him any fatisfaction, infifting upon fuch ridiculous and extraordinary terms, that no perfon can believe he could be in earneft or in his fenfes when he propofed them.

The arbitration being thus at an end, there remained nothing more for the rector to do but to bring the caufe to a trial, which he accordingly did at the next affizes holden at Maidftone, March 21, 1722, and very readily recovering his damages, Banifter was conftrained to pay both his own charges and thofe of the rector likewife.

Pending

Pending this difpute, an oppofition of another kind was fet up againſt the rector, who, April 10, 1721, having chofen a church-warden for the year enfuing, Wilkins and his affociates difputed his right of choice, affirming, that it lay in the pariſh, and that they themfelves would chufe another. They accordingly pro-ceeded, and pretended to choofe Wilkins. May 2 following was the vifitation, when the rector, who had been appointed to preach upon that occafion, coming down from the pulpit appeared in court, and when his pariſh was called, declared whom he had chofen for church-warden; againſt which the proctor for the adverfe party replied, averring from their information feveral falfities; to all which the rector anfwered, and the judge upon hearing both parties, as an expedient for peace, but without any detriment to the prerogative of the rector, propofed to him in court to name another perfon : the rector did fo, the perfon was fworn, and the judge would fuffer nothing to be alledged againſt it.

So unwearied were the knavery of thefe mifcreants, that, re-gardlefs of the determination of the quarter feffions abovemen-tioned, Jacob Baniſter, who fucceeded his brother as overfeer of the poor, at a veſtry holden April 30, 1721, produced a certain rate written by Wilkins, though no fuch rate had ever been granted by the pariſh, or indeed ever mentioned before, in which rate the parfonage houfe was again rated as it had been before. The rector, the church-warden, and others refufed to fign it.

At the fitting of the juſtices, May 4 following, the church-warden appeared and defired that the rate might not be con-firmed, at the fame time giving his reafons for it; that he had not figned it, neither could he, it being fo unequal and unfair ; and that as to the rector in particular, his cafe had been already heard and determined at the quarter feffions, and therefore his houfe ought not to be affeffed again, as the affeffment of it had

been

been fet afide before. All this appeared extremely reafonable to every body but Mr. Kenrick; who in a froward angry manner told the church-warden the rate fhould be confirmed notwithftanding the quarter-feffions : accordingly he figned it himfelf, and compelled another to fign it alfo.

By this act of dotage, the rector was reduced to the neceffity of purfuing the fame courfe again. But the event of the former bufinefs put an end to any further proceedings in this, and all vexation upon the fcore of affeffments ceafed. As to Wilkins, his fcurrility and diforderly behaviour encreafing, he was prefented by the church-warden to the ordinary, for wrangling and quarrelling in the church, and abufing the rector with opprobrious language there; which prefentment Wilkins appeared in court to anfwer, and denied the charge; whereupon an intimation was decreed to go forth for the rector or church-warden to appear and juftify, which they accordingly did; and divers articles were exhibited againft Wilkins for abufe, wrangling, and profanely fwearing in the church; and he would have received correction fuitable to his demerits, but, luckily for him, an act of general pardon was paffed at that very time, and he efcaped chaftifement. However, the difgrace fat heavy upon him, and to the great joy of the parifhioners he left the place, by his departure making room for a more worthy perfon.

By this means the combination was broken, and peace reftored to the parifh; nothing more being attempted by thefe people in their own perfons, 1724, except breaking open the church and ringing the bells at an unfeafonable hour; which extravagant action, the parties making a due fubmiffion, was readily pardoned by the rector.

But although no further vexation was given by thefe fellows in their proper perfons, yet, at the inftigation of Banifter, who was fteward to Sir John Hales, a fuit was promoted againft the

4   rector

rector by one from whom, upon account of his rank and quality, a better behaviour might have been expected.

When Mr. Mores firſt came to be rector of this pariſh, he found ſtanding at the eaſt-ſide of the church-yard a ſtately row of large and tall elms. The next year, being about to build a new parſonage-houſe, the carpenter mightily perſuaded him to take them down and uſe them in the building; but they being ſo very regular, ſo ornamental, and withal ſo great a defence to the church againſt high winds, he would by no means conſent thereto.

Notwithſtanding in the year 1714, Sir John Hales, pretending that they belonged to him as lord of the manor, ordered them to be felled, although it was with difficulty that he got any body to undertake the buſineſs. The trees were ſo generally ſuppoſed to be the property of the rector, that men of honeſty and civility refuſed to be concerned in the affair : preceding rectors were known to have lopped them without the leaſt diſturbance. The land on each ſide of the way was the rector's ; and the very man who was found to act in this buſineſs (Joſeph Caſtile) came firſt to entreat the rector's pardon for what he was about to do, pleading his dependence on his landlord Sir John, whom if he ſhould diſobey, he ſaid, it would prove his ruin, as he ſhould be infallibly turned both out of houſe and work. Old Mr. Baniſter, Sir John's ſteward, at that time aſſured the rector that himſelf had plainly refuſed to be concerned therein ; but Mr. Allen the rector of Murſton came and meaſured the diſtance of the trees from the church-yard wall, and finding it to exceed 18 inches, orders were given for their being cut down, and they were cut down accordingly.

But there were two aſhes, the one very ſmall, the other ſome-what larger, oppoſite to the church-porch, which ſtanding cloſer to the wall (i. e. within 18 inches) were for that reaſon left un-touched ;

touched ; and it was faid by the workmen, as Sir John's expreffion, that though he would take his own, they fhould not
take them becaufe they were the parfon's.

One of thefe afhes having a fpreading top, which was trou-
blefome to the waggons which came loaded down the road in
harveft, the rector was feveral times defired that it might be
lopped or cut upwards. But in the year 1724, having occafion
for a poft about fome repairs, the trees being inconvenient to
the road, the rector thought it better to remove them both ; the
value whereof did not exceed for the beft 2s. 6d. for the other 1s.

Near two years afterwards, in the beginning of March, 1726,
the rector being fick in his bed of a violent fever, came one
Mr. May into his chamber at London, and declared that he had
procefs againft him, at the fuit of Sir John Hales, for a trefpafs ;
but any farther particulars he knew not. His coming at a time
when the rector was in fo dangerous a ftate, and fo very unfit
to be difturbed upon fuch an occafion, feemed to import fomething very confiderable. The rector therefore fent to his attorney, who was then in town, defiring him to do what was
proper in the cafe ; and fo foon as he was able to go abroad,
was carried by a gentleman of fome eminence to Sir John, that
he might learn his offence. Sir John ftood at his parlour window reading, but fent out word that he was not at home. The
fervant was then required to go in again, and afk what other
time would be agreeable to his mafter to be waited upon about
bufinefs : the anfwer was, that he had no fuch time.

Being at a lofs what method to take after this treatment, the
rector was advifed by Sir Thomas Hales to write a letter to Sir
John, which he accordingly did, 18th March, 1725-6, telling
him, " that he knew not of any trefpafs againft him, and upon
" the utmoft ftretch of recollection could think of no caufe of
" action, except it was the taking two trees from the bank of
" his

" his church-yard fence, which trees, for many reafons, he be-
" lieved to be his own; and one of thofe reafons was, that Sir
" John himfelf had declared fo. Neverthelefs, if Sir John would
" now declare that he really thought the trees were his, the
" rector would very readily pay the value of them: otherwife,
" though the rector was by no means difpofed to litigate trifles,
" he would with equal readinefs try the right with him." To
this Sir John replied that he valued not the trees, but had been
informed that the rector had fpoken ill of him, mentioning the
expreffions which he had been told the rector had uttered
againft him; and fuch expreffions they were as none but the
moft defpicable of mankind ever make ufe of. But being
affured by the perfons who waited upon him with the letter,
that the rector was a perfon of no fuch behaviour, Sir John
appeared fatisfied, and faid that he would ftop any further proceedings.

The rector being informed of this accufation, was exafperated
greatly; and fcorning to be fuppofed a perfon of fuch language
(which, however common with Thomas Banifter, who was Sir
John's informer, was never ufed by him), wrote a fecond letter
to Sir John, vindicating himfelf as to that particular, which produced a meffage from Sir John, requefting the rector's company
at a time appointed; at which time the rector waited upon him,
Sir John repeated what he had before faid, and affured the
rector, that as he had before promifed to ftop any further
proceedings in the law, he had then actually done fo by a
letter to Mr. Lawkins, his attorney for that purpofe; adding
ftill further, that he was fenfible of Banifter's mif-reprefentations,
and upon what account thefe ill offices were attempted, and that
more might be attempted hereafter; but for the future, no refentment fhould be taken by him till he had firft written to, or
feen the rector.

L

With

With this affurance from a perfon of Sir John Hale's quality, who would not have been fatisfied ? But words are no deeds.
Some months after the rector found the fuit to go forward;
and the third of June, 1726, received a letter from Thomas
Banifter, purporting, that unlefs the rector paid 4l. and charges,
Sir John Hales would proceed. The 8th of June following,
the rector wrote to Sir John, reprefenting to him " how incon-
" fiftent this behaviour was with honour and his own affurances."
To which he was not pleafed to give any anfwer.

In what manner this affair ended, cannot certainly be faid.
It appears not to have come to a trial; and if it had, muft in all
likelihood have been determined in disfavour of Sir John Hales.
His demand feems to have been for two very fmall afhes which
grew clofe to the doors of the parfonage barn towards the road,
where was formerly a common well for the ufe of the poor
people in the adjacent cottages, before the inhabitants of thofe
cottages had feverally wells for their diftinct and particular ufe;
which they feem not to have had before the year 1680. Thefe
trees ftanding in the way of the barn were taken down by the
rector, on a prefumption that they were his own, in the year
1717, being then valued at 3s. after the carriage of them had
been paid to Sittingbourne; fo that with refpect to thefe, had
the rector been in an error, Sir John was precluded by the ftatute of limitations. And as to thofe growing by the wall of
the church-yard, if they were not the property of the rector,
it is doubtful whether Sir John could have any pretence to an
action for them, that part of the parifh being not in the borough of Tunftall, for which his borfholder is chofen (as the
parfonage houfe and barn is), but in the borough of Bredgar,
in the manor and hundred of Milton, and the borfholder of
Bredgar collects burrough-filver of Mr. Grove on one fide the
church, and of the ale-houfe on the other; from whence it
fhould follow that Sir John had nothing to do with them.

I   Monu-

12th May, 1740, Robert Tyler was collated to the rectory of Tunftall by archbifhop Potter, vacant by the death of Edward Mores*. Againft him the advertifement mentioned in p. 59, feems to have been levelled. He died June 12, 1766. He was alfo vicar of St. Lawrence in the Ifle of Thanet.

July 14, 1766, Tho. Pennington, M. A. on the death of Tyler was collated by abp. Secker.

* Regift. Potter, fol. 273, b.

Monuments

Monuments and Arms in Tunftall Church.

In the body of the church are three ftones whofe braffes are all loft. One had a fmall plate, with an infcription in the middle; the fecond a head with a like plate, and a fcrole now remaining in-fcribed **Jhu miferere me**; on the third were four fhields at the corners, and a plate in the middle.

On other ftones.

" Here lyeth interr'd
The body of Thomafin Gore,
Wife of the late Gerrard Gore,
Of Tunftall, efq. She was eldeft
Daughter of Edward Hales,
Of Chilfon, efq.
Only fon of Samuel Hales,
The fecond fon of Sir Edward
Hales, knight and baronet.
She departed this life on the
Twenty-firft day of January,
In the 49th year of her age;
And left iffue three fons
And two daughters,
Viz. ROBERT, Elizabeth,
Thomafin, John, and William.
MDCCVII."

In the chancel on white marble.

"ROBERT GROVE, junior,
Efquire, Juftice of
The Peace *(a)* (of
Tunftall) in the COUNTY
Of KENT, died October
The 10th, A^{no} D^{om} 1716,
Aged 24 years."

Arms: Ermine on a chevron Gules 3 efcallops Argent.

Adjoining to the above:
" Here lieth the body of
John Grove, eldeft fon
Of Robert Grove, of Tunftall,
Efq. who departed this life
Novr. the 20th, Ann. Dom. 1704,
Aged Twenty Years and
Eleven Months.
HERE
Alfo is interred the body of
Mrs. Elizabeth Grove (mother
Of the faid Mr. John Grove), who
Died the 29th day of July, 1722,
Anno Ætatis 64.

Engraven on a brafs plate, in capitals:
" Chriftophoro Webbes *(b)*, viro opt' integerrimo, Johannis Webbes de Gillingham in comitatu Cantii armigeri filio, in facra Theologia Baccha-
laureo, S^{ti} Johannis in Cantabrigia olim præfidenti dig-
niffimo, hujus ecclæfiæ, in qua nunc demum componitur, paftori
vigilantiffimo, 16 liberor', Jocofæ, Mariæ, Johannis, Elizabethæ,
Aliciæ, Thomæ, Edvardi, Katharinæ, Prifcillæ, Afræ, Chriftopheri,
Rogeri, Jacobi, Marthæ, Francifcæ, Matthiæ, partim fuperftitum, partim
defuctorū parenti piiffimo ; qui poftquam numerofam familiam et domum
apprime hofpitatem *(c)* fummā cū laude aluiffet, vitam inculpatam annos
natus 63, cum placida morte 7° Januarij 1610 comutavit *(d)*
Katharina pientiffima conjux hoc meritū moerens monumētū pofuit."

(a) and quorum has been erafed.
(b) See p. 56.
(c) S^{ic}. *for* hofpitalem.
(d) Sic. *for* commutavit.

Above

Above this on the fame ftone, but a feparate plate, are thefe arms :

Quarterly, 1 G. a fefs between 3 owls Or.

2 . . . . a fefs between 3 lozenges G.

3 Ermin, or rather fix fpots of ermine 3, 2, 1.

4 . . . . . a chevron G. between 3 eftoiles.

Creft, a dexter arm couped above the elbow holding an oak branch with leaves and acorns.

Clofe to the foregoing is an effigy in brafs of a prieft in his robes, with this infcription :

" Hic jacet dñs Radûs Wulf (*e*) nup rector ifti' ecclie qui
Obijt xx° die Junii A° Dñi MVCXXV° cui' aïe ,ppitiet' D'. Amen."

On a label iffuing from his fhoulder,
" Spes mea in deo eft."

Adjoining to which,

" Hic jacet Margareta filia dñi Jacobi Crowmer militis dudum vxor
Johis Rycyls heredis manerij de Eflyngham (*f*) quæ obiit fcdõ die dcẽbr.
Anno Domini millñio CCCCLXXXXVJ° cujus anime ,ppiciet Ie' Aẽ.

At each corner of this ftone are coats of arms, but too much defaced to be made out, except towards the right hand at the top may be feen, *Crowmer* impaling Argent, a fquirrel Gules, *Squirry* of Weftram (*g*), and at the bottom towards the left, Crowmer

---

(*e*) See p. 55.

(*f*) John Rykeld was tenant to the prior and convent of Rochefer for Æflingham here mentioned 1 H. VI. He was fheriff of Kent in the third year of this reign, anno 1425, and kept his fhrievalty at Æflingham. The fon or grandfon of this John Rykeld may probably be the John Rycyles of the infcription. See Year Books 11 H. VI. Pafc. 26. Wecver, p 532. 563. Pat. 21 R. II. m . . . commiffio directa Will° Rickhill de colloquio habendo cum duce Glouc' in villa Cales exiftent. See my extracts from the archbifhop's regifters, p. 126. 134. 170. 131. This Sir William Rickill was admitted ferjeant at law 7 R. II. and conftituted juftice of the bench 20 Maij 12 R. II. he was fent for into parliament touching this bufnefs of the duke of Gloucefter, 1 H. IV. See Hollis's Remains, p 48.

(*g*) Here the fquirrel ftands upright on his hinder legs.

4   impaling

impaling on the right . . . . 2 bars between 3 annulets . . . . On the left, Erm. on a chevron 3 *leopards* faces, ... as here engraved.

p 78

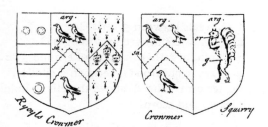

In the chancel.
" HERE LIETH THE BODIE OF JANE WOOD,
ONE OF THE DAUGHTERS OF JOHN ADYE OF
DONINGTON, WITHIN THIS COVNTIE, GENT.
AND LATE THE WIFFE OF JAMES WOOD ALIAS,
AT WOOD OF GRAYSE INN, GENT. OF THE
FAMYLIE OF SIR JOHN WOOD, OF SNAD . . .

❋ . ❋ ❋ ❋ ❋ ❋

[What fhould follow is hid by the communion rails.]
Certamen illud præclarum certavi
Curfum abfolvi."

Arms : Quarterly. 1. a chevron between 3 bulls heads. 2.
On a fefs 3 fleurs de lis. 3. On a fefs 3 roundels. 4. Gone.
Impaling, a chevron indented.

On the North fide of the communion table :

" Elizabetha Cayfar de Hollingborn,
Uxor Jacobi Dixon armigeri de Tunftall,
pia, modefta, eleganti formâ,
et ingenio vivaciffimo ;
unicam filiam duos filios relictos
habuit :
Alteram fobolem jamjam paritura
In ipfo conamine' fuccubuit,

Et

Et præmatura mors feipfam nobis,
Et nos feipfâ infeliciter eripuit,
Non fine ingenti amicorum luctu
pariter et difpendio
31 Maias
1680."

Arms : Gules on a bend O. between 6 plates ; three torteauxes ;
a chief of the 2ᵈ charged with 5 Ermine fpots impaling G. a
chevron engrailed Ermine ; on a chief Or 3 fleurs de liz Sable.

South of the communion table is a black marble thus infcribed :

" Here lyeth the body of John Putland, late of the county of
Stafford, gent. and one of the curfitors of the high court of chancery.   He married Ann daughter of John Grove, efq; of this
place, who, out of due regard to his memory, dedicates this
marble.   Natus Aug. 14, 1702, denatus Sept. 16, 1755."

Againft the north wall of the chancel, a monument of Dr.
Cheke, with his effigy in white marble, and the following infcription :

" READER Learne to live Learne to die by
this example of Patience, Humility, and all
Chriftian Virtues.
ROBERT CHEKE, (b) D. OF DIVINITY, OF SINGULAR PIETY
LEARNING : 4ᵗʰ SONNE OF JOHN OF THAMES-DITTON IN SURREY,
OF THE AUNTIENT FAMILY OF THE CHEKES OF BLOOD-HALL
IN SUFFOLK, ON THE 5ᵗʰ OF JULY, IN THE YEARE OF OUR
LORD 1647, OF HIS AGE 78, RETURNED TO HEAVEN.
TO WHOSE HAPPY MEMORY HIS EVER MOURNING AND MOST
LOVING WIFE MARY, DAUGHTER OF WILLIAM CLARKE,
OF FORD IN WROTHAM, ESQʳ. ERECTED THIS MO-
NUMENT, AND DESIRES HERSELFE TO BE BURIED BE-
SIDE HIM WITHOUT ANY OTHER REMEMBRANCE OF HER
THEN THAT SHE LIVED AND DYED ONELY HIS."

On a fillet of black marble over the head of the buft :
" I know that my Redeemer" &c.

(b) See p. 56.

Arms

Arms on this monument;

Or a cock G. beaked and membred Az.

Or a bend engrailed Az.   *Fekerham* of Berks.

Quarterly, 1 & 4, Or a cock G. beaked and membred Az. a crescent
for difference.

2 & 3 Barry of 8 Or and Gules.   *Fitz-Allen.*

Impaling

Or a bend engrailed Az.   *Fekerham* of Berks.

On the left of D^r. Cheke's, Mr. Mores's monument,

In a chapel on the south-side of the chancel

A very handsome monument against the wall with the effigy
of Sir James Crowmer and his wife praying before an altar, and
four of their children in the same attitude.

"MEMORIÆ SACRVM.

Scire viator aves istâ quis conditur urna :

Mors hominem dicit vita fuisse bonum.

Qualis erat? Miles, Crowmeri stemate clarus :

Nominis heu nunc est ultimus ille sui,

Quatuor hic genuit natas, at masculus hæres

Defuit ; hinc nomen, non tamen hoc periit.

Fallor enim, quicunque Deo sua nomina tradunt

In libro vitæ nomina scripta tenent.

Obiit 27 Martii, 1613.

LADY MARTHA
HIS DEARE AND
SORROWFULL
WIFE, FOR HONOUR
AND LOVE, NOT
WITHOUT MUCH
GREIFE HATH
ERECTED THIS
MONUMENT."

Over

Over one of the daughters, the arms gone,

" FRANCIS THE ELDEST DAUGHTER OF SIR JAMES CROWMER, OF TUNSTALL, KNIGHT, BY FRANCIS HIS FIRST WIFE, THE DAUGHTER AND HEIRE OF JOHN SOMERS, ESQ. MARRIED TO SIR MATHEW CAREW, KNIGHT, SONE AND HEIR OF SIR MA-THEW CAREW, KNIGHT."

Over the other three :

ELIZABEETH, MARTHA, AND CHRISTIAN, THE DAUGH-TERS OF SIR JAMES CROWMER, OF TUNSTALL, KNIGHT, BY MARTHA LADY CROWMER HIS SECOND WIFE, THE ONLY DAUGHTER OF SIR MATHEW CAREW, KNIGHT, AFORESAID.

Arms : Quarterly 1 & 4, Argent, a chevron engrailed be-tween 3 crows Sable. *Crowmer.*

2 & 3, Argent, a fquirrel erect Gules.
Squirry of Weftram.

Quarterly, as above, impaling

1 Or, 3 lions paffant guardant Sable. *Carew.*
2 Gules, a manche Ermine ; a fleur de liz for difference Or.
Delamar of Oxford.
3 Or, 3 torteauxes, a label of 3 points Az. *Courtney.*
4 Az. femée of fleurs de liz, Argent, a lion rampant Ermine.
5 Gules bezantée, a canton Ermine.
6 Per fefs and pale Or, and Gules, 4 efcallop fhells counter-changed.
7 Az. 3 bendlets Argent.
8 Ermine, a bend Gules. *Barnake.*
9 Gules, a bend Argent between 3 plates.
10 Gules, a fefs wavy Argent.
11 Gules, a chevron between 3 doves Argent.
12 Argent, a crofs floré Sable.

M

Upon.

Upon the floor before this monument lyes a ftone, with the following infcription upon a brafs plate :

" Here lyeth buried Henry Guyldeford, efquyer, captaine of her majeftie's forte of Artclyffe neere to Dover, the third fonne of Sir John Guyldeforde, knight, in Kent, who deceaf-ed the xxiiij[th] of Maye, 1595, beinge of the age of lvij yer-es, and in the yere of the raigne of our foverigne lady queene Elizabeath xxxvij."

Over which on a feparate plate are thefe arms,
A faltire between 4 mullets, a mullet for difference.
He was brother to Lady Elizabeth Crowmer, mother of Sir James

Upon each of the pinnacles of the monument have been fhields ; one is loft, the other ignorantly reverfed.

Weftward of this monument is a ftatue in white marble of Sir Edward Hales, lying at length in armour, reclining on his left arm on an altar of black marble ; on a fcroll of white marble this infcription :

M. S.
HERE LYETH SIR EDWARD HALES,
OF TUNSTALL IN THE COUNTY OF
KENT, KNIGHT AND BARONETT,
WHO DIED THE SIXTH OF OCTOBER,
1654, IN THE SEVENTY-EIGHTH
YEARE OF HIS AGE.

Arms : At one end of the altar ; Gules, 3 arrows Argent, headed Or. *Hales.*

At the other end, Or, 3 lions paffant guardant Sable. *Carew.*

In front, *Hales* impaling Or 3 lions paffant, Sable ; a finifter hand couped, G. on an efcallop Argent, a mullet Or.

I Quarterly,

Quarterly,
{
1 *Hales.*
2 A chevron engrailed ; colours worn out.
3 Argent, 3 lions heads erafed Sable, langued Gules.
4 Gules, on a chevron Argent 3 talbots paffant Sable, on an inefcotcheon Az. a fefs Ermine between 3 lions heads erafed Or.   *Harlakenden.*
}

Painted on vellum, and hanging againft a pillar in Mrs. Chambers' pew ;

Az. a fefs Ermin between 3 lions heads erafed Or,
    impaling
Per chevron Sable and Or 3 eagles difplayed counter-changed.

Underneath is this infcription :

" In the upper end of this ally lyeth interred the body of Sylvefter Harlackenden of Ufton, in the parifh of Tunftall and county of Kent, Efq. of the ancient family of the Harlackendens of Woodchurch, in the faid county, who departed this life the 19th day of March, 1659, being the 54th yeare of his age."

On the reading defk :
" W.   1588   C."

Arms in the windows.

In the eaft window of the chancel.
Crowmer, impaling Quarterly .... defaced *.

Ditto, impaling Quarterly, 1 & 4 per fefs and pale Or and Gules. 2 & 3. loft.

Ditto, impaling Quarterly, 1 & 4 Ermine .... defaced, but the fame as in the eaft window of the north ifle ; 2 & 3 Sable, a chevron between 3 mattocks Argent, as before : fome fragments of an infcription fcarcely legible.

* In the annexed plate the impalement is Quarterly, 1. Az. a lion rampant O. 2. 3. G. 3 croffes patée fitché Arg. 4. Arg. on a chief Sable a lion rampant Arg. impaling Arg. a faltire engrailed.

Weſt window of the north iſle :
Argent, 2 bars nebule Gules, or barry nebule of 6 Argent
and Gules.

In the next window :
Ermine a feſs nebule Gules.   Perhaps *Iſley*.

In the next window :
Crowmer impaling Or, a plain croſs Gules ; with others defaced.
Crowmer, with the creſt.   *Haut*.
Crowmer, impaling Or 3 chevronels Sable.
Some mutilated images of a dragon, a woman, and a great
ferpent.

In the next window :
Crowmer, impaling Or a plain croſs Gules, and
    Argent, on a chevron Gules between 3 bugle horns, Sable,
    as many mullets of 5 points Or.   *Haut*.
Crowmer, impaling Ermine on a chevron Gules, 3 leopards
    faces Or. *Cantelupe* ; and
    Sable, a chevron between 3 mattocks Argent.   *Moſeley*.
𝔒rate ro   om   ' 𝕮𝕮𝕮 𝕴𝕴𝕴.

In the eaſt window of the north iſle.
In the middle partition ſided by the roſe and ſceptre *France* and
    England.
Quarterly, 1 & 4, Az. 3 fleurs de lis Or.
            2 & 3, Gules, 3 lions paſſant Or.
            Crowmer.
            Az. 3 fleurs de lis Or, impaling *Crowmer*.

                                            Crowmer,

Pl. III. p84.

In the E. window of the chancel.

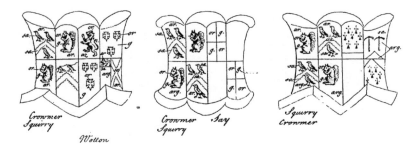

Cronmer
Squirry

Wotton

Cronmer
Squirry

Jay

Squirry
Cronmer

In the E. window of the N. isle.

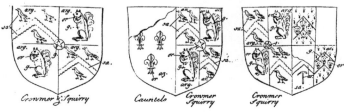

Cronmer & Squirry

Cauntelo Cronmer
Squirry

Cronmer
Squirry

In the S.W. wind. of the S. isle. p84.

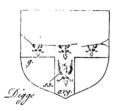

Digge

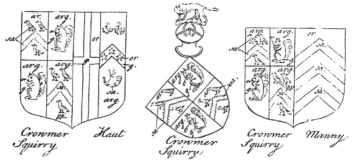

Cronmer   Haut   Cronmer   Cronmer   Manny
Squirry   Squirry   Squirry

In the NE. window of the N. isle.   p 84

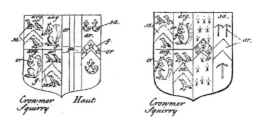

Cronmer   Haut   Cronmer
Squirry   Squirry

p 84

W. wind. of the N. isle.   NW wind. of the N. isle.

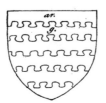
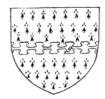

Crowmer, impaling Quarterly, 1 & 4 Ermine on a chevron Gules, 3 leopards faces Or.   *Cantelupe.*
2 & 3 Sable, a chevron between 3 mattocks Argent.
Mofeley.

In the fouth weft window of the fouth ifle,
Gules, on a plain crofs Argent, 5 eagles difplayed Sable. *Diggs.*

Atchievments.
In the chancel.
Gules on a bend Or between 6 plates 3 torteauxes, a chief of the fecond charged with five ermines Sable,
impaling
Gules, a chevron engrailed Ermine; on a chief Or 3 fleurs de lis Sable.
The firft coat impaling per pale Gules and Sable a lion paffant Argent.
Motto, " Ne me capiat jufticiæ oblivio."

Barry of 6 Argent and Sable, in chief 3 golpes.
Motto, " Vinco anima fponfa Chrifti."

In the fouth ifle.
Ermine on a chevron Gules 3 efcallop fhells Or.
impaling Argent a chevron chequy Or and Az. between 3 bucks heads erafed Gules, attired of the fecond.

In the chapel:
Hales, impaling on the right, Argent, a plain crofs between 4 crofs crofslets fitché Gules.
On the left; Ermine 2 bars Or, over all a lion rampant Azure, langued Gules.
Motto, " Unum eft neceffarium."

Over

Over the doors at the entrance of the chapel.
Hales impaling Argent a crofs wavy Sable.

In Mr. Mores' pew, Hales' creft with this motto.
" A folo ad cœlum."

In Mr. Grove's pew, Hales's arms.

In the north crofs ifle.
" Eleanor Chambers,
1729.
Aphra Chambers,
1731."

On the bells :
1 ROBERTUS MOT ME FECIT, 1596.
2 ROBERTUS MOT ME FECIT, 1600. } R. M. and 3 bells.
3 R. PHELPS FECIT, 1702.
4 PRAYSE YE THE LORD, 1573. A crown between 3 bells.
5 JOHN WILNAR MADE ME, 1630.

References

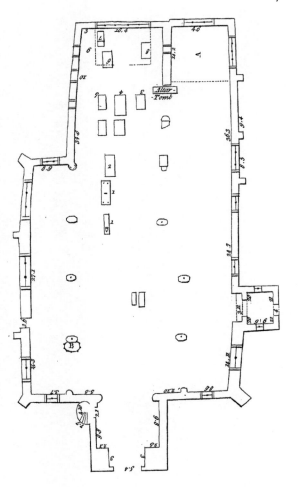

References to the Plan of the Church.

1. Three ſtones robbed of their braſſes.
2. Thomaſine Gore.
3.   Webbes.
4.   Wulf.
5. Margaret Rycyls.
6.   Wood.
7. Elizabeth Dixon.
8. John Putland.
9. Dr. Cheke.
10. Mr. Mores.

A. Addition by Sir Edward Hales, 1655.
B. Font.

Octogonal ſides of the pillars at the baſe 11 inches; at the ſhaft 8 inches; diſtance of each E. and W. taken from the ſhaft 9 feet 8 inches; from N. to S. 16 feet 4 inches.

The font is ſtone, but heightened with a rim of brick, and lined now with lead, from out to out at top 2 feet 7 inches; but the ſpace between the pilaſters will diminiſh them in the ichnography; height to the end of the ſtone 2 feet 7 inches; for the brick work add $3\frac{1}{4}$ inches.

The buttreſſes and the wall generally 2 feet 6 inches thick.

Lancet windows about 1 foot 5 inches.

Altar window, about a foot wider than the rails, muſt be placed exactly over them at the N. ſide, and a foot beyond them at the S. ſide.

Chapel E. window 5 feet 5 inches.

The next 6 feet 6 inches.

The

The next 5 feet 8 inches over Sir Edward Hales.
The next 4 feet 8 inches over Mr. Grove's pew.
The next 5 feet.
The next 4 feet 6 inches ⎫
The next or W. window of S. ifle, 4 feet 6 inches ⎬ and alike.

NOTES TAKEN 23 May 1760.

The Queen's arms erected 1708, Robert Grove, efq. then church-warden.

The altar monument pl. VI. in the chancel is made with one fide plain, and was therefore manifeftly intended to ftand againft a wall. Indeed it feems to have been made for the place where it now ftands, particularly from the appearance of the fouth end; if fo it was fet up fince the chapel was built. Upon it feveral idle perfons have cut the initial letters of their names; of thefe I obferve one in the year 1661.

On the fouth fide of the chancel ftill remains a lancet window fimilar in all refpects to the three in the north fide, and correfponding to the eafternmoft of them.

The lancet window remaining in the fouth wall of the chancel, and looking into the chapel, proves that the chapel was not built at the fame time with the chancel.

From

Pl VI p 61

From the Regifter.

A booke of all the weddings, chriftenings, and burienges, beginninge in the xxxth yeare of the reygne of Kinge Henrie the viii of famous memory, William Bounker being then parfon of this parifh of Tunftall.

Anno Domini 1538.

Mr. Symon Jenninges, parfon of Tunftall, fep. 27 Nov.

N. B. This gentleman built the pigeon-houfe belonging to the parfonage, as appears by his name cut on the walls thereof as follows:

1538

S. Jenyns: pries pour luy

1539.

Sʳ Wᵐ Cromer, Kᵗ. ob. 20 Jul. Sep. 21 die D.

1540.

Simeon Pottman, nat. & bapt. 5 Jul.

Joan Pottman, ob. Jul. 7. fep. 8.

Tho. Pottman & Eliz. Tournae marᵈ 22 Nov.

1541.

James Cromer, Efq. ob. 30 Maij fep. eodem die poft M.

Mary Pottman, nat. & bapt. 20 Aug.

Rob. Tong, nat. & bapt. 26 Sept.

1543.

Wᵐ Pottman, born & chr. 12 Maij.

John Bredgman & Godlie Chapnell marᵈ. 27 Maij.

1544.

Joan Pottman, nat. & fep. 7 Jan.

1545.

Rich. Pottman, nat. & bap. 25 Feb.

1547.

Ann Pottman, nat. & bap. 12 Feb.

N

1549.

1549.

Suſ. Pottman, nat. 31 Jan. bapt. 2 Feb.

1551.

Alice Tong, a good houſholder, æt. 52, ſep. 2 Feb.

Sara Pottman, nat. 16 Feb. bapt. 21.

1553.

Ann Pottman, nat. 10 Jan. b^p. 13.

1554.

Judith Hale, bapt. 5 Jun.

1556.

James Tonge, a good howſholder, æt. 71, worthy of perpetual memory, ſep. 18 Octobr.

James Tong & Agnes Henyter, nupt. 18 Jan.

1557.

James Tong, ſep. 15 Apr.

Marg. Pottman, nat. & bapt. 15 Maij.

Marg. Pottman, n. & b. 29 Jun.

Marg. Pottman, ſep. 22 Aug.

1558.

Wm Gore, ſep. 27 Apr.

Wm Pottman, bap^t. ap^d. Sittingb.

1559.

Mary Tong, n. & b. 9 Apr.

1560.

Wm Bunker, prieſt & parſon of Tunſtall, ſep. 15 Jun. fere.

Simeon Tong & Alice Bunker, nupt. 25 Sept.

1561.

W^m. Cromer, eſq^r. & Eliz. Gildeford, da. of Sr John K^t. mar^d. at Boughton Mallarde, 1 Octob.

Iſaac Tong, bapt. 13 Dec. ſep. 7 Feb.

1362.

James Cromer, f. W^{mi} n. b. & 1. 25 Maij.

Barbara Cromer, n. & b. eodem die.

Eliz.

Eliz. Tong, n. 22 Jun. b. 28.
Jane Cromer, f. W^{mi} n. 12 fep. b. 15.

1563.

Dorothy Cromer, f. W^{mi} nat. 5. Sept. b. 10.

1564.

Rich. Tong, n. 25 Maij.
J^{no} Pottman & . . . R . . . charden Peers, nupt. 29 Oct.

1565.

Zacheus Harlackenden, n. 3 Mar. b. 4.
Dorothy Tong, nat. 8 Mar. b. 10.
Tho. Pottman, yeoman, ob. 24 fep. 26 Mar.

1567.

From hence forw^d. I omitt the Pottmans.
Mary Cromer, fil. W^{mi}, n. 22 Oct. b. 23.
Dorothy Harlackenden, n. 3 Maij. b. 7. fep. 7 Jun.

1568.

Jonathas Harlackenden, n. 29 Maij.
J^{no} Tong, & Phillis Bull, nupt. 10 Jan.

1569.

Bridget Harlackenden, ux. Walteri 1. 28 Jun.
Nich. Tong, n. & b. 23 Sept.
James Cromer, f. W^{mi}, n. 24 Dec.

1572.

Tho. Thacker, late parfon of T. fep. 29 Sept.
Jone Thacker, his widow, 1. 5 Jan.

1573.

Suf. f. y^{ms} Tong, b. 30 Sept^r.

157$\frac{4}{3}$.

Hen. f. Walt. Harlackenden, b. 19 Mar.
J^{no} f. Simeon Tong, b. 2 Feb. 157$\frac{5}{6}$.
Ralph f. John Coldwall, parfon 1. 21 Jun:

1577.

Walt. f. Walt. Harlackenden, b. 21 Apr.

N 2

W^m f. Joh. Coldwall, parfon, n. 23 Apr. b. 26.

Wm Tylden of Wormfell & Eliz. Tong, n. 15 Jun.

Tho. Bifhop, gent. & Ann f. W^{mi} Cromer, nupt. 19 Sept.

Joan, wife of Mr Dr Coldwall, parfon, ob. 28 Dec. 1. 29.

1578.

J^{no} Sharpe & Joan Tong, nupt. 7 Jul.

Eliz ux W^{mi} Cromer, ob. 6 Jul. 1. 8.

Eliz. Harlackenden, f. Walt. b. 7 Dec.

1580.

Sara Harlackenden, f. Walt. b. 28 Maij.

Wm Shurland, Brafted arm. & Doroth. f. W^{mi} Cromer, nupt. 2 Nov.

1581.

Mich. f. Walt. Harlakenden, b. 17 Jun. fep. 3 Dec. 1596.

Peter Pott, parfon of Tunftall, occ. 17 Nov. ob. 10 Oct. 1584.

1583.

Doroth. Tong, fep. 14 Maij.

Geo. Wanderfon, & Ann T. mar^d 1 Jul.

J^{no} Harlakenden, f. Walt. nat. 12 Sept.

1584.

Pet. f. Pet. Pott. parfon of T. n. 3 Aug. b. 9.

Pet. Potts, parfon of T. ob. 10 Oct. fep. 11.

Chriftophe Webbes, Rect^r, ecclefiæ Tunftallenfis legis articulos illi lege ad legendum injunctos 21° Febr. hora p^r cum matutin. audientibus oibus parochis ann. R. R. E. 27, &c. coram his teftibus fubfcriptis

> Wm Cromer,
> Walt. Harlakenden,
> Wm Tonge,
> Simon Tonge,
> & others.

1586.

Ann f. Walt. Harlakenden, n. 2 Dec.

Suf.

Suf. f. Walt. n. eodem die, ob. 24 Dec.

Geo. Bynge, gent. f. Rob. Bynge, efq^r. & Jane f. W^{mi} Cromer, nupt. 22 Feb. $\frac{6}{7}$.

1587.

Suf. Harlakenden, ux. Walt. ob. 26 Maij 1. 27.

Sam. Boyfe de Hawkhurft gent. & Mary f.

W^{mi} Cromer, nupt. 12 Sept.

Hen. Clifford, efq^r. & Jane Harlakenden, nup. 26 Dec.

Walt. n. 19 Sept. 1590. fep. 3 Oct.

Urfula, n. 26 Nov. 1588. fep. 21 Sept. 1603.

Sam. Nichols, minifter, & Marg. Daye nupt. 30 Sept.

1588.

Rob. Tong & Eliz. Genet nupt. 30 Dec.

1590.

Eliz. f. W^{mi} Tong, n. 10 Apr.

159$\frac{1}{2}$.

James Tong & Alice Clarke, nupt. 2 Feb.

1593.

Mr Wm Tong, fep. 18 Jul.

Mr Ellis cur. of Milfted, ob. 9 Sept.

Wm Edw^{ds} & Eliz. Tong, wid^w. nupt. 17 Sept.

1595.

Mrs Anne Tong, ux. W^{mi} ob. 7 Dec.

1597.

Fr. Cromer, da. of James nat. 6 Apr.

Fr. ux. Jam. ob. 27 Apr.

1598.

Wm Cromer, Efq^r. juftice of the peace & quor. ob. 12 Maij, æt. 67. fep. 18.

Robt. Bradftreete, & Eliz. Tonge, nup. 9 Apr.

1599.

Jane Burftone, da. to Mrs Harlakenden 1. 24 Jan. $\frac{99}{100}$.

1600.

1600.

Wm Gilford & Eliz. Tong, mar^d. 16 Sept.

1601.

Martha f. Jam. Cromer, nat. 27 Apr.

Tho. f. Jam. Tong, b. 21 Jun.

Nich. Tong, & Tliz. Warrope, nupt. 27 Jul.

Hen. Harlakenden, f. Walt. fep. 18 Oct. being flain 15 of fame month tow^{ds} evening.

1602.

J^{no} f. Nich. Tong, b. 26 Sept.

Walt. f. Zach. Harlakenden, b. eodem die.

Tho. Awdley & Eliz. Harlakenden, nupt. 22 Febr.

1603.

Anne Harlakenden, fep. 13 Aug.

J^{no} f. Hen. Clifford, fep. 22 Sept.

Walt. Harlakenden, ob. & fep. 24 Sept.

Zach. f. Walt. ob. & f. 26 Sept.

Marg. ux. Zach. ob. & fep. 3 Octob.

1605.

Mich. Tonge, fep. 21 Octob.

1606.

Tho. Harlakenden, b. 4 Maij.

1607.

Chriftian Cromer, f. Jam. nat. 6 Octob.

1608.

Mr Wm Tong, ob. 14 Maij.

1610.

Mr Xpofer Webbes R^r. of T. fep. 15 Jan.

1613.

Sr James Cromer, ob. 27 Mar. f. 8 Apr.

1615.

Martha Cr. πότνα γυναικῶν f. Sr Jam. fep. 14 Apr.

Xpofer f. Dr Bennet bapt. 12 Jun.

1619.

1619.

Suf. ux. James Tong, jun^{rs} ob. Jul. 9. fep. 12.

Mrs Jane Paftrich, widow, da. of James Tong, fen^r. ob. Jul. 30.

1621.

James Tong, jun^r. & Joan Chalker nupt. 1 Nov.

1622.

James f. W^{ml} Tonge, b. 23 Jun. fep. 25.

1624.

J^{no} Hales, Efq. & Mrs Chrift^n. Cromer, nupt. 1 Mar.

1625.

M^r W^m. Tonge, fep. Sept. 13.

Edw. f. Sr J^{no} Hales, b. Feb. 12.

1626.

Dame Martha, wife of Sr Edwd Hales. 11 Maij.

1627.

James Tong, gent. fep. 11 Sept.

1630.

Edw. f. Sam. Hales, gent. b. 18 Apr.

1631.

Chriftian f. Sam. Hales, b. 10 Apr.

Mrs Eliz. Tonge, f. Feb. 2.

Eliz. f. Sam. Hales, b. Mar. 25. 1632.

1633.

Mrs Alice Tonge, ux. Tho. Tonge, f. 9 Ap. [fomething cut out.]

163$\frac{3}{4}$.

Suf. Harlakenden, fep. 14 Jan.

1634.

Deborah f. Sam. Háles, bapt. 5 Octob.

1635.

Eliz. f. Sam. Hales & Marthæ ux. ejus fep. 5 Apr.

1636.

[Something cut out, as before obferved.]

J^{no} f. Sam. Hales & M. fep. 1 Feb. $\frac{3}{7}$.

I   1638.

1638.

Sam. Hales, gent. fep. 18 Junij.

1639.

A child of Roger Harlakenden, fep. 21 Sept.

Sr J^{no} Hales, K^t. fep. 15 Octob.

1640.

W^m f. Silvefter Harlakenden, & Eliz^æ. ux. ej^s. bapt. 19 Aug.

Dame Chriftian, relict. Sr J^{no} Hales, fep. 23 Sept.

Wm Harlakenden, fep. 29 Jan.

1641.

Silvefter f. Silv. & Eliz. Harlakenden, bapt. 30 Dec

1646.

Rebecca, da. of Mr Harlakenden, bapt. 24 Maij.

Mr Wm Gell, A. M. curate of Tunftall fep. 20 Junij.

1647.

Robt. Cheke, D. D. Rect^r of T. fep. 8 Jul.

J^{no} f. Sylv. Harlakenden, & E^d. b.   Dec. fep. 7 Jun. 48.

Geo. & Jam. f. Rob. Dixon, A. M. R^r of T. b. 27 Jan. Geo.
ob. 4 Mar.

J^{no} f. Edw. Hales, Efq. b. 7 Mar.

1649.

Mary f. Sylv. Harlakenden, bap. 9 Nov.

1650.

Eliz. f. Rob. Dixon, A.M. b. 9 Jul.

M^n Mary Cheke, rel. of Dr Cheke, fep. 21 Octob.

Martha f. Sylv. Harlakenden, b. 3 Dec. f. 15. 4 Sept. 1653.

165$\frac{2}{3}$.

James Sylv. Harlakenden, b. 10 Febr. fep. 21 Nov.

James f. Jam. Tong & Helen ux^s. ej. b. 3 Nov.

Tho. f. Edw. Hales, efq^r. & Annæ b. 26 Dec.

1654.

John f. J^{no} Grove & Mildredæ, b. 2 Aug.

Sr Edward Hales, fep. 10 Octob^r.

                                                    Sarah

Sarah f. Sylv. Harlakenden, b. 26 Octob^r. f. 31.

Dame Ann Hales, ux. Sr Edwd. f. 8 Febr.

165$\frac{5}{6}$.

John f. Jam. Tong & Hel^æ. b. 3 Jan.

1656.

Sarah f. John Grove & Mildredæ, b. 29 Dec. fep. 7 Jan.

1657.

Edward f. Jam. Tong, & Helenæ, b. 23 Dec.

165$\frac{8}{9}$.

Robt. f. J^{no} Grove & M. b. Febr. 22.

1659.

Mary f. Sylv. Harlakenden, f. 22 Maij.

Eliz. f. Jam. Tong & Helenæ, b. 22 Dec.

Sylv. Harlakenden, f. 23 Mar.

1661.

Robert f. Jam. Tong, C. 12 Sept. f. 10 Octob.

1662.

Thomas f. Jam. Tong & H. fep. 7 Oct.

Charles f. ejufdem, bapt. 21 Febr.

1667.

Symon f. ejufdem, nat. 13 b. 17 Apr. f. 30.

1670.

Henry f. ejufdem, b. 15 Dec.

1673.

Edward f. J^{no} Grove & Mildr. f. 8 Nov.

1674.

Thomas f. Sylv. Harlakenden & Elizæ f. 10 Dec.

1675.

Jane f. Mr Hales of Roughton, f. 25 Sept.

1676.

Sylv. f. Sylv. Harlakenden & Eliz. ux. ejus b. 13 Junij, æt. 2 dierum.

O   167$\frac{7}{8}$.

$167\frac{7}{8}$.

John Grove, Gent. æt. 72 Jan 1. ob. 15 Jan. & fep. 16.

Mildredæ relict. ejus ob. 23 Febr. f. 24.

1678.

Silv. Harlakenden, gent. æf. 37 Dec. 30. ob. 22 Jan. $\frac{8}{9}$. f. 27.

Joel f. ejufd. & Eliz. rel. ejus b. 10 Feb. f. 10 Febr. $\frac{79}{80}$.

1679.

Rebecca f. Rob. Grove & Elize b. 25 Nov. æt. 10 dieth.

1680.

Eliz. ux. Jam. Dixon, efq^r. f. N. fide of the chancel, 3 Junij.

Eliz. f. Rob. Grove & Elizæ b. 23 Nov.

$168\frac{3}{4}$.

John f. ejufdem, b. 15 Jan.

1686.

Edward fon of Capt. Hales, f. 2 Sept.

1687.

Cicely, f. Rob. & E. Grove, b. 12 Apr.

1691.

M^{rs}. Sarah Dixon, widow of Dr. Robt. Dixon, f. 5 Maij.

1692.

Mrs Eliz. Tong, widow f. 18 Oct.

$169\frac{3}{4}$.

Lady Fr. ux. Honble Sr Edwd. Hales, f. 5 Mar.

1704.

John Grove, f. Rob. & Eliz. Tong, b. 15 Jul.

1708.

John f. ejufdem, b. 29 Maij.

1711.

Mr Robert Dixon, Rect^r. f. 25 Mar.

The laft entry in this regifter is

May 15, A^o. 1711—I was inducted into the rectory of Tunftall by Mr Robert Elwick, vicar of Bredgar, in the prefence of
Wm Lott then Church warden of the parifh, with feveral other of

4   inhabitants :

inhabitants: & on Sunday 10 June following I read the whole
fervice with the 39 articles, &c. & gave my affent & confent,
&c. as required by law having been collated into the faid parfonage
Maij 7 by the moft Rev^d. Father in God Tho. Ld Archb^p of Canterbury my good patron.

Edw. Mores.

On a blank leaf at the beginning of the regifter.

Francis Foxton was curate of this parifh 62 years. [The laft
time he figned the regifter was 22 Feb. 160⅔. The firft 5 Oct.
32 H. VIII.]

Nathaniell Jackfon, curate of Tunftall, 30 Aug. 1615 &
1612.

Onefiphorus Paul, A. M. curate of Tunftall 1965.—Ex aul.
Magd. Oxon. A. M. 5 Jul. 1664.

Thos. Brockbancke, A. M. cur. of Tunftall 1664.

Obadiah Paul, A B. cur. of Tunftall.

Robert Dixon, A. M. curate of Tunftall 1669.

Tho. Turner, A. M. curate of Tunftall 1671.

J^no Ballard, A. B. curate of Tunftall at the feaft of S^t. Mich.
1676.

Jofeph Hawling, A. B. curate of Tunftall 1678.

Will. Gell, A. M. curate of Tunftall, bur^d. 20 Jun. 1646.

From the new regifter.

1711.

Robert Gore, of Sittingbourne, efq. buried 25 Oct.

1712.

Eliz. da. of Rob. & Eliz. Tong, baptized 7 Mart.

1715.

Mary, da. of Rob. & Elizab. Tong, bapt. 18 Nov.

1716.

James

James Dixon, broth^r. to the rev. Rob. Dixon, late rector of this parish bur^d 26 Jul.

Rob. Grove, esq. son of Rob. & Elizab. Grove, bur^d 15 Oct.

1717.

Eliz. Gore of S^t. Paul's, Covent-Garden, Westminster, bur^d 12 Apr.

1720.

Thomas son of Will. & Eliz. Tong, bapt^d 26 Jul.

1721.

William son of Will. & Eliz. Tong, bapt. 25 Oct.

1722.

Eliz. wife of Rob. Grove from Kensington, but formerly of this parish, buried 28 Aug.

1723.

Robert Grove, esq. buried 13 Apr.

Eliz. da. of Will. & Eliz. Tong, bapt. 20 Dec.

1729.

Edward Hales, esq. buried 12 Oct.

1738.

Rebecca Grove, buried 12 Oct.

1742.

Robert Dixon of Town-Sutton, buried in linen 14 Aug.

1744.

Sr John Hales, bart. buried 20 Jan.

1746.

Mrs Thomasine Gore of the parish of Walton upon Thames, bur^d 19 Dec.

1749.

Mrs Ann Hales, mother of the present Sr Edward, bur^d 5 Apr.

Parifh Regifter of Tunftall.

Baptifmorum, nuptiajum & fepulturarum numerus quæ Tun-
ftalliæ fingulis annis contigere ab anno 30 H. VIII. 1538 ad
annum 23 G. II. 1750. ₁Mr. Mores had prepared column·
for each of thefe articles from the above period, but not
filled any till 1713.]

      Chr. m. bu.

	Chr.	m.	bu.	
1713	3	3	6	
1714	3	1	4	
1715	5	0	5	

Maria f. Rob. & Eliz. t. Nov. 18.   Robert Gore, of Sittingbourn,

1716	5	0	5	

efq. fep. Oct. 25, 1711.

1717	3	0	3	
1718	4	0	3	
1719	2	2	1	
1720	2	0	4	

James Dixon, brother to the
Rev. Robert Dixon, late rector
of the parifh, fep July 26,
1716.

Tho. f. Will. & Eliz. t. July 26.   Robert Grove efq. f. Rob. & Eliz.

1721	3	1	2	

Oct. 15, 1716.

Will. f. Will. & Eliz. t. Oct. 25.   Eliz. Gore, of St. Paul's Covent

1722	1	2	9	
1723	4	2	2	

Garden, Weftminfter, fep.
April 12, 1717.

Eliz. f. Will. & Eliz. t. June 6.   Eliz. wife of Robert Grove from

1724	3	0	0	
1725	2	2	5	
1726	6	0	3	

Kenfington, but formerly of
this parifh, Aug. 28, 1722.
Robert Grove, efq. April 13,

J. m. f. Will. & Eliz t. Dec. 20.   Edw. Hales, efq. Oct. 12, 1729.

1727	4	2	8	
1728	5	1	2	
1729	3	2	3	
1730	5	0	2	
1731	3	0	2	
1732	5	1	6	

Rob. Grove, Oct. 12, 1738.
Rob Dixon, of Town Sutton,
buried in linen Aug. 14,
1742.
Sir John Hales, bart. Jan. 20,
1743-4.

1733

1733	2	1	5
1734	3	1	5
1735	4	0	7
1736	2	0	3
1737	2	2	4
1738	4	0	5
1739	1	4	1
1740	8	4	4
1741	2	0	4
1742	6	0	6
1743	2	0	3
1744	2	2	3
1745	2	2	1
1746	4	1	2
1747	3	1	3
1748	3	2	4
1749	3	1	2

Mrs. Thomafine Gore, of the parifh of Walton upon Thames, Dec. 19, 1746.

Mrs. Ann Hales, mother of the prefent Sir Edward, April 5, 1749.

From

From the affefs books.

Affeffment made 27 Jul. 1679.
Fr. Kennet, ch. warden.

Rob. Dixon, re&tr	—	35	00	00
Rob. Grove, gent.	—	20	00	00
Edw. Hales, efq.—Mrs Segar	—	87	00	00
Mrs Harlakenden	—	24	00	00
Mrs Segar—Mary Hubbard, widw.		35	00	00
Edw. Hales, efq.—Wid. Brockhull		5	00	00
Mr Brockhull—Gerd Gatland		6	00	00
Mr Cobb—Jam. Sweetlove	—	5	00	00
Edw. Hales, efq.—Tho. Biggs	—	4	00	00
Rob: Kemp	—	4	00	00
Fr. Kennet	—	3	00	00
Joh. Sweetlove	—	2	00	00

Out dwellers.

Edw. Hales, efq. for Woodland	—	20	00	00
Joh. Grant	—	1·0		
Mr John Britcher for Piftock farm	—	34		
Mrs Allen—Will. Drury	—	20		
Ric. Tryer—Tho. Banifter	—	3		
Jacob Lane—Tho. Banifter	—	5		
Tho. Lake—Tho. Bauifter	—	1		
Mr Hales—Jam. Hubbard	—	8		
Mr Will. Slater, clerk	—	5		
Mr Tuck—Tho. Hunt	—	1		

Francis Kennet, churchwarden.

Affeffment

Affeffment made 6 Maij, 1745.

John Grove	—	37 00 00
Mrs Chambers	—	42
Mr Stanley	—	70
for the parfonage	—	80
for Mrs Thurfton's lands	—	6
Mr Will. Heyter	—	70
Mr John Southoufe	—	75
Mr John Denn late Oliver	—	86
Widow Love	—	12
Joh Fuller	—	12
Jeff. Dowle	—	4
Tho. Mitchell	—	6
Steph. Groombridge	—	6
Geo. Seely, late Hodges	—	6
Ric. Beele	—	4

Account

Account of the number of houſes and inhabitants in the pariſh of Tunſtall, taken 2 Jun. 1757.

Names of houſes and occupiers in my time, ſc. 1738.	Preſent tenants.	Landlords.	Number of the inhabitants.	
Tho. Mitchell	Empty	Sir Edw. Hales, bart.		
Grove-end	Joh. Southouſe	Ditto	himſelf, wife, 3 children, 4 ſervants	9
Gilb. Marſhall	Will. Hoby	Mrs. Quepſted of Canterb.	himſelf, wife and 4 children —	6
Goodwife Turner	James Spear	Ditto	himſelf only —	1
Steph. Gindar	Steph. Gindar	Himſelf	himſelf, da. her huſb. Ric. Beale, and 5 child.	8
Jeff. Dowle	Jeffry Dowle	Mr. Beckett of Charing	himſelf, Hodges's wid. and child, and Tho. Phillips, his wife and 5 children	10
Joh. Grove, eſq.	Ric. Grove, eſq.	Rev. Bland	himſelf and 5 ſervants —	6
Will. Hodges	James Phillips	Sir Edw. Hales, bart.	himſelf and his wife	2
Moſes Foods	Tho. Read	Ditto	himſelf, his wife and 4 children —	6
The parſonage			Will. Lake, his wife and 5 child. and Charles Mitchell, his wife and 2 child.	11
John Fuller	Matth. Wickenden	Sir Edw. Hales, bart.	himſelf and 6 children, and Will. Hartridge, his wife and 5 children	14
The old houſe	Geo. Sely	Ditto	himſelf, wife, 4 children and 3 ſervants	9
Margar. Love	John Love	Mr. Whitacre of Troſley	himſelf, wife and 2 children —	4
Gore-court	Tho. Stanley	Myſelf	himſelf, wife, 3 child. and 4 ſervants	9
Steph. Groombridge	Steph. Groombridge	Mrs. Chapman	himſelf, wife and 2 children —	4
Piſtock	Will. Heyter, gent.	Himſelf	himſelf, wife, 1 daughter and 6 ſervants	9
Ufton	Miſs Chambers	Mr. Hyde	herſelf, Mrs. Creek and her da. and 4 ſervants	7

Total 115

Mr. Southouſe, Mr. Sely (or more properly Mr. Den, whoſe ſervant only Sely is) Mr. Stanley, Mr. Hayter, and Miſs Chambers have teams.

P   APPEN-

A P P E N D I X.

P. 6.   Efc. 21 E. III. p. 1. n. 57.

Inq. capt. ap^d Ofpringe die Sabb. poft feft. S. Matth. poft Edm. de S. Joh. (fil. Hug. de S. Joh.)

Præ̃dcus Hugo tenuit die q° ob. unum feod. mil. in Tunftalle juxta Sydyng-bourne q^d Steph. de Cobham de eo tenuit, q^d valet ꝑ ann. xx libr.

P. 7.   Efc. 7 H. VI. 69.

Inq. capt. 16 Apr. ap^d Dertford coram Nic. Rykhull efcaet. poft mortem Tho. Ponynges de S. Johe chr̃. Tenuit d̃cus Tho. die q° ob. in feodo & jure talliato feoda fubfcript. ut ꝑcellas manerij fui de Bafyng & eid̃ m̃. pertinent. & appendencia; viz. &c. &c. &c. unũ feodũ mil. in Tunftall q^d Will. Crowmer tenet, q^d val. ꝑ ann. cũ accident. xl^s. m̃. de Bafyng tenetur in cap.

Obiit p̃dc̃us Tho. 6 Mart. ult. & Conftantia ux. Joh. Paulet, Alefia ux. Joh. Orell & Johes Bonevyle funt confang. & h. ꝑpinq. Conftantia æt. 20. Alefia 19 & ampl. Joh. Bonevyle 19 & ampl.

P. 8.   Efc. 17 R. II. n. 45.

Inq. cap. ap^d Erde die ☽ ante fm̃ S. Edm. poft mort. Ifab. ux. Lucae de Ponynges. Jur. dic. q^d p̃dc̃a Ifab. null. tenuit terr. feu ten. de rege in cap. fed q^d Rob. Knoles, chivaler, tenuit de p̃dc̃a Ifab. die q° ob. unũ feod. milit. in Tunftall preter alia feoda quorum quodlt valet ad accident. c s. ꝑdc̃a Ifab. ob. 16 Oct. ult. & Tho. de Pon-ynges chr̃ eft f. & h. ꝑpinq. æt. 36 & ampl.

P. 11. note n.   Cart. 29 H. III. m. 3.

Rex conc. Walfo de Gray fil. Rob. de G. nepoti W. arch. Ebor. int. alia quicquid juris habuit vel aliquo temp. here poffet in manerijs de Tunftall & Shepeye. Dat. ap^d Weftm. 12 Jun.

P. 12.   Cart. 11 H. III. m. 3.

R. conc. dilc̃o & fid. Hub. de Burgo & Marg. ux. & h. int. alia m̃. de Tunftall ex dono Rob. Arficke. Dat. ap^d Wind. 14 Sept.

P. 13.

P. 13.   Cart. 44 H. III. m. 4.

Rex conc. Joh. de Burgo fen⸢r⸣. & h. lib. war. in o͞ib̄z terris fuis de Dunſtall &
Newton com. K. Dat. ap⸢d⸣ Weſtm. 29 Jul.

Eſc. 44 H. III. n. 66.   Eſc. 3 E. III. p. 1. n. 67.

Inq. poſt mort. Joh. de S. Joh. capt. ap⸢d⸣ Alnodynton 15 Maij.

Kanc.   Et dicunt jurati q⸢d⸣ Steph. de Cobham jun. tenet m̄. de Tonſtall cū p̄tin. in
eod̄ com. de eodem Joh. de S. Joh. p̄ ſerv. 1 feod. mil. & val. ejuſd̄ m̄. p̄ ann. xᶫ.
Hug. f. &. h. ꝑpinq. æt. 19.

Eſc. 36 E. III. p. 1. n. 58.

Inq. capt. ap⸢d⸣ Newynton 24 Nov. 35 E. III. Joh. Douet qui ob. 22 Jul. ꝓx. præ-
terit. tenuit die q° ob. in d̄nico ſuo ut de feodo quod ten: ap⸢d⸣ Tunſtall de Pħa reg.
Ang. p̄ q⸢d⸣ vero ignoratur, & eſt ibi un. meſſ. q⸢d⸣ non val. p̄ ann. ultra p̄. & ſunt ibi
xl acr. paſt. quæ val. p̄ ann. xjˢ. viijᵈ. p̄ acr. ij den. vt in paſtur. p̄ viz. dent. it̄m eſt
ibi de firma ad fm̄ S. Mich. de duob̄s tenent. quorū no͞ia ignor. v q̄rt ordej vel in def.
iiijˢ. iiijᵈ. it̄m ſunt ibi ij acr. boſc. quæ ſemp in x annis poſſint amputari & tunc val.
acr. ijˢ & p̄dict. boſc. amputabatur trib. ann. jam elapſis.   Jacob. Donet æt. 11 fil.
& h. ꝑmiſſ. tent. in capite. & id̄ Jac. & Aver̄ fr̄ ejˢ (æt. ij ad feſt. purif. ꝓx.) ſunt
f. & h. ꝑmiſſ. tent. in Gavelkinde. Will' Simme & Guido Elys exec. teſtam. dc̄i
Joh. dc̄a ten. occupant.

P. 14.

Inter Recordas in Theſaurario Receptæ Scaccarij, viz. Placita de Juratis & Aſſiſis
coram Joħe de Regate & Socijs ſuis Juſtic. Itiner. ap⸢d⸣ Cantuar. in com. Kant. in
octab̄ Sc̄i Hillar̄ Anno Regni Regis Edwardi *Septimo* Septimo.

Rotulus Rex Regis.

Libertas Stepħi de Peneceſtr̄.

Stepħs de Penceſtre qui ħb. manerium de Tonneſtalle de dono Joħnis de Burgo
clamat habere in eodem manerio eaſdem lib̄tates quas ħuit idem Joħnes & ſine carta.
ſcilt infangenethef, furcas, aſſm̄ panis & cerviſ. tumber', viſum franci pleg', warennam, & tenere placita in cur̄ ſua de ſangūe fuſa. Et qd̄ hujm̄odi lib̄tatibus plene uſus
eſt. Et ſimilr̄ predc̄us Joħnes toto tempore ſuo. Et qd̄ niħil uſurpavit ſeu occupavit
ſup Dn̄m Regem vel antec̄ ſuos, petit qd̄ inquirat¹ p̄ patriam. Et milites ad hoc elc̄i
d̄nt ſup ſacr̄m ſuū qd̄ predc̄s Stepħus plene uſus eſt omnibus lib̄tatb. & qd̄ nihil
occupavit ſeu uſurpavit ſup Dn̄m Regē nec antec. ſuos ſic dc̄m eſt ei, q̄d ſine die cū
predc̄is lib̄tatibq̄ ſalvis ſemp Dn̄o Regi & ħer. ſuis jure & actōne cum inde loqui
voluint etc.

N. B. The *Septimo* above printed in italics muſt be a miſtake in copying, as
Stephen de Penceſter lived in the reigns of Edward I and II.

In

In Turri Londiñ inter Brevia Regum.

Placita Corone in com̃ Kant. facta apud Cantuar̃ coram Johe de Shrwre et Socijs fuis Juftic. Domini Reg·s itinerantibus in coñ prediĉto . . . . . . Poft feftum fanĉte Luciæ virginis Anno Regni Regis Edwardi tertij a Conqueftu feptimo.

Stephus de Cobeham de Dunftalle clamat in manerio fuo de Tunftalle habere furcas, pillord. tumberell. emend affize panis et cervif. fiaĉte de tenentibus fuis ejufdem manerij de Tunftalle, et libeiam warennam in omnibus dominicis terris fuis in eodem manerio.

Stephus de Cobeham clamat habere liberam warennam in omnibus dominicis terris fuis manerij fui de Redemeriigg.

P. 15. Ex Regiftro Albo 32 b.

16 Kal. Junii A. D. 1334, coram nobis Joh permiffione divina Cant. archiep. totius Anglie primate & aplice fedis legato in capella manerii de Otford dnis Philippo de Columbers mil. & Steph. de Columbers cleric. fil. et exec. teft. dnæ Alicie de Columbers defunĉt. perfonaliter conftitutis, idem Phil. et Steph. probationi diĉti teft. coram epo Roff. habite renunciarunt tamquam coram non judice: nam diĉta Alicia habuit bona in Cant. & aliis dioc. idcirco die prediĉto archiep. diĉt. teftamentum legitimum pronunciebat, & commifit adm. bonor. executoribus fupradiĉtis; Edmundo de Polle execut. in diĉto teft. nominato tunc prefente & onus adminiftrationis recufante, refervantes fibi (i. e. archiepo.) poteftatem committendi adminiftrationem dno Roberto de Shipton executori in diĉto teft. nominato cum eam petierit. Dat. ap. Otford.

Efc. 2 E. II. n. 66.
Bre regis dat. apd Byflet 22 Nov.

Inquif. de ris & tent. quæ funt Margarete quæ fuit vx. Steph. de Penefheft capt. cor. efcaetor. dni reg. apd Tunftall die ↄ in craft. Epiph. Dñi, regn. regis E. II. 2°, fecundm tenorem bris dni regis ad efcaetor. inde direĉt. p facr. Petr. le Coupere, Osbit de Swantone, Hen. de Grenehell, Walt. ate cherche, Rob. atte Caneme, Will. Robyn, Johñi Dodyr, Joh. ate Gore, Will. de Brodoke, Will. de Dungefelle, Joh. le Man, & Tho. atte Appeltone qui dic. qd pd. M. tenuit in feodo in villa de Tunftall Bradgare & Milftede die qo ob. vn. meff. cũ gardino qd val. p ann. iijs. iiijd. itm ten. feod. iiijxx x acr. terr. quæ val. p ann. xlvs p acr. vjd. itm ten. in feod. ij acr. dim. bofc. qæ val. p ann. xvd p acr. vjd. itm ten. feod. xvijd ob. & q. redd. cũ ptin. p ann. pcipiend. ad fñ S. Mich. & die qd pdĉa Marg. ob. feifita in dnico fuo vt de feod. de oĩbz terris pdcis. dicunt etiã qd pdĉa Marg. ten. oĩa pdĉa teñta in gavelkinde de dno rege in cap. p ferv. iij fol. vij den. q. & per ferv. vnius adventus

p ann.

p̄ ann. ad ꝑx. cur. dñj regis de Middletone poſt ſm̃ S. Mich. q̃ vocatᵣ Lagheday & p̄ ſerv. alterius advent. p̄ ann. ad cur. ejuſđ dñj regis de Middiltone ꝑx. poſt hakeday q̃ vocatᵗ Lagheday, & dic. q̃d Joh. de Orieby clicus c̄ fil. & h. ꝑpinq. ꝑdc̃æ Marg. & de æt. xxx ann. & ampl'.

Sm̃a totius extent. lijˢ ob. q̃. inde in cap . . . de redd. vt patet ſupra iijˢ vijᵈ q̃. et ſic valet de claro xlviijˢ vᵈ ob.

Ĩtm dicunt q̃d eađ. Marg. ten. die qᵒ ob. m̃ de T. q̃d extenditur ad lxˡⁱ p̄ ann. ad term. vit. ſue ex dim. Antonini Bek Dunelm. ep̄i q̃i Steph. de Peneſh'ſt quonđ viu ū ip̃ius Marg. & ip̃a Marg. feoffavit tenend. eiſđ S. & M. & h. ip̃ius Steph. de capit. đnis, &c. et dic. q̃d eađ Marg. tenuit p̄dc̃ū m̃. de Joh. de S. Joh. p̄ ſerv. feod. vnius mil. & faciend. ſeđ. ad cur. p̄dc̃i Joh. de Alnothintone de iij ſept. in iij ſept. & dic. q̃d Joh. ux. Hen. de Cobbeham de Rundale & Alicia q̃æ fuit ux. Joh. de Columberijs ſunt fil. & h. ꝑpinq̃. p̄dc̃i Steph. & dic. q̃d p̄dc̃a Joh̃a eſt de ætat. xl ann. & ampl. & p̄dc̃a Alicia de æt. xxx ann. & ampl. in cuj. rei teſt. p̄dc̃i jurati ſigilla ſua appoſ'.

p̄dc̃a Marg. nullas alias terras ſeu ten. tenuit in ballia mea die qᵒ ob. niſi terras & ten. in iſtis inquiſitionibus con.

P. 17. Eſc. 11 E. III. p. 1. n. 49.

Kanc. Inq. capt. apᵈ Eard 12 Febr. poſt mort. Hug. de Joh.

Steph. Cobeham tenet vm̃ feod. in Tunſtalle juxta Sydyngbourn, & valet p̄ ann. xx libr.

P. 37. Bund. Eſc. 10 E. I. n. 23.

Bře R. dat. apud Perſore 7 Jan. & diređ. vicec. Kanc. de inquirendo ſup libtatibz & conſuetud. quib. Rog. de Shyrlande & anteceſſ. qui tenentes m̃. de Sh. & V. uſi ſunt.

Inq. fađa apud Mydd. die 2 ꝑx' poſt ſm̃ Matth. ap̄li ann. 11 E. I.

Dc̃us Rog. & anteceſſ. ſui in m̃. p̄dc̃is uſi ſunt h̃ere wrecc. maris, blodwyte, childwyte & am̃ceiament. piſtor. & braciatorū de tenentib. ſuis propriis & qd nullus ball. đnj reg. ſolebat diſtringere in m̃. p̄dc̃is abſq. bedello vel ſervient. dc̃i Rog. ſeu anteceſſ. &c. & hoc a tempore cuj. non currit memoria, & dc̃us Rog. reddit annuatim regi xxx ſolid. redd.

Eſc.

Efc. 36 E. III. p. 1. n. 43.

Efc. capt. apud Midd. 12 Apr. 26 E. III.

Rob. Cheyne chivaler ten. in dnico fuo die q° ob. m̃i. de Vſton cũ ptin. in poch. de Tunſt. Midd. & Sidyngb. de Phꞑ regina Angl. ut de m̃i. de Midelton ut pcell. m̃i. de Shirlᵈ. p ſerv. ut fupradic. eſt. (fc. iiijˡⁱ annuatim folv. ad 4 anni term. p̃ncipal. pro m̃i. de Shiᵢlᵈ.) Rich. æt. 10. Rog. æt. 6. funt fil. & h. ꝓpinq.

P. 40.   Efc. 31 E. III. p. 2. n. 8.

Inq. capt. apd Midd. die Jovis ꝓx. poſt fm̃i S. Barnabæ 31 E. III. &c.

Jurati dic. qd n̄ ē ad dampn. regis nec alior. ſi id. dñs rex concedat Henº. atte Gore qd ipſe de xxviij acr. terr. ac ptin. in Sydingb. q̃æ tenentur de dno r. in cap. feoffare poſſit Hen. Willy capellanum ħend. eid. H. W. & h. de dno rege & h. p ſerv. inde deb. & eid. Hen. Willy qº ipſe, tute inde plene & pacif. feiſina refeoffare poſſit dc̃m H. atte G. & Aliciam ux. ej. ħend. dcũ H. & A. & h. ipſius Hen. de dno r. p ſerv. &c. in ꝓpet'.

Item dic. q̃d p̃dc̃a terra tenetʳ de dno rege in cap. p ſerv. 66 ptis vn. feod. mil. item q̃d valet juxta verum valorem ixˢ iiijᵈ. p't acr. iiijᵈ. item q̃d remanent eid Hen. atte G. ultra terram p̃dc̃am vnum meſſ. 80 acr. ter. cũ ptin. in Sydyngb. qd tenentʳ de Phꞑ regina Angl. ut de m̃i. fuo de Midd. in gavelkind p ſerv. 30 fol. p ann. item q̃d p̃dc̃a meſſ. cũ ptin. valet annuat. in oĩbz. exitib. juxta verũ valorem iijˢ iiijᵈ. p̃dc̃a 80 acr. cũ ptin. val. &c. xlˢ p't acr. vjᵈ.

From a furvey of the diocefe of Canterbury, made 12 May, 1578.

Muf. Brit. N° 1759. f. 416.

Sittingbourne deanry.

Sittingbourne, the parfonage impropriate to the Quene's Maj. the vicarage alfo in her gift, dwelling houfes 80, communicants 300, the tenths 20ˢ.

Newington (belonging to All Souls) dwelling houfes 77, communicants 236.

Bredgar, impropriate to Tho. Reader, gent. the vicaꞇage in his gift, dwelling houfes 50, comm. 155.

Borden, impropriate to dame Marg. Roche, wid. vicarage in her gift, dwelling houfes 53, comm. 160.

Milton,   —   dwelling houfes 108, comm. 374.

Tonge,   —   —   dwelling houfes 13, comm. 30.

Morſtone, the parfonage of the gift of Will. Cromer, efq. dwelling h. 10, comm. 42.

4   Bicknor,

Bicknor, — — dwelling h. 5 comm. 6.
Tunſtall, the paiſonage of the gift of archiep. Cant. dwelling h. 16, comm. 82. tenths 28ˢ.
Elmely, (belonging to All Souls) — dwelling h. j. comm. 6.

From a book of the tenures of land in Kent, penes Edv. Umfreville arm. This book belonged to Joh. Phillipot, *Blanch Lion.*

F. 4. a. Margaret que fuit ux. Steph. Pencheſtʳ tenuit in villa de Tunſtall, Bradgar & Milſted vn. meſſ. cũ gardin. 90 acr. terr. 8 acr. paſt. c acr. dim. boſc. et 18ᵈ ob. q. in gavilkinde de rege in cap. per ſerv. 3ˢ 7ᵈ. & per ſerv. ij adnat. p ann. ad cur. regis de Midleton 2 E. II.

F. 22. b. Man. de Tunſtall, Elmeley & Fogleſtone aîs Fulſtone ac diverſ. meſſ. terr. & tent. cognit. p nõia de Elmeley & Bynnen jacent. in Elmeley, Leiſdon, Morſton, & Tonge, ac diverſ. terr. cogn. p nõia de Grovende jacent. in Tunſtall, Bradgare, & Milſted; ac diverſ. terr. cogn. p nõia de Grovende jacent. in Tunſtall, Bradgare & Borden, ac diverſ. meſſ. terr. & tent. cogn. p nõia de Cutnell in Tunſtall, Brad-gare, & Borden, ac diverſ. meſſ. in Tunſtall, Bradgare, Borden, Milſted, Elmeley, Leyſbye, Morſton, & Bloxham, ac diverſ. terr. & tent. in Morſton, Tonge, Babchilde, Sittingborne, Milton, Etonbridge, Hever, Cowden, Weſtram, Chydingſtone, Stonebridge, and Braſted, dict. man. ſpect. et diverſ. meſſ. terr. & tent. cognit. p nõia de Church-court et Charpes-croſe jac. in Morſtone & Tonge ad manus R. devenerunt racõe attinct. W. Cromer, 4 p. or 1 & 2 Ph. & M. rot. 19 W. Cromer ten.

Abbreviament. omniũ tenurar. compert. p inquiſ. temp. H. VII. & VIII. remanet record. in cancellar.

F. 32. b. Man. de Vfton cũ ptin. tenetur in ſocagio de dño rege ut de fü. ſuo de Mydelton per fidelitatem, &c. ut compert. eſt p inquiſ. capt. ann. 4 H. VIII.

In the margin of the book is written *modo Aſheley juı e uxoris.*

From a folio MS. of Philipot's in the poſſeſſion of Edward Umfreville, eſq. containing the fines paſſed in this county temp. E. I.

P. 15. Fin. 34 E. I.

P. 297. Inter Aliciã que fuit vx. Joh. de Columbarys, quer. & Anton. ep. Dunelm. def. de med. mañij de Tunſtall cũ ptis. exceptis 50 acr. terr. vna acra boſc. xviij den. reddit. de pdict. mediet. qm Margareta q. fuit vx. Steph. de Penceſt, tenet ad term. vit. &c. ep. recogn. eſſe jus Aliciæ & conc. p ſe & h. qd pdict. med. cũ ptin. qm Margar. tenuit ad term. vitæ ex dimiſſ. iþius epi in pdca vill. die qº &c. poſt deceſſ. iþius Margar. integre remaneat eid Alic. & h. per ſerv. q. pertinent, &c.

Fin.

Fin. 35 E. I.

P. 320. Int. Hen. de Cobeham & Johannā vx. ej. quer. & Anton. ep. Dunelm. def. de medietat. maūij de Tunſtall cū ptin. exceptis 50 acr. terr. vna acr. boſc. & xviij den. redd. de p̄dc̄a med. q̃m Margar. quæ fuit vx. Steph. de Penceſtre tenet ad term. vit. &c. ep̄us recogn. eſſe jus Joḣæ & conc. ꝓ ſe & h. q̃d p̄dic̄t. med. cū ptin. ſicut p̄dc̄u eſt q̃m p̄dc̄a Margar. tenuit ad term. vit. ex dimiſſ. ip̄ius ep̄i poſt deceſſ. ip̄ius Margar. integre remaneat ijſc̄ Hen. & Joḣæ & h. ip̄ius Joḣæ ꝑ ſervic. q̃æ pertinent in ꝑpet'.

Fıom ſome collection for this county made in the reign of Q. Elizabeth. The book belongs to Mr. Warburton.

Maıgeria q̃æ fuit ux. Steph. Pencheſtr tenuit in villa de Tunſtall, Bradgare & Mılſtede vn. meſſ. cū gard. iiij×x acr. terr. 8 acr. paſtur. 2 acr. dim. boſci. & 18ᵈ ob q. in gavelkinde de r. in cap. ꝑ ſervic. iijˢ vijᵈ & ꝑ ſerv. ij adnat. ꝑ ann. adm̄. regis de Middleton, 2 E. II.—114. & 67.

Term. Mich. 14 Eliz. Ric. Thornhill ꝓ m̄. de Piſtocke.—f. 125.

M. de Tunſtall, Elmely, & Fogleſtone, aȴs Fulſtone, ac diverſ. terr. & ten. cognit. per nōıa de Elmely & Binnen jacent. in Elmeley, Leiſton, Morſton, & Tonge; ac div. terr. cognit. ꝑ nōıa de Grovende jacent. in Tunſtall, Bradgare & Mulſted; ac diṽſ. terr. cognit. ꝑ nōıa de Wrennes in Tunſtall, Bredgar & Borden; ac diṽſ. meſſ. terr. & ten. cognit. ꝑ ɾōıa de Cubnall in Tunſtall, Bredgar & Borden; ac diṽſ. meſſ. in Morſton & Bloxham; ac diṽſ. terr. & ten. in Morſton, Tonge, Babchilde, Sittingborne, Milton, & in alijs locis hujuſce com. ad man. r. deveñunt ɾone attinctus W. Cromer. f., 134.

Tranſcript. comp. collector. auxilij xlˢ de quolibet feod. mil. ad primogen. regis mil. faciend. 20 E. III. in ſcaccario remanentis emendatū in nōıb. poſſeſſor. ꝑ Rob. Maycote nuꝑ ſubviſ. Johannis Norton, mil. vicecom. Kanc. 5 H. VIII. prout ic̄ Rob. in turnia vic. p̄dc̄i dc̄o ann. tent. ꝑ inquiſic̄ōes jurator. colligere potuit ob colleccōem̄ expen. milit. com. p̄dc̄i ad ult. parl. exiſtent. melius ꝑficiend. & noviter emendatū per Ciriac. Pettyte, gen. feodariū d̄ni regis infra com. p̄dict. 35 H. VIII.

Hund. de Mydelton.

F. 75. b. viz. man. de Tunſtall.

De ān̄o Walt. de Manny pro vno feod. q̃d Margeria de Penceſtre tenuit in Tunſtall de Johanne de Sancto Johanne xlˢ.

nuper Will. Cromer, mil.*

modo hæred. ejuſdem †.

* Sc. ut opinor 5 H. VIII.   † Sc. ut opinor 35 H. VIII.

From

From another folio MS. in the poffeffion of the faid Mr. Umfreville, containing the fines paffed in the county of Kent, temp. H. III.

At the beginning is this note. 1633.

Pretium hujus libri ex archivis in thefaurario fcaccarij Weftm. extracti vjʰ. Jo. Phillipott, Someıfett.

The making the 2 kalendars [of perfons and places] and the bynding the bookes ⅺiijˢ. J. P. S.

P. 117. Finalis concordia facta ann. regn. regis H. fil. Joh. 55 inter Joh. de Wade-ton pet. & Barth. de Wadeton ten. de vno meff. octies viginti & 12 acr. terr. & paf-tura ad trefcentas oves, quatuor libratis & x folidatis redditus, & redditu xxiiij galli-narum cum p̃tin. in Menftre & Eftcherche in Schepeye hujus Joh. et pro hac recogn. id̃ Joh. conceffit eid̃ Barth. p̃dc̃a ten. cum p̃tin. fimul cum õib. alijs terr. & ten. quæ aliquando fuerunt Joh̃is de Wadeton patris p̃dc̃i Barth. in la Gore, Vppecherche, Renham, Nywenton, Bordenn, Stokyngebyr, Halweftowe, Myddelton, Sydingeborn, Tunftall, Rodmerfham, Bradgare, Mylftede & Hedecrone; ħend. eid̃. Barth. & ħedib. de corp' &c.

PEDIGREE of HENRY DE GREY, [See p. 12.]

Hen. de Grey.=

Walt. de Grey,
archiep. Ebor. (a)   Rob. de Grey.=

Walt. de Grey, =
ob. 52 H. III.(b)

Rob. de Grey,   =Avicia, fil.
f. & h. ob. 23 E. I.(c) | Will. de S. Lice.

Joh. de Grey, f. & h.=Margar. f. & coh.
æt. 24. 23 E. I. ob. | Will. de Odingsells.
5 E. II.(d)

Joh. de Grey, f. & h. =
ob. 1 Oct. 33 E. III.(e)

Joh. de Grey, f. & h.   Matilda. (g)
æt. 40. 33 E. I. (f)

(a) Esc. 24 E. I. 2. 104.   (b) Cart. 29 H. III. m. 3.   Cart. 30 H. III. m. 9.   (c) Fin. 52 H. III. m. 12.
Esc. 23 E. I. n. 60.   (d) Fin 23 E. I. m 12.   Esc. 5 E. II. 61.   (e) Clauf. 15 E. II. m. 20.
Cart. 4 E. III n. 44. l. War.   Cart 28 E. III. n. 15. l. War.   Esc. 33 E. III. n. 38.   (f) Esc. 41 E. III. p. 2. n. 35.
(g) Pat. 32 E. III. m. 13.   Clauf. 17 R. II. m. 18.

PEDI-

PEDIGREE of JOHN GROVE, [See p. 31.]

Arms; Erm. on a chevron G. 3 efcallops Argent.

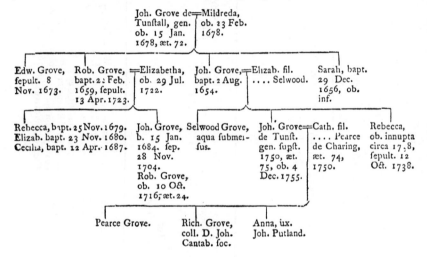

Joh. Grove de⊨Mildreda,
Tunftall, gen. | ob. 23 Feb.
ob. 15 Jan. | 1678.
1678, æt. 72.

Edw. Grove, | Rob. Grove, ⊨Elizabetha, | Joh. Grove,⊨Elizab. fil. | Sarah, bapt.
fepult. 8 | bapt. 2ᵉ Feb. | ob. 29 Jul. | bapt. 2 Aug. | .... Selwood. | 29 Dec.
Nov. 1673. | 1659, fepult. | 1722. | 1654. | | 1656, ob.
| 13 Apr. 1723. | | | | inf.

Rebecca, bapt. 25 Nov. 1679. | Joh. Grove, | Selwood Grove, | Joh. Grove⊨Cath. fil. | Rebecca,
Elizab. bapt. 23 Nov. 1680. | b. 15 Jan. | aqua fubmei- | de Tunft. | .... Pearce | ob. innupta
Cecilia, bapt. 12 Apr. 1687. | 1684. fep. | fus. | gen. fupft. | de Charing, | circa 17,8,
| 28 Nov. | | 1750, æt. | æt. 74, | fepult. 12
| 1704. | | 75, ob. 4 | 1750. | Oct. 1738.
Rob. Grove,		Dec. 1755.
ob. 10 Oct.		
1716, æt. 24.		

Pearce Grove. | Rich. Grove, | Anna, ux.
| coll. D. Joh. | Joh. Putland.
| Cantab. foc. |

Among the perfons who take their name from this place, Ofmund, fon of Edward de Tunftall gave 2s rent in Dya cum ptin. to the nuns of St. Mary Magdalen, at Devyngtone, co. Kent, 39 H. III. Monaft. I. 502.

In plac. de term. Mich, 45 H. III. rot. 13. dorf. Kanc. mention of John de Dunftall, clericus. Prynne's Pap. Ufurp. III. 119, b.

Tho. de Dunftalle, capellan. inftitut. in eccl. S. Mildredæ Cant. 8. cal. Apr. 1291. Regift. Peckham, f. 41, a.

Rob. de Tonftall, inftituted to the rectory of St. Dunftan in the Eaft, London, 8 id. Sept. 1322. ad prefentat. prior & cap. eccl. Ch. Cant. Newc. I. 333.

Rob. Tunftall, 1502. Ib. I. 585.
Ric. de Tunftall. Sa. 3 combs Arg. Ex arm. rot. antiq. p. 218.
Ric. de Tunftall de Bolton. Arg. on a chief indented Az. 3 bezants. Ib. p. 598.
Tho. Tunftall. Arms as the firft, Ib. p. 637.

PEDIGREE OF TONG.

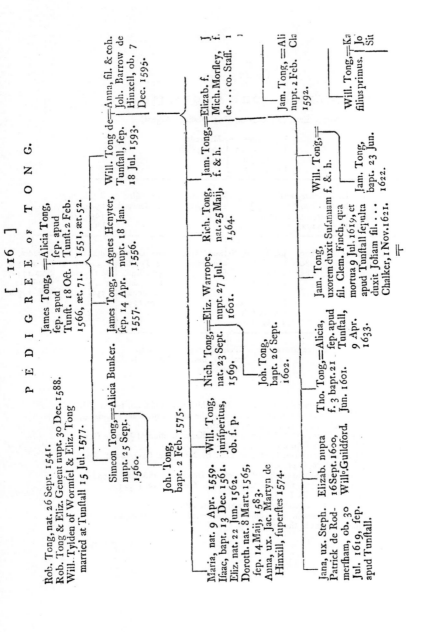

Rob. Tong, nat. 26 Sept. 1541.
Rob. Tong & Eliz. Genent nupt. 30 Dec. 1588.
Will. Tylden of Wormfel & Eliz. Tong
married at Tunftall 15 Jul. 1577.

James Tong, ⚭ Alicia Tong,
fep. apud | fep. apud
Tunft. 18 Oct. | Tunft. 2 Feb.
1566, æt. 71. | 1551, æt. 52.

Simeon Tong, ⚭ Alicia Bunker.
nupt. 25 Sept.
1560.

James Tong, ⚭ Agnes Henyter,
fep. 14 Apr.   nupt. 18 Jan.
1557.   1556.

Will. Tong de ⚭ Anna, fil. & coh.
Tunftall, fep. | Joh. Barrow de
18 Jul. 1593. | Hinxell, ob. 7
                 | Dec. 1595.

Joh. Tong,
bapt. 2 Feb. 1575.

Maria, nat. 9 Apr. 1559.
Ifaac, bapt. 13 Dec. 1561.
Eliz. nat. 22 Jun. 1562.
Doroth. nat. 8 Mart. 1565,
fep. 14 Maij, 1583.
Anna, ux. Jac. Martyn de
Hinxill, fuperftes 1574.

Will. Tong,
jurifperitus,
ob. f. p.

Nich. Tong, ⚭ Eliz. Warrope,
nat. 23 Sept.   nupt. 27 Jul.
1569.   1601.

Rich. Tong,
nat. 25 Maij,
1564.

Elizab. f. ⚭
Mich. Morfley,
de . . . co. Staff.

Jam. Tong,
f. & h.

Joh. Tong,
bapt. 26 Sept.
1602.

Jam. Tong, ⚭ Ali
nupt. 2 Feb.   Cla
1592.

Elizab. nupta
16 Sept. 1600,
Will. Guildford.

Jana, ux. Steph.
Patrick de Rod-
merfham, ob. 30
Jul. 1619, fep.
apud Tunftall.

Tho. Tong, ⚭ Alicia, fep. apud
f. 3 bapt. 21   Tunftall,
Jun. 1601.   9 Apr.
                 1633.

Jam. Tong,
uxorem duxit Sufanam f. & h.
fil. Clem. Finch, qua
mortua 9 Jul. 1619, et
apud Tunftall fejulta
duxit Joħam fil. . . .
Chalker, 1 Nov. 1621.

Will. Tong, ⚭
f. & h.

Will. Tong, ⚭ Ka
filius primus.   Jo
                 Sit

Jam. Tong,
bapt. 23 Jun.
1622.

⚭

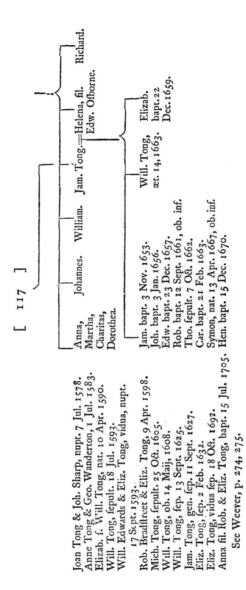

Anna,
Martha,
Charitas,
Dorothea.

Johannes. William. Jam. Tong.=Helena, fil. Edw. Osborne. Richard.

Will. Tong, aet. 14, 1663. Elizab. bapt. 22 Dec. 1659.

Jam. bapt. 3 Nov. 1653.
Joh. bapt. 3 Jan. 1656.
Edw. bapt. 23 Dec. 1657.
Rob. bapt. 12 Sept. 1661, ob. inf.
Tho. sepult. 7 Oct. 1662.
Car. bapt. 21 Feb. 1663.
Symon, nat. 13 Apr. 1667, ob. inf.
Hen. bapt. 15 Dec. 1670.

Joan Tong & Joh. Sharp, nupt. 7 Jul. 1578.
Anne Tong & Geo. Wanderton, 1 Jul. 1583.
Elizab. f. Will. Tong, nat. 10 Apr. 1590.
Will. Tong, sepult. 18 Jul. 1593.
Will. Edwards & Eliz. Tong, vidua, nupt. 17 Sept. 1593.
Rob. Bradfurct & Eliz. Tong, 9 Apr. 1598.
Mich. Tong, sepult. 25 Oct. 1605.
Will. Tong, ob. 14 Maij, 1608.
Will. Tong, sep. 13 Sept. 1625.
Jam. Tong, gen. sep. 11 Sept. 1627.
Eliz. Tong, sep. 2 Feb. 1632.
Eliz. Tong, vidua sep. 18 Oct. 1692.
Anna fil. Rob. & Eliz. Tong, bapt. 15 Jul. 1705.

See Weever, p. 274, 275.

[118]

F I N I S.

SECOND APPENDIX

TO THE

HISTORY OF TUNSTALL.

BEING

A LETTER FROM MR. BANISTER TO THE PRINTER.

S I R,   March 15, 1788.

IT was not till the other day (and then by mere accident) that I obtained a fight of the "Hiſtory of Tunſtall," compiled by the late Edward Rowe Mores, and publiſhed by you, ſo long ſince as the year 1780, in the firſt number of the "Bibliotheca Topographica Britannica." As I poſſeſs but a very ſlender portion of curioſity for antiquarian reſearches, I ſhould probably have thrown by the tract long before I had reached the concluding page, if my attention had not been excited by a kind of epiſode, or fabulous digreſſion, which, although it bore not the moſt diſtant relation to the Hiſtory of Tunſtall, was of much more intereſting concern to me, than the puerile and unimportant obſervations of Mr. Mores, reſpecting that ancient pariſh. This digreſſive narration formed an unjuſt and invidious libel on the character of a perſon long ſince numbered among the dead, and configned to that ſilent repoſitory which, one ſhould have hoped, might have ſecured his aſhes againſt the envenomed ſhafts of ſlander and detraction : but, in truth, theſe odious qualities ſeem to be the diſtinguiſhing features of his compilation. As I eſteem it an honour to have deſcended in an immediate lineal ſucceſſion from the perſon who has been thus unjuſtly calumniated, I have taken up my pen in his behalf; and this taſk I ſhould not have undertaken, notwithſtanding the near alliance in which I ſtand, and the filial piety which I bear to his memory, if I had not beeen well convinced of the falſity of the allegations brought againſt him : for he was a man of unblemiſhed honour, and uncorrupted integrity ; and, as ſuch, incapable of acting thoſe ſcenes of perfidy and corruption with which he is charged by the writer of this pamphlet. The wretch who could inhumanly fabricate an accumulation of falſhoods, tending to leſſen and depre-

R   ciate

ciate the character of a blamelefs individual, ought to be confidered as the peft of civil fociety. But as the original Compiler of thefe Anecdotes is now no more, I fhall forbear to treat his remains with that difrefpect which he has thought fit to beftow on thofe of the perfon in whofe behalf I have thought it my duty to ftand forth. Some kind of negative merit may be due to Mr. Mores in having with-held his collections from the eye of the public. But what will be faid of the perfon, who fhall prefume to unlock the efcrutoire of his deceafed friend *, and, by the publication of the pages in queftion, contribute to the difcrimination of a train of infamous falfehoods, fixty years after the events are pretended to have taken place, and when the perfon againft whom the attack is levelled had been more than thirty years in his grave ? Would not fuch conduct be juftly repro-bated, as proceeding either from a view to gratify the idle curiofity of fuperficial readers; or might it not be placed to a ftill more blameable fervice, the accomplifhment of his own mercenary ends? The refpectable clafs in which Mr. N. ranks, as a trader of piobity and liberality, acquits him of the latter of thefe charges; whilft his good tafte, and acknowledged abilities, as a man of letters, are a fufficient confutation of the former. I would therefore afk you, by what fatality did this flander find its way to your prefs? Perhaps you fcarcely knew that the Hiftory of Tunftall contained thefe offenfive pages : certain I am, from the character which you bear in life, that you would never have lent an helping hand towards the diffemination of them, if you could have conceived how much you have wronged the good name of the deceafed; for, if fuch infults are to be tamely acquiefced in, where is the perfon who can promife himfelf that reward which every man would wifh to merit from pofterity ; namely, the repu-tation of having paffed through life with credit? and what family dare promife themfelves the pleafing reflection of having defcended from anceftors of integrity and worth, if they are liable to have their ears wounded with injurious afperfions on the memory of a parent, from the production of fcraps of paper raked out of the drawers of fome invidious contemporary, and publifhed feveral years after the deceafe of each of the parties, when death has removed all thofe perfons who might have given the lye direct to fuch allegations; and all that remains for the injured defcendant is in fome meafure to fupply the lofs of oral teftimony, by circumftantial and analogous evidence? Happy am I to fay, that this latter mode of defence remains to me in its utmoft latitude. Yet, pafs but a few tranfitory years, and no traces would have been left to confute the idle tale; and the next generation muft tacitly have fubmitted to the imputation caft on the memory of their grandfather.

---

* This efcrutoire, as it is called, was unlocked by the family of Mr. Mores; and the work in queftion, fully prepared for the prefs, and even the plates engraved for it, were purchafed at a public auction. See the Preface, p. xxiv. The publifhing of the prefent letter, *literally* as it was received, is the faireft proof of our impartiality. EDIT.

Having

Having thus opened the nature of my complaint, and explained the motives which have induced me to addrefs you on the prefent occafion; I fhall, without further ceremony, proceed to the confideration of the pages that have afforded me fo juft caufe of offence.

It was very unfortunate upon me, that the pamphlet in queftion remained fo long unheard-of ; for, had it come to my knowledge at the time of its firft publication (feven years fince), I might have been able, from the recollection of more than one perfon of credit, then living, to have given a flat contradiction to every affertion hazarded in that part of the performance which relates to my family. Thefe aids are now, by the fubfequent deceafe of thofe ancient remembrancers, unhappily denied me ; and I muft content myfelf with reforting to teftimony of a more modern date, and to fome analogous circumftances, which will add as ftrong a proof as the nature of the cafe, at this diftance of time, can poffibly admit of, that the feveral allegations brought againft this injured perfon are founded in untruth, and owe their birth to the unjuft reprefentations of envy and malignity. The perfon, to whom I am indebted for the greater part of the facts I have collected, is an ancient inhabitant of an adjacent parifh, a venerable relation, near 20 years paft her grand climacteric, and who, to the entertaining loquacity of 83, happily unites the vivacity and chearfulnefs of 25.

The firft part of Mr. Mores's hiftory I have no concern in ; neither fhall I take under my confideration thofe curious anecdotes with which it is embellifhed, fuch as the ironical farcafm at p. 59, reflecting on the conduct of Mr. Tyler, the immediate fucceffor of Mr. Mores the father, and which, in truth, is a ftrong fpecimen of the fon's want of candour ; or the notice given in the Daily Advertifer to the creditors, of the payment of Mr. Hales's debts ; circumftances, doubtlefs, of the laft importance to pofterity. To fay the truth, thefe anecdotes remind me of my good old nurfe: fhe was a merry woman (reft her foul !), and many a long winter's evening have I beguiled in my boyifh years, by liftening to her wondrous ftories ; for fhe was moft circumftantially prolix, doated on a marvellous relation, and piqued herfelf upon the recollection of old wives' tales without number : pfhaw, how uncouthly have I expreffed myfelf ! I mean, fhe was like ROWE-MORES, rich in anecdote.

That part of the pamphlet wherein I am moft materially interefted commences at page 60, where it is faid, that " in 1717 Mr. Mores was advanced in the af-" feffment of the Land Tax, on his parfonage, from £.54 to £.100 *per annum*, " the tythes of the living being let at £.95, therefore, by a proper application, " the affeffment was reduced to £.90, which was £.36 *per annum* more than the " living was rated at when Mr. Mores firft received it." Then follows the weighty charge againft my honoured relation, which begins with this contemptuous obfervation. " About this time (after the affeffment on the parfonage had been " liquidated by the commiffioners) one Thomas Banifter came from Sittingbourn to " fettle here." Now, fince Mr. Mores, by this remark, has been pleafed to hint at the meannefs and obfcurity of Mr. Banifter's ftation in life, I fhall take leave, in this place, to correct his infinuation, and to inform fuch of the readers of that

account,

account, who may chance to look on this letter, that Mr. Banifter (who, by the bye, had been dead fourteen years before the time when Mr. Mores vifited the parifh in 1764) was defcended from anceftors who had refided in the parifh of Sittingbourn for a great number of years: that himfelf, his father, and grandfather, were feverally ftewards to the family of Hales, and were all of them men of confiderable note in their day; I mean, as wealthy yeomen, and large renters, and by the family whom they ferved each of them was beloved and refpected for the lengthened term of near a century; and there are written teftimonials yet remaining of the efteem wherein they were held, in letters under the fignature of the feveral baronets, from Sir Edward Hales, who followed the fortunes of the late King James, down to the prefent worthy poffeffor of the title and eftate. Many of thefe letters are at this day in the poffeffion of Mr. Banifter's family: one of them, fo far back as 1688, I have lately had the opportunity of perufing; wherein the then Sir Edward preffes his fteward to get in all the money he could raife, and fend to him in London with all imaginable difpatch. This was, no doubt, intended to fupply the exigences of the King, who had been ftripped of the greateft part of his moveables at Elmley Ferry, near Sittingbourn. Mr. Thomas Banifter rented land to the amount of more than a thoufand pounds *per annum*, and died in January 1750-1, with the reputation of an honeft man, and was well known and refpected by many gentlemen of rank and fortune in the Eaftern part of Kent. He left behind him a widow, who erected a handfome monument to his memory, in the chancel of the *Hales*, in the parifh church of Sittingbourn. Mrs. Banifter died in November 1784, defervedly lamented by her family and friends. Three children, their iffue, are all now living; " et nos turba fumus :" for a family in union within itfelf is an impenetrable fhield of defence againft every adverfary, how potent foever he may be; and, whilft this phalanx remains undivided, it will refift the fhock of an hoft of foes. Such was the man whom the original writer of this pamphlet, which you have thought fit to ufher into the world, has reprefented as a fellow of a bafe and low origin.

That Mr. Banifter never refided at Tunftall is moft probable, though I have not been able to meet with any living witnefs who can fpeak decidedly on this point; nor is this to be wondered at, as 70 years (the age of man) are now elapfed fince the time when this emigration is faid to have taken place. But, I fay, it is highly improbable that Mr. Banifter fhould quit a manfion-houfe well fituate for the conducting and management of his bufinefs, in favour of any farm houfe at Tunftall, where he had no concerns, except as fteward to Sir John Hales. The very unworthy manner wherein my family has been treated, by his contemptuous mention of my anceftor, will, I hope, plead in juftification of this piece of Egotifm, or (if I may be allowed to coin a new word) *Nofmetifm*. And now, having fketched out the general outlines of Mr. Banifter's ftation in life, I fhall mention a few anecdotes of Mr. Mores, the rector of Tunftall; which, though you have ftood forth the Biographer of his fon, may not probably have come to your knowledge: and this I am tempted to undertake, not from the ambition of increafing the literary ftore of anecdotes (the favourite diet of many of the readers

of

of the prefent age), or of ftamping a ridicule on his memory, for I fcorn a procedure fo mean. and illiberal ; but with the fole view of illuftrating my plain narrative.

Mr. Mores, as his fon has obferved in his tract, was for a feries of years rector of Tunftall, and built the parfonage-houfe at that place. His character, however his fon may have varnifhed it, was rather problematical. He was beyond meafure (I write not from my own knowledge, but from the information of thofe who were perfonally acquainted with him) querulous in his difpofition, ruftic in his carriage and addrefs, and in his temper vindictive and implacable. During his refidence at Tunftall, when he was already far advanced beyond the meridian of life, he married a young lady, the daughter of a citizen of London, who is reprefented as a female of exalted merit, and of many perfonal accomplifhments; and to this alliance Mr. Mores owed the refpect which he bore in the neighbourhood : though it fhould feem that his wife did not enjoy all that domeftic felicity in the connubial ftate which, from her many excellent endowments, fhe had reafon to expect; for, added to his other fingularities, Mr. Mores was at times poffeft with the dæmon of jealoufy, to the moft tormenting degree, in confequence of which he kept his wife within the moft rigid bounds of defpotic conftraint. Many ridiculous ftories are related in the neighbourhood refpecting this unhappy temper of the old man, fome of which are in themfelves fo truly comic, that the old lady *, from whom I had this relation, fhewed vifible marks of the impreffion which they made on her fancy; for, whilft fhe gave the account, fhe laughed, " fans intermiffion, an hour by the dial." As the infertion of every anecdote which has come to my knowledge, refpecting this fame rector of Tunftall, in this letter, could anfwer no very material end, I fhall content myfelf with a felection of thofe only, which have an immediate tendency to elucidate the fubject that I have taken in hand.

Mr. Mores, in his marriage, rather (as I before obferved) from the efteem to the fuavity which his lady's manners and converfation had conciliated, than from any intrinfic merit of his own, affociated with moft of the principal families in the vicinity of Tunftall, and among others with Mr. Banifter, with whom for many years he lived in terms of the moft unreferved familiarity ; as an inftance of which, take the following anecdote: In the winter, 1738, Mr. Tyler, the then vicar of Sittingbourn, having refufed to baptize a fon of Mr. Banifter, unlefs he would fuffer it to be brought to church, at the diftance of a quarter of a mile, which Mr. Banifter was unwilling to comply with, the child being in a weakly ftate, and the weather very cold ; application was made to the neighbouring rector of Tunftall (Mr. Mores), who readily complied with the requeft, and performed the ceremony at Glovers, Mr. Banifter's houfe. The circumftance of this chriftening, with the names of the difhes on the table, and the merry tales that were told by the different guefts, but more particularly the chearfulnefs and vivacity of Mr. Mores, who on this occafion of feftivity manifefted a more than ordinary degree of fprightlinefs and good humour, are all well remembered by my communicative friend ; and withal, that the old gentleman, being intent on a ftory which he was relating, paid too fmall regard to the coffee-cup that he held in his hand, by which

† We muft conclude fhe was our correfpondent's *good old nurfe*, p. 121.

neglect

neglect he fpilt the contents over her apron, the mark of which is to this day remaining, and was fhewn to the writer of this letter.

The flanderer having mentioned Mr. Banifter's name in the contemptuous manner
above related, proceeds to affert : " That Banifter, being defircus of a leafe of the
" Parfonage, in 1719 applied to the rector for that purpofe, offering a confider-
" able increafe of rent, if Mr. Mores would turn the then prefent tenant out of
" it, which he refufed; and therefore Banifter took the firft opportunity of ex-
" preffing his refentment; and, in the year 1720, being affeffor, he took upon
" him to raife the parfonage again to £.95; and from Banifter's giving in a wrong
" place for hearing the appeal, the rector was obliged to pay the money, though
" no more was paid into the hands of the receiver-general that year than for-
" merly, fo that the overplus ceded to the ufes of Mr. Banifter."

The accufation brought againft Mr. Banifter, in the preceding fection, is of a
very ferious nature indeed; and, could Rowe-Mores have brought any legal evidence,
to prove that Mr. Banifter offered an increafe of rent for his parfonage, if he would
turn out the old tenant, or that the increafe of the Land Tax affeffment ceded to
the ufes of Mr. Banifter; God forbid, that I fhould endeavour to palliate fuch
grofs and fraudulent impofitions ! But, fince Rowe-Mores has thought fit to bring
his own *ipfe dixit* only in fupport of thefe allegations, it is prefumed that Mr.
Banifter's refpectability in life, and the general character which he bore among
his neighbours (which, except from the poifoned arrows of this defamer, has remained always unimpeached), will fecure him from the imputation of this malignant
attack ; efpecially when it is confidered that the perfon, who hazarded this bafe
invective, is reprefented by you, his Biographer (fee Memoirs of the Author,
page xxiv.), as a man given up to habits of negligence and diffipation; but more
of this anon.   As to the latter part of this charge, refpecting the advance in the
affeffment, it appears to have been the concurrent and unanimous opinion of the
parifhioners, before Mr. Banifter came among them, that Mr. Mores was under-
rated at £.90 *per annum*; and therefore, allowing the truth of this latter part of
Rowe-Mores's allegation, Mr. Banifter (as affeffor) was defirous of making one
more effort towards fetting him on an equality with the reft of the land-owners.
As to the affeffor's giving in a wrong place for hearing the appeal ; this charge is
fo very futile, as fcarcely to deferve a ferious reply, and the bare mention of it
carries with it its own refutation : for, can it be imagined, that any man, endued
with a grain of common underftanding or difcretion, and Mr. Banifter was not de-
ficient in either, would hazard an impofition, whence he could derive no kind of
advantage, but which, on the contrary, would have fubjected him to immediate
detection? And, furely, if the affeffors had reafon to think that Mr. Mores was
under-rated in the affeffment, it would have been the higheft piece of injuftice towards themfelves, and the reft of the land-owners, not to have raifed him in his
valuation, by which the affeffment of every other land-owner in the parifh was
proportionably lowered.   And here permit me to offer a remark on the fly and
infidious manner in which Rowe-Mores introduces his affertion, that the two affeffors
ere abated £.10 *per annum*, that no more was paid into the hands of the receiver-
general

general that year than formerly, and that the overplus ceded to the ufes of Mr. Banifter. From this conclufion of Rowe Mores, it fhould feem, that to the two qualities of indolence and diffipation, he united that of the groffeft ignorance in matters of this kind, or that he wilfully fhut his eyes to an obfervation, which muft have occurred to any perfon of common difcernment, namely, that the af-feffors are limited as to the fpecific fum to be raifed on the parifh, the proportion which each man is to pay, towards making up this fum, being the only object left to them, and this to be fettled according to the rents. It therefore follows, that if Mr. Banifter, in conjunction with the other affeffor (for fimply in his own name he could make no legal affeffment); if, I fay, the affeffors had acted otherwife than they did, it would have been the greateft injury to every individual on their books, whofe affeffments were confequently lowered, as that of Mr. Mores was ad-vanced; and that the liquidation of thefe fums was properly arranged, was the duty of the commiffioners to infpect, and likewife that thefe fums made up the grofs amount heretofore levied on the parifh; and this being the cafe, where was the overplus to arife, which ceded (as Rowe-Mores pretends) to the ufe of Mr. Banifter? And although the commiffioners afterwards thought fit to reduce the affeffment of the parfonage; yet furely there refts no imputation on Mr. Banifter, or the other affeffor, for the part they took in this bufinefs; and fince this infinu-ation of Rowe-Mores, thus artfully and loofely worded, that Mr. Banifter applied any part of the money to his own ufe, falls to the ground, this is no bad argu-ment of the falfity of the former part of the charge mentioned in this fection.

Of equal validity is the accufation brought againft Mr. Banifter and moft of the other inhabitants (for on this occafion the greater part of the parifhioners are in-volved in the cenfure), of rating Mr. Mores, for his parfonage-houfe, in the parifh affeffments, and of making an alteration in the rate after it had been figned by the juftices. This charge, like the former, remains unfubftantiated; and therefore muft, by every candid and difpaffionate reader, be confidered as proceeding from a mind overflowing with fpleen and malevolence. As to the for-mer part of this charge, if divefted of the falfe glofs which Rowe-Mores has thought fit to give it in favour of his father, it amounts to no more than this: that the parifhioners, conceiving that Mr. Mores was under-rated, thought fit to lay an additional affeffment on the living; and if, in this bufinefs, the rector was affeffed beyond the true value of the living, he ought to have confidered, that the only method of arriving to the knowledge of the juft value of a difputed rent, is to make a charge in the affeffment beyond what is known to be its real denomination; nor is this any act of injuftice in the officer; nor ought Mr. Mores, in the prefent inftance, to have imputed any blame to Mr. Banifter, or his col-league, for this proceeding, fince Mr. Mores might eafily have obtained a reduc-tion, by fwearing to the true profits of his living: and here, as was pretended in the former cafe, he could form no plea that the officers had given him a wrong information, with refpect to the place where this redrefs was to be obtained, fince the houfe where the juftices hold their petty feffions is notorious to every perfon of the leaft confideration within the divifion for which they act. Thus you fee that
Mr.

Mr. Banister, however wickedly inclined, had it not in his power, either as affessor of the Land Tax, or as overseer of the poor, to commit an act of injustice on Mr. Mores; and, from what I have said in this and the preceding section, I hope that the impossibility of Mr. Banister's appropriating any part of the money raised by the Land Tax, or parochial affessments, will appear sufficiently clear to any one who will take the trouble of comparing the vague and indecent charge of Rowe-Mores with this defence.

That Mr. Mores (the rector) was not respected either by his own parishioners or the neighbourhood, is a fact that can be attested by numerous witnesses now living; though I think it needs no farther proof than his son's representations have yielded; and, upon this presumption, the conduct of Mr. Banister, however reprehensible it may appear upon a superficial view of the pamphlet (for we are all of us too apt to be led away by the glare of false colouring), will be found so far from meriting rebuke, that it stamps, in my opinion, a credit on his memory, since it demonstrates the impartiality of his proceedings, by not suffering one person to be screened in the adjustment of his rates, at the expence of every other individual in the parish. But I am inclined to think that the old gentleman, if he related this circumstance to his son *ore tenus,* told a monstrous great, what shall I call it? fib: and if the latter gleaned it from some scraps or memoranda of his father, the rector committed to writing much more than the truth; and I will tell you my reasons for thinking so; and, since I have related one anecdote, I shall here mention another. You are to know then, my good friend, that Mr. Banister was of manners gentle and inoffensive, and that he always avoided, as much as lay in his power, disputes of every kind, whether with individuals or with bodies of men. Of this pacific disposition I could give a variety of instances in both kinds, but shall content myself with one, which is the anecdote I promised you. About the year 1749, the then vicar of Sittingbourn caused a gate to be erected, opening out of his own premises into the church-yard, for the convenience of driving his chaise through the same, by which he avoided a very disagreeable piece of road. This alteration, though of no material injury to any person, was resented by many of the parishioners as an arbitrary act in the vicar, and much ill blood was occasioned between the worthy clergyman (for he was a man of real probity) and his flock, the latter having repeatedly demolished the gates erected by the former; and he, in his turn, persisting in his original design; till, at length, after many bickerings, the affair was amicably adjusted, though there were many individuals who never entertained a cordial friendship towards the vicar after this event. In the progress of this dispute, many vestries were held of the parishioners, and various meetings by the vicar and his friends, to confider of means to prosecute their several plans. Mr. Banister, from the love which he bore to peace and quiet, made it a point to absent himself from all these meetings, and could never be brought to enlist under the banners of either party, though vehemently solicited by both, and thus preserved the esteem as well of the clergyman as of the rest of his neighbours. Many people now living know this to be true, and will vouch for the general tendency of all his actions towards peace and good-will. I will therefore leave it to

the

the judgment of every unprejudiced reader; whether it be likely for such a person, in any part of his past life, to have deserved the epithets of a litigious and troublesome member of society, but especially the disgraceful appellation of knave and miscreant, which your friend Rowe-Mores has thought fit to bestow on him? These odious terms, I will be bold to say, were never more improperly applied than on the present occasion: and let me take leave to ask, whether a man of so placid a disposition as I have here described could, in two distant stages of his life, have acted so incongruously, as to have possessed the rancour and the implacability of a Blifil at 19 (which was the age of Mr. Banister when Rowe-Mores lays the scene at Tunstall); whilst at 49, when the dispute happened between the vicar of Sittingbourn and his parishioners, he had not only relinquished the unjust and knavish practices of his youth, but had deservedly gained the character of an honest, a mild, and a beneficent neighbour; and this too without quitting the station of his abode where he had practised the iniquitous arts of his youth? Such a character indeed would be not improperly adapted for the hero of a modern comedy, where the same person is often a very great rogue at the first act, and, before the end of the play becomes every thing that is praiseworthy: but this is by no means the case in real life. Mankind are with difficulty brought to lay aside the prejudices which they have imbibed against those by whom they have heretofore conceived themselves to have been hardly used; and I believe the instances are very rare, of a man having regained the general good opinion of his neighbours, who had once deservedly incurred their ill will by his repeated deviation from the paths of rectitude and virtue: whatever pains he may take for that purpose will be ranked under the disgraceful and contemptuous appellation of hypocrisy and deceit, and the man himself will be looked upon with a jealous eye, and avoided as a dangerous member of society.

The foul reproach, vented with so much confidence against Mr. Banister, of having made a seizure of Mr. Mores's goods, and converted the money arising from the sale of the same to his own use, is another charge of a very heinous nature; and which, I trust, I shall find little difficulty in refuting. And, although, in my own mind, I am perfectly convinced of the fallacy of this shameless accusation; and though, in the opinion of those who ever had any dealings or connections with him, such a charge will not obtain the smallest degree of credit, but will be looked upon as proceeding from a mind tainted with malice and envy: yet, to obviate any ill impression which may remain on the minds of those who were totally unacquainted with his person and his actions, I am unhappily driven to circumstantial evidence, by the decease of those people who, from their own recollection, might have spoken decidedly to the point. That Mr. Mores was a man of the most troublesome and litigious disposition appears most clearly from his having delayed the payment of his just dues, till it became necessary for the officers to resort to a legal method of obtaining that by force which they could not prevail on him to liquidate in a friendly and an amicable way; and to such a man little credit is due for any assertion which he may have made to his son concerning it, after the lapse of a considerable number of years, and when all animosities had

ceased

ceafed between Mr. Banifter and the rector of Tunftall (for the diftrefs is faid to have been taken in 1721, which was 9 years prior to the birth of Mores the fon, who was yet a boy when the friendly meeting took place between Mr. Banifter and old Mr. Mores, as mentioned in the former part of this letter): I fay; that a man of Mr. Mores's difpofition, who could carry peace and good will in his countenance at one time, and, at fome fubfequent period, inftil into the mind of his fon a rooted prejudice againft that perfon, by the relation of ftories which (if true) muft have ruined his character for ever, deferves not the leaft degree of credit. He muft have been actuated by the father of lyes; and his offspring the Hero of your romance) muft have been a man of a very depraved heart, to commit a notorious falfhood like this to paper with a view to publication. But, indeed, what better fruits could be expected from a mind long habituated, as you have informed us, to the vices of indolence and diffipation? But let us reafon a little longer on this charge. Does it feem confonant to the ideas of prudence and difcretion, that Mr. Banifter fhould act upon principles fo diametrically oppofite to his own intereft, as to conceit and carry into effect a plan of this nature, which muft have an immediate tendency to defeat its own end? What was the precife fum which would have been gained by this imputed fraud, Rowe-Mores has artfully with-held from the knowledge of his readers. In his relation of this affair, he fays; " that the rector was affeffed £.15. for the parfonage-houfe, which he " refufed to pay, and that the officers thereupon made a feizure of a large " quantity of pewter, and other utenfils:" but the quantum of the affeffment is not mentioned. Now I will give the utmoft fcope to his argument, and fuppofe that the poors-rate was two fhillings in the pound. The fum in difpute would in this cafe amount to thirty fhillings only; and is it probable (I had almoft faid is it poffible) that any man who was not at war with common fenfe, who like Mr. Banifter lived in credit with people of every denomination, and whofe bread depended on the prefervation of his moral character; would any man, I fay, thus circumftanced, have hazarded the lofs of friends, of fortune, and of reputation, in exchange for fo trifling, fo paltry a reward? Surely not. And fince the certainty of the allegation cannot be fubftantiated by irrefragable proof, which is the only evidence that ought to be allowed to give fanction to a calumny like this; let charity be fuffered to turn the balance, and let prefumption, together with thofe other circumftantial deductions before mentioned, incline every unprejudiced reader to judge favourably of the accufed.

As to Mr. Kenrick, the juftice of peace at Feverfham, whom you mention as having been in league with Mr. Banifter, refpecting the feveral affociations formed againft Mr. Mores by Mr. Banifter, Mr. Jacob Banifter, Mr. Wilkins, and others of the parifh of Tunftall; though I have made many inquiries, I have not been able to difcover any traces concerning him. His letter to Mr. Hunt (if fuch a letter was ever fent, for furely there is no herefy in doubting the veracity of every account, whereof there is no more credible voucher than the bare word of that diffipated author, Rowe Mores) exhibited, it muft be acknowledged, a flagrant deviation from the rules of orthography; but inftances of this kind, in country juftices of that date, are by no means rare or unprecedented, and I could furnifh you with fpecimens of ill fpelling in magiftrates of a much later period. But this letter proves nothing to the point in queftion : Mr. Kenrick, with all his deficiency in academical education, migh^r, for any thing that appears to the contrary, have been a very honeft man, and no contemptible adminiftrator of juftice.

With refpect to the letter which Rowe-Mores has thought fit to contraft againft that of Mr. Kenrick, this is equally inconclufive ; or, if it may be allowed to be given in evidence, will tend rather to impeach the conduct of the rector, than otherwife. Mr. Barman, it is true, laments that his friend fhould have fuffered through any improper conduct of his parifhioners, but at the fame time avoids giving any opinion upon the fubject of the difputes which may have originated between the rector and his flock, and urges a pious recommendation of the Chriftian virtue of patience. In truth, this letter, from the face of it, appears to have been written in anfwer to fome peevifh complaints which Mr. Mores had preferred in a former epiftle, and the reply of Mr. Barman can be underftood in no other light, than as referring to fuch letter, and a civil acquiefcence in the truth of the allegations : whereas, if Mr. Barman had conceived that Mr. Mores had been defrauded of his property by Mr. Banifter, and that the reft of the inhabitants had entered into an offenfive league to pillage him upon every occafion, which is the language held forth by Rowe-Mores, the letter under confideration would have been penned in terms much more forcible and energetic. He could, one fhould fuppofe, have recommended to his friend to have fought a legal remedy for thefe outrageous infults ; and this, not only with a view of recovering his own property, but as 'a retaliation of the public indignity offered to the clerical function ; for, if the rector had been treated with that afperity by his parifhioners which is imputed to them by Rowe-Mores in the pamphlet, it is very unlikely that any reverend gentleman, to whom Mr. Mores fhould think fit to prefer his complaint, would content himfelf by calmly recommending the lenient balfam of patience, which, although in fome cafes a virtue, would, in this inftance, have been highly culpable.

The pamphlet alledges further ; that an action was brought againft Mr. Banifter, for recovery of the money raifed by fale of the goods taken in diftrefs, after an ineffectual attempt to fettle the matter by arbitration, and that the rector recovered againft Mr. Banifter ; and, in the two following pages, an uninterefting account is given of a difpute between the rector and Mr. Wilkins, with which Mr. Banifter had no concern whatever.

It is a maxim in law, that the accufed can never prove a negative ; but it is no lefs univerfally allowed, that the bare affertion of a fact will in no cafe amount to a conviction. Hence it follows ; that though I am incapable of bringing any pofitive evidence to difprove this allegation of Rowe-Mores, with refpect to the action brought againft Mr. Banifter ; yet it refted with Rowe-Mores, or with you, as the publifher of that train of falfe and injurious afperfions with which the pamphlet abounds, to offer fome legal teftimony of what is advanced in this place ; and, till you fhall have done this, I fhould hope that the bare *ipfe dixit* of

Rowe-

Rowe Mores, or hi. Biographer, will have but small weight on the minds of every candid and unbiaffed reader, who will be very cautious of condemning any perfon upon fuch vague and unauthenticated relations.

The anecdote refpecting the trees felled by Sir John Hales, and likewife by Mr. Mores, is a curious fragment of topographical information; though I cannot agree with Rowe Mores, that Sir John was deferving of any cenfure for cutting down this timber, which by the rector himfelf is acknowledged to have grown on the baronet's eftate, and fo did likewife the two afhes felled by Mr. Mores. It feems, Sir John ordered an action to be brought againft the rector, as a punifhment for the commiffion of this illegal offence, for illegal it certainly was, let the in-trinfic value of the trees have been of ever fo fmall account; and this Mr. Mores well knew, for his fon tells us; " That when the rector waited upon Sir John, " on the 18th of March 1725-6, he told the baronet, that he knew not of any " trefpafs againft him ; and, upon the utmoft ftretch of recollection, could think " of no caufe of action, *except it was the taking the two trees from the bank of his* " *church-yard fence."* For the credit of his father, it would have been a mark of prudence in Rowe-Mores to have drawn a veil over this tranfaction, which expofes at once the weaknefs of his judgement, and the bafenefs of his heart. But, had he been filent on this head, there would have wanted matter to have furnifhed out another charge againft Mr. Banifter ; for (fays Rowe-Mores) " Sir John told " the rector, when at length he had gained admiffion to his prefence, that he " fhould not have proceeded againft him as he had done, if Banifter had not ad-" vifed him thereto." What! Are we to infer from this infinuation, that Sir John Hales took no concern in the management of his own affairs, but that he acted implicitly by the advice and direction of his fteward ? Such a fuppofition indeed is well adapted to the tafk which Rowe-Mores had undertaken, of heaping on the memory of Mr. Banifter a load of unmerited abufe, and this appears to be the conclufion that the fabricator of the account would with his readers to draw from the premifes. But, in the prefent inftances as well as in the foregoing, Mores reafons upon fallacious principles ; for you are to underftand, that Sir John Hales was a man of great good fenfe, and a gentleman, who, notwithftanding the fin-gularity of his behaviour in the latte part of his days, was alive to every thing which concerned his own intereft, and fearched into the very minutiæ of his af-fairs ; and, if this fact had been concealed from him by his fteward, I am well perfuaded, he would have paid dear for his breach of truft, as Sir John would moft affuredly have difcharged him from his office, the moment he had come to the knowledge of it. Mr. Banifter therefore acted wifely, and honeftly too, by giving the earlieft information to his employer, of the wafte that had been com-mitted on his eftate ; for, whether the intrinfic value of the trees was three fhil-lings, or three pounds, made not the fmalleft difference in the nature of the cafe. It was ftill an act of trover, as the law phrafes it, in Mr. Mores.

At page 74 it is pretended, " that Sir John proceeded in a fuit of law againft " Mr. Mores, though he had before engaged to give directions to his attorney, " that all proceedings might be ftopped ; but in what manner this affair ended
" cannot

" cannot certainly be f id, but that it appeared not to have come to a trial, and, if it
" had, muft, in all likelihood, have been determined in disfavour of Sir John Hales."
Perhaps it might ; but there was, in my humble opinion, at leaft, an equal probability that the event might have terminated in his favour. Be that as it may, Mr. Banifter
could have been in no degree affected by the decifion, though 1 cannot avoid remarking, that the fophiftry, and the Jefuitical cafuiftry, difplayed by Rowe-
Mores in this ftigma p ffed upon Sir John Hales, of having falfified his word
refp ct ng t e action brought againft Mr. Mores, on the fcore of the action of
Trov r co mi te d by hi n in cut ing down the timber, is a ftrong analogous proof
of t f t lt y of the various charges brought againft Mr Banifter ; for, fince Rowe-
Mo a knowledges that the caufe never came to a trial, and that it cannot certainly be fa d how the affair ended, does this imply that any blame refted on Sir
John and will it not be more candid to fuppofe, that Sir John adhered to his
promife a to the rector, of ftopping all further proceedings, than that he af-
te war s ot on with the fui , when there is no other foundation for this latter
conclufion, th n t e vague affertion above mentioned ? 1 repeat, therefore, that
this improbable ftort, refpecting Sir John Hales, invalidates the teftimony of
Rowe-Mores with refpect to the unauthenticated charges brought againft Mr.
Banifter.

I ave hitoert o confidered Mr. Banifter to have been perfectly innocent of every
charge brought againft him by Rowe-Mores, and have, in every inftance, fo far as
the length of time which hath elapfed fince the pretended commiffion of the
crimes alledged againft him would permit, given a negative, either by collateral
or analogous evidence, which, in the prefent inftance, ought in candour to be admitted as a proof of his innocence, to each fpecific charge exhibited againft him.
1 fhall now, for argument fake, fuppofe (what I by no means admit) that Mr.
Banifter, from the impetuofity of juvenile ardour, had exerted every nerve to
thwart and difappoint the rector; that he united with the major part of the parifhioners in raifing the parochial and other affeffments on the parfonage; that he
availed himfelf of the ignorance of Mr. Kenrick, the juftice, in procuring the
fanction of the magiftrates to thefe rates; and that the action, brought by
Sir John Hales againft Mr. Mores, was at his fpecial inftance. Yet were not any
of thefe acts illegal, but fuch as were naturally excited through the defpotic and
arbitrary fway of the rector, by wnich he expofed himfelf to the refentment of
his injured flock, who, it may be prefumed (for why fhould not I be indulged in
my prefumptions and furmifes as well as Rowe-Mores ?), were happy to meet with
a young man of fpirit, and, let me add, of refpectability and credit, to avenge the
affronts which were perpetually offered to them by Mr. Mores. Viewing the matter
in this light, the utmoft blame that can be imputed to Mr. Banifter is, that the
fire of his youth impelled him to ftand forth the champion of the infulted parifhioners, by which he became expofed to the mifreprefentation of a wafpifh and
malignant defamer.

At the time when Mr. Banifter is faid to have come from Sittingbourn to refide
at Tunftall, he had fcarcely completed his 19th year; and, therefore, if in that

early

early period of his life, he had fuffered his innate love of diftributive juftice to get the better of his difcretion, let not this, I befeech you, be imputed to him as a crime ; for that h's moral honefty was always unimpeached till the publication of Rowe-Mores' invectives, I have (I truft) brought fufficient inftances to fatisfy every candid inquirer ; and, if there were need of farther teftimony, no argument can be more to the point, than what I have frequently heard him mention : "That he em-
" barked in bufinefs long before he came of lawful age, and that he obtained
" truft, at that time, to a very large amount, when his creditors would have no
" other fecurity for their money, than what arofe from their confidence in his per-
" fonal integrity."

But there is yet another circumftance remaining, which, I fhould hope, will be alone fufficient to invalidate the odious afperfions brought againft Mr. Banifter by Rowe-Mores; and this is, the fmall degree of credit which is due to the author of thefe calumnies, who appears, throughout the whole tract, to have been actu-ated by a fpirit of malignity and ill nature, and to have fuffered no opportunity to efcape him of indulging his fatyrical vein. At page 59, this dealer in general invective prefents his readers with the tranfcript of an advertifement from the London Evening Poft of February 1752, reflecting on the char-cter of Mr. Tyler, as having neglected the duties of his facred function *, and who had been dead feveral years at the time of the republication of the advertifement in Rowe-Mores' fcandalous chronicle. With what virulence Mr. Banifter's character hath been treated by this Antiquary may be feen by referring to the tract, in which no lefs than 16 pages of a book, profeffedly written for general information, are ftained with the blackeft calumny on an individual. How far that perfon was deferving of the guilt imputed to him, I fhall leave to the judgment of every un-biaffed reader of this letter. When I fay, that fmall credit is due to the affertions of Rowe-Mores, I fpeak from the information of you his biographer. I have. faid that Mr. Banifter, at the time when he came to fettle at Tunftall, if he ever did remove thither, was fcarcely 19 years of age ; that he was then a young man of lively parts, and, in the hey-day of youth, might probably affent to fome acts

---

* This Mr. Tyler is the fame perfon mentioned in a former part of my Letter He was at that time vicar of Sittingbourn, and was much refpected by his parifhioners , but, if we may form a judgment from Rowe-Mores' farcafm, he became an altered man after his preferment to the parfonage of Tunftall. How far that farcafm may be founded in truth, I will not take upon me to determine ; though I well remember to have feen him more than once, during that time, at Sit-tingbourn, where his daughter (the wife of —— Cambell, Efq) then refided , and it feems very unlikely that he fhould come within little more than a mile of his rectory, and never once deign to vifit his flock, efpecially when it is confidered, that Mr. Tyler was one of thofe who paid the ftricteft regard to his canonical duties, and was known to be a rigid difciplinarian ; otherwife he would not have refufed to baptize the fon of one of his moft intimate friends at his own houfe, which he did with many apolgies, intreating his pardon for not complying with his requeft, and telling him, at the fame time, that, if he could procure another clergyman to per-form the ceremony, he fhould make no objection ; " but (fays he) my confcience will not fuffer me to relax in this particular."

which

which his riper judgement might afterwards reject; but, neither at this early period, or in the subsequent part of his life, did he ever depart from the laws of rectitude, of justice, and of truth. Now, mark the contrast! " Mr. Mores " (says his biographer) was a most indefatigable collector, and possessed great " application in the early part of his life; but, in the latter part, gave himself up " to habits of negligence and dissipation, which brought him to his end, by a " mortification, at his house at Low Leyton, Nov. 28, 1778." Shall then the reputation of a deserving member of society be sported with by one who had rendered himself infamous by a neglect of every praise-worthy action, and by a long continuance in the perpetration of the most blameable delinquencies; who, having attained to the vigour of his life, indulged himself in practices which would have disgraced the playful scenes of youth, a season which demands large allowances, on the score of inexperience, and when those are accounted trivial errors, and venial transgressions, which, 30 years afterwards, would justly expose the perpetrator of them to scorn and contempt? Can that author claim any credit with the publick, in the dissemination of artful fictions, of whom you (his biographer), who must be supposed not to have concealed any part of his good qualities, can urge no one circumstance in favour of his moral character; but, on the contrary, are driven to acknowledge, that, in the evening of his days, he gave himself up to habits of negligence and dissipation? Can a more severe satire be published against any man, than what is contained in this period? Does not universal negligence imply a neglect of every virtue; and habits of dissipation, an indulgence of every vicious practice? Does not the confession of every criminal confirm the justice of this inference? A neglect of their duty, and an indulgence in criminal excesses, proceeding from habits of dissipation, is the universal acknowledgement of every thief at the gallows. These generally make their exit in the zenith of their youth; and, it is possible, if their lives had been prolonged, that some of them might have returned to the paths of virtue and religion. But the compiler of the History of Tunstall had passed his ninth lustrum, when, according to your friend Horace, the animal passions begin to subside, and we are no longer perplexed by turbulent and unruly desires.

But I would ask; *Quorsum hæc tam putida tendunt?* Grant that the imputation cast on Mr. Banister had been as true as I am well convinced it is false, scandalous, and malicious; would the publication of it, at this distance of time, have answered any one good purpose? Has the History of Tunstall received any elucidation from it? or does it reflect any honour on the memory of Mr. Mores, the father? or did it contribute, in the small-st degree, towards reclaiming the errors of his son? If, in holding up to public scorn and derision, however unmerited, the reputation of this person, any one of these ends might have been accomplished, some little extenuation might be pleaded in behalf of the compiler. But, if the truth must be told, these unworthy censures apply to neither of these ends. The History of Tunstall would have been, at least, as complete, if Mr. Banister's name had not been mentioned; the reputation of Mr. Mores, the father, would have appeared not a jot the less conspicuous; and, as to the son, I should fear that, even with

so

fo evil an example before his eyes, he would ftill have remained obdurate. The young and vicious are with difficulty reclaimed by daily fpecimens of the inglorious ends which generally await the perpetration of unlawful acts: but when a man has grown old in fin, and when his exceffes (I fpeak the language of his biographer) are become habitual to him, all endeavours to call back fuch a finner from the error of his way to the paths of virtue would (I fear) be vain and ineffectual.

But although the diffemination of thefe flanders could anfwer none of the purpofes above mentioned, yet there are others which I can eafily conceive were moft effectually compaffed by it. Firft, it exercifed the malignity of the original fabricator, Rowe-Mores, who, from the character which you have given of him, could not but derive a pleafing fatisfaction fiom this aiabolical attempt; and his triumph would have been yet more complete, if his exceffes had permitted him to have lived to witnefs the publication of the pamphlet.

Thus have I endeavoured to refcue the character of this injured perfon from the unworthy and unmerited cenfures fo liberally beftowed upon it in the publication which you have been pleafed to ufher into the world; and I truft, that I have fulfilled the engagement I fat off with at the beginning of this epiftle, and have falfified, fo far as there remained a poffibility of doing it, after the lapfe of near 70 years, every injurious afperfon caft upon the memory of my deceafed relation. And in the reflection of having reftored the genuine and placid mien of the original picture, in the place of thofe diftorted features which difgrace the pencil of the copyift; and, in the confidence of having removed, from the mind of every candid and difinterefted reader, every ill impreffion which the perufal of thofe fabulous anecdotes might have excited, I feel a pleafure much more than adequate to the dread of the harfheft cenfures which may be paffed upon this humble attempt of an unexperienced writer, by any critical analyzers whatever.

You, Sir, I am perfuded, have too much liberality of fentiment, to wifh that the motives which induced you to publifh thefe anecdotes fhould be concealed: for my own part, I am well convinced, from the general reputation of Mr. N. as a writer and a trader, that he would never have fuffered any publication whatever to iffue from his prefs, which he could conceive had the moft remote tendency to injure the fame of the dead, or wound the feelings of the furviving part of his family. I am, Sir,

Your moft obedient Servant,

T. BANISTER.

2

P. 34, l. 4, for " 1634," read " 1654."

BIBLIOTHECA

TOPOGRAPHICA

BRITANNICA.

N° VI. PART I.

CONTAINING

Mr. THORPE's ILLUSTRATION of several ANTIQUITIES in KENT, which have hitherto remained undescribed.

———————

LONDON,
PRINTED BY AND FOR J. NICHOLS,
PRINTER TO THE SOCIETY OF ANTIQUARIES;
AND SOLD BY ALL THE BOOKSELLERS IN GREAT-BRITAIN AND IRELAND.
MDCCLXXXII.

[Price Three Shillings.]

ANTIQUITIES

IN

KENT,

HITHERTO UNDESCRIBED.

ILLUSTRATED BY

JOHN THORPE, of BEXLEY, Efq. M. A. F. S. A.

PART I.

a 2

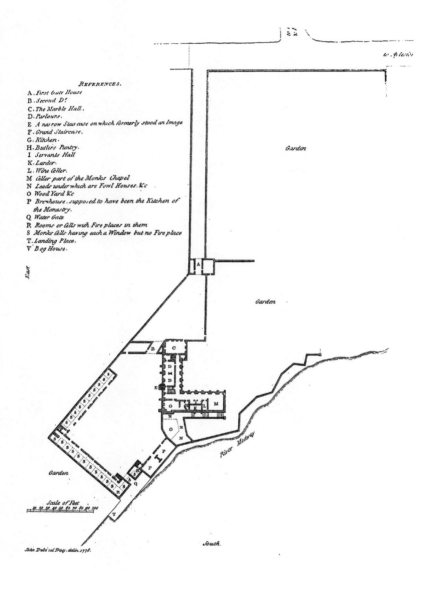

REFERENCES.

A . First Gate House
B . Second D?
C . The Marble Hall.
D . Parlours.
E . A narrow Staircase on which formerly stood an Image
F . Grand Staircase.
G . Kitchen.
H . Butlers Pantry.
I . Servants Hall
K . Larder.
L . Wine Celler.
M Celler part of the Monks Chapel
N Leads under which are Fowl Houses. &c
O . Wood Yard &c
P . Brewhouse. supposed to have been the Kitchen of
the Monastry.
Q . Water Gate
R . Rooms or Cells with Fire places in them
S . Monks Cells having each a Window but no Fire place
T . Landing Place.
V . Bog House.

East.

Garden

Garden

River Medway

Garden

Scale of Feet

South.

John Dubüvel Drap. delin. 1776.

ANTIQUITIES in KENT,

HITHERTO UNDESCRIBED.

AYLESFORD.

THE *Priory* here, commonly called the *Friers*, is pleafantly feated on the banks of the Medway above the town. Philipot calls it a fkeleton ; but certainly without reafon ; for even at this time the major part thereof remains very fair, and the leaft demolifhed of any conventual edifice in this part of the county ; owing to its having been, after the fuppreffion, the refidence of feveral eminent families. " It was founded by *Richard* Lord " *Grey of Codnor*, in the year 1240, 25 Henry III. for Car- " melites or White Friers in honor of the Virgin Mary [*]. " Many of his defcendants were buried in the conventual church " of this monaftery. It was granted with the royalty of it by " Henry VIII. to Sir *Thomas Wiat*; and on his fon's attainder it " efcheated to the crown, and was granted by Queen Elizabeth " to Mr. *John Sidley*, and he bequeathed it to his brother Sir " *William* Sidley, and from that family it paffed by fale unto " Sir *Peter Ricaut*, whofe heir Sir *Paul* Ricaut conveyed it to Mr. " *Caleb Banks* of Maidftone." Whofe fon Sir *John* Banks, Bart.

[*] Philipot, Villare Cant. p. 47. Tanner, Not. Mon. p. 223.

B

leaving

leaving two daughters, coheireffes, Elizabeth and Mary, *Elizabeth* carried it in marriage to the hon. *Heneage Finch*, fecond fon of the right honourable Heneage Finch earl of Nottingham, and lord high chancellor of England. It is now the property of his defcendant the right honourable the earl of *Aylesford*.

The great gate from the road is ftill entire, and the apartments over it, when I was laft there, ferved for the refidence of the fteward and his family. It opens to a large fquare court, in which are feen all the door-ways to the cells. The fide where the high buttreffes are on the left hand within the gate was the great hall or refectory, now divided into rooms. The kitchen was likewife on the eaft fide of the fquare, as appears by the large fire-places in one part of it. The chapel was that part of the building which ftands eaft and weft. The north fide of it fronts the garden, as the fouth does the river. The eaft window of it was where now is the dining-room or gallery-door with the iron balcony which fronts the town.

The principal parts of this convent, as the hall, chapel, cloifters, &c. were covered with plaifter; and converted into ftately apartments by Sir John Banks; and the cloifters were by him inclofed, and paved with black and white marble.

There is a fair high ftone wall which fronts the road on the north and weft fides, leading down to the gate, and inclofing the prefent garden, as it did originally the conventual.

The large ponds at the mill above belong to this eftate, and without doubt fupplied the monaftery with fifh.

A plan of the whole in its prefent ftate forms the firft plate of the prefent publication; plate VI. fig. 2. exhibits the front elevation of the gate, and fig. 3. a perfpective view of the court within the gate.

Thefe drawings, the more valuable as they have never before been taken, were made in 1778.

COBHAM

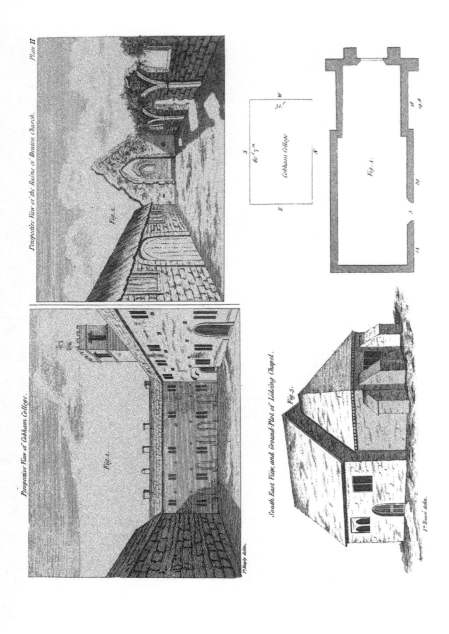

Plate II

Prospective View of the Ruins of Denton Church.

Fig. 2.

Prospective View of Cobham College.

Fig. 1.

J.ᵗ Busby delin.

Cobham College.

Fig. 4.

South East View, and Ground Plot of Luking Chapel.

Fig. 3.

I.ᵗ Tower delin.

COBHAM COLLEGE.

John lord Cobham, the laſt of the ſurname of that family, built Cowling Caſtle; and likewiſe founded and endowed a college here in the year 1362, for a maſter and chaplains to pray for the ſouls of him, his anceſtors and ſucceſſors. He alſo founded the chapel or chantry at the foot of Rocheſter bridge, and was a conſiderable benefactor to the ſaid bridge, as ſhall be more fully taken notice of when I come to treat of them in a Supplement to the Regiſtrum Roffenſe.

The college was valued at the ſuppreſſion at one hundred and twenty-eight pounds, ten ſhillings, nine-pence halfpenny *per annum* *.

It appears by the foundations and other remains to have been quadrangular; and part of the eaſt wall over-grown with ivy, and large chimney pieces of the kitchen or refectory yet remain at the ſouth-eaſt angle.

Between the north ſide of the new college and ſouth ſide of the church remains part of the north cloiſter; and the door-way from it into the church is ſtill viſible by the fair mouldings, though it is now ſtopped up. Through this door the maſter and brethren proceeded daily to their ſtalls, yet remaining on each ſide of the great chancel, to celebrate maſs for the ſoul of the founder and his noble family, whoſe graveſtones, with their effigies and inſcriptions, richly ornamented with braſs plates, paved a great part of the chancel of this collegiate church †.

Several of the maſters of the college were likewiſe buried in the church, whoſe portraitures, habited as prieſts, were on the braſs plates of their grave-ſtones, which, for the moſt part, are now torn off or deſtroyed. Two of the ſaid plates were in an

* Weever, p. 328. Tann. Not. Mon. 228. † Regiſt. Roff. p. 764.

B 2

old

old cheſt in the chancel when I was there. The inſcriptions are preſerved in the Regiſtrum Roffenſe *, and in Holinſhed †. The door-way, with its mitred arch, at the eaſt end of the cloiſter, yet remains, with the large iron hooks on which the door hung. This appears to have been the eaſt entrance of the college from the gardens.

John lord Cobham, the founder, married Margaret daughter of Hugh earl of Devonſhire, and had iſſue by her Joan his only daughter and ſole heir; who married Sir John De la Poole, Knt. and had iſſue by him Joan De la Poole baroneſs Cobham; who, by her ſecond huſband Sir Reginald Braybrooke, Knt, had iſſue one only daughter and heir likewiſe named Joan. She matched with Sir Thomas Brooke of Somerſetſhire, Knt. who was in her right lord Cobham, with all the honours appertaining to that great barony. From him, in lineal deſcent, was George Brooke lord Cobham, lord deputy of Calais, and knight of the moſt noble order of the garter ‡; who, after the diſſolution of religious houſes in the time of king Henry VIII, had a grant from the ſaid king, of Cobham college.

He lies interred in the middle of the chancel under a moſt ſtately tomb of white marble, with his effigies and that of his lady at full length, who was ſiſter and coheir of John lord Bray; and round it are the portraitures of their children kneeling. This ſumptuous monument was erected by his ſon William; but is now miſerably ſhattered and defaced by a large beam or timber falling on it many years ſince from the roof of the chancel.

William lord Cobham was conſtable of Dover Caſtle, lord warden of the Cinque-ports, knight of the garter, and lord chamberlain of the houſhold to queen Elizabeth. He founded and endowed the preſent college for the maintenance of twenty poor people; and appoints, under his will, Sir John

* P. 764.   † Caſtrations, p. 1503.   ‡ Pedigree penes me.

Leveſon,

Levefon, Knt. Thomas Fane, Efq. and William Lambarde, Efq. his executors and truftees to erect the faid college, requiring them to perform the fame within four years next after his deceafe; and to that end gave unto them and their heirs for ever, in and by his faid will, " all thofe edifices, ruined buildings, foil and ground, with the appurtenances, which fometime belonged to the late fuppreffed college; and wills the prefent to be called the *New College of Cobham.* He likewife gives unto them one hundred thoufand of fuch burning bricks as fhall be within his park or about his houfe at Cobham Hall, and forty tuns of timber to be taken in any of his lands within the county of Kent, his park at Cobham and Coolinge excepted *." By an act paffed after his deceafe in the above queen's reign, it is enacted, that the wardens of Rochefter Bridge for the time being, and their fucceffors, fhall from henceforth for ever be called by name, and fhall be in deed, the prefidents of the faid New College of Cobham, in the county of Kent, and fhall be from henceforth a body corporate, and have perpetual fucceffion by that name for ever; and that the faid college fhall from henceforth for ever be called the *New College* of Cobham in the county of Kent; and that the faid prefidents, and their fucceffors for ever, fhall have a common feal for the ufe of the faid college; and fhall and may, by the name of the Prefidents of the *New College of Cobham,* in the county of Kent, both fue and be fued, implead and be impleaded, &c. † Accordingly Sir John Levefon, Knt. and William Lambarde, Efq. being at that time wardens of Rochefter Bridge, were the firft prefidents of the faid college; and drew up moft excellent rules and ordinances for the election, maintenance, and well governing, &c. of the poor there. The number of the poor to be twenty married or unmarried, of which, one being a

* Regift. Roff. 242,   † Ib. 243.

man,

man, fhould be from time to time chofen, from any place whatfoever, without any reftraint, and prefented by the *Baron Cobham* for the time being, to be admitted and placed for *warden* of
this college.   Another, being a man alfo, fhould be from time
to time chofen from any place whatfoever, without any reftraint,
by the *prefidents* of the college, and their fucceffors, and placed
fubwarden of this college.   The eighteen refidue, being men or
women, married or unmarried, fhould be chofen from the refpective parifhes as mentioned in the rules and ordinances drawn
up by the above worthy prefidents.

The revenues belonging to this charity arife from lands in the
neighbouring parifhes of Shorne and Chalke; and in Weft
Thurrock and Stifford in Effex.

Among the MSS. in my poffeffion relative to the college of
Cobham is a lift of the prefidents in a long feries of years from
its firft erection; and likewife the accounts and difburfements,
&c. of the paymafters for the faid college, who are clerks of Rochefter Bridge; among which are the following articles.

Anno 1600, for two dayes worke in makinge the pewes for
the poore people in Cobham Church   —   VIIs.

For two locks for the iron door   ——   IXs. VId.

For XXIII Coguufaunces (Lions *) for the poore
there to weare   —   —   —   —   IVs. VIIId.

Anno 1603. Paid for a bell, to call the faid poore
people to morninge and eveninge prayer   —   IVs. VId.

Anno 1608. Elenor Newchurch expulfed for whoredome.

The excellent regulations eftablifhed by the firft prefidents,
agreeable to the pious intentions of the founder, were for a
while, duly obferved; but in length of time little if any regard
was had to them; a misfortune too frequently incident to chari-

---

* Arms of the founder, viz. Gules on a chevron Argent, a lion rampant Sable, langued and un-
guled Gules, crowned Or.

I   table

table inftitutions! for, through the inattention and neglect of many of the prefidents who refided at a great diftance, and their office being only for a year, improper people were made choice of for the office of *warden*, who is the principal perfon in the college, and is to fee to, keep an account, and inform of the behaviour of the reft; fuch a perfon being neceffary in order to reform the great irregularities, inform the prefidents, fee that prayers are obferved, church kept, contention avoided, fwearing, drinking, lying out in the night, etc. forborn. And for thefe reafons a perfon may be put into the office out of any part of the kingdom. Inftead of which, mean, dependant, day-labouring perfons, who could have no authority, capacity, or time to execute the office, were put into it; which was the caufe of all the irregularities in the college, and abufe of the charity. By which means the practice was to put into the college the moft abufive, wicked, vile, and obnoxious perfons, in order to free the parifhes from the trouble and difgrace of them, to the great difcredit of the college, and perverting the intent of the donor, who defigned it only for the poor and godly.

In the year 1733, Dr. Thorpe was elected one of the wardens of Rochefter bridge; the indefatigable pains and care which for many years he beftowed during his leifure hours for the benefit of this corporation; and the flourifhing ftate in which he left it, are fufficiently known, as the large collection of valuable manufcripts in my poffeffion relative to it will fully teftify. He was likewife, in the fame year, one of the prefidents of this college, and immediately fet about the reformation of it, by having an abftract containing the fubftance of the *rules and ordinances* of the college reprinted, together with the *morning and evening prayers*, as they are ufed in the faid New College of Cobham; and likewife the *form of a certificate* from the nominators and
eleêtors

electors of the poor perfons for the refpective parifhes upon any vacancy.

He had the feals of the office of prefidents re-engraved in a neat manner, with the arms of the founder properly blazoned; took care to have the buildings put in good repair; and the eftates of the college to be let nearly to the full value, or the beft bidder.

He fuffered no improper perfons to be admitted, and by frequently vifiting it, took notice if the warden and fubwarden did their duty, in having prayers duly obferved, and irregularities avoided. In fhort, he ufed his utmoft endeavour to reinftate every thing agreeable to the *rules* and *ordinances*, which were drawn up by the excellent pen of William Lambarde, Efq. one of the firft prefidents, and I hope they ftill continue to be obferved.

I fhall here fubjoin (from Strype's Annals) Mr. Lambarde's letter to lord Burghley concerning the will of William lord Cobham, relative to the endowment of this his *New College*.

William Lambarde, *a Juftice of Peace in* Kent, *a learned Antiquarian, that wrote the* Perambulation *of* Kent *and* Eirenarchia, *his Letter to the Lord Treafurer* Burghley, *concerning the laft Will of the Lord* Cobham *(who died this year), and fome of his Legacies. He was Conftable of* Dover Caftle, *and Lord Chamberlain to the* Queen *.

" Albeit, my moft honourable and gracious Lord, that my
" Lord *Cobham* will prefent your Lordfhip with a brief and large
" copy of the laft Will of that moft honourable and chriftian
" Lord both in life and death, his late departed good father; yet
" forafmuch as his laft difpofition ftandeth not only in his known

---

* Strype's Annals of Church and State under Queen Elizabeth, vol. IV. No. CCI. p. 270.

" teftament,

" teftament, but chiefly in the declaration of a fecret confidence
" repofed in Sir John Levefon, Mr. Fane the lieutenant of Dover
" Caftle, and myfelf; whereof he hath alfo in thefe his laft de-
" fires recommended the overfight to your good Lordfhip and
" Mr. Secretary, I take it to ftand both with his own good plea-
" fure and my duty to make known hereby (fince your lord-
" fhip's indifpofition of body permitteth not mine accefs) the
" heads and very contents of the fame.

" His lordfhip therefore minding an undoubted accomplifh-
" ment of his godly and fatherly intentions, as well towards the
" poor as his own children, did in his life-time put into the hands
" of Sir John Levefon the fum of 560l. almoft in ready money,
" over and befides rich furniture of his late lady's provifion,
" amounting in his own eftimation to the value of 2000 marks.
" His commandment to us was, that with 200l. or more of thefe
" monies, the late fuppreffed college of Cobham fhould be re-
" edified, and endowed with livelihood for the perpetual main-
" tenance of twenty poor. Next, that with 200l. or thereabouts,
" his fecond fon, Sir William Brook, fhould be freed out of debt,
" for to fo much he knew him to be endangered by mortgage of
" his lands and leafes, and by other bonds. And laftly, that an
" intereft for life in fome competent dwelling-houfe be procured
" for his third fon Mr. George Brook ; and that fome confideration
" fhould be taken of the poor eftate of his daughter's children by
" Mr. Edward Becker. And as for thefe furnitures, he would
" have them to be delivered to fuch of his three fons as fhould
" firft beftow himfelf in marriage.

" Give me leave, moft honourable lord, to add fomewhat of
" his, and of mine, concerning my now lord Cobham and his
" brethren, which neither it will grieve you to hear, nor I with-
" out their wrong may pretermit to write. We find them all
" not only to concur in moft chearful obedience to the utmoft exe-

C " cution

" cution of their good father's will and purpofes, but alfo to con-
" tend among themfelves whether of them fhall be more kind
" and bountiful to the other, whereof I moft humbly befeech
" your good lordfhip to take knowledge, and to confirm it in them
" with your good liking, their honourable father being moved
" by me to ufe them, or fome of them, now, for the execution
" of his will, however in the fetting down of his former wills he
" had pretermitted them, in regard, as I conceive, of their mi-
" norities. He anfwered thus, ' I would well to follow the exam-
" ple of my father herein, who, notwithftanding that I and other
" of my brethren were then of man's eftate, ordained Benedict Spi-
" nola and Mr. Ofborn to be his executors.'

" I have faid enough, if not too much, confidering the prefent
" weaknefs of your lordfhip's body, which I moft heartily pray
" the heavenly phyfician to re-cure; and fo moft heartily take
" my leave. *From* Lincoln's *Inn, the* xv*th of* March,
  " *Your good lordfhip's moft humble, and bounden,*
    " *by your manifold favours,*
      " WILLIAM LAMBARDE."

Cobham College is a neat quadrangular building, compofed of
fmall fquared ftones, containing twenty lodging-rooms for as
many poor families. The fouth and north fides within the quadrangle are in length fixty feet feven inches, the eaft and weft fifty-
one feet. On the fouth fide is the hall, which is a large room
with a fcreen at the entrance, and a raifed floor at the upper end,
as in other ancient halls, &c. On the right fide from the entrance, is a large fire-place with a ftone chimney-piece, at one
corner of which, in a plain fhield, are thefe arms: In chief
a Saltier, in bafe an efcallop-fhell. At the other corner is
a Saracen's head, one of the crefts of *Brooke.* In the windows
on the fouth fide are the arms of the founder in painted glafs, and
over the fouth portal or gate of the college next the gardens are
              likewife

likewife his arms, with the quarterings of *Cobham*, *Braybrooke*, *Delapole*, *Bray*, &c. (containing twelve coats within a garter) neatly carved in ftone ; and underneath thofe arms, on black marble, is an infcription in Roman capitals, which fee in Regift. Roff. p. 244.

The drawing was taken in the year 1774, and exhibits a perfpective view of the College, from the fouth-eaft angle, near the paffage to the hall.

Above the roof, on the north fide, appears part of the tower of the church. See plate II. fig. I.

The inftruments relative to the foundation and endowment, &c. both of the old and new college, fee in Regift. Roff. under *Cobham*.

D E N T O N,

In the Textus Roffenfis *Denituna* was, with other lands in different parifhes, given to the church of Rochefter by Brithric a rich Saxon, and Ælfswitha his wife, as appears by their famous will*. It was afterwards taken away by Odo bifhop of Bayeux and earl of Kent, but was reftored to that church by William the Conqueror, at the interceffion of archbifhop Lanfranc†. On the fuppreffion of the priory, it was granted by Henry VIII. to the dean and chapter of Rochefter. In the Cuftumale Roffenfe may be feen the ancient cuftoms and fervices belonging to this manor. The church was dedicated to St. Mary, a curacy in the patronage of the bifhop of Rochefter, whofe liberty claims here‡. At length falling to decay through the fmallnefs of the demefne, there being at this time but two houfes in the parifh, one of

---

* Regift. Roff. p. 26, 27.   † Hearne's Text. Roff. p. 142.
‡ Willis's Paroch. Angl. p. 19.

         which

which is the manor adjoining, together with the ſervice being diſcontinued, it is likely the bells, iron work, tiling, and other materials, were taken down and ſold, or otherwiſe diſpoſed of. Harris is miſtaken in ſaying it is down, for the outſide walls for the moſt part remain to this day, which muſt have been more entire when he publiſhed his hiſtory.   It was not a ruinated church in Kilburne's time[*] and many years ſince.   An ancient inhabitant of Graveſend informed my father that he remembered divine ſervice performed in it.   The whole is now encumbered with the falling in of the ſtones and rubbiſh, probably when the timbers were taken down, and almoſt choaked up with briars and nettles.   A cart-lodge has of late years been built againſt it on the north ſide for the conveniency of the farm-houſe, and the thatched roof reſts upon the wall, by which means the door-way and windows on that ſide are now ſtopped up, which an-ſwered to thoſe on the ſouth ſide, and ſhew it to have been a regular building.   The tower or belfrey at the weſt end is down to the foundations.   On the ſouth-eaſt human bones have at times been digged up where the cæmitery was, now part of the farm yard.

The perſpective view exhibited in plate II. fig. 2. ſhews the eaſt window of the chancel, and the arch mantled with ivy, which ſeparates it from the nave, and ſome portion of the win-dows and ſouth door.

It ſtands on a pleaſant bank by the road ſide, commanding a view of the Thames and Eſſex ſhore, on the left hand about half a mile diſtance from Milton church leading to Chalk, to which pariſh this of Denton now pays all dues and duties.

The drawing was taken in 1774.

* Survey of Kent, p. 72.

LIDSING

Plate III

No 2.

No 3.

No 1.
Sir Stephen de Pencheſter.

No 4.

Cath: Thorpe delin 1771.   Elevation of the Font in Penshurst Church.

Trevel delin 1777.   Front View of the Porch of Chiddle Church.

Rev.d Tho.s Baker delin 1735.

Cath: Thorpe delin 1766.   South West View of the Porch of Speldhurst Church.

L I D S I N G

Is a hamlet in Gillingham, which " in the reign of Edward III. was the property of Sir *Robert Belknap* the judge, who, by his deed bearing date the 8th of October, in the fecond year of king Henry IV. gave this manor to the priory of St. Andrew in Rochefter, for one monk who was a prieft, to celebrate mafs for ever for the foul of his father John Belknap, and for the foul of his mother Alice, and likewife for the foul of himfelf and all his fucceffors, in the church of Rochefter. This, upon the dif-folution of the priory, was by king Henry VIII. fettled on the dean and chapter of the cathedral church of Rochefter*." See the deeds relative to this manor in Regift. Roff. under *Chatham.*

Lidfing is now a chapel of eafe to Gillingham, and the vicar has the great tithes of it, who performs divine fervice here. The chancel or eaft end was rebuilt a few years fince with brick, at the expence of the late vicar, the Rev. Mr. John Jenkinfon. The drawing was taken in the year 1776. See plate II. fig. 3.

P E N S H U R S T.

This parifh is called in the Textus Roffenfis *Penneſherſt*, in the Regiftrum Roffenfe and fome antient records *Penceſtre* and *Pen-cheſter*. In the time of the Conqueror it is mentioned in the general furvey of Doomfday to have been the chief feat or re-fidence of a family who took their names from it. *Paul de Pen-cheſter* held lands here and at Lyghe. From him, it was by a continued feries brought down to the famous Sir *Stephen de Pen-*

* Philipott, p. 168.

cheſter,

chefter, conftable of Dover Caftle, lord warden of the Cinque Ports, and high fheriff of the county in the reign of Henry III. In the ninth year of Edward I. he had a licence granted by the king to him and *Margaret* his wife, to erect a caftle at *Alling-ton*; as it appears by the patent-rolls of that time. " Quod " Stephen de Penchefter et Margaretta ux. ejus poffint kernellare " domum fuam de Allington in com. Kanc." to fortify and em-battle their manfion-houfe at Allington in this county. Having thus eftablifhed this pile, he in the faid king's reign obtained a charter of free-warren to his manor of *Allington*, and alfo a mar-ket weekly on the Tuefday, and a fair yearly three days, on the vigil, the day, and day after St. Laurence, fo that it came to bear his name, and in fome old records to be called *Allington Pen-chefter**. By virtue of a commiffion iffued in the third year of Edward I. he and John de Rigate were the two juftices appointed by the king to hear and decide the controverfy relative to the ac-cufations brought againft Richard de Clare earl of Gloucefter for taking part with Simon de Montfort, in levying war againft Henry III. They, upon a ferious fifting the whole matter in debate, did finally determine it; and did abfolve the faid Richard from the crimes with which he was unjuftly charged†. In the eleventh year of Edward I. he amply granted and confirmed to the free-chapel or chantry founded by Sir *Thomas de Penefherft*, in his manor of *Penfherft*, within the bounds of the parifh of Lyghe, portions of lands out of his eftates in Penfhurft, Chi-dington, Lyghe, and Tunbridge, in pure and perpetual alms, for the health of his foul, of thofe of *Royce* and *Margaret* his wives, and all his anceftors.

He alfo granted and confirmed to the chapel of Groombridge, dedicated to St. John the Evangelift, lands in the parifh of Speld-hurft, in pure and perpetual alms, for the fame fervices. See

* Philipott, p. 41.   † Ibid. p. 345.

the

the inſtruments relative to the above grants, under the reſpective pariſhes, in the Regiſtrum Roffenſe.

He was a very learned man, and ordered all the muniments, grants, &c. relating to Dover Caſtle, to be written in a fair book, which he called *Caſtelli Feodarium*, out of which Darel compoſed his hiſtory of that caſtle *. *Penchester Tower* in the ſaid caſtle was named from him, and was kept in repair by lands given to the *Penchester* family by the crown for this purpoſe: they lay about Poſtling, Horton, Rucking, and Blackmanſtone †. Philipott, and Harris from him, are miſtaken in ſaying that *Margaret* his ſecond wife was daughter of the famous *Hubert de Burgh* earl of Kent, and chief juſticiary of England; whereas ſhe was daughter of *John de Burgh* his ſon ‡.

Sir Stephen had by her two daughters, *Joane* and *Alice* his coheirs; who, upon the death of Margaret their mother, divided his great eſtates in this county. *Joane* the eldeſt carried Allington caſtle to her huſband *Henry de Cobham* Lord of Roundal in Shorne; and *Alice* was matched to John de Columbers, who had with her the manors of Penſhurſt, Lyghe, &c.

Sir *Stephen de Penchester* was interred, ſuitable to his dignity, in the ſouth chancel of Penſhurſt church, under a tomb in a niche at the upper end near the eaſt window, with the portraiture of a knight compleatly armed, carved in a hard grey marble or Caen ſtone, his head reclining on a cuſhion, with a ſhield on the left arm, and the right hand graſping the ſword, ſimilar to the tomb of his ſon in law Sir Henry de Cobham of Roundal, in the ſouth chancel of Shorne church, ſtill called *Roundal* or Randal chancel, from his being lord of that manor ‖.

It was cuſtomary in that age for the lords of eminent manors, who were generally patrons of the churches and founders of the

* Harris, p. 485.   † Ibid. p. 373.   ‡ Bibl. Topogr. Britan. No. I. p. 14.
‖ Regiſt. Roff. p. 760.

chapels

chapels and fide ailes, to have burying places in them ; which were frequently endowed with chantries, to pray for the fouls of their founder and his defcendants ; and without a doubt there was one for Sir *Stephen de Penchefter* in his chapel at Penfhurft, as there were in the chapels abovementioned, which he endowed with lands for the fame purpofe. It was likewife then the prevailing fafhion to have their portraitures recumbent on their tombs armed and crofs-legged after the manner of knights Templars, agreeable to the rude fculpture of thofe times, and generally with French epitaphs. But as all fublunary matters have the fate of an uncertain inconftancy, fo had this great man's tomb ; for after his bones had refted in it for feveral ages, it was deftroyed to make room for the graves and monuments of the *Sidney* family, to whom this chapel appertained as lords of the manor of *Penfhurft*. His mutilated effigies, after being tumbled about, was at laft placed erect on a wooden block or treffel, on the fouth fide of the faid chancel, againft a door which has many years been faftened up, where it now remains with the words *Sir Stephen of Penchefter* painted over it on the wall *. His arms were, Gules, a crofs voided Argent. The vague defcription which Harris gives of this figure in faying, " it is of white marble, and hath a face of antiquity enough to be genuine †," fhews that he obferved it with little or no attention. The drawing (plate III. fig. 1) was taken in the year 1777.

The ancient font in this church is a neat piece of workmanfhip, and octangular. In each compartment is an antique fhield within a Gothic rofe, with the following devices.

In the firft are the letters IHΣ. In the fecond A. R. in Gothic capitals coronetted or flory. In the third XPΣ. In the fourth is the true and moft ancient crofs in Heraldry, or what Guillim calls a *crofs patible*. The fifth is as the

---

* Regift. Roff. p. 920.   † P. 485.

firft.

firft. In the fixth are the arms of the fee of Canterbury. The feventh is as the third. In the eighth is the crofs embellifhed with the inftruments of our Saviour's paffion, as the crown of thorns, fpear, fcourge, &c.

The compartments round the fhaft or column are ornamented with double Gothic arches neatly pointed.

This handfome font, like many others, is daubed over with paint; which was done many years fince, and at the fame time with the pillars and fcriptural fentences in the church.

The drawing, plate IV. fig. 2. was taken in the year 1775, and exhibits the elevation and compartments feparately.

C H A L K E.

The porch of this church is remarkable for its ftrange and whimfical ornaments, a tafte which often occurs in Gothic architecture, as may be feen on fome of the buildings in Oxford, and in various parts of the kingdom. Thefe chimerical dreffings convey little if any meaning or defign, and appear to have been merely the effects of rude caprice, and fantaftical humour of the architects and fculptors of thofe times.

Here the artift has indulged his fportive fancy in a manner too loofe and abfurd for a facred edifice. On the crown of the arch at the entrance is the figure of a man in the character of a jolly tippling fellow, holding a jug with both hands, and looking up with a moft expreffive laughing countenance to a grotefque figure in the attitude of a pofture-mafter or tumbler above the center of the moulding, as if pleafed with his pranks and performances, and about to drink to him. Between thefe figures is a niche or recefs ornamented with a neat pointed Gothic arch and rofes, in which formerly ftood the rood or image of

the Virgin Mary, to whom the church is dedicated. The impropriety if not indecency of its being placed between two such ludicrous figures one would wonder should escape the obfervation,
and not excite the difguft of the congregation, who, as good Ca-
tholicks, ufually made their reverence when they approached it.

The drawing (plate III. fig. 3.) was taken anno 1777, and
fhews the elevation or front view of the porch.

The niches and rood-lofts ftill remain in many churches and
monaftick buildings; but the roods or images were, after the
Reformation, taken down and deftroyed.

S P E L D H E R S T.

This church ftands on an elevated fituation, and is remarkable
for the loftinefs of its fhingled fpire, but more fo for the curious
porch, over which, in an antique fhield cut on ftone, are the arms
of *France*, with a file of three lambeaux, for *Charles* duke of
Orleans, general of the French army, who was taken prifoner at
the battle of Agincourt, by that famous foldier Sir Richard Waller,
for which fignal fervice king Henry V. affigned to him and his
heirs for ever an additional creft, viz. the arms or efcutcheon of
France hanging by a label on a walnut-tree, with this motto affixed, *Hæ fructus virtutis.* The king committed this noble prifoner to the cuftody of Sir Richard, who held him in honourable
reftraint many years at his feat at Groombridge in this parifh,
which the duke rebuilt for him on the old foundation. He likewife built the porch, and was a good benefactor to the repair of
Speldherft church. Sir *Richard Waller* * was fheriff of Kent the
fixteenth year of Henry VI. and kept his fhrievalty at Groom-

* Philpott, p. 320.

bridge,

bridge, and was before fheriff of Surrey and Suffex in the twelfth year of that prince*. From him, in a direct defcent, Groombridge came to Sir William Waller, who was fheriff of Kent in the twenty-fecond year of king Henry VIII. and lies buried in the church, at the upper end of the nave, in the year 1555, under a grave-ftone, on which are feveral brafs plates with the effigies of him, his wife and eight children. His fon Sir *Walter Waller* and *Elizabeth* his wife are interred in the chancel, to whofe memory, on the fouth wall, is a beautiful monument of alabafter, with great variety of work and ornaments, and over it are thefe arms, viz. two coats quarterly, firft, Sable, three walnut-tree leaves, Or, between two bendlets Argent; fecond, Azure, a chevron, Or, fretty Sable, between three croffes moline Argent; third as fecond; fourth as firft, impaling, Gules, three fwords bar-ways argent, pomelled and hilted Or, between eight mullets of the laft. In a canton parted per feffe, Argent and Or, a Lion paffant gardant Gules. Crefts, over baron, a walnut-tree; over femme, a hand holding a fword, the blade broken off by the hilt.

Underneath are two arches, in one a man kneeling in compleat armour, with the quarterings above defcribed hanging on the pommel of his fword, and three fons. In the other, the effigies of his wife (with her arms) and two daughters kneeling, in the drefs of the times, and on two tables of black marble are the following infcriptions:

" I'de prayfe thy valour, but Mars 'gins to frown;
" He feares when Sol's aloft that Mars muft down:
" Ide prayfe thy fourme, but Venus cryes amayne,
" Sir Water † Waller will my Adon ftayne:
" Ide prayfe thy learning, but Minerva cryes,
" Then Athen's fame muft creepe when Waller's flyes.

---

* Philpott, p. 320.   † Sic.

    " Affift

" Affift us England in our dolefull fong,
" When fuch limbs fade thy flourifh lafts not long.
" Earth hath his earth, which doth his corps inroule,
" Angells fing requiems to his bleffed foule.

" All worthy eyes read this that heather come,
" Never decaying vertue fills this tombe ;
" Never enough to be lamented here,
" As long as womankind are worth a teare ;
" Within this weeping ftone lyes lady Waller,
" All that will know her more a faint muft call hir :
" Life fo directed hir whilft living here,
" Leavell'd fo ftraight to God in love and feare ;
" Ever fo good, that turn hir name and fee,
" Ready to crown that life a lawrell tree *".

Of this family was defcended *Edmund Waller* †, efq. the celebrated poet, as is the prefent *Edmund Waller*, of Hall Barn, near
Beaconsfield, in Buckinghamfhire, efq.

Over the arms of the duke of Orleans, was a fmall nich or
recefs, now filled up, in which ftood the rood or image of the Virgin Mary, to whom the church is dedicated.

---

* Regift. Roff. p. 808.

† " Whofe famny," fays Dr. Johnfon, " was originally a branch of the Kentifh Wallers, and
" his mother was the daughter of John Hampden or Hamden, of the fame county, the zealot of
" rebellion." Our poet's occafional vifits to his relations at Groombridge were frequent in the early
part of life.. To this place he was attracted by its neighbourhood to Penfhurft. " Too young to
" refift beauty, and probably too vain to think himfelf refiftible, he fixed his heart, perhaps half
" fondly and half ambitioufly, upon the lady Dorothea Sidney, eldeft daughter of the earl of
" Leicefter, whom he courted by all the poetry in which Sachariffa is celebrated. His acquaint-
" ance with this high-born dame gave Wit no opportunity of boafting its influence ; fhe was not
" to be fubdued by the powers of verfe, but rejected his addreffes, it is faid, with difdain, and
" drove him away to folace his difappointment with Amoret or Phillis. She married in 1639 the
" earl of Sunderland, who died at Newberry in the king's caufe ; and, in her old age, meeting
" fomewhere with Waller, afked him when he would again write fuch verfes upon her, When you
" are as young, Madam, faid he, and as handfome, as you were then."

The

STARKEYS, in the Parish of WOLDHAM and County of KENT.

The noted chalybeate springs, though commonly called Tunbridge Wells, are in *Speldhurſt* Pariſh.

The drawing (plate III. fig. 4) exhibits the ſouth-weſt view of the porch, and was taken in 1776.

W O L D H A M.

In this pariſh, which derives the name from its ſituation under the wolds or downs, is an ancient houſe now called *Starkeys*, near the river Medway; but in times of remote antiquity, it had the repute of a manor, and was known by the name of *Woldham parva*, or *Little Woldham*. After ſundry deſcents it came to be the inheritance of Sir *Humfrey Starkey*, one of the barons of the Exchequer in the reign of Henry VII. who erected the preſent houſe called after his name. He was deſcended from the Starkeys of Wrenbery and Oulton in Cheſhire [*]; and lies interred, with *Iſabel* his wife, in the church of St. Leonard's Shoreditch, where was the following epitaph on his tomb; " Orate pro animabus " Humfredi Starkey militis, nuper capitalis Baronis de Scac rio " Domini Regis Henrici Septimi, et Iſabelle uxoris ejus, et om- " nium amicorum ſuorum, quorum &c†."

From him it came down to Sir *John Lewſon*, whoſe ſon Sir *Richard* Lewſon transferred his right in it to that learned baronet Sir *John Marſham*, and it is now the property of his deſcendant the right honourable *Robert Lord Romney*.

It is built with ſtone, and was in former times a handſome ſtrong edifice, and much larger than at preſent, being now only a farm-houſe; and, when this drawing was made, much out of repair, the great window of the hall being, for the moſt part, ſtopped up with bricks and plaiſter.

[*] Philpott, p. 3~4.   † Weever, p. 427.

Harris

Harris fays, that he " faw at Starkeys the remainder of a pretty " large chapel *." Of which only a fragment of the wall is now to be feen at the eaft angle of the houfe; but wnen I lived in this parifh, a larger portion of it was ftanding, and one of the fide windows with its mitred or pointed arch. In the church, on the north fide, is a fmall chancel belonging to Starkeys.

The drawing (plate IV.) was taken in the year 1769, and fhews the front or fouth-eaft view of the houfe.

GILLINGHAM.

The manor, now a farm-houfe, and called the *Court Lodge*, is feated near the church. It was, in very remote times, the property of the archbifhops of Canterbury, as appears by the books of Doomsday and Textus Roffenfis. They had here an eminent palace, in which they fometimes had their refidence. I have fubjoined the following account of its remains as they appeared when laft I vifited them, September 7, 1776.

The large building ftill remaining, which I judge to have been the great hall of the palace, and now converted into a barn and granary, is built chiefly with flint and fome ftone, and has been plaiftered over. The old windows, both on the eaft and weft ends, with their Gothic mullions and arches, yet remain, but fome are ftopped or filled with bricks. The great room has fire-places at each end; the plaiftering on the infide of the walls is ftill fair, and fhews no appearance of there having ever been either upper floors or any other partitions. The chimney jambs at each end projected into the room, and the funnels were worked up in the head walls, and came out at the ridge of the roof. There is no window at the fouth end; and the ancient

* Harris, p. 337.

door-

Plan of the Archbishops Palace at Gillingham.

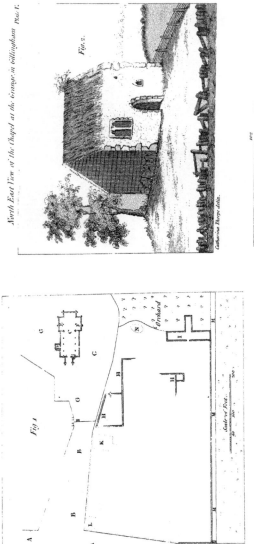

Fig. 1.

Scale of Feet.

Orchard

North East View of the Chapel at the Grange in Gillingham. Plate V.

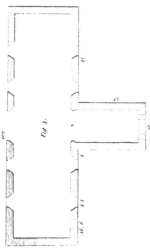

Fig. 2.

Catharine Thorpe delin.

Fig. 4.

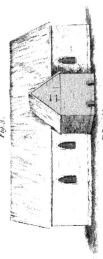

Fig. 3.

T. Brooe del.

The East View, and Ichnography of the Remains at Gillingham Palace.

door-way on the weſt ſide, no doubt, was enlarged to admit of the preſent pair of barn doors. Its loftineſs, and the above reaſons, incline me to think it was the *Hall*

The eaſt ſide was ſtrongly ſupported with ſhores, as it was much out of a perpendicular, and in danger of falling. On this ſide the building projects; and the tenant of the Court Lodge ſaid, that ſo long as he could remember (and he knew it was ſo in his father's and grand-father's time, who were likewiſe tenants) this part or projection of the barn is, and has always been, called the *Chapel*.

Notwithſtanding the appellation, however, it never could have anſwered the purpoſe of a chapel, as there are not the leaſt traces or ſigns of having ever been any window or door from without. I ſhould rather think it ſerved as a receſs for the uſe of the butler, or a withdrawing room or rooms for the company in the hall, as there are two Gothic arches or doorways leading out of the great room into it; which gives me ſome ground to think it was heretofore divided by partitions, and that the circular holes were made to convey away the dirty water, &c.

There is a door-way out of the barn into it, which you deſcend by two or three ſteps, as fully appears in the accurate plan of the whole taken in the ſame year by my ingenious friend Mr. John Treſſé of Brompton in that pariſh, and expreſſed in plate V. fig. 1, 3, 4. I find there have been heretofore two windows on each ſide; and it is now made uſe of as a granary; but to what purpoſe this, and the barn-part of the building, may have ſerved in ancient days, if not for a hall (or, according to the traditional account, a chapel) I will not preſume to determine. Without doubt there was a chapel, as it is recorded in the Textus Roffenſis, that the archbiſhops, during their reſidence in this palace, gave conſecrations to biſhops.

All

All the foundations of the palace that are at prefent vifb'e about the Court-Lodge yard are inferted in the plan, agreeable to the fcale; and the outer thick ftone wall on the fouth fide, covered with ivy, in great part remains, and may be traced on part of the weft fide as defcribed in the plan. Some workmen digging about two or three years before I was there, clofe by the foundations, found a large antique fpur almoft deftroyed by ruft, which was thrown afide and loft; and a Roman coin, which Mr. Treffé borrowed of the tenant for my infpection. It is copper, of the emperor Antoninus; the reverfe a woman fitting. Dr. Harris fays, a very large urn, containing fragments of burnt bones and afhes, was many years fince dug up in the falt marfhes of Gillingham *. Indeed, many difcoveries of curious Roman antiquities have very lately been made, in enlarging the military lines near Brompton, fomewhat fimilar to thofe difcovered on Barham and Chartham Downs near Canterbury, in the indefatigable refearches of that late learned antiquary the Rev. Brian Fauffet of Nackington, M. A. F. S. A. His noble collection is now in the poffeffion of his eldeft fon Godfrey Fauffet, Efq. at his feat called Hepington in that parifh. The Romans ufually had tumuli or barrows, &c. near their roads, and on the hills adjacent to their principal ftations.

* Hift. p. 131.

References

2

References to the plan of Gillingham, plate V. fig. 1.

A. The cross.

B. The cage, removed there 1663.

C. Parish church.

D. Vestry room built 1770.

E. Chapel belonging to East Court.

F. Chapel belonging to the Grange.

G. Church yard.

H. Foundations of the palace.

I. A large barn, formerly the hall.

K. The present farm-house.

L. Another farm-house erected also within the verge of the outer wall of the palace.

M. Road to the Grange.

N. A pond, apparently made since the decay of the palace.

East view, fig. 3. Wall two feet eight inches thick. Height of the building from the plinth to the eaves, fifteen feet. Ditto of the part that projects on the east side, ten feet.

THE GRANGE

Is an eminent manor situated about a mile east of Gillingham church. It is a large old brick building, and has a pound by the road side near the yard gate. Without doubt the house was much larger in more early times, and built with stone; for, as far back as the Conqueror's reign, it was in possession of the lords Hastings, ancestors to the earls of Huntington. In the reign of Edward III. it descended to John Philipott, Esq. alderman of London, and lord mayor temp. Richard II. who, for his signal services performed for the state, was knighted by that king, and had an augmentation to his paternal coat of arms. He was founder of the chapel here, as it was affirmed on its suppression in the reign of Henry VIII [*].

Harris says, "at this seat there was formerly a *church* or chapel, which was valued at 6£. per annum in the king's books: it was

[*] Philipott's Villar. Cant. p. 167.

E

built

built by Sir John Philipott, but is now only a barn *." From this vague defcription I am inclined to think he never faw it; for it could be no church, and certainly much too fmall for a barn. In former times, lords of eminent manors had frequently, by the permiffion and confent of their diocefans, oratories or chapels contiguous to their manfions, for the convenience of their houfhold and tenants. This chapel ftill remains; and ftands near the houfe, at the weft end. It is built with ftone, and very fair, and is now covered with thatch. The eaft end, within four feet of the ground, becoming ruinous, has been taken down, and is now weather-boarded. The door-way and windows on the fouth fide are only to be feen within; as they are outwardly concealed by a wooden fhed erected againft it.

The length of this chapel is 41 feet and a half; breadth at the eaft end 21 feet. When I was there, it was made ufe of as an outhoufe for implements of hufbandry, poultry, &c.

The drawing was taken the 7th of September, 1776. See plate V. fig. 2.

T W I D A L L.

From the Grange the road leads directly to Twidall, another eminent manor houfe about a mile diftant, at the extremity of the parifh. From the family to which it gave name, " it was paffed away by *Richard de Twidall*, in the fourth year of Richard II. to *John* the fon of Robert de *Beaufitz*. The chantry here was founded by *John* Beaufitz, who was fon of the above John, which he makes provifion for by his laft will the 22d of November, 1433, and orders it to be dedicated to John the Baptift, and likewife that one prieft fhould there celebrate mafs for the foul of him-

* Hift. p. 130.

felf,

East View of the Ruins of Halling Palace.
1. Chapel to the Palace. 2. Halling Church.

Perspective View of the court within the vaste at the river.

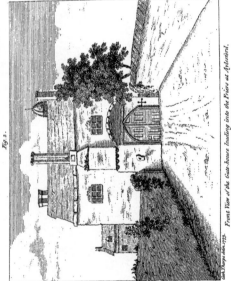

Front View of the Gate-house leading into the Friers at Aylesford.

Fig 2.

Fig 3.

felf, his wife Alice, his father John, his mother Ifabel, and his uncle William Beaufitz *."

The infcriptions on the brafs plates of the graveftones, together with an account of all the portraitures and arms of the above an-cient and noble family, which were in the fine windows of Gil-lingham church, and deftroyed in the time of the rebellion, are preferved in the Regiftrum Roffenfe, from the curious MS. of Baptift Tufton, prefented to my father by his friend Robert Paynter, Efq. the laft of the antient family of that name in this parifh, and lord of the manors of Eaft Court and Twydall, which eftates he bequeathed to the late Thomas Lambarde of Seven-oaks, Efq.

Philipott fays, " the feats in the chapel, and other remains, de-clare it to have been formerly a neat and elegant piece of archi-tecture †." Indeed, it even anfwered his defcription many years ago, when I faw it. However, its beauty did not preferve it, for it was pulled down in the year 1756, with a part of the old houfe; and if I miftake not, great part of the materials at pre-fent compofe the foundation of a large barn.

The chapel joined to the main building, was in that wing which run northward or north-weft, and was handfomely wainfcoted.

H A L L I N G.

The Bifhops of Rochefter had, from very early times, a palace here, in which they much refided; and many of their in-ftruments in the Regiftrum Roffenfe are dated from hence. The manor, wharfs, and ferry, are the property of the bifhop; and all leafed to *William Dalyfon* of Weft Peckham, Efq. but the tithes and prefentation to the vicarage belong to the dean and chapter.

* Philipott, p. 168.　　　† Ibid.

The

The palace was pleafantly feated on the banks of the Medway, and near the church. The learned antiquary William Lambarde, Efq. refided in it fome time, where he compofed the moft part of his work entitled " A Perambulation of Kent ;" and in my memory, there was a handfome row of ftone ftairs remaining, which reached the length of the palace, for the convenience of the bifhop's barge and other veffels to land. When I lived at Woldham, on the oppofite fide of the river, the roof of the chapel was deftroyed : but the walls, with the windows and door-way, remained entire ; and part of the hall, &c. was converted into a dwelling-houfe, and inhabited. There were likewife fome remains of the large kitchen, and out-offices ; but all thefe buildings have fince been totally deftroyed for the fake of the materials.

Concerning the ftatue of Hamo de Hethe, who was bifhop of Rochefter, and confeffor to Edward II. and built largely here, which ftood in a niche over the entrance, and was preferved by my father, and by him prefented to bifhop Atterbury ; the reader will find, with other curious matters relative to this palace, in the fecond volume of the Antiquities of England and Wales, by my friend Francis Grofe, Efq.

The drawing (plate VI. fig. 1.) fhews the eaft view of the remains of the palace, with the parifh church in the back ground, as they appeared in the year 1767.

END OF THE FIRST PART.

BIBLIOTHECA

TOPOGRAPHICA

BRITANNICA.

N° VI. PART II.

CONTAINING

Mr. THORPE's ILLUSTRATION of feveral ANTIQUITIES in KENT, which have hitherto remained undefcribed.

TO WHICH IS ADDED,

A Letter from Dr. PLOTT, intended for the ROYAL SOCIETY.

———————————

LONDON,
PRINTED BY AND FOR J. NICHOLS,
PRINTER TO THE SOCIETY OF ANTIQUARIES;
AND SOLD BY ALL THE BOOKSELLERS IN GREAT BRITAIN AND IRELAND.
MDCCLXXXIII.

[Price Three Shillings.]

Plate VII.

Drawn Publis. 1781.

A View of WHORNES PLACE on the Parish of CUCKSTONE.

ANTIQUITIES IN KENT,

HITHERTO UNDESCRIBED.

PART II.

C O O K S T O N E.

IN this parifh ftood the ancient feat called *Whorne's Place*, fo denominated from Sir *William Whorne*, knt. who erected it. He was Lord Mayor of London in the year 1487, and 3d of Henry VII. It was pleafantly fituated on the weftern bank of the Medway, commanding a view of the downs above Woldham on the oppofite fhore; and the meanders of that beautiful river down to the city of Rochefter, and upward to Halling, Burham, &c. on each fide. For a particular account of the defcents of this eftate, from Sir William Whorne to its prefent proprietor the Right Hon. Robert Lord Romney, I refer the reader to Mr. Hafted's Hiftory of this county, vol. I. p. 482.

Nicholas Lewfon, or *Levefon*, Efq. purchafed it about the be-ginning of Queen Elizabeth; for I find by an accurate furvey of the manor of Potynes in Snodland *, taken in the fecond year of

* MS. penes me.

F.

her

her reign, by order of Thomas Wotton, of Boughton Malherbe, Eſq. that ſome portions of the land of his ſaid manor of Potynes bounded to the lands of Nicholas and Thomas Lewſon, gentlemen. It ſhould ſeem that, while Whorne's Place was in the poſſeſſion of this family, they beſtowed much attention on it, by enlarging it and making great improvements, as appeared by the arms of *Leveſon,* quartered with three other coats hereafter mentioned, in a very handſome compartment over the weſt or back-door. I muſt confeſs, that as to the building itſelf, I ſaw no part except the large bow window towards the river, which could have been of Whorne's erection; and it may be obſerved in plate VII. that it breaks the regularity of the front. And I conceive that, on the re-erection or improvement of this manſion by the Leveſons, this window being curious, they ſuffered it to remain without deſigning their new work in any manner to ſuit it, the room which it lighted being little more than the window itſelf. A flight of ſtairs led from the river to a terrace walled in front; and on the ſouth ſide of the houſe were large gardens incloſed with brick walls, which produced a fine echo on the river, when oppoſite. On the north ſide of the houſe ſtood the magnificent ſtables, built with brick, in length 88 feet, in width 25 feet, with two fine towers, and pilaſters on each ſide the door-way. The whole front was enriched with a profuſion of work, and executed with excellent ſymmetry. The pediment over the door was ornamented with handſome ſtone mouldings and dental cornice, and three ſhields of arms. That in the center contained the following nine coats quarterly :

1. Three laurel leaves, the arms of *Leveſon.*

2. Two bends wavy, between 2 leopards heads caboſſed, with a border.

3. On a chevron between 3 cinquefoils, 3 roundles.

4. Ermine, a lion rampant, within a border ingrailed.

5. A

Plate VIII.

Trey delin. 1782.

A Front View of the Stables at **WHORNES PLACE** in the Parish of **CUCKSTONE** in Kent.

5. A cheveron between 3 cinquefoils.

6. A cheveron ermine between 3 buckles.

7. A cheveron between 3 cheffrooks.

8. Five martlets on a chief indented 3 crowns.

9. As the firft.

Sir John Levefon, of Whorne's Place, in Cookftone, married Margaret daughter of Sir Roger Manwood, knt. whofe arms were, Sable, two pallets Or, on a chief of the fecond a demi-lion naiffant of the firft.   Thefe arms are in a lozenge on the right-hand of the above quartered coat, and fhould imply that the faid Margaret was the firft wife of Sir John, the three lions rampant in the left-hand lozenge being probably his fecond wife's.   Wherefore I conclude the nine coats quarterly were the arms of Sir John Levefon, knt. and that the building was erected by him.   His brother Sir Richard Levefon, knight of the Bath, who was of Trentham in Staffordfhire, alienated all his lands in Kent to different perfons, and among them Whorne's Place, in the reign of Charles I. to that moft excellent hiftorian and antiquary Sir John Marfham, bart. author of the " Chronicon Egyptiacum," and other learned works.   Father Simon in his writings called him "the great Marfham of England;" and Anthony a Wood, in his Athen. Oxon. vol. II. p. 783, obferves, that all the great and learned men of Europe his contemporaries acknowledged him to be one of the greateft antiquaries, and moft accurate and learned writer, of his time.

I have been told, and from good authority, that his fine library was in this building, in the apartments raifed on the north-caft end of it, and another floor over *them*, with ftair-cafes on the outfide to each floor.   A pretty extraordinary circumftance, that no inconveniences from the feeding, &c. of horfes *under the ftudy* fhould be apprehended.   But the height and other reafons might be more regarded.   There were, I think, four rooms

above

above on each floor ; but of little ufe for many years paſt.   Mr.
Caleb Perfeét, the late reétor of this parifh,, informed me, that
fome years ago he often vifited poor fick people in fome of them ;
and there was a *window* in the ftudy, if I miftake not, that de-
ferved notice.   It is a great pity two fuch venerable buildings
fhould have been deftroyed : but only tenants and labouring
people having for many years lived there, and the noble and
worthy proprietor refiding altogether at his feat near Maiditone,
they were pulled down in the year 1782 ; and the whole, as
1 am informed, is defigned to be cleared away, except the granary
and barn ; the former is to be converted into a farm-houfe, and
the fcite of the old feat into meadows, &c.

Plate VII. exhibits a view of the houfe, and plate VIII. a front
view of the ftables of this curious old manfion.

The granary is a fmall building adjoining the road to Halling,
the fituation of which will be better underftood by the plan
annexed.

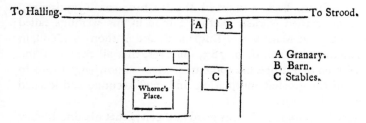

The way out of the road into the yard is between the granary
and barn.

Plate IX.

A View of the Roman Arch of Worthgate in Canterbury, from the Castle Yard

C A N T E R B U R Y.

N E A R Wincheap Gap in this city ſtands *Worthgate*, now diſ-
uſed and walled up, through which in ancient times the Roman
road continued in a direct line from Caſtle-ſtreet to Wincheap,
Chilham, &c.   The alteration of this road, which now makes
an elbow into Wincheap, and the different ſtations of the military
way, the reader will find amply treated of in Battely's edition of
Somner, p. 12, & ſeq.   Worthgate is without doubt the fineſt
remnant of antiquity in this city, and perhaps the moſt entire of
its kind in the kingdom *.   The preſervation of it is owing, as
Mr. Goſtling informed me, to the care and generoſity of Dr. Gray,
an eminent phyſician of this city (who died in 1737), through
whoſe interceſſion the corporation were prevailed on to let it remain, who otherwiſe would have taken it down.   And for its further ſecurity, the doctor, at his own charge, repaired the inſide wall
with new brick work and coping, and under it erected a commodious bench †.   The boldneſs of the arch, conſiſting entirely of Roman
bricks, ſtrikes the eye of the beholder with a kind of veneration.
In the inſide next the Caſtle-yard the ground has been raiſed
ſo much from time to time, that no more than one foot ſix inches
of the ſtone piers or columns to the ſprings of the arch are now
to be ſeen; but when viewed on the garden ſide in the city-
ditch, the gate makes a noble appearance, as the height of the

---

* Leland, in his Itinerary, ſays, " The moſt ancient buildinge of the toune ap-
" peareth yn the caſtel, and at Ryder's gate, where appere long Briton brikes."
The old way to London is found to have been along Caſtle ſtreet, and through this
gate; which Somner thinks took its name either from its vicinity to the caſtle, *Worth*
ſignifying a fort, or caſtle; or elſe from a corruption of *Wardgate*, from the watch
and ward kept in and about this fortreſs.   See Mr. Groſe, under his view of *Canterbury Caſtle.*

† This bench has been long removed, and the Roman bricks are now decaying
or rather falling out by the decay of the cement. A plan is alſo in agitation for
taking down the whole, and opening the old ſtrait road through the Caſtle-yard.

piers

piers is feven feet fix inches.   They are compofed of a kind of
rag-ftone, two feet fix inches in breadth, which appear to have
been fquared, but are now irregular and uneven, from being
much corroded and mouldered away through the great length of
time; whilft the arch, which confifts of a double row of bricks,
remains as firm and durable as ever, fo well had the Romans the
art of tempering and burning their clay.   The length of the
longeft brick on the caftle fide is one foot five inches, depth of
the thickeft three inches; and the number of the infide row 102
or 104*.   I took the meafurement of this gate-way in the year
1771, when the drawings in plate IX. were made, and find it
correfponds nearly with that fince publifhed by Mr. Goftling †;
which I fhall here give as follows.

In the infide,

	Feet.	Inches.
The diameter of the arch is	12	$3\frac{1}{2}$
It fprings from the piers	6	$0\frac{1}{2}$
The piers above ground	1	6

On the ditch fide,

Height of the plinth	1	0
From that to the fpring of the arch	6	6
Breadth of the gate-way from pier to pier	12	6
Height of the gate in the middle	13	$7\frac{1}{2}$
The thicknefs of the arch	2	4
The earth raifed on the caftle fide	6	0

As Mr. Goftling has given views of feveral gates in the city
and about the cathedral, it is a wonder that Worthgate, the moft
curious and ancient of any, fhould be omitted ‡; as are likewife

---

* Not more than 88 now remain entire.
† Walk in and about Canterbury, 2d edit. p. 365.
‡ A very fmall indiftinct view of it occurs in Mr. Grofe's plan of Canterbury
Caftle.

thofe

thofe which lead into the *White* and *Black Friers*.   It may be the fate of the two laft, one time or other, to be taken down, as many have been, to make more room; and as no draught of them has hitherto been made public, I have here given, in plate X. a front view of them taken in the year 1771.   The fmall niches or re-ceffes ftill remaining over the gates were formerly ornamented with figures of faints; which, on the fuppreffion of thefe mo-nafteries, were taken down and deftroyed.

C H A T H A M.

EGELRICUS, a prieft of *Cettham*, is mentioned as a bene-factor to the monks of St. Andrew in Rochefter, and was one of the fecular canons of that priory[*].   His being afterwards ap-pointed by his fraternity an officiating prieft in this parifh, im-plies that there was a church, or fome place of divine worfhip, which muft have been but a fmall mean building, as were moft of the facred edifices at that early period.   But after the Conqueft, when the Norman architecture prevailed, and lords of eminent manors built and endowed places of public worfhip on their de-mefnes, the buildings were upon a more enlarged and elegant plan.   *Chatham* was the principal manor which appertained to the barony of the potent and illuftrious family of the *Crevecoeurs*, and their place of refidence before they removed to Leeds Caftle; and they were frequently written *Domini de Cetham*[+].   *Hamon* de *Crevecoeur* was one of the knights who attended William I. to

[*] Text. Roff. p. 181.   [+] Phillipott, Vill. Cant. p. 104.

England, and was rewarded for his fervices by the king with the manors of Chatham and Leeds. Kilburne calls him *Hugh*, and fays, that he began the building of Leeds Caftle ＊. His defcendant, *Robert de Crevecoeur*, or *de crepito corde*, as he is ftyled in the Regiftrum Roffenfe, founded and endowed, anno 1119, the priory at Leeds for Black Canons regular, of the order of St. Auguftine, dedicated to St. Mary and St. Nicholas; which, at the fuppreffion, according to Dugdale, was valued at 362l. 7s. 7d. per annum.

Many of the founder's name and family were afterwards be-nefactors to this monaftery, by granting to it divers revenues and liberties; and fo great was his zeal, that he granted to it, for the repofe of his own foul and of the foul of his uncle Hamon Dapifer, feven churches at one time, fituated on his eftates; among which was the church of Chatham, with the rights and profits of the fair, &c. there †. This eminent family coming into England with the Conqueror, and being poffeffed of this manor, it is moft likely they enlarged if not re-edified the church; which, as before obferved, muft have been but a fmall edifice, and fre-quently liable to deftruction by the cafualties of fire and invafion of foreign enemies. It was no longer under the patronage of the canons of St. Andrew, but the cure of it was fupplied by a monk from the new monaftery at Leeds, whom the prior fhould appoint, and might remove at his pleafure; though it was en-joined that he fhould profefs canonical obedience to the ordi-nary‡. For when Gundulph was confecrated bifhop of Ro-chefter by archbifhop Lanfranc, March 19, 1077, who both likewife came from Normandy, and had been monks of the abbey of Bec in that province, he difplaced the fecular canons from the priory of St. Andrew, and filled it with monks of his own order,

---

* Survey of Kent, p. 164.　　　　　　† Regift. Roff. p. 209, & feq.
‡ Ibid. p. 214, &c.

who

South West View of the Parish Church, at Chatham.

Fig 1.

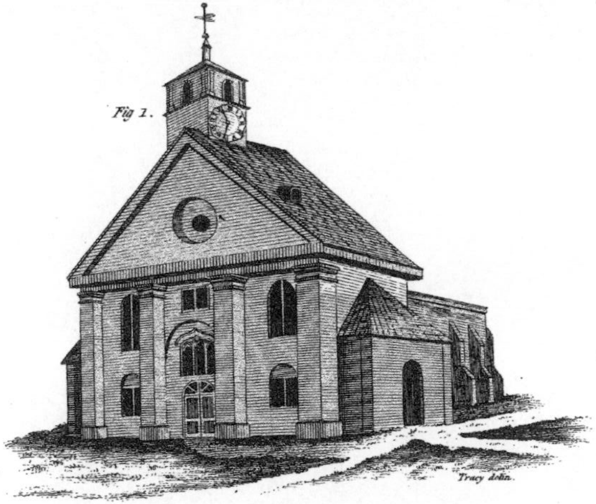

Tracy delin.

View of the Ruins of the Chapel in Milkhouse Street in Cranbrooke

Fig 2.

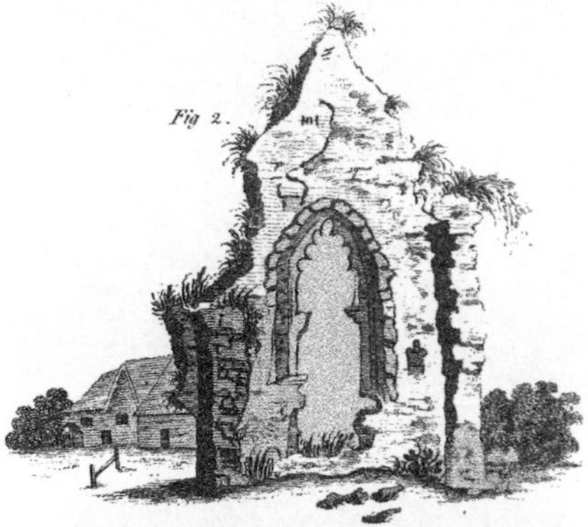

Fig 3.

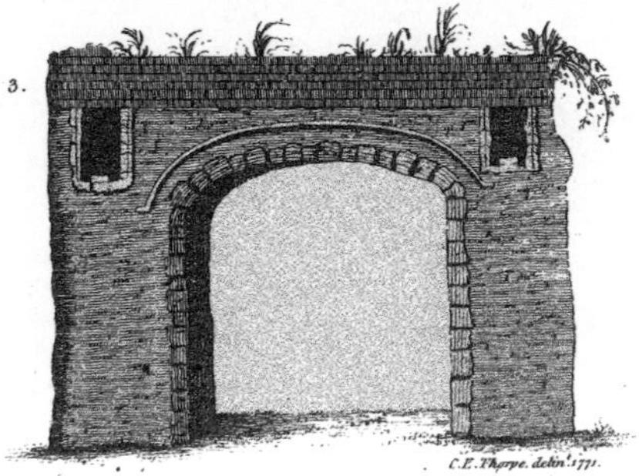

C.E. Thorpe. delin. 1771.

Front View of the Gate to the White-Friers, in Canterbury.

Fig 4.

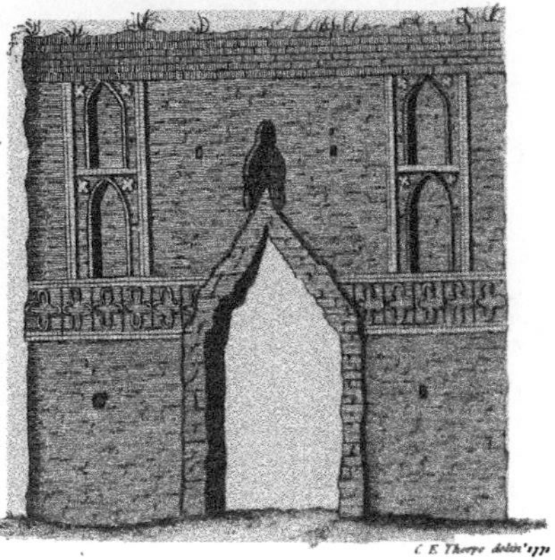

C.E. Thorpe delin. 1771

Front View of the Gate to the Black Friers, in Canterbury.

who followed the rule of St. Benedict.   The antient church of
Chatham being confumed by fire, the Pope granted a letter of
indulgence, anno 1352, of a year's relaxation of penance to all
perfons who fhould enable the inhabitants to rebuild it*.   It was
dedicated to the Virgin Mary, and Philipot fays it was repaired,
and the fteeple rebuilt by the commiffioners of the navy, in the
year 1635†.   According to a late Hiftory of Rochefter, p. 267,
the Eaft end of the church, now ftanding, is nearly all that remains of the building raifed by the Pope's brief, the North
and South ifles are of a latter date, and the faid commiffioners
rebuilt and enlarged the Weft end.   Philipot only fays they repaired the church, and erected the fteeple ; and indeed the
antient window over the door at the Weft end ftill remains
unaltered, and is now the only part of the church that
wears the face of antiquity.   The Weft end has been enlarged fince with a bold pediment fupported by pilafters, and
with a pigeon-houfe-like fteeple ; and the whole building is now
plaiftered, and fo much modernized, as to have, though a neat,
yet little appearance, of a facred edifice.   A South Weft view in
its prefent ftate is exhibited in plate X. fig. 1.

Some few years fince, in digging a grave in this church, a
hand was found intire and uncorrupted as far as the wrift or me-
tacarpal bones, griping the hilt of a fword ; the other parts of
the body were totally confumed, and likewife the blade of the
fword.   It was afterwards kept in a fmall box with bran, at the
fexton's houfe on *Chatham Bank* ; and when I faw it, I obferved
that the handle of the fword was, for the moft part, mouldered
away ; which being of brafs, the moifture had penetrated the
flefhy parts of the hand and nails, and tinged them of a verde-
greafe colour, which had preferved them.

* Regift. E. de Shepey, fol. 257. b.   † Villar. Çant. p. 104.

G   CRAN-

C R A N B R O O K E.

A T *Milkhoufe Street*, fo denominated from an antient feat in this parifh, ftand the ruins of a free chapel, founded and endowed by John Lawlefs, about the latter end of the reign of Henry VII. but on the general diffolution of the religious houfes, king Henry VIII. granted the lands belonging to it (then valued at 84l. 10s. 10½d.) to Sir John Baker, of Sifinghurft, in this parifh ; and among his other eftates it continued and defcended*. Kilburne fays, this chapel was in ruins in his time, and that it was dedicated to the Holy Trinity†.   All that now remains of it is part of the chancel end and great Eaft window, which make a venerable appearance, and fhew it to have been a handfome building.   See plate X. fig. 2.

C L I F F E.

A M O N G the communion plate appertaining to this large handfome church, is ftill preferved a very curious and antient *patine*, which, when the Roman Catholick religion prevailed here, covered the chalice, or contained the confecrated wafers at the facrament of the *mafs*, but is now made ufe of in collecting the *alms*.   It is of filver gilt, of the exact fize and dimenfion as the figure exhibited in plate XII. engraved from a correct drawing taken in the year 1774.   In the centre, moft beautifully embellifhed

* Philipott, Vill. Cant. p. 100.   † Survey of Kent, p. 65.

with

Tinbuck del.

J. Gry culp.

The South East Prospect of **FRINSBURY CHURCH** near Rochester.

Inside View of an ancient Patine _in_ Cliff _Church._

Bayly del.

North Elevation of the Font _in_ Frindbury _Church._

w. del. 1783.

with blue and green enamel, is reprefented the Deity fitting with his arms extended, and fupporting his Son on the Crofs, with an *olive branch* in the left-hand, and the *Gofpel* in the right. Round the verge or rim of the *patine* is the following infcription, in the ancient text letter, curioufly ornamented with fprigs of rofes between each word, alluding to the fubject:

𝕭enedicamus. 𝕻atrem. et. 𝕱ilium. cum. 𝕾piritu. 𝕾ancto.

The reft of the plate for the communion fervice confifts of two filver bread-plates, and one filver flaggon, with this infcription on them: " In minifterium Cœnæ Dominicæ, D. D. D. Q. Geor-" gius Green, S. T. B. rector et commiffarius de Cliffe."

F R I N D S B U R Y.

THIS church (fee plate XI.) ftands on a fine eminence, which commands a view of the river Medway, and on the oppofite fhore the city of Rochefter, the towns of Stroud and Chatham, to the right and left, with the circumjacent hills, &c. forming altogether a moft pleafing landfcape. The church confifts of two ailes, is neat, and in good repair, but has nothing very remarkable in it, except the *font*, which is a curious piece of gothic workmanfhip, and in good prefervation. It is octangular, with a taper elegant fhaft or column, and brackets at each angle from the bottom of the font to the fwell of the pedeftal. The compartments are excellently carved in relievo, containing the following fubjects: 1. The ancient text letter 𝕵. 2. In a fhield,

Gules,

Gules, two Bars argent, between three Annulets Or, in feffe a
Mullet for difference.   3. The letter 𝕽.   4. The fame arms.
5. The letter 𝕹.   6. The fame arms, with a Martlet in feffe
for difference.   7. The letter 𝕽.   8. A blank fhield.   Thefe
letters and infignia difcover the donor and time when erected;
for *John Rykeld* held the manor of *Eflingham*, in this parifh, of
the church of *Rochefter*, and was fheriff of Kent the 3d year of
Henry VI. and kept his fhrievalty at the faid manor*.   He was
likewife the fame year returned one of the knights in parliament.
Thomas Rykeld, of *Eflingham*, gent. died in the 18th year of Edward IV. leaving *John Rykeld* his fon and heir, a minor, the
cuftody of whom, as well as of this manor, during his minority,
was then granted by *John Langdon*, bifhop of *Rochefter*, to Sir
Thomas Seyntleger, knt. *Henry Merlande*, and *Henry Cantlowe* †.

The font being in part crouded by pews, which is generally
the cafe, rendered a drawing of it the more difficult.   It fhould
feem as if the arms had originally been painted, as their prefent
colours agree with the fame mentioned in the Regift. Roff. ‡, and
with the arms of *Rikhill* in Edmonfon's heraldry.   They likewife
elucidate, and fhew, that the perfon who lies interred in the north
chancel of Northfleet church, with his effigies in armour, and
that of his wife in the drefs of the times, with this imperfect infcription on the fragment of a brafs plate beneath them—*et Ka-
terine, uxoris ejus*—was of the fame family.   Above the figures
are thefe arms, viz. *Two Bars between three Annulets*; and the
fame again impaling a chevron between three columbines.
On another gravestone in the fame chancel is the following infcription on a brafs plate : " Hic fub pede ante altare jacent Wil-
" lelmus Rikhill, arm. filius Willelmi Rikhill militis primoge-
" nitus, et Katherina uxor ejus, que obiit 27 Aug. 1433. qui

---

* Philipot's Vil. Cant. p. 152.   † Regift. Roff. p. 372.   ‡ Ibid.

" quidem

" quidem Willelmus obiit . . . . . die . . . . . 1400. Quorum——*"
Weever, from Stowe's Annals, fays, that " Sir William Rikhill,
" the father, was one of the king's juftices, an Irifhman born,
" the vehement urger of accufations againft *Thomas* of Wood-
" ftocke, duke of Gloucefter, and *Thomas Arundell,* archbifliop of
" Canterbury, Ann. Reg. regis Ric. II. 21. 1397 †." Kilburne
mentions the two *Rickhills* buried in Northfleet church; one above
250 years, and another above 220 years before his time; but
does not give us their Chriftian names ‡. Philipott likewife fays
that *John Rykeld,* and *William* his fon, lay entombed in this
church; but ftrangely confounds both names and dates. For,
in page 255, he fays the four manors of *Ifield, Well, Cofington,* and
and *Shinglewell,* defcended to *John Rykeld,* about the reign of Henry
IV.; that *William* his fon deceafed without iffue male ; and *Rofe,*
his fole daughter and heir, was married to *Edward Limfey,* who
defcended from *Ralph de Limfey,* held the manor of Budbrook in
Warwickfhire, 20 William I. In the fubfequent page he fays,
that *Rofe* was fole heir of *John Rykeld,* and matched with *John
Limfey* ; and that the faid manors came to *Rykeld* about the beginning Henry VI.‖. How are we to reconcile thefe mifnomers
and miftakes? The confufion in the names certainly arifes from
his inattention, and of the hiftorians after him; nor will the
fhort period in which the family of the *Rykelds,* or *Rikhills,* exifted,
as the name came afterwards to be fpelt, allow for their being fo
many *Johns, Williams,* &c. and it fhould feem that Philipott's firft
acount of thofe in Northfleet muft be the true one; in fupport of
which I find that *Edward Limfey,* the father, was returned 12
Henry VI. one of the gentlemen of this county ; and Philipot,
p. 255, fays *John Limfey,* the fon, fifty years afterwards, viz.
1 Richard III. fold the *Rikhill* eftates. By all this it appears

* Regift. Roff. p 753. 756.   † Funeral Mon. p. 332.
‡ Survey of Kent, p. 204.   ‖ Villare Cant. p. 255, et feq.

Edward

Edward muſt have been the perſon who married *Roſe Rikhill*, and not *John*.

Richard II. cloſed his reign September 1399. Sir *William Rikhill* is ſaid to die in the next, and his ſon *William*, by the inſcription, in 1400; ſo that father and ſon muſt have both died within the year, if the ſon ſucceeded the father; but if he died in *vita patris*, then it is likely he might leave a ſon of the name of *William* to ſucceed his grandfather; which latter *William* (if there was any ſuch) was probably brother to *Roſe*, and the perſon who conveyed away the manor of *Ridley* 16 Henry VI. and likely died ſoon after, agreeably to the account given by Kilburne, of one of the *Rikhills* being buried at Northfleet about 1439. But I rather think there is a miſtake in the inſcription, in the placing the time of his death upon it, and that there were but two *Williams*. It is moſt likely the military perſon who lies interred under the imperfect inſcription, was the *John* mentioned by Philipott, and another ſon of Sir *William*. Without doubt there were originally other memorials of this family in the ſaid chancel, which may have been deſtroyed (as is too often the caſe) to make room for other graveſtones; and indeed I have ſome reaſon to think ſo from appearances. To conclude this matter, it is I think certain that the *Rikhills* of *Eſlingham* in *Frinſbury* deſcended from the family at *Northfleet*; and that *John Rikhill* of *Eſlingham*, who was ſheriff of Kent, was a younger ſon of Sir *William Rikhill* of *Northfleet*; and the arms, with a mullet for difference on the font, ſhew that he erected it. The coat differenced with a martlet, and the initials N. R. it is likely were for a younger brother, and the blank ſhield left in reſerve, or for want of another to fill it up. I find in Mores's Hiſtory of Tunſtall that *John Rykeld*, grandſon of the ſheriff, married *Margaret* daughter of Sir *James Crowmer*, of *Tunſtall*, knt. She is interred in that church under a braſs plate, with the following inſcription:

" Hic

" Hic jacet Margareta filia dni Jacobi Crowmer militis dudum uxor Johis Rycyls
" heredis manerii de Eſlyngham, quæ obiit feĉdo dcēbr' anno domini millmo
" CCCCLXXXXVI°. cujus anime ppiciet deus amē. *''

On the ſtone are the arms of *Crowmer*, viz. Argent, a chevron
engrailed Sable, between three Crows proper, impaling *Rykeld*.

The following ſhort pedigree may perhaps ſomewhat elucidate
the deſcents of the above family.

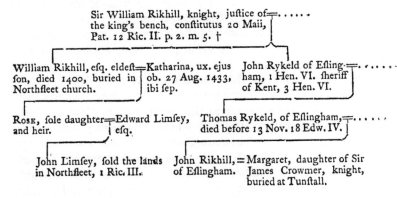

Sir William Rikhill, knight, juſtice of the king's bench, conſtitutus 20 Maii, Pat. 12 Ríc. II. p. 2. m. 5. †

William Rikhill, eſq. eldeſt ſon, died 1400, buried in Northfleet church.=Katharina, ux. ejus ob. 27 Aug. 1433, ibi ſep.

John Rykeld of Eſlingham, 1 Hen. VI. ſheriff of Kent, 3 Hen. VI.

Roſe, ſole daughter and heir.=Edward Limſey, eſq.

Thomas Rykeld, of Eſlingham, died before 13 Nov. 18 Edw. IV.

John Limſey, ſold the lands in Northfleet, 1 Ric. III.

John Rikhill, of Eſlingham.=Margaret, daughter of Sir James Crowmer, knight, buried at Tunſtall.

Plate XII. ſhews the elevation of the font, and its compartments
ſeparately.

Thus far I had written, when I was favoured by my learned
and ingenious friend the Rev. Mr. Denne with the following very
ſatisfactory particulars of this pariſh.

* Bibl. Topogr. Britan. N° I. p. 77.   † Dugdale's Origin. Judicial.

Frindſbury,

Frindſbury, or *Frendſbury*, is a pariſh in the weſt diviſion of the county of Kent. *Freondeſbirigh* is its denomination in ſome old deeds, and this word in the Saxon ſignifies, according to Lambard *, the Friend's Court. The church is ſituated about a mile from the weſt end of Rocheſter bridge, and the limits of the pariſh extend from the Medway to the Thames. Its other boundaries are the pariſhes of St. Werburgh in Hoo, Higham, Shorne, Cobham, and Strood.

Dr. Plott conceived that the Roman Watling-ſtreet, which, in his time, might be traced from the bank of the Thames a little above Lambeth palace as far as the north gate of Cobham park, went from thence over the hill where Frendſbury mill ſtands, and ſo to a point of land in Frendſbury marſh that was nearly oppoſite to Chatham church. He gave into this opinion becauſe there was here a ſhallow which made it the moſt fordable place through the Medway, and he adds its being a tradition, that, in the memory of our grandfathers, the river might have been paſſed here, there being not above three or four feet water upon a low ebb, and that in their paſſage over they uſed to tread upon the heads of horſes. The laſt circumſtance in this traditional tale certainly gives it the caſt of a vulgar notion, and it the leſs deſerves our paying an implicit credit to it, becauſe in the reigns of Elizabeth and James the royal dockyard was where the ordnance office now is.

If a judgment may be duly formed from preſent appearances, the narroweſt and the ſhalloweſt part of the river below the bridge

* Perambulation, p. 365.

was

was from the end of Strood-ftreet to Rochefter key ; and in an efiay concerning the four great Roman ways fubjoined to Leland's Itinerary, vol. VI. * fatisfactory reafons are affigned for this being the ancient place of fording. The parifh of Frendfbury, ought formerly to have contributed towards the repair of the firft pier and arch of Rochefter bridge; and it was probably for this reafon that William Saunder, whilft vicar of Frendfbury, was warden of the bridge †.

Offa king of the Mercians and Sigered king of Kent are mentioned to have given Frendfbury and Æflingham to the church of Rochefter (fee Textus Roffenfis, c. 92.) but there is a more circumftantial detail of this donation in two other chapters of this curious MS. In chap. 47, the title of which is of Æflingham, or Freondfbury, Offa, by a writing dated at Canterbury anno 764, is recorded (with the confent of archbifhop Bregewine, and Herbert king of Kent) to have granted to Eardulf bifhop of Rochefter twenty-one plowlands in Æflingham, with the appurtenances and advantages, in as ample a manner as they had been of old held by the earls, princes, and kings of Kent. Eardulf was alfo to have the liberty of difpofing of thefe lands in any manner he pleafed. Though this was termed a free gift by Offa, the bifhop feems to have made fome pecuniary acknowledgment, but probably not an equivalent. In the next chapter Sigered, who ftyles himfelf king of the half part of the province of the Kentifhmen, claims the merit of prefenting Æflingham to Eardulf, with the confent of the archbifhop of Canterbury ; and he is faid not only to have figned and fealed the deed, but to have eftablifhed the donation by the delivery of a turf of the land intended to be conveyed. Upon comparing thefe accounts, it is

---

* P. 118.

† He became afterwards rector of Hynton in Northamptonfhire, and died February 2, 1452. Brydges's Hiftory of that county, p. 177.

manifeft

manifeſt that Kent was at this time divided by the Medway into two regal provinces, and that both kings were in ſome degree dependent upon the victorious Offa. Three tracts of land called Denbers, in the common wood, were granted by Offa as appendant to Æflingham, and four more Denbers were added by Sigered.

When Domeſday ſurvey was made, the biſhop of Rocheſter held Frendſbury, rated in the time of king Edward for ten ſhillings, but then for ſeven. The arable land was fifteen carucates. In demeſne were five carucates, and forty villans with twenty-eight borderers, having eleven carucates. There was a church and nine ſervants, and a mill of twelve ſhillings rent, twenty acres of meadow, and *wood of five porcaries* (ſilva 5 porc). In the time of king Edward and after, it was valued at 8 *l.* but then worth 25 *l.* What Richard held in his own Lowy was valued at ten ſhillings. Whether by *ſilva porc.* was meant any ſtated meaſurement of wood, or what was ſuppoſed to be ſufficient for the pannage of a certain number of hogs, is a point that the gloſſaries leave doubtful; but it is moſt likely to be a word of the ſame ſignification with *denber*, and that it was in this place intended to denote *porcarium*, a porcary, and not *porci*, hogs. Mr. Haſted's conſtruction of the words is a pannage of five hogs †, which appears however to be too confined a range for ſo large a manor as Frendſbury was.

Richard here mentioned was Richard de Clare earl of Glouceſter, who had a grant from William I. of Tunbridge caſtle, and of a conſiderable tract of land denominated the Lowy of the ſame. Dr. Harris is of opinion that the earl had procured the eſtates which belonged to him in other parts of the county to be accounted within the juriſdiction of his lowy, and that this might

Regiſtrum Roffenſe, p. 370.　　　† Hiſtory of Kent, vol. I. p. 542.

be

be the reafon for our meeting with thefe entries in the Domefday inquifition of Frendfbury, Southfleet, Halling, &c. &c ". But the words ftrongly imply that the lands which Richard held of the bifhop as lord of thefe manors were in Tunbridge. It is particularly faid of Southfleet manor, that there is in Tunbridge as much wood and arable land as is valued at twenty fhillings; nor is it difficult to trace how the bifhops of Rochefter became poffeffed of lands within that diftrict. The denbers given by Offa and by Sigered are faid to be in a common wood, the term is *veald feuueftra* †; and as Tunbridge has ever been deemed a part of the *weald* of Kent, that the lowy fhould have within its extent one or more of thefe denbers is a highly probable fuppofition. The diftance of Tunbridge from Frendfbury can be no objection againft this furmife; becaufe, as Somner has remarked, there is fcarce any grant in the regifters of either the church of Canterbury or Rochefter of any confiderable portion of land from the king out of the weald, without a denber or woody valley in the weald, in which they were to have liberty of running and feeding cattle, particularly fwine. And it adds no fmall weight to this conjecture, that Gilbert de Tunbridge, the fon of Richard, is recorded to have reftored to the monks of St. Andrew in Rochefter their lands within his lowy of Tunbridge, viz. Uppringeberi, near Burne, which belonged to the manor of Frendfbury ‡.

Out of the profits of Frendfbury bifhop Gundulph at firft appropriated 5 *l*. 10 *s*. for cloathing the monks of St. Andrew ‖; but he afterwards fettled the manor itfelf upon this highly-favoured fraternity, referving only fome certain articles of provifion which were to be paid to the bifhops of Rochefter towards

* Hiftory of Kent, p. 127.   † Text. Roffen. c. 48.
‡ Roman Ports and Forts, p. 108.   ‖ Text. Roffen. c. 176.

keeping

keeping hofpitality, efpecially on the feftival of St. Andrew the Apoftle, to whom that cathedral was dedicated.

Ernulph, the compiler of the Textus Roffenfis, and who, after a fhort interval, was Gundulph's fucceffor in that fee, with the confent, and at the requeft of the monks, fettled the alms that fhould be diftributed in commemoration of Gundulph, and appointed what each manor belonging to the church fhould contribute for that purpofe. The whole allowance amounted to twenty fhillings and feven falmons, of which Frendfbury and three other manors were to give fix fhillings and two falmons. With the money the cellerar was to buy bread and fome fmall fifh as a dole for the poor; but the falmon were to be ferved up in the refectory of the convent. As Gundulph died in March, the lenten feafon would not permit the monks to feaft more luxurioufly on the anniverfary of their great benefactor *.

It appears from the Cuftumale Roffenfe †, that the eftate at Frendfbury was fo confiderable as to afford the priory of St. Andrew a firme or fubfiftence in provifion for three months in the year; and in the fame MS. is a particular account of the cuftomary fervices of this manor, of which the following is an abftract :—That there were 22 yoke (*juga*) of gave land of one fervice, and of one render—that the amount of the money-render for each yoke was 13*s.* 4*d.*—that the tenants were alfo required, upon notice from the bailiff, to do all work neceffary for fowing 21 acres of wheat; and that a forfeiture was to be incurred by each tenant who did not perform his proper fhare before the feaft of St. Martin (Nov. 11.)—that 16 only of the faid yoke were fubject to the plowing of the fame number of acres in the fpring

---

* Regift. Roffen. p. 7.

† Fol. 47. This curious old MS. is printed, and Mr. Thorpe propofes to publifh it as foon as a fuitable appendix to the Regiftrum Roffenfe, together with fundry plates of Antiquities.

feafon,

feafon, becaufe the five yoke of Bromhei were exempt from this plowing—that the tenants ought alfo to mow ten acres and a half of pafture, and to make, carry, and well ftalk the produce thereof; and likewife in autumn to mow, carry, and ftalk 21 acres. From the 21 yoke the following provifion-renders were alfo to be made.—At the *Xenium,* or hofpital entertainment on St. Andrew's day, 84 pullets and 21 geefe.—At Eafter 2100 eggs, of which the bifhop was to have 500, and the cellarer of the convent 500, and the remainder were for the court at Frendfbury. —To the bifhop were alfo to be delivered 21 lambs.—The monks are noticed to have had in demefne four carucates, and 28 hinds or cottagers *(ruftici),* who had an allowance of bread and cheefe only for fhearing the fheep.

From a MS. in the Cotton collection it is plain that the bifhop had fome other allowances befides thofe above recited, and which the compiler of the Cuftumale feems not to have recorded, as conceiving the bifhop's claim to them not to have been warranted by Gundulph's grant, viz. five and a quarter, *frefcingas,* fuppofed to be a certain quantity of bacon *, and three portions of fturgeon and of lampreys, and fixty bundles of furze. When the bifhop did not chufe to receive thefe articles in kind, he was to be paid in money for them according to the following prices; for each frefcinga 2 s.—for each goofe 2 d.—each pullet 1 d.—for a piece of fturgeon 4 d.—lampreys per hundred 8 d.—of ftraw or furze four bundles 1 d. The falmons paid by Frendfbury and fome other manors valued at 10 s. but thefe were changed for ftur-

* A fuitable difh with the eggs abovementioned; and it is obferved in the Antiquarian Repertory, vol. III. p. 44. that the cuftom of eating a gammon of bacon at Eafter, which is ftill kept up in many parts of England, was founded on this, viz. to fhew their abhorrence to Judaifm at that folemn commemoration of our Lord's Refurrection.

geon;

5

geon ; and eight pieces of sturgeon were considered as equivalent to one salmon [*].

The priory of St. Andrew held the manor of Frendsbury till the suppression of that religious house, when it became vested by act of parliament in the crown ; and king Henry granted the same to the dean and chapter of Rochester, in his charter of donation of that church. They are now possessed of it ; Mr. Philip Boghurst is their tenant, who a few years since erected the commodious and substantial courtlodge, which is situated near the church.

Antiently the advowson of Frendsbury was appendant to the manor, and so remained till Gundulph rendered it disappendant, by granting to the priory of St. Andrew the manor without the patronage of the church. The monks, however, by a grant from John archdeacon of Canterbury, who was confecrated bishop of Rochester 1125, obtained a temporary acquisition of the church of Frendsbury with the chapel of Strode belonging to it, and of all lands and tithes appertaining to the same ; which grant being deemed invalid by his successor in this diocese, John de Sues, he took from the monks the church of Frendsbury, as well as several other churches, and conferred the same, together with the archdeaconry of Rochester, on Robert Pollan or Pulleyne. With this spoliation of their rights, as the monks termed it, they being dissatisfied, applied to the Pope for redress ; and Asceline, who was appointed bishop of Rochester on the death of John de Sues, repaired to the court of Rome, in order to support their claim. Celestine II. was at that time Pope, and in the abfence of Pulleyne, against whom the appeal was made, he ordered all the churches, except that of Frendsbury, to be re-

* Regift. Roff. p. 133, 134. Haddenham in Bucks was rated for a fish of the value of twenty shillings; it must have been a large and a delicately flavoured fish to bear fo high a price in thofe days.

stored ;

ftored ; and Frendfbury not being included in the Pope's decree, there can be little room to doubt that the pretenfion of the monks to that church was entirely groundlefs.

It was fuggefted by the monks, that the non-appearance of their adverfary muft be attributed to his confcioufnefs of the injuftice of his caufe ; but it fhould feem that a due time was not allowed for him to attend, and that the queftion was determined with fome precipitation, becaufe the pontificate of Celeftine lafted only five months. After the death of Celeftine, Pulleyne procured from Lucius II. a re-hearing of the caufe, and a reverfal of the fentence given by his predeceffor, and had fo much intereft with the Pope, as to obtain a permiffion to refign, in favour of his nephew Paris, the archdeaconry of Rochefter, and the feveral churches, with their rights, claimed by the priory of St. Andrew. The monks, therefore, fent a deputation of their body to Rome, who carried with them a letter of earneft intreaty in their behalf from bifhop Afcelin to Pope Eugenius III. However, all their endeavours to recover the churches from the court of Rome were fruitlefs. Paris kept poffeffion of them ; but afterwards, in order to prevent all further litigation, he appears to have made a kind of acknowledgement of his having them by their gift, upon condition of their agreeing he fhould have quiet enjoyment of them as long as he lived *.

Very fevere were the monks in their reproaches upon bifhop John de Sues, pronouncing him to have acted more like a plunderer than a paftor ; nor could they forbear fhewing fome marks of their refentment towards Pulleyne. As the prelate was a foreigner, did not hold the fee of Rochefter more than five years, and might not probably often refide in his diocefe, little of his character is known ; but in beftowing thefe preferments on Pulleyne, he fhewed himfelf to be an encourager of a man of merit;

* Regift. Roffen. p. 8. 10.

for

for Pulleyne is univerfally agreed to have been a perfon diftinguifhed for his fuperior knowledge in moft branches of literature.
His name occurs in the lift of the chancellors of Oxford, and he
was worthy of that ftation.   Leland has extolled him as a reftorer
of learning there, and as one who omitted nothing that might
conduce to the inftructing of youth in the learned languages.
He alfo, for five years, read lectures upon the holy fcriptures,
the ftudy of which had been for fome time neglected by the members of that univerfity, and every Lord's day he preached to the
people, who were much edified by his doctrine.   His fame
fpread far ; and being fent for to Rome, Pope Celeftine made him
a cardinal, and Pope Lucius his chancellor, and by his intereft
with the court of Rome, he procured feveral bulls and charters of
privileges for the government and fecurity of the univerfity of
Oxford *.   Confidering the relation which fo eminent a man as
Pulleyne bore to Frendfbury, this fhort account of him will
hardly be thought an unfuitable digreffion from the hiftory of
this parifh, which fhall now be refumed.

   Though the monks failed in their attempt to keep poffeffion of
the church of Frendfbury, they eftablifhed a right to a penfion
of one mark a year out of it.   This was a grant to them from
bifhop John the firft, and was moft probably the whole of what
he really gave them.   The money was to be diftributed in alms
to the poor on the anniverfary of their benefactor †.

   From Gundulph the monks obtained an eafy compofition for
fome of the tithes of fome of the manerial lands they held, and a
total exemption for others, which privileges were confirmed to
them by feveral bifhops of Rochefter, and alfo recognized by
archbifhop Peckham on St. Mark's day 1281.   The compofition
for the demefnes of Frendfbury manor confifted of a field called
Nelgfield, formerly a part of the demefne, and one acre of wheat,

---

* Tanner, Bibliotheca, p. 602.　　　　† Regift. Roffen. p. 59.

one

one of barley, and one of oats, all to be grain of the middling fort in the time of harveſt; but for wool, milk, and all other ſmall tithes, nothing was to be paid. The church of Frendſbury was to have only the tithe of ſheaves from the grange of Chattindon, which was a member of Frendſbury manor; and at Rede, which was another member, the almoner of the convent received the whole tithe of ſheaves, but no tithe whatever was payable to the church *.

Anno 1193, Gilbert de Glanville, biſhop of Rocheſter, ſettled on his newly founded hoſpital in Strood the chapel of Strood, with all its emoluments, except the tithe of corn. In this grant he had the concurrence of William archdeacon of Rocheſter, who was at that time rector of Frendſbury, and with his conſent likewiſe Strood was then made an independent parochial diſtrict †.

Biſhop Laurence de St. Martin had, in 1256, the conſent of the priory of St. Andrew to an appropriation of the church of Frendſbury to the biſhop and his ſucceſſors, the ſame being then vacant. This appropriation was confirmed by Pope Clement IV. April 3, 1267, and has ever ſince been enjoyed, together with the advowſon of the vicarage, by the ſee of Rocheſter ‡. A vicar muſt have been ſettled not long after the rectory's being appropriated, as William is ſo denominated in 1289. The ordination of the vicarage is not extant; but the vicar by uſage, as the miniſter of Strood, under leaſe from the dean and chapter of Rocheſter by endowment, is entitled to all tithes except thoſe of corn and grain.

Thomas Inglethorp, biſhop of Rocheſter, granted to William, vicar of Frendſbury, and to his ſucceſſors for ever, the above piece of land called Nelegfield, the boundaries of which are ſet out in the grant. In conſideration of this donation, the vicars were always to retain a proper chaplain, who, when there was

* Regiſt. Roffen. p. 91, 92.   † Ibid. p. 632.
‡ Ibid. p. 66. 68.

occaſion,

occafion, was to affift the vicar in fupporting the burdens and difcharging the duties of the parifh. The vicars were alfo to be fubjeét to the expence of binding the books of the church, and to the repair of phials, furplices, and rochets.

19 Edward I. (1291) the church, i.e. the reétory of Frendsbury, with Strood included, was valued at 60 marks, and the vicarage at 100 s.* In 1535, 26 Henry VIII. the vicarage was rated for firft fruits at 10 l. 3 s. 11½ d. and for tenths at 1 l. 0 s. 4½ d. The procuration paid by the vicar to the bifhop when he vifits is 2 s. 6 d. i. e. after the proportion of 6 d. in the pound, according to the old valuation, and 7 s. 6 d. a year to the archdeacon. And in 1533, when a taxation was made in the diocefe of Rochefter, to defray the expences of Mr. Elifha Bayley, their proétor in con-vocation, 1 s. 4 d. was the quota for the vicar of Frendsbury †. The church of Frendsbury anciently paid 12 d. a year for the chrifm ‡.

The vicar has a manfion and fifteen acres of glebe land; but the vicarage houfe is at an inconvenient diftance from the church, and not in a very healthy fituation.

A church at Frendfbury is recorded in Domefday book, but it muft have then been fo dilapidated as to have fallen down foon after, if crèdit is to be given to a memorandum in Regiftrum Roffenfe§ of there being no church in the time of Gundulph. It was however rebuilt with ftone between 1125 and 1137 by Paulinus the facrift of the priory at Rochefter, who alfo furnifhed it with books and veftments ||. A view of this church is given. in plate XI.

* From the old valuation printed in the Hiftory of Rochefter by Rawlinfon, p. 79.
† Aét. Cur. Confift.
‡ Text. Roffen. c. 213.
§ P. 8.
|| Ibid. p. 118.

The

The church of Frendſbury, which is dedicated to All Saints, conſiſts of a nave and ſouth aile*, and is 64 feet in length and 48 in breadth. The chancel is in length 36 feer, and in breadth 26. At the weſt end of the church is a tower 20 feet ſquare and 40 feet high, upon which is a tower of nearly the ſame height. Richard Young, who was biſhop of Rocheſter from 1404 to 1418, made windows in Frendſbury church; and when Lambard wrote his Perambulation, a picture of this prelate was remaining in one of the windows.

In the tower are five bells, beſides the ſanĉte bell. The names of the benefaĉtors are not recorded; the names of the bell-founders and dates being the only inſcriptions, which are as follow: Date of the firſt bell 1637. On the ſecond, John Danbe made me 1656. The third could not be got at. On the fourth, William Reeve, bell-founder, 1584. On the fifth, Robert Watſon and John Rawlinſon, bell-founders, 1658. On the ſanĉte bell is inſcribed "Gerrit Schimmel me fecit Daventria, 1670."

Thomas Woldham, biſhop of Rocheſter, by his will, dated in September 1316, gave ten marks to his poor pariſhioners of Frendsbury †.

---

* Mr. Warton, in his deſcription of Kiddington church, p. 4, remarked that the old Norman-built parochial churches ſeldom conſiſted of more than one aile or pace: if the preſent church of Frendſbury is the ſame that was erecked between the years 1125 and 1137, and there is no reaſon to think otherwiſe, this is one exception to that author's obſervation.

† Reg. Roff. p. 113. The biſhop gave ten pounds to Ade of Frendſbury, and the ſame ſum to the ſons and daughters of the ſaid Ade; he alſo bequeathed to Ade one grey colt of two years old (*coloris grecei*).

The

The church and the poor of Frendsbury are ftill poffeffed of the following benefactions :

Seven acres of land, in two pieces, lying in this parifh, the donor unknown ; but the rent accruing from them has always been expended in repairing the church.

One acre of land, lying near Upnor, given by Bonham Penniftone, yeoman, towards the repairs of the church.

The green, containing one acre, the rent of it to repair the church.

A mill and 27 acres of land in Hoo, the joint purchafe of Robert Gunfley, clerk, and the parifhioners.   A part of the rent of this eftate to be applied in repairing the church, and the refidue to be divided among the poor.

A tenement and orchard in Higham, the gift of John Green, yeoman, the rent to be laid out in bread for the poor.

A tenement in Strood, given by Richard Watfon, the rent to be divided among ten of the pooreft people.

As the regifter of births and burials in Frendsbury does not commence till 1669, it will not afford any affiftance towards tracing the populoufnefs of this parifh at an earlier period, and difcovering whether any perfons eminent for their abilities or learning were natives of it.   But from Mr. Mafters's Hiftory of Ben'et college in Cambridge *, it fhould feem that Mr. Johnfon, vicar of Apuldore and Cranbrooke, in the weald of Kent, and author of the Clergyman's Vade Mecum, and of fome books in fupport of the notion he had conceived of the eucharift's being an unbloody facrifice, was born at Frendfbury 30th December, 1662, his father, Mr. Thomas Johnfon, being vicar of that parifh.

* P. 318.

Æflingham,

Æflingham, Chaddington, Goddington, Wainfcot, and *Brom-bei* are diftricts in Frendfbury, which formerly belonged to per-fons of fome confequence; but for the account of the genealogies of the families who were fucceffively poffeffed of them, and the tenures by which they held them, the reader is referred to the hiftories of Kent, and particularly to Mr. Hafted's very late publi-cation. So eminent was Æflingham as, at times, to have given its name to the whole parifh; and Hugh de St. Clare, when owner of it, had weight fufficient to obtain from bifhop Gun-dulph the grant of a free chapel within his manor *. A de-fcription of this chapel, with an account of the ancient privileges annexed to it, is not inferted, becaufe Mr. Thorpe propofes to pub-lifh an engraving of it from an accurate furvey, and to add a fuitable illuftration.

Lambard, in his Perambulation, p. 350, mentions a ftreet in Frendsbury called *Upnour,* from which, as adjoining to it, the caftle of Upnour took its name. This fortrefs was erected by queen Elizabeth in the third year of her reign, for the fecurity of her navy, as the infcription upon' it teftifies, in which are thefe words:

" Who gave me this fhew, to none other ende,
" But ftrongly to ftande, her navie to defende."

However, in 1667, when the Dutch fleet under Van Ghendt failed up the Medway, this caftle, by the neglect of Charles II. was in fo unprovided a ftate, that major Scott, who commanded in it, could but little annoy the enemy, fix of whofe men of war with firefhips having broke through the chain, were carried up as high as Upnor, and burnt fome, and damaged others of the king's capital fhips. The capital miftake and fault in the king

* Regiftrum Roffenfe, p. 370.

and

and his minifters confifted in not having a fleet properly prepared to repel the infults of an enemy ; for to the inhabitants of an ifland, floating and not fixed batteries are the beft defence.

An anecdote refpecting the father of the celebrated Sir Francis Drake is given by Lediard in his Naval Hiftory *, which, as it is connected with Upnor, ought not to be unnoticed. Lediard's account is, that in the reign of Henry VIII. whilft Sir Francis was a child, the father, who had embraced the Proteftant religion, being obliged to leave his houfe in Devonfhire, retired into Kent, and there inhabited the hull of a fhip, in which many of the younger of his twelve fons were born. This author adds, that Mr. Drake, in the time of Edward VI. got his livelihood by reading prayers to the feamen, was ordained deacon, and made vicar of the church of Upnor, on the river Medway †. That Mr. Drake officiated as a clergyman in the navy is probable, and he might have been curate of Frendsbury : but he certainly was not vicar of that parifh ; nor does it appear that there ever was a church, or even a chapel, at Upnor.

* I. 154.
† This ftory feems to be copied from Camden's Annals of queen Elizabeth *, who relates, as from Sir Francis' own mouth, that while he was yet a child, his father embracing the Proteftant religion, being called in queftion by the law of the fix articles made by Henry VIII. againft the Proteftants, withdrew into Kent. After the death of king Henry he got a place in the king's navy to read prayers to them, and foon after he was ordained deacon, and made vicar of the church of Upnore on the river Medway, where the royal fleet ufually rides. But, by reafon of his poverty, he put his fon apprentice to the mafter of a bark, his neighbour, who in reward for his induftry bequeathed his veffel to him. Dr. Campbell, in his Life of Drake in the Biographia Britannica, reconciles the chronology of this ftory, by referring it to queen Mary's time, fince the navy was not ftationed in the Medway till queen Elizabeth's reign. See alfo his Lives of the Admirals, I. 514.

* P. 351. Ed. Hearne.

WROTHAM.

Plate XIII.

J.B.Young delt.1773.

E.xter sculp.

South East View of WROTHAM CHURCH. Kent.

W R O T H A M.

T H I S parifh is large and extenfive, and takes in almoft the whole hundred to which it gives name. It is in the deanery of Shoreham, and a peculiar to the archbifhop of Canterbury, but in the diocefe of Rochefter. The manor is very confiderable, and is mentioned in Domefday book to belong to the archbifhops of Canterbury, and in their poffeffion it continued till **29** Henry VIII. when it was exchanged by archbifhop Cranmer with the crown for other lands. There are fix diftinct borfholderfhips within this manor, the borfholders of which, as alfo the confta-bles for the upper and lower divifion of the hundred, are all of them annually chofen at the court-leet of the faid manor. The borfholders likewife for the boroughs of *Ightham* and *Shipborne* are bound to pay *fuit and fervice* at the feveral leets of this manor, to which belong all royal franchifes, as being a liberty within it-felf; and the lord hath all *deodands, felons, waifs, ftrays, treafure trove,* &c *. The liberty of Wrotham claims likewife over *Plax-toole* and *Stanfted,* which are not valued in the king's books, be caufe they were antiently a part of the parifh; but in the year 1647, they were taken out of it by act of parliament, and made diftinct parifhes by themfelves †. The rectory, with the chapel of *Stanfted* annexed, is valued in the king's books at 50 l. 8 s. *per annum,* and the vicarage at 22 l. 5 s. 10 d. *per annum.* The rectory was formerly impropriated and leafed out by the arch-bifhops of Canterbury; but archbifhop Tenifon let the leafe run out, and then annexed the great tithes to the vicarage, by which

---

* Harris's Hift. of Kent, p. 341.   † Kilburne's Survey, p. 216. 255.

means

means Wrotham is now the beſt benefice in the diocefe of Rocheſter *.

The church is large, and kept in excellent repair, with a good
ſtrong tower, containing eight bells, accounted one of the moſt
tunable peals in this county.   There are many neat mural monuments, and ſeveral grave-ſtones with braſs plates, particularly
of the antient family of the *Peckhams* †.   From *John de Peckham*,
who attended Richard I. at the ſiege of Acon, defcended *Martin
de Peckham*, who married *Margery*, one of the three daughters
and coheirs of Sir *Thomas de Aldham*, defcended from *Thomas de
Aldham*, who likewife attended the ſaid king on that expedition;
and by this marriage, did increaſe his patrimony here with *Aldham*, a confiderable manor in this pariſh ‡.   The church muſt
be of very antient ſtanding, from the above families being interred in it, and from the archbiſhops of Canterbury being poſſeſſed of the manor at ſo early a period, and having a manſion-
houfe contiguous to the church.   Archbiſhop Simon Iſlip pulled
it, for the moſt part, down, and carried the materials to Maidſtone, towards building of the palace there, which his predeceſſor John Ufford had begun §.   A ſmall portion of this at Wrotham ſtill remains next the ſtreet; and without doubt the largeneſs
of the chancel, and the antient ſtalls on each ſide were, as Dr.
Harris obſerves, to accommodate the clergy when they attended
on the archbiſhops during their refidence here, and which I have
likewife ſeen in ſome other churches of the Peculiars, where
they had manſions.

When Dr. Potter was rector he new paved the chancel end,
by which means the grave-ſtones with braſs plates over two of
the old rectors were taken up, and not replaced, which ſurely
ſhould have been done either in ſome other part of the chancel or

---

* Harris's Hiſt. p. 341.   † Regiſt. Roff. p. 833, et ſeq.
‡ Philipot, p. 374.   § Kilburne, p. 297.
2   body

body of the church. When I was there in the year 1768, the said plates were then in a coal-hole in the church, at which time I copied their inscriptions, which are since inserted in the *Regist. Roff.* He likewise put in new plain semicircular windows, glazed with small squares, at Stanstead church ; and when I was there in the same year, the old stone window-jaumbs, with Gothic mouldings and mitred arches, lay scattered about the church-yard.

The two antient tombs near the church door at Wrotham, which long since have been robbed of their brafs plates, were erected, as Francis Thinne, who was Lancafter herald, faith, the one to the memory of *Martin Peckham,* esq. the other to *Margery* his wife, who brought ample revenues to the family of the *Peckhams.*

Robert Glover, Somerset herald, in his collections, faith, that *John Peckham,* esq. was lord of the manor of *West Peckham* in the first year of Henry III; and *John Peckham* archbishop of *Canterbury* in the reign of Edward I. left great eftates to his pofterity *.

Wrotham R. and V.
St. George.
cum *Woodland,*
Plaxtool, and
Stansted St. Mary. } cap. } In the patronage of the archbishop of Canterbury †.

The South Eaft view of this church exhibited in plate XIII. is from an accurate drawing in the year 1772.

It may be proper juft to obferve, that this fhort account of Wrotham church was drawn up, and partly printed off, before the publication of Mr. Hafted's fecond volume ; to which ufeful work the reader is referred for a more particular account of the parish, and for a view of the remains of the palace.

* Weever's Fun. Mon. p. 326. † Willis's Paroch. Aug. p. 12.

A N T I Q U I T I E S in K E N T,

Defcribed in a Letter from Robert Plott, LL.D. *keeper of the* Afh-molean Mufeum *in the Univerfity of* Oxford; *defigned to be fent to the* Royal Society *in* London.

GENTLEMEN,

Apledore, Sept..3, 1693.

O N Monday laft I went to Chilham, to view the tumulus of Quintus Durus Laberius, which is not in the form of any Roman barrow I ever faw, being more like one of our prefent graves; I paced it, and found it to be feventy of my paces in length, and twenty in breadth. This Laberius was a tribune, flain in one of Cæfar's engagements with the Britains; the country people to this day call it *Julaberries grave.* About half a mile from hence is a handfome feat of Mr. Diggs's, built within the trenches of Chilham caftle, the keep of which is yet ftanding, and made ufe for a brewing-houfe.

On Tuefday I went back again to Richborow, to make a more ftrict enquiry into fome particulars of antiquity; the one was, whether it was poffible that Richborow could ever have been part of the ifle of Thanet, as fome authors affirm. I found that the lands at Goffehall and Fleet, which lye on the weft fide of Rich-borow, are fituated lower than the lands which the Stower paffeth by; and while we were here, I met with feveral fea-fhells in the meadows.

On Wednefday I luckily hit on a double intrenchment in a wood, within three miles of the ancient city of Canterbury, a city honoured with the Englifh primacy; the inward trench con-tains an acre and half, the outward one about four times as much : it is very probable that this was the place where Cæfar met with the Britains in his fecond expediton; for he fays, that after he

had

had left Quintus Atrius to defend his ſhips, at that time lying above a mile and half wide off the town of Sandwich, he marched twelve miles up into the country, where he met with the Britains near a river, and forced them firſt of all to retire into one of their fortifications, and afterwards forcing their lines, beat them from thence. Camden contends this battle to have been at Chilham, though the diſtance does not agree, neither are there any ruins of a fortification to countenance his aſſertion.

On Thurſday I walked to Hyth, along a Roman cauſeway raiſed high, and paved with flint. This is one of the cinque-ports, and formerly contained ſix pariſhes : that of St. Nicholas only now remains; the chancel is raiſed extremely on grey marble pillars. In the charnel-houſe are great numbers of bones, and ſome of them very large. The inhabitants have ſeveral traditions of theſe bones, which, as fictitious, I ſhall omit. They are white and thin : I took the dimenſions of ſome of the largeſt. Two miles from hence are the ruins of Saltwood caſtle, formerly belonging to the ſee of Canterbury; it ſeems to have been a ſtately ſtructure, is of an oval form, and twenty-five rods in length. Within two miles of Folkſtone is a fortification of earth called *Caſtle*, which has one trench towards the ſea, and ſometimes one, at other times two trenches towards the con-tinent, according as the nature of the hill requires.

On Saturday I viſited Stutfall caſtle, a Roman ſtation. This was the *Portus Limenus*, whoſe ruins include eight acres of land, and are in form of an oblong ſquare; the walls are compoſed of a rocky ſtone, and a mortar made of the ſea-ſand and ſmall peb-bles; at two yards diſtance run double rows of Roman brick 14 or 15 inches long. Within a quarter of a mile from Lymne church is Shipway-court, a field where the lord warden of the cinque-ports is ſworn, and cauſes concerning the ports tried From hence I walked on the beach to Romney, and this morning
from

from thence hither, paffing moft of the way through the old channel of the Rother. Thefe are all the obfervations I have made in my journey through this part of the truly loyal county of Kent, which wil no ways recompence the time loft in the perufal of this from, Gentlemen,

Your humble fervant,

R.   PLOTT.

ADDITION to p. 28.

Anno 1529. Concordatum fuit inter dominum Johannem Bodyll, rectorem eccle-fie parochialis de Coxfton, et dominum Thomam Snydall, vicarium de Hallyng Roffen' dioc', fuper quibufdam litibus pro decimis fupvenientibus in parte boriali cujufdam tenementi vocat' Hornes places prope ecclefiam parochialem de Coxfton predicta fituati. In prefenciis magiftri Ricardi Scharpe, facre theologie profefforis, magiftri Roberti Johnfon in legibus bacallarii, et domini Johannis Wright, vicarii fancte Margarete juxta Roffam, in hunc modum ut fequitur.

The faid Sir John Bodle, parfon of Coxfton, fchall have paide to hym by Sir Thomas Snydall, vicar of Hallyng, for the tithes of fuche perfones and fervaunts lying in the north fide of Hornes Place, everi Yeftre duryng ther liffes xviɗ.

Prefente me Johe Bere, notario, cum partibus predictis.

E libro vifitat' et actor' anno predict'. fol. 1. a.

END OF THE SIXTH NUMBER.

⁎ Number VI. confifts of Two Parts, and contains Thirteen Plates, Six in the Firft Part, and Seven in the Second.

BIBLIOTHECA

TOPOGRAPHICA

BRITANNICA.

N° XVIII.

CONTAINING

The Hiſtory and Antiquities of RECULVER and HERNE, in the County of KENT. By the Rev. JOHN DUNCOMBE, Vicar of HERNE.

In the Press,

The HISTORY and ANTIQUITIES

OF

The Three ARCHIEPISCOPAL HOSPITALS

at and near CANTERBURY; viz.

St. NICHOLAS, at HERBALDOWN;

St. JOHN's NORTHGATE;

AND

St. THOMAS, of EASTBRIDGE.

THE

HISTORY AND ANTIQUITIES

OF THE

TWO PARISHES

OF

RECULVER and HERNE,

In the County of KENT.

By JOHN DUNCOMBE, M.A.

VICAR OF HERNE.

ENLARGED BY SUBSEQUENT COMMUNICATIONS.

———————

" Inter hæc conventus religioforum multis in locis aguntur, cœnobia fabricantur, abbatiæ conftruuntur. Apud *Raculfe*, quo in loco fibi rex Ethelbertus fedem regni præparaverat, cœnobium conftruitur, cujus abbas ultimus fuit Wen-redus." MS. Chron.

———————

LONDON,
PRINTED BY AND FOR J. NICHOLS,
PRINTER TO THE SOCIETY OF ANTIQUARIES;
AND SOLD BY ALL THE BOOKSELLERS IN GREAT BRITAIN AND IRELAND.
MDCCLXXXIV.

[Price Five Shillings.]

A D V E R T I S E M E N T.

The Editor of the BIBLIOTHECA TOPOGRAPHICA BRITANNICA prefents this number to the publick with the more pleafure, as it gives him an opportunity of acknowledging his obligations to a number of very refpectable friends. For the ground-work of the Hiftories of RECULVER and HERNE, he is indebted to Mr. DUNCOMBE ; and for many of the embellifhments therein to his accomplifhed Lady. Sir JOHN CULLUM, Mr. GOUGH, and Mr. BOYS, have each largely contributed towards the illuftration of the Antiquities of RECULVER; and Mr. JACKSON has happily exerted his elegant poetic talents in lamenting the probable demolition of " The Sifter Spires."

When the work was far advanced at the prefs, the Editor having accidentally mentioned it to Dr. DUCAREL, that gentleman very kindly communicated the inftruments printed in p. 129, and the following pages; which were long fince taken by him from the archiepifcopal records and regifters at Lambeth, the parifh of RECULVER being exempt from the archdeacon's jurifdiction, and, as fuch, immediately under that of the Commiffary of Canterbury. From the fame fource the Editor has been enabled to give the names of the incumbents of RECULVER and HERNE as far as the beginning of this century, which have been completed by Mr. DELASAUX, Regiftrar of that diocefe.

For the curious defcription of FORD-HOUSE, from the Parliamentary Survey, the Editor is indebted to Mr. SAMPSON, the archbifhop of Canterbury's receiver. And it is greatly to be lamented that no plan or view of that ancient building when in its fplendour has yet been any where difcovered.

ANTIQUITIES in KENT.

HISTORY of RECULVER.

By JOHN DUNCOMBE, M.A..

OF RECULVER, or, as it is ftill pronounced by the inhabitants, RACVLFAR, the Latin name is *Regulbium**, and the Saxon *Raculf-cefter*, or *Raculf-minfter*, which Lambard fancies to be derived from the Britifh word *racor*, which fignifies " forward ;" becaufe this place projects towards the fea. Harrifon, however, derives its name from one Raculfus, who built, he fays, a monaftery there. But the Saxon Chronicle afcribes the building of it to Baffa, one of the nobles of king Egbert, then a prieft, to whom that prince, A.D. 669, gave fome lands, and the place was called *Raculf* before that time†. Mr. Archdeacon Battely, in his *Antiqui-tates Rutupinæ*, thinks that it rather takes its name from the Britifh word *rhag*, which fignifies " before," and *gwylfa*, " watch-

---

+ Twyne, De rebus Albionicis, p. 16, cited by Battely Antiquitates Rutupinæ, p. 59, fays, " Regulbium quafi *Reculfum* a *recelio* derivandum."

† An. DCIXIX. Þeɲ Ecbyɲ t cyning ɼealbe Baɼɼe mæɼɼe pɼeoɼt Racult mynɼteɲ oɲto tymbɲianne. p. 40.

Reculver, *Raculf* Bede, Reauculɼe Saxon. *Taculf* Floril. falfely for *Raculf*. King Egbright gave to one Baffa a prieft the land at Racult ftanding on the North fide of the water fometime called Genlade, to build a monafterie upon. Shortlie after Brightwolde beinge abbot of the houfe was made archbifhop of Canterbury, and fucceffor to Theodore the Grecian. It is in Kent, at the fide of Tanet, and called at this day *Keculver*. Lambarde, Dict. p. 291.

M.   ing,"

ing," or perhaps from *golen*, " a light ;" and hence, he fuppofes, the Latin word *Regulbium* * may be derived ; it having very early a watch-tower, where, no doubt, lights were kept to direct fhips in the night †. The caftle alfo commanded a view not only of the open fea, or the German ocean, but of the mouths or thofe noble rivers the Thames and the Medway ; on which account it was ufed as a watch-tower, to difcover the approaches of an enemy, and alfo as a light-houfe to guide mariners, by fires kindled every night ; and this purpofe ufed to be anfwered by the two fteeples of the church‡, called the Sifters, or the *Reculvers*, which formerly ferved as a fea-mark for avoiding the flats or fhallows in the mouth of the Thames ; but by the fhifting of the fands they are now faid to be no longer ufeful, and mariners rather depend on St. Nicholas church, or Monkton mill.

" The countenance of the fort doubtlefs (as Dr. Salmon obferves §), encouraged a fettlement of inhabitants where they might be fecure. And the ground was fo well chofen for a Pharos, that the remaining towers of the monaftery built afterwards on the fame fpot are at this day a fea-mark and a rule for failors."

It is fituated in the north part of Kent, 9 miles N.N.E. from Canterbury, 65 from London, and 12 eaft from Margate, in the diocefe of Canterbury and deanery of Weftbere.

It was annexed to Chrift church in Canterbury, A.D. 949, by the grant of king Edred, in the prefence of archbifhop Odo, being then eftimated at 26 caffates, with all appurtenances on the fhore, in the field, meadows, forefts, &c‖. The liberty of

---

* Dr. Battely, from the mention of this place in the Notitia only, fuppofed it was at firft called *Rutupiæ*, as well as the other ftation of that name on the coaft. Antiq. Rutup. p. 52.

† Mr. Baxter derives it from *Reg ol vion*, q.d. the point againft the waves.

‡ See the views annexed, Plates I. and II.

§ New Survey of England, p. 45.

‖ Mon. Ang. I. 21. This grant may be feen in the Appendix, tranfcribed from the original in the Cotton library.

the

S. Benzenbek de. 1799

1. A High view from Crecca

down by the Sea

West View of Perediver Church. ² Part of the Fortress

Flough.

the archbifhop of Canterbury claims over the manor of Reculver, and the liberty of St. Auguftine over the reft of the parifh,
as being in the hundred of Blengate, which belonged to that
abbey But anciently Reculver was an hundred of itfelf*, So
in Domefday, l. 3 b.

In Rocvlf hvnd.

Ipfe Archieps ten *Rocvlf* . p . viii . folins † fe
defd . Ira . e . xxx . car . In dnio funt . iii . car.
7 qt xx . 7 x . uilli cu xxv . bord hnt . xxvii . car.
Ibi æccla 7 i . molin de xxv . den . 7 xxxiii . ac pti.
Silua . xx . porc . 7 v . falinæ de lxiiii . den . 7 una
pifcaria . In totis ualent . T.R.E . ualuit . hoc ⊙ . xiiii.
lib . Qdo recep. fimilit . 7 m . xxxv . lib . Sup hæc
ht archieps . vii . lib 7 vii . folid.

Ipfe Archieps ten *Nortone* in dnio . p xiii . fo
lins fe defd . Ira . e . xxvi . car . In dnio funt . ii.
car . 7 qt xx . 7 xii . uilli cu . xl bord . hnt . lix.
car 7 dimid . Ibi æccla . 7 x . ac pti . Silua . l . porc.
In totis ualent . T.R.E . ualuit hoc ⊙ . xxiiii . lib
7 v . fot . 7 poft tntd . 7 m redd archiepo . l . lib.
7 xiiii . fot 7 ii . den . 7 archidiacono . xx . fot.
De hoc ⊙ ten Vitalis de archiepo . iii . folins.
7 un jug 7 xii . acs tiæ . 7 ibi ht . v . car . 7 xxix.
bord 7 v . feruos . 7 vii . falinas de . xxv . fot 7 iiii . den.
Ibi . e æccla 7 una parua dena filuæ . Int totu ual
xiiii . lib . 7 vi . fot 7 vi . den.

* Kilburne's Kent, p. 221.

† *Solinum* was a meafure of land peculiar to the county of Kent, equal to feven carucates ; for fo Du Cange *in voc.* corrects Coke upon Littleton, § 1. or 17. Somner confounds it with *fwothynga*, a plough land, from ruth, a plough. Du Cange *in*
voc. Mr Hafted, without afcertaining its contents, defines it " a larger meafure
than a carucate."

Philipot, and Somner after him, gave Domefday account of this place thus :

"Raçulf eft manerium archiepifcopi in T.R.E. fe defendebat pio viii. full. & eft appretiatum x & ii. lib. & v. fol. tres minutes minus."

Minutes, fays Philipot, was a coin equivalent to our now Englifh pence. But this extract is fo different from the original record, that little ftrefs can be laid on it.

The church, dedicated to St. Mary, is now a vicarage, and valu-ed, with Hoath chapel, an adjoining parifh which is annexed to it, at 9 *l.* 12 *s.* 3 *d.* in the king's books; together about 100 *l.* a year. It is exempt from the jurifdiction of the archdeacon of Canterbury, was very anciently of the archbifhop's collation, as appears by a record in a note below *, and fo continues.

The prefent vicar is the rev. Richard Morgan.

It was of old a mother-church, on which depended four chapels of eafe, *Hoath, Herne,* and in *Thanet,* St. *Nicholas* and *All Saints.* Upon the three laft was impofed, for the mother-church's greater ho-nour and dignity, or *in fignum fubjectionis,* as the inftrument ex-preffes it, an annual penfion to the vicar of Reculver on the found-ing of that by archbifhop Winchelfea, 1310, with thofe other vi-

---

* " Rex ex merâ graciâ conceffit papæ fructus archiepifcopatus Cantuarienfis,
" necnon jus prefentandi ad ecclefias ejufdem durante vacacione, *falvâ prefentatione*
" *ad ecclefiam de Reculver,* quam rex prius conceffit Nicho de Tingewicke, medico
" fuo. 12 Sept. Rot Rom. de annis 24 & 25 Ed. I. m. 8 & 9. E collect. Jo.
" Anftis." Lewis, Hift. of Tenet, p. 31.

" The parfon or rector, when in being, and when petty ecclefiaftical jurifdic-
" tions under *foreign commiffaries,* as they called them, were in afhion, now 300 years
" ago and upwards, had the fame jurifdiction within his own parifh and chapelries
" annexed as afterwards, and at this day the commiffary of Canterbury exercifeth
" there. I have feen commiffions to this purpofe to the rector there for the time
" being, both from the archbifhop *fede plenâ,* and from the prior and convent *fede*
" *vacante.* And it was indeed a common practice with it, and fuch other exempt
" churches as, like it, were mother-churches in the diocefe, in thofe days." Somner's Roman Ports, p 85.

carages

carages of Herne and St. Nicholas, the vicarage of St. Nicholas and All Saints being charged with 3 *l.* 3 *s.* 4 *d* per annum, and that of Herne with 40 *s.* per annum *. And as the vicars of thefe dependent and annexed chapels were under this charge and burthen to him of the mother-church, fo the parifhioners and people of thefe chapelries, however gratified and accommodated with chapels of eafe for leffening their trouble by fhortening their way to church, whether for divine fervice in their life-time or interment after death, yet were, it feems, left as liable and fubject to the repairs of the mother-church of Reculver, as the peculiar and proper inhabitants of the place and themfelves were before the chapels were erected: a matter controverted between them of Herne and Reculver in archbifhop Stratford's time, who, after cognizance taken of the caufe, and evidence of all parties, paffed a decree in the year 1335 (which Mr. Somner had feen under feal, and had a copy of it), in behalf of the Reculverians, condemning and adjudging thofe of Herne to the repair of the mother-church. Much conteft about this matter happened afterwards, till by a decree (which Mr. Somner had alfo feen) of archbifhop Warham in the reign of Henry VIII. the difference was by and with the confent of all parties thus finally adjufted: that the people of each chapelry (Herne and St. Nicholas) fhould redeem the burthen of repairs by the payment of a certain moderate annual ftipend, or penfion, in money 3 *s.* 4 *d.* (now 5 *s.*) by the church-wardens of Herne and St. Nicholas to thofe of Reculver, on a certain fet day in the year (Monday in Whitfun-week); but with this provifo, that if they kept not this day, but overflipped it, they were then laid open and expofed to the law, and muft fall under as full an obligation to the repairs of the mother church as if the decree had never been †. Hoath ftill remains liable to the repairs of the mother-church,

* See the endowment of Herne in the Antiquities of that parifh.
† Somner, ib. p. 85—87. Lewis's Hift. of Tenet, p. 30.

by a decree of archbifhop Fitz-Alan, dated at Ford, Jan. 20, 1410 *.

The great tithes, formerly given by archbifhop Kilwarby to the hofpitals of Harbledown and St. John's North-gate, were appropriated by king Edward III. at the requeft of archbifhop Stratford, to the archbifhoprick of Canterbury, and are now held on leafe by Richard Milles, efq; late one of the members for that city, to whofe family they have been demifed ever fince the reign of king James I†.

Kilburn fays, it was once a cathedral church; but this does not appear. He was probably mifled by the governor being ftyled, not an abbot, but dean ‡. But that was common in thofe monafteries which had fecular canons.

A. D. 747, Egbert II, king of Kent, gave to the church of *Reculfre*, in the time of archbifhop Bregwin, the toll of one fhip in the town of Fordwich §. Eardulf, king of Kent, gave, A. D. 943, to Heahberth, abbot of Racul, and his family, the monks refiding in the place called *Raculfre*, the produce, or land, of one plough ||, in a place called *Perbamftede* **. In a MS. Cartulary of the archbifhop of Canterbury, in the Bodleian library, p. 11. is a grant of Lothair, king of Kent, of *Weftanea* and *Sturige* to this monaftery, A. D. 679; and of Eadmund, king of Kent, of *Scilwith*, A. D. 784 ††. Bifhop Tanner fuppofes ‡‡ that the abbot and black

---

* Chartæ Antiquæ, C. 188.   Archiv. Cantuar.
† The great-grandfather of this gentleman, Chriftopher Milles, efq. of Herne, by his will, dated May 28, 1638, left four pounds annually to the poor of this parifh, to continue as long as the leafe of the parfonage fhould be cortinued to any of his furname.   See the claufe in the Antiquities of Herne.   He died on the 13th of November following.
‡ See Somner's Roman Ports, &c. p. 82.
§ Mon. Ang. I. 19.   See allo a MS. Cartulary of the archbifhop of Canterbury in the Bodleian library, p. 14.
|| The original is imperfect, *et etiam unius aratri.*
** Ib. 20.   MS. Cartul. archiep. Cant. p. 27.
†† Ib. p. 27.   Mon. Ang. p. 19.   ‡‡ Not. Mon. p. 207.

5   monks

monks were removed when it was annexed to Chrift-church; yet it feems to have remained a church of more than ordinary note, and under the government of a dean, till A. D. 1030.

In Philipot's time the church was " full of folitude, and lan- " guifhed into decay; yet when Leland made his perambula- " tion, it was in a more fplendid equipage."

Leland calls the chancel here by the name of choir, and fays, that at the entrance of it was one of the faireft and moft ftately croffes that ever he faw; it was nine feet in height, and ftood like a fair column. The bafis was a great unwrought ftone. The fecond ftone was round, and had the images of Chrift, and fome of his apoftles, curioufly wrought, with labels from their mouths painted in large Roman letters. The next ftone contained the paffion of our Saviour. The next above that had the twelve apoftles. The fifth had our Saviour nailed to the crofs, with a *fuftentaculum* under his feet; and the uppermoft ftone was in the form of a crofs. Leland faw alfo in the church a very anci-ent book of the Gofpels in large Roman letters, and in the boards thereof a cryftal ftone, infcribed CLAVDIA ATEPICCUS; probably a Roman feal found here. On the north fide of the church was then the figure of a bifhop painted under an arch *. Leland adds, in digging about the church-yard were found old buckles of girdles and rings *(fibulæ)*. The whole precinct of the mo-naftery, as appeared by the old wall and the vicarage-houfe, was made of ruins of the monaftery. There was a neglected chapel without the church-yard, which, fome faid, was a parifh-church before the abbey was fuppreffed and given to the archbifhop of Canterbury ‡. There was alfo a hermitage.

At the upper end of the fouth aile, Weever fays ‡, he faw a monument of an antique form, mounted with two fpires,

* Itinerary VII. 127.   † Ib.
‡ Funeral Monuments, p. 260.

in

in which, as tradition fays, lay the body of Ethelbert I. the
fifth Saxon king of Kent, and the firft Chriftian monarch, who,
after giving his palace at St. Auguftine's in Canterbury to the
monk of that name, the Englifh apoftle, retired to his palace at
Reculver, where he died, and.was buried in this church under an
arch. No remains either of. the crofs above mentioned, or of this
monument, are now to be feen; but in the place of the latter, on
the wall, was, a few years ago, the following old infcription,
now inaccurately tranfcribed on a wooden tablet :

> Here, as hiftoriographers have faid,
> St. Ethelbert, Kent's whilome king, was laid,
> Whom St. Auguftine with the Gofpel entertain'd,
> And in this land hath ever fince remain'd ;
> Who though by cruel Pagans he was flain,
> The crown of martyrdom he did obtain.
> Who died on the 24th of February, in the year 616.

The Annals of St. Auguftine fay, that the body of king Ethelbert II. was alfo interred there A. D. 760.

In the chancel, within the communion rails, is a handfome
monument reprefenting Sir Cavalliero and Lady Maycote, with
their eight children, all in alabafter figures, kneeling, and over
them the family arms, with this infcription :

Here under waite for a joyful resurrection, the bodyes of dame Marie and of
her husband Sir Cavalliero Maycote, knight, who lived together in great
contentment (from St..Andrew's day, anno 1586) full 20 yeares, in which
time they had 8 fonnes and one daughter, namelye Jhon, Thomas, George,
Richarde, Thomas, William, Harbert, George, and Elizabeth, wharof 5
fonnes dyed before them. She was the daughter of Thomas Monninges,
gent. and Ales Crifpe, fumetime dwellers at Swanton in Liddon, and dyed on
Chriftmas-daye, anno 1606. He was the fonne of George Maycote, gent.
and of Margarette Brooker (long dwellers in this parifhe) who dyed———
To all whome the Lorde be mercyful at the latter daye.

He lived at Brook, in this parifh (now a farm-houfe belonging
to Sir Henry Oxenden, fo named probably fiom a brook that
runs near it), where is a curious old gateway with brick pillars.

On

Perry del.

Monument of Ralph Brook, York Herald, in the
Chancel of Reculver Church. See the Epitaph, p. 73.

Cook sculp.

To Dr. DUCAREL, F.R. and A.S.S. Commissary and
Official of Canterbury, this Plate is Respectfully inscribed.

On a flat ftone in the chancel are two brafs figures [fee plate V. fig. 6], with this infcription engraved :

Hic jacet Johannes Sandewey armiger, et Johanna uxor ejus ; quorum animabus propitietur Deus. Amen.

Which feems to be thus given by Weever :

Here lieth . . . . . Sandwey efquire, and Joan his wife, who died 1437, 6 Henry VI.

On a brafs plate againft the fouth wall, with a herald's coat (engraved in plate II.)

Here under quitt from worldly miferies
Ralph Brook, efquire, late Yorke Herald, lyes ;
Fifteenth of October he was laft alive,
One thoufand fixe hundred twenty and five.
Seaventy-three yeares bore he fortune's harmes,
And forty-five an officer of armes.
He married Thomfin daughter of Michaell Cobb of Kent,
Serjeant at Armes, by whome two daughters God him lent ;
Survyvinge, Mary, William Dickins wife,
Thomafin, John Exton's—Happy be their life.

Weever alfo gives the following epitaph :

Hic jacet dominus Thomas . . . . qui ob . . . . .
Vos qui tranfitis Thomam deflere velitis,
Per me nunc fcitis quid prodeft & gloria ditis.

The arched weftern door-way (plate V. fig. 2.) is a beautiful remain of Saxon architecture, but being much expofed to the weather, is mouldering away.

A fair was anciently held here on St. Giles's day, September 1 *; and William †, archbifhop of Canterbury, procured it a grant of a market on Thurfdays, 1279, 7 Edward I‡.

* Kilburne.
† Philipot. There is an error in this name. Robert Kilwarby was the archbifhop who procured the market.
‡ Here again Philipot miftakes, by faying that it was obtained " 7 Edward II."

N   Reculver,

Reculver, in Leland's time, was near half a mile from the fea-fhore : but it is to be fuppofed that in times paft the fea came up to Gore-end, two miles from Northmouth ; as at Gore-end was a little ftair, called Broadftaires, to go down the cliff; and about this fhore was good taking of mullets. The great Raguïeis lay for defence of wind at Gore-end* .

The great antiquity of this place is apparent from the vaft num-ber of Roman coins (chiefly of the lower empire), medals, vafes, &c. that have been, and ftill continue to be, found here.   For Reculver (or *Regulbium*) no doubt was one of the five Roman watch-towers, or forts, as Richborough caftle (or *Rutupiæ*) was another, each of them commanding one of the mouths of the river Genlade, or Wantfume, which, as Bede fays, then di-vided the ifle of Thanet from the continent of Kent.   This caftle †, which guarded the north mouth, was the Roman ftation of the Vetafii ‡, and was certainly on the hill where now ftands the church, and where formerly ftood the monaftery; though between the time of the Romans and its monaftic ftate it was alfo (as has been related p 72.) the fite of a royal palace, not only for Ethelbert I. but for all his fucceffors, kings of Kent.   The confular denarii, and the coins of all the Roman emperors from Julius to Honorius, and fharp, fine, new-coined medals of Tiberius and Nero, which have been found here in great numbers, prove that the Romans had not only an early fettlement here, but that they long continued it.   Many globules have been alfo found unftruck, which, with other circumftances, have given Dr. Battely reafon to fuppofe

---

* Itin. VII. 137.

†Kilburne afcribes the building of this caftle to the emperor Severus.

‡ " Tribunus cohortis primæ *Vetafiorum Regulbio*" under the count of the Saxon fhore. Notitia Imperii. Horfley, Brit. Rom. p. 476. 487. Thefe foldiers are called Bætasii in an infcription on an altar at Elenfoot fort in Cumberland.   They were a people of Belgic Gaul, written in Pliny *Betafi*, in Tacitus *Betafii* or *Betbafu*. Horfley, ibid, 281.   Cumberl. LXVI.

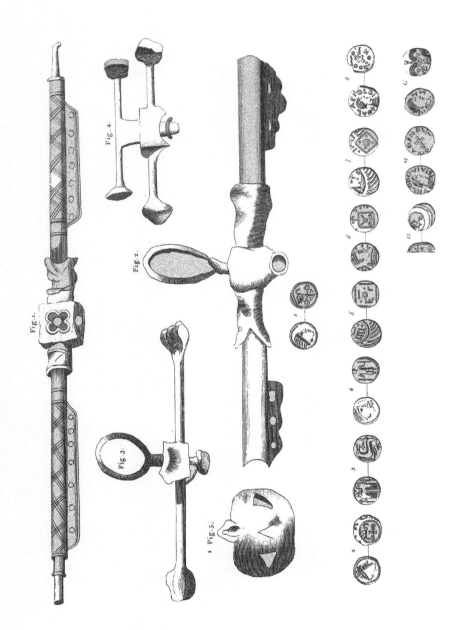

Fig. 1.

Fig. 2.

Fig. 3.

Fig. 4.

Fig. 5.

that this place was formerly fo confiderable as to have had a
mint, as vaft maffes of a mixed metal, formed by the melting of
fome brafs and gold coins which lay contiguous, have occafioned
Dr. Plot alfo reafonably to conjecture that Reculver was formerly
burnt, either by accident or by an enemy.   Britifh coins, of the
metal called *electrum*, one-fourth gold and the reft brafs, and
fome others of filver, with odd characters on them, neither
Britifh nor Gothic, but perhaps Gaulifh, (fee pl. III. and p. 76.)
fome with Chriftian croffes, many quarter-pieces of the old Englifh pennies, and others of king Henry III. and his three fucceffors, have alfo been found here, with Roman urns, *patera*,
vafes, &c. broken by the falling of the cliffs.   The antiquities
engraved in Pl. III. found at Reculver, were communicated by
the late Mr. Goftling to the Society of Antiquaries June 8, 1738.
They are fuppofed to be the *antennæ*, or crofs bars, of the Roman
vexillum, or ftandard *. Fig. 1. is engraved by fcale from a
drawing of Mr. Holmes †, and is 9 inches ⅝ thin length, befides
being a little crooked. The colours being laced to it through the
feveral holes, which are on each fide of a larger one, through
which, it appears by another (fig. 3.) found fince by the fame
curious gentleman, went a fwivel, with an oval loop, or ring, at
top to faften it by to the pole, or pike, held by the ftandard-
bearer; a reprefentation of which is very common in the allocu-
tions on the Roman medals, only with this difference, that in
them the pole, or ftaff, feems to have gone through this hole.
By the Tau, or crofs, on the fide oppofite, which in our plate has
a rofe, it may be fuppofed to be one of the ftandards of the emperor Conftantine, whofe coins have been fo frequently met with
where this was found. Fig. 2. is feven inches long, and has but

---

* Mr. Stennit of Bofton, and fome members of the Society of Antiquaries, fuppofed them yards of a fhip; referring to Bayfius de re navali, p. 164—168.
Others imagine them the beams of fcales or ftilliards, which perhaps is the moft
probable opinion of the three.

† Lewis on feals, p. 7, where it is engraved.

three

three holes to lace the standard to it.   Fig. 3. is four inches long, and may have ferved as a fibula, as our fpring fwivels do now; the ring hanging to a belt, and the antennæ paffing through a flit in the accoutrements.   Fig. 4. is a double pair, of two inches and two inches and a half in length.   The bell, or ornament, fig. 5. has five triangular holes.

In the fame plate are reprefented 15 of thofe fmall rude coins mentioned by Dr. Battely (fee p. 75), who had them engraved on a fcale larger than the originals, which were more faithfully executed on a feparate plate, with many others found in and near the ifle of Thanet, at the expence of Mr. John White, in order to obtain fome account of them.

The two firft are not unlike the coins of *Clovis*, engraved by Bouteroue, p. 195, who calls the bird a *peacock*.

The crofs on the eighth occurs on others of the fame prince, ibid. p. 199. 201, and in Bouteroue's feven plates at the end of his work.

The reverfe of the laft may be paralleled with that in the fame author, p. 209 and 237.

N° 14 may belong to *Theodoric*, fon of Clovis, ibid. p. 210.

N° 5, and perhaps N° 7, is more perfectly reprefented in Bouteroue, p. 215, and referred to by *Clodonur*.   *Vicus*, or *Quantovicus*, was a confiderable town near the river Authie, with a good port, famous for its trade, and frequently mentioned in the reign of Dagobert, though now reduced to a village named *Quain-le-vieil*. Perhaps N°⁵ 9 and 10 are of the fame kind.

A clofe comparifon with the coins engraved in Bouteroue's book, allowing for the difference of draughtfmen, and with varieties in other cabinets not yet engraved, might perhaps afcertain all thefe coins to be Gaulifh.

The

The Roman town has been long covered by the fea, which laft winter threw down the remains of the north fide of the old Roman wall which furrounded the caftle, and makes fuch rapid inroads on the cliff (great part of it, with a houfe, ftanding when the view in plate I. was taken, and which in the memory of man had a farm-yard adjoining to it, being lately thrown down), that it has long been apprehended that this noble ftructure and. fea-mark, with all the level below it, notwithftanding the great attention and expence beftowed in planking, piling, &c. by the commiffioners of fewers, will in a few years fhare the fate of the Roman town above mentioned. Reafonable hopes, however, are now entertained that both the church and the level will be faved by the fkill and efforts of captain (now Sir Thomas Hyde) Page, of whofe abilities as an engineer the public have had a remarkable proof, by his fupplying Sheernefs with water from the depth of 328 feet, in July, 1782.

For a flight fketch of the works at Reculver, propofed by Sir Thomas Page, and defcribed in a note, p. 90, fee plate V. fig. 8. in which

a a a are Fafcines.
b b b High-water mark.
c c Return at each end.
d d Jettees.
e e e Cliff.
f Church.

For a farther account of the antiquities of this place, the reader muft be referred to Dr. Battely's *Antiquitates Rutupinæ* (mentioned above) of which an Englifh abridgement was publifhed by the compiler of this article in 1774.

HELBURGH

HELBURGH was an ancient feat in this parifh.   The firft that
Philipot found poffeffed of it was *Nicholas Tingewike,* originally defcended from Tingewike in the county of Buckingham, and who
likewife held large poffeffions at Dartford.   He died poffeffed of
it, 14 Edward II.* 1321.   After this family deferted the poffeffion,
Pines became its proprietors, of which family was *James de la
Pine,* who was fheriff of Kent 26 and 27 Edward III.   He was in
poffeffion of this place at his deceafe, 33 Edward III †. and left it
to his fon *Thomas Pine* ; to whom fucceeded another *James Pine,*
who about the beginning of Henry IV. paffed it away to *Cheyney,* in which family it continued till the beginning of Elizabeth ;
when the lord *Henry Cheyney,* who then began to retail himfelf
and his eftate out to ruin in parcels, alienated this to *Maycott,*
whofe fon, Sir *Cavaliero Maycott* (mentioned p. 72) an eminent
courtier in the reigns of Elizabeth and James, on the entrance
of that prince into his government, paffed it away to Sir *Chriftopher Clive;* and he immediately after conveyed it away to *Contry,*
whofe fon, Mr. *Thomas Contry,* fold it to Sir *Edward Mafters* of
Canterbury; and his fon, *Richard Mafters,* efq. was heir to it
when Philipot wrote ‡.   This is the fame manfion that is now
called *Brook* § (fee p. 72) ; which name was fubftituted by one of
the mafters, taken, I am informed, from the feat where they refided (now pulled down), near Wingham, and not, as I fufpected,
from the adjoining brook.   From the heirs of that family it came
to the late Sir *George Oxenden,* bart. father of Sir *Henry,* the prefent poffeffor.

* Rot. Efc. N° 182. This was probably the laft rector at Reculver, who confented
to the impropriation of it in 1310. See the endowment in the Antiquities of Herne.
One of the fame name was phyfician to Edward I. and had a grant of the prefentation, from that king, during the vacancy of the fee.   See p. 68.   Could he, in
confequence, take orders and prefent himfelf?

† Rot. Efc. N° 13.   ‡ Philipot's Kent.   § Harris's Hift. of Kent.

The

The oyfters taken on this coaft are well known to have been
a luxury at Rome in the time of Juvenal.

Circeis nata forent, an
Lucrinum ad faxum, Rutupinove edita fundo,
Oftrea, callebat primo deprendere morfu. Sat. IV. 140.

He whether Circe's rock his oyfters bore,
Or Lucrine lake, or the Rutupian fhore,
Knew at firft tafte. DUKE.

" The oifters that be dredged at Reculver, are reputed as farre
" to paffe thofe of Whitftaple, as Whitftaple doe furmount the
" reft of this fhyre in favorie faltneffe *."

The beautiful fpires of Reculver have furnifhed Mr. Keate
with an ingenious legendary tale in his *Sketches from Nature,* and
they are alfo introduced in two poems, with which I fhall clofe
this article ; the one by the lady who drew the Weft view of the
church in plate I. the other by my friend Mr. William Jackfon
of Canterbury.

* Lambard's Kent, p. 261.

To

To Anna Maria D.

How happy, thus free from the trouble of drefs,
In this rural retreat, this quiet recefs;
Where you walk with a book, and furnifh your mind
(" Leaft alone, when alone") with ideas refin'd;
Where hiftory, poetry, fable and fong
Alternately haften time fwiftly along:
Too fwiftly, O time, for improvement and joy,
The hours pafs away that you thus may employ!
Here, thick branches around yield a fheltering fhade,
There, a bench beneath firs invites to yon glade.
Here no vifits of form our ftudies moleft,
Untortur'd your hair, unadorn'd flows your veft.
Yet here with the warmeft reception of love
We enjoy our friends' converfe in bower or in grove;
A few chofen friends, who by friendfhip fincere
Are invited to gladden our folitude here;
Where learning's purfued, and philofophy fought,
And you, my dear child, are infenfibly taught
How to value the world, its good to refpect,
Its vices abhor, and its follies reject:
Yet chearful and playful, befitting your age,
I wifh not to check, by my precepts too fage,
Any innocent fallies infpir'd by youth,
Since I fafely can truft your difcretion and truth.
And when winter advances, with reverend pace,
The languifhing charms of cool autumn to chafe,
When forc'd by the feafon reluctant you move,
And leave the fea-fhores, cliffs, and fields that you love,
And high Reculver fpires, the mariners' mark,
Fair fight to behold from their far diftant bark;
(O ftop, mighty Neptune, now ftop thy dread wave,
And fave from deftruction thefe fifters, O fave!)

Then

Then haste, dear Maria, this villa to quit,
Society seek, and to fashion submit,
Avoid all extremes, and let modesty guide,
And carefully shun affectation and pride.
At home, and abroad, in the dance, at the play,
Not prudishly grave, nor coquettishly gay,
Your manner polite to all ranks and degrees,
Insensibly sweeten'd by wishing to please ;
Let your heart to your friends be open and kind,
And may friendship reward your ingenuous mind!
Of your principles sure, and goodness of heart,
I tenderly venture those hints to impart,
For you only, Maria, my lays can inspire,
Maternal affection awakens the lyre ;
Hapless lyre! forgotten, unsought, and unstrung,
'Midst heaps of old poetry carelessly flung,
'Till for you, in soft accents, once more I essay,
By the Muse's assistance, advice to convey,
Ever anxious to see, in each ripening year,
Improvements in wisdom and virtue appear.

Methinks a prophetical spirit I feel,
Which tells me, this instant, what Time shall reveal ;
Something more than the Muse now attends to my prayer,
And your future character seems to declare,
When judgment mature shall chase childhood away,
Like mists of the morning before the noon-day.

Herne, Sept. 5,
1781.

S. D.

The SISTERS: an ELEGY.

Written on the Shore at HERNE Bay.

By Mr. W. JACKSON.

By the white margin of the tide,
  Lone wand'rer, as I ſtray,
How free from care ! how tranquil glide
  My morning hours away!

Yet here my not inactive mind
  What various ſcenes employ !
For in this ſolitude I find
  Variety of joy.

Whether amid thoſe ſons of toil,
  Who plough the ſwelling ſea,
On yonder bench I reſt awhile,
  And join their jocund glee ;

And briſkly whilſt from gueſt to gueſt
  Goes round the nappy ale,
I liſten to the peaſant's jeſt,
  Or hear the ſailor's tale :

Or whether on the pebbly beach,
  Eugenio by my ſide,
At length my liſtleſs limbs I ſtretch,
  And watch th' approaching tide.

And ſometimes by the winding ſhore
  I meditate alone,
And liſten to old ocean's roar,
  And hear the ſea-bird's moan.

And oft as by the rolling ſea
  In penſive mood I ſtray,
The fav'ring Muſe will deign to be
  The partner of my way.

And oft, regardleſs of the ſhore,
  She turns my wand'ring eyes,
To where, yon brown cliff peering o'er,
  The ſiſter ſpires ariſe *.

Ye ſiſters then, alas the while,
  A pitying tear I pay,
To view your venerable pile,
  Now haſt'ning to decay.

For Ruin, ill betide the deed !
  Uſurps each mould'ring ſtone,
And haſtes with unobſtructed ſpeed
  To claim you for his own.

But oh, nor let me plead in vain,
  The impious deed forbear !
Ye waves, reſpect the holy fane,
  And you, ye wild winds, ſpare !

But yet, if neither wind nor wave
  Reſpect the tottering wall,
O ſon of commerce, haſte and ſave
  The ſea-mark from its fall !

Leſt, homeward bound, thy luckleſs crew
  Attempt this dang'rous ſhore,
And all in vain with anxious view
  The ſiſter ſpires explore !

And thou, with fruitleſs grief, behold
  Thy good ſhip ' dock'd in ſand,'
And all thy ſtores of future gold
  Beſtrew the length'ning ſtrand !

But oh, to winds untaught to hear
  I pour the fruitleſs lay,
And waves regardleſs of my prayer,
  And men more rude than they !

Ye ſiſter ſpires, though (laſting ſhame !)
  Your ruins ſtrew the plain,
To blot the mem'ry of your fame
  Oblivion ſtrives in vain !

For that, to lateſt times conſign'd,
  Shall live, ſhall flouriſh long,
Your fame in Keate's ſoft tale † enſhrin'd,
  And Stella's moral ſong ‡.

And aye, perhaps, if right I ween,
  This little lay ſhall tell
To future times ye once have been :
  So, Siſters, fare ye well !

* See the view of Herne Bay, with the ſpires as here deſcribed, in plate VI.
† See Keate's Sketches from Nature, 2 vols.
‡ Mrs. D's Verſes, printed in p. 80.

For

For the following additional Account the Editor is obliged to WILLIAM BOYS, Efq. of SANDWICH, F. S. A.

SIR,

Sandwich,
July 7, 1783.

THE remaining walls of Reculver caftle fkirt a hill of pit-fand, which is higher in every part than the ground without the walls. The earth has fallen, perhaps has been wafhed, away from the bafe of the hill, and the foundation of the wall is thereby expofed to view in many places, which correfponds exactly with that at Richborough, being laid on fmall fmooth pebbles in the natural foil. The facing of the wall both within-fide and without, as far as I can examine, is deftroyed; except at the eaft end of the north wall, where it is perfect for a few yards in length, but not to a fufficient height from the bafe to comprehend a row of tiles; none of which are to be feen entire in the wall, though numberlefs fragments lie on the ground, which, moft probably, were originally worked up in the facing of the wall, in rows, as at Richborough; where the firft row of tiles appears about five feet from the foundation. Many pieces of tile are introduced, in the moft irregular manner, into the mafonry of the church, efpecially under the windows on the north fide. The wall is no where more than ten feet high; and it is obfervable, that it never rifes above the level of the ground within the caftle. It muft have been originally higher, and the upper parts have been thrown down, feemingly, on purpofe to bring the remains to their prefent level. But then, what is become of the fragments? At Richborough, the fallen maffes have withftood every effort of thofe who have been interefted, for ages,

to

to remove or deftroy them ; nor has the weather operated with much effect upon their texture.   On the other hand, the fragments that fall into the fea from the north wall of Reculver caftle, by their alternate expofure every day to air and moiflure, and by the action of the waves, are foon decompofed, and the detached materials are fpread to a great diftance over the furface of the fhore.   May we not infer from hence, that the fea has heretofore wafhed the foot of Reculver hill on the eaft, weft, and fouth fides alfo, and that the fragments there have been difperfed by the fame operations as take place now on the north fide ?   And might not this encroachment of the fea, by alarming the monks who occupied the area of the caftle, give rife to the embankments, which fhut out the fea from the marfhes, at the back of the caftle ? Upon meafuring the large fragment that fell lately, I found it to be between eight and nine feet in thicknefs ; fo that, with its two facings, the wall muft have been originally about eleven feet through, as at Richborough.

The fig-tree, *ficus carica*, appears among the bufhes along the fouth wall; and the dwarf elder, *fambucus ebulus*, abounds there.

The fhore before Reculver is nearly covered with large maffes of fand-ftone, which are collected and arranged under the direction of the commiffioners of fewers, with a view to check the encroachments of the fea.   But thefe, and all other expenfive operations of the commiffioners, though well defigned and properly conducted, have been hitherto ineffectual to prevent its ravages, which now begin to be truly alarming.   The houfe marked (A) in the plan * has been damaged by the fea, and taken down fince the year 1781, when my furvey was made ; and the church will, moft probably, foon be in the fame predicament, if meafures cannot be adopted to keep off the fea.   In Leland's time, between 1530 and 1537, the village of Reculver ftood† "withyn a quarter of a myle, or

---

* See plate IV. This houfe appears in place I.   † Leland's Itin. 3d ed. p. 1-9·

"a little

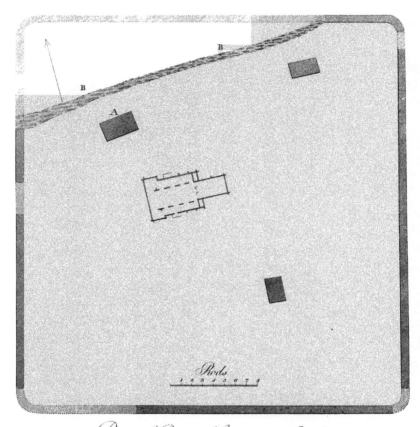

Plan of Reculver Church and Castle

The shaded part B B shews the direction of the Cliff in 1780.
The parts of the wall, shaded lightly, are either wholly destroyed, or concealed from view by the Soil

Plate V

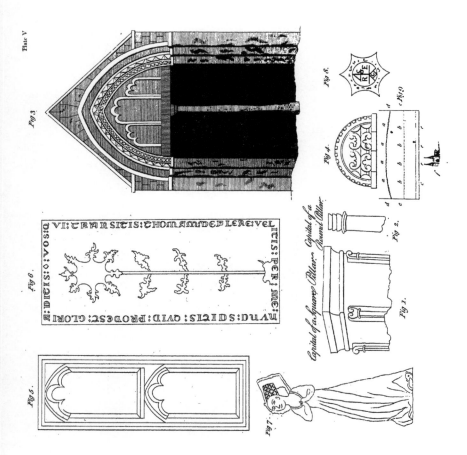

Fig 3

Fig 6

VI : TRANSITIS : THOMAM DEPLERE : VEL

R : DICIS : O : VOS : Q

ICIS : PER : ME :

NVNC : SITIS : QVID : PRODEST : GLORI : R

Fig 5

Fig 8

Fig 4

Fig 9

Fig 2.

Capital of a square Pillar. *Capital of a Round Pillar.*

Fig 1.

Fig 7

" a litle more, of the fe fyde;" and Leland's miles were none of the fhorteft.

The caftle, when entire, occupied 8 acres, 1 rood, 1 pole of ground; and the area within the walls meafured 7 acres, 2 roods, 26 poles.

The church does not appear to be a very ancient ftructure. It confifts of a nave, two ailes, and a chancel. The arches in the body of the church are pointed, and their pillars fquare. The fides of the two wefternmoft pillars are 8 feet by 15 inches; of the reft 3 feet 10 inches by 1 foot 3 inches *. The paffage from the nave into the chancel is under three circular arches, whofe pillars are round, with capitals of a fingular kind, as in fig. 2. The great weftern door is of Caen ftone, much corroded and mouldering away. The arch is pointed and ornamented, as at fig. 3. The arch over the north door is circular, fig. 4. In the fouth wall of the chancel have been three double windows, as at fig. 5, two of which are bricked up.

In the chancel, on a graveftone, is the following infcription, fig. 6, cut in the ftone round its verge:

> Vos qni tranfitis, Thomam deflere velitis:
> Per me nunc fcitis, quid prodeft gloria ditis.

Which may be thus tranflated, without much difgrace to the elegance of the original:

> All you that come near, upon Tom drop a tear:
> From whom 'twill appear, that the rich are poor here.

Clofe by this ftone is another with figures, on brafs plates, of John Sandwey, efq; and Joan his wife, eight fons and feven daughters†. The arms, in brafs, over the man, are three boars heads

---

* Figure 1. in plate V. is the capital of one of thofe fquare pillars.
† This epitaph is given in p. 73. and alfo in p. 89.

couped

couped at the neck; over the woman, three rams heads couped. Her head-drefs being fomewhat remarkable, I have figured it at N° 7. On a ftone fixed in the north wall of the chancel is a fhield carved and coloured, bearing Gules, femée of crofs croflets and a Lion rampant, Or.

In one of the fouth windows painted on glafs is Azure a Crofs patée, Or, between four Martlets (the glafs of the latter removed). In another window, Gules, three Lions paffant, Or.

The external figure of the church is from actual admeafurement: the internal parts are moftly from memory.

W. BOYS.

Fig. 8. in plate V. was found in a field near Reculver, fticking to the tine of a harrow; and is now communicated by John Thorpe, efq. F. S. A.

Fig. 9. is explained in pp. 77 and 90. The defcription and fketch, however, of Sir Thomas Page's works having been given from the plan only, before they were begun, their pofition is different to what is there apprehended. They are placed very near to the cliff, and not " much below high-water mark."

Plate VI. *p.86.*

View of Herne Bay with Reculver Spires.

Ruins of the Archiepiscopal Palace of Ford.

CAMDEN's account of this place may be thus tranflated:

" Proceeding along an open fhore abounding with fhell-fifh
and oyfters and plenty of oyfter-pits, we come to *Reculver*, called
by the Saxons Reaculf; but by the Romans and Britons REGUL-
BIUM, as in the Notitia, which places here the Tribune of the firft
cohort of *Vetafii*, under the Count of the Saxon fhore, by which
name all this coaft went at that time, and this its antiquity appears
by the coins of Roman emperors dug up here. Ethelbert [*], king
of Kent, after he had given Canterbury to Auftin the monk,
built himfelf a palace here. Baffo, a Saxon, embellifhed it with
a monaftery, from which Brightwald the eighth bifhop of Canterbury was called to that fee. Hence it was alfo named *Raculf-
minfter* from the monaftery, when Edred, brother to Edmund the
elder, gave it to the church of Canterbury. At prefent it is only
a fmall country village, and owes all its confequence to that monaftery, whofe church fpires are of ufe to mariners to avoid the
fhoals and fands in the Thames' mouth. For, as the author of
the Philippeis [†] fings,

> *Cernit oloriferum Tamifim fua Doridi amaræ*
> *Flumina mifcentem———*

> It fees the fwanny Thames unite its ftreams
> With bitter Doris."

---

[*] Creffy, p. 300, afcribes the monaftery to this prince ; but he only built a palace here. See Tanner, Not. Mon. 207.

" Inter hæc conventus religioforum multis in locis aguntur, cœnobia fabricantur,
abbatiæ conftruuntur, apud *Raculfe*, quo in loco fibi rex Ethelbertus fedem regni præparaverat, cœnobium conftruitur, cujus abbas ultimus fuit Wenredus." MS.
Corp. Chrifti Coll. Camb. Mifc. G. p. 307, in Dugd. Mon. Angl. I. 26.

† *Hadrian Junius,* Holland.

NOTES

NOTES taken at RECULVER, September 9, 1782.

By the Rev. Sir JOHN CULLUM, Bart. F.R. & A.SS.

RECULVER church ftands on the higheft part of the cliff, within a little of the fea, and at a diftance is a ftriking object, from the two fpires at its weft end; but, upon a nearer view of it, one is much difappointed. As a fpecimen of beautiful architecture, for which it has been extolled, it deferves but little notice. Its weft end, which from its ftyle muft have been built fome time after the Conqueft, feems never to have been very elaborate; and the mouldings of the door-cafe, where the chief work was beftowed, being of a foft ftone, and greatly expofed to the weather, are much decayed. The reft of the mafonry was never excellent, confifting of irregular ftones intermixed with Roman bricks. The coins, however, are of fquared ftone.

The body of the church is about 60 feet long, the chancel 48; the latter has at the eaft end a handfome triplet of lancet windows, and four fingle ones of the fame form on the north and fouth fides. It is feparated from the church by three round arches fupported by two lofty round pillars, with plain capitals. The floor of the church was formerly laid with terras, made of coarfe ftone and mortar; the furface quite fmooth and even polifhed, being thinly encrufted with a red compofition, as appears by fome parts ftill entire that are not in the tread of feet. This floor is ftill of exceffive hardnefs, the clerk being with difficulty able, even with a pickaxe, to get me a fmall piece of it as a fpecimen.

At

At the eaft end of the fouth aile of the church is this infcription, on a newly-painted tablet of wood, copied (and I fuppofe
with fome faults) from an old one near it, almoft effaced :

> Here, as hiftoriographers have faid, &c. (as in p. 72.)

On a tablet of black marble in the fouth wall of the chancel is
fcratched (for it is fcarcely more), in the neateft manner, the por-
trait of a man in a herald's furcoat, cloak, trunk-breeches, boots
with the tops turned down, fpurs, head with fhort hair and fhort
beard, and a ruff about a foot high *.   Beneath him is this infcription :

> Here under quit from worldly miferies, &c. (as in p. 73.)

His arms are Or, a Crofs engrailed party per pale Gules and
Sable, in chief Gules a Lion paffant guardant Or.   The creft, an
arm holding a fword wreathed with fome plant.   This with
the pediment and fome of the upper ornaments are tumbled
down, and lie in a corner of the chancel; and the reft will probably foon follow.

Under a man and woman with feven fons and one daughter,
all of marble, kneeling, affixed to the fouth wall of the chancel,
is this :

> Here under waite, &c. (as in p. 72.)

On a flip of brafs on a flat ftone in the chancel, beneath two
figures in brafs, the woman with the immenfe head-drefs of the
time of Edward IV. (fee plate V. fig. 6.) is this :

> Hic jacet Johannes Sandewey armiger, et Johanna uxor ejus; quorum animabus
> propitietur Deus.   Amen.

Near the laft is a ftone † thus circumfcribed in Saxon characters :

> Vos : qui : tranfitis : Thomam : deflere : velitis :
> Per : me : nunc : fcitis : quid : prodeft : gloria : ditis.

* See plate II.   † See plate V. fig. 5.

The

The cliff is continually crumbling away (particularly in the winter time) and falling on the beach, where the children of the neighbourhood pick up several Roman coins. I was offered a handful of them, at no high price; but they were all so corroded that they were not worth purchasing. They were all small, some extremely so.

The crumbling away of the cliff on which the church stands is become so alarming, that I am informed this year (1783) some means are to be employed to stop the evil *. I am not willing to think that this edifice being a sea-mark is the only reason of this attention to its preservation †.

---

* See p. 77. and plate V. fig. 8. Sir Thomas Page proposes to construct much below high water mark a breast-work of long fascines fixed together and strongly secured, each end to have a return up to the cliff, and, if necessary, two jettées also to be carried out farther into the sea. Over this breast-work, being in deep water, the waves will have much less power than when breaking on the shore, and it is hoped it will also collect the beach, and thereby receive additional strength, as has been the case at Sheerness. The present works, though very expensive, have been found insufficient, and being near the cliff, the waves, by dashing over them, form a back-water, which undermines and throws it down. D.

† Certainly not; the Trinity house having totally disregarded it, and the commissioners of sewers, and the occupiers who pay scots, having no view nor interest but to secure the level, which must be overflowed when the hill is washed away. D.

APPENDIX.

A P P E N D I X.

Carta Eadredi R. de cœnobio Raculfenfi cum omnibus ad id
pertinentibus ecclefiæ Cantuarienfi conceffis et collatis.

✠ MULTIS itaque vitiorum preftigiis mentes humanas incentor fraudulen-
ter perjugulando deludit, nunc inquam promiffis quafi prolixioris vitæ
ftadiis decipit, nunc rebus migrantibus pervicaciter quafi neceffarius inlicit. Interea
etiam ftigia inferni fupplicia tanquam levia et tranfitoria fuggerit quatenus mifero-
rum coida in cupiditate lafciviaque enerent * diffolvat fecumque cabeata ✠ ad tartara
ducat. Sed fancti viri præfago fpiritu beftiales precognofcentes infidias fcuto bonæ
voluntatis coronati quicquid in femet ipfis terrenum fentiunt indefinenter atque
naviter operibus fanctis exauriunt, unde defcoriatis coram Chrifto Jhefu meritis ruti-
lantes fimillima Titanii fulgoris luce præfententur. De quorum præconio tuba
fanctæ fcripturæ rebohans inter alia teftimonia propenfius intelligenda noftris hæc
geminis auribus refultando profudit. " Beati quorum veftimenta alba funt in con-
fpectu domini," et alibi, " jufti fulgebunt fint fol in regno patris eorum." Hujus
ergo dominici confpectus & pater in amore regni perfufus, unde nobis victus reftat
fine dubio certus, de victuque dominus dixit " Beatus qui manducabit panem in
regno Dei;" Ego Eadred rex divina gracia totius Albionis monarchus, et primi-
cerius Chrifto regi meo in throno regni perennis perpetualiter fubthronizato, et conceffis mihi ab eodem labilium gazis rerum accepti tirocinii, quarto mei terreftris
regni anno ad templum fuum incomprehenfibili dedicatum numini in urbe Doro-
berniæ Odone archiepifcopo metropolitanam cathedram præfidente, et regni cæleftis
fuper arva Britannica claves præportante, monafterium Raculfenfe bis denis fenif-
que eftimatum caffatis interius exteriufque cum omnibus ad hoc rebus rite pertinentibus, five litorum, five camporum, agrorum, faltuumve, ficut inferius territoria
promulgantur, humillime atque devotiffime fincero corde in perpetuum jus quamdiu
Chriftianitas vigeat pro meis abluendis exceffibus indeterminabiliter impendo. Si
quis autem, quod abfit, tiranica fretus poteftate, regalis, epifcopalis, five homo
alicujus dignitatis, hoc decretum a Deo mihi conlatum infringere temptaverit, five
hujufive donationis a præfata ecclefia vel paffum pedis fegregaverit, nifi prius hoc
enorme fcelus pænitendo deterferit fe facrilegii culpam incurriffe et a domino Jhefu
Xto in perpetuum fine ullo fubtractionis refocillatu dampnaturum perfentiat.

* *Lege* inherentia.　　　　　† *Sic.*

P 2　　　　　　　　　　　　　　　Hæc

Hæc enim fingrapha anno dominicæ incarnationis DCCCCXLIX orthodoxorum fcripta eft unanimi confenfu, quorum inferius nomina literaria qualitate diftingui videntur.

✠ Ego *Eadred* rex divina protegente gratia Albionis fummam præfidens agiæ crucis hanc caitulam notamine perftrinxi.

Ego *Odo* archiepifcopus metropolitana præfidens gubernacione hoc donum regia conceffum munificentia figno crucis fixi.

Ego *Wulfftan* aichiepifcopus metropolitici honoris faftigio Eboracenfis civitate fuffultus huic largitati crucem afcripfi.

Ego *Ælfhean* epifcopus Wintonenfis ecclefiæ hoc donum figno crucis confirmavi.

Ego *Æthelgar* Cridianenfis ecclefiæ præful hanc largitatem corroboravi.

Ego *Ælfric* epifcopus hujus donationis conftipulater fignum crucis depinxi.

Ego *Wulffige* epifcopus hujus largiflui muneris domini figno falubri adnotavi.

Ego *Theadred* epifcopus piodigam hanc impenfionem patibuli confirmatu addidi.

Ego *Ælfred* epifcopus hoc Deo inftigante donum crucis Xti conftipulatu munivi.

Ego *Birhtfige* epifcopus hujufce donationis corroborationem contuli.

✠ Ego *Coenwald* epifcopus confenfum adhibui.

✠ Ego *Cynefige* epifcopus unanimitatem præbui.

✠ Ego *Wifbelm* epifcopus promiffionem profudi.

✠ Ego *Eadbelm* abbas devotus in hoc piæftiti.

✠ Ego *Ofulf* dux c nfenfi et humiliter adititi.

✠ Ego *Eadmund* dux libens confilio aderam.

✠ Ego *Athelftan* dux promto animo confenfi.

✠ Ego *Eadgifu* regis genitrix piæfati animo hanc præfatam lætabundo in Xto largitionem ob optabilem remunerationem conceffam figni corroboratione falutiferi humillime confignavi.

✠ Ego *Dunftanus* indignus abbas, rege Eadredo imperante, hanc domino meo hæreditariam kartulam dictitando compofui, et propriis digitorum aiticulis perfcripfi.

✠ His inquam limitibus hæc telluris particula circumgirari videtur.

Ꝼepꝼc on nopð healꝼe ꝼðelleꝼðeꝼ lonðe. ꝼıa ꝼopð beꝼande oð Noꝼðmvðan to Ɱeanbꝺioce ðonne to æꝼneꝼeȝe, oꝼ æꝼneꝼeȝe to Eanꝼlæðemuð o. oꝼ Eanꝼlæðemuðan on Ɱeaꝼe ꝼleoteꝼmuꝼan. Cꝼ Ꝺeaꝼe-ꝼleoteꝼmuꝺan epð on Eanꝼleðmuꝼan. ðonne on eaꝼt healꝼ to mylenꝼleoteꝼemvꝼꝥn oð ꝺvðt n oꝼ ꝺvðtvn anðlang bꝺoceꝼ to ꝺæðemæꝼınȝe, ðonne on ꝺvðhealꝼe oꝼ hæðemæꝼınȝe to ꝼcocccm. oꝼ ntoccum anðloı ȝ ꝼtæte oð ꝼce Aȝuꝼtıneꝼ meaꝼce. Ꝼnom ꝼce Aȝuꝼtıneꝼ meaꝼce oð bꝺoc, anðlang bꝺoceꝼ oꝼ ꝼtanbꝺˑȝe ꝼvð Ꝼnom ꝼtanbꝺvȝe oð pıꝼelınȝ to Cꝼıꝼteꝼ cıꝺıcan ȝemæꝺe ꝼnom Cꝺıꝼteꝼ cıꝺıcan ȝemæꝺe oð ealðan hæȝe on ꝼeꝼt healꝼ ealðan heȝe to ꝼeaxum. ðonne ꝼeꝼt ꝼnom ꝼeaxum to celðan to Cınȝeꝼȝemæꝼe. ꝼnom Cınȝeꝼȝemæꝼe oð ȝata ȝehæȝȝe. ðonne ꝼıenðan ꝼeoꝼeꝼ ꝼꝼvlınȝ bınnan ea ꝼæꝼ lonðeꝼ ꝼe ȝebypeð ınto Raculꝼe. on Teneꝼ ꝼeoꝼeꝼ ꝼꝼvlvnȝ ouð an læꝼ on paꝼvð ȝebypeð ınto Raculꝼe. ðonne ıꝼ ealleꝼ ꝼaꝼ lanðeꝼ xxv ꝼꝼvlvnȝ ꝼ an ꝼꝼvlvnȝ en Lꝺeolvꝼınȝtune ꝼvð be pealða ꝼæpe cıꝺıcan to boꝼe.

Hoc

Hoc eſt.

Primo, ab aquilone *Æthelferthi* terra ; ita prorſum per arenam uſque ad North-mutham [a] ad [rivulum] *Meanbroc* [dictum] ; inde ad priſcam viam ; a priſca via ad *Eanfledæ* oſtium ; ab Eanfledæ oſtio ad *Mearcfleotam* [b] · a Mearcfleota iterum ad Eanfledæ oſtium, ab oriente vero ad molendinarii fluenti oſtium uſque ad *Suth-tunam* [c] : a Suthtuna per longitudinem rivuli ad *Hæthemæringam* [d] : ab auſtro vero ab Hæthemæiinga ad ſtipites, a ſtipitibus per longitudinens viæ aduſque Sɛ̄i Auguſtini limitem ; a Sɛ̄i Auguſtini limitem uſque ad rivulum ; per longitudinem rivuli uſque ad pontem lapideum auſtrum [verſus]; a ponte lapideo uſque ad *Wiſe-lingam* [e], ad ecclefiæ Xti [Cantuarienfis] limitem ; ab ecclefiæ Xti limite uſque ad veterem ſepem ; ab occidente veteris ſepis ad *Feaxum*. Tunc occidentem veiſus a Feaxum ad *Celdan*, ad regis limitem ; a regis limite aduſque portæ ſepem. Sunt autem quatuor carucatæ terræ intra aquam quæ pertinent ad *Raculfe*. In *Thaneto* quatuor carucatæ [terræ] et unum paſcuum in littore pertinent ad *Raculfe*. Sunt autem de tota terra illa xxv carucatæ et una carucata in *Coelulfingtuna* [f] ex auſtro ſaltus ad eccleſiam reparandam [aſſignatæ].

[a] Oſtium fluminis aquilonare. [b] Limitaris fluenti oſtium. [c] Auſtralem villam.
[d] F. portum celebrem. [e] F. curculionum locum. [f] Ceolulfi villa.

A grant

A grant or demife of part of the demefnes of Reculver Monaftery made by Archbifhop Agelnoth to two of his minifters.

From Somner's Antiquities of Canterbury, Append. p. 424. 4to.

IN nomine domini noftri Jhu Xti ego Aegelnothus peccator, fervus fervorum Dei et minifter ecclefiæ Xti, Anglorum quoque licet indignus archiepifcopus, notum volo effe omnibus noftræ mortalitatis fuccefforibus quod quandem terram dominicam ′ Scæ Mariæ Raculfenfis monafterii L. fcil agros in præftariam annuo duobus miniftris meis Alfwoldo et Aedredo ex confenfu fratris ñri Givebardi decani ejufdem ecclefiæ fcæ matris Dei, ut illam terram habeant non longius quam ipfi placuerit decano, vel ejus fucceffori. Quamdiu vero eam tenuerint fingulis annis dent in ipfo monafterio deo famulantibus ratam decimam frugum et omnium pecorum quæ in ipfa terra nutriunt, et pro cenfu L denarios, et de fubjectis pafcuis I penfam cafeorum et fi quid fracturæ contigerit. Ubi vero eidem fratri ñro decano vel ejus fucceffori vifum fuerit ut illam terram poffint fructificare dominicatui fuo recedant ab ea abfque querela et contradictione, quia dominica eft Scæ Mariæ, nec eam fibi vel pofteris ullo modo poffint defendere. Quod fi præfumpferint et ipfi et fautores fui iram Dei et excommunicationem omnium Dei fidelium incurrant, & legem patriæ domino fuo folvant. Hujus præftariæ traditionis teftes funt fratres ejufdem monafterii et quidam milites mei qui fubter funt ordinate defcripti.

Ego Givehardus fubfcripfi.
Ego Frefnotus mon. fubannotavi.
Ego Tancrad mon. recognovi.
Ego Milo mon. affignavi.
Ego Siwad miles conteftificavi.
Ego Godiic miles teftis fui.
Ego Wlfi miles.
Ego Wlfige miles.
Ego Radwine miles.
Ego Orduoth miles.
Ego Alfric miles hog'.
Ego Ofward miles.
Ego Aelfhelm miles.
Ego Lefsona miles.
Ego Aelfric miles quatin'.

* *Dedi* or *conceffi* omitted.

Ego

Ego Sibriht miles.

Ego Aelwine miles.

Ego Hericus presbiter, jubente domino Agelnotho archiepiſcopo, hanc cartulam conſcripſi die nativitatis Sēi Johannis Baptiſtæ.

Evidentiæ eccleſiæ Xti Cant. ex MS. in collegio C. C. Cant. dicto *Thorn.*

Inter Decem Scriptores, col. 2207.

A. dnicæ inc. DCLXXIX. Ego Lotharius rex Cantuariorum pro remedio animæ meæ concedo terram in inſula Thanatos in loco qui appelatur *Weſtanea* tibi, Burthwolde abba tuoque monoſterio cui nomen Raculfe, cun omnibus ad illam rite pertinentibus, campis, paſcuis, maudeis. Adjeci adhuc eidem eccleſiæ tuæ terram xii manſionum in loco qui dicitur *Sturete*, liberam ut ſuperiorem ab omni ſeculari ſervicio, exceptis iſtis tribus, expeditione, pontis et arcis conſtructione.

Ex eodem MSto. Ib. col. 2211.

Anno dnicæ incarnationi, DCCXLVII. Ego Eadbertus rex Canciæ cum conſenſu optimatum meorum Bregowini archiepiſcopi et cæterorum principum meorum concedo eccleſiæ quæ eſt apud Reculf et tibi, Deneah abba, tuæque familiæ pro ſalute animæ meæ vectigal et tributum unius navis in portu ac villa quæ dicitur *Fordewic* ad opus ut præfatus ſum Scæ Mariæ quæ in jam nominata eccleſia Deo ſervit: ſimulque præcipio in nomine omnipotentis Dei præfectis, præpoſitis, actionariis, et omnibus fidelibus qui habent vel habituri ſunt aliquam poteſtatem ut hæc mea donatio ſit ſtabilis & firma imperpetuum.

Anno incarnati domini DCCLXXXIIII. Ego Ealhmundus rex Cantiæ do tibi, Wetrede, honorabili abbati tuæque familiæ degenti in loco qui dicitur Raculf Ceſtre terram xii aratrorum quæ dicitur *Schyldwic*, cum univerſis ad eam rite pertinentibus, liberam ab omni ſeculari ſervitio et ab omni regali tributo, exceptis expeditione, pontis et arcis conſtructione *.

Ex eod. MSto. Ib. col. 2220.

Anno dnicæ incarnacionis DCCCCXLIX. Ego Eadredus rex, præſente Odone archiepiſcopo et Edina matre mea, dedi eccleſiæ Xti in Dorobernia monaſterium Raculfenſe, cum tota villa et omnibus ad eam rite pertinentibus, liberam ab omni ſeculari ſervitio, exceptis expeditione, pontis et arcis conſtructione. Ego Dunſtanus indignus abbas cartulam inde imperante domino meo rege compoſui, cartulam et propriis digitis perſcripſi.

Ego Eardulfus rex Cantiæ tibi, venerabilis Eadberte abba, tuæque familiæ conſiſtenti in loco qui dicitur Raculf concedo terram unius aratri in loco qui nominatur *Berhamſtede,* cum omnibus ad eam pertinentibus liberam ab omnibus ſecularibus ſerviciis †.

---

* See this alſo in Leland's Collect. II. 55.   † Ibid.

ABBOTS

A B B O T S of R E C U L V E R.

BERTHWALD, or BRITHWALD [a], monk of Glaftonbury, was elected archbifhop of
Canterbury July 1, 692, after two years vacancy of that fee on the death of Theodore. Bede [b] fays, he was well verfed in fcripture, and in ecclefiaftical and monaftic
difcipline, though not comparable to his predeceffor in the fee. He was equally
inveterate againft Wilfrid archbifhop of York, till the pope pronounced him innocent of the charges brought againft him, and obliged his adverfaries to fubmit to
his reftoration. Having fat longer than any other archbifhop of Canterbury, viz.
near thirty eight years [c], he died 9 Jan. 731, and was buried in St. Auftin's monaftery [d]. Lambarde [e] obferves he was not the firft, as Polydore faith, but the fecond man of all the Saxon nation that afpired to that dignity.

HEAHBERT [f].
DENEAH, A. D. 747 [g].
WETRED, A. D. 783 [h].
HWITREDE [i], A. D. 784.
EDBERT, A. D. 949 [k].

[a] Mat Weft. *Breetzwald,* Hoved. *Britwold,* Huntingd. *Brithwold,* Brompton. *Brichtwald,* Diceto. *Be-
reehtwald. Bertwald* Bede. *Beretuald* Malsmb. *Bribtwald* Flor. Wig. *Berchtwald* Chron. Mailros et
S. Crucis. *Brithewald* Mat. Par. *Brichwald* Birchington vit. archiep. Cantuar. Angl. Sac. I. 3. " Abbas
in monafterio quod juxta oftium aquilonare fluvii *Tencloude* [*f.* Tenet loade] eft pofitus in Reculfre."
MS. Trin. cited by Godwin.
[b] V. 9.   [c] 37 Gervas. Chron. Chron Mailros 135 Huntingd. IV. 194. b. 17.
[d] Godwin de præf. ed Richardfon 43.   [e] Kent. p. 261.   [f] MS. E. R. Mores.
[g] Carta Eadberti regis.   [h] Carta Ealhmundi regis.   [i] MS. E. R. Mores. "
may be the fame with the foregoing.   [k] Carta Eardulfi regis.

HISTORY OF HERNE,

BY JOHN DUNCOMBE, M.A.

HERNE, or HEARN, is fituated in the North part of Kent, fix miles North of Canterbury, 12 Weft of Margate, and 14 Eaft of Feverfham, in the Weft divifion of the lath of St. Auguftine, and Eaft divifion of the county, in the upper half-hundred of Blengate, the deanery of Weftbeer, and diocefe of Canterbury.

This parifh, which is bounded North by the German ocean, North-Weft by Swacliff, or Swalecliff, Weft by Whitftable, South and South-Eaft by Chiflet and Hoath, and North-Eaft and Eaft by Reculver, is in length from North to South about two miles, and in breadth from Eaft to Weft about fix miles. It is divided into five boroughs, viz. Hampton, Thornden, Stroud, Haw, and Beltinge, each of which has a borfholder fubordinate to the conftable of the upper half-hundred of Blengate, who is chofen at the court-leet two years from this parifh, one from Reculver, one from Hoath, and one from Stourmouth. It is in the archbifhop's manor of Reculver, whofe fteward holds a court-baron there every year.

It probably derives its name (as does alfo Herne-hill) from the number of herons that ufed to frequent thefe parts; and the family of Knowler, who have been fettled in this parifh fome centuries, have that bird for their creft.

P   Places

Places of note are, or were, 1. *Haw-Houſe*, formerly belonging to the family of *Apuldrefeild*, a daughter of which carried it in marriage to Sir *John Fyneux*, in whom it continued till another daughter of the ſame carried it to Sir *John Smyth*, of Oſtenhanger, anceſtor to the preſent viſcount Strangford, from whoſe grand-father it deſcended to the Hon. Mr. Roper, of whoſe heirs it was purchaſed about 20 years ago by the late Rev. *Francis Hender Foote*, LL. B. whoſe eldeſt ſon, *John Foote*, eſq. of Charlton in Biſhopſbourn, is the preſent poſſeſſor. It ſeems to have been a large venerable manſion, but is now only a farm-houſe. 2. *Seas* or *At-Seas Court*, now called *Stroud-Houſe*, which belonged to the family of *At-Sea* till the reign of queen Elizabeth, when it was ſold to Mr. *Knowler*, in whoſe lineal deſcendant *Gilbert Knowler*, eſq. it is now veſted. It is a regular brick manſion*, with a pleaſant garden and grounds adjacent, and is at preſent occupied by Iſaac Bargrave, eſq. of Eaſtry-Court, one of the commiſſioners of bankruptcy, who has in his poſſeſſion there ſome valuable original portraits remarkably well preſerved, particularly thoſe of his anceſtor, Dr. Iſaac Bargrave, dean of Canterbury, 1625—42, and his lady, a daughter of Sir Cholmondeley Dering, bart. by Cornelius Janſen, Sir Henry Wotton, and Father Paul, both painted in Italy, and collected by the dean, a ſmall whole length of lord Wotton, &c. 3. *Underdown*, formerly the ſeat of *John Sea*, eſq. as appears from his monument in the church, was rebuilt by the late Sir *George Oxenden*, bart. who purchaſed the eſtate, but is now only a farm-houſe, belonging to the preſent Sir *Henry*. 4. The rectorial houſe, formerly the manſion of the *Milles's* (afterwards mentioned), now much contracted, and occupied by the maſter of one of the hoys. The vicarage-houſe, an ancient building†. It has no glebe, but only an orchard and large garden.

* See a view of it, plate VIII.   † See a view of it, plate VII.

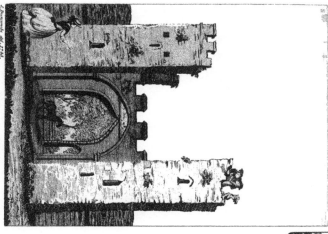

S. Duncombe del. 1785.

N. View of Danadeion Gateway taken from the House.

Fig. 1.

S. Duncombe del. 1775.

West View of Herne Church.

a. The Porch.
b. The School.

Fig. 2.

Fig. 3.

Plate III. p. 91

LADY PHELIP.

Fig. 2. p. 105.

JOHN DARLEY, B.D.

Fig 4 p 98.

Fig. 3. p. 98.

J. Duncombe del. 1783.

View of Stroud House, in Herne the Seat of Gilbert Knowler Esq.

F. Gary sculp.t

Sarah Highmore del. 1777

Herne Vicarage House.

In the reign of Edward III. a market was obtained to be held there on a Monday, and a two days' fair, by the intereft of the archbifhop, on the feaft of St. Martin, to whom the church is dedicated. It has now a fair on Eafter Tuefday.

The parifh-regifters, which are well preferved, commence with November 1558, 1 Elizabeth. In the firft 20 years were baptized 544, buried 651, married 162 couple. In the laft 20 years, ending with 1782, were baptized 742, buried 507, married 149 couples. By this it fhould feem to be more healthy now than formerly.

Little fo material as what follows occurs in the regifters :

" 1565. John Jarvys had two woemen children baptized at " home joyned together in the belly, and havynge each the one " of their armes lyinge at one of their own fhoulders, and in " all other parts well proportioned children. Buryed Aug. 29."

" 1566. Stephanus Sawyer, vir piæ memoriæ, annos natus " 92, Martii 30 vitâ fuâ finiit, cum 30 annos continuos purâ " Chrifti religione contra Romanam tyrannidem profeffus fuiffet."

" 1567. *Ould* Arnold, a *cryfomer*, buried February 8."

This word, fometimes fpelt *chrifomer*, often occurs afterwards for about a hundred years, but not fince. Dr. Johnfon defines *chrifom* (from chrifm) to be " a child that dies within a month after its birth. So called (he fays) from the chrifom-cloath, a cloath anointed with holy unguent, which the children anciently wore till they were chriftened." *Chrifm* is applied in the Gloffaries to the popifh facrament of Confirmation. *Ould* Arnold might therefore, in the firft appearance of Proteftantifm in England, be firft confirmed late in life, or perhaps on his converfion to Proteftantifm : as anciently perfons who were recovered from any herefy, if not already confirmed, were *anointed with Chrifm.* Du Cange.

" 1567.   William Lawſon, an infant, chriſtiend *by the woe-men*, buryed 21 Martii."

This remnant of popery, it ſeems, then remained.

The church is a large ancient handſome ſtructure, having a tower of flint and ſtone, containing ſix bells.   It confiſts of a nave, two ſide ailes, and three chancels, of which the great chan-cel, repaired (as appears by the endowment in the Appendix) by the vicar, has ſix ſtalls for the ancient popiſh miniſters of the church like a cathedral, and was formerly divided from the nave by an open carved ſcreen of oak, as the two other chancels are ſtill.   The nave is in height 33 feet, in length 70 feet, the chancel 43; total 113.   The north chancel is in breadth 23, nave 30, ſouth chancel 16; total 69.   The whole roof is leaded, and embattled, except that of the great and ſouth chancels, which are tiled.   The ſtone font is very ancient, with ſeveral eſcutcheons of arms; now plaiſtered over.   The wooden frame ſtill remains of a ſmall organ, which, tradition ſays, was ſold to Feverſham; and two large tables of benefactions, hung up in 1777, ſhew that the annual donations to the church and poor amount to 15 *l.* 10 *s.* 9 *d.* in money, and 17 *l.* 5 *s.* in land.   Total 32 *l.* 15 *s.* 9 *d.*   The vicarage is rated in the king's books at 20 *l.* 16 *s.* and is worth about 150 *l. per annum.*

A weſt view of the church is annexed, in plate VI.

By the endowment of the vicarage, taken from the regiſter of archbiſhop Winchelſey, A. D. 1310 (which, by the favour of Dr. Ducarel, will appear in the Appendix), the vicars of Reculver, Herne, and St. Nicholas are entitled, among other things, to *omnes minutas decimas quæ ad altaragium* * *ſpectare*

---

* The word *altaragium* ſignifies all tithes, offerings, oblations, &c. becoming due to a miniſter by virtue of his office, or for officiating at the altar, and conſequently has ſuch a latitude as to comprehend every tithable matter not expreſsly mentioned in the endowment amongſt the tithes appropriated.   *Bateman on Agiſtment Tithes.*

dicuntur.

dicuntur. The two latter are directed alfo to keep the great chancels in repair, or even to rebuild them if neceffary *, and to pay annually, Herne 40*s.* and St. Nicholas four marks, and 10*s.* to the vicar of the mother-church.

Befides thefe payments, the church-wardens of each of thofe parifhes pay alfo to thofe of Reculver five fhillings annually, in confequence of a decree of archbifhop Warham, exempting them, on that condition, from the repairs of the mother-church, to which before they ftill remained liable, as the chapelry of Hoath is ftill. On default of payment on a fet day, the ancient obligation remains in force.

Extract from the laft will and teftament of Chriftopher Milles, efq; of Herne, bearing date May 28, 1638.

" I will and beqeath to my children the poor of Herne 3*l.* of Reculver 4*l.* of Hoath 2*l.* of Weftbeer† 1*l.* a year, in all 10*l.* to be paid the laft day of Auguft every year from year to year after my deceafe, which was the day of my birth; to continue as long as it fhall pleafe his grace and fucceffors to continue the leafe of the parfonage of Reculver, Hoath, and Herne, to any of my fur-name, that one after another fhall fucceed me in the faid parfon-age and tytheries; and therefore pray the vicars and minifters of Reculver, Hoath, and Herne, and parfon of Weftbeer, for the time being, and the chief of every parifh it concerns, to be petitioners, as caufe fhall require, to his grace and fucceffors for the poor in that behalf, as they tender the well-doing of their own children they fhall leave here behind them, and would not the guilt of

---

* His grace furely exerted here a fingular and unwarrantable ftretch of authority; as otherwife thefe repairs by common law would have belonged to the archbifhop himfelf, or his tenant of the great tithes, whom he thus took upon him to exonerate. It is alfo remarkable that the prefent incumbent of Herne, contrary to the ufual cuftom and practice, not only has a vicarage in which he repairs the chancel, but two rectories (in Canterbury) whofe chancels he does not repair.

† Why Mr. Milles left this benefaction to Weftbeer, which is not an appro-priation, like the others, does not appear.

confcience they elfe fhall hence carry with them for neglecting to gain the charity of the dead towards the living poor, fo adopted my children."

The leafe of the faid parfonage ftill continues in the fame family, being now held by Richard Milles, efq; of Nackington near Canterbury, and North Elmham in Norfolk, the lineal defcen- dant of the above teftator. Mr. Milles is interred under a flat marble in the great chancel, with the following infcription :

" In memory of Chriftopher Milles, efq. fometime clerk of queen Anne's robes; afterwards fucceffively fworne of king James and king Charles's moft honourable Privy Chamber. With whom is here interred Mary, his fecond wife, on his left fide, and Edward, his eldeft fon, on his right.

> Wee fleepe fecure, as haveing loft but breath,
> And gain'd the life which never fuffereth death.

Edward died the 28th of February, 1627.
Mary the 3d of October, 1631.
Chriftopher the 13th of November, 1638.
In the fame grave with Edward lyes buried Alicia, firft wife of Chriftopher Milles, gent. who died March 21, anno 1664 ; and Sarah his fecond wife, who died January 29, 1675."

On the North fide of the fame chancel is a handfome marble monument furmounted by the creft and arms of the family. Below them another efcutcheon, under a canopy held by two weeping cherubim, on each fide a flaming pillar, and under them two other efcutcheons, reprefenting in all the four different bear- rings of Mr. Milles's four wives ; and on the table beneath a La- tin infcription to the memory of Chriftopher Milles, efq; (grandfon of the former) who died January 22, 1706, aged 61, and of his four wives, viz. Alice, daughter of Robert Saunders of Maidftone, in Kent, gent. Sarah, of Samuel Difborow, of Elfworth, Cam- bridgefhire, efq; Margaret, of John Boys, of Betfhanger in Kent, efq; and Elizabeth, of Cheney Colepepper, of Leeds-Caftle in Kent, efq; by all whom he had children, but left only Samuel furviving by the fecond.

On

On the South fide of the fame chancel is a black and white marble pyramidical monument, on the bafe of which is a Latin epitaph on the abovementioned Samuel Milles, efq. fteward of the temporal courts of the archbifhop and dean and chapter of Canterbury, and of the monaftery of St. Auguftine's, and member of parliament for the neighbouring city in the reign of king George I*. He married Anne, fifter of Sir Thomas Hales, bart. by whom he had fix fons and fix daughters, of whom Chriftopher the eldeft erected this monument. He died Dec. 10, 1727, aged 70. Arms of Milles quartering Hales.

Againft the Eaft wall, on a white oval marble, in a frame of Sienna, is an infcription to the memory of the Rev. Charles Milles, M. A. rector of Harbledown in Kent, and minifter of Great and Little Walfingham in Norfolk (a younger fon of the above Samuel), who died June 24, 1749, aged 42, and of two of his daughters, Catherine aged three years, and Anne aged 25, who are all buried in the family vault near that place. Above is an urn, with the letters A.M. under a weeping willow, and beneath the arms of Milles and Brooke, and Milles fingle in a lozenge. This monument was carved by Moore.

Under the brafs figure of a warrior in armour and his wife,

Hic jacet Petrus Hall, armig. & Elizabeth uxor ejus, filia Dom. Wilhelm. Waleys, militis, et Dom. Margaretæ uxoris (without date.) Mater Dei, miferere mei.

Hic jacet Anto. Loverick, armig. et Conftantia uxor ejus, qui obiit 10 Octob. 1511.

Hic jacet Wilhelmus Fineux, fil. & heres Johannis Fineux, militis, qui obiit ..... regis Henrici VIII.

Sir John Fineux was one of the juftices of the King's Bench to Henry VII. and a benefactor to the Auftin Friars at Canterbury †.

---

* His grandfon, the prefent Richard Milles, efq; reprefented this city alfo in the three firft parliaments of the prefent reign.

† Appendix to Somner's Canterbury, N° 22.

Others

Others of that name (Weever says) lie here entombed, but without any infcription to preferve their memory.

On a brafs plate, however, near the communion-table, under the brafs figure of a lady in the drefs of the times, is an infcription in old charaċters to the memory of Elizabeth the wife of John Fyneux, efq. who died Auguſt 22, 1539.

And on another,

John Fyneur, late of Hearne, efq. and Margaret his wife, daughter of Thomas Morley, fometime of Glyne, in the county of Suffex, efq. She died * Dec. 9, 1591; and he July 31, 1592, leabing one only daughter, Elizabeth, who married John Smith, efq. fon and heir of Thomas Smith, late of Oftenhanger, in Kent, efq.

On a flat ftone,

" To the memory of the Rev. William Rogers, B. A. vicar of Hearne, who died Auguſt 28, 1773, aged 52."

Againſt the North wall of this chancel is an old marble monument, reprefenting a warrior in armour kneeling on a cufhion at a table, under a pediment fupported by two Corinthian pillars. Above are the arms of *Thornhurſt*, Ermine on a chief Gules, two leopards heads Argent ; under a pediment fupported by two pilafters ; and over them hang the banners, and are placed the helmet, creft, &c. Below is the following infcription :

" Here lieth buried the body of Sir William Thornhurſt, knight, fonne and heire to Sir Stephen Thornhurſt, of Foorde, in this countie, knight, which Sir William married Ann, daughter unto the Right Honourable Thomas lord Howard, vifcount Howard of Bindon, and by her had iffue one fonne, named Gifford Thornhurſt, and two daughters, Frances and Grace. He dyed the 24th daye of July, 1606, and in the 31ft year of his age."

Under the North window of this chancel in the wall, with three efcutcheons on it almoſt defaced by whitewafh, is an old tomb without any memorial, probably of the founder of the church.

* This lady in the Regiſter is buried the fame day, December 9.

On

On a flat ſtone near the communion rails is a braſs figure in a batchelor of divinity's gown (ſee plate VIII. fig. 2), with this inſcription, in old characters:

> Siſte gradum, videas, corpus jacet, ecce, Johannis
> Darley, qui multis fuit hic miratus in annis:
> Ille pater morum fuit et flos philoſophorum,
> Qui via norma legis patriæ fuit anchora gregis;
> Pagina ſacra cui dedit inceptoris honorem.

Round the margin,

Hic jacet magiſter Johannes Darley, baccalaureus in ſacra theologia, quondam Vicarius * * * * [The reſt illegible.]

In the South-Eaſt corner of the South chancel is a mural marble monument, with two kneeling figures, between them *Memoriæ Sacrum*, under an arch with a pediment ſupported by pillars, and the arms of *Knowler* in the cornice, and below is an epitaph on

Robert Knowler, gent. of Herne, who died May 1, 1635, aged 62, and Suſan his wife, who died July 18, 1631, aged 57.

On ſeveral black marbles are reſpectively commemorated, in the ſame chancel,

Richard Knowler, M. A. of Pembroke college, Oxford, ſecond ſon of the above Robert, who married Anne, daughter of Richard Sandwell, of Minſter, in the Iſle of Thanet, and died Feb. 20. 1659, aged 59, leaving four ſons and three daughters:

Thomas Knowler, gent. and batchelor, fourth ſon of the ſame Robert, who died March 27, 1658, aged 39, and gave 10*l.* to buy a pulpit-cloth and a communion-cloth, 10*l.* to be diſtributed upon the day of his burial to the poor, 2*l. per annum.* for ever to repair this iſle, and 5*l. per annum* for ever to cloath the poor of this pariſh, out of his farm at Beltinge, in Hearne:

Elizabeth Knowler, ſecond daughter of Richard, who died Nov. 29, 1724, aged 51:

Gilbert Knowler [*], of Stroud, in Hearne, grandſon of Richard, who died Feb. 16, 1729, aged 67. He married 1. Elizabeth, daughter of Elias Juxon, M. A. 2. Honywood, daughter of Vincent Denne, ſerjeant at law. 3. Suſanna, daughter of Martin Liſter, M. D.

* William Knowler, LL. D. of S. John's College, Cambridge, and rector of Boddington, Northamptonſhire (who died in Dec. 1773, and of whom an account is given in the "Anecdotes of Mr. Bowyer," p. 448), was the third ſon of this gentleman.

R And

And on a mural monument of two Corinthian pillars of Sienna marble, fupporting a pediment, is an infcription,

To the memory of Gilbert Knowler, efq. (eldeft fon of the laft) who died Feb. 23, 1737, aged 45. and of Mary his wife, daughter of William Blandford, citizen of London, who died June 28, 1735, aged 43, leaving Gilbert* their fon ftill furviving.

On a flat ftone in this chancel is the following :

Here lies a piece of Chrift, a ftar in duft, ⎫
A vein of gold, a China difh, which muft ⎬
Be us'd in Heaven, when God fhall feed the juft. ⎭
Approv'd by all, and lov'd fo well,
Though young, like fruit that's ripe, he fell.

In the North chancel are feveral brafs plates, figures, and in-fcriptions, well preferved ; in particular one with a figure in the drefs of the times, and a gold chain, of lady Philip, wife of Sir Matthew Philip, lord mayor of the city of London in 1463 (fee plate VIII. fig. 1.) fon of Arnold Philip of Norwich, with this infcription :

Orate fpecialiter pro anima Domine Ætine dudum uroris Mathei Phelp, aurifabri, ac quondam majoris civitatis London', que migrabit ab hac valle
miferie EEU° die Maii A° D'ni milleſimo CCCC°LEE° ; cujus an'e propitietur
Deus. Amen.

Which Weever gives thus :

Hic jacet corpus Chriftine dudum uxoris Matthei Philip, aurifabri, ac maioris Londonenfis, quæ obiit . . . . . 1470 ; pro cujus animæ falute velitis Deum orare.

This lord-mayor was created a knight of the Bath at the coronation of Elizabeth, queen of Edward IV. together with Sir Ralph Joceline, and Sir Henry Weever; and after that, with other aldermen, was knighted in the field, anno 1471.

---

* The prefent Gilbert Knowler, efq. who married, in 1754, Barbara, daughter of William Prefgrave, efq. furgeon, of Weftminfter. Having no iffue, he has fold the reverfion of this eftate, after his life, to Samuel Whitbread, efq. M. P. for Bedford, and refides at Canterbury.

The

The following account of bifhop Ridley's connection with this parifh is taken from Dr. Ridley's Life of that prelate.

" Mr. Nicholas Ridley was collated by archbifhop Cranmer to the vicarage of Herne, in Eaft Kent, April 30, 1538, vacant by the death of John Warren. Here he was diligent to inftruct his charge in the pure doctrines of the Gofpel as far as they were yet difcovered to him (not from the fchoolmen and popifh doctors) except in the point of Tranfubftantiation, from which error God had not yet delivered him. And the good fruits of his miniftry were feen in the effects it had, particularly on the lady Fiennes [rather Fineux] whom he converted to the Gofpel truths; which fhe afterwards teftified by her future exemplary life and good works. And to enliven the devotion of his parifhioners, he ufed to have the Te Deum read in his parifh-church in Englifh; which was afterwards urged in accufation againft him.

" For two years Mr. Ridley refided at his parifh of Herne, getting new lights himfelf by a clofe application to his ftudy of the holy Scriptures and the Fathers, by friendly conference with his patron the archbifhop [who frequently refided in the neighbourhood at his palace of Ford*], and faithfully communicating to his people the word of God. And while he was at Herne, he fo well difcharged his paftoral office, that he gained the general applaufe of the people in the adjacent parifhes, who, neglecting their own teachers, for many miles round would come to hear his fermons.

" In 1543 Dr. Ridley [being then alfo mafter of Pembroke-hall, Cambridge, and a prebendary of Canterbury] was prefented at the archbifhop's vifitation, for preaching at St. Stephen's againft auricular confeffion, and for having Te Deum fung in Englifh at Herne, where the faid " Mafter Doctor" was vicar.

---

* Of this palace a particular account may be feen in p. 152.

" Dr.

" Dr. Ridley fpent a great part of the year 1545 in retirement at Herne, and probably carrying with him an apology publifhed by the Zuinglians for their exploding the doctrine of Tranfubftantion, ftill in fome degree maintained by Luther and his followers, gave the queftion a fair examination, and difcovered its fophiftry. In point of authority too his eyes were opened by a fmall treatife written about the year 840 by Ratramus, or Bertram, a monk of Cologne, at the requeft of the emperor Charles the Bald, which had been publifhed at Cologne in 1532, and fully vindicated the doctrine from the charge of novelty. Dr. Ridley was no fooner convinced, than he ftrengthened his brethren, firft convincing archbifhop Cranmer, and in the following year, by Cranmer's means, old Latimer. And this was laying the axe to the root of popery.

" In May 1547 Dr. Ridley was prefented by the fellows of Pembroke-hall to the vicarage of Soham in Cambridgefhire, and in September following he was advanced to the fee of Rochefter, with which he held the vicarage of Herne in commendam, nor quitted it till he was tranflated to the fee of London in 1550, when Thomas Brooke (one of the fix preachers of Canterbury cathedral) fucceeded him."

In his laft farewell, when under fentence of death, to all the places with which he had been any way connected, Herne is thus diftinguifhed : " From Cambridge I was called into Kent by the archbifhop of Canterbury, Thomas Cranmer, that moft reverend father and man of God, and of him by and by fent to be vicar of Herne in Eaft Kent. Wherefore farewell, Herne, thou worfhipful and wealthy parifh, the firft cure whereunto I was called to minifter God's word. Thou haft heard of my mouth oft-times the word of God preached, not after the popifh trade, but after Chrift's Gofpel : Oh that the fruit had anfwered to the feed ! And

yet

yet I muſt acknowledge me to be thy debtor for the doctrine of the Lord's Supper, which at that time God had not revealed unto me : but I bleſs God in all that godly virtue and zeal of God's word, which the Lord by preaching of his word did kindle manifeſtly both in the heart and the life of that godly woman there my lady Fiennes * : the Lord grant that his word took like effect there in many more !"

Biſhop Ridley was burnt at Oxford, with biſhop Latimer, October 16, 1555.

Herne having a commodious bay and two ſworn, meters, ſeveral colliers frequent it from Sunderland, &c. and two hoys, of about 60 tons each, ſail alternately every week with corn, flour, hops, &c. to London   The ſoil is clayey.   Thirty-ſeven teams are kept in the pariſh.   It has about 17 acres of hops ; had lately double that number, and theſe are continually diſplanting.   It alſo produces much canary, of which it ſometimes has had 100 acres.

The pariſh raiſes to the land-tax, at 4*s.* in the pound, 342*l.* 16*s.*   To the poor-rate, at 3*s.* 486*l.* 18*s.*   Its annual rents, as rated to the latter, are 3179*l.* 10*s.*   It appears by the endowment that Reculver, Herne, St. Nicholas, Hoath, and All Saints, contained in the year 1310 above 3000 ſouls ; and theſe were continually increaſing.

In queen Elizabeth's reign a beacon was fixed in this pariſh on the hill where ſtands the windmill, as appears by a chart of the beacons in Lambard's Perambulation, drawn by the direction of Sir William *Brook*, *lord Cobham*, lord lieutenant of the county.

* This lady I ſuppoſe to be the ſame who was buried in the great chancel in 1539. See p 104.

EPITAPH

EPITAPH mentioned in p. 102.

M. S.

CHRISTOPHORI MILLES, armigeri;
qui, fexagefimum et alterum jam annum agens,
vicefimo fecundo Januarii, anno falutis 1700,
animi deliquio inter legendum correptus,
puncto temporis fato conceffit:
aliis quidem (quorum in rebus adverfis commodiffimum fe præbuit)
præmaturo:
fibi, ob vitam pulcherrimè actam,
fatis opportuno.
Erat fide, probitate, conftantiâ, atque imprimis continentiâ fingulari.
Juftitiam, ut privatus femper, ita non minus in magiftratu coluit.
Paterfamiliâs diligens, ac prudens;
ut fui non profufus, ita nec alienî appetens:
amicis beneficus, ac propter mores facillimos gratus omnibus,
fuis egregiè charus.
Ingenio ingens, judicio non minor,
quidquid ufui erat comparaverat fe magiftro;
præcipuè rerum gerendarum prudentiam;
Sermo pro moribus, proque indole fuit;
lenis, promptus, expeditus, ante omnia comis, modeftufque;
inerat cum gravitate lepos, fine dicacitate facundia,
recte præcepta verbis non invito, fed nec temere fequentibus.
Atque hæc vel folus, vel cum paucis habuit.
Sunt et alia communia, fed pro more memoranda tamen.
Uxores quatuor in matrimonium duxit,

Aliciam Roberti Sanders, de Maidftone in com' Cant. gent.
Sarah Samuelis Difbrowe, de Elfworth in com' Cantab. ar.
Margarettam Johannis Boys, de Betfhanger in com' Cant. ar.
Elizabetham Cheney Colepepper, de Leeds Caftle in com' Cant. * eq.
} Filiam.

Cumque ex omnibus parens factus effet,
ex fecundâ et tertiâ plures liberos fufcepiffet,
unum Samuelem ex fecundâ fuperftitem reliquit;
qui hoc quale quale pietatis in optimum patrem monumentum pofuit.
De primis duabus uxoribus loquitur marmor propinquum:
hoc ergo noluit defunctâ de tertiâ filere (quartâ fuperftite)
cui vir cordi, privigni ac fui in deliciis erant.
Virtus memoriam confecravit, et pofteris exemplum. Ob. Dec. 10, 1679, æt. 31.

---

* In the Englifh, therefore, p. 102, for 'Cheney Colepepper, efq.' read 'Sir Cheney
Colepepper, knt.'

EPITAPH mentioned in p. 103.

Posteris sacrum,
et felici memoriæ SAMUELIS MILLES, armigeri ;
quem siluisse et illi et tibi, lector, fuerat injurium ;
pulcherrimum enim defuisset exemplar
viri in omnibus tum civis, tum hominis, officiis probati :
qui scientiam juris, præcipuè municipalis,
(et erat cum paucis scientissimus)
ad sanctissimos usus accommodavit,
Inopiæ et innocentiæ paratus semper advocatus.
Cæteras laudes, quas angusta non capit tabula,
tuam quam honestissimè vitam instituendo,
tu, lector, quóvis melius epitaphio, supplebis.
Dum rebus interfuit humanis,
in curiis temporalibus dom' archiep' dec' et cap' Cantuar',
et monasterii divi Augustini,
cognitor præsedit ;
et a civitate vicinâ,
regnante Georgio primo,
ad parliamentum delegatus est.
Uxorem duxit Annam, sororem dom' Thomæ Hales, baronetti,
ex quâ sex filios et sex suscepit filias ;
quorum Christophorus natu maximus,
pietatis et gratitudinis ergo,
monumentum hoc optimo parenti dicavit.
Ob. 10 Decembris, A. D. 1727, suæqué ætatis 70.

F O R D.

F O R D - H O U S E.

This palace, which lies partly in the adjoining parifh, or borough, of Hoath, and partly in Chiflet, was the moft ancient feat belonging to the fee of Canterbury; being given to it by Ethelbert I. king of Kent, who, as has been faid, refided in the latter part of his reign at Reculver: but it was demolifhed about the year 1658, and the bricks, timber, and other materials fold to any purchafer*. Archbifhop Cranmer refided much at Ford. In particular we find him there in 1537, when the plague raged at Lambeth, and the Bible was firft publifhed in Englifh. And king Henry VIII. in one of his excurfions to the Continent, went in his barge to Gravefend, where he landed, and proceeded on horfeback to Ford, where he lodged that night with the archbifhop, and then continued his journey to Dover, where he embarked. Cranmer was there alfo in 1552, when he reviewed the Articles of Religion. And it is remarkable, that though he had had an ague that fummer at Croydon, he removed to Ford in October; a low fituation, and fo unhealthy, that archbifhop Parker would have pulled it down to repair and improve the palaces at Beakfbourn and Canterbury, but met with fuch delays in his fuit to the queen for that purpofe, as made him drop the defign †.

In 1613, November 2, archbifhop Abbot granted the office of keeper of Ford park to Sir Peter Manwood, knt. ‡; and it was confirmed to him by the dean and chapter of Canterbury ‖.

---

* Harris's Hift. of Kent, p. 157.   † Ibid.
‡ Chartæ Mifcellaneæ, in the MS. Library at Lambeth, vol. I. N° 34.
‖ Ibid. N° 33.

In

In 1620, Dec. 8, the fame archbifhop granted the cuftody of the manor and palace of Ford to Sir Thomas Perryn, knt. *; in 1625, July 15, to William Ayfone †; in 1628, April 12, to Sir Matthew Mennes, knt. ‡; to whom it was again granted Auguft 21, 1632 ‖; and in 1634, June 4, to Nicholas Robinfon §.

In 1627, on archbifhop Abbot's refufing to licenfe a fermon preached by Dr. Sibthorpe at Northampton affizes, in juftification of a loan which the king (Charles I.) had demanded, he was ordered by his majefty (July 5) to withdraw to Canterbury; which the archbifhop declined, becaufe he had at that time a law-fuit with that city, and defired he might rather have leave to go to his houfe at Ford, which was granted; and on the 9th of October a commiffion was given to five bifhops to exercife the archiepifcopal authority. But about Chriftmas his grace was fent for, and reftored to his power **.

An exemplification of all the archbifhop of Canterbury's privileges, eftates, and manors (granted to archbifhop Sheldon by king Charles II. October 31, in the 10th year of his reign ††) is preferved in the MS. Library at Lambeth; with an exemplification of a decree concerning the perpetual freeing of the fee of Canterbury from rebuilding Canterbury Palace, Ford Houfe, and Beakefbourn, 19 Charles II ‡‡.

I know of no view of this palace now in being. From the ruins of walls and the foundations that remain (fee plate VI.) little can be collected, but that the buildings were extenfive. The archiepifcopal records at Lambeth have, however, fupplied the following defcription from the Parliamentary Survey of 1647.

" The gate-houfe, or lodge, ufually the houfekeeper's, of four
" ground-rooms and three above, and two bays of outhoufing,

---

* Chartæ Mifcellaneæ, in the MS. Library at Lambeth, vol. I. N° 31.
† Ibid. N° 26.   ‡ Ibid. N° 44.   ‖ Ibid, N° 32.   § Ibid. N° 37.
** Rufhworth's Collections, vol. I.
†† Chartæ Mifcellaneæ, vol. XIII. N° 2.   ‡‡ Ibid. N° 1.

" all

" all built with brick, a fmall orchard and garden, with a dove-
" houfe, timber-built, covered with tile; in the whole, eight
" acres broad, with the park unftored with deer, containing
" 166 acres of gravelly and fandy land;   *l.   s.   d.*
 " Value *per annum,*   -   -   -   -   43 10 0
 " Broomfield, in the parifh of Herne, at 4*s.* per ⎱
  " acre *per annum,*   -   -   -⎰ 0 16 0

                44 6 0
 " Rent referved to the archbifhop,   -   -   20 0 0
 " Neat value,   -   -   -   -   24 6 0

 " Timber and pollards, about 300, valued at 90 *l.*
 " All the materials of all the buildings worth, to be fold,
  " 820 *l.*

 " The premiffes are within feven miles of Canterbury, and
" three from the fea.

 " The keeper of the houfe, ponds, and gardens, the park and
" the woods, in the lordfhip of Herne and Reculver, had a patent
" for three lives, with all pannage and herbage for fix cows and
" four horfes or geldings; the gate-houfe, or lodge, with dove-
" houfes, &c.; 2 *d. per diem*; and four cart-loads of wood out of the
" faid woods, and a livery with the gentlemen; and a claufe of
" diftrefs for the 2 *d.* per day of the herbage and pannage upon
" the manors of Herne and Reculver, or Chiflet, except the young
" pidgeons of the dove-houfe when the archbifhop refides at Can-
" terbury, or within twelve miles of it.

 " Belonging to the faid manor are two free commons lying in
" the parifh of Herne, one called Hunter-ftreet *, and the other
" Belting-green †, which are for the lord's tenants and any travel-
" lers and drivers to reft their cattle, containing in the whole fe-
" ven acres.

  ⁎ Now Hunter's-borftal.   † The prefent name.

                   " There

" There are two fairs; one at Reculver at Lady-day, and the
" other at Herne on the Friday before Easter yearly; and all
" worth 2 *d. per annum* each.

" Issuing out of the said manor a yearly pension of 2 *l.* to the
" vicar of Reculver *; and an acre of land, parcel of the manor ad-
" joining to Lord's mead, worth *per annum* 10 *l.*"

It appears by the register-book of Reculver that the archbishop
had a chapel there; "Francis, sonne of Sir Thomas Perryn, knight,"
being baptized in it " September 28, 1620†." Though why he
should be registered in Reculver rather than in Hoath, in which
the palace stood, I know not. Some of the walls have flues in
them, the use of which cannot be ascertained. Part of the old
gateway still remains. There seem also to have been fish-ponds,
a vineyard, and a park; which latter retains the name. And tradition says, that a turning in the Reculver road leading to Chislet
is called *Oxenden's corner*, from some of that family in ancient
times there making depredations on the archbishop's game, and
having frays with his keepers.

* ee p. 128.   † See p. 113.

D A U N D E L I O N,

A fashionable place of resort in the parish of St. John the Baptist in Thanet, was once the seat of a family in elder times called *Dent de Lyon** (lion's tooth), as appears by ancient deeds *temp.* Edw. I. About the reign of Henry IV. the name was changed to *Dandelion, Daundelyoun,* or *Daundeleon*; i. e. they wrote their name as it was pronounced or spoken, not as it was originally spelt. In that prince's reign this estate belonged to *John Daundelion,* as appears by several deeds of that age. He had issue *John Dandelion,* or *Daundelyon* (whose heiress about the beginning of the reign of Edward IV. married to —— *Petit,* of Shalmesford, near Chartham), and lies buried in the North chancel of St. John the Baptist's church, Margate, with his portraiture in brass, and this inscription :

Hic jacet Johannes Daundelyon, gentilman, qui obiit in die Invencionis Sancte Crucis, anno ab incarnatione Domini nostri Jesu Christi millesimo ccccxlv; cujus anime propicietur Deus.

From this alliance the ancient seat descended at last to Captain Henry Petit, who died Feb. 23, 1661, being then 30 years old, and by his two wives having had ten children, of whom five sons survived him. His epitaph, and those of several of the name, may be seen in Lewis's History of the Isle of Thanet, Col. p. 86—88.

It seems as if this seat was anciently walled round very strongly, according to the fashion of the age, for a defence against bows and arrows. Part of this wall is still standing with the gate-house †, built with bricks and flints in rows, with loop-holes and battlements at top. Over the gate are the arms of *Daundelyoun* (as in plate VII. fig. 2.) *viz.* Sable, three Lions rampant, between two bars dancette Argent. On the right hand of this gate is a smaller one for common use, at the right corner of which is a blank es-

* Philipot's Villare, p. 386.   † See a North view of it in plate VII.

cutcheon,

cutcheon, and at the left corner a demy lion, with a label out of his mouth, out of which is written *Daundelyon*, as reprefented in fig. 3. Under the right fide of it, as you go out of the gate from the place, was found in 1703 a room large enough to hold eight or ten men, in which were a great many pieces of lachrymatories of earth and glafs. Under the other fide of it is a well-prifon. Over this gate-houfe, betwixt the towers, has been erected a building of pannel-work for a pigeon-houfe. In the window of the manfion-houfe are the arms of *Daundeleon* quartered with thofe of the *Petits*, as reprefented in fig. 1 *.

The farm now belongs to Mr. *Bowers*; and the fpot being very picturefque, having a pleafant grove adjoining (a fingularity in Thanet), and a bowling-green fkirted with trees and flowers, open to the fea, is now become a kind of public place, as his fon-in-law, Mr. Thomas Staines, allures to it two mornings at leaft in every week, during the feafon, the principal company of Margate and Ramfgate, by adding to its natural beauties a band of mufic from London, and every accommodation for breakfaft and dinner, heightened by a courteous and obliging behaviour. The South view of this gateway, which has more work in it, particularly feveral layers of cut flints, is in Lewis, and has been frequently taken. The North view was alfo very neatly drawn, and prefented to the proprietor, in 1782, by George Cumberland, efq. of London.

* Lewis's Hiftory of the Ifle of Thanet, p. 149, 150.

COLLECTIONS relating to RECULVER and HERNE;

Extracted from the Records, Registers, &c. at Lambeth;

Communicated to the Editor by Dr. DUCAREL.

A. D. circa 1180.   BY a deed executed during the pontificate of Richard archbishop of Canterbury*, a pension of twenty pounds a year was settled on the Hospitals of St. Nicholas at Harbledown, and St. John's, Northgate, to be paid out of the church of Reculver, by the confent of Hugh the rector, in addition to the yearly fum of 140 pounds before granted by archbishop Lanfranc, the founder of thofe hofpitals, out of his manors of Raculfe and Boctun †.

1284.   In 1284, on a complaint from the parifhioners of the chapelry of All Saints, the vicar of Reculver was directed, by archbishop Peckham, by a deed dated at Aldyngton, v kal. May, to provide a refident prieft to officiate in that chapel. It was at the fame time decreed that the chapels of All Saints and St. Nicholas fhould be kept in repair at the joint expence of the whole parifh ‡.

1290.   By a charter of king Edward the Firft, dated Dec. 18, in the 19th year of his reign, and reciting letters patent of archbishop Peckham, dated at Otteford, non. Julii 1290, it appears that archbishop Kilwarby had appropriated the great tithes of Reculver to the hofpitals abovementioned, by way of exchange for the fums before that time paid to them by preceding archbifhops.

* Who had formerly been prior of Dover, and enjoyed the primacy from 1171 (according to fome writers) to Feb. 16, 1183; or, as others fay, to Feb. 17, 1184. See Le Neve.   † This curious deed is printed in p. 129.
   ‡ See this decree in p. 130.

This

This appropriation being found inconvenient to all parties, the church of Reculver was, by the charter abovementioned, restored to the fee of Canterbury in 1291 *.

In 1296, occurs a decree of archbifhop Winchelfea, dated at Reculvre, 3 id. April, concerning the oblations and alms in a certain cheft near the great ftone crofs between the church and chancel at Reculver †.

A. D. 1296.

In the fame year the archbifhop's mandate was iffued to the commiffary of the church of Reculver, directing what punifhment fhould be inflicted on perfons convicted of adultery, fornication, witchcraft, and other offences ‡.

1296.

In 1297, an inquifition occurs concerning the bounds of the parifhes of St. Nicholas and All Saints, in the ifle of Thanet, and the mother church of Reculver ‖.

1297.

In the fame regifter is a decree about the way or path belonging or leading to the chapel of All Saints, in Thanet §.

In 1299, 8 id. March, John de Langton, canon of Lincoln, who had intruded himfelf into the rectory of Reculver, was removed by archbifhop Winchelfea **.

1299.

In 1310, the vicarage of Reculver was endowed; and alfo the vicarages of St. Nicholas (with All Saints chapel) and Herne ††. An exemplification of this endowment, dated April 9, 1481 ‡‡, and another, June 17, 1598 ***, occurs in the archiepifcopal regifters. Archbifhop Secker alfo gave an exemplification of it to the late Mr. Rogers, which Mr. Duncombe now has.

1310.

* See this decree in p. 131. † See this decree in p. 133.
‡ See this order in p. 134.
‖ Inquifitio fuper finibus parochiar' Sci Nicholai et Omnium Sanctorum capell Infulæ de Taneto, et matrice eccl' de Reculver dependentium. Dat. 2 id. Mait. 1297. Reg. Winchelfea, fol. 240. a.
§ Ordinatio ftrate peitinentis ad capellam Omnium Sanctorum in Thaneto. Ibid. fol. 193. a. ** Reg. Winchelfea, p. 274. b. †† See this inftrument, p. 135.
‡‡ Exemplificatio ordinationis dictarum titum vicar' per Johannem Parmentai, commiffar' general'. Dat. 9 April. 1481. Reg. Bourchier, fol. 100, b.
*** Alia exemplificatio dictæ ordinationis per Johem Whitgift, Cant' archiep'. Dat. 17 Junii, A.D. 1598. Reg. Whitgift, pars III. fol. 93. a. b.

4 On

A. D.
1313.

On the 17th of February 1313, archbifhop Reynolds ob
tained from Edward II. the grant of a market *, to be holden
every Thurfday throughout the year, at his manor of *Reicolvre* †.

1314.

In 1314, 12 kal. Julii, Nicholas de Tyngewyck obtained a
difpenfation from archbifhop Reynolds for holding the rectory o
Reculver, together with that of Calelhull in the diocefe of Sarum ‡

1315.

In 1315, a decree of archbifhop Reynolds occurs, concerning
fome tithes in the parifh of Stourmouth belonging to the recto
of Reculver ‖.

1325.

In 1325, 5 id. Dec. the fame archbifhop gave full power t
Nicholas de Tyngewyck to hear and determine all complaint
and offences that came within the archiepifcopal jurifdiction a
Reculver and its dependent chapels §.

1332.

In 1332, Richard atte Broke granted to Henry de Suthreye anc
Chriftian his wife one acre of land in the parifh of Herne an
burgh of Thorndenne ** ; and in the following year John th
fon of Walter atte Broke renounced claim to half the faid acre ††.

1334.

In 1334, archbifhop Stratford, by an order dated at Cherrynge
10 kal. Nov. decided a difpute which had arifen between th
vicars of Reculver and Herne, on the right of burying the arch
bifhop's tenants in capite, by directing that they fhould in futur
be buried in the cemetery of the mother-church ‡‡.

1335.

In 1335, the fame archbifhop, on a complaint that the pa
rifhioners of Herne had refufed to bear their proportion of th
repairs of the mother-church, enjoined, by a decree dated at Lam

---

* Two miftakes may hence be corrected above, in the notes on p. 73. Th
error was originally occafioned by Philipot's miftaking the name of the archbifhop
which was *Walter*, not *William*. He was right in the name of the king, Edw. II.
 † This charter may be feen at large in p. 138.   ‡ See p. 139.
 ‖ Walteri Reynold, Cant' archiep', ordinatio fuper quibufdam decimis in parochi.
de Stourmouth, ad rectorem de Reculver pertinen'. Dat. apud Lambeth, 14 kal
Aprl. 1315. Chartæ Mifcellaneæ, inter MSS. Lambeth, vol. VI. N° 66.
 § See this commiffion in p. 140.
 ** Herbaldown Private Deeds, N° 77.   †† Ibid. N° 78.   ‡‡ See p. 145
                                                                          bet

beth on the ides of March, that they fhould in future be punc-
tual in their compliance, on pain of excommunication *. This
was followed by a fimilar decree, Lambeth, March 15, 1335†.

In 1330, archbifhop Stratford obtained a grant ‡ for a market A.D.
and fair at his manor of St. Nicholas, in the ifle of Thanet; 1336.
the market to be holden every Monday, and the fair on the
morrow of the Nativity of Saint Mary (Sept. 9.) and the following day.   In the fame deed is contained alfo a grant of a market
and fair at the archbifhop's manor of Gyllingham in Kent, the
market to be on Thurfdays, and the fair on the day of the Invention of the Holy Crofs, and feven following days.

In 1338, Walter Bayli granted to Henry, fon of Richard de 1338.
Sutherye and his wife, two acres in Thorndenne borough ‖.

In 1345, a grant occurs from James Bate to Nicholas de Under- 1345.
doune, of one acre and two roods at Gateheye, in Herne §.

In 1347-8, on the 16th of March, a licence was granted to 1347-8.
archbifhop Stratford ** (who died in the courfe of that year) for
appropriating the church of Reculver to the archbifhop's table;
and for payment of 160 l. a year out of the revenues of the fee
of Canterbury to the hofpitals of Harbledown and Northgate,
notwithftanding the ftatute of mortmain, &c.

In 1348, king Edward III. confirmed to the above hofpitals 1348.
their annual payment of 140 l. in cafe of a vacancy in the fee of
Canterbury ; and alfo the payment of a penny a day from the
archbifhop's manor of Limenge ††.

In 1356, Oct. 18, an affignment was made from Thomas de 1356.
Wiltone to Philip de Northwode of all his lands and tenements at
Henneford, in Herne, paying 40 s. to the hofpital of Northgate,
and 20 s. to Harbledown hofpital ‡‡.

---

* See p. 145.   † See p. 146.   ‡ See the charter in p. 140.
‖ Harbledown Private Deeds, N° 79.   § Ibid. N° 80.   ** See p. 141.
†† Harbledown Charters, N° 18.   The manor of *Leminge* was holden by the
archbifhop of Canterbury in demefne at the making of Domefday Book.
‡‡ In 1400 Thomas Sprynget demifed his manor of Henneford to John Barry ;
and in 1411 releafed to James Twitham all claim in that manor ; and in ten acres,
fix of them at Hare's in Childe, two at William's at Halkes, and two at States-
londe ; all purchafed of Philip Northwode. Northgate Private Deeds, N° 147, &c.

A.D.   In 1357, Ifolda, widow of Henry de Frokyngove, granted t
1357.   John Sewale two pieces of land at Frokyngove in Herne, contain
ing two acres *.

1359.   In 1359, John Sewale of Herne granted to Ifolda Southerye on
verft in Herne †; and Gedeline, the wife of John Sewale, renounce
claim to the faid land ‡.   Thomas Sewale made a like quit claim|
        In the fame year, John Sewale granted two fhillings a year t
Harbledown hofpital, out of the fame land §.

1361.   In 1361, a grant of John Arynburg, fenior, and others, con
cerning one quarter of barley iffuing out of a grange, one ftable
and 12 acres of land, at Weftbrooke.   Dated at Herne, 5 Sept
35 Edw. III. **.

1364.   In 1364, Salamon Butt granted to William atte Welle and other
three acres of land in Reculver, April 18, 38 Edw. III, which
were the fame day re-conveyed to feoffees ††; who fettled the
again on Salamon Butt, June 12, for the yearly rent of " one fea
" of barley," *unius fumme ordei* ‡‡.

1368.   In 1368, a commiffion of penance was given to the vicar c
Reculver, like that recited from archbifhop Winchelfey's regifter
p. 134; but to remain in force for one year only ||||.

1379.   In 1379, Nov. 1, Thomas Bargrave and others demifed to Ri
chard and John Lucas one acre in Herne, for their natural lives §§

1389.   In 1389, an exemplification was made of certain deeds relatin
to the church of Reculver ***.

1395.   In 1395, Robert Baker renewed the grant of a quarter of bar
ley †††, which in 1399 was releafed by Dionyfius atte Stone ‡‡‡
and in 1401 was again granted by J. Prowde and J. Chirche||||||.

---

* Harbledown Piivate Deeds, N° 81.   † Ibid. N° 82.   ‡ Ibid. N° 83
|| Ibid. N° 84.   § Ibid. N° 85.   ** Ibid. N° 86.
†† See p. 143.   ‡‡ See p. 143.
|||| Item facta fuit commiffio pœnitentiar' vicar' de Recolvre pro parochianis fuis
dat' apud Heggefton, non' Marcii, 1368, per ann' tantummodo duratui'.   Reg. Wit
tlefey, fol. 4. b.   §§ Northgate Hofpital Private Deeds, p. 146.
*** See this exemplification at large, p. 142.
††† Harbledown Private Deeds, N° 87.   ‡‡‡ Ibid. |||||| Ibid. N° 88.

In 1415, June 15, Henry Gate was collated to the Hermitage A.D. of Reculver *. 1415.

In 1445, archbifhop Stafford granted to his faithful fervant John 1445. Pawlyn fix acres of land in Billing +.

In 1452, Oct. 29, Matthew Phelip, alderman of London ‡, 1452. affigned to Henry Harder fix acres near the rectory at Herne, for the ufe of Northgate hofpital ||.

In 1461, Hugh Cherlton, clerk, and William atte See, 1461. gave to the two hofpitals one acre in Herne, called Goldland, late Robert Byfmer's §.

In 1466, Oct. 14, a leafe was granted from the hofpital of 1466. Northgate to Robert Hunt, of Hothe, in Reculver, of two acres and three roods, called Brotherynlond, for ten years; rent 3 s. 4 d. ⁑

In 1477, William Taylore, otherwife Paramour, and others, 1477. granted to Richard Dererd two acres of land in Thornden bo- rough in Herne ++; which Dererd afterwards granted to Harble- down hofpital ‡‡.

In 1492, a grant of James Chirche to Harbledown hofpital of 1492. fixteen pence a year at Le Platts in the burgh of Strode, and pa- rifh of Herne |||| ; and another grant from the fame Chirche of eight pence a year out of a meffuage and three acres of land in Strode burgh at Herne §§; and alfo of eight pence a year and two acres and a half at Stockgrove in Thornden in Herne ⁂.

In 1528, an agreement between Thomas Nightingale, vicar of 1528. the parifh and mother-church of Reculver, John Coke and John Cobbe, churchwardens of the faid church, and Henry Holande,

* 15 Junii, 1415, apud London' Dñs contulit Henrico Gate ad hermitagium de Reculver, vacant', ut dicitur, et ad fuam collationem pleno jure fpectant'. Reg. Chicheley, fol. 64. b.

† See p. 153. ‡ Afterwards lord mayor. See his wife's epitaph in p. 106,
|| Northgate Hofpital Private Deeds, N° 153.
§ Ibid. N° 156. ** Ibid. N° 162.
†† Harbledown Private Deeds, N° 89. ‡‡ Ibid.
Ibid. N° 92. §§ Ibid. N° 93. *** Ibid. N° 94.

vicar

vicar of St. Nicholas in Thanet, and John Everard and Robert Abraham, chapel-wardens and inhabitants of that parifh, before archbifhop Warham, concerning the repairs of the faid mother-church *.

A.D.
1589.   In 1589, a decree of archbifhop Whitgift concerning the faic compofition, dated 31 Aug. 1589 †.

1632.   In 1632, April 2, John Welby, junior, affigned to the hofpita at Northgate two acres and a half of arable in Haweburgh, and a tenement, garden, and two acres adjoining, at Childforftal, alia Herft, near the common in Herne, for 60l. ‡

1637.   Letter to archbifhop Laud, from the lords of the council requiring him to proceed with all expedition in a caufe depend ing before him, between the inhabitants of Reculver and thof of the chapelries of St. Nicholas and Herne, touching th repair of the church and fteeple of Reculver; dated from White hall, the laft day of December, 1637 ‖.

A lift of the rectors and vicars of RECULVER, from the archi epifcopal regifters, may be feen in p. 154—156; and of th chantry priefts there, p. 157, 158.

The vicars of HERNE will be found in p. 159, 160.

---

* Compofitio inter Tho' Nightingale, vicar' eccl' paroch' et matricis de Reculver Joh' Cocke & Jo' Cobhe, economos, five bonorum cuftodes, eccl' predict', et mag Hen' Holande, vicar' capellæ Sci Nicholai in Thanet, et Joh' Everard et Rob' Abra ham, economos, five bonorum cuftodes, ejufdem capellæ, & parochianor' inhabitant' coram dno Will' (Warham) Cant' archiep', de annua folutione III s. IIII d. et fupe confectiione et reparatione dicte matricis eccl'. Dat' apud Cant', 24 Aug' 1528 Reg. Whitgift, pars 1. fol. 257. a. b.   † Ibid. fol 261.

‡ This purchafe was probably with a fine paid by the countefs of Winchelfea in confequence of an agreement made (by allowance of archbifhop Abbot) betweer her ladyfhip and the prior and brethren, after a verdict given at a trial in the Guild hall, Canterbury, in 1626, in favour of the countefs; who engaged to pay annuall 13s. 4d. to the hofpital, with arrears from 1564, amounting to 44l. 13s. 4d. and t add 20l. provided to l. wete laid out for the benefit of the hofpital; the prio and brethren, in return, renouncing all claim on the lands at Herft. Privat Deeds of Northgate Hofpital, Nos 33. and 147.

‖ Reg. Laud, pars 1. fol. 286. a. b.

T W

TWO LETTERS from the Rev. Mr. GREEN* ;
Communicated by Dr. DUCAREL, from a MS. in the Lambeth Library,
intituled, " Notitia Parochialis," and marked N° 1605, 1606.

IT is certain the church of RECULVER is one of the moſt ancient churches in
Kent ; and, if any credit may be given to an inſcription written upon the ſouth-
eaſt part of the ſaid church, in old Engliſh†, over a ſmall chancel or cemetery, king
Ethelbert was buried there. By whom it was founded is uncertain: whether the church
now ſtanding was the ancient pariſh church ſeems to me doubtful. Reculver,
being once the ſeat of a king, was ſo populous, that it ſeems to me improbable that
the preſent church could contain the people ; and the current tradition of the
place is, that the pariſh church ſtood about a mile into the ſea, upon a place called
by the inhabitants " The Black Rock;" which ſhews itſelf at low water. The preſent
church ſeems to me to be built for the uſe of the religious houſe within the walls.
The ſea has ſwallowed up one half of the pariſh ; and, with the *terra firma*, the
ancient pariſh-church that ſtood upon it. This tradition of the place ſeems to me
not improbable. About the year 1271, Archbiſhop Kilwardby appropriated
that church and the hoſpitals of Harbledown and Northgate, " ſalvo perpetuo
" vicario qui in dictâ eccleſiâ curam haberet animarum congruâ porcione."
About the year 1279, Archbiſhop Peckham diſappropriated that church, " &
" revocabat eam in priſtinum ſtatum." In the book of taxations of eccleſiaſtical
livings made in 1281 it is mentioned, that the church of Reculver had theſe
chapels thereunto annexed, viz. Hoath, St. Nicholas, All Saints, and Herne.
It is very probable that, for many years before that taxation, thoſe chapels were
annexed to that mother-church. In the year 1310 Archbiſhop Winchelſey, reciting
that one Nicholas de Tyngewyk was then rector of that church, did ordain three
vicarages, " unam videlicet in eccleſiâ de Reculver, cujus vicarius perpetuus in
" ipſâ & capellâ adjacente de Hoth, & aliam in capellâ Sci Nicolai in Thaneto, cu-
" jus vicarius in ipſâ & capellâ Omnium Sanctorum, necnon & tertiam in capellâ de
" Herne, cujus vicarius in ipſâ animarum ſub rectore qui pro tempore fuerit curam
" gerent & perſonaliter exercebunt ;" and appointed that the vicar of Reculver ſhould
in that church, and in the chapel of Hoath, have " decimas fœni, lini," and all
ſmall tithes, " cum decimis garbarum in hortis clauſis, & a pede foſſis," and certain
yearly penſions from the vicars of St. Nicholas and Herne ; and that the vicar of
St. Nicholas ſhould have the like tithes in St. Nicholas and All Saints, and the
vicar of Herne ſuch tithes in Herne. In the year 1311, Clement VI. granted to
the then Archbiſhop of Canterbury [Reynolds], that, " cedente vel decedente rectore de
" Reculver," the ſaid church, with the chapels, ſhonld be appropriated " menſæ

* It does not appear to whom the above letters are addreſſed, nor have they any date ; but it
muſt have been between 1695 and 1716, the time of Mr. Green's incumbency. See p. 156.
† See it, p. 72.

" aſ-

" archiepifcopali Cant';" and that the archbifhop fhould appoint a congruous portion for the vicar to be there maintained, with this provifo, " Quod ecclia parochia-
" lis & capellæ prædictæ debitis obfequiis non frauderentur, & quod in eis cultus
" divinus & confuetus miniftiorum numerus non minuerentur." In the ftate the
faid Clement put the church of Reculver it continues to this day. The archbifhop
collates. It is endowed with a vicarage-houfe, and about three acres of glebe;
one acre of which is marfh land. It is alfo endowed with all fmall tithes, and
the great tithes of all land lying within the walls that environ the church and the
fite of the monaftery *, which I compute to be about eleven or twelve acres. It
has alfo an augmentation granted of twenty pounds a year, paid out of the parfonage of Herne, Reculver, and Hoath, in the hands of Samuel Milles, Efq paid
half yearly; ten pounds at Lady-day, and the like fum of ten pounds at Michaelmas. Herne pays annually a penfion of forty fhillings, the one half at Lady-day,
the other at Michaelmas. The parifh of St. Nicholas, with the chapelry of All
Saints (now dilapidated) thereto annexed, pays to the vicar of Reculver yearly the
fum of three pounds; and this penfion is paid alfo half yearly at Lady-day and
Michaelmas. I muft not forget alfo to add, that, when the faid vicarages were ordained, there were certain penfions ordained yearly to be paid by the parifhes of
Herne and St. Nicholas, towards the keeping of the mother church of Reculver in
repair. Herne pays annually the fum of five fhillings, and St. Nicholas the annual
fum of three fhillings and four pence. Thefe fums the parifhes aforefaid are obliged
to pay on Monday in Whitfun-week; and for default or nonpayment of the
faid fums upon the faid day, they are liable to be equally rated and affeffed with
the parifhioners of Reculver and Hoath, towards the repairs of the faid church.
About threefcore years ago the parifhes aforefaid neglected or refufed to pay the
faid penfions; whereupon the churchwardens of the parifh of Reculver made an
equal affeffment upon all the lands in Herne, St. Nicholas, and Reculver, towards
repairing the faid church; which affeffments, as appears by the church books now
extant, were punctually paid by the faid parifhes for three years together (fo long,
I prefume, the fuit betwixt the parifh of Reculver and the parifhes of Herne and
St. Nicholas lafted); but afterwards they complied to pay the penfions, and fo have done
(as they have good reafon) ever fince. The fuit was managed, on the part of Reculver, by one Mr. Cobb of Bifhopfton in Reculver, one of whofe anceftors was
York herald at arms, and lies buried in the chancel of Reculver†. I think myfelf
obliged in gratitude to mention this gentleman's name; becaufe it is in a great
meafure owing to his indefatigable care and application in fearching records and
managing this fuit, that thefe penfions were not then loft. And here I cannot well
forget the piety of John Hills, a farmer, who lived at Brooke in the parifh of Reculver, partly to preferve his memory, and partly to provoke others of ability to

---

* Agreeably to the original endowment. See p. 137.
† See h s epitaph, p. 73.—He married a Cobb, of this county, and feems to have been the
man who made the remarks on Camden's Britannia; which poffibly he did out of fpite and re-
venge, becaufe he miffed the place of Clarencieux. The author of Camden's Life faith, this
man's name was in reality Brookfmouth, but that he contracted it to Brook, becaufe he thought it
founded better.   Dr. HARRIS.

follow

follow his example. This good man, befides three pounds a year and upwards'
which he gave to the labourers of Reculver for ever, gave to the church a large
Bible and a pulpit cloth, a large filver flaggon, chalice, and falver, for the communion fervice, and a very fine damafk table-cloth to fpread upon the altar.

The church of Reculver is lofty and well built; it has two fteeples in front, in one
of which hang four bells; thefe fteeples were built, if we believe the tradition of
the place, by two fifters; and, as appears by all the fea charts I have feen, are of great
ufe in carrying fhips over the flats, to and from London. The chancel is large and
lofty; it has two ftately pillars to fupport its entrance, and a curious afcent to the
altar; fo that it is exceeded by few in Kent. I could fend you the infcriptions that
are in the church, if I thought them neceffary; and you may command them at any
time by letter. I have given you the beft account of my church and chapel I am
able; and am, Sir, Your very humble fervant, F. GREEN.

My church, by the ill neighbourhood of the fea, and being too indulgent a mother, in giving large portions to her two daughters Herne and St. Nicholas, is
now left the pooreft of the three.

L E T T E R II.

THE chapel of HOATH, alias Hoth, annexed to the vicarage of Reculver,
was dedicated " in honorem gloriofæ virginis Mariæ genetricis Dei & fuæ cru-
" cis vivificæ;" and the feaft of its dedication was yearly celebrated on the 19th day
of December. The chapel is diftant from Reculver about four miles; and fo probably was built at the charge of the inhabitants, to fave themfelves the trouble of
going to the mother-church to hear divine offices. The chapel is very ancient; built,
when Reculver was a rectory, long before the Reformation, in the year 1303 Boniface VIII. in a faculty which he granted concerning the faid chapel of Hoath,
after he had therein recited that he was informed by fome of the parifhioners that
many of them dwelt three miles, or thereabouts, from the church of Reculver, and
that in the winter-time they could hardly bring their dead bodies to that church,
and that the chapel of Hoath was canonically founded within the parifh, " & cum
" fontibus baptifmalibus erecta in quâ," they heard divine fervice and received the
holy facrament, " per facerdotes ad hæc per rectorem dictæ ecclefiæ deputandos,"
did, upon their petition, give leave that they might make and have a church-yard
near that chapel to bury their dead in. In the year 1410, Archbifhop Arundel
dedicated this chapel, and granted " fepulturam" there; and ordered that the vicar
of Reculver fhould not by that ordinance be prejudiced in the oblations or other
rights to him due or accuftomed: " nec ipfum vicarium ad capellani alicujus in-
" ventionem, feu ad aliqua alia onera in eâdem capellâ ultra folitum aftringi
" nolumus vel teneri." He and the then inhabitants there bound themfelves,
with their fucceffors, to obey thefe ordinances. In the year 1360, one Thomas
Newe *, being vicar of Reculver, for the perpetual difcharge of himfelt and fuccef-

* In 1354 he was rector of Aldington, and is defcribed in Abp. Iflip's regifter (fee p. 157) as
" dudum vicar' eccl' paroch' de Raculvre." In 1371 he occurs in Abp. Wittlefey's regifters (fee
p. 157) as " rect' eccl' de Godmerfham."

fors from officiating in the cure of Hoath, and for furnifhing the burghers with a conftant and refident prieft, to attend them at all needs, founded in Hoath chapel a perpetual chauntry to be ferved by a refiding prieft; who, befides the duty of the chauntry, fhould officiate in the cure there; which chauntry was endowed with competency of means, and the prieft accommodated with a houfe and glebe.   From the foundation of the chauntry till the diffolution, the cure of Hoath became duly ferved " in divinis" by the chauntry-prieft thereof; the vicar of Reculver in the interim being quit of all care thereof, or attendance thereon.   Since the diffolution of the chauntry, frequent difputes have happened between the burghers of Hoath and the vicars of Reculver; the vicars often neglecting the cure of Hoath for fome years together; holding and pleading themfelves acquitted of the cure by that ancient provifion made touching the fame by Newe, their predeceffor: and this their plea was allowed by the vifitors in Queen Mary's days, and by Archbifhop Abbot in his time, after a fuit between the burghers of Hoath and one Mr. Barnabas Knell *, vicar of Reculver; which depended fome years.   The chauntry houfe and lands may be eafily traced.

Query,   Whether there be no way to recover the revenues of the chauntry, and to revive the chapel therewith?   And whether the ftatute 37 Henry VIII. could reach or rightly feize the fame; in regard they were not given principally to a fuperftitious end, but towards the maintaining of divine fervice?

There is a penfion of 40 s. paid by Ford, a feat of the Archbifhops of Canterbury, demolifhed in the late unhappy times of rebellion.   Its patron and tithes the fame with Reculver; they do not amount to 14 l. a year.

* Who became vicar in 1602. See p. 155.

Among the Private Deeds of Harbledown Hofpital, Nos. 65, 66, and 67, are terriers; in which occur,

De terra de *Reycolfer*, Robert Clay folvit IIII s. p an. & John Littelle II s. Alfo Solomon Hachard and Thomas his brother II s.

The land in *Reculv'* of Sand' Hallet to pittance III s. iv d.

Ifolda wife of Henry Southereye II s. out of a croft called Brokesfeld in *Herne*.

The land of John a Churche in *Herne* to pittance III s.

The lands in *Herne* to pittance XXII s. II d.

Harbledown Hofpital receives at prefent, from 50 acres rented in *Herne* by Mr. Tucker (one third of the rent)   4 l. 13 s. 4 d.
And from fome other lands in that parifh   10

Northgate Hofpital receives, from lands there called Childforftal,	2	10	0
From the 50 acres rented by Mr. Tucker (two thirds of the rent)	9	6	8
From 28 acres and a half, Mr. Hubbard's,	6	11	0
From 1 acre and a half, Mr. Pembroke's,	0	10	0
From 3 acres and three quarters in *Reculver*,	1	15	0
From Brotherhood clofe, in *Hode*,	0	10	0

3   C H A R T E R S

CHARTERS and other RECORDS
relating to RECULVER and HERNE.

Charta Ricardi Archiepi Cant'. Dat' inter A. D. 1171 & 1184.

(In dorfo.) Donatio xx librarum ex ecclia de Reculver ultra cxl li. prius conceff' ex maneriis de Raculfe & Boctun.

From the Charters of Harbledown Hofpital.

An old copy of this charter begins, " Copia fcripta ex libro antiquo de Recol-
" vere, qui quidem liber dicitur Textus quifitus p fres de Northgate."

RIC' Dei gra Cant' archiep'*, tocius Anglie primas, univ̄fis-s̄ce m̄ris ecclie filiis ad quos littere ifte pvenerint, eīnam in Dūo falt'. Res gefta fc̄pto pvide
commendat' ne pceffu tēporis aut a memoria decedat, aut aliqua malignantium verfu-
tia infirmetur. Eappter ad omnium notitiam volum' pvenire, quod cum olim bone
memorie Lanfranc' pdeceffor n̄r duo hofpitalia, unum fcilicet apd Herebald', &
aliud apd Cant' extra Norgate, inftituiffet, & ad fuftentationem fr̄m hinc leproforum,
illinc claudorum, cecorum, & debilium, fepties viginti libras fterling' de duob'
maneriis, videlicet de Raculfe & Boctun, annuatim pcipiendas affignaffet, tandem ad curam & regimen s̄ce Cant' ecclie, licet indigne, Dūo tam' difponente vocati, cum pdictas
fepties xx libras ad fuftentationem hofpitalium minime fufficere, & fres eorundem
hofpitalium graviffima pauptate & inedia videremus laborare, defiderio defideramus
eor' paupertati & infufficientie fubvenire : Quod quidem diu in animo volventes &
revolventes, commodius & plenius adimpleri poffe non credidimus quam in ecclia de
Raculve, que in manerio de Raculve fundata eft, de quo ex parte maxima reddit'
pdictar' fepties xx librarum annuatim pvenire debet : Cum ergo dilectus filius
nofter Hugo, perfona ejufdem ecclie, fuper hoc diligenter admonitus, reverenter &
devote divina pveniente gra ammonicionibus āris obtemperando eccliam ipfam libere nob' refignaffet, pdictis hofpitalib' & frib' eorundem hofpitalium in fupradicta ecclia viginti libras fterling' in fefto Sci Johis annuatim pcipiendas, in liberam &
perpetuam elemofinam conceffimus & affignavimus, ita quidem quod refiduum fructuum ipfius ecclie in n̄ra & fuccefforum ārorum manu & poteftate refidebit fecūm

* See p. 118.

U

dm

dm ficut nob' placuerit difponendum. Un' volumus & ea qua fungim' auctoritate pcipimus quod pdicta hofpitalia & fres in eis degentes habeant & percipiant annuatim ficut diximus in pnoiata eccla xx libras fterling'. Et ut hec ura donatio firma & incolvulfa pmaneat, eam pfenti fcripto & figilli uri appone decrevimus confirmare; ftatuentes & fub interminatione anathematis phibentes ne quis hanc ure confirmationis paginam infringere aut ei aliquatenus temere contrarie pfumat. Teftibus hiis, Gerardo [a] epo & Moyfe priore Coventr', magro Petro Bleffen' [b] Bathon', Willo Gloceftr' archidiaconis; magro Henr' Northampton, Willo de Honorio, capellanis; magro Rob' de Ingleham, magro R. de Rulveftun', magro Rad' de Sco. Martino, magio Rog' Norwic', Rogo Decano, magro Armico, Thoma de Newefole, Ric' Lundon', Galfr' Forte, Euftachio elemofinario, Michale de Burnes, Willo Sotewaene, & pluribus aliis.

Ordinatio inter Parochianos Capellarum Omnium Sanctorum & Sancti Nicholai in Thaneto, 1284.

From the Regifters of Archbifhop Peckham, fol. 206. b.

UNIVERSIS, &c. frater Johannes [c], &c. intelligimus nuper dilectis filiis ecclefie feu capelle Omnium Sanctorum in Thaneto parochianis nobis informantibus quod vicarius ecclefie de Racolvre aftrictus, tam de jure quam de confuetudine approbata & hactenus optenta pacifice & quiete, ad inveniend' unum presbyterum celebratione in capella Omnium Sanctorum in Thaneto commorantem affidue & etiam pernoctantem, ad preftand' facramenta & facramentalia ecclefiaftica parochianis ibidem, necnon & ad faciend' fervicium divinum, matutinas, vefperas, & alias horas canonicas, presbyterum & fervicium hujus propria auctoritate fubtraxit minus jufte, quodque ex hoc contingit quod parochiani dicte capelle Omnium Sanctorum, que per ceteros fines five limites divifa fuerat antiquitus, ut dicitur, capellam ipfam deferere, & vicinas ecclefias adire, divina audituri, ac facramentalia ecclefiaftica recepturi, funt coacti. Nos, volentes periculis in hac parte iminentibus obviare, & animarum nobis fubditarum faluti induftria quanta poffumus providere, inquifitionem fuper hiis ex officio noftro per viros fide dignos fieri fecimus fpecialem; verum tranfmiffa nobis inquifitione eadem & tam parochianorum capelle Sancti Nicholai quam eciam

---

[a] According to Le Neve, Gerard la Pucelle was confecrated Bp. of Litchfield and Coventry, Sept. 25, 1183.
[b] Le Neve likewife mentions, on the authority of Gervafe, col. 1464, 1490, that Henry fucceeded Peter Blefenfis in the Archdeaconry of Bath in 1182. But it appears from this inftrument, to which he is a witnefs, that he enjoyed that Archdeaconry in 1183.
[c] Archbifhop Peckham.

Omnium

Omnium Sanctorum nec non procuratoris dicti vicarii specialis ac aliorum quoru n intererat ad hoc notatorum presencia publicata clerici & commissarii nostri negot i circumstantiis & articulis in dicta inquisitione consideratis, ac etiam discussionibu, habitis inter procuratorem & capellarum parochianos antedictos ; ordinarunt vice nostra, decreverunt, & etiam pronunciarunt juxta tenorem inquisitionis supradicte, quod vicarius de Racolvre qui pro tempore fuerit suis proprus sumtibus inveniet unum presbiterum in dicta capella Omnium Sanctorum, matutinas, vesperas, ac alias horas canonicas celebrantem, & in eadem parochia assidue pernoctantem, ipsius loci parochianis, prout in inquisitione eadem plenius continetur, ecclesiastica sacramenta & sacramentalia prestiturum. Decreventes insuper ut quociens altera capellarum Omnium Sanctorum & Sancti Nicholai predict' reparacione indigeat in futurum, utriusque parochiani ad reparacionem hujus pro rata porcionis contribuant in perpetuum, & quodnam vicarius de Racolvre quam eciam parochiani supradicti ad premissa in posterum facienda & etiam observanda per quemlibet loci ordinarium per quamcunque censuram ecclesiasticam quociens opus fuerit sine judiciali strepitu compellantur, ipsorum procuratoris & parochianorum capelle utriusque consensu ad hoc expresso accedente. Nos autem quod per clericos & commissarios nostros ac procuratorem & parochianos in hac parte actum est & consensu ratum habentes & firmum id auctoritate nostra confirmamus. In quorum omnium testimonium, & eorundem perpetuam firmitatem, has literas utriusque capelle parochianis concessimus sigilli nostri munimine roboratas. Dat' apud Aldyngton, v kal' Maii, anno Dñi MCCLXXXIIII, Ordin' ñri sexto.

Confirmatio Edwardi I. de Revocatione Ecclie de Reculver ad cameram Archiepiscopalem Cant'; et ut Hospitalia sustineantur ex redditibus ipsius Archiepi, 1291.

From the Charters of Harbledown Hospital.

EDWARDUS Dei gra rex Angl', dominus Hibernie, & dux Acquitanie, omnibus ad quos presentes littere pervenerint saltm. Inspeximus litteras patentes venerabilis patris Johis Cantuar' archiepi, super revocatione ecclie de Racolvere in statum pristinum, in hec verba : " Universis sancte matris ecclie filiis ad quorum noti-
" tiam presens scriptura pervenerit, frater Johes[a] permissione divina Cantuar' ar-
" chiepus totius Anglie primas salutem in Domino sempiternam. Dudum bone
" memorie dñs Robtus[b] predecessor noster ut cameram archiepalem ab onere presta-
" tionis cujusdam magne quantitatis pecunie quam de Herbaldon leprosor' & de
" Northgate pauperum hospitalia nostre diocef' pro sustentatione infirmorum & pau-
" perum ipsorum hospitalium ex antiqua consuetudine consueverunt annuatim perci-

---

[a] Abp. Peckham.   [b] Abp. Kilwardby.

U 2

" pere,

" pere, & tam beati Thome ᵃ quam alior' archiᵉpor Cantuar' fucceffor' ipfius tem-
" pore ufque ad tempus ejufdem Roberti continue perceperant, liberaret, eccliam
" de Racolvere ejufdem diocef' ad liberam collacionem Cantuar' archiepi perti-
" nentem in proprios ufus ipfis hofpitalibus in compenfationem ejufdem quantitatis
" conceffit, capituli Cantuar' ad hoc procurato confenfu : Nos autem prefato Ro-
" berto immediate permittente Dño fuccedentes, ac advertentes follicite memoratam
" appropriationem in ecclie ac hofpitalium predictor' grave prejudicium & jactu-
" ram multipliciter redundare ; cum & ecclia ipfa ex hoc debitis & ab antiquo
" confuetis defraudetur obfequiis, & animarum curam non abfque gravi periculo
" in eam dampnabiliter negligatur ; quodque parochiani ejufdem ecclie ipfam
" leprofis fubeffe, ac hujufmodi appropriationem molefte ferentes, pro eo quod ipfis
" rectoris folacio deftitutis, per eam fuffragia fpualia fubtrahuntur, eis de viribus ip-
" fius ecclie non refpondent, ficque dca hofpitalia de redditibus ipfius ecclie, licet
" plus valere dicantur, debitam nequeant percipere quantitatem. Volentes quo-
" que animar' faluti & dictor' hofpital' utilitat.bus in hac parte confulere, & tam
" in fpualibus parochianorum, quam in temporalibus hofpitalium predictor' com-
" modius providere, fanctiffimi pa'ris Dni Nichi Pape quarti ad hoc per litteras
" apoftolicas concurrente beneplacito & mandato, ac etiam pronunciato per execu-
" torum litterar' earundem hoc debere fieri, conceffaque nobis ab eo fuper revoca-
" tione hujufmodi libera faculate, necnon capituli ñri Cantuar', dictor' hofpitalium
" parochianor', & ipforum Cuftodis hofpitalium accedente confenfu, eccliam de
" Racolvere fupradictam in ftatum priftinum revoc·mus, & archiepalem cameram
" juxta priftinam ordinationem & confuetudinem predictam ad eandem pecunie quan-
" titatem quam ante appropriationem hujufmodi ab ipfo percipere confueverant
" dictis hofpitalibus annis fingulis perfolvendam pro nobis & fucceforibus noftris
" inperpetuam obligamus. In cujus rei teftimonium, prefentem fcripturam figilli
" ñi fecimus appenf'one muniri. Dat' apud Otteford non' Julii, anno dni Mcc
" nonagefimo, ordinacionis ñre duodecimo." Nos autem predictam revocationem
& oneracionem camere archiepalis (ant' ad fuftentationem infirmorum predictor'
fic ordinatam igras habentes & gratas, eas pro nobis & heredibus noftris quantum in nobis eft concedimus & confirmamus, ficut littere predicte racionabiliter teftantur. Tefte meipfo apud Weftmon', decimo octavo die Decembr', anno regni ñri
decimo nono.

(Broad feal very well preferved.)

ᵃ Abp. Becket.

Ordinatio inter Vicar' de Reycolvre & Parochianos ejufdem, fuper Oblationibu in trunco in Ecclefia reponend', & de delatione clavium ejufdem & ceteris que patent', 1296.

From the Regifters of Archbifhop Winchelfey, fol. 185, b. 186, a.

IN nomine Domini, Amen. Cum nos Robertus [a] Dei gratia Cantuar' archiepifcopus, totius Anglie primas, ecclefiam de Reculvre cum fuis capellis noftre dioc' vifitantes inter cetera inveniremusquafdam contentiones inter ecclefie fupradicte vicarium & parochianos ejufdem fuiffe fubortas, videlicet, fuper oblationibus feu elemofiris in quodam trunco juxta magnam crucem lapideam inter ecclefiam & cancellum repofitis, & de modo hujufmodi oblationes feu elemofinas colligendi, confervandi, ac eciam erogandi, ipfis parochianis afferentibus obventiones eafdem per eos & non per alios recepi, colligi, confervari, & tam ad ecclefie & cancelli fabricam ac reparationem defectuum ipforum ecclefie, & cancelli, & librorum, ornamentorum, & veftimentorum ejufdem, quarum fabrice & reparationum onus de confuetudine iidem parochiani agnoverant hactenus & agnofcunt, & non per alium colligi, nec ad ufus alios erogari debere prefato vicario conquerenteac etiam afferente quod dicti parochiani per feipfos fine vifu alicujus miniftri ecclefie dictas obventiones colligunt, & per varias fuafiones populum imbi confluentem, ac etiam ejufdem ecclefie parochianos, follicitant & inducunt ut oblationes quas ad' magnum altare facere vellent, & quas tam in purificationibus mulierum quam in fponfalibus & pro defunctis fepeliendis confuetum eft fieri, ad crucem offerant antedictam; ipfum vicarium, & vicariam fuam predictam fuo jure, per fuafiones hujufmodi defraudentes, quodque obventiones hujufmodi profua voluntate in ufus alios, non ad premiffa, diftribuunt & convertunt: Nos demum volentes tam ecclefie quam perfonis fervata in omnibus ut convenit debita honeftate profpicere; de premiffis precipimus, ac etiam ordinamus, ut dictus truncus fub quatuor clavibus conferratur, quarum unus ecclefie fupradicte vicarius, & duo parochiani loci ejufdem ad id p communitatem parochianorum electi duas alias, & quartam unus parochianus ecclefie feu capelle de Herne electus fimiliter a communitate parochianorum ejufdem, habeant, & in fefto nativitatis beate virginis unus ipfius ecclefie clericus indutus fuperpellitio, una cum duobus vel tribus parochianis dicte ecclefie fibi affiftentibus fi voluerint, obventiones colligant antedictas, & eas ftatim in prefato trunco reponant, nulla fuafione aut folicitatione ipfo die vel diebus aliis quibufcunque modis facta aut etiam procurata per que oblationes ad magnum altare ex voluntaria devotione vel de confuetudine ut fuperius tangitur faciende aliqualiter fubtrahantur, minuantur, aut in dicto trunco ponantur. Nec aliquis vel aliqua de parochianis dicte ecclefie ab ob-

[a] Archbifhop Winchelfey.

Y2

lationibus confuetis ea ratione fe fubtrahant, aut oblationes ipfas in dicto trunco
reponant, fub pena excommunicationis majoris, quam ipfo facto contra premiffa vel
eorum aliquod venientes incurrunt, tanquam juris ecclefie notorii offenfores.   Cum
vero dictum truncum aperiri contigerit, pecunia in eodem exiftens per vifum vicarii
& aliquorum parochianorum exinde recepta, cujus quantitas in aliquo memoriali
fcribatur, ad dictas fabricam & refectionum defectum, & non aliis ufibus, per duos
parochianos electos per totam parochiam, & de fidelitate juratos, per vifum vicarii
applicetur, & poft modum tempore competenti faltem femel in anno in ipfius vicariis & aliquorum parochianorum prefentia ad id per parochianos deputatos fidelis computus exinde reddatur ut fit factum parochianorum quoad id per vicarium
teftificari valeat & videri.   Dictus vero vicarius & ceteri miniftri ecclefie de pecunia eadem in aliqua curialitate refpiciantur prout parochianis videbitur opportunum.
Inhibemus eciam, fub pena excois predicte, nequis contra noftram ordinationem premif-
fam in quocunque fui articulo quicquam facere feu clam vel palam procurare prefumat,
nec obventiones premiffas aliquo modo colligere, feu in alios ufus quam fupra tan-
guntur committere, quoquo modo. De legatis quoque, relictis, & ceteris bonis quacumque devotione collatis ad luminare, videlicet, ad fuftinendum feptem cereos in
cancello ecclefie fupradicte, de quibus fimiliter inter eofdem vicarium & parochianos
erat contentio ; taliter ordinamus ut duo parochiani ejufdem ecclefie, per communitatem ceterorum comparochianorum electi & ad fubfcripta jurati, prefatas obventiones ad luminare hujus colligentes per vifum vicarii, prenotati recipiant ; & ipfum
luminare exinde fuftineant.   Ac etiam computum de fic receptis & erogatis femel in
anno fimiliter reddant, ut fuperius eft expreffum. Idem etiam vicarius vi cereos &
duos proceffionales fumptibus fuis fuftineat in cancello. Parochiani vero, ut fuperius tangitur, eligendi coram commiffario rectoris ecclefie fupradicte, aut dicto vicario,
ac etiam in aliquorum comparochianorum prefentia, de fideliter ac diligenter faciendo premiffa, juramentum innovent omni anno.   Act' & dat' apud Reculvre III
Idus Aprilis, anno Dñi MCC nonagefimo fexto, & confecrationis noftre fecundo.

Commiffario Rectoris Ecclefie de Raculvre ut fuper diverfis criminibus & exceffibus
diffamati & convicti Pœnitentias fubeant que fibi per Archiepifcopum & fuos Commiffarios fuerunt indicte. 1296.

From the Regifters of Archbifhop Winchelfey, fol. 189. b.

ROBERTUS permiffione, &c. Dilecto filio commiffario rectoris ecclefie de
   Reculvre & perpetuo vicario loci ejufdem falutem, gratiam, & benedictionem.
Quia nuper in noftra ibidem vifitatione plures comperimus fuper diverfis criminibus
& exceffibus diffamatos, quorum aliquibus ut convictis certe pœnitentie per noftros
commif-

commiffarios funt indicte, & de aliis eft plenius inquirendum, vobis cum cohercio-
nis poteftatem committimus & mandamus in virtute obediencie, & fub pena excõis
majoris firmiter injungentes, quatenus omnes illos quibus pœnitentie taliter indicun-
tur per fufpentionis & majoris excõis fententias in perfonas eorum de die in diem
fi in hac parte rebelles extiterint, ut ipfas pœnitentias fubeant premiffa monitione
canonica compellatis, quorum nomina & pœnitentie fepedicte in quadam cedula figillo noftro fignata quam vobis tranfimittimus plenius continentur.   De aliis vero
in alia cedula vobis fub eodem figillo tranfmiffa contentis volumus & mandamus ut
ipfis perfonaliter coram vobis citatis & objectis eifdem per vos criminibus feu exceffibus de quibus fic nobis feu commiffariis noftris denunciatum extiterat, fi ea ne-
gaverint, inquiratis fuper hiis per viros ydoneos ad de veritate dicenda juratos, dili-
gencius veritatem eis purgationum canonicam juxta qualitatis exceffuum indicentes,
contra quos inquifitio non de veritate facti fet de fama duntaxat aftruet feu deponet:
de adulterio quoque vel fornicatione fponte confeffis, pro adulterio duas fuftigationes per mercatum proximum, & duas alias circa fuam parochialem ecclefiam ; pro
fornicatione autem fimplici duas alias circa ecclefiam parochialem per dies do-
minicos ante proceffiones ejufdem, in fuis duntaxat camefiis ac femoralibus
fubeundas; convictis vero per inquifitionem aut purgationis defectum, pro
adulterio tres fuftigationes per mercatum, & tres circa ecclefiam fuam parochialem, pro fornicatione vero fimplici tres circa ecclefiam modo quo fuperius tangitur
indicatis; fet convictis de fortilegio fex fuftigationes per mercatum, & fex circa
fuam ecclefiam parochialem ut fupra ; ufurariis vero convictis tres circa ecclefiam &
unam per mercatum modo fimili injungatis ; compellentes ut premittitur omnes &
fingulos fic convictos ut pœnitentias faciant fic indictas; contra illos fiquidem qui
fe in noftra vifitatione hujufmodi abfentarunt, & quos videritis de criminibus fupradictis notatos, quam cito redierint in forma qua in fupra tangitur acrius procedatis.
Quid autem feceritis in premiffis, & de pœnitentiis fic completis, ac etiam de re-
bellium quoad ea feu excommunicatorum nominibus fi qui fuerint, nos plenius certificetis quas cito poteritis oportune. Anno Dñi MCCXCVI.

Ordinatio Vicar' in Ecclefia de Reculver, & in Capella de Hothe adjacen', in Capella Sti Nicholai in Thaneto, & in Capella Omnium Sanctorum; necnon in Capella
de Herne.   Dat' apud Chering, 9 non. Aug. 1310.

From the Regifters of Abp. Winchelfey, fol. 30.

ROBERTUS permiffione divina Cantuar' archiepifcopus, tocius Anglie primas,
ad perpetuam rei memoriam * * * * * * * * * * * * Sufcepti regiminis cura
folicitat' ut utilitatibus fubjectorum in illis per quæ animarum faluti confulere, follicite providere, ac, paftoris more vigilis, gregem unicum ñræ vigilanciæ creditum,
                                                                           quan-

quantum nobis ex alto pmittitur, falubria obfervancia cuftodire curemus; ne illum lupus rapax, antiquus ferpens, humani generis inimicus, invadat, ejufque fanguis de iiris, qd abfit, manibus requiratur ; fed ut ad laudem divini nominis de illo poffumus dignam in extremo judicio reddere rationem : Sane bonæ memoriæ quondam dñs Robs ᵃ olim predeceffor' ñr' volens cameram archiepifcopalem a pftatione annua ducentar' & quadraginta marcar' fterlingorum de Herbaldoune leproforum, & de Noithgate paupeium hofpitalibus, juxta antiquam confuetudinem, ab eadem camera perfolvend' totalitei liberare, ecclefiam de Reculvre ñre dioc' oum fuis juribus & ptin' in proprios ufus ipfis hofpitalibus in compenfacione dictæ quantitatis, ñri capituli ad hoc pcurato confenfu, ꝓ fua voluntate conceffit ; falva perpetuo vicario qui in dicta ecclefia curam haberet animaium congrua porcione quam in proventibus certis taxavit, ꝓut in ordinatione ipfius plenius eft contentum. Sed recolendæ memoriæ quondam dñs ᵇ J. pdeceffor ñr, & ipfius dni R. fucceffor immediatus, ppendens quod ꝓpter appropriacionem pdictam, dicta ecclefia debitis obfequiis fuerat defraudati, & animarum cura non abfque ipfarum gravi periculo quodammodo derelicta, unius hois follicitudine non fufficiente ad regimen tantæ curæ & parochiæ trium millium vel amplius animarum, auctoritate apoftolica fibi fpecialiter in ea parte conceffa, hofpitalium & capituli ñri pdictor' interveniente confenfu, ecclefiam de Reculvre pdictam in ftatum priftinum revocavit, & archiepalem cameram in penfione annua fupradicta in perpetuum obligavit, prout in literis ejufdem pdefefforis ñri plenius vidimus contineri. Verum cum ex hoc adhuc non fit fuccurfum falubiit' aut fufficient' tantæ multitudini, quæ poftea crevit non modicum, & in dies augmentum recipit animarum, rectore & vicario uno tum propter dcam multitudinem, tum propter capellarum ipfius ecclefiæ & locorum diftanciam, fufficere ad curam non valentibus, ad ipfam ecclefiam & falutem animarum ñræ follicitudinis ftudia ac intuitus converfentes ; ut in ipfa matrice ecclia de Reculvre & capellis ejus non fimplex facerdos ad placitum removend' plerumque forfitan idiota ut fieri confuevit curam exerceat animarum ; fed vicarius ppetuus idoneus qui de cura animarum fit follicitus, & in celebratione divinorum ac collacione facramentorum fe viriliter exerceat & honefte, Xpi nomine invocato & adjutorio virginis gloriofæ in cujus nomine & honore eft dicta ecclia de Reculvre dedicata, in ipfa ecclia & capellis ejus, de confenfu dilecti filii magri Nicholai de Tyngewico ᶜ, rectoris ipfius ecclie, tres ppetuas ordinamus, ftabilimus, & facimus vicarias ; unam videlt in ecclia de Raculvre, cujus vicarius ppetuus in ipfa & capella adjacente de Hothe ; & aliam in capella Sci Nicholai in Taneto, cujus vicarius in ipfa & capella Omnium Sanctorum ᵈ; necnon & tertiam in capella de Herne, cujus vicarius in ipfa, animarum fub rectore qui ꝓ tempe fuerit curam gerent & perfonaliter exercebunt : Decreventes & ftatuentes, ut de proventibus ipfius ecclefiæ & capellarum fuarum dicti ppetui vicarii has competentes & congruas ex nunc habeant porciones. Habeat & pcipiat ppetuus vicarius ecclefiæ

ᵃ Abp. Kilwardby.   ᵇ Abp. Peckham.
ᶜ See above, p. 78. This rector died 14 Edw. II. 1321.
ᵈ All Saints chapel is now dilapidated and annexed to St. Nicholas.

        de

de Reculvre in ipfa ecclefia & capella de Hothe omnes oblationes, decimas fœni, lini, lanæ, & lactis, agnorum, ortorum, & omnes alias minutas decimas, que ad al-taragium [a] fpectare dicuntur, cum decimis garbarum in ortis cl.aufis crefcenciu n & pede foffis, ac pratis, ad ecclefiam de Reculvre & capellam de Hothe pdcam fpec-tantibus, necnon & cum quadam area apud Reculvre in qua domus effe confueve-rat rectoriæ [b].   Et nihilominus a ppetuis vicariis capellarum Sti Nicholai & de Herne annuas de quibus infra fit mentio pcipiat penfiones.   Vicarius autem ca-pellæ Sti Nicholai in ipfa & capella Omnium Sanctorum confimiles illationes & de-cimas ad ipfam & ad capellam Omnium Sanctorum fpectantes, cum terris ad ipfas capellas fpectantibus, habeat & obtineat ejufdem nomine vicaiiæ.   Sed de eifdem proventibus perpetuo vicario de Reculvre, in fignum fubjectionis perpetuæ, & ut ip-fius porcio augeatur, quatuor marcas & decem folid' quos eidem vicarie perpetue imponimus, perpetuo vicario de Reculvre in perpetuum perfolvend' folvat annis fingulis nomine perpetuæ penfionis.   Habeatque & percipiat perpetuus vicarius ca-pellæ de Herne in ipfa capella oblaciones & decimas confimiles ad ipfam capellam fpectantes fuæ noie vicarie.   Sed quadraginta folid' quos ipfi vicariæ ppetue fimiliter imponimus, ppet' vicar' de Reculvre annuat' pfolvat, prout de pcedente vicario fu-perius duximus ordinand'.   Has autem in feftis natalis Dni & beati Johis Baptiftæ folvent dci vicarii p equalibus porcionib' penciones.   Porro habebit quilbt dcor' vicar' unum presbyterum idoneum fuis fumptib' fibi focium ad melius regimen fuæ curæ. Et facient omnes vicarii prædicti obedienciam canonicam rectori ecclefiæ de Reculvre, qui eft in quafi poffeffione in parochianos fuos & fua parochia jurifdictionem ordina-riam exercendi, ac fibi obedient in canonicis mandatis & licitis, prout confon' erit jur'.   Et perpetui vicarii capellar' Sti Nicholai & de Herne prædictar' perpetuo vi-cario de Reculvre qui pro tempore fuerit, propter reverenciam matricis ecclefiæ cujus eft vicarius, obfequium conveniens impendent cum reverencia & honore.   Et ad pro-ceffiones Pentecoftales juxta morem ecclefiæ faciendas, cum fuis prefbyteris & minif-tris ac parochianis, venient ad fuam prædictam matricem ecclefiam, faltem annis fin-gulis in craftino Pentecoftes, necnon ad proceffionem & officium miffæ iidem vicarii venient in die nativit' Virginis gloriofæ.   Ad decimam infuper cum fuerit perfolven-da, quæ a perpetuo vicario ecclefiæ de Raculvre pro proventibus vicariæ dum una tan-tum fuerat ad viginti quinque marcar' taxata integraliter exigetur, contribuet vica-rius capellæ Sti Nicholai undecim folid' & quatuor denar'; et vicarius capellæ de Herne novem folid' & undecim denar' pro fua quam recipiunt porcione, & pro ea-dem rata quam juxta fingulas porciones predictas fibi duximus moderandam contri-buent in aliis hujus oneribus extraordinariis indicendis.   Et volumus ac ftatuimus ut vicarii capellarum Sci Nicholai & de Herne, fi in exhibendis obfequiis reverencia & honore, in non veniendo ad proceffiones prædictas, aut con ribucionibus fupiadictis,

[a] See Hiftory of Herne, p. 100, note *.
[b] By this the area in which the rectory-houfe ftood was charged with vicarial titles; which may account for what is faid in Mr. Greene's letter, p. 126, of the corn growing in the field, near the church paying tithes to the vicar.   This augmentation remains to this day.

X   rebel-

rebellionem fecerint, feu ab eis ceffaverint fine caufa, ex hoc eo ipfo a fuis vicariis amoveri perpetuo, valeant & privari Onus infuper miniftror', libror', ornamentor', cancellor' reficiendor', feu conftruendor' de novo, & alior' hujus onerum ordinariorum, in capellis Sti Nicholai & Omnium Sanctorum ad perpetuum vicarium Sti Nicholai, & in capella de Herne ad ipfius vicarium pertinebit. In ecclefia autem de Reculvre, in qua parochiani ejufdem de confuetudine laudabili approbata cancellum conftruunt & reficiunt, & libros & ornamenta, ut dicitur, inveniunt cum eft opus, necnon & capella de Hothe, vicarius ecclefiæ de Reculvre illa onera fuftinebit quæ vicarii ipfius ecclefiæ olim in eis confueverant fuftinere *. Volumus infuper & eciam ordinamus quod ad omnes prædictas vicarias perpetuas in quibus tres perfonas idoneas nobis nuper poft ordinacionem noftram prædictam per prædictum· magiftrum Nicholaum prefentatas inftituimus, videlt, dominum Johannem de Hoo in vicaria ecclefiæ de Reculvre, dñm Andream de Grantefete in vicaria capellæ Sti Nicholai prædict', & dñm Hugonem de Godyneftre in vicaria capellæ de Herne predict', cum ipfas vacare contigerit, idem magr Nicholaus & fucceffores fui nobis & noftris in perpetuum perfonas prefentent idoneas infra tempus a canone limitatum ordinatione quondam dni Roberti predeceffor' noftri prædicti, quam fi & inquantum præmiffis obviat & per bonæ memoriæ J. predeceforem noftrum prædictum non fuerit revocata, ex caufis prædictis revocamus totaliter non obftant'. Et ut hæc noftra ordinacio perpetuum robur obtineat firmitatis, ipfam, per dñm Galfridum de Brampton, notarium publicum & fcribam noftrm, in publicam formam redigi fecimus, & figilli noftri appenfione muniri. Et capitulum noftrum eidem procuravimus confentire. Acta funt hæc apud Charinge, ix kalend' Augufti, anno Domini·1310, conf' noftri xvi, Indict' viii, in prefentia magiftrorum Michis de Bereham cancellar' ñri, Phi de Turvyke, Hen' de Derby, Roberti de Mallyng, caufarum ñræ curie auditor, ac Nichi de Tyngewico prædicti &.Will' de. Swanton, clericorum noftrorum, ad hæc fpecialiter vocatorum.

Grant of a Market at Reculver; 7 Edw. II. 1313.   (From the Original.)

EDWARDUS, Dei gra, rex Angl', dominus Hibnie, & dux Aquitanie, archiepis, epis, abbatibus, prioribus, comitibus, baronibus, jufticiariis, vicecomitibus, prepofitis, miniftris, & omnibus ballivis & fidelibus fuis, falutem.. Sciatis nos de gra ñra fpeciali conceffiffe, & hac carta ñra confirmaffe, venerabili patri Waltero [b] archiepo Cantuar', tocius Anglie primati, quod ipfe & fucceffores fui imperpetuum habeant unum mercatum, fingulis feptimanis, p diem Jovis, apud manerium fuum

---

* Thus as the parifhioners of Reculver ufed to repair the chancel, the vicar of that parifh was exonerated. For a long time paft it has been repaired (as ufual) by the leffee of the great tithes.
[b] Walter Raynold, abp. 1313—1327.

de Reicolvre in com' Kanc', nifi mercatum illud fit ad nocumentum vicinorum mercatorum. Quaꞇe volumus & firmiter p̄cipimus, ꝑ nobis & heredibus n̄ris, q̄d p̄dꞓus
archiepiſcopus & ſucceſſores ſui p̄dꞓi impeꝛpetuꝛin habeꝛnt p̄dꞓum mercatum, cum
ōꞁbus libertatibus & liberis confuetudinibus ad hujuſmodi mercata peꝛtinentibus, uiſi
mercatum illud fit ad nocumcntum vicinorum meꝛcatoꝛum, ficut ꝑdcum eſt.
     His teſtibus, veñalib' patribus H. Wynton'[a], W. Coventrien' & Lichefelden'[b], J.
Ciceſtren', J Bathon' & Wellen'[c] c̄pis; Gilbeꝛto de Clare[d] comite Glouceſtꞇ' & Hert-
ford, Humfredo de Bohun[e] comite Hereford & Eſſex, Adimꝛro de Valencia[f] comite
Pembroch', Hugone le Deſpenſer, & Edmundo de Malolacu ſeneſcallo hoſpitii n̄ri,
& aliis. Dat' ꝑ manum n̄r̄m apud Cantuar', decimo ſeptimo die Febꝛuarii, anno regni n̄ri ſeptimo.
     [The ſeal is loſt; but the holes for it remain.]

Dimiſſio pro magiſtro Nicholao de Tyngewyk, 1314.

From the Regiſter of Abp. Reynolds, fol. 105. a.

PATEAT univerſis per preſentes, quod cum coram nobis Waltero, permiſſione
divina, &c. archiep' Cant', viſitationis noſtre officium actualiter exceꝛcenti-
bus, fuiſſet mag' Nich' de Tyngewico, rector eccleſie de Raculvꞇe, noſtre dioc', ſuper
pluralitꞇte beneficiorum ſuorum duorum, curam animarum habencium, ſcilt, eccle-
ſiarum de Caleſhull Sarum dioc' primo, & de Raculvre predicta poſterius aſſecuta-
rum judicialiter impetitus; idem magiſter Nich', coram nobis comparens, munimenta
& privilegia quibus ſe in hac parte munitum aſſeruit exhibuit in termino ſibi ad hoc
aſſignato : Nos igitur, hujus exhibitis per nos inſpectis diligenter ac
eciam examinatis, quia invenimus eundem magiſtrum Nicholaum ſuper retentione beneficiorum predict' fuiſſe & eſſe ſufficienter munitum, ipſum ab examine noſtꞇo, quatenus ad noſtrum officium attinet, dimittimus per decretum. In cujus, &c. Dat' apud
Lambeth, 12 kal' Junii, anno Dñi 1314.

[a] Henry Woodloke, bp. of Wincheſter 1305—1316.
[b] Walter de Langham, lord treaſurer and lord chancellor, bp. of Coventry and Litchfield 1295
—1322.
[c] John Drokensfoꞇd, keeper of the king's wardrobe, and deputy to the lord treaſureꞇ, bp. of
Bath and Wells 1310—1329.
[d] The laſt earl of Glouceſter of that family. He was ſlain at Stirling Caſtle in the ſame year
that he witneſſed this chaꝛter
[e] Lord conſtable of England. He married Elizabeth daughter to king Edward I.
[f] Earl of Pembroke 1296—1323. Mary his thirdlady was the founꝺꞇeſs of Pembroke Hall, Caꝺ-
bꝛidge, and alſo of Denny-abbey in that county. She died April 17, 1377.

Commiffio ad exercend' Jurifdictionem de Racolvre, 1325.

From the Regifter of Abp. Reynolds. f. 146. b.

WALTERUS, &c. Dilecto in Chrifto filio magiftro Nicholao de Tyngewico, rectori ecclefie de Racolvre, falim, &c. Ad procedendum, cognofcendum, & firmaliter terminandum quafcunque caufas & quecunque negocia in parochia de Racolvre predict' cum fuis capellis emergent', necnon ad debite corrigend' & puniend' commiffa quofcunque fubditorum noftrorum inibi delinquencium, vobis, de cujus circumfpectione & induftria fidem plenam gerimus, vices noftras committimus, cum coherfionis canonice poteftate, donec eas duxerimus revocandas. In cujus, &c. Dat' apud Lambeth, 5 id' Decemb', 1325.

Grant of a Market and Fair at St. Nicholas in the Ifle of Thanet, and alfo at Gillingham in Kent, 10 Edw. III. 1336. (From the Original.)

EDWARDUS, Dei gra, rex Angl', dominus Hibnie, & dux Aquitan', archiepis, epis, abbatibus, prioribus, comitibus, baronibus, jufticiariis, vicecomitibus, prepofitis, miniftris, & omnibus ballivis & fidelibus fuis, falutem. Sciatis nos de gra nra fpeciali conceffiffe, & hac carta nra confirmaffe, venerabili patri Johi 8 archiepo Cantuai', tocius Anglie primati, quod ipfe & fucceffores fui archiepi loci pdci imperpetuum habeant unum mercatum, fingulis feptimanis, p diem Lune, apud manerium fuum Sci Nicholai in Thaneto in com' Kanc', & unam feriam ibidem fingulis annis p duos dies duratur', viz. in craftino Nativitatis beate Marie Virginis & in die prox' fequenti ; & unum mercatum, fingulis feptimanis, p diem Jovis, apud manerium fuum de Gillyngham, in com' predict', & unam feriam ibidem fingulis annis p octo dies duratur', videlicet, in die Inventionis Sce Crucis & p feptem dies prox' fequentes ; nifi mercata illa & feriæ illæ fint ad nocumentum vicinor' mercator' & vicinar' feriar'. Quare volumus & firmiter pcipimus, p nobis & heredibus nris, qd pdcus archiepifcopus & fucceffores fui pdci imperpetuum habeant dicta mercata & ferias apud dicta maneria fua, cum oibus libertatibus & liberis confuetudinibus ad hujufmodi mercata & ferias pertinentibus, nifi mercata illa & ferie ille fint ad nocumentum vicinorum mercatorum & vicinarum feriarum, ficut pdcum eft.

8 John Stratford, who had been bifhop of Winchefter and lord chancellor, enjoyed the fee of Canterbury from 1333 to 1348.

Hiis teftibus, veñalib' patribus Henr' Lincoln'ᵃ eᵽo thefaurario ñro, Riĉo Dunelm'ᵇ eᵽo, Joĥe comite Cornub'ᶜ fratre ñro cariffimo, Wiltmo de Monteacuto, Roberto de Ufford fenefcallo hofpitii ñri,.& aliis. Dat' ᵽ manum n�̃m apud Wodeftok, tricefimo die Maii, anno regni ñri decimo.

[The great feal, as engraved in Sandford, well preferved.]

Licence of King Edward III. for appropriation of the Church of Reculver to the Archbifhop's Table, and for payment of CLX l. per ann. out of the Revenues of the See of Canterbury to the two Hofpitals, notwithftanding the Statute of Mortmain, &c. 1348.

From the Harbledown Charters.

EDWARDUS, Dei g�;a, rex Anglie & Franc', & dominus Hibernie, omnibus ad quos pi efentes littere pervenerint falutem. Sciatis quod cum dudum Cantuar' archiep� hofpitalibus fuis de Northgate & Herbaldon de elemofinis fuis fundatis, ab olim & a tempore cujus contrarii memoria non exiftit, ad fuftentacionem fratrum, foror' & alior pauperum in dictis hofpitalibus degencium de bonis fuis temporalibus centum & quadraginta libras certis terminis per equales porciones annuatim exfolviffent ut dicitur fede plena; Nofque & progenitores ñri, quociens & quando dĉa fedes vacabat, pro rata vacationis temporis hujufmodi de proficuis temporalium in manibus ñris & ipforum progenitorum noftrorum exiftencium ipfis pauperibus portiones fumme predicte folviffemus ficut per certificacionem thef' & baronum de Sĉĉio ñro in cancellar' noftram ad mandatum n�e;m miffam plene liquet, & ut accepimus rectores qui pro tempore fuerant ecctie de Recolvre que de archiepᵉ;i Cantuar' exiftere dinofcitur patronatu viginti libras eifd' pauperibus annuatim folviffent per tempora fupradicta; Nos ad requificionem venerabilis patris Joĥis de Stretford archiepᵉ;i Cantuar' qui circa ñror' & regni ñri negotior' directionem diucius & efficacius laboravit, & quem eo pretextu, ac eccttiam Xᵽi Cantuar' fuo commiffam regimini ob finceram dilectionem quam ad locum illum gerimus favore benevolo profequentes, de g�e;a ñra fᵽali concef-fimus & licentiam dedimus, pro nobis & heredibus ñris, quantum in nobis eft, prefato archieᵽo, quod ipfe & fucceffores fui corporalem poffeffionem dicte ecti e de Recolvre ac capellar' eidem ecctie connexai', rectore ipfius ecctie cedente vel decedente, vel alias ipfam ecctiam dimittente auctoritate aᵽlica apprehendere & habere poffint,

ᵃ Henry Burwefh, lord treafurer and lord chancellor; bp. of Lincoln 1320—1343.
ᵇ Richard de Bury, otherwife Angervil, lord privy feal, afterwards lord chancellor and trea-furer, bifhop of Durham 1333—1345.
ᶜ John de Eltham, fecond fon of Edward III.

taf.

eafdemque eccliam & capellas cum fuis juribus & pertin' univerfis in proprios ufu: ipforum & menfe fue archiepalis imperpetuum retinere. Ita tamen, quod vacante fede archiepali nos vel heredes occafione temporalium archiepatus illius in manibus ñiis vel heredum ñror' exiftencium, feu alia occafione quocunque ad folucionem dictor' fummar', in toto vel in parte, minime teneamur ; fet quod dictus archiepus & fucceffores fui, qui fede plena, & alii qui fede vacante fructus & emolumenta dictor' ecclie & capellar' funt percepturi, ad folucionem dictar' fummar' dictis pauperibus faciend' firmiter teneantur, prefatoque archiepo & ejus fuccefforibus, ac aliis fructus & emolumenta hujufmodi fic percepturis, quod ipfe predictas centum & fexaginta libras maĝris, five cuftodibus, & fratribus & fororibus, hofpitalium predictor' annuatim, in fumma predicta imperpetuum folvere, & eifdem maĝris, five cuftodibus, fratribus & fororibus, quod ipfi eandem fummam annuatim a prefatis archiepo & ejus fuccefforibus, feu aliis, fructus & emolumenta predicta fic percepturis percipere & habere valeant fibi & fuccefforibus fuis imperpetuum ut eft dictum tenore prefentium fimiliter licentiam dedimus fpalem ; ftatuto de terris & ten' ad manum mortuam non ponend' edito non obftante. Nolentes quod predictus archiepus, vel fucceffores fui, feu alii fructus & emolumenta hujufmodi percepturi, vel dicti maĝri five cuftodes, aut fratres, feu forores, vel eorum fucceffores, ratione ftatuti predicti, feu pro eo quoù advocatio dicte ecclie de Recolvre tenetur de nobis in capite, per nos vel heredes noftros, juftic', efcaetores, vicecomites, aut alios ballivos, feu miniftros nŕos quofcumque occafionentur, moleftentur in aliquo, feu graventur. In cujus rei teftimonium has litteras ñras fieri fecimus patentes. Tefte meipfo apud Weftm' fextodecimo die Martii, anno regni in Angl' vicefimo fecundo, regni vero ñri Francie nono.

Carta Salamon But de tribus acris terre in Reyculver, 1357.

From the Private Deeds of Harbledown Hofpital.

SCIANT prefentes & futuri quod ego Salamon But de Halyberg de parochia de Recolvre dedi conceffi & hac prefenti carta mea confirmavi Willmo atte Welle capllo, Willo Chilham, Robto Bernard, Rico Lorkyn, Johi Motoun & Simoni Godhayt tres acras terre mee cum pertin', jacent' in poch' de Recolvre apud Sperkyn in campo vocato Brounyngefton inter terram heredum Willi Loue verfus eaft, & terram Thome Dunfton verfus fouth & weft, & terram Jacobi Lapyn verfus north ; habend' & tenend' predictas tres acras terre cum fuis pertin' prefatis Willmo, Willmo, Robto, Rico, Johi, & Simoni, heredibus & affign' fuis, libere, quiete, bene, & in pace imperpetuun, de capit' dno feodi per fervicia inde debita & de jure confueta. In cujus rei teftimonium prefenti carte figillum meum appofui. Dat' apud
Re-

Recolvre decimo octavo die menf' April', anno regni reg' Edwardi Tercii poft conqueftum Ang' tricefimo octavo. Hiis teftibus, Thoma Dunfton, Hamone Hycke, Thoma Herwoldyngg, Willo Chepman, Johne Sely, Thoma Symeon, Johne de Eftwyk clerico, & aliis.

Carta ejufd' Sal' But de predictis tribus acris terre in Reculver, 1357.

From the Private Deeds of Harbledown Hofpital.

SCIANT prefentes & futuri quod ego Salamon But dé Halyberg de parochia de Reculver dedi, conceffi, & hac prefenti carta mea confirmavi Willo atte Welle capellano, Willo Chilham, Robto Bernard, Ricardo Lorkyn, Johi Moton, & Simoni Godhayt, feoffatis, ad ufum prioris, fratrum & foror' hofpitalis Sci Nicholai de Herbaldown tres acras terre mee cum pertin' in parochia de Reculver apud Sperkyn in campo vocato Brownyngefton inter terram heredum Willi Lowe verfus eaft & terram Thome Dunfton verfus fouth & weft & terram Jacobi Lapyn verfus north, habend' & tenend' predictas tres acras terre cum fuis pertinen' prefatis Willo, Willo, Roberto, Ricardo, Johi, & Simoni, modo & forma predict' hered' & affign' fuis libere, quiete, bene, &. in pace imperpet' de capit' dno feod' per fervicia inde debita & de jure confueta. In cujus rei &c. Dat' apud Reculver 18 April', an' regni reg' Edwardi Tertii 38. Hiis teftibus, Thoma Dunfton, Hamone Hyck, Thoma Herwoldyng, Willo Chepman, Johe Sely, Thom' Symeon, Johe de Eftwyk clerico, & aliis.

Carta indentata predictis feoffatis concedens predictas iii acras terre predict' Solamon But fub annuo redditu unius Summe Ordei, 1357.

From the fame Deeds.

HEC indentura teftatur quod Wills atte Welle caplis, Wills Chilham, Robtus Bernard, Ricus Lorkyn, Johes Motoun, & Simon Godhayt, dederunt & hac prefenti carta fua indentata confirmaverunt Salamoni But tres acras terre cum pertin' fuis jacent' in poch' de Recolvre apud Sperkyn in uno campo vocat' Brounyngefton. Habend' prefato Salamoni heredibus & affign' fuis imperpetuum, reddend' inde annuatim prefatis Willo atte Welle, &c. heredibus & affign' fuis, unam
fummam

summam ordei palmal'* annui redditus juxta melius precium except' duobus denarr-
is in summa in festo Sci Michis archangeli apud Herbaldown. Et predictus Salamon vult & concedit pro se, heredibus, & assign' suis & obligat dictas tres acras
terre cum pertin' suis districtione predictor' Willi atte Welle, &c. hered' & assign'
suor': ita quod bene licebit eisdem in dictis tribus acris terre cum pertin' suis dis-
tringere quocienscunque dictam summam ordei palmal' annui redditus aliquo termino
a retro esse contigerit, & districtiones penes se retinere quousque de omnibus arrerag'
una cum dampnis & expensis ea occasione habitis & incursis plenarie fuerit satisfactum,
vel predictas tres acras terre cum pertin' suis retinere & eas pacifice possidere sibi,
heredibus & assign' suis sine contradictione predicti Salamonis & hered' suor'
imperpetuum. In cujus rei test' partes predicte huic carte indent' sigilla sua alternatim apposuerunt. Dat' apud Racolvre duodecimo die mens' Junii, anno regni
reg' Edwardi tercii post conquestum tricesimo octavo. Hiis testibus, Thoma Dun-
ston, Johne atte Welle, Willo Gilbert, Andr' Grenehame, Thoma But, Johe Symeon, Johe Sely, Johne Loue, Simone Loue, & aliis.

Exemplificatio antiqua [1384] continens varia instrumenta ad ecclesias de Reculvre et
Herne spectantia, hodie (A. D. 1756) penes Decan' et Capit' Cantuar'.

From a transcript made by the Rev. Mr. Hall.

UNIVERSIS Christi fidelibus ad quos presentes litteræ pervenerint Robertus
de Bradgare, commissarius Cantuarien' generalis, salutem in Domino sempiternam. Noverit universitas vra quod novem litteræ patentes quarum sex litteræ sigillo
bone memorie quondam dni Johannis Stratford, Dei gratia, archiepi Cantuariensis, ac
duæ litteræ earum sigillo commissarii Cantuariensis generalis a c alio sigillo bone
memorie quondam Petri Durant audientiæ venerabilium virorum dnor' prioris et
capituli eclesie Cantuariensis (sede Cant' vacante) auditoris cera viridi eisdem
appendentibus sigillatæ non abolitæ non rasæ non cancellatæ sed sane & integre ac
omni vitio et suspicione sinistra carentis. Nobis in judicio pro tribunali sedentibus
pro parte discreti viri magistri Johannis de Montecuto, perpetui vicarii ecclie de
Reculvre, Cant' diœc' extiterant presentatæ, fuitque pro parte dicti vicarii nobis
judicialiter propositum quod ipsum vicarium tam in diversis regni Angliæ quam
extra ipsum regnum partibus etiam in Curia Romana fidem saltem summariam
facere opertebat de eisdem litteris, et propter viarum discrimina et alia pericula que
ratione delationis litterarum ipsarum si eas ad partes hujusmodi deferri contingeret
possint in hac parte de facili verisimiliter evenire prefatas litteras originales ad par-

---

* If this word is rightly copied, it is not to be found in the Glossaries in any sense applicable to
barley, unless it means *large sized* grain.

tes hujus fecure deftinare non audcbat, quaproptei ex parte ejufdem vicarii nobis
cum inftantia debita extitit humiliter fupplicatum quatenus hujufmodi litteras re-
fpicere diligenterque infpicere tranfumi et examinari facere omnem juris effectum
qui exinde fequi poterit curaremus, etiam ut hujufmodi tranfcripto cum litteris orig-
nalibus fupradictis fides indubia adhiberetur, quarum vero litterarum tenores per ordinem fequuntur et funt tales.

1. Johannis Stratford, Cantuar' archiepi, nominatio III auditorum caufarum in curia
audientie dicti domini archiepi, dat' apud Dovor', 21 die Feb. A. D. 1334.

2. Sententia dni Johannis Stratford, Cant' archiepi, in controverfia orta inter vicarios de Reculver et Herne, fuper fepultura tenentium in capite dni archiepi, apud
Herne decedentium, quod dicti tenentes in cemeterio matricis ecclefie de Reculver
fepelire debent in futuro.   Dat' apud Cherrynge, 16 kal' Nov', ann' Dñi 1334.

3. De reparationibus ecclie de Reculver. "Johannes permiffione divina Cant' archiepus totius Angliæ primas, et aplice fedis legatus, dilecto filio commiffario ũro Cant.
generali fal', gram, et ben'. Cum, in vifitatione ñra Cant' dioc' per nos facta, pochiani
ecclie pochialis de Reculvere hamlettum feu villam de Herne ejufdem dioc' inhabitantes, una cum aliis dicte ecclie pochianis, conftructioni et reparationi ipfius ecclie et
aliis ejus neceffitatibus, ficut alii parochiani ejufdem, cum neceffitas imminebat, contribuere denegantes, ac in termino eis ad proponendum canonicum fi quod haberent quare
fic contribuere non deberent auctoritate ñra peremptorie affignato nihil in ea parte effectuale feu canonicum proponentes ad contribuendum juxta fufficientiam eorundem
conftructioni et reparationi et aliis neceffitatibus ecclie fupradicte, una cum aliis pochianis ejufdem, quotiens opus fuerit, ex decreto noftri in ea parte commiffarii fuerant legitime condemnati, que condemnatio et decretum in authoritatem rei tranfierant judicate,
tandemque poft proceffus varios fuper executione condemnationis et decreti predictorum authoritate ñra facta dictis pochianis coram ũro vicario (nobis tunc in remotis agentibus) in fpiritualibus generali fufficienter comparentibus, et de ftando altæ et baffæ
ordinationi ũri fuper his et variis inobedientiis fuis et contemptibus in hac parte
fe fponte et fimpliciter fubmittentibus et ordinationi ñre promittentibus parituros
fub debito juramenti corporalis præftiti per eofdem : Nofque poftmodum,
ponderatis undique ponderandis ordinavimus, in hunc modum, ñra authoritate ordinaria femper falva, quod dicti pochiani apud Herne ut præmittitur commoran-
tes dictis condemnationi et decreto pareant cum effectu, ac conftructioni et reparationi hujus aliifque dicte ecclie neceffitatibus, una cum ceteris pochianis ejufdem, ficut et illi juxta conditiones perfonarum et quantitatem facultatum fuarum, futuris contribuant temporibus, quotiens opus erit, ad eos ad hoc faciendum decrevimus canonice compellendos, refervantes nobis punitionem dictorum pochi-
anorum pro ipforum inobedientiis et contemptibus fupradictis, vobis commi-
timus et mandamus quatenus dictos pochianos omnes et fingulos hameletum de
Herne ut præmittitur inhabitantes, quotiens opus erit, et per partem rectoris dicte
ecclie de Reculvre, feu cuftodis ejufdem, fueritis requifiti, publice et folemniter moneatis & effectualiter inducatis, quod ipfi dictis condemnationi et decreto pareant cum
effectu, et ut premittitur contribuant conftructioni et reparationi ac aliis neceffitatibus
ecclie fupradicte; quod fi hujufmodi monitionibus ũris parere contempferint, ipfos ad

Y   id

id per quafcunque cenfuras ecclefiafticas canonice compellatis; ad quod faciendum vobis cum coliercionis canonice poteftate committimus vices ñras, et quod faceritis ac ipfi facere duxeritis in premiffis, cum per partein rectoris feu cuftodum dicte ecclie de Reculvre fueritis requifiti, certificetis per litteras ñras patentes harum feriem continentes. Dat' apud Lambeth, id' Martii, ann' Dñi 1335, et ñre tranflationis ann' tertio."

4. In Dei nomine, amen. Cum in vifitatione Cant' dioc' per nos Johannem permiffione divina Cant' archiepum totius Angliæ primatem et aplice fedis legatum actualiter nuper facta, pochiani ecclie pochialis de Reculvre ñre dioc' antedicte hameletum feu villam de Herne inhabitantes, una cum aliis dicte pochianis fabrice ejufdem reparatione neceffaria indegentis contribuere denegantes, ac in termino eifdem ad proponendum canonicum fi quod haberent quare fic contribuere non deberent peremptorie affignato nihil in ea parte effectuale feu canonicum proponentes ad contribuend' juxta fufficientiam eorundem ex tunc conftructioni & reparationi ecclefie fupradicte una cum aliis paiochiis ejufdem quotiens opus fuerit ex decreto ñri in ea parte commiffarii fuiffent legitime condemnati, que condemnatio & decretum in authoritatem rei tranfieiant judicate, tandem iidem parochiani poft proceffus varios fuper executione condemnationis & decreti prediétor' authoiitate ñra faét' coram ñro vicario (nobis tunc in remotis agentibus) in fpiritualibus generali fufficienter poftea comparentes de ftando alte & baffe ordinationi ñre tam fuper contributione hujufmodi facienda quam pro variis inobedientiis fuis & contemptibus in hac parte taétis facrofanctis evangeliis corporaliter juraverunt & fe ad hoc faciendum fponte & fimpliciter fubmifferunt. Nos fiquidem Johannes archiepus fupradictus, ponderatis undique ponderandis, taliter ordinamus quod dicti parochiani apud Herne ut premittitur inhabitantes dictis condemnationi & decreto pareant cum effectu, ac conftructioni & reparationi & aliis dicte ecclefie neceffitatibus una cum ceteris parochianis ejufdem ficut & illi juxta fufficientiam perfonarum & quantitatem facultatum fuarum futuris contribuant temporibus quotiens opus erit & eos ad hoc faciendum per cenfuras ecclefiafticas decernimus fore canonice compellendos, refervantes nobis punitionem dictorum parochianorum pro ipforum contumaciis, inobedientiis, & contemptibus fupradictis. In quorum omnium teftimonium figillum ñrum fecimus hiis apponi. Dat' apud Lambeth, 15 die Martii, A. D. 1335.

5. Confirmatio fentente fuprafcripte, dat' apud Cherryng, 16 kal' Nov', A. D. 1334, fuper fepultura tenentium dni in capite apud Herne deeendentium, per dñm Johannem de Stratford Cant' archiep'. Dat' apud Lambeth, 9 die Feb', A. D. 1339.

6. Johis Stratford Cant' archiepi mandatum fuper executione fententie olim late pro vicario de Reculvre contra vicar' de Herne fuper oblationibus datis & miffis in funeribus tenentium capital' dni archiepi apud Herne decedentium celebratis. Dat' apud Cantuar', 15 kal' Maii, A. D. 1341.

7. Compofitio facta inter parochianos eccl' de Reculvre & parochianos eccl' de Herne, Sti Nicholai, & Omnium Sanctor', fuper reparationibus eccl' de Reculvre.

Memorandum quod inter nos parochianos ecclie de Reculvre Cant' dioc' ex parte una, parochianos ecclefiar' feu capellar' de Herne & Sancti Nicholai & Omnium

3   Sanc-

Sanctorum ab eadem eccfia de Reculvre dependentium, fupra quota feu quahtitate
& modo contributionis faciend' conftructioni & reparation ipfius ecclie de Reculvre
& aliis neceffitatibus ejufdem per dictos parochianos de Herne, Sancti Nicholai, &
Omnium Sanctorum, ad quam contributionem (ut premittitur) faciendam per commiffarium ven' patris dni Johannis Dei gra Cant' archiepi totius Anglie primatis
nuper fuerant rite & legitime condemnati, mota fuiffent difcordia et materia quefti-
onis, tandem comparentibus coram nobis Thoma de Cantuar' commiffario Cant'
generali in eccl' Chrifti Cant', 6 Idus Junii, anno Domini 1336, omnibus parochianis de Reculvre, Herne, Sancti Nicolai, et Omnium Sanctorum predict' pro
bono pacis et concordie inter eofdem in premiffis habendo, per nos commiffarium
predict' de ipforum authoritate et expreffo confenfu ita extitit ordinatum, quod fin-
guli oboli de fingulis acris terrarum parochianorum omnium predictorum infra
dictas parochias exiftentium folverentur, colligerentur, & expendantur hac vice inre-
parationem dicte ecclie de Reculvre neceffario faciend', et quod fex viri fide digni
electi et nominati per parochianos predict', videlicet, Johes Love et Johes Hugelot
de parochia de Reculvre per parochianos ejufdem, Johes de Helwoldynge et Johis Baker de parochia de Herne per parochianos ejufdem, Johes Leneye et Johes Strodere
de parochia Sancti Nicholai & Omnium Sanctorum per parochianos ejufdem, eque,
fideliter, et jufte taxarent quemlibet parochianum de Reculvre, Herne, Sancti Nicolai, et Omnium Sanctorum, juxta quantitatem terrarum fuarum in ejufdem parochiis exiftentium et numerum acrarum eorundem de fingulis obolis fupradictis, et
pecuniam juxta taxacionem hujufmodi quemlibet concernentem ab eifdem exigerent
levarent et colligerent, ac cuftodibus operis ecclie de Reculvre predict', vidit, Johi
Sewale et Simoni Love plene et integraliter folverent in reparationem ejufdem ne-
ceffariam per dictos cuftodes fideliter et utiliter convertendam ; dictique cuftodes pecuniam hujufmodi per ipfas receptam periculo eorum cuftodirent, et prout optis erit
in reparationem ejufdem ecclie fideliter expenderent, et fidelem computum inde red-
derent omnibus quorum intereft cum fuper hoc effent congiue requifiti ; ad quod
bene et fideliter faciend' tam dicti fex viri per dictos parochianos ut premittitur electi
feu nominati quam cuftodes operis antedicti quatenus ad ipfos pertinet juramentum
ad fancta Dei evangelia per ipfos tacta corporaliter preftiterunt.   In cujus rei teftimonium figillum officii nri prefentibus appofuimus. Dat' Cantuar', 4 kal' Julii, anno
fupradicto.

8. Inftrumentum continens libellum et fententiam per commiffarium Cant' latam pro
vicario de Reculvre contra vicario de Herne fuper fepultura tenentium capitalis dni
archiepi in Herne infra eccl' paroch' de Reculvre decendentium, et inhibitionem
commiffarii predicti contra vicarium de Herne ne corpora predict' tenentium in
eccl' de Herne fepelientur in futuro ; necnon compofitionem factam inter vicarios
de Reculvre et Herne fuper miffis pro animis defunctor' celebrandis, viz. quod vicar
de Reculvre oblationes ad primam miffam, et vicar' de Herne oblationes ad fecundam
miffam, recipiet. Dat' in eccl' Chrifti Cant', 4 die Mart', A. D. 1356.

9. Mandatum auditoris caufarum prioris et capit' eccl' Chrifti Cant' (fede Cant'
vacante) contra vicar' de Herne, et condempnatio ejufdem ad folvend' vicario de Reculvre iv fol' ab eo receptis pro celebratione miffe temporis fepulture Phil' And:
in

in cemiterio de Herne dum vixit capital' tenent' dni archiepi; et monitio eidem facta fuper obfervatione fententie olim per dnm Ricardum Cant' archiep' late contra vicar' de Herne olim in premiffis delinqnent'. Dat' Cant', 2 id' Jan' A. D. 1333.

Conclufio predicte Exemplificationis.

Nos vero Robertus commiffarius Cant' fupradictus attendentes hujufmodi fuppli-cationem confonam fore juri litteras predictas pro parte dicti vicarii, in notariorum publicorum et teftium fubfcriptorum prefentia, ut premittitur, publice et judicialiter prefentatas, recepimus, infpeximus, vidimus, perlegique et examinari fecimus dili-genter. Et quia litteras hujufmodi reperimus in ea parte fanas, integras, ac omni vitio et fufpicione carentes, eas per difcretos viros magiftrum Johem Bedell confif-torii Cantuarienfis regiftrarium, et Ricardum Water dicti confiftorii procuratorem, clericos Cantuar' dioc' notariofque publicos infrafcriptos tranfcribi et copiari man-davimus, et eas fic tranfcriptas et copiatas in prefenti publico inftrumento de ipfis tranfcriptis fideliter . . . . . . in nra et dictorum notariorum et teftium fubfcriptorum prefentia legi et collationem fieri, dictafque litteras publicari fecimus ac etiam publici juris forma, et demum quia prefentes litteras fic tranfcriptas . . . . . . litteris originalibus invenimus concordare, decernimus quantum in nobis eft . . . . tranfcripto quod eifdem litteris originalibus tam in judicio quam extra, etiam ubique, fidem plenam et indubiam fore adhibend'. In quorum omnium et fingulorum fidem et teftimonium prefentes litteras . . . . . . publicum inftrumentum per prefatos no-tarios fcribi et publicari mandavimus, et figillo officii nri appofitione communiri. Dat' et act' Cantuar' tertio die menfis Decembris, fub anno 1389. Indictione 13 pontificatus fanctiffimi in Chrifto patris et Domini Domini Urbani divina provi-dentia pape anno 12.

Hec Exemplificatio, cum figillo valde obliterato, hodie (A. D. 1756) remanet penes dec' & capit' Cantuar'*.

Order of Abp. Iffip, 8 Id. Feb. 1355, directing that clx li. p an', due from the Archbifhoprick to the Hofpitals of Harbledoun and Northgate, fhould be paid for the future out of the church of Reculver.

From the Harbledown Charters.

OMNIBUS pfentes lras vifuris Simon pmiffione divina Cantuar' archiepus, tocius Angl' primas & aplice fedis legatus, falutem in Auctore falutis : Nove-rit univerfitas vra qd cum pauperes hofpitalium de Herbaldoun & de Northgate, ta   ar' dioc', fuper & de elemofina Cant' archiepor' fundator', ab olim necnon ab

---

* See Somner's Treatife of the Roman Ports and Forts, p. 84, in edit. Oxon. 1693.

omni tempore & prefertim cujus contrarii memoria hōium non exiftit, de elemofina archiepor' Cant' qui fuerunt centum & quadraginta libr', necnon de ecclia de Reculvre jam menfe archiepali aucte aptica novit' unita & rectoribus ejufdem, viginti libr' ftirlingor', tam ₽ fuftentatione fua & alior' infirmor' ad ipfa hofpitalia confluencium quam aliis fibi incumbentibus oneribus comodius fupportand' continue pcepiffent: Principes infuper excellentiffimi reges Angl' onus pftacois dictar' centum & quadraginta libr' quotiens & quando fedes archiepales vacaffet, & temporalia dictor' archiepor' ea occafione feu alias in fuis manibus jure regio extitiffent pro temporibus quibus temporalia hujufque tenuerant agnoviffent, & eafdem centum & quadraginta libr' ₽ rata terminorum in eifdem vacacoibus feu temporibus quibus in eorum manibus temporalia predicta extiterint qualicumque currentium infuper perfolviffent, ab omni tempore fupradicto: Bone tamen memorie dñs Johnes de Stretford ūr pdedeceffor, confpiciens dictos pauperes fupradictas pftacoibus nullam ₽bacoem aliam quam poffeffionem pdci temporis habuiffe, que eis diverfa afferebant incommoda dum fingli archiepi in fuis creacionum principiis pro fuis confcientiis ferenand' ₽bacoes de antiquis temporibus exigebant; que fine magno ipforum pauperum incommodo pt' expenfas non modicas nequiverant expedire: Quodque contingencium vacacionum temporibus quandoque immo pcrebius ₽ captanda folucoe predicte fumme centum & quadraginta libr' ipfius ptem magnam & notabilem expendebant: Et quod magifter Thomas de Aftele, ultimus rector pdce ecclie, quibufdam quefitis coloribus fuper pftacione dearum viginti libr' moleftacoes varias eifdem pauperibus intuliffet: Volens pietatis intuitu dictis pauperibus ubius & utilius pfpicere, & de pfatis fummis fecuritatem facere per quam poffent dno quiecius famulari; & ne a quoquam fucefforum fuorum impoftum de eifdem poffit quicquam in dubium revocari, pdcam eccliam de Reculvre, ut de fructibus ejufdem imperpetuum folverent, fumme memorate, tam ad exoneracionem archiepórum Cant' fede ipfa plena, quam nobilium regum Anglor' fuccedentibus vacacionum hujus temporibus, in recompenfacionem confenfus regii in appropriacione pdicta & fub eadem cordicione adhibiti fibi & menfe fue archiepali in perpetuum aucte aplica appropriari optinuit, & univit. Set idem pat' revendus ante finalem expedicionem fecuritatis hujus ficut Dño placuit ab hac luce migravit. Nos vero Simon archiepus pdcus fibi quamvis immeriti fuccedentes, confiderantes hec ad laudem Dei, neceffitatum pauperum pdictorum fublevacionem piiffimam, de intencione puriffima ₽ceffiffe: ipfius pris cupientes ftudiofis inherere veftigiis; receptis pmit' fuper pmiffis omnibus actis in formacoibus atque veris, tractatu infuper cum capitulo ūro Cant' diligenti, eo ₽pterea evocato, habito fpiritualiter fuper pmiffis, caufis pdcis difcuffis, & decreto p nos interpofito fuper eis, ad laudem Dei & quietem dictor' pauperum neceffitatumque fuorum relevacoem congruam, exoneracoemque Cant' archiepórum de fructibus ecclie predicte memoratas fummas vidl' ad centum & fexaginta libr' fe extendentes, per nos, & fucceffores ūros ipfa fede plena, & ipfa fede vacante per manus eorum qui fruct' & emolumenta dicte ecclie & capellarum eidem annexarum funt percepturi, juxta diftincionem inferius annotatam quamdiu menfe archiepali appropriata duraverit, fore decernimus in perpetuum exfolvend': Ad quarum quidem folucoem quatuor anni temporibus p equales porciones; vidl', feftis Sti Martini in yeme, purificacois

beate

beate Marie virginis, apoſtolor' Pĥi & Jacobi, & Sc̄i Petri quod dicitur ad vincula, de fructibus ecclie p̄c̄e, quamdɪu ſic unita menſe archiep̄alɪ fuerit fidideliꝉ' faciend', deliberac̄oe provɪdo p̄uptenta de conſenſu p̄dc̄ɪ capiꝉli ūrɪ, ꝓpt' cauſas ꝓdc̄as, & utɪli- tatem archiep̄atus evidentem, obligamus dc̄am eccham de Recolvre ſic menſe ūre archɪe- p̄alɪ ut p̄'nɪttɪꝉ' unɪtam, nos ecɪam & ſucceſſores ūros, p̄fatɪs hoſpɪtalɪbus & pau- perɪbus ɪn eɪſdem degentɪbus, & que ſibɪ ſuccedent ɪn perpetuum, quocunque nomɪne ·cenſeant, pɪefata vero aproprɪacɪone qualɪꝉcumque ceſſante ſeu, quod abſit, revocata, vel qualɪꝉcumque diſſoluta, decernɪm' volum' & ecɪam ordɪnamus, quod temporæ- lɪa dɪctɪ archɪep̄atus ad ſoluc̄oem dictaɪum centum & quadragɪnta lɪbr' & p̄fata ec- cha de Reculvre ad ſoluc̄oem vɪgɪntɪ lɪbr' ſicutɪ p̄mɪtus fuerant, redeant & remane- ant onerata, hoſpɪtalɪaque predɪcta & pauperes tunc degentes ɪn eɪs quocumque nomɪne cenſeant, ad jus ſuum pcɪpɪendɪ & habendɪ dɪctas ſummas ut p̄fert' redeant antɪquum, & eo extunc lɪbere utant' & gaudeant', ſicut ante ɪpſius ecclie unɪonem & approprɪac̄oem p̄mɪſſis utɪ ſolebant qualɪꝉcumque ſeu gaudere, dɪcta approprɪac̄oe & tempɪs fluxu non obſtantɪbus, nec ɪmpedɪmentum afferentɪbus quovɪſmodo : Et ne ꝓpt' mortem archɪep̄orum dɪverſis temporɪbus decedencɪum de ſoluc̄oe ɪn p̄fatɪs ꞇmɪs facɪenda dubɪum alɪquod orɪat': Volumus & ordɪnamus quod quicumque archiep̄us poſt pceptos p eum annales fructus dc̄e ecclie & capellar' eidem annexar' poſt feſ- tum Sc̄i Micĥis & ante feſtum Paſch' tunc ꝓx' ſequens ex nunc deceſſit, quod ipſe & executores ſuɪ ad p̄ſtac̄om dɪctar' ſummar' quatuor ꞇmɪs dɪctam pcepc̄om ɪmmedɪ- ate ſequentɪbus integralɪꝉ' teneat', lɪceatque prɪorɪ dɪctɪ capɪtulɪ quɪ' fuerɪt fructus dumtaxat ɪn dɪcta ecclia & ejus capellɪs exɪſtentes tempore mortɪs ſue ſi ad ſo- luc̄oem p̄dɪctar' ſuffɪc̄e potɪnt ſummarum : Alɪoquɪn cetera bona dɪctɪ archiep̄ɪ ubɪ- cumque exɪſtentɪa uſque ad concurrentem quantɪtatem ꝓ ɪpſɪus ꞇmɪs a retro exɪſtent ſequeſtrare & ſub arto cuſtodɪre ſequeſtro, quouſque dɪctɪs pauperɪbus de prefatɪs ſummɪs fuerɪt integralɪꝉ' ſatɪsfactum : Si vero archiep̄us hujus poſt feſtum Paſche & ante feſtum Sc̄i Micĥis ꝓx' tunc ſequens deceſſit, cum ɪn hoc caſu de conſuetudɪne ec- clie Cant' notor' fructus majores & autumpnales ejuſdem annɪ ad ɪpſum ptɪnere de- bebunt : ſi ejus executores fructus dɪctɪ ecclie & capellarum hujus juxta conſuetudɪnem ɪpſam integre pcepɪunt : & de eɪs habuerɪnt facultatem lɪb̄am dɪſponendɪ, ad ſolu- c̄oem pro quatuor ꞇmɪs pcepc̄oem hujus ɪmmedɪate ſequentɪbus quatenus fructus hu- jus ad hoc ſe extenderɪnt & non ultɪma, ɪnſuper defunctɪ archiep̄ɪ nomɪne teneant': Quod ſi ſoluc̄oem hujus non fecerɪnt, lɪceat tunc dɪcto prɪorɪ, ſi vacatɪo ɪpſa uſque ad pcepcɪonem fructuum hujus duraverɪt, porcɪonem fructuum ecclie p̄dɪcte dc̄m defunctum contɪngentem & nulla alɪa bona dɪctɪ defunctɪ ſequeſtrare & ſub arto ſɪ- mɪlɪter cuſtodɪre ſequeſtro : quouſque de dɪctɪs ſummɪs ꝓ ꞇmɪs hujus debɪtɪs, ipſis pauperɪbus fuerɪt ɪntegralɪter ſatɪsfactum. Et ſi porcɪo dɪctum defunctum contɪngens non ſuffɪcɪat, reſɪduum de porcɪone futurɪ pontɪfɪcɪs ſuppleat': Noſtre tamen ɪntencɪo- nɪs non exɪſtɪt', quod ſi ſede plena temporalɪa dɪctɪ archiep̄atus quacumque ocaſɪone ad manus regɪas applɪcent': ɪta quod archiep̄ɪn de ſpɪrɪtualɪbus vɪvere & regɪ op- teat, ꝓ tempore hujus ecɪam ad ſolucɪonem alɪquam dɪctɪs pauperɪbus facɪend' ar- chiep̄us quɪ ꝓ tempore fuerɪt alɪqualɪt' teneat': Set ɪn eo caſu temporalɪa ſicut ɪp- ſius remaneant on̄ata. In cujus reɪ teſtɪmonɪum ſigɪllum noſtrum fecɪmus hɪɪs ap- ponɪ. Dat' apud Otteford, vɪɪɪ id̄us Febr', anno D̄nɪ Mɪlleſɪmo trecenteſɪmo quin- quageſɪmo quɪnto, & noſtre conſecratɪonɪs ſeptɪmo.

Copy of the Mortmayn of the lands in Reculver and dyverfe other placys,   1426

From the Harbledown Private Deeds.

HARY be the grace of God kyng of Ingelond and of Fraunce, and lorde of Erllond, to all peple in hoys pfent lettẽ behyt knowen fendyth gretyng. Knowe ze þᵗ wᵗ we fchull take wel belovyd to us in Criſt õ brodryn and fuſteryn of the hofpitall of Herbaldowne fchal have of the geſtys of dyṽfe pſonys to hem an-aᶜtyd aftyr þe ſtatute of þe londye ⅋ þe tenẽmt to þe hondys of þe mortemẽt and not put fro but enduyd thoo meiuagys v fchopys en gardyn xxx acris ⅋ to by the pecis of lond on zerde of wode ⅋ xxv fchelynges ⅋ the halfin dell of an fferdyng of rente, and rente zeldynge of a quat' of berr' *, ⅋ an henne ⅋ half a certell ⅋ þe III parte of a certell, and xL of eggs wᵗ hys ptinence in Reculvre and Herne, Herbaldoune, Goodneſton, fuburbz of Cauntburi, Weſtgate nexſt Cantburi ⅋ in the Ilde of Herteye de whyche of us fchul not holde in fee ⅋ is wurth be zer an c fchellynges ; that ys to feye, of John Roper of Weſtgate on mefuage and III fchopis in the parfche of Seynt Dunſtanys in þe fayde towne of Weſtgate ; of Thomas Inglot on mefuage ⅋ on a gardine in the parfche of Seynt Paulys in fub-urbz forfayde ; of John Eldyng of Weſtgate II fchoppis in þe forfayde parſhe of Seynt Dunſtanys ; of Solomon But III acris of londe in Reculṽe ; of Richard Lu-cas on acre of lande in Herne ; of Thomas Fog, knyt, III aciis ⅋ on zeide of londe ⅋ an half in Herbaldoune; and of Richard Mellar on pece of londe in Goodneſton ; of Phylypp Northwoode xx fchelynges of rente comyng of diṽfe londis ⅋ tenẽmts in that forfeyde towne of Herne ; of John Sewale II fchelynges of rente, and of zefte of II acr' of londe ⅋ half in þe forfayde towne of Herne; of John Harewell of Goodneſton vi pence of rente and of a mefuage in Goodneſton ; of Willyam Ive, John Halle of Sandwyche, and William Buttone of ho Ofprenge IIII fchelynges and vi pence, and the half of a fferdyng of rente, and rente of two certellis, and the III parte of a ceitell, and an henne ⅋ an half, and xv eggys of diṽfe tenẽmts in the Ielde of Heſtaye ; of John Ainyngbury and Alice his wyff, William Gybbard ⅋ Walt' Pymme rente of a quart' of ber', and too acris of londe in Herne, in the fame mefuage, fchopas, gardine, londe, woode, ⅋ rente forfayd to hem fo þe date aft' þe ſtatuyt forfayd in growyng have bene our licence or for our pgenitors upon thefe fchal nayt be wⁱdrawe : We, of our grace fpecialle ⅋ of our fupplication of the forfayde broderyn ⅋ foſtyn be þe zettys of the fame brodryn ⅋ foſtyn trefpas contemptys be hem in þᵗ parti made, in alfo moche as in us ptynes of occafyon forfayde, and furdyemor', of eny oþr in our grace we have zeve ⅋

* Quarter of barley.

ygrauntyd

ygrauntyd & yconfermyd how moche in yow is he þe fame biodryn & fostyn mefu-
agis, fchopys, gardins, londs, wode, & rente toifayde with hys pryntee havyng &
holdyng in pece to hem & iho here fuccefforis for evermore, wᵗoute ony pediment
of oure heyerys or of oure mynyftrys, or of mynyftrys of oure heyerys wherefoū
ev̄ hit be. In hijs witneffe heur letirs ben' made we have made patente. Wyt-
neffe me hymfelf at Weftm' þe xiii daye of Juni, de zere renyng of oure kyng xiii
zere.

Litera Pardonatûs Henrici Sexti; Jun. 13, 1426.

From the Harbledown Private Deeds.

HENRICUS Dei gratia rex Anglie & Francie & dominus Hibnie, omnibus ad
quos prefentès litere pervenerint falutem. Sciatis quod cum ut accepimus
dilecti nobis in Chrifto fratres & forores hofpitalis de Herbaldoune habeant, & prede-
ceffores fui habuerunt, de donis diverfar' perfonar' eis factis poft ftatutum de terris
& tenementis ad manum mortuam non ponend' editum, duo mefuagia, quinque fchopas, unum gardinum, triginta acras & duas parvas pecias terre, unam rodam bofci,
viginti & quinque folidatas & medietatem unius quadrantate redditus, & redditum
unius quarterii ordei, unius galline, & dimid' unius farcelle * & tertie partis unius farcelle, & quadraginta ovor' cum pertinenciis in *Recolvre, Hierne*, Herbaldoune, Gwode-
fton, fuburbiis Cantuarie, Weftgate juxta Cantuar', & Infula de Hertaye, que de
nobis non tenentur in capite, & valent per annum centum folidos; videlicet, de
Johe Roper de Weftgate unum mefuagium & tres fhopas in parochia Sc̄i Dunftani,
in predicta villa de Weftgate; de Thoma Inglot unum mefuagium & unum gardinum in parochia Sc̄i Pauli, in fuburbiis predictis; de Johe Yelding de Weftgate
duas fhopas in predicta parochia Sc̄i Dunftani; de Salomone But tres acras terre in
Recolvre; de Ric̄o Lucas unam acram terre in Hierne; de Thoma Fogg chivaler
tres acras & unam rodam terre & dimid' in Herbaldoune; de Ric̄o Mellere unam
peciam terre & unam rodam bofci in eadem villa; de Willo Mortone & Johanna
uxore ejus tres acras terre in eadem villa; de Robto Dodyngton unam peciam terre
in Guodnefton; de Pho Northwode viginti folidatas redditus provenientes de diverfis
terris & ten' in predicta villa de Hierne; de Johe Sewale duos folidos redditus exeuntes de duabus acris terre & dimid' in predicta villa de Hierne; de Johanne Narnhell
de Gwodnefton fex denariatas redditus exeuntes de uno mefuagio in Gwodnefton;
de Willo Yoe, Johe atte Hall de Sandwych, & Willo Bottone de Ofprenge, quatuor folidatas & fex denariatas ac medietatem unius quadrantate redditus, & redditum duar' farcellar' ac tercie partis unius farcelle, unius galline & dimid' & quin-
decim ovor' exeunt' de diverfis tenementis in Infula de Herteye; de Johe Aryng-
burge, juniore, & Alicia uxore ejus, Willo Gilbert, & Waltero Symme, redditum

---

* The only fenfe of *farcellus* and *fercellus* in the Gloffaries is *the fgi of an hoop, indicating that wine is fold* at the houf: where it hangs out. Q. If it can bear that fenfe here?

unius

·unius quarteril ordei exeunt' de una grangea & uno stabulo ae duabus acris terre in Hierne; & eadem mesuagia, shopas, gardinum, terram, boscum, & redditum predicta, sibi sic data post statutum predictum ingressi fuerint, licentia nostra aut progenitor' nostror' super hiis non optenta: Et nos, de gracia ñra speciali, & ad supplicationem predictor' fratrum & sororum, pardonavimus eisdem fratribus & sororibus transgressiones, contemptus, & forisfacturas per ipsos in hac parte factos, & quicquid ad nos pertinet occasone predicta. Et ulterius, de uberiori gracia nostra, dedimus, concessimus, & confirmavimus, quantum in nobis est, eisdem fratribus & sororibus, mesuagia, shopas, gardinum, terram, boscum, & redditum predicta, cum suis pertinentiis; habend' & tenend' quietè sibi & successoribus suis imperpetuum, absque impeticoe ñri, heredum vel ministrorum nostrorum, sive ministror' heredum ñror' quorumcumque. In cujus rei testimonium has literas nostras fieri fecimus patentes. Teste meipso apud Westm', tertiodecimo die Junii, anno regni ñri tertiodecimo. Per breve de privato sigillo. WAKE.

Abp. Stafford's Grant to John Pawlyn, of divers Escheats at Reculver, &c.

From the Register of that Archbishop.

OMNIBUS Christi fidelibus ad quos presentes littere pervenerint Johannes * permiss' divina Cant' archiep' totius Anglie primas & apostolice sedis legatus salutem in Dño sempeternam. Noveritis nos concessisse dilecto & fideli servienti Johi Pawlyn pro bono & laudabili servicio nobis & ecclesie nre Cant' multipliciter impenso quandam escaetam apud Reculvre ad manus ñras devenientem per mortem Johis Clere, alteram escaetam ad manus ñras similiter devenientem per mortem cujusdam mulieris vocat' Lap' Wyncheslove, sex acr' terre in Rolling que ad dictas manus ñras devenerunt ut escaet' per mortem Johanne que fuit uxor Michaelis Downer, duas pecias terre vocat' Hunterslonde in Tenterden, & unum messuagium in Senitmauchurche que ad dictas manus ñras devenerunt similiter ut escaeta; habend' & tenend' omnia predict' escaet' terras & messuagium cum eorum redditibus & proficuis quibuscunque prefato Joh' Pawlyn, heredibus & assignatis suis, a dat' presentium usque ad finem quadraginta annorum extunc prox' sequentium & plenarie complet' absque aliquo nobis vel successoribus nostris inde reddend' per presentes. In cujus, &c. Dat' apud Lambeth, xvi Nov. Anno Domini MCCCCXLV.

* Abp. Stafford 1443—1452, lord chancellor and lord treasurer.

Z

INCUMBENTS of RECULVER,

INCUMBENTS.	REGISTERS.
RECTORS.	
Hugh occurs rector, between 1171 and 1184 (fee p. 129.)	
1299, 8 Mâr. John de Langeton, rector, (fee p. 119)	Winchelfey, f. 274. b.
1310. Nicholas Tyngewicke, rector, and the firft vicar. (fee pp. 78, 136.)	Ibid. f. 39.
VICARS.	
1351, 8 May. John de Iflip,	Iflip, f. 260. b.
Thomas Newe *. See p. 157.	
1356, 14 July. Hugh Power †, on the refignation of Niewe.	Ibid. f. 273. a.
1361, 25 Oct. William de Blytheworth, on the death of Power.	Ibid. f. 292. b.
1376, 8 Oct. Richard Skeene, by exchange with Blytheworth.	Sudbury, f. 119. a.
1384, 2 Oct. John Langham, by exchange with Richard Skeene.	Courteney, f. 255. a.
1386, 23 May. Thomas Attkyn, on the refignation of John Langham.	Ibid. f. 265. a. b.
1387, 18 Oct. John Montagu, on a legal vacancy.	Ibid. f. 267. b.
1392, 3 Aug. John Bedell, alias de Sancto Dionyfio, by exchange with Montagu.	Morton, Dene, Bourchier, and Courteney, fol. 205. b.
1392, 11 Oct. John Bradley, on the death of Bedell.	Ibid. fol. 207.
1393, 15 June. Robert Langton, on the refignation of Bradley.	Ibid. fol. 212.
1402, 24. Nov. John Bulwyk, by exchange with Langton.	Arundel, vol. I. fol. 292.
1403, 13 Jan. William Wenlyfton, by exchange with Bulwyk.	Ibid. fol. 292. a.
1414, 3 Jan. John Spifer, on the death of Wenlyfton.	Chicheley, vol. I. f. 62. b.
1416, 10 Dec. John Palmere, by exchange with Spifer.	Ibid. fol. 80. b.

* I'e refigned it for the rectory of Aldington, and was alfo rector of Godmerfton. See p. 127. He founded two chantries at Reculver, and another at Hothe, in 1354, and a fourth at Harbledown in 1371. See p. 157.

† In 1357 Thomas de Aftele is mentioned as " ultimus rector ;" fee p. 149.

INCUMBENTS.	REGISTERS.

VICARS.

1421, 3 Aug.	Henry Befet, by exchange with Pal-mere.	Ibid. fol. 128. a.
1431, 14 Mar.	John Whitinge, on a legal vacancy.	Ibid. fol. 194. b.
1433, 20 Jan.	John Fcurnes, by exchange with Whitinge.	Ibid.
1449, 9 Oct.	—— Kelfey, on the death of Fournes.	Stafford and Kemp. f.01.
1452, 17 Dec.	John Cooke, on the refignation of Kelfey. Thomas Thorp.	Ibid. fol. 322.
1479, 17 Nov.	John Bedell, on the death of Thorp.	Bourchier, fol. 122. b.
1482, 8 Feb.	John Nutkin, on the refignation of Bedell.	Ibid. fol. 132. a.
1495, 29 April.	Leonard Eglesfeld, on the refignation of Nutkin.	Morton, Dene, Bourchier, and Courteney, fol. 158. a.
1519, 25 June.	John Penyton, M. A. Lawrance Miller, on the death of Penyton.	Warham, fol. 368. a.
1556, 12 July.	Thomas Hewitt, on the death of Miller.	Pole, fol. 69. a.
1560, 10 May.	William Vele, on the refignation of Hewitt.	Parker, vol. I. fol. 343.
1575, 11 Feb.	Joshua Hutton, by lapfe, on the prefentation of the Queen.	Ibid. vol. II. fol. 118. a.
1584, 4 Jan.	William Baldok, on the refignation of Hutton.	Whitgift, vol. I. fol. 457. b.
1594, 18 Jan.	Robert Hunt, on the death of Baldok.	Ibid. vol. II.
1602, 5 Oct.	Barnabas Knell, on the refigna-tion of Hunt.	Ibid. vol. III. fol. 272. b.
1661, 5 Sept.	Robert Goddin, M. A. on a legal vacancy.	Juxon, fol. 127. b.
1672, 29 Oct.	Henry Hughes, B. A. on the death of Goddin.	Sheldon, fol. 252. b.
1679, 10 April.	Alexander Innes, M. A. on a legal vacancy.	Sancroft, fol. 377. b.
1688, 22 April.	Theophilus Beck, on the refignation of Innes.	Ibid. fol. 385.
1688-9, 15 Mar.	Adam Reeves, M. A. on the refig-nation of Beck.	Ibid. fol. 427. a.

1695,

VICARS.	REGISTERS.
1695, 7 Mar.	Francis Green *, on the death of Reeves.	Tillotfon, fol. 159. b.
1716, 6 Mar.	William Squire †, M. A. on the death of Green.	Wake, vol. I. fol. 299. b.
1726, 17 Nov.	Peter Vallavine ‡, LL. B. on the refignation of Squire.	Ibid. vol. II. fol. 235. b.
1729, 24 Oct.	Thomas Clendon ‖, M. A. on the refignation of Vallavine.	Ibid. fol. 235. b.
1757, 26 Aug.	Thomas Thompfon §, M. A. on the death of Clendon.	Secker.
1762, Feb.	Anthony Lukyn **, B. A. on the refignation of Thompfon.	Ibid.
1779, 13 Feb.	Richard Sandys ††, on the death of Lukyn.	Cornwallis.
1782, 16 April.	Richard Morgan, on the death of Sandys.	Ibid.

* See p. 125.

† Refigned this vicarage for that of Herne. See p. 160.

‡ Alfo vicar of Monckton, afterwards one of the minor canons of Canterbury cathedral, and vicar of Prefton near Wingham, for which he refigned Reculver. Died in 1767.

‖ Alfo vicar of Sturry.

§ Refigned this for the vicarage of Elham, where he died in 1773. He was alfo one of the fix preachers in Canterbury cathedral, and had been miffionary on the Coaft of Africa; in defence of which inhuman and unchriftian traffic he publifhed a pamphlet in 1772, intituled, " The African " trade for Negro Slaves fhewn to be confiftent with the Principles of Humanity, and with the " Laws of Revealed Religion."

** Afterwards M. A. holding with this vicarage, by difpenfation, the united rectories of St. Mildred's and All Saints in Canterbuiy.

†† He married, March 27, 1781, the right hon. Lady Frances Alicia Aflong, relict of William Aflong, efq. and youngeft fifter to the earl of Tankerville. He had kept his terms and exercife for the degree of LL. B. at Cambridge; and died Feb. 27, 1782.

RECULVER CHANTRIES.

ORDINACIO cantarie in eccl' de Racolvere, directa Tho. Nyewe * deWolton, rectori eccl' de Aldington, dudum vicar' eccl' paroch' de Raculyre, Cant' diœc'. Dat' apud Maghfield, 23 Mart', 1354. Regist. Illip, fol. 104. a.

Condemnatio per mag' Will' de Wyttlesey, cancellar' et commissar' dni archiepi,. in causa detentionis et subtractionis redditus eccl' de Racolvere, Will' Gilbert parochian' dicte eccle, comparentem omnes terras in paroch' de Raculvere et Chiftlet dicte Cant' dicec' ad se per obitum Alicie de Brouke devolutas ex pia causa in xiii sol' et iiii den' annui redditus ad subsidium suftentationis unius capellani divina in eccl' de Raculvere pro anima dicte Alicie et animabus omnium fidelium defunctorum celebraturi imperpetuum rite et legitime esse onoratas; et petentem se in dict' xiii s̃ iiii d̃ solvend in eccl' de Racolvere in feftis nativitatis Dñi et nativitatis S. Johannis Baptifte annis fingulis capellano predicto sententialiter et diffinitiva condempnata. Dat' et Oct' in eccl' paroch' de Maghfield, 8 kal' Maii, 1354. Regift Illip, fol. 114. a.

Confirmatio ordinationis trium cantariarum; duarum videlicet in eccl' de Reculver, et tertie in capella de Hothe eidem annexe, per Dñm Tho. Niewe rect' eccl' de Godmersham fundat'. Dat' apud Saltewode, 4 kal' Junii, 1371. Regifter Wittlesey, fol. 45, a, b. 46, a, b.

Declaratio dni archiepi cujusdam clausule non residentie super ordinatione duarum cantariarum in ecclesia de Recolvre. Dat' Cantuar', 1 April. 1377. Regifter Sudbury, fol. 35. a. b.

Submissio Johis Oxendenne de paroch'de Wingham, Cant' dicec', propter subtractionem annui preftationis xiii s̃ iiii d̃ a capellano cantarie beate Marie iu eccl' de Reculvre, ex eo quod ipse Johes Oxendenne certas terras et tenementa que olim fuerint cujusdam Will' Gilbert defuncti in parochiis de Chiftlet et Racolvre ejusdem Cant' dicec' protunc habebat, possidebat, et occupabat; quas quidem terras et tenementa idem Johes Oxendenne adquisierat de heredibus sive executoribus vel feossatoribus cujusdam Laurentii Buckvell defuncti. Quodque occupator et possessor quicumque dictar' terrar' et tenement' pro tempore exiftens unum annuum redditum sive unam preftationem spualem tresdecem solidorum et quatuor denariorum capellano cuicunque cantarie beate Marie in eccl' de Reculver fundat' et ad collationem propriam dni Cant' archip' pleno jure spectantis pro tempore exiftenti solverit fingulis annis imperpetuum absque contradictione aliqua in hac parte. Tamen idem Johes non ignarus dictar' terrar' et tenement' possessor sive occupator prefatum annuum reddit' de xiii s̃. iiii d̃. diu subtraxit et detinuit. Dat apud' Cant' 6 Junii, 1420. Regifter Chicheley, Pars 2. fol. 338. b. 339. a.

* In a MS. Hiftory of Eaftbridge Hofpital, by Nicholas Battely, M. A. it appears that this person was nominated mafter of that Hofpital Dec. 18, 1351, and continued so till 1382. In different deeds he is called Thomas de Wilton, Thomas de Wolton, and Thomas Newe de Reculvre. He is ftyled by Somner "vir veie infignis, rector ecclefiæ de Aldington, dudum vicarius ecclefiæ de Raculvre." See pp. 127, 154.

The

The following Names of Incumbents of the Chantries at RECULVER occur in the Archiepifcopal Regifters at Lambeth.

	CHANTRY PRIESTS.	REGISTERS.
	William Drogby, chaplain of Trinity chantry.	Iflip, fol. 297. a.
1382. 4 Jan.	Thomas Webb, chaplain.	Courteney, f. 248. a.
1383. 27 Aug.	John Wengrave, by exchange with T. Webb.	Ibid. f. 251. a.
1384. 18 Nov.	John Cherchgate, by exchange with Wengrave.	Ibid. f. 255. a.
	Thomas Faunt.	
1425. 28 Julii,	William Caldewell, on the refignation of Faunt.	Chicheley, pars 1. 156. b.
	William Speere.	
1459. 8 March.	John Furbour, on the refignation of Speere.	Reg. Bourchier, f. 5. b.
1462, 16 Nov.	William Kirkeby, on the refignation of Fourbour.	Ibid. p. 856.
1464, 16 Feb.	Robert Afhford.	Ibid. fol. 90. a. b.
	Simon Flegard, by exchange with Afhford.	
1466, 3 Oct.	John Hunter, on the refignation of Flegard.	Ibid. fol. 94. a.
1466, 15 Jan.	Alex. Syddy, on a lawful vacancy.	Ibid. p. 94. b.
	John Bonaunteer.	
1480, 19 April.	Thomas Ballys, on the refignation of Bonaunteer.	Ibid. fol. 125.
1480, 8 Jan.	Simon Wareyn, on the refignation of Ballys.	Ibid. fol. 127. b. a.
1495, 19 April.	John Michell, on the death of Wareyn.	Morton, Dene, Bourchier, and Courteney, fol. 158. a.
1531, 18 Sept.	Thomas Dale, on the refignation of Michell.	Warham, fol 405. b.
1538, 4 July.	Thomas Hewett, on the refignation of Dale.	Cranmer, fol. 365. a.

I N.

INCUMBENTS of HERNE.

	VICARS.	REGISTERS.
1310.	Hugh de Godyneſtre *, firſt vicar.	Winchelſey, f. 30.
1321, 27 Oct.	Henry Rouhall, by preſentation of Nicholas Tyngewicke.	Reynolds, f. 29.
1350, 7 Jan.	Richard Medeborne.	Iſlip, f. 255. a.
1357, 15 Oct.	Will. Kac, on the reſignation of Medeborne. John Hawe.	Ibid. f. 279. a.
1376, 9 July.	Nich. de Farneham, on the death of Hawe.	Sudbury, f. 114. a.
—— 28 Oct.	Roger Sutton, by exchange with Farneham.	Ibid. f. 119. a.
—— 28 Oct.	John Chert, by exchange with Sutton.	Ibid. 119. b.
1376, 31 Dec.	Will. Graunt, by exchange with Chert.	Ibid. f. 123. a.
1393, 19 March.	Will. Goſſe.	Courteney, in Morton, Dene, Bourchier, and Courteney, f. 216. b.
1431, 10 Feb.	Henry Baſſett, on a legal vacancy.	Chicheley, p. 1. f. 194. a.
1432, 5 May.	John Derby.	Ibid. 195. b.
1446, 12 Aug.	John Bedale, on the reſignation of Derby.	Stafford, f. 90. a.
1464, 9 Oct.	Chriſtopher Warmyngton, by exchange with Bedall. Richard Bonaventure.	Bourchier, f. 89. b.
1489, 2 July.	John Caton, on the reſignation of Bonaventure.	Morton, Dene, Bourchier, and Courteney, f. 146. a.
1511, 29 March.	Andrew Benſtede, on the death of Caton.	Warham, f. 342. a.
1531, 14 Aug.	John Warren, on the reſignation of Benſtede.	Ibid. f. 405. b.

* This vicar is named in the endowment, but whether he ſucceeded to it is not certain.

1538.

VICARS.	REGISTERS.
1538, 30 April. Nicholas Ridley *, S. T. B. on the death of Warren.	Cranmer, 364. b.
1549, 16 Jan. Tho. Broke †, clerk ‡.	Ibid. f. 410.
1562, 21 Dec. John Brydges, on a legal vacancy.	Parker, 358. b.
1590, 5 Sept. Richard Colfe, on the resignation of Brydges.	Whitgift, f. 488. b.
1613, 22 June. Isaac Colfe, on the resignation of R. Colfe.	Abbot, 396. b.
1616, 19 Sept. Jacob Colfe ‖, on the resignation of Isaac Colfe.	Ibid. 420.
1617, 12 Feb. Tho. Harward, on the death of Jacob Colfe.	Ibid. 429. b.
1620, 2 March. Alexander Chapman §, on the death of Harward.	Ibid. p. II. f. 326. a.
1629, 12 Sept. Francis Ketelby, D. D. on the death of Chapman.	Ibid. p. III. f. 185. a.
1634, 11 Oct. John Reader, on the resignation of Ketelby.	Laud, p. I. f. 310. a.
John Webb, died 1689.	
1689, 16 Oct. Will. Foache **.	Sancroft, f. 41. b.
1713, 4 Dec. John Ramsey, on the death of Foache.	Tenison, p. II. f. 219. a.
1724, 26 Oct. Henry Archer, D. D. †† on the death of Ramsey.	Wake, p. I. f. 333. a.
1726, 29 Oct. William Squire, M. A. on the resignation of Archer.	Ibid. p. II. f. 235. a.
1739, 29 March. Rob. Gascoyne ‡‡, B. A. on the death of Squire.	Potter, f. 267. a.
1752, 4 Nov. Henry Hall ‖‖, M. A. on the resignation of Gascoyne.	Herring, f. 294. b.
1756, 7 July. William Rogers §§, B. A.	Ibid.
1773, 12 Nov. John Duncombe ***, M. A.	Cornwallis.

* Bishop of Rochester 1547, bishop of London 1550, martyred 1555. See p. 106.
† One of the six preachers in the cathedral.
‡ Per resignat' rev' pat' Nicholai Roffen' episcopi ejusdem vicarie commendatarii vacantem.
‖ Third son of Dr. Richard Colfe, prebendary of Canterbury. See Wood's Ath. Ox. I. 257. II. 189. Fasti, 179, 180.
§ Also rector of Deal.
** Presented by the king, during Abp. Sancroft's suspension.
†† He quitted it for the rectory of Mersham.
‡‡ He quitted it for the rectory of Evershot in Bedfordshire.
‖‖ Mr. Hall resigned this vicarage on being presented to that of East Peckham in the same county, 1756, which he held with Harbledown. A particular account of him will be given in the History of the Hospitals of Harbledown and St. John's Northgate.
§§ Died Aug. 28, 1773.
*** The present incumbent, rector of St. Andrew's and St. Mary Bredman's, Canterbury, master of Harbledown and St. John's Hospitals, and one of the six preachers in the cathedral.

7 HERNE

H E R N E, Cantaria B. MARIÆ.

Chantry Priests.	Registers.
William Burke.	
1377, 3 non. Jan. John Kyngg, on the refignation of Burke.	Sudbury, fol. 123. b.
1385, 28 Dec. Nich. Crek, prefb. John Robyn.	Courteney, fol. 259. a.
1440, 14 Oct. Tho. Curteyfe, on the refignation of Robyn.	Chicheley, p. 1. fol. 226. a
1443, 19 March. John Florens, on the refignation of Curteyfe.	Stafford, fol. 76. b.
1460, 20 Aug. Rich. Wyram.	Bourchier, f. 78. a.
1489, 4 Jan. John Caton, on the refignation of Wyreham. Richard ap Gryffythe.	Morton, Dene, Bourchier, Courteney, f. 145. a. b.
1506, 10 Oct. Will. Mychill, on the refignation of Gryffythe.	Warham, f. 328. b.

END OF NUMBER XVIII.

₊ This Number contains Eight Plates, all regularly paged.

E R R A T A.

P. 73. l. ult. r. ' 1313, 7 Edward II. ;' and in note †, for ' Robert Kilwarby, r. 'Walter Reynolds.'

P. 77. l. 18. r. ' fig. 9.' And fee the defcription corrected in p. 86.

P. 99. l. 6. r. ' Eafter-Monday.' There is another fair at Broomfield in this parish on Whitfon-Monday.

P. 114. note *, r. ' Hunters-forftal.'

P. 128. l. 6. from bottom, r. ' Chilforftall' (from the cold), now Herne common.

BIBLIOTHECA

TOPOGRAPHICA

BRITANNICA,

N° XLV.

CONTAINING

An APPENDIX to the HISTORIES of RECULVER
and HERNE;

AND

OBSERVATIONS, by Mr. DENNE, on the Archiepifcopal
Palace of MAYFIELD in SUSSEX.

LONDON:

PRINTED BY AND FOR J. NICHOLS,

PRINTER TO THE SOCIETY OF ANTIQUARIES.

MDCCLXXXVII.

[PRICE THREE SHILLINGS AND SIX PENCE.]

AMONG the various Labours of Literary Men, there have always been certain Fragments whose Size could not secure them a general Exemption from the Wreck of Time, which their intrinsic Merit entitled them to survive; but, having been gathered up by the Curious, or thrown into Miscellaneous Collections by Booksellers, they have been recalled into Existence, and by uniting together have defended themselves from Oblivion. Original Pieces have been called in to their Aid, and formed a Phalanx that might withstand every Attack from the Critic to the Cheesemonger, and contributed to the Ornament as well as Value of Libraries.

With a similar view it is here intended to present the Publick with some valuable Articles of BRITISH TOPOGRAPHY, from printed Books and MSS. One Part of this Collection will consist of Re-publications of scarce and various Tracts; another of such MS. Papers as the Editors are already possessed of, or may receive from their Friends.

It is therefore proposed to publish a Number occasionally, not confined to the same Price or Quantity of Sheets, nor always adorned with Cuts; but paged in such a Manner, that the general Articles, or those belonging to the respective Counties, may form a separate Succession, if there should be enough published, to bind in suitable Classes; and each Tract will be completed in a single Number.

Into this Collection all Communications consistent with the Plan will be received with Thanks. And as no Correspondent will be denied the Privilege of controverting the Opinions of another, so none will be denied Admittance without a fair and impartial Reason.

This NUMBER contains EIGHT PLATES;

In Continuation of those already given in Nº XVIII; viz.

Plate IX. p. 162.

West Front of the Church at RECULVER, taken October 11. 1781.

* The Remains of a Chapel, now converted into a Cottage.
† The arch over the Window on the South side is composed of Roman bricks.
‡ The North Porticus Lighthouse, or Tower.

|| Margate.
§ Birchington.
¶ The Isle of Thanet.

The Rev. John Brydon F.S.A. completes this Plate.

——————

LETTER to Mr. JOHN NICHOLS,

From the Rev. JOHN PRIDDEN, M. A.' F. A. S.

S I R,   Fleet-ftreet, March 30, 1787.

AFTER the very learned and ingenious communications
with which the publick have been favoured refpecting the
HISTORY of RECULVER, little can indeed remain to attract its
attention to a fubject fo feemingly exhaufted; nor would the
following memoranda have ever been liable to its cognizance,
did not the repeated attacks of the relentlefs ocean threaten a
fpeedy demolition to a place venerable for its antiquity, and to a
fabric not lefs admired for the peculiarity of its ftructure, than
affuredly ufeful as a fea-mark to navigators, among the numerous
fands and fhoals that infeft this coaft.

Reculver, whatever may have been its priftine grandeur, is
now dwindled into an infignificant village, thinly decked with
the cottages of fifhermen and fmugglers. The ruins of its caftle
are only fufficient to convey a faint idea of its original magnificence, while the fea, with gradual but frequent approaches,
baffles every effort to refcue from deftruction this devoted territory.

Of Queen's College, Oxford, Minor Canon of St. Paul's Cathedral, Vicar of
Heybridge juxta Malden, Effex, and Curate of St. Bride's, London.

A a   The

The church of this place, when viewed from the Ifle of Thanet, appears fo peculiarly majeftic and fingular in its ftructure, that it draws many vifitors during the bathing-feafon to contemplate its beauties. The difappointment is as great as general. The man of tafte, who expects to fee an elegant and ornamental pile, meets with nothing but a weather-beaten building, and the few embellifhments that once graced it mouldering away by the fury of the elements.   The citizen, who vifits the ifland for the exprefs purpofe of indulgence, and who, by the accidental obfervance of the Reculver fpires, is prompted to faunter as well here as elfewhere; after a ride of twelve miles [1], finds to his forrow no well-ftored larder, and, unlefs he can relifh dry bifcuit, bad ale, four cheefe, or weak moonfhine, he muft return to Margate to repair the damage his curiofity has impofed on his fenfitive affection.

The principal remaining curiofities at Reculver are, the church, an old chapel near it, part of a religious building, and the walls of the caftle.

The church, though compofed of common materials, is tolerably regular.   The weft front, flanked by two towers, each furmounted by a fpire, covered with lead, affumes a dignity uncommon to moft churches, and by its fymmetry, though deftitute of much ornament, commands a veneration fuperior to its merit.   The view of it in plate IX. was taken from a ftation fomewhat elevated, to introduce the profpect of the diftant country.   The north and fouth fides have little worthy of notice in them, and are nearly alike.   In plate X. I have given a north-

[1] There is a nearer way, over the Sands, when the tide is out; but it is by no means recommended for ftrangers to attempt it without a guide, as there are feveral pieces of quick-fand on the flats between St. Nicholas and Reculver.

eaft

Fig. 1. p. 165.

Inside of Reculver Church from the west end
Fig. 2. p. 165.

Fig. 3. *p. 165.*
Arms in the Chancel.

Fig. 6. p. 170.

Remains of an ancient building

Fig. 5. Effigies of Sandway &c. p. 167.

Alden delin. 1785.   Cook sc.

eaſt view [1], as being the moſt picturefque.   The roof of this church was formerly more pointed than at preſent, as will appear by the finiſhing of the eaſt and weſt walls, and by the upper part of the two windows over the weſt door being bricked up ; it has lately been repaired, and the following memorandum is raiſed on the lead :

A.   S A Y E R,

CHURCHWARDEN,

1775.

The inſide of the church and chancel, when viewed from the weſt door over which a ſtone gallery communicates to each of the towers, has a very regular and pleaſing effect (ſee plate X. fig. 2.) The pavement or flooring is in moſt places of very peculiar firmneſs, being compoſed of a very ſtrong cement ; and where that does not prevail, it is formed of the painted tiles which are ſo common in old churches.

On the north ſide of the altar are theſe arms carved in ſtone and blazoned ; Gules, ſemee of crofs croflets a lion rampant, Or, (ſee plate X. fig. 3.)

Againſt the ſouth wall of the chancel, within the altar rails, is the beautiful monument of Sir Cavaliero Maycote (ſee plate X.

---

[1] See Plate X. fig. 1.   While I was taking this view (about ten in the forenoon of April 17, 1781), a ſhock occaſioned by the exploſion of a powder-mill at Faverſham was ſo fenſibly felt here, as to alarm the whole village. The day was perfectly ſerene; not a ſingle cloud interrupted the azure beauty of the horizon. The vaſt body of fmoke, natural on ſuch an accident, kept a ſtationary appearance from eleven to three, in the ſhape given in the view ; it then aſſumed the ſhape of two eggs placed horizontally on each other, and towards five it formed a long ſtream, which ſeemed to reach ſeveral miles ; the appearance of this immenſe maſs of fmoke was viſible the next morning.   The ſhock was alſo felt at Margate.   This view alſo ſhews part of the vicarage, the foundation of the caſtle wall, the neglected chapel, now con-verted into a cottage, and the houſe, whofe foundations were ſo fapped by the fea in the ſtorms of the winter of 1782, as to be taken down to prevent its fall over the cliff.

A a 2

fig.

fig. 4.) The figures of himſelf, wife, and nine children, are well executed; the monument is ſurmounted with the creſt and arms of Maycote; creſt, a ball ſpiked; arms, quarterly, 1. 4. Ermine, in a canton, Argent, a ſtag ſeiant Gules; 2. 3. party per pale Sable and Ermine, a chevron engrailed Gules.

On the pedeſtal of the reading-table, between Maycote and his Lady, are the arms of Maycote impaling Moninges; Gules, three creſcents, Argent.

A little below the figures is the following inſcription:

HERE VNDER WAITE (FOR A JOYFVL RESVRRECTION) THE BODIES OF DAME
MARIE AND OF HER HVSBAND SIR CAVALIERO MAYCOTE, KNIGHT,
WHO LIVED TOGETHER IN GREAT CONTENTMENT (FROM St. ANDREW'S DAY,
ANNO 1586), FVLL 20 YEARS, IN WᶜH TIME THAY HAD 8 SONS AND
ONE DAVGHTER, NAMELY, JHON, THOMAS, GEORGE, RICHARDE, THOMAS, WIL‐
LIAM, HARBERT, GEORGE, AND ELIZABETH, WHEAROF 5 SONNES DYED BEFORE
THEM. SHE WAS THE DAVGHTER OF THOMAS MONINGES, GENT. AND ALES
CRISPE, SVMETIME DWELLERS AT SWANTON IN LIDDEN, AND DYED ON
CHRISTMAS-DAYE, ANNO 1606. HE WAS SONNE OF GEORGE MAYCOTE, GENT.
AND OF MARGARETTE BROOKER (LONG DWELLERS IN THIS PARISHE) AND DYED *
TO ALL WHOME THE LORDE BE MERCYFVL AT THE LATTER DAYE.

The only braſſes left in the church (except that of Ralph Brooke, whoſe monument is much ruined) are thoſe of the *Sandeweys*, on a flat ſtone in the chancel, near the altar rails. He is repreſented in armour with his feet reſting on a greyhound. She (with a label iſſuing from her mouth, on which is written, **fiat miſericoꝛdia tua Dᷠne ſuper nos**) is dreſſed in a looſe habit; her waiſt is exceedingly taper, and the ridiculous enormity of her head-dreſs fully reſcues our modern belles from every imputation of abſurdity in this part of their decoration. A little lower are the effigies of their numerous progeny; viz. 8 ſons and 7 daughters; over the man are 3 boars heads couped at the

---

* The date of his death is not inſerted on the monument.

neck,

neck, and over the woman 3 rams heads couped (fee plate X. fig. 5.) and this infcription:

Ijic jacet Johannes Sandewey armiger, et Johanna uxor ejus; quorum animabus propicietur ã eus. Amen.

The label iffuing from the mouth of the man, and two efcutcheons near the foot of the ftone, are loft.

Befides the infcriptions in the chancel already noticed in Nº XVIII. of the " Bibliotheca Topographica Britannica," is one on a. fand ftone near the entrance, thus fingularly infcribed :.

Here lieth the Body of Robert
Godden, gent. late Vicer of
Reculver; hee died Auguft
the 22d, 1672.

In the body of the church are feveral ftones to the memory of the families of *Cobb* and *Hills*. They are all in the middle aile, and are as follows :

Arms, a chevron between 3 cocks, impaling, on a bend eotized, a lion paffant :

HEERE LYETH BVRYED, THE BODYES OF
BENJAMIN COB, OF RECVLVER, IN THE COUN-
TYE OF KENT, GENT. AND OF ALICE HIS WIFE,
THE DAVGHTER OF ROBERT KNOWLE, ESQ.
OF HEARNE, IN THE SAID COVNTYE, GENT.
HE HAD ISSVE BY HER, TWO SONNES, ROBERT
AND FRANCIS, AND FOWRE DAVGHTERS, SVSANNAH,.
MARY, ANNE, AND MARGARET; HE DEPARTED
THIS LIFE ON THE 10TH DAY OF JVNE, 1642,
IN THE 38TH YEARE OF HIS AGE : SHE DYED
BEFORE, VPON THE 7TH DAY OF JVLY, 1641,
IN THE 33D YEAR OF HER AGE.

HERE ALSO LIETH BVRIED THE BOBY OF ROBERT COBB,
OF RECVLVER, IN THE COVNTY OF KENT, GENT. SONNE
OF BENJAMIN COBB; HE MARRIED MARY
DAVGHTER OF JONAS HVNT, GENT. SOMETIMES
OF CHISLET, BY WHOM HE HAD ISSVE 3 SONNES,
VIZ. BENJAMIN, ROBERT, AND JOHN, AND 2 DAVGHTERS,
ANNE AND MARY: HE DIED JVNE THE 17TH, 1676
AGED 42 YEARS.

Here

Here lieth buried the Body
of MARY COBB, daughter
of Robert and Mary Cobb :
Shee departed this life the
23d day of April, in the
Year of our Lord 1681,
aged 10 years.

Here lyeth the body of
BENJAMIN COBB, of Chiſlet, gent. ſon
of Robert and Mary Cobb, of Reculver,
who married Frances, late wife of
William Whiteing, of Chiſlet, by whom
he left iſſue one daughter, Mary
Cobb : He was buried the 10th of July,
1683, aged 21 years.

Arms.   On a feſs, between 3 cinquefoils pierced, a lion paſſant.

Here lyeth the body of
MARY late wife of ROBERT COBB,
of Reculver, gent. She was daughter
of Jonas Hunt, gent. ſometime of
Chiſlet. She was buried May the 29th,
1684, aged 45 years.

HERE LYETH THE
BODY OF HENRY
HILLS, WHO
DIED FEBR. 16,
1664.

HERE LYETH
THE BODY OF
MARY HILLS,
WHO DIED
MARCH 25,
1665.

HERE LYETH THE BODY OF HENRY
HILLS; HE HAD ISSUE BY HIS WIFE
CATHERINE TWO SONS AND TWO
DAUGHTERS, HENRY, JOHN, MARY, AND
CATHERINE. HE DIED IN DECEMBER,
1684, AGED 62 YEARS.

HERE

HERE LYETH THE BODY OF JOHN
HILLS, SON OF HENRY HILLS,
WHO HAD TO WIFE ELIZABETH.
HE DEPARTED THIS LIFE THE 20th
OF JUNE, 1685, AGED 30
YEARS.

On a ftone next the weft-door, much broken :

Here lieth interred the Body of Catherine Hills, who
departed this life the 25th day of January, 1696-7,
aged 72 years and odd months.
She had iffue by her hufband abovefaid, 2 fons,
and 2 daughters, Henry, John, Mary, and Catherine, all
buried near this place; fhe was daughter to
Vincent W--lderdown of Birchington, in the Ifle of
Thanet, yeoman; and her hufband Henry Hills gave
the poor men of Reculver the rent of 3 pounds 10s.
a year, payable the 24th day of June, for ever.

The following particulars are enumerated on a table fixed to
one of the fouth pillars in the middle aile.

From the parfonage, bequeathed by Chriftopher Milles, efquire, by his laft will, bearing date May 28, 1638, to be paid the laft day of Auguft every year, as long as the leafe fhall be continued to any of his fur name.	4	0	0

In May - Street.

An annuity arifing from one acre and five perches of pafture land, now or late in the occupation of Mr. Thomas Reynoldes.	0	-	-
Fifteen perches of wood-land, lying contiguous to the above.			
From two rods and twenty-four perches of pafture-land, now or late in the occupation of Vincent Harrifon.	0	6	0
From twenty-five perches of arable-land, now or late in the occupation of Stephen Sayer.	0	2	6

In Chiflet.

A meffuage or tenement, with one acre, three rods and twenty-fix perches of pafture and wood-land, now or late in the occupation of Benjamin Morris.	3	0	0

In Herne.

One acre, one rood, and eleven perches of pafture-land, now or late in the occupation of the faid Benjamin Morris.	1	-	-

1785.   RICHARD MORGAN, Vicar.

STEPHEN SAYER,
WILLIAM STAINES,   } Church-wardens.

The

The parochial Regifter of Reculver begins at 1602; but the following entries are all that the fhortnefs of my time admitted me to feleɛt.

1605, June 9, Chriftopher, fon of ⎤
1606, Oɛt. 9, Elizabeth, daughter of ⎰ Sir Chriftopher Clyve, knight, baptized.
1609, Sept. 10, Barbara, daughter of Thomas Thornhurft, efq; baptized.
1620, Sept. 28, Francis, fon of Sir Thomas Perryn, knt. was baptized in the chapel of Forde.
1672, Oɛt. 31, Robert, fon of Robert Cobb, gent. and Mary his wife, baptized.
1672, Aug. 25, Mr. Robert Godden, Vicar of Culver, buried.
1676, June 20, Robert Cobb, gent. buried.

Having an opportunity at the fame time of perufing the Regifter of the adjoining chapel of *Hoath*, I alfo feleɛted fuch entries as appeared obfervable. This regifter begins anno 1563.

1576, April 24, Mr. Spracklin, of St. Lawrence, and Joan Linch, widow, of Elm-ftead, married.
1624, April 15, Humfryd Peryent, gent. and dame Mary Peyton, widow of Sir Samuel Peyton, Knt. and Bart. married.
—— July 8, James, fon of Sir Thomas Peryent, Knt. baptized.
1679, April 1, Mr. John Webb, Vicar of Hearne, and Mrs. Joyce Roafe, of Chiflett, married.
1702, Richard Mantle, chofe clerke of Hoath.

A little north of Reculver Church, within a few paces of the edge of the cliff, are remains of an ancient chapel, now converted into a cottage ; many Roman bricks are worked in the mafonry of the walls, and in the fouth wall is an arch entirely compofed of them (fee plate X. fig. 1.) About 40 yards W. W. N. of the church, is a building which has the appearance of having been part of fome monaftic ereɛtion. (See plate X. fig. 6.) Of the Caftle, nothing remains but the maffy foundations of its walls, which are apparent on three fides of the hill, the north afpeɛt has, together with the fite thereof, been wafhed down ; fome huge fragments yet remain on the beach.

A

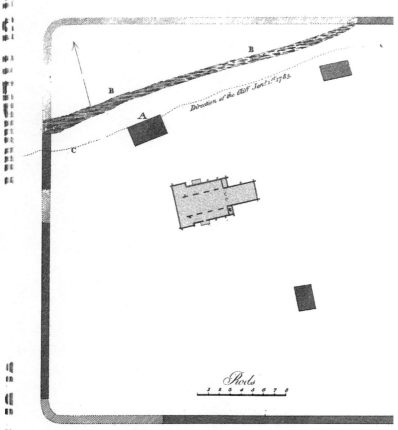

Direction of the Cliff Jan.ʸ 1.ˢᵗ 1785.

B

A

B

C

Rods
1 2 3 4 5 6 7 8

Plan of Reculver Church and Castle.

The shaded part B B shews the direction of the Cliff in 1780: CC in 1785.
The parts of the wall, shaded lightly, are either wholly destroyed, or concealed from view by the Soil.

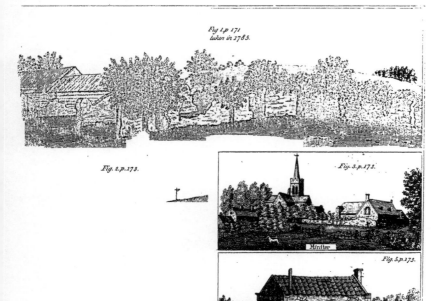

Fig. 1 p 171
taken in 1785.

Fig. 2.p.173.

Fig. 3.p.173.

Minster

Fig. 3.p.173.

Chantry at S? Laurence

ridden del. 1781.

A comparifon of plate XI. (here annexed) with the fame plan as it ftands marked N° IV. in your XVIIIth Number, will fhew the incroachment of the fea between 1780 and 1785.

The little mark where I have placed an afterifk, in the plan of the church, is not unlikely to be the fpot where the remains of Ethelbert were depofited. (See p. 72.)

Such are the trifling memorabilia, which I have been able to add to the more important communications the publick have already been indulged with from abler hands. The probability that within a very few years the church and town will become a prey to the fury of the waves, fully juftifies what is now fubmitted to its infpection, however infignificant, by   Yours truly,

JOHN PRIDDEN.

P. S. The following drawings will perhaps form a mifcellaneous plate or two of Kentifh Antiquities, not wholly unconnected with the neighbourhood of Reculver.

Plate XII. Fig. 1. Is a perfpective view of Ford Palace, taken in September 1785. Some account of it has been given in N° XVIII. to which Strype's Narrative may ferve as a companion :

" There belonged antiently to this great Archbifhoprick, many noble feats, and they of a firft and fecond rank. Of the former fort, were thefe palaces * following : That at Canterbury, that at Otford, at Knol, at Croydon, and Lambeth. Of the latter, were the country and manor-houfes at Ford, at Charte, Charing, Charteham, Tenham, Wingham, Bekefborn, and elfewhere. But before this Archbifhop's time, they were almoft all paft away from the fee. His predeceffor Cranmer ufed to be much at Ford, towards the latter end efpecially of King Edward : which was one of the oldeft feats of the archbifhops of Canterbury; a magnificent manfion, as Philpot calls it ; given by Ethelbert King of Kent, who granted alfo the whole parifh, called Chiftlet, wherein Ford ftandeth, unto the faid fee. It had a certain proportion of land impaled round it, in form of a park, as if they had judged it meet thereby to juftify the firft donation. But Bekefborn, a far lefs houfe, but more healthfully and conveniently fituated, pleafed Archbifhop Parker better. It was a fmall, yet an elegant houfe, very commodious for the Archbifhop's retirement and recefs, and the river brought fo convenient about it, that the trouts,

* Of Mayfield, another archiepifcopal palace, an account will be given in a future page.

the

the principal fifh there, are plentifully ufeful to it. But our Archbifhop found Bekefborn too ftrait for him. Ford was larger, as he wrote to the lord treafurer, but very inconvenient, being an old, decayed, waftful, unwholefome, and defolate houfe. To that cafe, it feems, it was come in his time. He therefore was minded to enlarge his houfe at Bekefborn, with the materials of the former. This enlargement he thought needful and requifite, as well for the foreigne friends, as for the foreigne enemies. Ford was in fuch a corner, and the foil fuch, as he thought no man would have any delight to dwell there, if he had any other place nigher the church. He would alfo, with the ruins of that, have repaired his palace at Canterbury, and fupplied it with fome better lodging. This, he faid, he thought honeft, and yet would leave houfes enough at Ford, to fuch as fhould have the overfight of his grounds there. Now, for the compaffing this, it was convenient he fhould have the Queen's confent. For this, he made ufe of the Lord Treafurer; intreating him to wait his opportunity to move her Highnefs in this fuite: That he might make a deed of gift of it to her; and then that fhe might grant it again to him and to his fucceffors; not meaning, as he profeffed, one penny of advantage to himfelf, but to the commodity of the fee, if it fhould ftand in any tolerable ftate. This was compounded in March. But he had it in his mind the December before; but was difcouraged from making the fuit, the Queen having denied him in fome things before: no queftion occafioned by fome of his back friends at court. "He "had thought," as he told the Lord Treafurer in that month, "to have uttered a "fmall fuit, that fhould not have been in honour hurtful to her Majefty, nor to her "purfe chargeable; but that he was too unlucky and unfortunate to win any thing "for himfelf, or his friends. Which made him refolve hereafter, to crave little, "as he had not ufed much importunity, he faid, in a dozen years before: although "moft of his predeceffors had things of more importance granted them by the "Prince's favour in their time. But he would hold himfelf within his bounds, "and take the times as they were; and would yet do his duty in confcience, and "ferve to his uttermoft power, till the day of his diffolution." And fo he waved wholly the mention what his requeft was at this time. But his requeft, when he afterwards difcovered it, feemed to find a favourable admiffion; for I find in April following, the writings were drawn concerning the tranflation of Ford Houfe, and fent to the Lord Treafurer for his approbation. But there they ftuck till the latter end of the year, and how long after I cannot tell: for in the month of November, he put his lordfhip in mind again of this bufinefs; telling him, "that if "his lordfhip would comfort him with her Majefty's grant, he would yet affay to "amend Bekefborn building." And in the fame month, he again told him, " that if "he knew her Majefty's contentation, he would prepare towards the reparation of "Bekefborn; meaning to do," as he faid, "while he lived, as though he fhould live "ever: and yet he trufted, being ready in all the ftorms of the world, to depofe "his tabernacle to-morrow; doubting not but his lordfhip was fo framed for "both: *Per bonam famam & infamiam, per convitia & laudes*, to go forward in his "vocation, as God had placed him." But the reafon of the delay of this bufinefs, was, I fuppofe, occafioned, partly by the Queen's going her progrefs this fummer;

fo

fo not at leifure to be fpoken to about leffer bufinefs; and partly by the oppofition of fome of his court enemies.   This in fine came to nothing.   Ford Houfe ftood till of late years it was pulled down by Sequeftrators.   And the Archbifhop finifhed Bekefborn this year, though not with that largenefs and magnificence his good heart intended."   Strype's Life of Parker, p. 406.

Fig. 2. Salmefton Grange, vulg. Samfon, was formerly a Grange belonging to the monaftery of St. Auftin, Canterbury ; much of the original building yet remains, particularly the chapel, infirmary, and fome of the inferior offices.   A South-weft view is here given.

Fig. 3. This view fhews an Eaft profpect of the church and manor-houfe of Minfter ; the front of the manor-houfe is much modernized fince the drawing given in Lewis's Antiquities of Thanet was made.   The ruins of a tower at the South angle of the building is part of the chapel belonging to the nunnery of this place.

Fig. 4. Dene Chapel, near Margate, ftands in a little valley, called Chapel-bottom, in the road from Margate to Minfter, a little S. W. of Salmefton ; it is a perfect ruin (the South wall being quite down), built of field flints rough cafted over ; on the North fide are the remains of two rooms, which (as they have no communication with the chapel) were probably the apart-ments of the officiating prieft   The chapel part meafures about 40 feet by 30 ; the above rooms and chapel as viewed from the North-weft are here fhewn.

Fig. 5. A North-eaft view of the remains of a little chapel, a fmall diftance eaftward from St. Lawrence, now turned into a cottage.   It was dedicated to the Holy Trinity, and in it was founded a chantry.

Fig. 6. South view of Quekes, a venerable manfion, about three quarters of a mile E. S. E. of Birchington, which town was antiently the manor, as this was the feat of the Quekes,

which

which family ended in a daughter, who was married to Mr.
Crifpe, of Stanlake, in Oxfordfhire. Henry Crifpe was fheriff
of Kent, and had fuch influence in thefe parts, that he was
ftyled *Regulus Infulæ Thaneti :* he died in 1575, leaving two fons;
one of which, Sir Nicholas, dying in 1651, gave his eftate to
his nephew Henry Crifpe, efquire, who was commonly called
Bonjour Crifpe, on account of his being carried into France, where
he was fome time, and learned no more French than *bonjour,* or
good-morrow. He, having one only fon, Sir William Crifpe, who
died before him, gave this feat and the eftate belonging to it to
his nephew Thomas Crifpe, efquire, who died in 1680, and left
four daughters, coheirs. At his houfe king William III. ufed
to refide, till the winds favoured his embarking for Holland. A
room, faid to be the bed-chamber of the royal gueft, is ftill
fhewn. His guards encamped in an adjoining enclofure. This
ancient feat, like moft others of the fame rank, is going faft
to ruin ; the weather penetrates into moft of the apartments
(particularly weftward of the porch), which have been the principal ones ; the tiles are blown off in many places, the windows
demolifhed, and no part of it inhabited, or indeed fit to be,
except a fmall portion at the end, which is occupied by a farmer.
A few years will probably reduce this building to what may be
feen Eaftward of the porch, as it is in agitation to pull the remainder down ; a very fine fuite of apartments at the North-weft
corner has been demolifhed this fummer (1781); and as any of
the inhabited part of the building may want repair, or purchafers
for the materials can be procured, the reft will fhare the fame fate.
The whole of this building is of brick, except the large ftone
window at the South-eaft corner, and the bottom of the South-weft
window. From this houfe, Henry Crifpe, efquire, a man of
great property, who had been high-fheriff for the county, was

furprifed,

furprized, and carried prifoner to the Spanifh Netherlands. As this was an undeniable fact, and the only inftance of the kind ever known in this kingdom *, it fhould feem to deferve notice. I could, therefore, wifh to perpetuate (as far as a publication of this fort may prefume to perpetuate) the memory of fo fingular an event. They who do not think themfelves interefted in the ftory, are at full liberty to pafs over it. I gave it in the words of the author of The Margate Guide."

" Henry Crifpe, efquire, of Quex, in the Ifland of Thanet,
" in Kent, was, in Auguft 1657, forcibly and violently, in the
" night-time, without his will, taken and carried out of his then
" dwelling-houfe at Quex, in the parifh of Birchington, near
" the fea-fide, by certain Englifhmen, and others, and by force
" carried to Bruges in Flanders, and detained there as a prifoner,
" till three thoufand pounds fhould be paid for his ranfom.
" Henry Crifpe, a few days after his arrival at Bruges, fent to his
" brother's fon, Thomas Crifpe, efquire, who then lived near
" Quex, to come over to him at Bruges, to give him affiftance
" in thofe great exigences and extremities ; and accordingly he
" went over to him, and after fome advice taken there, Henry
" Crifpe difpatched his nephew, Thomas Crifpe, into England,
" there to join his endeavours, together with the endeavours of
" his fon, Sir Nicholas Crifpe, knight, then in England, for his
" ranfom and enlargement, and to raife money for that purpofe ;
" both which they found great difficulty to effect, becaufe
" that Oliver Cromwell having, at that time, taken upon him
" the government of the nation, and fufpecting that the taking
" away Mr. Henry Crifpe was only a collufion, whereby to

* A like attempt was made, but fortunately prevented, on the famous Sir Thomas Spencer. See the Hiftory of Canonbury Houfe, Iflington.

" colour

" colour the lending or giving three thoufand pounds to King
" Charles II. then beyond the feas: Oliver Cromwell and his
" Junto did call a council, and made an order that the faid
" Henry Crifpe fhould not be ranfomed; whereupon much diffi-
" culty arofe to procure a licence to ranfom Henry Crifpe, which
" put Sir Nicholas Crifpe, and the faid Thomas Crifpe, to great
" trouble and expence to obtain. Sir Nicholas Crifpe died before
" his father was ranfomed, and then the whole care devolved
" on Thomas Crifpe to obtain the licence and to raife money.
" And after the death of Sir Nicholas Crifpe, he returned back
" to Bruges, to acquaint Henry Crifpe, that he could not raife
" fufficient money in England for his ranfom to be fuddenly
" done without the fale of fome part of his eftate ; and there-
" upon he impowered his nephew Thomas Crifpe, and one
" Robert Darrel, efquire, to make fale of fome lands for that
" purpofe, and all care and diligence was ufed to haften the
" ranfom ; and Thomas Crifpe, in the winter's dangerous feafon
" of the year, fix times paffed the feas, to comfort and confer
" with his uncle Henry Crifpe, in order to remove all obftruc-
" tions, and to raife money to redeem him out of his imprifon-
" ment at Bruges, where he was eight months before releafed,
" and then returned to England, and died at Quex, July 25, 1663."

" The above memorial (continues the author already quoted)
was communicated to me in Auguft 1766, by the late Hon. Mrs.
Rooke, of St. Lawrence, near Canterbury. It was found among
the writings of the eftate at Stonar in this ifland, of which fhe
was then the proprietor, but which formerly belonged to Mr.
Crifpe, and was mortgaged for his ranfom.

" Such other anecdotes as I have been able to obtain relative to
this matter, by the moft cautious and diligent enquiry among
perfons of good credit, are to the following effect :

7   " The

" The enterprize was contrived and executed by captain Golding of Ramfgate; he was a fanguine Royalift, and during the time that King Charles II. had taken refuge in France, he ran away with a very valuable merchant-fhip which he commanded (the Blackamoor Queen); and having fold both fhip and cargo for a large fum of money, he gave it all to the King, to fupply his neceffities. Golding was ever after in great favour with him; he was brought into England at the Reftoration, and had the command of the Diamond man of war, on board of which he was killed, in an engagement with four Dutch frigates, in May, 1665. Echard makes honorable mention of him, by the name of " the brave captain Golding." The affair was thus conducted: The party landed at Gore-end, near Birchington, and at Quex took Mr. Crifpe out of his bed without the leaft refiftance. They conveyed him in his own coach to the fea-fide, where he was forced into an open boat, without one of his domefticks being fuffered to attend him, although that favor was earneftly requefted. He was conveyed firft to Oftend, and from thence to Bruges, both which places were in the power of Spain, which had been at war with England for more than two years. It appears that Mr. Crifpe (for what reafon it is not known) had been for fome time under apprehenfions of fuch an attack. Loop-holes, for the difcharge of mufquets, were made in different parts of the houfe; and he is faid to have afforded very generous entertainments to fuch of his neighbours as would lodge there to defend him. But all his precautions had no effect.

" The knowledge of fome other little incidents relating to this matter was obtained, but they were too trifling to deferve notice. No care was taken to preferve the memory of this event, in the parifh of Birchington, and it coft me infinite pains to inveftigate the traces of a fact, which had, for fo many years, been almoft buried in oblivion. I am well convinced of the truth of the

relation

relation myfelf, or it never fhould have been publifhed, to impofe on the credulity of others."

Plate XIII. Fig. 1. A South-eaft view of the Gateway at Daun de Lyon, as it appeared in 1781.

Fig. 2. DUNGEON HILL, juft within the city wall at Canterbury, and not far from the caftle; which Somner fuppofes to be fo called, corruptly for *Danian Hill*, or Danes Hill, being raifed by the Danes when they befieged and took the city, in King Ethelred's [1] reign, A. D. 1011. He alfo fuppofes both the hill and outwork, or moft part of it, to have been originally caft up without the city-wall, but, " for the city's more fecurity," to have " been taken and walled in fince [2]." With this drawing I was favoured by Mrs. Duncombe.

Mr. Grofe, in the Preface to his Antiquities, p. 69, fays, " the efcutcheons, over the pillars of the entrance to the Strangers' Hall at Canterbury, are remarkable, not being cuftomary at the time of its erection ;" and in his plate has reprefented them as exact fhields with charges on them. The rough fketch in fig. 3. fhews their appearance, Auguft 18, 1779, and proves that they could never be intended for efcutcheons of arms.

Fig. 4. Is a reprefentation of the font in the very ancient church of St. Martin, near Canterbury.

Fig. 5. A feal of the hofpital of St. James, or St. Jacob, in Canterbury. See Bibl. Topog. Brit. N° XXX. p. 428.

The feal of Birchefter [3], fig. 6, is now in the poffeffion of John Thorpe, of Bexley, in Kent, Efq; M. A. and F. S. A. It was found in the year 1755, in a garden at Stroud, oppofite the church, near Rochefter.

---

[1] Mr. Goftling, by miftake, ftyles it King " Ethelbert," who reigned 860—866. Walk, p. 7.

[2] Antiquities of Canterbury, p. 75.

[3] See Kennet's Parochial Antiquities, and Fifher's Hiftory of Rochefter.

On

Plate XIII. p.178

J. Hadan del.

Fig 1. South-East, or Front View of the Gateway at Daun de Lyon, in the Isle of Thanet, Kent, Oct. 26. 1781.

S. Duncombe del.

Fig. 2. View of the Dungeon Hill, Canterbury. p.178.

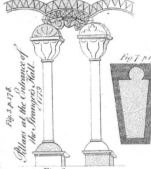

Fig. 3. p.178. Pillars at the Entrance of the Swangers Hall. 1779.

Fig. 6.

Fig 7. p.17.

Fig. 5. p.178.

Seal of Binchester. p.178.

Fig. 8. p.179.

Fig. 4. Font, at St. Martin's near Canterbury, p.178.

On removing the prefent pavement of Canterbury Cathedral, in February 1787, at a fmall diftance from the tomb of Archbifhop Iflip, was found a ftone coffin, or cyft (the lid of which was fuppofed to be ftolen at the Reformation) fitted to the fhape of the human body, like the fketch in fig. 7.

The Dimenfions.		feet.	inch.
Cavity of the head		1	11
Breadth of the fhoulders		2	0
Breadth at the feet		1	3
Length within from fhoulders to feet		6	3
From out to out		6	10
Depth of the coffin		0	10½

There is no doubt (though fome imagine this cannot be Iflip's grave *, as ftone coffins were of much earlier date, and therefore then out of ufe) that this curious coffin contains the remains of Archbifhop Iflip, who died in 1366, and according to Somner

---

* May not the doubt refpecting this ftone coffin not having been the repofitory of Iflip's corpfe be fully obviated, by fuppofing that it had been primarily ufed many years before, but was unoccupied at the time of the Archbifhop's death? Lanfranc, Anfelm, and Ralph, the three firft Archbifhops after the Conqueft, were certainly buried in the nave, and the two former towards the upper part of it ; for Lanfranc was interred *ante crucifixum* (Godwin de Præful. pag. 61.); and Anfelm *ad caput prædeceſſoris fui Lanfranci* (W. Malm. de Geft. Pontif. p. 130.) But the crucifix called the holy crofs, and the great crofs, was placed by the fteps of afcent into the choir. (Somner's Antiq. p. 93. and Battely Cant. p. 9.) After the fire of Canterbury cathedral, A. 1174, the bodies of Lanfranc and Anfelm were taken up and re-interred. The ftate of Lanfranc's is particularly defcribed by Gervafe in X Scr. c. 1301 ; and I think it may be inferred that he had been put into a ftone coffin. It can, however, hardly be fuppofed that the perfons who directed the removal of thefe bodies would chufe to be at the trouble of digging up thefe large ftone coffins. Of Lanfranc's body it is particularly related: " Lanfrancus levatus. " eft *de farcofago* fuo in tabula plumbea," X Scr. 302. It alfo appears that the monks at the fame time removed the body of Archbifhop Theobald, which they found in high prefervation, out of his fepulchre, and caried into the veftry upon a bier ; and that this fepulchre was a ftone coffin ; *fublato farcofagi lapide fuperiore.* (X Scr. c. 1301.) S. DENNE.

C c

was

was buried in the middle of the body at the upper end, inclining to the north fide, under a fair tomb of marble, which was afterwards removed and placed between two pillars, where it remained till taken down in February, 1787. The bones had been difturbed, the fkull much broken, and lying upon the breaft, but the teeth nearly perfect.

On the fouth fide of the nave, between two pillars, under a large raifed tomb, were found the remains of Archbifhop Wittelfey, who died in the year 1374. He was buried in the folid foundation, cut out partly in the fhape of a coffin; the fkeleton was entire; the body had been lain in wood afhes. A leaden feal of a papal bull (fee fig. 8.) was found near the hand, and is now in the poffeffion of the Rev. Dr. Berkeley, Vice-dean of Canterbury.

Of the *autennæ* engraved in plate III. of this Hiftory, p. 75, it fhould have been obferved, that fome ingenious antiquaries, among whom are Mr. Jacob of Faverfham, and Mr. Gardner, differ on very plaufible grounds from Mr. Goftling, Mr. Stennit, &c. in their idea of them, being of opinion that, as fo many of them remain, they could not be made for military, but eccle-fiaftical ufe. In particular, Mr. Jacob has not lefs than fourteen or fifteen of different fizes in his own poffeffion, and has given feveral away. And Mr. Gardner, in his hiftorical account of Dunwich (4to, 1754), who had many in his poffeffion, found there, fays, p. 96, that " the fculpture AVE MARIA, &c. on one " fide, and on the reverfe, A. DOMINY TECUM (as in the Roman " Rofarium) on N° 5. pl. IV. fhews it to be done fince the time " of Conftantius; thefe very likely were ufed to be borne in pro- " ceffions with the four Evangelifts thereon. They may have " been expofed, with the fhrines, in former times to the populace " on grand feftivals."

P. 155. Omitted in the Lift of the Incumbents of Reculver. GEORGE FRENCH, M. A. 1652. LET-

LETTER to Mr. JOHN NICHOLS,

From the Rev. Mr. SAMUEL DENNE,

SIR, *Wilmington, March 22, 1784.*

IN the entertaining, and, in many points, fatisfactory account of Herne, printed in N° XVIII. of the Bibliotheca Topographica Britannica, Mr. Duncombe, at p. 99, has inferted the following curious extract from the Regifter Book of that parifh, with a remark upon it, which I have alfo tranfcribed.

" 1567, *ould* Arnold, a *Cryfomer*, buried February 8th.

" This word, fometimes fpelt Chrifomer *, often occurs after-
" wards for about a hundred years, but not fince. Dr. Johnfon

---

* A *Chryfome* was a cloth which covered the child's face when brought to be baptized, and not the prieft's fee for chriftening it; but in cafe the child died in the month, the prieft had only two-pence, and the cloth was to bury the child in. And by the manual *in ufum Sarum*, it is ordered, that godfathers and godmothers fee that the mother bring the Chryfome at her purification or churching, with other accuftomed offerings.

In the earlieft regifter of St. Bride's parifh, in London, beginning in 1587, and ending in 1653 (a regifter the more curious as having been preferved from the great fire which deftroyed fo many others in the laft century), the term frequently occurs under a variety of fpelling; as *cryfome, cryzome, criffom, cryzom, crefom,* &c. but the entry is regularly, either " a cryfum," or " one cryfome," or " the cryfomer," of fuch and fuch a perfon. The earlieft that occurs in this regifter is in 1614, and the lateft in 1652. In the fame period the " ftill-born" and the " bafe-born" children are carefully diftinguifhed.

On a flight infpection of St. Bride's regifter, I met with the two following articles, here thrown out for the ufe of future commentators on Shakfpeare.

" 1590. xviith of May, Ifabell the wife of *Hamblet* Panketman, was buried.
" 1592. *Hamlet* Evans, buried ixth of Nov." J. N.

C c 2 " defines

" defines *Chrisom* from (Chrism) to be *a child that dies within a*
" *month after its birth, so called, he says, from the Chrism cloath,*
" *a cloath anointed with holy unguent, which the children antiently*
" *wore till they were christened.*   Chrism is applied in the glossaries
" to the Popish Sacrament of Confirmation.   *Ould* Arnold might,
" therefore, in the first appearance of Protestantism in England
" be first converted late in life, or perhaps, on his conversion to
" Protestantism : as anciently persons who were recovered from
" any herefy, if not already confirmed, were anointed with
" Chrism."   Du Cange.

Of the justness of his conjecture respecting the signification
of Cryfomer, the ingenious historian, by his manner of expref-
sing himself, seems to be diffident ; nor am I clear that I can
propose a more plausible surmise.   But, if you are of opinion
that the hints I have to offer may help to elucidate the meaning
of the word, you will be so obliging as to give them a place in
a future number.

The Chrism was an unguent compounded of oil and balfams,
confecrated annually on Maundy Thursday by the bishop of every
diocefe in his cathedral, where the parochial clergy, on paying
the customary fee, were supplied with a sufficient quantity for
the enfuing year.   Anointing children at their baptifm was one
of the ufes to which it was applied.   Dr. Johnfon (as quoted by
Mr. D.) fays, that the cloth, styled the Chrifom, was worn by
children till they were christened.   This I apprehend to be a
miftake, and that it was not put on till after they had received
the facred unction, nor do I recollect having obferved that the
cloth itself was previoufly anointed.   If the child died within
the month, it was, when buried, wrapt in this baptifmal veftment ; otherwife the Chrifom was to be brought to the church
by the mother when she returned thanks for her fafe deliverance ;

or

or fhe was to make an offering in money inftead of it *.   The
veftment the child had on at its baptifm retained the name of
Chrifom, after the practice of anointing ceafed, but it was alfo
called the face-cloth.   This is the term in the account of the
dues belonging to the vicar of St. John's, in Tenet, mentioned
by Mr. Lewis, in his Hiftory of that ifland, p. 145, and he has
fubjoined an explanation by John Hunte, curate of Herne, in
1621. Among the notes for reformation of the church, A 1560,
publifhed in Strype's Annals, vol. I p. 208, is this direction :
" To avoid contention, let the curate have the value of the
" Chrifm, not under the value of 4d. and above, as they can
" agree, and as the ftate of the parents may require." It was
reafonable that a compofition fhould be made for the face-cloth,
becaufe in the valuation of the livings under the Stat. of 25

---

* This feems to be confirmed by the following fentence in Mr. Reed's edition of
Dodfley's Old Plays, 1780, vol. IX. p. 352.
   " Madam, the preacher,
   Is fent for to a churching, and doth afk,
   If you be ready; he fhall lofe, he fays;
   His *chryfome* elfe !"
   And Mr. Steevens, in his edition of Shakfpeare, 1778, in a note on Falftaff's
making " a finer end, and went away, an it had been any chrifom'd child;" fays,
" The *chryfom* was no more than the white cloth put on the new baptifed child."
See Johnfon's Canons of Ecclef. Law. 1720.
   " I have fomewhere (but cannot recollect where) met with this further account
of it; that the *chryfom* was allowed to be carried out of the church, to enwrap fuch
children as were in too weak a condition to be borne thither; the *chryfom* being
fuppofed to make every place holy. This cuftom would rather ftrengthen the al-
lufion to the weak condition of Falftaff. The child itfelf was fometimes called a
chryfom, as appears from the following paffage in *The Fancies*, 1638: " — the boy
furely I ever faid was a very *chrifome* in the thing you wot."
Again, in *The Wits*, by Sir W. Davenant, 1637:
   " ——— and would'ft not join thy halfpenny
   " To fend for milk for the poor *chryfome*."
Again, in fir W. Davenant's *Juft Italian*, 1630.:.
   " ——— and they do awe
   " The *chryfome* babe."

Again,

Henry VIII. according to which the incumbents were to pay firſt-fruits and tenths, the profits ſuppoſed to accrue from the Chryſoms were rated, and in ſome caſes particularized. In the return of the rectory of Lambeth, was the following article :

" Item oblationes per mulieres inquinatas, et in pannis Chriſ-
" matoriis. ijs. viiid."

From the practice of burying an infant in the Chryſom, it is imagined that the word *Chryſoms* was printed in the weekly bills of mortality among the caſualties and diſeaſes, though, from the ignorance of Pariſh Clerks, or their informants, it was latterly put to denote children who died unbaptized [1]. The tranſition from Cryſom to Cryſomer being ſo eaſy and obvious, it might be concluded, that the perſons entered in Herne Regiſter, were thus denominated, did not the advanced age of Arnald render this notion very queſtionable, there being reaſon to think that, till about the year 1600, there were few, if any, of the Engliſh nation who had objections to Infant Baptiſm [2]. They were indeed ſo diſſatisfied at women's being reſtrained from chriſtening

---

Again, in his *Albovine*, 1629 : "Sir, I would fain depart in quiet like other young *chryſomes*." Again, in *Your Five Gallants*, by Middleton : " —— a fine old man to his father, it would kill his heart i'faith : *he'd away like a chryſom*."

Mr. *Tyrwhitt* addꜱ, " In the Liturgie, 2 E. VI. *Form of private Baptiſm*, is this direction." " Then the miniſter ſhall put the white veſture, commonly called the *chri-* " *ſome*, upon the child," &c. The *Gloſſary* of Du Cange, voce *Chriſmale*, explains this ceremony thus : " Quippe olim ut et hodie, baptizatorum, ſtatim atque chriſ- " mate in fronte ungebantur, *ne chriſma deflueret*, capita *panno candido* obvolvebantur, " qui octava demum die ab iis auferebatur." During the time therefore of their wear- ing this veſture, the children were, I ſuppoſe, called *chriſomes*. One is regiſtered under this deſcription in the regiſter of *Thatcham, Berks*, 1605. [Hearne's *Append. to the Hiſtory of Glaſtonbury*, p. 275.] " A younge *criſome* being a *man child*, beinge found drowned, &c."   J. N.

[1] Wheatly on the Common Prayer, p. 498.
[2] Some account of Dr. Wicliff, by Lewis, p. xxiii.

children

children in cafes of neceffity, when no clergyman was to be had immediately, " that a homily was compofed purpofely to teach " people that they need not to ftand in any fcrupulofity about the " delay of baptifm [3]." It is alfo obfervable, that there is no form for the baptifm of perfons of riper years in the Liturgies of either Edward VI. or of Elizabeth, and that in the rubrics and prayers of the offices of public and private baptifm in the book of Elizabeth, " children and infants" are the words which always occur.

Unction by the Bifhop having been a branch of the ceremony of Confirmation, inclines Mr. D. to imagine, that, though the practice had been difufed, a word that had formerly a relation to it might give an appellation to confirmed perfons. I am dubious about the validity of this furmife, becaufe, at an early period of the Reformation, it was generally agreed, that the impofition of hands was confirmation, and the chrifm not practifed, as being without any foundation in Scripture [4]; and becaufe Confirmation and Bifhoping were the words conftantly ufed for this religious obfervance [5].

Another Chrifm was the anointing of the fick in their laft hour. In compliance with a deep-rooted prejudice of the age, by the firft Book of Common Prayer of Edward VI. anointing was allowed to fuch patients as defired it. And though, in the fecond Book of the fame King, and in the Liturgy of Elizabeth, this indulgence was omitted; it is not unlikely, that many dying perfons, as well as their friends, might not acquiefce in being deprived of what they had been taught to confider as neceffary to a tranquil and fafe paffage out of life.

---

[3] Strype's Annals, vol. I. p. 183.   [4] Burnet's Hift. Part I. Book III. Coll. 211.
[5] Among the expences of the Archdeacon of Lincoln, occurs :
" Item in pretio Balfami quam idem Archidiaconus propriis expenfis annuatim " miniftravit Epo die cœnæ ad Crifma confecrand'   x li."

Mr.

Mr. D's explanation is founded upon the idea that the perfons regiftered Cryfomers, were Proteftants; but as Papifts were not debarred the right of being interred in the church-yards and churches of their refpective parifhes, might not Cryfomer have been a term by which the Papifts were characterifed? We may, at leaft, be affured, that as they were perfuaded that extreme unction would ferve as a viaticum, they would not depart un-anointed, if a prieft could be procured to adminifter it; nor, probably, was there any period, fince the Reformation, when there were not Romifh priefts in moft parts of the kingdom. It is mentioned by Mr. D. that the word often occurs in his regifter for about a century after the burial of Arnold. Poffibly, from an attention to the names of the perfons recorded, and from other local circumftances, he may be able to trace, whether the perfons fo ftyled, or their families, were Proteftants or Papifts. Should they have been Papifts, it will add fome weight to my conjecture, that, at Herne, Cryfomer was a mark of diftinction for the people of that perfuafion, on account of their obfervance of the rite of extreme unction. But, fo far from having it in my power to cite any authority for this opinion, I frankly own that the word is new to me. And this is my inducement for defiring to have the queftion fubmitted to the confideration of your more intelligent correfpondents, it being a little mortifying not to comprehend what one reads, though it be only an extract from the regifter of a country parifh *.   Yours, &c.

S. D E N N E.

* After all, I fhould be ftrongly inclined to imagine, that the word meant a chriftened child that died within the month; for in 1567, the practice certainly was to bury fuch children in the chryfome. How *chryfomer* could be applicable to a child that died unbaptized, not a little puzzles me. In your citations from Old

3
Plays,

To the foregoing Obfervations, the Editor is enabled to annex the Opinions of two other refpectable Antiquaries on the fame fubject.

The late excellent Sir JOHN CULLUM, in a letter, dated Hardwick-houfe, Jan. 19, 1784, fays, " The firft Prayer Book of Edward VI. fet forth in the fecond year of his reign, in the Office of Baptifm, after the child has been dipped, thus directs : " Then the god-fathers and god mothers fhall take " and lay their handes upon the childe, and the minifter fhall " put upon hym hys *white vefture*, commonly called, the " *Crifome*, and fay, Take thys white vefture for a token of " the Innocency ;" &c. afterwards, " the minifter fhall com- " maunde, that the *Crifomes* bee broughte to the churche, " and delyvered to the prieftes, after the accuftomed manner, at " the purificacyon of the mother of every chylde ;" hence a child that died between its chriftening and mother's purification,

plays, and in the explanatory notes, *chryfome* plainly refers to a baptized babe. And yet Mr. Boys feems to be firmly perfuaded, that though the word *chryfomer* fo perpetually occurs in the regifters he has examined, it conftantly means a child or perfon that had not been baptized. The number of inftances that gentleman has met with, adds to the difficulty. For mothers of the Church of England, I believe, always were (as they undoubtedly at prefent are) extremely anxious that their children fhould be, as the vulgar phrafe is, *half baptized,* and not die without a name. In the regifters to which Mr. Boys alludes, there is not, I conclude, any entry of what is called the Chriftian name, nor in the regifter of chriftenings any entry of a furname, correfponding as to date, with the entry in the regifter of burials. If baptized infants who died within the month were meant, it is eafy to account for this mode of entry in the regifter of burials ; becaufe the term *Chryfomer* would authenticate thofe children for whom no compofition was to be made by the mother to the minifters for the Chryfome or Face-cloth. The names of children who died within the month, might not be entered in the regifter of chriftenings, as having been only privately baptized, and not received at the font. S. D.

was

was called a Crifom. Where Dr. Johnfon learnt, that the Crifom-cloth was " a cloth anointed with holy Unguent, which the " children antiently wore till they were chriftened," he has not informed us.

" Among the dues belonging to the vicar of St. John's, Margate, in 1577, is, " for churching a woman, but muft compound for the *Face-cloath*, 1s." upon which, Mr. Lewis, in his hiftorical notes, obferves, " the ancient duty for chriftening was a *Cryfome*, or the *Face-cloath*, that covered the child at its baptifm, if it lived; but if the child died, the minifter was to have but 2d. for baptifing [which was the woman's offering at her churching], and was to lofe the Face-cloath, for that was to wind the child in. By the manual *in ufum Sarum*, it is ordered, that godfathers and godmothers fee that the moder bring agen her Cryfom at her purification. Hift. of Ifle of Thanet, p. 145.

" In Penfhurft Regifter, between the years 1633 and 1665, the burials of feveral children occur, that are called *a Crifom*, a *Crifom fon*, a *Crifom daughter*, of fuch and fuch a perfon, the father only being mentioned.

" Hence I fufpect that " ould Arnold *, a *Cryfomer*, buried," means only, with fome little variety of expreffion, a *Crifome Child* of old Arnold buried.

" *Chrifoms* occur in the weekly bills of mortality at leaft as late as 1722, about one in a week.　　　　　JOHN CULLUM."

* Another gentleman conjectures " *ould* Arnold " to be a miftake for " *one* Arnold;" but the interpretation of Sir John Cullum is undoubtedly right.

Mr.

Mr. Boys, of Sandwich, in a letter, dated January 4, 1784, obferves, that " the word Chryfomer perpetually occurs in old Regifters, and conftantly means a child, or perfon, that has *not* been baptized. I have fometimes met with it more properly written, an *A*chryfomer, where the *a* is privative, and fully explains the meaning. The Chrifm is the holy oil, formerly made ufe of in Baptifm, and was fo effential to the ceremony, that the word Chrifmatio denoted baptifm. Thus, in Charta Johannis Redonenfis Epifcopi anno 1240 apud Auguftinum *du* *Pas*, p. 594. ' Nullum ejufdem ecclefiæ parochianum ad jura parochialia admittens, nifi in duobus cafibus neceffitatis, videlicet ad baptifmum, five chrifmationem, & confeffionem [1]."

" There are a few miftakes," Mr. Boys adds, " in your elegant little volume of the Hiftory of Reculver and Herne, which may be corrected, if you think proper, in a fubfequent number.

Page 73 prodeft *et* glorie—dele *et*.

77 for figure 8 read 9.

78 for *mafters* (I fhould think) MASTERS.

144 *Ordeum palmal*, is undoubtedly *Ordeum palmare*, the beft barley.

152 *Sarcella*, from the French *Sarcelle*, a Teal, and perhaps means here any wild fowl. There might probably then be decoys upon the coaft about Reculver and Herne, as there are now near Faverfham.

I hope foon to be able to fend you fomething illuftrative of the Kentifh Antiquarian Hiftory. I have materials and inclination, but I want time; otherwife you would hear frequently from me; as I heartily approve your plan, and think myfelf indebted to you for much pleafure and information I have received from it. I am, Sir, yours, &c.   WM. BOYS.

[1] Du Cange in *voce* *Chrifmatio.*

D d 2   E P I-

EPITAPHS AT HERNE.

In the Body of the Church.

STEPHEN KNOWLER, late of this parish, gent. died Sept. 19, 1675, aged 55. Here lieth the body of MARY the wife of Mr. STEPHEN KNOWLER, of the city of Canterbury, Chirurgeon, son of the abovesaid STEPHEN KNOWLER, gent. She was the daughter of WILLIAM MONINS, late of Dover, esq. and died October 2d, 1735, aged 83 years. Also here lieth the abovesaid Mr. STEPHEN KNOWLER, Chirurgeon, who died Nov. 7, 1737, aged 88 years.

Here lieth the body of WILLIAM KNOWLER, Woollen Draper, late of Canterbury, son of STEPHEN KNOWLER, of the same, Chirurgeon, and of MARY his wife. He died March 2, 1714, aged 29 years. By this pew lieth his grandfather STEPHEN KNOWLER, of Herne; also a brother and two sisters adjoining to the head of this stone; also here lieth ELIZABETH wife of ABRAHAM LEGRAND, daughter of STEPHEN KNOWLER, and of MARY his wife; she died October 11, 1721, aged 29 years; and her two daughters, MARY KNOWLER aged 8 days, and ELIZABETH aged 11 days, were buried with her. She left surviving one son STEPHEN LEGRAND. Also here lieth the body of the abovesaid ABRAHAM LEGRAND, who died January 19th, 1742, aged 60 years.

Here lieth the body of ELIZABETH the wife of JAMES CONYERS, of Feversham, daughter of STEPHEN KNOWLER, of Herne, gent. She died September 26, 1721, aged 66 years. In the same place, and near unto, lie her father and mother. Also in the same grave lieth here one son, THOMAS CONYERS, who departed this life aged 17 years.

In the great Chancel, against the South Wall.

Here lieth the body of EDWARD EWELL, gent. who married ELIZABETH sister of Bishop Gauden, deceased; after, Ann, daughter of Sir THOMAS EDEN, deceased; after, he married KATHERINE, daughter of Sir EDWARD BOYS, of Fredville; anno Dom. 1686, ætatis 82.

North Chancel.

Here lieth interred the body of ELIZABETH wife of JOHN STEPHENS, of Canterbury; she was daughter of RICHARD GILLOW, of Woodnerburrough, gent.; also near this place lie 9 of her children, viz. 6 sons and 3 daughters; she departed this life the 16th day of September, 1743, aged 63 years.

Here lieth the body of MARTIN RIGDEN, son of DAVID and ANNE RIGDEN, who departed this life Nov. 4, 1742, aged 5 years.

Sleep on, sweet child; till
Christ his power thee rise
And meet thy parents
When they end their days,

o   Here

Here lieth the body of WILLIAM FOCHE, of Chrift Church, Canterbury, gent. who had iffue by his wife 7 children; died Auguft 1, 1713, aged 56 years. Here alfo lieth the body of ELIZABETH his wife, daughter of JOHN WHEATLEY, of Margate, in the Ifle of Thanet, gent. who died Nov. 21, 1747.

Here lieth interred JOHN SEA, of Underdowne, in the parifh of Herne, efquire; who tooke to wife MARTHA HAMOND, daughter of THOMAS HAMOND, of St. Alban's, in Eaft Kent, efquire, by whome he had iffue VI fonnes and III daughters; and after her deceafe, married SARA BOYS, eldeft daughter unto THO BOYS, of Barefreflon, gent. by whom he had one fonne and one daughter. He lived and died in peace; obiit 23 Februarii, anno Domini 1604.

South Chancel.

Here lyeth buried the body of GEORGE KNOWLER, gent. the fonne of GEORGE KNOWLER, late of this parifh, who departed this life the 2d day of Nov. in the year of our Lord 1659.

Here lieth the body of GEORGE FAIRMAN, the fon of THO. and MARY FAIRMAN; he died April 29, 1772, aged 25 years.

> Without a name I am loft to every age;
> Duft, afhes, and nought elfe lie within this grave:
> Alive I was once, but now I am not.
> Afk no more of me; 'tis all I am,
> And all that you fhall be.

Here lieth interred the body of RICHARD KNOWLER, of Hearne, in the county of Kent, gent. and Mafter of Arts in Pembroke College, in Oxford, the 2d fonne of ROBERT KNOWLER, late of Hearne, gent. who tooke to wife ANN SANDWELL, daughter of RICHARD SANDWELL, of Minfter, in the Ifle of Thanet, in the fame county. They had iffue 4 fonnes, viz. ROBERT, RICHARD, THOMAS, and JOHN; and 3 daughters, MARGARET, ANN, and SUSAN: he departed this life the 20th day of February, 1659, and in the 59th yeare of his age.

> To fuffer patiently is a greater gift, then to raife the Dead,
> The Juft fhall live by Faith.

Here lies the body of JOHN GILBERT, of the precinct of Chrift Church, Canterbury, gent. who departed this life Auguft 7, 1749, aged 47 years.

Here lieth depofited the remains of THOMAS FAIRMAN, late of this parifh, Bricklayer, who departed this life Dec. the 8th, 1782, aged 73 years: he left furviving one daughter ELIZABETH.

> His latter days were burthenfome,
> His foul was fore oppreft;
> But God, I hope, has took him home,
> To his eternal reft.

2

Here

Here lieth the body of MARY FAIRMAN, the wife of THOMAS FAIRMAN, Bricklayer of this Parish, daughter of THOMAS KNOWLER, of Herne, yeoman. She died July 8, 1769, aged 57 years. By him she had issue 3 sons and two daughters, viz. KNOWLER, FRANCIS, and GEORGE; ANNE and ELIZABETH; and left surviving GEORGE and ELIZABETH.

<blockquote>
O Death, thou haft from this age of flesh
Sunk my fainting head;
Here lie the ruins in this grave
Among my kindred dead.
</blockquote>

H. S. E.

GILBERTUS KNOWLER, de Stroud, in parochia de Hearne, arm. uxorem primam duxit ELIZABETHAM filiam unicam. . . . JUXTON, A. M. et de Aldington in com. Cantii Rectoris, cujus cineres ad dextram quiefcunt. Secunda fponfa fuit HONEYWOOD nata VINCENTII DENNE ad legem fervientis; ipfius exuvias hic etiam invenies. Tertiam habuit SUSANNAM MARTINI LISTER, M. D. fobolem, quæ fupervixit. Vita deceffit 16 Februarii, anno ætatis 67, Salutis 1729. Tres filii et totidem natæ poft funera vivunt.

Here lieth the body of ELIZABETH KNOWLER, fecond daughter of ROBERT KNOWLER, gent. who died Nov. 24, A. D. 1724, aged 57; and, out of refpect to the memories of her anceftors, defired it fhould be here added, that in the fame grave and adjoining thereto, lie the remains of her Grandfather,

JOHN KNOWLER.	} died	May 18, 1655,	} aged	53
ROBERT, her Father,		Nov. 1, 1693,		62
ELIZABETH, her Mother,		March 22, 1693,		61
KATHERINE, her eldeft fifter,		Sept. 5, 1708,		50

<blockquote>
All muft to their cold graves,
But the religious actions of the Juft
Smell fweet in death, and bloffom in the duft.
</blockquote>

Arms of *Knowler*. Argent, on a Bend between 2 cotizes Sable, a lion paffant, guardant of the field, crowned Or.

Arms of *Stevens*. On a Cheveron 3 crofs croflets between 3 demi-lions rampant.

Arms of *Wheatley*. Party Fefs, 6 pales counterchanged, 1, 4 and 5, charged with a Lion rampant.

Arms of *Conyers*. Azure, on a mantle Or.

Arms of *Juxton*. Or, between a crofs Gules 4 blackamoors heads.

Arms of *Denne*. Azure, 3 Saracens heads Or.

Arms of *Lifter*. Ermine, on a fefs Azure 3 mullets Or.

Arms of *Gillow*. A lion rampant, and on a chief 3 flower de luces.

Arms of *Foche*. Between a fefs indented, 6 lozenges, 3 & 3.

Arms of *Monings*. 3 Crefcents.

Arms of *Gilbert*. A faltire and chief Verrey.

P. 75.

P. 75. In the eighth volume of the Archæologia, p. 79. is a Letter from John Pownall, Efquire, to Mr. Douglas, containing a defcription, accompanied with an engraving, of a Roman Tile, found in September 1785, at Reculver.

" I have the honour to fend you herewith," fays Mr. Pownall, " a very rude and imperfect fketch of one of the tiles which cover fome ducts, or drains, now difcernible in the cliff at Reculver in Kent, about eight feet below the furface of the Roman ftation.

" I call thefe ducts, or drains, becaufe I am unable to determine whether they were merely drains or fewers to the camp, or whether they were ducts to a bath.

" From the fimilitude of the tiles in fize and fhape to thofe defcribed by Mr. Lyon as ufed in the ducts of the Roman bath difcovered under St. Mary's church at Dover *, and to thofe ufed for the like purpofe in the Roman bath difcovered near Brecknock, as defcribed by Mr. Hay †, and from the whole of the fpace occupied by thefe ducts or drains being covered above the tiles with a thick coat of very hard plafter compofed of mortar mixed up with bruifed brick, exactly fimilar to that ufed for the fame purpofe in thofe baths, as defcribed by Mr. Lyon and Mr. Hay; I fay that from thefe circumftances I am inclined to believe that thefe alfo are ducts belonging to a Roman bath, and that the coat of plaifter laid over the tiles was the floor of fome room above; but I fay this only on the ground of conjecture, as my vifit to Reculver was too fhort to purfue that mode of inveftigation which might have afcertained the fact; nor fhould I have troubled you with thefe obfervations, had it not been for the very curious rude fcrawl on the tile I brought away with me, a fac fimile of which is upon the drawing inclofed ‡.

" If thefe are really letters, and the Romans ever wrote in fuch characters, of which I never yet faw any fample, I fhould be inclined to think that the infcription refers to the Legio fecunda Britannica, which, after having been removed by Valentinian from amongft the Silures, was ftationed at their different pofts in Kent, for the defence of the coaft againft the Saxons.

" I examined a great number of the fragments of tiles lying amongft the rubbifh at the foot of the cliff, underneath where thefe ducts or drains appear; but that which I brought away is the only one that has any infcription upon it, though every one has invariably that femicircular mark upon it which is defcribed in the fketch, and which feems to have had no other meaning than as a guide to the workmen in laying the tiles with greater exactnefs."

Gray's Obfervations on the Foffils of Reculver Cliff, with a note by Sir Hans Sloane, may be feen in Phil. Tranf. XXII. 762. or in the Abridgement, IV. 461.

P. 115. Another proof of there having been a chapel at Ford, is the following entry in the regifter-book of Herne: " Thomas, the fon of John Knowler, baptized " at Ford, 26 April, 1607."

P. 154. Note *, l. 1. r. Godmerfham.

* Archaeologia, vol. IV. p 325.   † Ibid. vol. VII. p. 205.
‡ See the Archaelogia, vol. Viii. plate II.

P. 160.

P. 160. add to note +*, This vicar was of the fame family with the laft abbot of St. Auguftine's, John Effex, whofe family name was Foache, ftyled VOCHIUS by Twyne, in his Commentarius *de rebus Albionicis*, in which this abbot bears a diftinguifhed part. One of the vicar's daughters was married to Mr. Newman, of Weftbeer, by whom fhe had the late Daniel Newman, efquire, Recorder of Maidftone and Faverfham.

Slight *Memoranda*, taken in a Kentifh Tour, 1785.

HALDEN PLACE.   Manfion-houfe demolifhed.
An old building ufed as a ftable and lumber-rooms at the eaft-end.
Creft.   On a wreath a Porcupine paffant, chain'd.
Arms.   Quarterly 1ft and 4th a Pheon.
                2d & 3d Barry of 8, over all a Lion rampant ducally crowned.
    Date 1563.

On the north fide of the fame building.

Arms.   1ft as before.   Impaling 10 coats, viz.
1ft.   A Lion rampant.
2d.   A Lion paffant.
3d.   Barry of 6 in chief 3 Torteauxes.
4th.   Within a bordure ingrailed, a Lion rampant, a crefcent for difference.
5th.   A Fefs between 6 crofs Fitchée's.
6th.   Checquy a Chevron ermine.
7th.   A Fefs between 2 Chevronels.
8th.   A Saltire engrailed, between 4 martlets.
9th.   A Chief, over all a bend engrailed.
10th.   Much broken.   It feems to be, Barry of 8; over all an efcutcheon Ermine, on a chief.—Date 1563.

BIDDENDEN.

Here is a free-fchool founded by one of the family of Mayney, of this place, in 1522, endowed with a houfe, and 20l. a year, in the gift of feoffees. A farm called by the name of *The Bread and Cheefe Farm*, rented many years ago at 6l. a year, at the beginning of this century at 18l. and in 1785 at 32l. 10s. is ftill known by the appellation of *Bread and Cheefe Land*; the rents having been originally appropriated to a free gift of bread and cheefe on every Eafter-day, which is thus beftowed; to all the poorer fort a three-penny loaf of bread and nuncheen of cheefe; and to the richer, a little manchet and bit of cheefe; the remainder to be diftributed in money to the poor.   The donation is fuppofed to have been made by two
                                        women,

women, who were twins, and joined together in their bodies, who are faid to have lived together till they were betwixt 20 and 30 years old. The eftate is in the hands of feoffees, and the bread and cheefe is diftributed by the parifh officers to all that are at church on Eafter-day after divine fervice; and the Tuefday following to all perfons who pafs through the village +.

200 Loaves (each Loaf 3¼lb. ⎱ were given on Eafter Sunday and Tuefday,
200 Weight of Cheefe ⎰ 1785.
Twin Cakes (according to the clerk's account) were firft inftituted as a Dole, A. D. 1011, by one Chalkhurft, or during the miniftry of a perfon of that name.

ROLVENDEN.

INSCRIPTIONS on Brafs Plates in the poffeffion of JOHN BEARDSWORTH, Efquire, at the Hole, in the Parifh of ROLVENDEN, and taken from that Church.

HERE RESTETH ROBERT GIBBON, SONNE AND
HEIRE OF THOMAS, SONNE AND HEIRE OF
GIBBON SACKFORD, LINEALLY AND LAWFULLY
DESCENDED FROM THE FAMILYS OF SACKFORD-
HALL IN SUFFOLKE, AND CLAN GIBBON IN
IRELAND. OBIIT XIII° DIE JVNII ANN° D'NI MDCXVIII.

HERE VNDERNEATH RESTETH IN ASVRED
HOPE OF A JOYFVLL RESVRRECTION
LIDIA, THE DEARLY BELOVED WIFE OF
EDWARD CHVT OF BETHERSDEN, ESQVIRE,
WHO DEPARTED THIS LIFE THE 12TH OF
NOVEMBER, ANN° DO'INI 1631, AGED 46.

STAPLEHURST.

Over the Weft Door of the Church are 3 efcutcheons, much crufted over with mofs, &c.

1ft. On a Chevron 3 quarterly.
2d. A Lion rampant.
3d. A crofs engrailed.

* See in Ducarel's " Repertory of Endowments," 8vo, p. 137, an engraving of one of the cakes.

E e

A SE-

A SECOND LETTER from Mr. DENNE.

SIR,   June 23, 1787.

A PERUSAL of the Regifter of Burials in the parifh of
Maidftone, occafions my communicating to you a few more laft
words concerning a *Cryfomer*. The regifters in this church
being perhaps originally as accurate, and now as perfect, as thofe
of any parochial diftrict, it was fome furprize to me not to difcover the term during the reign of Elizabeth, nor for feveral
years after; and the omiffion is the more extraordinary, becaufe
Mr. Robert Carr, who, there is fufficient reafon to conclude, was
minifter for about thirty-feven years, feems to have paid a conftant attention to them.

. Mr. Newton (fee Hiftory and Antiquities of Maidftone, p. 64.)
fuppofes Mr. Carr to have been minifter or curate from the firft
year of the Queen's reign to 1602; but, according to the regifter,
" Mr. Richard Storer, a reverend preacher and minifter of the
" holie Word of God, and curate of this parifh, was buried 24
" Eliz. Dec. 4." And it appears from the Regifter, that " Robert
" Carr, Mafter of Arts, our reverend paftor, was buried October
" 15, 1620."

In his time the Regifters were tranfcribed on vellum; not
having, however, feen a lift of the church-wardens, I am not
able to afcertain the date of the tranfcripts. For the firft forty
years of the reign of Elizabeth, every page is fubfcribed by
Robert Carr, minifter, and William Bafeden, and William Emiott,
church-wardens. And, after " Finis of the fortithe yeare," there

are

are the fame fignatures, together with thofe of two other church-wardens, Thomas Bargarve and William Henman. The pages of the following years are regularly fubfcribed by Mr. Carr, and William Lorrymer, church-warden, and the enfuing pages by Mr. Carr only.   No otherwife can I account for the omiffion of a word fo frequently to be met with in other regifters, than that, when the tranfcripts were made from the old regifters, or from the day-books, Mr. Carr might think it unneceffary to per-petuate the burial of children, whofe Chriftian names are not inferted in other regifters.

But whatever might be the reafon, in 1621, is this entry, " *A Cryfan* of Robert Belman's," was buried Sept. 21 ; and for almoft fixty years the term is to be met with under the wonted variations ; fuch as *A Crifam, Crifom, Cryfom, Crifome, Cryfome, Crifomer, Cryfomer*. Inftead of *A, One* is often prefixed, and now and then *two*, which being mentioned to be *Cryfomers* of the fame perfon muft denote their being twins [1]. And in a few entries the age of the infants may, I apprehend, be deduced from this circumftance, that the burial of the mother imme-diately precedes, or follows their burial—thus—

1628. One Crifome of John Eftery, Sept. 17.
       Jone the wife of John Eftery,   24.

1632. One crifome of Robert Brooke, October 3.
       Sarah wife of Robert Brooke,   27.

1636. Sufanna, the wife of William Auften, } Oct. 23.
       One cryfome of the fame William Auften, }

---

[1] 1626. Two crifomes of Thomas Dons, Feb. 22.
1636. Two cryfomes of Chriftopher Belfon, March 21.
1658. A crifome, fon of Richard Blundell, March 9.
    Another crifome, fon of Richard Blundell, March 17.
1659. Crifomes, fon and daughter of Thomas Smeething, Jan. 2.

1641. Urſula, wife of William Bridgeman, ⎫
         One cryſome of the ſame Bridgeman, ⎬ Sept. 24.

1655. A criſome, ſon of Richard Pierſon, April 7.

         Judith, wife of Richard Pierſon, April 11.

The preſumption is, that the mothers of theſe cryſomers died in childbirth.

If the cryſomer was baſe-born [2] this was noticed; and to the mother's name is ſometimes added that of the reputed father [3]. Whether the cryſomer were a ſon or a daughter is not ſpecified till 1554, when we meet with ' a cryſome, ſon of Edward Goffe, April 25.' Afterwards the ſex of the deceaſed is commonly diſtinguiſhed, as is likewiſe the trade, or rank of the father [4]; and the place of abode, if the father was not an inhabitant of Maidſtone [5]. Except in one inſtance the Chriſtian name of the cry-

---

[2] In the regiſter of Hinckley in Leiceſterſhire, in 1583, this entry occurs:
  " Agnes filia Bartholomæi Iley fornicatoris, bapt. 26 Jan."

[3] 1627. One cryſome baſe of Rebakca Dunning, March 16.
  1635. One cryſome of Ann King, the reputed father Stephen Auſten, March 30.
  1639. One baſe criſome of Elizabeth Auſt, April 3.
  1655. A criſome, ſon of Suſan Owen, widow; the reputed father Thomas Matthew, Hair-dreſſer, baſe, May 3.
  1658. A criſome, ſon of Alice Knowle, priſoner in Bridewell, Dec.

[4] 1652. A criſome of John Cary, Hatter, Nov.
  1653. A criſome of John Carter, Barber, Nov 25.
    A criſome of John Goare, Threadtwiſter, Feb. 24.
  1654. A criſome, ſon of John Rolfe, Labourer, Sept. 8.
    A criſome, ſon of George Longley, Baſket-maker, July
    A criſome, ſon of William Smith, Swingler, October 5.
  1657. A criſome, ſon of Mr. Richard Bills, Jurate, October 21.

[5] 1627. One cryſom of Thomas Mylles, of Gillingham, Oct. 2.
  1640. One criſomer of Thomas Lake, London, Sept. 13.
  1639. One cryſom of James Fowle of Tunbridge, Sept. 14.
  1654. A criſome, ſon of William Heely, of Hedcorne, Jan.
    A criſome daughter of Francis Spratt of Rocheſter, May

fomer

fomer did not occur to me, and that fo late as 1658. Theophilus Tilman, the cryfome fon of Chriftopher Tilman, Sept. 28.

The following table [6] will fhew, that after the fufpenfion, by the parliamentary commiffioners in 1643, of Mr. Robert Barrell, who was the fucceffor to Mr. Carr in this curacy, the term is more frequently to be met with than in the foregoing years; and it ought to be obferved, to the credit of the perfon who was the regifter in thofe days of confufion, that he appears to have difcharged the office with exactnefs [7].

After the Reftoration the term was difcontinued; and in 1661 are thefe entries.

May 4. Robert Gifford, labourer, had two children buried' which were not baptized.

7. George Bills, Wheeler, had a child buried, not baptized.

From which may it not be inferred, that, not being baptized, they were not allowed to have any pretenfion to the appellation of Cryfomers?   S. DENNE.

[6]

1622	3	1634	11	1646	10
1623	3	1635	8	1647	16
1624	2	1636	7	1648	15
1625	4	1637	6	1649	12
1626	7	1638	10	1650	14
1627	8	1639	9	1651	17
1628	9	1640	10	1652	17
1629	5	1641	14	1653	6
1630	7	1642	7	1654	11
1631	4	1643	12	1655	16
1632	9	1644	13	1656	8
1633	5	1645	17	1657	12

[7] His appointment is entered in the Regifter of Burials, and is as follows; "The 29th of September, 1653."

"Henry Pierce, of the towne of Maidftone, in the countie of Kent, being chofen by the parifhioners to bee Regifter for the faid towne and parifh, was this day fworne before me John Saunders, Maior of the fame towne and parifh, and Juftice of peace there, and I doe approve of him to be Regifter, according to an act of this prefent pailament, intituled, an Act touching marriages and regiftring thereof, and alfo touching births and burials."

Obfer-

Observations on the Archiepiscopal Palace of MAYFIELD, in Suffex, in a Letter from Mr. D E N N E.

IT was the wifh of Mr. Stephen Vine, an ingenious correfpondent in the Gentleman's Magazine *, to receive a fuller account
of Mayfield *Palace* than he has favoured the publick with. Not
much intelligence concerning this venerable manfion can now
probably be obtained; but to the little I have collected relative
to it, and to occurrences in that diftrict before the alienation of
the manor from the fee of Canterbury, he is welcome ; as are
likewife thofe readers who find any amufement from a fubject
of this kind, which to be fure is not very interefting, or enliven-
ing to the uninitiated in the fecret of antiquarian free-mafonry.

No proof direct can, I fufpect, be produced of the time when
the Archbifhops firft became poffeffed of Mayfield. Among the
donations of manors and lands to Chrift-church, Canterbury,
printed in the Appendix to Somner's Antiquities, N° xxxvi. are
the following articles in Suffex.

Anno Domini DCLXXX, Pageham, with its appendages, Slindon,
Scrippaneg, Cereum, Bucgrenora, Beorghamftede, Chrif-
meamme, North Mundanham, and another Mundanham,
given by king Cedwall to Archbifhop Wilfric.

A. D. DCCCXXXVIII. A reftoration by Ecgbert and king Athel-
wolf, his fon, of Malling, which Baldric had given, but
the donation invalid, becaufe the nobles had not confented
to it.

* Vol. XLVI. p. 464.

A. D.

A. D. DCCCCXLI. The village of Terrings near the Sea, given by king Athelſtan.

Mayfield being at a greater diſtance from both Pageham and Terrings than from Malling, it is more likely to have been a parcel of Malling, than an appendage to either of the other two manors: weight is added to this ſurmiſe from its being one of the ten pariſhes within the peculiar deanry of South-Malling; and though the archbiſhops of Canterbury have long been deprived of the manor, they are ſtill patrons of the vicarage of Mayfield, and of ſix of the other pariſhes.

In the time of Archbiſhop Dunſtan, Mayfield was made parochial, it being recorded of him by Edmer, that he there built a church of wood, as he did in others of his villages remote from Canterbury, where he had places of abode, and which he diſpoſed at convenient diſtances. (*Idem pater a Cantuaria in remotiores villas ſuas opportunis ſpatiis diſponens, apud Magavellam, ſicut in aliis hoſpitiorum ſuorum locis, ligneam eccleſiam fabricavit.* Eadmerus de vita S. Dunſtani, &c. Anglia Sacra, v. II. p. 217. Mr. Vine, by conſulting Domeſday Book, may be informed of the ſtate of this manor when that ſurvey was taken.

Mayfield continued in the ſee of Canterbury till Archbiſhop Cranmer, averſe as he was to diminiſh the revenues of it, judged it expedient, or rather found it neceſſary, to relinquiſh this manor, with other eſtates, to his arbitrary and rapacious ſovereign. The alienation was dated November 12, 27 Henry VIII. [1] A kind of compenſation was promiſed, but none obtained before Auguſt 31, 1547, when Edward VI. in conſideration of his father's promiſes, and in performance of his laſt will, and for the exchange of the manor and park of Mayfield, &c.

[1] Battely Cantuar. Sacr. p. 56.

granted

granted to Thomas Archbiſhop of Canterbury the rectories of Whalley, Blackborn, and Rochdale, &c. [1].

The number of inſtruments dated at Mayfield, which. are extant, ſhew that the archbiſhops frequently reſorted to that place. In Wilkins's Concil. Mag. Britan. many are inſerted that were iſſued by Peckham, Winchelſey, Mepeham, Iſlip, Langham, Sudbury, and Courtney. One of them is intituled Concilium Maghfeldenſe, 13 Aug. 1332, in which is recited the conſtitution of Mepeham concerning holydays and feſtivals, vol. II, p. 565. And another in 1368 (4 non. Jul.) contains a prohibition of Langham againſt holding a market in the Iſle of Shepey on the Lord's-day, v. III. p. 73. Iſlip was at Mayfield the greater part of the ſummer, in the firſt year of his primacy ; for there are in Wilkins ten inſtruments executed by him in the months of May, July, Auguſt, and September, 1350. The firſt was an injunction to Capellans, to ſerve cures for moderate ſtipends ; the ſecond for ſettling the ſtipends of Capellans; the third, an order iſſued in obedience to the king's commands to offer up public prayers for ſuccefs againſt the Spaniſh fleet. The other ſeven inſtruments relate to the memorable controverſy between the univerſity of Oxford and Biſhop Synwell of Lincoln, who had refuſed to confirm their election of William de Palmorna to be their chancellor.

Though the conſtitutions for the eſtabliſhment and govern- ment of Canterbury-hall, founded in Oxford by Iſlip, which are printed in Wilkins, under the year 1362, do not ſpecify either time or place, they were probably drawn up by him before his removal from Mayfield, after his paralytic attack, becauſe it is certain that he there executed the charter of foundation, and the

[1] Strype's Ecclef. Memor. v. ii. p. 76.

grant

grant to the Society of the manor of Woodford in Northampton-shire [1], on the 6 Id. of April, 1363. He was also resident on . Dec. 9, when he collated Wicliffe to the wardenship [2].

Bishop Godwin has advanced, and he has been followed by Battely, that Islip appropriated to Canterbury-hall the rectories of Pagham and Mayfield. His authority for this suggestion does not appear. Stephen de Birchington, whom he has cited for other facts, says, that the Archbishop had determined to appro-

[1] Mr. Battely [*] has fallen into an error, in stating Essex for the county in which Wodeford was situated ; and I am suspicious there is an inaccuracy in his account of the Archbishop's having purchased of his nephew William Islip this manor, which he gave to Canterbury Hall. In the charter of Foundation, the Archbishop only says, that he procured the manor of Wodeford belonging to his nephew to be assigned to the college (*manerium ad perdilectum nepotem nostrum Willelmum de Islep, spectans eidem collegio procuravimus assignari*); and I am rather inclined to believe, that, in order to elude the statutes of mortmain, the Archbishop might, as was a very common practice, have conveyed the manor to his nephew in trust, and that, in pursuance of this trust, William passed it to the college. The charter is dated April 13, 1363, the confirmation of the grant by William de Islip not till the 4th of June. It may also be remarked, that the manor of Wodeford is not inserted in the licence of mortmain from Edward III. To the Archbishop's granting to his intended college a parsonage belonging to the see of Canterbury the King might have no objection, though he might have disapproved of his alienating in mortmain a manor that was not an ecclesiastical possession. Wodeford manor is not noticed, either in the mandate of Pope Urban to execute the sentence of his legate confirming Archbishop Langham's ejection of Wicliffe, and the three secular fellows appointed by the founder, or in the royal pardon to the prior and the convent of Christ Church, for having violated by this adjudication the licence of mortmain ; a favour they obtained from the King about two years after, on their paying a fine of two hundred marks [†].

Bishop Tanner, in Biblioth. Britan. p. 447, says, that Archbishop Islip was of the county of Oxford ; inferring this, as I suppose, from his being called Simon de Islip. He might, however, acquire this surname because he was a native of Islip, in Northamptonshire. That the family were connected with this county is plain, from their being possessed of the manor of Wodeford, which is not far from Islip.

[2] Lewis's Life of Wicliffe, p. 238. 240.

[*] See Cantuar. Sacr. p. 107.   [†] Lewis's Life of Wicliffe, p. 241. 246.

priate

priate the churches of Pageham and Ivechurche for the fupport
of his new foundation, but that he was prevented by death.
*Ecclefias de Pageham et de Ivechurche pro fuâ fuftentatione appro-
priari decrevit. Sed morte præventus, hujufmodi opus imperfeĉtum
reliquit.* Ang. Sac. ii. p. 46. This might be true as to Ivechurch,
but Pageham is mentioned in the licence of mortmain granted
by king Edward III. Oĉt. 20, 1361, and the members of. Canterbury-hall were for fome time poffeffed of it. However,
during the litigation which enfued upon the difplacing of Wicliffe from the wardenfhip, Archbifhop Langham fufpended the
revenues of this parfonage. It is obfervable that Pageham does
not occur in the charter of foundation [1]; and a fubfequent conveyance of it, if not confirmed by the prior and the chapter
of Chrift-church, Canterbury, would not be valid. Poffibly it
might be owing to fome fuch defeĉt in the title, that Pageham
parfonage was not ever fully vefted in Canterbury College ; it
is certainly mentioned as being annexed to that manor when
alienated by Cranmer [2].

With regard to Mayfield reĉtory, Bifhop Tanner [3] has referred
to a deed of Archbifhop Stephen (Langton), by which the church
of Maghfeld was granted for the endowment of a fifth prebend
in the church of South Malling ; but I have my doubts whether
that eftablifhment took place, becaufe one of the charitable deeds
recorded of Archbifhop Winchelfey is, his having given to the
poor of Mayfield, and to other indigent perfons, all the profits

[1] In the archives of the church of Canterbury is an inftrument confirming the
appropriation of Pageham to Canterbury College, with the Bull of Pope Urban
concerning the fame. Cantuaria Sacra, p. 107.
[2] Cantuar. Sacra, p. 64.
[3] Notit. Monaft. p. 549.

of

of that rectory then appropriated to his fee [1], except what was referved for the repair of the houfe and church [2]. Mayfield is alfo entered in a valuation of the fpiritualities of the Arch-bifhopric of Canterbury in 1426 [3]. And, as before obferved of Pageham, the rectory of Mayfield was granted by Cranmer to Henry VIII. as an appendage to the manor, though reftored, if, as mentioned by Ecton, the Archbifhop is the impropriator.

The legendary compiler of the miracles faid to have been wrought by Archbifhop Winchelfey after his death, and which, in the opinion of his zealous and fuperftitious friends, entitled him to canonization, has recorded the cure of William Andrew of Mayfield, who had been totally blind upwards of three years. It was effected by his wife's bringing him to the tomb of that prelate; and, left a doubt fhould be entertained of its authenticity, it is related not merely upon the common fame of perfons in and near Canterbury, but attefted by the oaths of the wife, of Peter Poteman, a cook, and of others, who were convinced of the fact by true and probable experiments [4].

In Wilkins are two inftruments figned by Archbifhop Court-ney at Mayfield. The latter in 1391, May 14, is an inhibition to the clergy of all denominations, not to hear, nor encourage the preachings of William Skynderby, of the diocefe of Lincoln, an heretick convicted, and who, after having abjured his erro-neous doctrines, relapfed [5]. The former, in 1385, Sept. ult.

---

[1] " Ecclefia de Maghefeld in Decanatu de Southmalling 1 x lb." A fum fo high as to render it doubtful whether it did not include other fpiritualties which the Archbifhop had in that deanry. He had the appropriation of the rectory of Wadhurft. Ecton, Lib. Val. John Kirby, clerk, was patron and incumbent in 1780. Bacon, Liber Regis.
[2] Wilkins, Concil. v. II. p. 489.
[3] Cantuar. Sacr. Supplem. N° xi. a.
[4] Wilkins, v. II. p. 438.
[5] Id. III. p. 215.

relates

relates to a matter which the prelate, from his manner of expreffing himfelf, probably judged to be of high importance,
however trifling and ludicrous the fubject may appear to us.
When the Archbifhop was making a metropolitical vifitation,
the abbot and the convent of the canons of St. Auftin, in Briftol,
complained that their habit, being white, was much foiled and
otherwife damaged by the dirt and greafe of the black leather
boots which they were obliged to wear by a rule of their eftablifhment. In order therefore to obviate this indecorum, his grace
was pleafed to grant them a licence to ufe, within the precincts of
their monaftery, ftockings, or hofe, of cloth of a black or brown
colour, fo that the price of it did not exceed twenty pence a
yard. But, left fuch an indulgence fhould afford an occafion for
their growing luxurious and finical, when they went abroad they
were to appear in boots, and not in ftockings without the fpecial
leave of their abbot [1].

No entries occur in Wilkins of deeds executed at Mayfield by
either of the archbifhops Mepeham or Stratford. But, as obferved by Mr. Vine, Mepeham died there in 1333, Oct. 12;
and Stratford, Auguft 23, 1348. According to Birchington [2],
Stratford was at Maidftone when taken with the fevere illnefs
that proved fatal to him, and not at Mayfield, as mentioned by
Godwin. Finding, however, that he daily declined, he was by
fhort ftages removed to Mayfield, where he made his will; and
was indeed nearly his own executor, by diftributing to his do-
meftics their refpective legacies. Probably a grateful remembrance of his charitable donations long prevailed at Mayfield, as
it was his practice to give with his own hands, three times every

[1] Wilkins, V. III. p. 193.
[2] Birchington, Ang. Sac. ii. p. 41.

day,

day, money or provifions to thirteen poor perfons in different claffes.   To each of the thirteen, in the morning and evening, a penny and a loaf of bread, and at noon a loaf of white bread, a pottle of ale, with broth, and a good plate of fifh or flefh.

Dr. Harris [1] has related, that archbifhop Iflip, whilft at his palace at Mayfield, was feized with a fit of the palfy, which *foon* carried him off; *foon* I fuppofe to be a tranflation of the words *paulo poft.* in Godwin, from which book the Doctor's memoirs of the archbifhops of Canterbury feem to have been principally drawn.   But it conveys an idea of a more fpeedy departure of Iflip than was really the cafe.   For it appears from Birchington [2] that the Archbifhop furvived the paralytic ftroke above three years.   The account he gives is, that about the end of January, 1362, when Iflip was travelling from Otteford towards Mayfield, between Sevenok and Tonebregg, he had a fall from his horfe in a miry and water-place, by which he was thoroughly wet, or, as Birchington's expreffion is, *Adeo quod ipfe quàm fub equo, quàm defuper fuerat penitus madefaElus*; that he not only proceeded in his journey, but alfo on his arrival at Mayfield, went to fleep in a *certain ftone chamber*, without changing his cloaths, the confequence of which was a ftroke of the palfy after he had dined, which rendered him almoft incapable of utterance; that he continued at Mayfield till the beginning of July, when he was removed, with eafe to himfelf in a horfe-litter, to Charing; that he paffed fome time at Canterbury and Charing alternately; and in Auguft returned to Mayfield, where he ftayed a year and half; but at length he died at Mayfield, on the morrow of St. Mark, 1366.

[1] Hiftory of Kent, p. 549.
[2] Ang. Sac. v. I. p. 46.

There

There was a park at Mayfield when granted to Henry by Cranmer, and a mark of such an inclosure is delineated in the maps of Suffex, published by Speed, and in Bishop Gibson's edition of Camden's Britannia, though perhaps no vestiges of it may be now discernible. The archiepiscopal manors of Slynden in that county, and of Saltwood [1], Otteford, and Aldyngton, in Kent, had also parks appertaining to them, and to the last was annexed a chafe for deer. Supposing all these parks to have been stocked with deer, Islip, in selling to the Earl of Arundel an antient claim appendant to Slynden manor of twenty-six deer out of the Earl's forest, was no otherwise blameable than that he applied, as it is infinuated, the money to his private use. These deer, or stags, were to be delivered half-yearly, thirteen in the fat season " in tempore pinguedinis" and thirteen " in tempore *deffermefoun* [2]," a word not noticed in any dictionary that I have met with [3]. Bishop Fleetwood in Chronicon Preciosum, has specified the prices of oxen, sheep, hogs, &c. at this period; but as deer were not so openly sold in the 14th as they are in the 18th century, the relative value of them cannot be so clearly ascertained. As the Earl, however, paid CCLX marks sterling to discharge his estate from this venison rent, the purchase of the fee-simple of it may, on an average, be estimated at the rate of something more than six pounds and two shillings per head, which is said to be under the price that a London dealer will give for a fat buck. How great cause Archbishop Parker had to regret the alienation of parks, and of such a number of deer from the fee payable in kind, as it inclined a friend to believe that even sodden venison might be an acceptable

[1] Saltwood was well stored with deere. Philipott. Villar. Cant. p. 298.
[2] Birchington, in Ang. Sac. I. p. 45.
[3] It is probably *fence* month. *Tems de fermesoun*, time of shutting up.

present

prefent to his grace, appears by a curious letter from Robert Duddeley to him, remaining in his collection of MSS. in Bennet College Library, and publifhed in the Antiquarian Repertory, v. II. p. 166. For in this letter Mr. Duddeley acquaints the Archbifhop with his having fent to him by the Queen's command a great and fat ftag, killed indeed with the Queen's own hand; but which, " becaufe the wether was woght, and the dere fome-" what chafed, and daungerous to be caryed fo farre w'owt fome " helpe he had caufed him to be parboyled in this fort for the beft " prefervation of him."

According to Mr. Vine's reprefentation [1], Mayfield-houfe muft, in its profperity, have been a fpacious ftone fabric. If Dunftan was the firft edifier of a houfe here (and that he was may be inferred from the paffage before cited from Eadmer's life of that prelate), it may be prefumed that it was in his time only a wooden building, as he would hardly have erected a church with lefs durable materials than what he employed for his own dwelling. The defcription of the aparment (in quadam lapidea camera) in which Iflip unwarily repofed himfelf after his ride from Otford, implies that a part only of the houfe was then built with ftone. Whether the age of the prefent ruins can be deduced from the ftyle of architecture is fubmitted to the con-

---

[1] " It was in a much more perfect ftate," fays Mr. Vine in 1776, " about forty or fifty years ago, when the roof and floors were taken down, and a great deal of ftone and other materials put to other ufes ; but the lofty ftone arches which fupported the roof are ftill left ftanding, not with any intention of fhewing to pofterity its antient grandeur, but becaufe the materials were judged inadequate in value to the expence and danger of throwing them down. The eaft end is now, and has been for many years, converted into a farm-houfe ; and on a ftone mantle of one of the chamber chimneys is this date, 1371. In this houfe is kept for a fhow what they call Dunftan's tongs, anvil, and hammer, which appear to have been FORGED long fince Dunftan's time."

fideration.

fideration of Mr. Urban's correfpondent, who has fo often furveyed them ; and I beg leave to add, that the noble arches, which he fays are ftill remaining, feem to merit a copper plate [1]. If the figures 1371, infculped on a chimney-piece, denote the year of its being originally put up in the houfe, it muft have been done by the direction of Archbifhop Wittlefey, who was Iflip's nephew, and who, after an interval of little more than two years, was his fucceffor in the fee of Canterbury.　As Iflip unqueftionably refided much at Mayfield, it is likely that he erected fome, and might intend to build other commodious additional apartments, which, from a regard to his uncle's memory, Wittlefey might be the more folicitous to compleat.　It was indeed requifite and juft, that Iflip, or his reprefentatives, fhould expend very confiderable fums in repairing and improving the buildings of the fee; he having recovered from the brother of Archbifhop Ufford 1100l. [2] for dilapidations, and having obtained from the Pope a bull to levy upon the clergy of his province, after the rate of four-pence in the mark towards the fupport of his charges, but under which, by a collufion, a tenth was extorted from the clergy of his diocefe [3].　It is alfo related of Iflip, that he committed a greater wafte of timber in the Dourdennes in the Weald of Kent, than had been done by any of his predeceffors.　Birchington mentions his having nobly repaired the

[1] Two views of them are here annexed (fee plates XIV. XV.) from the Supplement to Mr. Grofe's Antiquities.　And fee p. 212, 213.

[2] So Godwin de Præful. p. 113. 1000 marks.　Birchington, Ang. Sac. I. p. 43: According to Godwin, the whole of this money was expended in repairing the palace at Canterbury; but, qu. as the fum recovered was for the dilapidations of all the houfes.　Palatium Cantuarienfe, receptis—pro deftructionibus *domorum mille marcis,* fecit nobiliter reparari.—Barchington.

[3] Cantuar. Sacr. p. 73.

palace

ST DUNSTAN'S PALACE.

Pl. IV. p. 21.

S.ᵗ DUNSTANs PALLACE, MAYFIELD SUSSEX.

Published the 26 of December 1783 by S. Hooper.

palace at Canterbury [1], and his finishing the house at Maidstone, which Ufford had begun to build, making there a new chamber. That he should therefore pay almost an equal attention to his house at Mayfield, which was a favourite villa, is a very probable supposition.   S. DENNE.

Further PARTICULARS of MAYFIELD PALACE; from the SUPPLEMENT to GROSE's ANTIQUITIES.

IN 1332, a provincial council was assembled here; and a constitution passed relating to holidays, their number, and the observance of them; and in 1362, another was held here on the same subject.

In 1259, Archbishop Boniface obtained a charter from Henry III. for a market and fair to be held here; and in 1382 Archbishop Courtney obtained from Richard II. a grant of a market and two fairs; or perhaps rather a comfirmation of the former charter.

In 1389, a great fire happened here, which consumed the church and almost all the town.

The manor and mansion was granted by Archbishop Cranmer in 1525 to King Henry VIII. who gave it in the same year to Sir Edmund Worth, by whom it was shortly after alienated to Sir Thomas Gresham; who had the honour of entertaining Queen Elizabeth in this mansion in her Kentish progress of 1573. A large room in the habitable part of the building, still retains the appellation of " Queen Elizabeth's room." In the Life of Sir Thomas Gresham, in the Biographia Britannica, are the following particulars respecting the furniture of the mansion : " But " his chief seat (meaning Sir Thomas Gresham's) seems to have " been at Mayghfield in Suffex, one room of which was called " the Queen's chamber, and the goods and chattels belonging to " it, were estimated at seven thousand five hundred and fifty-

[1] Hist. & Antiq. of Rochester, p. 36.   Biblioth. Topogr. Britann. N. VI. P. I. p. 22.   Wilkins's Concil. v. II. p. 253.

" three

" three pounds, ten fhillings and eight-pence." This eftimate, from an original note, appears to have been extracted from Sir Thomas Grefham's Journal in manufcript. Whether the goods of the Queen's chamber only, or thofe of the whole manfion, were here eftimated, is not clearly expreffed; but probably the latter; and a very confiderable fum it was, efpecially in thofe days.

The manfion was bequeathed by Sir Thomas Grefham to Sir Henry Nevil, who fold it to Thomas Bray, of Burwafh, efq; whofe widow difpofed of it to John Baker, efq; to the widow of one of whofe defcendants it ftill belongs for life. The manor is the property of Mr. Pelham.

The remains of this antient manfion are very confiderable; the great hall retaining its magnificence even in ruins. The infide of it in the prefent ftate is fhewn in plate XVI. It is 68 feet long, 38 broad, and in height fully proportionable; its roof was taken off within the memory of perfons now or lately living. The crofs arches are, however, ftill remaining, and give it a moft venerable and picturefque appearance. The part appearing like a Gothic door or arch, near the centre of the upper end of the room, is the back part of the archiepifcopal chair of ftate; and confifts of a number of little fquares, each containing a rofe, elegantly carved. Near the top are what feem to be traces of a Gothic canopy with which it was covered; over it is a niche, fuppofed to have either contained, or been intended for, a ftatue. The window near it, over the doors belonged to the Archbifhop's chamber; whence he could fee what was paffing in the hall without being prefent; a common circumftance in many of the ancient manfions. The gate-houfe and porter's lodge remain entire; and there appears to have been a covered way from the manfion to the church-yard.

END OF NUMBER XLV.

Pl. XVI. p. 222

London Published by J. Harper No 12 Leyd Holborn, June 24 1798.

Engraved by J. Newton.

Great Hall,
Mayfield Palace Sussex.

BIBLIOTHECA

TOPOGRAPHICA

BRITANNICA

N° XXX.

CONTAINING

The History and Antiquities
of the THREE ARCHIEPISCOPAL HOSPITALS,
and other charitable FOUNDATIONS,
at and near CANTERBURY.

By Mr. DUNCOMBE, and the late Mr. BATTELY.

[Price Ten Shillings and Six Pence.]

AMONG the various Labours of Literary Men, there have always been certain Fragments whofe Size could not fecure them a general Exemption from the Wreck of Time, which their intrinfic Merit entitled them to furvive; but, having been gathered up by the Curious, or thrown into Mifcellaneous Colleƈions by Bookfellers, they have been recalled into Exiftence, and by uniting together have defended themfelves from Oblivion. Original Pieces have been called in to their Aid, and formed a Phalanx that might withftand every Attack from the Critic to the Cheefemonger, and contributed to the Ornament as well as Value of Libraries.

With a fimilar view it is here intended to prefent the Publick with fome valuable Articles of BRITISH TOPOGRAPHY. from printed Books and MSS. One Part of this Colleƈion will confift of Re-publications of fcarce and various Traƈs; another of fuch MS, Papers as the Editors are already poffeffed of, or may receive from their Friends.

It is therefore propofed to publifh a Number occafionally, not confined to the fame Price or Quantity of Sheets, nor always adorned with Cuts; but paged in fuch a Manner, that the general Articles, or thofe belonging to the refpeƈive Counties, may form a feparate Succeffion, if there fhould be enough publifhed, to bind in fuitable Claffes; and each Traƈ will be completed in a fingle Number.

Into this Colleƈion all Communications confiftent with the Plan will be received with Thanks. And as no Correfpondent will be denied the Privilege of controverting the Opinions of another, fo none will be denied Admittance without a fair and impartial Reafon.

THE

HISTORY AND ANTIQUITIES

OF THE

THREE ARCHIEPISCOPAL HOSPITALS

At and near CANTERBURY;

VIZ.

St. NICHOLAS, at HARBLEDOWN;

St. JOHN's, NORTHGATE;

And St. THOMAS, OF EASTBRIDGE.

WITH SOME ACCOUNT OF

The Priory of St. GREGORY, the Nunnery of St. SEPULCHRE,
the Hofpitals of St. JAMES and St. LAWRENCE,
and MAYNARD's Spittle.

By JOHN DUNCOMBE, M. A.

Vicar of HERNE, and Mafter of the Hofpitals of St. NICHOLAS and St. JOHN;

and the late NICHOLAS BATTELY, M. A.

Vicar of BEAKSBOURN, and Editor of SOMNER's Antiquities of CANTERBURY.

——— *Juvat* antiquos *accedere fontes,*
Atque haurire ———

LONDON,
PRINTED BY AND FOR J. NICHOLS,
PRINTER TO THE SOCIETY OF ANTIQUARIES.
MDCCLXXXV.

TO

THE MOST REVEREND FATHER IN GOD,

J O H N,

BY DIVINE PROVIDENCE,

LORD ARCHBISHOP OF CANTERBURY, &c.

P A T R O N

OF THE

HOSPITALS OF ST. NICHOLAS,

ST. JOHN, AND ST. THOMAS,

THE FOLLOWING HISTORY

O F

THOSE ANCIENT FOUNDATIONS,

COLLECTED CHIEFLY FROM THEIR OWN ARCHIVES,

IS, WITH GREAT ESTEEM AND RESPECT, INSCRIBED,

BY HIS GRACE'S

OBLIGED AND DUTIFUL SERVANT,

J. DUNCOMBE.

Arthur Nelson del. 1766.

W. View of St. Nicholas Hospital, Harbledown.

1 *Brotherhood Farm-house.* 2 *Parish church of St. Michael.* 3 *Hospital Chapel.* 4 4 4 *Hospital house.* 5 *Hall or Porter-house.*
6 6 *Mill in the Mint.*

H E R B A L D O W N.

THE hofpital of HERBALDOWN, that is, " the pafture-down, or the down of herbage or tillage*," (commonly called HARBLE-DOWN), about a mile from the Weft gate of Canterbury, is dedicated to St. Nicholas, and was anciently fituated in the Blean-wood, of which king Henry I. in one of their moft ancient charters†, allowed the hofpitallers to " grub and clear away ten perches of wood on all fides." It was fo ftyled, as Mr. Somner with reafon fuppofes, " to diftinguifh it from the neighbouring hills, or downs, " as yet continuing wild or woody." It was built, as was St. John's, by archbifhop Lanfranc, about the year 1084, and was originally intended for a lazar-houfe, of which there were two others near Canterbury, St. James's‡, and St. Laurence's ||, both, like this, without the city, from which all leprous perfons were excluded. Inftead of lands, he endowed each hofpital with 70 l. per annum, payable out of his manors of Reculver and Boughton under Blean, to which archbifhop Richard, Becket's immediate fucceffor, about 1180, added 20 l. more, payable out of the rectory of Reculver § : which 160 l. or 240 marks (80 l. to each) remained unaltered till the time of

---

* Sommer's Antiquities of Canterbury, p. 46. The fpot where this hofpital is fituated has been remarked as peculiarly healthful ; and it is well known that herbalifts come regularly every year to collect medicinal plants that grow only on this particular fpot. † See p. 204.

‡ Or St. Jacob's, founded before 1188, fuppreffed in 1551.

|| Founded in 1137 by Hugh the Second, abbot of St. Auguftine's, for the reception of the leprous of that abbey; fuppreffed in 1557. On the fite of this now ftands a manfion-houfe, the property of vifcount Dudley, let to Mrs. Bridges. St. James's was public. The frequency of the leprofy (fo called) in thofe times, and its unfrequency in thefe, deferve inveftigation.

§ See p. 208. This charter is inferted in the Hiftory of Reculver, p. 129.

B b

arch-

archbifhop Kilwardby, who withdrew their stipend, and inftead of it appropriated to them his parfonage of Reculver, with the chapels annexed *. But a tithery, and that fo remote, being very inconvenient to fuch infirm and difeafed people, his immediate fucceffor, archbifhop Peckham, revoked this grant, and reftored the hofpitals to their former ftate †. And this was confirmed by Edward I. in 1291 ‡. Archbifhop Winchelfey, in 1298, gave them a body of ftatutes ||, the firft they had. But, having no written endowment, they were obliged, at the acceffion of every archbifhop, to petition for the continuance of this cuftomary allowance. At length, the parfonage of Reculver being held *in capite* of the king, Edward III. by his charter §, at the defire of archbifhop Stratford, appropriated it to the archbifhop's table, charged with the ancient ftipend above-mentioned, which was afterwards fecured to them by his fucceffor archbifhop Iflip in a written charter **, 1355, confirmed by the prior and convent of Chrift-church, by which, with very little interruption, it has been ever fince peaceably enjoyed ††. This was equally divided between the two hofpitals, and was at that time a moft liberal provifion, but, from the gradual decreafe of the value of money, it is now reduced to a very flender ftipend. It, however, was very fortunate for them that Lanfranc did not endow them with lands, as he did his other foundation of St. Gregory; for their efcape at the general fuppreffion feems owing to their having no lands of value fufficient to tempt the rapacity of Henry VIII's courtiers. At different times their revenue has been

---

* One cannot but obferve, 1ft, how very large this endowment was fo many hundred years ago; and 2dly, that it feems unaccountable, confidering its prefent value, how the manor, or rectory, of Reculver could be adequate to fuch an expence, though much of it, we know, has been fwallowed up by the fea.

† See the Hiftory of Reculver, p. 131.   ‡ Ibid. || See p. 214.
§ See this alfo in the Hiftory of Reculver, p. 141.   ** Ibid. p. 148.
†† Mr. Somner's fuccefsful application for the continuance of their penfion in the laft century is mentioned, p. 202.

augmented

augmented by feveral other donations, fome of which have been
made to both hofpitals conjointly, fome to one alone.   There
do not appear to have been any other ftatutes previous to the
time of archbifhop Parker, who gave them, Sept. 15, 1560,
the book of ftatutes by which both hofpitals are at prefent governed, to which he made additions Aug. 20, 1565, and May
20, 1574*.   Some additions have alfo been occafionally made by
his fucceffors, particularly archbifhops Whitgift, Laud, and San-
croft†, as it feems to be in the power of any archbifhop to make
what alterations he may think proper in their number, government, or maintenance.

Among the ancient fecular benefactors to Herbaldown, Somner
mentions Eilgar of Bourne, and John of Tonford, two neighbouring gentlemen; but the principal was king Henry II. (not III.
as he fuppofes) who gave it 20 marks a year out of his fee-farm
rents in the city of Canterbury ‡, a large fum too at that time,
which continues to be paid to this day by the chamberlain in half-
yearly payments of 6l. 13s. 4d. each.   Total 13l. 6s. 8d.

Nothing remarkable is recorded of this hofpital till it is
thus introduced by Erafmus in his *Peregrinatio Religionis ergo*,
1510.   " OG. In the road to London, not far from Canterbur y
" is a way extremely hollow, as well as narrow, and alfo ? eg
" the bank being on each fide fo craggy that there is no efcaping;
" nor can it by any means be avoided.   On the left fide of that
" road is an alms-houfe *(mendicabulum)* of fome old men; one of
" whom runs out as foon as they perceive a horfeman approach-
" ing, and after fprinkling him with holy-water, offers him the
" upper-leather of a fhoe bound with brafs, in which a piece
" of glafs is fet like a gem.   This is kiffed, and money given
" him.   ME. I had rather have an alms-houfe of old men
" on fuch a road than a troop of fturdy robbers.   OG. As Gra-
" tian § rode on my left hand, nearer to the alms-houfe, he was

* See p. 219.   † All thefe may be feen in the Appendix, pp. 220—225.
‡ See Appendix, p. 205.   § Dr. John Colet, dean of St. Paul's, 1505—19.

                    B b 2   " fprinkled

" fprinkled with water; to this he fubmitted; but when the
" fhoe was held out, he afked what it meant.   And being told
" it was the fhoe of St. Thomas, he was fo provoked, that turn-
" ing to me, ' What! (fays he) would this herd have us kifs the
" fhoes of all good men? they may juft as well offer their fpittle
" to be kiffed, and other bodily excrements.'   I took compaffion
" on the old man, and gave him fome money by way of con-
" folation."

There feem at prefent to be no remains of Lanfranc's building,
except the church or chapel.   The houfes which the brothers and fifters inhabit, were rebuilt in the latter end of the
laft century, as will be mentioned hereafter.   The church, which
adjoins to the hofpital, a large ancient ftructure, confifts of a
nave and two ailes, with a font, and a turret containing four
bells *, having of old been the parifh-church of St. Nicholas,
Herbaldown, and as fuch pays procurations to this day †.   Some
curious painted glafs remains in the windows.   In 1292 it
was valued, as a parfonage, at nine marks per annum (more
than moft of the neighbouring livings), and accordingly the tenths
were fet at 12s.   The ancient incumbent was a rector.   To
this church, and its prefbyter, of St. Nicholas, archbifhop Theobald granted, by charter, the tithes of his manor of Weft-gate:
and thus improved, archbifhop Stratford, in 1342, when he new-
founded Eaft-bridge hofpital in Canterbury, by his charter appropriated to it this rectory ‡, and in confequence Mr. Bridges, the
leffee of that hofpital now holds it, and repairs the chancel. But
this having been alfo the church of the poor, or, as archbifhop
Parker fays, " built for them by their founder Lanfranc," Stratford
in his charter obliged Eaft-bridge hofpital to provide them a chaplain.   Inftead of which, archbifhop Wittlefey, in 1371, erected a

---

* Ringing being charged three times in the prior's account, 1709, 1s. each time,
an order was made by the mafter, Mr. Paris, that " no ringing fhould be allowed
" on any account for the future."   † See p. 183.
‡ See the appropriation of Eaftbridge Hofpital, p. 225.

perpetual

perpetual chantry*, the prieſt of which reſided at Clavering near
the hoſpital.   And this continued till the Reformation, when
both chantry and chantry-prieſt were aboliſhed ; and the church
continuing to the hoſpital †, prayers are read there once a week,
and the ſick occaſionally attended, by a reader, ſo called, who at
preſent is the rev. John Goſtling, M. A. eldeſt ſon of the late
worthy " Walker."   The ſtipend is 8l. a year, and a houſe.
The maſter, through whom petitions for corrodies are preſented
to the archbiſhop, and who has the care of both hoſpitals, under
his grace, their patron and viſitor, has no ſalary.   The number
of in-brothers and ſiſters in this hoſpital is 15 of each ; beſides
which there is the ſame number of out-brothers and out-
ſiſters, who have only a penſion of 6s. a quarter.   The number maintained in each hoſpital ſeems to have been variable.
In 1398 there were in Herbaldown about 80, in St. John's
in 1375 there were 100; in 1464 there were 80; now there
are 60 (in and out) of each, in all 120;   By archbiſhop
Winchelſey's ſtatutes, no corrodies were allowed to any who
did not reſide in the hoſpital ; nor is there any mention of out-
brothers and ſiſters before archbiſhop Parker's ſtatutes.   Theſe
receive only their ſhare of the archbiſhop's penſion, and the
other revenues of the hoſpital are divided among the reſident
members.   The allowance of out-brothers and ſiſters was probably occaſioned by the want of lodgings as well as the ſmallneſs
of income.   In Herbaldown there are only 26 houſes; in St.
John's 31.   They at firſt lived in the ancient conventual manner,
and had their common halls for dining, and their dormitories for
ſleeping; but as the buildings fell to decay, and no proviſion was
made for repairing them, the in-dwellers were neceſſarily obliged
to be leſſened.   Of theſe one is annually choſen prior, whoſe
principal office is to collect the rents, and one of the ſiſters

* See p. 183.   † Battely's Somner, p. 145.

prioreſs,,

priorefs, with fome particular perquifites to each.   The hofpital ftands (as defcribed by Erafmus) on the South fide of the London road, in the village, and adjoining to the parifh, of St. Michael, Herbaldown, and is pleafantly fituated on the fide of a hill, with a fpring of fine water, called from ancient times " The Black Prince's Well." A Weft view of the hofpital, chapel, &c. is annexed (fee plate I.)

Its poffeffions were valued, 26 Hen. VIII. at 112*l*. 15*s*. 7*d*. in the whole, or at 109*l*. 7*s*. 2*d*. per annum clear, including the archbifhop's ftipend of 80*l*.

Among the benefactions previous to thofe of this century, Mr. Somner devifed by will an eftate in Romney Marfh to this hofpital, after the death of his fon, in cafe he had no iffue ; but the fon paffed a fine, barred the entail, and defeated the benefaction.

October 24, 1674, the following account of this hofpital was given to archbifhop Sheldon : " The hofpital of St. Nicholas, Herbaldown, confifts of 15 in-brothers, and as many in-fifters, who have 4*l*. apiece yearly, befides two loads of wood. Out-brothers and out-fifters in like number have yearly 1*l*. 14*s*. a piece. The whole revenue is 160*l*. 1*s*. 8*d*."

In the fame year (1674) the lodgings of the brothers and fifters of this hofpital being ruinous, archbifhop Sheldon gave 200*l*. and Mr. John Somner 50*l*. and in 1685 archbifhop Sancroft gave 67*l*. and Dr. Thorp, prebendary of Canterbury, mafter of the hofpital, 20 *l*. by which benefactions chiefly thofe lodgings, together with the common-hall of the houfe, and the Brotherhood farm-houfe, were rebuilt, and the barns, ftables, and out-houfes repaired.

This is commemorated in a tablet hung in the hall, where the brethren and fifters have an annual feaft (for which, in moft of their leafes, fome payments, now inadequate, are referved) on the name-day of their patron-faint (St. Nicholas) Dec. 6. In the hall alfo the members are admitted and fworn to the obfervance of
the

the ftatutes, and the ancient charters and other deeds are depofited in a ftrong cheft. All thefe (as is more particularly mentioned p. 201.) were carefully examined, forted, and labelled in both hofpitals, and an account of them tranfmitted to archbifhop Secker, in 1764, by the rev. Dr. Beauvoir, in a book which he entitled *Liber Hofpitalium Archiepifcopi*, now preferved in Lambeth library, to which the compiler of this article has great obligations. The number (as may be feen in the appendix) is large, and the royal and archiepifcopal charters (in particular) very curious.

For the repairs of the buildings there is no allowance, but what is provided by the reparation-purfe, which fund arifes thus : From each perfon at admiffion a reparation noble, or 6s. 8d. ; the ftipend that accrues during each vacancy ; 6d. a month from every non-refident, and 5s. feal money on fealing every leafe. Several places alfo are kept vacant at Lambeth, and the ftipend fent annually to the mafter, as a farther fupply. By the ftatutes they are enjoined to repair their own houfes, but from this they are now difabled by their poverty. Some late benefactions fhall be recapitulated. Mrs. Elizabeth Lovejoy, of Canterbury, relict of the Rev. George Lovejoy, mafter of the king's fchool, by her will dated in 1694, among many other donations, gave to the mayor and commonalty of that city, her leafe of Callis Grange, in the parifh of St. Peter, in Thanet, held under the dean and chapter, in truft, to pay this hofpital 5l. per annum, which is divided among the refident members. Ralph Snowe, gent. of Lambeth, fteward to the archbifhop, by his will dated in 1707 *, bequeathed each hofpital 200l. in truft, with which archbifhop Tenifon purchafed for this of Herbaldown part of an eftate at Mitcham in Surrey, which now lets for 12l. per annum clear. And archbifhop Secker, by his will dated in 1769, left

* See p. 175.

them

them 500*l.* each in reverſion, in 3 per cent. annuities, after the deaths of Mrs. Talbot and her daughter, both of whom being now deceaſed, the former dying Jan. 9, 1770, and the latter Jan. 19, 1784, aged 97, that deviſe, of which the preſent biſhop of Cheſter is the ſurviving-truſtee, is expected ſoon to take place.

Among the original deeds belonging to this hoſpital is an old leathern caſe for holding ſome of them, of which a ſketch is given in plate IV. fig. 9. inſcribed " 𝔈𝔫 𝔇𝔦𝔢𝔲 𝔢𝔰𝔱 𝔱𝔬𝔲𝔱."

And in the cheſt is a curious maple bowl, uſed on their feaſt days, of great antiquity, the rims of which are ſilver gilt; and in the bottom is faſtened the medallion engraved in plate V. The ſtory is evidently one of Guy earl of Warwick; the motto.

GY DE WARWYC : ADANOVN : FEEI OCCIS : LE DRAGOVN [*].

John Shurley, in his " Renowned Hiſtory of Guy earl of Warwick [†]," 4to, tells a ſtory of his ſeeing a dragon and lion fighting together in a foreſt bordering on the ſea, as he was returning to Europe from the relief of Byzantium. He determined to take up the conqueror; and after the lion was fairly ſpent, Guy attacked the dragon, and after many hard blows on his adamantine ſcales, ſpying a bare place under his wing, he thruſt his ſword in to the depth of two feet, and with a dreadful yell the dragon expired. No ſcene of action is aſſigned; but we ſuſpect ſome real or fictitious place is concealed under the name of *Danoun*, perhaps for a rhyme ſake, and then the inſcription will ſignify that " Guy of Warwick at *Danoun* ſlew the dragon."

The hoſpital-ſeal is engraved in plate III. fig. 1.

---

[*] Some have thought that the third word may be ɪᴄᴄɪ or ʏᴇᴄɪ, for " here;" ſome that the fourth may be ᴀᴅᴏʀᴠɴ, " on the back of a roan horſe," but that the letters evidently will not bear; and others that ᴅᴀɴᴏᴠɴ might be the name of Guy's ſword, as *Durindana* was that of Orlando, &c.

[†] This Hiſtory has no date; but was " printed by A. M. for C. Bates and " J. Foſter," about the beginning of the preſent century.

The

Plate IV. p. 180.

The prefent revenue of this Hofpital (1784) is as follows:

Paid Quarterly.	l.	s.	d.
The Archbifhop's penfion *,	80	0	0
Rents of lands and houfes,	88	0	0
Half-Yearly.			
Rents, &c.	21	6	0
Penfion from the city of Canterbury †,	13	6	8
Mrs. Lovejoy's legacy ‖,	5	0	0
Yearly.			
Rent of lands at Mitcham, purchafed with Mr. Snowe's legacy §,	12	0	0
Two acres of wood (in hand) about,	12	0	0
Penfion from the Exchequer ‡, (clear)	3	4	9¼
Fines for renewing leafes, on an average,	10	0	0
Feaft rents, and collected from the guefts, ufually about,	3	0	0
Annuities.			
Mr. Charles Palfrey, for land at Herne,	0	10	0
Lady Hardres's heirs, for Hardres meadow,	0	2	0
John Lade, Efq. for land at Grayney,	0	2	0
Total	248	11	5¼
Ded.	59	3	1
Clear	189	8	4¼

which is not 6l. 10s. each.

Difburfements.

	l.	s.	d.
To the reader, per ann **.	8		
To three out-brothers and two out-fifters, at or near Canterbury, (paid quarterly).	6	0	0
To twelve out-brothers and thirteen out-fifters, at or near Lambeth ††,	30	0	0
Quit-rents, viz. to Weftgate manor, 15 2			
to Reculver, 3 4			
to Hall and Beverley, 12 5	1	13	1
to Grayney, 0 10			
to the city of Canterbury, 1 4			
Towards the charges of the feaft on St. Nicholas day, ufually about,	3	10	0
Other expences, at leaft,	10	0	0
	59	3	1

* Of this 50l. is paid by the Archbifhop's regiftrar, Mr. Delafaux, at Canterbury, and 30l. is referved to pay the out-brothers and fifters at Lambeth.

† See p. 175. ‖ See p. 179. § Ibid. ‡ See p. 227.

** 8d. per quarter is referved out of every ftipend to make up this fum. The reader has alfo of late 2l. more for the rent of one of the houfes.

†† See note * above.

Rev. George Thorp, D. D. prebendary of Canterbury.
1708. —— John Paris, M. A[1]. rector of St. Andrew's and St. Mary Bredman's, Canterbury.
1709. —— John Bradock, M. A. one of the fix preachers.
1711. —— Elias Sydall, D. D[2]. prebendary.
1731. —— John Lynch, D. D[3]. prebendary.
1744. —— Thomas Lamprey, M. A. rector of St. Martin's, and vicar of St. Paul's, Canterbury.
1761. —— John Head, D. D[4]. archdeacon and prebendary.
1770, Sept. 15. —— John Duncombe, M. A. one of the fix preachers.

The following Inftruments relating to Herbaldown are preferved in the Regifters at Lambeth.

HEREBALDOUNE juxta Cantuar' Hofpital'.

INJUNCTIONES a priore, prioriffa, fratribus & fororibus dicti hofpitalis ob-fervandæ; dat' in predict' hofpitali, 6 kal' Mart' A. D. 1298. Reg. Win-chelfea, fol. 69. a.

Mandatum dni archiepi fuper perceptione eleemofyne archiepi; dat' Hofpital' de Harbledown & de Northgate Cant' dat' apud Otteford, 3 id. Feb. 1355. Reg. Iflip, fol. 111 b. 112. a.

Confirmatio Roberti[5] prioris eccl' Chrifti Cant' & ejufdem loci conventus litteræ precedentis; dat' in domo fira capit', 10 Feb. 1355. Ibid. 112.

A leafe granted by Sam. Parker, D. D[6]. Archdeacon of Canterbury, and Maf-ter of the hofpital of Eaftbridge, alias St. Thomas, in the City of Canterbury, of the tithes, &c. belonging to the Hofpital of St. Nicholas Harbledown, within the bounds of Harbledown, to Simon Lowth[7] of the parifh of St. Cofmas and Damian in the Bleane in the County of Kent, for the term of 21 years; dat' 25 Dec. 1682. Reg. Sancroft, fol. 359. a.

Confirmatio Dni archiepi locationis prædict'; dat' 12 Sept. 1683. Fol. 360. a.

[1] Alfo mafter of Eaftbridge Hofpital.
[2] Dean 1728, Bp. of St. David's and afterwards of Gloucefter, 1731.   [3] Dean 1733—60.
[4] Afterwards Sir John, Bart.
[5] Robert Hathbrand, who died in 1370.   [6] Bifhop of Oxford, 1686.
[7] See p. 186. note 1.

4   CHAN-

CHANTRY of St. NICHOLAS, HERBALDOWN.

REGISTERS-

1371, 4 Nov.	Fundatio & Ordinatio Cantarie in Eccl' Wittlefeye, fol. 51. b. 52. a Sči Nich' in Hofpitali de Herebaldon * per D'n'm Wittlefeye Cant' Archiepifcopum; dat' apud Croydon,	
1376, 24 Féb.	John Halgheton.	Sudbury, fol. 121. a.
1386, 16 Feb.	John Vagge.	Courtney, fol. 265. a.
	Walter Setryngton.	
1399, 3 Mar.	John Martyn, on the refignation of Setryngton.	Arundel, fol. 265. b.
1400, 2 Jan.	John Bray†, on the refignation of Martyn.	Ibid. fol. 273. a.
	Thomas Barbour.	
1426, 25 Jan.	John Wellyng, on the death of Barbour.	Chicheley, p. I. fol. 167. a.
1429, 11 Oct.	Hugh Nobul, on the refignation of Wellyng.	Ibid. fol. 178. a.
	Walter Gilbert.	
1468, 3 Sept.	William Robert, on the refignation of Gilbert.	Bourchier, fol. 99. a.
	Robert Lafungby.	
1488, 27 Oct.	Thomas Cottebery, on the refignation of Lafungby.	Morton, Deene, Bourchier, and Courtney, fol. 136. a.
	Thomas Porter.	
1524, 30 Sept.	George Hyggis, on the death of Porter.	Warham, fol. 382. b.

RECTORS of St. MICHAEL, HERBALDOWN.

From the Regifters at Lambeth.

	RECTORS.	REGISTERS.
1316, 6 Jan.	Nicholas Burnell.	Reynolds, fol. 19. a.
1324, 15 June.	Edmund de Newenton, by exchange with Burnell.	Ibid. fol. 253. a.
	Hugh de Birton.	
1361, 10 Sep.	John Lacey, on the refignation of Birton.	Iflip, fol. 289. b.

* Founded by Thomas Newe, rector of Godmerfham, under the patronage of Abp. Wittlefey. See the Hiftory of Reculver, p. 157.

† The chantry-prieft mentioned in the exemplification of Abp. Arundel, 18 May, 1402. See p. 211.

1361,

INCUMBENTS.	REGISTERS.
1361, 17 Dec.	Robert Flemyng, on the resignation of Lacey.	Ibid. 293. b.
1371, 10 Dec.	William Savage. John Montague.	Wittlefeye, fol. 88. a.
1406, 30 Oct.	Richard Hilley, by exchange with Montague.	Arundel, fol. 311. b.
1410, 23 Oct.	Matthew Edenham, on the death of Hilley.	Arundel, p. 2. fol. 60. a.
1412, 15 June.	John Orwell, by exchange with Edenham. Richard Baron.	Ibid. fol. 64. a.
1422, 9 Feb.	Walter Gorge, by exchange with Baron. William Palmer.	Chicheley, p. I. fol, 137. b.
1446, 18 Jan.	William Cleve, B. A. on the death of Palmer.	Stafford, fol. 91. b.
1448, 5 Nov.	William Leake, on the resignation of Cleve. Thomas Symond.	Ibid. fol. 98. a.
1470, 26 Feb.	Edmund Lychefeld, on the death of Symond. Henry Barradon.	Bourchier, fol. 103. a.
1493, 8 May	Robert Curfon, M. A. on the death of Barradon.	Morton, Dene, Bourchier, and Courtney, fol. 154. b.
1507, 2 April.	Thomas Bafchurche, on a legal vacancy.	Warham. fol. 330.
1507, 30 Aug.	John Thorneton *, Epifcopus Cironen', on the refignation of Bafchurche.	Ibid. fol. 326. b.
1513, 28 March.	Michael Vaughan, on the refignation of Thorneton.	Warham, fol. 348. a.
1516, 9 Sept.	John Oxley, by the ceffion or difmiffion of Vaughan.	Ibid. fol. 361.
1517, 3 Feb.	Thomas Dodyng, on the refignation of Oxley. John Boneton.	Ibid. 364. b.
1521, 12 April.	Philip Taylor, on the refignation of Boneton.	Ibid. 372. b.

* Or Thornden, D. D. and feveral times commiffary or vice-chancellor of this univerfity [Oxford], while Archbifhop Warham was chancellor, viz. between the years 1506 and 1514, in which time he is often ftyled " Epifcopus Syrynenfis" and " Syrymenfis" (perhaps the fame with Sirmium in Hungary) as being a fuffragan to the archbifhop. He was prior of the black monks at Dover, and fuffragan of Dover, 1508. Wood's Athen. Oxon. I, 654.

1528,

RECTORS.	REGISTERS.
1528, 10 May. Arthur Strewike, on the death of Taylor.	Ibid. 395. b.
1534, 16 Nov. Richard Croſſe.	Cranmer, fol. 353. b.
1557, 15 Nov. Robert Moubrey, on the death of Croſſe.	Pole, fol. 74. b.
1562, 21 March. Robert Pownall, on the death of Moubrey.	Parker, fol. 360. a.
1571, 17 Sept. Henry Murrey, on the death of Pownall.	Ibid. fol. 406. b.
1579, 22 July. John Bridges[1], on the reſignation of Murrey.	Grindal, fol. 526.
1589, 1 Sept. Andrew Peerſon[2], B. D. on the reſignation of Bridges.	Whitgift, fol. 259. b.
1594, 23 Nov. Francis Wormeal[3], on the death of Peerſon.	Ibid. p. II. 324. b.
1596, 9 March. Robert Hemynges, M. A.[4] on the death of Wormeal.	Ibid. p. III. fol. 265. b.
1601, 9 July. Humphrey Aylworth, B. D. on the death of Hemynges,	Ibid. fol 267. b.
1601, 5 Feb. William Swift[5], M. A. on the reſignation of Aylworth.	Abbot, p. II. fol. 340.
1624, 23 Feb. Robert Say, D. D. on the death of Swift.	Ibid. p. II. fol. 340.
1628, 22 May. Robert Auſten, D. D. on the death of Say.	Ibid. fol. 357. b.
164 , Richard Culmer, M. A.[6]	
1661, 12 Sept. John Bargrave[7], D. D. on a legal vacancy.	Juxon, fol. 127. b.

[1] Probably the ſame who was alſo vicar of Herne from 1562 to 1590. See the "Hiſtory of that pariſh," p. 160.

[2] Chaplain to Abp. Parker, rector of Braſted, Chidingſtone, and Wrotham, maſter of the faculties, one of the tranſlators of the Bible, &c.

[3] Chriſtopher Wormeal was at this time Archbiſhop Whitgift's principal ſteward and receiver at Lambeth. See the "Hiſtory of Croydon," p. 152.

[4] Of Cambridge. Incorporated at Oxford in 1590. Wood's Faſti, I. 141.

[5] Great-grandfather to the famous Dean of St. Patrick's, and rector of St. Andrews, Canterbury, where he was buried. Dr. Swift by miſtake calls him "a prebendary."

[6] The name of this fanatic, commonly called Blue Dick, from his wearing blue in oppoſition to black, does not occur in the Regiſters, but is ſupplied from Wood's Athen. Oxon. He was miniſter of Goodneſton, from which he was ſuſpended for not reading the Book of Sports on the Lord's Day, was alſo vicar of St. Stephen's, a bitter enemy to Archbiſhop Laud, author of "Cathedral News, &c." and diſtinguiſhed himſelf by breaking the great north window of the cathedral. He died and was buried at Monkton.

[7] Prebendary of Canterbury. He died May 11, 1680.

RECTORS.	REGISTERS.
1670, 8 Dec. Simon Lowth, M. A[1]. on the ceffion of Bargrave.	Sheldon, fol. 346. a.
1690, 10 Feb. Simon D'Evereux, prefented by the king and queen.	Sufpenfio Sancroft, fol. 51. b.
1733, 6 Aug. John Frances[2], M. A. on the death of D'Evereux.	Wake, p. II. fol. 271. a.
1734, 27 Nov. Charles Milles[3], M. A. on the death of Frances.	Ibid. fol. 274. a.
1749, 4 July. Thomas Herring[4], M. A. on the death of Milles.	Herring, fol. 282. b.
1750, 26 March. Henry Hall[5], M. A. on the refignation of Herring.	Ibid. fol. 285. a.
1764, 20 March. John Benfon[6], M. A. on the death of Hall.	Secker.
1780, 18 Dec. William Nance[7], LL. B. by exchange with Dr. Benfon.	Cornwallis.

[1] Dr. Caftilion, dean of Rochefter, dying Oct. 21, 1688, King James II. nominated Mr. Simon Lowth to fucceed him, but he not being then D. D. and not in a poffibility to obtain that degree before the King left the nation, King William III. gave it to one Dr. Henry Ullock, canon of Rochefter. Wood's Fafti Oxon. II. 138. This Mr. Lowth therefore was probably deprived of this rectory. Q. Whether for not taking the oaths? He feems to have been the fame who was leffee of the tithes of Harbledown hofpital in 1682. See p. 181. He is there ftyled " of St. Cofmas and Damian in the Blean."

[2] Head-mafter of the King's School, Canterbury, where he was buried in the cloifters of the Cathedral.

[3] Alfo minifter of Little Walfingham in Norfolk, a younger fon of Samuel Milles, Efq. M. P. for Canterbury. See the " Hiftory of Herne" (where he was buried), p. 103.

[4] One of the neareft relations to Archbifhop Herring, who alfo appointed him one of his executors. He married a daughter of Sir John Torriano, and died at Kenfington, April 18, 1774, being then rector of Chevening in Kent, and Cullefdon in Surrey, precentor of Chichefter, a prebendary of Southwell, and one of the principal regifters of the prerogative court of Canterbury.

[5] Of whom fee a particular account in the fucceeding page.

[6] Nephew to Bifhop Benfon, one of the fix preachers in Canterbury Cathedral, vicar of Shepherd's Well, and rector of Great Chart, which latter he held by difpenfation with this rectory, and exchanged both for the vicarage of Boxley. He is now alfo D. D. one of the prebendaries of Canterbury, regiftrar of the diocefe of Gloucefter, and rector of St. Michael Royal, College Hill, London.

[7] The prefent incumbent, who is alfo rector of Great Chart.

The

The Rev. HENRY HALL, M. A.

Was the fon of a tobacconift in Bifhopfgate ftreet, where he was born in 1716. He was fent early to Eton, was admitted on the foundation in 1729; and elected to King's College, Cambridge, in 1735, where of courfe he became a fellow in 1738, and took the degrees in arts. Being recommended by Dr. Chapman * to Archbifhop Potter, his Grace appointed him his librarian at Lambeth in 1744, on the refignation of Mr. Jones. In that ftation he continued till the death of his patron in 1747; when Archbifhop Herring, who fucceeded to the primacy, being fenfible of his merit †, not only continued him in that office, but, on his taking orders, appointed him one of his chaplains, and in April 1750 collated him to the rectory of Harbledown (vacant by the promotion of Mr. Thomas Herring ‡ to the rectory of Chevening); in November 1752, the Archbifhop collated him alfo to the vicarage of Herne, which he held by difpenfation; to which his Grace afterwards added the finecure rectory of Orpington in the deanry of Shoreham, one of his peculiars. In 1756 Mr. Hall vacated Herne, on being prefented to the vicarage of Eaft Peckham by the Dean and Chapter of Canterbury, by whom he was much efteemed, having greatly affifted their auditor in digefting many of the records, charters, &c. preferved in their regiftry ||. In return, the late Dr. Walwyn (one of the prebendaries, who vacated that vicarage) was collated by the Archbifhop to the rectory of Great Mongeham, void by the death of Mr. Byrch. On the death of Abp. Herring in 1757, he refigned the librarianfhip of Lambeth, and from that time refided chiefly at Harbledown, in a large houfe §, which he hired, now the feat of Robert Mead Wilmot, Efq. only fon of Sir Edward. Soon after the death of Archbifhop Herring, Mr. Hall was prefented by his executors to the treafurerfhip of the cathedral of Wells, one of his Grace's options. He was alfo at firft a competitor for the precentorfhip of Lincoln, an option of Archbifhop Potter

* Fellow of King's College, and now archdeacon of Sudbury, treafurer of Chichefter, &c. who in 1742 was very near being elected provoft of King's.
† His Grace, in one of his letters to Mr. Duncombe, faid, " I have an excellent young man for " my librarian, who never did and never can offend me."
‡ Of whom fee p 186.
|| For which, among other prefents, they gave him, in December 1762, a fine copy of the Oxford edition of Bp. Hooper's Works, 1757, on large paper and elegantly bound; which copy, after his death, having been fold with his other books, was purchafed by his intimate friend Dr. Ducarel, in whofe library it now remains. Mr. Hall had two excellent ftained drawings of Wimbledon and St. Mary Cray churches by Skelton, a very ingenious young painter, patronifed by Archbifhop Herring, who died at Rome. Thefe are now in the collection of the Rev. Dr. Beauvoir, being prefented to him by Mr Hall's aunt and executrix.
§ This houfe, in 1757, when the late Duke of Marlborough commanded the camp on Barham Downs, was lent by Mr. Hall to the Dutchefs and her family; and in it their eldeft daughter, Lady Diana Spencer, (now Beauclerk) was married, Sept. 9, 1757, to Lord Vifcount Bolingbroke, by the prefent Archbifhop, at that time domeftic chaplain to the Duke of Marlborough. It has fince been occupied by the late Gen. Belford.

(which

(which Dr. Richardfon gained in 1760 by a decree of the Houfe of Lords) but foon withdrew his claim, well-grounded as it feemed. His learning and abilities were great, but not fuperior to his modefty; and by his fingular affability he obtained the love and efteem of all who knew him. His charitable attention to his poor parifhioners, efpecially when they were ill, was conftant and exemplary. At Archbifhop Secker's primary vifitation at Canterbury in 1758, Mr. Hall was "pitched upon" (his Grace's official expreffion) to preach before him at St. Margaret's Church, which he did from Acts xvii. 21. "For all the Athenians and ftrangers which were there, fpent their "time in nothing elfe, but either to tell or hear fome new thing." He died a bachelor, at Harbledown, Nov. 1, 1763, in the 47th year of his age, after a fhort illnefs, occafioned by a violent fwelling in the neck, which could not be accounted for by the eminent phyficians who attended him. He was buried under the communion-table of Harbledown church, without any epitaph to preferve the memory of that moft worthy and valuable man, who lived univerfally beloved, and died much regretted.

Extracts of Letters from Mr. HALL to Dr. DUCAREL.

Harbledown, Dec. 6, 1760.

" I have at prefent in my poffeffion fome very ancient and curious writings, which I will detain, if poffible, till I have the pleafure of feeing you here. I received them in a confufed heap, but you will find them in fome order, and perhaps an abftract of them. What I mean, are the old deeds, &c. belonging to the hofpital here, which the Archdeacon * has defired me to look over; and, that I might do fo to the better purpofe, I had them brought hither. It is very neceffary for the mafter of the hofpital to have a particular account of them, and I intend to give the Archdeacon the beft I can. There is amongft them a grant by Archbifhop Richard, immediate fucceffor to Thomas a Becket, of xx l. per ann. to the hofpital, out of the parfonage of Reculvre, which is mentioned to have been refigned on this

* John Head, D. D. (afterwards Sir John, bart.) then mafter.

occafion by Hugo the Rector +. In the inftrument, Archbifhop Lanfranc is faid to have founded the two hofpitals; the one at Herebaldown, the other at Canterbury extra Northgate. The writing is very fair and frefh, and two thirds of the feal (viz. the upper and lower parts of the reverfe, and the upper half of the other part) are ftill remaining. But the moft curious impreffion of a feal is at the bottom of an inftrument of Archbifhop Arundel's +, which I believe you will think deferves to be engraved by your Society of Antiquaries. There are likewife the impreffions of the feals of Archbifhop Iflip ‡, William of Wickham ||, and of fome broad feals, very well preferved."

Harbledown, Feb. 9, 1761.

" Mr. Somner found "virgultum" in a bull of Pope John § (which he quotes in his Antiquities of Canterbury [p. 44.], under the article of Harbledown hofpital); but, as he has not tranflated that word, I fuppofe he was doubtful of it's meaning. The Pope intended to exempt the poor people from the payment of certain tithes; viz. " de ortis & virgultis & animalium nutrimentis:" the firft article is very plain; the laft relates to the pafture for 12 kine and a bull **; which were kept in the hofpital, as appears by their writings. It likewife appears, that they had an orchard, containing about three or four acres. The land ftill preferves that name, though all the trees are grubbed up, and it is planted entirely with hops; and by its name of " an orchard," it is privileged and exempted from the payment of tithe. The reft of the tithes, by a grant from Archbifhop Stratford, belong to Eaftbridge hofpital, and are let for 21 years by leafe from the mafter thereof ++, in the following words; " all the tithes of corn, grain, pulfe, pafture, hay, and all " other tithes whatfoever, growing on the lands belonging to the hofpital of St. " Nicholas Harbledown; except the tithes of the common garden or orchard be-" longing to the brothers and fifters of the faid hofpital." An exception in favour of the fodder is omitted, having been unneceffary ever fince they kept no cattle. But the other exceptions, and the practice accordingly, I take to be the beft comment upon the Pope's bull; and from thence I conclude, that " virgultum" fignifies " an orchard." I have further to obferve, that underwood being a fpecies of great tithe, it is not likely that it fhould be placed between two articles of fmall tithes."

* See the Hiftory of Reculver, p. 129. + See plate III. fig. 14. ‡ Ibid. fig. 11.
|| Ibid. fig. 12. § XXII. See this bull at large p. 235.
** "Ten cows and a bull" in the Survey, p. 18. ++ See p. 176.

D d

" The

Harbledown, April 26, 1763.

" The ancient church of St. Nicholas in this village has generally been considered to be no more than a chapel to the hospital; but it appears to me
to have been as much a parish church, as the other of St. Michael in the same
place; and if it be not one at present, for want of its minister and parish-officers,
it seems capable of being put upon its ancient footing. If this should be done, a
parish will be added, or at least restored, to your jurisdiction. In Battely's Appendix to Somner, p. 57. m. 29. you will find " Ecclesia S. Nicolai de Herbal-
" doune, in decanatu Canterbury," among those which are exempt from the Archdeacon, and of consequence, as I presume, subject to the Commissary. You may have
taken notice of a place called " the Mint *," situated between the two churches here.
It belonged to the chauntry of St. Nicholas, founded † by Archbishop Wittlesey;
and since the dissolution of the chauntry, by which it was severed from the hospital,
it has been deemed extraparochial. It seems to me to be otherwise, and that the
master of Eastbridge hospital is liable to be charged with the stipend of a curate,
to be nominated by him for the benefit of such of the inhabitants of the parish as
are not included in the hospital. Mr. J. Gostling ‡ is in hopes of being curate, if
the Archbishop should think proper to appoint one."

* In Easter-week 1773, on an application from Gen. Belford and some other inhabitants of the
adjoining parish, St. Michael's, suggesting the inconveniences resulting to them from this extraparochial place, two neighbouring justices, in pursuance of an act 13 and 14 Charles II. appointed
two inhabitants of the Mint overseers of St. Nicholas. But Mr Duncombe, the master, apprehensive
of the burden that would be brought on the poor of the hospital by being subjected to parochial taxes,
laid the case before the late Abp. Cornwallis, and with his Grace's approbation (as expressed in the
letter annexed) directed the Prior to appeal at the next Quarter Sessions against the appointment,
where, upon hearing the arguments of counsel, it was quashed. In the Mint are now eight houses,
or tenements, and a wind-mill. If that alone had been made a vill, or parish, there could have
been no objection.

" Revd. Sir,   Lambeth, June 26, 1773.
" I was absent from home when your letter came here, and did not return till two days after, which
" has prevented my answering it sooner. I think your objections to the proceeding of the justices well
" founded, your reasons against it just, and I much approve of the method you propose towards to-
" wards redressing the grievance. My being from home was unlucky; but, as you say the appeal
" must be entered this week, I hope you did not wait for my answer.
                                                 " Sir, your faithful humble servant,
" Rev. Mr. Duncombe.   " FRED. CANT."

† See p. 183.
‡ Reader, or chaplain, to the hospital. See p. 177.

NORTH-

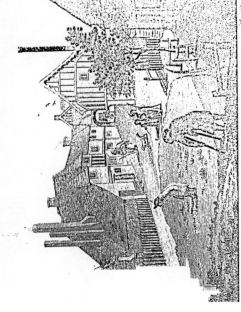

A. View of St. John's Hospital Canterbury.

1. The Chapel.   2. The Gateway.   3. John Banks. } Inhab.ts of the Brethren.
4. William Miles. }

S. Raymond del. 1784.

N O R T H G A T E.

This hofpital, dedicated to St. John the Baptift, is juftly ftyled by Somner the "other twin" of Herbaldown*, being founded and endowed by archbifhop Lanfranc, at the fame time, and in the fame manner, about the year 1084. In the words of Edmer †, "With-" out the North gate of this city (Canterbury) archbifhop Lanfranc " built a fair and large houfe of ftone, and added to it for the va-" rious wants and conveniencies of its inhabitants feveral apart-" ments, with a fpacious court. This palace [fo it is called] he di-" vided into two parts, one defigned for men labouring under va-" rious diftempers, the other for infirm women. He provided them " with cloaths and daily food at his own expence. He appointed " alfo officers and fervants, who fhould by all means take care that " they wanted nothing, and that the men and women fhould " have no communication with each other." Its original en-dowment (70l. per annum), and fubfequent ftatutes, being the fame as thofe of St. Nicholas, little more need be faid of them here. This hofpital ftands on the Weft fide of the ftreet, or road, leading to Herne, Reculver, and the ifle of Thanet, and has a garden and orchard behind it extending to the river. It fuffered by fire in the reign of Edward III. as appears by a kind of brief under their feal, directed to all prelates in general, de-ploring "a lamentable fire, which had wafted their houfe and " adjacent buildings, in which more than a hundred poor " people were fuftained, intreating their charitable affiftance,

* Antiquities of Canterbury, p. 50.   † Hift. Novor. lib. I.

" and

" and informing them of the feveral indulgences that had been
" granted to their benefactors by former archbifhops and
" bifhops *." Archbifhop Stratford, in the fame reign, when
he erected and endowed the adjoining vicarage of St. Mary,
Northgate, exprefsly referved and excepted from it " the ob-
" lations and obventions of the hofpital of Northgate." Its revenues were valued, 26 Henry VIII. at 94*l.* 16*s.* 8*d. ob.* clear ;
of which 80*l.* was the ftipend paid by the archbifhop. Oppofite
to this hofpital was the priory of St. Gregory, founded alfo by
archbifhop Lanfranc for fecular priefts†, but made a priory of
black canons by archbifhop William ‡, and diffolved at the Reformation.

St. John's Hofpital has an ancient church, or chapel, which
was larger formerly than at prefent ; but fince Somner and even
Battely wrote, all the bells but one, as being indeed ufelefs,
have been fold ; and the fteeple and North aile, to diminifh
the expence of repairs, were taken down in 1744 by a faculty from archbifhop Potter. Mr. Goftling, who gives this
account, ironically adds : " fo, by way of improvement, were
" many of the old houfes, and fmaller and lefs convenient ones
" erected in their room ; a ftone wall was alfo taken away, which
" fheltered the whole from the cold North-Weft wind blowing
" over the river and the meadow land, and being pentifed over-
" head, was called by the poor people their cloifters, under which
" they ufed to walk, or fit, and converfe with each other, on the
" benches ‖."

To return to the chapel. The Eaft window, in Somner's
time, was " a very brave" one, " having," he fays, " in fo many

---

* This letter is not now in the hofpital-cheft. See p. 203.
† Leland's Collect. vol. I. p. 84.   ‡ Tanner's Notitia Monaftica, p. 209.
‖ Walk in and about Canterbury, p. 29.

" panes

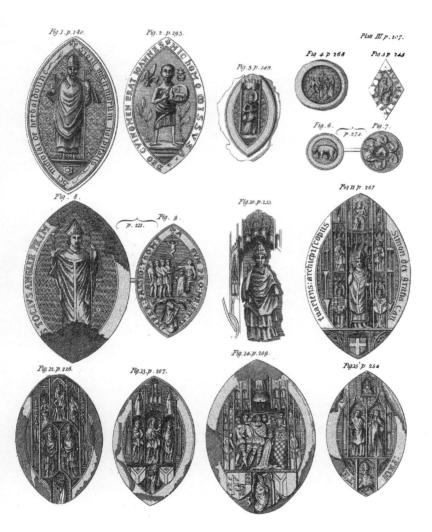

Fig. 1. p. 180. Fig. 2. p. 193. Fig. 3. p. 149. Plate III. p. 207.

Fig. 4. p. 268. Fig. 5. p. 245.

Fig. 6. p. 274. Fig. 7.

Fig. 8. Fig. 9. Fig. 10. p. 253. Fig. 11. p. 267.

p. 221.

Fig. 12. p. 226. Fig. 13. p. 207. Fig. 14. p. 209. Fig. 15. p. 254.

" panes every of the twelve apoftles pourtrayed, with the feveral
" articles of the creed that they are faid to make." At prefent it
is much broken and mutilated, but fome old heads that remain are
remarkably well expreffed.   Somner alfo mentions the monument of Alice Afhburnham (now no more), with this infcription : *Orate pro animâ Aliciæ Afhburneham, filiæ et hæredis Willielmi Tooke, armigeri, et Aliciæ Woodland, uxoris ejus, et antea fuit
uxor Thomæ Roper, gent. quæ obiit* XVII *die April. anno R. R.
Hen.* VIII. XV. *et anno Domini* 1524. *Cujus animæ,* &c.   And
in the Eaft window of the fame fide-chancel (now taken down, as
above-mentioned), *Orate pro* —— *Rooper, et pro bono* —— *Tho-
mafinæ uxoris ejus* —— *Domini* 1529.   In the South window,
Orate pro animabus Domini Willielmi Septvans, et —— *confortis
ejus,* &c.   And in the choir window, *Orate pro bono ftatu* ——
*Hyllys, fratris iftius Hofpitalis, et prior. qui ab hoc feculo migravit, qui
feneftram iftam fieri fecit, anno Domini* 1474.   As at Herbaldown,
this is the principal, if not the only part of Lanfranc's building that
now remains; as all the lodging-houfes (of which there are 31) are
modern edifices.   A Weft view of the hofpital is annexed, plate II.
There is a hall here (as at Herbaldown) now only ufed for the annual feaft on St. John the Baptift's day, the admittance of members,
and the reading and fealing of leafes.   And there, in a ftrong cheft,
the ancient charters, &c. are depofited.   The hofpital feal is engraved, pl. III. fig. 2.   On the North fide of the chapel is a
burying ground for the members of the hofpital.; and prayers are
read twice a week by a chaplain or reader, who has a ftipend
of 8*l. per annum.*   The prefent is the Rev. George Hearne,
rector of St. Alphage, and vicar of St. Mary Northgate, and one
of the fix preachers in the cathedral.   The mafter is the fame
as of St. Nicholas ; and as the mafters from the beginning of
the prefent century have been. the fame, their fucceffion may be

feen

feen there, p. 182. To Mr. William Somner, the eminent antiquary, both hofpitals were indebted for the continuance of their penfion in the laft century (as is mentioned p. 202) ; and being appointed mafter of this hofpital by archbifhop Juxon, in 1660, by his intereft and courage he recovered fome part of the endowment of which it had been fleeced by the ftatute 37 Henry VIII *.

At a vifitation made by archdeacon Harpsfield, in 1557, it was prefented that the ornaments of the chapel had been taken away by the mayor. " Memorandum, Delivered again one chalice, with " the paten of filver, four table-cloths, four furplices, two " towels, three bells in the fteeple. Memorandum, They fay " they are of no parifh, but a parifh of themfelves."

In the account of this hofpital given to archbifhop Sheldon, Oct. 24, 1674, its ftate was as follows : " The hofpital of St. John " the Baptift contains a prior, a reader, 18 in-brothers, 20 in- " fifters, and the like number of out-brothers and out-fifters. " The revenues in the whole are 195l. 8s. 9d†." At prefent it confifts of the like number of in-brothers and fifters ; but there are only 22 out-brothers and fifters, who have only a penfion of 1l. 4s. per annum each, paid quarterly, of whom 20, refident in and near Lambeth, are nominated by the archbifhop, and the other two are recommended by the mafter.

After the Reformation, archbifhop Parker, in the firft year of his confecration, vifited this and Herbaldown hofpital, and framed very wholfome ftatutes ‡ for their better government. Thefe were

* Bifhop Kennet's Life of Somner, p. 116. To this our antiquary alludes in his account of this hofpital, publifhed in 1640, where he fays, " I fufpect a fleecing " of it, as of other like places, by the facrilegious pilferers of thofe ravenous and " wretched times, fet upon the fpoil even of (what the proverb might have ftaved " them from) the very fpittle itfelf. I could inftance in fome particulars wherein " it fuffered." Antiquities of Canterbury, p. 51.   † Ibid. part II. p. 169.
‡ Printed in the Appendix, p. 214.

delivered

delivered to the prior and priorefs of St. John's (no doubt, in the chapel above-mentioned) by Dr. Yate, his grace's commiffary in this vifitation, and his vicar-general. The fame were alfo given about the fame time to the hofpital of St. Nicholas. Aug. 20, 1565, the archbifhop took fome farther cognizance of his hofpitals, upon fome difagreement for precedence between the prior and the reader, and fome other matters, and added five articles to the faid ftatutes ; and again May 20, 1574, he added two more ; all which may be feen in the Appendix*. And by thefe good ftatutes the hofpitals are governed at this day.

In modern times Mrs. Elizabeth Lovejoy of Canterbury, by her will, dated in 1694, bequeathed to this hofpital 10l. annually, from her eftate in Thanet (paid half-yearly), to be divided among the refident members. Ralph Snowe, gent. of Lambeth, by his will, dated in 1707, left to this hofpital (as he did alfo to St. Nicholas) 200l. of which 160l. was laid out by archbifhop Tenifon, Aug. 10, 1714, in the purchafe of 14 acres of marfh-land in the parifh of Wickham-breux, which now let for 8l. per annum †.

* Pp. 219—225.

† The archbifhop affigned this eftate in truft to Dr. Thomas Greene, archdeacon, Dr. George Thorp, and the Rev. Elias Sydall, prebendaries (the latter mafter of the hofpitals), Dr. Thomas Wife, rector of St. Alphage, William Turner, efq. William Deedes, M.D. and Paul Lukyn, gent. all of Canterbury, for the benefit of this hofpital, with directions to the four furviving truftees always to chufe three more. On Feb. 2, 1730, Dr. Greene (then bifhop of Ely), Dr. Sydall (then dean of Canterbury), and Dr. Deedes, made a new feoffment, and put in four feoffees, Dr. John Lynch (afterwards dean of Canterbury), Mr. Julius Deedes (afterwards prebendary of Canterbury), William Crayford, efq. recorder of Canterbury, and Samuel Norris, gent. auditor to the dean and chapter. And all the above-named truftees having died without having made a conveyance of the premifes to any new truftees, by which means they became vefted in William Lynch, efq. (now Sir William, K.B.) as eldeft fon and heir at law to the faid Dr. John Lynch, the laft furvivor of the deceafed truftees, in order to perpetuate the faid charity, &c. Mr. Lynch, by indenture bearing date July 16, 1767, fold, delivered, and releafed the faid parcels of land to Dr. John Head (archdeacon and mafter), the Rev. Ofmund Beauvoir, the Rev. Thomas Hey, William Deedes, efq. and Thomas Benfon, gent. in the furvivors of whom, Dr. Beauvoir, Mr. Hey, and Mr. Deedes, with Sir William Lynch, the eftate is now vefted.

6   Mrs.

Mrs. Mary Mafters, of Canterbury, by her will, dated Jan. 11, 1711, left 5 *l.* per annum each to this hofpital and five others in that city, charged upon her eftate; but having appointed Sir Harcourt Mafters, one of the South Sea directors, her fole executor, and his eftate being fubjected by an act 7 George I. to raife money on a public account, was found infufficient to divide more than 6 *s.* 6 *d.* in the pound on the claims of thefe hofpitals, which being fixed at 660 *l.* by Mr. Borrett, one of the mafters in chancery, at that rate came to 214 *l.* 10 *s.* with which fum (law charges deducted) amounting to 183 *l.* 9 *s.* 4 *d.* was purchafed in Jan. 1736, in the names of Dr. Lynch, dean of Canterbury, and John Knowler, efq. recorder, 163 *l.* 16 *s.* 3 *d.* capital ftock in old South Sea annuities; which fum (that part which was paid off by act of parliament at Michaelmas 1737 having been replaced) is now ftanding in the faid ftock in truft for the hofpitals of St. John, Eaft-bridge, Maynard, Boys, Cogan, and Smith, from which this hofpital has of late received annually no more than 7 *s.* 6 *d.*

Archbifhop Secker, in 1769, left by will to this and St, Nicholas hofpitals 500 *l.* each, in three per cent. Bank annuities, in reverfion after the deaths of Mrs. Talbot and her excellent daughter, both of whom being now dead (as has been mentioned p. 180), that bequeft is expected foon to take place.

And Thomas Hanfon, efq. of Crofby-fquare, London (who died in 1770), left by will in truft to this hofpital, Eaft-bridge, and Maynard's, 500 *l.* each, which being invefted in 3 per cent. reduced Bank annuities (583 *l.* 6 *s.* 8 *d.*) divides to the refident members of this hofpital 17 *l.* 10 *s.* per annum, paid half-yearly.

The

The prefent revenue * of this Hofpital (1785) is as follows:

Paid quarterly.	l.	s.	d.
The Archbifhop's penfion †,	80	0	0
Rents collected by the prior,	95	9	0
Rents collected by the porter,	23	5	0
Half-Yearly.			
Rents, &c.	32	19	0
Mrs. Lovejoy's ‡ legacy,	10	0	0
Mrs. Mafters's ‖ legacy (5d. each),	0	7	6
Mr. Brown's § legacy,	0	10	0
Rent of lands at Wickham-breux, purchafed with Mr. Snowe's legacy ** (clear),	7	0	0
Mr. Hanfon's †† legacy,	17	10	0
Yearly.			
Northgate burying-ground,	0	5	0
The Hofpital chapel-yard,	0	5	0
Two bufhels of wheat from Rowling farm,	0	10	0
Rent of Brotherhood Wood (now in hand)	12	0	0
Fines for renewing leafes (on an average),	10	0	0
Penfion from the Exchequer (clear) ‡‡,	2	18	5½
Feaft rents,	5	2	0
Annuities.			
Earl Cowper, for lands at the Moat, called Wyke ‖‖,	0	13	4
Sir Edward Hales, for the conduit in Brotherhood Wood,	0	6	8
Mrs. Allen, for Barnfield at St. Thomas's Hill,	0	4	2
Mr. Roberts's heirs, for Prieft-field at Sturry (not paid fome time),	0	3	4
Mr. Whitfield, for Nafh Marfh in Sturry (not paid fome time),	0	1	4
Mr. Tilbe, for two houfes in St. Dunftan's,	0	3	4
Mrs. Strouts, for a houfe in Weftgate,	0	0	10
Mrs. Delmar, for two tenements in North-lane,	0	0	8
Sir Hewet Aucher's heirs, for Millfield in Bifhopfbourn §§ (not paid fome time),	0	3	0
	299	17	7½
Difburfements (on the other fide) 52	13	9
Clear 247	3	10½

which is above 6l. 10s. to each perfon.

* This confifts chiefly of houfes, but that of Herbaldown of land; therefore the latter is more valuable, the fines being larger, and the repairs lefs.

† Of this 56l. is paid at Canterbury, and the reft is referved to pay the out-brothers and fifters at Lambeth.   ‡ See pp. 195, and 280.   ‖ See pp. 196, and 280.

§ See p. 281.   ** See p. 195.   †† See p. 196.   ‡‡ See pp. 230, 249, and 252.
‖‖ See pp. 202, 284, &c.

§§ Afterwards Dr. Corbet's, now Stephen Beckingham's, Efq. But it has not been paid fince 1709 or 10, though the payments appear, from the hofpital accounts, to have been made to that time ever fince the year 1614.

E e

Disbursements.

		£	s.	d.
To the reader*, p ann.		8	.	_
To two out-brothers at Canterbury, and ten out-brothers and ten out-sisters, at Lambeth		26	8	0
Towards the feast on St. John Baptist's day, usually about,		6	0	0
Quit-rents, viz. to Blean and Hoth Court manor,	5 4			
Westgate,	12 2			
Barton,	1 10			
Reculver,	8 0			
Chislet,	1 8	2	5	9.
Dean and Chapter of Canterbury†,	11 5			
Ditto, for the Hermitage, Surrey ‡,	3 8			
Dean and Chapter of Rochester §,	1 4			
City of Canterbury,	0 4			
Other expences about,		10	0	0

Total　52　13　9

* See p. 193.—8d. per quarter is reserved out of the stipend of every brother and sister to make up this sum.　　† For houses in the manor of Caldecot.

‡ In the manor of Vaux-hall. See p. 273.　§ For a tenement in Loader's lane, Canterbury.

P. 180. note, l. 1. r. " the *fifth* word."—The description of the curious bowl at Herbaldown. having been communicated to the editor of the Gentleman's Magazine for April 1784, p. 257, produced the following remarks from an anonymous correspondent : "I take shame and sorrow to myself, to think that I passed a week close to the hospital at Herbaldown without knowing a tittle of the very curious article in your last. I read NECI OCCIS, *Nece occidit.* Dragons and lions do not grow naturally in England now, else I should be tempted to guess that by *Ad Danum* " at Don-" caster" was meant; at least the scene of action is most likely to be commemorated, and Nor-thumberland grew dragons *. May one beg the favour of any one of the many intelligent and curious residents at Canterbury (and I know no town or neighbourhood that has more), to tell us the width, depth, and capacity of the bowl; of what materials (whether metal or wood) the medallion is made ; for as such things were rare, I should guess it was a seal cut in metal or wood a-top of the foot, and so screwed in ; yet if it was a seal, the figures and letters would all stand wrong †. I am so pleased with the bowl, that I think of sending to Canterbury, and get-ting one turned of the size and shape."

* In Dr. Percy's very valuable Collection of Ancient Ballads, vol. III. p. 106, Guy says,
" A dragon in Northumberland
" I also did in fight destroye,
" Which did both man and beast oppresse,
" And all the countrye fore annoye."
But this seems to have been a different dragon, and in the famous Romance " of Bev and Sir Guy," quoted by Chaucer is said to be
" a fowle dragon,
" That sleath men and beastes downe."

† The top diameter is 8 4 inches, depth at the edge of the medallion 3.4 inches. The solid contents = 6 wine pints, or 173¼ cubic inches. Diameter of the medallion 3.6 inches, of the top of the foot 3 inches and ½ a tenth Height of the foot 1.7 inch
The medallion, foot, and several plates and cramps, to strengthen or mend the bowl, are all (like the rim) of silver, gilt. The medallion cannot have been a seal, being in basso relievo, nor is it screwed in (as appears by the measurement) but rivetted at the top.

P. 187.

P. 187. Inftead of the firft note, read, John Chapman, D.D rector of Merfham, and alfo of Aldington, with the chapel of Smeeth, all in the county of Kent, ever fince the years 1739 and 1744, being then domeftic chaplain to Abp Potter. He was alfo archdeacon of Sudbury, and treafurer of Chirhefter, two options. Being educated at Eton, and elected to King's, 1723, he was a candidate for the provoftfhip of that college, with the late Dr. George, and loft it but by a fmall majority. Among his pupils he had the honour to clafs the prefent Lord Camden, Jacob Bryant, Efq. Dr. Cooke (now provoft), the late Dr. Afhton, Dr. Barford, James Hayes, Efq. (now a Welfh judge), and, for a fhort time, the Hon. Horace Walpole. His remarks on Dr. Middleton's celebrated letter to Dr. Waterland were publifhed in 1731, and paffed through three editions. In his " Eufebius," 2 vols. 8vo, he defended Chriftianity againft the objections of Morgan, and againft thofe of Tindal, in his " Primitive Antiquity explained and vindicated, being remarks on a book intituled " Chriftianity as old as the Creation " The firft volume of Eufebius, publifhed in 1739, was dedicated to Archbifhop Potter, and when the fecond appeared, in 1741, Mr. Chapman ftyled himfelf " Chaplain" to his Grace. In the fame year he was made archdeacon of Sudbury ; was honoured with the diploma of D.D. by the univerfity of Oxford; and publifhed " The Ancient Hiftory of the Hebrews vindicated ; or, Remarks on " the third Volume of the Moral Philofopher ; wherein a particular account is given of the Shep- " herds in Egypt, and the origin of Circumcifion in that Country, by Theophanes Cantabrigien- " fis," 8vo. He publifhed alfo two tracts relating to Phlegon, in anfwer to Dr. Sykes, who had maintained, that the eclipfe mentioned by that writer had no relation to the wonderful darknefs that happened at our Saviour's crucifixion. In 1738 Dr Chapman publifhed a fermon preached at the confecration of Bifhop Mawfon. He printed four other fingle fermons, 1739, 1743, 1748, and 1752. In a differtation written in elegant Latin, and addreffed to Mr. (afterwards Dr.) Tunftall, then public orator of the Univerfity of Cambridge, and publifhed with his Latin epiftle to Dr. Middleton concerning the genuinenefs of fome of Cicero's Epiftles, 1741, Dr. Chapman proved that Cicero publifhed two editions of his Academics ; an original thought, that had efcaped all former commentators, and which has been applauded by the (prefent) Bifhop of Exeter in his valuable edition of Cicero's " Epiftolæ ad Familiare, 1749." In 1744, Mr. Tunftall publifhed " Obfervations on the prefent collection of Epiftles between " Cicero and M. Brutus, reprefenting feveral evident marks of Forgery in thofe Epiftles, &c." To which was added a letter from Dr. Chapman, on the ancient numeral characters of the Roman Legions. Dr. Middleton had afferted, that the Roman Generals, when they had occafion to raife new legions in diftant parts of the empire, ufed to name them according to the order in which they themfelves had raifed them, without regard to any other legions whatever. This notion Dr. Chapman controverts and confutes. According to Dr. Middleton, there might have been two thirtieth legions in the empire. This Dr. Chapman denies to have been cuftomary from the foundation of the city to the time when Brutus was acting again Antony. Dr Chapman affirms nothing of the practice after the death of Brutus. To this Dr. Middleton made no reply. In 1745, Dr. Chapman's affiftance to Dr. (afterwards Bifhop) Pearce in his edition of " Cicero " de Officiis *," was thus acknowledged in the Preface. " Ne quid vero huic editioni deeffet " quod à me parari poffet à doctiffimis quibufdam viris, amicis meis, impetravi, ut hos libros de " officiis relegerent, & mecum fua quifque annotata communicarent. Gratiæ igitur tibi, Lector, " illis referendæ funt, in primis eruditiffimo Joh. Chapmaano, cujus non paucas notas & utiles " & doctas meis adjunxi, ejus nomine ad finem unius cujufque appofito. Multum debet illi viro " Refpublica literaria qui nonnulla alia lectu digniffima jam in lucem protulit, plura (ut fpero) " prolaturus, cum omni fere doctrinæ generi fe tradit, incredibili pene & eadem felici diligentia." Dr. Chapman introduced Mr. Tunftall and Mr. Hall about this time to Archbifhop Potter, the one as his librarian, the other as his chaplain, and therefore had fome reafons to refent their taking an active part againft him in the option caufe—though they both afterwards dropped it. Dr. Chapman's above mentioned attack on Dr. Middleton, which he could not parry, and his

* This Dr. Chapman always called " our edition." Its excellence was mentioned with high encomium, by a Cardinal at Rome to Mr. Guthrie.

interpofition

interpofition in defence of his much efteemed friend Dr. Waterland, provoked Dr. Middleton
to retaliate, in 1746, by affailing him in a much more vulnerable part, in his charge delivered
to the archdeaconry of Sudbury. In 1747, to Mr. Mounteney's * edition of fome Select Orations
of Demofthenes Dr. Chapman prefixed in Latin (without his name) " Obfervations on the
" Commentaries commonly afcribed to Ulpian, and a map of ancient Greece, adapted to
" Demofthenes." If Archbifhop Potter had lived to another election, he was intended for
Prolocutor. As executor and furviving truftee to that prelate, his conduct in that truft, particularly his prefenting himfelf to the precentorfhip of Lincoln, void by the death of Dr. Trim-
nell (one of his Grace's options), was brought into chancery by the late Dr. Richardfon,
when Lord Keeper Henley, in 1760, made a decree in Mr. Chapman's favour, but, on an
appeal to the Houfe of Lords, the decree was reverfed, and Dr. Richardfon ordered to be prefented. When Mr. Yorke had finifhed his argument, in which he was very fevere on Dr. Chapman, Mr. Pratt (now Lord Camden), who had been his pupil, and was then his counfel,
defired him, by a friend, not to be uneafy, for that " the next day he would wafh him as
" white as fnow." Thofe were his words. Thinking his cafe partially ftated by Dr Burn
in his " Ecclefiaftical Law," vol. I. (Article BISHOPS) as it was taken from the briefs of his
adverfaries, he expoftulated with him on the fubject by letter, to which the Doctor candidly replied, that " he by no means thought him criminal, and in the n   edition of his work would
" certainly add his own reprefentation."

P. 289, note ‡ add, In the year before.(1622) a turkey, which c   vs. had been given to the
fame counfellor.

* Who had been fchool-fellow with Dr. Chapman at Eton, and went to King's College in 1725.

⁎ As the two following Letters from the Rev. Mr. LAMPREY *⁎*,
   Mafter of St. John's and Harbledown Hofpitals, to Archbifhop
   SECKER, give fome additional information relating to the Hofpitals of St. John and St. Nicholas, it has been thought proper to add them here.   Though the Archbifhop's Letters do
   not appear, the fubjects of his enquiries may be collected
   from the anfwers.

L E T T E R I.

MY LORD,   *Canterbury,*   1759.

At length I humbly offer to your Grace the beft information I am able to procure, concerning the prefent ftate of the two hofpitals committed to my care.

The original number of brothers and fifters maintained in each hofpital was 60 ;
and that they were all obliged to refide there, may, I think, be concluded from the

* Thomas Lamprey, M. A. rector of St. Martin's, and vicar of St. Paul's, Canterbury, and
one of the minor canons of the cathedral. He alfo took out the feals for the rectory of Stonar,
a dilapidated church, near Sandwich, and in confequence was involved in an expenfive and un-
fuccefsful fuit (which was tried at the affizes) with the late Mrs. Rooke, the widow *Blackacre* of
her day. He died in 1760.

fiⁱft of Archbiſhop Parker's ſtatutes; [ſee p. 214.] not more than 20 (that is, as I apprehend, of the whole original number of 60) being permitted to live out of the houſe at once. In time, upon the diminution, as I conceive, of their revenues, the number of in-brothers and ſiſters at St. John's was reduced to 38, and at Harbledown to 30 ; but at what particular time this was done, I cannot ſay. The outbiothers and ſiſters of each receive only a ſtipend of 6 s̃. 8 d̃ *. per quarter from the Archbiſhop, and are not, as far as I know, obliged to the obſeⁱvance of any ſtatutes, or required to be poſſeſſed of any ſpecial qualifications with reſpect to age †, celibacy, &c. Theſe are admitted at Lambeth, without the leaſt account taken of them here ; ſave only, that two out-brothers only are admitted at St. John's, and two out-brothers and three out-ſiſters at Harbledown. But the reaſon of this appointment, and at what time it was introduced and took place, I am yet to learn. The emoluments of the 38 in-brothers and ſiſters at St. John's, and of the 30 in-brothers and ſiſters at Harbledown, ariſe partly from the yearly penſion of 1 l̃. 6 s̃. 8 d̃. paid to each of them by your Grace, and the remainder from the rents of their lands and houſes, and fines upon the renewal of leaſes ; to which may be added a ſmall yearly penſion from the Crown ‡, and two private benefactions given, not many years ago, to each hoſpital by Mr. Snowe and Mrs. Lovejoy §. Theſe ſtipends, and rents, amount yearly to the following ſums in each.

[Theſe have already been given pp. 181 and 197.]

There are at preſent but 32 ‖ dwellings at St. John's and 24 at Harbledown, for the in-brothers and ſiſters ; ſo that the reſidue muſt neceſſarily be admitted to live elſewhere. To whom this leave of abſence ſhould be indulged, Archbiſhop Potter was pleaſed to intruſt to my diſcretion. I generally diſpenſe it according to ſeniority, unleſs I find ſome ſpecial reaſon to the contrary. In purſuance of the general truſt repoſed in me, I have conſtantly made it a part of my care to preſerve the peace. and good order, and to advance (as far as in me lies) the proſperity of both theſe fraternities. I keep a watchful eye not only to the maintenance of their eſtates and buildings, but likewiſe over the manners of the people, obliging them to conform, as nearly as may be, to the obſervation of their ſtatutes. Several of theſe ſtatutes, it muſt be confeſſed, were better accommodated to the former, than to the preſent ſtate of the hoſpitals. Some of them are become obſolete, and others hardly practicable, as things are now circumſtanced. And yet the in-brothers and ſiſters are ſworn, at their admiſſion, to the obſervance of them. Upon the whole, I humbly conceive, that they are capable of being

---

* Of this and all the ſtipends, 8 d. per quarter is reſerved to make up the ſtipend of the readeⁱ. D.

† Yet a young, healthy, or wealthy, perſon could not be admitted conſiſtently with the terms of the corrody, which is always granted " in conſideration of poverty, old age, and bodily infirmities." D.

‡ See pp. 239, 240, and 252.

§ Mr. Hanſon's to St. John's may now be added. See p. 196. D.

‖ There are now but 31, one of them, which was uninhabitable, being converted into a ſtorehouſe. D.

altered

altered much for the better in many particulars, and I fhall readily (whenever a opportunity offers of delivering my thoughts to your Grace *ere tenus* on thi fubject,) point out feme inftances wherein I apprehend certain alterations to be moft needful, together with fome orders which, I think, would prove conducive to the benefit of the hofpitals. This being an end laudable in itfelf, I fhall the more chearfully take fome pains in it, efpecially if I find your Grace difpofed to encourage it.

I humbly thank your Grace for the calculations you have taken the trouble of making with refpect to the hofpital fines in general. They will be a good rule of direction to me in particular inftances. The fees for leafes in both hofpitals are the fame, and in both (as they ought to be) very moderate §. Five fhillings, out of every fuch leafe, are put into the reparation purfe, there being no ftated provifion for the reparation of the public buildings but what arifes from admiffion fees and vacancies; and therefore I have found it fometimes neceffary (with the confent of the Archbifhop) to apply fome part of the fines, efpecially when large, to thefe purpofes. And Mr. Parry + will inform your Grace that ordinarily 12 l. and upwards hath been yearly remitted from Lambeth for the fame purpofes; arifing from reparation-nobles, and vacancies of out-brothers and fifters places.

Herewith I tranfmit to your Grace another certificate. I have often wifhed that poor perfons from the country might, for the moft part, be appointed to fupply the vacancies at Harbledown; thofe who have lived in the city being generally defirous (under various pretences) after admiffion there, to fpend their time here, whereby their houfes, by not being conftantly inhabited, run fafter into decay.

I am, &c.

THOMAS LAMPREY.

§ The expence, fince the date of this letter, is much increafed by the additional ftamps. Five fhillings are alfo paid for regiftering, a practice, which, though highly ufeful and expedient, was till 1772 neglected, and of courfe feveral leafes, having been loft or deftroyed, have, for want of renewal, expired, fo that not only the fines, but the lands themfelves, have been loft; a fmall unimproveable annual payment, originally a referved rent, only remaining. Such doubtlefs was the origin of the 10 s. "for land" at Herne paid annually by Mr. Charles Palfrey, the 2 s. paid by Mr. Lade at Grayney (fee Herbaldown Rental, p. 181), &c. and fuch would probably have been the fate of 2 acres, 3 roods, held of St. John's at Hoath by John Sennock, at 1 l. 15 s. referved rent, had not a leafe to his great-grandfather, dated in 1686, been lately difcovered, in confequence of which he has been obliged to renew and take a 21 years leafe of the premifes. Such loffes are now prevented by regiftering. D.

+ Thomas Parry, efq. receiver to five fucceffive Archbifhop. He died Sept. 12, 1773.

LETTER II.

LETTER II.

MY LORD,   *Canterbury,*   1760.

In obedience to your Grace's commands, I now humbly offer the moſt ſatisfactory account in my power, concerning thoſe enquiries made by your Grace in relation to the hoſpitals of St. John and St. Nicholas.

It does not appear to me that the in-brothers and ſiſters of theſe hoſpitals are, by any eſtabliſhed rule or cuſtom, required to be natives or inhabitants of this or any other county. Indeed, as this city and the parts adjacent can furniſh an abundant ſupply of fit objects for all vacancies, the choice has not uſually extended farther. But yet probably there have been inſtances, at moſt times, of ſome who were ſelected from places more remote. I remember one ſuch who was appointed by Archbiſhop Wake, two by Archbiſhop Potter, and four by Archbiſhop Herring, two of them even his own menial ſervants *. Whenever ſuch perſons have been admitted at Lambeth, Mr. Parry uſually makes an entry upon the corrody (tranſmitted to me), that they have been ſworn to the obſervation of the ſtatutes; upon which their names are enrolled in the hoſpital-book. But whether the ſtatutes ſhould be recited to them, and the oath to obſerve them adminiſtered, previouſly to their admiſſion, or may be deferred till they come to reſide in the hoſpital, your Grace will moſt ſurely collect from the third and fourth of Archbiſhop Parker's ſtatutes †.

2. It is a caſe which rarely or never happens, that any of thoſe who deſire to reſide in the hoſpitals, are forced, for want of room, to live out ‡. Their living abroad is generally looked upon as a matter of privilege and indulgence; and the method taken of diſpenſing this indulgence according to ſeniority (unleſs where peculiar circumſtances require it to be otherwiſe) will, I truſt, be approved of by your Grace, as an equitable rule of proceeding.

3. I ſhall look upon your Grace's next query as a direction for the future to ſpecify, in the notice of a vacancy, whether the brother or ſiſter departed, made his or her abode in the hoſpital, and alſo to ſignify to your Grace, from time to time, to whom leave of abſence may be moſt properly granted.

4. The order againſt the admiſſion of married perſons into the hoſpitals hath been in my time conſtantly obſerved; but was not always (though for the moſt part) attended to by one of my predeceſſors §.

* Viz. Elizabeth Lodder, who died in 1768, and Elizabeth Mynton, in 1769. To the latter, who was one of his houſekeepers, his Grace alſo left an annuity of 10 l. Archbiſhop Secker too appointed ſome from diſtant counties; in particular, Rebecca Hobday, in 1762, a near relation of the Rev. Mr. Etough, of Therfield, Herts, at the recommendation of Mr. Archdeacon Plumptre, to whom that eccentric character left his fortune.

† See p. 215. They are now never ſworn to obſerve the ſtatutes till they come to reſide.

‡ This caſe now happens frequently in St. John's, all the houſes being inhabited.

§ This order hath not of late been obſerved, celibacy not being enjoined in Archbiſhop Parker's ſtatutes.

6

5. The

5. The dividends arising from fines are ordinarily very inconsiderable. I do not think they yield to each person 10 s. *communibus annis*. There is too a small allotment of wood, which may amount to about 6 or 7 s. yearly to each in-brother and sister [and also some fruit]; so that, upon the whole, their annual income may be estimated at about 6 l. besides the accommodation of a dwelling.

8. The fees for lease and counterpart are only 20 s *. besides the stamps; out of which, 5 s. are put into the reparation purse, 5 s. are laid out upon a small refection to the brothers and sisters, and the remaining 16 s. are paid to the clerk of the hospitals, who draws the leases, and reads the statutes to the brothers and sisters yearly, on Midsummer-day, &c.

I shall, with your Grace's permission, note all such particulars in relation to the statutes and customs, as appear to me capable of being improved to the benefit of the hospitals; and at a proper time submit them to your Grace's consideration.

I am, &c.

THOMAS LAMPREY.

The attention bestowed on these hospitals, by this truly benevolent prelate, appears not only by the above, but by the reversionary bequest of 500 l. (mentioned pp 180 and 196) which he left, by a codicil to his will, to each, contingent on the deaths of Mrs. Talbot and her daughter. But though both these events have now taken place, the legacies have not yet been paid, for which it may be proper here to account.

The bishop of Chester, his Grace's surviving trustee, having been advised by his counsel, that he could not with safety transfer the stock appropriated to the several charitable purposes mentioned, without the direction of the court of chancery, unless Thomas Frost †, Esq. the residuary legatee of the testator, would give his consent and authority to the said transfer, and Mr. Frost not agreeing to give this consent, and expressing a desire that the opinion of the court might be taken upon all the legacies; the bishop has been under the necessity of applying to the court of chancery, for a decree to establish the will, codicils, and legacies, and to direct his future conduct. An amicable bill therefore has been filed by his lordship's solicitor, Mr. Burn, in which the charities interested (16 in all) have concurred. Mr. Frost's principal objection seems to lie to the sum left to repair, &c. the houses of poor vicarages in the diocese of Canterbury, which is supposed to be by void by the mortmain act; but of this the archbishop was aware, and noticed it in another codicil, leaving the sum given for that purpose to be disposed of as his trustees should approve.

Archbishop Cornwallis was desirous, and had an intention, of making some alterations in the statutes of these hospitals (as he informed Mr Duncombe in a letter, dated Sept. 20, 1770); but finding it would take more time than he was aware of, that design became abortive.

* These fees are now 1 l. 1 s. registering included. The stamps are 12 s. See p. 200, note §

† Of Nottingham. One of the principal registers of the province of Canterbury, and nephew to the archbishop, being his sister's son.

APPEN-

A P P E N D I X

OF

CHARTERS AND PRIVATE DEEDS

relating to the Hofpitals of HERBALDOWN and NORTHGATE.

From the ORIGINALS; and Two MSS. in the LAMBETH LIBRARY, viz.

Nº 1131, fol. containing the Rev. Mr. HALL's rough draught of his intended Chartulary of Herbaldown Hofpital; and,

Nº 1132. quarto, intituled, " Liber Hofpitalium Archiepifcopi, hoc eft, Sancti " Nicholai de Herbaldown, & Sancti Johannis Baptiftæ de Northgate juxta Can- " tuariam, MDCCLXIV." drawn up by the Rev. Dr. BEAUVOIR, (then) of Can- terbury: The Preface to which is here printed at large, as the propereft intro- duction to the following inftruments.

MR. HENRY HALL, late rectorof St. Michael, Herbaldown, having undertaken to put in order the charters and other deeds belonging to the hofpital of St. Nicholas, in Herbaldown, which were in the greateft confufion in the hofpital-cheft, propofed to tranfcribe them all, but died before he had perfected his intention. He had tranfcribed all the charters, and a great part of the private grants, which tran- fcripts are in a book by themfelves. It was thought proper to finifh the account which he had begun, but not in fo laborious a manner. A knowledge of what is the purport of each deed, it was apprehended, would be fufficient, if the deeds themfelves were fo difpofed, that recourfe might readily be had to them if there fhould be occafion. This has been attempted; and further, an account has been taken of every thing that was contained in the cheft of the other hofpital of St. John the Baptift in Northgate, where alfo every thing was in the greateft diforder; for a compleat knowledge of either is not to be obtained but from both, on account of their common foundation, ftatutes, and eftates; fome things refpecting which are depofited in one hofpital, and fome in the other.

The method, which has been followed, is this. Each deed is wrapped up in a piece of paper by itfelf, which is indorfed with a number correfponding with the numbers in this book, and hath written upon it the fame account of its contents as is contained in this book. This account was copied from the titles prefixed by Mr. Hall to each in his tranfcript, as far as that went. The deeds are difpofed under the names of the refpective parifhes in which the eftates lie, and all the deeds refpecting the fame eftate are put together, and feparated from the next donation by a black line. It was not found poffible to do this, but by making tables of the bounds defcribed in each deed. And, to render this collection more ufeful, as good an account as could be procured is added of the prefent revenues of each hofpital.

F f

The

The number of thefe deeds is much increafed by the practice, which obtained, of collecting and preferving title-deeds, as far backwards as they could go ; and yet the greateft care of this fort has not been able to preferve all their eftates to them, as may appear from the lofs which St. John's Hofpital has fuftained of the eftate of Wyke [*], confifting of 32 acres, and other things, out of which they retain only the quit-rent of 13s. 4d. which had been at firft referved to the monaftery of St. Auguftine, the lords of the manor ; although there are ftill in the hofpital-cheft the original donation, the king's licence of mortmain, and the confirmation of the abbey of St. Auguftine, befides an ancient map of the land and other evidences ; and this was loft after a trial at law [†].

Many deeds that are here do not appear to have any reference to the hofpitals, and very poffibly either did belong to fome of the members, or were depofited there for fecurity by other perfons. It feems to have been the cuftom to make the donation to fome one or more of the brethren of the hofpitals, who transferred the truft to other perfons, or to the hofpital. Thomas de Wolton [‡], of whom there is frequent mention, was mafter of Eaft-bridge Hofpital from 1351 to 1381.

The charters of Herbaldown Hofpital are put into an old ftrong oaken box, guarded with iron plates ; and the private deeds into a box, which is divided into four partitions : and both are put into the hofpital-cheft. There are drawers within the cheft belonging to St. John's Hofpital for this purpofe ; and all the writings belonging to this hofpital are depofited in them, each drawer being properly labelled with its contents.

It is not neceffary to give any hiftory of thefe hofpitals, becaufe little can be added to the account which Mr. Somner has publifhed in his Antiquities of Canterbury. It will, however, be but juftice to him to take notice of one thing not mentioned either by him or his editor ; That the continuance of their penfion to the hofpitals after the lands of the fee of Canterbury were feized by the parliament was owing to a petition which he drew up for them, which is alfo inferted at the end of the book [‖] intituled, " The Prior's accounts from 1605 to Sept. 14, " 1647." Nor may it be improper to obferve two miftakes which he has made. The charter of Archbifhop Richard [§] is not in St. John's Hofpital, as he fays, p. 43. but in Herbaldown. He fays too, p. 44. " this hofpital's (Her-" baldown) ancient governor, now called a mafter, was a dean," and quotes the fubfcription of Benedict with this addition, " tunc temporis decani de Sancto Nico-" lao :" whereas Algar was at that time prefbyter of St. Nicholas, and Benedict writes himfelf only dean, as may be feen in the fubfcriptions to the deed, which is here copied at large :

" Noverint prefentes & futuri quod ego Elueus Pinnefloue conceffi Deo & fratrib' hof-" pital' de Sancto Nicholao vi denarios annuatim de domo & de manfione quam Lithe " filia Canteuel tenuit & mi folebat reddere illos vi denar' annuatim Litha. Tefti-" monio Bnd' tc tepis decani, qui s has litteas fepfit, & dni Algari prbri de Sancto " Nichol' & dni Ade prbri, & Simonis de Sancto Andrea. Concedentib' etiam duob'

* At the Moat, now belonging to Earl Cowper.
† The extracts relative to this eftate will be printed in the Appendix to Northgate, Chap. V.
‡ Otherwife called Thomas New, vicar of Reculver. See the Hiftory of that parifh, p. 157.
‖ See an account of this book in the Appendix to Northgate, Chap. VI.
§ Printed in the Hiftory of " Reculver," p 124.

" filiis

" filiis meis Barthol' & Robe." Benedict was moſt probably the rural dean of Canterbury at that time. This deed, which is without date, ſeems to be the moſt ancient in the hoſpital.

He quotes, p. 50, a letter under the ſeal of the hoſpital, requeſting alms, to prove that St. John's Hoſpital was fired in King Edward the Third's time. There is no ſuch letter now in the cheſt of the hoſpital. There is one beginning with the ſame addreſs: " Omnibus ſanctæ matris eccleſiæ prælatis, ad quos literæ iſtæ per-
" venerint, fratres & ſorores hoſpitalis de Northgate de Cantuar' ſalutem & apoſ-
" tolicam benedictionem: domus ſiquidem noſtra in tanta conſiſtit paupertate &
" neceſſitate quod cum maxima miſeria vitam indubitanter ſuſtinemus." In this no mention is made of fire, but the recital of their indulgences immediately follows. Yet this ſeems to be the ſame that Mr. Somner quotes, p. 51.; for it ſays, " Et ſunt in
" hoſpitali noſtro centum [the number which he gives] fratres & ſorores cæci, clau-
" di, ſurdi, & aliis diverſis infirmitatibus languidi." It was cuſtomary for ſome of the brethren to be ſent about the kingdom to collect alms twice a year, for one month before the Nativity and before the Feaſt of St. John the Baptiſt, and for three weeks after each ; and this continued to be done in Queen Elizabeth's time, ch. III, N°s 12, and 13 *. At theſe times they carried letters under the ſeal of the hoſpital, reciting the indulgences granted them by popes, archbiſhops, and biſhops (which they were very diligent to obtain) and beſtowing a ſhare of them upon their benefactors. In this let-ter, which ſeems to be the only one of this ſort, they ſay, " Si quis dicto hoſpitali noſtro
" anulum, firmaculum, aurum, vel argentum, vaccas, juvenculam, bidentem, agnum, vel
" vitulum dare vel tranſmittere voluerit, tradat & liberet procuratori noſtro præſenti, &
" eum recipiemus in fraternitatem hoſpitalis noſtri prædicti, concedentes eidem par-
" ticipationem omnium bonorum operum quæ in prædicto hoſpitali fient in per-
" petuum." And afterward it is ſaid that theſe 100 brothers and ſiſters ſay daily 30,000 Paternoſters and Ave Marias, the benefit of which, and all other religious exerciſes, they freely impart to their benefactors. But the brethren of Herbaldown ſet theirs at a cheaper rate, N° 9. They were in number about eighty, ſaid daily 4000 Pater noſters, Ave Marias, and Credos; and any one might have the benefit of them for giving them any thing of the value of one penny, or even one half-penny. They had indulgences from 53 cardinals and biſhops; and this bears date 1398, about 300 years after their foundation; and in this manner they every where hawked about theſe indulgences. Such was the miſerable ſtate of religion that then prevailed!

In an archiepiſcopal charter in Herbaldown Hoſpital +, directions are given for ſettling the payment of the penſion to the hoſpitals, which at that time was charged upon the parſonage of Reculver, ſo as to prevent diſputes be-tween the executors of any archbiſhop and his ſucceſſor: and in this mention is made of a cuſtom of the ſee of Canterbury, That if any archbiſhop ſhould die be-tween Eaſter and Michaelmas, " in hoc caſu, de conſuetudine ecleſie Cantuarien.
" ſis notorie fructus majores & autumpnales ejuſdem anni ad ipſum pertinere de-
" bebunt." OSMUND BEAUVOIR.

* Two licences were granted for this purpoſe, in 1572 and 1585. See the Appendix to Northgate, Chap. V.
† Printed at large in the Hiſtory of Reculver, p. 148.

ROYAL

ROYAL AND ARCHIEPISCOPAL GRANTS.

1. Grant from King Henry I. of ten perches of land in Blen Wood *.
[Seal worn out, filk bag remaining.]

HENRICUS rex Angl' archiepo Cantuar', & vicec', & omnibus baron', & miniftr' & fidelibus fuis de Chentt, Francis & Anglis, fal'. Sciatis me dediffe & conceffiffe, ꝓ Dei amore & anima patris & matris mee, & Matilde regine & Willi filii mei, & ꝓ redemptione peccatorum meorum, in acrementum hofpitalis, de bofco de Blen, x perticatas terre de bofco ad exfartand' & excolend' undique circa hofpitale. Et volo & firmit' pcipio ut habitantes in loco illo habeant meam firmam pacem, ne aliquis eis injuriam aut contumeliam faciat. T. Willo elemofinario capllo meo, & Pagano fil' Johis, & Gaufr' fil' Pagan', & Pagan' Peur' ‡. Apd Odeftoc ‖.

2. King Henry the Second's Charter of protection. [Seal much decayed.]

HENRICUS Dei gra rex Angl', & dux Norm' & Aquitan', & com' And', archiepis, epis, abbatibus, archidecanis, decanis, comitib', baronib', juftic', vic', & omnibus ballivis & fidelibus fuis Angl', falutem. Sciatis qd infirmi de Cantuar', & oms res & poffeffiones fue funt in manu & cuftodia & protectione mea. Et ido pcipio qd eos & omnes res & poffeffiones fuas cuftodiatis & manuteneatis, & protegatis fic' meas proprias, ita qd nullam violentiam aut injuriam aut gravamen eis faciatis nec fieri pmittatis. Et fiquis eis fuper hoc in aliquo forisfacere pfumpferit plenariam eis inde fine diloe jufticiam fieri faciatis. T. Willo clico de Cam', apud Windefor'.

---

* Printed in Battely's edition of Somner's Antiquities of Canterbury, part I. Appendix, N° XIV. b. p. 11.
† Kent.
‡ Perhaps. Peverel.
‖ Woodftock.

3. King Henry the Second's writ for one carriage every day in Short [Sorotta] wood. (There is an attested copy of this writ by Somner.) [See N° 5.]

HENRICUS rex Angl', & dux Norm' & Aquit', & com' And', vic' suo de Kent, & minist'r' suis, sal'. Concedo leprosis de Herbandona quod habeant singulis diebus unum sumarium * in boscho de Sorotta, ad attrahenda ligna ad op' eor' quamdiu placuerit. T. Tom' ᵃ Canc', apud Canth'.

4. Grant of twenty marks, " ex reditibus regis in Cantuaria, 19 Hen. II." [1173.] [This king made another grant to the same effect; 18 Feb. anno regni 23. Seal, much broken, in a yellow laced silk bag.]

HENRICUS Dei gra rex Angl', & dux Norm' & Aquitan', & com' And', archiepis, epis, abbatibus,. com', baron', justic', vic', & omnibus ministris & fidelibus suis Angl', salutem. Sciatis me dedisse in ppetuam elemosinam, & presenti carta confirmasse, leprosis de Herbaldona xx marcatas ᵇ reddit' singulis annis habendas de redditu meo Cantuarie donec eas assignó alibi suscipiendas, ut in ecclia, et in aliis redditibus. T. G.ᶜ epo Lond', R.ᵈ epo Wigorn', R.ᵉ electo Wint', R.ᶠ electo Hereford', magistro Waltero de Insula, com' Willo de Mand', Willo fil' Andr' Hug' de Creissi. Apud Westm'.

5. Grant of Richard I. for one carriage every day in Short ᵍ [Sorotta] wood, November 9. [With an attested copy by W. Somner.]

RICARDUS, Dei gra, rex Angl', dux Norm', Aquit', & com' And', vice-com' & baillivis suis de Kent, salutem. Concedimus leprosis de Herebaldona, quod habeant singulis diebus unum sumaium in bosco de Sorotta, ad attrahenda

---

* " Summaimus" was probably a cart drawn by one horse. Thus in " Decem Scriptores," p. 572, 65. " five plaustris, five quadrigis, five bigis, five summariis comportata." This was to fetch timber for their buildings, " ad attrahenda ligna ad opera eorum." See Nᵒ 5.

That it could not be " a load of wood" appears from a charter of the same king, p. 1575, by which he had previously given all his Blenwood (" totum boscum nostrum de Blen") to the monks of Christ Church, excepting one horse-load given by his father to the canons of St. Gregory's, and confirmed by his charter.

In the " Decem Scriptores," p. 1574, Gervas mentions a perambulation, on the oaths of 24 men of the vicinage, of the boundaries of this same wood (" boscum de Blen quod Srutte cognomina-" tur)," made 29 Aug. 1192, 3 Rich. I. by G[eoffry] Prior of Christ Church, with six monks, and Reginald sheriff of Kent, with several soldiers and others, by virtue of a mandate from the chancellor [Longchamp Bp. of Ely,] justiciary of the realm, and the barons of the Exchequer; when all the King had previously given to the monks on each side of the highway was assigned to them. D.

ᵃ Supposed to be Thomas Becket, who was made chancellor in the beginning of this king's reign, and resigned the great seal upon his being made archbishop of Canterbury. This writ must therefore have issued before the 9th of H. II. [H. HALL.]

ᵇ This payment remains to this day—now 13l. 6s. 8d.

ᶜ Gilbert Foliot was bishop of London from 1163 (9 H. II.) to 1187.

ᵈ Roger was bishop of Worcester from 1163 (9 H. II.) to 1179.

ᵉ Richard Trotclive, alias More, was elected bishop of Winton 1173 (19 H. II.)

ᶠ Richard Foliot, bishop of Hereford, was consecrated 6 Oct. 1174 (20 H. II.) [H. H.]

ᵍ At the end of a copy of this, and the like grant of H. II. is written, " Concordat hæc copia " cum originalibus chartis, facta invicem collacione fideli per me,

" Willelmum Somner, Notarium Publicum."

ligna

ligna ad opera eorum, p̃ falute n̄ra & p̃ aïa patris n̄ri, in liberam & ppetuam elemofinam; & precipimus quod non permittatis quod monachi Cantuar' aut aliquis alius eis
aliquam moleftiam faciant aut gravamen: precipimus aut' & vol' quod cuftodiatis &
protegatis ipfa domum & leprofos, & non permittatis quod eis faciat aliquis moleftiam aut gravamen; & faciatis eis habere integre redditus fuos quos habere debe-
bant & folebant tempore d̃ni regis patris n̄ri in baillivis n̄ris. T. meipfo, apud Rupe *
And' ix die Novembris. [Great part of the feal remains. H. H.]

6. The King's writ, "Pro infirmis Hofpitalis de Herebandon," 1 March, 1
Hen. III. [1217. A writ to the bailiffs of Canterbury, for payment of xx marks
with the arrears granted by K. Henry II. 18 Feb. 23 year of his reign. Seal
much broken.]

7. Exemplification of King Henry the Second's grant of twenty marks a year,
12 Oct. 31 Edw. III. [1358. Seal almoft perfect.]

8. Breve regium baïlivis Cant', pro folutione prædict' xx marc' p̃ an' cum arrerag'. 10 Nov. 1 R. II.
A writ to the baïliffs of Canterbury, for payment of xx marks p̃ ann. and the arrears, agreably to the grant of K. Henry II. 8 Feb. 23d year of his reign. [Seal
broken. 1378.]

9. Exemplification and confirmation of grants of xx marks p̃ ann. from K. Henry
II. in the 19th year of his reign, and 18 Feb. in the 23d year of his reign, with
an exact copy. [1 March, 1 Hen. V. 1414.] (The broad feal perfect, and extremely well preferved.)

10. A confirmation of the twenty marks to be paid out of the chamber of Canterbury, 28 May, 1 Hen. VI. 1423. [not, as it is indorfed, 1 H. VIII. Seal
fomewhat broken.]

11. Carta de xx marcis, 8 Julii, 12 Hen. VI. [1435. Seal much broken.]

12. Exemplification and confirmation of King Edward the Third's exemplification
and confirmation of King Henry the Second's grant of Feb. 18, an. regni 23;
dated 14 Oct. 1 Edw. IV. [1461. Seal fomewhat broken.]

13. Exemplification and confirmation of King Henry the Second's grant of xx
marks a year, 30 Nov. 2 R. III. (The broad feal entire, and extremely well
preferved.) [1484. Reciting the exemplifications of E. IV. E. V. and R. II. the
exemplifications of the Houfe of Lancafter.]

14. Exemplification and confirmation of the grant in N° 12; 20 Nov. 1 H. VII.
[1485. Seal broken.]

15. Another confirmation, 14 April, 2 H. VIII. [1511.] (The feal entire, and
well preferved, except the horfe's head a little rubbed.)

* Probably *Rupes ad Yonem*, Rochefur Yon in Poitou, or fome other place abroad.

16. Quieta

16. Quieta clamatio in perpetuum de decimis & primis fructibus, 2 Maii, 29 H. VIII. [Difcharge from payment of firft-fruits and tenths *.]

17. Exemplification and confirmation of King Henry the Second's grant of xx marks; and of King Henry the Eighth's difcharge from tenths and firft-fruits, 2 Dec. 2 Edw. VI.

18. Confirmatio regis Edwardi III. de cxl li. ex reditibus archiep' Cant' folvendis [fede vacante] ipfi Hofpitali ; & de uno denario fingulis diebus ex manerio de Liminge percipiend'; & ulterius ut liberi fint ab oĩbus taxis, &c, 1 Dec. 9 Edw. III. 1335.

19. Copia cujufdam [prædictæ fcil'] cartæ antiq' ex conceffione d͠ni reg' Angl' nunc, que eft in cuftodia fratrum & fororum de Herbaldoune.

20. A true tranflation of the faid letters patents.

21. Copia cujufdam cartæ novæ ex conceffione d͠ni reg' Angl', in cuftodia fratrum & fororum Hofpital' de Northgate. 6 Mar. 1371, 4 Edw. III.

22. Copia mandati d͠ni Willͫi Wittlefey, Cant' Archiep̄i, ad declarand' omnes excommunicatos qui jura & libertates Hofpitalibus per cartas d͠ni Edwardi regis conceffas infregerint, 13 kal. April. 1370 *.

WILLIELMUS, permiffione divina, Cantuar'archiep̄us, tocius Anglie primas, & ap̄lice fedis legatus, dilect' filiis commiffario n͠ro Cantuar' generali offic' n͠ri Cantuar', ac omnibus & fingulis rectoribus, vicar', & capellan' poch', p̄ n͠ras civitatem & dioc' conftitut', faltͫ, gͬam, & b͠n'. Cum nuper excellentiffimus in Xp̄o princeps & d͠nus n͠r dominus Edwardus, Dei gͬa, rex Anglie & Franc' illuftris, ac d͠ns Hib͠n', p̄ fuas patent' literas, ꝓ fe & heredibus fuis, concefferit pauperibus frͥbus & fororibus hofpitalium n͠ror' de Northgate & Herbaldownͤ juxta Cant', quod ipfi & fucceffores fui imperpetuum de tallagiis fingulis & contribuc.onib' quibufcunque effent quieti ; quodque conceffionem fuam p̄ alias fuas patentes literas ad duo mefuag', &c. poft conceffionem p̄dict' adquifit' etiam innovatam ; & concefferit ꝓ fe & heredibus fuis, quatenus in ipfo eft, quod ipfi fͬes & forores & fucceffores fui, tam de contribuc͡one t͠re maritime qͫ aliis tallagiis, auxiliis, & contribucionibus fupͥus fpecificatis, racione t͠rar' & tenementor' fuor' faciendis, omni quiete in perpetuum.   Ex parte tam' dͤor' frͫ & foror' nobis exiftit intimatum, quod nonnulli maledictionis & perditionis filii dicte n͠re dioc', quorum nomina ignorantur penitus & perfone, dͤos fͬes & forores racione bonorum catallorum tenementorum & terr' horum fatagunt tallagiaruͫ, & ad contribucionem cuftodie teri'maritime & ad contribuciones alios fup̄fcript'compellere quam dͤos ipfos racione p̄miffa talliarunt & contribuere fecerint, jura & libertates p̄ cartas dͤi n͠ri regis eis ut p̄mittitur conceffas infringendo, in dͤor' frͫ & foror' p̄judicium non modicum & regie libertatis lefionem manifeftam : Vobis igitur conjunctim, & unicuique veftrum divifim & in folid' committimus & mandamus, firmiter injungentes quamque in fingulis ec-

* Enrolled in the Exchequer, 29 H. VIII. and in the Firft Fruits Office, 24 May, 33 H. VIII.
† See the feal in plate III. fig. 13.

cliis

cliis ñr' civitat' & dioc' pdict' & in locis aliis in quibus viderit expedire, & p partem eoïdem fïm & foror' fueritis congrue requifit', diebus dnicis & feftivis inter miffar' folempnia, cum major in eifdem convenerit ppli multitudo, & divina moneatis & efficaciter inducatis moneri & efficaciter induci p alios faciatis publice & in genere omnes & fingulos qui dcos fïes & forores occafione bonorum, catall', ten', & terrar' horum talliarunt, feu ad fupradict' contribuere fecerint publice & occulte, aut jura & libertates ut pfertur eis conceffas enervare moliuntur, quod a pdict' injuriis & gravaminibus in pofterum faciend' penitus defiftant, & ab attemptat' hactenus per eofdem eifdem fatisfaciant competent', fub pena fententie excoïcationis majoris, quam in ipfos malefactores omnes & fingulos viis monitionibus non parentes & eis in pmiffis feu pmiffor' aliquo confilium dantes auxilium vel favorem clam vel palam p vos & veftium quemlibet volumus amone fulminare, ipfosque fuiffe & effe excoïcat' occafione pmiffa publice & ingeñe in eccliis & locis predict' vos infuper pmandari quociens & viderit quando oportunum. Prefentes quoque literas, cum p aliquem vïm execut' fuerint, retenta ear' copia penes vos fi volueritis dict' fïibus & fororibus libet'. Dat' apud Otteford xiii kal' Aprilis, anno Dñi millmo cccfeptuagefimo, et ñre tranflat' tercio.

23. Acquittance for lxxix s. viii d. (two fifteenths) due from the hofpitals, and of their lands in Kynghampford, Wyngham, Weftgate, and Eftry. 1 R. I. 1189.

24. Copy of a writ of King Richard II. to difcharge the hofpital from payment of a tenth and fifteenth, and half a tenth and fifteenth, in confequence of King Edward the Third's exemption from taxes, 26 March, 3 R. II. 1379.

25. Exemplificatio & confirmatio Reg. H. IV. chartæ Reg. Ric. II. per quam charta Regis Edw. III. an. regni fui 45, de tallagiis, &c. non folvendis exemplificatur & confirmatur, 6 Dec. 1 H. IV. 1399.

26. Exemplification of the preceding charter, 14 July, 1 H. V. 1413.

27. Vera copia brevis dni regis, p exonerat' hofpital' de Northgate & Herbaldoune, in com' Kanc', unius integr' xvme & xme. 12 Oct. 9 H. ....

28. [Pardon from K. H. VI. 13 Jun. 15th of his reign, to the Hofpital, for having purchafed certain lands contrary to the ftatute of mortmayn; and] Lïa perdonat', 7 Maii, 15 H. VI. 1457. This is a general pardon.

29. 1. Charta Ricardi Archiepi Cant', dat' inter A. D. 1171, & 1184. In dorfo, Donatio xx librarum ex ecclia de Reculver ultra cxl li. prius conceff' ex maneriis de Raculfe & Boctun. (Hic mentio fit fundationis per Lanfrancum.) This charter is printed by Mr. Battely *, App. 61. Part of the counter-feal remains, infcribed RICA.....PRIMAS

29. 2. Copia antiqua prædictæ chartæ.

29. 3. A Copy of N° 29, in the hand-writing of Mr. Somner; and the fame tranflated into Englifh.

* And alfo in the Hiftory of Reculver, p. 129.

30. 1. Con-

30. 1. Confirmatio Ed. I. de revocatione ecclie de Reculver ad cameram archie-p̄atus Cant', & ut hospitalia suſtineantur ex reddiubus ipſius archiep̄i, 18 Dec. 19 Edw. I. 1291*. See hereafter, p. 240, N° 71.

30. 2. Licence of K. Edw. III. for appropriation of the church of Reculver to the archbiſhop's table; and for payment of 160 l. p an. out of the revenues of the fee of Cant' to the hoſpitals, notwithſtanding the ſtatute of mortmain †. 16 March, 22 Edw. III. 1348. See hereafter, p. 241, N° 72.

30. 3. Order [rather letters patent] of Abp. Sim. Iſlip, that 160 l. per an. due from the archbiſhoprick to the Huſpitals of Herbaldown and Northgate ſhall be paid for the future out of the [appropriation of the] church of Reculver ‡, 8 id. Feb. 1355. [which uſed to be paid out of the temporalities of the fee of Canterbury, with the confirmation of the prior and chapter of Canterbury.] (The ſeal; ſee plate III. fig. 11. is entire.)

31. Charta Simonis Iſlip Archiep̄i Cant', ejuſdem tenoris & dat'. (Part of the ſeal remains.)

32. Alia charta predicti Archiep̄i ejuſdem tenoris & dat'.
(In dorſo.) " Herbald more auncient than St. John's by this, dated 1255 ; ſo that " it appeareth that this yere 1617 it is ſince 262 yeres." (The ſeal loſt.)

33. Confirmatio predictæ chartæ per prior' & capit' Cant'. (In dorſo.) " For our " wageſſes. Herbaldoune perquiſitū p fr̄em Willm de Chyleham tunc p̄orem ibid'."

34. Tho. Arundel Archiep̄i exemplificatio & confirmatio fundationis Cantariæ § in hoſpitali Sc̄i Nicħi de Herebaldoun ‖. (The ſeal, which ſee in plate III. fig. 14. is entire, and repreſents the martyrdom of Thomas Becket.) [18 May 1402.]

(In dorſo.) The Confirmation of a chauntry for a pryeſte to ſerve the hoſpitalls.

THOMAS, permiſſione divina Cantuarien' archiep̄s, totius Anglie primas [& Ap̄lice ſedis legatus* *] dilectis in X p̄o filiis priori & prioriſſe ac fratribus & ſororibus hoſ-pitalis noſtri de Herbaldoune ſalutem, graciam, & benedictionem. Scrutato regiſtro bone memorie dn̄i Willelmi Wittleſeye predeceſſoris noſtri dotacionem ſive ordinacionem per-petue cantarie in hoſpitali n̄ro predicto reperimus in eodem tenorem qui ſequitur

* Printed in the Hiſtory of Reculver, p. 131.
† Printed in the Hiſtory of Reculver, p. 141.
‡ Printed in the Hiſtory of that pariſh, p. 148.
§ A chantry founded by Abp. Wittleſey, 4 non. Feb. 1371. See p. 183.
‖ This exemplification is printed in Battely's edition of Somner's Antiquities of Canterbury, p. 1. Appendix N° XIV. p. 10.
** Theſe words have a line drawn through them in the original.

G g

conti-

continentem. "Univerfis fćé matris ecclefie filiis prefentes literas infpecturisWillelmus, permiffione divina Cantuarien' archieps, totius Anglie primas, & apoftolice fedis legatus, falutem in dno fempiternam. Cum cuftos quilibet hofpitalis noftri de Eftbrigge in Cantuaria qui pro tempore fuerit fuis fumptibus & expenfis invenire teneatur facerdotem ydoneum, qui jugiter divina celebret coram pauperibus alterius hofpitalis noftri. de Herbaldoune in ecclia Sći Nicholai ibidem, & eorum confeffiones audiat, eisque diebus & noctibus prout oportebit ecclefiaftica miniftret facramenta; fitque de prefenti & erit verifimiliter in futurum difficile ftipendiarios reperire facerdotes ydoneos qui inter dictos pauperes taliter converfari voluerint, prefertim cum ipforum pauperum nonnulli lepra fint infecti; ac pro infectis hujufmodi ipfum hofpitale principaliter fit fundatum, nifi forfan manfionem ab eis feparatam habuerint & vicinam, cantariamque non mobilem ppetuam obtineant ad victum eorundem capellanorum dotatam competenter: Nos, premiffa debito confiderationis intuitu penfantes, cureque animarum dictorum pauperum & hofpitalis predicti utilitati providere volentes, quandam perpetuam cantariam unius capellani, ut premittitur, divina apud Herbaldoune celebraturi fundamus, dotamus, & ut fubfcribit' ordinamus. Habebit fiquidem facerdos hujufmodi ipfius cantarie perpetuus, in partem dotis ejufdem, unam manfionem fufficientem & honeftam edificatam ex oppofito porte dicti hofpitalis de Herbaldoune, cum prediis & gardinis adjacentibus, ac quodam columbari ibidem jam conferend' dicto hofpitali de Eftbrigge per dnum Willm atte Welle capellanum, de regis licentia jam obtenta, ut inter benefactores habeatur utriufque hofpitalis fupradicti. Necnon quandam aream prefato hofpitali ńro de Herbaldoune contiguam vocatam Claveringge *. Habebit etiam facerdos ipfius cantarie de fratribus & fororibus hofpitalis de Herbaldoune duas marcas de claro p equales porciones annuatim in ppetuum. Reputabitur infuper & erit facerdos ipfe, abfque ńro aut fuccefforum noftrorum novo onere, unus de numero pauperum in hofpitali ńro de Herbaldoune requifito, propter ipfius converfationem, celebrationes, & orationes quas quafi continue faciet coram eis & inter eos, tantum pcipiens, & taliter, ficut eorum unus, incedens, fi voluerit, veftitus, pro reverentia fui ordinis, ut facerdos fecularis. Habebit infuper quinque marcas liberi & fecuri redditus in denariis tempore dni Thome Elton, jam cuftodis dicti noftri hofpitalis de Eftbrigge, eidem hofpitali adquifitas apud Herne, quas folvent quid' Thomas de Court, heredes & affignati ejus, pro terris & tenementis dimiffis eis p factum in hac pte fufficiens de folvendo. Ac etiam duas mareas cum dimidia annuat' de cuftode quocumque ipfius hofpitalis ńri de Eftbrigge p tempe eid' capell' pfolvend' ad quatuor anni terminos ufualit' principales, quas cuftos ipfe cum ulteriori fuma annis fingulis de certis terris, reddit' & paftur' libere habere poterit quas

---

* "Where before, fpeaking of this hofpital, I faid the chantry prieft dwelt over againft the hofpital, I find I was miftaken: for the account of the chantry's endowment, given to the commiffioners about the time of the fuppreffion, faith he had his dwelling here at Clavering." Somner, Marginal Note.

After Claveringge, in archbifhop Wittlefeye's Regifter, is contained as follows, "que manfio cum ipfis prediis, gardinis, columbar' & area, eftimatione communi, duas marcas de claro valebit impeipetuum annuatim. Reputabitur infuper, &c." [HALL.]

dictus

dictus dominus Thomas cuftos, eciam fue cuftodie tempore, adquivifit de domino
Thoma de Ros, milite, apud Hothe; fuper quibus teriis & pafturis libere dif-
tringere facerdos ipfe valeat p omni tempe ipfar' duar' marcai' & dimid' poft unum-
quemque tm fupradictum, per menfem fi poftea in folucione hujufmodi fit ceffatum.
Et fic dos ipfius cantarie undecim marcas cum dimidia vel circit' verifimilit' in pofterum valebit annuatim. Ad ipfam autem cantariam, quociens eam vacare contigerit
cuftos dicti hofpitalis de Eftbrigg, qui pro tempore fuerit, facerdotes ydoneos, qui in
ea refidere voluerint, & cotidie coram ipfis pauperibus, ceffante impedimento legitimo,
juxta canonum exigentiam, celebrare divina, aut per alium facere celebrari, & aiar'
curam gerere eorundem, ut eft dictum, ad que omnia & fingula facerdotes hujufmodi
teneri volumus & artari, nobis & fuccefforibus noftris prefentabit. Ad fumptus autem
reparacionis domorum prefate manfionis & columbaiis, ac exhibitionem panis, vini, &
luminariorum honeftorum p celebrationibus miffarum predictarum neceffariorum, tenebitur facerdos ipfe ratione predicte dotis fue. Si autem facerdos ydoneus haberi non
poterit qui ipfam cantariam habere velit, & ad celebrationes & curam predictam ac
alia predicta oña artari noluerit, ut eft dictum, ex tunc cuftos memorati hofpitalis de
Eftbiigge, qui p tempore fuerit, poffeffiones dicte dotis fupius defcriptas ingrediatur
& teneat, ac de dictis celebrationibus & cura difponat, ficut prius tenebatur, & prout
melius videbitur fibi expedire. In quorum omnium teftimon' has literas noftras fieri
fecimus patentes figillo noftro confignatas. Dat' apud Croydone, iiiiⁱᵒ non' Februarii, anno Domini MCCCLXXI, et noftre tranflationis quarto." Nos igitur Thomas,
pmiffione divina Cantuarien' archiepus, totius Anglie primas, & aplice fedis legatus
predictus, predictam dotacionem, five ordinationem, ratam habentes pariter & acceptam fimiliter approbando & quantum in nobis eft confirmantes, vobis coit' & divifim
firmit' injungendo mandamus quatenus dūm Johannem Biay, capellanum predicte
cantarie modernum, tanquam unum de numero pauperum in hofpitali predicto admittatis, tantum & talit' ficut alicui alteri pauperi ejufdem, in quibufcumque pecuniar'
fumñis, feu aliis vite neceffariis, effectualit' miniftrantes. Dat' in palatio noftro Cantuarie XVIII die menfis Maii, anno Dñi millmo quadragentefimo fecundo, et noftre
tranflationis anno fexto.

35. Abp. Winchelfey's Statutes, Feb. 24, 1298.

The feal (fee plate III. fig. 8.), almoft entire, reprefents a Bifhop at full length, holding a crofs in his left hand; his right hand lifted up, and his mouth open.
...... S. TOCIVS ANGLIE PRIM...... The reft of the infcription broken off.
Reverfe (fig. 9.) reprefents the martyrdom of Tho. Becket; archbifhop praying
underneath. Infcription, AuxiliVM PRO ME SIT SEMPER PASSIO THOME.

ROBERTUS, permiffione divina Cantuar' archiepus, tocius Anglie primas,
dilectis filiis Priori & Prioreffe, fratribus ac fororibus, Hofpitalis de Herebal.
doune juxta Cantuar', ad perpetuam rei memoriam. Quia nuper in ñra vifitacione
comperimus ipfum hofpitale per liberaciones extra conceffas, & habitas, ex toto
difformes, ac etiam fratrum & fororum ejufdem inordinatos inceffus, & modis aliis a

ftatu

ftatu congruo multipliciter jam eductum, neceffarium ac honeftum effe confpicimus ut id modo debito reformemus.

In primis quoque ftatuimus, ordinantes, ut omnes fratres & forores hofpitalis ejufdem habitum habeant uniformem ; videlicet, tunicam feu fupertunicam claufam, & fratres fcapularium cum capucio, ac forores mantellum de groffo ruffeto unius precii & coloris. Fururis infuper & penulis agninis, dumtaxat nigris, levis & ejufdem precii, eofdem fres & forores uti volumus & precipimus in futurum. Habeant etiam tam fres quam forores de bovino coreo foculares, ultra medium tibie coreo circa tibiam laqueatos, aut de eodem coreo nodulatos, vel botas, non de alio coreo quam bovino. Infuper nec fres fine fcapulario, nec forores fine mantello, portam exeant quoquo modo. Sorores etiam caput coopertum habeant duplici velo, videlicet albo inferius, & fuperius nigro, non de fubtili panno (fc. groffo), ejufdem precii & coloris.

Item ftatuendo precipimus impofterum firmiter obfervari, quod nullus frater aut foror in dicto hofpitali de cetero admittatur, nifi perfona admittenda in eodem, diligenter prius examinata, Oracoem dominicam, Patrmnr, cum Salutacione beate virginis, Ave Maria, & fimbolum Credo in Deum fciat prius fufficienter inftructa edicere diftinctius & aperte. Item quod ex nunc muti, qui omnino loqui non poterunt, in dicto hofpitali, nec etiam loqui valentes, nifi fuum habitum prius habeant, ut preordinatur, preparatum, nullatenus admittantur.

Quicunque vero frum & foror' confueta fuffragia & debita in eodem hofpitali inftituta ex antiqua ordinacione quolibet die dicenda negligenter omiferit, in proxima fexta feria peccatum fuum hujufmodi, coram fratribus & fororibus omnibus hinc fexta feria congregandis, publice fateatur, & fres a Priore, & forores a Prioriffa, vel ipfis abfentibus a tenentibus ipforum loca, penitentiam fubeant falutarem ; videlicet quod fabbato pximo fequente, ceffante impedimento, hujus fuffragia per ipfos omittentes duplicentur.

Fratribus etiam & fororibus hofpitalis ejufdem omnem alienacion' terrar', reddituum, ac quorumcumque immobilium poffeffionum, inpignoracionem etiam mobilium hofpitalis ejufdem, fine archiepi licentia, faciendam, interdicimus, fub pena exconis majoris, in quam contravenientes incidant ipfo facto.

Ceterumque nuper in vifitacione dicti hofpitalis invenimus quod corrodia quibufdam uxoratis, & aliis divitum fervientibus, ac miniftris aliunde vite neceffaria fibi querere valentibus extra ipfum hofpitale commorantibus, contra fundatoris illius intencionem, qui voluit omnes de bonis ejufdem hofpitalis victualia habentes, ad cetera fuffragia infra ipfius loci fepta dumtaxat dicenda fingulis diebus aftringi, vendita & conceffa, pauperes & infirmos prefati hofpitalis debitis alimoniis, ipfumque hofpitale, & ejus miniftros, confuetis & ab antiquo inftitutis orationibus & fuffragiis, folitifque obfequiis, propter facultatum diminucionem hujus temere defraudari, in ipforum vendentium & concedentium grave animarum periculum, & fcandalum manifeftum ; ftatuendo diftrictius inhibemus, ne unquam aliquibus perfonis extra prefatum hofpitale in feculo commorantibus vendantur hujus corrodia, vel concedantur, vel aliqualiter folvantur, fc. talibus dumtaxat qui in dicto hofpitali continuo ftare voluerint, & Deo Altiffimo, fecundum antiquam obfervacionem,

6   ora-

oracionum reddere fuffragia confueta, fub pena excôis majoris, quam ex nunc in-
quofcunque contravenientes proferimus in hiis fcriptis, quorum abfolucionem nobis
fpecialiter refervamus.

Fratres infuper aut forores hofpitalis ejufdem, fine Prioris aut Prioriffe licentia,
ex caufa dumtaxat legitima concedenda, exterius non vagentui. Caufas autem
hujufmodi taliter declaramus, ut ᵱ negotiis utilibus domus, perfone ad hoc idonee
& experte, aut pro infirmitate graviffima, vel morte, aut gravi infirmitate parentum feu amicorum, vel pro aliqua recreatione modica, aut pio negociis propriis ad
victum neceffariis hiis que indigere nofcuntur, hujus exeundi, licentia concedatur,
dum tamen bini & bine nullo modo fufpecte fimul incedent, & exeuntibus ipfis terminus brevis & competens ut domi redeant ftatuatur ultra nullatenus moraturis.
Quod fi voluntarie fecerint, puniantur graviter protinus redeuntes. Et fi trina vice
fic illicenciati exierint, vel in termino fibi ad redeundum ftatuto redire contempferint, per fuperiorem ipfius hofpitalis cuftodem a domo perpetuo amoveantur. Et
hoc idem quibufcumque fratribus & fororibus domus ejufdem, qui trinis monicionibus
aut coireccionibus factis de eorum exceffibus incorrigibiles fuerint, diftricte precipimus obfervari.

Item fratres & forores garrulofi, contentiofi, aut rixofi, fi primo, fecundo, & tertio moniti fe non correxerint, penis prius eis impofitis pro commiffis ad quartum
exceffum fuper hoc, feu dictum per fuperiorem cuftodem ut fupra, a domo perpetuo
ejiciantur. Idem de inobedientibus, fi in rebellione perftiterint, diftricte precipimus
obfervari.

Item nullus frater, aut foror, in civitate Cantuar', vel ipfius fuburbio, extra domum fuam fupradictam pernoctet, nec de confuetudine comedat, aut diu fine caufa
evidenti, & ex conceffa, ut fupra, licentia, diucius moram trahat. Et fi fuper hiis,
vel eorum aliquo, inveniatur incoirigibilis, amoveatur a domo poft trinum exceffum,
prius tamen correptus & monitus ficut prius. Item quod aliquis vel aliqua conju-
gatus, vel conjugata, in fratrem vel fororem dicti hofpitalis de cetero non admittatur diftrictius inhibemus.

De incontinentia vero fufpecti, ftatim coram Priore & Prioriffa, & fratribus duobus & duabus fororibus non fufpectis, exinde conveniantur, & arguantur. Et convicti ftatim ᵱ fuperiorem cuftodem ejiciantur a domo, nullatenus poft modum redi-
turi; quanquam enim iidem fratres & forores certam religionem canonem pficiendam
non habeant, obedientiam tamen, ac continentiam ab eildem fratribus & fororibus,
dum ibidem morari voluerint, ftatuimus, & diftricte precipimus obfervari. Ad que
etiam in fuo ingreffu juramentum preftent, coram fratribus & fororibus fpeciale
✳ ✳ ✳ ✳ ✳ ✳   [N. B. *Two lines of the original are erafed.*]

Hec vero ftatuta & ordinaciones noftras legi fecimus, & publice recitari, in hofpitali predicto de Herebaldoune, in prefentia Prioris, Prioriffe, ac aliorum fratrum
& fororum ejufdem loci, & aliorum quampluiium congregatorum ibidem, die Martis, in fefto Sancti Matthie apli, vidiet fexto kaln' Martii, anno Dñi мссnona-
gefimo octavo, confecracionis noftre quinto, ut extunc robur obtineant firmitatis,
& in fingulis fuis articulis impofterum, fub interminacione anathematis, fideliter obfer-
ventur. Dat' die, loco, & anno predictis.

36. Abp,.

56. Abp. Parker's Statutes (with part of the feal remaining) on paper.
Sept. 15, 1560 *.

MATTHEW, by the fufferance of God, Archbifhop of Canterbury, Primate and Metropolitan of England; to all Chriftian people fendeth greeting in our Lord : Whereas amongft other things that do concern our paftoral office, wee have before our eyes the charitable affeThis and godly zeal that was in divers our predeceffors, archbithops of Canterbury, who founded and erected two feveral hofpitals; th'one of St. John's in Northgate, in the fuburbs of Canterbury, and the other of St. Nicholas of Harbaldown, nigh unto our fee, the city of Canterbury ; for poor, fick, impotent, and needy people to be relieved and fuccoured in the fame; wee, knowing the provifion for the poor to be a thing very acceptable to God in this world, have, for the difcharge of our confcience, thought it our duty unto God to fee, as nigh as wee can, and the law of God doth fuffer, that the faid hofpitals be ufed and ordered according to the minds of the founders, our predeceffors.

1. Wherefore wee ordain and appoint, That according to the firft foundation, there be in our hofpital of St. John's in Northgate xxx † men, whom (after the ancient cuftome) we will to be called Bretheren, that by this name they may be the rather put in mind of their duty to live together like bretheren in unity, concord, godly agreement, and brotherly love : and xxx † women, whom after the like manner wee will to be called Sifters, which all fhall be bound to make their abode, and to dwell, within our faid hofpital, except they have for their abfence a fpecial grant and difpenfation by writing, from us or our fucceffors, archbithops of Canterbury, for the time being. Providing, and alwayes forefeeing, that there dwell not out of the houfe above the number of x bretheren and x fifters at any time ‡.

2. Alfo we ordain, That upon every vacation or avoydance of any of the rooms of the brethren or fifters, whether it be by death, deprivation, ceffion, voluntary departing, expulfion, or by any other lawful means; the elder, or the prior, fo commonly called, for the time being, with three of his bretheren, within x dayes next after fuch avoidance, if the brother dwelt in the houfe, or in the city of Canterbury, and of others that are further off, fo foone as he or they have certain knowledge thereof, fhall intimate and give in writing unto us and our fucceffors, archbifhops of Canterbury, or elfe to the dean and chapter, *fede vacante*, as well the perfon's name and manner of departing, as alfo the day, month, and year of fuch departing, that wee may eftfoones appoint fome other to the faid roome.

---

* Thefe are the fame, *mutatis mutandis*, at both Hofpitals, and are therefore inferted here, though they mention only St. John's.
† Viz eighteen in and twelve out brothers, twenty in and ten out-fifters.
‡ In this Hofpital there are thirty-one houfes, of which thirty are now occupied. D.

Alfo

Alfo we ordain, That henceforth none be admitted brother or fifter, but fuch as fhall be named by fome certificate from or to our fuccefors under our fignet, elfe fhall perfonally exhibit to the prior for the time being, and to his bretheren, or unto four of them at the leaft, a grant of a corrody, under feal from us or our fuccefors, or under the feal of the dean and chapter, *fede vacante*: and the elder or prior, upon fight of every fuch grant, fhall within two dayes next following, in the prefence of four of his bretheren at the leaft, admit any fuch brother and fifter without further delay, til there be the full number of xxx bretheren and xxx fifters. And every brother and fifter, at his or her admiffion, fhall pay towards the maintaining and repairing of the church and other houfes 6 s. 8 d. and have their names written in the table appointed for the fame purpofe. And the prior fhall caufe thefe ftatutes to be read to every brother and fifter, at his or her admiffion to dwell within the hofpital: And alfo to be read yearly on Midfummer-day before all the bretheren and fifters.

4. Alfo wee ordain, That every brother and fifter, at his or her admiffion to dwell in the houfe, fhall take a corporal oath upon a book in manner and form following: "I A. B. brother or fifter of St. John's in Northgate, fhall bear true
" faith and due allegeance unto the Queen's highnefs, her heirs and fuccefors;
" and fhall obferve and keep all fuch ftatutes and orders and rules. which now be,
" or hereafter may be made and given by Lord Matthew, Archbifhop of Canter-
" bury, or by his fuccefors, concerning the ftate of the hofpital, not repugnant
" to the laws of God, nor to the laws of this realm. And I fhall obey the el-
" der or prior for the time being, in all things lawfull and honeft; and I fhall
" not confent nor agree to fell, to give, to change, to pledge, or by any kind
" of wayes to alienate any lands, tenements, buildings, paftures, woods, cattle,
" utenfils, ftock of money, deeds, charters, or other writings, or any other thing
" appertaining or belonging to the faid hofpital, without the confent and affent
" of the faid Lord Matthew or his fuccefors, archbifhops of Canterbury, firft had
" and obteined; fo God me help, and by the contents of this book."

5. Alfo wee ordain, That none, having the ufe of reafon and fpeech, be admitted brother or fifter, but fuch as can fay the Lord's Prayer, the Articles of the Faith, and the X Commandments of God, in the Englifh tongue: and that after admiffion, within a convenient time, they endeavour themfelves to learn by heart the brief Catechifme inferted in the book of Common Prayer.

6. Alfo wee ordain, That all the bretheren and fifters, dwelling within the faid hofpital, fhall diligently come to the church twife in the day, morning and evening, except there be lawfull caufe to be abfent, and allowed by the prior, there to offer up their common prayers unto Almighty God, and attentively to hear God's Holy Scripture read; and if any be abfent, not having fufficient caufe, or be flack and negligent in coming to the church; or being there, do ufe to jangle, to talk, or to fleep in the time of Common Prayer, the Adminiftration of the Sacraments, reading of the Holy Scriptures, or the Homilyes; if after two admonitions given by the prior to amend that fault, the party eftfoones commit the like offenfe, that
brother

biother or fifter, whither it be, fhall be punifhed in the ftocks * one half day or more, at the difcretion of the prior, for his or her correction. And if that brother or fifter, after fuch punifhment, will not amend, but continue ftill that lewd beha. viour and example, wee will, that the prior, with the affent of four of his bretheren, do give knowledge unto us, our fucceffors, or lawfull deputyes, of the evil quali. tyes of that brother or fifter, that wee, following the example of a good furgeon, may eftfoones cut off that member, which is not only unprofitable, but alfo huit. full to the whole body.

7. Alfo wee oidain, That no brother dwelling within the faid hofpital, goe abroad without the precincts and limits of the fame, except he firft fhew to the pri. or a juft caufe of his going, and the prior do allow the fame; the fifters in like fort fhall not goe forth without a juft caufe firft fhewed to the prioreffe, and by her al. lowed. Whofoever fhall do contemptuoufly to this order, fhall (after three mo. nitions given him by the prior, if it be a brother, and by the priorefs, if it be a fifter) be punifhed in the ftocks * at the difcretion of the prior. Provided, That no brother or fifter being in the houfe, dwelling, be abfent more than two months in the year, jointly or feverally, except in common caufes of the houfe, &c. and that the prior do make a note of their going and returning again, for the more certainty.

8. Alfo wee will and ordain, That there be a prior chofen yearly within one month next before the feaft of·All Saints, or within one month next, and immedi. ately following the faid feaft, in fuch form and order as of an old cuftome hath been ufed: and as the bretheren do choofe their prior, fo wee will and ordain, that the fifters fhall choofe a priorefs. At which day the prior is chofen, fhall be allfo chofen four of the fkillfull, fober, and difcreet bretheren, to be affiftants and coun. fells to the prior that year, as well in things appertaining to the ftate of the houfe, concerning the lands, tenements, and reparations, as alfo in the due execution of the ftatutes.

9. Alfo we will, that the prior fhall underftand, that his office is to fee that his bretheren keep and obferve the ftatutes and ordinances of the houfe; as of the pri. oreffe, to call upon her fifters in like manner to do the fame. The prior, and one of the bretheren with him, or elfe two of the four bretheren, fhall every year twife at the leaft, that is to fay, at Eafter and Michaelmas, fee and view their church, their houfes both at home and abroad otherwayes, that, where need is, reparations may be done in time; and to take diligent heed, that neyther any of their lands be changed, nor ftript, ne waft upon their grounds, nor in their houfes, be made by any of their tenants. The prior himfelfe, or fome one of his bretheren, muft have from time to time a diligent eye to the woods which ferve for provifion of the houfe, that no fpoil, ne waft, be made of them; and that the fprings be fuffi. ciently fenced, and kept from cattle.

10. Alfo we will and ordain, That the prior, and one of the bretheren, as hath been aforetime accuftomed, fhall faithfully collect and gather up the rents and fums

---

* Q. Whether this can be juftified by law, thefe ftatutes not having been confirmed by act of parliament? Certain it is that this punifhment is never inflicted. D.

of

of money due to the houfe: and every year once, in the prefence of all the bretheren, or of ten at the leaft, make a true, and perfect, and plain accompt of the
fame, in fuch form and order as fhall be prefcribed by us; and in the end of the
accompt fhall deliver up there that money which fhall be found to be in his or
their hands, which money fhall be layd up in a treafury-houfe, in a coffer with
three feveral keys and locks: in which coffer we will the foundation of the houfe,
the charters and grants, and confirmations of charters, the ftatutes, all leafes,
and the common feal, be warily kept: and the prior to keep one of the three
keyes, and two of the brethren the other two, and no one man to have two of
thofe keyes in his cuftody at one time; but if any of the keepers go from home,
he fhall leave his key with a brother that hath no key; and the prioreffe fhall keep
the key of the treafure-houfe door.

11. Alfo we will and ordain, That if any brother fhall, by the teftimony of
fix of the bretheren, or any fifter, by the teftimony of fix of the fifters, be convict
before the prior, to be a common drunkard, a quarreller, a brawler, a fcold, or
a blafphemous fwearer; every fuch offender, fo convict, fhall for the firft time fit
in the ftocks ~ one day and a night with bread and water; and offending in that
fault again, fhall the fecond time be punifhed in the ftocks * two days and two
nights; and for the third offence in the fame crime, three days and three nights
with bread and water only * ; but if, after the third punifhment, he or fhe do eftfoones offend in the like offence, then to be expulfed and driven out of the houfe
for ever.

12. Alfo we ordain, That if a brother or fifter be accufed before the prior, of
fornication or adultery, or that he or fhe receiveth or maintaineth fornicators,
adulterers, or any fuch leud perfons, he or fhe, whether it be, fhall within one
month next after any fuch accufations, make his or her purgation, before the
prior and his four bretheren, after this manner : The brother accufed fhall bring
fix of his brethren, who fhall depofe upon a book before the prior, that in their
confciences they think that man not faulty in that crime that he is accufed of. The
fifter fhall bring fix of her fifters, which, by virtue of an oath, fhall teftifie, that
in their confciences they think fhe is not faulty in the crime objected againft her ;
which if they do, the prior fhall pronounce the party accufed to be clear and free from
that fault. But if either brother or fifter faileth in his or her purgation, then
the prior fhall pronounce that perfon to be faulty and convict of the crime, and
immediately for the fame expulfe that perfon out of the houfe.

13. Alfo we will and ordain, That no leafe of any lands, houfes, tenements,
or ftocks of cattle, fhall pafs under the common feal for term of years, without
the affent of us, and our fucceffors, firft had and obtained to the fame: and no
reverfion to be given before the leafe be fully expired, or within one year of ex-
piring †.

* See note, p. 216.
† A concurrent leafe, by the law of the land, may be granted three years before the former leafe
expires. D.

14. Alfo

14. Alſo we will and ordain, 'That every of the LX brethren and ſiſters quarterly, out of the VIS. VIIId. paid unto every of them by us and our ſucceſſors,
ſhall allow and leave in the prior's hand VIIId. amounting in the whole to the
ſum of VIIIl. which ſhall be imployed to the ſtipend of an able prieſt *, to be
nominated, appointed, and admitted by us and our ſucceſſors, to be their curate,
to inſtruct them how to live in the love and fear of God, and to miniſter unto
them Chriſt's Holy Sacraments.

15. Alſo, if any brother or ſiſter ſhall willingly or wittingly do contrary to the
oath taken at his or her admiſſion, for the due obſervation of theſe ſtatutes; we
will and ordain, that every ſuch perſon, upon a ſufficient proof thereof made, ſhall
be accepted, reputed, and taken as perjured; and for his offence ſhall be expulſed
out of the houſe, never after to enjoy any alms thereof.

16. Furthermore we will and ordain, That it ſhall not be lawful for the brethren and ſiſters of the ſaid hoſpital, at any time, to abrogate or change, or by any
means hereafter to alter, theſe ſtatutes, rules, and ordinances, or any of them, or
any part of them, without our aſſent in writing under our ſignet firſt obtained and
had.

17. And if any ſcruple or doubt ſhall hereafter ariſe about the ſame, or any of
them, we reſerve the interpretation of them to us and our ſucceſſors; and that
we during our life, may, if we ſee juſt cauſe, put to, change, abrogate, and diſ-
annul them, and every of them, at our will and pleaſure.

18. And for the more authority, and better confirmation, of theſe ſtatutes, we
the ſaid Matthew have put to our ſeal; and the brethren and ſiſters, for a ſure
band for the due obſervation of the ſame on their partie, have put to their common
ſeal.

Given in our manner at Lambeth, the 15th day of September, in the 2d year
of our ſovereign Lady Elizabeth, by the grace of God, Queen of England
France, and Ireland, defender of the faith, &c. and of our conſecration the firſt'

---

* The following note is entered in the margin: " This ſtatute had bene fraudulently razed,
and VI pence quarterly by the brothers detained from their prieſt's ſtipend; but the fraud being
diſcovered by a collation of thes ſtatutes [viz. of Herbaldown] with the ſtatutes of St. John's; it
was ordered by my Lord's Grace, March 20, anno 1611, that this ſtatute ſhould be reſtored,
and the ancient ſtipend unto the prieſt revived.   Sic teſtor, MARTIN FOTHERBY †."
The ſame ſtipend is paid to the chaplain, or reader, to this day. D.

† " Son of Maurice Fotherby, of the ancient and genteel family of his name living at Grimſby in Lincoln-
ſhire, which Martin having been bred Fellow of Trinity College in Cambridge, was, after he had been Prebendary of Canterbury 22 years, conſecrated at Lambeth on the 18th of April, 1618, [Biſhop of Saliſbury]. He
ſurrendered up his laſt breath on the eleventh of March, an. 1619, and was buried in All-Saints Church in
Lombard Street within the city of London. Soon after was a very fair monument erected over his grave, with
a large inſcription thereon, but deſtroyed by the great fire that happened in London in the beginning of September, 1666. He hath extant at leaſt four Sermons, beſides his ' Atheomaſtix,' which being put into the
preſs before his death, was not publiſhed till 1622, fol." Ath. Ox. I. 726.

Additions

Additions * to the former Statutes, made by the said Reverend Father in God, August 20, 1565.

[19. ITEM, We will that the minister, to whom we have committed the charge of your soule, shall be no underling to the prior, or at his commandment, but, for his office sake, equal with the prior; and the minister to assist the prior with counsel, and the prior to assist the minister in executing our statutes; that as in name ye be called, so in the whole conversation of your lives, ye may live together like bretheren and sisters before God and the world.]

20. Item, We will that none, having our dispensation to be an out-brother or sister, be suffered to be an in-brother or sister, until he or she hath surrendered to us or our successors his or her dispensation: and then to have a new warrant from us or our successors, to be received an in-brother or sister.

[21. Item, We do ordain, that all and every of the bretheren or sisters, being at home and in health, do go every Sunday together in seemly order, to hear the sermon at Christ's Church.]

22. Item, We will that every brother or sister do keep clean and sweet their dorter-chambers †, and do lie in the same two weeks in the year at least, between the feast of the Annunciation of our Lady, and the feast of St. John the Baptist.

23. Item, We will the prior to see, from time to time, that the said dorters * be sufficiently repaired; or else, after two admonitions given by the prior before the bretheren and sisters in the common hall, and yet not amended, to stop so much of his or her wages, as he by the advice of two or three of the bretheren shall think reasonable for the sufficient repairing of the same.

MATTHEW CANTUAR'.

Additions again, May 20, 1574.

24. ITEM, We will and ordain moreover, that whatsoever brother or sister shall hereafter offer his or her corrody to sell, or shall lay the same to mortgage, the same person shall immediately for the same fault or offence, upon a sufficient proof thereof by two witnesses, cease to be taken any longer for a brother or sister, and shall lose his or her living in this our hospital, by expulsion out of the same house, and be deprived from all the commodities of the same. And also, that he

---

* "N. B. That in thes additions here wanteth one, wherby the priest is made equall to the prior, and adjoyned unto him as an assistant in the government of the howse, as may be seen in the statutes of St. John's hospital, p. 16." The omission noticed by Dr. Fotherby are here supplied from Strype, being the first of the additions, and numbered 19. He has also supplied another omission, which is numbered 21.

† There was formerly a large building in St. John's Hospital, called the Dorter (or Dormitory) which was taken down by the order, or consent, of Archbishop Potter in 1744. D.

or fhe, which is not a brother or fifter, and hath bought any fuch corrody, fhall never have grant or other corrody to be admitted into any of the fame rooms fo bought and bargained for.

25. Item, We will and ordain, that every in-brother and in-fifter, and fo many of the out-brothers and out-fifters as be dwelling within the city of Cant', or near thereunto, and having the ufe of fpeech and reafon, fhall once every year in the time of Lent, before Eafter, being called thereunto, come and fay over the catechifme, either before the minifter of your houfe, or before him whom we or our fucceffors fhall appoint for the fame matter; and that brother or fifter which fhall refufe to be obedient to this order, and doth not learn the catechifm againft the fame time, or elfe doth negligently forget the fame, after he or fhe hath once learned it, that brother or that fifter fo offending fhall want or lofe his or her quarter's ftipend at the next quarter-day following, for the fame offence, and be further punifhed, as we or our fucceffors fhall appoint, if they do not conform themfelves to this order afterwards. And the faid quarters ftipend, or ftipends, in fuch fort abridged, and taken from fuch unorderly perfons, fhall go to the reparation of the houfe to be immediately imployed upon the fame.

MATTH. CANTUAR'.

37. A parchment book in quarto (with an iron box, in which was formerly, as fuppofed, the Archbifhop's feal) containing the fame ftatutes of Abp. Parker, with obfervations in the margin in the hand-writing of Dr. Fotherby, and the following injunctions of fucceeding Archbifhops.

Order of Archbifhop Whitgift, 1591.

WHEREAS I have received very certeine information, that divers inconveniences have already growen, and are likly to growe dayly, to the two hofpitalls of Harbaldowne and St. Johns, by the children of fuch brothers and fifters as have lived in them, for that after the death of their parents they are left as orphanes in the fayde hofpitalls, to the greate difquiet and charge of the poore bretheren and fifters there: I have thought good to fet downe this order and decree, for the redreffe of this diforder and inconvenience, that hereafter there be noe children admitted into the fayde hofpitalls. But in cafe the parents be admitted as brethren or fifters into them, they fhall otherwife provide for the bringinge upp of their faid children, and not charge or trouble the faid hofpitalls with them; which order and decree I doe will to be inviolably kept, and to be regiftred in eyther of the faid hofpitalls, for the better obfervacon thereof. Yeoven under my hand and feale at Lambehith the xxth of May, MCCCCCXCI, anno regine Elizabethe XXXIII. JOH. CANTUAR'.

2* WHERE-

Regulations of Abp. Abbott, 1618.

2*. WHEREAS the pryors of Harbaldowne, together with theyr affiftants, and others of the brotherhood, have, by an unfufferable boldneffe, worthye of punifh- ment, prefumed to make leaffes of theire lands without my confent, where- unto the letter of the ftatute dothe neceffarilye binde them, which confent of myne in thefe cafes I doe not otherwife paffe then under my owne hand, whatfoever fome have otherwife conceyved, becaufe fuch grantes, beinge allredye paffed under theire common feale, cannot well be recalled or anulled : For preventing the like inconveniences for the tyme to come, my order is, that none prefume to ex- change or demife theyre lands, in ether of the hofpitalles, without my fpeciall affent and confent therunto required. And forafmuch as there hath bin a ftocke of XII kine and a bull, which now is no longer in beinge, but is alienated from the hof- pytall at Harbaldowne, and the lands and houfes which wear made over to the hofpitall to fecure the fayd ftocke have of late bin releafed ; my order is, that the matter be throughe examined, and that wee may be certified. And feeinge ther is a new farmer of late admitted, which hathe taken upon him to make good ther ftock at the end of XXI years; I hold it neceffarye that he give in good cau- tion to the hofpitall, and that fubfidie men be bound with him and for him.

3. I think it fitt and convenient that the mafter of the hofpitalles have a coppie of theis ftatutes ; and therfore doe foe ordayn, that for the prefearving of the letter of the ftatute from defacinge or razinge, and for which the brothers of Harbal- downe have bin heretofore challenged by my predeceffor, that the mafter by offer- ing the coppies of bothe bookes, the ftatutes beinge the fame in bothe hofpittales, tranfcribe a perfeft copie of all ftatutes and injunftions therin contayned, for his direftio :.

4. I doe furthermor injoyne that the mineftre in either of the hofpitalles, acording to my Lord Archbyfhoppe Parker's injunftions, be equall with the prior in all thinges. And confequently that he be called to all fraternities and meetings; and that noe bu- fynefs of the hofpitalls be tranfafted without him.

5. That in regard that the evidences and writinges of the hofpitall at Harbaldown have bine lofelye kept, and fom embeayzeled ; as it is thoughte, which if ther be good proofe, I will furely punifh ; I doe likewife appoint, that the minefter of Harbaldown, in regard that he is a fworne in-brother, and is otherwife made equall to the prior in all refpeftes, have one of the three keyes of the muniment chefte.

6. That the prior and his affiftants at Harbaldowne produce theyre ancient original rentall in parchment, which is ufuallie kept in everie hofpitall, and hathe the lyke lat- lye bin fhewed to the mafter by the brothers of St. John's ; which if they fhall fayle to exhibite, I fhall have jufte caufe to fufpeft that thay have loft or embeazeled it, amonge other writinge, or els that thay doe on purpofe conceale it to cover theire mifdemeanours in defraudinge of the bretheren of their right, for which thay have bin fufpefted and challenged, and fhall be by me condignely punifhed.

* So numbered in the Original.

7. Further-

7. Furthermore, becaufe that the treafure or ftocke of mony belonginge to the hofpitall at Harbaldowne is now in the hands of needy perfons, whofe wants and neceffities may drive them to unlawfull practices; I doe enjoyne them to give an account quarterlie of all their refytes, and particularlie to fhew what hath bin expended; and their feveral items and reckonninges to be alowed by a competent number of the brothers.

8. Wheereas their hath bin a cuftome amongft the brothers of St. John's, that the executor of a deceafed brother doth claime fomtimes a quarters, fomtimes halfe a yeares profit, after his death, to the prejudice of the next fucceffor; I doe utterlye abolifh that order, as unjuft, uñlawful, and unconfcionable; and doe appoint the brother or fifter prefenlye upon his admiffion to enter upon all profitts and emoluments that maye accrew unto him by the houfe.

9. The lyke cuftome at Harbaldowne of exactinge xv s̃. vi ď. of a brother to be admitted *, befydes his reparation noble, I doe utterlye abolifh as a meer extortion; as a'fo that St. John's of exacting x s̃. at admiffion; and whatfoever payments for drinking at burialles, wherwith the poor are wrongfully burthened.

10. I doe precifelie forbid forrainers and ftrangers, who are not members of the houfe, to be lodged in either of the hofpitalls; and if any fuche have hertofore out of indulgence bin admitted, that thay prefentlye voyd the houfe.

11. Wheras yt is not the true meaninge of the ftatutes, nor the practife of anye well-ordered hofpitall, that marryed couples fhould cohabit and lodge together within any of our hofpitalles, the place beinge cheefly intended to fingle perfons, and fuch as have a purpofe fo to continew (to which form I purpofe, God willinge, hereafter to reduce them); yet, becaufe fuche married couples are now harbored within our fayd hofpitalles, upon good advife I doe order, that the hufbands or wives of fuch as are in-brothers or in-fifters, fhall give bond to voyd the houfe immediatelye upon the death of the faid in-brothers or in-fifters.

12. Furthermor, wheareas there are children borne in our hofpitalles, and others are nurfed and brought up there, to the annoyance of the places, and with which the hofpitalles are lyke to be burthened; becaufe I knowe that to be agaynft the intent and meaninge of the ftatutes, that woemen that are breeders, and within the age of childbearinge fhould be admitted in-fifters; I doe therfore cõmand that my Lord Whiteguiftes injunctions in this behalfe mad and fet downe in both ther ftatute-bookes, concerninge the forbiddinge of children to be brought into the hofpitalles †, be forthwith put in execution, and that the hofpitalles be ridde and freed from thes incombrances.

13. Laftlye, touchinge the fucceffion unto the voyd houfes or gardens of any in-brothers or fifters deceafed, I am contented thay paffe accordinge to fenioritie, unles, by beinge a difordered perfon, the next fenior be thought unworthie and uncapable of this favour. Provided alwayes, that I referve unto myfelfe a power freelye to give houfe and garden when I fhall thinke it fitt, this my confent herein delivered notwithftandinge. Auguft 17, 1618.

---

* 3s. 4d. is all that is now paid (in bread and beer) to the brothers and fifters, at each hofpital, on admiffion. D.

† See p. 220.

By

By the Lorde Archbifhope of Canterbury [Sheldon] his Grant, 19th of February 1663.

BEING given to underftand that the in-brothers and fifters of my two hofpitalls of Northgate and Harbledowne, after there admiffion, doe fometimes
marry, and that to ftrangers, perfons not members of the houfe, nor fubjeft or
fworne to the orders and goveinment of the fame, and fuch fometimes as bringe a
traine of children alonge with them, to the great incumbrance of the houfe, and
the defeating the founder's intention :

For remedie, therefore, and prevention of this abufe and corruption in time to
come, I doe hereby order and decree, that if any in-brother or in fifter of either of
my faid hofpitalls, already admitted or to be admitted, fhall heereafter marry to
or with any perfon that fhall not then be a member of the houfe, hee or fhee foe
marrying fhall ipfo fafto forfeite and forgoe his or her in-brothers or in-fifters place ;
and fhall forthwith quitt or be expelled the houfe. And that this my order and
decree may have its full effeft, my further will and pleafure is, that it bee forthwith entred and regiftred in the ftatute-booke of each hofpitall, that every brother
and fifter may take notice of it, and conforme unto it as a ftatute, which by there
oath they fhall bee obliged to obferve equally with the reft. Given under my
hand and figne manuall att Lambeth, the nyneteenth day of February, 1663.

GILB. CANT.

Archbifhop Sancroft's Regulations, 1686.

To the Mafters, Priors, Brothers, and Sifters of the Hofpitalls of St. Nickolas in
Harbledowne, and St. John's Norgthgate, neere Canterbury, refpeftively,

WILLIAM Lord Archbifhop of Canterbury fends greetinge in our Lord God.
Wheareas wee have bin informed that fom of the in-brothers and in-fifters
of our hofpitalls of St. Nicholas in Harbledowne, and St. John's Northgate, neare
Canterbury, doe live and vend in other places, and not in the houfes allotted to
them in the faid hofpitalls, without any leave or difpenfation from us had, contrary to the ftatuts of the faid hofpitalls, whereby, and befides many other inconveniences, the faid houfes goe much to decay and ruine : For the prevenfion of
thefe mifchiefes, wee do heareby decree and ordaine, that all fuch perfons before
menfhoned, who at prefent live out of the faid hofpitalls, and have houfes there,
doe, before the feaft of St. John Baptis next enfewing, repair to and dwell in
theire faid houfes, except thay obtaine our difpenfacion according to the ftatuts
of the fayd hofpetalls : And that the priors of the refpeftive hofpitalls fhall, upon
the receipt heareof, forthwith give notis to the perfons confernd, that if thay doe
not obey this order, the prior fhall detaine theire ftipend for the publick ufe of the
hofpitall ; and if thay doe not perform this order within fix monts after the feaft
of St. John Baptis, there places fhall be pronounced in the Frater-hall by the mafter

ter and prior of each hospitall to be actually void, of wich the prior shall give notis to us and our succeslors, under his hand as usealy.. And if heareafter any in-brother or in-sister that shall be admitted into ether of the said hospitalls shall not dwell in their respective houses within one month after there admittance, then there stipends shall be detained as before for the publick use; and if within six monts aft that thay shall not com and actually inhabit there, that then their place shall be actually void, as in case of death. And case wee or our succeslors shall see reson to grant any such dispensasion to any person, yet the prior of each hospitall shall detaine after the rate of sixpence a month, during there absence, out of the pension of each person soe dispensed with, to be layd out one the repaires of their sayd hoses soe uninhabited, in case thay want any, and if not, for the publick repairs of the hospitall. And for the better keeping of the said houses in repaire for the time to com, we doe heareby order and decree, that twice in the yeare, to wit, in the month of March and September, the master, or such persons as he shall apoint, with the prior of each, shall take a perticuler survay of the wants of repaires of all the houses and bildings in both hospitalls; and in case any of them neede repairing, the prior shall forthwith give notis to the respective persons concernd therein, that within two month thay make good such repaires; and in case thay neglect to make good such repaires within the said time, the prior of each hospitall imediate-ly, with the approbashon of the master of the hospitall, set men one worke to make good such repaires, and deduct the charges of doeing thereof out of the stipends of the sayd partis; and the prior shall take care that the publique bildings, such as the chappell and hall, and other bildings, of each hospitall, be repaird; and that the master of the said hospitalls give us and our succeslors notis of the observation of this decree every year in the month of October.

And whearras som persons, by reason of age and imfermite, cannot be suffi-chently provided for alone by the stipends of the respective hospitalls, wee doe heareby further decree and ordaine, that, before the admishon of any in-brother or in-sister, ether the officer of the parish from whence thay com, or som other sub-stantiall person, shall give security-by bond to the respective priors for the time be-ing, in case the master of the respective hospitalls require the same, that, by reson of sicknes, age, or other infirmites, such persons admited cannot live and be main-tained by the stipend of the said hospitalls only, that then such further resonable alowance shall be made to them, out of the respective parishes whence such pear-sons com, as the Deane of Christ Church Canterbury, or the Mayor of Canterbury for the time being, or any one of the justices of peace, not being of the said pa-rish, shall think fit to order to be alowed *. And wee doe allsoe heareby injoyne the strict performance of the statuts of each hospitalls, against the admishon of

* Certificates, which had been usual, being ineffectual as the Hospitals are extra-parochial; such a bond as is above required is now given, on every admission, by some friend of the pauper, obliging himself, under a penalty of 20 l. to pay weekly whatever two justices of the peace for the county may order, in case the person admitted should by accident or infirmity be unable to subsist on the stipend of the Hospital. D.

          I

chilldren and grand chilldren, or other perfons to dwell with the faid in-brothers or in-fifters in ether hofpitall, unles it be found needfull by the mafter of the hofpitall for any of the in-brothers or in-fifters to have fom com of theue chilldren or relations to nurs them in their infirmities and ficknes, and that the mafter of the hofpitalle doe imediately examin what perfons in each hofpitall now refiding are concerned in this decree, and fee it imediately put in execufion, and certifie this allfo to us and our fucceffors in the month of October every yeare, as before.

And wee doe heareby further order and decree, that all payments and ftipends, payable to any in-brother or in-fifter, or out-brother or out-fifter, that fhall dy or depart this life at any time heareafter fhall goe and be payd from the time of there death into the reparacōn purfe of the refpective hofpitalls untill the day of admittance of fum other perfon or perfons into there refpective place or places; and once in a yeare, in the month of October, the faid reparation purfe fhall be caft up, and acount made by the prior to the mafter of all the payments and difburfments relating to the fame, which account fhall be made apart by itfelfe.

And wee doe allfoe heareby injoyne and command, that the readers of each refpective hofpitall fhall ftrictly obferve the ftatuts of the fame hofpitalls, in catechifing the in-brothers and in-fifters, efpefhaly in the time of Lent; and in cafe he be remis therein, the mafter of the faid hofpitalls fhall informe us thereof; and in cafe any of the in-brothers or in-fifters fhall be neglygent in their duty hearein, thay fhall be feverly punefhed acording to the ftatutes. And our will and command is, that thefe feverall decrees and orders, and things contained, be forthwit tranfcribed into the boock of ftatuts of the refpective hofpitalls, and forever heareafter be performed and kept as the reft of theire ftatuts are and ought to bee. Given under our archiepifcopal feal, this fourth day of March, in the third yeare of the reain of our foverin Lord James the Second, by the grace of God, over England, Scotland, France, and Ireland king, defender of the faith, and of our confecrafione the tenth, anno Domini 1686.

38. Sequeftration of Eaftbridge Hofpital by Abp. Courtney, 25 July, 1394. This feems to be an ancient copy.

WILL'M'S, permiffione divina Cantuarien' archiepus, tocius Angl' primas, & aplice fedis legatus, dilectis in Xpo filiis magro Wilto Savage, in legibus baccalaureo, & Johi Bedell, notario publico, ac rectori ecclie beate Marie de Biedman ire dioc', falutem, gratiam, & benedictionem. Ad nrm nuper pveñit auditum quod nonnulla onera hofpit' Sci Thome martyris de Eaftbregge, ire civitat' Cantuar' incumbencia, minime fupportant', hofpitalique pdict' nonnullis punic' & accoib' tam in domibus quam in rebus aliis ad ipfum hofpital' pertinentibus abinde nofcitur in prefenti: Nos igitur, ex caufis predictis & aliis nos in hac parte moventibus, omnes & fingulos fructus, redditus, & pvenciones hofpit' pdci tam pfentes quam futuros dirigimus fequeſtrand', prout tenore p̄ſencium fequeſtramus, vobis committim' & veſtrum alter' diviſim coinmittim' & mandam' quacumque fequeſtr' nr̄m h̄moī publi-tantes & ad ipſor' pro *mteſos* * notitia deducentes fructus, redditus, & provenc' hoſpi-tal' p̄di' ſub arta & ſalva cuſtodia fequeſtr' ſicun p̱ eiſdem v̄ro volueritis periculo ſpondere, donec aliud a nobis ſuper hoc h̄ueritis in mandatis ; contradictores quoſcun-que auctoritate n̄ra apoſtolica compeſcendo. Et q̄m̄d' in p̄miſſ' feceritis, ſeu v̄rm alt' fecerit, nos, cum ex pte n̄ra fueritis requiſiti, diſtincte & aperte certificetis lris v̄ris patentibus habentibus hunc tenorem ſigillo autentico conſignatis. Dat' in ma-nerio noſtro de Maydenſtan, xxv die Julii, anno Dn̄i millo ccc nonogeſimo quarto,. & n̄re tranſlationis xiii.

39. An Indulgence from William (of Wykeham) Bp. of Wincheſter to this Hoſ-pital to aſk alms through his dioceſe, 22 Jan. 1355. The ſeal very fair. (ſee plate III. fig. 12.)

WILL'S, permiſſione divina, Wynton' epūs, dilectis filiis univerſis abbatibus,. prioribus, archidiaconis n̄ris Wynton' & Surr', & eorum offic', decanis, tem-poralib' rector', vicariis, & capellanis parochianis nobis ſubditis p̱ n̄ras civitatem & dioc' conſtitutis, ſalutem in amplexibus Salvatoris. Indigenciis pauperum fratrum & fororum hoſpitalis Sc̄i Nicholai de Herbaldown paterno comparentes affectu ; uni-verſitatem veſtram rogamus & oramus, cum fratres p̄dc̄i vel eorum veri nuncii ad vos, venerint, pro elemoſinis Xp̄i fidelium petendis ac eciam colligendis, ipſos pauperes ſeu nuncios admittatis benigne, eiſdemque ad ſuſtentacōem eorum gratia capiatis, ſubſidia erogetis, & pauperes erogari & ſubditam vobis plebem hujuſmodi ſubſidia eiſdem liberar' integral' facientes. Et ut ad id mentes v̄re ac aliorum fidelium ppen-ſius excitentur, de Dei omnipotentis miſericordia,. beate & glorioſe ſemperque vir-ginis Marie genitricis ejuſdem, necnon & beatorum apoſtolorum Petri & Pauli, ſanctorumque, confeſſorum, virginum, S. Mich' Archangeli, omniumque ſanctorum & precibus confidentes, omnibus Xp̄icolis p̱ n̄ras civitatem & dioceſim confitentes, & aliis p̱ n̄ram dioceſem, hanc n̄ram indulgentiam ratam habuerunt & acceptam, peccatis ſuis vere pœnitentibus & confeſſis, que de bonis ſibi a Dei collatis quicquam contu-lerunt, legaverint, ſeu quoviſmodo aſſignaverint fratribus & fororibus ſupradictis, ac. pro ſtatu, tranquillitate, & pace eccleſie, regis, & regni Angl', ac animabus omnium fidelium defunctorum, devote oraverint, quadraginta dies indulgencie concedimus p̱ p̄ſentes ; ratificantes inſuper, quantum in nobis eſt, omnes indulgencias in hac parte pro conceſſis, & n̄ris temporibus concedendas. In cujus rei teſtimonium, ſigillum nr̄m fecimus huic apponi. Dat' apud Suthwerk, xxii° die menſis Januar', anno Dn̄i millo ccc° quinquageſimo quinto, & n̄re conſ' decimo.

* This word,. though certainly wrong, we cannot better decypher.

40. A

40. Copy (with an interlined Tranflation) of the Survey of Herbaldown Hofpital, taken by K. Henry VIII's Commiffioners, by virtue of his Commiffion. Dated 14 Feb. ann' reg' 37, 1546.

The Tranflation (abovementioned) is as follows:

County of Kent.   The Hofpital of St. Nicholas of Harbaldowne.

IN the furvey, or yearly value, of all and fingular colledges, free-chapels, chanteries, hofpitalls, brotherhoods, guilds, and ftipendiaries whatfoever, having any perpetuall ftipend or perpetuity, fcituat and being in the faid county of Kent, and charged or chargeable to the payment of firft-fruits and tenths, taken and had before the reverend Father in Chrift Thomas [Cranmer] archbifhop of Canterbury, Henry [Holbeach] bifhop of Rochefter, Thomas Cheyney, John Baker, Thomas Moyle, Richard Longe, John Guildeford, and William Finche, knights, Anthony Aucher, —— Sydley, Paul Sidney, Richard Modye, Thomas Spylman, and Thomas Greene, efquires, ohn Ofborne, Thomas Walton, and John Wyte, gentlemen, commiffioners of our lord king Henry VIII. by vertue of his commiffion dated 8th day of February in the year of his reign 37th, to enquire as well of the true yearly value of the faid colledges, and other the premiffes, as in divers other articles in the faid commiffion fpecified, according to the tenor and effect of a certaine act in parliament at Weftminfter in the faid 37th year of the forefaid king holden, in that behalfe publifhed and provided, amongft other things is contained as followeth:

> The fcite and one gardin, with one orchard*, conteining by eftimation III acres, in the tenure and occupation of the prior and brethren, prioriffe and fifters of the hofpitall, to their and the common ufe of the hofpitall, now extended by the yeare   xx ̈s.
>
> A farme † of one meffuage, two barnes and one ftable, within the faid fcite, and of one clofe of arrable land, called XVIII acres, and of another clofe to the fame adjoyning,

* This old orchard, containing two acres and a half, 20 perches, and Ifabel Mead (afterwards mentioned) containing 13 acres and a half, are now let on leafe to Mrs. Elizabeth Lanfell at a referved rent of 14 l. per ann.

† This farm, now called The Brotherhood Farm, with Brentsfield, Lawrence Tenement, Ladder's Croft, the Grove, &c. in the whole 41 acres, and 9 roods, are now let on leafe to Mrs. Elizabeth Young at a referved rent of 43 l. 10 s.

I i 2

con-

conteining VIII acres, as also of one croft, called The Ladder, conteining IIII acres, and also of one close called Greate Brents, conteining V acres, and of one croft, to the same adjoyning, called Little Brents, conteining II acres, and of one close arrable, with a peece of land adjoyning, called Dunland, conteining VII acres, and of one pasture called The Grove, conteining II acres, [in the whole XXXVI acres,] so demised to John Bynge by indenture dated   day   yeare   VII l. XV s. IIII d.

of the now king Henry VIIIth, for the terme of seven yeares, yeilding therefore at the feasts of th'Annunciation of the blessed Virgin Mary and of St. Michael th'Archangell, in moneyes VI. and in the price of II quarters of greene pease XIII s. IV d. ten measures of wheate or corne VIII s. IV d. five quarters of oates X s. one hogge II s. and the pasture of ten cowes and of one bull with straw to be fedd, between the feast of St. Andrew th'apostle, and St. George the martyr, XXI s. VIII d. and XX d. the head. In all by the yeare

The scite of the said hospitall, with the demesnelands, and with diverse quit-rents apperteining to the same.

Rents of assize of diverse tenements in the parishes underwritten, to wit, The going out of a tenement in the tenure of John Codington lying in the parish of St. Margaret of the said city, V s. the going out of a tenement in the tenure of Thomas Dandye in the Isle of Hartey, III s. for the quittrent going out of lands called Westbroke felde in the tenure of John Churche within the parish of Hearne *, III s. IV d. for the like rent issuing out of the lands of Alexander Howlett in the parish of Reculver, as in the price of one quarter of barley, II s. for rent going out of a tenement in the parish of Stelling in the tenure of the heirs of Lente.   In the whole by the yeare   XIV s. I d.

* Heron in the Latin throughout.

The

The farme of one tenement within the said scite in the tenure of   Carter at will. By the yeare ⟩ XVI s.

The farme of one clofe, paftur, heath-ground, call d Ifabel meade [*], conteining twenty acres, XL s. of one pecce of land in Devington mede, conteining three rods, II s. in the tenure and occupation of the faid prio[r] and prioriffe, for the common ufe of the hofpitall, but valued in the whole by the yeare ⟩ XLII s.

The parifhes of St. Michael of Harbaldowne, St. Dunftan, St. Paul, Goodnefton, and Chiftlet.

The farme of one tenement and gardin in the parifh of St. Michael of Harbaldowne, lying nigh the well there, in the tenure of Giles Allyn at will, by yeare ⟩ VII s.

The farme of diverfe tenements in the parifh of St. Dunftan of the faid city, in the tenure of [George Hunt, x s. Henry Maye, VI s. VIII d. John Bold, VI s. VIII d. Robert Capper, VI s. VIII d. John   , IIII s. Agnes   , III s. and Thomas   , VIII s.[†]] fo to them dimifed at will. The whole by yeare ⟩ XLV s

The farme of three tenements in Ivelane in the parifh of St. Paul, at will dimifed ⟩ X s.

The farme of one acre of land in the parifh of Goodnefton lying neer the tenement of   Bull, in the tenure of John Bull, at will, by the yeare ⟩ XXII s.

The farme of two crofts called Devell's Gate, in the parifh of Heron or Chiftlett, conteining IIII acres, III rodds, in the tenure of John Churche, at will. By yeare ⟩ VII s.

The farme of xx acres of land in the parifh of Herne, to wit, of the third part of LX [‡] acres of land in three parts divided, in the tenure of John Byngeham, as by the indenture above, among the lands of the hofpital of St. John without Northgate, Canterbury, is remembered. By the yeare ⟩ XXV s. I d.

* See note † p. 227.
† Omitted in the tranflation.
‡ Now 50 acres, more or lefs, let on leafe to Mrs. Jane Tucker, at a referved rent of 14 l. of which the third part is 4 l. 13 s. 4 d.

The

Farmes in diverſe pariſhes.	The farme of the moyety of a tenement and lands in the pariſh of Goodneſtone called Rowlinge, conteiring xciv acres of land*, in the tenure of William Joley, by indenture above, among the lands and poſſeſſions of the ſaid hoſpital of St. John recited. By the yeare	xli ſ. viii d.
	The farme of the paſturing of fourteen ſheepe, and one rodd of merſh-land, in the pariſh of Graveney, in the tenure of John Okeden, by indenture, dated day yeare of the now king Henry VIIIth. By yeare	iiii ſ.†
	Part of the fee-farme of the citty of Canterbury, by the grante of Henry [II.] ſometime king of England, &c.	xiii l. vi ſ. viii d. ‡
Annuities and penſions.	A certaine annuitie, iſſuing out of the lands of the late monaſtery of the Church of Chriſt, Canterbury, yearlie allowed, by decree of the counſell of the Court of Augmentations, and by the hand of the receiver of the ſaid court in the county of Kent. Paid by yeare	lxviii ſ. vii d. ‖
	A certaine like annuity, iſſuing out of the lands of the late priorie of Leeds, allowed by the aforeſaid decree, and by the hands of the ſaid receiver. Paid by yeare	x ſ. ‖
	A certaine annual penſion, or annuity, iſſuing out of the manors of Reculver and Boughton, and out of the rectory of Reculver, by the Archbiſhop of Canterbury. Paid by the yeare	lxxx l.

* Now let on leaſe to Sir Narborough D'Aeth, Bart. at a reſerved rent of 16 l. per ann. to each hoſpital, and three buſhels of wheat. By a map in the hoſpital-cheſt, taken in 1617, there were then only 80 acres and a half, and 29 perches, at 16 feet and a half to the rod. Now by eſtimation there are 88

† This is now probably dwindled into an annuity of 2 s. per ann. paid by John Lade, Eſq. See p. 179.

‡ The ſame ſum is ſtill paid by the chamberlain. See the grant, p. 205, N° 4.

‖ For theſe two ſums, now making together 3 l. 18 s. 6 d. two debentures are annually delivered to the maſter, or his order, ſoon after Michaelmas, by the auditor of the king's land-revenue (or fee-farm rents) by virtue of which it is paid as above, by the receiver-general of that revenue for Kent, Surrey, and Suſſex; at preſent James Beſt, Eſq.

```
      7 s.  4 d.  two debentures.
      4     2    receiver's fee.
      ─────────
     11     6
      ─────────
      3    7   0 clear.
```

See the Appendix to Northgate, Chap. II. N° II.

5

De-

Deductions.

Fees.

Fees to the collector of the rents of the lands and poffeffions of the 'forefaid hofpi-tall. By the yeare — xxvi s. viii d

Rents re-ferved.

Rents paid out, iffuing out of diverfe lands and tenements, parcell of the poffef-fions of the aforefaid hofpitall, to wit, to the maner of Weftgate, for rent of the fcite of the faid hofpitall and parcell of de-mefne lands, xv s. 11 d.* to the maner of Tunford, for rent of parcel of the demefne lands xviii s. x d. to the maner of Thytche for rent of land called Ifabel Meade viii s. 1111 d. to the deane and chapter of Canterbu-ry, for rent of a parcell of wood-land there, 11 d. to William Fyneux, Efquire, for rent of land called Devell'sGate [in Herne], xv d. to the king's majefty, for rent of tenements in Ive lane, xvi d †; to the church-wardens to St. Dunftan, for rent of tenements in the parifh there, xii d. to John Freeman, for rent of two tenements in the fame parifh, called Blanket Houfe, vi d. to the manor of Wyngeham, for rent of land called Rol-lynge, xiii s. 1111 d. and to the manor of Herne, for rent of twenty acres of land there, iii s. and to the manor of Welcourte v s. ix d. In the whole by the yeare — lxviii s. viii d.

And it is clerely worth, above all the de-ductions aforefaid, by the yeare — cxii l. ‡

Woods and under-woods.

One wood, called The Hofpitall Wood, lying on the fouth part of the king's highway leading towarde Canterbury, nere the Hermi-tage there in the parifh of St. Michael of Harbaldowne, contein-ing by eftimation xx acres.

One other wood, called Brotherhood Wood, lying on the north fide of the faid way, nere Bofomden Wood, in the parifh aforefaid conteining by eftimation x acres ‖.

Ten acres are of age fufficient to be cutt downe, every acre being of the value of xxvi s. viii d.

* The fame fum is ftill paid to that manor.
† This quit-rent is now paid to the city of Canterbury.
‡ The exact fum is 112 l. 19s. 3 d.
‖ The North Wood now contains 15 acres, the South Wood 48.

he

41. The Anſwere of the Brothers and the Curate or Chauntrie Prieſt * of the Hoſpital of Saynte Nycoles of Herbaldowne to certen Articles to them mynyſtred by the Kyng's Majeſtie's Commiſſioners. Hen. VIII. (Not dated.)

TO the fyrſt we anſwere, that we have a chauntrie prieſt which hathe the care of all the brothers and ſuſters within the ſaid hoſpitall, and mynyſtreth unto us all the ſacraments when need requyreth, and ſaithe devyne ſervice, according to his foundacyon; and the ſaid prieſt is one of the number of the brothers of the ſaid hoſpitall in part of his ſtypend. Alſo the ſaid prieſt hathe exhybyrid a rentall, wherein is conteynid all the revenues, profyts unto the ſaid chauntre prieſt of the ſaid hoſpitall, and the yerly reſolving and deductions beying goyng owt of the ſame.

Impiimis, a howſe where the prieſt dwellith callid Clavering, and an orchard adjoinyng to the hoſpitall, be eſtimacõn worth yerly,   XIII ſ. IIII d̃.

Item, a tenement aginſt th'hoſpitall of Harbaldowne and a gardin at IIII acres and halfe acre of lande thereto adjoynyng by eſtymacion, worth yerly,   XXII ſ. VIII d̃.

Item, divers lands callid Mekynbroke lyeng in the pariſhe of Herne, whiche lands perteynethe to the maſter of th'hoſpitall of Eaſtbryg in Canterbury, and payeth yerly to the ſaid prieſt,   III l. VI ſ. VIII d̃.

Item, owte of Hoth corte lying in the pariſhe of Coſmas Blean, the whiche lands parteyneth to the maſter of th'hoſpitall of Eaſtbryg in Canturbury, and paithe yerly,   XXXIII ſ. IIII d̃.

Item, the ſaid prieſt is one of the numbre of the poor brothers of the ſaid hoſpitall, and recevythe yerly for his porcyon as other doth ther by eſtimacion   XXXIII ſ. IIII d̃.

Summa VIII l. XIII ſ. IIII d̃.

Whereof is paid yerly to m̃r Fynyx of Herne for quyt rent for a tenement, above wryttyn   III ſ. VI d̃.
And III hens and a koke for the ſame tenement,   XIIII d̃. ob̃.
Diſſolved anno ſ lo Ed. Sexti.

42. 1. An order for the recovery of certain lands to the Hoſpital at Herbaldown, 17 June, 12 Char. I. 1637.

42. 2. A writt of execution of a decree of charitable uſes for the Hoſpital of St. Nicholas Herbaldoune, in Kent. It is to Mary Counteſs of Weſtmoreland and Arthur Ruck her tenant, to reſtore three acres and a half in Larons tenement, and one in the field called Rede, formerly given to the Hoſpital by John de Thongford, 21 April, 14 Charles I. 1639.

43. Letter of Attorney to William Oliver the prior to collect the rents granted to the Hoſpitals by Capt. Charles Bowles (which rents had been purchaſed by him of the Parliament's feoffees) in lieu of their augmentation money, 8 July, 1659.

* Then probably George Haggys. See p. 183.

44. A

44. A Remonftrance of ill ufage from a tenant (of and to whom is not faid) in behalf of the Hofpital, dated from Chrift Church, Canterbury, 18 Aug. 1591, by John Hyll *.

MY duty and commendations to your worfhip remēbred, &c. The poore bro-thers of Harbaldowne Hofpitall do mofte humbly crave your worfhip's fa-vour in the matters that are in controverfye. They thinke themfelves to be hardly ufed at your farmers handes,

Dunlands.

Firft, for Dunlande, where theire deedes do manifeftly leade them to have an aker, a roode, and the eight parte of an aker, and yet your worfhip's farmer doth wytheholde the fame from them and occupieth it, before there be any determination of the controverfye, for he wolde neaver yet, fince the meafurynge of it, lett them underftande what the quantitie of it was. Howbeit, by there owne meafurynge of it, they fynde that there is ynowghe in the peece to allowe to your worfhip nyne acres and xxx perches, and 1 aker, 1 roode, and ix perches to remayne to the Hofpitall, befydes that whiche lyeth betwyxte the Burne and the edge of the eightyne akers as parte of the xviii akers.

Lauron's Tenement.

Secondly, For Larones tenemente, the pece as it now lieth con-teyneth, by their meafuremente, eight akers and eight perches, for the whiche they have divers deedes of fundry parcells, whiche, by great probabilitie, do leade them to thinke that to be theire owne lande, as firfte one deede of 1111 acres dī, gyven by John of Tun-forde, wherof 111 acres dī. lye in a fielde called by the name of La-rones Tenemente, and 1 acre lyeth in a fielde called the Rede †, and 11 acres were gyven by Peter Durante and Felix his wyffe, whiche alfo were confirmed by Joane of Dufhington. Alfo in the before named dede of John of Tunforde (wherin he gyveth them 1111 acres dī.) he furthermore gyveth them the halfe of that lande whiche he purchafed of the tenemente of Levenote, lyinge in the fame fielde called Larones tenemente; whiche halfe parte, if it be efteemed at 1 acre dī. and viii peerches, added to the reft, will make up viii acres viii perches. And that this fhowlde be theire Larones tenement, it hathe this probabilitie for prooffe, the Rede and Larones Tene-ment do joygne togeather; but it is certen that the Rede is parte of this viii acres which they call Larones Tenement, for it lieth in the northweft corner of it: yea, your worfhip's owne note under Sir Ch. Hale's hande (unles I be deceyved) doth by an interlyne note the Rede to be Larones Tenement, or in Larones Tenement, whiche if it

* B. D. prebendary of Canterbury, which he obtained by exchange with Dr. John Pory for a canonry of Weftminfter, in 1568. By this letter it fhould feem that he was alfo mafter of the Hofpital. He died in 1595.
† See p. 232, N° 42, 2.

be

be granted, then is there no dowbte but that fielde muſt neades be Larones Tenemente. And to proove that that fielde is not Northbygberye (as your worſhip ſuppofeth) the brothers ſay, that they have inquired of the awncinteſt inhabitantes therabout, who do affirme that Northbygbery lyeth above the bowndes of that fielde weſtwarde, and Sowthbygberye lyeth ſowth from Larones Tenement and Northbygberie, and that the two Bygberies are devyded by a footepath betwixte them. And therfore they humbly crave of your worſhip, that you wolde fearche amonge youre owne evydences how the ſayd Northbygbery is bownded, for thereby the truthe wolde appeare. For if your Northbygbery be bownded any way as is that pece of viii acres viii peerches, whiche they call Larones Tenemente, then hath youre worſhip great probabilitie on youre ſyde, otherwyſe the probabilitie is greate for them.

Theire thirde grieffe is towchinge Lokers Crofte, which your worſhip claymeth from them, only by a bownde mentioned in an indenture of exchange betwixte Sir Tho. Fogge, Knyght and them, whiche myght be ſett downe by ſome error of the wryter of the ſayd indenture, or by overſyght and unſkilfulnes in takynge of the bowndes; but if it myght pleaſe your worſhip to ſhew ſome deede that bowndeth the ſame, they wolde quietly ſtand theruntoe, for that wolde put all owt of dowbte, otherwyſe they think theire deede to carry more probabilitie than that indenture. That fielde bowndeth upon Goldhill northe, upon the way leadynge from Canterbury to Chilham eaſte, upon Dunlande ſowth and weſt, whiche bowndes, if they be mentioned in any of youre worſhip's deedes, the matter wil be cleare. But this they complayne of in the meane while, that your worſhip putteth them to make evydent prooffe by theire deedes, and for lack therof do take the lande from them, and yet youreſelfe do ſhew no deedes to proove it your owne by any bowndes mentioned therin.

Lockyer's Crofte.

Youre worſhip's note ſayth that Lokeres Crofte is the ſame that is called Lader Crofte, whiche you proove by a rentale, thus noted in the margyne, " Loker's Crofte p rentale modo vocat' Lader Crofte." But that this conjecture ſeemeth not to be true, it thus appeareth: There are two ſeverall deedes of the two croftes, and Loker's Crofte in the deede therof is bownded only upon the higheway leadynge from Canterbury to Chilham; but Lader Crofte, in the deed therof, is bownded not only upon the ſayd highewaye ſowth, but alſo to the eightyne akers eaſt, and to Parnels Croſſe Lane north and weſt. If they were all one, they wolde be alyke bownded; but ſo they are not, and therfore it is lyke that they are ſeverall peces. Wherfore the note ſeemeth to be but an erroneous conjecture of him that made it.

Theire fourth and laſte gryeffe is the takynge of the wheat ſowen upon the overplus of grownde in Turnforde fielde, wherin notwythſtandynge, they hope to fynde more favor at your worſhip's handes than is pretended by your farmer, the rather
Theire

becaufe the lande was fowen before this controverfy was mooved ; for if the farmer had knowne that he fhowlde have byne inhibited to take the croppe, it is not lyke that he wolde have cared it and fowen his feade upon it. They humbly crave therfore of youre worfhip, that it myght pleafe you to take fome refonable re-compence for the lande for this tyme, and herafter they wyll abfteyne from inter-medlynge upon youre lande and kepe wythin theire owne bowndes, and fhew them-felves thankfull for your worfhip's favor.

Thus have I delivered unto your worfhip the fumme of theire grieffes, and wyth-all the growndes and reafons whiche they alleadge for themfelves, whiche I have done to th'end youre worfhip may confider of them, and therupon refolve as fhall feeme good unto your wyfdome. And whatfoever it fhall pleafe your worfhip to returne for anfwere to thofe four poyntes, either for the overthrowynge of theire clayme and reafons, or for the eftablifhinge of youre owne ryghte, I fhall fayth-fully delyver unto them, to fatisfie them as muche as fhall lye in me, and to kepe them quiett and contented. And thus, wyfshinge and prayinge for your worfhip's health, I commend the fame unto the Lorde. Canterbury, from Chrift Churche, the 18th of Auguft, 1591.   Youre worfhip's to his power, JOHN HYLL.

45. Bull of Pope John * confirming the poffeffions of Herbaldown Hofpital, and exempting them from Tithes. [1319.]

JOHANNES epus, fervus fervorum Dei, dilectis filiis Priori & fratribus hof-pitalis leprofor' Sci Nicholai de Herbaldon', Cantuarien' dioc', falem & aplicam benedictionem. Sacrofancta Romana ecclefia devotos & humiles filios ex affuete pietatis officio propencius dirigere confuevit, &, ne pravorum hominum mo-leftiis agitantur, eos tanquam pia mater fue protectionis munimine confovere. Ea-propter, dilecti in Domino filii, veftris juftis poftulacionibus grato concurrentes affenfu, perfonas veftras, & locum in quo fub communi vita degitis, cum omnibus bonis que impfenciar' raconabiliter poffidetis, aut in futur' juftis modis, dante Do-mino, poteritis adipifci, fub beati Petri & fira protecone fufcepimus ; fpecialiter au-tem terras, domos, pratum, pafcua, grangias, maneria, nemora, molendina, pif-carias, jura, jurifdictiones, vineas, ortos, & alia bona fra, ficut ea jufte ac pacifice obtinetis, nobis, & per nos hofpitali veftro aplica auctoritate confirmamus, & pfentis fcripti patrocinio munimimus ; diftriccius inhibentes ne quis de ortis & virgultis† vris, feu de fror' aialium inftrumentis decimas a vobis exigere vel extorquere pfumat. Nulli ergo omnino homini liceat hanc paginam fire pteccionis, confirmationis, & in-hibiconis infringere, vel ei aufu temerario contraire. Si quis autem hoc attemptare pfumpferit, indignaconem omnipotentis Dei & beatorum Petri & Pauli aplorum ejus fe noverit incurfurum.   Dat' Auinion' ‡, id. Junii, pontificatus firi anno tertio.

* XXII. as he was the only Pope of that name who refided at Avignon, where he governed the church from 1316 to 1334; confequently this muft be dated as above. "He was a man of " underftanding, had prodigious activity, immenfe wealth, and great conftancy in purfuing what " he once undertook." See Mrs. Dobfon's Life of Petrarch, vol. I. p. 92.

† See a letter of Mr. Hall's, p. 189.   ‡ The Roman See was fixed at Avignon by a Gafcon Pope in 1313, and continued there above 70 years.

fcripti

PRIVATE DEEDS.

1. (In dorſo, manu antiqua.) Carta Eilgar de la Burne filii Godefridi de una acra & quarta parte unius acie terre q̄ jacent in campo q̄ vocatur *Gore* *. Sans date.

2. (In d. m. a) Charta Eilgar' de la Burne filii Godefridi de quatuor acris terre & ſex pcatis que jacent in campo q̄ vocatur *Gore*. Sans date.

3. (In d. m. a.) Carta Petii & Walteri fil' Roberti de Beregethege de quatuor acris terræ que jacent in campo qui vocatur *Gore* inter Elfgar de la Burne. Sans date.

4. (m. a.) Carta Terri' aurifabri de quatuor acris terre que jacent in campo qui vocatur *Gore*. Sans date.

5. Releaſe from Tho. Athonworde, to the Hoſpital, of a quit rent of one penny p an. iſſuing out of [a piece of land called] *Combe* † in the pariſh of St. Michaels Herbaldoune, 29 Edw. I.

6. (m. a.) Carta Richardi fil' Guidonis de una acra & quarta parte unius acre terre que jacet in campo qui vocatur *Clenlinge*. Sans date.

7. (m. a.) Carta Ris de Weſtgate de decem den' liberi redditus ſui de una acra terre & dimid' que jacet in campo qui vocatur *Brodeſole*. Sans date.
(The impreſſion of the ſeal, which is perfect, repreſents a flower de luce. Inſcription round it, SIGILV RIIS DE WESTGATE.) (See plate IV. fig. 7.)

8. (m. a.) Carta Eilgar' de la Burne de una virgata & dimid' virgata teire ‡, que jacent juxta terram que vocatur *iealde hamſtall*. Sans date.

9. xx d̄. a year near the bourne Southward, and the downe Northward. By Walter ſon of Robert de Beregethege.

* *Binnegore* is at preſent called the 18 acres, and contains 19 ; in 1761 it was entirely planted with hops.

† *Combe* is part arable, part hop-ground, without any wood.

‡ The bounds are thus deſcribed, " que jacent in longitudine ſua a ſtrata regia uſque ad ter" ram quam predicti fratres tenent *in gavelikend* de Petro & Waltero de Bergetee, & in latitudine " ſua inter teiram predictorum fratrum quam tenent de me *in gavelikend* et terram que vocatur ialde " hamſtall que fuit Eadmundi." The land held *in gavelikind* was ſo called, ſays Sir Edward Coke, from " Gave all kynd; for this cuſtom giveth to all the ſons alike." This derivation, howevr, Mr Somnei rejects. See his Treatiſe of Gavelkind, p. 6. And p. 38. he quotes the above or a ſimilar donation of land to this Hoſpital " in perpetuam eleemoſynam, and to *Gavelkind*," as, 1. being held by deſcent, and theiefore deviſable, and 2. as reſerving a quit-rent. D. So in Nº 11, " inter teiram quam predicti fiatres tenent in Gavelikend de Eilgaro de la Burne." This Elgar gave the lands in Nᵒˢ 1 and 2, in both which a rent is ieſeived payable to himſelf and his heirs " in cuiia eorum de H'baldune."

10. Carta Ifembard' fil' Eilgar' de la Burne, de una virgat' terre que jacet in campo que vocatur *Gore* & aquam que vocatur *Burnam*. [Grant of one yard of land adjoining to the Bourn by Ifembard de la Burne.]

11. Carta Anfrid' fil' Salomon' de Turifoid, de fex acris & tres peiticatis terre in campo qui vocatur *Gore*.

12. Carta Gileberti filii Rogeri Talebot le Draper de quatuor acr' terre & dimid' acr' terre; que tres acr' & dim' vocantur *Tenementum*, & una acr' terr' vocatur la *Rede*; [as fuppofed in Laron's tenement.] 1 Edw. III. 1327.

13. Laron's Tenement *, and [1 acre in] Rede, and a moiety of [his land in] Levenote, 16 Edw. I. 1288. [A grant from John Thonyford of 3 acres and a half in.]

14. *Upfeld* (in a modern hand, inftead of *Brentche*, erafed) at *Croydene*, in the parifh of St. Mich' Herbald. [From Peter Durant, and Felicia his wife, an. reg. H. III. 55. with a confirmation thereof de Johanna de Dunftintone Mart. 19 E. I.]

15. Carta de duabus acris in *Hupfielde*. Mar. Edw. I. 19. 1291. Nota de *Chalfeham*.

16. Releafe of vi d̃. p an. out of two acres in *Breinths*, 6 Edw. II. 1312.

17. Releafe of iii d̃. p an. due from two acres in *Breinths*, 8 Edw. III.

18. Copy of a grant from Algar fon of Godefry de la Burne of three acres and a half in *Bingore*, and [one acre and] one yard in *Dunland*.

19. *Denftede*. Grant [from Hamo de Denftede] of a quit-rent of viii d̃. and two hens, p ann. out of half an acre in Denftede.

20. *Denftede*. Grant [from William de Morton and his wife] of iii d̃. p an. out of a meffuage there.

21. *Hégham*, als Hyham, in Tonford field. Releafe of three acres, [from Roƀt. de Denftede, clerk.] 32 Edw. III.

22. Willm atte Crowche releafeth to Tho. Priefte all his right of lands [tenements, &c.] in Herbaldoune, 1439. [17 Nov.] 18 Hen. VI.

Ifabelle Mead.

23. Carta Richard' Sut' de una acra terre in puram & perpetuam elemofynam dedit, q̃ jacet in campo q̃ vocatur *Yfabele Mede*, inter terram hofpital' de Herbaldune q̃ eft verfus Suth & terram Alani Pocok q̃ eft verfus Noith. [Grant from Rich. Levechild of 1 acre in Ifabel Mead.]

24. Carta Richardi Sut' de quatuor denar' redditus fui, ... quos foleb' annuaim reddere ei de quod' tenemento quod vocatur *Yfabele Mede*.

25. Grant from Will' de Vaus to Gilbert de Wenchepe of [two acres of] his land in the pa.ifh of Herbaldune at Ifabelle Med, with the crop thereon. 18 Edw. I. 1279.

* Now called in the leafe to Mrs. Young (fee p. 227.) 'Lawrence Tenement.'

26. Grant

26. Grant from the said Gilbert de Wenchepe of the said two acres to the hospital, 26 May, 1289.

27. [Grant from Loretta daughter of Robert Ateburne of 5 perches and a quarter of land] In dorf. v virgat' terre cum ptin' & una via de octo pedibus. 1 virgat' prati cum peitin' & una via de VIII ped'. 8 id. Nov. 1289.

28 In doif. Donatio trium pticar' & 1 quarterii pticatæ. [Grant from Vincent Fonte of a cioft containing 5 yards and a way to it, and of a meadow and a way to it.]

29. Grant (by indenture) from Rob' German [Roper] to Walter Gylbert, clerk, John Swayn, and John Caldham of half an acre in *Isabelle Med.* 22 Martii, 31 Hen. VI. 1453.

30. Grant from Simon Guy to John Pardoner of one acre and one rood of wood in the parish of Herbaldoune. 15 Nov. 13 Hen. IV. 1412.

31. Releafe from Sampfon Colman to Richard Wellys of his claim to five roods of wood. 20 Oct. 1 Edw. IV. 1461. This and N° 30 fhould be placed after N° 40.

32. *Long Mead.* [Grant from Silvefter Baker to Richard Roper of] A croft befide *Isabelle Med.* 24 April, 7 Hen. IV. 1406.

33. Releafe from John Roper, John Swayn, John Chamberlayn, Will' Bygge, and Thomas Bayly, to Robert Germyn Roper, of a piece of land in Longmed. 3 Edw. IV. 1463.

34. Grant of the said land from Robert Germyn Roper, to William Bygge, 14 Aug. 3 Edw. IV. 1463.

35. Grant of the aforefaid land from William Bygge to John Caldham, William Luton, and John Cropham. 6 Sept. 5 Edw. IV. 1465. [Containing 3 acres and a half.]

36. [Grant from Reymund Roper of a] way to Longmead, 12 Aug. 1 Hen. V. 1413.

37. Ifabell mead. Exchange between John Monger and the hofpital, of two pieces of land, each containing half an acre *; and releafe of the rent of wax due from the hofpital, 1 April, 25 Eliz. 1592.

38. Simon Tannere to John Bryan, 5 yards of wood land, 13 Ric. II.

39. John Bryan to Walter Bernard, the said 5 yards of wood-land, June, 22 Ric. II. 1399.

40. Walter Bernard to Simon Gy, the said 5 yards of wood-land, 25 July, 3 Hen. IV. 1402. N° 30 and 31 ought to have followed this deed.

41. Clement ate Welde to Peter ate Welde and [Anice] his wife, 5 yards of wood-land in Harbledoun, 3 Edw. II. 1310.

* See N° 29.

42. Smale-

42. *Smalebores.* Tho. Liefhelm to Edmund Hogg, one rood of wood-land. [in the parifh of St Michael Harbaldoun] 24 June, 20 Ric. II. 1397.

43. Johanna widow of John Elmer, and daughter and heir of Edmund Hogg, to Wm. Holeweye, the faid piece of wood-land in Smalebores. 27 May, 8 Hen. V. 1421.

44. Will. Holeweye to John Rykard, al' Bocher, the faid wood-land at Smalebores, 18 Nov. 4 Hen. VI. 1425.

45. Warrant of attorney of faid W. Holeweye to deliver feifin. 18. Nov. 4 Hen. VI.

46. John Rycard, al' Bocher, to Thomas Herewarde, the aforefaid wood-land in Smalebores. 20 Oct. 13 Hen. VI. 1435.

47. Tho. Hereward to Will. Palmer clerk, all his lands and tenements in Herbaldowne. 1 Sept. 17 Hen. VI. 1439.

48. Will. Palmer to Simon Colyn and Julian Horne, the laft mentioned piece of wood-land. 24 Oct. 18 H. VI. 1440.

49. Vincent atte Welle to Reymund Roper 5 roods of wood-land in Herbaldown apud Le Well. 1 Oct. 12 Hen. IV. 1411.

50. John Chycche, efq. to Rob. German and others a piece of wood-land called Northwoode. 16 Jan. 25 Hen. VI. 1445.

51. Richard Fille and John Sothereye to John Martyn, efq. and others, the faid wood-land. 4 Dec. 3 H. VII. 1487.

52. Declaration of Richard Fille and John Sothereye, that the laft mentioned conveyance was on condition that the faid Northwoode fhould remain to the hofpital. 4 Dec. 3 Hen. VII. 1487.

53. Releafe from Margaret, widow of John Swayne, to John Martyn, efq. and others, of the faid wood land called Northwode. 10 Dec. 3 H. VII. 1487.

54. Grant of 5 roods from Luke [Son of William ate] Nethereche, made 7 Sept. 7 Ed. I. 1279, then under age, and confirmed by him 19 April, 21 Edw. I. 1293.

Tenements in Herbaldown.

55. John Elmer, fmith, and Joan his wife, to Thomas Charles of Herbaldon, a meffuage and garden at Herbaldoun. 12 Oct. 12 H. IV. 1411.

56. Houfe and garden next the Duke's head [late the White Horfe.] Releafe from W. Arderne, clerk, W. Puxtone, and John Feverfham, to John Bedel and John Plonket, 10 Jan. 6 H. V. 1419.

[Eight other deeds relating to the fame] In dorf. A deed of the houffe next the Whyt Horfe. 10 June 6 H. V. 1411. viz.

57. Tho..

57. Tho. Charles to John Perdour, and John Yaldyng, a meſſuage and garden in Herbaldoun, Nov. 7 H. VI. 1427.

58. J. Perdour and J. Yaldyng, to Richard ſon of Tho. Charles and his wife and their iſſue, the ſaid meſſuage and garden. Jan. 8 H. VI. 1430.

59. Rob. Charlys to Henry and Richard Wellys the beforementioned meſſuage and garden. 21 June, 4 Edw. IV. 1464.

60. Releaſe from W. Rychefeld and others, to ſaid Henry and Richard Wellys. 23 June, 4 Edw. IV. 1464.

61. Richard Wellys to Chriſtian widow of Hen. Wellys, the ſaid meſſuage and garden. 19 April, 7 Edw. IV. 1467.

62. Richard Wellys to Henry Beald and others, the ſaid meſſuage and garden. 22 Dec. 2 R. III. 1484.

63. Releaſe from John Beald to Henry Beald and others, of ſaid meſſuage and garden. 19 Jan. 3 H. VII. 1488.

64. Henry Beald and others, to John Johnſon and others, the ſaid meſſuage and garden. 7 May, 4 H. VII. 1489.

Terriers.

65. Terrarium primum. Reddit' . . . . . ſolvend' Hoſpit'. (This title, written in red, is almoſt worn out. It is a terrier containing 44 articles.)

66. A ſecond terrier, conſiſting of two rolls, of different breadths, ſewed together. 50 Ed. III. 1376.

67. The rents of the brothers and ſiſters of Harbaldoune.

68. A third terrier.

69. The copy of the mortmeyn of the lands in Recolver and dyverſe other placys. 13 June, 13 H. VI. 1435 *. This is a tranſlation of N° 70.

70. The ſame in Latin †. 13 Jun. 13 H. VI. 1435.

71. Confirmatio Edw. I. de revocatione eccſie de Reculver ad cameram Archieṗalem Cant'. Et ut Hoſpitalia ſuſtineantur ex redditibus ipſius Archieṗ. 18 Dec. 19 Edw. I ‡. 1291. See before, p. 209, N° 30. 1.

* Printed in the Hiſtory of Reculver, p. 151.

† Ibid. p. 152. The ſeal, which is almoſt entire, is different from that which is fixed to the General Pardon, dated 7 Man, an. 15 H. VI. 1437. See Royal Grants, N° 28.

‡ Ibid. p. 131. The broad ſeal is very well preſerved. There is alſo an ancient copy of this inſtrument.

2

72. Licenfe of K. Edw. III, for appropriation of the church of Reculver to the Aichbifhop's table ; and for payment of 160 l. a year out of the revenues of the fee of Cant' to the two hofpitals, notwithftanding the ftatute of mortmain. 16 March, 22 Edw. III. 1348 *. See before, p. 209, N° 30. 2.

73. Carta Salamonis But de tribus acris terre in Reculver, apud Sperkyn, in campo vocato Brounyngefton, Willmo atte Welle Capello, aliifque. 18 April, 38 Edw. III. 1364 +.

74. Carta ejufdem Sal' But iifdem de predictis 111 acris terre in Reculver, 18 April, 38 Edw. III. 1364 ‡.

75. Carta indentata predict' feoffat' concedens predict' 111 acras terre predict' Salamoni But fub annuo redditu unius fumme ordei. 12 Jun. 38 Edw. III. 1364 ||.

76. Pars altera predicte carte indentate.

Herne.

77. Ricus atte Broke 1 acr' in Thorndenne Henr' de Suthreye & uxori ejus, Maii, 6 Edw. III. 1332.

78. Quieta clamacu Johis filii Walteri atte Bioke, Henrico de Sothereye, & Chriftine uxori ejus de dimidia acre predicte, Jun, 7 Edw. III. 1333.

79. Walter Bayli to Henry fon of Richard de Suthereye and his wife, two acres at Rokyngrove, in Thorndenne borough, in Herne, 1 Nov. 12 Edw. III. 1338.

80. James Bate to Nich' de Underdoune 1 acre, 111 roods, at Gatekaye in Herne. 19 Edw. III. 1345.

81. Ifolda widow of Henry de Frokyngone, to John Seuale, 2 pieces of land at Frokyngone, containing 2 acres. 21 Dec. 31 Edw. III. 1357.

82. Carta Johis Sewale de Hierne de uno crofto vocat' Brokesfield in Hiern. March 33, Edw. III. 1359.

83. Quieta clamatio Gedeline ux' Johis Sewale de predicta terra Ifolde nuper uxori Hen. Southereye. 33 Edw. III. 1359.

84. Quieta clamatio Thome Sewale eidem de predicta terra, 33 Edw. III. 1359.

85. Carta John Sewale concedens Hofpital' 11 s. p an. exeunt' de pdca terra, 18 Nov. 33 Edw. III. 1359.

86. Carta Johis Aryngburg junior' & alior' concernens un' quarter' hordei exeunt' de una grangia, uno ftabulo, & x11 acr' terre apud Weftbroke in Strodeburg'. [Herne] 5 Sept. 35 Edw. III. 1361.

* Ibid. p. 141.
+ Hiftory of Reculver, p. 142.   ‡ Ibid. p. 143.
|| Ibid. p. 143. Thefe are all mifdated in the Hiftory of Reculver, ' 1357.'

87. 1. Redd'

87. 1. Redd' unius quaterii ordei provenientis de una grangia, uno ftabulo, & xii acris terre jacent' in paroch' de Herne. 25 July, 18 Ric. II. 1378.

87. 2. (In dorf.) Releafe from Denis atte Stone, nephew and heir to Henr' atte Stcne (one of the grantees in Nᵒ 86) to John Wylk, of the faid quarter of barley, agreeably to the laft will of the faid Henry atte Stone, 1 Nov. 1 Hen. IV. 1399.

88. Grant, by indenture, from J. Plowde and J. Cherche, of the faid quarter of barley to the hofpital, 14 Sept. 2 Hen. IV. 1400.

89. Grant from William Tayloure, alias Paramour, and others, to Richard Dererd, of two acres of land in Thornden borough in Heine. 10 Jan. 17 Edw. IV. 1477.

90. Grant from Richard Dererd of the faid two acres of land to the hofpital. 20 Jan. 18 Edw. IV. 1478.

91. Carta Jacobi a Churche de xvi denar' apud le Platts in burg' Strode, in paroch' Herne. 13 March, 1492, 8 Hen. VII.

92. Grant from James a Chirche to the prior and priorefs of the Hofpital of viii d. p an. out of a meffuage and three acres of land in Strode borough in Herne. 23 March, 1492, 8 Hen. VII.

93. Grant from John a Chirche of viii d. p an. out of two acres and a half at Stockgrove in Thornden in Herne, to the prior and priorefs. 23 March, 8 Hen. VII. 1492.

St. Dunftan's near Canterbury.

1. Carta Ivo fil' Salamonis filii Eadvardi Bifet de duobus denar' liberi reddit' fui de uno mefuagio qd jacet in parochia Sci Dunftani.

2. Carta Johis Binnewiht de duodecim denar' liberi reditus fui, quos ei reddere folebat Hamo le Waudes ad med' Quadragefim' annuatim, de quodam mefuagio qd jacet in parochia Sci Dunftani in perpetuam elemofinam.

3. 1. Carta Syronis molendinarii extra Weftgate Ricardo de Berekote de uno tenemento quod jacet in parochia Sci Dunftani emptum. (The firft witnefs to this deed is, dno Petro de Mekalonde tunc temporis capello curie dni Archiepi Cant.)

3. 2. In dorfo. Carta Ricardi de Berekote de uno meffuagio quod jacet in parochia Sci Dunftani emptum.

Grant from Richard de Berekote to the brothers of the hofpital of the faid meffuage.

4. Carta Stephani filii Willi le Cocker in perpetuum quietum clamavit de duabus denar' quos reddere confueverunt fratres de fuo garnario in parochia Sci Dunftani. 41 Hen. III. 1256.

5. Carta

5. Carta de la Gerner de Weſtgate. Feb. 12. Ed. . . .

6. For a ſhop in the paiiſh of St. Dunſtan's. Feb. 1. Ed. II. 1308.

7. 1. In dorſo. Evydence of Plunket's releaſe from Ingerim Carpenter to Tho. Plunket and Matt. Cramber of a meſſuage and garden. 7 Jan. 12 Ed. IV. 1473. [It ſhould be 17 Jan.]

7. 2. In dorſo. Evydence of Plunket's grant from Ingerim Carpenter to Thomas Plunket and Matt. Cramber of the aforeſaid meſſuage and garden. 16 Jan. 12 Ed. IV. 1473.

7. 3. In dorſo. Evydence of Blanket (lege Plunket) houſes. Releaſe from Matt. Cramber to Tho. Plunket of the ſame. 25 Sept. 13 Ed. IV. 1473.

7. 4. In dorſo. Evydenſſe of Plunket's grant from Tho. Plunket, brother of Herbaldoune Hoſpital, to W. Bromley of St. Dunſtan's and Julian his wife, of the ſaid meſſuage, &c. for their lives, and after to the hoſpital. 4 Oct. 13 Ed. IV.

7. 5. Pars altera predicte carte indentate, cum duobus figillis.

8. 1. In dorſo. Carta de Bedel. Grant from Matilda Glovere to John Tyete of two ſhops in St. Dunſtan's. 19 Oct. 37 Ed. III. 1363.

8. 2. In dorſo. Carta de Joh' Tyete Joh' Heldyngge de duabus ſhoppis in Weſtgate. 20 Oct. 37 Ed. III. 1363.

8. 3. In dorſo. Carta Johis Yelding de (predictis) duabus ſhoppis Tho. Wolton clerico, aliiſque. .. Jul. 1 Ric. II. 1377.

8. 4. In dorſo. Carta indentata Rici Skynnere & alior', concedens dictas ſhoppas Joh' Gryffyn & uxori ejus, pro termino 101 annorum. 30 Ap. 5 R. II. 1382.

8. 5. Grant from J. Gryffyn to Tho. Kent of the remainder of the ſaid term of 101 years. 11 Feb. 16 R. II. 1393.

9. 1. In dorſo. De tribus ſchopis in parochia Sci Dunſtani. Grant from John Roper to John Wylk, Adam de Drove, and others, brethren of Herbaldown Hoſpital, of one meſſuage and three ſhops in St. Dunſtan's. 25 Jan. 22 R. II. 1399.

9. 2. Releaſe from Edmund Roper to Adam de Drove and Will' Hall of the ſaid meſſuage and three ſhops. 24 Maii, 11 H. IV. 1410.

9. 3. Carta Ade de Drove & W. atte Halle, Rob' Omer, aliiſque, de predict' meſſuag' & 111 ſhopis. 31 Maii, 11 H. IV. 1410.

10. 1. Quieta clamatio Edithe Berthilmewe Barthol' Rygdon de uno ten' in paroch' S. Dunſtani. 7 Dec. 13 Ed. IV. 1473.

10. 2. Carta Barthi Rygdon, Johi Webbe, & Hamon' Fuller, de predicto & alio ten'. 10 Dec. 13 Ed. IV. 1473.

10. 3. In dorſo. Grant from John Jakes and Ingerim Carpenter to John Martyn, Eſq. and others, of the corner houſe in St. Dunſtan's. 29 Sep. 4 H. VII. 1488.

11. 1. Grant of three tenements and gardens in St. Dunſtan's, by Will' Roper of Eltham, to the hoſpital. 1 May, 12 Eliz. 1570.

11. 2. Feoffamentum de prediċtis III ten' & gard'. 20 Oċt. 25 Eliz. 1583.

11. 3. Feoffamentum aliud. 18 Jan. 39 Eliz. 1597.

11. 4. Feoffamentum aliud. 15 Oċt. 4 Ja. I. 1606.

Here end the titles of the charters and other evidences which Mr. HALL *had tranſcribed. In the "* Liber Hoſpitalium" *of Dr.* BEAUVOIR, *theſe are all methodically copied ; and, in addition to them, a regular liſt is made out of private deeds belonging to the Hoſpital of* Herbaldown, *relating to their poſſeſſions in the following places :*

Rollyng in Godwynſtone near Wingham.

.1. Grant from Robert Goldfynch to John and Alice Gerard of 3 roods in a field called Hokedefelde. Feb. 15 Edw. II. [1321].

2. Releaſe from Chriſtian atte Halle to Walter Tykenherſt of one half acre and one rood. Oċt. 24 Edw. III. [1350].

3. Grant from Walter Tykenherſt to Robert and John de Bourbach of three roods and an half of land. 11 Oċt. 24 Edw. III. [1350].

4. Grant of half an acre of land, cum dimidia aula & quinta parte unius porte muri arbor' foſſis & foſſatis ſuperſtantibus from Henry Creche to Iſabelle daughter of Richard Pyrie. 6 Edw. III. [1332].

5. Grant from William Werebald to Robert and John de Burbach of one acre at Rollyng called Crecchefcroft. 1 Dec. 23 Edw. III. [1349].

6. Releaſe from Henry Crecche to Robert and John de Burbach of claim on one acre in Crecchefcroft in Rollyng. Dec. 23 Edw. III. [1349].

7. Releaſe from John Granger to Robert and John de Burbach of 2s 7d ob from a tenement of Thomas Granger for 5 years enſuing. 22 Jan. 20 Edw. III. [1349].

8. Releaſe of John le Clerk of Sandwich, to Sir Robert de Burbach and John his brother, of all claims on the lands and tenements which had been his father's in Rollyng. 5 Jan. 22 Edw. III. [1348]. Oval ſeal, red wax, a figure ſtanding habited in a long garment holding up ſomething in one hand.

9. Agreement from Robert de Burbach and John with John le Clerk, that the aforeſaid releaſe ſhall be void, on payment of 40 marks ſterling. The ſame date and ſeal as N° 20. Seal broken.

10. Grant

10. Grant from John Granger to Robert and John de Burbach of 0 a. 3 r. 0 p. of arable. 22 March, 23 Edw. III. [1349].

11. Grant from William de Tykenherſt to Robert and John de Burbach of one acre of arable. April, 23 Edw. III. [1349].

12. Releaſe from Matilda widow of William de Tykenheiſt to Robert and John de Burbach, of all claim on the acre granted them by William de Tykenherſt. 15 Nov. 23 Edw. III. [1349].

13. Grant from Thomas Tebbe to Robert and John de Burbach, of 1 a. 0 r. 14 p. of arable. 3 April, 23 Edw. III. [1349.. Seal red wax. Virg. & ch. in a lozenge, AVE MARIA GRATIA. (See plate III. fig. 5.)

14. Grant fiom Thomas Tebbe to Robert and John de Burbach, of 2 acres and a half of arable. 10 Dec. 23 Edw III. [1349]. Seal ſame as the laſt.

15. Indenture of partition of a meſſuage and 2 acres between John Granger and Alice his ſiſter. 14 Aug. 24 Edw. III. [1350].

16. The counterpart of Nº 15.

17. Grant from John Granger to Robert Berbach, chaplain, of one meſſuage &c. in Rollyng. 24 Edw. III. [1350]. The ſeal is of green wax; oval. Legend. S. IOHANNIS GRANG . . .

18. Grant from Thomas ate Sole to Sir Robert de Berbache, chaplain, and John his brother, of 1 acre in Rollyng, at a place called ate Berghe. 23 Edw. III [1349]. Seal round; white wax; obliterated.

19. Grant from Henry Creeche to Robert and John de Burbach, of 2 acres of arable. Oct. 23 Edw. III. [1349]. A round ſeal, the virgin with a crown on, and child. AVE MARIA GRATIA.

20. Grant from Thomas de Peddyngge of Sandwich, to Henry ate Pende de Peddyngge, of all his lands at Rollyng. 20 Nov. 23 Edw. III. [1349].

21. Grant from Henry at Pende de Pendyng, to Robert and John de Burbach, of all his lands at Rollyng, given by his brother Thomas. Dec. 23 Edw. III. [1349].

22. Releaſe from John Attebrok Sen. and Jun. and Thomas Attebrok, to John and Robert Burbach, and J. Clarke of Sandwich, concerning 3 acres in Rollyng. 27 Oct. 24 Edw. III. [1350].

23. Grant from Thomas Attebrok, to Robert and John Burbach, of one acre. March, 28 Edw. III. [1354].

24. Grant from Robert de Burbach, to dnus Thomas de Wolton, and others, of one meſſuage and 74 acres and a half, and 1 rood of arable land, late John le Clerk's, and

and of one meſſuage and 12 acres of arable more, both in Rollynge. Dec. 29

Edw. III. [1355]. Seal round, red wax; 彐ᛒᚦ round s. ROB'TI DE BORBACH.

25. Copy of a licence of mortmain from Edw. [III.] to William atte Welle chap-lain, and others, to aſſign to the two hoſpitals, 86 acres and two meſſuages in Rollyng, which are held of the Archbiſhop of Canterbury. Indorſed. "Irrot' in tertia paite patentium aº intra ſcripto." 6 Aug. 31 Edw.   [1357]. The original is in St. John's Hoſpital. See p. 251.

26. Releaſe from John ſon of late William Clerk of Sandwich, to both the hoſpi-tals, of all claim on the lands granted by Robert de Burghbage chaplain in Rollyng. April, 35 Edw. III. [1361].

27. Grant from Thomas de Woltone, clerk, and others, to the two hoſpitals of the lands granted to them by Robert de Burbach. 1 April, 36 Edw. III. [1362]. Five Seals.

28. Grant from Robert Dodynton and Alice his wife, to William atte Welle and others, brethren of Harbledown hoſpital, of a piece of land in Godneſton, called Whitefeld. 29 Aug. 49 Edw. III. [1375].

29. Grant from John Adams, to John Blake, of half an acre in Rollyng, called Somerleſe. Oct. 8 Ric. II. [1384].

30. Grant from John Blake at Weſtgate, of half an acre at Rollyng, called le Teghe. 1 Dec. 4 Hen. VI. [1425].

31. Grant from Richard Duglas, to both hoſpitals, of one yard of land in Gud-neſton, and of one other yard of land in the ſame. 2 Jan. 15 Hen. VII. [1499].

32. Releaſe from Griſella Byllys of Sandwich to the hoſpitals of a quit rent &c. due from their lands at Rollyng. 5 March, 6 Hen. VIII. [1515].

33. Indenture, ſpecifying what the hoſpitals are to pay out of their lands at Rollyng to the courts of Wyngham, of St. Sepulchre's Canterbury, of William Tyte-combe, of Twitham, of the abbot of Langedon, of Chiltone, of Akholte, of John de Harleſtone, and to Gwodneſtone Church. Sans date.

34. A terrar of Rollyng, containing xxɪx articles. Sans date. In the ſame hand-writing as Nº 33. Sum of acres ₓₓₓᵥᵢ a. 1 r. and half, with a curtilage.

35. A terrar of Rollyng. The ſame as Nº 34. Sans date.

36. 1. A terrar of Tabeder's land (the ſame land), containing xxvɪɪɪ articles. Sum total ₓₓᵥɪɪɪ a. xɪx p. 1674. In Engliſh.

36. 2. Another copy of the ſame.

37. A terrar of Rollyng, containing xxɪ articles. Sum total ₓₓ a. 11 r. xxɪɪɪ p. Sans date. In Engliſh.

38. 1. A terrar of Rollyng. The fame as N° 37, with the neceſſary changes of the names of occupiers. 24 July, 1706.

38. 2. A map of Rollyng. There is another, a duplicate, in St. John's Hoſpital, done 1617.

Borſtalle.

39 Confirmation by Mariotta Synages de Borſtalle of a diviſion of three acres of land between her daughter Cecilia and herſelf, in the pariſh of St. Margaret near Suthgate. 30 Sept. 15 Edw. II. [1324.] Seal oval, legend s. MARIOT FL' WI . . . . .

40. Grant from Ric' Dryvere of Borſtalle to Ric' Kebbel of a curtilage [yard or garden plot]. 29 Sept. 7 Edw. III. 1333.

41. Grant from John Suthereye of Borſtalle to Ric' Kebbel of a tenement and 1 a. III r. and ef 11 r. 14 Jan. 22 Ed. III. 1348.

Chalſloke.

42. Grant from Stephen and John, ſons of Roger Rhondes, to Chriſtian de Oxeneye of one acre in Chalſloke. 21 Edw. I. 1291.

Chilham.

43. Grant from William Maycock of Herbaldown to the hoſpital of a piece of land in Chilham in the borgh of Eaſture. 2 Mar. 1 Ric. II. 1378. In dorſ'. A piece of land in Chilham in the borowghe of Eaſture, now called Eaſt Stuarde.

Canterbury.

44. Burgate. In dorſ. Carta Elueue Pinneſlaue de v denar' libri reddit' ſui añuatim pcipiend' ad feſt' Sc̄i Mich' de dono Leticie filie Cauuel in parochia Sc̄i Michael' apud Burgate. (See p. 202.)

45. St. Margaret. Grant from Alice daughter of Wiulph of XIII đ. rent from the houſe of William de Welles in St. Margaret's, paying out of it III đ. II đ. and a pair of gloves worth I đ. annually. Sans date, but it is 26 vel 27 Hen. III. 1243 vel 1244.

46. Indenture between the prior, &c. and Thomas Whychylynge, releaſing to him the payment of IV đ. per ann. out of XIII đ. per ann. due to the hoſpital from an houſe in St. Margaret's, once William de Welles's, 24 Nov. 3 Hen. V. 1415.

47. St.

47. St. Paul, Ivy Lane. Grant from Thomas Ingelet of Thanet to William atte Welle, chaplain, and others, of a meſſuage and garden in Standfaſtlane in St. Paul's. 4 Oct. 37 Edw. III. 1363.

48. Grant from Thomas Godhayt of Merſham to John Frowde and J. Cherche of an houſe and garden in Standfaſtelane. July 17 Ric. II. 1393.

49. Grant from John Lovel and others to John Newman and others of two ſhops in Standfaſtlane. 4 Jan. 3 Hen. VI. 1424. This is indorſed, Evydence of two houſes in Ive Lane in Canterbur'.

Elham.

50. Grant from John Ilent, a brother of the hoſpital, of one acre and a half in Elham. 1 Jan. 5 Hen. VIII. 1514.

51. Releaſe from John Proude and J. Cherche of lands and tenements in the hundred of Weſtgate, in Wodneſberg, and in Elham. 24 Jun. 7 Ric. II. 1383.

Graveney. Pettyt.

52. Indenture between the hoſpital of Herbaldown and Ciriac Pettyt, of Boughton ſubtus le Blean, of exchange of the paſturage of fourteen ſheep, eſtimated at fourteen acres of Saltmarſh in Graveney, and one rood in Southfield in Graveney, for two acres in Herbaldown. ult' Feb. 13 Eliz. 1571.

Herbaldown.

53. Grant of a cloſe from Thomas de Waleſham to William (brother of Gilbert) rector of St. Nicholas de Herbaldun. 37 Hen. III. 1253.

54. Grant from the prioreſs of Davintun of xi s. rent, which was due to that convent out of Davintun Mead from the hoſpital. 3 Ed. I. 1274. and a tranſcript.

55. Releaſe from John Monger of London of a rent of one hen iſſuing out of half an acre called Iſabel Mead, and arrears, on condition that he enjoys half an acre in Iſabel Mead, received from the hoſpital by exchange. 20 May, 25 Eliz. 1583.

56. A map and deſcription of on capitall meaſuage, known by the name of St. Nicholas Hoſpitall, liying at Harbaldoune, neere the cittie of Canterbury, with twelve parcells of errable thereunto belonginge, contayninge ... acres, on quarter, two perches. *Gulielmus Boycot deſcripſit*, 1621. This map is 15 inches and a quarter long, and 14 inches and one eighth broad; and the number of acres, which he has omitted above, is 67 a. 3 r. 13 p. In red 57 a. 1 r. 12 p.; and in black 10 a. 1 r. 31 p.

Hertey.

Hertey.

57. Grant from William Yue and others to Thomas Smyth and others of ɪv s̄. vɪ đ. ob. two cercells * and one third of one hen, and one third of half an hen, and xv eggs. July, 3 Ric. H. 1379. Two feals perfect.

58. Grant from John and William, fons and heirs of brother William Skynner, to Adam Grove and others of the rent as in N° 70. 6 Jun. 18 Ric. II. 1395.

Lodenham.

59. Grant from John Roper of Whistapell to John Caldyng of Goodneston of one meſſuage and garden and xxxɪɪ acres and ɪ acre in Lodenham. 21 Hen. VI. 1442.

Stellyng.

60. Grant from John Ilent of 11 s̄. yearly out of a tenement and two acres at Weſt-meneſſe in Stellyng. 7 Jun. 6 Hen. VIII. 1515.

Woodneſborough.

61. Grant from the prior and convent of Ledes to the hoſpital, to receive at their grange in Worneſburgh three feams of barley, which uſed to be paid to them out of the tithes of Summerfeld in Worneſburg. Sans date.

62. An ancient copy of the fame.

63. A true copy of the patent or grant to the two hoſpitals for 6 ɪ. 17 s̄. 2 đ. ob. p ann. (which they uſed to receive from the monaſtery of Chriſt Church, Canterbury, before the diſſolution); and to Herbaldown Hoſpital for 10 s̄. p ann (inſtead of the 3 feams of barley N° 74) to be paid by the king's receiver of the Augmentation (Office). 1 May, 37 Hen. VIII. 1545. See pp. 230 and 252, 3.

---

* From the French " cercelle," the water wild fowl, denominated by us a teale. Somner's " Gloſſar. ad finem X Scriptorum." Of theſe birds there probably was always an abundance in Herteye Iſland. Two teale, and the third part of another, was a whimſical kind of reddend', and if delivered in kind, with exactneſs, would probably require the hand of a dextrous carver.
W. and D. in Gent. Mag. for 1784, p. 174.

In the Hiſtory of Reculver, p. 152, is a mortmain grant from Henry VI. ſecuring this and other payments to Herbaldown hoſpital, but there, inſtead of " ob." as above, we read " medietatem unius quadrantate" (half a farthing), which has drawn ſome ſhrewd remarks from the ingenious writer quoted above. Inſtead of " the third part of a hen, and the third of half a hen," this grant has alſo " the third part of a teale, a hen and a half."

STATUTES, CHARTERS, PRIVATE DEEDS, &c.

RELATING TO NORTHGATE HOSPITAL.

From the " Liber Hofpitalium," compiled by Dr. Beauvoir.

C H A P. I.

STATUTES and ORDINANCES.

1. An Indenture containing Archbifhop Matthew Parker's original Statutes under his Seal, but not figned by him. Dated 20 May, 2 Eliz. 1560. See p. 214.

2. Archbifhop John Whitgift's decree that no children be kept in either hofpital : on paper, figned by him, and fealed with his private Seal. 20 May, 1591. See p. 220.

3. Licence from Abp. Whitgift to let by leafe, for 21 Years, all their fmall parcells of land and houfes, fuch as have ufually been let for 20 fhillings or under by the year, on certain conditions. (They ufed before to be let from year to year.)

   1. Notice to be given to the Archbifhop of the quantities, &c. reparations, the old rent, the new, fine, term.

   2. The rent to be paid half yearly or quarterly.

   3. The tenants to bear all charges, repair and build.

   4. The boundaries and abutments to be expreffed in every leafe always.

   5. No edifice, garden, or ground, belonging to the fcite of the Hofpital, to be demifed by virtue of this licenfe. 28 Sept. 1596.

4. Archbifhop William Sancroft's orders to both Hofpitals. See p. 223.

   1. Orders forbidding non-refidence of the In-brothers under certain penalties.

   2. The mafter and prior, annually, in March and September, to furvey and order repairs; and the mafter to report to the Archbifhop in October.

   3. Security to be taken from the refpective parifhes from which they come for the fupport of the aged, infirm, &c.

4. No

4. No children or grandchildren to be in-dwellers with their parents, unlefs as nurfes, &c. And this to be certified every October to the Archbifhop.

5. Stipend from the time of death, to the day of the next admittance, to go to the reparation-purfe, and to be caft up every October.

6. The reader to catechife, efpecially in Lent. Signed by the Archbifhop and fealed. 4 March, 1686.

5. Archbifhop John Potter's faculty for pulling down the North fide of the Chapel, with a plan of the Chapel, under the Archbifhop's Seal. Signed John Haynes, Regifter. 9 June, 1744.

6. A parchment book in quarto, containing Archbifhop Parker's Statutes; Archbifhop Whitgift's Decree, Number 2 at the beginning; and, at the end, the copy of a decree forbidding the marriage of any in-brother or in-fifter, on pain of expulfion. Dated 19 Feb. 1663.

7. Another parchment book in quarto, containing the fame as Number 6. And a copy of Archbifhop Sancroft's Orders, Number 4.

C H A P. II.

LICENCES OF MORTMAIN — EXEMPTIONS FROM TAILLAGE — INSPEXIMUS — EXEMPTIONS FROM FIRST FRUITS AND TENTHS.

EDWARD III.

1. Licence of mortmain, to hold lands, tenements, and rents to the value of 100 s per ann. tam de feodo fuo proprio quam alieno, exceptis terris, tenementis, et redditibus, que de nobis tenentur in capite. 10 Jan. a. r. 1. 1328. (The feal almoft whole. The king fitting; one fleur de lys on each fide the throne; on the reverfe, three lions only on his fhield and furcoat.) This was granted " ad requifitionem dilecti Valletti noftri Johannis de Deen hoftitiarii came fire."

2. Another to hold 5 a. 1 r. 0 p. in Hakyngton, of the yearly value of 21 pence, given by Margaret atte Helde, Richard Fox, Robert Knyght, and John Crocker. 4 Jan. 1329. (Seal broken. The king fitting in the regal chair, as before.)

3. Another to William at Well and others, to affign to both hofpitals two meffuages and 86 a. 0 r. 0 p. in Rollyng, holden of the Archbifhop ut dicitur, 6 Aug. a. r. 31 1357 *. (The feal very fair and almoft whole.)

* The fame farm that is now let to Sir Narborough D'Aeth. See p. 230.

4. Another

4. Another to Thomas de Wolton, to give 46 acres of land, 6 acres of pasture, 10 acres of underwood and brushwood in St. Cosmas ard Hakyngton, worth (ultra redditum resolutum) 11 s. 6 d. per ann. and to Richard de Meddeburne. to give 40 s. rent in Herne, to be holden by the hospital as of the value of 4 marks (2 l. 13 s. 4 d.) in satisfaction for part of the 100 s. granted by Number 1. 30 Nov. a. r. 39, 13'5. (The seal lost.)

5 Another. Confirmation of Number 1, 3, and 4; and grant to be free tam de contribucione custodie tre maritime, quam tallagiis, auxiliis, et contributionibus. To both hospitals. 6 M. a. r. 45, 1370. (Seal white wax ; almost destroyed ; torn out.)

RICHARD II.

6. Iaspeximus and confirmation of the grant of Edward III. to both hospitals, 1 Dec. a. r. 9, 1335, of freedom from talliage, and licence of mortmain, 28 Jan. a. r. 1, 1378. (Seal lost.)

HENRY V.

7. Inspeximus and confirmation of former grants. 11 Jan. a. r. 8, 1421. (Seal lost.)

EDWARD IV.

8 Inspeximus and confirmation of former grants. 20 March, a. r. 8, 1468. (Seale much broken.)

HENRY VIII.

9. Inspeximus and confimation. 14 April, a. r. 2, 1511. (Seal perfect, but cracked.)

10. Grant of exemption from first fruits and tenths. a. r. 29. 1538. This is much worn. The revenues of this hospital, as delivered in and upon the survey, amounted to 91 l. 16 s. 8 d. ob. (Seal rubbed and broken.)

11. Patent exemplifying a decree of the chancellor and council of the court of augmentations, by which 6 l. 17 s. 2 d. ob. which used to be paid to both hospitals by way of alms by the prior and convent of Christ Church, Canterbury, now dissolved, shall *for ever* be paid them by the general receiver of the augmentations. And,
That the hospital of Herbaldown *shall have of the King's Highness for ever the some of ten shillings yerely* from the said receiver, for and in recompence of three semes or quarters of barley which they used to receive of the Monastery of Ledes, now dissolved. 1 May, a. r. 37, 1545 *. (The seal is torn off, and much broken.)

* See p. 230, and p. 249.

F. D.

EDWARD VI.

12. Infpeximus and confirmation of all the former grants. 2 Feb. a. r. 3. 1550. (Seal broken.)

COMMONWEALTH.

13. Captain Charles Bowles's affignment of certain rents to the hofpitals, amounting to 4 l. 2 s. 9d. in fatisfaction for 3 l. 8 s. 7d. q. due out of the augmentation office. 10 June, 1654.

It appears by this deed, that by a decree of the Chancellour and Court of Augmentations, dated 24 April, 37 Henry VIII. 1545 (which is not among the deeds in the hofpital cheft) 3 l. 8 s. 7 d. q. was to be paid from the receiver of that office to this hofpital; and Captain Bowles covenanted with the truftees appointed by the parliament to fell the fee farm rents belonging to the Commonwealth to pay it : and he here affigns to the hofpital 14 different fmall rents lying in different parifhes chiefly in the Weald of Kent, which were old obits, &c. for the fatisfaction of this demand on him. This Deed is much hurt by damp.

14. A copy of the Deed, Number 13. imperfect.

15. A letter of attorney fiom the prior, empowering John Biffet to receive the rents due to the hofpital, by virtue of Captain Bowles's affignment. 20 Feb. 1659. Reference is made for particulars to fchedules not here. Thefe rents are now loft; and the whole fum vi l. xvii s. 11 d. ob. is now paid by the Crown, according to N° li.

Archbifhop WILLIAM WITTLESEY.

16. Confirmation of Edward III's grant of exemption from talliage, Number 5. by excommunicating the infringers of it, " Sententiâ excommunicationis majoris. Dat' ap' Otteford, xiii kln' Aprilis, (20 Mar.) 1370."

17. A copy of the fame, tranflated into Englifh.

CHAP. III.

INDULGENCES—LICENCES FOR ALMS-GATHERING.

1. INDULGENCE from Archbifhop John (Stratford) of 40 days to encourage the giving alms to them when they made their collections through his Diocefe, 14 April, 1341. (Only the middle part of the feal remains *. It is torn off. The archbifhop in his habit bleffing.)

* See plate III. fig. 10.

2. Ralph

2. Ralph (de Stratford) Bishop of London, Indulgence of 40 days to all benefactors to the Hospital. 19 July, 1348. (The middle part of the seal pretty whole. A bishop blessing.)

3. Archbishop Simon (Islip) 40 days. Dat' apud Maghfeld, 14 Julii, 1350.

4. Simon (Langham) Bishop of Ely, 40 days. Dat' apud Cant', 2 non. (6) Oct. 1364. (Seal pretty perfect, excepting round the rim; torn off.)

5. Archbishop William (Wittlesey) 40 days, 18 June, 1369. (Seal lost.)

6. Archbishop William (Wittlesey) 40 days, 19 June, 1369. (Seal quite broken.)

7. King Edward III. A letter of protection, general; and particularly of their proctors collecting alms, 23 Oct. a. r. 48, 1374. (Seal much broken.)

8. A letter sent about with the brother that went about asking alms, containing the indulgences granted to them, 29 June, 1375. (Seal is lost.)

OMNIBUS sancte matris ecclesie prelatis ad quos lre iste pvenerint fres & sorores hospitalis de Northgate de Cantuar' saltm aplicam benedictionem: domus siquidem ura in tanta consistit necte & paupertate quod cum maxima miseria vitam indubitanter sustinemus. Ista vero fuerunt beneficia ab archiepis oibus benefactoribus uris concessa; scil, Lanfranc' archieps fundator ejusdem hospitalis XL dies relaxationis concessit; Scus Thomas archieps Cant' XL dies; Stephus [Langton] archieps Cant' XL dies; Theobaldus archieps Cant' XL dies; Ricus archieps Cant' XL dies; Stus Edmund' archieps Cant' XL dies; Bonifacius archieps Cant' XL dies; Johnes de Peccham archieps Cant' XL dies; Robtus Kilwardby archieps Cant' XL dies; Robtus de Winchelse archieps Cant' XL dies; Waltus [Reynolds] archieps Cant' XL dies; Symon de Mepeham archieps Cant' XL dies; Johns [Stratford] archieps Cant' XL dies; Itm Hamo eps Roffens' XL dies; Robert' eps Cicestren' XL dies; Ricus eps Roffen' XL dies; Johns eps Elmessen * XX dies; Willms eps Wynton' XX dies; Henric' Roffen' eps XX dies; Petrus eps Hereforden' XX dies; Willms eps Cicestren' XXX dies; frater Gilbert eps Giadmes de Hybnia XXX dies; Radulphus eps London' XL dies; Stephs eps London' XX dies; Thomas eps Wygorn' XX dies; Henric' eps Lincoln' XX dies; Henric' eps Wynton' XX dies; Adam eps Herefordens' XX dies; Thomas eps de Dureham XX dies; Symon [Islip] archieps Cant' XL dies. Ratificantes insuper omnes indulgencias in hac parte rite concessas & nris temporibus concedendas. Frat' Ricus, Dei apostolice sedis, gratia Dei, archieps de Nazareth, XL dies; preterea XII Cardinales de Curia Romana, qlibet eor' concessit omnibus vere penitentibus & confessis qui ad pdcm hospitale pium manum adjutrices porrexerint, vel in extremis laborantibs aliquid de bonis suis legaverint dicto hospitali, causa devocois accesserint, XL dies de injunctis tibi penitenciis. Omnino diocesanis ejusdem habeant indulgentiam ratam, habint misericorditer in dno relaxavit & unusquisque relaxat. R.tificans omnes & singulas indulgencias nobis hacten' in hac parte rite concessas & temporibus suis in futurum conce-

* E'meham.

dendas.

dendas. Propterea Johnes papa vicefimus fecundus omnes libertates & immunitates & predecefforibus fuis Romanis pontificibus privilegia feu alias indulgentias dicto hofpitali concefsis, necnon libertates & exemptiones fecularium exactionum a regibus & principibus aliisque Xpi fidelibus nobis & dicto hofpitali indulgencias jufte & pacifice optentas auctoritate apoftolica & bulle fue patrocinio ratificavit & communivit. Et quod nulli homini liceat hanc paginam fue confirmationis infringere, vel eam aufu temerario contemnere. Et fi quis hec attemptare prefumpferit, gloriofe virginis Marie & beator' Petri & Pauli apoftolor' ejus fe noverit curfui'. Conceffit eciam idem Johannes papa omnibus benefactoribus ñiis ftationes curie ratione x.iiii annor', eciam feptimam ptem de injuncta fibi penitentia mifericordit' relaxavit. Et qui aliqua bona habuerint, & cui vel quibus ea reftituere ignorant ; & qui votum fecerunt except' Jherol', Scor' Jacobi, apoftolor' Petri & Pauli, & caftitat', vel fi aliquis, vel aliqua fecerint delictum erga priorem vel matrem except' manuum injectione; faciant elemofinam dicto hofpitali Sancti Johis Baptifte de Northgate. Et dñs papa eos abfolvat ; exceptis aliis beneficiis & indulgenciis in dicta Romana ecclefia in diebus factis & fiend' imperpetuum. Et fi quis pdicto hofpitali ñro anulum, firmaculum, aurum, argentum, vaccas, juverculam, bident', anferem vel vitulum dare & tranfmittere voluerit, tdet & liberet pcuri ñio prefenti, & eum recipiem' in fraternitatem, hofpitalis ñii predicti : concedentes eidem participacoem omnium bonor' operum que in hofpitali predicto fient imperpetuum. Et funt in hofpitali noftro centum fratres & forores ceci, claudi, furdi, & aliis divrfis infirmitatibus langdi, qui qualibet die concefferunt & dicunt xxx mille Pat' noft' & Ave Maria cum difciplinis, & orationibus innumerabilibus que ibm fiut: & cum jejuniis & omnium alior' beneficior' innumerabilium benefactores ñios participes effe conftituim' p prefentes. Summam dier' indulgencie de divifis archieps, epis, & cardinalibus conceff' excentis a fumis pontific' curie Romana conceff' mille liiii annor' cxl dies qui qualibet die miff' de diverfis domibus & aliis bonis opibus miffar' celebrationibus que dicto hofpitali ffit quor' ŝm' nemo noverit nifi folus Deus. Idcirco ad colligendas elemofinas ñras latorem prefentium frar' & frm nrm fidelem clemencie vre deftinamus. Rogantes p Deo quater' de temporalibus bonis vris ad vite ñre fuftentationem fi placeat & ad dicti hofpitalis edificior' ñror' qutaemque portionem put Deus in cordibus vris deftinavit nobis p eum tranfmittere velitis. Prior eciam & convent' ecclefie de Cricherche in Cant', prior & conventus Sci Gregorii Cant', concefferunt omnibus ñiris effe pticipes omnium bonor' que fuerit in eadem domo. Fres & forores de ñiris bonis concefferunt illis effe pticipes omnium bonor' que fuernt in eadem domo. In cujus rei teftimonium cre figillum dom' ñre p porem & conventum fecimus hiis apponi. Dat' apud Cant' in fefto apoftolor' Pet' & Pauli Anno Dñi mjllmo ccc feptuagefimo quinto.

(It is written in a fair fquare text, the firft letter illuminated, red paragraphs, and is much worn).

9. A like letter from the brethren at Herbaldown, 5. June, 1398.

10. Another letter from the brethren of St. John's, empowering fifter Mariana Swetman to receive alms, 12 Sept. 1465. (Seal perfect.)

11. Arch-

11. Archbiſhop Thomas (Bourchier) indulgence of 100 days. 14 June, 1474. (Seal loſt.)

12. A licence from four juſtices, to go about to collect alms at the cuſtomary ſeaſons. 4 Jan. 14 Eliz. 1572.
Theſe ſeaſons were, one month before and three weeks after Chriſtmas and St. John Baptiſt.

13. A like licence from five juſtices. 12 Jan. 27 Eliz. 1585.

C H A P. IV.

ORIGINAL ENDOWMENT.

1. **H**EN·RY de Eſtria, prior of Chriſt Church, Canterbury. Inſpeximus, recital, and confirmation of the inſtrument by which Aichbiſhop John (Peckham) revokes the appropriation of the church of Reculver, and ſettles the maintenance of the hoſpitals to be out of the archiepiſcopal chamber as before, 21 July, 1291, (the archbiſhop's inſtiument bears date 7 July, 1290) under the conventual ſeal. The ſeal is but little broken, and is very fine. It is engraved by the Society of Antiquaries, and called The third Seal of the Convent.

2. An ancient copy of the ſame.

3. King Edward III. Licence for appropriation of the parſonage of Reculver to the archbiſhop's table, and for payment of 160 t. out of the revenues of the ſee of Canterbury, notwithſtanding the ſtatute of mortmain, to both hoſpitals. 16 Mar. a. r. 22, 1348.
The broad ſeal is ſomewhat broken. It is exactly engraved in " La Genealogie des ʼ "Comtes de Flandres, par Olivier de Wrée," p. 46.

4. An ancient copy of the ſame.

5. Archbiſhop Simon (Iſlip). An order that the 160 t. per annum, due from the archbiſhoprick to the hoſpitals, be paid, for the future, out of the church of Reculver. Dat' apud Otteford, 6 Feb. 1355. The ſeal is ſomewhat broken. The middle part repreſents the martyrdom of Becket, over which is the ciucifixion, and under it the archbiſhop kneeling (ſee plate III. fig. 11.). The legend is almoſt all broken off.

6. Archbiſhop Thomas (Chichley)*. Exemplification of N° 3. and of N° 1. and of N° 5. and of the confirmation of Pope Nicholas (I ſuppoſe V.) Dat' Romæ, 13 Feb. a. p. 2. (1447.)

* Chichley's Chriſtian name was ' Henry,' not ' Thomas,' and he died in 1443. John Stafford was archbiſhop in 1447.

5

The

The truth of this exemplification is attefted by the archiepifcopal feal, and the atteftations of two notaries public. Dat' in ecclef' de Hakynton, anno 1447, 5 Maii.

7. An authentic extract from the " Parliamentary Survey of the Manor of Bough-" ton, parcell of the Poffeffions of the late Archbifhop of Canterbury;" mentioning the payment of fevenfcore pounds per ann. to the two hofpitals, out of the manors of Boughton and Reculver, appointed by Archbifhop Lanfranc, and 20 l. per ann. more, out of Reculver, by Archbifhop Richard.

8. Copy of an order for the continuance of the payment of 160 l. per ann. to the two hofpitals.

By the Truftees for maintenance of Minifters, June 25, 1652.

WHEREAS there is due unto the brothers and fifters of the two hofpitalls of St. Nicholas in Herbaldowne and St. John's without Northgate, in Canterbury, in the county of Kent, the yearely fumme of one hundred and fixty poundes, payable by the Archbifhop of Canterbury for the time being to the priors of the faid feverall hofpitalls, to bee by them diftributed among the brothers and fifters of the faid hofpitalls, according to theire proporcons: Now, in purfuance of an act of this prefent parliament, for the fale of gleablands of bifhops, and deanes and chapters; it is ordered that the faid yearly fumme of one hundred and fixty poundes bee, and the fame is hereby, allowed and continued to the faid brothers and fifters of the faid hofpitalls refpectively, the fame to be accompted from the firft day of November laft.

JOHN THOROWGOOD.
FRA. WEST.
RICHARD YOUNG.
Jo. POCOCK.

Ex. WM. STEELE.
Vera Copia.

C H A P. V.

PRIVATE DONATIONS.

Aſh.

1. Grant from Thomas and John Hochon of xvi ꝺ. annual rent out of a meſſuage and one acre and a half of land at Naſh in Aſh. 25 Feb. 33 Hen. VI. 1455. (Much periſhed.)

2. Tranſlation of the ſame.

Biſhopsbourn.

3. Grant from Thomas Myles of Bourne to John Broun of Bourne of one place of a meſſuage in Biſhoppeſbourne. Apr. 11 Edw. III. 1337.

Brabourne.

4. Grant from John Schottewade to John Andrews and Bartholomew Vade of all his lands and tenements in Braborne. July, 18 Ric. II. 1394.

5. Grant from Stephen Andrewe of Braborne to Peter Tanner and others of all his lands (excepting xii acres), tenements, and reverſions in Braborne and Haſtingleghe. 8 Hen. V. 1420.

6. Grant from John Marchant of Braborne to Stephen Andrewe of one toft called Clokeſhaghe, containing half a rood, 4. Jun. Hen. V. 1421. (Much worn and torn.)

7. Grant from Elis Bakere to Stephen Andrew and others of all his lands and tenements in Braborne and Demecherche. 12 H. VI. 1433.

Canterbury.

8. St. Alphege. Copy of a clauſe in Matthew Brown's will giving x s̄. yearly to each of the hoſpitals of Eaſtbridge, Maynard's, St. John's, and Herbaldown, out of two meſſuages in Staplegate, dated Dec. 12, 1717, proved Aug. 26, 1721.

9. St. Andrew. Confirmation by William de Aula and Amabilla his wife of a bequest of William le Brewere of IV s. p ann. charged on a tenement in St. Andrews, to buy peafe for their potage. 20 Apr. 1275. (Worn to pieces)

10. St. George. ·Releafe from Clementia widow of Stephen Merile to Thomas de
Prey of all claim on a meffuage in Bertha de Newyngate in fuburbio, which he
had bought of her hufband. March, 1 Edw. I. 1273.

11. Releafe of all claim from Agnes daughter of John Brewere to Thomas de Percy
on a meffuage in Richerchepe in St. George's in the fuburbs of Canterbury. 1
Edw. II. 1307.

Quod quidem meffuagium Alicia quondam uxor prædicti Johannis le Brewere, &
mater mea mihi & .... forori meæ in teftamento fuo fecundum confuetudinem
civitatis Cantuar' legavit. (Seal very fair, round ✠. s. AL..IE FILE JOHIS
BREVER.)

12. Grant from Thomas de Percy to John de Selvefton of one meffuage in St.
George's in the fuburbs. 1313. (The feal is remarkable,   on a field fable
two combatants with fword and very fmall buckler, round s. THOME HER C....

13. Grant from John Sythe to Roger Barham of a tenement in Retherchepe. Apr.
6 Hen. IV. 1405.

14. Grant from Roger Barham to Martin Chefman of the fame. July, 9 Hen. IV.
1408.

15. Releafe of claim on the fame from William Harry of Bifhoppefbourne to Martin Chefham. 9 Hen. IV. 1408.

16. Grant from Martin Chefham to John Nafh of the fame tenement. 22 July, 1
Hen. VI. 1423.

17. Releafe from John atte Neffche to Martin Chefham of claim on the fame.
May, 3 Hen. VI. 1425.

18. Grant from Martin Chefham to William Skot and others of the faid tenement.
20 Apr. 4 Hen. VI. 1426.

19. St. Mary at Bredene. Grant from John Ordwy of Stelling to Thomas de Wolton *, clerk, and others, of one acre in St. Mary at Bredene apud Doddifdane.
Nov. 1 Ric. II. 1377. (Seal

20. St. Mary de Caftro. Grant from Joan wife of the late John de Selveftone of
Eaftry, to the hofpital of 11 s. annual rent out of the fouthern part of a capital
meffuage in St. Mary de Caftro, which John de Monck ufed to pay her. 5 Aug.
16 Edw. III. 1342.

* Thomas de Wolton was mafter of Eaftbridge Hofpital from 1351 to 1381.

21. Letter of attorney from Joan wife of late John de Silveſtone to William her ſon to put the hoſpitall in poſſeſſion of the above annuity of 11 s. 5 Aug. 16 Edw. III. 1343.

22. Releaſe from John Byrcholte of vi d. rent from a piece of land called Readacr, at Reydowne, which the hoſpital uſed to pay to him. 7 Feb. 27 H. VI. 1449.

St. Martin and St. Paul. Wyke.

23. Thomas de Garwynton, Jun. to the hoſpital 32 acres, and a penſion of 15 s. 3 d. ob. and eight cocks and nineteen hens, with reliefs, &c formerly belong-ing to the chantry of Lukedale in Littlebourn, of his own patronage: which 32 acres lay at Wyke. 11 Aug. 30 Edw. III. 1356.

24. Indenture from the abbot and convent of St. Auguſtin, permitting the hoſ-pital to take the aforeſaid from Thomas de Garwynton, and hold it by the ſervices therein recited: paying 13 s. 4 d. to the convent for the land, as lords of the fee, and doing ſervice at the court at Longe Port. 38 Edw. III. 1364. much worn. The ſeal is pretty well preſerved.

25. Edward III. Licence of mortmain to Thomas de Garwynton to make the fore-going aſſignment. 25 July, a. r. 38, 1364. Broad ſeal ſomewhat different from the others.

26. Extract from a terrier of the parſonage of St. Paul, made 5 June, 33 Hen. VIII. 1542. In the archives of the Cathedral, Canterbury, and from an exemplification under the broad Seal, 28 Jan. 8 Eliz. 1567, both to ſhew that five acres, lying in St. Paul's pariſh, were part of a Field called Brethren Field. See the Map, Ch. 6. 1.

27. A copy of the petition from the hoſpital to Archbiſhop Whitgift, touching Sir Moyle Finch's detaining Mote lands from them. Poſt 1583.

28. Exemplification of a recovery in an ejectment between Abraham Hartwell, leſſee of the hoſpital, plaintiff, and William Brown, defendant, of 27 acres lying in St. Martin's pariſh near Canterbury, parcel of 32 acres contained in their demiſe to him, and of judgment for the defendant for the reſidue. 5 Feb. 41 Eliz. 1599.

29. Extract from the Survey of Colleges, &c. in Kent, " onerat' ſeu onerabilia ad " ſoluconem primiciar' & decimar'," made 37 Hen. VIII. concerning the hoſpi-tal of St. John. Extracted 11 Auguſt, 1624. It was taken to ſhew, among other particulars of their poſſeſſions, the following, " cert' terr' ibm cont' xvi " acr' terr' in tenur' Willmi Fynch, milit', jacen' juxta veñell apud Fourhcde " Croſſe, xiii s. iiii d. & ultra redd' reſolut'."

30. Copy of a petition from the hoſpital (after being caſt in a trial at law) to Archbiſhop Abbot, to permit them to accept Lady Finch's offer of 40 l. for arrearages,

arrearages, 20 l. towards cofts, and 13 s. 4 d. annually for ever, and to permit them to releafe all claim on the lands. 1627.

31. Archlifhop Abbot's confent to the petition, and decree thereupon. Signed by him, Oct. 3, 1627.

32. The petition of the prior and bethren to the Countefs of Winchelfea, figned by them, and her declaration of agreement with them, according to the termes N° 31. Signed by her, 7 Feb. 7 Car. I. 1631.

33. Indenture of agreement between the Countefs of Winchelfea and the hofpital, by which the hofpital renounces all claim on the lands at Moat, and the Countefs engages for the payment of 13 s. 4 d. annually for the future, with arreats from 1.64; amounting to 44 l. 15 s. 4 d. and to add 20 l. more, provided 60 l. be laid out in a purchafe for the benefit of the hofpital *. This agreement was in confequence of a verdict given at a trial in the Guildhall, Canterbury, in 1616, in favour of the Countefs, and was made with the allowance of Archbifhop Abbott, 8 Feb. 7 Car. I. 1633. The feal is rubbed off. This is figned by the Countefs.

34. St. Mildred. Grant from John de Pyywode to Thomas atte Hecche of a meffuage in Stour Streate. 25 Mar. 15 Edw. III. 1361.

35. Grant from Sufan atte Bore widow, and Sibella daughter of Hugh Turnour, to Thomas Cobits and Alice Overyes his wife, of one meffuage in Northgate: in length XLVIII feet, in breath from Broadftreet XVIII feet, in breadth front Foffam XVI feet. Jan. 1, Ed. II. 1308. Damaged by wet.

36. Leafe from John Heneper and Robert Wade to the prior, &c. of a meffuage in Northgate, juxta regiam foffam, for the term of 100 years. 23 Edw. III. 1349. Almoft oblirerated.

37. Leafe by indenture from John Heneper and Robert Wade to the hofpital of a tenement for 100 years. 23 Edw. III. 1449.

38. Grant from Robert Colt and John Tygge of Weftgate without to Richard Dunkyn of a tenement and garden in Broadftreet. 3 June, 14 Hen. VI. 1436.

39. Indenture of conveyance from Richard Dunkyn to John Spencer and others of one tenement and garden in Brodeftrete. 20 Aug. 26 Hen. VI. 1448.

40. Releafe from John Skot, Efq. and others to Richard Dunkyn of all claim on a tenement and garden in Brodftrete. 4 Sept. 27 Hen. VI. 1448.

41. Indenture of conveyance from John Spencer and others to Simon Bird and Thomas Hempftede of a tenement in Broadeftrete on payment of IV l. 14 Oct. 37 Hen. VI. 1458.

42. Counterpart.

* See p. 202.

43. Grant:

43. Grant from Nicholas Churchman and others, feoffees of William Brokynden and others, feoffees of Simon Bird, to Hamo Lambard and others of a tenement in Broadſtreet. 30 May, 1 Edw. IV. 1451.

44. Grant from John Rowe to John and Joan Clerke of Lyminge of a tenement in Brodeſtrete. 3 Jun. 4 Edw. IV. 1464.

45. Indenture from John and Joan Clerke of Lymynge granting to Jacob and Alice Colyn one tenement in Brodeſtrete, reſerving a rent of vii l. p aun. for the term of their own lives. 4 July, 4 Edw. IV. 1464.

46. Counterpart.

47. A pair of indentures by which William Kendall, and others, confirm to John Aſbourn, R. Grove, and R. Exbregge one meſſuage and one garden on payment of the ſums therein ſpecified. 5 Nov. 21 Hen. VII. 1481. Endorſed. The upper houſe in Broadſtreet.

48. Releaſe from Alexander Bokyngham to Nich. and Ag. Wade of all claim on two tenements and gardens contiguous in Brodeſtreet. 15 Dec. 7 H. VII. 1491.

49. Indenture of conveyance from Nich. and Agnes Wade to John Wade and others of a tenement and garden, on payment of viii l. xiii s. iv d. 24 July, 9 Hen. VII. 1494.

50. Indenture from Robert Hynkſell and others, feoffees of Nich. and Agnes Wade, granting, at the requeſt of Edmund and Agnes Wylcock, late wife of John Wade, to John Poyle and others a tenement and garden in Broadſtreet for the uſe of Johanna the wife of John Wattys and his heirs for-ever. 27 June, 12 Hen. VII. 1498.

51. Releaſe from Agnes widow of Nich. Wade to Robert Hynkſell and others of all claim on a tenement and garden. 15 Feb. 12 Hen. VII. 1449.

52. Grant from James Downe, clerk, to Ralph Browne, Pargrave, and others, of a meſſuage and garden in Northgate. 14 Apr. 19 Hen. VII. 1504.

53. Grant from Ralph Browne and others to William Kendall and others of one meſſuage and garden in Northgate. End of the upper houſe in Broadſtrete. 14 Apr. 20 Hen. VII. 1505.

54. Grant from Ralph Browne and Richard Exbregge to William Michell, clerk, and two others, of one meſſuage and garden in Broadſtreet. 27 Feb. 13 Hen. VIII. 1522. Almoſt periſhed.

55. Grant from William Michell, clerk, and others, in compliance with the will of William Pargrave, to Nicholas Reynolds and others of a meſſuage and garden in Broadſtreet. 30 Oct. 21. Hen. VIII. 1530.

56. Grant

56. Grant from Thomas Laurence and others, at the requeſt of Matilda widow of William Pargrave, who ordered it to be ſold by his will, of a meſſuage and garden in Broadſtreet, to R. Reynolds, P. Richemont, R. Frognall, and R. Chaundler. 31 Oct. 21 H. VIII. 1530.

57. Warranty from John ſon of James Baker and Suſan his wife, to William and Iſabelle le Centurer, of two ſhops and a piece of land in Broadſtreet, which they had from Nicholas-de Acriſe, clerk. 16 Edw. I. 1287. Seal, a ſtar of ſixteen points, s. IOHIS FIL. IACOBBII. Seal, a ſtar of ſixteen points, s. SVSANNE FIL. IOHIS.

58. Grant from John Payne to . . . . atte Leaſe and Thomas K'ypping, and one tenement. Endorſed. Of one of the houſes in Broadſtreet. 1 Ric. II. 1377.

59. Smith. George Smith of Chelsfield, Kent, enfeoffed John Boys, and eleven more of their heirs, of one meſſuage newly made, two dwellings backwardes, and gardens in Northgate, to pay one-fifth of the rent to himſelf during life, and to whom he ſhall appoint, end two-fifths to ten, nine, eight, ſeven, ſix, or five poor houſeholders of St. Paul's, and two-fifths to St. John's Hoſpital. This is an indenture from the feoffees empowering the prior and his four aſſiſtants, and the churchwardens of St. Paul's for the time being to appoint a perſon to receive and pay the above rents. 10 Sept. 1622.

60. New enfeoffment from Thomas Mills, Jonas Waters, and John Evernden, ſurvivors of the firſt 12 feoffees to 12 new ones, ſix of Northgate, and ſix of St. Paul's. 3 Sept. 1645. It is here ſaid theſe tenements were purchaſed of Edward Robarts, Gent. and their boundaries are deſcribed.

61. New enfeoffment by George Young, Ric. Pyſing, Nich. Fowle, and Paul Gilmer, ſurvivors of the ſecond enfeoffment, to 12 new feoffees. 17 Mar. 16 Char. II. 1663.

Shrottynton Lane, vulgo Ruttington Lane.

62. 1. Grant from Nicholas le Gardener to William de Wy of a piece of land ten feet long and ſeven feet broad. March, 8 Edw. II. 1315. Seal round, a ſtar with eight points, s. NICOLAI GARDINIR.

62. 2. Grant from Alice, widow of William de Hortone, to William de Aſkelby of a meſſuage and a piece of land. 13 Edw. II. 1320. Seal s. AINCIE UXOR WIL.

63. Grant from Clement Thomas to John Bret and John Weryn of all his lands and tenements in Throtyngton Lane. 18 Ric. II. 1389.

64. Releaſe from John Gate Wever to John Park . . . . of all claim on one tenement and garden. 3 Oct. 18 Hen. VI. 1439.

65. 1. Grant

65. 1. Grant from John Farintevn of Fordwich to Sampfon Colman and John Burbage of a tenement and garden. 10 Dec. Ed. III. Much perifhed.

65. 2. Grant from Thomas Sheder to Salomon Halke of a tenement and garden. 15 Mar. 24 H. VI. 1446.

Bertha de Northgate, Ducklane.

66. Grant from Henry fon of Thomas le Cliter, and Matilda his wife to William le Bukeler and Ifabella his wife of a meffuage, &c. in Bertha de Northgate. 21 Edw. I. 1292. Endorfed. In Duklane. Seal round, white wax, ftan. broken.

Le Boar.

67. Grant from Ad. Baleys to John atte Hecche of a meffuage at Le Bor. 14 Ed. III. 1340.

68. Grant from John atte Hecche to Ric. Godeman of the faid meffuage. 41 Edw. III. 1367.

69. Grant from Ric. Godeman to Thomas de Wolton and others of the faid meffuage. 18 Oct. 41 Edw. III. 1367. Much perifhed.

70. Grant from John Arumper, brother of John Mylftede, to William Wells of a meffuage apud Le Bor. Jan. 14 Edw. III. 1340.

Froxpole Lane.

71. Grant from John Snil Chaloner, and Sarah widow of Adam Robert, to William Stabler de Stebbregge of two fhops in Froxpole. 24 Edw. III. 1350. Much perifhed.

72. Grant from William Stabler to John and Margaret Gardiner of one fhop and garden in Froxpole. 32 Edw. III. 1358.

73. Leafe from the hofpital to John Tournour of an houfe and land in Froxpole lane for the term of 100 years, rent x d̄. fterling. 18 Oct. 14 Ric. II. 1390. Almoft perifhed.

74. Grant from Patricius Clerk to Joan Byrdys, fifter of the hofpital, of a fhop and garden in Froxpole lane. 6 Hen. IV. 1405.

75. Releafe from Joan Byrdys to John Knyght and others of all claim on the faid tenement and garden. Mar. 6 Hen. IV. 1428.

76. Grant from John Ledys to Thomas Feefte of III r. in Northgate. Mar. 13 Hen. VI. 1435.

77. Letter

77. Letter of attorney from John Ledys to Thomas Sturmyn, to put Thomas Feefte in poffeffion. Mar. 13, Hen. VI. 1435.

78. Grant from Thomas Feefte to William and Robert Engelard of the faid III r. 15 Feb. 16 Hen. VI. 1438.

79. Grant from William and Robert Engelard to Thomas Palmer of the faid III r. 4 Oct. 23 Hen. VI. 1444.

Poldrefield.

80. Grant from Cecily Halcok to William Wygge, vicar of St. Dunftan, of a piece of land at Poldrefield in Northgate. 12 June, 15 Ric. II. 1392.

Sturry Road.

81. Confirmation by Stephen Frende of the devife made by John Fremyngham of II a. I r.* to the hofpital in Northgate, after the death of his wife Joan and Thomas Chyldemell. 5 May, 16 Ed. IV. 1477. Indorfed, "Juxta viam que ducit ad Sturry."

82. Grant from John Lameherft to John Starkey and others, feoffees, of II a. I r.* in Northgate. 15 Nov. 19 Hen. VIII. 1528.

83. Releafe of claim from John de Grenehew and others to Lawrence . . . . and Julian his wife, on a meffuage in Northgate, once Walter Fryblod's. Jan. 19 Ed. II. 1326. Very much worn. The fituation is not defcribed.

Lexis Lane.

84. Releafe from Dionyfia, relict of Reginald Counger, and Margaret his daughter, to Sir Andrew Byford, chaplain, of a piece of land and the buildings thereon at Lexiflane in Northgate, xxxi feet long, xix feet broad. 24 June, 1 Edw. III. 1327. Indorfed, " De tenemento Konegh."

85. Grant from Thomas de Efkilby to Robert and Collette Cook of two pieces of land in Northgate. 33 Edw. III. 1358.

86. Fragment of a grant of William Engelard to Roger . . . . . . of a tenement and garden in Northgate. 24 Hen. VI 1445. See Nº 79.

87. Copy of the will of brother P. Ruffel, bequeathing his gret houfe, after his wife's deceafe, to the hofpital. 20 June, 1502.

* This muft probably be the III roods of meadow or pafture land now leafed to Mr. George Frend, at a rack rent of 1 l. 10 s. as it is defcribed in the leafe as " bounding to the king's " highway leading from Canterbury to Sturry."

O o

St. Paul.

St. Paul.

88. Grant from Thomas and Agnes Yngelot of Tanet to Margery Rufshelyn, priorefs of the fifters of the Almonry of St. Auguftin, of xii d, rent out of a tenement in St. Paul's. 25 Edw. III. 1352. Seal, virgin and child. Legend very fair.

89. Grant from John Lovel, clerk, and others, feoffees of the late Henry Webbe, to William Benet and others, of two fhops in St. Paul's. 28 Jan. 8 Hen. VI. 1430.

90. Parcell of St. John's Jerufalem, copied and attefted by Mr. Somner. This is a copy of part of a rentall, by which it appears that they received from St. John's Hofpital, for the rent of a tenement in Loderflane, p ann. xii d. ⁓ for do of Herbaldown Hofpital x d. and paid to both hofpitals p ann. viil. viis. iid. ob.

Weftgate without.

91. Grant from Elueua ate Melne, late wife of Elyas Marefcal, to the hofpital of iii s. annually out of a tenement there. Sans date. Indorfed, " Croker Leane Ende †."

92. Grant (on payment of xv s. iid. fterl.) from John, fon of Hugh, fon of Edward, of xxvii d. annually to the hofpital, to be paid, xiii d. by Edward Pottere out of a meffuage, one acre of land, and wood on it, and xiv d. by Robert the carter. Sans date.

93. Another grant of the fame annually, from John, fon of Hugh, &c. in which the lands are more clearly fpecified. Sans date. The feal is broken ; the outer coat is green, the inner red wax.

94. Grant from Reginald, prior, and the convent of St. Martin, Dover, with the confent of Archbifhop Stephen (Langton), to Northgate Hofpital of eight acres and a half of wood without Weftgate, of the tenement of the Archbifhop, which was given to them by Peter, fon of Salomon, fon of Ulric de Sandwich, paying to the convent xii d. annual rent. Sans date. A very fine deed. Between 1207 & 1228.

95. Grant from Richard de Bernefole, fon of Turg' de Hyllegh, to the hofpital of xx s. and i d. fterling rent, and one cock and four hens, without Weftgate and Northgate, from the perfons therein named, for which the hofpital paid xii marks fterling. 55 Hen. III. 1271. Seal is fewed up in a piece of leather.

---

* Though no fuch tenement or lane can now be found, this xii d. efcheating probably to the crown, on the fuppreffion of the Knights of St. John, and being granted as a fee-farm rent to the Dean and Chapter of Rochefter, is ftill paid annually to their receiver, with iv d. for acquittance. But who pays in return the " vii l. vii s. ii d. ob." alfo mentioned above ?

† Mr. Tilbe now pays for a houfe in Crocker Lane a like annuity of iii s. and Mrs. Strouts, for a houfe there, x d.

96. Another copy of Richard de Bernefole's grant, of the fame date. In this he writes himfelf " Ric' de Dovor, fil' Turgif' de Yll*gh*." In the date, " anno regni reg' Henr' fil' reg'. " Jo*h*is" is omitted. Seal oval.

97. Releafe from Stephen de Fyndon of Canterbury to Stephen de Horfham of all claim on a rent of viii đ. out of a tenement without Weftgate. 37 Edw. III. 1363. Almoſt periſhed. Seal, broken, has an infcription round the arms *.

98 Releafe from John Proude of Canterbury of . . . . . . for which John Smyth and himfelf were made feoffees by Conſtance [Bertyn]. In part periſhed. 20 May, [1487].

99. Confirmation from William Hope, grandſon of Conſtance Bertyn, of three ſhillings annually † out of certain tenements in Crocker lane. 28 Feb. 19 Edw. IV. 1479. Tho. atte Wode [Atwood] Efq. maior.

Priory of St. Gregory, and Archbiſhop Simon Iſlip ‡.

100. Compofition between St. Gregory's Priory and the hofpital concerning a fewer going from St. Gregory's under the king's highway, and a fhop called the Goterfhope and a curtilage of the hofpital, going from thence in a ſtrait line to the great ditch where now clothes are wafhed, being in length from the king's highway xviii rods, and in breadth three feet. Confirmed by Archbiſhop Simon *Iſlip*. Sealed with the feal of the priory, and under this feal, 17 Sept. 31 Edw. III. 1358. The Archbiſhop's feal, almoſt entire, has the Archbiſhop in the middle, over his head and under his feet broken §. Upper compartments, crofier fide, St. Paul; other fide, St. Peter (as legate of the apoftolical fee). Under, two angels, one fupporting the arms of England ‖, the other of the fee, in which are inferted two crofiers. St. Gregory's feal has in the middle St. Gregory; on his right hand St. Mildred; the other fide is broken.

Chiſtlet.   Park Street.

101. Grant from Henry Holte to Thomas Walware of one meſſuage at Park ſtreet in Chiſtlet. 12 Hen. IV. 1352. Small round Seal.

102. Anicia Hughes, widow of John Middleton, of one meſſuage here. 20 April, 10 Hen. V. 1422. The feal the fame as 101.

103. Letter of attorney from Robert Holyman, empowering Thomas Deryng to put Hamon and Joan Bregge in poſſeſſion of a feeding of four cows in a marfh called

---

* This is the fum ſtill paid by Mr. Tilbe.
† See N° 91.
‡ This, by miſtake, is labelled "Archbiſhop Simon Mepham."
§ See this feal in plate III. fig. 11 fiom the inſtrument defcribed in p. 209.
‖ Archbiſhop Iſlip had been fecretary and keeper of the privy feal to K. Edward III.

Salt-

Saltkynesbrok, and two pieces of arable. 2 April, 19 Hen. VI. 1451. Much worn.

104. Releafe from Nicholas Gylbert to Hamo Bregge of all claim on a meſſuage, garden, and xxix a. 11 r. of land, wood, meadow, and paſture, lying ſeparately in Chiſtlet, granted to him and the late Robert Kennet by Robert Holyman. 10 Feb. 36 Hen. VI. 1457.

105. John Parſoun of Chiſtlet to Ric. Hoke of two pieces of land. 45 Ed. III. 1472.

Forſtalfield.

106. Robert, ſon and heir of Thomas Conſant, to John Ive of three acres in For-ſtalfield, below the curtilage de Hacche. 8 Oct. 6 Hen. VII. 1490.

Coſmus Blean.   Foxholes.

107. John, ſon of Robert Lapyn, to Thomas Braunche of a piece of land at Foxholes. 26 Nov. 22 Edw. III. 1348.

108. Thomas Adam de Helde in Hakynton to Thomas Kywhit and Peter Botevi-layne, brothers of the hoſpital, of a piece of land at Foxholes in Coſmus Blean. 3 Feb. 25 Edw. III. 1352.

109. Releaſe from Thomas Adam of Hakynton to Thomas Braunche of all claim on one croft and one acre of wood-land at Foxholes. 32 Edw. III. 1359. Seal oval a half moon between two ſtars.

110. Grant from Thomas Braunche of Canterbury of one croft in St. Coſmus Blean, called Foxholes, 8 Nov. 33 Ed. III. 1360. Seal (ſee plate III. fig. 4.) round, fair, and the impreſſion from the murder of Becket.

111. Walter and Conſtance Boner and John Taborer to Sir Thomas de Wolton, clerk, and others, of a croft at Foxholes, and part of one meſſuage and one croft in Hakynton. Mar. 30 Edw. III. 1358.

112. Walter Bonere to the hoſpital of a piece of land at Lithiſfelde in ſaid pariſh. 34 Edw. III. 1360.

113. William Martyn of Hakynton to John Hurtyn and others, of a piece of land at Scherthe in Coſmus Blean. 27 Dec. 11 Hen. IV. 1410.

114. Nicholas Pende to Robert Cauſton of half an acre in Coſmus Blean called Shep-perdyſcroft. 18 Sept. 18 Hen. VI. 1439.

115 Robert Cauſton to the hoſpital of the ſaid half acre. 2 Jan. 24 Hen. VI. 1446.

God-

Godwynſtone. Rollyng.

116. John Stour to Simon Philpot of a meſſuage and four feet of land. 11 June, 15 Ric. II. 1392.

117. Thomas Copedok to Giles Nyker of . . . . . . and one acre at Elmynton . . . . . Almoſt obliterated.

118. Thomas, ſon of Richard Sedeges, to John and Emma Sedeges of one rood of land at Heryngodes, and his part of a meſſuage, late Richard Sedeges's. 13 Edw. III. 1339.

119 John Sedeges to Thomas and Joan Copedok and their iſſue, of one meſſuage and half an acre of land diviſim; if no iſſue, to revert. 31 Edw. III. 1357. Much worn.

120. Hamo and Thomas, ſons of Stephen atte Steghele of Aſh, to Thomas Copedok of one rood and a half. 39 Ed. III. 1355.

121. Thomas Cheeſman of Bourn to Thomas Copedok of half a rood of land. 50 Edw. III. 1376. See T. Ch. 183.

122. William Tebbe to Thomas Copedok one rood at Rymerſtoun. 25 Mar. 6 Ric. II. 1383.

123. Thomas Copedok and Simon Philpot to John Copedok of two acres and one acre, in all three acres, in a field called Attemede. 10 June, 20 Ric. II. 1397.

124. William Couper to John Copedok of Sandwich two acres and one rood and a half at Northdane. 20 April, 22 Ric. II. 1399.

125. Releaſe from Alice Dowele and Conſtance Chapman, daughters and heireſſes of John Copedok, and Thomas Shereman, couſin and heir, to both hoſpitals, of all claim on a tenement and ten acres, late John Copedok's. 3 May, 4 Edw. IV. 1463. Almoſt periſhed.

126. Another releaſe from the ſame, dated 1 June 4 Edw. IV. 1463.

127. Acquittance from Thomas Sherman of London for xx s. in full payment of all demands on the ſaid tenement and ten acres. 9 May, 6 Ed. IV. 1466.

128. John Coppedok to John Fiede and others of one meſſuage and garden. 6 Feb. 5 Hen. VI. 1427.

129. Henry Chapman to both hoſpitals of two acres. 10 April, 4 Edw. IV. 1464.

130. Henry Chapman's letter of attorney, empowering William Jacob to put the priors in poſſeſſion. 12 April, 4 Edw. IV. 1464.

131. Simon Leyceſtre of Sandwich to both hoſpitals of a tenement and eight acres, late John Coppedok's. 12 May, 4 Edw. IV. 1464.

132. Si-

132. Simon Leyceſtre's letter of attorney to William Jacob for livery and ſeiſin 12 May, 4 Edw. IV. 1464.

133. John Baker of Chyllendon to John Johnſon and Thomas Warde of a tenement and ten acres, late John Coppedok's. 25 July, 8 Hen. VII. 1492.

134. John Johnſon and Thomas Warde to both hoſpitals of the ſaid tenement and ten acres. 31 July, 8 Hen. VII. 1492.

135. Richard Duglas to bothe hoſpitals of two yards of land ſeparate. 2 Jan. 15 Hen. VII. 1500.

136. Releaſe from Richard Duglas of all claim on the ſame. 20 Aug. 20 Hen. VII. 1505.

137. Affidavit before the mayor of Sandwich, by Griſſell Bills, that her late huſband John left to the hoſpital an annual rent goyng yerlie out of the lands of the ſaid brethren, called Taberland at Rollyng, as by dede of releaſe appears. Under the common ſeal, 21 Feb. 28 Hen. VIII. 1537.

Graveney.

138. William de Beyrdeſtone to the hoſpital of half the rent of a ſaltwork there *. 10 Edw. I. 1281. Much periſhed. Seal oval, red wax. s. IACOBI FIL' VIL-ELMI.

Hakinton, vulgo St. Stephen's.

139. James ſon of William de Colewenewode, to the hoſpital of a tenement in Hakinton and ſome land, late belonging to Maſter Hugo de Clervans, with an annuity of xxxvii d̄. from different perſons, on payment of xL marks ſterling. 55 Hen. III. 1260.

140. Releaſe from John, ſon of Terric of Canterbury, to the hoſpital of all claim on ſix acres in the tenure of the Archbiſhop, which the Archbiſhop had by the feofment of Lucia de Hakinton. 4 Edw. I. 1275. Torn.

141. Margaret, daughter of Arthur atte Helde, to the hoſpital of three acres and a droveway at Stonrokks. Sept. 10 Edw. II. 1317.

142. Walter and Conſtance Bonere of Coſmus Blean to the hoſpital of one meſſuage and toft. 34 Edw. IV. 1360. (See 111.)

143. John Ropere of Weſtgate to Thomas de Wolton and others, of houſes and land at Teghelerſhelde. 28 May, 36 Edw. III. 1362.

* Now probably reduced to a penſion of 2 s. per ann. paid by John Lade, Eſq.

144. Wil-

144. William Fox to the hofpital of two acres for xcix years by indenture. 7 Oct. (1477.) 17 Edw. IV.

145. Indenture between the hofpital and Sir Roger Manwood, granting a water-courfe from the fpring-head in their wood called St. John's, alias Brotherhood wood, unto his houfe at Hakinton, in a leaden pipe, on payment of vi s. viii d. annually; confirmed and figned by Archbifhop John (Whitgift), and figned and fealed by Sir Roger Manwood. 13 March, 30 Eliz. 1588*.

Herne.

146. Affignment from Thomas de Woltone to Philip de Northwode of all his lands and tenements at Henneford †, paying to this hofpital XL s. and to Harbledown hofpital xx s. annually. 18 Oct. 30 Edw. III. 1356.

147. Thomas Bargve and others to Richard and Joan Lucas of one acre for their natural lives. 1 Nov. 3 Ric. II. 1379.

148. Thomas Sprynget to John Barry of his lands and manor called Henneford †, and two acres at Hampton, which he had from Barry. Sept. 1 Hen. IV. 1400.

149. Releafe from Thomas Sprynget to James Twitham of all claim on Henneford †, purchafed of John, fon of Philip Northwode, and of ten acres, fix at Hares in Childe, two William at Halkes, two at Stateflonde, purchafed of the faid Northwode. 8 Jan. 12 Hen. IV. 1411.

150. James Twitham to William Benet and others, of all his three tenements, woods, &c. in Herne, which he had by feofment from John Yong, ... on fome condition which is worn out. 6 June, 4 Hen. VI. 1426.

151. Copy of the will of Nicholas Rydere, granting to certain feoffees a capital meffuage and lands for the term of ten years, with certain entails, paying for that term vi s. viii d. a year to the hofpitals, and after other contingencies fome other fums to thefe and other religious houfes. 10 Feb. 1437. Almoft obliterated.

152. Fragment. Thomas Nowthorpe to John Bette of a meffuage at Onderdowne. 28 Aug. H. . . . .

153. Matthew Philip, alderman of London, to Henry Harder fix acres near the rectory. 29 Oct. 30 Hen. VI. 1452.

154. Probate of the will of Johane Harder, widow, fyfter of the hofpital, ordering (befide bequefts at her funeral, &c.) her feoffees to deliver an account of her lands ‡ at Herne to the prior, and the filling up the feofment. 25 Jan. 3 Hen. VIII. 1512.

155. Feoffment from John Martin and others to John Lamberherft and others for the purpofes of Joan Harder's will. 26 May, 3 Hen. VIII. 1512.

* The fame fum is ftill paid by Sir Edward Hales, bart. the prefent poffeffor of the Hackington houfe and eftate.

† Thefe are the 50 acres now let by both hofpitals to Mrs. Tucker. See N° 216.

‡ This muft be the land mentioned in N° 216, now let to John Hubbard, as in the leafe it is ftyled " Mayes, fome time called Sifter Harding's land."

156. 1. Thomas and Charity Marten to Thomas Peeffe of Grove of two acres of woodland, late Joan Sanders's, mother of Charity Marten. 4 April, 27 Eliz. 1585.

156. 2. Hugh Cherlton, clerk, and William atte See, to both hofpitals of one acre called Goldhord, late Robert Byfmer's. 39 Hen. VI. 1461.

157. Conveyance from John Welby, jun. to the hofpital of two acres and a half arable in Haweburgh, and of a tenement, garden, and two acres adjoining at Childforftal *, alias Heift †, near the common in Herne, for fixty pounds. 2 April, 8 Char. I. 1632. This feems to have been purchafed with Lady Winchelfea's money. See N° 33.

158. Bond from John Welby, jun. to warrant the conveyance. 2 April, 8 Char. I. 1632.

London.

159. Affignment from Ifabelle and Joan Lytelgram to Hugh Lytelgram of the remainder of a leafe for fifty years, from Trinity Convent, London. 20 May, 5 Hen. V. 1417.

Littleborne.

160. Robert Couper, natural fon of John Couper, late of Littleborne, to Andrew and Joan Mowre of St. John's Hofpital, of one annuity of vi l. xiii s. iv d. and two quarters of wheat from lands in Littleborne for their lives. 4 May, 7 Eliz. 1565.

Reculvre.

161. John Goldyng to John Knyght and John Baldewine of two acres, three roods ‡. 23 Sept. 1 Hen. V. 1413.

162. Leafe from the hofpital to Robert Hunt, of Hothe in Reculver, of two acres, three roods, called Brotherynlond ‡ for ten years, rent iii s. iv d. 14 Oct. 6 Edw. IV. 1466.

---

* "Forftal," in the laws of King Canute, (Chron. Bromton. apud X Scriptores, 923, 51.) fignifies "prohibitio itineris," and in Chron. Thorn, 2031, 9. "quietus effe de amerciamentis "de catallis areftatis infra (Q. intia) tertiam veftram, &c." At prefent it feems fynonymous to "common," and perhaps may be derived from "fofter-noth, pafture grounds, or places where "cattle feed." See Somner's Saxon Dictionary. And the above poffibly might be ftyled "Chil-"forftal," from the cold, that common being expofed to the N. and N. E. winds from the fea. D.

† Now let to Mr. Anthony Jennings, at a referved rent of 2 l. 12 s. per ann.

‡ Thefe together are probably the iii a. iii r. now let to Mr. Sennock, tenant at will, for 1 l. 15 s. per ann. and the 1 a. 1 r. called Brotherhood Clofe in Hoath, let to Mr. Anthony Jennings at a referved rent of 8 s. per ann.

Rochefter.

Rochefter.

163. An indenture of partition between Thomas and Johanna Godet, his wife, and Mary Morel, of Rochefter, her fifter; Joan to have a tenement, &c. by St. Clement's Church, Rochefter, and Margaret a tenement bought of the Countefs of Pembroke, and another tenement in Horflane. 32 Edw. III. 1359.

Sellynge.

164. Indenture of exchange of five acres for five acres between Robert Morris and John Proude. Sept. 23 Ric. II. 1399.

Stourmouth.

165. William dĉs Poťier de Beyrdeftone to the hofpital of four bufhels of white falt, which Thomas de Stagno ufed to pay him out of a faltwork at Stourmouth, called la Hokot. 26 Dec. 7 Edw. I. 1278. See N° 138.

Stowting. Lyminge. Storton.

166. Letter of attorney from Simon Inkepette to Stephen Andrews to deliver poffeffion to Henry Seymour and John Fraunceys of all his lands in thofe parifhes. 1 July, 34 Hen. VI. 1455.

Streatham.

167. Leafe from the Dean and Chapter of Chrift Church Canterbury, of the Hermitage at Streatham in Surrey for 21 years, rent III s̃. IV đ. dated Dec. 7, 1676. Defcribed in the leafe under the name of " All that their meffuage or tenement " fituate and ftanding in Streatham, in the county of Surrey, upon the common " called Streatham Common, and commonly known by the name of The Hermi- " tage, with the appurtenances; and alfo one half acre of the faid common ly- " ing next the faid meffuage, called The Hermitage, as it is taken in and inclofed " for an orchard by and with the confent of the Dean and Chapter, of the tenants " of the faid manor of Vauxhall in the faid county of Surrey, whereof the fame is a parcel." (Seal of the Dean and Chapter partly preferved. See plate IV. fig. 8.)*

Sturresfeld.

168. Leafe from the hofpital to John Frymyngham of three roods for XL years, rent XX đ. 10 Jan. 14 Edw. IV. 1475.

* The meffuage, defcribed as above, is ftill held in the fame manner, and for the fame referved rent, and is now let on leafe by the hofpital to Mr. John Rofs, at a referved rent of 2 l. 3 s.

P p   *Thanyington.*

Thanyngton.

169. Gilbert and Alifcia de Cokeryng to Thomas Pope of Winchepe of two acres at Ung hɔlbetel in Cokeryng borgh † for XL ṡ. paid to them by Thomas Pope. 19 Edw. II. 1325.

170. John atte Fryth to Sir Henry de Norton, rector of St. Alphege, Canterbury, of two acres and a half in Tanington. 28 Oct. 42 Edw. III. 1368.

171. Indenture by which Henry de Norton (above mentioned), chaplain, exchanges with Thomas de Alkham de Wenchep a piece of land in Northfield, Tanyngton, lately bought of John atte Fryth, for one acre in Cokerynsfield. 44 Edw. III. 1370.

172. Thomas Alkham, baker in Wenchepe, to Walter Cours and others, of four acres apud le Sandpette. June, 3 Ric. II. 1379.

173. Another grant of the fame. 29 June, 3 Ric. II. 1379.

174. The fame to the fame of two acres and a half at the Sandpette. Feb. 9 Ric. II. 1385.

175. Thomas de Merfham to Agnes Paniter of Sevenok of two acres at Shaftyndone. 20 Dec. 15 Edw. III. 1342.

176. William de Betefhamme to John Pyk, two acres. Feb. 19 Edw. III. 1345.

177. Henry Coupere to John de Romene of one acre. 4 March, 7 Edw. III. 1334.

178. John de Romene, citizen of Canterbury, to John Pyk of one acre. 19 Edw. III. 1346.

179. John Couper of Winchep to John Pyk of one acre, three roods. 31 Edw. III. 1357.

180. Releafe from Margery, late wife of John Couper, of Hamildown, to John Pyk of all claim on one acre, three roods. 40 Edw. III. 1366.

181. Grant from Thomas and Agnes Perot to John Pyk of three yards of land at Citeryng, 12 Mar. 32 Ed. III. 1358. Two feals; an elephant; and a rofe of fix leaves, with fix letters round it, plate III. fig. 6, 7.

182. John Pyk to William Farnham of a meffuage and five acres, two roods, of land. 26 Nov. 46 Edw. III. 1372.

183. Thomas de Norton, chaplain, to John Chefman of one acre at Shaftyndoun. 20 March, 47 Edw. III. 1373.

184. John Chefeman to Thomas Broggaue and others, [brethren of the hofpital] of four acres at Shaftindoun. 21 Sept. 1 Ric. II. 1377.

† Edward Sankey now holds on leafe from the hofpital XII acres of land at Cockering, at a rack rent of 4 l. 2 s. per anr.

158. Re-

185. Releafe from John Dovor to Thomas Broggaue and others of claim on the faid four acres. 21 Sept. 1 Ric. IL. 1377.

186. Leafe from the hofpital to William Arnold of xiii acres in Thanington. 16 Dec. 37 Hen. VIII. 1545. Almoft obliterated.

Thanet.

187. John Eadmond, fenior, of St. Lawrence, Thanet, to Walter Conrs and others, of an annual rent of iii d. fterling, from one acre of land by the For-ftall * in faid parifh. 5 Ric. II. 1381.

188. Laurence atte Nynne to Thomas Brokgrave and others, brethren of the hof-pital, of a rent of xii d. iffuing out of one acre in the manor of Menftre. 30 June, 6 Ric. II. 1382.

189. Grant by indenture from the prior, &c. to Thomas Waldyn of Eaft Clivef-end of one acre, one rood, (which was given them by Stephen Elifander) on payment of xii d. perpetual annual rent. 8 Feb. 3 Hen. IV. 1402. With an Englifh tranflation by Somner.

Monkton.

190. John Helk and John Elkyn, feoffees of John Miles, to Thomas Bergrave and others, of one acre, two roods †, in the tenure of Chrift Church, Canterbury. Feb. 1 Ric. II. 1376.

Menftre.

191. Matilda, daughter of John Ho, to the hofpital of 11 s. annual rent out of a meffuage and one rood and a half of land. 1 Edw. I. 1272.

192. Leafe from the hofpital to John Hamon of three yards of land in Mynfter ‡ for xl years. 5 May, 6 Hen. VII. 1492.

Sarre.

193. 1. Richard and Agnes Tayllor to Thomas Baldewyn and others of fix acres in St. Giles's. 1 Nov. 2 Hen. IV. 1401.

194. 1. Thomas Baldewyne and others to the hofpital of vi a. xx p. divifim in St. Gyles's. 1 Nov. 3 Hen. IV. 1402.

* See note * p. 272.

† 1 a. iii r. at Monkton are now held by the heirs of Sir John Sabine, at 1 l. per ann.

‡ Whether this be the land now let on leafe to the Rev. William Byrch, at a referved rent of 10 s. per ann. or that called Culverhoufe Garden, let to Mary Wotton for 6 s. 8 d. cannot ea-fily be afcertained, as the quantity of both is the fame, viz. three roods.

Weftbere.

Weſtbere.

193. 2. Laurence and Joan Menchar to William and Mary Carpenter of a piece of land. Sept. 10 Ric. II. 1386.

194. 2. John Herryng to John Soklyng of three roods. 16 Ric. II. 1393.

195. William Haute and others, feoffees of John Helar, to Richard Michell of two acres. 7 April, 13 Hen. VIII. 1522.

196. Richard Michell, brother of the hoſpital, to Peter Pemble and others, of the ſaid two acres. 5 Jan. 26 Hen. VIII. 1545.

Wye.

197. Releaſe from Thomas Kempe of Wye to William Smith of claim of a meſſuage in Wye. 9 Jan. 14 Ric. II. 1391.

Wickhambreux.   Mr. Snowe's Benefaction.

Ralph Snowe of Lambeth, Gent. left by will, dated 13 June, 1707, 200 l. to be laid out for the benefit of St. John's Hoſpital by the Lord Archbiſhop. Archbiſhop Teniſon bought with 170 l. of this money xiv acres of marſh-land in Wickhambreux, 20 Aug. 1714, and aſſigned it to Archdeacon Thomas Greene, Dr. G. Thorpe, Dr. Elias Sydall, Prebendaries of Canterbury, Dr. T. Wiſe, Rector of St. Alphage, William Turner, Eſq. William Deedes, M. D. and Paul Lukyn, Gent. of Canterbury, for the benefit of the Hoſpital, with directions to the four ſurviving truſtees always to chuſe three more.   Dr. Greene, then Biſhop of Ely, Dr. Sydall, then Dean of Canterbury, and Dr. Deedes, 2 Feb. 1730, made a new feoffment, and put in as feoffees, Dr. J. Lynch, afterwards Dean of Canterbury, Mr. Julius Deedes, afterwards Prebendary, William Crayford, Eſq. recorder of Canterbury, and Samuel Norris, gent. auditor to the Dean and Chapter.   The title-deeds of this eſtate are as follows:

198. Conveyance from George Auſtin of Canterbury, to Valentine Auſtin of Adiſham, of xiv acres of freſh marſh-land in Wickhambreux, with the boundaries deſcribed. 20 Dec. 1628.

199. Conveyance from Valentine Auſtin of Upper Hardres to Robert Auſtin of Adiſham. 20 A. 1631.

200. Probate of Robert Auſtin's will.   He gives (inter alia) theſe lands to his ſon Michael Auſtin; made 7 April, 1653; proved 2 Sept. 1653.

201. Deed of gift from Michael, ſon of Robert Auſtin, to his brother William of the ſame. 29 Dec. 1664.

202. Mort-

202. Mortgage of the fame from William Auftin to Thomas, afterwards Serjeant, Hardres. 9 Dec. 1668. Within it a bond to perform covenants.

203. Affignment of William Auftin's mortgage from Serjeant Hardres to George Gilbert Pierce. Aug. 26, 1671. Signed by William Auftin, with his bond to perform covenants within it.

204. Copy. Affignment of William Auftin and other mortgagees, from George Gilbert Pierce to Serjeant Hardres. 1 Feb. 1671-2.

205. Conveyance of thefe lands from William Auftin to John Enfett of Sturry. 26 Feb. 1680-1. Within it are put, 1. William Auftin's Affidavit of his title. 2. Covenant to fell. 3. Bond to perform covenants; and, 4. His receipt for 180 l. the purchafe money.

206. Affignment from Serjeant Thomas Hardres of the mortgage N° 203. to Alexander Enfett. 11 Aug. 1681. It is endorfed on N° 203.

207. Affignment from Alexander Enfett to John Enfett of the fame mortgage. 11 Aug. 1681.

208. Probate of John Enfett's will, giving (inter alia) his lands in Wickhambreux (and elfewhere) to his fon William and his heirs; on failure, to his brother Alexander and his heirs for ever. 26 May, 1695. Proved 8 June, 1695.

209. Mortgage from Alexander Enfett to Ed. Gibbs for l. 24 Jan. 1704.

210. Releafe from Alexander Enfett to the Lord Archbifhop [Tenifon] of thofe lands. 20 Aug. 1714. Within it is the leafe for a year. 19 Aug. 1714.

211. Affignment of Ed. Gibbs's mortgage to Dr. Sydall, in truft to attend the inheritance. 20 Aug. 1714.

212. Affignment from Dr. Sydall to Mr. Sawkins, to attend the inheritance. 10 Sept. 1714.

213. Releafe and conveyance from the Lord Archbifhop to Dr. Greene and others, in truft for the hofpital. 8 Oct. 1714; and leafe for a year. 7 Oct. 1714.

214. Releafe and conveyance from Dr. Greene, Bifhop of Ely, to Dr. Lynch and others. 2 Feb. 1730.

215. Releafe and conveyance from William Lynch, Efq. (now Sir William, K. B.) eldeft fon and heir at law of Dr. Lynch, to Dr. Head and others, in truft. 17 July, 1767. (Copied into the hofpital account book.)

C H A P.

C H A P. VI.

MAPS, TERRIERS, RENTALS, BOOKS.

MAPS.

212. THE platform of a parcel of land lying before the gates of the Moate Houſe, neere Canterburie in Kent, called the Brotherhoode Lande.
It is on parchment, two feet ſquare, coloured, and contains the land (as it ſeems) given by Thomas de Garwyntone, ſee Nº 23, &c. Wyke, and ſhews the boun. daries of the pariſhes of St. Martin and St. Paul. It ſeems to have been drawn in the time of Henry the Eighth.

213. A ſketch on paper of part of the ſame lands by William Boycote, who mapped the Moate eſtate about 1620.

Rollyng.

214. Map of a tenement and 21 pieces of land at Rolinge in the pariſh of Goodneſ. ton, containing LXXX a. II r. XXIII p. at XVI ft. VI in. to the rod, or LXXXIII a. XXIII p. by the ſhort rod of XVI ft. (See Nº 116, &c.) By William Boycote, 1617*.
It is on parchment, XX inches by XI.

Chiſlet.

215. Ruſhley Wood, contayne VIII a. III r. XXX p†. By William Boycote, 1639. It is on parchment, XIII inches and a half by V inches.

Herne.

216. The deſcription of XV pieces of land in the occupation of John Nottingham, contayning LVI a. I p‡. whereof Th. Smith claym . . . . . . *The reſt is torn off.*
On the ſame parchment is the deſcription of three pieces of land called Mayes, in the occupation of G. Hellet, contayning XXXI a. II r. XIV p. whereof, in the field, having this mark ⚥, Sir James Oxenden claymeth two acres; the bo thers of Herbaldown claym three acres; the reſidue (being) XXVI a. II r. XIV p. (belong) only to the hoſpitale§. Sans date. It is on parchment, XXII inches by XIV and three quarters. See Nº 154.

* Now let on leaſe to Sir Narborough D'Aeth, bart.
† Now let on leaſe to Mr. Anthony Jennings at a reſerved rent of I l. 12 s. per annum.
‡ Now eleven pieces, containing 50 acres, let to Mrs. Jane Tucker for 14 l. per ann. two-thirds to this hoſpital, and one third to Herbaldown, and known by the name of Hensford.
§ Now XXVIII a. II r. belonging ſolely to this hoſpital, and let on leaſe to John Hubbard for a reſerved rent of 6 l. 11 s. per ann.

2

217. A

217. A map of nine pieces of arable land demifed to Mrs. Mildred Knowler, widow, by the two hofpitals, contayning LIII a. 1 p. by Henry Maxted and Edward Randall, 1729. It is on parchment xxvii inches by xviii. It is of the land in the occupation of Nottingham in the former map. N° 216.

TERRIERS.

Rollyng.

218. A terrier of Tabeder's land, belonging to the brothers of St. John and Herbaldown, made July the 20th, 1674. It is a parchment roll, containing xxviii articles; the fum total is LXXXVIII a. xix p. [It is now let to Sir Narborough D'aeth.]

219, A true and perfect terrier of feveral pieces and parcels of land lying in Roling in the parifh of Goodneftone in the county of Kent; belonging to St. John's Hofpital, and St. Nicholas Herbaldowne, containing LXXX a. II r. XXIII p. It is a parchment roll, and has xxi articles. No date. Between 1674 and 1706.

220. Another terrier, exactly the fame as N° 219, excepting the alterations of occupiers names. Made the 24th day of July, 1706.

RENTALS.

221. An old prior's rental beginning, "Item, three tenements in Ivy Lane."

222. The janitor's accounts of repairs from Michaelmas 1462 to Michaelmas 1463, in Latin.

223. Another. Sans date.

BOOKS.

224. The Chapel Regifter, containing five baptifms, from 1635 to 1698-9; xiii marriages, from 1638 to 1676; and cix burials, from 1635 to 1689. On ten folio pages.

225. Regifter of admiffions, from March 26, 1559, to May 12, 1658.

226. The prior's accounts of the pittance-money; beginning 1521, ending 1549; and the prior's admonitions.

227. The prior's accounts from Michaelmas 1510 to 1563.

228. The prior's accounts from 1605 to Sept. 14, 1647. Mr. Somner's petition is at the end in his own hand writing. (See it in Chap. IX. p. 281.)

229. The prior's accounts from 1701 to Michaelmas, 1727.

CHAP.

C H A P.   VII.

AN ACCOUNT OF MRS. LOVEJOY'S, MRS. MASTERS'S, AND MR. BROWN'S LEGACIES.

MRS. LOVEJOY.

ELIZABETH Lovejoy, widow, by her will, proved about April 1695, gave to the mayor and commonalty of the city of Canterbury the leafe of the parfonage of Callis Grange in St. Peter's Thanet, holden from the Dean and Chapter of the Cathedral, Canterbury, charged with the payment (inter alia) of one annuity of ten pounds to St. John's Hofpital.

MRS. MASTERS.

Mrs. Mary Mafters, formerly of the city of Canterbury (fpinfter), by her laft will, dated 11 Jan. 1711, appointed Sir Harcourt Mafters her executor; and by a codicil gave five pounds a year to each of the poor hofpitals in Canterbury.

By an act of parliament 7 Geo. 1. Sir Harcourt Mafters's eftate was forfeited to make good the lofies of the South Sea Company, of which he was a director; and all who had claims on his eftate were directed to claim before Dec. 5, 1721.

Sept. 14, 1721, the fix hofpitals in Canterbury and its fuburbs, by a letter of attorney, empowered Richard May, Gent. to claim for them, which he did Sept. 21, 1721, which claim was allowed; and the faid yearly fum of five pounds to each hofpital were valued by Mr. Borrett, a mafter in Chancery, at DCLX l. But Sir Harcourt Mafters's eftate being not fufficient to anfwer all the claims thereon, was found able to pay but VI s. VI d. in the pound.

May 13, 1735, The hofpitals petitioned to have their dividend of the DCLXl. which was granted.

July 4, 1735, They impowered the faid Richard May to receive it.

July 22, 1735, He accordingly received for the faid hofpitals CCXIV l. X s. out of which was deducted a bill due to him for charges and trouble, XXXI l. VIII d. and there remained in his hands CLXXXIII l. IX s. IV d.

October 23, 1736, The hofpitals, by a letter of attorney, empowered Dr. Lynch, Dean of Canterbury, and John Knowler, Efq. recorder of Canterbury, to receive the faid CLXXXIII l. IX s. IV d. and to place it in the public funds, which they did Jan. , 1736, and with it purchafed CLXIII l. XVI s. III d. capital ftock in old South Sea annuities, for the ufe of the faid hofpitals.

At Michaelmas, 1737, the annihilation on VI l. XVI s. VIII d. was paid to the truftees, and at Michaelmas 1740 they repurchafed the fame fum. So that the capital is ftill CLXXXIII l. IX s. IV d. old South Sea annuities.

Mr.

Mr. Knowler, the furviving truftee, transferred the truft to the mayor and aldermen of the city of Canterbury; and the chamberlain regularly pays the dividends to the hofpitals. They are Eaftbridge, St. John's, Maynard's, Jefus, Cogan's, and Smith's.

MR. BROWN.

Matthew Brown, by his will, dated 12 Dec. 1717, and proved 26 Aug. 1721, gave to the hofpitals of Eaftbridge, Maynard, St. John, and St. Nicholas; to the charity fchool in Canterbury, and to the parifh of Weftgate for two poor people, to each of them refpectively ten fhillings, to be paid to them on the 10th of March yearly for ever, iffuing out of two houfes in the borough of Staplegate, at that time in the occupations of Paul Whitehurft and Matthew Derby, with power to enter and diftrain: xvi s. is to be paid to Weftgate yearly.

But thefe houfes not being fufficient for the payment of thefe fums, they are untenanted *.

* This is not the cafe at prefent, the ftipends above mentioned having been regularly paid for fome years paft to each of thofe charities. D.

CHAP. VIII.

THE PRESENT STATE OF THIS HOSPITAL, 1765.

[THIS chapter is omitted, as the ftate of the Hofpital in the prefent year (1784) has been already given in p. 197.]

[*Here ends the MS. of Dr.* BEAUVOIR.]

CHAP. IX.

The Cafe of the Hofpitalls of Herbaldowne and Northgate neer Canterbury, concerning their Annual Penfion of 80 l. apiece from the Archbifhop of Canterbury, ftated.

[Drawn up by Mr. Somner (fee p. 279.). The notes in the margin are the Author's.]

I. THAT the faid hofpitalls were refpectively founded more then 500 yeares ago, by Archbifhop Lanfrank, in the Conqueror's dayes (1), and that their faid founder endowed [them] with maintenance for poore, aged, and difeafed
† 60 in each houfe, people of both fexes †, is clear by the teftimony of Eadmerus, a
120 in both. monke of the cathedral at Canterbury of the very fame time (1), in the hiftory which he wrote of his owne times, called "Hiftoria Novorum," pag. 9. where, relating their foundation, he fayes of the one (Northgate), "Ordinavit etiam eis de fuo veftitum & victum quotidianum;" that is, "he allotted to "them, out of what was properly his owne, dayly food and rayment:" of the

(1) Viz. about 1084.

other

other (Herbaldowne), " His pro qualitate fui morbi omnia quibus egerent de fuo
" miniftrari conftituit ;" that is, " to thefe, according to the quality of their difeafe
(which was the leprofy), " he affigned, of his owne, what might fupply them with
   * Of late yeares   " all neceffaries." Thus Eadmerus * ; who gives no further ac-
fet out by Mr.   count of their endowment, what it was, either in groffe, or in
John Selden.   particular.

II. But within, or neer upon, 100 yeares after, to wit, in Hen. II's, or Rich.
I's time, a fucceffor of Lanfrank, one Richard (1), taking into confideration and
commiferation the great indigence of the faid hofpitalls, for want of competent endowment, for remedy thereof, by his deed or charter, yet extant (2), under his
archiepifcopal feale (after recitall therein made of the faid hofpitalls endowment with
140 l. fterling per ann. by his predeceffor Lanfrank their founder, payable out of
his manours of Reculver and Boughton in Kent), grants them an augmentation of
20 l. per ann. payable out of the parfonage of Reculver.

III. From and after which time of augmentation the faid hofpitalls, for about
100 yeares together, conftantly received the faid 160 l. accordingly, namely, untill
the time of Archbifhop Kilwardby (3) in Edward I's dayes, who, in lieu thereof, granted unto them the whole parfonage of Reculver; which grant his next fucceffor Archbifhop Peckham (4) (in regard of fundry inconveniences by experience
founde to follow thereupon), taking along with him the confent of the Pope, the
Prior and Convent of Chrift Church, and the refpective governors of each hofpitall, revoked, charging the fee with the payment of the wonted maintenance, as
by his charter, alfo extant (5), will further appeare.

IV. And thus it continued untill Archbifhop Stratford's time (6), who, in Edw.
III's dayes, finding the hofpitalls defective of fecurity by writing for their faid
penfion of 160 l. per ann. and being minded to fuccour them with better fecurity
for time to come, obteened an appropriation of the faid parfonage of Reculver to
him and his fucceffors, annexing it :" menfæ archiepifcopali," or " to the archbi-
" fhop's table;" from and out of the fruits of which parfonage fo appropriated
the faid hofpitalls penfion fhould afterwards arife ; but the faid Archbifhop dying
ere the perfecting the fecurity intended, his fucceffor, Simon Iflep (7), by his charter (8), charged himfelfe and his fucceffors, and in the vacancy the collectors of
the profits of Reculver parfonage, with the faid penfion, during the continuance of
the faid appropriation ; which if at any time ceafing, the penfion to be afterwards
raifed out of the Archbifhop's temporalities ; as by his faid charter (8), and the
charter under the broad feal of Edw. III. in confirmation of the forementioned
appropriation, yet extant (9), will further appeare.

V. And accordingly (for ought appeares by any recorde in either of the faid
hofpitalls, or elfewhere, now extant, to their knowledge), the matter ftood with

---

(1) Archbifhop Richard was archbifhop from 1174 to 1184.
(2) See it in the Hiftory of Reculver, p. 129.   (3) 1272—1278.
(4) 1278—1294.   (5) See it in the Hift. of Reculver, p. 131.   (6) 1333—1348.
(7) 1349—1366. Iflip was not Stratford's immediate fucceffor. Bradwardin and Ufford in-
tervened.   (8) See it in the Hiftory of Reculver, p. 148.   (9) Ibid. p. 141.

the

the faid hofpitalls in point of maintenance untill the time of the diffolution of religious houfes by Hen. VIII. and Edw. VI. At that time the faid hofpitalls were both kept up undiffolved, and their faid maintenance, according to their charitable foundation, continued, as by the furvey taken of either, and recorded in the Court of Augmentations (1), whereof they have copies ready to produce, appeares : wherein (amongft other things) expreffe mention is made of a penfion of 80 l. per ann. due and payable unto each of them by the Archbifhop of Canterbury, which indeed they have ever fince conftantly received from the Archbifhop's receiver generall, or his affigne authorifed from time to time to pay the fame out of the rents due to the Archbifhop from St. Gregorie's neer Canterbury, the demefnes of Chiftlet manor, and the parfonage of Reculver, quarterly, as the faid rents come in.

VI. Truth is, the faid furvey intimateth the one (that of Northgate) to be payable out of the Archbifhop's coffers, the other, from the manors of Reculver and Boughton, and the parfonage of Reculver. But this difference in their pay at that time how it came to paffe, or by what meanes afterwards the faid rents of St. Gregorie's, Chiftlet, and Reculver, became charged with it in fpeciall, they are altogether ignorant. For, being poore, fimple people, they alwayes thankfully received it, without regard or queftion from whence it rofe ; being never driven, for lacke of payment, either to conteft for it, or to fhew any evidence to juftify their claime thereunto ; ever peaceably enjoying it without any interruption. Howbeit, by what is prealleaged, they conceive their claime and title to the faid perfion to be fo fully and fufficiently cleared and afferted, and the archbifhopricke fo apparently liable unto it, as they fhall not neede to doubt of a confirmation and fettlement thereof, by authority of parliament, upon them and their fucceffors to all perpetuity, according to the laudable intention of their pious founder, and for encouragement of others in like acts of charity.

The feverall particulars in this cafe are truly and faithfully alleaged.

Will'm Somner, Notary Publicke.

This cafe was drawne and prefented, with a copy thereof, to the furveyors of the Bifhops, &c. lands in the yeare 1646 (2), to the end they might take notice of the hofpitalls right and claime to that penfion of 160 l. per ann. out of the Archbifhop's revenews, and might certify the fame to the truftees, whereby fome timely provifion might be made for the conftant payment thereof in time to come, by referving fo much of the yearly revenew from fale, or otherwife.

(1) In the Prior's Difburfements for 1647 is this article,
" Item, laid out for the furvey which wee had out of the Augmentation Courte, xxiiii s. vi d.
(2) And in thofe for 1646, are the following :
" Spent when wee went to Wingham to prefent a pettition to the deputie leiuetenants, ii s. iiii d.
Item, paid for hors hire when wee went to the lords, v s.
Item, paid for a pettition to fend to London, ii s.
Item, paid for writtinge of a pettition to prefent to the lords, ii s.
Item, paid to George for his journey to London, v s.
Item, paid for two other petitions which were fent to London, vs. iii d."
With feveral other charges of journeys to London, and elfewhere, " about getting off their feffes."

C H A P.

C H A P.   X.

The MOAT LANDS, or WYKE; Suit concerning them.

THE ftate of the controverſy relating to the Moat Lands, or Wyke (briefly mentioned, p. 260.) will appear from the following petition, which was preſented to Archbiſhop Whitgift ſoon after 1583.

"To the moſt Reverend Father in God and our dreade patron, the Lorde Archbiſhoppe of Canterbury his Grace, Primat and Metropolitan of all Englande, and one of his Majeſtie's moſt honourable Pryvie Counſell.

IN moſt humble and lamentable wiſe ſhewethe and enformeth your grace your poore bounden orators and dalie beadmen, the brothers and fiſters of your grace's hoſpitall of St. John the Baptiſt nere Canterburye; that whereas your ſaide orators and there predeceſſors ever ſince the foundation of the ſaide hoſpitall were feaſed in there demeaſne, as of fee, as in the righte of the ſaide hoſpitall, of certen lands called the Moat Lands, containing xxxii acres lyinge at ·the Moat nere Canterburye, worthe per ann. xvi l. nowe in the occupation of Sir Moyle Fynche, knighte ┌, for whiche lande your ſaide orators have bin yerelie anſwered for the farme thereof xiii s. iiii d. by Sir Thomas Fynche, Sir·William Fynche deceaſed, and diverſe, whoſe eſtate they had, without deniall, untill about xxi yeres· paſt the gardaines [guardians] of the ſaide Sir Moyle Fynche, in his minoritie, felled the tymber trees growinge uppon the ſaide lande, which your ſaide poore orators perceyveinge, caryed awaye parte thereof ; whereuppon your ſuppliants exhibited a ſupplication unto the Lorde Archbiſhoppe Parker's grace, who, by aſſent of the ſaide Sir Moyle Fynche, referred the judgemente of the righte thereof unto Sir Roger Manwood, knighte, now L. Chiefe Baron, who, upon the ſighte of our evidence, willed Sir Moyle Fynche to ſatisfie the atrerages of the rent, but made no finall end, for that the ſaide L. Archebiſhoppe died *, ſince whoſe deathe the ſaide Sir

---

* Sir Moyle Finch was afterwards a baronet, being advanced to that title 9 Jam. I. but he did not long enjoy that and his ample fortune, as he died in December, 1614, while this ſuit was litigating. Eaſtwell houſe and manor, &c. was derived from his mother, daughter and coheir of Sir Thomas Moyle; the Moat from his father Sir Thomas Finch, as deſcended from Philip Belknap.

† In 1575.

Moyle

Moyle Fynche hathe denyed and yet dothe denie to paie the fame, unles your faide orators will receave the fame as a drie rent out of the faide lande, whereby the fee fymple thereof fhoulde be in him and not in your faide orators, who have verie ancient evidence to prove the fame. Since which your fade orators exhibited one other fupplication to the late L. Archbifshoppe Grindall his grace touchinge the premiffes, who, by affent of Sir Moyle Fynche, appointed Mr. Redman now archdeacon of Canterbury, and Mr. John Boys, efquire, to here and determine the caufe, who, perceyveinge a manifefte righte in your faide orators, required him to paye the rent and the rerage, and he fhoulde have fuche leafe for terme of yeares as they coulde make, but he refufed to paye it but as drie rent, and ymediately the faide Archbifhoppe died †. Forafmuche, therefore, as the arrerage of the faide rent of the lande dothe amount unto xiiii l. or thereaboute, and yerelye increafethe, to the greate impoverifhinge of your faide poore orators, beinge parte of theire ftipend, and prejudice of there inheritaunce, if it fhoulde thus longe continewe litigious; and forafmuche as your faide poore orators have no other to appeale unto, but only to your grace's ayde and defence in there juft quarrell, beinge of themfelves aged, impotent, and poore, unable any waie to releve themfelves, muche leffe to mayntaine futes with fuche a perfon; moft humblie befeche your grace of your accuftomed clemencye to have fome commifferacion uppon your faide poore orators, to take there caufe into your grace's protection, to order and decide the fame accordinge to your orators' righte, as beft fhall feme to your grace's moft approved wifdome. Or ells, that, with your grace's affent, to whome we humblie fubmitt ourfelves, your faide poore orators maye take fuche courfe by lawe for tryall of the title thereof as to your grace fhall feme expedient. And your faide poore orators fhall accoidinge to our bounden dutie praye unto God for your grace longe to contynewe in moft happie eftate."

By the petition inferted p. 290, they feem in 1596 to have had a verdict in their favour. It came to a trial, however, again in 1615, of which the progrefs and event will beft appear by the following extracts from the Prior's books, which are alfo curious as they give the particulars of law-charges 170 years ago.

"Here begineth the charges of the fewt between Sir Moyll Fynche, Knight, and his hayres, and our Houfpetall of St. Johne's; fyrft Markes Hyfoll, pryor, in the yeare of our Lord God 1614, and continuing in Renell Bourn's tyme, being pryor in the yeare 1615, and ending in Jefper Wreeke's tyme, being pryor in the fame yeare 1615, being the xviiith of September, with thefe charges that foloweth, all for our land at the Mott [Moate] before the gatt.

* 1583.

"Li

" In Markes Hyffol's tyme.

Ĥm, payd for a horffe hyre for on of our brethren to Eyftwell,	II ŝ. VI đ.
———— to Mafter Groves our atorny,	IV ŝ. II đ.
———— for the feeking out of the prambulatyon of St. Paulle's,	VI đ.
———— for a copy of the juryes names,	IV d.
———— unto Strydicke * going to Loundon to my Lorde's Grace with a petityon,	XVII ŝ.
———— unto Mafter Denn [counfellor] for his fee,	X ŝ.
———— for the making of the petityon,	IX đ.
	XXXV ŝ. III đ.

" In Renold Bourne's tyme.

———— for a fupyne [fubpœna] to fetche in III witneffes,	II ŝ.
———— for the farving of them upon three of them, VI đ. apiece,	XVIII đ.
———— unto Kellfo for him and his horfe to Lydd unto Mafter Henden the counfelar's,	VI ŝ.
———— for a quart of wynne [wine] opun the layyours [lawyers] at their metyng at Mafter Dennes,	XII đ.
———— for two fupynes [fubpœnas] for fix witneffes,	VI ŝ. VI đ.
———— for Thomas Taylore and the brothers that kept him company the XVIIIth daye of September for their dynors,	III ŝ. VIII đ.
———— for his fupper the fame daye at nyght,	II ŝ. II đ.
———— unto Mafter Henden the counfeler,	XX ŝ.
and for a quart of facke,	XII đ.
———— unto Mafter Pebett the counfeler the XIX of Sept. for his fee,	X ŝ.
———— for our drinking for the company when they came from the court, being in number tenn of our brethren,	XXII đ.
———— the XIX daye of September at nyght for Thomas Taylor's fupper and the reft of our brethren at the requeft of him,	IIII ŝ.
———— unto Thomas Taylor the XX daye of September in recompence of his gorny [journey] commyng and going home agayne [to Lambeth],	XVI ŝ.
———— unto Mafter Dennes man for making out the learfees [leafes] and the letter of atorny,	VIII ŝ. II đ.
———— unto Mafter Leder our atorny his fee in the feut at Loundon agaynft Sir Moyll Fynche, knyght,	III ŝ. III đ,
———— at the takinge of the newe pofefion the tenth of October to a man for a witnefs at the fam tyme	VI đ.
———— for the executyon that was farvid upon Strydick * touching the nonfuting of our feut,	XXXIX ŝ. VII đ.

* See p. 288, laft note.

" Here

" Here begineth a newe feutte for our land nere the Motte.

Ĩtm, payd unto Andrew Banke for his paynes at the taking of the newe poffefion, — vi đ.

————— unto Banke and Bourne on another daye to pout off the catell from the groune, — II š.

————— for the arefting of the tenant, — xvi đ.

————— the atorney's fee, — II š. vi đ.

————— for the letter fending to Lambeth to Thomas Taylor, — vi đ.

————— for the mappe of the groune, — II š. vi đ.

————— for mending of it, to Mafter Ryder, — IIII đ.

————— for bread and drinke for our brothers for twifs going to Herbouldowne and their comyng hyther, — VIII đ.

————— for the makyng of too petityons, the fyrft not too our mafter's licking, wherefore we were dreyen too make another to fend unto my Lordes Grace, — xvi đ.

————— for the making a new petityon the III daye of Aprell, — xII đ.

————— for removing of Carpenter to St. Nycoleffe, — III š.

————— unto Martaye for his going to Loundon for the Coiedes [Corrodies] for the removing of the brothers, — vi š.

————— unto Mafter Leder for ferching out of the Court Bookes at Loundon, — III š. VII đ.

————— unto Mafter Ryder for the making of a petytyon to deliver unto my Lordes Grace, — vi đ.

————— unto Mafter Smyth, my Lordes Graces fecrotory, for a letter to fend unto Mafter Scot, and to Richard Smyth, and to the other exectors *, and to his mane [man], — VII š.

————— unto Mafter Groves for warring [warning] of the jury, — VIII š.

————— unto Mafter Leader for the fearching out of other Court Rowlles at Loundon and bring' home of them, — II š.VI đ.

————— for the taking out of nottes out of a regifter book, and for paper, — IIII đ.

————— fpent about bufines of our feule, — VI đ.

————— for fending a letter unto Thomas Taylor, — xII đ.

————— unto John Groves for making of a letter, — xII đ.

————— for the carring of a letter unto Mafter Henden[coun'ellor], — II š. vi đ.

————— unto Mafter Hendry Halle, — xx š.

————— for another letter fending unto Thomas Taylor the xI of September, — xII đ.

————— unto Mafter Denn the counfeler for his fee, — x š.

————— unto Mafter Pettet for his fee, — x š.

————— unto Mafter Leder for his fee, — v š.

————— unto the fargant + for his fee, — II š.

————— fpent in feeking out of witneffes, — II đ.

* Of Sir Moyle Finch, no doubt.

+ The town ferjeant, probibly, as the trial was in the Guildhall of Canterbury.

" In

." In Jefper Wreeke's tyme being pryor.

Item, payd for too fubpines [fubpœnas] to fetche fartayn witneffes for our feute, that is to faye, Adam Bourcke [and feven more], IIII s.

———— for their charges, IIII s.

—— fpent upon Mafter Halle at his comyng, for his welcom, in wine and cakes, XVIII d.

—— payd unto Mafter Hennden for his fee, XX s.

———— unto Thomas Tayllor for his commyng doune, XX s.

———— his charges at Thomas Bourne's, III s. x d.

———— unto Andrew Rouke for his going to the Motte [Moat] to know of my ladyes * going awaye, IIII d.

———— at the tryall daye for beere for the gentellmen, VI d.

" Here endeth the charges of our houfpetall in the feut agaynft Sir Moyll Fynch, knyght, in his liff tyme, and his lady * after his defeefs, for too yeares feut, being in thre pryeres tyme, as is to faye, Markes Hyffold, pryor, Renold Bourne, Jefper Wreeke, pryor, ended the XVIII of September, 1615, with this fom as foloeth, to our oufpetall's loffe and henderance.

" The holl fom of this laft charges of feut, XV l. XI s. VI d †."

This fuit, however, did not end here; for in a fubfequent account are the following articles:

1618. " Item, payd for making of a peticion, XII d. and for another petion to delyver unto my Lordes Grace the VI of Auguft, againft our Lady Fynche conferning our land at the Mott in her wrong delyng to the Houfpetall, XVIII d. II s. VI d.

And on September 20, 1620 (17 Jam. I.), the prior (George Stredwicke ‡), brothers, and fifters, gave a leafe (ftill extant) for 21 years of the 32 acres in queftion (defcribing them as " lyeing and beeing at or neere a place called the " Mote, and in the pifhes of St. Marten and St. Paule neere the cittie of Canter-" bury, or elfewhere, nowe or late in the occupacõn of Sir Moyle Finche, knight,

* Elizabeth fole daughter and heir to Sir Thomas Heneage, knight, advanced by James I. in 1623 to the dignity of Vifcountefs Maidftone, and by Charles I. in 1628 to that of Countefs of Winchelfea. From her fourth fon by Sir Moyle Finch are defcended the prefent Earls of Winchelfea and Aylesford.

† I make this total rather lefs. Be that as it may, fmall as it may now feem, it was a large fum in thofe days for the hofpital to pay, added to the lofs of their fuit and land. It is obfervable that thefe paupers, as they might juftly be deemed, did not fue, however, in formá pauperis, as in particular 20 s. to each of their counfel, and 5 s. to their folicitor, may be deemed equivalent to the fees that would be paid on the like occafion at prefent—though I hope that in fuch a cafe counfel might be found to plead without a fee.

‡ This prior gave no account either of his receipts or his payments. And in 1621 is this article, " Payd unto Mr. Courtet for writing of fartayn artickelles againft Strydwicke, Appull 2, VIII d."

" and

" and baronet, or of his tenants, farmers, or officers"), to Edward Norris for the annual rent of xiii s. and iv d. the same to be void on their paying or tendering to him or his assigns, &c. the sum of vi d. And accordingly, on September 27, John Claringbell, by virtue of a letter of attorney from the prior, brothers, &c. entered on the premises, and delivered them to the said Edward Norris, who on Aug. 7, 1623, on the receipt of vi d. (covenanted as above) surrendered up his rent and interest in them to the prior *, &c.

This was followed by another trial that year, as appears by these entries:

1623. " Item, spent when we measured our land at the Moat,   ii d.
—— spent when we gave instructions to the jury at the court-hall in Canterbury,   ii d.
—— paid to William Boycott † for measuring of our land at the Moat, and plotting of yt oute,   ii s. vi d.
—— spent when we went to informe the jury concerning the Moat land,   ii d.
———— when we went to the court-hall to give our attendance upon the said jury,   ix d.
—— paid for waxe to seale the letter of attorney and the lease for the Moat,   ii d.
———— to the two witnesses for their traveil to the Moat to see the lease sealed,   xii d.
—— to Richard Marble for his traveile to the Moat to take the said lease,   vi d.
—— spent when we went to the Moat aboute the said busines,   iiii d.
—— paid for making a peticion to Mr. Serieant Henden, and for writing of a coppy of the record out of the Court of Augmencon to send to our Lords Grace,   vi d.
———— to Mr. Denn's clerke for making the letter of attorney and the lease for the entry uppon our land at the Moat,   v s.
———— for a sugar loafe weieng ix lb. at xi d. the pound ‡, which was given to Mr. Denn for his counsell,   viii s. iii d.
———— to our brother Norton for his expenses and his leyinge out in a jorney to London to the Court of Augmentacon about the house busines,   xx s.

* This appears by an endorsement, and also by the following entry: " Paid to Edward Nor- ris for to redeem a lease which he " had of our lands at a place called the Moat, in the parishes " of St. Martin's and St. Paule's, vi d."

† See an account of this map, p. 278.

‡ This shews the comparative dearness of sugar in those times, and would be thought an un- common fee to counsel in these days.

In 1627 alſo ſome other expences occur, of "going to Foorde to my Lord's Grace," and "to the Lady Fynche above our buſineſſe," &c.

For in this year her ladyſhip having offered to pay them XL l. for arrears, with xx l. more towards their coſts, &c. the hoſpital preſented the following petition to Archbiſhop Abbot:

To the moſt Reverend Father in God, our Right Honourable good Patron, the Lord Archbiſhop of Canterburie his Grace, Primate of all England, and Metropolitan.

The humble Petition of your Grace's Almeſmen and Almeſwomen, the Brothers and Siſters of your Grace's Hoſpitall of St. John neere Canterburie.

SHEWETH, That whereas in a tryall concerning a ſuite for certayne lands, betweene your graces petitioners and Sir Moyle Finch, knight, the veredict of XII ſufficient jurors paſſed on the behalfe of your petitioners the ſeaventeenth day of July, in the 38th yeare of the raigne of Queene Elizabeth *. And where your graces petitioners being fruſtrated, by ſiniſter meanes, of the poſſeſſion of the ſayd lands, then adjudged them by the ſaid veredict, were conſtrained to commence a new ſuite, which received a tryall in Canterburie † at your grace's being there, at which tyme the ſayd ſuite paſſed againſt your petitioners: neverthleſſe, ſo it is, if it may pleaſe your grace, that, ſince the ſayd tryall, the Lady Finch ‡ hath offered unto your petitioners, in lieu of their arrerages of thirteene ſhillings and four pence per annum, by them heretofore received, to give them fourty poundes, and twenty poundes towards their coſte and charges diſburſed, together with a graunt and confirmation of the ſaid annuall rent of thirteene ſhillings and four pence to the ſaid hoſpitall for ever, ſo as your grace's petitioners will releaſe the land formerlie queſtioned, to the ſaid Lady Finch, and to her heires for ever, under their common ſeale; which to doe your petitioners utterlie refuſe, unleſſe it may ſtand with your good pleaſure and liking to give approbation thereunto. Your grace's petitioners therefore doe moſt humblie beſeech your grace to ſignifie your pleaſure, whether you will vouchafe to ſtand their gracious patron, in caſe they ſue for the ſaid lands againe, or that they ſhall accept of the ſaid motions and offers of the ſaid Lady Finch, and doe as ſhee requireth, as above. And your grace's petitioners ſhall (as in dutie they are bounden), continue their daylie prayers for the right honorable proſperitie of your grace in this life, and for your eternall happines in the life to come.

---

* In 1596. See p. 285.

† Probably in 1615, as it appears, p. 293, that the archbiſhop was that year at Ford.

‡ She was then Viſcounteſs Maidſtone, being ſo created in 1623. See p. 288, note †.

To

To this the Archbifhop returned an anfwer, with his confent and decree, as is here expreffed:

THAT the brothers of St. John's Hofpitall doe accept of my Lady Finch * hir offer, in fuch manner as hath bin reprefented unto mee by theire peticōn, that is to fay, of fortie pounds, in leiu of theire arrerages of thirteene fhillings and foure pence per annum, by them heeretofore receyved. And twenty pounds towards their cofts and charges difburfed in theyre fuite. Together with a grant and confirmation of the faide annuall rent of thirteene fhillings and foure pence to the faide hofpitall for ever, fo that the brothers and fifters of the faide hofpitall doe releafe the lands formerlie queftioned to the Lady Finch * and to hir heyres for ever, under theire cōmon feale. And I doe further decree, that thefe fommes of monny thus receyved fhall not pafs into a divident among the brothers and fifters now in beeing; but that, for the good of them and theire pofteritie, it be imployed in fome purchafe. By meanes whereof they fhall not only have their former rent of xiiī s. iv d. per annum; but an addition and increafe alfoe of three pounds by the yeare accordinge to twentie yeares purchafe.

So that thefe conditions bee performed by the advife of learned counfell, that there may be no further queftion heereafter, I give my confent that all thinges fhould be effected as heere is fpecified. October 3, 1627.

G. Cant.

Yet after this, it feems, there was another trial at the Guildhall of Canterbury, as it appears to have been after the Countefs was fo created, which was in 1628. And then, in 1631, the prior, &c. prefented to her ladyfhip the following petition:

To the Right Honorable the Counteffe of Winchelfey, widdowe, late wiefe, of Sir Moyle Finch, Knight and Baronett, deceafed.

The humble Peticōn of the Pryor, Brothers, and Sifters †, of the Hofpitall of St. John the Baptift neare and without the Walles of the Cittie of Canterburie.

WHERAS wee have heeretofore brought feveral fuits againft your honour's faid husband in his liefe tyme, and one fuite in your honour's widdowhood, for certeyne lands, parcell of your mannor or lands called the Moate, neare Canterburie, which fuits wee were induced to cōmence and profecute by fome entries in our bookes, and by fome other evidences. Nevertheles, upon the late long tryall of that fute brought in your widdowhood, after feaven or eight houres fpent in deliverie of the evidence on both fides the verdict was on your honour's parte. And it then appeared, and our councell at lawe and wee reft fatisfied, that wee have onlie right to a rent of thirteene fhillings, and fower pence per annum, iffu

---

* That the archbifhop fhould not give this lady her proper title of " Maidftone" is a little furprifing. See p. 290, note ‡.

† No " fifters," however, have figned it.

R r 2

inge

inge out of Moate lands, and noe tytle at all to any the faid lands, which rent
hath not been payed fince Michaellmas one thowfand five hundred fixtie and fower,
which was in the feaventh yeare of the raigne of the late Queene Elizabeth. We,
therefore, by the advice of our counfell, and by the good liking and approbation of the moft reverend father in God, the lord's grace of Canterburie, our moft
honorable patron, humblie befeech your honour, that the faid arrerages may be
paid unto us, and the faid rent of thirteene fhillings and fower pence may for ever,
from henceforth, be yeerlie payed unto us and our fucceffors out of the faid lands.
And wee fhall be reddie to doe any acte that your honour fhall require for the re-
leafinge and renouncinge all pretence of clayme or tytle to any of the faid lands,
other then the faid annuall rent of thirteene fhillings and fower pence. And wee
fhall daylie praye for your longe lief with increafe of honour and all happines.

The marke of
John Carr ⊥ prior.
James Coppen.

The marke of	Adrian Mighell.
The marke of A	Adam White.
The marke of Ϫ	William Rooke.
The marke of	William Rude.
The marke of ⌒	John Berte.
	William from Fryps.
	Joh. Halte.
	Joh. Flactun.
The marke of V	Henrye Pribles.
The marke of +	Reynold Shipleye.
	William Barles.
	Joh. Blowfeild.
	Joh. Harward.

To which the Countefs returned the following anfwer :

THE profecution of this cawfeles and uniuft fuite I doe willingly paffe by,
and fhall willingly from henceforth pay the thirteene fhillings and fowre
pence rent annually to the brothers and their fucceffors, the non payment of which
hath bene occafioned by their pretence of tytle to the land. But the . . . . *
moft of them incurred before the tyme of theis petitioners, of which it is no reafon
they have the benefitt ; but, upon conferring with my lord's grace, I am willing
the money behind be layed owt in buying landes or rent in perpetuity to the peticoners and their fucceffors; and at my lord's grace his requeft, I am alfo content to geve twenty poundes more to the peticoners, fo as with the faid twenty
poundes and forty poundes of the arrerage fome fitt landes of the yearely valew
of three poundes be purchafed for the brotherhood to continew for ever to the
hofpitall, and the refidew of the arreres may goe to the peticoners towards their
charge.

Secundo die Februarii, anno   E. WINCHELSEY.
regni Caroli feptimo, 1631.

* Worn and illegible in the MS.

With

With this fum the four acres and a half on Herne Common, or Childforftall, and probably fome land at Hoath, were purchafed, now let (together) to Mr. Anthony Jennings for 11 l. xviii s. per ann. and thus the matter ended. The firft mention of " an annuity from the Countefs of Winchelfea of xiii s. and iv d. out of " certaine lands at the Moate, due at Michaelmas, which is yeerly paid than to the " pittance," is in 1632.

In 1643 they delivered a note to Mr. Maior and Sir William Man " for to receive their money due out of the Mott lands." But it has been regularly paid ever fince.

C H A P. XI.

Farther Extracts from the Prior's and Reparationer's Account Books.

" 1615. Payd unto the payntors for [archbifhop] Lanfranck's armes,   ii l s. iv d.
Item, payd unto Wickel for the Denne's * armes, planing of the bourd, and making the verfe,   viii d.

———— unto Mafter Drury for his paines in helping us to Lanfrancke's armes,   xii d.

———— unto Andrew Rouke [clerk] for ringeng twifs at the going of my lorde's grace + to Fourd,   vi d.

The fucceeffion of mafters in this century was Dr. Martin Fotherby (bifhop of Sarum, 1618), Dr. Clarke, Dr. Jackfon ‡, and Mr. Somner (the antiquary), 1660, but when the others fucceeded I cannot afcertain. It appears that in the laft century the hofpital had two feafts, one at Chriftmas, and the other at Midfummer, towards the former of which was paid in 1638,   ii l. v s. vi d.
Expence of it,   iii l. x s. x d.
Towards the latter,   ii l. ix s. vi d.
Expence of it,   iii l. vi s. x d.
The latter bill, to fhew the price of provifions at that time, fhall be added.

" Payd to the woman that helped in the kitchen,   vi d.

———— to the two turnfpets,   viii d.

———— for beere at diner,   iiii d.

———— for beere to make the ferveing men drinke that brought meat to our feaft,   ii d.

* Dean's, then Dr. Charles Fotherby.
+ Archbifhop Abbot.
‡ Thomas Jackfon, D. D. prebendary of Canterbury, 1614, and rector of Ivychurch in Romney Marfh. He died in 1646, in which year is this article, " Spent upon the ringers when Dr. Jackfon was buried, 1 s. 1 d." though he does not appear to have been buried in the hofpital church.

2

" Payd

"Payd for 80 pound * of beefe at v ſ. the ſcore,　　　　　　　　i ł.
———— for a calfe,　　　　　　　　　　　　　　　　　xviii ſ.
———— for two lambs,　　　　　　　　　　　　　　　xviii ſ.
———— to the cooke for driſſing of diner,　　　　　　　iiii ſ. ┼
———— for beere for the kitchen,　　　　　　　　　　iiii ð.
———— for putter wee borrowed,　　　　　　　　　　vi ð.
———— for a gallon of facke,　　　　　　　　　　　iiii ſ. iv ð.
———— for a pottle of claritt ‡ and a pottle of white wine §,　ii ſ. viii ð.
———— for a buſhell and a pecke of meale,　　　　　　v ſ.
———— for halfe a barrel ‖ of beere,　　　　　　　　iiii ſ. ii ð.
———— for three coople of chicken,　　　　　　　　ii ſ. vi ð.

　　　　　　　　　　　　　　　　　　　　iiił. viſ. x ð.

They had alſo at that time three communions in the year, viz. at Eaſter, Lam-
mas, and Chriſtmas, beſides one occaſionally " for thoſe of St. Gregories;" at each
of which the uſual expence of " three quarts of muſcadell" was " iii ſ. vi ð. bread
ii ð." That there were alſo ſermons occaſionally, appears from the following entries:

1642. " Payed for a pinte of facke when Dr. Peake ** did preach, March 12,
vii ð. Item, for a pinte of muſcadell and a biſcett, when our maſter did preach,
viii ð.††
1647. " Spent upon Mr. Lovell when he gave us a ſermon, i ſ. iv ð." which
by a ſubſequent account (" when Mr. Dellmay preacht"), ſeems to have been
" for a quart of facke and biſcetes." But when Mr. Lovell gave them a ſermon
again, the expence " in cakes and beere" was only x ð. At preſent their communion-table and their pulpit are never uſed.

* This in 1642 was increaſed " to 177 pounds, ii l. i s. iv d."
† This expence the year before was only ii s. and in 1634 only xii d.
‡ That all red wine was at that time called " claret" is pretty certain, and that the " fack"
was not canary, but rheniſh, is as evident, if it were the ſame wine with which Falſtaff thought it no
ſin to mix ſugar. Even when they agreed with a carpenter to repair their church ſteeple in 1640,
their beverage was " a pint of facke, viii d." Thus theſe hoſpitallers were more expenſive than
their ſucceſſors, who are contented with one feaſt in a year, and with beer only at that; and even
this the increaſed price of proviſions, and the decreaſed value of money, the feaſt-rents ſtill continuing the ſame, would render " more honoured in the breach than the obſervance."
§ This in 1642 was increaſed to " three quarts of facke, a gallon of claret, and a gallon of white
" wine, viii s. ii d."
‖ And this to a " barrel of beer, ix s."
** Humphry Peak, D. D. prebendary of Canterbury, 1632.
†† This on the ſame occaſion in 1643 was " a quarte of facke, i s. iv d."

In

In 1609 is this entry: " Payd unto Mafter Edwards for wryting out of our Laten rentoll into Eynlefh [Englifh], 11 s. viii d."

" In the yeare of our Lord God 1611 the Porter's Logge [Lodge] was newe built in the month of September and October by the pryer and his fouer affiftants, not only by the charges of the Hofpetall, but only the greter part by the Right Wor-fhepfulles and·other well defpofed peopell.·

" The names of the gyvers.

Sir Peter Manod·*, knight.	Docter Newman:
Sir John Boyffe +, knight.	Mafter William Mau, Counfeller:.
Sir William Lovlefs ‡, knight.·	Mafter Edward Gardner, Efquyre..
Sir Thomas Hartlei, knight.	With many other·gentellmen more."
Docter Fothersbe §..	

In 1631 Sir Peter Hayir' 1 gave x s. " towards the repayringe of the greate windowe in the churche," d in the fame year his daughter and afterwards others of his family were buried the.c.

In 1636 is a difburfement " for wine,. when our church-yard was confecrated;. xx d."

In 1637 is another " for pitch and terr to burne in the church, and about the houfe, vii d." and in 1641 " for frankenfence about our church and hall, 1 d." This, I fuppofe, muft have heen from an apprehenfion of the plague ||. In 1643 they feem frequently to have attended " the committee," to get off their feffes, for the writtinge of a releafment for their lands laid out," &c. In 1646, is this article, " Spent when wee runge for ioy of the king's cominge to London, 1 s. 11 d."

In the fixteenth century are feveral entries in a book for, that purpofe of pur-gations before the prior and his affitlants, punifhments by the ftocks, and expulfions for fornication and other crimes,. according to the ftatutes ; but fcarce any of thefe occur fince.. The Regifter-book of the laft century has feveral baptifms and mar-riages, as well as burials,. both of the hofpital and the liberty of St. Gregory's, &c. Among the burials is that of " Mr. Ralph Groves, towne-clarke of Canterbury, Dec. 23, 1635." And June 15, 1648, is the following entry, " That fatal yeare was the beft of kings taken from off the earth, and by cruel hands fuffered. mar-tirdome, being falfly accufed, declared, and judged."

* Manwood, of St. Stephen's, keepei of Ford Park, &c.
+. Boys, recorder of Canterbury and founder of Jefus Hofpital.
‡ Lovelace, of Biddenden.
§ Martin Fotherby, mafter of the hofpital, prebendary, 1596, bifhop of Salisbury, 1618.
|| " This year" (1636), fays Echard, " proved calamirous by the plague, which broke out at London in the beginning of it, and reigned in fome meafure the whole fummer and autumn."

The

The following letter was from Henry Grey, feventh Earl of Kent, who died without iffue in 1615.

To my very loving frends the Prior of the Hofpitall of St. John's in Canterbury, and his Colleagues there. Thees.

AFTER my very hearty commendacōns. Whereas one John Kite[*], a poor old man, who by the guyft of doctor Mathew Parker, late Archbifhop of Canterbury, to whom he was fervant, had graunted and confirmed unto him out of your howfe for tearme of his lyfe an annuity or penfion of foure nobles per ann. which for a long tyme has been neglected and not received, is now dead: I have therefore thought good in his behaulf, having lyved in my fervice for more then xxx yeares paft, to certify that he departed this world the xxiiii[th] of this inftant month of September at my howfe in Beddfordfhire, to the ende that fuch order may be taken with thofe arrerages of his fayd annuity or penfion which upon accompt fhall appeare due, as may beft ftand with charity and good confcience, and the entent of the fayd guiver and guifte, which alfoe I could not but commend to your good and Chriftian confiderations. And foe, not doubting of that good care to be had therein which is meete in that behaulfe, I bid you hartily farewell, refting your very loving frend,
Wreft, 27 Sept. 1610.   H. KENT.

I doubt not, but in your Regyfter Booke it will appeare how long fince John Kite was admitted into that fociety, and that from the tyme of his admittance for how many yeares his penfion hath been anfwered, and to whofe hands, and thereupon what was remayninge in your cuftodye as due unto him unto the tyme of his deathe, which ys to be fatysfyed accordingly.

[*] It appears by the appointment of his fucceffor that this John Kyte was an out-brother. In the prior's account-book is the following entry, made probably as foon as Kite's death was known: "1610. Delyvered unto the brotheres and fifteres the xiii daye of Defember of John Kytte's mony the fom of xiii l. xii s." which to 34 perfons, whofe names are added, was 8 s. each. "Remaynyng to the Reperatyon the fom of vi l. xii s. vi d." But annexed is the following order of the then mafter: "Whereas there hath been taken out of the coffer 13 l. 12 s. and divided amongft the brothers and fifters above named, being part of the wages of one John Kyte, which had bene referved in the coffer untill it arofe unto the fumme of twenty fower pounds: forafmuch as the brothers aforefayd had noe right unto the fayd mony; therefore it is by me ordered, Auguft 25, 1612, that fo many of the brothers and fifters as be yet living fhall pay back their eight fhillings a piece which they had received, by two fhillinges a quarter. And that the reft of the mony (which they have taken out upon prætence of reparations and joineys to London) fhall be made up, untill it come to twenty fower pounds, out of the yerely rent of a howfe in Ruttenton lane, now in the occupation of William Baker, renting yerely 3 l. 6 s 8 d. And that this mony fhall be putt into a box with three locks, wherof one key fhall remaine with myfelfe, and a note truly kept what mony is quarterly putt into the box, untill the whole fumme be againe fupplyed. MARTIN FOTHERBY." This probably might be owing to the powerful interference abovementioned. At 1 l. 4 s. per ann. the arrears muft have been accruing twenty years, viz. from 1590. Archbifhop Parker died in 1575. And Kyte had been in Lord Kent's fervice from 1580.

EAST-

Engraved &c.

View of East Bridge Hospital, Canterbury, taken from King's Mill.

A. The Chapel.
B. The short Nun's House.
C. King's House.
D. Relief of the late Archbishop's Arms.
E. Relief of A.B.'s Arms.
F. King's Bridge.

The ANCIENT and MODERN STATE of the HOSPITAL of EASTBRIDGE, in the City of CANTERBURY.

Collected chiefly from the Records and other Writings now remaining in the Cheft of the faid Hofpital, &c,

By NICHOLAS BATTELY [1], M. A.

THE DESIGN OF THESE COLLECTIONS.

IN the hofpital of Eaftbridge, there was a leiger-book, containing an account of the whole ftate of the faid hofpital, in which were written at length all the feveral grants, donations of lands and benefactions, anciently given to the faid hofpital, &c.

This book Mr. Somner ufed, and frequently mentions it, in his Treatife of the Antiquities of Canterbury, by the name of *Liber Hofpit. de Eaftbridge.*

But this book is now loft, and thereby many things belonging to the faid hofpital may be alfo loft.

---

[1] Vicar of Beakfbourn, 1685, editor of Somner's Antiquities of Canterbury, 4to, 1703, and brother to the Rev. John Battely, D. D. Mafter of this Hofpital, archdeacon ·and prebendary of Canterbury, and author of *Antiquitates Rutupinæ.* Mr. Battely died in 1704.

The

The lofs of this book makes me fufpect, that feveral records and other writings belonging to the hofpital may be alfo wanting, efpecially becaufe the mafters of the hofpital have from time to time taken the liberty to keep in their private libraries fuch writings concerning the hofpital, as they chofe; and it is a queftion whether their executors have been as careful to reftore all thofe writings to the fucceeding mafter, as they were to preferve and keep them fafe: Alfo fuch writings as the feveral mafters did not care to preferve in their own cuftody, are kept in a publick cheft belonging to the hofpital, and ftanding in the chapel there. The key of this cheft hath been ufually kept by the reader or fchool-mafter; and of his care or faithfulnefs there was not fuch fecurity as there ought to have been.

By this means it is more than probable, that feveral records and writings are at this day miffing: for I cannot now find fome leafes, which I faw in the cheft within lefs than fix years laft paft.

Hereupon I was firft inclined to make thefe collections, to preferve fuch writings as are ftill extant from being loft for ever.

THE SITUATION, NAME, AND FOUNDATION, OF THE HOSPITAL.

T H E river Stour runs through the city of Canterbury in two branches [1]; the leffer of thefe branches runs juft by Weftgate, and the bridge over it is called Weftgate-bridge.

The larger branch runs eaftward of the former, and more in the middle of the city, and the bridge over it is called Eaft-bridge; upon which bridge, and on each fide of it [2], is fituated the ancient hofpital, commonly called *The Hofpital of Eaftbridge*; which was the firft name by which this hofpital was called: for fo I find it named, in fome of the moft ancient writings, *Hofpitale de ponte de Eaftbridge*, before ever it was honoured with the addition of St. Thomas the Martyr.

[1] Somner's Antiquities of Canterbury, p. 37, 38.
[2] Rather " at each end of it." On the north fide is the mill. D.

The

Plate VIII p. 293

J. Pratt. del.

South View of Kings-bridge and Mill, and of the Church of All-saints at Canterbury, according to the late improvements taken (from the Parlour window of the Kings-head inn) March 11.1760.

The bridge is fometimes called *King's Bridge* [1], and the mill, which ftands by it, *King's Mill*, becaufe it was fome time *The King's:* In particular, Thorn relates a remarkable ftory concern- ing it [2], That king Stephen being in great ftraight at Lincoln, where he was furprized and taken prifoner by Robert earl of Gloucefter, and put to a great fine for his ranfom, towards his relief in that neceffity, borrowed of Hugh, the fecond of that name, Abbot of St. Auguftine, one hundred marks, and in con- fideration thereof, by his charter, gave to the monaftery this mill. Concerning this, fee more in Mr. Somner's Antiquities of Canter- bury, p. 43. It was called *Molendinum de Eaftbridge*, aliter *King's-mill* [3]. From hence the hofpital hath been commonly called *King's bridge Hofpital*.

It was alfo called the *Hofpital of St. Thomas the Martyr*; the reafon of which name will fufficiently appear from the follow- ing collections.

It ftands in that divifion of the city, which is called *The Ward of Weftgate*.

By whom, and in what year this hofpital was founded, is altogether unknown.

Archbifhop Lanfranc (who founded the hofpitals of St. John the Baptift without Northgate [4], and St. Nicholas Herbaldown without Weftgate [5], and the Priory of St. Gregory, in Canterbury,

[1] Somner, p. 42.
[2] Thorn, in vitis Abbatum Sancti Auguftini.
[3] A view of this mill and bridge, taken by the Rev. Mr. Pridden in 1780, is here annexed. See plate VII. The following infcription is copied from a ftone now on this bridge:
"For the greater fafety and convenience of paffengers, this bridge was widened x feet, in the year MDCCLXIX, Jofeph Royle, Efq; being mayor.
The expence was fupplied by voluntary contributions from the city and its neigh- bourhood. Fifty-five miles, fix furlongs, from London-Bridge."
[4] The late capt. Stephen Riou was the architect. Eadmer. Hift. Nov. l. I. p. 9.
[5] See the Hiftories of thofe Hofpitals.

and

and endowed the fame bountifully out of his own revenues) is
by fome fuppofed to have been the founder and endower of this
hofpital alfo [1]. This archbifhop Lanfranc is famous for his great
buildings and works of piety; which are at large recorded by Eadmer, in Hiftor. Novor. l. I. and in the book called, *Dies obituales
Archiepifcorum Cant.* But the hofpitals which he built, are faid to
be *extra civitatem* [2]; of which thofe two above-named, the hofpitals of St. John the Baptift and of St. Nicholas Herbaldown,
continue to this day monuments of his excellent piety and
charity; but that he built the hofpital of Eaft-bridge, I never
could find mentioned by any writer. Lanfranc died 1089.
The forenamed *Dies obituales Archiepifc. Cantuarenfium* fays of
him, " *Memoratur, quod multas et honeftiſſimas domos præpa-*
" *ravit* [3];" which is the moft, that I can find, why he fhould
be fuppofed the founder of this hofpital, and this at beft is but
a weak conjecture.

The next four archbifhops, Anfelm, Ralph, William, and
Theobald, have not left us any grounds to fuppofe that any
of them erected this building. To thefe fucceeded Thomas
Becket, by whofe name this hofpital was called; but whether
becaufe it was built by him, or whether becaufe it was dedicated
to him after his martyrdom (which was A. D. 1170), is ftill a
great queftion; for it is not improbable, that this hofpital was
built before his time, and afterwards dedicated to him : if it was
not built by Lanfranc, yet it was certainly built before or at leaft
about the time of Thomas Becket; for fome time after his death,
we have records, ftill extant, of grants made to this hofpital, as.
will appear afterwards.

[1] Somner's Antiquities of Canterbury, p. 82, 83;.
[2] Anglia Sacra, vol. I. p. 55.
[3] Ibid.

Mr.

Mr. Somner is of opinion, that it was " firft eiected and endowed by the charity and piety of St. Thomas Becket, in the time of Henry II. and that from thence it was called *The Hofpital of St. Thomas, the Martyr, of Eaftbridge.*"

His opinion is grounded on the ordination of archbifhop Stratford (dated A. D. 1342), which was 172 years after the martyrdom, and 121 years after the tranflation, of St. Thomas, in which ordination are thefe words :

> Hofpit' de Eftbreg per beatum et gloriofum martyrem Thomam olim Cant' archiepifcopum, predecefforem noftrum, fundatum antiquitus et dotatum, &c. — idem hofpitale per beatum martyrem antedictum, pro pauperum peregrinoium Cantuar' confluentium receptione nocturnâ, et fuftentatione aliquali ab olim, et pro jam incumbentibus eidem oneribus dotatum exiliter, &c.

And this is certainly the beft evidence we can find for the foundation of the hofpital, it being given by an archbifhop within 172 years after Becket's death : and it feems, the other records, either of the foundation or of the inftitution thereof, could not be found in his days. Hereupon,

This return was made by the commiffioners to queen Elizabeth, of her writ touching this hofpital [1] :

> " Imprimis. Quod reverendiffimus pater et dominus dominus Thomas Becket Hofpitale de Eftbrig in civitate Cant' inftituit et fundavit pro receptione pauperum peregrinantium et Cantuariæ confluentium, &c." [2]

But when he founded, or how he endowed, this hofpital, we know not. Neither do I find any writer of his life who makes mention of his founding this or any hofpital. His troubles and banifhment feem to give him no time to erect fuch a building.

Archbifhop Whitgift doubted, whether Thomas Becket founded the hofpital [3] ; for when the lawyers (whom he employed to that

---

[1] Somner, p. 111.
[2] A paper in the hofpital cheft.
[3] A writing in the hofpital cheft.

2

purpofe)

purpofe) had drawn up the beginning of the act of parliament for the better foundation of this hofpital (in the time of queen Elizabeth), and had put thefe words into the beginning of the bill, *The Hofpital of Eaftbridge*, alias *the Hofpital of St. Thomas the Martyr, founded, as yt ys reported in ancient writings, by Thomas Becket, fometime Archbifhop of Canterbury*, &c. he altered this paffage with his own hand, and inferted thefe words, *The Hofpital of Eaftbridge, founded and endowed, as it is alledged, by certain Archbifhops of Canterbury*, &c.

But probably this alteration was not fo much becaufe he doubted whether Thomas Becket founded the hofpital, or no; but rather to erafe the name, and to eclipfe the memory, of one who at that time was held in too much honour and veneration, and even adored and worfhiped by the people.

I have feen the regifter of Arundel cited, That the hofpital of Eaftbridge was founded by archbifhop Becket [1], &c.

OF THE ENDOWMENT OF THE HOSPITAL, &c.

Mr. Somner, Antiquities of Canterbury, p. 120, declares, that " he will not fpeak much of the endowment of the hofpital."

The firft endowment, to which I can fix any date [2] was beftowed in king John's time, by archbifhop Hubert, who died, A. D. 1205. He gave it the tithes of Weftgate-mill, of a mill and two falt-pits at Herewick (which Mr. Somner fuppofeth to be in or near Whitftable), of a windmill in Reculver, and of another windmill in Wefthalimot, in Thanet.

[1] Reg. Arundel, Part II. fol. 16.
[2] A. D. 1193.

The

The words of his grant are these :

" Hubertus, Dei gratiâ, Cant' Archiepifcopus, totius Angliæ primas, omnibus Chrifti fidelibus ad quos prefens fcriptum pervenerit, æternam in Domino falutem. Ad omnium notitiam volumus pervenire nos, divinæ pietatis intuitu, et confideratione neceffitatis et egeftatis quâ dilecti filii noftri fratres hofpital' Sancti Thomæ de Eftbruge nofcuntur laborare, conceffiffe et dediffe eidem hofpitali in fubfidium fuftentationis fratrum ipfius decimam molendini, de Weftgate in Cant' et decimam molendini et duarum falinarum de Herewick. et decimam molendini ad ventum in Raculfre, et decimam molendini ad ventum in Wefthallimot in Tenet ; quas decimas nuper confueverunt ecclefiis dari. Quare volumus et precipimus ut idem hofpitale Sancti Thomæ eafdem decimas integre habeat, precipiat, et poffideat. Quod ut ratùm in perpetuum permaneat et inconcuffum, hac prefentis fcripti ferie et figilli noftri appofitione duximus confirmandum. Hiis teftibus, magiftro Ric' Cancell' noftro, Rann' Thefaurar' Sarum, Galfrido de Bocklande, Magiftro Symone de Sywell, Magiftro Willielmo de Calne Decano de Codenham, Magiftro Willielmo de Summercote, Magiftro Reifero, Magiftro Fulcherio, et multis aliis."

Copia vera, ex ipfo originali, per me Nic' Battely.

This grant was confirmed alfo by the then prior and chapter of Chrift-Church, in thefe words :

" Univerfis Sanctæ Matris ecclefiæ filiis ad quos prefens fcriptum pervenerit, J. Prior [1] humilifque conventus ecclefiæ Chrifti Cantuar' falutem in Domino æternam. Noverit univerfitas veftra nos chartam venerabilis patris Huberti, Dei gratiâ, Cant' archiepifcopi, totius Angliæ primatis, infpexiffe fub hac forma, " Hubertus Dei gratia," &c. [ut fupra] Nos igitur dictam conceffionem et donationem, ficut jufte et rationabiliter facta eft, quantum in nobis eft, falvo jure cujuflibet, confirmamus. In hujus rei teftimonium prefens fcriptum fecimus fieri, et figilli noftri appofitione fignari. Valete.

[1] This " J. Prior" muft be John-de Chetham, who was prior in archbifhop Hubert's time. And hence Mr. Somner muft be miftaken, who gives a true account of the death of archbifhop Hubert ; viz. in July, 1205 ; but, in his relation of the priors, makes John the prior to fucceed Galfridus, A. D. 1206 ; for this confirmation of John, the prior, and convent of Canterbury was before the death of Hubert, otherwife it would have called him nuper Archiep'. See this at large contefted in the hiftory of the priors of Canterbury, in Anglia Sacra, vol. I. p. 140. et 797.

I have tranfcribed this charter of Hubert, and the confirmation of it by John, prior, and the chapter of Chrift-Church, partly to correct the miftake above-named in the year when John fucceeded Galfridus, and partly to prove, that this grant and the confirmation of it was made, A. D. 1205, a little before the death of Hubert ; but chiefly to take notice, that all the benefactions conveyed to the hofpital by this firft benefactor are at this day alienated ; and hence I will further fearch, what is become of thefe gifts, when they were alienated, and whether it be poffible to recover them again.

COKYN'S HOSPITAL ANNEXED TO THE HOSPITAL OF EASTBRIDGE,
IN THE TIME OF ARCHBISHOP HUBERT.

NEAR to the hofpital of Eaftbridge was another hofpital,
built and founded by one William Cokyn, a citizen of Canterbury, and from him called Cokyn's Hofpital [1]. This hofpital was
dedicated to St. Nicholas and to St. Catherine the Virgin and
martyr; and ftood in the parifh of St. Peter's, almoft directly oppofite to the Black-Fryers gate; having had a lane by it aforetime
called Cokyn's-lane, but now fhut up and built upon. This lane
is often mentioned in the writings of the hofpital of Eaftbridge.

William Cokyn, for 18 marks *de gerfumâ*, or for the confideration of 18 marks, purchafed of Stephen the prieft, and
Godefman, the fons of Richard Mercer, of Canterbury, with
the confent of their widow-mother Cicely, a meffuage next adjacent to his own; thus in the deed or charter defcribed:

"Totum illud meffuagium, cum ōīb̄s pertinentiis fuis, quod habet in latitudine
verfus cheminium domini regis 42 pedes, et in longitudine quantum extendit a
cheminio domini regis ufque ad aquam que dicitur Sture. Quod vero meffuagium
adjacet proximo meffuagio lapideo predicti Willielmi et meffuagio Walteri mercatoris in parochiâ Sancti Petri."

This meffuage was either converted into an hofpital, or elfe he
built an hofpital upon the ground where it ftood.

This done, Godefman, one of the fons of Richard the merchant, claiming an intereft in the foil where this hofpital ftood, was
bought out of it for the confideration of 7 s. And he made a
charter to archbifhop Hubert, acknowledged in a full burghmote
of the city, of releafe of all his right to it. The words are thefe:

[1] Somner's Antiquities of Canterbury, p. 116, 117.

This muft be diftinguifhed from a houfe in the fame ftreet, fituated alfo on the
fouth fide, devifed in 1657 by Mr. Cogan, its owner, to the ufe of fix clergymens
widows, which, from the fimilarity of its name and fituation, has been confounded
with the other, even by Mr. Goftling, in his intelligent "Walk," but corrected by
another able hand (Dr. Beauvoir) in the Addenda to the fecond edition. D.

"De

" De terrâ in quâ hofpitale fundatum eft, quod Willielmus Cokyn fecit, quæ jacet inter terram quæ fuit Willielmi Cokyn et terram Thomæ Mercatoris, fc. a magna via regali ufque ad Sturam '."

The prior of St. Gregory alfo had fome intereft here ; for Robert the prior of St. Gregory, and his convent, did by their charter confirm

" Donationem quam Willielmus Cokyn fecit fratribus hofpitalium Sancti Nicholai, et Sanctæ Katharinæ, et Sancti Thomæ Martyris de Eaftbridge, de illo meffuagio quod eft in parochiâ Sancti Petri proximè adjacen' hofp' Sancti Nicholai et Sanctæ Katharinæ verfus Weft, quod eft in tenura noftrâ," &c.

on confideration of paying yearly 18 d. to the faid priory of St. Gregory [2].

This hofpital was united to the hofpital of Eaftbridge in the time of archbifhop Hubert, and probably by his confent : And this union was confirmed by a bull of pope Innocent III. which bears date " 16to kalend' Februar', pontificat' anno 6to," which was in the year 1203.

The words of the bull are thefe :

" Innocentius [3] Eps, fervus fervorum Dei, dilectis filiis rectori et fratribus hof-pitalis Sancti Thomæ Cantuarienf' falutem et apoftolicam benedictionem. Cum a nobis petitur quod juftum eft et honeftum, tam vigor æquitatis quam ordo exigit rationis, ut id per folicitudinem officii noftri ad debitum perducatur effectum : Ea propter, dilecti in Domino filii, veftris juftis poftulationibus grato concurrentes affenfu, hofpitale ipfum in quo divino eftis obfequio mancipati, cum iis quas impræ-fentiarum rationabiliter poffidetis, aut in futurum, Deo propitio, juftis modis poteritis adipifci, fub beati Petri et noftra protectione fufcipimus. Specialiter autem hof-pitale Sancti Nicolai et Sanctæ Catharinæ, poffeffiones et terras pertinentes ad ipfum, ficut eas juftè et pacificè poffidetis, vobis et per vos eidem hofpitali autoritate aplica confirmamus et prefentis fcripti patrocinio communimus. Nullo ergo omnino ho-minum liceat hanc paginam noftræ protectionis et confirmationis infringere, vel ei aufu temerario contraire : fi quis autem hoc attemptare prefumpferit, indignationem omnipotentis Dei, et beatorum Petri et Pauli, apoftolorum ejus, incurfurum fe fciat. Dat' Anagniæ [4], xvi kal' Februarii, pontificatus noftri anno fexto."

[1] The Hofpital writings.
[2] The charter is ftill extant.
[3] This pontiff was only 37, and a deacon, when he became pope, on Jan. 8 or 9 1198. He held the general council of Lateran, at which he prefided, 1215, and died at Perugia in 1216. He wrote feveral works, enumerated by Moreri and others.
[4] A city in the *Campagna* of Rome, of which this pope was a native, formerly the capital of the Hernici, whofe country was very fruitful ; whence *divis Anagnia*, Virg. Æn. VII. 684.

T t

Afterwards William Cokyn, by his charter (wherein he mentions the union of thefe hofpitals) entitles the faid hofpitals to all his lands, poffeffions, and chattels, and makes them his heirs.

The words of the faid charter are thefe :

" Univerfis Chrifti fidelibus, ad quos prefens fcriptum pervenerit : Willielmus Cokin, civis Cantuarienfis, falutem in Domino. Noverit univerfitas veftra me pro falute animæ meæ, et pro animab' parentum meorum et benefactorum et omnium fidelium, Dominum noftrum Jefum Chriftum et membra ejus, videlicet, pauperes et infirmos fratres hofpitalium Sancti Nicholai et Sanctæ Katherinæ, et Sancti Thomæ martyris de Eftbrigge in Cantuaria, quæ fimul funt unita, et a felicis recordationis papa Innocentio confirmata, omnium terrarum et poffeffionum ac catallorum meorum, falvo omnibus dominis, de quibus terram teneo, redditu et fervitio fuo, meos conftituiffe in perpetuum hæredes et affignâffe. Ut ergo hæc conftitutio et affignatio rata fit et ftabilis in perpetuum, illam in prefens fcriptum redactam figilli mei munimine corroboravi. Hiis teftibus, magiftro Joanne Pœnitentiario, magiftro Willielmo de Leiceftre, magiftro Waltero officiale domini Cantuar', magiftro Thoma de Fracham, magiftro Willielmo de Herbaldune, Hugone de Craule, Willielmo Wilárd, Arnoldo Ferre, Joanne filio Roberti, Joanne Turte, Henrico Le Jay, Eudone filio Eudonis, Philippo filio Terrici, Roberto de Stureya, Joanne filio Lefwini, Roberto Colle, Jofeph' Clerico, et multis aliis."

Copia vera ex ipfo originali per me Nic' Battely.

Eaftbridge Hofpital being thus united to Cokin's Hofpital, not long after it became poffeffor and owner thereof : And (as we may fuppofe) it was not long before Cokin's hofpital ceafed to be ufed as an hofpital, and the manfion-houfe thereof was let and rented out ; for,

A. D. 1238, Peter, the then rector, or keeper, of Eaftbridge Hofpital, and the brothers of the fame, granted and demifed to one William Samuel a parcel thereof, viz.

" Totum tenementum cum ædificiis fupra pofitis, tam ligneis quam lapideis, et omnibus pertinentiis fuis, quod jacet in parochia Sancti Petri Cant' inter domum Ofmundi Polre quæ eft ex parte orientali, et venellam quæ appellatur Cockynes-lane, quæ eft ex parte occidentali, et regiam ftratam quæ eft ex parte Aquilonari, et Sturam quæ eft ex parte Auftrali."

The lane called Cockin's-lane was then open, and not built upon ; and in the fame charter it was covenanted, that the fame lane fhould remain free and open ; for thefe words follow in the fame deed :

" Præ-

" Præterea ita convenit inter partes predict', quod nec predict' Petrus, nec fratres, nec succeſſores eorum, nec predictus Willielmus, nec hæredes sui, nec sui aſſignati, poterint predictam venellam obſtruere, quin utraque pars poſſit uti commode via predictæ venellæ eundo et redeundo."

There is an ancient deed or charter ſtill in being, by which,

" Vivianus Mercer, primus filius Ordnothi tinctuaiii, dedit 24 placatas terræ apud Hackington Willielmo Cockyn fundatori hoſpitalis Sanctæ Catharinæ virginis et martyris, et fratribus ejuſdem hoſpitalis," &c.

This deed or charter was made in archbiſhop Hubert's time at leaſt, before the two hoſpitals were united; and the writing ſhews itſelf to be of great antiquity. One of the witneſſes to it was, " magiſter Radulphus de ponte Eaſtbregge," who was one of the firſt maſters of the hoſpital.

Robertus de Cockering dedit 3 acras terræ et modicum amplius apud Cockering, &c.

This, by the writing and witneſſes, was about the ſame time with the former.

Nicholaus filius Baldwini dedit Willielmo Cockin procuratori hoſp' Sancti Nicolai confeſſ' et Sanctæ Katharinæ virg', et fratribus et fororibus ejuſd' hoſp', 5 acras terræ et dimidium in Cockering.

Witneſs among others is " Mag' Radulp. procur' hoſpit' de " Eaſtbrigge." This was before the two hoſpitals were united.

Nicolaus filius Baldwini Flandrenſis dedit 9 acras terræ in Cockering.

About the ſame time.

Willielmus parvus filius Henrici dedit Willielmo Cockin 62 acras terræ in parochia de Hackintune, &c.

About the ſame time.

Robertus de Cockering dedit 13 acras terræ in Cockering.

About the ſame time.

Henricus de Swoleford dedit 5 acras et unam rodam, &c. in Cockering.

Stephanus Harengod miles dedit 3 acras terræ in Cockering. Dat' A. D. 1243, menſe Aug. Teſt. Henrico de Minſtre, tunc Seneſchallo curie archiepiſcopalis Cantuar', ſede archiepiſcopali tunc vacante [1]; Willielmo de Burnes clerico, &c.

[1] See Anglia Sacia, vol. I.

This

This vacancy of the archiepifcopal fee was after the death of Edmund, and before the confecration of Boniface.

Henricus et Aluredus, filii Roberti de Cockering, confirmaverunt donaconem 13 acrarum terræ quas pater dederat.

A. D. 1252. Hamo filius Joannis de Cokering, et Matildis filia Richardi Aldermanni de Cockering, dimiferunt et quietum clamaverunt redditum fex denariorum, &c. anno r. R. Hen. filii Joannis regis 36to.

A. D. 1269. Matild. filia et heres Richardi Aldermanni demifit totam terram prediti patris, &c. anno r. R. Hen. filii Joannis 53°.

A. D. 1258. Henricus filius Roberti de Cockering remifit 5s. redditus ex 13 acris terræ quas pater demifit hofpitali, anno r. R. H. filii Joannis 42.

A. D. 1237. Hamo filius Joannis de Cockering, et Matildis et Agnes filiæ et hæredes Ricardi Aldermanni de Cockering, dederunt 5 acras e tdimidi.m terræ in Worth, &c. Anno r. R. H. filii Joannis 21°.

A. D. 1242. Hamo filius Joannis de Cockering, Matildis filia Ricardi Aldermanni deCockering, Matildis et Alicia filiæ Agnetis filiæ diti Ricardi, dimiferunt 9 denar' et obolum, partem redditus de 5 acris et dimid. terræ prius deditæ hofpitali. Sexto kal' Maii.

Amifius Capellanus filius Roberti de Malaffe, intuitu Dei et beatæ Mariæ et gloriofi martyris Thomæ, dedit 2s. et 6d. lib. reddibus, quos recto. et fratres hofpitalis folvere folebant, et quos accepit jure hereditario de Roberto filio Hamon.s de Cockering, in puram et perpetuam elemofinam, &c.

A. D. 1268. Matildis filia Walteri remifit unum denarium de forifgabulo pro. parte unius acræ terræ in Cockering, &c. Anno r. R. H. filii Joannis 52.

A. D. 1270. Walterus de Kenefrilde warrantizat 13 acras terræ apud Cockering, &c.

A. D. 1272. Edmundus filius Roberti. de Cambio Cant' confirmavit hofpitali 3 acras et dimidiam terræ in Kokering, pro qurbus dictus Edmundus recepit 4 acras terræ in parochia Sancti Martini, &c. Actum erat hoc exchambium anno r. R. H. filii regis Joannis 56, menfe Julii.

OF THE ENDOWMENTS IN BLEAN, BELONGING TO THE HOSPITAL.

STEPHEN LANGTON, the next archbifhop after Hubert, by his and his convent's charter, confirms to the hofpital the gift of Blean church or parfonage, made to it by the patron Hamon Crevequer [1], after the refignation of it by the till then

---

[1] Properly Crevecœur.

incumbent

incumbent and parfon, William Crevequer: whereupon the Mafter or Keeper of the hofpital became afterwards parfon there[1]; and continues to this day patron of the vicarage.

By another deed, the faid Hamon Crevequer grants the parfonage-houfe to the mafter and brothers of the hofpital, in thefe words:

" Totum meſſuagium cum pertinentiis, quod fuit Lefwini facerdotis perfonæ ejufdem ecclæ, et quod poftea fuit archidiaconi de Petters perfonæ ejufdem ecclæ, et quod poftea fuit Willielmi de Crevequer perfonæ ejufdem ecclæ."

Hamon Crevequer, in his charters, is commonly called " Hamo de Blen, filius Etardide Crevequer;" and on his feal, which is a man in armour on horfeback, engraved in plate VI. fig. 5, is this infcription, " Hamo de Crevequer." He lived in archbifhop Langton's time; for to one of his charters, Henricus de Sandford, archidiaconus Cant', and Willielmus Curteys, are witneffes. This Henry Sandford was confecrated bifhop of Rochefter, A. D. 1227; and William Curteys, called " Decanus Cantuari- " enfis," was official of Canterbury at the time of the death of Langton, which happened A. D. 1228; for, " vacante fede per " mortem predicti archiepifcopi[2] capitulum Cantuarienfe omni- " modam jurifdictionem exercebat per Willielmum Curteys offi- " cilem fuum[3]."

Another of his charters runs in thefe words:

" Sciant prefentes et futuri, quod ego Hamo de Blen, filius Etardi de Crevequer, dedi et conceffi, et hâc prefenti mea charta confirmavi, Waltero[4] Priori ecclæ Chrifti Cant' et magiftro Henrico de Sandford, archidiaconi Cant' executoribus teftamenti dnæ Agnetis de Clifford," &c.

[1] A. D. 1206. Somner, p. 113.
[2] Sc. Stephani Langtoni.
[3] Anglia Sacra, vol. I. p. 150.
[4] This Walter, the prior, contemporary with Hen. Sandford, is not mentioned by Mr. Somner among the priors. See his Antiquities of Canterbury. p. 282. where he makes Rogerus de la Lee immediately fucceed John Sittingborn. and when he fpeaks of archdeacon Sandford (ibid. p. 309), he fays, that " he was co-executor with the prior of Chrift Church, of the lady Agnes Clifford's will." And in the margin, he quotes, for his authority, the leiger book of the hofpital of Eaftbridge. It is ftrange that he fhould not take notice of the prior's name, which is written at large, " Waltero Priori." This Walter, the third of that name, was made prior A. D. 1217, and died 1222. See Anglia Sacra, vol. I. p. 140.

The

The moſt noted witneſſes to the charters and deeds of Hamon Crevequer, beſides thoſe already named, were,

"Willielmus de Cluſe, Lambinus de Blen, Simon de Blen, Robertus Lupus,. Henricus Jay, Radulphus de Porta, John Crevequer, Thomas Speciarius, Euſta- chius de Natindune, Saiomona de Fraxino."

Robertus, filius Hamonis de Blen, had theſe witneſſes to a deed:

"Willielmus de Cluſe, Robertus Lupus, Rad' de Porta (ut ſupra), Robertus de Wrotham, Hamo et Bartholomæus filii Simonis de Blen."

I take notice of theſe witneſſes, becauſe they were witneſſes to divers charters and deeds which are not dated, as well as to ſome that are dated; as the firſt ¹ charter of Hamo de Crevequer was A. D. 1225; and about that time divers.gifts and charters were beſtowed upon the hoſpital.

Mr. Somner, in his Antiquities of Canterbury, p. 309, ſays of Henry Sandford, that, " being archdeacon, he took a reſig- nation of Blean Church, by the title of *vices gerens Domini Stephani Cantuarienſis*, meaning archbiſhop Langton:" and for this he quotes the Leiger-book of the hoſpital.

There are ſeveral other charters or grants of lands or rents given to the hoſpital, lying in Blean: as,

Robertus Lupus, A. D. 1245.

Robertus filius Richardi de Wrotham, anno 34to Henrici filii regis Joannis; i. e. A. D. 1250.

Willielmus filius Stephani de Hoth, 1268, &c.

Avicia filia Radulphi de Baldwerd dedit 3 acras, et quartam partem acræ, terræ, in campo de Reyfeild' Rad' cuſtos hoſpital' witneſs.

The ſaid Avicia, and Reginald her huſband, confirmed the ſame grant. " Witneſs, Mag' Rad' cuſtos hoſpital'."

Cicilia filia Radulphi de Balverd dedit unam acram et tres partes unius acræ de nemore in campo de Reyfeild.

The ſaid Cicily and Bartholomew de Hiwecham confirmed the ſame grant, as is ſet down among Canterbury endowments.

Ralph, maſter of the hoſpital, was witneſs to all theſe grants.

¹ Viz. The firſt which was entered in the old book of the hoſpital.

Feugerius

Feugerius filius Simonis de Hocke dedit tres acras, et quartam partem acræ, terræ, de nemore, &c.

Hamo de Crevequer dedit 14 acras, et quartam partem acræ, terræ, et 4 acras de bosco.

Idem dedit totum campum de Willelmesmed in Blen.

Idem dedit tenementum, &c. et 14 gallinas, &c.

Idem dedit terram, &c. intra Nigreth et Middleditch, et clausturam prioris et conventus Christi Cant' et aquam quæ currit ad Fishmansbregge et Prestekote, &c.

Idem dedit diversos redditus et gallinas, &c.

Most of these donations were made before the hospital of Saint Nicholas and Saint Katherine was united to Eastbridge hospital.

Item dedit 6 acras de bosco, quæ vocatur Nigreth.

Wlwardus, filius Walteri Huppehoth, dedit quandam terram, &c.

Agnes filia Anserii dedit 2 acras et 3 virgatas terræ, &c.

Simon et Petrus filii Estermanni dederunt boscum et fundum qui jacent ad caput campi quod vocatur Weterled, &c.

Richard de Bromfeild Senescallus Curiæ Christi Cant' dedit 6d. redditus, A. D. 1242.

1243. Willielmus de Suthfolk dedit de terra, quæ vocatur Slippesfeld, 12d. et de terra quæ vocatur Linhere 5d. ob. &c. Dat' anno r. R. Hen' fil' Joann' 27° hiis testibus Martino tunc vicario de Blen, &c.

1268. Willielmus filius Stephani de Hoth dedit terram illam in villa de Blen, quæ vocatur Slippesfeld. Anno r. R. Hen' fil' Joann' regis 52.

Joannes de Fraxino, parochianus Storum Cosmi et Damiani de Blen, dedit 5d. redditus de terra quæ vocatur Godlendlend. A. D. 1272.

Willielmus, filius Hammonis de Lekel de Blen, dedit 8 acras terræ, sc. 4 acras nemoris, et 4 acras terræ arabilis, in Blen. Dat' anno r. R. Hen fil' regis Joannis 56; id est, A. D. 1272.

A. D. 1280. Abreda, filia Roberti de la Hoth, dedit 2 acras et unam virgatam terræ in Blen, &c. anno r. R. Edw' filii regis Henrici 8°.

A. D. 1289. Robertus Scot' dedit 3 acras et dimid' terræ in Blen. Dat' die Martis in vigilia Sti Laurentii martyris, anno reg. R. Ed. I. 17°.

A. D. 1299. Marabilia filia Joannis Atei Hearth remisit duas perticas terræ in Blean, unam sc. in campo qui vocatur Merchotefeld, alteram in campo qui vocatur Orfeld. Dat' anno r. R. Edw' filii Henrici 27mo.

Prior et conventus ecclesiæ Christi Cant' habent boscum unam de venditione magri et frat' hospitalis de Estbrig, A. D. 1278. Registrum ecclesie Christi Cant. (A) fol. 217.

A WIND-

A Wind-mill in Little Foxmold.

THE priorefs and nuns of the church of St. Sepulchre made an agreement with the mafter and brothers of the hofpital of Eaftbridge [1], thereby granting them

Quartam partem unius acræ teriæ fuæ in Parva Foxmold in parte occidentali, ad conftruend' molendinum fuum ad ventum:

Mr. Somner adds, *in hundredo de Ridingate*; which he took out of the Leiger-book of the hofpital: but thofe words are not in the charter or original agreement. The conditions of the agreement were thefe:

" That the faid mafter and his brethren of the hofpital fhould hold the faid land *jure hæreditario in perpetuum.*

" That they fhould pay to the faid priorelle and her nuns every year fix-pence on Midlent Sunday.

" That the faid priorelle and her ñuns fhould bear a fourth part of the charge of building, repairing, and maintaining the faid mill, and fhould receive the fourth part of the profits thereof, and have their own corn ground there whenfoever they pleafe." And,

" That the mafter and brethren of the hofpital fhould find a way *a magno cheminio per terram fuam ufque ad præfatum molendinum,*" &c.

It is not " *a cheminio magno regali,*" as Mr. Somner hath it.

About the fame time Richard de Bramford, fteward of Chrift-Church, paffed over all his right in a mill in Foxmold to the hofpital [2]; the words of his charter are thefe:

" Sciant prefentes et futuri, quod ego Richardus de Bramford, fenefcallus ecclefiæ Chrifti Canr', dedi et concelli, et hâc prefenti meâ chartâ confirmavi, magiftro et fratribus hofpitalis Sancti Thomæ Cant' quicquid habui in molendino ad ventum apud Foxmolde in liberam et perpetuam elemofinam, ad faciendum anniverfarium meum et uxoris meæ et omnium antecefforum et fuccefforum noftrorum in predicta don o in perpetuum. Et ut hæc donatio et concellio et confirmatio mea robur obtineat, prefentem chartam figilli mei munimme roboravi. His teftibus, magiftro Wilhelmo pænitentiario, Hamone facerdote, Willielmo Crevequer, Ofmundo Pollie [3]," &c.

---

[1] About the year 1200.   [2] Ibid.
[3] Ofmund Pollie lived 1238, in the houfe next but one to the hofpital. See p. 3c6.

Some

Some of thefe were witneffes alfo to the agreement between the nunnery and the hofpital.

Not long after, Lambin the Fleming [1], the fon of Adam de Berghes, gave to the brethren of the hofpital of Eaftbridge *unam fummam* [one feam] *frumenti*, from his mill called Medmilne [2], on St. John Baptift's day, and 14 *perticatas terre, que jacet Binnewytt*, (which is the ifland *With* in Canterbury) *et tres denarios de redditu de Alwardetune*, &c.

This benefaction being afterwards withheld from the hofpital, the mafter and brethren fued for it in the fpiritual court, and obtained this decree againft Thomas, the fon of Lambin the Fleming:

" That whereas Lambin, the father of Thomas, had given (as above) *unam fummam frumenti* to the hofpital *in puram et perpetuam eleemofynam*, he fhould pay the fame accordingly every year; and that he fhould deliver to them about Eafter *tres fummas frumenti*, in fatisfaction of arrears due to them, *fub penâ excommunicationis*."

This decree was made *die Lune poft feftum Sancti Valentini*, A. D. 1253, *in ecclefiâ Chrifti, Cant*.

Grant above-mentioned, p. 312.

" Omnibus Chrifti fidelibus ad quos prefens carta pervenerit, Juliana, prioriffa, et conventus ecclefie Sancti Sepulchri, Cant', falutem. Sciatis nos dediffe et conceffiffe, et hâc prefenti cartâ mea confirmâffe, rectori et fratribus hofpitalis Sancti Thome Martyris de Eaftbridge, in Cantuariâ, quartam partem unius acre terre in Parvâ Foxmolde, in capite occidentali, tenendam et habendam in perpetuum de nobis, reddendo inde annuatim nobis fex denarios fterlingorum in Dominicâ mediâ quadragefime pro omnibus fervitiis, et omnibus rebus, &c. Hiis teftibus, Henrico archidiac' Cant', magiftro Rogero pœnitentiario, Herberto perfonâ de Plukeley, Martino perfonâ ecclefie Sancti Alphegi, Ofmundo Polre," &c.

This was before the year 1227, when archdeacon Henry de Stanford was confecrated bifhop of Rochefter; perhaps it was

[1] So " firnamed," fays Somner, " from either his birth-place or parentage." His houfe was afterwards the hofpital of the poor priefts, who alfo fucceeded him in this mill, charged, however, by a decree, in 1325, with four bufhels of wheat to Eaftbridge hofpital.

[2] Of Medmilne, " *quafi Middlemilne*, as ftanding about midway between St. Mildred's mill and Eaftbridge," or Medmilne, " *quafi Mead'milne*, becaufe fituate by the meadows." See Somner's Antiquities of Canterbury, p. 138. 1ft edition.

U u

in

in the time of his predeceffor Henry de Caftilion, who was archdeacon in archbifhop Hubert's and king John's time.

By the following Bull of Pope Honorius III. the hofpital was
privileged of and from paying tithes of their gardens:

A. D. 1210. " Honorius [1] epifcopus, fervus fervorum Dei, dilectis filiis, rectori
et fratribus hofpitalis Sancti Thome Cantuarienfis, falutem et apoftolicam benedictionem. Juftis petentium defideris dignum eft nos facilem prebere confenfum, et
vota que a rationis tramite non difcordant, effectu profequente complere: Ea
propter, dilecti in Domino filii, veftris juftis poftulationibus grato concurrentes.
affenfu, perfonas veftras ac hofpitale ipfum quo divino eftis obfequio mancipati, cum
omnibus bonis que in prefentiarum rationabiliter poffidetis, aut in futurum juftis modis,
preftante Domino, poteritis adipifci, fub beati Petri et noftra protectione fufcipimus.
Specialiter autem poffeffiones, redditus, et alia bona veftra, ficut ea ōia jufte et
pacifice poffidetis, vobis, et p̃ ṽro prefato hofpitali, noftra auctoritate apoftolica confirmamus, et prefentis fcripti patrocinio communimus, diftrictius inhibentes, nequis a
vobis de ortis veftris decimas exigere vel extorquere prefumat.   Nulli ergo omnino
hominum liceat hanc paginam noftre protectionis, confirmationis, et inhibitionis infringere, vel ea aufu temerario contraire. Siquis autem hoc attemptare prefumpferit,
indignationem omnipotentis Dei, et beatorum Petri et Pauli, apoftolorum ejus, fe
noverit incurfurum. Dat' Rome, apud Sanctum Petrum, xiiii kal' Januarii, pon-
tificatûs noftri anno primo."

A. D. 1269. John of Adifham gave two acres and a half in
the parifh of Saint Martin, abutting on an acre of his own
land towards the Eaft, on his brother's land towards the Weft,
on the king's highway towards the North, and on the lands of
the abbot and convent of Saint Auguftine towards the South, to
the mafter and brothers of the hofpital of St. Thomas of Eftbrigge, dated *Anno r. R. Hen' filii Joannis regis*, 53°, &c. (See
the charter at large among the writings of the hofpital). For
this they were to provide him a chamber in the faid hofpital, with
meat, drink, cloaths, and fhoes, fo long as he fhould live.

GUILDHALL LAND IN ROMNEY, GIVEN TO THE HOSPITAL.

" Omnibus hoc fcriptum vifuris, vel audituris, barones portûs de Romeny falutem.
Noveritis quod nos, communi affenfu noftro, pro falute animarum noftrarum et ante-

---

[1] This Pope reigned from July 17, 1216, to March 18, 1227. Confequently this Bull muft have
been dated in 1216, or 1217. " On all occafions," fays Moreri, " he gave proofs of a zeal really acting
" for the good of the Church, and the advantage of the Faithful."

cefforum et fuccefforum noftrorum, fc. ut fpecialiter participes fimus omnium bene-factorum que in hofpitali beati Thome martyris de Eaftbridge in Cantuariâ in per-petuum fient, conceffimus et quiete clamavimus Deo, et beate Marie, et dicto hof-pitali, et fratribus ibidem Deo fervientibus, totum jus et clamium noftrum quod ha-buimus in terrâ que vocatur Gildehalle land in villâ de Romeney, in liberam, puram, et perpetuam eleemofinam, ità quod predicti fratres terram predictam abfque ca-lumpniâ vel impedimento noftro, vel heredum noftrorum, in perpetuum libere et quiete teneant et poffideant : ut autem hec conceffio et quieta clamatio ftabilis et inconcuffa in perpetuum permaneat, fcripto prefenti commune figillum univerfitatis noftre appofuimus. Hiis teftibus, Domino Heremanno, capellano, Richardo, ca-pellano," &c.

Afterwards, the rector and brethren of the hofpital, with the confent of Edmund [1] lord archbifhop of Canterbury, paffed over by indenture to

" Thomas, the fon of Humphrey, all that land in Romney, upon which Guildhall ftood, which lyes over-againft the church of St. Laurence [2], towards the north-eaft : upon condition, that he payes yearly to the hofpital of Eaftbridge, in Canterbury, the fumme of two markes, that is to fay, one mark at the feaft of the Nativity of Chrift, or within twelve days after, and one mark at the feaft of the Nativity of St. John the Baptift : And in cafe he or his heirs do make default in payment of the faid money at the appointed times, that then he fhall pay double fo much as he hath not paid according to the appointed times : And if he failes to make pay-ment for one whole year, then the mafter and brothers of the hofpital fhall enter and feize upon the faid land, and take full poffeffion of it, without any further confideration. And for this grant the faid Thomas gave to the faid mafter and brethren 40 l. fterling *in gerfumiam*, by way of fine," &c.

See the leafe at large among the writings of the hofpital.

IN CANTERBURY.

A. D. 1257. CHRISTIANA, the daughter of William Silveftre, the relict of William Samuel, gave to the mafter and brethren of the hofpital, and their fucceffors for ever, the fum of three fhillings and fix-pence a year, free rent, which the heirs of Kerloms Le Mercer ufed to pay her, at two times in the year, viz. at Midlent one-and-twenty pence, and at the Feaft of St. Michael one-and-twenty pence, out of a certain fhop in the Mercery [3] before the gate of the church of the Holy Trinity [4], i. e. between the tenement of Thomas the fon of Lambin Fleming [5], and the tenement of the heirs of Richard Bigges, and the highway leading to the church of the Holy

[1] Archbifhop Edmund was confecrated, A. D. 1234.
[2] St. Laurence's church was in New Romney.
[3] Now Mercery-lane.
[4] Now Chrift Church.
[5] See above, p. 313.

Trinity

Trinity on the one part, and the tenement of Henry Le Furmger on the other part.
This rent to be held *in liberam, puram, et perpetuam eleemofynham*, &c. Dated anno
regni regis Henrici, filu regis Joannis, 41°. Hiis teftibus, Gregorio Palmigero, et
Roberto Burre, tunc Ballivis Cant', Willielmo Cokin, Joanne Digges," &c.

This rent is paid at this day out of the houfe where Mr.
Kingsford the milliner now lives, viz. A. D. 1690 [1].

Maynerius Le Waydur, civis Cant', was bound to maintain a
waterfpout which went from his houfe to the river, and was
joined to the roof of the kitchen belonging to the hofpital; and
that he and his heirs, and whoever fhould own his houfe,
fhould be bound to pay to the hofpital the fum of xii pence yearly,
at the feaft of St. Michael [2].

" Hiis teftibus, Willielmo Samuel, Huberto Mercerio, tunc prepofitis, Henrico Jay,
Ofmundo Polre [3]," &c.

This is the houfe of Mr. Lefroy, the dyer, now joining to
the hofpital on the Eaft fide of it [4]; of the fame houfe Mr. Somner
writes, p. 120, that, " one Creffy, a Jew, built the forepart of it
againft the head of the chapel belonging to the hofpital :" And
that " when the Jews were expelled Canterbury, this houfe, with
others, were given by the king to Chrift-Church." This Creffy
was forced to agree with the hofpital, that his houfe might be
fuffered to ftand, and had a charter in writing for it, which
bears date 1236. It is in a leiger book belonging to the Church,
called *Charta Remiffionis*, made by Peter the then rector, and
the brethren of the hofpital of Saint Thomas of Eaftbridge, to
Creffy the Jew,

" De omnibus querelis occafione domûs, vel fundamenti, vel muri, quam in parte
orientali in capite capelle noftre edificavit, ut nunquam queftio movebitur in
curiâ Chriftianitatis vel feculari," &c.

---

[1] Now, 1784, occupied by Mr. Richard Elwyn, eutler.
[2] This was foon after A. D. 1200, in the time of Archbifhop Hubert.
[3] " Or Poller, as we now write it," fays Somner. He lived in the houfe next to this. See above,
p. 312.
[4] Now, 1784, in the occupation of James Ronolds, gun-maker.

IN

IN AND ABOUT CANTERBURY.

Ivo [1] filius Ade, textoris, de Holeſtreet, dedit tres denarios redditûs fratribus et ſororibus hoſpit' beati Thome Martyris de Eaſtbregge in Cant' ex meſſuagio in parochiâ Sanſti Dunſtani, &c.

Among other witneſſes is *Magiſter Radulphus, tunc cuſtos jam dicti hoſpitalis*, &c. This was about the time of archbiſhop Hubert; the writing ſhews it to be old.

Mattheus, filius Thome, filii Sunewinni, **extra** Weſtgate, dedit hoſpitali Sanſti Thome Martyris de Eaſtbrigge in civitate Cant' 26 denarios, viz. 12 denar' ex meſſuagio extra Weſtgate in parochiâ Sanſti Dunſtani, et 14 d. de meſſuagio illo extra Weſtgate, quod jacet in venellâ que vocatur Northlane.

This ſeems to be about A. D. 1230.

Hamo de Lutterwood dedit duos denarios de redditu, et omne jus in meſſuagio in parochiâ de Northgate, &c.

About 1220.

Alicia, filia Hammonis, filii Arnoldi, Tinſtoris, de Eaſtbrigge, dedit rectori et fratribus hoſpit' Sti Tho' Cant' tres denarios de redditibus que ſolebant ſolvere, &c.

Aſcelina, filia Rad' filii Arnoldi, de ponte Eaſtbrig, dedit rectori et fratribus hoſpit' Sanſti Tho' Mart' oēs terras illas, cum pertinentiis ſuis, que jacent inter pontem de Eaſtbrigge et meſſuagium Gawen Tinſtuarii, datum anno MCCXXXIX, ſecundo quo dominus rex Henricus, filius regis Joannis, deſponſavit reginam filiam Comitis Provinciæ.

Ricardus, filius Radulphi, filii Arnoldi, Tinſtoris, dedit domui hoſpitali Sanſti Tho' Martyr' et ejuſd' domûs fratribus ſucceſſorib', illam terram in parochiâ Omnium Sanſtorum, que jacet juxta Sturey, et habet in latitudine ſuâ ſuper cheminium domini regis 42 pedes, et in longitudine ſuâ 77.

Richard Calvil dedit fratribus et ſororibus hoſp' Sanſti Tho' Martyr', et ſucceſſoribus eorum, in perpetuum, illam terram, cum domib' et pertinentiis ſuis, que habent in latitudine ſuâ verſus Suth 29 pedes, in latitudine ſuâ 32 pedes, et in longitudine ſuâ de chemino regis verſus North 200 pedes.

Gode, filia Wiberti, Carnificis, extra Weſtgate, dedit hoſpit' Sanſti Thome Martyris, et fratribus et ſororibus ejuſdem loci, duodecem denarios redditûs de meſſuagio extra Weſtgate, quod adjacet proximè Sture.

Robertus Pyn, et Beatricia uxor, dederunt duos ſolidos de redditu ex meſſuagio in parochiâ Sanſti Petri, &c.

Among the witneſſes is *Magiſter Radulphus, tunc cuſtos jam dicti hoſpitalis.*

Joannes Chopeleſe, extra Weſtgate, filius Admeri Clerici, dedit fratribus et ſororibus hoſp' beati Tho' Mart' tres ſolidos de redditu extra Weſtgate, &c.

[1] This Ivo, and his father Adam, the dyer, are afterwards ſaid to have given a penſion of 9d. a year to the hoſpital in 1200. See p. 310.

To

To this one of ·the witneſſes is *Magiſter Radulphus, tunc cuſto[s] dicti hoſpitalis.*

1200. Avicia, relicta Lamberti Weyderi, dedit hoſp' beati Tho' Martyr', et fratribus et fororibus ejuſdem, totum illud meſſuagium, cum omnibus pertinentiis ſuis, quod adjacet proximè meſſuagio lapideo predict' hoſpital' et meſſuagio quod fuit Aluredi, mercatoris, et venella que vocatur Venella Judeorum, in parochiâ ecclefie Omnium Sanctorum [1].

One of the witneſſes is *Mag' Radulphus, cuſtos dicti hoſpital'.*

1200. Bruningus, Molendinator, extra Weſtgate, dedit fratribus et fororibus hoſpitalis beati Thome Martyris 16d. redditûs de meſſuagio extra Weſtgate, in parochiâ ecclefie de Weſtgate.

Witneſs, *Magiſter Radulphus, dicti hoſpitalis tunc cuſtos.*

1200. Bartholomæus de Hiwecham, et Cicilia uxor, dedit unam acram et tres partes unius acre nemoris in campo de Reifeld.|

I ſuppoſe this is in Blene. Witneſs, *Radulph' cuſtos hoſpitalis dicti.*

1200. Rogerus Vachier, et uxor ejus, dederunt 6 denarios de redditu, extra Weſtgate, de meſſuagio in capite venellæ quæ vocatur Crokere-lane. Teſte M'ro Rad.

Hugo Godeſhalt dedit Deo et fratribus hoſpit' Sancti Tho' Mart' totam illam terram, cum pertinentiis ſuis, que jacet inter terram Radulph' filii Willielmi verſus Weſt, et regiam ſtratam verſus Eaſt, &c.

A. D. 1269. Arnoldus Bedellus, de Weſtgate, in Cant', dedit rectori et fratribus hoſp' duos denarios, et tres quadrantes, redditûs de tenementis lapideis que ſita ſunt inter ecclefiam Sancti Petri in Cant' et domum Joannis filii Roberti.

Petrus, filius Stephani de Dene, dedit meſſuagium illud, cum pertinentiis ſuis, quod eſt ſuper Sturam, et duo meſſuagia illa verſus Weſt proximè illi adjacentia.

Wlfredus, filius Eſtrilde de Herebaldune, dedit Deo et fratribus et fororibus hoſp' Sancti Tho' Martyr, 2s. redditûs pvenientes de 6 acris terre ſup Derindele, &c.

Salomon de Tuniford dedit 6 denarios liberi redditûs magiſtro procuratori dicti hoſpitalis, &c.

Ante 1241. Thomas Aurifaber, filius Gervaſii de Witherinbrook, dedit totam illam terram que fuit Willielmi filii Hamonis fratris uxoris Alicie, que jacent inter Sturam et terram heredum Garwi, Tinctoris, in civitat' Cant'.

The ſame was before given by Aſcelina, filia Radulphi filii Arnoldi, as above, p. 317.

Petrus de Burleg dedit 6 ſolidatas et 2 denariatas redditûs Mro' et fratribus hoſpit' quas predicti Mag' et fratres reddere ſolebant annuatim de tribus meſſuagiis que jacent in civitate Cant' juxta pontem de Eaſtbridge, verſus Weſt, &c. Act' anno Domini 1241, &c.

---

[1] The houſe " adjoining to Jewry-lane," no part of which is in the pariſh of All Saints, is that which is now, 1784, the coffee-houſe. D.

Hence

Hence the donations and confirmation of Thomas Aurifaber, p. 318. and Afcelina, filia Radulphi, p. 317. were before that date.

Ante 1241. Lodovicus, filius Willielmi de Machelii, dedit 6 denarios redditûs quos emit a Robert Vach et uxore ejus, de meffuagio extra Weftgate, in capite venelle que vocatur Croker-lane, &c.

This is the fame that Roger Vàch gave before; as abovementioned, p. 318.

Adam, filius Wlfredi, dedit 37 denarios redditûs de domo lapideâ extra Weftgate [1].

Joannes, filius Viviani, dedit quandam terram in Cant' &c. in parochiâ Omnium Sanctorum, &c.

Aldhienna, filia Thome, dedit 20d. redditûs de terrâ extra Weftgate in parochiâ Sancti Dunftani, &c.

Hugo de Redegate dedit meffuagium quoddam extra portam de Radegate.

Margareta, filia Randulfi de Geddings, dedit 12d. redditûs, quos Godefredus dedit recipiendos in dicto hofpitali, &c.

A. D. 1254. Henricus, filius Nicolai, filii Baldwini, dedit octo et decem denarios redditûs pvenientes de quodam meffuagio, cum fuis pertinentiis, in parochiâ Sancte Marie de Northgate, quod fuit Radulfi de Littleburn, quod fuit juxta terram monachorum Sancte Trinitatis Cant' verfus Weft, et regiam ftratam verfus Eaft, ad duos terminos anni, fc. 9d. ad feftum Sancti Michael', et 9d. ad mediam quadrageffimam. Actum anno regis Henrici, filii Joannis, 38.

A. D. 1246. Thomas Lock, filius Ade Cementarii, dedit quandam terram in parochiâ Sancti Petri, &c. anno r. R. Henrici, filii domini Joannis regis Anglie, 30mo.

Guido et Joannes, filii Sufanne, filie Roberti des Ewer, dedit terram in Bramdune, &c.

Simon, filius Willielmi, ⎱ dederunt feptem acras terre in Bromedune in' tenemento
Adam de Saxingherth, ⎰ de Weftgate, &c.

Gunnora, filia Euftathii de Merewith, dedit tres folidatas liberi redditûs ex meffuagiis tribus juxta pontem de Eaftbridge.

There are feveral other charters to confirm the donations of the faid meffuages.

1200. Walterus de Safford capellanus dedit decem denarios liberi redditûs ex meffuagio quod jacet in parochiâ Sancte Margarete in Cant' [2].

This was about archbifhop Hubert's time, or foon after.

Arnoldus Aurifaber refignavit, et in perpetuum quietum clamavit, Magiftro et fratribus hofpit' Sancti Thome Martyris, totum jus et clamium in toto illo meffuagio, cum pertinentiis fuis, quod de iis tenuit in parochiâ Omnium Sanctorum Cant'. Quod quidem meffuagium jacet inter meffuagium quod fuit Joannis de Adifham,

---

[1] This houfe belonged to Mr. Thomas Walker in 1740. Now occupied, 1784, by Mr. Thomas Delafaux, jun. filk mercer.
[2] Mr. Thomas Hollingbery, 1740.

quod

quod eft verfus North, et viam que ducit ad molendinum regium verfus Suth, &c.
Dat. A. D. 1256.

This meffuage is alienated at this day.

1245. Rogerus Aldermannus, filius Joannis, Aldermanni de Readingate [1], dedit
duos folidòs redditûs de 4tuor acris terre in Foxmold, &c.

Rogerus Aldermannus, filius Joannis, &c. dedit 7 acras terre, viz. v acras in
Foxmold, et duas acras juxta viam ex alterâ parte, &c.

Wilhelmus de Readingate, filius Joannis Aldermanni, dedit 3s. redditûs, viz.
1s. quem fratres hofpit' folvere folebant de acris terre in Foxmold, &c. 2s. quos
fanĉte moniales Sanĉti Sepulchri folvere folebant, &c.

About the year 1245, as may be colleĉted from the witneffes.

Willielmus, filius Joannis, Aldermanni de Readingate, dedit 24 folidos redditûs, et
oĉto denarios et obolum annui redditûs, fc. de Jofepho, textore, 3s. de hered'
Roberti de Rodericume, 8d. de priore et conventu ecclefie Chrifti, Cant', 2s. 1od. de
hered' Walteri Boel, 23d. de Warino de Burgate, 6d. de hered'. Terrici Aurifabr',
2s. 4d. de meffuagio Siwardi, piftoris, 4s. de Warino de Niole, 23d. de monial' ecclefiæ Sanĉti Sepulch', xiid. de Joanne, filio decani de Hakintune, 2s. de Rudulpho
de Leghe, 1s. de Reginaldo de Cornhill, 8d. de eleemofynariis ecclefie Sanĉti Auguftini, 4d. de Thomâ Arcioniario, 1od. de Mro Simone de Thaneto, 6d. de
W'mo de Cockin, 6d. ob. de heredibus Thome Aldermanni, 1s.

A. D. 1227. " Dat' coram jufticiariis itinerantibus, fc. Martino de Patefhell,
Ric' Duketh, Willo de Infulâ, Thoma de Kamullâ, apud Cant', anno r. R. Hen.
fil' reg' Joannis, 11mo."

The other charters, which were made by the fons of Aldermannus de Readingate, muft have been of more ancient date.

Henricus de Ofpring dedit 16d. de libero redditu ex tenemento in Natindune, &c.
1200. Adam, textor, de Holeftreet, et Ivo filius ejus, dederunt 9d. redditûs.

Witnefs to it, *Magifter Rad' tunc cuftos hofpital.*

An agreement between the prior and brethren of the hofpital
of Herbaldown, and the mafter and brethren of the hofpital
of Eaftbridge, to pay out of a meffuage in St. Peter's parifh, 4s.
yearly, to the mafter and brethren of the hofpital of Eaftbridge:

[1] This father and fon, and alfo another fon, William, (mentioned afterwards)
feem to have been fucceffively " aldermen of the ward of Riding-gate" (as it is
now ftyled), that being one of the fix ancient wards of the city (which ftill continue), and the aldermanries being faid by Somner, to be " as ancient as Richard
" Ift's time," but to have been originally, " freeholds, either demifeable or de-
" vifeable, or defcending, if indifpofed of at death, to the next heir at law." D.

Quod

Quod eſt inter meſſuagium monachorum Sanƈte Tri itatis, quod verſus We l; et regiam ſtratam, que verſus North, &c.

An agreement between the maſter and brethren of the hoſpital of Eaſtbridge, and John, the ſon of Ralph Bernigadarere, that the ſaid maſter and brethren granted unto the ſaid John, his heirs and aſſigns, a meſſuage, with all its appurtenances, which lies in the pariſh of St. Peter's, and adjoins to a meſſuage of the monks of the Holy Trinity, which is towards the Eaſt, &c. And they are to receive for the ſame yearly, for ever, 3 s. 6 d. viz. 21d. *ad feſſ Sanƈti Mich'*, *et* 21d. *ad dominicam mediam quadrageſime.*

" Eccleſia Chriſti ſolvit abbati de Faverſham v'd. pro terrâ de quâ magiſter hoſpit' Sanƈti Thome reddit nobis (i. e. Priori et Capi̅lo eccleſie Chriſti Cant') tres ſolidos, et eſt in parochiâ Sanƈti Petri."

In Herbaldown.

MICHAEL, filius Heylye de Blen, dedit totam illam terram, que vocatur Bromthiache, et jacet inter Bromdunama et la Herſte, et eſt in parochiâ Sanƈti Nicolai.

Idem dedit terram, que fuit Lamberti Guarderii, &c.

A. D. 1280. Joannes, filius Rogeri Criſtmiſſe, dedit domino Joanni, vicario de Wycham, magiſtro hoſpit' &c. unam peciam terre in parochiâ Sanƈti Dunſtani extra Weſtgate, jacentem inter terram Petri Durant verſus Eaſt, et terram hered' Tho' Abot verſus Weſt, et terram domini archiep' Cant' verſus North, et regiam ſtratam verſus Suth, &c. Dat' anno r. R. Edw' filii R. Henrici 14.

This is the piece of land called Lompitts.

A. D. 1297. Willielmus Cryke & Suſanna uxor ejus remiſerunt ſex denariatas annui redditûs de Lompitts. Anno r. R. Edw. primi 25.

Joannes Holt dedit meſſuagium cum domibus deſuper conſtruƈtis, &c. quod jacet inter hoſpit' de Eaſtbridge verſus orientem, et tenement' Roberti Polre verſus occidentem, et inter regiam ſtratam et rivum Sturam.

This, by the writing and witneſſes, appears to be ancient.

A. D. 1354. Joannes Godard remiſit 2s. redditûs de peciâ terre, vocate Lompits, quos magiſter hoſp' ſolvere ſolebat, &c. Dat' apud Cant', vigil' Epiphan', anno r. R. Edw' tertii a conqueſtu 28vo.

Petrus de Wurt dedit 18 denar' liberi redditûs quos ei ſolvere ſolebant magiſter et fratres hoſpit'.

This was very ancient, as appears by the witneſſes and writing.

X x   A. D.

A. D. 1547. " Magifler hofpitalis de Eaftbregge, pro 7 acris terræ ad terras manerii
de Thanington verfus North et Eaft, ad terras nuper monialium Sancti Sepulchri
vocat' Mynchyncroft verfus South, et ad regiam viam verfus Weft, folvit annuum
redditum viid. per Tho. Hales ', anno 1 Edw. VI."

The land of the manor of Thanington, to which thefe feven
acres did abut, are called Long Crow Down; and the highway
on the Weft is, *via equeftris quæ ducit ab Holoway ufque Petham.*

This money was paid by the mafter of the hofpital to Mr.
Tho. Hales, &c.

Ex libro ms. ecclesiæ Christi Cant', circiter A. D. 1300.

Redditus quem debemus certis nominibus pro terris quas tenemus:

Ad purificationem beatæ Mariæ.
Hofpitali Sancti Thomæ de Eftbrugge, viii d.
Item hofpitali de Eaftbrugge, vs. ix d.
Ad annuntiationem beatæ Mariæ.
Hofpitali de Eftbrugge ———— ii d.
Item eidem ———— — ii d.
Ad Pentecoften.
Hofpitali de Eftbrugg .—— ii d.
Item eidem ———— v d.
Ad feftum Sancti Michael.
Hofpitali de Eftbrug ——— vi d.
Eidem hofpitali ——— vs. ix d.
Item eidem — — viii d.
Item eidem — — ii d.
Item eidem —— — iii d.

xivs. viid.

In Beaksborn, alias Livingsborn.

THE hofpital was formerly endowed with feveral parcels of
land in this village, which at this day are alienated.

William de Becco fold unto William de Sancto Eadmundo, rector of Livingfborn, 26 acres of land, which are plainly fet out in the charter by fuch abuttalls
as are known at this day, viz. 14 of them, " verfus orientem ad regiam viam que
ducit de Patricfburn ad Livingfburn, verfus occidentem ad terram Hugonis le
Noble; in breadth, verfus aquilonem, ad meffuagium et terram prædicti Hugonis
le Noble; verfus auftrum, ad terram Euftathii de Burne, militis." And the other
14 acres " jacent in longitudine verfus orientem ad ftratam regiam, verius occidentem ad terram que vocatur Woppin, in latitudine verfus aquilonem ad regiam
ftratam quæ cucit de Livingfburn ad Cantuariam; et verfus auftrum ad terram et
meffuagium Hugonis le Noble," &c.

' Ex libro MS. Tho. Hales.

Richard

Richard and William, the fons of the faid William de Becco ' confirmed this charter of fale by their refpective charters to the faid William de Sancto Edmundo, rector of Livingfborn. And to thefe charters one of the witneffes was Peter, who was mafter of the hofpital of Saint Thomas the martyr, A. D. 1236-1242.

That any of thefe lands were afterwards given by William de Sancto Edmundo to the hofpital, there is no deed or charter now extant to prove; but that either fome part of thefe or fome other pieces of land, did belong to the hofpital doth appear; becaufe, in another charter of Richard de Becco, *filius Willielmi de Becco*, the 10 acres of Wopping land in Beakfborn are mentioned to abutt *inter terram dicti hofpitalis, que eft verfus Eaft.* This charter is dated A. D. 1250.

A. D. 1240. An agreement was made between William del Bec de Livingfburn, et William de Sancto Eadmundo, cler', rector de Livingfburn, that William del Bec did let by leafe to Willielmo de Sancto Edmundo 10 acres of land, *in campo qui vocatur Wopping,* for the term of 25 years; beginning *ad Epiphaniam Domini anno* MCCXL°, *fc. anno r. R. Hen' filii Joannis regis* 24*to,* to the full term of 25 years compleat; and after that term of years compleat, the faid 10 acres of land to return again to William del Bec, &c. Witnefs to this leafe was Peter, (abovementioned) *tunc magifter hofpitalis Sancti Thome Martyris, &c.*

This leafe William de Sancto Edmundo affigned to the mafter and brethren of the hofpital of St. Thomas in Canterbury; and becaufe in the firft year they fuftained a great lofs in their crop of oats, William del Becco added one year to the faid 25 years, by way of increafe.

At length Richard, the fon of William del Becco, gave the faid 10 acres in Wopping to the faid hofpita for ever. The words of the charter are thefe:

" Sciant

" Sciant prefentes et futuri, quod ego Ricardus del Becco de Livingefburne, filius Willielmi del Becco, militis, dedi et concceffi, et hâc prefenti chartâ meâ confirmavi, magiftro et fratribus hofpitalis Sancti Thome Martyris de Eftbrigge in Cant', pro falu:e anime mee, et antecefforum meorum, et heredum meorum, in liberam, puram, et perpetuam elemofinam, decem acras terre mee, cum fepibus et foffatis, et ōibs aliis pertinentiis fuis, que jacent in campo qui vocatur Wopping, juxta acram ecclefie de Livingfburn que eft verfus North, et terram que fuit Euftachii, militis, de Burnes que eft verfus Suth ; et inter terram dicti hofpitalis que eft verfus Eaft, et terram dicti Richardi del Bec que eft verfus Weft. Tenend' et habend' dictis fratribus, et eorum fuccefforibus, de me, et heredibus meis, liberè, quietè, et jure hereditario, et pacificè in perpetuum, ficut aliqua eleemofina liberius et fecurius poffidetur : Et ego Richardus, et heredes mei, warrantizabimus et defendemus dictis fratribus et eorum fuccefforibus omnem predictam terram, cum omnibus fuis pertinentiis fuper dictis, contra omnes homines et feminas, tam Judeos et Judeas quàm Chriftianos et Chriftianas. Et ut hec mea donatio, et charte mee confirmatio, et hujus dicte eleemofine mee facta et recordata in curia mea apud Livingfburn conceffio, rata et ftabilis permaneat in perpetuum ; hanc prefentem cartam meam figilli mei appofitione roboravi. Actum fc. nono kalend' Maii, die Sancti Georgii, anno Domini 1250.—His teftibus, domino Philippo, tunc vicario de Livingefburn : Nichola de Burne, Ric' fratre ejus, Henrico magiftro, Willielmo de Bec, Joanne de Dudintune, Will'o filio Thome, Henrico Noble, Henrico Peynot, Roberto de Woltune, et aliis."

Copia vera ex ipfo originali, per me Nic. Battely.

Willielmus de Sancto Edmundo did give,

" Domui Sancti Thome Martyris de Eaftbrigg in Cant', et magiftro et fratribus ejufdem loci, in puram, liberam, et perpetuam eleemofinam, &c. omnes terras, redditus, &c. anno Domini 1240."

The charter of this was entered fol. 38. of the book belonging to the hofpital. In the fame book was another charter of the fame William de Sancto Edmundo : *Domui hofpitali Sancti Thome Martyris de. Eaftbreg, et pauperibus et infirmis illuc confluentibus, et magiftro et fratribus ibidem Deo fervientibus, &c.* But thefe and the book are now all loft.

Page 43 and 44 of this book, king Edward, confirms by his letters patent the 26 acres of lands which William de Burnes gave to the hofpital, and the 10 acres of land that Richard de Bec' gave, which lie in Wopping field.

IN BIRCHINGTON, IN THE ISLE OF THANET.

" WALTERUS, filius Eilmeri, filius Aldithe, dedit fratribus domûs hofpitalis Sancti l'home de Eaftbreg in Cant. et eorum fratrium fucceftoribus, in perpetuum, unam acram terræ in Huppedune, &c.—in Burchetune."

THE MANOR OF MONKTON.

" By a rental made for the faid manner the 22d of June, 1545, Mr. Henry Crifpe has to ferme certain lands called Eaftbridge Lands, and this land pertains to Eaftbridge Spittle, in Canterbury, that is, the Spittle that is on Kingfbridge, befides Allhallon Church. Thefe lands bound to the lands of Mr. Henry Crifpe, befides Quekis, Eaft, South, and Weft, and contein three acres dī rowde xii perches. And another peice lying to the land of Mr. Crifpe South and Weft, to the king's highway North, and to Mr. Dingle Eaft, and it contains one acre three perches: and another peece lynge by Adrian's Croft to the lands of Mr. Crifpe North and Weft, and to Mr. Crifpe, late Boucher's, and to the lands of Mr. Dingle South, and contains one acre and 5 perches. Another peece lying at Farthinge, downe to the lands of Mr. Crifpe, Weft, Eaft, and North, and to the highway South, and containes one acre di and 5 perches.

" And another peece lyes in the lands of Mr. Petit, called Highhams, befides Blithes Croffe, and this peice is dowled out with 4 dowells, and lyes on the northfide of the way leading from Quekes to Blight's Croffe, a little befide a deel or hoole, with a hawthorn growing on the bank, and bounds to Mr. Pettit Eaft, South, and North, and to Den lands Weft, conteins by eftimation 5 acres and a halfe refid', and fo contains in two l. of Eaftbridge land in the hands of Mr. Crifp, and at his hering out xi acres, 3 roods, v perches, 2s. the acre, xxiiis. ob."

Extract out of the Court Rolls.   Examined by John Coppin, Steward.

" Sciant prefentes et futuri, quod ego Gilbertus de Clare, comes Gloceftrie et Hereford, conceffi et confirmavi fratribus hofp' Sancti Thome Martyris de Eftbrug in Cantuar' terram illam que fuit Willielmi. filii Roberti Edith, cum pertinentiis, et terram illam cum pertinentiis que fuit Wulwardi tegulatorii, et terram illam que vocatur Elfledeftune, et terram illam cum pertinentiis quam tenent de Lambino, et Michaele, et Joanne, filiis Elizæ de iblen, et tres folidos, et quatuor denarios, et tres gallinas, redditûs cum pertinentiis que, tenent de Willielmo fratre Hamonis de Blen de terra que vocatur Aikland, et 12 denarios redditûs, cum pertinentiis, quos tenent de dicto Joanne filio Elye, tenend' et habend' fecundum formam in confirmatione Hamonis de Blen contentam; falvo fervitio mihi debito. His teftibus, Willielmo de Hubrig, Baldwino de Ver, Mich' de Foffa, W'mo de Clufe."

This laft witnefs lived about 1225.

" Sciant prefentes et futuri, quod ego Gilbertus de Clare, comes Gloc' et Heref', conceffi et confirmavi fratribus hofp' Sancti Tho' Martyr' de Eaftbrug in Cant' terram.

terram illam cum pertinentiis que vocatur Nigrethe, et terram illam que vocatur Williams Mede, et terram illam que vocatur Benethewe, et unam acram que jacet juxta aquam verfus North, ex oppofito de Prefticote, et domum illam que fuit Willielmi et Joannis fratrum Hamonis de Blen, et 20 folidos, et 3 denarios, et 3 quadrantes liberi redditûs, et 17 gallinas, et liberum exitum et communiam, in pafcuis, forinfecis, et cheminiis, et femiftis, et aquis, ad omnia negotia fua facienda, fecundum formam in chartis Hamonis de Blen contentam, in puram et perpetuam elemofinam. Hiis teftibus, Willielmo de Hobrug, &c."

These are the confirmations of the gifts of Hamo de Blen, by the Earl of Gloucefter, *capitalis domini feodi*, and whofe confent was required to the alienation of them.

" R. Comes Leğræ [1], baillivis fuis, et omnibus hominibus fuis Francis et Anglis, tàm prefentibus quàm futuris, falutem. Sciatis quod ego, pro falute anime mee et Petronille comitiffe, uxoris mee, et pro animabus patrum et matrum noftrorum, et antecefforum et fuccefforum noftrorum, dedi et conceffi hofpitali beate Thome martyris, quod fitum eft Kantuarie fuper pontem Eaftbrigie, unam marcam argenti in prefectura mea de Leğra, ad fuftinendos pauperes in predicto hofpitali Kantuarie, recipiend' fingulis annis ad feftum Sancti Michael'. Quare volo et precipio quod predicta domus hofpitalis Kantuarie, et fratres ibidem Deo fervientes, hanc predictam marcam in liberam, puram, et perpetuam, eleemofynam fingulis annis abfque omni impedimento ad predictum terminum percipiant. Tefte Petronilla comâ: Wilfo de Wivill, Rogero de Halmo, Willielmo Sanfon, Gileberto de Chernil, Galfrido de Turkitt, Raðo Mall, Roberto Wibto, capellano.

King Edward I, by his letters patents under the great feal, confirmed the hofpital revenues [2].

Ex ipfo originali.

" Edwardus, Dei gratia, rex Angliæ, dominus Hiberniæ, et dux Aquitaniæ: Omnibus ad quod præfentes literæ pervenerint falutem. Conftitutionem et affignationem, quas Willielmus Cokyn, quondam civis Cantuar', fecit per fcriptum fuum, conftituendo et affignando pauperes et infirmos fratres hofpitalium Sancti Nicholai, Sanctæ Katerinæ, et Sancti Tho' Martyiis de Eaftbrigge in Cantuar' quæ fimul font unita, hæredes fuos in perpetuum omnium terrarum et poffeffionum, et catallorum ipfius Willielmi; et donationem, conceffionem, et confirmationem, quas Hamo de Blen, filius Etardi de Creveceur, fecit per chartam fuam rectori et fratribus præd' hofpit' Sancti Tho' Mart' Cantuar', de terrâ illâ quæ vocatur Nigreth, cum pertinentiis, et de terra illa quæ vocatur William's Med, et de terra illa proxima quæ vocatur Benetewee, et de una acra quæ jacet juxta aquam verfus North ex oppofito de Prefteecote, et de domo illa quæ fuit Willielmi et Joannis fratrum predicti

[1] Robe   of Leicefter. See Bibl. Top. Brit. N° VII. p. 9.
[2] Printed in the Monafticon, Vol. II.

3

Hamonis,

Hamonis, et de 20 folidis, et 3 denariis, et 3 quadrantibus, liberi reditûs, et de 17 gallinis, folvendis fingulis annis prefatis rectori et fratribus per manus diverforum hominum de terris quas idem homines tenent in villa de Blen, ficut præfato Hamoni reddi folebant, cum omni jure de predictis terris et predicto redditu et predictis gallinis, in releviis, cafibus, efcaetis, in fectis curiarum et omnibus rebus ad præfatum Hamonem et hæredes fuos omnibus modis pertinent' : Ita quod licitum foret prædictis rectori et fratribus tenere curiam fuam de prædictis hominibus in villa de Blen ubicunque vellent in tenemento fuo: Et etiam conceffioni quam predictus Hamo fecit per eandem chartam fuam eifdem rectori et fratribus de libero exitu et communiâ in pafcuis forenfecis et cheminiis, femitis, et aquis in villâ de Blen ad omnia negotia fua facienda : Et fimiliter donationem, conceffionem, et confirmationem quas predictus Hamo de Blen fecit per quandam aliam chartam fuam rectori et fratribus predictis de terra illa cum omnibus pertinentiis quæ jacet in tenurâ de Blen inter Nigrethe et Middleditch: Et infuper 'remiffionem et quietam clamantiam, quas Ricardus de Becco, filius Willielmi de Becco, militis, fecit per cartam fuam magiftro et fratribus hofpit' præd' de fex denar' redditus, quos eidem Ricardo de 26 acris terræ cum pertinentiis, quas habuerunt de dono Willielmi de Burnes, annuatim reddere confueverunt : Necnon donationem, et conceffionem, quas præd' Ricardus fecit eifdem fratribus per eandem cartam fuam de decem acris terræ cum pertinentiis in campo qui vocatur Wappings, et fimiliter donationem, conceffionem, et confirmationem, quas Radulphus filius Arnoldi tinctoris fecit per cartam fuam fratribus et fororibus hofpit' præd' de terrâ quæ fuit ipfius Radulphi in parochiâ Omnium Sanctorum inter terram quæ fuit Hamonis fratris ipfius Radulphi et aquam Sturye, ratas habentes et gratas eas pro nobis et heredibus noftris, quantum in nobis eft, magiftro et fratribus hofpit' præd' et eorum fucefforibus, concedimus et confirmamus, ficut fcriptum et cartæ predictæ rationabiliter teftantur. In cujus rei teftimonium has litteras noftras fieri fecimus patentes. Tefte meipfo, apud Cantuar', vicefimo fecundo die Februarii, anno regni noftri feptimo '.

W. SUTTON."

Having thus collected feveral gifts and charters given to the hofpital in the firft hundred years after its foundation by Thomas Becket, the firft of them beginning about the year 1200 ; I will now proceed in the following benefactions given to the hofpital from the year 1300 to about the year 1500 ; of which I find the following account.

From the firft foundation till the year 1342, there appears no evidence to what intent this hofpital was erected by its firft founder ; neither can there be found any ftatutes, or rules, by

' Viz. R. Edw' I. A° 7°, i. e. A. D. 1279.

which

which this hofpital was to be governed. To fupply this defect, John Stratford, archbifhop of Canterbury, in the year 1342, gave his charter, by which he prefcribed laws and a form of government to it, whereby he reftored the foundation, and preferved it from that confufion, in which the concerns thereof were ready to be involved for want of fuch rules and laws of government.

This feemed to be a concern of fo great importance, that the commiffioners upon the ftatute of 37 Henry VIII. cap. 4. afcribed the foundation of the hofpital to this archbifhop. And we may truely fay, it was built by Thomas Becket, endowed and augmented by archbifhops Hubert Walter and Stephen Langton, and refounded or reftored by archbifhop Stratford.

I have feen two MS. copies of this ordinance of archbifhop Stratford ; one of them is in an ancient regifter belonging to Chrift-Church, Canterbury; and the other is among the writings of the hofpital : but Mr. Somner having printed it at large in his Antiquities of Canterbury, hath fpared me the pains of tranfcribing it.

It begins, " Joannes permiffione divinâ Cantuar' archiepifcopus, totius Angliæ primas, et apoftolicæ fedis legatus. Dilecto in Chrifto filio domino Rogero de Rondes, prefbytero, magiftro hofpit' pauperum de Eftbregg in civitate Cantuar' patronatûs noftri, falutem, gratiam, et benedictionem. Et fi votivus noftri invalefcat affectus," &c. (See Antiquities of Canterbury, p. 111. &c.) It is dated, " in capitulo dictæ noftræ Cantuar' ecclefiæ, xxiii° die menfis Sept. A. D. 1342, et noftræ tranflationis nono."

This charter was confirmed by the prior and chapter, which, becaufe Mr. Somner hath omitted it, I have added :

A. D. 1342. " Et nos frater Robertus ', permiffione divinâ, prior ecclefiæ Chrifti Cantuar' metropolic' fupradict', et ejufdem loci capitulum, habito primitus cum venerabili patre domino noftro Joanne Dei gratia Cant' archiepifcopo antedicto folemni et diligenti, ut præmittitur, tractatu, qui de jure exigitur in appropriatione

---

' This muft be Robert Hathbrand, who fucceeded Richard Oxinden in 1338, and died in 1370. See Somner's Catalogue of Priors, Antiq. of Cant. p. 290.

con-

concessione, annexione, et unione dicte parochialis ecclesie beati Nicolai de Harbaldowne hospitali predicto ac ipsius magistro et successoribus ejusdem in proprios usus
factis et causis eorundem, concurrentibusque oib' et singulis que hujusmodi con-
cessionibus perpetuis et ecclesiarum alienationibus requirebantur devenire qu·n um
in nobis est, pro nobis et successoribus nostris, in perpetuum una cum dicto p·tre
nostro venerabili consentimus; et appropriationem, concessionem, annexionem, et
unionem hujusmodi, et prefatas ordinationes hospitalis predicti, approbamus, ratifi-
camus, &c. etiam confirmamus. Salvis nobis et ecclesie nostre predicte juribus,
libertatibus, dignitatibus, privilegiis nostris et consuetudinibus quibuscunque. In
cujus rei testimonium, sigillum nostrum commune fecimus hiis apponi. Act' et dat'
in caplo nostro, die et anno supradictis."

Thefe ordinations continued the ftanding rules for the government of the hofpital, until the time of archbifhop Parker, who
framed new ftatutes and ordinations; and they contain alfo a
benefaction done to the hofpital by annexing the parifh-church (or
rectory) of St. Nicholas Harbledown to the fame. I have therefore hereto annexed the particular parts of the faid charter or
ordination; the fum of which is comprehended under thefe
heads.

The ftatutes, ordinations, and charter, which John Stratford,
    Archbifhop of Canterbury, made for the government of the
    hofpital of Eaftbridge.

" 1. As his defire was to take a particular care of fuch places as are deputed
and defigned for the reception and relief of poor and miferable perfons, and for
the increafe of divine worfhip, efpecially fuch as were under his tuition and government; above all, his earneft defire was to defend, preferve, and afford neceffary
relief to the hofpital of Eaftbridge, founded of old time, and endowed by the
bleffed and glorious martyr Thomas formerly archbifhop of Canterbury, our predeceffor, *qui fuis veneratoribus opem porrigit.*

" 2. By the petition of Roger de Rondes, then mafter of the faid hofpital, it
did appear, that the hofpital aforelaid was built for the reception and fuftentation
of poor pilgrims that fhould come to Canterbury; and that at that time a far greater
number of pilgrims than formerly did refort to Canterbury, fince the glorious
triumph and canonization of the faid bleffed Saint, the founder thereof.

" 3. By the neglect and fault of fome of the mafters of the faid hofpital, the
woods belonging thereunto were alienated, or deftroyed, with all their poffeffions,
goods and chattels, moveables and immoveables; that great debts were brought
upon the faid hofpital, fuch as they were unable to difcharge; that the edifices of
the

the faid hofpital, which before were a fair and goodly building, were fuffered to run to ruin, and fhamefully to decay; and that the hofpital was by thefe means become fo poor, in fuch a ruinous condition, as neither to be able to repair their ruins, nor to receive and fuftain poor pilgrims reforting thither. And that, under the reproach of fo great poverty, no man can be found to undertake the care and government of the fame as he ought to do.

" 4. For thefe reafons, he annexed and united the parifh-church of St. Nicholas Harbledown for ever to the ufe of the mafters of the faid hofpital, to be employed for the relief and fuftenance of the poor pilgrims that reforted thither; and that the right of the patronage of the faid church of St. Nicholas, in Harbledown, fhould belong to the mafter of the faid hofpital, and to his fucceffors for ever.

" 5. He had lately vifited the hofpital, and was fufficiently informed of the forefaid defects and decays, both in the edifices and in celebration of divine worfhip, and in the charitable reception of poor pilgrims; all which appeared from his own view, and from the teftimonies of feveral credible perfons upon oath, who were examined according to form of law. He had alfo a folemn and diligent confultation with his religious fons, the prior and chapter of the church of Canterbury, as is required in granting perpetual alienations of churches by law; and with their confent he granted and annexed the church of St. Nicholas aforefaid.

" 6. The mafter of the hofpital is appointed to allow a competent maintenance for a prieft, who fhould take care of the fouls, and perform divine offices in the faid parifh church, whom alfo the faid mafter might put in or turn out at pleafure; and the faid mafter is to bear all charges and burthens belonging to the church aforefaid, out of the profits and revenues of the fame.

" 7. That, for the more orderly government of the hofpital, thefe rules be obferved:

" 1. There fhall be one mafter, who fhall be in priefts orders, maintained and appointed by the archbifhop for the time being; who, within a month after his admiffion, fhall take a full and perfect inventory of all the goods belonging to the hofpital, and deliver it to the prior of the church of Canterbury; and who fhall, every year between the Feafts of St. Michael and All Saints, deliver to the prior, for the time being, a full and true account of his miniftering the goods and revenues of the hofpital.

" 2. The mafter fhall keep with him *facellanum*, a chaplain, in the faid hofpital, whom he may put in and remove out at pleafure; and the mafter and chaplain fhall conftantly celebrate divine fervice, and fuch particular maffes and offices, as the faid ordinations do at large direct and appoint.

" 3. That all the profits, rents, and revenues of the faid hofpital, fhall be difpofed of by the care and appointment of the mafter.

" 4. That there fhall be no ¹ common feal belonging to the hofpital.

" 5. That the poor fick pilgrims, which fhall happen to die in the hofpital, fhall be buried in the church-yard belonging to our church in Canterbury, in the place antiently affigned for that purpofe; and that poor pilgrims falling fick in their pilgrimage (if fo be they be not leprous) fhall be provided for in the hofpital.

¹ Sic.

" 6. Poor

" 6. Poor pilgrims in good health shall be entertained only for one night; and poor, sick, and well pilgrims, shall have daily 4d. expended for their sustenance, out of the revenues and profits of the hospital; greater regard should be had to sick than to well pilgrims.

" 7. That if there be not a sufficient resort of pilgrims in any one day to require the whole 4d. for their sustenance, that what is so spared in one day, shall be laid out freely in another day when the number of pilgrims shall be larger; and for every day of the whole year the entire summe of 4d. shall be carefully and faithfully expended.

" 8. That there shall be 12 beds convenient to lodge the pilgrims in the said hospital; and a woman, of honest report, aged above 40 years, who shall take care of the beds, and provide necessaries for the poor pilgrims; and who shall be maintained out of the revenues of the hospital.

" 9. That every master upon his admission shall, before the archbishop, promise upon his oath, that he will observe these ordinances as far as he is able; and that he will not alienate, or destroy, any of the lands, possessions, woods, goods, or other things belonging to the hospital.

" 10. That no admission of a master shall be firm and valid, until he is in priests orders, and hath taken the foresaid oath.

" 11. He reserved to himself and his successors, the archbishops of Canterbury for ever, a full power to add to, or to detract from, or to change, or to amend these ordinations, as they shall from time to time see convenient [1]."

LANDS, &c. GIVEN IN BLEAN.

THE manor of Blean and Hoath-court, is the principal and chiefest revenue that belongs to the hospital. This was given 33 Edward III. to the hospital, by Thomas de Roos de Hamlack, probably the same whose death Walsingham thus mentions in the year 1399:

" Eodem anno dominus Thomas de Roos, dum reverteretur a terrà sanctâ in insulâ de Cypro, civitate Papho, tactus aeris regionis incommodo, diem clausit exremum."

---

[1] Somner, p. 111. The Statutes of archbishop Stratford, printed by him, I have compared with the register of Christ-church, Canterbury; and I find these variations. Somner, p. 111. l. 21. lege, " et re-"ceptione;" l. 35. " fet," lege, " fed."—p. 112. l. 11. " ordinati,' lege, " ordinato."—p. 113. l. 18. lege, " per successores nostros."—p. 114. l. 23. lege, " in eo recipiantur,"—l. 27. lege, " peregri-"nos tamen."—l. 31. " peregrinantes," lege, " peregrinos."—l. 34. dele hæc verba, " præd' ib'm, " quod minus diebus præd' est expensum in ampliori receptione subsidiorumque vitæ necessariorum et " ministratione pauperum peregrinorum."

Of

Of whom, Mr. Somner adds thefe further conjectures, that
" he dwelt at Chilham Caftle ; from whence, the year before,
his mother Margery, lady Roos, daughter of Bartholomew lord
Ladlefmere, and widow of William de Roos de Hamlak, who,
as a benefactor to the work, hath his name and effigies fet up,
and pourtrayed in a window of the Chapter-houle at Chrift-
church ', dates a charter of hers to the mafter of this hofpital ;
and at her prefentation, as patronefs, in the year 1349, the fee of
Canterbury being then void, one Ofbertus is admitted by the
prior and chapter, " *ad liberam capellam beatæ Mariæ in caftro
de Chilham*, there perfonally to ferve and officiate, as a perpetual
chaplain ²." The above are Mr. Somner's words.

Charta MARGARETE Domine de Roos.

" Sciant prefentes et futuri, quód nos Margareta domina de Roos tradidimus,
conceffimus, et dimiffimus, totum manerium noftrum de la Bleen, juxta Cantuariam, Thome de Welton, et Roberto de Denton, capellanis, pro quadam fumma
pecunia nobis, pre manibus, perfolute, per eofdem tenend' et habend' totum
predict' manerium noftrum, cum omnibus terris, pafturis, bofcis, redditicus, cum
fervitiis tenentium ad idem manerium pertinentibus, et aliis quibufcunque pertinentiis fuis, prefatis Thome et Roberto, heredibus et affignatis fuis, ad totum terminum vite noftre, reddendo inde capitalibus dominis feodi illius debita fervitia,
et confueta. Et nos vero dicta Margaretta eifdem Thome et Roberto et affignatis
fuis totum manerium predictum, cum omnibus et fingulis pertinentiis ejus, ad totam
vitam noftram, contra omnes gentes warrantizabamus. In cujus rei teftimonium,
prefentibus figillum noftrum appofuimus. Hiis teftibus, Willielmo Saure, Edmundo Stapulgato, Roberto Capyn, Thoma Everard, Joanne Elys, Joanne de
Brigge, Henrico de Sturey, et multis aliis. Dat. apud Chilham, 1° die Julii,
anno r. R. Edwardi tertii poft conqueftum Angliæ 32º. A. D. 1358."

" Omnibus Chrifti fidelibus ad quos prefentes littere pervenerint, Thomas de
Roos de Hamelak, falutem in Domino. Cum Robertus de Denton, capellanus,
teneat fibi et affignatis fuis manerium de la Blen, juxta Cantuar', de hereditate
noftra ad totam vitam Margarite matris noftre et fuam, ex dimiffione matris noftre
et confirmatione noftra, quod quidem manerium cum pertinentiis poft mortem ipfius
matris noftre et predicti Roberti ad nos et heredes noftros reverti debet : Noverit
tamen univerfitas veftra, nos prefatum Thomam de Roos conceffiffe per prefentes

---

¹ Antiquities of Canterbury, by Somner, p. 118.   ² Lib. Eccl. Cant.

quod

quod manerium predictum cum fuis pertinentiis, quod idem Robertus fic tenet de hereditate noftra, et quod poft mortem ipfius matris noftre et prefati Roberti ad nos et heredes reverti deberet, remaneat Thome Wolton, magiftro feu cuftodi hofp.-talis Sancti Thom- martyris de Eaftbrigge, Cantuar', et fucceforibus fuis in per-petuum, in fubfidium cantariar' et elemofynar' faciend' in eodem hofpital:, fecundum ordinationem reverendi in Chrifto patris domini Simonis Dei gratia Cantuariens' archiepifcopi totius Anglie primatis, pro animabus patris et fratris noftri et omnium anteceforum noftrorum ac anima matris fue atque noftra, cum migraverimns ab hac luce, tenend' de capitalibus dñis feodi p fervit'a inde debita et confueta. Et nos predictus Thomas de Roos et heredes noftri predictum manerium, cum omnibus et fingulis pertinentiis fuis, predicto Thome de Wolton, et fucceforit us fuis, contra omes gentes warrantizabimus in perpetuum. Hiis teftibus, Thome Chicche, Ra-dulpho filio Radulphi Sentleger militis, Roberto Vineter, Willo Gervays, Thoma atte Gate, Willo de Eftwell, Joanne de Bregge, Joanne de Hoke, et aliis, In cujus rei teftimonium, figillum noftrum prefentibus eft apprentum. Datum apud Maghefeld, 17 die menfis Septembris, 1359, anno r. R. Edwardi tertii poft conqueftum 33".

There is another charter, the fame with this, dated at Weft-gate, juxta Cant', anno r. R. Edw' tertii 32, primo die Octobris.

The firft charter was of Margaret, mother of Thomas de Roos, dated at Chilham, July 1, A. D. 1358.

The fecond charter was of Thomas de Roos, dated at Weft-gate, juxta Cantuar', October 1, 1358.

The third charter was of the faid Thomas de Roos, the fame with the former, dated at Maghefeld, Sept. 17, A. D. 1359.

John the mafter, and the brethren of the hofpital, did grant by leafe unto John ate Hatch, an acre and a half of land in Bleen, in a place called Alotes, for ever, on condition to pay yearly to the mafter of the hofpital ten pence at Michaelmas-day, and ten pence at Lady-day, and two hens on Chriftmas-day. And for default of payment, the mafter and brethren of the hofpital were to re-enter, or to diftrain, &c. Dated anno r. R. Edw. filii Edw. 17, A. D. 1324.

They alfo let unto the fame John ate Hatch another piece of land in Blean, called Ullery, on condition to pay yearly to the mafter and brethren at Lady-day 15d. and at Michaelmas-day 15d. and at Chriftmas-day two hens. And for default of pay-ment,

ment, diftrefs to be taken, and re-entry, &c. Dated the fame
year with the former.

The church of SS. Cofmus and Damian, in Blean, was appropriated to the hofpital; (fee Reg'rum Sudbury, fol. 6.)

" Johannes de la Lee, miles, dedit unum mefTuagium, 180 acras terre, fex
actas prati, fex acras bofchi, 27 folidatas redditus, et redditum 9 gallorum et 21
gallinarum, in villâ de Fleen, habend' et tenend' pred et mefTuag' in terras, &c.
Thome de Wolton, et fuccefioribus fuis magnis hofpit' de Faftbregge, in Cantuar', ad
cer a opera pietatis in eodem hofpitali p animabus dñe Ifabelle nuper regine Anglie,
et noftri regis nunc, et aliorum progenitorum fuorum, ac meâ, cum ex hâc luce
migravero, et omnium aliorum benefactorum dicti hofpitalis " &c. A. D. 1360.

The witneffes are the fame that were witneffes to the charter
of Thomas de Roos.

Dat. " apud Cantuar' die Jovis in craftino Sti Martini, Anno r. R. Edw' tertii
poft conqueftum 34to."

There is another charter, granting the fame donations, and
dated the fame day and place, having the fame witneffes; only
with this difference; inftead of " *Thome de Wolton, et fuccefforibus fuis, ad certa opera pietatis,*" are thefe words, " *Thome de
Wolton, magiftro hofpitalis predict', ad totam vitam fuam, et fuccefforibus fuis, in augmentum operum pietatis* [1]·

HERNE, RECULVRE, WALELYVE, WHITSTAPLE, AND CHISTELET.

" ADAM le Heir dedit Tho' Wolton, magro five cuftodi hofp' beati Thome
martyris de Eaftbrigge, omnia tenementa, et terras, et redditus, marifcos, et pafturas,
cum omnibus pertinentiis, que et quas nuper perquifivit apud Mekembroke in Herne,
habend' et tenend' dicto Thome et fuccefioribus fuis magiftris five cuftodibus hofpit'
pred' in fubfidium fuftentationis eorum, et pro uberioribus elemofynis in prefato
hofpit' occafione poffeffionum predictarum largiendis. Dat' apud Herne, die Veneris
proxime poft feftum tranflationis B. Thomæ martyr', anno r. R. Edw' tertii poft
conqueftum 30."

" Adam le Heir, civis Londini, dedit omnia tenementa, et terras, redditus, pafturas, bofcos, fepes, et foffatas, que et quas dudum acquifivit in villis de Whitftaple, et

[1] Mr. Somner (Antiq. of Cant. p. 119.) gives an imperfect account of this benefaction, by omitting
to mention " the fix acres of meadow, and the fix acres of wood," which are expreffed in the faid
charter, in both the original writings of it.

Swalclive,

Swalclive, cum omnibus pertinentiis, in fubfidium fuftentationis eorum, et p uberioribus elemofinis in prefato holpit' occafione poffeffionum prediétarum largiendis,
&c. Datum apud Whitftaple, die et anno fupradiétis."

He gave lands alfo in Reculvre and Chiftelet, but the charters
by which he granted them are loft. However, the licence of
mortmain ftill remains, and will fupply the defeéts of the loft
charters. And for that reafon, I have tranfcribed it at large.

" Edwardus III. Dei gratia, rex Anglie et Francie, et dominus Hibernie,
omnibus ad quos prefentes littere pervenerint, falutem. Licet de communi concilio
regni noftri Anglie ftatutum fit, quod non liceat viris religiofis feu aliis ingredi
feodum alterius ita quod ad manum mortuam deveniat fine licentia noftra et capitalis dñi de quo res illa inimediate tenetur ; tamen p 10 libris quos Adam le Eyr ',
civis Londin' nobis folvet, conceffimus et licentiam dedimus pro nobis et heredibus noftris, quantum in nobis eft, eidem Ade, quod ipfe centum acras terre,
centum acras pafture, et 20 folidatas redditus cum pertinentiis, in Reculvre, Herne,
Swalclive, Whiteftaple, et Chiftelet dare poffit et affignare dileétis nobis in Chrifto
magiftro et fratribus hofpitalis Sti Thome de Eftbrugge, Cantuar', habend' et tenend'
eis magiftro et fratribus et fucceffioribus fuis ad inveniend' certas cantarias et elemofinas juxta ordinationem prediéti Ade in hac parte faciend' in perpetuum. Et
eifdem magiftro et fratribus, quod ipfi terram, pafturam, et redditus prediét' cum
pertinentiis a prefato Adamo recipere poffint et tenere fibi et fucceffioribus fuis ad
inveniend' cantar' et elemofynas pred' in perpetuum, ficut prediétum eft ; tenore
prefentium, fimiliter licentiam dedimus fpecialem, ftatuto prediéto noftro obftante.
Nolentes quod prediétus Adam, vel heredes fui, aut prefati magifter et fratres, feu
fucceffores fui, ratione ftatuti prediéti per nos vel heredes noftros inde moleftentur
in aliquo vel graventer. Salvis tamen capitalibus dñis feodi illius fervitiis inde
debitis et confuetis. In cujus rei teftimonium, has litteras noftras fieri fecimus patentes. Tefte meipfo, apud Novum Caftrum fuper Tynam, 20 die Januarii, 1355,
anno regni Anglie 29, r. vero noftri Francie 16."

" Helena atte Park de Roth, de parochia de Reculvre, dedit Thome de Wolton,
magiftro hofp', &c. omnia terras et tenementa fua cum patris bofcis, &c. Dat.
anno 1360, r. R. Edw. tertii 34."

King Edward III. granted licence of mortmain to John de
Mayton, clerk,

" Quod ipfe quandam plateam terre cum pertinentiis in Cant' ordinatam pro
tentis five tentoriis, continent 17 perticatas terre in latitudine, dare poffit five affignare
magiftro et pauperibus hofpital' Sti Thome Martyris ad inveniend' et fuftentand'
annuatim quendam cereum in ecclefiâ Chrifti Cant' coram feretro diéti Sti thome
certis temporibus ardend', et ad alia pietatis opera p animabus magiftri Edmundi
de Londin', quondam aichia' Bedeford, et prefati Joannis, cum ex hac luce migraverit." Dated " apud Sandwicum, 25 Junii, 1345, anno regni noftri Anglie 19."

¹ Le Heir in the two former charters.

King

King Edward alfo granted licence of mortmain for 40s. to William atte Welle :

" Quod ipfe unum meffuagium et 8 acras terre cum pertinentiis in Harboldown, juxta Cant' dare poffit vel affignare magiftro five cuftodi hofpit' de Eaftbrugge in Cant', et de Harboldown juxta Cant', in auxilium fuftentationis cujufdem capellani divina fingulis diebus in ecclefiâ dict' hofpit' de Harboldown pro falutari ftatu ipfius Willi dum vixerit, et pro anima fua cum ex hâc luce migraverit, et pro animabus omnium benefactorum dictorum hofpitalium, et omnium fidelium defunctorum," &c. Dated " apud Weftm', 22 Jan', anno regni 35."

The fame king feized upon 40 acres of land in Cockerings, belonging to the hofpital, on pretence that the faid lands were appropriated to the ufe of the hofpital after the ftatute of mortmain; but it did appear that all the faid lands were given before that ftatute, except five acres and one rode, which Walter le Tanner gave after the faid ftatute. Letters to William Truffel, efcheater, were directed, and dated *apud Turrym London', Maii* 3, *anno regni* 11°, 1337.

Acquietantia facta dño Thome de Wolton, magiftro feu cuftodi hofpit' de Eft-bregge Cantuar', de compoto adminiftrationis fue facto in bonis pred' hofpitalis. Ex regiftro ecclefie Chrifti Cant', K. fol. 73.

" Nos Robertus [1], permiffione divina, prior ecclefie Chrifte Cant', omnibus prefentes lias infpecturis, falutem in Dño fempiternam. Cum ad priorem dicte ecclefie pertineat auditio compoti magri feu cuftodis hofpitalis B. Thome de Eaftbrigge, in civitate Cant', qui p tempore fuerit, p ordinationem bone memorie dñi Johannis de Stratford, nuper Cant' archiepi [2] ; et dñus Thomas de Wolton, magr feu cuftos hofpitalis pred', fe fufficienter obtulerit ad reddendum nobis compotum adminiftrationis fue in bonis prefati hofpitalis; nos fufficienter didifcimus quod ipfe pauperibus ad id confluentibus hofpitalitatem, capellanis etiam et miniftris aliis requifita in eodem neceffaria, miniftravit, novas conftruxit domos, et reparavit collapfas, poffeffionefque ejufdem hofpitalis in prefens redditibus in bonis aliis notorie et modo . . . . . ex bonis aliis, ut firmiter credimus, quam ipfius hofpitalis ampliavit, et conatur in dies, ut afferitur, ampliare : Non curavimus ipfius audire compotum quem in premiffis eidem hofpitali tam utiliter intelleximus providentem, fed ut eum excitemur ad fimilia in futuris temporibus promptius facienda, ipfum cuftodem, quantum poffumus, ab ulteriori compoto dicte fue adminiftrationis p tempore tranfacto quietamus per prefentes. In cujus rei teftimonium figillum noftrum fecimus hiis apponi. Dat. Cant', primo die menf' Nov', A. D. 1367."

[1] Robert Hathbrand.   [2] See above, **p. 330.**

Of

Of the CHANTRIES, removed from LIVINGSBORN, alias BEAKS-
BORN, to the Hofpital.

Mr. Somner gives this fhort account of it; " with leave
and liking of archbifhop Langham [1], a certain chantry in the
church of Livingfborn, that is Beaksborn, founded in the year
1314, by one James of Bourn [i. e. Livingfborn], with the
revenues of the fame, was tranflated to this hofpital by one
Bartholomew of Bourn."

And in his Appendix to his Antiquities of Canterbury, p. 16.
he hath fet down at length the foundation of the chantry of
Eaftbridge, as follows :

" Sancte Matris ecclefie filiis univerfis," &c.

The inftrument was made by Simon, " archbifhop," who fays, that " he had
feen the letters patent of his predeceffor, Simon de Iflip," " nuper archiep'," &c.
He then relates the caufes of the foundation, " ad honorem Dei, cultufque divini,
et pro falute animarum quorundam benefactorum ipfius hofp', et omnium fidelium
defunctorum."

" He appoints the falary to be ten marks.

" He enjoins daily celebration of divine fervice, and care to be taken of ad-
miniftering " facramenta et facramentalia" to the poor pilgrims that refort thither.

" He appoints a chamber for the chanter within the hofpital, to be kept in repair
at his own charge.

" King Edward (viz. the Third) gave the meffuage in the city, which is called
" La Chaunge," to the hofpital, to help them to fuftain a chaplain to pray for him,
and for the foul of his deareft mother Ifabella, deceafed.

" The Change being, at the time when it was given, much out of repair, it
was put in good repair by the executors of Simon Iflip, and the rent of it was
raifed to 7 marks a year.

" That it was hard to find a good and worthy chaplain to perform daily offices
for 10 marks a year; and that the gift of king Edward had been hitherto fruftrated;
he, therefore, with the confent of Thomas Wolton, then mafter, did increafe the
former falary of ten marks a year, by adding 5 marks and a half yearly out of
the rent of the Change, to the falary of the chaplain.

" That whereas the chantry in Bourn was united to the chantry of the hofpital,
by his predeceffor; and whereas, before the union, the prefentation of the chantry

---

[1] This foundation-inftrument was not made by Simon Langham, who was archbifhop 1366, but by
Simon Sudbury, who was archbifhop 1375, and, according to the date of the inftrument, was that fame
year tranflated from London to Canterbury, fo that Mr. Somner is miftaken in faying, that " archbifhop
" Langham gave leave to remove the chantry from Bourn to the hofpital."

of

of Bourn did belong to Bartholomew of Bourn, and his heirs and affigns; he did appoint and ordain, that the archbifhop for the time being, or the prior and chapter of Canterbury, *fede vacante*, and Bartholomew of Bourne, his heirs and affigns, fhould collate and prefent to the fame by turns; and that the next turn did belong to the archbifhop, the prefent chaplain being nominated and prefented by Bartholomew of Bourn.

" That the chaplain, before his admiffion, fhould make oath to obferve the rules of the chantry, &c.

" Dated at Wingham, xv kal. Nov. A. D. 1375, et tranflationis noftre anno primo.

" Sciant prefentes et futuri, quod ego Bartholomeus de Bourn patron' cujufdem Cantarie perpetue quam Jacobus de Burne progenitor meus fundavit in ecclefia de Livingfburn, et dotavit de uno meffuagio, viginti quatuor acris terre arabilis, et dimidia marca annui redditus, ibidem ex certis caufis falutem anime ejus, mee, et progenitorum meorum concernentibus, alibi in ordinatione quadam venerabilis patris domini Simonis [1] Dei gratia Cantuar' archiepi, totius Anglie primatis, et apfce fedis legati, plenius expreffatis, dedi et conceffi, et hac prefenti mea charta confirmavi, eidem venerabili patri patronatus ejufdem Cantarie alternis vicibus vacationes Cantarie dicte, habend' et tenend' eundem patronatum alternis vicibus vacatione ipfius predicto venerabili patri et fuccefforibus fuis in perpetuum. Ita quod collatio ipfius Cantarie ad dictum reverendum patrem et fucceffores ejus in proxima vacatione ejus pertineat, et fic alternis vicibus pertinebit in futurum. Ita quod facerdos quilibet, cui fic illa Cantaria per ipfum patrem reverendum aut fucceffores fuos conferatur, five facerdos fuerit prefentand' per me, heredes et affignatos meos, noftris alternis vicibus celebret in hofpitali de Eaftbrugg Cantuarie, qui etiam facerdos percipiet in eo fex marcas per ordinationem dicti patris ultra valorem dicte dotis quam dictam Cantariam de confenfu meo dictus pater adunabit et incorporabit in perpetuo, eamque, quantum in me eft, aduno et incorpero dicto hofpitali caufa exilitatis ipfius dotis, prout in ordinatione dicti patris plenius continetur. Reddet infuper dictus facerdos, aut magifter dicti hofpitalis pro eo, mihi, heredibus et affignatis meis, in feflo Sti Michaelis in perpetuum apud Burne unum par calcarium, vel fex denarios pro eifdem, pro quibus mihi et eis licebit deftringere fuper terras dicte Cantarie apud Burne. Et ego predictus Bartholomeus, heredes et affignati mei, dictum patronatum alternis vicibus, ut dictum eft, eidem patri et fuis fucceffibus warantazibumus in perpetuum. In cujus rei teftimonium huic prefenti charte figillum meum appofui. Datum apud Levingefborne, die Dominica proxima poft feltum purificationis beate Marie, anno r. R. Edw' tertii a conqueftu 37. His teftibus, Johanne Brode, Martino Petit, Reg' Digge, Rogero Faulkham, Thoma de Garwinton, Thomas Bolle, Joanne Bolle, et aliis."

" Omnibus Ste Matris eccle filiis ad quos prefentes littere, five prefens tranfcriptum, pervenerint, Willielmus Hunden commiffarius Cantuar' generalis falutem in diu.n Salvatore. Quum p difcretum virum Thomam Bultire Capellanum Cantarie

[1] Simon Iflip.

3   perpetue

perpetue beate Marie in hofpitali Sti Thome Martyris juxta Eſtbrugge Cantuar' fundate nobis in capella dicti hofp' pro tribunali fedentibus, fuit cum inſtantia non modica fupplicatum, ut cum ipfe dominus Thomas qualdam litteras originales figillatas re' me' [1] Simonis Iſlip et Simonis Sudbury dudum eccle Cant' archiepiſcoporum, nec non Roberti quondam dicte eccle prioris et ejuldem loci capituli figillatas, ipfum dominum Thoma mratione Cantarie predicte concernentes, quas non habuit, ut afferuit, duplicatas neceſſe habeat in diverſis mundi partibus et non modice diſtantibus, pro jure ipſius domini Thome ac Cantarie fue predicte perfequend' et confervand' alias ut dixit deſtinare, prefentare et exhibere, que quidem littere poſſent, dum fit pro earum deſtinatione, prefentatione, vel exhibitione peitarentur, five transferentur, propter viarum difcrimina et maris periculum, et alios adverfos et diverfos cafus qui frequenter accidunt, feu verefimiliter contingere poterunt, deperire; aut ipfe dominus Thomas, propter dictam litteraium feu munimentorum difficilem feu forfan impoſſibilem exhibitionem fimul et femel in diverfis mundi partibus et multum diſtantibus ut prefertur faciend' periculum incurrere ñ modicum et gravamen quatenus predictas litteras, et eam figilla eildem appoſita infpicere, et ea fic ꝑ nos primitus infpecta poſtea auctoritate noſtra per notarium infra fcriptum tranfumi, exemplari, fubfcr bi et in publicam formam redigi, precipere et mandare, ut ex hoc tanta fides prefentibus litteris noſtris five tranfcripto ubi libet adhibeatur, ficut litteris originalibus antedictis et tantam auctoritatem faciant, ficut littere oiiginales predicte curaremus. Quarum quidem litterarum originalium tenores fequuntur in hiis verbis :

" Simon, permiſſione divina, Cantuarienf' archiep', totius Anglie primas et aprice fedis legatus, univerfis prefentes litteras infpecturis falutem in omnium Salvatore. Significavit nobis dominus Bartholomeus de Bourne, clericus, patronus cujufdem Cantarie in eccla parochiali de Levyngefburn quod quidam Jacobus de Bourn progenitor fuus ipfam Cantariam fundaverit de confenfu domini regis et eorum quorum interfuit, et dotaverat eam de una manſione 24 acris terre arabilis et dimidia marca annui redditus in villa de Bourne, quorum verus valor ad 4 marcas vix afcendit annuatim, refervando fibi, heredibus et affignatis fuis, ex dote illa unum par calcarium, vel fex denarios annui redditus pro eildem a facerdote ipfius Cantarie, de quo quidem annuo redditu manfio et terre predicte retroactis temporibus fuerant onorate, et quod modernis temporibus facerdotem ydoneum reperire non poteſt, qui eidem Cantarie tam exiliter dotate velit defervire in dicta eccla juxta mentem prefati fundatoris. Supplicavit igitur nobis quod ipfam Cantariam cum dote fua predicta que adjacet terris hofpitalis de Eſtbreg Cantuar' in prefata villa de Bourne eidem hofpitali adunare, annectere, et incorporare dignaremur, de confenfu fuo, ipfamque dotem augmentare in eodem hofpitali ad victum unius facerdotis competentem, qui poſſet in eo, ut miniſter loci, continuo miniſtrare ad Dei laudem et requiem animarum fubfcriptarum, viz. domine Ifabelle nuper regine Anglie, Jacobi predicti fundatoris, Joannis filii Euſtachii de Bourne, domine Margarette de Bourne, progenitorum dicti domini Barthofomei, domini Roberti de Burbach, et Willielmi de Bradele, nec non pro falute dñi noſtri regis, noſtra, dñi Joannis de la Lee,

[1] Reverende memorie.

domini

domini Euſtachii de Ambrithcourt, et conſortis ſue, dñi Thome de Wolton, Willmi de Coppeclyne, et Ricardi de Wodeland, et omnium benefactorum dicti hoſpit' et animabus noſtris, cum migraverimus ab hâc luce. Et ut hoc libentius et ſecurius faceremus, dedit nobis et ſucceſſoribus noſtris in perpetuum per factum ſufficiens patronatum ipſius Cantarie alternis vicibus vacationis ejuſdem, ità quod ea jam in principio conferamus, reſervando ſibi, et heredibus ſuis et aſſignatis, preſentationem ad eam in ſecunda vacatione ejus, et ſic in alternis vacationibus ejuſdem in futurum, volens quod de morâ, modo miniſtrandi, ſtipendio ſacerdotis, dicte Cantuarie, quam in dicto hoſpitali conceſſit fore perpetuum, nec non de aliis quibuſcunque in hac parte neceſſariis ſeu opportunis, noſtrâ autoritate, prout nobis viſum fuit, ordinemus. Nos autem ex ea exilitate predicta et pro numero miniſtorum in dicto hoſpitali, augmentando ad majorem Dei laudem et ob predictarum animarum medelam, ſupplicationi dicti domini Bartholomei favorabiliter inclinati, dictam Cantariam ad dictum hoſpitale de conſenſu ejus expreſſo auctoritate noſtra ordinaria transferrimus, ipſamque, cum tota ſuâ dote predicta, et omnibus ejus pertinentiis, eidem hoſpitali perpetuo aduniamus, annectimus, et incorporamus. Volentes et ordinantes quod ſacerdos qui deſerviet eidem Cantarie (quam in iſto hoſpitali volumus eſſe perpetuam, et Cantariam de-Beatâ Virgine nominari) a magiſtro ſeu cuſtode ipſius hoſpitalis, qui pro tempore fuerit, ultra iv marcas ad quas annuus valor dicte dotis dicitur aſcendere, de quâ dote diſponet liberè, ipſe cuſtos ſeu magiſter, ſicut de poſſeſſionibus aliis ipſius hoſpitalis, de magiſtro dicti hoſpitalis bonisque et proventibus ejuſdem ſex marcas percipiet annuatim, quarum ſex marcarum annuatim ſolvendarum ad terminos infra ſcriptos, omnibus ejuſdem magiſtro hoſpitali, de conſenſu magiſtri ipſius expreſſo, etiam autoritate noſtra ordinaria in perpetuum ex cauſis predictis imponimus, ut ſic ſacerdos ipſe in dicto hoſpitali ſecundum preſentem ordinationem deſerviens, in futuro decem marcas habeat pro victu ſuo competenti ſibi ad feſta Natalis domini, Paſche, nativitatis Sti Joannis Baptiſte et Sti Michis, equalibus portionibus ſolvend' annuatim in capella dicti hoſpitalis, et ſi forte item mager ſive cuſtos aliquo dictorum feſtorum in ſolutione hujuſmodi deficiat in poſterum, vel in parte, vel in toto, de conſenſu magri autoritateque noſtra predictâ licere volumus eidem ſacerdoti ſuper omnibus terris de dote dicte Cantarie apud Bourne, et in omnibus aliis terris et tenementis adquiſitis et appropriatis dicto hoſpit' de novo in villa de Hern apud Mekynbrook, et Akermel, per Adam le Eyer, que jam ad firmam dimittuntur pro decem libris, et in omnibus aliis terris et tenementis adquiſitis eidem hoſpitali, ſimiliter de novo apud le Blean, juxta Cantuariam, de domina de Roos, et de domino Thoma filio ejus, per Thomam de Wolton, nunc cuſtodem ejuſdem hoſpitalis, que ad firmam conſueverunt tradi pro x marcis, libere diſtringere et diſtrinctiones retinere, quouſque ſibi de arreragiis debitè fuerit ſatisfactum. Celebrabit autem ipſe ſacerdos cotidiè per ſe, vel alium capellarum, vel ſaltem quinquies ſingulis ſeptimanis, in ſuperiori vel inferiori capella prefati hoſpitalis, hora competenti, prout magr ſeu cuſtos ejuſdem hoſpitalis imponet ei, et in aliis officiis divinis, ſi cum nota dicantur per alios ipſius hoſpitalis miniſtros, preſens erit cum illis per ſe aut alium ſcientem competenter legere et cantare, adjutor ſedulus et devotus Dei celebrius perſolvendas. Exceptis duntaxat annuatim feſto Sti Michis, ſexto die hebdomade Natalis Dñi, 4to die hebdomade,

Pentecoſt

Pentecoſt, ac feſto Sẗi Petri apli, in quibus per ſe vel alium in dicta eccla de Bourne miſſam celebrabit, morabitur etiam ipſe ſacerdos perſonaliter et continuè in civitate Cantuar' aut ejus ſuburbio, et non ablentabit ſe ab ea per ſpatium unius diei continue, niſi de licentia maḡri dicti hoſpitalis, ſeu tenentis locum ejus.   Proviſo ſemper quod in ejus abſentia faciat dicte Cantuar' in dicto hoſpitali in forma ſupradicta honeſtè deſerviri, obediet etiam prefato hoſpitalis maḡro, et tenenti locum ejus, in ipſius abſentia, in licitis et honeſtis.   Non autem tenetur ipſe maḡr ſacerdotem hujuſmodi ad menſam ſuam nec ad moram in hoſpitali recipere, niſi quatenus ſibi videbitur èxpedire.   Solvet preterea predictus ſacerdos de ſuo predicto ſalario dicto domino Bartho, et heredibus et aſſignatis ſuis, dictum par calcarium, vel ſex denarios por eiſdem apud Bourne in feſto Sẗi Michis annuatim prout in fundatione ipſius Cantarie, ut prius, fuerit ordinatum, pro quibus ipſe et ipſi diſtingrere poterunt apud Bourne ſuper terris de dote primaria ipſius Cantarie.   Et ſi forte maḡer hoſpitalis, qui terras ipſas tenebit, per diſtrictiones hujuſmodi calcaria aut ſex denarios pro eiſdem cogatur ſolvere, deducat ipſe maḡer ipſos ſex denarios de dicto ſalario ejuſdem ſacerdotis.   Quilibet inſuper ſacerdos ad dictam Cantariam in poſterum aſſumendus·in inſtitutione ſua, ſeu ſaltem antequam corporalem poſſeſſionem ejus aſſequatur, jurare tenebitur ad ſancta Dei evangelia, quod iſtam ordinationem, quatenus ad eum attinebit, ceſſante impedimento legitimo, plenè per omnia obſervabit. Alioquin ſit ipſius Cantuarie poſſeſſor minus canonicus ſeu injuſtus, nec tenebitur ſibi magiſter dicti hoſpit' quicquam pro victu ſuo ſolvere de dicta ſumma quouſque coram nobis, aut noſtris ſucceſſoribus, noſtro aut eorum comiſſario ad hoc ſpecialiter deputato, prefatum preſtitent juramentum; poſſeſſionem autem ipſius Cantuarie dicto ſacerdoti ſemper tradi et aſſignari volumus auctoritate noſtra et ſucceſſorum noſtrorum in inferiori capella dicti hoſpitalis per manualem apprehenſionem hoſtii ſeu altaris ejuſdem, poſtquam predictum preſtit juramentum, de quâ preſtatione maḡro loci per literas noſtras et ſucceſſorum noſtrorum, aut alias certitudinalitates innoteſcat, antequam ei quicquam teneatur ſolvere de ſuma memorata.   In cujus rei teſtimonium, ſigillum noſtrum his apponi fecimus.   Datum apud Mayherfeld, ſexto kalendas Martii, A. D. M.CCC°.LXII. et noſtre conſecrationis quarto decimo."

" Omnibus Sancte Matris eccle filiis, ad quos preſentes littere pervenerint, Robertus [1] permiſſione divina prior eccle Chriſti Cantuar' et ejuſdem loci capitulum ſalutem in Chriſto.   Litteras venerabilis patris dñi Simonis Dei gratia, Cantuarienſ', archiepi, totius Anglie primatis, et aptie ſedis legati, non obiltas, non cancellatas, nec in aliqua ſua parte vitiatas, inſpeximus, tenorem qui ſequitur continentes. Simon, permiſſione divina, &c. ut ſupra, uſque ibi et noſtre conſecrationis XIIIIto. Nos vero hujuſmodi donationem et aſſignationem, quantum in nobis eſt, approbantes, ad Cantariam predictam perpetuo (ut premittitur) cuſtodiend' noſtram autoritatem et conſenſum tenore preſentium impartimur, jure et dignitate eccle noſtre Cantuar' in omnibus ſemper ſalvis.   In cujus rei teſtimonium ſigillum noſtrum hiis litteris, apponi fecimus dat' in capťo noſtro 26 die menſis Septemb', anno ſupradicto.

[1] Robert Hathbrand.

" Sancte

" Sancte matris eccle filiis universis, ad quos presentes litere pervenerint Simon, permissione divina Cantuar' archieps." &c.

as in Mr. Somner's Appendix to his Antiquities of Canterbury, p. 16. is printed at large.

" Nos igitur commissarius antedictus, supplicationibus dicti domini Thome nobis (ut premittitur) factis inclinantes, et annuentes, dictas iras originales ac corum sigilla eis, ut prefertur, apposita palpavimus, inspeximus et examinavimus diligenter; et quoniam prefatas Iras, non ratas, non abolitas, non cancellatas, nec in aliqua parte earum vitiatas, sed oĩ vitio et suspitione sinistris carentes invenimus, ne dicto domino Thome propter pericula feu caufas predictas, feu aliquem eorundem, damnum vel prejudicium aliquod. in pofterum generetur, ad omnem juris effectum qui inde sequi poterit, vel in cafu verisimiliter debebit autoritate noftra prefatas iras originales publicavimus, et tantum fidens prefentibus literis noftris five tranfcripto ficut predictis iris originalibus in quantum de jure potuimus ubilibet adhibendum fore decrevimus per magrum Adam Body, publicum aplica autoritate notarium, fubfcriptum tranfumi, exemplari, fubfcribi, et in hanc prefentem formam redigi, et ejus figno confueto fignari mandavimus et fecimus, ac figilli officii noftri, viz. commiffariatus Cantuar' generalis fecimus appenfione muniri. Dat' et act' ut premittitur, per nos commiffarium antedictum in capella antedicta primo die menfis Decembr', A. D. 1397. Indicatione fexta pontificatus fanctiffimi in Chrifto patris et domini noftri domini Bonefacii divina providentia pape IXi anno nono ; prefentibus difcretis viris Thome Bourne, clerico, et Ricardo Fifh literato, Cantuar' diocef', teftibus ad premiffa vocatis et fpecialiter rogatis.

" Et ego, Adam Body, clicus, Sarum diocef' publicus apoftolica autoritate notarius, predictarum Irarum, exhibitioni, infpexioni, examinationi, et publicationi, ceterifque omnibus et fingulis, dum fic ut premittitur agerentur et fierent fub anno indict' pontific' menf' die et loco fupradictis, unà cum teftibus antedictis, prefens interfui, eaque fic vidi fieri et audivi, prefentes fcripfi, et in hanc prefentem formam redigi, fignoque ¹ et nomine meis folitis et confuetis fignavi, rogatus et requifitus in fidem et teftimonium permifforum ².

¹ See his mark in plate VI. fig. 10.

² Somner, p. 403. l. 18. una, lege, unam. l. 22. ejufque, lege, cujufque. l. 29. predictas, lege, predicte. p. 403. l. 5. fuerit per fe, lege, fuerit in eodem per fe. l. 18. ipfius, lege, fuis. l. 19. celebranti, lege, celebraturi. l. 31. afcendit, lege, afcendet. p. 404. l. 29. jurabit quilibet, lege, jurabit infuper quilibet. l. 33. fint, lege, fit.

" I compared the above written charters with a fair copy of them in the Regifter of Canterbury ; as alfo with Mr. Somner's book, p. 402, &c. where one of the charters is printed ; and they do agree, only the above named various lections in Mr. Somner's book are to be corrected out of the fame Regifter, viz. Regiftium R.— Nic. Battely."

Of

Of Blean;

Archdeacon Harpsfield's Vifitation made this return, A. D. 1557.

" Cofm' et Dam' de Blean. Rectoria impropriat' mgro Willo Sworder."

" Vicar', Dr. Georgius Higges. Familiæ, 30. Communicantes, 94."

Out of the Archdeacon's black book.

" Taxacio dioc' Cantuar'. Ecclia Cofmi et Dami, 6s.

" Temporalia Hofpitalis de Eftbregge, in Cant', Lyvyngborn et Mounketon, " viiil. ixs. viiid.

" Bulla de denariis Sti Petri p Gregorium papam de ecclia de Blen, xiid."

King Edward the Third proved a royal benefactor, by giving a meffuage, called *la Chaunge*, as appears from the foundation of the chantry, by the charter of the archbifhop Simon Sudbury, in which are thefe words :

" Dominus nofter excellentiffimus dñus Edwardus rex Anglie et Fiancie illuftris qui nunc eft quoddam meffuagium fuum in civitat' Cant' fitum, la Chaunge vulgariter nuncupatum, in magna parte tempore donationis ejufdem collapfum ex pia donatione fua domino Thome Newe de Wolton, nunc magro pred' hofpit' ad terminum vite fue donavit, ita quod poft mortem fuam ipfum meffuagium fuccefforibus ipfius, magris viz. hofpit' predict' remaneret in perpetuum in auxilium fuftentationis unius capellani perpetui,' &c. '

Concerning the Change, I refer myfelf to Mr. Somner, and to an abftract he hath tranfcribed out of the book belonging to the hofpital. I have feen the original records which he cites concerning this matter, in his Antiquities of Canterbury, p. 63, and p. 64.

The foundation of Harbledown chantry was firft by archbifhop William Wittlefey, " 4to nonas Feb. A. D. 1371, et tranflationis 4to," altered and amended by Thomas Arundel, archbifhop, " 18 of May, anno 1402, et tranflationis fexto." The whole is fet down at large by Mr. Somner, in his Appendix to his Antiquities of Canterbury, p. 10.

' See Somner, p. 17.

Litera

Litera miffa dño archiepo de lris confirmatoriis eccliarum de Stratford et Sti
Nic' de Harboldown eidem per nos tranfmiff :

"Ad tanti patris bene placita paratum obfequium cum oi reverentia et honore :
Pater et dñe reverende, lras confirmatorias ordinationis vre fuper cantaria in ecclia
de Stratford, ac lras confirmatorias appropriationis ecche Sti Nic' de Harboldown,
hofpitali vro Sti Thome de Eaftbridge, p vos facte figillo capitlo confignatas p
magrum J. de Wymbue latorem prefentium vobis mitto, &c. Dated in the year
1342." Copia vera ex regro ecche Chrifti Cant', p me, Nic' Battely.

The parfonage of Blean being affigned and confirmed *in
proprios ufus* to the hofpital, Mr. Somner fays, " Archbifhop
Iflip afterwards, induced by many reafons, founds a perpetual
vicarage there, indowing it in fuch wife, as the charter thereof
demonftrates."

Here Mr. Somner is under a miftake; for it was not Simon
Iflip, but Simon Sudbury, who founded this vicarage, as ap-
pears from the date of the inftrument, which was in Auguft,
A. D. 1375, " et tranflationis primo." The fame year that he
founded the chantry in the hofpital, which was not done, as
Mr. Somner fays, " by Simon Langham," but " by Simon
Sudbury."

The inftrument is fet down at large by Mr. Somner, in his
Appendix to his Antiquities of Canterbury, p. 10, which inftrument contains,

" 1. The caufe of the foundation," viz. " Becaufe the church of Blean was
appropriated to the hofpital, and was diftant from the hofpital above a mile, &c.

" 2. The endowment of the vicarage," viz. " A manfion-houfe, erected by
Thomas Newe, mafter of the hofpital, the tithes and oblations under-written, which
amount to 10l. a year or more: i. e. decime prediales apud Natyngden ¹, due of
old to the hofpital, to the clear value of 5 marks; the predial tithes of Blean, except the lands belonging to the hofpital, &c. alfo the tithes of calves, lambs,
geefe, flax, wool, milk, cheefe, hay, herbage, woods, &c. and all oblations in
the faid parifh, except from Hoth-court, &c.

" 3. The burthens of the vicarage. To repair the chancel at his own coft and
charge, from time to time, and his own dwelling-houfe. And to pray for the
health of Simon the Archbifhop, and Thomas Newe, Mafter of the hofpital, while
they live, and for their fouls after they are deceafed, and for the fouls of Thomas

¹ Nackington. This portion of tithes is ftill paid to the vicar of Blean.

de

de Roos, a great benefactor to the hospital, and Beatrix his wife, and of Eustachius de Dapleckecourt and his wife, who have been great benefactors to the hospital: and to provide wine and bread, and candles, necessary to celebrate in the said church, at his own cost and charges.

" 4. Continual residence, and obedience to the master in lawful things, is required of the vicar.

" Dated at Otteford, 3° nonas Augusti, A. D. 1375, et translat' anno primo [1]."

" Universis Ste Matris eccle filiis Hamo de Blen, filius Etardi de Crevequer, salutem. Noverit universitas vestra me dedisse et concessisse, et hac presenti cartâ meâ confirmasse, intuitu Dei et Beate Marie et gloriosi martyris Thome et sanctorum martyrum Cosmi et Damiani, pro salute anime mee, et pro animabus parentum meorum, et uxoris mee, et Joannis fratris mei, rectori eccle sanctorum Cosmi et Damiani de Blen, et fratribus hospitalis Sti Thome martyris de Eastbrig in Cantuaria, totum messuagium cum pertinentiis quod fuit Lefwini sacerdotis, persone ejusdem eccle, et quod postea fuit archidi de Petters, persone ejusdem eccle; et quod postea fuit Willielmi de Crevequer, persone ejusdem eccle, et unam acram terre que jacet versus North, juxta aquam ex opposito de Preftecote, et extendit se in longitudine sua a capite nemoris mei juxta novum cursum aque quem Wlwardus fecit usque ad cheminium per quod itur ab eccla Sanctorum Martyrum Cosmi et Damiani usque ad Cantuariam, et tres denarios liberi redditus mei quos Wlwardus tegulator solebat michi reddere de terra juxta aquam de Preftecote, et de terra supra nemus meum versus Est de Preftecote, in liberam, puram, et perpetuam elemosinam. Et ego et heredes mei guarantizabimus pariter et defendemus predictum messuagium et predictam terram et predictum redditum, sicut prenotatum est, in omnibus et de omnibus contra omnes homines et omnes feminas. Et ut hec mea donatio et concessio et confirmatio stabilis permaneat in eternum et firma, presentem cartam meam sigilli mei munimine roboravi. Hiis testibus, magistro Henrico de Sandford, archido Cant', magro Thomâ de Fracham offic' Cant', mro W'mo Curtys, decano Cant', Hugone persona de Tanterdene, Baldrico Capellano, Simone le Scot, Willmo de Cluse, Salomone de Fraxino, Lambino de Fonte, Hamano de Bosco, Gilberto de Blen, Galfrido de Blen, Wlwardo Tegulario, et multis aliis."

This charter was dated before the year 1227, in archbishop Langton's time, when Sandford was archdeacon, and William Curtis official.

The parsonage thus given to the hospital, the vicarage was afterward founded, as before.

[1] Reg. Sudbury, fol. 66. in the Lambeth MSS.

At Milkhouse Street, in this parish, was built, a little before the general suppression of religious Foules, a free chapel (now in ruins) dedicated to the Holy Trinity, to which were given lands for its endowment, which were valued at its demolition, at 84l. 7s. 10 ½d. per annum, which lands were granted to Sir John Baker of Sisenhurst. Ducarel's Repertory, from MS. Lewis.

" Sciant

" Sciant præsentes et futuri quod, ego; Simon de Blen, dedi, et conceſſi, et hac præsenti carta mea confirmavi, intuitu Dei, et Beate Marie et Sanctorum martyrum Cosmi et Damiani, et pro salute anime mee et juxoris mee Godelef, et pro animabus patris mei Roberti et matris mee Reynild, et Wlwardi, et Brigthere Siwardi, Randwiſi, et Bartholomei, et omnium parentum meorum et succeſſorum, in liberam, puram, et perpetuam elemosynam, capellano miniſtranti in ecclâ Sanctorum Cosmi et Damiani de Blen, 14 denarios liberi redditus mei quos Willmus de la Beche et heredes sui solvent eidem capellano pro una acra terre, et unâ hameleth, cum pertinentiis, quas tenet de me in villa de Blen, que jacet inter terram meam et terram ejusdem Willi, ad duos terminos, sc' ad annunciation' dominican' 7d. et ad feſt' Sti Mich 7d. Et ego Simon et heredes mei warrantizabimus et defendem us eidem capellano celebranti miſſas pro animabus noſtris prædictum redditum contra omnes homines et feminas in perpetuum ; et ut hec mea donatio et conceſſio, et confirmatio et warrantizatio et defensio, firma sit in perpetuum et ſtabilis, præsentem cartam sigilli mei munimine roboravi. Hiis teſtibus, Dominô Radulpho celerar), Philippo theſaurario, Samsone Grevethario, monachis, Dominis Waltero et Roberto ſacerdotibus, Ricardo Seneſcallo, Wilhelmo de Cluse, Lambino de Blen, Salamone, Willo de Fraxino, Roberto Lupo, et multis aliis."

By the witneſſes this is about the fame date with the former, that is, about Archbiſhop Langton's time, A. D. 1222.

Vicars of St. Cosmus and Damian in the Blean ; communicated by Mr. Delasaux.

1560. Thomas Makaride.

1569. John Cowper.

1586. Nicholas Simpson, M. A.

1609. William Thurgar, M. A.

1632. Stephen Sackett.

1679. Simon Lowth [1], M. A.

[1] Rector of Harbledown, 1670, and leſſee of the tithes of the hoſpital, 1682. See the Hiſtory of that Hoſpital, pp. 182. and 186.

" Simon Lowth, vicar of this church, received the king's letters patent for the deanery of Rocheſter, in November, 1688. He took the degree of D. D. at Cambridge, on the 18th day of January [enfuing] in the fame year. The expulſion of king James II. from his kingdom, and the acceſſion of the new king William to his throne, have prevented his being inſtalled, till the preſent 29th day of March, 1689, and perhaps he never will.

" At the beginning of Auguſt, in the fame year, Simon Lowth above-mentioned was ſuſpended from his prieſtly function for refuſing to ſwear faith and true allegiance to king William and queen Mary.

‹ In

" In the month of February following, he was for the fame reafon deprived; and of his reftoration he remains doubtful and uncertain to this prefent day of April, 1690.

" Though the above mentioned Dr. Simon Lowth, vicar of this church, refufed to fwear allegiance to king William and queen Mary, yet, after James II. had abdicated his kingdom, and gone to France (with his queen and their fon), who gave him royal letters patent for the deanry of Rochefter, and after William afcended the throne, and was crowned king of Great Britain, France, and Ireland, Dr. Simon Lowth, the above-named vicar, prayed publickly, in his church of St. Cofmus and Damian in the Blean, for William and his wife Mary, as king and queen of England, Scotland, France, and Ireland, according to the form of prayer prefcribed in the Liturgy, or book of Common Prayer, for the king: he prayed not only in general (as mentioned above) for the king and queen, but exprefsly named king William and queen Mary, and ufed all that form for them, from beginning to end, not once only, but on every Sunday, till king William gave his royal letters for the deanery of Rochefter to another doctor in divinity. And when that other doctor was inftituted and inducted dean of Rochefter, at length and not before, he refufed both to pray and fwear faith and allegiance to king William. And when I myfelf afked him, after he was fufpended and deprived, whether he had ever publickly prayed for William as king of England, &c. and had ufed the form in the book of Common Prayer for the king and queen, he owned that he had fo prayed; and when I again afked him, why therefore he refufed to take the oaths of faith and allegiance to the king's majefty? he anfwered, in this very houfe, the firft time that I faw him, " An oath is a facred thing." I replied, " Public prayer is alfo a facred thing. As you have confeffed in your
" prayer that William is king of England, &c. you owe him allegiance. As be-
" tween the regal power and the fubjects allegiance there is a tranfcendent relation,
" and the one, namely, the regal power, being placed and acknowledged in William,
" the other neceffarily follows, namely, the allegiance due to him ; and unlefs you
" would act inconfiftently, you are bound to fwear faith to him. If you act other-
" wife, your hearers will think you guilty of hypocrify and the utmoft diffimu-
" lation, as you had ftyled William king in your prayers, yet have refufed to
" fwear the fubjection due to the king, and will judge that you did not believe
" William to be king, though you had confeffed him to be king in a public
" prayer offered to the omnifcient God, but intended king James the IId, which
" is moft abfurd." I therefore advifed him to remain in his houfe, and to keep his church, by praying, as he had been accuftomed, for king William, and by taking the oath of fidelity due to him, &c. At that time I had the great feal appending to a prefentation to this church, which I exhibited to him ; neverthelefs, I told him, that I would not ufe it, not doubting that God would provide for me and my family. If he would remain there and qualify himfelf, I wifhed him the utmoft happinefs in this church. But he faid, that he would never take the oath of allegiance to king William; and if I fhould refufe to take this church, without doubt another would take it ; he therefore advifed me to accept it, and to fuffer him to remain with his family in this houfe till Eafter, and that I would fub-

fcribe

1690. JAMES WILLIAMSON [1], M. A.

scribe the sequestrator's account, and acquit him of all the tithes collected in the two preceding years allowed him ; which I willingly promised him, and afterwards did, not doubting that he had paid the curate, who supplied his place, out of the tithes, for those two years while he was suspended and deprived, and also the tenths due to the archbishop, and all the procurations due to the archdeacon. But I was circumvented ; for after I had subscribed the sequestrator's account, and was inducted into this church, on the 24th of March, 1690, the curate, Mr. Thomas, junior, school-master of Sandwich, made me pay fifteen pounds due to him, which the sequestrator Whyt, or the vicar South, was bound to pay him, if I had not subscribed that account, which mentioned only four pounds being paid to him, and this induced me to believe that all were due to him. I was also obliged to pay the tenths to the archbishop, and the procurations to the archdeacon, for the two preceding years, which were due before I left Scotland. When I represented this to Dr. Oxenden, vicar-general to archbishop Tillotson, though the archbishop promised and intended to give me a recompense, yet Dr. Oxenden said, that Dr. Lowth was the deprived incumbent, and would not suffer me to seek in court a resolution from him of all those pounds which I paid to my own detriment; nor have I ever received a farthing from Dr. Lowth for those fifteen pounds, or for the tenths, procurations, or dilapidations; which is very hard. But that all which I have written is most true, I attest, on the word of a priest, and subscribe with my hand,

JAMES WILLIAMSON."

[1] " Master of Arts, both in the university of St. Andrew in Scotland, and in that of Oxford in England, Vicar of the church of St. Cosmus and Damian in the Blean, and of St. Dunstan's, and formerly parson or rector of Kirkaldie in Scotland, for many years. Though I prayed for William and Mary, as king and queen, on the very day prescribed to all ministers, yet their power could not protect me in that church from the oppression of persecutors ; for it was notorious that I was persecuted on account of the divine right and apostolical discipline of episcopacy; and though I was twice acquitted of their calumnies by the king's most honourable privy council, yet the provincial synod of Fife, and a conventicle of preachers, and lay elders, for no other reason, deprived me, and gave that desirable church of mine to that fanatic pastor of a conventicle, Robert Rule, who, like another Ahab, irregularly seized it, and also the stipend of that whole year, above eighty pounds English, due to me. And they forced me to fly my country, to leave my church, my wife and family and all my friends, and to go to England (where I had not one acquaintance) within fourteen days, on pain of imprisonment and rebellion. I departed from my family, recommending that, with my dear parish, to God and the word of his grace, on the 15th of September, 1690, and embarked on board a ship bound to London. Many tears were shed, amidst the embraces and adieus of all the principal inhabitants and many friends, who escorted me to the ship, which lay near the shore. I arrived at London October 3, and trusted in

God

God that I fhould return whenever he fhonld pleafe; but now I fear that the epifcopal difcipline will never hereafter be reftored, and that I fhall never return, or that difcipline be reftored,

————While life thefe limbs infpires;

as I am now old, being feventy-two * years of age, and been banifhed my country twenty-five. I believe, however, that Almighty God both can and will in his own good time reftore that difcipline of his divine church which I long have earneftly defired; with fubmiffion to the divine will, his will, not mine, be done. The Lord, who has the king's heart, and thofe of all his fubjects, in his hand, knows the time, and can turn them as he pleafes; and when he pleafes, our extremity is his opportunity. When the tale of bricks was doubled, came Mofes, fent by God, who delivered the Ifraelites from the houfe of bondage. Who knows what God will do for the epifcopal church in Scotland? O that, as an union was made by our moft gracious queen Anne, of bleffed memory, between the two nation's, uniting the long diftinct kingdoms of England and Scotland into one kingdom of Great Britain, and under one civil government, fo I pray that our moft gracious king George the Firft, king of Great Britain, France, and Ireland, may, with his par-liament, make an union in ecclefiaftical difcipline, by bifhops having the fole but the principal and fuperior power both of rank and jurifdiction over the prefbyters, fubordinate to them by the divine law; and fo there will be one national church and one epifcopal government throughout all Great Britain; and thus a national civil union will be confirmed and continue for ever. And if fuch an union be not fettled, the civil union, I fear, cannot well be lafting. O that all in Great Britain would repent, and fear God, and their fovereign king George, and acknowledge him now at leaft to be the true, lawful, and fupreme governor of this great king-dom of Britain, and would pay him true allegiance; *nor meddle with thofe who are given to change*, Prov. xxiv. 21. with thofe who tranfgrefs the commands of God and their princes, *for their calamity fhall rife fuddenly*, ver. 22. and they who oppofe their fupreme power *refift the ordinance of God, and they who fo refift fhall receive to themfelves damnation. Let every foul*, whether it be of clergy or laity, *be fubject* therefore to king George. And becaufe I have fworn faith and true allegiance to him and his fucceffors, and have abjured all papifts who pretend to have a right to reign, and by God's affiftance will keep my oath, and intreat all his people to be faithful and fubject to him, efpecially that thofe who have folemnly promifed their allegiance will ferioufly perform what they have fworn, fo I doubt not that God is willing to blefs us all, and that our king, who is the defender of the Faith, will both defend our reformed religion, and that when it fhall feem good to God, the king, and his parliament, that ancient and apoftolical epifcopal difcipline will be reftored to the Scotch, and to my native country, Scotland, where it is now abdi-cated. That this may be happily accomplifhed, I pray *the God of patience and confolation, according to his will*, that all we Britons may *be like-minded one towards another, that we may with one mind, and one mouth, glorify God, even the Father of*

* As Mr. Williamfon lived till Aug. 1728, he muft therefore have been 82 at the time of his death.

our

1728. RICHARD LEIGHTONHOUSE ', M. A.

1771. RICHARD NEILD, M. A.

1781. JAMES SMITH ', M. A.

1784. WILLIAM THOMAS ', M. A.

ST. NICHOLAS HARBLEDOWN.

Ex libro MS. in ecclâ Chrifti Cant', fic intitulato, " Taxatio beneficiorum ec-
clorum p totam Angliam et Walliam."

" Eccla Sti Nicholai de Harboldown.——ix marcas."

A like taxation is in another MS. of the faid church, thus
intituled,

" Ex libro taxationum beneficiorum in Angliâ, Ranulphus Ceftrenf' A. D. 1289.
17° Edw. I. Circa hunc annum, jubente papa Nicolao, taxate funt eccte Anglie
fecundum verum valorem," &c.

In turre Londin', ex Rotulo taxac', &c. A. D. 1291, 20 Edw. I.

And the fame taxation is in the archdeacon's black book.

---

our Lord Jefus Chrift. And thus I conclude this writing with the words of St. Paul
to the Romans, xv. 5, 6, in the year of our Lord 1717, September 9.
                                        JAMES WILLIAMSON,
     Vicar of the parifh of St. Cofmus and Damian in the Blean ; and alfo of St.
     Dunftan's, near Canterbury, fubfcribed with my own hand +."

 ' One of the minor canons of Canterbury Cathedral, where he is buried in the
cloyfters. He died Sept. 13, 1770, aged 80.

 ' Mr. Smith was alfo rector ot Eaftbridge in Romney Marfh, and vicar of Alkham.
He was born at Lifbon of Englifh parents, was educated there a Romifh prieft, and
had a narrow efcape in the earthquake in 1755; and having foon after renounced
the errors of the church of Rome in Lambeth chapel, in prefence of Archbifhop
Secker, being patronized by that prelate and his fucceffor Archbifhop Cornwallis ;
he, in 1767, publifhed by fubfcription (infcribed, by permiffion, to the latter) ten
dialogues, intituled, " The Errors of the Church of Rome detected ;" which have
gone through two editions, and been well received by the public. He died fuddenly at Canterbury, after officiating at Harbledown (of which he was curate), Feb.
8, 1784.

 ' Fellow of Chrift's College, Cambridge, and fon of the late Dean of Ely,
Mafter of that college.

     + This is tranflated from the Regifter-bock, where it is inferted in Latin.

REPAIR

REPAIR OF THE BRIDGE, DONE BY THE HOSPITAL.

The city chamber hath a record, dated 7 Richard II. A. D. 1391, whereby it appears, that the mafter of the hofpital ought to repair, erect, and fuftain the neighbour-bridge, i. e. King's-bridge. The account of the hofpital eftate given up to the commiffioners upon the ftatute 37 Henry VIII. chargeth the mafter with the paving alfo of the great ftreet there [1].

Out of an old account-book of the hofpital.

	l.	*s.*	*d.*
Imprimis dño Alano Blunt, capellno Cantar' de Eftbregg, ꝑ falario fuo per annum	x	vi	viij
Et folut' dño Waltero capellno, ꝑ falario fuo ibid' per annum		c	
Et alio capeltno divina celebranti in hofpitali pred' ꝑ 3 dies in feptimano nil hoc anno, tamen folebat habere per annum		xxx	
Et folut' cuidam mulieri cuftodienti pauperes in hofpit' predict', per annum		xx	
Et in cervifia empt' et dat' pauperibus pred', per ann', ꝑ feptimanam vj d.		xxvi	
Et in cera, pane, et vino empt' ꝑ capella			
Et in expenf' fenefchalli curie de Blen			xx
Et folut' Joanni Thornbury, pro redditu terre apud Denne lefe hoc anno		xiij	iiij
Et folut' dñe Duciffe de Buckingham et ferv' dñi feodi militis in le Blen hoc anno		ij	
Et folut' pro expenf' militar' ad milites parliament' hoc anno		iij	ij
Et folut' prioriffe et monial' de Scapeia pro redditu de Eftbrugge hoc anno		vi	
Et folut' firmar' de Whitftaple, pro reddit' eis debitis hoc anno		ij	
Et folut' Bernardo Brokey, pro redditu de Pettsfalfes hoc anno			xiiij

£. xx xii

Comput' vet' Hofpitalis.

	s.	*d.*
Recep' de Willo Audele ꝑ redditu ten' qui nuper Joannis Bertlet, dyer, per annum	xx	
De executor' Joannis Bertlet, junior', ꝑ redditu tenementi fui, nuper Scoles, per annum	xiij	iiij
De Hamone Bele, ꝑ redditu tenementi Balfham, in parochia Omnium Sanctorum, per annum	iiij	
De Tho' Deynold, ꝑ redditu tenem' Hawkwode, militis, per annum	iij	iiij
De relicta Lynde, ꝑ redditu nove taberne in paroch' St. Andree in le Merceray, per annum	iij	vj
De figno Stelle in parochia Ste Margarette, per annum		x

De

[1] Somner's Antiquities of Canterbury, p. 129.

De Joanne Whyte, botcher, ꝑ redditu ten' ſui juxta caſtrum, per   *l.*   *s.*   *d.*
annum   viij

De execut' Joannis Langle, ꝑ redditu tenem' ſui juxta Radyngate
in paroch' Beate Marie de Dunghil, per annum   vj

De Joanne Gray, ꝑ reddit' ten' ſui in paroch' Sti Alphagi, per
annum   xij

De Ricardo Willis, ꝑ reddit' ten' ſui in paroch' de Northgate,
per annum   iiij

De Theſaurar' eccle Chriſti Cant', per annum   xxiij

De Rogero Layborn, ꝑ redd' terre in crofto juxta rectoriam de
Harbaldown, per annum   vj

In Cantuaria.

De Michae Flandr', ꝑ firma ten' ſui vocat', le Chang, ꝑ 4tuor partes,
viijs. 4d. per totum annum   xxxiij   iiij

De Joanne Sharp, coco, ꝑ firma ij tenement' per annum   xxxiij   iiij

De Willo Seban, ꝑ firma tenem' ſui ibid'   xvj

De Milo Denne, ꝑ firma ten' ſui, per annum   xxvj   viij

De Joanne Hope, leache, ꝑ firma ten' ij ibid   x

De alio ten' juxta portam fratrum minorum nil hoc anno ꝑ defectu
tenentis

De Willmo Bigg, ꝑ firma cujuſdam prati in Medlane, per annum   v

De Thoma Banoak, ꝑ firma   juxta le Longwall, per annum   vj   viij

De M° Rico, ꝑ firma   in hoſpit' Sti Tho' Martyris, per annum   vij

Firme extra Cantuar'.

De Willo Olyve, ꝑ firma terre ſue apud Bleen et Stoke, per annum   xliiij   viij

De eodem, ꝑ firma terre nuper Parker's, per annum   vj   viij

De eodem, ꝑ firma terre nuper Bathers, per annum   xiij   iiij

De Thoma Colyn et Henrico Balnot, ꝑ firma de Hothcourt, per
annum   iiij   vj   viij

De terra nuper Willi, nil hoc anno ꝑ defectu tenentis   vj

De terra nuper in manu Nich Rich, nil hoc anno ꝑ defectu tenentis   xx

De Thoma Vydel, ꝑ firma de Salefeld, per annum   ij

De Bernardo Brokay, ꝑ firma de Petfalles, per annum   vj

De Joanne Sewain, ꝑ firma de Bromedewne, per annum   x

De Roberto Coleman, firmario de Cockering   xxxiij   iiij

De Joanne Iſaack, armigero, ꝑ firma Cant' de Bekyſborn, per
annum   lx

De Willo atte See, firmario de Mekyngbrook, per annum   lxvj   viij

De Joanne Roper, ꝑ firma de Lompett, per annum   vij

De decima mol' de Weſtgate, xxd. per annum, ſed iſto anno quo
molendinum ſtetit vac' ꝑ iij quart' per defectum reparacionis
ejuſdem hoc anno   xij   vj

De Rogero Brent, ꝑ hordio firmar', per annum, viij quarters

De relicta Joannis Aldelener ꝑ firma terre jacen' in parochia de
Byrchington, et Omnium Sanctorum in Thaneto, per annum   vj   viij
   Decima

Decima de Westgate.

De Joanne Swaine, firmar' de Westgate, pro decimis.
Pro 2 porcellis, viijd.
Pro decimâ vitulorum, ijs. vijd.
Pro decimâ xv vaccarum, ijs. iijd.
Pro viij agnellis, viijd.
Pro 1 quartier et dimid' lane xviijd.
Pro decimâ cannabi, nil.
Pro firmâ de Bromedown, xs.

Summa totalis redditus, xxvjl. xjs. ijd.

A rental made in the 21st year of Henry VII. A. D. 1506,
agrees in almost all particulars with the following rental, made
A. D. 1509; except, in this first rental,

	£.	s.	d.
The rent of Cockering	1	13	4
The rent of Westgate is	9	6	8

A rental of the lordship of Hoath and Bleen, in the 1st year of Henry VIII.

	£.	s.	d.
Lord prior of Christ-church, for Monkland	0	6	3
Item, my said lord, for Cliff's land	0	0	4
Item of Ralfe Simon, for Oxendine his love	1	2	9
Item, John Bovyar, ob.	0	1	2
Item, the brethren of Northgate	0	4	6
Item, the vicar of Bleen, for John Gentiles his love	0	1	0
Item, of Vydel his love	0	1	9
Item, of my lord's Beeham	0	0	2
Item, of Robert a Mayton	0	1	7
Item, of John a Mayton for William Bovyar	0	0	9
Item, of William Took	0	13	4
Item, John Wynter	0	0	8¼
Item, John Roper for Butiller's Court	0	6	8
Item, John Winter for William Sellewer, tenant on the Bleen	0	0	4
Item, of Mr. Walter Langley for Well-court	0	10	0
Item, Robert Cobherd	0	0	6
Item, Robert Elnore	0	4	6¼
Item, Ralfe Simon for John Clif	0	2	5
Item, John Elner the younger	0	3	5
Item, Robert Bowyer, for Christian Cadman	0	0	2

B b b

Item,

	£.	s.	d.
Item, John Philpot for the same Christian	0	0	4
Item, Nic' Sheldwick	0	3	2
Item, George Belsyr	0	0	11
Item, Ralfe Simon for his fader	0	2	9
Item, Robert Cowerd	0	0	6
Item, Ralfe Simon for John Clyff	0	0	5
Item, Robert Bobyar	0	0	4
Item, Thomas Elinor 2d. et pro 9 gallinis 5s.	0	5	2
Item, John a Mayton	0	0	9
Item, William Bobyar	0	0	3
Item, John Winter for Thomas Procter	0	0	9.
Item, John Cooper the younger	0	0	4
	5	4	0¼
Item, John Bobyar	0	1	0
Item, for himself, 6 gallinas			
Item, John Philpot, servant	0	0	4
	5	5	4½

and vj gallinas

Fee farms in the Bleen, 1mo Henry VIII.

	£.	s.	d.
Videl his love	4	0	0
John Winter	3	0	0
George Belsyr, for 2 acres, half, and 3 perches	0	1	6
Widow Thomas, pet for pit fallyes	0	7	0
John Cooper	0	9	0
Robert Mayton for John a Mayton	0	8	0
William Geree	0	7	0
	8	12	6

Seynt Dunstonys.

	£.	s.	d.
The heirs of Belsyr for Bushy-lane	0	2	0
The parson of Harboldown, for a croft besides the parsonage	0	0	6
Mr. John Roper for Lomepitte	0	2	0
John Temple for Bromedune	0	10	0
	0	14	6

Westgate

Weftgate Parifh.

	£.	s.	d.
The heirs of Mr. Ramfey	0	3	0
Baker, for tent of Cokering	1	6	8
Tho' Percy Baker, for R. Welles, in Crokker-lane	0	1	0
Robert Copar, for tents called Swaynes and Philpots	0	0	6
Stony-ftreet, for the tenement in North-lane	0	1	6
The manner of Weftgate	8	0	0
	9	12	8

Parochia S'ti Petri.

Mr. William Kudele	1	0	0
Mr. John Mayton	0	13	4
Harry Sworder	0	12	0
William Geree, for a meadow in Medelane	0	4	0
iiij tenements in the faid parifh	1	5	0
Romefcot	0	0	0
Nicolas Miller	0	2	0
The vicar of Hern, for John Plumpton, in St. Peter's-lane	0	2	0
John Rand for Miles Denne	0	0	4
	3	18	8

Parochia Omnium Sanctorum.

Thefaurarius eccle Chrifti Cantuar' p Stillicidio	0	1	11
Thomas Beel	0	4	0
Joannes Bellyng	2	1	0
Joannes Dryfton	1	10	10
Wiltus Geree	1	0	0
Joannes at See de Hern	2	6	8
Firmar' de Bekyfborn	2	13	4
John Baker de Harboldown for Richard Hart	1	6	8
John Coleman p tento juxta rectoriam Omum Sanctorum	0	1	0
	11	5	5

Parochia

Parochia S'te Marie de Northgate.

	£.	s.	d.
Joannes Saunder	o	4	o

Parochia S'ti Andree.

| Thomas Fokys [Fox] pro le Borys [Boar's] head | o | 3 | 6 |

Parochia S'te Margarite.

Robertus Sturdy, pro Joanne Bradkerk	o	o	10
Joannes Crifpe de Tenet	o	6	8
	o	7	6

Cocks in le Blene and le Hoath?

Ralfe Simon, vj gallinas.   George Belfyr, 9 gallinas.
Ric. Elnother, 9 gallos, 4 gallinas, et tertiam partem unius galline
Wm. Bovyar, 2 gallin* et dimid'.   John a Mayton, 9 gallinas.
Walter Langly, 9 gallos, 12 gallinas.
Cowherd, 9 gallos et 9 gallinas.
W. Woodland, 9 gallos, 8 gallinas.
Fratres hofpitalis Sti Joannis de Northgate ij gallinas.
Hered' Nich' Sheldwich, 9 gallos, iij gallinas.
John Bowyer, 9 gallinas.

Summe total of the cocks and hens 119, and a third part of a hen, and a half hen.

Gate Silver in Le Blene.

Walter Langly, 4d.	Nic' Rich, 1d.
Walter Tuck, 2d.	George Belfyr, 4d.
Rafe Simon, 1d.	Nic. Sheldwich, 4d.
Hered' Oxenden, 8d.	In all, 2s.

Item venditio bofci.

| Summe total of this rental is | 40 | o | 1½ |

Befides venditio filvarum, and
Cocks and hens 119, and a half and a third part of a hen.
Anno Domini 1509.

TWO

Two other rentals, the one made A. D. 1528; the other made 1529.

	£.	s.	d.
Imprimis, of William Weeks, and for a farm of Hoth and Blen	4	0	0
In the former of these the rent is 8 0 0			
Item, of Wm Alen for the farm of Tunfeld and Maytons	0	10	0
In the former of these it is 0 18 0			
De priore eccle Cant'	0	6	8
De Joanne Roper, armigero	0	6	8
De Joanne Norton, milite	0	10	0
De Salomone Mayton	0	2	7
De Joanne Littlecot	0	3	2
De Roberto Mayton	0	1	8
De Joanne Roper pro terris Oxenden	1	3	9
De eodem p terris vocat' Woodland, nup Willi Took	0	13	4
De hofpitali Sti Joannis extra Northgate	0	4	6
De Joanne Winter	0	0	4
De Chriftophero Winter	0	0	8½
De Elienora Winter	0	0	1
De Georgio Elnor	0	2	0
De Thoma Proctar	0	0	3
De Radulpho Simon	0	7	2
De heredibus domini Rogeri Downfield	0	2	8
De Joanne Lamberherft	0	0	6
De Joanne Fodolfo p incremento jd. ob' terrarum nuper Willi Cluer	0	1	11
De Elenora vid' Will' John et Thomas	0	3	0
De Roberto Bomar	0	0	3
De Henrico Copar	0	0	4
De herede Belgar	0	0	11
	9	2	5½
De Joanne Norton, milite, p uno gallo et 12 gallinis	0	3	2½
De Rogero Downwill, p una gallina	0	0	3
De magro Joanne Roper p Woodland, p gallo et 8 gallinis	0	2	2½
De hofpitali Sti Johannis extra Northgate p 2 gallinis	0	0	6
De Radulpho Simon, p xi gallinis dimid'	0	2	10½
De Roberto Mayton, pro una gallina	0	0	3
De Roberto Bomar, p 36 gallinis et dimid'	0	0	10½

De

	£.	s.	d.
De relicta Copar, 1 gallina		o	3
De M'io Joanne Roper, ⫞ 1 gallo et 5 gallinis		1	5½
De Joanne Littlecot, ⫞ gallo et tribus gallinis		o	11½
De hered' Georgii Belfyr, ⫞ gallina		o	3
De Roberto Symis pro gallina		o	3
De Lambeherft, herede Cowherd, ⫞ 1 gallo et 1 gallina		o	5½
De herede Elnor, vidue, ⫞ gallina	8	o	3
De Salomone Mayton, ⫞ 1 gallo, 2 gallinis, et 3ia parte galline		o	o 10¼
De Georgio Elnor, ⫞ una gallina		o	o 3
	o	15	2¼

The cock is 2d. ob. the hen is 3d. every one

Gate Silver.

De Joanne Norton, milite,	o	o	4
Joanne Roper	o	o	10
Radulpho Simon	o	o	3
Joanne Roper, armigero	o	o	4
Joanne Littlecote	o	o	4
——Belfyr	o	o	4
	o	2	5

Add this 4l. 8s. in the 2 firft fums of the rental	4	8	o
	14	8	5¾

The rental is thus fummed up.
Sum total of all the whole lordfhip of Blen
and Hoth £. 15 17 5 qu.
Whereof the rents of affize with cocks and
hens is £. 5 3 5 ob. qu.

Here follow the tenements in Canterbury.

In parochia Omnium Sanctorum.

De Henrico Gyre, p annum	1	10	o
De Umfry Wales	1	10	o
De Joanne Guftenbury	o	10	o
De Joanne Waffel	1	o	o
De W'mo Penjoy, ⫞ tenemento annex' janue hofpit'	o	8	o

In

In Parochia S'ti Petri.

	£.	s.	d.
De Sandero, pro tenemento annex' hofpital'	o	5	o
De Joanne Afhby, pro domo juxta domum predict'	o	5	o
De Thoma Belman, pro tenemento annexo	o	6	o
De Henrico Maning, pro teñ'to juxta portam fratrum	o	5	o
	5	19	o

Quit Rents in Canterbury.

All-Hallows Parifh.

Mr. Beal, for the garden where he dwelleth, called the tenement of Baafhman, per annum	o	4	o
Of the Treafurer of Chrift Church	o	1	11
Of the Garden which Sir Thomas Hale hireth within the Eaftbridge			

St. Peter's Parifh.

Of William Eaft p̄ tenements annexed to Grey Frier's Gate	1	o	o
Of the tenement next, now John Fowle	o	13	4
Of the tenement next to the houfe of John Aucher	o	4	o
Of two tenements in St. Peter's Lane	o	4	o
Of tenements now in Coleman's Garden	o	o	8
Of Coleman for his tenm̄t annexed to the parfonage of Allhallowes, now Mr. Coleman's maulthoufe, fometime Sworder, formerly Raygats	o	1	o
Of a tenement over-againft the faid parfonage, now Lucas	o	o	4
Of a tenement in Brokepot Lane, fometimes Sworder, now Coleman's Stone Yard	o	o	8
	2	16	11

Quit-

Quit-rents in St. Dunstan's Parish.

	£.	s.	d.
A piece of land called Deering's Dale, or Bushelmes	o	2	o
Of the chaplain of Christ's church for a piece annexed to the parsonage of Harboldown	o	o	6

Westgate Parish.

	£.	s.	d.
Of the widow of Ralfe Brown	o	1	6
Of Garard Reed, for a house in North-Jane	o	1	6
Of John Barbet, for a house late-John Elnor	o	3	1
Of John Hills, of London, for a house annexed to the bridge	o	o	6
Of Thomas Wood, for the parsonage of Westgate	9	o	o
Summed in the rentals 9l. 9s. 6d.	9	9	1

St. Andrew's Parish.

	£.	s.	d.
Of Thomas Fox, for the house called the Boar's-head	o	3	6

St. Margaret's Parish.

	£.	s.	d.
Of Geo' Rotherham, for a brewhouse called the Star, sometimes Winter's, now Geo. Haselherst	o	o	10

Northgate Parish.

	£.	s.	d.
Of Thomas Mallard, for the house against the Ambre [Almony] of Christ's church, sometimes Wills and Saunders	o	4	o
	o	8	4

Farms.

	£.	s.	d.
For a close at St. Thomas Hill	o	9	o
For a meadow in Myde-lane	o	4	o
Of John Boker, for lands lying in Nackington	1	6	8
For Lompits	o	2	o
Of the prior of St. Gregoryes for Long Harriscroft	o	10	o
Of Tho. Bing, for Cockering-lane, in Thanington	1	10	o

Of

	£.	s.	d.
Of John Auſten and Robert Simmes of Livingſborn, for lands there	2	16	8
Of Mr. John Criſpe, for lands lying in Thanet, and for tithes	0	6	8
Of Mr. Beal, for a little cloſe lying at the poſtern	0	4	0
	7	9	0

Farms which the prieſt of Harbledown doth receive.

Of Robert At Sea, for lands lying in Herne	3	6	8
Of John Fadalfe, for lands in Coſmus Blean	1	13	4
	5	0	0

Summe total of lands   47l. 0s. 2d. qu.

Diſburſements by the maſter of the hoſpital.

To my lady [prioreſs] of Shepey, for a rent of a garden uſed by the hoſpital	0	,	—
Rent for land at St. Thomas's hill; to the lord of the manor	0	1	2
To my lady [prioreſs] of Saint Sepulchre	0	9	0
Item, quit-rent for lands in North Blean	0	2	0
Item, for wood, ale, and other neceſſaries for the relief of poor men in arms	6	1	4
Item, to the keeper and his wife to attend about the poor men, beſides his ſallery	2	6	8
To Mr. John Morys, prieſt	10	6	8
To Sir George Higges [1], [chantery prieſt] of Harboldown	6	0	0
To the court of Thornbury, for rent	0	13	4
	26	7	2

This was annexed to one of the foreſaid rentals.

[1] Alſo vicar of Blean. See p. 363.

Other

Other rentals about the fame time agree with thefe; only Quit-
rents in St. Dunftan's Parifh.

	£.	s.	d.
Deering's Dale, or Bufhelmes, is faid to contain vj acres	0	2	0

In Parochia [de] Weftgate.

De Glover, carnifice, p tento angulari quod tenet juxta Bartonis-lane	0	3	1
—p tento juxta pontem de Weftgate ex parte Auftrali	0	0	6
The fuma totalis of the other rentals is	44	7	10
Of another rental the fume total was	49	6	2
The farmes at Bekyfborn rented at 3l. p annum.			

A terrier of the lands belonging to Eaftbridge-Hofpital, taken
Nov. 26, 1713, by George Cadman, leafed to Mrs. Boys, &c.

	Acres.
Hoth-Court 6 pieces	62
Two woods adjoining to Hoth-Court	30
Ben Horn, 8 pieces	90
Horfe Downs, 2 pieces	40
Roothams, 11 pieces	50
Thomas Nickolls, 8 pieces	30
Henry Cullen, 2 pieces	7
John Fleet, 2 pieces	7
Thomas Cullen, 6 pieces	17
Denge Lees	60
	395

There is one farm that lets for 45l. per annum, whereof the houfe and clofes
except of the land (about 10l. per annum) are fee-fimple; the reft belongs to the
hofpital.

Anno 37° Henrici VIII. The king directed his commiffion to
Thomas [Cranmer] archbifhop of Canterbury, Henry [Hol-
beach] bifhop of Rochefter, Thomas Cheney, John Baker,
Thomas Moyle, Richard Long, William Finch, knights, Anthony Aucher, and others, &c.; who certified as enfueth [1].

---

[1] Out of the papers which G. Hayes fent to archbifhop Whitgift.

Reddit'

Reddit' Affiz' exeunt' de diverfis terris et tent' in civit' Cant', viz. in *l.   s.   d.*
the parifh of Hallowes, for divers tenements there—xiij *l.* xii *s.* vij *d.*
In the parifh of St. Peter's, for divers tenements there, lxx *s.* viij *d.* In
the parifh of St. Margaret's, x *d.* In the parifh of Weftgate, xj *s.* vj *d.*
In the parifh of Northgate, iiij *d.* In the parifh of St. Andrew's,
iij *s.* 6 *d.*   x\ii xix v

Item, firm' diverfar' terrar' ad voluntatem dimiff', viz. cert'-terr' in
Bekefborn continent' per eftimat', 60 acras, per ann' lvj *s.* viij *d.* cert'
terr' apud Cockering, in Thanington, per ann' xxx *s.* Claufura vocat'
Long ·Harris, in Harboldune, x *s.* cert' terr' in Birchington, nec non
certar' decimarum predialium, ibid. ꝑ annum, vj *s.* viij *d.* claufura
vocat' Pytfylds, ꝑ annum, x *s.* ij *d.*   v xiij vj

Item, firm' diverf' terrar' et tent' ad voluntatem dimiff' in diverfis
parochiis in dicta civit' Cant', ꝑ annum   vj x viij

Item, firm' xi acr' terr' in camp' vocat' St. Laurence Feild, ac 4 acr'
terre in pred' campo   xxvj vii

Item, firm' fcitus manerij de Blene et Hoth court, ac omnium do-
mor' ac edific' cum diverfis pafturis et claufuris`continent' ꝑ annum
154 acras, nec non et omnium decimarum perfonalium et predialium
omnium premifforum in parochia Cofmi et Damiani de Blene, in
tenura Thome Higham ad voluntatem, per annum   x xiij iiij

Portio decimarum predialium de ōibs terris dominical' manerii archiepi
Cantuar' de Weftgate in tenura Thome Ligham, per annum   ix

Porcō decimarum predial' omnium terrarum intra parochiam Sti Nicolai de Harboldown in tenura Thome Ligham, ꝑ annum   xiij iiij

Porcō decimarum predial' in parochia Storum Cofmi et Damiani in
le Blene vocat' Foxholes, in tenura Thome Ligham   ij

Summa li *l.* xviij *s.* x *d.*

In the fore-named accompt are omitted the 200 acres, and xxx *s.* rent that Adam
le Heir gave in Herne, Reculvre, &c.

Item, 25 quarters of corn to be paid yeerly.

Item, except the 60 acres of land in Bekefborne, all the reft of our Lady's
chantery lands, rented at 7 *l.* 0 *s.* 4 *d.* ꝑ annum, are omitted.

" Ecta Storum Cofmi et Damiani de Blen appropriatur magro hofpit' Sti Thome
de Eftbrugge, Cantuar';" as may appear in the office of firft fruits and tenths,
anno 26 Henry VIII.

" Geo' Higges, vicar there, receiveth for tyth-corn, ꝑ annum,   v *l.*
" for tythes predial and perfonal, oblations, and other fpiritual profits, iv *l.*

" In all ix *l.*

The parfonage of Harbeldown was appropriated to the hofpital, anno 16 Edw.
III. and was charged with perpetual tenths, per annum, 12 *s.* 6 *d.*

Item,

Item, in the office of firſt fruits and tenths, the hoſpital of Eaſtbridge is charged
with perpetual tenths, at 47*l.* o*s.* 10*d.* ob.

Salaries paid out of the Hoſpital Rents.

	£.	s.	d.
To Stephen Morrys, chantery-prieſt in the ſaid hoſpital	10	6	8
To Sir George Hygges, chantery-prieſt of Harboldown	5	0	0
Item, there was one Nicolas Chapman, chantery-prieſt of our Ladyes chantery in the ſaid hoſpital, per annum	10	11	8

Salaries and diſburſements paid by the maſter of the hoſpital,
as are ſet down in two rentals, as I ſuppoſe, in the time of
king Henry VII. viz.

	£.	s.	d.
Imprimis, To Thornbury	0	13	4
To my lady Bokingham	0	2	0
To the prioreſs of Sheepy	0	7	0
To the fermer of Whiteſtaple	0	2	0
To Brocas of Banerlay	0	1	2
To my lady prioreſs of St. Sepulchre	0	9	0
To the chantery-prieſt of Eaſtbridge, .Sir H. M.	10	6	8
To Sir Walter of Harboldown	5	0	0
To a woman to keep the ſpittle	1	0	0
For ale for the poor people	1	6	8
For wine and wax for the chapel	0	10	0
For making and carrying 1000 fagots to the ſpittle for the poor men	1	0	0
	20	17	10

There is put down alſo for mending a black veſtment
of velvet, xij*d.*

Ancient rents at the bottom of an old rental, about the time of
king Henry VII. added to the former.

In Parochia S'ti Michaelis.

De Theſaurario Sti Auguſtini de terra que fuit Rogeri de Cornhil; que jacet apud Burgate ex oppoſito eccle Sti Michaelis	( ) 4

In Parochia de Chartham.

De caria de Chartham de tenente Mich' Foreſtar'	1 10

S'ti

S'ti Sepulchri.

	£.	s.	d.
De monialibus Sti Sepulchri de 4 acris terre apud Foxmold	o	2	o

Weſtgate.

De heredibus Roberti Bereberd de domo ſua extra Weſtgate ſuper Sturam proxime pont' ex parte Aquilonari	o	o	6
De monachis Ste Trinitatis de terr' ſupradict' in Taneto	o	6	8
De monachis Ste Trinitatis ꝑ terra quam emerunt de Willielmo et Róberto Halfeyaſt in Bleen	o	4	10½
Prior et conventus Ste Trinitatis tenent terras et tenementa que fuerunt Adæ Storey vel Theobalds de Thanet, per ſervitium, ꝑ annum	o	11	6

Thanet, Wood, et Birchington.

Firma de terr' et tenement' in Thaneto dimiſſ' Joanni Motte, et Joanni Miller, et Hamoni Brewer, ꝑ annum, reſolut' Jacobo Heoſyng in parochia de Wood et Birchington	o	6	10
De elemoſynario Sti Auguſtini de terrâ que fuit Willmi de Eſſetreford extra Radyngate	c		.

The return of the commiſſion delivered to king Henry VIII. did conſiſt of theſe particulars, viz.

" That the hoſpital was a pariſh church."

Then followed a particlular of all the rents and revenues belonging to the ſaid hoſpital.

Then an account of the annual diſburſements, viz.

" To Sir Nicolas Chapman, chantery prieſt, ꝑ annum	10	6	8
To Sir George [Higges, chantery prieſt of] Harboldown	1	13	4
To the keeper of the hoſpital for looking to the poor	1	0	0
For carrying wood to the hoſpital	o	10	0
For cutting and making the wood	o	5	11
Fee to the ſteward	o	13	4
Fee to the rent-gatherer	1	6	8
For beer to the poor	1	6	8
Quit-rents to Sir James Hale, for rent ſometimes belonging to the nuns of St. Sepulchre's	o	9	0
To the maſter of the College of Noſk	o	2	0
Item, for rent of the 4 little houſes, and for the garden within the hoſpital	o	7	0
Item, for rent to the lord of the manor for Cockering	o	7	0

	£.	s.	d.
King's money, tenths, and fubfidy for the hofpital,	4	10	6¼
To the dean and college of St. Stephen, in Weftminfter	0	13	4
For quit-rents of the Pitholes	0	1	1

" The mafter alfo ftands charged, befides the charges above rehearfed, with the focking fheets, and the burying of poor people that die within the hofpital; the which of late hath been very chargeable, and like to increafe during his majefty's prefent wars.

" Befides, the faid mafter ftands charged not only with the reparations yearly of the tenements belonging to the faid hofpital, with his manfion-houfe, and the chapel, but alfo with the reparations of the King's-bridge, and the paving of the ftreet."

The inventory of the goods belonging to the hofpital.

" Two bells to ring to fervice.

" Item, within the houfe a cheft bound with iron, wherein remaineth all the evidences belonging to the faid hofpital.

" Item, that the faid hofpital is a parifh-church, wherein there is continually adminiftered all facraments, and facramentally to the poor people thither reforting, and to the keeper of the faid hofpital, and his houfehold, and all others remaining within the precincts of the fame, by the faid chantery prieft. And it is diftant from the parifh-church of Allhallows the breadth of the ftreet, by eftimation of xxi feet.

" Item, there is in the faid hofpital a chantery prieft, having a foundation, receiving for his ftipend by the year 10l. 6s. 8d.

" Item, We find that the faid chantery prieft, notwithftanding his foundation, hath ever fince Chriftmas laft paft fung and celebrated maffe at St. Andrew's for Mr. Naylor, not doing his duty at home, nor any for him, according to the foundation in that behalf [1]."

Lands in Herne, Reculvre, Swalcliff, Chiftelet, alienated, when, by whom, &c. [2]

" Anno fecundo regis Edwardi VI. Annoque Domini 1547, by an act of parliament chanteries were diffolved; and thereupon, the lands given to thefe chanteries, which belonged to the hofpital, were difpofed to feveral perfons, to

---

[1] Taken out of one of Mr. Somner's MSS. belonging to the library of Chrift-church, Canterbury.
[2] Ex literis G. Hayes to Archbifhop Whitgift.

whom the king was pleafed to grant the fame ; and, together with the chantery lands, fome other lands were fraudulently alienated from the hofpital, which never did belong to the chantery, but were given before any of thefe chanteries was founded ; of which I find thefe following inftances.

"The lands in Herne, Reculvre, Chiftelet, &c. which Adam le Heir gave anno 30 Edw. III. being 200 acres, and 20s. rent, were not given wholly for the ufe of the chantery, but for other pious and charitable ufes, and to fuftain the charge of the poor in the hofpital. (See p. 334. fupra. "Dedit magiftro et fratribus "hofpital' in fubfidium eorum fuftentationis et ‚P uberioribus elemofinis in prefato "hofpitali occafione poffeffionum predictarum largiendis.") Thefe are the exprefs words of the charter : only in the licence of mortmain by king Edward thefe words are added to the other ; " ad inveniend' cantar'," &c.. The rent of thefe lands was 3l. 6s. 8d. which was paid out of Making brooks lying in Herne, by one Henry Oxenden ; who, as it is reported, hath all the reft of the faid lands, and the 20s. rent, that the faid Adam le Heir gave to the hofpital of Eaftbrigge. And fince the ftatute, anno 27 regni Eliz. upon the refervation of 7l. 10s. to the queen, to be paid by the hofpital, the faid rent of 3l. 6s. 8d. hath been alfo kept back from the hofpital, and fo continues to this day."

Lands alienated from the hofpital, lying in Beaksborn.

Francis Gill and Lodowick Gryvil purchafed certain lands to themfelves, belonging to the hofpital, lying in Beaksborn, under pretence that they were chantery-lands, viz.

Spytil-field, containing 11 acres. Snote, 7 acres. Wapping, 10 acres. Nobells-bill, 19 acres. A piece called vj acres. The yearly rent 56s. 8d.

Though fome of thefe did belong to the chantery which James de Bourne founded and endowed, yet great part of them belonged to the hofpital, and had no relation to the chantery.

It appears plainly from the charter, or deed, above written, that Richard de Becco, A. D. 1250, gave 10 acres, called Wapping in Beaksborn, to the mafter and brethren of the hofpital, *in puram, liberam, et perpetuam elemofinam*, long before the chantery was founded [1]. Alfo

William de Sancto Edmundo, rector of Livingsborn, gave 26 acres of land, lying in Beaksborn, long before the chantery was founded [2]: yet all thefe were alienated from the hofpital

[1] See p. 324.   [2] Ibid.

under

under the pretence of chantery-land.   Thefe were confirmed by
the record of king Edward II. in anno 7°, A. D. 1314.

The like is probable of fome other lands, &c.

Lands and Tenements in Canterbury, alienated from the Hofpital.

The tenement juxta hofpitale, in quo incumbens ibidem modo inhabitat, per
annum, 5s.

Item, firma unius meffuagii cum gardino et pomario, vocat' Clavering Hofpital,
in quo incumbens ibidem inhabitat, valet per annum, 13s. 4d.

Item, firma unius tenti cum gardino et 4 acris terre et dimid' fcituat' ex
oppofito hofpital' predict', valet per annum, xxvjs. viijd.

Thefe three parcels were granted by king Edward VI. to Mr.
Cartwright and Mr. Hyde; and were lands and tenements given
before the chantery was founded.

The third parcel feems to be that which Arnoldus Aurifaber
gave to the hofpital, A. D. 1256; and the other two were
given long before the chantery was founded.

There are two rentals, one dated in the 3d year of king
Edward VI. anno Domini 1548, Oct. 6.

The other dated April 4, anno primo et fecundo Philippi et
Marie, Mr. William Sworder being mafter.

Rents of Affize with cocks and gates.

	£.	s.	d.
Wellcourt, for rent, 10s. for xij hens, 3s. for gate filver and a cock vjd. ob.	0	13	6¼
John Roper, by the hands of John Weeks, 23s. 4d. for rent of Woodland, 13s. 4d. for one cock and viij hens, 2s. 9d. ob. gate filver, 10d.	2	0	1¼
Prior of St. John's, 4s. 6d. and 2 hens, vjd.	0	5	0
Ralfe Simons, for rent, 6s. 11d. ob. for one cock and xij hens, 3s. 2d. ob. for gate filver, 4d.	0	10	6
Widow Mayton for rent, xxd. a hen, 3d.	0	1	11
Winter, or Weeks, for rent	0	0	8
John Winter, for rent	0	0	4
John Weeks, or Denys Hall, for rent	0	0	2
Widow Alen, rent 4d. a hen 3d.	0	0	7

Thomas

	£.	s.	d.
Thomas Miles, rent	0	0	3
Mr. Roper, for Ruther's court, rent 6s. 8d. a cock and 5 hens, 17d. ob. gate filver [1] 4d.	0	8	5½
John Fidal	0	1	11
Robert Symnes, rent 4d. a hen 3d.	0	0	7
William Lamberherft, or John Harrifon, for rent, 6d. a cock and hen 5d. ob.	0	0	11½
George, or Robert Elnor, rent, 2s. a hen 3d.	0	2	3
Jamys Chapman, executor of Roger Domflede, rent, 2s. 8d. a hen 3d.	0	2	11
William Hart, for rent	0	0	3
R. Weeks, heir of William Eluer, rent 2s. 10d: ob. qu. a hen 3d.	0	3	1¾
Auften Eften, for rent,	0	3	5¼
Mr. William Roper, for rent,	0	4	5½
	5	1	4¼

Rent Charge in Allhallows Parifh.

William Parker, for a gutter	0	1	11			
Simon Barret, for Hardres malt-houfe	0	1	0			
Mr. William Oxendine, for a houfe and garden, 4d.	0	0	4	0	7	3
Mr. Beles, or Mr. Clark, or Mr. Drayner, for rent of a garden	0	4	0			

Rent Charge in St. Peter's Parifh.

Stephen Scot	0	13	4			
John Eton, or William Hart	0	4	0	1	1	4
Mr. George Bingham	0	4	0			

Rent in Weftgate Parifh.

John Bell	0	1	6			
John Cuthbord, or Phil' Jervace	0	1	6	0	6	7
John Onyon, or William Swift	0	3	1			
Mr. Hills, by the hands of John Winter	0	0	6			

Rent Charge in St. Margaret's Parifh.

John Trot	0	10

[1] Q. The meaning of " gate filver," mentioned here and elfewhere ?

Rent

Rent Charge in Northgate Parifh.

John Walſtal, for a houſe late Thomas Mallard's   ɔ 4 c

Rent in St. Andrew's Pariſh.

Roger Bere, or Peter Naylor   3 6

Rent in St. Peter's Pariſh.

Stephen Scot

Tynet.   [Thanet.]

Mr. Harry Criſp, for rent of certain lands and tithes   ɔ 6 8

Harboldown.

Thomas Lyham, for tithes   o 13 4
Tithes of Foxholes   o   2 o

Suit of Court.

William Roper, 8*d*. Robert Mayton, 4*d*. Auſtin Eſton, 8*d*. William
  Roper, 4*d*. Mr. Gremer, 4*d*. William Roper, 4*d*. Roger Dom-
  flede, 4*d*. Prior of St. John's hoſpital, 4*d*. Robert Simmes, 4*d*. ɔo 6 8
  George Elner, 4*d*. John Fedal, 8*d*. Chriſtopher Winter, 4*d*. John
  Winter, 4*d*. Widow Allen, 4*d*. Ralfe Simon, 8*d*. William Hart, 4*d*.

Perquiſites of court   4 12 2

Rent of Fermes.   [Farms.]

Of Bonaventure Fryder   1 10 o
Of John Paſhly   1   6 8
Another houſe next adjoining   o 10 o
Of Peter Wilkinſon   1   o o
Of Stephen Scot   o   8 4
O Walter Trot, for a meadow in Meadow-lane   o   1 6
Of Walter Scot   o   6 8
Of John Ford, a meadow   o   1 8
Of John Thetcher, a piece of land   o   2 6
Of George Hunt   o   2 6
Of Mr. George Bingham   o 13 2
Of Mr. William Bingham, for Cockering   o   7 6

Theſe regiſters are imperfect.

Dr.

Dr. Nicolas Harpsfield, archdeacon of Canterbury, visited all parish churches, hospitals, &c. within his archdeaconry; and the return was made, concerning this hospital, in these words [1].

" Hospitale de Eastbrigge.

" Mager Willielmus Sworder, Mager hospitalis.

" *Memorandum*, They are bound to receive wayfaring and hurt men, and to have viij beds for men, and four for women, to remain for a night or more, if they be not able to depart; and the master of the hospital is charged with the burial, and they have xx loads of wood yearly allowed, and xxvj s. for drink.

" *Memorandum*, There was 10 l. land a year, with a mansion, which the priest always had to serve the chapel, taken away by the king; and that it is the head church to Cosmus Blene; but they have no ornaments but organs.

" This visitation was Aug. 14, A. D. 1557."

Mr. Somner (p. 63.) calls this " Cardinal Pole's visitation," by a mistake; for it was the archdeacon's visitation in the time of Cardinal Pole; and he gives an imperfect account of it.

MASTERS, RECTORS, or WARDENS, of this Hospital.

1200	1. RALPH, or RADULPHUS [2].
1236	2. PETER.
1242	3. JOHN.
1261	4. GEOFFRY.
1264	5. WALTER.
1280	6. JOHN [3].
1320	7. JOHN, of Tynoden.
1323	8. JOHN, of Thuighden.
———	9. WILLIAM BURGOOS.

[1] Ex originali in officio Regrarii Cant'.

[2] The first master (*Custos* or *Procurator*) whose name occurs in the most ancient charters of this house. He was master before the hospital of St. Nicolas and St. Catherine, i. e. Cockyn's Hospital, was united to Eastbridge: He was witness to an ancient deed or charter made to Cockyn's hospital before the union of it, and to several other charters of Blean, &c. By the hand writing, which is the same character with the deed or charter by which Archbishop Hubert gave the tithes of the mills to the hospital, he seems to have lived in Archbishop Hubert's time, and about the year 1200

[3] Vicar of Wycham.

1334		10. RICHARD [1] of Ivingho [2] [Bucks].
1342		11. ROGER de Rondes.
1349	18 June,	12. WILLIAM of Farham [3].
1351	1 Aug.	13. WILLIAM GRADEEL.
1351	18 Dec.	14. THOMAS NEWE [4]; of Wolton, or Wilton.
1381		15. JOHN OVINGS.
1382		16. JOHN LUDHAM.
1383	9 Apr.	17. JOHN WHITTICLIFF.
1383	25 Nov.	18. WALTER CAUSTON [5].
1395		19. JOHN MONTAGU.
1400		20. THOMAS PELICAN.
1405		21. THOMAS BURTON [6].
1429		22. THOMAS CHICHELEY.
———		23. THOMAS KEMP.

[1] Rector of Fawkinge, and afterwards of Brook.
[2] He was a monk probably of that convent.
[3] Instituted by the prior and convent of Christ-church, Canterbury, the fee being vacant by the death of Archbishop Bradwardin.
[4] Rector of Aldington, and vicar of Reculver, where he founded and endowed a chantry in 1354. See the History of that parish. He also endowed a chantry at Herbaldown. During his mastership, the vicarage of St. Cosmus and Damian in the Blean was, with his consent, founded and endowed by archbishop Sudbury, in 1375. See the endowment in Somner's Appendix. This Mr. Newe, it appears by it, built the vicarage-house. In his time king Edward III. gave Le Change to the hospital, archbishops Islip and Sudbury founded the chantry of the hospital. John de la Lee gave 180 acres of land, &c. Adam le Eyr gave the lands in Reculvre, Herne, Chistelet, &c. and Thomas de Roos gave the manor of Blean. He is often mentioned from 1354 to 1371. In the charter of the foundation of the chantry of Herbaldown, he is called Thomas Elton. In two ancient charters he is called Thomas Newe de Reculvre; and Mr. Battely was not certain whether this Thomas Newe was the same with Thomas de Wolton; for in the same deed he had seen Thomas Newe de Wolton and Thomas Newe de Reculvre mentioned; and rather supposed that Thomas Newe de Reculvre succeeded in 1372.
[5] Monk and precentor of Christ-church, Canterbury, afterwards prior of St. Martin's in Dover.
[6] Rector of Snargate. He succeeded on the resignation of the former master.

1445		24. THOMAS CHICHELEY [1].
1467		25. JOHN BOURGCHIER [2].
1469		26. JOHN FITZ WARREN.
1494		27. THOMAS HALLIWELL.
1538		28. PETER LYGHAM [3], LL. D.
1538		29. WILLIAM SWORDER.
1562		30. WILLIAM MORPHET.
1569	18 Feb.	31. THOMAS LAWES [4], LL. D.
1595	25 Aug.	32. RICHARD ROGERS [5], D. D.
1596	18 June,	33. ISAAC COLFE [6], M. A.

[1] Great nephew to archbishop Chicheley, being grandson of his younger brother William. Feb. 18, 1429, he was collated to the prebend of Cadington minor in St. Paul's; and to the archdeaconry of Canterbury, December 13, 1433. February 10, in the same year, he had licence under the privy seal to take and execute the office of prothonotary to the pope. But it is supposed he resigned the archdeaconry some years before his death, for Thomas Winterbourn is styled archdeacon of Canterbury, Sept. 1, 1448. He died Jan. 26, 1446, and was buried in the church of Wingham in Kent. Stemmata Chichleiana, Pref. ix. where his mastership of this hospital is not noticed. Q. Did he resign this last place and resume it again; for no other person of his name occurs earlier.

[2] Archdeacon of Canterbury, provost of Wingham College, 1463, and prothonotary to the pope; brother, or near kinsman, Somner supposes, to archbishop Bourgchier. He died Nov. 6, 1469.

[3] He was made dean of the arches by archbishop Cranmer, by letters dated " in " manerio ñro de Ford, 30 die mensis Octobris, anno 1535, et confecrationis tertio."

[4] A native of Norwich, prebendary of Canterbury, 1568, and the archbishop's commissary. This master was taxed with making some concealments of lands belonging to the hospital, and with leasing them out at low rents, by the connivance of archbishop Whitgift. See Strype's Life of that archbishop, p. 498; and Masters's History of Corpus Christi College, Cambridge, p 333. He died August 9, 1595.

[5] The last suffragan bishop of Dover, to which office he was consecrated by archbishop Parker 1569, and in 1584 made dean of Canterbury, where he was buried in the Deans' chapel. See Wood's Athen. Oxon. 686. He was also rector of Great Chart, to which he was inducted Jan. 19, 1567. See Lewis's Essay on Suffragan Bishops, p. 15.

[6] Fourth son of Amandus Colfe, alias Coulte, of Calais in France, and of the city of Canterbury in England, was born in Kent, probably in that city; and was educated at Oxford a commoner in Broadgates-hall, 1576. He died July 15, 1597, and was buried in the chapter-house of the cathedral church of Canterbury. See the register of the hospital.

3

1597	14 Aug.	34.	JOHN BOYS [1], D. D.
1625	25 Oct.	35.	ROBERT SAY [2], B. D.
1628	27 May,	36.	JOHN SACKETTE [3], B. D.
1664	20 Oct.	37.	EDWARD ALDEY [4], M. A.
1673	10 Apr.	37.	SAMUEL PARKER [5], D. D.
1688	1 Sept.	38.	JOHN BATTELY [6], D. D.
1708		39.	JOHN PARIS [7], M. A.
1709	Jan.	40.	JOHN BRADOCK [8], M. A.

[1] Fourth fon of Thomas Boys, efquire, of Eythorn, in Kent, and nephew to Sir John Boys of Canterbury, was admitted of Bene't, or Corpus Chrifti. College, Cambridge, 20 April, 1586; fellow of Chelfea College, 1610, rector of Bettfhanger, and dean of Canterbury, 1619. He died Sept. 28, 1625, and was buried in the Deans' chapel near the fermon-houfe in the cathedral church, where he has a monument. See a lift of his works in Mafters's Hiftory of Corpus Chrifti College, p. 241.

[2] Rector of Herbaldown. He died April 8, 1628.

[3] Rector of Great Mongeham. He died Auguft 24, 1664, and was buried in the chancel of his church.

[4] Prebendary of Canterbury, and rector of St. Andrew's and St. Mary Bredman's. He died July 1, 1673, and was buried in the chancel of the parifh church of St. Andrew, in Canterbury, now taken down, but his monument is preferved in the veftibule of the new church.

[5] Archdeacon and prebendary of Canterbury, and rector of Chartham and Ickham; afterwards bifhop of Oxford, 1686. He died at Oxford, March 20, 1687.

[6] Archdeacon and prebendary of Canterbury, rector of Adifham, author of *Antiquitates Rutupinæ*, and *Sti Edmundi Burgi*; the former printed 1711, 8vo and the latter Ox. 1745, 4to. He was a great benefactor to this hofpital. His picture hangs in the hall.--The queftion being put, Whether a mafter of the hofpital, upon his collation, ought to compound for firft-fruits; this anfwer was returned. " All " hofpitals, whofe revenues are difpofed to charitable ufes are to be difcharged by " the ftatute; and we fend out no proceffes againft mafters of any hofpital what- " foever, concluding the revenues thereof to be difpofed to pious ufes, and there- " fore you need not trouble yourfelf about compofition for the fame. I am
" Oct. 1, 1688. " Your humble fervant,
" To Dr. BATTELY." " ROBERT URWYN."

[7] Rector of the united parifhes of St. Mary Bredman and St. Andrew, in Canterbury, and vicar of Beakfborne.

[8] Vicar of Hackington, or St. Stephen's, near Canterbury, and one of the fix preachers in that cathedral. He died Auguft 14, 1719, and was buried in the chancel of St. Stephen's church.

1719

1719 16 Dec. 41. JOHN LEWIS [1], M. A.
1746 14 Mar. 42. JOHN SACKETTE [2], M. A.
1753 2 July, 43. HENRY HEATON [3], B. D.
1777 23 Sept. 44. WILLIAM BACKHOUSE [4], D. D.

[1] A learned antiquary, rector of Acryfe 1690, of Hawkinge 1702, vicar of St. John's Margate 1705, rector of Saltwood and Eaftbridge 1706, and vicar of Min-fter in Thanet 1708. See a lift of his numerous works in Mafters's Hiftory of Corpus Chrifti College, Cambridge, Appendix, p. 102. His picture, from which there is a print prefixed to the 2d edition of his " Hiftory of Thanet, 1736," 4to, hangs in the hofpital hall. He died Jan. 16, 1746.

[2] Grandfon to the 36th mafter, minifter of Folkftone, and rector of Hawking, 1699; known as an antiquary, by his letter dated 18 Nov. 1702, giving an account of the chapel in Dover Caftle; as a naturalift, by a paper in the Phil. Tranf. N° 349, on the finking of ground near Folkftone; and as an epigrammift, by his *Lufus Poetici*, in the early volumes of the Gentleman's Magazine. See a farther account of him in Mafters's Hiftory of Corpus Chrifti College, p. 363.

[3] A native of Doncafter in Yorkfhire, admitted of Bene't, or Corpus Chrifti Col-lege, Cambridge, 1730, B. D. 1745, fucceffively fellow and tutor of the college, minifter of St. Benedict, Cambridge, and one of archbifhop Herring's domeftic chaplains, by whom he was collated to the rectory of Ivy Church, and the vicarage of Boughton under the Blean; and his Grace bequeathed to him a prebend of Ely, an option. Mr. Heaton's claffical abilities would have been known only to his pupils and particular friends, had not his connection at college with the prefent earl of Hardwicke and his brothers (to three of whom, and alfo to the prefent earl of Briftol, and his youngeft brother, &c. and " laft " and " leaft," to the writer of this note, he was tutor), induced him to take an active part in the *Athenian Letters*, in which he wrote the fifteen, figned H. His epitaph alfo on his friend Dean Caftle (mafter of the college) in Barley Church does equal credit to his heart and head. He died July 7, 1777, and was buried in his church at Boughton. See an epitaph on him in the Gentleman's Magazine for that year, p. 499.

[4] The prefent worthy mafter, who, after having been many years one of archbifhop Cornwallis's domeftic chaplains, is now alfo, by his Grace's favour, archdeacon of Canterbury 1767, rector of Ickham 1771, and of Deal 1779.

BENEFACTORS to this HOSPITAL.

Thomas Becket, archbishop of Canterbury, was the first founder and endower of this hospital. See p. 301.

A. D. 1200. Hubert, archbishop of Canterbury, gave the tithes of Westgate mill, of a mill and two salt-pits at Herewic; of a windmill in Reculvre, and of a windmill at Westhalimot in Thanet. See p. 302, &c.

1203. William Cocking, citizen of Canterbury, founded the hospital of St. Nicolas and St. Katherine, which was united by Pope Innocent III. to the hospital of Eastbridge; after which he gave all his lands, possessions, and chattels, to the hospital, whom he made his heirs. See p. 304, &c.

Vivian le Mercer, eldest son of Ordnothus the dyer, gave 24 perches of land in Hackington, to Cockin's hospital. See p. 307.

Nicolas, the son of Baldwin, gave 5 acres and a half in Cockering, and about the same time 9 acres more. See p. 307.

William, the son of Henry, gave 62 acres in Hakintune.

Henry de Swoleford gave 5 acres and a rode in Cockering.

1243. Stephen Haringod gave 3 acres in Cockering.

Robert de Cockering gave 3 acres and 13 acres.

Hamo, the son of John de Cockering, gave 5 acrs and a half. See p. 308.

Walter de Kenefield gave 13 acres.

All these lands lie in Cockering.

Hamo de Crevequeur granted the parsonage of Blene, &c. to the hospital, and many pieces of land, and was a most considerable benefactor. See p. 308, &c.

Archbishop Langton confirmed the grant thereof, and annexed the parsonage of Blene to the hospital.

Wlwardus gave the hospital a certain prebend in Blene.

Agnes the daughter of Anferius gave two acres and three roods of land. See p. 309.

Simon

Simon and Peter, the fons of Efterman, gave a wood and a farm. See p. 309.

Richard de Bromfeld gave 6d. rent.

1243. William de Suthfolk gave 17d. ob. rent.

1268. William, the fon of Stephen of Hoth, gave the land called Sheepfield.

1272. Joannes de Fraxino gave 5d. rent.

—— William, the fon of Hamon le Lekel, gave 8 acres of land.

1280. Abida, the daughter of Robert of Hoth, gave two acres and a rod of land.

1289. Robert Scot gave three acres and a half.

1299. Mirabilia, the daughter of John At le Heart, gave two pieces of land.

Avie, the daughter of Ralfe de Balward, gave three acres and a quarter of land in Reyfield.

Cicily, the daughter of Ralfe de Balward, gave an acre and 39 acres of land.

Feugerius, the fon of Simon de la Hocke, gave three acres and a quarter of wood.

Robert Lupus, Robert the fon of Richard Wrotham, and William the fon of Stephen of Hoth, and many others, gave lands and rent.

All thefe lie in the Blean.

1210. Pope Honorius the Third freed the hofpital from paying tithes. See p. 314.

John of Adifham gave two acres and a half. Ibid.

The barons of the port of Romney gave the lands called Guildhall lands in Romney. Ibid.

Chriftiana, the daughter of William Silveftre, gave 3s. 6d. yearly rent out of a meffuage in Canterbury. See p. 315.

1230. Matthew, the fon of William Sunewine, gave 2s. 6d. out of two meffuages lying in Canterbury. See p. 317.

Afcelina, the daughter of Radulphus, the fon of Arnoldus,

E e e   gave

gave certain lands and meſſuages adjoining next unto the hoſpital. See p. 317. Richard, the ſon of Radulphus, joined with
his ſiſter in the ſaid gift.

Richard Calvel gave certain lands and houſes, &c. Ibid.

Gode, the daughter of Wibertus, gave 12d. rent out of a
meſſuage without Weſtgate. Ibid.

Robert Pin and Beatrix his wife gave 2s. a year rent out of a
meſſuage in St. Peter's pariſh. Ibid.

Joannes Chopeloſe gave 3s. rent without Weſtgate. Ibid.

Avice, the widow of Lambert Weyder, gave a meſſuage by
Jury-lane, in All Saints pariſh. See p. 318.

Bruningus the miller, gave 16d. rent out of a meſſuage
without Weſtgate. Ibid.

Hugo Godeſhalt gave certain lands.

Peter, the ſon of Stephen de Dene, gave three meſſuages
nigh the hoſpital.

Wlfrede, the ſon of Elſtrede, gave 2s. rent out of 6 acres
of land at Deeringdale.

Solomon de Tuniford gave 6d. rent.

Adam, the ſon of Wlfred, gave 3s. 1d. rent out of a houſe
without Weſtgate.

John, the ſon of Vivian, gave certain lands in Canterbury.

Aldhiena, the daughter of Thomas, gave 20d. rent in St.
Dunſtan's.

Hugo de Radingate gave a meſſuage without Radingate.

Henry, the ſon of Nicolas, the ſon of Baldwin, gave 18d.
rent out of a meſſuage in St. Mary's pariſh of Northgate.

Thomas Lock gave certain lands in St. Peter's pariſh.

Guido and John, the ſons of Suſan, gave lands in Brumdune.

Gunnora, the daughter of Euſtathius de Merewith, gave 3d.
rent out of three meſſuages nigh unto Eaſtbridge.

Simon, the ſon of William and Adam, of Saxenherth, gave
7 acres of land in Brumdune.

6   Walter,

Walter, the fon of Safford Capellanus, gave 10d. rent out of a meffuage in St. Margaret's parifh. See p. 319.

Arnoldus Aurifaber gave the meffuage over-againft the hofpital. Ibid.

Rogerus Aldermannus gave 2s. rent out of 4 acres of land in Foxmold, &c. He gave alfo 5 acres of land in Foxmold, and two acres over-againft Foxmold. See p. 320.

William, the fon of John Alderman, without Readingate, gave 24s. 8d. ob. rent out of certain meffuages, &c. Ibid.

Henricus de Ofpring gave 26d. rent out of a meffuage in Na_tingdune. Ibid.

Adam Textor de Holeftreet gave 9d. rent.

Michael, the fon of Helie de Blen, gave land in the parifh of St. Nicolas Harbledown. See p. 321.

John, the fon of Roger Chriftmafs, gave the piece of land called Lompette. Ibid.

William de S'to Edmundo, rector of Livingsborn, gave 26 acres of land in Livingsborn, alias Beaksborn. See p. 323.

William de Becc gave 10 acres of land, called Wopping, in Livingsborn, alias Beaksborn. See p. 322.

Walterus, the fon of Eilmery, gave land in Burchentune [Birchington]. See p. 325.

Gilbert de Clare, earl of Gloucefter and Hereford, gave certain lands and rent in Blene, and confirmed the gifts of Elias and Hamo de Blen. Ibid.

1342. Archbifhop Stratford gave laws and ftatutes for the government of the hofpital. See them, p. 329. He alfo united and annexed the parifh church of St. Nicolas Harbledown to the hofpital.

1359. Thomas de Roos de Hamalalk gave the manor of Blene.

1360. Joannes de La Lee, miles, gave 180 acres of land, 6 acres of meadow, and 6 acres of wood, 27s. rent, 9 cocks, and 21 hens.

1355. Adam le Heir gave 200 acres of land and 20s. rent in Herne, Swalclive ¹, Whitftaple, and Chiftelet. See p. 355.

¹ Mifprinted " Watelyve", p. 334.

E e e 2

1360,

1360. Helena atte Park de Hoth gave all her lands, tenements, &c.

1345. Johannes de Mayton, cleric', gave a certain piece of land in Harbeldown.

1362. Simon Iſlip, archbiſhop of Canterbury, founded the chantry, and united the chantry of Beaksborn to the hoſpital.

1363. Bartholomeus de Bourne (de Beakſborn) tranſlated the chantry, which James de Bourn founded in Livingſborn, and endowed to the hoſpital, together with the endowment of the chantry.

1375, Simon Sudbury, archbiſhop, refounded the chantry, and founded the perpetual vicarage of Blean.

William Wittleſey, and Thomas Arundel, archbiſhops, founded the chantry of Harbledown.

King Edward III. gave the chaunge in Canterbury to the hoſpital; and is to be numbered among the benefactors.

Archbiſhops Matthew Parker and John Whitgift may be eſteemed as the greateſt benefactors, and founders, and reſtorers of this hoſpital.

1585. The dean and chapter of Chriſt-church, in Canterbury, did give one ſmall bell, called the Wakerel, to the uſe of the hoſpital, to be hanged up in the chapel, for the calling together the brothers and ſiſters to the appointed ſervice there.

1614. Mr. Nevil, brother to Dr. Nevil, gave 10s. to the poor of this hoſpital.

1615. Dr. Nevil, dean of Chriſt-church, Canterbury, gave 40s. to the poor of this hoſpital.

" There are, without doubt," ſays Mr. Battely, " other bene-
" factions, which have not come to my knowledge."

1648. Mr. Avery Sabin gave ten marks per annum to the ten poor in-brethren and ſiſters, to be paid quarterly.

1660. Archbiſhop William Juxon did contribute bountifully towards the repair of the brothers lodgings next the bridge. The particulars of his benefaction are not recorded.

1676.

1676. Dr. Gilbert Sheldon, archbifhop of Canterbury, contributed towards the repairing of the fifters lodgings: for, as Dr. Parker wrote to his grace William lord archbifhop, "By the help of "your grace's predeceffor's benevolence, I have repaired the houfe."

1688. William Sancroft, lord archbifhop of Canterbury, gave the large Bible, which is now in the chapel, and a large Common Prayer book, for the ufe of the reader in the chapel.

1694. Mrs. Elizabeth Lovejoy gave five pounds per annum to the ten in-brothers and fifters.

1708. The rev. Dr. John Battely, D. D. archdeacon of Canterbury, new-built three of the fifters lodgings, and did feveral other great repairs; and at his death left to the in-brothers and fifters 100l. the intereft of which to be proportioned by Mr. John Bradock and Mr. Somerfcales, vicar of Doddington.

1710. Dr. Thomas Tenifon, archbifhop of Canterbury, gave towards the repair of the bridge belonging to this hofpital, 20l.

1710. The dean and chapter of Chrift Church, Canterbury, for the fame ufe, 10 pounds.

1711. Mrs. Mary Mafters left 5l. per annum to this hofpital, now much reduced. See Hiftory of St. John's Hofpital, pp. 196 and 280.

1719. Mr. John Bradock, mafter of this hofpital, gave 25l. 13s. 4d. for the better payment of the poor people at Lady-day and Michaelmas.

1721. Mr. Matthew Brown, of St. Peter's, Canterbury, Carpenter, by his will, dated Dec. 12, 1717, gave 10s. per annum for ever, to the in-brothers and fifters of this hofpital. See p. 281.

1768. Thomas Hanfon, efquire, late of Crofby-fquare, London, by his laft will and teftament, dated April 30, gave the intereft of 500l. for ever, to the in-brothers and fifters of this hofpital, which being now invefted in the 3 per cent. reduced bank annuities. produced 17l. 10s. per annum. See p. 196.

The

The mafter of the hofpital laid claim to certain tithes of meadows, or paftures, called Cowbrooks, or Cowmedys, in Hakington, &c. The whole of which will appear from this following in-ftrument, which I have tranfcribed out of a book, commonly called, " The Archdeacon's Black Book," fol. 25.

" Univerfis Sancte Matris ecclie filiis ad quos prentes litere five prefens publicum inftrumentum pvenerint five pvenerit. Johannes, permiffione divina, prior ecclie Chrifti Cant' ac reverendiffimi in Chrifto patris ac Dñi Dñi Henrici Dei gratia Cantuar' archiepi, totius Anglie primatis, et apoftolice fedis legati in remotis agentis, vicarius in fpiritualibus generalis, falutem in Domino fempiternam et fidem indubiam prentibus adhiber'. Veftre univerfatis notitie deducimus p prentes, quod orta nuper difcentionis materia in quodam negotio de jure et poffeffione pcipiendi et habendi decimas quafcunque de quibufdam pratis, pafcuis, et pafturis, Cowbrokys alias Cowmedys majori et minori vulgariter nuncapatis, infra fines et limites ecclie parochialis de Hakynton notor' adjacentibus provenientes, moto inter venerabiles et difcretos viros dnum Thomam Burton, magrum five cuftodem hofpitalis beati Thome martyris de Eaftbregge, civit' Cant', ex pte una, et magrum Willum Byngham, clericum, reverendi viri magri Henrici Rumworth, archidiac' Cant' procuratorem fe dicentem, ex pte altera; dictis ptibus coram nobis in quadam capella in honore beate Marie Virginis, infra dictam eccliam Chrifti dedicata, in negotio fupradicto inter eafdem partes ad jura reddend' pro tribunali fedentibus, comperentibus, prefatus Thomas Burton, mager five cuftos hofpitalis fupradicti, fue rbm compitionis et intentionis affectum nobis intimavit, quod ex certis caufis ipfum, ut afferuit, moventibus, etiam pro eo et ex eo quod ipfe probationes legitimas ad proband' jus et poffeffion' de jure aliqum in pceptione decimar' pediciar' p jure fuo et hofpitalis fui pdicti munimine habuit aut habere potuit cuicunque liti ea de caufa materia in pofterum et movende omnino cedere et renunciare voluit, palam, publice, et expreffe. Qui quidam Thomas et mager fupradictus infuper quandam renuntiationem in quadam cedula papiri fcriptam in manu fua tenens fecit et legit publice et expreffe fub forma que fequitur tenore verborum :

" In nomine Dei, Amen. Coram vobis reverendo in Chrifto patre et Dño Dño Johanne pmiffione divina priore ecclie Chrifti Cant' et rev'mi in Chrifto patris et Dñi Dñi Henrici Dei gratia Cant' archiepi totius Anglie primatis et apoftolice fedis legati in remotis agenti vicario in fpiritualibus generali: Ego, Thomas Burton, clericus, magr et cuftos hofpit' beati Thome Martyris de Eftbregge civitatis Cant', dico, allego, et in his fcriptis propono, quod licet orta nuper fuerat quedam difcentionis materia fuper jure et poffeffione pcipiendi et habendi decimas de quibufdam locis et pratis vocatis Cowbrokys, majori et minori, provenientes qualitercunque et pventuras infra fines et limites ecclie parochialis de Hakynton, Cant' diocef', adjacentibus, inter me Thomam Burton, magiftrum five cuftodem hofpit' fupradicti ex pte una, et magrum Willum Bingham, reverendi viri magri Henrici Rumworth, archiepi Cant' pcuratorem generalem, ex pte altera: Ego tamen Thomas Burton, magr maḡr et cuſtos hoſpital' p̄dict', omni juri, titulo, et poſſeſſioni, quod, quem, et quam habui, aut habeo, ın eiſdem decimis aliqualiter vel ad eas ex certis de cauſis me in hac parte moventibus, vi nec metu inductus neque compulſus, ymmo ex mea propria et ſpontanea voluntate pur' liber' ſimpliciter, et abſolute, ex certa mea ſententia renuntio, et ab eıſdem re et verbo totaliter recedo, ipſaſque decimas et poſſeſſionem earundem, quatenus ad me nomine hoſpitalis mei p̄dicti attinent, dimitto in hıs ſcriptis : Nos inſuper Johannes, vicarius iñ ſpiritualibus ſupradictus, volentes prout ad ñrum pertinet officium partibus p̄dictis in p̄miſſis facere juſtitie complementum, et in eodem negotio ex earundem p̄tium petitione procedentes, ex ıpſius dıcti Thome Burton, maḡri et cuſtodis hoſpital' p̄dicti conſenſu expreſſo, p̄ jure reverendi viri dn̄i archidiac' ſupradicti nomine ecclıe parochialis de Hakynton, p̄dict' decimas feni et agiſtament' animalium et alias decimas quaſcunque de pratıs, paſcuis, et paſturis ſupradictis, infra fines et limites dicte ecclıe de Hakynton notor' adjacentibus p̄venientes et p̄venturas p̄cipiend' et habendi ipſas vero decımas ad dıctum d̄num archıdıaconum nōıe ecclıe ſue de Hakynton, p̄tinuiſſe, pertinere, et pertinere debere in futurum p̄nuntiamus et declaramus, dictas etiam decimas lite ſive controverſia inter p̄tes p̄dict' pendente ſequeſtratas et ſub arto ſequeſtro in ſalva cuſtodia ex conſenſu p̄tium p̄dictarum pariter et aſſenſu repoſitas in quorumcunque manibus exiſtant p̄fato d̄no archıdıacono ſive ipſius nōıe p̄curatori ſuo p̄dıcto reſtituendas et deliberandas fere p̄ jure et poſſeſſione ipſius dn̄i archıadıaconi ſupradicti ipſas decimas ſic p̄cipend' et habend' ut p̄fertur decrevimus judicialiter tunc ıb̄m, .que ōıa et ſingula, ad quorum intereſt ſeu intereſſe poterit in futuram volumus notitiam pervenire. In quorum omnium fidem et teſtimonium p̄miſſorum ſigillum quo in ñro utimur officio, unà cum ſigno et ſubſcriptione Adam Body publici autoritate apoſtolicâ notarii et in p̄fato negotio actorum ſcrıbe p̄ſentibus duximus apponendum. Data et acta ſunt hec, prout ſupra ſcribuntur et recitantur, ſub anno Domini milleſimo ccccmo xvIII°, indictione xıı, pontificatus ſanctıſſimi in Chriſto patris et Dn̄i ñri Dn̄ı Martini Dei p̄videntia pape quinti anno ſecundo, menſe Decembrıs dıe decima, in capella ſuperıus recıtata ; p̄ſentibus diſcretis viris Johanne Dennys, domicello, Rogero Rye, et Henrıco Lynde, literatis, et aliis Cant' dioc' teſtıbus, ad p̄miſſa vocatıs ſpecialiter et rogatis.

Et ego Adam Body, clericus Sarū dioceſ', publicus autoritate apoſtolica notarius Cant', p̄miſſıs ōıb' et ſingulis dum ſic ut p̄mittitur ſub anno indıct' pontif' menſ' dıe et loco p̄dıctıs ꜳgebantur et fiebantur, unà cum p̄nominatis teſtıbus p̄ſens interfui, eaque oм̄a et ſingula ſic fieri vidi et audivi, ſcripſi, publicavi et in hanc publıcam formam redegi, ſignoque et nōıe meıs ſoliti et conſueti demandatis p̄efatı dn̄ı vıcariı in ſpiritualibus generalis ſignavi rogatus et requiſitus, in fidem et teſtımonıum p̄miſſıor', et conſtat mıhı in nōrio ſubſcripto de iſtarum; dictıonum " cuıcumque ſuper" in decima et undecima lıneis iſtius inſtrumenti a capite ejuſdem computandıs, quos approbo ego notarius antedictus.

Ex

Ex archivis ecclefiæ Chrifti, Cantuar'. Of Bourn-Chantry.

Omnibus Sanѐe Matris ecclie filiis ad quos p̄fentes littere p̄venerint : Henricus, p̄miffione divina, prior ecclie Chrifti Cant', et ejufdem loci captum, falutem in Chrifto. Litteras venerabilis patris Dm Walteri, Dei gratia, Cant' Archiepi, totius Anglie primatis, non abolitas, non cancellatas, nec in aliquâ fuâ parte vitiatas, infpeximus, tenorem qui fequitur continentes. "Walterus, p̄miffione divina, Cantu., archiepus, totius Anglie pri nas, falutem et pacem in Dño fempiternam. Inftrumentum quoddam litteras five cartam p Jacobum de Burr' confe𝔠t fuper donatione et affignatione te rarm et reddituum ad quandam Cantariam in ecclia B. Petri de Lyvyrgefburn perpetuo conftituendam per eundem Jacobum, quod hujus donationem et affignationem approbemus ac hujus Cantarie conftituend' ñram ñri p ianus auori-tatem et confenfum cum nftant' poftulantium nobis exhibitas, non abolitas, fed omni fufpicione carentes infpeximus, fub eo qui fequitur tenore verborum.

"Univerfis Chrifti fidelibus ad quos p̄fentes litteræ p̄venerint, Jacobus de Burn falutem in Dño. Noverit univerfitas v̄ri quod cum fereniffimus dñus ac rex ñi dns Edwardus, filius Edwardi, Dei gratia, rex Angli, dñus Hibernie, et dux Aquitanie, michi Jacobo p̄ed' concefferit et p cartam fuam regiam Licentiam dederit fpecialem, quod poffim unum meffuagium, certas terras et ei de ei us meus in Lyvengefburn, dare et affignare cuidam capellano divina in ecclia Sti Petri de Lyvynfburn celebraturo, prout in carta regia p̄dicta continetur, cujus tenor talis eft.

"Edw. Dei gratia, rex Anglie, dñus Hibernie, et dux Aquitanie, omnibus ad quos p̄fentes litere p̄venerint falutem : Licet de comuni confilio regni ñri ftatutum fit quod non liceat viris religiofis feu aliis ingredi feodum alicujus ita quod ad manum mortuam deveniat fine licentia ñra et capital' dñi de quo res illa imediate tenetur, p finem tamen quem Jacobus de Burn fecit nobifcum, conceffimus et licentiam dedimus p nobis et heredibus ñris quantum in nobis eft, eidem Jacobo, quod ipfe unum meffuag', vigint' et quatuor acras terre, et fex folidatas, et octo denariatas redditus cum pertinentiis in Lyvyngefburn dare poffit et affignare cuidam capellano divina fingulis diebus in ecclia Sti Petri de Lyvyngefborn, p animabus ipfius Jacobi et Joannis filii Euftathii de Burn, et animabus patrum et matrum et antecefforum et heredum fuorum, et omnium fidelium defunctorum, celebraturo; habend' et tenend' eidem capelino et fuccefforibus fuis capellahis divina fingulis diebus in ecclia p̄dict' p animabus p̄dict' celebratrur' in perpetuum : Et eidem capelino quod ipfe p̄dicta meffuagium, terram, et redditum cum pertinentiis a p̄fato Jacobo recipere poffit, et tenere fibi et fuccefforibus fuis p̄d' in ppetuum, ficut p̄dictum eft, tenore p̄fent' fimiliter licentiam dedimus fpecialem. Nolentes quod p̄dictus Jacobus vel heredes fui, aut p̄dictus capellanus, feu fucceffores fui p̄dicti, ratione ftatuti p̄dicti per nos vel heredes ñros inde occafionentur, moleftentur in aliquo, feu graventur. Salvis tamen capitalibus dñis foedi illius fervitiis inde debitis et confuetis. In cujus rei teftimonium has iras ñras fieri fecimus patentes. Tefte meipfo apud Weftm' 2do die Decembris anno regni ñri feptimo."

Ego Jacobus p̄dictus, Dei nomine invocato, pro falute anime mee et corporis mei et p falute animarum Joannis filii Euftathii de Burn, patrum et matrum, anteceftorum et heredum ñrorum, et omnium fidelium defunctorum, do et affigno uni capellano divina fingulis diebus in ecclia p̄dicta, pro anima mea et animabus no-
minatis

'minatis fuperius celebraturo, unum meffuagium meum quod habeo in Lyvynfburn. Item, 24 acras terre in Lyvynfburn pdicta. Item, fex folidatas et octo denariatas redditus cum pertinentiis, qui redditus exfurgit de talibus locis exiftentibus in Lyvynfburn pnominata, viz. inter meffuag' Nicholai Rauf verfus Weft, et terram heredum Wilti Champeneis verfus Eaft, habend' et tenend' dict' meffuag' cum teriis et redditibus pdictis eidem capeltho et fucceffolibus fuis capeltnis divina fingulis diebus in ecclia pd' p animabus pd' celebratur' in ppetuum; falvis tamen capitalibus dnis feodi illius fervitiis inde debitis et confuetis. Donationem autem et affignationem pdictam factam fub modo et forma fubfcriptis, viz. quod liceat mihi prius donationem et affignationem meam pdict' primum capeltnium ad pmiffa ydoneum, et fic deinceps fucceffores ipfius capellan' quam diu vixero infra menfem a tempore vacationis dno Cant' archiepo qui pro tempore fuerit, loci dyocefano, fede plena, et dnis priori et capitlo Cant', fi fedes Cant' vacare contigerit, pfentare, poft deceffum vero meum volo, quod liceat heredibus meis infra hujus menfem ad ipfam Cantariam, cum eam vacare contigerit, dicto dno archiepo, fede plena, ac ea vacante, ipfis dnis priori et captlo, perfonam ydoneam pfentare; et fi forte contigerit, quod ego pd' Jacobus infra dictum menfem, dum vixero, aut heredes mei poft mortem meam infra menfem hujufmodi fic ut pdiximus non duxerimus pefentare idoneum capeltnum, tunc volo, confentio, ftatuo, et ordino, quod pd' dnus archiepus fede plena, ac pfati dni prior et capitulum fede vacante, ipfam Cantariam conferant capeltno ydoneo, qui fciat, velit, et valeat diebus fingulis, ficut pmittitur, divina in ecclia pd' celebrare illa vice. Ita tamen, quod falva femper fit pdicto Jacobo et heredibus fuis pfentatio dicte Cantarie in forma pdicta. In cujus rei teftimonium figillum meum pfentibus appofui: Hiis teftibus, Hen' de Burn, Joanne de Shelwyngge, Joanne filio Euftathii de Burn, Willo de Hegham, Willo filio fuo, Thoma de Northington, Alano de Nobles, Thoma Pykeril, Radulpho Patrick, Joanne, Willo, Rogero, et Thoma, filiis Thome de Grenehill, Joanne de Walmer, clerico, et aliis."

Nos vero hujufmodi donationem et affignationem, quantum in nobis eft, applicantes ad Cantar' pdict, ut pmittitur, conftruend' nram autoritatem et confenfum tenore pfentium impartimur, jure et dignitate ecclie nire Cant' in omnibus femper falvis. In cujus rei teftimonium figillum noftrum hiis iris apponi fecimus. Dat' apud Northfleet, vj kal. Maii, A. D. M.CCC.XIIII.

Nos autem hujus donationem, affignationem, et approbationem, quantum in nobis eft, ratas habentes pariter et acceptas eas, prout in iris originalibus rationabiliter continentur, tenore pfent' confirmamus: Salvis in oibus juribus dignitatibus privilegiis et libertatibus niris et eccle nire Cant' pd' tam fede plena quàm vacante. In cujus rei teftimonium pfentibus iris figillum nrum duximus apponend': Dat' in capitulo niro fexto die menfis Maii, A. D. fupradicto.

Ex Archivis ecclefie Chrifti Cant'.
Vifitatio hofpitalis per Thomam Priorem, &c.

THOMAS, permiffione divina, prior eccle Chrifti Cant', et ejufdem loci conventus, dilecto nobis in Chrifto 'lhome Chichele Archipo Cant', falutem in Autore falutis. Cum vacant' ecclia antedicta p mortem fmi in Chrifto Patris et Dni Dni Joannis miferacone divina epi Ste Ruffine, S. Ste eccle Romane Cardinalis, Cant' Archiepi, totius Angliæ primatis, et Aplice fedis beati, univerfa ae omnimodo jurifdictio eccle Chrifti pd' que jam dicto fmo Patri ceterifque ejufdem eccle Archiepis ante eum et p tempore exiftentibus ptinuit, nobis p nunc competere dinofcatur. Nofque dicta durante vacatione capitulariter congregati, de firo unanimo confenfu, decrevimus put decreveffimus, ecclam Chrifti antedict' civitatemque atque dioe' Cant' ex caufis rationalibus p tunc animum noftrum ad hoc moventibus p nos noftrofve fakem commiffarios fori vifitandas, eafque tunc actualiter vifitavimus. Atque inter cetera in dicta fira vifitatione compta invenimus ac plenius intelleximus prout meminerimus atque intelleximus, fructus, redditus, pventus, ac emolumenta hofpitalis beate ac gloriofe virginis Marie atque Sti Thome martyris de Eaftbrigge vulgariter nuncupati civitat' Cant' pd', cujus magr feu cuftos ee dinofceris : quod quidem hofpitale p tunc realiter vifitavimus multipliciter decreviffe. Nec non memorati hofpitalis confiderate fundationis tempore, onerumque in ipfa fundatione ae de poft eidem hofpitali ac magris feu cuftodibus ejufdem impofitorum, in pofterumque p ipfum hofpitale, dictive hofpitalis magros feu euftodes fupportandum non mediocriter diminuta, dyrumperata ac minorata exiftere, prout in nonnullis aliis dict' Cantuar' diocef' locis cognovimus, ac in locis dominiifque firis propriis plus fatis expti fumus ; ac infra ambitum five fepta dicti hofpitalis firis oculis p tunc confpeximus domos diverfas. onerofas fupervacuas, defertas, inutiles, atque fuperfluas confiftere, et quas depauperatione et diminutione emolumentorum pdict' ac onerum fupportandorum quantitate ponderatis atque diligenter p nos penfatis plus nocere quàm prodeffe, plus confumere quàm pficere, plenius p tunc cognovimus. Et pfertim duas ex capelle dicti hofpitalis pte auftrali conftitutas et eidem capelle contiguas : Quafque fervatis in hâc parte fingulis de magro fervandas fupfluas, fupvacuas, onerofas, et inutiles tunc p firum decretnm atque fententiam ibm tunc pronunciavimus exiftere. Tibi igitur ut jam dictas domos dicti hofpitalis fupfluas et inutiles demoliri et de reliquiis et refiduis earundem ceteras dicti hofpitalis domos neceffarias reficere, reparare, ac emendare, reliquias ac refidua hujufmodi in ufus dicti hofpitalis neceffarios committere lceat tunc ibm declaravimus, et ex fuper abundanti tenore pfentium plenius declaramus, et fuper pmiffis pte fiendis firas autoritatem et licentiam concedimus fpeciales. In cujus rei teftimonium figillum firum quo utimur ad caufas pfentibus duximus apponend'. Dat' Cant', 4to die menfis Maii. A. D. 1354.

Univerfis Ste matris ecclie filiis ad quos pfens fcriptum pvenerit frater Petrus, rector hofpitalis Sti Thome de Eaftbridge in Cant', falt'. Noverit univerfitas vra me de confeniu fratrum firorum remififfe Creffeo Judeo et heredibus fuis omnes querelas et actiones mihi et fratribus firis contra eum vel fuos competentes occafione domûs

vel

vel fundamenti vel muri quem in parte orientali capite capelle ñre edificavit, ita quod occasione p̄dict' edificii nunquam de cetero ex pte ñra vel successorum ñrorum illi vel heredibus suis aliqua questio movebitur in curia Christianitatis vel seculari : facta autem fuit ista remissio vel quieta clamatio, A. D. 1236, mens' Maii; salvis nobis actionibus ñris, si in posterum contra nos vel domum ñrum deliquerit. Valeat universitas ũra semper in Dño. Interfuerat autem huic remissioni mag̃r Wills penitentiarius, Wills rector de Livyngesborn, &c.

Hoc scriptum ñ tradatur Cresseo Judeo nec heredis' suis, n̄ rector et fratres hospitalis Sti Thome Martyris eos impetierint de muro vel edificiis domus Mainerii ; et si eum super hec impetierit, reddatur ei vel suis ad sui defensionem.

In the beginning of the reign of queen Elizabeth, the land and tenements belonging to the hospital, yea, the very hospital itself, being converted into tenements, were seized upon, and let out by private persons, till archbishop Parker, in the 20th year of her reign, by his pious and prudent care, restored it again to pious and charitable uses; and made new statutes and ordinances for the better government of the same, such as in wisdom he did contrive, being not only suitable to the then times, but also agreeable to the first design of the foundation of the hospital; and to the former statutes of Archbishop Stratford, as far as could be; of which I have transcribed this following copy out of the original, now in my hands.

" UNIVERSIS Sancte Matris eccle filiis, p̄sentes literas inspecturis, visuris, vel audituris, Matheus divinâ p̄videntia Canturiens' Archiep̄s, totius Angliæ primas et metropolitanus, verus et indubitatus patronus hospitalis pauperum de Eastbridge civitatis Cantuarie, salutem in Domino sempiternam.

" Pastoralis officii debitum meritò nos solicitat ut locorum piorum nobis potissime subditorum commoditatibus, his p̄sertim que ad divini cultus augmentum ac miserabilium p̄sonarum sustentationem ptinent, quantum cum Deo possumus, opportune provisionis remedio subveniamus, ut ea que ab initio piè fundata et stabilita, vel temporum mutatione et diuternitate vel rectorum negligentiâ in abusum vergere dinoscuntur, vel in pristinum statum et decorem (quantum convenit) restituantur et restaurentur, vel pro tempore, &c. p̄sentis rerum statûs racōne in melius convertantur, et reformentur.

" Inter alia autem dicti hospitalis patronatus cura nos solicitos reddit eò quod hospitale p̄dict' p quosdam p̄decessores ñros pro receptione nocturna ac aliqua sustentationem pauperum perigrinantium ad dictam civitatem confluentium fundatum,

ac

at dotatum exſtitit, ac nonnullis legibus, ſtatutis, ac ordinationibus ſtabilitum e confirmatum, quorum aliqua p̄ſentibus temporibus minimè conveniunt, alia ve tuſtate et mutatione temporis a priore inſtituto fiunt aliena, nonnulla rectorum ſive mag̃rorum dicti hoſpitalis incuriâ, fraude, ſive negligentia in diſſuetudinem abierunt. Bona etiam (ſicut accepimus) nemora, poſſeſſiones, ac alia jura dicti hoſpitalis de veriſimile dilapidationi et diſſipationi ſubjiciuntur. Et, quod miſerrimum eſt, pauperes juſtis elemoſynis iōm defrauduntur.

" Nos igitur debito officii n̄ri excitati, zeloque charitatis accenſi, ſuper ſtatus dicti hoſpitalis ac ad reformationem dictorum defecuum procedere intendentes, fundationes, ordinationes, dotationes, ſtatuta, ac munimenta dicti hoſpitalis, et p̄ſertim quaſdam ordinationes Johannis Stratford quondam Cantuar' Archiep̄i p̄deceſſoris n̄ri ſub dát' xxiii° die menſis Septemb' A. D. 1342, et tranſlationis dicti patris anno nono, in medium proferri juſſimus, eiſque diligenter ac maturè inſpectis, penſatis, et intellectis, ac cum p̄ſentium rerum ſtatu collatis, interponentes eam autoritatem addendi et detrahendi dict' ordinationibus, eáſque mutandi et corrigendi, que nobis et ſucceſſoribus n̄ris Archiep̄is Cant', in literis dictarum ordinationum reſervata eſt, habito primitus ſuper hoſpital' p̄dict' diligenti tractatu, comunicatione, ac matura deliberatione, ſervatis p̄ nos omnibus de jure in hac parte ſervandis, ad honorem Dei, ppetuam rei memoriam, ac dict' hoſpitalis comodum et utilitatem, ſic duximus ordinandum et ordinamus in hunc, qui ſequitur, modum.

" 'Imprimis, viz. Quod p̄ nos et ſucceſſores n̄ros Cantuar' archiepiſcopos talis vir nominetur et p̄ficiatur talis mag̃er hoſpital' p̄dict', qui pro tempore hujuſmodi admiſſionis fuerit Comiſſarius generalii in civitate Cantuar' p̄ dictum archiep̄um qui pro tempore fuerit nominandus, qui etiam in ſacro presbyteratûs ordine conſtitutus fuerit (niſi aliter ſecum diſpenſatum fuerit) et non diutius iōm mag̃r hoſpitalis p̄dict' ſit, niſi quam fuerit Comiſſarius archiep̄i.

" Et quod infra unum menſem poſtquam dict' hoſpital' adeptus fuerit de ſingulis ipſius hoſpitalis bonis ſigillatim et ſpecificè plenum conficiet' inventorium; cujus veram copiam nobis et ſucceſſoribus n̄ris quàm citò comodè poterit exhibebit, atque ſingulis annis inter feſtum Sancti Michaelis archangeli et duodecimum diem menſis Novembris proximè ſequentis, de adminiſtratione bonorum, fructuum, proventionum, jurium, et reddituum dicti hoſpitalis pro anno finito in feſto Sti Michaelis antedicto nobis et ſucceſſoribus n̄ris, ſeu alicui alteri ad hoc p̄ nos deputato, plenam et diſtinctam racōnem reddat cum requiſitus fuerit.

" Volumus p̄terea quod ad dicti mag̃ri diſpoſitionem et curam ſolicitam fructus, redditus, et proventus, dictique totius hoſpitalis regimen, quàm diu iōm p̄dictus mag̃er fuerit cum moderamine ptineant infra ſcripto; viz. quod ad placitum domini archiep̄o pro tempore exiſtentis manebit et reſidens erit in domo manſionali hoſpitalis p̄dicti, vel in manerio ſuo de Blene vel Hoth Court, et de reddit' et proventionibus terrarum et poſſeſſionum hoſpit' p̄d' p̄cipiet et habebit ſingulis annis ſex hōras, tredecim ſolidos, et quatuor denarios, et xii caractat' boſci de nemoribus ptinentibus manerio ſive firma de Hoth Court.

" Et quamdiu in pace vivitur ſine bello ſingulis diebus Veneris non feriatis horâ nonâ, et ſi feriati fuerint, horâ duodecima p̄ totum anni circulum abſque aliqua omiſſione iōm p̄dictus mag̃r hoſpitalis predicti p̄ ſe vel p̄ legitimum deputatum ſuum triginta pauperibus et maximè indigentibus de civitate Cantuarienſi oriundis vel iōm diu habitantibus in aliquo loco convenienti intra limites hoſpitii pauperum

2   p̄dicti

p̄dicti congregat' ad oftium five in domo hofpitii firi Cantuarienfis, omni carnal affectione femotâ, fupra quo confcientiàm ejus oneramus, triginta denarios dabit' partim habendo refpectum ad commendationem pretoris oppidi Cantua renfis ꝑ tempore exiftentis.

" Hoc tamen obfervatum volumus, quod nullus dictorum triginta pauperum eo tempore fit in altero ñrorum hofpitalium de Harboldown vel Sti Joannis apud Northgate in civitate p̄dict': illos enim (quoniam aliàs ñre eleemofyne ꝑticipes funt) ab ifta diftributione penitùs excludemus.

" Verum-fi tempus inciderit quando bellum gerendum eft, ità quod milites ꝑ civitat' Cantuar' tranfire contigerint, quàm primum hujufmodi bellum publice fuerit denuntiatum dict' diftributio trigiuta denariorum quolibet die Veneris protinus ceffabit quamdiu hujufmodi bellum duraverit, et ad tres menfes poft, et ad fublevandos milites valetudinarios bellove lefos ꝑ dictam civitatem proficifcentes et redeuntes in dicto hofpitali quotidie ad fumam quatuor denariorum pro numero fingulorum dierum in anno de exitibus, redditibus, ꝓventibus, et bonis hofpitalis p̄dicti volumus expendi.

" Sani vero illuc accedentes non habentes de fuo ꝑ noctem unam recipiantur. Valetudinarios autem (modo ne leprofi fint) cum fanis confluentes tam ad moram, quàm ad vite fubfidia juxta eftimationem p̄dictam ꝑcipiendam fanis volumus anteferri. Quod fi dierum aliquo in ufus p̄dictos pauperum militum de exitibus, redditibus, proventionibns, et bonis hofpitalis ipfius, quia nullos vel paucos hujufmodi illuc contigerit declinare ad eftimationem p̄dictam non expendatur ordinamus et volumus quod diebus aliis feu temporibus copiofioris adventus pauperum p̄dict' ibm, quod minus diebus p̄cedentibus effe expenfum, in ampliori receptione fubfidiorumque neceffariorum et miniftratione pauperum hujufmodi juxta modum fuperius annotatum fuppleatur taliter cum effectu ut quotannis tàm pacis quàm belli temporibus in ufu tam pio et laudabili de exitibus, redditibus, proventionibus, et bonis hofpit' p̄dict, ad fumam quatuor denariorum ꝑ quolibet anni tempore die difcretione previa, integraliter et fideliter erogetur.

" Qui in fata ibm decedent in cemiterio ñra Cantuar' ecclie fepeliantur loco ad hoc antiquitus defignato.

" Cautum infuper efto ne dictum hofpitale, quod folummodo in pauperum peregrinorum ufum primitus fundatum eft, oneretur aliquando quod habitationem pauperibus in civitate Cantuar' vel fuburbiis ejufdem degentibus aut illis, qui ꝑ aliquod tempus proximè p̄teritum in eifdem aut intra feptem miliaria a dictâ civitate habitâffe comprobentur.

" In hofpitali autem p̄dict' duodecem lectos competentes cum fuis pertinentibus ordinamus debere perpetuò confiftere ad ufum confluentium pauperum militum hujufmodi, ac mulierem aliquam honefte vite, que quadraginta annorum etatem ad minus excefferit, minifterio hujufmodi pauperum pro eo tempore tam in lectis quàm vite neceffariis, ut p̄mittitur, miniftraturam effe volumus, cui mulieri miniftretur de exitibus, redditibus, proventionibus, et bonis dicti hofpital' prout magro videbitur opportunum.

" Sint p̄terea in dicto hofpitali duo libri, quorum alter fit inftar kalendarii in quo numerus pauperum ibm pernoctantium, eorum valetudo, et pecunie illis erogate affiduè annotentur, quem librum magr exhibebit fingulis annis nobis et fuccefforibus.

cefforibus ñris, unà cum computo ſuo de terris, tenementis, et aliis profictis ad dictum hoſpitale ptinentibus, tempore ſuperius expreſſo et limitato: In altero dies, nienſ', annus, et nomina in hoſpitali, p̃dicto morantium, diligenter inſcribantur.

" Volumus inſuper et ordinamus quod in domo aliqua dicto hoſpital' ſpectant' cuſtodietur ſchola p magrum hoſpitalis p̃dict' p tempore exiſtent' vel aliquem alium ſubſtituend': p eum ad hoc officium idoneum, in quâ ipſe liberè et gratis docebit et inſtruet, ſeu doceri vel inſtrui faciet de tempore in tempus pueros ſupra etatem ſeptem annorum et infra etatem octodecim annorum ad legendum, cantandum, et pulchrè ſcribendum, et p̃ſertim in cantando et ſcribendo dumodo quilibet hujuſmodi puer in ſcholâ p̃dicta ultra quatuor annos non manebit, et quod in ſchola p̃dicta ñ inſtruatur ſeu doceatur ſimul ultra numerum viginti puerorum. Et hoc liberè aut gratis, prout dicto magro hoſpitalis p̃dicti placu' it, et cum ſubſtituto ſuo concordatum fuerit.

" Volumus etiam quod in diebus ferialibus ter quâlibet hebdomadâ omnes pueri p̃dicti precationes in capellâ hoſpitalis p̃dicti altâ voce canendo dicent, vel litaniam vel alias ſolemnes orationes breves juxta ordinationem magri qui pro tempore fuerit.

" Volumus etiam quod poſtquam ſolutio decem librarum p annum Wilhelmi Sworder nuper magri hoſpitalis p̃dict', quam jam ex conceſſione quâdam occupat, legitime ceſſabit, feu determinata fuerit, ex tunc in ppetuum dictus mager dicti hoſpitalis dabit et ſolvet ſupradictis pueris ſufficientia papyrum, calamos, et atramentum, et alios libros maxime congruentes p eorum uſu in ſecello.

" Proviſo quod inſtructor puerorum tam in ſcribendo quam in legendo et cantando p magrum ſemper deputandus ſit collector reddituum dicti hoſpitalis, qui pro tempore ſuo p hujuſmodi collectione p ſingulis annis recipiet xxvj s. viiid. cum una liberatura p magrum illi quotannis donanda tali qualem aliis ſervis ſuis in futurum daturus eſt, et quod recipiet p labore inſtructionis ſue p̃dicte quatuor libras annuatim ſibi ſolvendas.

" Proviſo etiam, quod p̃dict' magr hoſpitalis p̃dicti, ſi ipſe in edibus hoſpital' p̃dict' habitare vel noluerit, vel non poſſit, quod tunc rector eeclie Sti Andree in civitate Cantuarienſ' vel ſubſtitutus ſuus pferatur ad habitationem in eiſdem domibus pro annali redditu xxvis. viiid. et non amplius: modo idoneus ad idem officium inſtructoris puerorum fuerit p magrum hoſpitalis et decanum eccle Cant' qui p tempore fuerit, ſemper examinandus et approbandus.

" Volumus pterea quod ex redditibus annuis hoſpitalis p̃dicti ſolvatur duobus ſcholaſticis in collegio Corporis Chriſti et beate Marie in Cantabrigia inſtruendis, juxta eam firmam que in denturis quibuſdam convenit inter magrum hoſpitalis p̃dicti, et magrum et ſocios collegii p̃dicti, quamdiu terminus annorum hujuſmodi indenture durabit, et eo modo eligantur et pficiantur, quomodo in p̃dictis indenturis exponitur et declaratur.

" Et ne hec ñra ordinatio poſthac veniat in oblivionem, vel negligatur, quin ſemper temporibus futuris ſumma ſex librarum et decem ſolidorum ad uſus pauperum tam pacis quam belli tempore quotannis expendatur, et quod oibus expenſis et receptis rite computatis, tam p oneribus ſupra dictis, quam p reparationibus dicti hoſpitalis et aliis rebus eidem ptinentibus, quod reſiduum fuerit ſemper inter
pauperes

pauperes diftribuatur, ita ut diftributio eorum vel augeri vel diminui poffit, juxta eftimationem bonorum pvenientium hofpitalis pdicti.

" Volumus etiam quod magr dicti hofpitalis qui pro tempore fuerit p fe vel p alium fingulis annis uno aliquo die dominico inter feftum Omnium Sanctorum et feftum Natalis Domini ante diftributionem pauperibus erogandam clare et diftincte pronunciabit Anglice hanc nram ordinationem incipiendo ab eo loco, *Volumus præterea quod ad dicti magiftri difpofitionem et curam follicitam fructus*, &c.—legendo ad iftam ufque claufulam, *Volumus etiam quod magifter*, &c.

"· Et ad ordinationem pfentem in fingulis fuis articulis, prout eft poffibile, fideliter obfervandam, et quatenus in eo eft facere fieri obfervandam, nec non de corrodiis, penfionibus, terris, poffeffionibus, nemoribus, aut bonis mobilibus, immobilibus, feu juribus ipfius hofpital' non vendendis, concedendis in ppetuum, vel ad tempus donandis vel ad firmam dimittendis et locandis, vel alio quovis alienationis titulo non alienandis, nobis et fucceffioribus nris archiepis Cantuar' inconfultis et non confentientibus ad hoc expreffe p fcriptum nrum hoc teftan' p quofcunque magros hofpitalis pdict' quibus ejus regimen comittetur, in pofterum volumus et ordinamus in comiffionibus fingulis de ipfo faciendis eifdem corporale ad fanctum Dei Evangelium preftari juramentum.

" Provifo femper, quod fi magis expediens videbitur Archiepo qui pro tempore fuerit, ut fuffraganeus ejus ad idem hofpitale promoveatur, quod tunc ex eo cafu ipfe fuffraganeus pferatur omnibus aliis ad ejufdem hofpitalis pfecturam, cum conditionibus fupradictis, etiamfi comiffarius qui p. tempore fuerit habeat firmam manerii de Blene et Hothe Courte ad comodum et ufum fuum. Comiffionem autem hofpitalis pdict' fi facta fuerit alteri quam fuffragraneo vel comiffario qui p'tempore fuerit, vel pdicto non exacto feu pftito juramento, fore volumus ipfo jure irritam et inanem.

" Refervata nobis et fucceffioribus nris archiepis Cantuar' hujufmodi ordinationi nre addendi, detrahendi, eamque mutandi et corrigendi, prout expedire videbitur, plenaria poteftate.

" Actum et datum in manerio nro de Lambhith vicefimo menfis Maii, A. D. 1569, et noftre confecrationis, a. xe.

MATTHEUS Cantuar".

Thefe Ordinations and Statutes were contrived to agree, as far as might be, with the original foundation of the hofpital, and with the former ftatutes made by Archbifhop Stratford, as will appear by the following particulars, in which they are compared together.

STRATFORD.	PARKER.
Et fi votivus nr invalefcat affectus, decus et comodum locorum ad miferabilium pfonarum et pauperum receptionem et	Paftoralis officii debitum merito nos follicitat ut locorum priorum nobis potiffime fubditorum comoditatibus his pfertim

STRATFORD.

fuſtentationem divinique cultus augmentum providè deputatorum nobis potiſſimè ſubditorum quatenus poſſumus p curare: Tamen conſervatio et relevamen neceſſarium hoſpit' de Eaſtbridge p beatum et glorioſum martyrem fundati antiquitus et dotati—pro pauperum peregrinorum Cantuar' confluentium receptione noſturnâ, et ſuſtentatione aliquali.

— p ipſius hoſpitalis incuriam magrorum, qui nemora ejus proſternunt, eaque et alia jura, poſſeſſiones, et bona illius tam mobilia quam immobilia variis alienari modis temere pſumunt—in domibus etiam ſuis deformitates evidentes in tantum patitur et ruinas—
— peregrinos admittere non valebit—
—Nos ad ppetuam rei memoriam ſuper his certos modum et formam in hoſpit' pd' in perpetuum obſervandos edere ſeu conſtituere duximus, et taliter ordinamus, viz.

Quod in ipſo hoſp' p nos et ſucceſſores ñros archiep' Cant' pſonatur ſeu pficiatur talis magr, qui tempore, quò ponetur ſeu pficietur eidem, ſit in ſacerdotali ordine conſtitutus.

Magrum etiam quemlibet hujuſmodi cum ipſum hoſp' primo adeptus fuerit intra menſem ſeq' prox' de ipſius hoſp' bonis ſingulis ſigillatim et ſpecifice inventarium plenum conficere, ipſiuſque copiam infra menſem eundem tradere.—

Annis ſingulis inter Sti Mich' et Omnium Sanctorum feſta de adminiſtratione ſuâ reddere plenam et diſtinctam volumus rationem.

PARKER.

pſertim que ad divini cultus augmentum ac miſerabilum pſonarum ſuſtentationem pinent, quantò cum Deo poſſumus opportuno proviſionis remedio ſubveniamus, ut ea que ab initio piè fundata vel ſtabilita.—

Inter alias autem hoſpit' patronatus cura nos ſolicitos reddit—
—pro receptione nocturna et aliqua ſuſtentatione pauperum peregrinantium ad dictam civitatem confluentium fundatum.

—Bona etiam, ſicut accepimus, nemora, poſſeſſiones, ac alia jura dicti hoſpitalis de veriſimile dilapidationi et diſſipationi ſubjiciuntur—
—et, quod miſerrimum eſt, pauperes juſtis elemoſinis ibm defraudantur.

—Ad perpetuam rei memoriam, ac dicti hoſpitalis commodum et utilitatem, ſic duximus ordinand', et ordinamus, in hunc qui ſequitur modum, viz.

Quod per nos vel ſucceſſores ñros Cantuar' archiepos vir nominetur et pficiatur futurus magr hoſp' pd', qui p tempore hujuſmodi admiſſionis—in ſacro presbyteratus ordine conſtitutus fuerit.

Et quod infra unum menſem poſtquam dictum hoſp' de ſingulis ipſius hoſp' bonis ſigillatim et ſpecifice plenum conficiet inventarium, cujus veram copiam, quam cito commode poterit, exhibebit.

Atque ſingulis annis intra feſtum Sti Mich' Archi, et 12 diem Novembr' proxime ſeq' de adminiſtratione bonorum, fructuum, proventionum, jurium et reddit' dict' hoſp' p anno finito in feſto Sti Mich' antedicto, nobis et ſucceſſ' ñris, ſeu alicui alteri ad hoc per nos deputato, plenam et diſtinctam raconem reddat, cum requiſitus fuerit.

Ordi-

Ordinamus p̄terea quod ad dicti magri difpofitionem et curam folicitam, fructus, redditus, et proventus, dictique totius hofp' regimen pertineant, cum moderamine infra fcripto in peregrinorum ufus, ad ipforum vite fubfidium, diebus fingulis ad 4 denarium eftimationem de bonis hofp' p̄dict' volumus expendi.

In fata decedentes ibm in cemiterio ñre Cantuar' eccle fepeliantur in loco ad hoc antiquitus fignato.

Sani peregrini pauperes accedentes ibm p noctem unam recipiantur, duntaxat p peregrinos valetudinarios pauperes illuc confluentes cum fanis tam ad moram quàm ad vite fubfidia in eftimationem p̄dictam pcipienda fanis anteferri volumus.

Quod fi dierum aliquo in ufus p̄dict' peregrinorum de bonis hofp', &c. verbatim.

In hofpit' autem p̄dicto 12 lectos competentes ordinamus.

Ac mulierem aliquam honefte vite, &c. verbatim.

Et ad ordinationem p̄fentem in fingulis fuis pticulis, &c. verbatim.

Refervata nobis, &c. verbatim.

Volumus etiam quod ad dicti magri difpofitionem et curam folicitam, fructus, redditus, et proventus, dictique totius hofp' regimen pertineant, cum moderamine infra fcripto ad fublevandos milites valetudinarios bellove lefos p dictam civitatem proficifcentes, vel redeuntes, ad fummam 4d. p numero fingulorum dierum in anno.

Qui in fata ibm decedent in cemiterio ñre eccle Cant' fepeliantur in loco ad hoc antiquitus fignato.

Sani illuc accedentes, ñ habentes de fuo, p noctem recipiantur unam, valetudinarios autem, modo ne leprofi fint, cum fanis confluentes tam ad moram quàm ad vite fubfidia juxta eftimationem p̄dictam fanis volumus anteferri.

Quod fi dierum aliquo in ufus p̄dict' pauperum militum de bonis hofp', &c. verbatim.

In hofp' p̄d' 12 lectos competentes, &c. verbatim.

Ac mulierem aliquam honefte vite, verbatim.

Et ordinationem p̄fentem in fingulis fuis articulis, &c. verbatim.

Refervata nobis, &c. verbatim.

Inftead of " poor pilgrims," Archbifhop Parker provides for " poor and maimed foldiers, that fhould pafs forward and back- " ward through Canterbury;" after the fame manner in which pilgrims were provided for; which was a fit and feafonable alteration; becaufe now pilgrims ceafed to refort hither; but the frequent wars between England and France caufed frequent marches of foldiers to pafs through the city.

Some

Some brief Remarks upon the Statutes and Ordinances
of Archbifhop Parker.

1. He had a particular regard to the intention of the founder
of this hofpital, and in correfpondence thereunto he appointed
4d. a day, for every day of the year, to be expended in the
lodging and entertaining of poor, fick, and maimed foldiers,
inftead of poor pilgrims; and in thofe times there were frequent
marches of foldiers through Canterbury, by reafon of the wars
between England and France.   But becaufe wars fometimes
ceafe, and in times of peace fuch objeᵈts of charity feem more
rare, and thereby, for want of fick foldiers to be relieved, the
money raifed by the hofpital-rents might be employed poffibly
to private ufes, and the charity defigned thereby might be altogether perverted; he prevents this by appointing in times of
peace 30d. to be paid every week to 30 poor people at the hofpital-door on Fridays, at nine in the morning, if it be no
holyday, and at twelve, if it be a holyday; the reafon was,
that the poor might not wait for alms at the hofpital-door at
fuch hours as prayers were celebrated in the cathedral church [1].

He appoints alfo xii beds, to be maintained in the hofpital
for the convenience of fuch poor or fick foldiers as fhould refort thither; and an aged woman, of honeft report, to look
after the beds, and to provide neceffaries for the poor and fick
that fhould lodge in them.

2. He had a fingular regard to the quality of the mafter
who fhould prefide in the hofpital, and be intrufted with a faithful difpenfation of fo great charities as this hofpital did afford;
he muft be one ordained in the holy priefthood; he muft be a
prieft of great note and dignity, either the commiffary-general,
or the lord bifhop fuffragan for the time being; he muft, at his
admiffion, take an oath for a faithful difcharge of his office

---

[1] By this it appears, that in queen Elizabeth's reign divine fervice was performed in the
cathedral on holydays only.

in

in governing the faid hofpital; he muft make and deliver a perfect inventory of all the goods belonging to the hofpital; and he muft once a year (if it be required of him) pafs his accompts concerning his faithful adminiftration of his truft.

3. That the goods and rents of the hofpital may feem at the mafter's own pleafure, he is limited by the ftatutes to a certain falary; namely, 6l. 13s. 4d. which is properly his own; and he cannot honeftly take to himfelf any more of the hofpital rents to his own private ufe : only, befides this fum, he is allowed 12 loads of wood, a fmall and poor falary for the undertaking fo great an office! fo that the mafter by this fmall falary fhews, that he undertakes the care and trouble of this hofpital more for charity-fake than for the fake of gain and profit to himfelf.

4. For fuch as die in the hofpital, he confirms the grant of being buried in the church-yard belonging to the cathedral, as of old before was granted unto them.

5. He appoints two books, in one of which were regiftered the number, names, &c. of fuch as fhould lodge within the hofpital, at the charge of the hofpital. In the other, the day, month, year, and names of thofe that die in the hofpital were to be regiftered.

6. Becaufe ignorance had univerfally overfpread the face of the world, for the promoting of learning and knowledge, he appointed a fchool to be kept in the faid hofpital, wherein 20 poor children were to be taught to read, fing, and write, gratis, and to be furnifhed with books, pens, ink, and paper accordingly, at the charge of the hofpital; and he appoints a competent falary for the teacher of the faid children.

7. He enjoins thrice a week prayers to be faid in the chapel of the hofpital; and the children to be prefent at the fame, and to fing the prayers with a loud voice.

8. He appoints exhibitions for two fcholars in Bene't College,

in Cambridge, to be paid out of the hofpital revenues towards the maintaining of them in the univerfity.

9. After all thefe payments and charges, as alfo the charges of reparations and other neceffary expences, the remainder of the money, which fhould arife from the hofpital-rents, was to be diftributed among poor people, be it more or lefs.

10. That he fhould once a year read thefe ftatutes publickly, and with a loud voice, in prefence of the poor people that meet together to take the alms.

11. The mafter was not to make leafes of the lands, &c. without the confent of the Archbifhop for the time being.

12. He referved a power to himfelf and his fucceffors, to alter, amend, diminifh, or increafe thefe ftatutes, as he or they fhould fee fit.

Dr. Lawfe's [1] opinion concerning the burying of the poor brethren and fifters that dye in the hofpital of Eaftbridge, in the city of Canterbury.

" The words of the ordinance of Archbifhop Stratford, made anno 1342, and confirmed by the prior and convent the fame day and year, are thefe :

" Peregrini fiquidem valetudinarii pauperes quos arripit infirmitas in fue peregrinaconis itinere, non leprofi, in hofpitali fufcipiantur eodem : et in fata decedentes ibm in cemiterio ñre Cantuar' eccla fepeliantur in loco ad hoc antiquitus affignato."

" The words of my lord's grace of Canterbury his ordinance that now is, and confirmed by act of parliament, anno Elizabethe nunc regine 27°, are thefe :

" Alfo it is ordered, that if any of the in-brethren or fifters, mafter or fchoolmafter aforefaid, fhall fortune to dye there, then the perfon fo deceafing fhall and may be buried within the church-yard of Chrift, in Canterbury, according to a former agreement made between the Archbifhop, his predeceffor, and the prior and convent of the faid church.' faid

" The place is well known to divers now belonging to the church, and the hofpital poor have by your confent been buried,

_____

[1] The 31ft mafter. See p. 373.

ever

ever fithence the faid act of parliament; and touching the altering of the ftate of the church and hofpital, fithence the prior and convent there, I take it that all interefts and rights in this behalfe have been referved from time to time.

" THOMAS LAWSE."

Queen ELIZABTH fent her writ to certain commiffioners, to enquire into the ftate of the hofpital of Eaftbridge; which commiffioners made the following return :

" 1. Imprimis, Quod reverendiffimus pater et dominus, dominus Thomas Becket, hofpitale de Eaftbrydge, in civitate Cant', inftituit et fundavit ,p receptione pauperum peregrinantium ad Cantuariam confluentium.

" 2. Item, Quod deinde dominus Joannes Stratford, olim Cantuar' archiepus, xxiii° die menfis Septembris, A. D. 1342, fuper difpofitionem bonorum dicti hofpitalis inter alia conftituit, et ordinavit, prout fequitur, viz.

" 3. Quod in dicto hofpitali effent 12 lecti competentes cum ptinentiis ,p receptione pauperum peregrinantium et illuc confluentium, tam fanorum quam valetudinariorum ppetuo confiftentes.

" 4. Item, Quod de et ex bonis hofpitalis juxta eftimationem 4 denariorum ,p numero fingulorum dierum in anno in ufus pauperum fuorum neceffarios ·viteque fubfidia quotannis impenderetur et erogeretur.

" 5. Item, Quod in dicto hofpitali effet ppetuo mulier quedam etatis quadraginta annorum vel fupra, que de bonis ejufdem hofpitalis in fingulis vite fue neceffariis victum et amictum haberet, comperietur ; dictis lectis et pauperibus miniftratura femper intendens.

" 6. Item, Quod pdicta omnia et fingula eodem anno primo regni domine fire Elizabethe regine in brevi ejufdem domine regine mentionata, anteaque et retro a die ordinationis pdicta ufque ad et in vicefimum diem Maii, 1569, p fingulos annos fideliter pimpleta, obfervata, et cuftodita fuerunt.

" 7. Item, Quod de nominibus et cognominibus dictorum pauperum in quorum gratiam pecunie pdicte impendebantur, non conftat pro eo quod nulla ordinatione feu fundatione, ut pfervantur, vel regiftro cuftodirentur, cautum erat.

" 8. Item, Quod poftea, viz vigefimo die Maii, 1569, reverendiffimus pater et dominus, dominus Mattheus providentia divina nunc Cantuar' archiepus, ex certis rationibus animum fuum moventibus, cum confenfu capli eccle Chrifti Cant' ordinacionem pdictam mutavit, et de et fuper difpofitionem bonorum ejufdem hofpitalis ftatuit et ordinavit, prout fequitur.

" 9. Imprimis, viz. Quod tempore pacis fingulis diebus Vereris, cujuflbet anni, triginta pauperibus infra civitat' Cantuar' habitantibus, et maxime indigentibus de et ex bonis ejufdem hofpitalis erogetur et diftribuatur in foribus ejufdem 30 denarii.

" 10 Item,

" 10. Item, Quod in eodem hofpitali fint 12 lecti cum ptinentiis ppetuo confiftentes ad ufum et p̃ recepcione militum valetudinariorum tempore belli.

" 11. Item, Quod tempore belli fum̃a predict' 30 denariorum in ufum hujufmodi
militum illuc confluentium p̃ fingulas feptimanas expendatur.

" 12 Item, Quod in eodem hofpitali 20 pueri fupra etatem 7 annorum et infra
etatem 18 annorum ad legendum, cantandum, et pulchrè fcribendum gratis ppetuo
educeantur.

" 13. Quod de redditibus dicti hofpitalis folvatur duobus fcholafticis in collegio
Corp' Chrifti et Marie in Cantabrigia quotannis libre xiii et iiii denarii.

" 14. Item, Quod hec omnia et fingula a dicto vicefimo die Maii, una cum
aliis in dicta ordinatione penes magiv̄m ibm remanend', contentis, fideliter quotannis pimpletis, obfervata et cuftodita fuerunt et funt in p̃fenti.

" In cujus rei teftimonium, &c."

By this laft claufe it appears that this return was made in favour of the hofpital, and probably by the direction of Archbifhop Parker, who in them is called " nunc Archiep'us."

Archbifhop Parker, befides his care of preferving and -
ftoring the hofpital and the revenues thereof to pious and charitable ufes, did not only make wife and good ftatutes for the
well government thereof, but alfo he himfelf for feveral years
took the accounts of the hofpital, ordered the laying out of
money for the neceffary reparation of the edifices and tenements
which belong to it, and paid the receiver of the rents, June
16, 1569 (in which year he made the new ftatutes for the
government of the hofpital) the fum of 10l. 17s. 4d. which,
as far as I can difcern from the faid accounts, feems to be a free
gift out of his own pocket. The words are thefe.;

" Received of my Lord's Grace, June 16, 1569, the fum of 10l. 17s. 4d."

He alfo received of the mafter of the hofpital, and paid to
Bene't College in Cambridge, the yearly penfion for two fcholars,
as appears from feveral acquittances under his own hand. Hence
it appears that he took a particular and fingular care for the
benefit of the poor to be relieved by the hofpital.

No fooner was archbifhop Parker dead, than this hofpital, with
its revenues, was immediately feized upon, and became a prey
to

to one John Farneham, one of her majefty's gentlemen-penfioners, to whom the queen gave it in fee-farm upon confideration of fervices : The method was this ;

Anno R. R. Eliz. 17. Notwithftanding the favourable return of the former writ, and good accompt certified thereby concerning the hofpital, that all popifh and fuperftitious ufages were abolifhed, that great and excellent charities were duly obferved and performed by relieving the poor and needy, by teaching of young children, and maintaining two fcholars in the univerfity, and the like ; yet a new commiffion was now granted to Sir James Hales, Sir George Hart, knights, Mr. Wotton, and others, to enquire and certify the eftate of Eaftbridge hofpital in Canterbury, who accordingly certified into her Majefty's court of Exchequer,

" That the fame hofpital-houfe ftood then ruinated, and neyther mafter nor
" brethren were regynt or dwelling of long time : the houfe let out into
" tenements for yearly rent : the beds, that were there wont to lodge and
" harbour poor people reforting thither, were gone and fold, contrary to the
" old order and foundation of the fame : and the faid hofpital to be re-
" linquifhed and concealed from her majefty, &c."

Whereupon, by her letters patent under the great feal, dated July 20, A. R. R. Eliz. 18, fhe gave the faid hofpital to the faid John Farneham.

John Farnham did not long keep poffeffion of the hofpital ; but fold and conveyed her majefty's faid gift thereof, in as large and ample manner and form as her highnefs had given and granted the fame, unto one G. Hayes, in confideration of money owing to him the faid G. Hayes from the faid J. Farneham, and more paying in hand, to the value of 550 l. ; and for fome time it remained in his poffeffion.

2.

For proof of her majesty's title to difpofe of the hofpital and the revenues belonging thereunto, this was pretended.

" The faid hofpital was founded a corporation of mafter and brethren, for the maintaining of " pauperum peregrinorum illuc " confluentium," with lodging, fire, bread, and drink, for a night, two or three, wherein were maintained in the faid hof-pital-houfe viij beds, furnifhed, in one chamber, for men, and iiij beds in another chamber for women ; all which beds, at the time of the vifitation of the faid commiffioners, were fold and gone; and no hofpitality or relief for the poor, neither mafter nor brethren there recyent or dwelling, &c."

" To prove the faid corporation, the governors of the faid hofpital have been, time out of mind, incorporated by the name of " Mafter and Brethren ;" and were fo accepted, re-puted, known and taken, from time to time ; and were fued, charged, and diftreined by that name ; and under and by that name of " Mafter and Brethren," all their lands were purchafed, given, and taken : And all their licenfes of mortmain were fued out under and upon that name, as may appear by divers records, as enfueth ; the copies whereof are extant, under the officers hands, to be feen.

" p donacõnem certarum terrarum quas Hamo de Blene, Ricardus Creviquer, et alii dederunt magro et fratribus hofpit' pdict', ut patet de recordo in anno 17 Edw' IIdi.

" p donationem quam Adam Eyer fecit de certis terr' magro et fratribus hofpit' pd', ut patet de recordo anno 29 Edw' III.

" p donacõnem quam archiepus Stratford fecit de rectoria de Harbaldown magro et fratribus hofpit' pd', ut de recordo anno 17 Edw' tertii."

The faid archbifhop in his ordinances inhibits them to have a common feal [1] from thenceforth ; which argueth they were a corporation, and had a common feal.

[1] This common feal having been loft or purloined, the prefent mafter, Mr. Archdeacon Backhoufe, has lately, at his own expence, fupplied the hofpital with another.

" Item

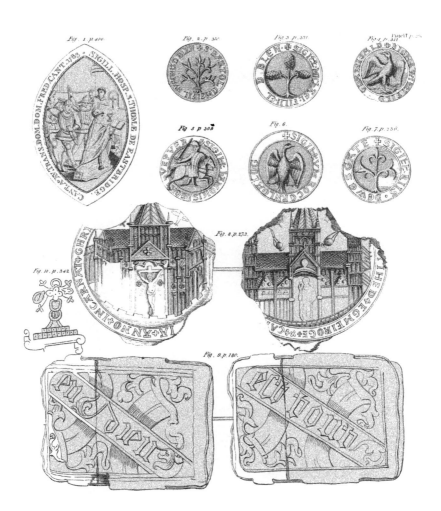

Fig. 1 p. 400.

Fig. 2. p. 311.

Fig. 3. p. 371.

Plate II p. 270.
Fig. 4. p. 311.

SIGILL. HOSP. S. THOME. DE EASTBRIDGE. CANT. A. TRANS. DOM. FRED. CANT. 1782.

Fig. 5 p. 308.

Fig. 6.

Fig. 7. p. 256.

Fig. 8. p. 273.

Fig. 10. p. 342.

Fig. 9. p. 180.

" Item, They were fued, charged, and diftrayned by the name of Mafter and Brethren, *ut patet de recordo*, anno xii Ric. IIdi.

" Item, They were licenfed and protected by the king, by the name of Mafter and Brethren, *ut de recordo*, *in anno* 17 Edw' IIdi.

" Item, They had a common feal fince the inhibition of Arch-bifhop Stratford's ordinance, as may appear by an old deed, dated in A. D. 1474.

" The queftion hence is this, —Whether is the faid cor-poration diffolved or not? viz. at the time of the certificate of her faid Majefty's' commiffioners, when there was neither mafter or brethren there recyent or dwelling; but the hofpital-houfe let out into tenements for yearly rent, as aforefaid?

" If the corporation be then diffolved, whether the queen's Majefty have not title to the lands given to the body incorporate, as well by efcheat, relinquifhment, or otherwife, by the ftatutes of the realm?"

This was the argument in law ufed and urged in behalf of Mr. Hayes, to maintain his titles to the faid lands by the grant of queen Elizabeth; which argument may be thus anfwered.

The hofpital was not founded a corporation of mafter and brethren, as is afferted; but a fpittle under the government of a mafter, who was to relieve poor pilgrims reforting thither, out of the revenues of the faid hofpital, &c.

" All the beds, at the time of the vifitation of the commif-fioners, were fold and gone." This might be true; and yet no argument of the diffolution of the government thereof; but only of the male adminiftration of the fame: it does not prove that there was no mafter, but rather that there was a bad mafter, who fold and made wafte of the hofpital goods; and it feems ftrange, that no fooner was archbifhop Parker dead, who took

H h h   a fpecial

a fpecial care of the hofpital, but immediately it is certified, that the beds were fold and gone, and no hofpitality or relief was given to the poor.

"Neyther mafter nor brethren there recyent or dwelling."

The non-refidence of the mafter doth not argue that he did relinquifh or abdicate his charge; but only that he was defective in his duty, fo far as concerned refidence. He was ftill mafter, and was then mafter.

No ordinance required the refidence of brethren; for refident brethren were contrary to the foundation and ordinances of the hofpital, which was built and endowed for the entertainment of ftrangers and travellers, not permanent, but of tranfient brethren; and not of brethren only, but of brethren and fifters.

His proof of the corporation:

"That the governors of the hofpital have been time out of mind incorporated by the name of Mafter, and were fo accepted, reputed, known, and taken, from time to time, &c. of which he brings particular inftances; as by and under that name of Mafter and Brethren all their lands were purchafed, given, and taken."

Anfwer to this:

It is a great miftake; for under the name of Mafter and Brethren, a very fmall portion of their lands were given; for the name and title varied according to the particular fancies of the donors and benefactors; of which take inftances.

The firft charter of archbifhop Hubert is, "Hofpitali S'ti "Thome de Eftbrug:" and he calls the inhabitants or governors "Fratres hofpitalis" [S. Thome.]   See p. 303.

The bulls of pope Innocent and Honorius are directed "Rec-"tori et fratribus hofp' &c."   See pp. 305, and 314.

The

The charter of William Cokyn makes heirs to all his estate,
" Dominum nostrum Jesum Christum, et membra ejus, viz.
" pauperes et infirmos fratres hospit' S'ti Nicholai, S'te Katherine,
" et S'ti Thome Martyris de Eastbrig." See p. 306.

Most of the charters, or grants, of lands before the union of this
hospital with Cokyn's hospital, were directed " Procuratori
" hosp' S'ti Nicolai confessoris et S'te Catherine virginis, et fra-
" tribus et sororibus hospit' S'ti Thome, &c." See p. 307.

Guildhall land in Romney was given " Deo, et beate Marie,
" et hospit' beate Thome, et fratribus ib'm Deo servientibus, &c."
See p. 315.

In brief, the grants are, " Custodi, rectori, magistro hosp' ;"
sometimes, " hospital' domui hospit'," sometimes, " fratribus,"
sometimes, " fratribus et sororibus," sometimes, " rectori, fra-
" tribus et sororibus, &c." After this manner they vary.

The licences of mortmain were sued out under and upon that
name, viz. " Master and Brethren."

The letters of king Edward I. anno 7, recite Cokyng's gift
as above mentioned ; and the gift of Hamo Creveceur, " Rectori
" et fratribus," and the gift of William de Becco, " Magistro et
" fratribus ;" and the gift of Ralphe the son of Arnold the dyer,
" fratribus et sororibus hospit'." All these varieties are in the
same letters patent.

The donation of Adam le Heir was not " Magistro et fratribus,"
but " Thome Wolton, magistro sive custodi hospit', &c. et succes-
" soribus suis, magistris sive custodibus hosp' pred'." See p. 334.

The donation of archbishop Stratford was, " Domino Rogero
" de Rondes, magistro hospit' pauperum, &c. successoribus suis,"
without any mention of the brethren. See p. 328.

King Edward III. gave *La Chaunge*, " Domino Thome Newe,
" magistro hospit', ad terminum vite sue, et post mortem suam
" successoribus ipsius, magistris hospit' pred', &c." See p. 343.

Licence

Licence of mortmain fued out by William atte Well, was to grant land, " Magiftro hofpit' et fuccefforibus fuis."

Johannes de Le See gave " Magiftro et fuccefforibus fuis. " magiftris hofpit,' &c." This may fuffice to anfwer all his particulars.

The feal, which is objected, was a feal ufed by the mafter of the hofpital, and was called " Sigillum —— Magiftri hofpitalis " de Eaftbridge."

But archbifhop Whitgift put a ftop to the objections of the learned lawyer, and reftored the hofpital to its revenues again, by procuring an act of parliament, and by making new ftatutes and ordinances for the better government of the fame, and by fixing of it in the fame ftate in which it remains to this day, being a lafting monument of his piety, prudence, and exceeding great charity.

The Copy of the ordinance he made, here followeth :

An Ordinance of the moft Reverend Father in God John Whitgift, Archbifhop of Canterbury, Primate and Metropolitan of all England, touching the Hofpital of Eaftbridge, in Canterbury, and the government of the fame, made July 20, 1584.

" Whereas the hofpital of Eaftbridge in Canterbury, before the time of memory of man, was founded and endowed by fome of the predeceffors of the now archbifhop of Canterbury, patrons of the fame, for one mafter and his fucceffors, which mafter hath been alway fince of the collation of the archbifhop of Canterbury for the time being, and inftituted and inducted into the fame, and for the relief of brethren not permanent, but wandering and wayfaring, by reafon whereof eyther the profits of the lands have been often detained in the mafter's hands, for that fome fuch have come thither, or elfe in the time of pilgrimage or wars the houfe hath been furcharged; and for that John Stratford, fometime archbifhop of Canterbury, and divers others his fucceffors, have, from time to time, by their ordinances in writing, referved to themfelves and their fucceffors power and authority to change the orders and foundation of the faid hofpital, and have often changed the fame:"

" Now,

"Now, for the better government of the said hospital, and for rhe greater relief of the poor inhabiting within the city of Canterbury, and the suburbs of the said city; and to the end that a number of certain persons may be provided for, and the state and right of the present master not impugned, nor much impaired, and the interest of the present leases of the lands of the said hospital, which are to have continuance not above the term of 21 years from the date hereof, to them and every of them, saved.

"It is by the said most reverend Father in God John Whitgift, now Archbishop of Canterbury, primate and metropolitan of all England, patron of the said hospital, ordered and decreed as followeth; that is to say,

"That the said archbishop and his successors, from time to time, so oft as the mastership of the said hospital shall be void, as patron thereof, shall or may collate upon a sufficient man (being within holy orders) the mastership of the said hospital, who shall be instituted and inducted as hath been accustomed, and shall have a convenient lodging in the said hospital, now known by the name of the Master's Lodging, and shall take and have for his yearly stipend vj l. xiij s. iiij d. to be taken and received quarterly, by equal and even portions, and twelve loads of wood, to be taken out of the profits of the lands of the said hospital, and brought unto his lodging, at the charges of the said hospital, according to the late former ordinance.

"Item, It is ordered, that the master of the said hospital shall appoint one school master, from time to time, who, in the chapel within the said hospital there, by himself or his sufficient deputy, shall freely instruct 20 poor children of the city of Canterbury, being above the age of seven years, and not above the age of sixteen years, to write, read, and cast accompt, which said children, and every of them, shall have books, pens, ink, and paper, provided for them, by the appointment of the master, out of the profits of the said hospital, provided that none of the said children shall remain in the said school above three years.

"And the said school-master shall read morning and evening prayers on Mundayes, Weddensdayes, and Frydayes, being not otherwise appointed to be observed as holydays, weekly, at six o'clock, morning and evening in the summer, and at seven in the morning, and between four and five in the afternoon in winter, unto the brothers and sisters and scholars there; for the doing whereof, the said schoolmaster shall have a lodging within the said hospital at the master's appointment, and yearly out of the profits of the said hospital four pounds, to be paid quarterly, by even proportions; and for his further relief he shall be from time to time (if the master shall think it convenient) receiver of all the revenues, commodities and profits, of the said hospital, and shall likewise have and receive for such his collection yearly twenty-six shillings and eight-pence, to be paid at the feast of the Annunciation of St. Mary the Virgin, and St. Michael the Archangel, by even portions, and two loads of wood, yearly, brought and laid at the said hospital, without any his charge, and one summer lyvery coat cloth.

"Item, It is ordered, that out of the profits of the said hospital, there shall be paid for ever unto two scholars, to be taken out of the common school in Canterbury, commonly called the Mynt, by the master of the said hospital, with the

consent

confent and affent of the Archbifhop of Canterbury for the time being, to be fent and placed in the college of Corpus Chrifti, and the Virgin Mary ', in Cambridge, three pounds, fix fhillings and eight-pence, yearly, according to the laft former ordinance in that behalf made.

" Further, whereas by former ordinances, the mafter of the faid hofpital is only tied to pay in the time of peace unto the poor paffengers, or to fuch other poor people as the mafter fhall think good, thirty-pence a week, and in the time of war, that payment ceafing, to provide xii beds for the lodging of poor foldiers paffing through the fame city, within the faid hofpital, for one night's fpace only, which are now grown wholly out of ufe, efpecially fince the lofs of Calais; now for the better relief of the poor inhabiting within the city of Canterbury, and the fuburbs thereof;

" It is ordered, that the former laft recited order fhall ceafe, and that inftead thereof there fhall be five in-brothers and five in fifters, from time to time, to be nominated and admitted as hereafter is fpecified, which fhall be permanent, and have their habitation within the faid hofpital.

" And after the end of twenty years next enfuing, there fhall be five other called out-brothers, and five other called out-fifters, to be alfo nominated and admitted, from time to time, as hereafter is mentioned.

" And every of the faid in-brothers and in-fifters fhall have a feveral dwelling and lodging within the faid hofpital, and twenty-fix fhillings and eight-pence by the year, to be paid quarterly, and one load of wood, to be laid at the faid hofpital yearly, between Midfummer and Michaelmas, without any charge unto the faid brethren or fifters, or any of them.

" And every of the faid out-brothers and out-fifters, after the end of twenty years next enfuing, fhall have twenty-fix fhillings and eight-pence by the year only, likewife to be paid quarterly.

" Item, It is ordered, that the mayor of the city of Canterbury, for the time being, fhall and may, from time to time, nominate unto the mafter of the faid hofpital, for every the faid brothers and fifters rooms at fuch time as they or any of them fhall be void and unfurnifhed, and not otherwife, two poor perfons, men or women, as the places fhall require, being lame, impotent, blind, or aged, and above fifty years; and which fhall have inhabited within the city of Canterbury, or the fuburbs thereof, by the fpace of feven years laft before their nomination, of the which two being fo qualified and nominated, the mafter of the faid hofpital fhall choofe and admit one, and none other, to the place void, unlefs the mayor for the time being fhall refufe or neglect to nominate fuch perfons as are in this ordinance appointed, by the fpace of three months after notice to him given by the mafter for the time being, of the vacancy of any fuch room or place; in which cafe only, the mafter fhall have full power of his own choice to admit any that fhall be qualified as is abovefaid.

" Provided always, That for the room or rooms of every out-brother and fifter, the faid mayor of Canterbury for the time being fhall nominate and appoint two fuch perfons as are before fpecifyed, whereof one at the leaft fhall be fuch as hath dwelt within the faid city or fuburbs thereof as aforefaid, but not within the county

---

' Now commonly called ' Bene't College.'

of

of the faid city, by the fpace of three whole years at leaft before the faid nomination, to the end that pooi people dwelling within the city and fuburbs, and not within the county of the faid city, might [may] receive fome benefit by this ordinance, according to the true meaning thereof.

"Alfo it is further decreed, That if any of the faid brothers or fifters after their admittance fhall ufually go abroad a begging, either within the city or elfewhere, without licence under the hands and feals of the mayor of Canterbury, and the mafter of the faid hofpital, for the time being, which licences fhall not be granted but upon fome manifeft and extreme neceffity, or fhall be otherwife offenfive in life, the faid mafter fhall call him or her before him, and admonifh them to defift from fuch demeanour; and if after admonition they fhall not amend, then fhall the party fo eftfoons-offending forfeit and lofe one quarter's wages, which fhall be divided and beftowed upon the in brothers and in fifters that fhall live orderly. And the faid mafter for the time being fhall admonifh the fecond rime the party fo offending; but if after the fecond admonition it fhall be juftly proved to the mafter, that he or fhe hath again offended in the like, then fhall the faid party be by the mayor and mafter difplaced without further delay, and another fhall be chofen into the room [1]. But if the offence be notorious or enormous, as inceft, adultery, fornication, and fuch like, the mafter fhall remove the party fo notorioufly offending, without any admonition. And thefe admonitions and fentences of difplacing, with the caufes thereof, fhall be regiftred by the fchoolmafter in a book for that purpofe, wherein the names of every brother and fifter, and the time of their admittance, fhall be alfo entered, immediately after they fhall be admitted.

"And it is alfo ordered, That the mafter of the faid hofpital for the time being fhall, of the profits of the faid hofpital, repair and fuftain the faid hofpital, and all the houfes and edifices belonging to the fame, and within the circuit thereof; and alfo fufficiently fuftain and maintain the bridge, called the King's-bridge, alias Eaftbridge, within the city of Canterbury, and pay to the queen's majefty, her heirs and fucceffors, vij l. and x s. yearly, due to her highnefs for a penfion of a chantery, fometime within the faid hofpital, and all other rents due unto the feveral lords, and all other duties and payments whatfoever, going out of the faid hofpital.

"Item, It is further ordered, That the mafter of the faid hofpital for the time being fhall not let for years, life, or lives, any of the faid lands or tenements of the faid hofpital, nor make any wood-fales of the woods thereunto belonging, without the exprefs confent and affent in writing of the archbifhop of Canterbury for the time being, and fhall yearly, between the feafts of St. Michael and St. Andrew, make a true account of all the iffues and profits received of the faid hofpital for the year paft, if it fhall be demanded, to the faid archbifhop; fo that of the furplufage (all the charges defalked) the portions of the faid brethren and fifters may be increafed, at the will of the archbifhop, as heretofore hath been ufed.

---

[1] The laft inftance of expulfion by this ftatute was, "Sept. 9, 1738," when "James Hofkins having been twice admonifhed, according to the ftatutes of this hofpital, by the mafter, for the fin and vice of drunkennefs; and having been feveral times guilty of the fame vice after the faid admonitions, was, according to the directions of the abovefaid ftatutes, expelled the hofpital, by us,

JOHN LEWIS, Mafter of Eaftbridge Hofpital.
THO. DAVIS, Mayor."

Admiffion Book, &c.
"And.

" And it is ordered, That if any of the in-brethren or fifters, mafter or fchool mafter aforefaid, fhall fortune to dye, then the perfon fo deceafing fhall and may be buried within the church-yard of the cathedral and metropolitical church of Chrift, in Canterbury, according to a former agreement made between the faid archbifhop's predeceffors and the then prior and convent of the faid church.

" And it is further ordered, That whofoever fhall hereafter be inftituted and inducted mafter of the faid hofpital fhall take a corporal oath upon the holy Evan-gelifts, before the faid archbifhop for the time being, to obferve, perform, or caufe to be obferved and performed, all the ordinances aforefaid, and fuch as fhall be hereafter fet down by the archbifhop of Canterbury for the time being, as much as in him lieth; and it fhall be lawful for the faid archbifhop for the time being, from time to time, to make new decrees and ordinances tending to the increafe of the revenue, further relief, and better government of the faid hofpital, or of the goods, lands, tenements, or other hereditaments, thereto belonging, fo as the faid decrees and ordinances be not repugnant to thefe ordinances, or to the common laws or ftatutes of this realm. In witnefs whereof we have hereunto put our feal, dated at our manor of Lambeth, the day and year firft abovefaid, anno confecrationis noftre fecundo.".

Thefe ordinances are confirmed by act of parliament, which act was obtained by the fole care and induftry of archbifhop Whitgift; and he not only procured the act to be paffed, but had the chief hand in framing and contriving of the fame : for he gave directions to fome eminent lawyer to draw up the bill to be prefented to the parliament; and when he had done this, he reviewed and ftrictly confidered the feveral claufes of the faid bill, and with his own hand made feveral confiderable amendments; the particulars whereof are thefe, which I have taken out of the original itfelf.

The bill drawn up by the lawyer.	The amendments of it by the arch-bifhop's own hand-writing.
" No title.	" An act for the better foundation and relief of the poor of the hofpital of Eaftbrridge, within the city of Canterbury.
" Whereas a certain hof-pital within the city of Canterbury, commonly cal-led or known by the name —Hofpital of St. Thomas the Martyr, founded as yt ys reported in ancient writ-ings, by Thomas Becket, archbifhop of Canterbury, of a mafter and fucceffors.	" Whereas a certain hofpital within the city of Can-terbury, now commonly called or known by the name — Hofpital of St. Thomas, founded and endowed, as it is alledged, by certain archbifhops of Canterbury, of one mafter and his fucceffors.
	" A free

" A free-fchool for certain children.

" The archbifhop of Canterbury that now is.

" After the expiration of certain leafes.

" Wherein are xxj years to come, or thereabouts.

" The faid number of poor, and portion.

" Is but xxiij l. per annum.

" The yearly charge.

" Will amount to 60 l.

" For the relief of the faid poor.

" A free-fchool for a certain number of poor children.

" John, now archbifhop of Canterbury.

" After the expiration, or determination, of certain leafes.

" Wherein are not above xx and one years to come.

" The faid number of poor, and the faid portion.

" Is but xxiij l. xviij s. ix d. per annum.

" The charge yearly.

" Will amount unto 60l.

" For relief of the faid poor.

The bill drawn up by the lawyer.

" Be it ordained and enacted, by the authority of this prefent parliament.

" That the faid ordinance made of the faid hofpital by the now archbifhop, and every claufe.

The bill amended by the Archbifhop.

" Be it ordained and enacted, by the queen's moft excellent Majefty, with the affent of the lords fpiritual and temporal and the commons in this prefent parliament affembled, and by the authority of the fame.

" That the lands, tenements, and hereditaments, and other poffeffions, now belonging to the faid hofpital, or reputed as part or parcel thereof, may and fhall for ever remain unto the mafter of the faid hofpital, and his fucceffors, mafters of the fame, and be employed to the godly and charitable ufes limited and appointed by the faid ordinance of the faid moft reverend father the archbifhop of Canterbury that now is; and that the faid ordinance [1] made of the faid hofpital by the faid prefent archbifhop, and every claufe.

The lawyer's opinion.

" This is provided for in the ordinance.

Memorandum, the Oath added by the Archbifhop.

" Memorandum, To procure a form of corporation for the faid hofpital, to be drawn of a mafter and his fucceffors, and for a feal of the faid hofpital.

" [1] Bearing date the 20th of July, 1584. And that the faid ordinance, together with this prefent act, fhall be enrolled in the courts of chancery and exchequer, within 40 days after the end of this feffion of parliament.

" He

" He can make no leafe by the ordinance, without the confent of the arch-bifhop.

" Item, A claufe to make void all leafes for a longer time than the continuance of the granter, unlefs fuch leafes be confirmed by the archbifhop of Canterbury for the time being, under his feal; and fuch fo to be confirmed not to exceed 21 years, or three lives at the uttermoft.

" It is enacted, That he fhall prefent, &c.

" Item, A claufe to authorife the archbifhop of Canterbury, and his fucceffors, to be patrons and vifitors of the faid hofpital from time to time, and as oft as need fhall require; yet at his or their own proper cofts and charges, and not of any the charges of the faid hofpital.

An Act for the better foundation and relief of the poor of the hofpital of Eaftbridge, within the city of Canterbury.

" Whereas a certain hofpital within the city of Canterbury, now commonly called or known by the name of the hofpital of Eaftbridge, alias the hofpital of St. Thomas, founded and endowed, as it is alledged, by certain archbifhops of Canterbury, of one mafter and his fucceffors, which mafter hath been always fince of the collation of the archbifhop of Canterbury for the time being, and inftituted and inducted into the fame; and by the firft ordinance hath and might take all the profits of the faid hofpital to his own ufe, beftowing only for the relief of wandering and wayfaring brethren and poor, in bread and drink, after the rate of 4d. the day, and one night's lodging for 12 perfons (if fo many come thither at one time), in the whole not above fix pounds, two fhillings and fix-pence per annum, until the time of the moft reverend Father in God Matthew Parker, late archbifhop of Canterbury, who, by authority in a former ordinance, concerning the difpofition of the profits of the faid hofpital to him and his fucceffors archbifhops of Canterbury, referved to alter and change the fame, did, by his ordinance in that behalf made, under his hand and feal, not only increafe the faid fum of fix pounds two fhillings and fix-pence to be from thenceforth beftowed weekly upon poor uncertain inhabiting within the county and city of Canterbury, but alfo appointed other fums of money thereout yearly, to be paid towards the keeping of a free-fchool for a certain number of poor children of the county of the city of Canterbury, to be taught to write and read freely within the faid hofpital, and towards the finding of certain fcholars in the univerfity of Cambridge, and other like good ufes. And whereas the moft reverend Father in God John, now archbifhop of Canterbury, finding the yearly profits of the faid hofpital to be greater than the yearly charges of thofe good ufes, appointed by the faid ordinances, hath, by his ordinance, made under his hand and feal, concerning the government of the faid hofpital, and difpofition of the yearly profits thereof, not only decreed thofe former laft recited good ufes to have continuance for ever, but alfo hath greatly augmented and increafed the portions of thofe former ordinances appointed for poor uncertain inhabiting within

within the faid city of Canterbury, and converted the fame to the relief of certain poor brethren and fifters, to be permanent within the faid hofpital, with a competent yearly ftipend for their maintenance, and with a provifo, that after the expiration or determination of certain leafes of the lands of the faid hofpital, wherein are not above twenty and one years to come, the faid number of poor, and the faid portion, fhall be further increafed; that is to fay, from ten to twenty poor brethren and fifters, and from the now allowance of thirteen pounds, fix fhillings and eight-pence per annum for their relief, then after the expiration of the faid leafes, to twenty-fix pounds thirteen fhillings and four-pence per annum for ever. After which proportion, whereas the valuation of the whole hofpital, by record in the exchequer, is but twenty-three pounds, eighteen fhillings, and nine-pence, the charges yearly out of the profits of the faid hofpital, then to be employed to good and charitable ufes, will amount unto fixty pounds per annum, or thereabouts, befides a further increafe of relief for the faid poor brethren and fifters, after the expiration of the faid leafes. Therefore, to avoid all fcruples, ambiguities, and queftions which hereafter may be moved againft the good perpetuity and continuance of the faid hofpital, Be it ordained and enacted, by the queen's moft excellent Majefty, with the affent of the lords fpiritual and temporal, and the commons, in this prefent parliament affembled, and by the authority of the fame :

" That the lands, tenements, and hereditaments, and other poffeffions now belonging to the faid hofpital, or reputed as part or parcel thereof, may and fhall for ever remain unto the mafter of the faid hofpital and his fucceffors, mafters of the fame, and be employed to the godly and charitable ufes limited and appointed by the faid ordinance of the faid moft reverend Father the archbifhop of Canterbury that now is, bearing date the 20th of July, one thoufand five hundred eighty and four; and that the faid ordinance, together with this prefent act, fhall be enrolled in the court of chancery and exchequer, within 40 days after the end of this feffion of parliament ; and the faid ordinance made of the faid hofpital by the faid archbifhop, and every claufe, article, and thing therein contained, fhall and may remain and continue in full force and virtue according to the tenor, purport, and true meaning thereof, to all intents and purpofes, and in manner and form as if the fame were in this prefent act efpecially and particularly mentioned and rehearfed, and by the authority aforefaid enacted and confirmed, any thing to the contrary notwithftanding.

" Saving to all and every perfon and perfons, other than the queen's majefty, her heirs and fucceffors, and other than the donors, founders, and fuch as may claim from, by, or under them, or any of them, all fuch eftate, right, title, intereft, rents, and fervices, as they have, or may have, into the fame, or any part thereof, any thing herein contained to the contrary notwithftanding.

" Provided always, That whereas there is a yearly rent of feven pounds ten fhillings iffuing out of the lands of the faid hofpital, and paying yearly unto the queen's majefty, her heirs and fucceffors, by reafon of a chantery that was founded in the fame hofpital :

" Be it therefore enacted, by the authority aforefaid, That her Highnefs, her heirs and fucceffors, fhall and may have, receive, and enjoy the faid yearly rent of

feven

feven pounds ten fhillings, any thing in this act above-mentioned to the contrary notwithftanding.

" Provided alfo, and be it enacted, by the authority aforefaid, That it fhall not be lawful to any archbifhop of Canterbury to make any ordinance or decree to be obferved by the mafter of the faid hofpital of Eaftbridge, or any other under the jurifdiction of the faid mafter, which fhall be contrary or repugnant to the laws or ftatutes of this realm, now in force; and that the oath to be adminiftered to the mafter of the faid hofpital, mentioned in the faid ordinance, fhall be fuch as here-after enfueth; viz.

" That he fhall, as much as in him lyeth, duly obferve all the ordinances and decrees contained in an ordinance ratified by parliament, in the twenty-feventh year of the reign of queen Elizabeth, and all other which be or fhall be made by any archbifhop of Canterbury for the time being, which fhall not be contrary or repugnant to the laws or ftatutes of this realm in force, the laft day of the feffion of parliament, held in the 27th year of the reign of queen Elizabeth.

" And be it likewife enacted, That none hereafter fhall be collated to the mafter-fhip of the faid hofpital of Eaftbridge, except he be a preacher allowed according to the laws and ftatutes of this realm now in force.

" *Exam', Vera Copia.*
" JOHN WALKER, Deput'
" JOHN BROWN, Cleric' Parliament'."

An order, that the brethren and fifters of the hofpital of Eaft-bridge may refort to the parifh church of Allhallows, to prayers, preaching, and the facraments.

" Hofpital' de Eaft-bridge.
Decimo feptimo die Januarii, anno Domini juxta computationem eccle Anglicane 1585, coram vene-rabili viro magro Stephano Lakes, legum doctore, civitat' et diocef' Cantuar' comiffario generali legitime deputato in eccla parochiali dive Margarete intra civi-tatem Cantuar' judicialr feden' in pfentia mei Leonardi Sweeting, Notarii publici, propter abfentiam magri Francifci Aldric, Notarii publici regeftrarii affumpti.

Quo die comparuerunt pfonaliter Thomas Bateman, et Johannes Charitie, fratres in hofpital' de Eaftbridge, in civitate Cantuar', exempte jurifdictionis r'mi Cantuar' archiepi qui tàm nominibus fuis quàm aliorum pauperum fratrum et fororum dicti hofpitalis allegaverunt fe hactenus ad nullam ecclam parochialem affignari et admitti, unde humiliter petierunt fe per dom judicem affignatam admitti in aliquam ecclam parochialem arbitrio domini judicis affignand' unde dominus ad eorum petitionem decrevit et affignavit in forma fequenti; viz. Quod quilibet pauperum fratrum et fororum dicti hofpitalis ecclam parochialem Omnium Sanctorum in civitate Cantuar', vocat' vulgariter Alhallowes, ad audiend' divina diebus dominicis

et

et feſtivis frequentabunt, et ad pticipand' Euchariſtiam in eadem, juxta jura, con-
ſtituta, et confuetudinem hujus regni Anglie modo ſtabilit' nec non injunxit eis ad
folvend' miniſtro dicte eccle pro tempore exiſten' feoda facramentaria prout juris
eſt et equitatis (falvis femper r'mo archiepo Cantuar', et ejus comiſſario generaḷi
civitat' et dioceſ' Cantuar' et aliis ſuis officiariis teſtamentorum approbationibus ibm
decedentium ac bonorum hujuſmodi defunctorum adminiſtrationis comiſſionibus de
tempore in tempus, ac feodis conſtitutis, &c.) Et dominus, ad eorum petitiones,
decrevit hoc decretum intimand' fore cunctis intereſſe habentibus dictis fratribus
confenſ' et acceptan', &c.

> " Concordat cum actis curie penes regrum curiæ comiſ' archiepalis
> Cantuar' remaïnum, fact' diligenti collatione p me Willm Somner, notarium
> publicum, magri Franciſci Aldriche, regrarii, deputat'.

Lib. Actorum, 1584, folio 24.

Oct. 11, 1587. Ex regiſtro hoſpitalis.

" It was ordered, That every of the in-brothers of the hoſpital, in courſe, ſhall weekly lock the door of the hoſpital every
night after the corfeu bell hath rung, immediately, and deliver
the key unto the fchool-maſter of the the faid hoſpital; and that
none of them ſhall burn any wood but in the chimney and
common place appointed for that purpoſe, upon pain of admonition, according to ordinance.

" Thomas Lawse, [Maſter.]"

" Thoſe who dye in the hoſpital, and are to buried in the
church-yard of the cathedral church, according to the ſtatutes of
the hoſpital, are to be buried on the weſt-ſide of the cloyſters ; as
the ancient accuſtomed place." See the regiſter, A. D. 1614.

In Mr. Battely's MS. in this place follows.

1. A rental of the revenues belonging to the hoſpital of Eaſtbridge, made anno
29, R. R. Eliz. A. D. 1587, Oct. 10.

2. A terrier of lands belonging to the hoſpital of Eaſtbridge, made June 10, 1596,
with a letten by leafe, to John Cheefe, which lie in Cockering, containing by eſtimation 30 acres, and lie in 8 ſeveral parcels.

This terrier was made, after the deceafe of the faid John Cheefe, by Edward Strong,
who married the wife of the faid John Cheefe, who hath her life in the faid leafe.

3. Aricles

3. Articles of agreement made the 12th of July, in the 31st year of our fovereign lady queen Elizabeth; between John Boys, efquire, and John Rofe, alderman of the city of Canterbury.

Sealed and delivered in the prefence of   Jo. CANTUAR' [1]

               R. DOVER [2].

               WM. AUBREY.

4. Memorandum, That the dean and chapter of the cathedral church of Chrift, in Canterbury, by decree in their chapter-general, holden at the Feaft of St. John the Baptift, 1585, did give one fmall bell, called a Wackerel, to the ufe of the hofpital of Eaftbridge, to be hanged up in the chapel, for the calling together of the brothers and fifters to their appointed fervice there. (Taken out of the regifter book of the hofpital.)

5. Quit-rents belonging to the manor of Blean and Hoath-court.

6. Quit-rents unpaid for many years, 1724.

7. Quit-rents of Blean manor, 1725.

8. An account of the feveral leafes of Cockering farm.

9. Leafes of Pitholes in Harboldown, and Lompits in St. Dunftone's parifh.

10. Leafes of two tenements in St. Peter's parifh, and half an acre of meadow in Medlane.

11. Leafes of the King's-head, in All Saints parifh.

12. Leafes of two fmall pieces of land in St. Peter's parifh.

13. Leafes of Mrs. George's houfes in High-ftreet, in All Saints parifh.

14. Leafes of Bromedune, or Long Harris Croft, in Harboldown.

15. Leafes of the tithes of Harboldown,

16. Leafes of the eleven acres of land in St. Laurence-field, in the parifh of St. Mary Bredin.

17. Five tenements and a fhop.

18. Leafes of Hoath Court and Eaftry Lees, &c.

19. The Mafter's houfe.

1630. John Sacket to John Jacob Vander Slaert   9 0 0

   Since that it let to Mr. Tuck, for   6 0 0

   Let to Mr. Tuck, at the rent of   8 0 0

20. At a Court Baron holden the 8th day of October, in the 15th year of the reign of our fovereign lady Elizabeth, &c.

At the faid court it is ordered, that the furveyors appointed fhall monthly drive the common, and put all ftrangers cattle, and fuch cattle of the tenants and their farmers as be there kept above their rates limited, into the pound, until fatisfaction be made for the trefpafs done, viz. for every horfe, gelding, mare, cow, or ox iiij d. and for every fheep ob. thone moiety to the lord, and the other to the furveyors.

Item, That it is ordered, that if eny perfon do keep eny hogs upon the common unryngled, after the feaft of St. Luke next, that then the owner of every hog fo taken, or found unryngled, [pay] iiij d.

     p me, GILB'TUM HYDE,

      Senefcallum ibm.

   Copia vera, ita teftor NIC. BATELY.

---

[1] Archbifhop Whitgift.

[2] Dr. Roger, fuffragan bifhop, dean of Canterbury, 1584.

4

21. BLEAN et ⎱ Vifus franc' pleg' cum cur' tent' i̇ƀm xmo die menfis Aprilis,
    HOATH. ⎰ anno regni dn̄e n̄ri Elizabethe Dei gratia, Anglie, Francie, et Hibernie, regine, fidei defenf', &c. xmo.

Thomas Qweyffe, Joħes Pyrkyn, Stepħus Baffock, Henricus Crippin, Thomas Hunt, Joannes Smith, Thomas Coping, Willus Wix, ħent diem p̃ mandatum d̃ni citra prox' vifum ad c̄tificand' quot catalla quilet debet depafcare fuper c̄oe de Blean, et fi hoc non poffunt quod tunc c̄tificant quot catalla p̃d' c̄oe poteft depafcare in anno.

Copia vera, ita teftor ego NIC. BATTELY.

22. BLEAN et ⎱ Vife franc' pleg' cum cur' tent' iƀm 17 Octob. anno R. R. Eliz.
    HOATH. ⎰ undecimo.

Elegerunt ad fupvidend' c̄oe de Blene quod nullus p̃mittat porcos fuos iƀm depafcare nifi prius fint annulati et quod nullus occupat c̄oe cum pecoribus fuis nifi fit tenens hujus manerii, viz. Willus Morrys, et Joannem Tredfoffe.

23. Mr. Sabine's Gift to the Hofpital.

Mr. Avery Sabine, late alderman of the city of Canterbury, did, by his laft will, give and bequeath a certain annuity, or rent charge, of 20l. per annum, for certain charitable ufes, as by his will may appear more at large : for the faithful difcharge of this truft, he appointed certain feoffees, viz. Thomas Hardres, Edward Roberts, Robert Kitchel, Thomas Gold, Thomas Treffar, William Whiting, and Leonard Brown; and when the major part of thefe fhall dye, the feoffment is to be renewed; and then follow thefe words :

" The faid truftees fhall for ever hereafter pay ten marks a year, parcel of the
" annuity or rent-charge of 20l. a year, unto ten poor in-brothers and fifters for
" the time being of the hofpital called Eaftbridge, within the city of Canterbury,
" by equal payments, every year quarterly, at the Feafts aforefaid, or within 21
" days next after every of the faid feafts, that is to fay, every quarter 3s. 4d. a-piece
" to every of the ten brothers and fifters." Alfo,

They fhall lay out 12l. parcell of the faid 20l. to cloath ten poor people in the city of Canterbury, on the Feaft of St. Andrew, yearly; and the overplus fhall bear the charges of renewing the faid feoffment, or be divided between the poor people of the city of Canterbury, as by the will is more fully expreffed.

All the lands of the faid Mr. Avery Sabine, lying in Monketon, in the Ifle of Thanet, are bound for the payment of this rent-charge. The will was dated Nov. 22, A. D. 1648.

Excerpt' ex ipfo originali,
p̃ me, NIC. BATTELLY.

24. A claufe taken out of Mr. Somner's will.

" As to my meffuages and hereditaments in St. Margaret's, Cant', St. Andrew's, and St. Mary Bredman, in cafe my fon dyes without iffue of his body lawfully begotten, I give the fame to Elizabeth wife of Mr. John Lukener, of the city of Canterbury, Hatter, and the heirs of her body : and for the want of fuch heirs, to the prior, brothers, and fifters, of the hofpital of Kingfbridge, and their fucceffois for ever."

On the like conditions he gives his lands in Chartham, and in Romney Marfh, to the hofpitals of Northgate and Harbledown.

The will is dated Aug. 26, 1679.

25. An

25. An account of the real and extended value of the feveral lands, meffuages, &c. which are let out by leafe, belonging to the hofpital, being directions for the renewing of the leafes.

26. Captain Terry's houfe, the King's-head in High-ftreet, lets to the prefent tenant, at p annum   16 c

Mr. Stredwick, 11 acres in St. Laurence Field, now worth above 22 l. p annum   22 0 0

Mrs. George, at full or rather more than   37 0 0

Mrs. Green, 5 tenements and a fhop

		£	s	d			
1. To Ruglton, p annum		5	0	0			
2. Goodm' H.		4	10	0			
3. Goodw' Pofly		3	10	0	24	10	c
4. Eaftman		3	10	0			
5. Willmot		3	0	0			
6. Beverton		5	0	0			

Mr. Turner, 2 tenements in St. Peter's, to Brown   10 0 0 } 15 c ͻ
                  to Mr. Peter's   5 0 0

Cockering rents formerly (but now they are fallen)   16 c
Now not above 10 l. p annum
1753, at 12 l. p annum

Pithôles, p annum   4 0 0
Lome pits, p annum   8 0 0
Mudhoufe, p annum   8 10 0
Mr. Hall's garden   3 10 0
Harboldown tithes, of 36 acres of hop-ground, and 24 acres of arable land, about   20 0 0

27. A true account of the revenues of the hofpital of Eaftbridge, as it is at this day, A. D. 1691.
Rents received.

Leafe of Hoath-court, to the lady Head, for 3 lives   48 () ()
Leafe of Nicolas Stredwick for 21 years, for 11 acres in St. Laurence-field, p annum   3 0 0
Leafe of Mrs. Green for 21 years, for Cockering lands   3 0 0
Leafe of Mr. Lowth for 21 years, for Lompits and Pitholes, and the tithes of Harboldown   3 12 c
Leafe of Mr. Hall for land in Harboldown, and two pieces of land in St. Peter's, for 21 years   3 2 0
Leafe of Mrs. Green for 40 years, for 5 tenements   3 0 0
Leafe of Mrs. George for feveral tenements, for 40 years   3 2 0
Leafe of Mrs. Turner for 2 tenements in St. Peter's, for 40 years   1 12 0
Leafe of Mr. Terry for 40 years, for the King's Head, a tenement in High-ftreet   3 0 0

                               71 8 0

Rent

Rent upon leafes, p annum, quarterly paid.

	£	s	d
Befides, the vault lets for, p annum	1	6	8
Mr. Hall pays for a piece of the mafter's garden, and for the royalty of fifhing, p annum	0	6	8
Mr. Crifp's eftate in Burchington	0	11	8
Mrs. Petib's eftate in Burchington	0	8	4
Dry rent iffuing out of certain tenements in and about Canterbury, (See p. 358.)	2	9	1
Quit-rents belonging to the manor of Blean (See p. 353.)	4	15	4
24 loads of wood, at 10s. p load, out of the manor	12	0	0
Hay and ftraw to the mafter out of the manor of Blean	2	0	0
	95	5	9
The mafter's houfe lets for	6	0	0
	101	5	9

Befides thefe, are the fines upon the renewing of the leafes; and alderman Sabine's gift of 13s. 4d. a-piece by the year; which gift comes not into the mafter's hand, but is paid by one of the aldermen of the city.

28. A true account of the difburfements.

				£	s	d
To the in brothers and fifters, p annum				28	0	0
To the out-brothers and fifters, p annum				13	6	8
To the fchool-mafter—his wages, p annum	4	0	0			
Livery-coat	0	13	4	6	16	0
Rent-gathering	1	6	8			
Additional falary upon increafe of rent in Mr. Hall's leafe	0	16	0			
Brooms to fweep the chapel, 6d. p quarter				0		
Books for the fcholars, pens, ink, and paper, formerly p annum 1l. the fcholars now increafing, comes to				2	0	0
				50	4	8
Exhibition to Bene't College				6	13	4
Charge of fending the money to London				0	1	0
Penfion to the king				7	10	0
Acquit and return of money				0	3	0
Tenths at Chriftmas				2	7	10½
Acquit				0	0	4
Mafter's falary	6	13	4			
Rent of his houfe	6	0	0	13	0	0
Rent of Mr. Hall's garden	0	6	8			
Wood to the mafter and the poor				12	0	0
Making of the wood				1	4	0
Hay and ftraw to the mafter				2	0	0
Leafe in the dry rents and quit-rents, about				1	10	0
Formerly for fweeping the bridge (which of late hath been paid by the poor), and is now again paid by the mafter				0	10	0
				97	4	2½

So there remains about 3l. p annum for the maintaining of reparations, and keeping of the court at Blean, and other extraordinary

" 29. Bene't College, Cambridge.

The foundation of two Scholars by Archbifhop PARKER, out of Eaftbridge Hofpital, in Canterbury.

" THIS indenture, made the twenty-fecond day of May, in the eleventh year of the reign of our fovereign lady Elizabeth, by the grace of God, queen of England, France, and Ireland, defender of the Faith, &c. betwixt William Morphet, clerk, mafter of the hofpital of the poor of Eaftbridge, in the city of Canterbury, on the one part, and John Pory, Dr. of Divinity, and keeper of the college of Corpus Chrifti and the bleffed Virgin Mary, in Cambridge, and the fellows and fcholars of the faid college, on the other part, witneffeth, that the faid parties, and every of them, for them and their fucceffors, do covenant and grant, with the other and his or their fucceffors, in manner and form following : Firft, the faid William, mafter of the faid hofpital, with the confent of the moft reverend father, Matthew, Archbifhop of Canterbury, metropolitane of all England, and primate, and patron of the faid hofpital, covenanteth and granteth, for him and his fucceffors, to and with the faid John, mafter and keeper of the faid college, and the fellows and fcholars of the fame, and their fucceffors, that he, his fuc- ceffors and affigns, fhall yearly pay unto the faid mafter or keeper, fellows or fcholars, or their affigns, to the ufe of the faid college, at the quire door of the church of Weftminfter, on the weft part of the faid church, at the feaft of St. Michael the Archangel, or within thirty days next following the faid feaft, the fum of fix pounds, thirteen fhillings, and four-pence, of lawful money of England, for and during the term of two hundred years next enfuing the date hereof. And further, that if it happen the faid yearly payment to be behind unpaid, at the place aforefaid, after the faid term of thirty days, and there lawfully demanded by the fufficient deputy of the faid mafter or keeper, and fellows or fcholars, then the faid mafter of the hofpital and his fucceffors fhall pay unto the faid mafter or keeper, and fellows or fcholars, for every fuch default of payment, three pounds fix fhillings and eight-pence, of lawful money of England, in the name of a pain, over and befides the fum of fix pounds, thirteen fhillings, and four-pence, of yearly payment, with the reafonable cofts and charges of fuit and travail for the fame, during all the faid term of two hundred years : In confideration whereof the faid mafter or keeper, and fellows or fcholars, covenant and grant for them and their fucceffors, to and with the faid mafter of the hofpital and his fucceffors, that they the faid mafter and keeper, and fellows or fcholars, and their fucceffors, fhall and will admit and receive into the faid college of Corpus Chrifti, and the bleffed Virgin Mary, for the increafe of the number of fcholars there, over and befides the ordinary number now in the faid college, two fcholars, to be chofen, named, ex- amined, and approved, by the mafter of the faid hofpital, and the dean of Chrift Church, in Canterbury, for the time being, and their fucceffors, if any dean fhall then be, or elfe by the mafter only, and to be taken by him or them out of the free-fchool in Canterbury, being fuch of the fcholars there as are or fhall be born within the county of Kent, and fent to the faid college at Cambridge, which two fhall be called Canterbury Scholars : And that after fuch admittance and receipt, the faid fcholars fhall remain and continue in the faid college, according to the orders, decrees, and ftatutes of the faid college, and fhall have of the provifion of the faid mafter or keeper, fellows or fcholars, and their fucceffors, convenient chamber, commons, barber, launder, reading, and other neceffaries as other fcholars

in

in the faid college have had and enjoyed, and fhall have and enjoy in the faid college, according to common cuftom, or otherwife, for and during the term of two hundred years next enfuing the date hereof. And further do covenant and grant, that when and fo often as it fhall happen, any of the faid fcholars fo named and admitted in form aforefaid, to be expulfed, or otherwife removed from the faid college, or benefits aforefaid, by any manner of means, that then they the faid mafter or keeper, fellows or fcholars, and their fucceffors, will and fhall receive and admit, from time to time, into the faid college, other fuch fcholar or fcholars, to enjoy the rooms, fcholarfhips, and benefits aforefaid, as fhall be from time to time chofen, examined, and approved by the mafter of the faid hofpital and his fucceffors, for the time being, with the confent of the faid dean of Chrift Church, in Canterbury, and his fucceffors, for the time being (if any dean fhall be then), or elfe by the mafter only, out of the faid fchool of Canterbury as aforefaid, to the faid college, which fcholar or fcholars fhall have and enjoy all fuch profits and commodities as the other did and fhould have had and enjoyed, by the cuftoms, orders, and ftatutes of the faid college, during all the faid term of two hundred years. And that if default at any time fhall be had or made by the faid mafter or keeper, fellows or fcholars, and their fucceffors, in refufing to admit or receive the faid fcholars, or any of them fo chofen, examined, and approved of in form aforefaid, and fent to the faid college by the letter fubfcribed by the hand of the faid mafter, and dean of the faid church, or their fucceffors, if any dean be, or elfe by the hand of the faid mafter only; or in allowance of neceffaries in form above-mentioned, that then for every refufal of fuch fcholars, or any default by them contrary to the covenant in thefe indentures expreffed, they fhall pay to the mafter of the hofpital, and his fucceffors, the fum of twenty fhillings of lawful money of England, with the reafonable cofts of fuit and travail in and about the fame : And further do covenant with the mafter of the faid hofpital, and his fucceffors, that within fix weeks after every expulfion, or removing of any fcholar admitted or received from the faid college, the faid mafter or keeper, fellows or fcholars, and their fucceffors or affigns, fhall make notice to the mafter of the faid hofpital, or his fucceffors, of the faid expulfion or removing. In witnefs whereof, as well the mafter of the faid hofpital, for him and his fucceffors, as alfo the faid mafter or keeper, and fellows or fcholars, for them and their fucceffors, to thefe indentures have interchangeably fet their feals. Dated the day and year firft above written."

30. A perfect and true terrier of all the lands and other commodities belonging to the manor of Blean and Hoth Court, in the parifh of St. Cofmus and Damian on the Blean, in the county of Kent, declaring the names and contents in the feveral fields, with the tenements belonging thereunto, of the demife and grant of John Lewis, clerk, of Minfter, in the Ifle of Thanet, mafter of the Hofpital of Eaftbridge, alias St. Thomas in the city of Canterbury, unto John Boys, of Hoth-Court, efquire, and Elizabeth his wife, now farmers of the faid manor, made and delivered unto the faid mafter, according to a compofition and article comprized within the faid demife on the part of the faid John Boys and Elizabeth his wife, their executors and affigns, to be done and accomplifhed at or before the fealing of the faid demifed leafe, which was from the day of the date thereof, as plainly appeareth in the faid demife, dated the twentieth day of March, in the fifth year of the reign of our fovereign lord George the Second, &c. annoque Domini 173¾.

31. Copies of feveral leafes of lands belonging to Eaftbridge hofpital.

Kkk 2

The

The Priory of St. GREGORY, in Canterbury.

In the Northgate-Street, over-againſt the Hoſpital of St. John, Archbiſhop Lanfranc founded [a church, in honour of St. Gregory, the Pope], for ſecular prieſts, A. D. 1084; but Archbiſhop William [*temp.* Hen. I.] made it a priory of [Black Canons, or] Regulars. *Leland*.

Eadmerus ſays, ⸱theſe canons were to " adminiſter to the infirm " people of St. John's hoſpital whatſoever was neceſſary for the " good of their ſouls, and to take care alſo of their burial." And Somner ſuppoſes it to have been " the firſt houſe of Regular " Canons in the kingdom." On July 2, 1145, the church, we are informed by Gervaſe, was burnt.

Archbiſhop Hubert confirmed this priory and its revenues. See Dugdale's Monaſticon, vol. II. p. 373, where theſe Charters are printed.

The names of ſome of the priors.

1. Dunſtan, A. D. 1187. Gerv. col. 1497.

2. Thomas, A. D. 1227. ⎫
3. Nicolas, A. D. 1244. ⎪
4. Hugh, A. D. 1263. ⎬ Regiſt. Cant.
5. William, A. D. 1271. ⎭

6. Henry, A. D. 1278. He was prior alſo the xth of kal. Apr. 1276 ; alſo A. D. 1275, when he and Nicolas [Thorn] abbot of St. Auſtin's ſealed a writing, or certificate, of ſome grants made to the church of Canterbury.

7. Guy, A. D. 1293. Thorn, col. 1961.

8. Elias of Sandwich, 1294.

9. Robert of Winchepe, died A. D. 1349.

10. William atte Thorn, inſtalled June 10, 1349.

11. Thomas, A. D. 1403.

12. William of Canterbury, 1413.

13. Thomas, A. D. 1443.

14. Dr. Thomas Wellys, Biſhop of Sidon, Sept. 26, 1515, and Jun. 28, 1521.

15. William,

Plate VIII. fig. 1.

F. Perry del.

View of S.ᵗ Gregory's Priory, Canterbury

fig. 2.

F. Perry del.

Ruins of S.ᵗ Thomas's Chapel, Canterbury,
as they appeared in 1781.

15. William, 1531.   He was at the convocation in that year,
and was one of thofe that gave a negative voice to the queftion
then propofed.   See the Specimen of Errors in Burnet's Hiftory
of the Reformation, p. 195.

16. John Symkins, the laft prior [1].

At cardinal Bourchier's vifitation there were only five canons,
befides the prior; but [about the time of the Diffolution, here were
thirteen religious, who were endowed with the yearly revenue of
121l. 15s. 1d. per ann. *Dugdale*. 1661. 4s. 5½d. *Speed*. Lambard
reckons it only 30l.   The fite was granted, 28 Henry VIII. to the
archbifhop of Canterbury, in exchange for Wimbledon.   *Tanner*.

It is now held, on a leafe from his grace, by George Gipps, efq.
one of the prefent members for Canterbury.   The precinct, or
vill, maintains its own poor, and is extra-parochial.

Mr. Goftling's account of its prefent ftate is as follows:

" Part of this priory is now ftanding, but not a great deal,
only one large room, unlefs the buildings of the ftreet may be
looked on as the lodgings of the poor and fick, who were provided for there.   The ground belonging to its precinct is almoft
entirely laid out in gardens for our market.   The chapel of St.
Thomas (whofe ruins are there) had over the door, at the weft
end of it, a handfome old arch, which the archbifhop's leffee
took down fome years ago, to make a portal to his own dwelling-
houfe, at St. Thomas's-hill; but that being fold and rebuilt, a
curious gentleman [2] in the country, by adapting the front of one
of his out-buildings to it, has preferved this piece of antiquity,
and added to the beauties of his feat."

The little that remains of this ancient ftructure may be feen
in the view of it given in plate IX. fig. 1.; and the ruins of St.
Thomas's chapel in fig. 2.]

[1] On the diffolution of the priory, he had a penfion of 20l. per ann. from the
king, till, on the foundation of the collegiate church of Rochefter, he was admitted one of the firft prebendaries, and lived there till March 14, 1553, when he
was deprived for being married.   He had been a monk of St. Bartholomew's, in
London.   Dr. BATTELY.

[2] The late reverend Mr. Brockman, of Beachborough.

Indentura

Indentura inter priores ecclesiarum Chrifti et Sti Gregorij, Cantuar', de quibufdam jocalibus legatis dicte ecclie Sti Gregorii, p dnum Rogerum Herun, quondam rectorem five magrum ecclie collegiate de Maydeftan, non aliendis, ut patet inferius.

PRESENS indentura facta 26to die Maii, anno r. R. Henrici fexti, Anglie et Francie vicefimo primo, inter venerabilem patrem Johannem, priorem ecclie Chrifti, Cant'; et ejufdem capitlum (fede vacante) ex parte una, et Thomam priorem ecclie Sti Gregorii Cantuar' pd' ex parte altera, teftatur, quod pd' Joannes, prior ecclie Chrifti Cant', et ejufdem capitlum, ex affenfu et confenfu omnium executorum Rogeri Herun, clerici, cujus corpus in eccla Sti Gregorii pdict' fepelitur, tradiderunt et deliberaverunt pfato Thome, priori Sti Gregorij, quedam jocalia argentea, viz. duas pelves argent' cum ij lavacris argent ponderant' cxxvi unc' et j quart' ij potellers argent' ponderant' lxvi une' et dimid': et unum magnum cyphum argent' cum co-opculo ad eundem ponderantem clxviii unc' et dimid' ad laudem et honorem Dei, et in ppetuam rei memoriam, p falute anime pfati Rogeri in prioratu Sti Gregorii pd' ad ufum refectorij ejufdem prioratus imperpetuum remanfura. Ita quod non licebit pfato Thome priori, neque fuccefforibus fuis, pdicta jocalia, nec aliquod eorundem, vendere, alienare, feu cuicunque quovifmodo impignorare, nifi magna et urgens caufa illud requirat, et in cafu illa impignorentur, five aliquod eorundem impignoretur, fufficienti perfone p confenfum capitli ejufdem eccle Sti Gregorii, ac etiam licentia et affenfu prioris ecclie Chrifti Cant', qui pro tunc fuerit, et aliter non. Et fi contingat pd' Thomam, modò priorem, aut fucceffores, aliquo tali cafu urgente, pdicta jocalia feu aliquod eorundem alicui impignorare, quod pd' nunc prior et omnes fucceffores fui jocalia illa fic impignorata, feu jocale illud fic impignoratum, infra annum poft impignorationem illam ad prioratum pdict' rehabeant feu rehabeantur, et ad ifta fideliter p fe et fucceffores fuos obfervanda pfatus Thomas, prior Sti Gregorii, coram pdicto venerabili patre Joanne, priore ecclie Chrifti, corporale fuum pftabit juramentum. Et omnes fucceffores ejufdem prioris Sti Gregorii in fuâ primâ creatione eidem venerabili priori ecclie Chrifti Cant' et fuccefforibus fuis confimile pftabunt juramentum. In cujus rei teftimonium hiis indenturis pdicti venerabiles paeres Johannes, prior ecclie Chrifti, et Thomas, prior ecclie Sti Gregorii, figilla fua alternatim appofuerint, die et anno fuprafcriptis.

Henry, prior, and the convent, granted to William de Hunt a chantry in the chapel of Wadenhal, in the parifh of Waltham, dated 1276, 10 kal. Apr.

The

The lands and rents anciently belonging to the priory of St. Gregory, out of the leiger-book of the priory of St. Gregory.

Goldſtanton. A leaſe was made by the prior and convent 13ᵉ Henry IV. of the grange of Goldſtanton, and all the tithes thereto belonging.

Northfleet. Certain corn, &c. for tithe out of the archbiſhop's demeſnes of the manor of Northfleet, viz. 8 acr' ſuccis' meſſis', 4 frumenti, et 4 ordei, in terra meliori de manerio archiepi in Northfleet. There are two receipts of 40s. p annum, by the prior and convent for 4 acres of wheat, and 4 acres of barley, for tithes of the manor of Northfleet.

Beatriſden. Hadingfeld, 43 acres ½.   Holmis, 14 acr. ¼.
           Horſenlees, 17 acres ¼.   Buttervale, 3 acr.
           .Courtwood, 3 acres ½ and ¼. Burckmede, 3 acr.

Berham. vi marc' p annum de rectoria de Biſhopſborn, p decimis dominis de Berham.

St. Gregoreyes poſſeſſions, out of an old taxation.

Ecclia de Tanington.   Ecclia de Northgate.
Ecclia de Weſtgate.   Ecclia Sti Dunſtani.
Ecclia de Natinden.   Ecclia de Walther.
Ecclia de Elmeſtide.   Ecclia de Betheriſden.
Ecclia de Stratesfeld.   Ecclia de Oreſni decanatu de Auſprig.
Ecclia de Lethingeſborn, alias Bekeſborn, in decanatu de Bregge.
Decime de Richbourn.   Decime de Biſhoppeſbourn.
Decime apud Goldſtanton, Gooſhall, et in campo vocato Hartſland, et Holdam juxta Wingham.   Decime in Pluckley.
Portio in Northfleet.   Temporalia.
ij marks penſion p decimis dominij de Pluckley.
Decime in Hawle in Eaſtenham.
In eodem libro.
Compoſitio vicarie de Elmſtede.   Compoſitio vicarie de Northgate.
Compoſitio vicarie Sti Dunſtani.   Compoſitio de Weſtgate.
Pro patronatu vicar' de Weſtgate.

A recovery of the parſon of Harboldown, unius ſume frumenti, et duarum ſummarum hordei, p decimis in Harboldown ſpectant' priorat' de Sto Gregorio: exceptis decimis majoribus dominij de Denſted, que ſpectant dictu prioratui.

This recovery was, anno 42° Edw. III.

An account of the poſſeſſions of the priory, 4 Hen. V.

Inter alia, p decimis in Weſtbery, p rector' de Orty [Hartey] near Feverſham, p molendino vocato Spaffet Mill, p xvj acris terre, vocat' Oker, et 8 acris in Northgate, p decimis in Yldenton in parochia de Adiſham, p ij tenementis in civitate Roffenſi. Alſo rents of aſſize and penſions.

Decime prioris et conventus Sti Gregorij, Cant', in feodo de Goldeſtaveſtone, cum decimis eorundem que pervenerint de quodam campo domini archiepi, qui vocatur

catur Hodame, jacente juxta Wengham, xv marc'. Ex libro MS. in Biblioth' ecche Chrifti, Cant'.

Fcche appropriate priori Sti Gregorij regiftrantur in regro Henrici, prioris ecclefie Chrifti, Cant', p. 141.

Ex libro MS. Tho. Hales. Domino archiepifcopo Cant', pro uno meffuagio et terris apud Cokeryng, in parochia de Thanyngton, nuper prioratûs Sti Gregorii, extra Northgate civitatis Cant', ac antea Johannis Ramfey, folut' anno 1 Edw' VI. ad Thomam Hales——vj l.

Carta Lanfranci archiepifcopi de fundatione prioratus Sti Gregorij. Vide Monaftic' Anglic', vol. II. p. 373.

Carta Huberti archiepi 'Cant' de eodem. Ibm, p. 374.

Taxatio temporalium et fpiiitualium prioratûs St. Gregorii. Ibm, p. 374.

Lanfrancus archiepus, primus fundator, inftituit canonicos feculares; Gulielmus archiepus canonicos regulares induxit. Lelandi Collectan' Vol. I. p. 84. Monaft' Anglic', vol. II. p. 375.

[" The chapel of St. Thomas (mentioned p. 421) was called (as I find by the will of one William Harry, of St. Martin, A. D. 1461, who gave a legacy to it,) *The Chapel of the Brotherhood of St. Thomas the Martyr, fituate in the garden of St. Gregory's.*" So fays Somner, who clofes his difcourfe of the priory with the following *memorandum,* touching the water-courfe of Chrift-church running through this part of it. " *Memorandum,* faith a " Book of Chrift-church, concerning a charter of the prior and " convent of St. Gregory's by Canterbury making particular " mention of this matter, wherein it is expreffed, That they fhall " preferve, as far as they can, a water-courfe of the prior and " convent of Chrift-church in Canterbury, which runs through " their orchard, fafe and free from damage; and that they fhall " grant free liberty of ingrefs, egrefs, and regrefs through their " court and gate to the workmen of Chrift-church as often as it " fhall be neceffary for them to repair the fame water-courfe. " [In the fame agreement it is further added, That they fhould " fend in dinner-time into the refectory of Chrift-church a bafket " of the beft fruit on or before the 15th day of September, every " year; and fhould further pay the fum of eight pence, as a yearly " rent for a fmall piece of land there, belonging formerly to the " archdeacon. N. B.] Dated in July, A. D. 1227."

Their

Plate IX. fig. 1.

W. View of St Sepulchre's Nunnery, Canterbury   a. Road to Dover.

fig. 2.

N.E. View of Maynard's Spital, Canterbury.   a. Stour street.

Their temporalities in the year 1292, in Canterbury, Natyn-don [Nackington], Hugevelde, Chertham, Tanynton, and Herbaldoun, were together valued at xxvl. xvs. Their titheries, in the fame year, were the parfonages at Taynton [Thanington], Weftgate, Northgate, St. Dunftan, Natindon, Livingsborn [Beakf-bourn], Waltham, Elmftede, Betherfdenne, Stallesfield. Together with certain titheries in Goldftanefton [Goodnefton], Berham, Plukele [Hluckley], and Rifleburn [Rufhbourn?]. *Lib. Eccl. Chr. Cant.*

·Nunnery of St. SEPULCHRE.

In the fouth-eaft part of Canterbury was a Benediᴄtine nunnery, founded by archbifhop Anfelm about A. D. 1100. It was called St. Sepulchre's, and had [a priorefs, and] five or feven nuns. *Speed.*

Its principal benefaᴄtors to it were William Calvel, citizen of Canterbury, King Richard I. ', and the prior and convent of Chrift Church.

A. D. 1184. The parfonage of St. Edmund of Ridingate was granted to it by the abbot and convent of St. Auguftine's, which church was afterwards united, with the confent of the nuns, to St. Mary Bredin, A. D. 1349. To the vicar of this parifh they paid a yearly penfion of 60s.

This nunnery was diffolved 28 Henry VIII. and valued then at 38l. 10s. 7¼d. *Speed.* 29l. 12s. 5¼d. *Dugd.*

The fite was granted, 30 Henry VIII. in lieu of fome other lands, to the archbifhop of Canterbury, but afterwards, 30 Henry VIII. to James Hales. *Tanner.*

' After this prince had given the wood, or foreft, of Blean to Chrift Church, W. the prior and convent of the fame granted to this nunnery, and the priorefs and convent thereof, as much wood as one horfe going twice a day could fetch thence, where the church wood-reeves fhould appoint; which uncertainty, in the year 1270, the nuns releafing, had in lieu, and by way of exchange for it, a certain part or portion of the faid Blean wood [90 acres] affigned and made over to them, as appears from the words of the deed; the which wood retains to this day the name of *Min-cnen-wood*, taking its name from the nuns, which our anceftors, from the Saxon Mynecena, called *Minchens. Somner.*

Regrum

Reḡrūm H. ecclie Chriſti, Cant', fol. 118.
Moniales Stĩ Sepulchri ſolvebant ecclie Chriſti, Cant'.
Pio Petro Columbvn et Ricardo Mercatore ad feſtum Stĩ Joarnis, vs. iijd.
Pro Joanne, filio Morini, ad feſtum Stĩ Michaelis, vjd.
Pro eodem ad feſtum Stĩ Joannis Baptiſte, vjd.
Item ibm extra tarram ad feſtum Stĩ Michaelis, iiis. jd. &c.
Redditus quos debent Theſaurarii monialibus Stĩ Sepulchri.
Ad feſtum Stĩ Mich. ixs. iijd. Ad Natale [Chriſti] ixs. iijd. Ad Paſch' ixs.
iijd. Ad feſtum St. Joan' Bapt' ixs. iijd.
Item eiſdem in Cantuaria.—Ad feſt' Stĩ Mich' x ¼d.
Ad medium xLme [Mid Lent] —xijd. Item ad eundem terminum, x¼d.

In 1365, Cecilia Thornford, prioreſs of St. Sepulchre's, reſigned
her place into the hands of Simon [Langham] archbiſhop of Canterbury, who ſent his letters, dated at Maghfeld, Feb. 19,
A. D. 1365, to Robert [Hathbrand] Prior of Canterbury, com-
miſſioning him to elect a new prioreſs. Accordingly, on March
3, he went to the priory or church of St. Sepulchre's, and calling all the nuns together, he elected, confirmed, and inſtalled
Joan de Cheriton, one of the ſiſters of that houſe, and in all
reſpects rightly qualified to be the prioreſs.

Archbiſhop Morton, by his laſt will, gave lands near Maidſtone,
in the Mote park, and a mill near the ſame park, to the church
of Canterbury, the archbiſhop and his ſucceſſors, to the end that
he and his ſucceſſors for ever ſhould pay yearly to the prioreſs
and nuns of St. Sepulchre's eight marks to find a prieſt to celebrate
maſs within the ſaid nunnery, in a chantery founded in the ſame
by John de Bourn, formerly rector of Frackenham, in the time of
archbiſhop Wittleſey.

In the taxation in the archdeacon's black book, A. D. 1292,
the temporalities of theſe nuns were thus rated: " In Canterbury
and the ſuburb, Biſhopesbourn, Taynton, [Thanington] Hackyn-
ton, and Little Hardres, xiil. xs. vd. tenths xxvs. ¼d."

" At this place," ſays Somner, " ſometime one Elizabeth
" Barton, more vulgarly known by the name of the Holy Maid
" of Kent, that great impoſtor of her time, was a vailed nun
" and votareſs. Whoſe pranks and practices, or rather the
" monks and other papaliis, by her agency, are obvious both in
" our ſtatutes and ſtories. . . .   " It

" It feems the parifh church of St. Sepulchre was born down
" in the fame fall with the nunnery.   For however frequent
" mention may be found, both of parifh, church, and church-
" yard alfo before, yet fince the fuppreffion, the place of the two
" latter is unknown, the limits of the other uncertain, and the
" memory of all three almoft extinct.   Only that ftone-gate by
" the turning on your left hand to Dover-ward, feems to have
" been the weftern door of the church ', as I collect by this
" boundary": " Of the land which lieth over againft the church
" of the Holy Sepulchre, nigh a ftreet by which they go toward
" Dudendale [now Morton-farm], on the fouth-fide of the faid
" church." " The boundary of the piece of ground directly over-
" againft it. The laft lady priorefs of this houfe, by name Dame
" Philip John [Philippa Joan], lies buried in the north-ile of
" St. George's church, which in her will fhe calls The Chappel of
" the Bleffed Mary."

Juliana, priorefs, and the convent of St. Sepulchre's, granted a
fourth part of an acre of land to the hofpital of Eaftbridge. See
the Grant, p. 313.   This was before the year 1227.

Mynchyncroft appertinentia eft monafterii Sti Sepulchri.   Lib. MS. Tho. Hales.
Anno 1184. Rogerus, Abbas, et Conventus Sti Auguftini concefferunt eccliam
B. Edm' de Redingate in puram et perpetuam elemofynam monialibus S. Sepulchri,
Cant'. Ita tamen quod moniales pred' in recognitionem juris quod S. Auguft' habet
in ppo ecclie de Redingate xij denarios de ipfa ecclefia fingulis annis reddent fuper
altare Sti Auguftini in die ipfius Sancti ad organa reparanda : et fuper hec tunc
prioriffa, tunc fubprioriffa in capitulo noftro fidelitatem juraverunt. Prefentibus
multis teftibus.
Regiftrarium archidiaconi Cant. In MS. Catalogo domorum religiofarum, in
totâ diocefi Cantuarienfi fic recenfetur—Prioratus S. Sepulchri Cant' moniales nigre.
Moniales S. Sepulchri non ingrediantur poffeffiones S. Auguftini. Vide Thorn,
col. 1893.
Harum fundator fuit Anfelmus archiepifcopus, et quanquam infra limites feodi beàti
Auguftini fint conftitute, tamen in folo archiepifcopatus fite funt. Erat namque ibi
ecclefia in honorem S. Sepulchri, de patronatu archiepifcopi, exiguis terris circum-
cincta, ubi in prefenti conftat eas effe fundatas. Thorn, ibm.

' A view of this weft gate (or rather gate-way) with part of the wall of the nunnery, is annexed.
That it could not have been the " door of the church," but merely the gate-way to the nunnery, feems
obvious on infpection, as it leads to a court, in which fome old arches and ruined walls ftill remain.

[Tradition fays, that thefe fifters were fo indigent, that they were ftyled the poor nuns of St. Sepulchre's.]

Hofpital of St. JAMES, or St. JACOB, near Canterbury.

This was an ancient hofpital, dedicated to St. James, for xxv leprous fifters, a priorefs, three priefts, and one clerk, founded, before 1188, in the fuburbs of Canterbury, at the end of Win-cheap, near Thanington, and thence fometimes called " *Hofpital's* " *de Wincheap*." Lambarde and Weever have faid by miftake, that it was founded by queen Eleanor, wife to king Henry III. But long before that, viz. in king John's time, " the prior and con-vent of Chrift Church, Canterbury, took it into their cuftody and protection." See the charter cited by Somner, *ex archiv. eccl'ie Chrifti, Cant'*.

" Afterwards Henry III. gave the parfonage of Bradegate [1] towards the augmentation of its endowment.

" Its revenues were Firmin's Barton, fo called from Firmin, once governor of it ; the reft lay at Egerton, Charing, Merfham, Blean, Hakynton, Natindon [Nackington], Thanington, Sha-doxherft, Kingfnoth, Roking, and in and about Canterbury, valued *de claro*, at 46l. 6s. 3d. in Henry VIIIth's time, by the commiffioners.

" It payed no tithes at all.

" It efcaped the general diffolution ; but foon after [Feb. 28, 1551,] Young [the farmer] faith, that Freeman and one Dartnall caufed the fifters to furrender the houfe to the king, and Robert Dartnall, by the king's letters patents, got poffeffion. The lands were worth 100 marks per annum, &c. The fifters have xlvi s. viii d. by the year penfion. Mr. Freeman's widow hath the

[1] Now Bredgar. See Hafted's Hiftory of Kent, vol. II. p. 587.

writings,

writings, and Sir Edw. Walton hath bought a great part of the lands, and hath a manfion-houfe, &c. There was but one fifter then alive. Cardinal Pole's [1] vifitation, 1557." Thus far Mr. Somner.

A. D. 1414. John [Woodnesburgh [2]] Prior of Canterbury, vifited the hofpital of St. James, and gave feveral ftatutes and ordinances to regulate the fervices of the chapel, and the well government of the hofpital. And he calls himfelf *Hofpital' S'ti Jacobi juxta Cant', ab ejufdem fundatione, cuftos atque vifitator.* Thefe Statutes are omitted by Somner; but fee them, p. 431.

I have examined the charter cited by Somner, p. 77, the two laft lines, and p. 78 [3]; and it is true, except p. 78, line 16. [4] read, *appofitione illa roboravimus.*

Bulla Alexandri pape ad confirmationem carte ꝓtectionis p̄dicte, dated Anagniæ [5] 13 kal' Jul' pontiff' 5to extat' in archiv' eccḽe Chrifti, Cant'.

Rex H. dedit eccḽam de Biadgate, &c. In archiv' eccḽe Chrifti, Cant'.

Witneffes to the abovefaid charter, made in archbifhop Hubert's time, were Gilbertus Roffenfis, i. e. Gilbert Glanvil, who was confecrated Sept' 29, 1185, and died June 24, 1214.—H. Cant' archid', i. e. Henry de Caftillion.—Rogerus abbas Sti Auguft', Algarus, the 3d abbot of Feverfham.

Littere ꝓ hofpitali Sti Jacobi de ꝓ . . . . . ma̅gri hofpit' de Eaftbrigge, Cant'.

"Salutem : Quia quidam clericus, p̄tendens fe effe ma̅grum [6] hofpitalis Sti Thome Eaftbrigge, Cantuar', ob favorem inceptum quem habet coram auditore caufarum curie venerabilis patris n̅ri d̅ni archiep̄i [7], nos et eccḽam n̅ram et miferabiles p̄fonas in hofpitali n̅ro Sti Jacobi extra Cant', multipliciter nititur fatigare laboribus et expenfis ; n̅ miremini fi propter importunitatem hujus auditoris, ꝓ defenfione juris n̅ri et eccḽe n̅e et hofpitalis n̅ri p̄d', ad fuperioris examen' previa occafione convolemus: proinde confiderantes, quod ex hoc forfitan fumus flam̅am ignis ꝓducit qui im̅eritos arderet. Vale in eo qui femper valet et viget femper. Dat' Cant', die Om̅ium Sanctorum, 1329."

---

[1] Rather archdeacon Harpsfield's. See p. 371.

[2] This prior Mr. Goftling fuppofes to have been an eminent architect, as his face and name are on a key-ftone in the roof of a chapel (now the finging-fchool] over St. Michael's in the cathedral. "Walk," p. 251, 252.

[3] Appendix, p. 9, (2d edit.)

[4] p. 9. l. 8. from the bottom.

[5] See p. 305, note 1, and 4.

[6] In the lift of mafters of Eaftbridge Hofpital, p. 371. William Burgoos appears to have been then mafter.

[7] Simon Mepham was then archbifhop.

6

Prioriſſæ hoſpitalis S. Jacobi pro ſitu ejuſdem hoſpitalis ac pratis et terris ejus in Thanington de redditu p annum, vijs. ijd. et pro gallinâ 4d. in toto vijs. vj d. ſolut' 1° anno Edw' VI. MS. Tho. Hales.

Mr. Somner, p. 77. in his own book, [1ſt 'edit.] hath added in writing. " In archbiſhop Baldwin's time I find expreſs mention of this hoſpital, and of the then maſter and founder (as an old book calls him), Magiſter Feramin [or Firmin] by name; to whom, with the prior of Feverſham, letters were directed from pope Clement III. about the then differences between the ſame archbiſhop arid his monks, touching the college at Hakinton, as may be ſeen in Gervas Dorobern '."

p. 79. Mr. Somner adds, That " archbiſhop Baldwin was diſpleaſed with this hoſpital, becauſe Mr. Feramin, the then maſter, was one of thoſe that were commanded to execute the pope's decree in favour of the monks againſt the archbiſhop. Gervas Dorobern '."

Thus there were three hoſpitals near the city for lepers, Herbaldown, St. James, and St. Laurence, all without the walls, of which ſee Joſephi Antiq. Judaic. l. ix. c. 4, 5. The Samaritans had a law that leprous perſons ſhould go out of the city; and Choppine de Sacra Politia, l. 3. tit. 5. ſays, that the phyſicians excluded leprous perſons from the city. Of ſuch lazar-houſes, ſee alſo Coke upon Littleton, fol. 135, 136.

In the council at London, under Hubert Walter, archbiſhop of Canterbury, A. D. 1200, there was a particular canon made,

" Ut leproſi cœmiterium et propriam habeant capellam ²."

" Affectu pietatis inducti, concilii Lateranenſis etiam inſtitutione ſuffulti, decernimus ut ubicunque tot leproſi ſimul fuerint congregati qui eccleſiam cum cœmiterio ſibi conſtruere, et proprio valeant gaudere preſbytero; ſine contradictione aliquâ habere permittantur, &c."

This ſhews the number of lazars in thoſe days to have been very many.

' Theſe paragraphs were afterwards inſerted by Mr. Battely in his improved edition.

² Concil. Brit. T. II.

Litera teftimonialis quod forores Sti Jacobi non funt profeffe.

Regrum eccŀe Chrifti, Cant'. K. fol. 57. Univerfis Chrifti fidelibus pfentes fras infpecturis Robertus [Hathbrand] pmiffione divina prior eccŀe Chrifti, Cant' : Salutem et finceram in dno caritatem. Univerfitati vre notum facimus p pfentes, quod licet prioriffa et forores hofpitalis Sti Jacobi in fuburbio Cant', vulgariter nuncupato, quod quidem hofpitale ad iirum patronatum et difpofitionem ptinet, tanquam religiofe mulieres comuniter ibm vixerunt, ad religionem tamen vel regularem ordinem approbatum inibi obfervand' nullatenus funt adftricte, nec profiteri tenentur tacite vel expreffe, fed ab eodem hofpitali libere recedere poterunt, prout ipfis placuerit, ficut alie feculares. In cujus rei teftimonium figillum iirum fecimus hiis apponi. Dat' Cant', A. D. 1349.

In the 9th year of Henry VII. Sept. 6, Joan, priorefs, and the fifters of the convent of St. James, demifed by leafe to William [Selling], prior and the convent of Chrift Church, Canterbury, for the term of 40 years, their lands, tenements, and appurtenances, lying near Filernhil [Tyler-hill], in the parifhes of St. Stephen de Hakynton, near Canterbury, and of St. Cofmus and Damian in La Blean, containing 93 acres of land, 3 roods, and 33 perches, at the yearly rent of 33 s. 4 d. (all timber excepted.) Regiftrum Cant' R.

In catalogo domorum religiofarum in tota diocefi Cant', fic recenfetur;
" Domus fororum Sti Jacobi extra Cant'."

Statuta hofpitalis Sti Jacobi, juxta Cantuariam, A. D. 1414, fecundum ecclefie Anglicane curfum.

JOANNES [Woodnefburgh] pmiffione divina Ste Cant' ecclie prior, hofpitalis Sti Jacobi juxta Cantuariam ab ejufdem fundatione cuftos atque vifitator, dilectis nobis ipfius hofpitalis fratribus et fororibus falutem : ut iira vifitatio, nuper in dicto hofpitali facta, fiat connuente dno fructuofa ad correctionem et reformationem ejufdem hofpitalis, tam in fpiritualibus quam in temporalibus, infra fcripta iira mandata, ftatuta, et ordinationes, in virtute obedientie, pcipimus p vos inviolabiliter ppetuis futuris temporibus obfervari.

Imprimis, ftatuimus et ordinamus quod omnes fratres et forores ad oratorium, five eccliam inibi fcituatam, fingulis diebus horâ confuetâ conveniant, horas canonicas et miffas in ipfo oratorio dicendas et celebrandas integraliter audituri, nifi ratione officii, vel alia caufa rationabili, pfidenti ejufdem hofpitalis infinuanda, dictis tempo_ ribus contigent abfentari.

Statuimus

Statuimus p̄terea quod numerus capellanorum ab antiquo in ipſo hoſpitali ſta. tutus, quàm citius facultates dicti hoſpitalis ad hoc poterunt ſufficere, obſervetur et cuſtodiatur. Quodque ipſi capellani in oratorio dicti hoſpitalis divina horis com. petentibus cotidiè, legitimo ceſſante impedimento, celebrent. Atque horas canonicas alta voce, ita quod a fratribus et ſororibus tunc p̄ſentibus audiri poterunt, ſimul dicant in eodem, pulſatis primitus ſignis, ſeu campanis, juxta morem in ipſo hoſpi. tali ab antiquo uſitatum.

Inſuper ordinamus quod fratres et ſorores ipſius hoſpitalis in ipſorum oratorio a confabulationibus penitus ſe abſtineant: Ipſorumque ſinguli ſingulis diebus nu. merum orationum dominicarum cum ſalutationibus B. Marie Anglicis, alias eiſdem p̄ p̄deceſſores ñros in eorum viſitationibus injunctum et aſſignatum, ſi com̄odè fieri poterit, compleant, in ipſo oratorio dicant, et cum devotione.

Item quod nullus recipiatur in fratrem, aut aliqua in ſororem, dicti hoſpitalis ſine conſilio et aſſenſu ecclie Cant', qui pro tempore fuerit, prioris.

Idemque ſtatuimus de capellanis in ipſo hoſpitali celebraturis.

Ad hec ordinamus, quod de cetero deputetur una ciſta in loco ſecuro infra dictum hoſpitale ponenda, tribus ſeris tribus diverſis clavibus ſignata; quarum clavium unam habeat prioriſſa, ſecundam habeat unus fratrum ejuſdem hoſpitalis, ſi quis fuerit, p̄ confratres ſuos eligendus: alioquin una ex ſororibus p̄ majorem partem conſororum ſuarum ad hoc nominanda. Tertiam autem habeat ipſius hoſpitalis celeriſſa. In ipſa verò ciſta reponantur ejuſdem hoſpitalis ſigillum com̄une, ac ejuſdem hoſpitalis evidentie, carte, et munimenta quecunque.

Itemque in viſitatione antedicta comperimus quod prioriſſa ipſius hoſpitalis, que nunc eſt, ſolebat et ſolet ões-redditus et proventus dicti hoſpitalis ſola, abſque ſcientia conſororum ſuarum, clam recipere, et ipſis inconſultis de eiſdem diſponere; volumus et ordinamus, quod ex nunc dicta prioriſſa, et que erit p̄ tempore in hoſpitali p̄dicto, nullas pecuniarum ſum̄as, abſque ſcientia confratrum,(ſiqui ſint, habitum juxta ipſius hoſpitalis fundationem deferentium, et majoris partis conſororum ſuarum, recipiat quoquo modo. Pecunias verò ſic receptas, ſi eas tempore receptionis earundem expendi non oporteat, in ciſta memorata deponi volumus et mandamus. Item ordi. namus quod nullus cuſtodum clavium p̄dictarum clavem ſibi com̄iſſam alio tradat cuſtodiendam.

Item, quod ipſa prioriſſa quatuor ſingulis annis terminis ſubſcriptis, viz. in feſtis Sti Hillarii [1], inventionis Sancte Crucis [2], Sti Petri ad Vincula [3], et Omnium Sanctorum [4], de ōibus redditibus et proficuis ipſius hoſpitalis per eam vel ejus nomine receptis ipſo anno fratribus habitum, ut p̄dicitur, geſtantibus, et ſororibus ſuis, plenum compotum in forma compoti reddere, ipſumque compotum poſt dictum feſtum Omnium Sanc. torum priori ecclie Cantuarienſis, qui erit p̄ tempore, aut ipſius deputato, ante feſtum Nativitatis Dñi quolibet anno tradere teneatur.

Ordinamus etiam quod de cetero quantum fieri poteſt alique recipiantur juvencule literate, aut alie juvenes dociles et capaces in literatura imbuenda.

Item, quod fratres et ſorores dicti hoſpitalis eccliam de Bradgare eiſdem unitam ad firmam non tradant; nec etiam aliquas eorundem poſſeſſiones vel tenementa; nec boſcum aut ſubboſcum vendant aut donent: nullamque lram ſub eorum ſigillo com.

[1] Jan. 14. [2] May 3. [3] Aug. 1. [4] Nov. 1.

muni

muni figillent, feu faciant figillari, quovis modo, fine affenfu prioris Cantuarienfis, qui fuerit p tempore.

Item, Ordinamus quod fi contingat prioriffam dicti hofpitalis ab eodem p unum diem abfentari, quod rpfa deputet unam ydoneam ex confororibus fuis, qui durante abfentia fua ipfius poterit fupplere vices.

Item, quia in ipfa vifitatione nobis extitit detectum fingulos fratres et forores dicti hofpitalis decem folidos annuatim in pecunia numerata de exitibus dicti hofpitalis ultra panem et cervifiam eis in communi miniftratum, P eorum veftitu, qui eis nullatenus miniftratur in communi, ac aliis diverfis eifdem incumbentibus oneribus, duntaxat recipere ; quodque bona ejufdem hofpitalis mobilia infra paucos annos adeo effe augmentata, quod ad uberiorem diftributionem pecuniarum inter fratres et forores antedictos occafione pmiffa annuatim faciendam commode prout etiam ipfis fatis a diu eft novimus poterunt fufficere ; idcirco matura deliberatione phabita, attenta dictorum fratrum et fororum fingulorum penuria, ftatuimus et ordinamus, quod fingulis annis futuris cuilibet fratri habitum, ut pdicitur, gerenti, nec non fingulis fororibus dicti hofpitalis, ultra x folidos pdictos, in fefto Omnium Sanctorum folvantur tres folidi et quatuor denarii monete Anglicane de bonis communibus hofpitalis memorati, in dictorum fratrum et fororum penurie fubductionem, ac victus augmentationem, cum ipforum nulli p oibus diebus cujuflibet anni, in quibus ipfos aut carnibus aut pifcibus vefci deceat vel oporteat, ultra unum porcum recipere confueverant femel in anno.

Item, quia facris obviat inftitutis mulieres etiam facratas facra vafa contingere, aut circa altaria miniftrare, ordinamus, quod nulla fororum dicti hofpitalis, aut alia quevis mulier, dum divina in dicto hofpitalis oratorio celebrantur, quovis modo inibi circa et prope altaria ftare vel federe, aut pbyteris divina celebrantibus, vel horas canonicas dicentibus, miniftrare pfumant, cum, fecundum dicti hofpitalis primariam fundacionem, ejufdem capellani five facerdotes habere debeant unum clericum, qui eifdem debeat in pmiffis officiare, cui volumus de bonis communibus dicti hofpitalis, ut convenit, miniftrari, atque de fuperpelliceo, ejufdem hofpitalis fumptibus, dum fibi commiffum pagit officium, provideri.

Ordinamus etiam pterea, et ftatuimus, quod quotiefcunque fiet in coi diftributio panis et cervifie p fratrum et fororum dicti hofpitalis fuftentatione, quod prioriffa et celeraria ejufdem hofpitalis (aliqua ex fororibus ipfius hofpitalis p fratres, fi qui fuerint, et forores ejufdem hofpitalis, vel majorem partem eorundem, nominanda et eligenda) que cum prioriffa et celeraria predict' vel earum altera ad tollendam dem fufpicionem inequalis diftributionis communis panis et cervifie, aut aliorum, fiqua fuerint inter fratres et forores hofpitalis antedicti dividenda, ceffante collufione, adjungatur pmiffis, quoque ftatuendo adjicimus, quod prioriffa dicti hofpitalis nulla communia negotia abfque confenfu fratrum, fiqui fint, et majoris partis fororum dicti hofpitalis, diffiniat vel expediat, nullafque penitus faciat circa reparationem dicti hofpitalis aut domorum quarumcunque eidem hofpitali ptinentium expenfas voluptuofas, nec etiam utiles vel neceffarias, circa eas, que fummam xx folidorum in anno excedunt, fine confenfu fratrum hofpitalis fupra nominati, fiqui fuerint, et fororum, aut majoris partis eorundem. Premiffis quoque pcipiendo fubjungimus, quod pri-

oriffe

orifta dicti hofpitaliś, que eft, et que erit p tempore, nullos infra fepta dicti hofpitalis peregrinaturos five moraturos recipiat fine confenfu fororum fuarum, vel majoris partis earandem, et licentia ñra et fuccefforum ñrorum petita et optenta.

Ceterum quia comperimus nonnullas ordinationes, injunctiones, et monita falutaria p pdeceffores ñros in ipforum vifitationibus in dicto holpitali exercitis facta fuiffe et effe; nos tam ea quam etiam hec ñra ftatuta et ordinationes p vos, quibus pfentes ñre diriguntur ire, ac quemlibet veftrum, fub majoris excomunicationis pena mandamus inviolabiliter oblervari.

Volentes infuper tam pdecefforum noftrorum ordinationes, injunctiones, et monita, quam etiam ñra pfcripta, fub pena inobedientium et contemptus, fexies in anno temporibus interpolatis publicè coram vobis in domo illa, ubi horum orationum veftrarum fingulis diebus legere foletis, legi, atque in vulgari etiam exponi, fub pena proxime fuperius nominata. In quorum omnium teftimonium figillum noftrum fecimus hiis apponi. Dat in prioratu ñro Cautuar' quoad pfentium confignationem, 18 die menfis Februarii, A. D. 1414.

[All that now remains of this building is part of a ftone wall, the boundary of an orchard, on the eaft fide of the road, juft without Wincheap, near the turnpike.]

MAYNARD'S SPITAL.

[This, properly fpeaking, though one connected building, is two hofpitals, having two different endowments. The firft was founded in 1312, by John Maynard, or Mayner, a citizen of Canterbury, who, Somner fays, was called " The Rich, an addition which was continued alfo to his defcendants." He dedicated it to the Bleffed Virgin, and endowed it with eftates in the city to the value of 3l. 7s. per ann. a wood of nine acres, called Brotherhood Wood, and a meadow adjoining of an acre and half, called Brotherhood Clofe, in the parifh of Fordwich, for the maintenance of four brothers and three fifters, fingle perfons, of the age of fifty or upwards. The other owes its origin to Leonard Cotton, an alderman of the city, who, by his will, dated in 1604, fome years before his death, left fome eftates in truft (which has been ever fince continued), for the maintenance of one additional brother and two fifters,

a widower

a widower and widows, of St. Margaret's parifh, if proper objects there; if not, of St. Mildred's; if not, of any parifh in Canterbury; in thofe tenements which, it feems, he had then erected and annexed to Maynard's building.

In 1666, the records of thefe two hofpitals, being fent to London, on account of a law-fuit then depending, were deftroyed in the great fire, except the old leafes of their eftates from the time of queen Elizabeth. In 1711, Mrs. Mary Mafters, of this city, of whofe donation an account is given p. 280, left this hofpital, and five others, 5l. a year each. But, for the reafons there affigned, they receive only 16s. 4d.

Mr. Matthew Browne, in 1717, bequeathed to it ten fhillings a year, iffuing from two houfes in the borough of Staplegate (fee p. 281); and an abftract of his will is annexed, p. 442.

50ol. left to it by Thomas Hanfon, efq; (who died in 1770), being now invefted in 3 per cent. bank annuities, produces (fee p. 196) a dividend of 17l. 10s. per ann. And there being no fund for repairs, Mr. William Rigden, brewer, who died in 1776, fettled in truft and conveyed for that purpofe, in 1771, a meffuage and fmith's forge in Hawk's-lane, which let for 6l. per ann. The hofpital has a common feal, whofe device is the Virgin and Child. See it engraved in plate X. fig. 2.

It ftands in a lane in St. Mildred's parifh, leading from Caftle-ftreet to Stour-ftreet, and confifts of ten tenements, with a chapel near the centre, as reprefented in the plan, plate IX. fig. 2. where prayers are read twice a week by the prior. On the chapel is this infcription:

"This houfe and chapel was founded by John Maynard, for 3 brothers and 4 " fifters, *Anno Domini*, 1317, in the 12th year of the reign of king Edward the " 'fecond. This work was finifhed, and the chapel repaired, in the year of our " Lord 1617, by Jofeph Colf, efquire, Alderman of the city of Canterbury, and " M. of this hofpital. William Gray, M. 1776." This is not now ftrictly true, as in the great ftorm on Nov. 3, 1703, that building was blown down, ar' fcription fet on foot in the neighbourhood, the prefent hofpital was erected in 1708.

The

The mayor, for the time being, is patron; the mayor and aldermen are perpetual vifitors; and one of the aldermen is mafter. The prefent is William Long, efquire, to whom I am obliged for moft of the above particulars, and alfo for a farther detail of the eftates of this hofpital in the Appendix, fubftituted to a very brief and imperfect account given by Mr. Battely].

The Hofpital of Poor Priests.

An hofpital, for the relief of poor, infirm, and aged priefts, in St. Margaret's parifh, was founded, Tanner fays, by archdeacon Simon Langton, before 1243. Thorn fays, " he founded it with the alms and charity of feveral benefactors [1]."

Soon after its foundation, the abbot and convent of St. Auguftine's [at the inftance of the founder] granted to it the parfonage of Stodmarfh. The grant of it is in Thorn, col. 1892.

A. D. 1249, before St. Margaret's church was united to the hofpital, a compofition was made with the rector for tithes, &c. preferved in Thorn, col. 1897.

A. D. 1271, that church was given to it by Hugh Mortimer, archdeacon, with confent of the patrons, the abbot and convent aforefaid. See the grant in Somner. See alfo Thorn, col. 1920.

A mill belonged to it, out of which 4 bufhels of wheat were yearly paid to the hofpital of Eaftbridge. See more of this in Somner, p. 138.

Thomas Wyke, mafter of the hofpital, new-built it of ftone, A. D. 1373.

This hofpital was fpared at the general diffolution; and in queen Mary's reign, Hugh Barret was prefented to it by archdeacon Harpsfield, patron of it.

[1] Quod hofpitale idem Simon' archidiaconus diverforum elemofinis dicitur fundaffe. Thorn, col. 1892.

5.

Masters

Mafters of the Poor Priefts Hofpital, with the rectory of St.
Margaret's annexed, prefented by the archdeacons.

1494. May 5. HENRY HARVY.

1497. Apr. 22. THOMAS WATER, by exchange with Harvy,
for Arundel's chantry in Chrift Church.

1511. Nov. 14. PHILIP TAYLOR, chaplain. Water refigned.

1528. April 25. NICHOLAS LANGDON, M. A. Taylor deceafed.

1554. HUGH BARRET. Langdon deceafed.

1560. March 8. ROBERT BACON [1].

1575. May 12. BLASE WINTER [2].

Extracted from the Regifter by JOHN. DRAKE, Notary Public.

The hofpital of poor priefts paffed over their right in a houfe
and land at Hottewell [near the bridge, on the N. fide] to the
prior and convent of Chrift Church, and fealed the grant with
the feal of archdeacon Langton, *huic prefenti fcripto figillum
magif' Simonis de Langetune, archidiaconi Cant', e' appenfum
eò quod tunc temporis commune figillum non habebamus.
Actum, A. D. 1242. 4to non' Martii.* The imprefs of the feal
was the murder of Thomas Becket, and about it, *Sigillum
Simonis archidiaconi.* On the other fide, a head, with a hand
from above over it, and round about it, *S. magiftri Simonis
Langtune, i. e. Sigillum magiftri Simonis Langtune,* with the S on
the reverfe, which fignifies, in the old feals, that the hofpital
was dedicated to the Virgin Mary.

Though it efcaped the general diffolution, as mentioned above,
it was furrendered by the then mafter, patron, and ordinary,
17 Eliz. and granted by the queen, with all its lands and appurtenances, to the mayor and commonalty of the city for the
ufe of the poor, as an hofpital and bridewell. " It is now the

---

[1] Styled by archbifhop Parker, in his account, 1562, " a temporal man, who is
not refident, nor maketh any diftribution.". Strype's Life of that archbifhop, p. 113.
[2] The laft mafter, who furrendered it foon after.

general.

general workhoufe, being fo appointed by act of parliament in 1728, for the maintenance and employment of the poor of the city, under guardians incorporated for that purpofe [1]."

Anno 1296. Maḡr Guido de Well, rector ecclie de Swalclyve, tunc fyndicus feu procurator hofpitalis pauperum facerdotum Cantuarie, venit in capitulum monafterii S. Augultini, et ibidem preftitit publice facramentum fidelitatis ratione ecclefiarum S. Margarette in Cantuaria et beate Marie de Stodmarfh, fecundum confuetudinem, &c. Thorn, col. 1966.

ST. LAURENCE.

The hofpital of St. Laurence in the S. E. fuburb, on the right hand of the road from Canterbury to Dover, was founded (fays the private Leiger [2]), in 1137, by abbot Hugh II. of that name, and the convent of St. Auguftine, for the reception and relief of lazar or leprous monks, and of the parents and relations of fuch as were reduced to beggary [3]. The names of grants at the beginning were *Fratribus S. Laurentii; Fratribus et Sororibus S. Laurentii*; and afterwards, from the 47 Edward III. they granted and received by the names of priorefs and fifters, and there were no brothers. Nine acres of land within the lordfhip of St. Auguftine were given by the founder (as appears by the charter annexed) on the right fide of the road to Dover, with all the tithes of the manor of Longport, and all the tithes of wheat and peas adjoining on the left fide. The tithes of the whole manor of Dodingdale [now Morton] were afterwards added by Richard de Marci, the lord of it (fee his charter), with many other benefactions

[1] Goftling's Walk, p. 60.
[2] Somner's Antiq. p. 38.
[3] " For fixteen brothers and fifters, and for one chaplain, and one clerk, ferving in the faid hofpital," are the words (in Latin) of the Leiger.

needlefs

needlefs to recapitulate. 26 Henry VIII. the revenues were valued at 39l. 8s. 6d. in the whole. *Tanner.*

30 H. VIII. A leafe was made by the priorefs and fifters to Sir Chriftopher Hales, knight, of the fcite of the faid hofpital, and of all the poffeffions for 9 years, yielding no yearly rent, but finding the fifters and priorefs during their lives. The intereft was vefted in Mr. Lovelace.

May 26, 3 and 4 Philip and Mary. This hofpital was granted, by letters patent under the great feal of England, to Sir John Parrot, in fee, in confideration of a fum of money, *ac gratiâ noftrâ fpeciali, et mero motu, et certâ fcientiâ.*

6 Edward VI. A feoffment was made from the priorefs, and fifters to one Tipfell of London, of this hofpital, in fee; the eftates of which Sir John Parrot and Tipfell, by the appointment of Serjeant Lovelace to keep the leafe in force, conveyed to Hoveden and Bingham.

In the account given up to the vifitors, "feven fifters, a priorefs, and a prieft, were faid to be maintained by the produce of the lands, which was eftimated at 20l." This ftatement was figned by " Joanne Francys, prioriffa, Elizabeth Oliver, Florence Younge, *nondum foror, nomine fororum.*" The chief governor (as ufual) was called keeper, or maiter *(cuftos),* and he was always one of the monks of St. Auguftine's. The chief of the feven fifters was called priorefs.

In 1562 [by archbifhop Parker's account], the houfe was " lamentably mifufed [by reafon of the above-mentioned leafe]," and had only two fifters then in it, [who received from the farmer there only 40s. per ann.]

In May, 1574, 16 Elizab. it was found by inquifition, *virtute officii,* before the efcheator of Kent, that this hofpital was concealed, and worth yearly 4l. which being returned into the exchequer, one Honywood took a leafe of it for xxi years,

yielding

yielding 4l. yearly, after he fhould have poffeffion of the premifes by virtue of the faid leafe ; and in default of payment for a certain fpace, the leafe was to be void.

This eftate and manfion-houfe, built on or near the fite of the old monaftery, being vefted in Sir George Rooke, and afterwards in his fon, were bequeathed by the latter to his relict, fifter to the late vifcount Dudley and Ward. And Mrs. Rooke, at her death, devifed them to her nephew, the prefent vifcount. On one of the flinty piers of the old gateway, a figure of St. Laurence on the gridiron may be difcovered, with a man ftanding at his head, and another at his feet [1]." Tanner, however, queries " whether it was not rather built in memory of St. Laurence [as he ftyles him] the archbifhop, fucceffor to St. Auguftine, than of the broiled martyr, as Somner terms him [2]." But where does it appear that archbifhop Laurence was ever canonifed ?

Circa hec tempora idem abbas (viz. Hugo 2dus) fundavit hofpitale Sti Laurentii. Ad cujus fundationem contulit novem acras terre, in quibus ipfum hofpitale fitum eft. Contulit eciam eidem totam decimam de dominico de Langeport, et tres carectatas feni; unam de Langeport, aliam de facriftiâ, et terciam de camerario. Fuit autem illud hofpitale ad hoc fpecialiter inftitutum et fundatum, ut fi contingat quod aliquis monachus iftius monafterii morbum contagiofum, et precipuè lepram, incurrat, ratione cujus morbi infra fepta monafterii abfque fcandalo fratrum converfari non poterit, providebitur illi in loco predicto de camerâ competenti, et ibidem habebit victum et veftitum, non de bonis hofpitalis predicti, fed de monafterio ifto, ficut et alius frater. Si verò contingat, parentem alicujus monachi, patrem, videlicet, aut matrem, fororem aut fratrem, ad tantam inopiam devenire, ut cum fcandalo monafterii et illius fratris oportuerit ipfum hoftiatim mendicare, providebitur ipfi in eodem hofpitali competens fuftentatio fecundum facultatem illius domus, per confiderationem abbatis et magiftri hofpitalis predicti qui pro tempore fuerit ibm.

Notum fit omnibus Dei fidelibus, tam prefentibus quam pofteris, quod ego fecundus Hugo, Dei gratiâ, abbas Sti Auguftini, ejufdemque loci conventus, pro redemptione aïarum ñrarum, predecefforum ñrorum, atque fucefforum, conceffimus ac dedimus in elemofinam vii acras terre de dominio ñro precio quondam adquifitas, ad faciendum hofpitale in illis vii acris fupra memoratis juxta viam que a Canterburiâ ducit ad Dovre, in dextra parte vie. Contulimus eciam illi loco, ad fuftentationem infirmorum aut pauperum, decimam tocius annone de totâ terrâ illâ quam habemus

[1] Goftling's Walk, p. 21, 22.   [2] Notit. Mon. p. 213.

in

in dominio, in dextra parte vie, et ōem decimam frumenti et pifarum tocius terre, que adjacet ad Langeport, de dominio ñro in finiftrâ parte vie. Quicunque ergo pro amore Dei benefecerint infirmis illic habitantibus, et locum illum manute. nuerint, benedictionem Dei habeant, et gratiam fimùl et commune beneficium loci. noftri.

Richardus ¹ de Marci omnibus fuis hominibus Francis et Anglicis, tam prefentibus quam futuris, falutem. Sciatis me conceffiffe et dediffe decimas terre mee de Dodingdale hofpitali S. Laurentii, quod eft juxta Cantuariam, in ppetuam ele- mofinam, p falute animarum predecefforum meorum, et mei, et uxoris mee, et meorum infantium. Quare volo et precipio quatenus pd' hofpitale decimas preductas habeat et poffideat, benè, et in pace, et libere; precipioque, ex parte Dei, et ex parte mea, ut fratres et forores pd' hofpitalis habeant decimas illas nōiatim ad lir.eum pannum emendum in fefto S. Johannis Baptifte, quia credo quod tunc mei et me- orum memores erunt.

A claufe drawn up by archbifhop Wake's direction, to be in ferted in Eaftbridge hofpital leafes.

" And the faid A. B. doth for himfelf, his heirs, executors, adminiftrators, and affigns, and for every of them, covenant, promife, and grant, to and with the faid John Bradock, mafter of the faid hofpital, and his fucceffors, by thefe prefents, That he the faid A. B. his executors, adminiftrators, and affigns, fhall not, nor will, at any time hereafter, during this demife, do, commit, or wittingly or willingly fuffer any wafte, fpoil, or deftruction, in or upon the premifes, or any part thereof; but fhall and will, to the utmoft of his and their power, keep and preferve the fame from all wafte, fpoil, and deftruction whatfoever. And alfo, that he the faid A. B. his executors, adminiftrators, and affigns, fhall and will from time to time, and at all times, during this demife, order and manage the faid lands and premifes in good and hufbandlike manner, and fhall and will, at all times during this demife, imbarne · ftack, and lay all the corn and hay growing or arifing in and upon the demifed premifes, in the barns or other convenient places belonging to the premifes; and the faid hay, and the ftraw, and chaff, arifing from the faid corn, fhall and will fodder out and fpend in and upon the premifes, and the dung, fullage, and com- poft arifing therefrom, fhall and will, in good and hufbandlike manner, lay, fpread, fpend, and beftow in and upon the faid lands, or fome part thereof, where moft need fhall be, and fhall not elfewhere lay, fpread, fpend, or beftow the fame, or any part thereof.

WM. TURNER.
18 November, 1718."

Memorandum, To ftrengthen the claufe to prevent the tenants from cutting down timber, &c.

¹ " Rogerus," in Thorn.

N n n

A claufe

A clause taken out of Mr. MATTHEW BROWNE's will, dated December 12, 1717, proved at Canterbury, August 26, 1721 [1].

"Item, I give, devise, and bequeath unto the several hospitals of Eastbridge, alias St. Thomas, Maynard Spittle, St. John, and St. Nicholas Harbledown, in and near the city of Canterbury, and to every of them respectively, the sum of ten shillings apiece, of lawful money of Great Britain, yearly, and every year, for ever, out of the rents, issues, and profits of my two messuages, or tenements, with the appurtenances, situate and being in the borough of Staplegate, and now in the several occupations of Paul Whitehurst and Matthew Darby, or their assigns.

"Which said several and respective sums of ten shillings, I will, order, and appoint, shall be respectively paid to the prior, brothers and sisters of the said respective hospitals, upon the twelfth day of March yearly for ever. And my will and mind is, that if default shall happen to be made in payment of the said several sums of ten shillings, or any of them, to the said several hospitals, or any of them, at the day and time herein before appointed for the payment thereof, that then, and at all times afterwards, it shall and may be lawful to and for the priors, brothers and sisters of the said respective hospitals, to whom the said sum of ten shillings shall be so unpaid, to enter into and upon the said two messuages or tenements, or either of them, to distrain, and the distress and distresses there found to have, take, carry away, keep, retain, possess, and enjoy, until the said several respective sums of ten shillings, and all arrears thereof, and all charges in and about taking such distress, shall be fully satisfied and paid."

Vera copia excerpta ex testimonio MATTHEI BROWN,.   per JOS. WEBB [2].

[Besides the above, and the two great Benedictine and rival monasteries of Christ Church and St. Augustine's, whose history and antiquities have been amply discussed by Somner, Battely, Gostling, &c. the other religious and charitable foundations in and near Canterbury, were,

1. St. MILDRED's abbey, mentioned by Dugdale [3], within the walls, on the south side of the city, whose last abbot's name was Alfwic; " of which," says Bishop Tanner, "neither Mr. Somner nor Mr. Battely give us any account [4]."

---

[1] An abstract of this was given, p. 281. And see p. 135.
[2] Late reader of Eastbridge hospital. He died in 1771.
[3] Monast. I. p. 26.   [4] Notit. Mon. p. 208.

2. A priory

2. A priory of Dominican, or Black, Fryars, in St. Alphage's parifh, founded probably not long after 1221, by king Henry III. who, it is faid, built them a monaftery on the banks of the Stour, on land given them by archbifhop Langdon, of which fome venerable ruins remain, particularly the Gothic arches of a bridge, drawn by Mr. Grofe and others, and the fouth gate-way, faced with fquare flints, in St. Peter's-ftreet, built not long before the 30th Edward III. This is engraved in Mr. Thorpe's Kentifh Antiquities, the VIIth number of this work, pl. X. fig. 4. It had two other gates, or paffages, one in the ftreet near St. Alphage's church, and the other in Beft's-lane near the Water-lock, oppofite Prince of Orange-lane, then the Rufh-mar-ket, which led directly to their church, as appears by a very exact ftained drawing of that and the monaftery, with its pre-cinct, and a meafurement, by Thomas Langdon, 1595, in the poffeffion of the rev. Mr. Byrch, the prefent proprietor of the manor and principal manfion, which, we are informed, will be engraved in the IIId volume of Mr. Hafted's Hiftory of Kent. Part of the hall is now the Baptifts meeting-houfe, and the other is the houfe of Mr. John Haward; there are no veftiges of the church but part of the north wall, and part of the church-yard is the Baptifts burying-ground.

An indenture is ftill in being, made by thefe fryars only five years before their diffolution, of which the following is a copy:

" This indenture, made the vith day of the month of February, yn the xxvth yere of the reigne of kyng Henry the viiith [A. D. 1534] witneffeth, that John Wenar, ꝑor of the houfe of Frers ꝑrcheurs, yn the citie of Canturbery, and the covent of the fame houfe, of their hole mynde, affente, and confente, have dy-myfed, graunted, and letten to ferme unto Richard Burchard, of the ꝑrfhe of Saynite Elphe yn the fayde citie of Canfbery, drap, all that their gardyne [1], with the apꝑtenns, lyeing and beyng within the fite of the faid place, whiche gaidyne John Edward, vyntenar, late had and occupied yn ferme of the ꝑor and covent of

_____
[1] This, by the defcription, appears to be the orchard lately purchafed of Mr. Detanoy by Mr. Cyprian Bunce.

the faide houfe, boundyng to the comyne ryvare towards eafte, to the orchard
of the faid Freres towards northe, to the comvne way ledyng from Saynéte Peter's
paryfhe to the churche of the faid Freres, and the gardyne of the fame Freres,
occupied by James Thomfon and Marke Olford, towards fouth, and to the houfe
and gardyne of Xtofer Cornewall, and the lane leading from Saynéte Petre's
chuiche into the fayd orchard, towards weft: To have, hold, and occupye the
forefaid gardyne, with the apprtenances, to the faid Richard Burchard and his
affignes, from the fefte of the Annunciation of our I adye the Virgine next coming
after the date of thefe prefents, unto the end and term of fourtye yeres [1] then
next enfuing, and fully to be cõpleted, yeldyng and payeng therfor to the põr and
cõvent of the faide houfe, for the tyme beyng, yerely, by the fpace of the firft
twenty yeres of the faid teime, xiiis. iiiid. of lawful money of England, and
yerely by the fpace of the other xx yeres of the faid terme, xvs. of lawful money
of England, at the fefts of the nativity of Saynéte John Baptift, Saynéte Myghell
the Archangell, the byrthe of our Lord God, and the Annunciation of oure Ladye
the Virgyne, by evyn porcyons, duryng the faid terme to be payd. And if it happen
the faide yerely ferme of xliis. iiiid. by yere duryng the faid fyrft xx yeres, or of
xvs. by yere duryng the other xx yeres, to be behynd yn parte, or yn all not
payde, the fpace of xiii dayes next after any fefte yn the whiche it owyght to be
paide, as it is above lymyted, fo that it be duely afked and requyred at any daye
within the faid xiii dayes, then it fhall be lefull to the prior and cõvent aforefaid,
and theyr fucceffors, after the xiii dayes expyred, into the forefaid gardyne, with
the apprtences, holy to re-entre, and the fame to repoffede, and have agayne and
enjoye, as yn theyre former poffeffion, and the faid Richard Burchard and his
affignes from the fame uttrely to expell, put outt, and amove, this indenture yn
any wyfe notwithftanding. And the faid Richard Burchard convenanteth and
graunteth by thefe prefents- to make and maynteyne, by all the faid terme, at his
ppre coftes and charges, with pale or otherwife fufficiently, fuche claufures as
fhall belong to hym for his parte about the faid gardyne. In witneffe whereof, as
well the convent feale as of the faid põr and convent, as the feale of the aforefaid
Rychard Burchard, to thefe indentures enterchangeably do fett. Geven the day
and yẽr above wrytten. It is further agreed and covenanted between the faid pties,
that the faid Richard Burchard, by all the faid time, fhall fufficiently repair the
houfe nowe beyng within the faid gardyne, at his coft and charge, and leve the fame
gaydyne and hous, at the end of the faid time, in as good condition as it now is; and
that he and his affigns, by all the faid time, fhal have free coming into the faid
gardyne, and going out of the fame, at all tymes lawful and convenient."

It is fairly written on parchment, indented.

Both the feals are loft: That of the friars was Az. on a crofs
Arg. between four mitres labelled Or, a text t, furmounted
with the letter S. fable [2].

---

[1] *Nefcia mens hominum fati fortifque futuræ.* Virgr.
[2] See Edmondfon's Heraldry, vol. I.

After

After the diffolution, this fryary was granted [30 Henry VIII.] to Thomas Wifeman, and then to John Harrington, 2 Eliz. *Tanner*. The next proprietor was Hoveden, who was fuccceded by Mr. Peter Peters, great-grand-father of Mrs. Barrett, 3d wife of the late Thomas Barrett, efq; of Lee, mother of Mrs. Byrch, who brought it in marriage to the rev. Mr. Byrch, now poffeffor of the manor and principal manfion; the other tenements having been alienated. In 1685, a fuit for fubftraction of tithes was inftituted in the court of exchequer, by the rev. John Stockar, rector of St. Alphage, but, after a full hearing, the exemption was allowed. Weever mentions Robert and Bennet Browne, efquires, and Bennet, wife of Sir Wm. Wendalls, knt. as buried there.

3. The Francifcan, Minor, or Grey Fryars, nine of whom came into England in 1224, of whom five, by the direction of Henry III. ftayed and fettled in Canterbury. Alderman Digges, in 1273, removed them to an ifland in the weft part of the city, then called Binnewith, or Binney ifland, now Bingley, where they continued to the diffolution, when this priory was granted, 31 Henry VIII. to Thomas Spilman. Mr. Hartcup is the prefent proprietor. A quit-rent of 4s. per ann. is payable out of it to the crown. Of this building, nothing but ruined walls and fome arches remain. It had two gates, one, the eaft, in Stour-Street, the other, the north, in St. Peter's-Street. Lord Badlefmere, hanged for treafon, 1321, Sir Giles his fon, and 17 other knights and ladies, were interred there.

4. The White Fryars, or Heremites, of the order of St. Auguftine, who obtained a fettlement and houfe by the gift of Richard French, baker, in St. George's parifh, about the year 1335. King Edward III. and others added their benefactions. Their north ftone gate-way, ftill remaining in that ftreet, is alfo engraved in Mr. Thorpe's Antiquities, pl. X. fig. 3. It was

granted,

granted, 33 Henry VIII. to G. Harper. *Tanner.* The manfion and fite are now in the poffeffion of David l'apillon, efquire.

5. A houfe of the Knights Templars, in the parifh of St. Mary, Northgate, fays Somner, but more probably St. Alphage, as all that remains of it, viz. an ancient ftone door-cafe, is in that parifh, near Brown's (formerly the Abbot's) Mill, fuppofed by Mr. Goftling to have been a back door to it [1]. In an adjoining ftore-houfe, belonging to Mr. Tremaine, a woolcomber, is a very fubftantial rafter of chefnut, a foot and a half thick, and feventeen feet long, which probably belonged to the building.

6. A houfe in the fame parifh, belonging to the priefts of a chantry eftablifhed by the Black Prince in 1363, in the under-croft of the cathedral, whofe creft, or feather, may ftill be feen on a ftone, inferted in the wall, at the turning oppofite to Befts'-lane. The " ancient ftone-porch," mentioned by Somner [2] or " ancient door-way of ftone," as Mr. Goftling terms it [3], over which thefe arms in Somner's time were placed, has been long removed, the prefent being a modern wooden door-cafe. But the old wall, of flint and ftone, into which it opens, and which extends weftward towards the river, was probably part of this chantry-houfe. It was of the yearly value of 20s. and was kept in repair by the prior and convent of Chrift-church.

To thefe may be added, as foundations now exifting,

8. JESUS, more commonly called Boys's, Hofpital, from Sir John Boys, recorder of Canterbury, &c. the founder of it, who died in 1612, of which Mr. Goftling gives the following account:

" Sir John endowed this for eight poor men, and four women, viz. a warden, who has a houfe to himfelf, feven brothers, of whom one is claviger, or porter, with 40s. addition to his falary, and four fifters : their apartments form three fides of a little

Walk, p. 62.   [2] Antiquities, p. 71.   [3] Walk, p. 62.

fquare,

fquare, on a bank clofe by the much frequented road from Canterbury to Thanet, and the coaſt from thence to Herne. The
entrance is by a gate, four ſteps above the road, in the middle of
a dwarf wall, which completes the fquare, and gives the fraternity a near view of all that paſſes. The warden and brothers.
ufually attend the cathedral in gowns every Sunday morning.
Sir John, in his book of ordinances of this hofpital, directs that
the warden fhall be appointed by fuch of the furname of the
founder as fhall be owner of Bettefhanger (if not under age) ;.
or, in default of them, by fuch of the fame name as fhall be
owner of Fredville [thefe were two of the numerous feats of
that ancient family in our neighbourhood] ; in default of thefe,,
by the dean of Canterbury for the time being ; if no dean, by
the mayor of the city; if thefe fail to nominate in two months,,
then, after proper notifications, by the archdeacon.

" The feats being now in other names and families, our deans·
have for many fucceffions been mafters here, and as fuch, on any
vacancy of brethren or fifters places, nominate two perfons,
ftatutably qualified to the mayor, who chufes one of them."

9. COGAN's HOUSE, in St. Peter's-ftreet, which was given by will,
July 27, 1657, by a citizen of that name, in truft to the mayor
and corporation, for the habitation of fix poor widows of clergymen of the diocefe of Canterbury, and endowed with the lands
of the late archbifhop in Littlebourn; but thefe being refumed
at the Reftoration, the houfe alone remained, unendowed. This
was, however, in 1696, in fome meafure compenfated by the
benefaction of Dr. Aucher, a prebendary of the cathedral; who
vefted an eftate in truftees for the payment of ten pounds a year
to fix clergymens widows, and gave a preference to thofe in
Cogan's houfe. Five guineas a year are alfo given to each widow
by the Society for the relief of the widows and orphans of
clergymen

clergymen of the diocefe.   This houfe was very lately put into fubftantial repair from private fubfcriptions.   The prefent truf-tees are the rev. Heneage Dering, D. D. John Benfon, D. D. John Lynch, LL. D. (Prebendaries), Thomas Hey, M. A. and Francis Gregory, M. A.

10. SMITH's Hofpital, in Longport, from the name of the founder, John Smith, efquire, in 1657, for four poor men, and four poor women, who are nominated by William Hougham, efquire, of Barton-Court.

11. HARRIS's Alms-houfes in Wincheap, built by a gentleman of that name in 1726, for five poor families, nominated by Richard Harris Barham, efquire, one of the aldermen of the city, grandfon of the founder.   And,

12. Some alms-houfes near Riding-gate, founded in 1778, by the rev. Mr. Byrch, above-mentioned, for fix poor women of his nomination.

APPEN-

Plate X p 411

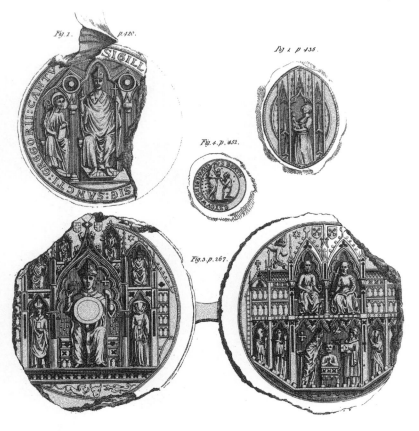

Fig. 1. p. 420.

Fig. 2. p. 435.

Fig. 4. p. 452.

Fig. 3. p. 267.

APPENDIX X.

MAYNARD'S SPITAL, founded 12 Edward II. A. D. 1317, in Love-lane, now called *Hospital-lane*, in the parish of St. Mildred, in Canterbury.

	l.	*s.*	*d.*
Revenues of the estates at the foundation, *per ann.*	3	7	0

Besides Brotherhood Wood, of nine acres, and Brotherhood Close, of one acre and a half adjoining, in the parish of Fordwich.

	l.	*s.*	*d.*
The income of these estates in 1600 was	20	4	0

March 21, 1604. Leonard Cotton, gent. (mayor of the city in 1580), by his will, of this date, recites, that " he meant to increase the number of poor in Maynard's Spital, and had erected three rooms, or lodgings, in the said Spital, for three poor persons, viz. one poor man, and two poor women, to be placed therein by the mayor for the time being, out of the parish of St. Margaret, if any there capable; and if none such there, then out of the parish of St. Mildred; and if none capable there, then out of the county of the said city capable thereof. And such poor to be a widower and widows of good and honest conversation; merely poor, and of the age of 50 years at least." And for the perpetual maintenance of such poor, the testator gave to trustees " a tenement, with the appurtenances, in St. Margaret's in the said city, and another tenement, with the appurtenances, in St. Margaret's aforesaid, and another tenement and orchard, with the appurtenances, in Winecheap, in the parish of St. Mildred, in the said city; in trust to continue the same for the use and maintenance of such three poor persons in the said hospital for ever," as by the said will fully appears.

This

This truft has been faithfully difcharged and perpetuated.

The eftates given by the teftator are leafed out, and produce a clear income of 4l. 17s. 6d. per quarter (or 19l. 10s. per ann.), for which the mayor gives his receipt, and the money is collected by the prior of Maynard's-Spital, and paid to the three poor in Cotton's foundation quarterly.

N. B. The three houfes founded by Cotton are the uppermoft next Caftle-ftreet.

November 3, 1703. The houfes of this hofpital were blown down by the great ftorm. And foon after, the mayor, aldermen, and common-council drew up a petition in behalf of the poor brothers and fifters, for a fubfcription to rebuild the fame. To this the mayor and commonalty, collectively and individually, were large contributors; as were the archbifhop, dean and chapter, members for the city, the principal inhabitants, and many of the neighbouring gentry; and alderman Oughton, then chamberlain, received the fubfcriptions, amounting to 301l. 6s. 6½d.

Sept. 23, 1707. At a court of Burghmote, the mayor and four aldermen were appointed to forward and overfee the work.

The prefent houfes and chapel were erected in 1708, and coft 299l. 4s. 2d. as appears by the faid chamberlain's accounts.

April 30, 1768. Thomas Hanfon, of Crofby-fquare, London, efquire, by his will of that date (proved March 10, 1770), bequeathed to this, Eaftbridge and St. John's hofpitals in Canterbury, the intereft of 500l. each to be invefted in the funds, which amounts to 17l. 10s. each a year, and is half-yearly divided among the refident brothers and fifters, by the mayor, and aldermen who have been mayors, purfuant to the faid will.

April 23, 1771. William Rigden, of the city of Canterbury, brewer, by bargain and fale (enrolled in chancery, 29th of the fame month) vefted in truftees a meffuage and fmith's forge in

the

the said city, in Hawk's-lane, in trust, to apply the rents in the reparations of Maynard's and Cotton's hospitals: And if any surplus should remain, the same to be yearly paid and divided among the brothers and sisters of Maynard's 7 houses, who should be constantly resident, as the said trustees should think fit to divide the same among them.

The said William Rigden died November 29, 1776, aged 82.

The annual rents of these two hospitals (including the above-mentioned 7l. paid by the city), in the year 1712 amounted to 36l. 12s. per ann. and continued nearly the same to 1770; when it appearing that several abuses had been committed in the management of the revenues, the mayor and commonalty, in their court of Burghmote, appointed a committee to examine into them, which committee made many regulations and alterations for the benefit of the hospitals; and a like committee is still continued. The annual rents (including the 7l. paid by the city) amount to 46l. 4s. on the old foundation. The fines, on renewal of leases, have been, from the year 1770, very considerably increased. And there is no doubt but that, if the mayor and commonalty continue to patronise and protect the poor of these hospitals with the same attention, its salutary effects will be farther extended.

All leases granted by the prior, brothers and sisters are [as in the archiepiscopal hospitals] with the advice and consent of the master, who signs them, and affixes the common seal.

A complete account of all the revenues of both these hospitals will soon be made out, and hung up in the chapel.

May 28, 1785,   W. L.

The

The feal of St. Gregory's priory (fee p. 420.) is exhibited in plate X. fig. 1. The fecond feal in the fame plate is that of Maynard's hofpital (fee p. 435.); the third is that of archbifhop Iflip, defcribed in p. 267; the fourth is a feal found fome years ago in the garden of Mr. Lacy, town clerk, in Hawk's-lane, Canterbury.

The few ruinous remains of St. Thomas's Chapel in St. Gregory's, mentioned p. 421. and drawn by Mr. Perry in plate VIII. fig. 2. have within thefe two or three years been removed to make way for the plough.

——— *Seges eft ubi* facra *fuerunt.*
——— *Ipfæ periere ruinæ.*

Page.
78. add, archbifhop Courtney gave to this hofpital 5 marks; and left St. John's hofpital 5 marks, by his laft will, as a legacy. (Ex Reg. eccl. Chrifti, Cant'.)
179. note, for " p. 175" read pp. " 195 and 276."
180. l. 8. for " plate IV." r. " plate VI." and l. 11. for " V." r. IV."
181. In Difburfements, l. 2. r. " two" out-brothers and " three" out-fifters and l. 4.—" thirteen" out-brothers and " twelve" out-fifters
199. l. 3. from bottom, r. " reafon"
200. l. 2. for " or" r. " viz."
    l. 10. for " Mr." r. Dr."
    note * for " went" r. " was elected"
236. l. 18. for " plate IV." r. " plate VI."
    Dr. Chapman died Oct. 14, 1784; and his valuable library has been fince fold by auction (1785), by Meff. Leigh and Sotheby.
273. l. 27. for " plate IV." r. " plate VI."
295. note II. l. 1. r. " calamitous"
321. after l. 18. add " See his feal, plate VI. fig. 3."
345. note, add, This ruined chapel is engraved in Mr. Thorpe's Kentifh Antiquities, plate X. fig. 2.
360. l. 20. r. " almonry "
421. l. penult. for " plate IX." r. " plate VIII."
443. note, r. " Delanoy"

END OF NUMBER XXX.

BIBLIOTHECA

TOPOGRAPHICA

BRITANNICA

N° XLII.

CONTAINING

I. The Hiftory and Antiquities of SAINT RADIGUND's, or BRAD-SOLE ABBEY, near DOVER.

II. A Collection of Tradefmens Tokens iffued in the Ifle of THANET, and in fuch of the Cinque Ports as are within KENT.

III. A Defcription of the MOAT, near CANTERBURY.

IV. Sketch of HAWKHURST Church.

V. Original Letter from Mr. ESSEX, on CANTERBURY CATHEDRAL.

VI. Differtation on the URBS RUTUPIÆ of PTOLEMY, by Mr. DOUGLAS.

VII. Memoirs of WILLIAM LAMBARDE, Efq; the eminent Lawyer and Antiquary.

LONDON:

PRINTED BY AND FOR J. NICHOLS,

PRINTER TO THE SOCIETY OF ANTIQUARIES.

MDCCLXXXVII.

[PRICE THREE SHILLINGS.]

AMONG the various Labours of Literary Men, there have always been certain Fragments whofe Size could not fecure them a general Exemption from the Wreck of Time, which their intrinfic Merit entitled them to furvive; but, having been gathered up by the Curious, or thrown into Mifcellaneous Collections by Bookfellers, they have been recalled into Exiftence, and by uniting together have defended themfelves from Oblivion. Original Pieces have been called in to their Aid, and formed a Phalanx that might withftand every Attack from the Critic to the Cheefemonger, and contributed to the Ornament as well as Value of Libraries.

With a fimilar view it is here intended to prefent the Publick with fome valuable Articles of BRITISH TOPOGRAPHY, from printed Books and MSS. One Part of this Collection will confift of Re-publications of fcarce and various Tracts; another of fuch MS. Papers as the Editors are already poffeffed of, or may receive from their Friends.

It is therefore propofed to publifh a Number occafionally, not confined to the fame Price or Quantity of Sheets, nor always adorned with Cuts; but paged in fuch a Manner, that the general Articles, or thofe belonging to the refpective Counties, may form a feparate Succeffion, if there fhould be enough publifhed, to bind in fuitable Claffes; and each Tract will be completed in a fingle Number.

Into this Collection all Communications confiftent with the Plan will be received with Thanks. And as no Correfpondent will be denied the Privilege of controverting the Opinions of another, fo none will be denied Admittance without a fair and impartial Reafon.

This NUMBER contains SIX PLATES; and a PEDIGREE.

HISTORY AND ANTIQUITIES

OF

SAINT RADIGUND'S

O R,

BRADSOLE Abbey, near DOVER.

In a LETTER from the Rev. Mr. LYON to J. NICHOLS.

SIR,   Dover, June 4, 1785.

ON the high ground about three miles north-weſt from Dover ſtand all the remains (which have eſcaped the rage of reformers and the deſtructive hand of time) of a religious houſe, formerly belonging to the order of the Præmonſtratenſes; and now known by the name of Saint Radigund's, or Bradſole [1].

The ſituation of this houſe, in the time of its proſperity, appears to have been peculiarly adapted for rural pleaſures, meditation, and health; it being on a lofty and retired hill, free from the noiſe of the buſy crowd, and well planted with wood, which ſerved to defend the inhabitants of this ſolitary manſion from the chilling cold of winter's blaſts, and the ſcorching heat of the ſummer's ſun.

The trees which for ſo many years have afforded ſhelter for this ancient ſtructure againſt the fury of the howling tempeſts,

[1] By Weever (p. 269, 281.) miſtaken for two diſtinct monaſteries.

P p p   are

are taken down by the prefent proprietors; and the few fcattered ruins are now left expofed to the fierce attacks of every ftorm.

There is no faying with any certainty, where, or by whom, this abbey was founded; as authors feem very much divided upon the fubject; and many of them appear to be only barely tranfcribers of their predeceffors' errors and doubts.

Weever [1] fuppofes this abbey was built by Hugh de Flori, or Floriaco, by birth a Norman, and nearly related to William the Conqueror; while Tanner [2] and others after him, think it was founded by Richard the Firft, about the year 1191; or by Jeffery earl of Perch, and Maud his wife, the parents of Henry de Wengham. The charter in the Monafticon feems to affect all thefe; but though it is not directly faid who was founder, it could not be Hugh I. abbot of St. Auguftine, for he died 1124. A MS. in the Afhmolean Mufeum at Oxford (n. 1519.) refers the foundation to Richard I. Certain it is, that king gave to the abbey and canons of St. Radigund's of Bradfole 100 acres of wafte on the hill adjoining to their houfe, as king John did 100 more of land and brufh-wood (*brufcia*), all which were confirmed to them by Henry III. and Edward II. [3]

By an extract from a will of Thomas Poinyngs, knight, baron Poynings, we have reafon to conclude that this abbey was built by fome of his family; for he directs his body to be buried in this abbey of Saint Radigund's, in Kent, which, he fays, is of my foundation, in the middle of the choir, and before the high altar [4].

[1] Ubi fupra.
[2] Not. Mon. p. 218.
[3] Cart. 2 Hen. III. p. 1. m. Cart. 8 Edw. II. m. 17, 18. n. 33 per infpex. Mon. Angl. II. 244.
[4] See p. 462. Dugd. Bar. II. 134. See the Pedigree annexed.

King

King John by charter, dated Rouen, 24 April, in the firſt year of his reign, by the hand of H. [1] archbiſhop of Canterbury his chancellor, confirms to this houſe the ſite of Bradeſole, with all lands and tenements given to them by his brother Richard and others; and grants in frankalmoign all his demeſne land in River by Dover, lying on the weſt ſide of Splintrindonhill, between the lands of the prior of Dover and of Fulbert de Dover, in breadth and in length from Potton-wood to the White-way road [2].

There ſeems to have been a deſign of tranſlating this abbey to the neighbouring church of Ryvere. Our records inform us, that in the ninth of John, theſe monks, either by their intereſt, or their complaints, procured of the king a grant of his manor of River, with the church, pleas of court, and every other emolument and advantage ariſing from his ſaid manor, to build their monaſtery there; but, after having obtained this addition to their revenue, they were probably better ſatisfied with their ſituation, as we hear no more of their attempting to remove their buildings to a more convenient place.

It is difficult at this diſtant period of time from the foundation of the abbey, and from the different appearance which the face of the country has aſſumed by cultivation, to aſſign the true reaſon why this community wiſhed to change the ſite of their monaſtery, from the hill, to the valley. Whether it was a ſcarcity of good water [3]; whether it was inconvenient to procure the common neceſſaries of life through the badneſs of the roads; whether ambition had fired the breaſts of the ſeveral members of this ſociety to approach nearer the road of prefer-

---

[1] Hubert Walter.

[2] Mon. Angl. III. P. I. p. 69. from the Regiſter of Bradſole in the hands of Wm. Pierpoint, eſquire, f. 3.

[3] Leland's Itinerary, vol. VII. p. 103.
"There is on the hill a fayre wood, but freſh water laketh ſum tyme."

ment;

ment ; or, whether envy annoyed their peace, on feeing the rays
of royalty fometimes fhining on their more happy brethren in the
town of Dover ; it is now impoffible to determine, as hiftory has
caft the veil of filence over each particular.

King John gave River church to build there the abbey,
which was at Bradfole. Teft. P. [1] bifhop of Winton, by the hand
of Hugh de Wells, archdeacon of Wells, at Porchefter, 26
Mar. a. r. 9. [2]

Thomas earl of Perche [3] confirmed the grant in frankal-
moigne of his father Geffrey and mother Maud, of all the
land of his fee in Bradefole, held by Wm. Hecket and Emma
his wife, with confent of Wm. de Polton and Stephen his heir,
and pafture in all Polton's land, with that part of Bradefole
moor [4], which Stephen Polton allowed them to enclofe, and all
the land below the moor to the north, as far as the marfh [5],
marked by the new ditch, and all the eafements, and the marle-
pit called Chamelettes Chalkpot, by Eftedefcumbe, and a way
through Wm. Polton's land. The earl further confirms all the
land in his fee given them by Stephen Polton his knight, viz. a
piece of land called Edfredefcumbe, between the caufeway [6]
leading to Hautam and Lovefheld, and another piece reaching
from Edfredefcumbe towards Bernett, between the land called
Shortfurlong and the faid caufeway, and through the valley
called Stodes Edfredefcombe, to the land of the monks of Dover,
called Bernett, and the land called Littlecumbe and Heaggh Knoll,
and the land called del Teghe, containing 6 $\frac{1}{2}$ acres lying towards Gorefeld and the Ofrilo, called Radeweye, and part of the
field called Lovefheld, and a little piece of ground lying between

---

[1] Pater de Rupibus.
[2] Regift. f. 47. Rot. Cart. 1 J. p. 1. m. 22. n. 130. Cart. 5 J. m. 3. n. 16. Cart.
9 J. m. 2. n. 13. Cart. 17 John m. 6. n. 44.
[3] Pertici.   [4] Moura.
[5] Morreffa.   [6] Catia.

the spot where was the messuage of Robert Strode and Bradsole moor, and the rent and occupation of a field called Straholefeld, and 4d. rent from the Lepers of Dover for land lying in Pultone vale, and all the tenements which Walter Pannentar holds of Stephen aforesaid, and the rent, service, and homage, and that acre formerly belonging to Brichtine and Malote, which the said canons inclosed, and the acre wherein is the place called Swine-sole [1].

Robert Polton gave his manor of Polton cum pertinentiis. Testibus Bertramo de Criolio tunc constabulario and sheriff of Kent, Simon his brother, &c. [2].

Hubert de Burgh, earl of Kent, chief justice of England, gave the canons the church of Portslade for their support and for the relief of poor pilgrims that visited them, saving only to Robert the parson and Robert the vicar their pensions for life. Given by the hand of Luke, in the chapel at *Evering*, 28 Nov. 6 Hen. III. [3].

He also gave them the church of St. Leonard, at *Alderthorn*, for the building of their church, and afterwards to the use of the saints, to find lights for ever, saving to David the parson his pension for life [4].

Hamo de Crevequer, for his own soul and that of Maud d'Abrincis his wife, gave them the advowson of the church of Altham (Alkham), and the chapel of Mauregge thereto belonging [5].

---

[1] Mon. Angl. Ib. ex eod. reg.
[2] Ib. f. 40. Cart. 19 Hen. III. m. 2. Pat. 35 Hen. III. m. 5. Fin. 6 Hen. III. de ½ parte manerii de Polton. Pat. 3 Ed. III. p. 2. m. 8. Pat. 15 Ed. III. p. 4. m. 30. Pat. 22 vel 23 E. III. p. 3. m. 11. MS. Edw. Rowe Moies.
[3] Regist. f. 594.
[4] Ib. f. 622.
[5] Ib. f. 598.

Bertram

Bertram de Crioll gave his manor of Combe for the maintenance of 5 canons chaplains to fay mafs for his foul and the
fouls of all his predeceffors; he alfo bequeathed his body to be
buried in their church [1].

Henry the Third gave them all that land in his manor of
River near Dover lying on the north-fide of Spiltrindone-hill,
between the hills of the priory of Dover, and of Fulbert de
Dover, breadthwife, and from Poltone-wood to Whiteway road,
in length, together with the church of Revere, which they held
by grant of his predeceffors in pure and perpetual alms; alfo
the church of St. Michael of Porteflade, which they held by
gift of Hubert de Burgh, earl of Kent, chief juftice of England;
the church of St. Clement at Leifdone in Shepey, by gift of
Robert Arficke, confirmed by Stephen archbifhop of Canterbury [2]; a mill near the manor-houfe of Rivere, and other lands
purchafed by the king of Blan Corbel; lands granted by Stephen
Polton in Polton, with the chapel of the faid place; and 2 $\frac{1}{2}$
acres of land formerly belonging to two women, Brittuna and
Malota, and one acre of land near them, and all the land lying
under their garden, and 9 acres, and a virgate of land lying on

[1] Ib. Reg. f. 205.

[2] Omnibus, &c. S. * permiffione divina Cant' epus, et S. Rom' eccl' cardin', falut'.
Noverit univ' veftra nos intuitu Dei, et ob favorem religionis, et pio neceffitate et
utilitate novelle plantationis domus scæ Radegund de Bradefole, conceffiffe dilectis
filiis ñris abbi et conv' ordinis Premonftr' ejufd' domus eccliam S. Petri de Riveria
cum pertin'. fuis, quam illuftris rex Angliæ J. eis mifericorditer conceffit; habend' et
tenend' in perpetuum in proprios ufus; falvo tamen jure Johis de Riveria clerici
quamdiu vixerit, et falva vicaria c folidos a nobis vel fucefforibus ñris in ead' ecclia
affignand' capellano qui ad eorund' abbis et conv' prefentationem ab archiepo in
eadem inftitutus miniftrabit.   Hiis teftib', mag. o W. de Barden Wellens', magro W.
de Tiln' Elienf' archidis, magro Elia de Derham, Rob' de Briftoll, magro Tho' de
Frettum, magro Waltero de Eynefham, magro Willo de Beanton, Auron de Kent †.

* Stephen Langton.   † Reg. Cant. MS. e coll. Wh. Kennet.

the

the weft fide of Polton wood; tenements and homages which
Walter Pannetar and Ofbert Swyfith held, and the field called
Deltegee, and Sudholefeld, and Nordholefeld, and Eldemede, and
ín Wemede, and Grenefale, and two acres of land lying along-
fide of Aldemede ditch, 3 acres given by Stephen de Polton
aforefaid,.lying before the faid canon's gate.   The fáid king alfo
confirmed. the grant of Philip fon of Philip de Columbariis, of
the church of Poftlinges ¹, and that of Henry de Wengham, dean
of St. Martin's, London, of the church of Sibertefwand.   This
confirmation by infpeximus is dated at Wodeftoke, on the vigil
of St. Mildred, 1257.

Another infpeximus of the fame king, dated Weftminfter,.
2 February, confirms the grant of Hamo de Crevequer, of his
garden at Alkham, with the church of Alkham, and the chapel
of Maurigge thereto belonging ².

The king's barons of Hee ³ certify to the abbot of the Præ-
monftratenfes, that a certain fpot of ground among them called
Blakewofe ⁴, formerly fubject to the houfe of their order of
Lavendene ⁵, wherein were five canons and one convert, who,
being unable to fubfift, were taken under the protection of the
abbot of St. Radegund, and by him amply relieved, and their
houfes repaired, which he did a fecond time after the war

---

¹ Omnibus, &c. Hubertus Dei gratia Cant' archiepus falut'. Noverit univ' veftra
nos cartam nobilis viri Philippi de Columburiis infpexiffe; ex cujus infpectione per-
pendimus ipfam ecclam B. Mariæ de Poftling Deo et eccliæ B. Radegund de Bradfole, et canonicis ibidem contuliffe; unde et eadem pia ipfius donatio perpetuam
obtineat firmitatem cum authoritate qua fungimur confirmamus. Hiis teftibus :
H. de Caftellion, archido Cant'; Ranulfo, thefaurar' Sarum; Magro S. de Sywel!;
thefaur' Lichfield'; Wilt. de Bofco. Ib. ex iifd. collect.
² Mon. Ang. II. 244, 245.
³ Quere Hithe.
⁴ A priory of white or Premonftratenfian canons, or a cell, firft a cell to Lavendene Priory, after united to St. Radegund. Tanner, p. 218.
⁵ A Premonftratenfian priory in the county of .Bucks. Tanner, p. 29.

had

had ruined them ; the barons therefore defired to have the cell of Blakewofe reftored to the abbey of Lavendene [1].

They had a rent in Rochefter, by grant of William Gernon, whofe original charter was in bifhop Tanner's collection, in the volume marked *Jackfon*, p. 53.

Their poffeffions in *Haveking, Polton, Rifing,* &c. appear from Pat. 18 E. I. m. 25. 50 acres in *Pifing* from Plac. ap. Weftm. 20 E. I. rot. 49 Pat. 21. E. I. m. 12. vel 13. Pat. 33 E. I. p. 2. m . . . Pat. 35. E. I. m. Pat. 21. 2 vel 3 Fin. 49 H. III. in *Newenton, Alkham,* &c. Pat. 27 H. VI. p. 1. m. ult. vel penult. *Sutton, Halemede,* and *Paddlefworth,* Fin. 42 H. III.

Other records cited by bifhop Tanner relative to this houfe are Breve 6 E. II. Trin. rot. 6. Cart. 8 E. II. and Bifhop Kennet

[1] Viro venerabili dno abbi Præmonftratens', Barones dni regis Angliæ de Hee falutem. Eft quidam locus apud nos qui dicitur *Blakewofe,* quem aliquando vidimus fubjectum domui de *Lavendene* quæ eft de Vro ordine, et fuerunt ibi tunc temporis quinque canonici et unus converfus : qui quidem locus eorum non potuit eos exhibere, et ipfi penitus oculo paftoris longe pofito deftituebantur, et auxilio per provinciam inordinate vagantes fanctæ religioni et maxime ordini Vro multimoda fcandala generabant. Quod quidem poftquam capitulo veftro fuit præfentatum locum illum quam pauper et perfonis oneratus et fine cuftodia, contulerunt ecclefiæ S. Radegundis quæ fatis eft vicina. Abbas vero S. Radegundis dictos fratres de Blakewofe ab obedientia abbatis de Lavendene per preceptum ordinis abfolutus ad obedientiam fufcepit et difperfos revocavit, domos eorum reparavit, debita folvit, et locum tam in fpiritualibus quam temporalibus nec fine propriæ domus gravi difpendio laudabiliter ampliavit. Tandem tamen ingruente guerra quæ patriam firam penitus vaftavit locus ille ad nichilum valde redactus eft, quem quidem domus S. Radegundis poftea de bonis fuis plurimum reftauravit, et fupra priorem ftatum in poffeffionibus, redditibus, et edificiis locupletavit; unde rogamus attencius, et in Domino confulimus, quatenus non fciat veftra difcrecio quod dicta domus S. Radegundis dicti loci de Blakewofe aliquatenus privetur poffeffione, quia femper vidimus dictam domum S Radegundis dictum locum de Blakewofe in fpiritualibus ampliantem et domum de Lavendene eundem locum fpoliantem. Satis autem veftra novit difcrecio quod facro docemus evangelio quod auferendum eft talentum a pigro fervo qui non fecerit fructum et dandum fervo bono qui ftuduerit illud multiplicare. Valeat fanctitas veftra in Domino *.

* Regid. Bradefole, f. 258. Mon. Angl. II. 71.

refers

refers to others in Dr. M. Hutton's Collections from Chrift Church priory regifter [1].

Befides the regifter before referred to in the Monafticon, bifhop Tanner [2] mentions Cartularies, in the hands of Henry Hamon of Seling, in the county of Kent, efquire, and another in the poffeffion of Sir Cholmondely Dering, of Survenden.

Though it does not appear that king John ever vifited Saint Radigund's in his journey to Dover, yet Edward I. [3] in the 30th year of his reign, in the month of September, and on the Sunday preceding Saint Michael, after mafs, received the great feal with his own hand, in the king's chapel [4] at St. Radigund's, and delivered it to William Grenefield, dean of Chichefter, his chancellor.

Though Madox mentions the chancellor's ufing the great feal next day at the maifon de Dieu at Dover, I do not find that Rymer has recorded any public act, as figned and fealed there, at the time above-mentioned.

The king's bufinefs was probably to confult [5] with his barons of the five ports, and their ancient towns, concerning the forces he fhould want to go againft the Scots; as I find in November following, letters were fent to Robert de Burgherfh [6] conftable of Dover caftle, and to the mayors and bailiffs of the Cinque-Ports, and their ancient towns, demanding them to be ready

[1] W. Kennet, 1223. Coll.

[2] P. 218.

[3] Madox's Hiftory and Antiquities of the Exchequer, vol. I. p. 72. John de Drokensford, keeper of the wardrobe, John de Caen, Robert de Bradelbey, Walter de Winterburn, Hary de Blanotefden, the king's almoner, the chaplains, and clerks, attended him on this journey.

[4] Madox's Hiftory and Antiquities of the Exchequer, vol. I. p. 72. Cl. 30 E. I. m. 6. dorf.

[5] See Hiftory of England, 30 E. I.

[6] Rot. Clauf. 30 E. I. m. 1. or, Rymer's Fœdera, vol. II. p. 911,

with

with their men and ſhips, at Berwick upon Tweed, the place of
rendezvous, by the Feaſt of Pentecoſt; in order to aſſiſt in quel-
ling the rebellion in Scotland.

Among the perſons who deſired to be buried in the church, we
meet with Bertram de Crioll, who died . . . . In the archiepiſcopal
regiſtry at Lambeth, Reg. Sudbury, f. 84. a, is preſerved the
will, " d'ni Thomas de Ponyngs militis," dated at Slagham on St.
Simon and St. Jude's day, 46 Edw. III. and directing his body to
" be buried en l'abbie de feint Radigundis, en Kent, q'eſt de ma
" fundacion droit en my le coer devant le haut alter;" that a
fair tomb ſhould be placed over his grave with the image of a
knight thereon made of alabaſter, and 100l. to be given to
that abbey, part for the doome therof, and the remainder to be
diſpoſed of in maſſes and prayers for his ſoul. This Thomas
was maternal great grandſon to Bertram de Criol, who was alſo
buried here, as appears by the pedigree annexed.

The revenues of this houſe were returned into the Exchequer
25 Henry VIII. at 98l. 9s. 2d. per ann. as Dugd. 1421. 8s. 9d.
as Speed. At the diſſolution it was granted to the archbiſhop of
Canterbury and his ſucceſſors, in exchange for ſome of the old
eſtates of the fee [1].

The following abbots of this houſe are from Mr. Mores's
collection.

> Richard,   6 Hen. III.
> Henry,   25 Hen. III.
> Henry,   42 & 49 Hen. III.
> John,   1 Ed. I.

J. abbas S. Radegundis adſtitit arch'epo Cant' ap Liminge, 18
kal' Jul' 1279 [2].

---

[1] Tanner, ubi ſup.
[2] Reg. Peckham.

                                                          Saint

Brachole, or St. Rodiquents.

Pub. 2 July 1784, by S. Hooper.

Bradfole Abbey, Kent.

Malm. Sc.

Saint Radigund's Abbey has fhared the fate of many other monafteries in this kingdom fince the Reformation, as part of it is now fitted up for a farm-houfe, barn, and other neceffary conveniencies, and the remainder is left to crumble away. See plate II. here annexed, from Mr. Grofe.

The gateway which leads through the Tower (fee plate I.) on the north fide of the buildings, appears to have been the principal entrance to the quadrangles, hall, chapel, and offices. There are ftill to be feen on the right, going crofs the quadrangle from the fame tower to the hall, the remains of feveral apartments, and on the left feveral ruins.

The tower (fee plate I.) is built with flint, and is now about 40 feet high, and as many wide, and is covered with ivy in feveral parts of it. By the holes remaining in the walls, which formerly received the ends of timbers, we cannot doubt but there were two ftories, and the middle room in each, about 17 feet fquare; with apartments at each fide of different dimenfions.

Between the tower and that part of the building now converted to a farm-houfe there are two quadrangles. The firft, which extends to the fragment of the wall, as feen through the arch, is 27 feet wide, and 40 feet long; and the fecond, which is bounded on the fide oppofite the gateway by that part of the building now the farm-houfe, is 65 feet wide, and the window is feen in the back front of it through the arch.

It is generally fuppofed, that the church ftood on the left going from the tower to the hall, as the burying-ground, belonging to the Society, was on the fame fide of this quadrangle.

Perhaps the inquifitive antiquary, upon a bare infpection of the feveral parts of the buildings now remaining, may endeavour to affign to each apartment its original ufe; but as this at the beft will be but conjecture, I do not think it

6   prudent

prudent to enter into fuch a wild field of fpeculation, where the wifeft may err, and where the incautious muft be loft.

St. Radigund was daughter of Berthier king of Thuringia; fhe was taken prifoner when very young, and falling into the hands of Clothair I. king of France, he caufed her to be carefully educated at Ath, in Virmondois, and afterwards married her. She was a princefs of great beauty, but of greater virtue, being continually occupied in works of charity and devotion. Such was her mortification, that fhe conftantly wore in Lent a fhift of hair-cloth under her robes, befides iron chains, collars, and even hot plates of iron; vifited lepers, and perfons afflicted with the moft naufeous diftempers, and abftained not only from flefh, but even from fifh, eggs, and fruit. Six years after her marriage fhe privately withdrew from court, and at Noion fhe obliged St. Medard to confer on her the veil. She then retired to a religious houfe at Poitiers, where fhe fixed her refidence, and built the abbey of Holy Crofs. The king her hufband would have forced her from her retreat, but was diffuaded from his defign by St. Germain, bifhop of Paris. After fuftaining a kind of continual martyrdom, fhe died in peace, Auguft 13, A. D. 587, on which day her anniverfary is kept, and was buried in St. Mary's church at Portiers [1].

To her, jointly with the Virgin Mary, was dedicated the nunnery founded at Cambridge by Malcolm king of Scots, 1260, converted by Alcock bifhop of Ely into Jefus College.

If you think the view of the tower worth preferving, and the few remarks I have made worthy a place in the next number of your Kentifh Antiquities, they are at your fervice.

Yours, &c.

JOHN LYON.

[1] Martyrolog. Vitæ fanctorum.

PEDIGREE of POYNINGS, from DUGDALE's BARONAGE, II. p. 133—137.
With MS Notes of LE NEVE.

ADAM DE POYNINGS, of Poynings, of the county of Suffex.

Adam.   William.   John.
from one of whom defcended
Michael.
To whom fucceeded
Thomas.

₊....:.. Margaret=Michael   Lucas fummoned to =Ifabel, widow of Henry de Burgherfh,
Bartholomew or   fummoned to   parl. from 47 E. III.   da. of Hugh and fift. of Edm. St. John
Bertram de Criol.   parl. 22 E. I.   to 9 R. II. incl.   baron Bafing, d. 17 R. II.

Eleanor = John.

Agnes = Thomas flain in the fea fight   Thomas ld. St.=1 Philippa countefs of Arundel
    near Slufe, 13 Ed. III.   John d. 1428.   & Pembroke, da. to Edmund
                Mortimer earl of March.
                2. Maud, d. 31 H. VI

Joan da. of fir Rich'd =Michael d. 43 Ed. III. Richard,   Hugh,   Conftance,   Alice,   Joan,
Rokfley, widow of   d.v.p. m John Paulet   m. John   m. Boneville
ld. Molyns d. 1369.   Orrell   John

Blanch de Moubray   =   Thomas   Margaret,   Elizabeth,   Richard,   Agnes
remarried to John de   d. 49 E. III. bd. at   One of the daughters married to   mar. Ifabel, da. of Sir
Worthe, d. 10 H. IV.   St. Radegund's.   Bardolf, another to lord Dacom.   Robert de Grey lord
                    FitzPayne d.1387, 10
                    R. II. fhe d. 17 R. II.

Joan   Robert fummoned to parl. from 5 Hen. IV. to 23
        H. VI. incl. flain at the fiege of Orleans 25 Hen. VI.

        1 - - - - - - =Richard   Robert died = Eliz da.
    2 Eleanor da. of fir John   died 1430.   49 H. VI.   of John
Eleanor   Berkeley of Beverton,   Pafton,
mar. Sir   knt. remarried 1. John   of Pafton,
Regin.   earl of Arundel.   Eliz. da. of fir = Edward dep. of   c. Norf.
Grey of   2. Sir Walter   J. Scot, knt.   Ireland, 10 H. VII.
Ruthin.   Hungerford, knt.   d. 14 H. VIII. of a
                    peftilential fever [A].
    Sir Henry Percy, knt. = Eleanor.
                John, d. v p.

[A] By 4 concubines he had Sir Thomas and Sir Adrian; Edward flain at Bologne, 38 H. VIII., and 4
daughters. 1. Mary=Tho. Clinton. 2. Margaret=Edm. Barry, of Semington, co. Kent. 3. Rofe=Sir
Thomas Wilford, knt. 4. ....=.... Leukner. Sir Thomas was created baron of the realm, married
Catherine daughter and coheir of John lord Marney, and died 37 H. VIII. Under his adminiftration,
10 Hen. VII. was paffed a fett of ftatutes called *Poyning's Laws*, to reftrain the power of Parliament in
Ireland, fubjecting their acts to the revifal of the parliament of England. Thefe, with the act of 6 Geo. I.
enacting the dependency of Ireland on England, were repealed 25 G. III.

The following Letter was read before the Society of
Antiquaries, 1766.

S I R,

INCLOSED is an account of what I have seen and can recollect
concerning St. Radegund's Abbey. If the ivory book and
figure therein mentioned should be thought worth further inspection, they shall be produced whenever you please. An account of the Seal lately found in a garden at the antient town of
Winchelsea, of which I herewith send you the impression[1], the
skeleton of three persons found buried and standing upright,
with each a stake at their backs, near a chapel of mine of the
Augustines at Rye (now a malt-house), and the stones I shewed
you taken out of the intestines of a miller's horse, &c. &c. must,
for want of time, be postponed to a further opportunity.

I am,

S I R,

Yours, &c.

Red Lion Square,
June 5, 1766.

THO. OWEN.

[1] This we have not been able to recover. EDIT.

ON a vifit not many years fince to a Captain of one of the
King's packets at Dover (a man of fome fpeculation), he entertained me with the following account: That two ftrangers had
then lately appeared at St. *Radigund's* abbey, who brought with
them hazel rods, pretending that treafure was oftentimes found
in the ruins of fuch old buildings; and if there was any, by thofe
rods they could difcover it; and begged leave of the farmer, who
lived in the old porch of the abbey, to make the experiment.
On entering a little parlour on the right hand of the porch, they
declared, if he would let them dig under that room, they fhould
certainly find riches, of which they offered him a fhare.   The
farmer wanting faith, they declared they were fent from Rome,
where it was regiftered that the image of the Virgin Mary in folid
gold was hid there.   The floor was prefently taken up, and they
dug feveral nights.   Whether the object of their fearch was
found, is not known.   But the farmer fold off his ftock, and
bought a commiffion in the army.   Soon after thefe ftrangers
were gone, my friend the Captain obtained leave to fend his failors
to dig among the ruins.   Near the E. end of the abbey chapel,
they found, in a wooden box which mouldered away, an ivory
book[1] with gold clafps and hinges, about the fize of a fmall octavo,
on the infide of which is carved the wife men's offering, and on the
other fide the crucifixion.   They alfo found the figure of a man
of the fize of a large print on earthen ware glazed green, a fox
and goofe on the fide of it, and underneath it 60. IAR. ABE GAN
The failors kept the clafps and hinges, but gave the captain the
book and figure, which he gave to me, and afterwards conducted
me to the place.   It is fituated, as near as I can guefs, about a
mile on the right hand of the road from London to Dover, and
three miles on this fide of it, and a mile to the left of the road

---

[1] See an engraving and defcription of fuch a book (poffibly the very fame) in
Gentleman's Magazine, 1785, page 849.

from

from Folkftone to Dover on the ridge of a hill; the lands fertile round it, though the adjacent country is barren. It is almoft furrounded with a wood of large and high timber trees, fo as not to be feen at any diftance, there being no publick road to it except from Dover. Paffing through a fmall wood you are at once prefented with a view of its fpacious and venerable ruins. In front is a large fquare tower covered with ivy. On the right and left of it, part of the walls of the abbey facing the tower, ftands the gateway, now a farm houfe, in which I was fhewn by pulling up the parlour floor (which has never been re-laid fince the fearch) a vault ten feet deep, nine long, and four or five wide, cafed with ftone like that of Portland. On the fouth fide of the gate are the walls of the chapel, where the book, &c. were found. On the right and left of it appear feveral other ruins, and many other large vaults.

THO. OWEN.

Red Lion Square,
June 5, 1766.

*** The manor, farms, and wood-lands, called *St. Radigund's* and *Poulton*, within two miles of Dover, containing about 800 acres lying together, with 80 acres of land at Dimchurch in Rumney marfh in Kent, were advertifed in the London Gazette, Auguft 3, 1710, to be fold by decree of the High Court of Chancery.

TRADEMEN'S

ſuch of the Cinque Ports as are ſituated in KENT. (See Plate III.)

1. James Coſton, of Deale, 1653.
2. Richard Stutly, in Dell, 1653.
3. John Lobdell, in Deale, his half peny, 1669.
4. John Pittock, in Deal, 1660.
5. William Brothers, his half peny, in Deale, 1669.
6. Peter Underwood, in Lower Deall.
7. Edward Chambers, in Dover, 1649.
8. John Brian, in Dover, 1652.
9. Thomas Kite, in Dover, 1656.
10. David Adamſon, in Dover, 1657.
11. Robart Woodgreen, of Dover, 1658.
12. Martha Fford, in Dover, 1659.
13. John Haynes, Baker, in Dover, 1655.
14. Dover Farthing, 68.
15. Roger Rogers, in Dover, 1665.
16. Robert Woodgreen, in Dover, 1666.
17. Katharen Gardner, in Dover, chanler, 1667, her halfe penny.
18. For the Poore of Dover, a halfe penny, 1668.
19. Thomas Piearce, junior, of Dover, 1669, his dubble token.
20. Pines Kite, in Dover, 1670, his half peny.
21. James Homard, Baker, in Dover.
22. Thomas Sharnal, in Dover.
23. John Thomas, Grocer, in Dover.
24. At the Queene of Bohemia in Dover, $\frac{c}{I \, M}$.
25. Edward Franklin, his half-peny, of Foulſton in Kent, 70.
26. David March in Hythe, 1669, his half peny.
27. Joᵃ. Baſſett his half peny, 1670, in Hythe in Kent.
28. Richard Langley, at Marget in Kent, his halfe peny, 1667.
29. Steven Greedier, his half peny, of Marget in Thannet.
30. Chreſton Houdgben, of Marget in Kent.
31. Joſeph Mackſith, Margeret in Kent.
32. John Dyer, his half peny, of Minſter, in Kent.
33. Richard Baker, in New Romney.
34. Hen. Noldred, in Romans Get in the Iſle of Tennet, his half peny.
35. Clement March, at Romans Gat in Thanet.
36. Richard Criſp, in Sandwich.
37. Ralph Robins, in Sandwich, 1655.
38. David Rogers, in Sandwich, 1666.
39. Richard Aſherniden, of Sandwich.
40. John Revell, in Sandwich, his half peny.
41. Thomas Sandum, in Sandwich, 1667, his half peny.
42. Henry Furnice, in Sandwich, his half peny.
43. John Vandebrouck, in Sandwich, 1656.
44. Thomas Thomſon, at Stoowry, 1650.
45. Thomas Parſoen, in Dell, 1658.
46. Richard Langley, of Ramſgate, 1657.

Nᵒˢ 1, 2, 5, 6, 7, 9, 11, 14, 19, 24, 26, 27, 29, 30, 34, 35, 36, 37, 38, are engraven from the collection of my late excellent friend Mark Cephas Tutet, Eſq. F. A. S. whoſe valuable collection of curioſities is ſoon to be diſperſed by public auction, in conſequence of the expreſs directions of his laſt will.

Nᵒˢ 3, 4, 8, 10, 12, 13, 15, 16, 17, 18, 22, 23, 32, 39, are from the collection of another friend who died whilſt this plate was engraving, the late Dr. Ducarel, F. R. and A. SS. whoſe catalogue mentions alſo " a token of Wm. Fillet, of Dover, " miſlaid." This gentleman's large collection of antiquarian books, prints, coins, &c. is alſo deſtined to the auctioneer's hammer, by the nephew of the Doctor, who fondly hoped they would have been preſerved as " heir-looms" in his family.

Nᵒˢ 20, 21, 25, 28, and 33, are from the cabinet of the Rev. Mr. Southgate.

Nᵒˢ 40—46 were obligingly communicated by William Boys, Eſq. of Sandwich, F S. A. long after the other part of the plate was engraven.

Plate III. p.468.

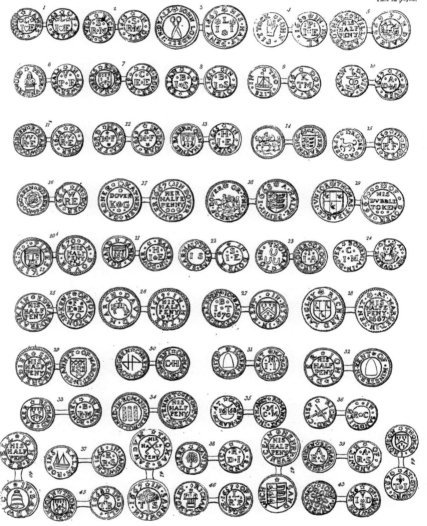

R. Thomas delt.

The Moat, near Canterbury; late one of the Seats of Earl Cowper.
Taken down in 1785.

A corresponding view is concealed by the trees.

THE MOAT near CANTERBURY; Plate IV.

IN St. Martin's parifh at Canterbury, is the *Moat*, antiently called the *Wyke*, either from Fordwich, adjacent, for it adjoins to it, faith Somner, p. 3. at a place called Wyking Smerke, or rather, perhaps, becaufe formerly a place of ftrength. It is a houfe of note, and formerly had owners of the name of *Wyke*. Stephen de Wyke poffeffed it 20 Henry III. paying aid for it at the marriage of Ifabel the king's fifter. But in the beginning of the reign of Richard III. it came into the hands of Sir Richard *de Hoo* and William *Skippe*, who fold it to Simon *Spencer*, and he to John *Sandford*, gent. from whom it went the fame way to Richard *Smith*, and thence to John *Eaftfield*, efquire, fon of Sir William Eaftfield, K. B. and Lord Mayor of London, 1438. From him it went by fale to William *Rogers*, who by a fine levied 23 Henry VI. fold it to Philip *Belknap*, efquire, mayor of Canterbury, 1458, and fheriff of Kent the year after. He married Elizabeth daughter of John Woodhoufe, efquire, whofe only daughter and heir, Alice, carried it in marriage to Henry *Finch*, of Netherfield, efquire, and hence it came down to John Lord Finch, who was created baron of Fordwich, by Charles I. when he was keeper of the great feal. From him it came to be in the poffeffion of the right honourable the earl of Winchelfea.

It had antiently a chapel belonging to it, in which divine fervice was celebrated by licence from Richard Oxenden, prior of Chrift Church, 1333 [1].

[1] Richardus permiffione divina prior ecclefiæ Chrifti de Cantuar' dilecto fibi in Chrifto Domino Stephano de Wyke, capellano, falutem, &c. Ut in capella tua apud Wyke, decenter ornata in parochia S. Martin, juxta Cantuar' & jurifdictionis ecclefiæ noftræ immediatæ miffas celebrare poffis ac tibi & tuis ydoneis abfque parochial' juris quoad oblationes & parochialia jura hujus ecclefiæ præjuditio canonice facere celebrari devotioni tuæ (fede Cantuar' vacante) autoritate noftra & capitule qua fungimur in hac parte tenore prefentium licentiam in Domino concedimus fpecialem. In cujus rei teftimonium, &c. Dat. A. D. 1333. (Ex Archiv. in eccl. Chrifti Cant.)

Appendix to Batteley's edition of Somner's Canterbury, I. Appendix, N° IX.

This

This feat and eftate were purchafed of the Earl of Winchelfea, by Lord Chancellor Cowper, before he was ennobled; the neighbouring corporation of Fordwich being his fecond title.   It was drawn by a friend of the late Mr. Duncombe, juft before it was taken down, in the fummer of 1785.

Plate V. contains a View, by Serres, of the famous monumental ftones in the grounds of Mr. Bartholomew, at Addington Place in Kent, defcribed by the late Mr. Colebrook, in Archæologia, v. II. p. 107; and in Mr. Thorpe's " Antiquities in Kent, within the diocefe of Rochefter," p. 68.

Plate VI. is an exact Sketch of Hawkherft Church, in the Weald of Kent.

Hawkherft is a large, pleafant, and well-inhabited village, particularly defcribed by Kilburne in his Survey of Kent, who was a refident at the place; the church was an appendage of the abbey of Battele, till the Reformation, and is fuperior in architecture to moft of the village churches in the vicinity, moft probably from its connexion with that magnificent religious houfe [1].

Letter from the late ingenious Mr. Essex to Dr. Ducarel, containing Obfervations on Canterbury Cathedral.

S I R,   Cambridge, Feb. 1, 1760.

If I may judge by the queftion you propofed to me (in your letter to Mr. Webb) concerning the different thicknefs of the outer walls of the choir at Canterbury, you have fome fufpicion that thofe walls have been altered fince they were built, which alterations may have been the caufe of their extraordinary thicknefs.   If this is your opinion, *as it is mine*, then I fancy we are both in the fame opinion about other particulars relating to this church, though the fhort opportunity I had of feeing it did

[1] See Gent. Mag. July, 1787.

not

Jones del.

Eliza sculp.

Monumental Stones in the Grounds of . W.ᵐ Bartholomew at Addington Place in Kent.

Plate VI p. 47.

HAWKHERST Church, Kent

not furnish me with all the materials neceffary to fupport my opinion.

Soon after my return from Canterbury, I took an opportunity of examining my memoranda made in and about that cathedral; and uponcomparing what I there obferved with Gervais's account of the burning and re-building the choir of Conrad (as it is publifhed, with Edwin's plan, by the Antiquarian Society), I had fome reafon to doubt whether that account might be entirely depended upon.

In the defcription which he gives us of Conrad's choir, and in Mr. Batteley's plan made from that defcription, there were 24 columns in that choir, 9 of which ftood in a direct line on each fide, and fix more which formed a femicircle : I doubt not but he is very right in his account of thofe that ftood in direct lines ; but, if my obfervations are not wrong, there were no more than 4 in the femicircle, which makes the number of columns in Conrad's choir but 22 in all. I have reafon to believe that this was not Gervais's miftake, but in copying his manufcript where IV might eafily be taken for $\hat{V}I$.

After defcribing the church, he fays, in the year 1174, the glorious choir of Conrad was confumed by fire ; *and that this choir was re-built from the very foundations* ; which work was undertaken by William of Sens, a French architect, who was a whole year in taking it down.

Now I have fome reafon to doubt whether this account is altogether true ; for by my obfervations it feems, that as much of the prefent choir as is comprized between the great tower and the two little towers of St. Gregory and St. Anfelm is the greateft part of the original choir of Conrad, and that all the columns, if not all the arches above them, with the vaulting of the fide ailes, as far as the eaft-crofs, belonged to that choir.

And it is my opinion, that the fire deftroyed no more of the building than the Monks' ftalls, and the roof of the choir, which

7   at

at that time was only cieled with wood, and painted; but that the said ailes were not much hurt, being vaulted with ftone; nor do I fuppofe that any more of the choir was taken down than the femicircular end and chapel adjoining; and it is probable Gervaife meant no more, as the ancients often diftinguifhed that part by the name of *Chorus*.

The taking down of this, with a pillar and two arches on each fide, for enlarging the openings into the Eaft-crofs, and fecuring the remaining arches, might be the work in which William of Sens, the firft architect employed the firft year; and if this conjecture is true, then the pieces of wood which have been fixed in thofe arches were tyes of his fixing to fecure the work till the whole was finifhed, as the arches could not well ftand without fome fuch continuance.

If the building was not taken down, many alterations muft neceffarily have been made in it, not only to make it conformable to the new work, but for the convenience of vaulting the middle aile; and fome of thefe alterations may be the caufe of that extraordinary thicknefs you obferve in the walls. I cannot fay that I obferved the different thicknefs of them, but that the inner part was of a different ftile from the outfide, I noted in my pocket-book at that time.

As I had not an opportunity of examining this building fo completely as I could wifh, I will not pretend to fay that I may not be miftaken in my opinion, though I have other obfervations that feem to confirm it; but, as you have an opportunity of tracing the whole throughout, you may find fome pleafure in examining it. And if any obfervations that I have made upon the building can further your enquiry, I fhall be ready to anfwer, as far as they can affift me, any queries you pleafe to propofe upon that fubject; and am, Sir, your humble fervant,

JAMES ESSEX.

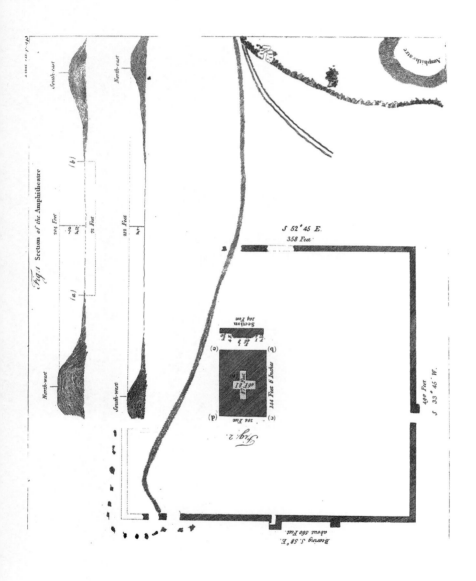

Fig. 1 Section of the Amphitheatre

North-west   South-west

South-east   North-east

(a)   (b)

204 Feet   213 Feet

Fig. 2.

S 52° 45' E.
358 Feet

490 Feet   S 33° 45' W.

Bearing S. 58° E.
about 565 Feet

Section 104 Feet

(b)   (c)

(d)   (e)

104 Feet

144 Feet 6 Inches

Amphitheatre

PLATE VII. here annexed was originally intended to have accompanied " Some Account of the AMPHITHEATRE and CAS- " TLE at RICHBOROUGH; in a Letter from WILLIAM Boys, Efq. " of Sandwich, F. S. A. dated Feb. 22, 1773," and addreffed to the late Dr. DUCAREL. But, in delicacy to the very ingenious writer, from whom there is daily reafon to expect a particular hiftory of this famous Caftle, no more of his Letter fhall be ufed than barely to explain the references in the Plate.

" I have carefully meafured the Amphitheatre, for fo I am inclined to call it, and the dimenfions are as you will find in the drawing *. The plow has been fo often over it (for the land is in conftant tillage), that it is impoffible to afcertain the extent of the arena, as there is no part of the bottom now level; and for the fame reafon, it is impoffible to be exact as to the figure and capacity of the whole. The plow has broken down, and thrown within and without the crater all the higher and thinner part of the rim, fo that its prefent form muft differ confiderably from the original. My method of taking the circumference was this: I found out the centre, and, ftanding there with my eye about 5 feet 8 inches above the ground, I directed my affiftant to fix fticks in the ground, where a line from my eye was a tangent to a convex part of the rim, fo that I could well difcern the bottom of every ftick; and as my eye was below the hori- zontal level of the rim in every part of it, I think I cannot have made the circuit too large †.

The plan of the caftle (plate VII. fig. 2.) is taken by my eye from a correct one. The numerals and bearings are correct; the bearings not corrected for the variation.

* See Plate VII. fig. 1.
† The circumference is 565 feet. If any part of the bottom of the hollow is more level than the reft, it is the fpace between (a) and (b), 72 feet in diameter.

N° XLII.   S s 3   a. The

a. The building within the walls, which I traced out laſt ſummer, is a ſolid maſs of maſonry. The ſurface around the croſs is perfeſtly level. It is a compoſition of flint ſtones and coarſe mortar; over the whole is a coat of the ſame ſort of mortar about ſix inches thick, extending to the edge of the platform all round, ſo that probably there was never any wall or other building ereſted on it, excepting the croſs, which is compoſed of the ſame materials, with ſome ſquared ſtones remaining in the facings, and riſes from three to four feet above the ſurface of the platform. In the angle at *(a)*, ſomebody with infinite labour has endeavoured to penetrate into the croſs and platform; but was obliged to deſiſt on account of the hardneſs of the materials, after however getting about two feet below the ſurface. I dug quite below the building, and got in about 11 feet underneath it. It was like a ſolid rock, impenetrable by any inſtrument whatever. By taking the level with an inſtrument, I find the upper ſurface of the platform to be about two feet higher than the foundation of the walls of the caſtle. At *(b)* the ſame ſurface is ſix feet under ground; at *(c)* five feet; at *(d)* and *(e)* two feet nine inches.

The view of RICHBOROUGH CASTLE in Plate VIII. is from a drawing communicated by Mr. DOUGLAS.

Plate VIII. p. 190.

View of Richborough Castle from the Amphitheatre; and of the Isle of Thanet.

On the URBS RUTUPIÆ of PTOLEMY, and the Limben-pic of the Saxons. By the REV. JAMES DOUGLAS, F. S. A.

Μεθὰς ἄναῖο λικώτοῖοι ΚΑΝΤΙΟΙ, ἐν οἷς πόλεις.
Λονδίνιον. κ. νδ.
Δαρούενον. χα. υγ. γε.
Ῥυτήπιαι. κα. νδ.

Poſt quos maxime Orientales CANTII, in quibus urbes;
Londinium	20	54	0	London.
Darvenum	21	53	40	Dover.
Rutupiæ	21 45	45	44 0	Canterbury.

THE antients had a city in Kent, which they ſpeak of under the name of the city of the *Rutupine Ports*; the ſituation of which has not been ſatisfactorily eſtabliſhed by any of our antient or modern writers.

The words of Ptolemy are ʿΡυτήπιαι, *Urbs Rutupiæ.* Our Bede ſays, *civitas quæ dicitur Rutubi portus, qui portus a gente Anglorum nunc corruptè Reptuceſter vocatus.* And from this, Leländ, Camden, Burton, and Lambarde affirm, that Richborough was a city, which they ſet down as the *Urbs Rutupiæ* of the Antients.

Ruthuby, or *Rutubi*, is a monkiſh perverſion of the plural *Rutupiæ*, under which was conſidered the Rutupine Ports; and which is not to be confounded with *Reptaceſter*, a port at ſome diſtance from the city: near to which was a *caſtrum*, as the word *ceſter* evidently implies [1] : to be more clear as to the diſtinction

---

[1] See *Regulæ Generales*, Chron. Saxon. Terminationes *caſter, cheſter, ceaſter*, &c. ortæ funt a ᵹ. ceaᵹcen, *urbs, civitas, oppidum; caſtrum, caſtellum.* See alſo in Burton's Itinerary, where *cheſter, ceaſter, caſter*, &c. are proved to be derived from *caſtra,* or places where the Romans had formerly a walled ſtation.

of

of the Ruthuby and Reptacefter of Bede, let us confider the root of *Reptacefter.*

Reptacefter derives its name from the Britifh word *Rhyd Tufith,* reach or creek, which perfectly agrees with its fituation; and which Camden calls a fandy-bay, from which Sandwich derived its name.

Cefter was indifcriminately called by the Saxons Beᵱ, Beᵱiᵹ, Beoᵱᵹ, Buᵱᵹ, *Urbs, Oppidum, Burgus* [1]; hence the *Peptacefter* of Bede, and *Richburg* or *Richborough* of more modern times. I muft likewife add, that in the *Regula Generalis* of the Saxon Chronicle, *Burg, burrow,* or *burh,* fignifies *civitas, arx, caftrum, municipium, oppidum,* &c. On the advent of the Saxons, but more efpecially when they made a conqueft of the ifland, they gave the name of *Berg,* an hill, to the commanding camps of the Romans, whether caftellated or not; but if we adhere to the text of Bede, *Reptacefire* or *Richborough* only imply a caftle on a hill, a defence of a poft, which is now actually to be feen by the prefent ruins of *Richborough,* and which muft not be fuppofed to have any affinity with *Ruthuby.* Mr. Somner, who was more a theoretical or fpeculative than a practical antiquary, as may be feen by his works, believes *Sandwich* to be this city. Dr. Batteley, who had a local opportunity of grubbing up a few antiquities of the lower empire at *Reculver,* the old *Regulbium* and twin port with *Richborough;* and to fupport an elegant Latin hypothefis, fixes the city where he made his collection; by which means he enhanced the value of his difcoveries, and gained over many very learned profelytes. Thefe kind of *deliria* are extremely pleafing; and they conftitute a principal delight, efpecially when they are feemingly authenticated by a concur-

[1] See Spelman's Gloffary.

rence

rence of materials, which an ingenious antiquary can foon wreft to the text of his favourite fubject; or, to fpeak with more indulgence, the fanguine antiquary will, on a curfory furvey of the materials before him, without any imputation of fallacy, be infenfibly cajoled by a fpecious appearance of things into an erroneous furvey of the plan he is methodizing. It was for want of this caution, that this excellent claffick Dr. Batteley was extremely indeliberate when he fpoke of thofe writers who furmifed that Canterbury was the *Urbs Rutupiæ*. " As to thofe perfons," fays he, or fomething to this purpofe ', " who fix the place at " Canterbury, though in other refpects men of learning, it " would be only loft labour to confute them."

I fhall bring forward fome reafons in the face of this antiquary's affertion, and attempt to prove that the *Urbs Rutupiæ* was at Canterbury.

I make a diftinction between the *Urbs Rutupiæ* of Ptolemy, and the *Ruthubi* or *Reptacefter* of Bede. With the greateft propriety, and well fuiting the elegance of a claffic writer, Canterbury might be called by Ptolomy the city of the Rutupine ports, for which purpofe, in a fubfequent paffage, I fhall advert to the importance of the place, and fhew that it had challenged from the earlieft time the refpectable name of a chief town, or *caput Imperii.*

Civitas qui dicitur Rutubi portus, qui portus a gente Anglorum nunc corrupte Reptacefter vocatus. *Rutubi* and *Reptacefter* here feem to imply the fame place. The miftake is in the acceptation of the word *civitas*, which, inftead of *city*, fhould be read *town*. The precife letter of the text has been the occafion of all the controverfy and difagreement of Lambarde, Leland,

---

' See Dr. Batteley's Antiquitates Rutupinæ.

5   Twine,

Twine, Somner, Batteley, and others, concerning the locality
of this place, for Bede had certainly confounded the *Urbs*
of Ptolemy, with the haven or port. A learned monk of
his age, well-verfed in the Greek tongue, cloiftered all his life
at a diftant quarter of England in the North, near Durham,
might eafily be, indued to apply the *civitas* or *urbs* of Ptolomy,
to the haven town of *Rutubi*, which I have fhewn before is a
monkifh corruption of the *Rutupiæ*, the Rutupine ports; and
this we fhall actually find to be the cafe, for in an old and curious tranflation of Bede by Stapleton, printed 1565, the above
paffage is thus tranflated; *the firft haven towne whereof to arrive
at, for a man coming out of England, is called* Ruthuby; *the haven
whereof is now corruptively called* Reptacefter. Can any thing be
more clear? Again, we have the diftance marked from Calais,
the port of the Morini, to this town, which is here by Bede confounded with the *Urbs Rutupiæ* of Ptolemy; it is computed at
forty miles [1], *fome fay fixty*. This diftance fhould be applied
to the *Urbs*, not to the haven near the town; for prefently we
fhall find, that as there was a city of the Rutupine ports [2], fo there
was a town to the haven, and which were by the old credulous
Durham monk [3] funk into the fame name; to the confufion of
many of his honeft readers, who placed too much confidence in
the miracles he has recorded, and the correct naration of his
hiftory which he has tranfmitted to us. The different accep-

[1] Richard of Cirencefter calls it 46 miles in his Itinerary.

[2] I conceive Dover to have been called one of the Rutupine ports.

[3] Lambarde, with fome humour, fays, " I wote well this writer is called *vene-*
" *rabilis*; but when I read this, and a number of fuch (meaning his miracles),
" which make the one half of his work, I fay with myfelf as fome time did the
" Poet,

    " Quandocunque oftendis mihi fic,
   " Incredulus odi."

tations

tations of the diſtance from the Rutupine ſhore, to this *haven town* of Bede, but which is the *city* of Ptolemy, perfeⅽtly accords with the different acceptation of authors of the *Portus Itius* of Cæſar [1], who have been as much at a loſs where to fix this port of the Morini as Antiquaries the *Rutubi* of Bede, ſome fixing it at Calais, ſome at Boulogne [2]. In Bede's time I

---

[1] See Cluverius, Somner, Battely, and others.

[2] The real ſituation of the Portus Itius we ſhall find to be at Calais; and this will perfeⅽtly accord with the diſtance of the port of the Morini to the *Urbs Rutupiæ* or Canterbury. Cæſar ſays, he ſet ſail from a part of the Morini, " quod inde erat " breviſſimus in Britanniam transjeⅽtus," and arrived on the coaſt of Britain; but not judging it expedient to land where he found the enemy on the *Clifts*, which place was undoubtedly Dover, he ſaid ſailed, to uſe his own words, " circiter millia " paſſum, viii ab eo loco progreſſus, aperto ac plano littore naves conſtituit." Thus the diſtance of this port of the Morini to the place where he landed is thirty miles; therefore adding the diſtance from Calais to Dover, and from thence to Deal, the thirty miles are aſcertained. The quotations from Strabo and Pliny, to prove that St. Omer's was the *Portus Itius*, only confirm the abſurdity of this ſuppoſition; for Cæſar again ſays, " Atque omnes ad Portum Itium convenire jubet;" and that from thence to Britain he knew was the ſhorteſt way. He calls it thirty miles; but it is evident, he means to the place where he was to land; for of what advantage would it be for him to talk of the ſhortneſs of the diſtance, if he could not arrive at that diſtance? Dover he could not, but Deal he could; therefore Deal was the ſhorteſt paſſage from the Portus Itius, and which exaⅽtly correſponds with Cæſar's thirty miles. Thus eſtabliſhing Calais to be the Portus Itius, and taking the diſtance from thence to Canterbury, it will, with ſome little variation in the meaſurement of old and modern Engliſh miles, produce the forty miles mentioned in Bede. I have had occaſion to print this remark before: I ſhall therefore uſe my own words, by obſerving, that it is impoſſible for St. Omer's, or Boulogne, as ſome have imagined, to be the Portus Itius of Cæſar; for his Commentaries ſay, " that eighteen ſhips of large burthen, with cavalry on board, were wind-bound at a place eight old Engliſh miles diſtant from the Portus Itius; which, with Dr. Halley, I believe to be Graveline, or the Γεσοριακον επινιον of Ptolomy. It is obvious, that no port, or harbour, that meaſures eight miles from this port of Cæſar, can be found near St. Omer's or Boulogne. Why not therefore ſupport Mr. Horſley; and, with all ſubmiſſion to the learned Somner, Battely, Cluverius, and other Antiquaries, who have written on the ſubjeⅽt, fix the Portus Itius of Cæſar at Calais?"

am

am inclined to think that *Richborough* was difufed as a port, being blocked up in part with- fand; which we find now to be the cafe in a great meafure with Sandwich, as year after year much accumulation of mud is thrown up in the haven.   In Stapleton's tranflation there is a note, which fays, *that this haven, meaning* Reptacefter, *is loft by the irruption of the fea*; this in a great meafure alfo clears up the mift of this confufed paffage.

The place which modern Antiquaries now call *Richborough*, or *Reptacefter*, is an elevated fpot of ground, on which is fituated the remains of a walled ftation of the Romans, built in the time of Theodofius, as a defence for the *littus Saxonicum :* it is a fquare of 105 paces on one fide, and 150 the other, according to the Roman order of laying out camps, a third part longer than their breadth.   It is impoffible this place could have been the haven by its elevated fituation; and, I am fure, by its want of fupply of water, it could never have been inhabited by a peaceable or a civil community as a town.   The haven, therefore, was at a little diftance towards the confluence of the river or æftuary, and fallen into decay by the choaking up of the channel, and fo in time finally loft.   I do not by any means think it improbable that Sandwich might have arifen from the decay of this haven.   According to Lambarde, fome writers conceived this place to be the *Reptachefter* of Bede, againft whom this Antiquary does not produce a reafon of the fmalleft cogency; but, be this as it may, it feems this haven, to which the *caftrum* of the Romans, now vulgarly called *Richborough*, was a mural defence, is now not known; and were it known, I am perfuaded, it would only be proved to have been the fimple haven, a *trifling* landing-place for paffengers, which, as I have before obferved from Camden, was called *Rhyd*, a creek, harbour, or berg, and

to

to which the *cefter* or *berg* at a little diftance from it was a military depôt, or protection to it ; hence we have *Ryd-cefter*, *Repta-cefter*, *Rhyd-burg*, *Richborough*, or *Richborow* ; but which is in every acceptation, and in every rational conception, totally different to the *Civitas Rutubi*, or *Urbs Rutupiæ*, the city of thefe ports.

Let us now fhew where Bede has confufed his readers by his mifconception of the *Urbs Rutupiæ*. In his time the *caftra* of *Reculver* and *Richborough* were deftroyed, their confequence forgotten ; confequently their real name perverted by the Saxons. In the Itinerary of Richard of Cirencefter, we find the ftation under the name of *Rhutupium Colonia*, where the II Legio Aug. was ftationed, and which Richard, from the error of his time, alfo calls a city. What affinity is there in this to *Repta-cefter ?* It implies one of the Rutupine ports, *Rhutupium* being the fingular number : but *Repta-cefter* is the vulgar perverfion of *Rutubi*, fays Bede. *Rhutupium* he fhould have faid, if he had faid any thing. According to Lambarde, Repraceaʏcep. is a Saxon name. What confufion ! he fays it is derived from *Rwyd*, *a net*, a Britifh word ; doubtlefs it was fo named by the Britons after the departure of the Romans, prefixing their name to the *caftra*, the *cefter* of the Romans. Hence we get a clear definition of the *cefter* and *Burgh* or *Burrow*, the Britons prefixing the name of *cefter* to the caftellated ftations which they occupied on the departure of their friends the Romans; while the Saxons, on the capture of the fame ftations from the Britons, called them *Burgh* or *Bergs*, in their own language, the fame implication, as I have before remarked, as *Cefter* or *Caftra*. Hence we have the *Repta-cefter* of the Britons, and the *Richborough* of the Saxons : the true Roman name of places

U u u 2   being

being tranfported by the Romans themfelves; and not obliterated by fucceeding conquefts, or the manifeft intention, as fome authors have fuppofed, of the Saxons to change the real names of places, and to tranfmit their own names to pofterity, as the hereditary owners of them.

It may now be reafonably afked, why in Bede's time Canterbury did not retain its claffical name among the Saxons? which would have caufed Bede to have been clear in his *civitas* and *portus*. Bede lived an. Dom. 720; St. Auguftine arrived in Britain an. 582. Shortly after, I conceive the name of *Cantuaria* to be given to it, *Cantuaria, Ædes facra* [1], from the magnificent church he caufed to be erected. " At Auguftinus con-" fertim ut Doroverniæ fedem pofuit, templum quod ibidem " magnificum erat, a Romanis, ut fama eft, olim fuis diis con-" ditum Chrifto dedicavit, in eoque metropolis pontificis cathe-" dram locavit [2]." One hundred years and more is fufficient to change the name of a place; and efpecially in thofe barbarous times, when letters were fo confined, a name would be foon forgotten. But it is to be remarked from Matthew of Weftminfter, and alfo from Bede, that, at the arrival of St. Auguftine, it was called *caput Imperii* [3], the chief town of the empire, and moft likely had the Britifh name of *Caer Kent*, the chief city in Kent. Hence, from thefe few examples, compared with the ftate of the times, it is not likely that it would have fuffered its claffical name of *Dorovernum*, or *Dorobernia*, to be torn away from it by the Romans, who gave it the name of the *Urbs Rutupiæ* of Ptolemy;

[1] See Spelman.
[2] See Polyd. Verg. lib. III. p. 64.
[3] By the Monks in the time of Matthew of Weftminfter, and Richard of Cirencefter, who certainly copied the errors of Bede, it was called *Cantiopolis* from *Caput Imperii*. See Richard's Itinerary, by Stukeley, p. 41.

6   a name

a name of equal importance to the Caput Imperii, which the sequel will prove, there being no such place in Kent to challenge so respectable a name as Ptolemy has prefixed to it. I hope I have sufficiently explained where Bede has committed the blunder, in translating *Civitas Rutupiæ*, and confounding it with *Reptacester* or *Richborough*. Had he been cloistered at Canterbury or in the neighbourhood, and not lived at the distance of 300 miles from the spot concerning which he has written, I conceive the nature of the coast, and the locality of abode, would have taught him better. His readers have also been led blind-folded into the mire, when they read his *Civitas* a City, when it evidently implied a Town. Bede has blundered, and his readers have blundered more.

I shall now return to the text of Bede. " Qui portus a gente " Anglorum nunc corruptè *Reptacester* vocatur." Somner [1] supposes that it lost its name of *Rutupium*, and was called by the Saxons Lunden-pic, the haven or port of London.

I should think it was not possible for so learned a man as Somner confessedly was, to lose sight of common sense in this instance? How could this port lose its name, if it was called *Reptacester*, or *Richborough*, by Bede, who lived in the Saxon æra? Is it not also very remarkable that he did not in this case make a very natural inference, and fully establish the following principle, which arises from the disagreement of the passages : *That the name of* Lunden-pic *was not confined only to one haven or port, but was also common to several on the coast of Kent; perhaps towns as well as ports, that led to London ?* Mr. Somner, in citing a passage from the Textus Roffensis, confounds the Lunden-pic of

See his Treatise on the Roman ports and forts in Kent.

Rutupium

Rutupium with *Regulbium*, evidently another port to London, which we shall hereafter clearly find. Let us confront these passages. " Milthredæ vero abbatissæ de Menstre, in Insula Thaneti, " dedit libertatem thelonii ac totam exactionem navigiorum, sibi " et antecessoribus suis jure publico in Londinensi portu primitus " competentem, cartâque suâ confirmavit." This port of London is evidently *Reculver*, situated in the Isle of Thanet. The extract was made by Mr. Somner from a book in St. Augustin's abbey at Canterbury, which relates to a charter granted to Minstre abbey in that island by Ethelbert, one of the Kentish kings. The other passage is from the Textus Roffensis, to this purpose: *If any Kentish-man shall buy any thing in* LUNDEN-WIC, *let him take with him two or three honest men, or the king's portreeve, to witness, &c.* Mr. Somner confesses, by this passage in the laws of Lothaire and Eadrie, that the place here meant was not only a market, but the emporium, or chief market-town, in Kent, which he concludes to be Sandwich, where he fixes the *Rutupium* or *Ruthubi* of Bede ; but it was evidently Canterbury [*]. We will now turn to the *Lunden-wic* of the East Saxons, of which place Mellitus was made bishop, an. 604. Bede says, " In this year " Austin, Archbishop of Britain, consecrated two bishops, Mel- " litus and Justus. The former to preach to the province of " the East Saxons, which is separated from Kent by the Thames, " and joined to the East sea ; the chief city of which is London, " situated on the banks of the Thames, a princely mart, and " much frequented by people from sea and land." This is confirmed, by all the five manuscripts, to be London, and not Sandwich, without Bede's authority. The Cottonian reads Lunða-pic.

---

[*] See Lib. II. Cap. III.

I am

I am alſo inclined to believe the Lunꝺen-pic cited alſo by Mr. Somner, from whence Boniface ſailed to Frieſland to convert the Heathens in the reign of Ina the Weſt Saxon king, to be *Reculver* or *Regulbium* [1]. *Immenſis peragratis terræ partibus*, he traverſed the country to the eaſtern parts of England, to the aforeſaid port, and not to *Richborough*, *Rutupium*, or *Sandwich*, which have no ſpecified name of *Lunden-wic*, as *Reculver* is found to have from Mr. Somner's extract of the grant of king Ethelbert · to Minſtre abbey in the iſle of Thanet. From an argument of this concluſive nature, I ſhall therefore, in my own judgement, eſtabliſh this Saxon name of Lunden-wic at *London*, *Canterbury*, and *Reculver*, the port to which the caſtle of *Richborough* was a defence; being at this æra difuſed or blocked up; and Sandwich only opened perhaps a century or more after it. The *Lunden-wic* where Mellitus was biſhop, was *London*. The *Londen-wic* cited from the Textus Roffenſis, concerning commerce at that place, was *Canterbury*; and the *Lunden-wic* ſo called in Ethelbert's grant, *Reculver*. *Sandwich* does not appear to have been mentioned before an. 979, three hundred and ſeventy-five years after the above mention of *Lunden-wic*. I think, therefore, with great reaſon, we may put this place out of the queſtion. Thus we find there has been as much confuſion and unintelligible diſcuſſion raiſed on the ſubject of *Lunden-wic* [2], as of the *Urbs Rutupiæ*; the whole ariſing from various acceptations of thoſe places by the antients, and to which a previous locality has not been eſtabliſhed by them.

---

[1] Willibaldus de vita S. Bonifacii, p. 354.

[2] Ponꞇ and pic, or wich, are ſynonymous in the Saxon; nor do they always mean havens or ſea-ports; this is evident in Þamꞇun-ponꞇ uſed in the Saxon annals as Northampton, *Portland near Shrewſbury*, Nortwich, Nantwich, and Droitwich, the north of England, and ſeveral other places, where they mean *Urbs, Oppidum*.

Let

Let us now confider Canterbury as the *Urbs* ʿΠάϊεπαι of Ptolemy.

The Romans had three ports of eminence on the coaft of Kent, *Dover*, *Lymne*, and *Richborough*; from each of thefe was a military way to the city of Canterbury. The road to Richborough is not to be traced at this day; but it is doubtlefs the Romans had fuch a way, fince the *Itinerary of Antoninus* gives the diftance of miles from Richborough to Canterbury, as well as from the other two ports [1]. Hiftory does not only, as we fhall find, affign high antiquity and great importance to Canterbury as a city; but thefe three principal ways, traverfing and concentring themfelves in it, add validity to the affertion, and prove that in the remoteft periods it muft have been a populous and much-frequented place.

According to Dr. Somner, the fpeedy and miraculous progrefs of Chriftianity penetrated into this ifland as early as king Lucius [2], paffing through thofe places that were inacceffible to the Romans [3]; it alfo had infinuated herfelf in every place among the legions [4]. We have therefore every reafon to believe, that wherever they had their military eftablifhments, there the caufe of religion would be favoured, by the erecting of temples, or places of Chriftian worfhip. From this confideration, and as Chriftianity was promulgated in this country on the earlieft advent of the Romans, according to Bede, an. 156, when Pope Eleutherius confirmed king Lucius, at which time the Britons received their faith; we muft conclude this city to have been

[1] See alfo the Iter of Richard of Cirencefter.
[2] See Lambarde's Peramb.
[3] Tertull. adverf. Judæos I.
[4] Hefterni fumus et veftra omnia implevimus, Urbes, Infulas, Caftella, Municipia, Conciliabula, Caftra ipfa, Tribus, Decurias. Vid. Tertull. Apologet. II. from Somer.

a populous

a populous place and much reforted to; indeed, we are not wanting in authors who attempt to prove it a city 900 years before the birth of Chrift.

If, from the great fertility of its fituation, healthy air, its being fituated in a valley, through which the river Stour branches itfelf into feveral courfes, and uniting again, one branch of which runs through the city, advantages which muft ever tempt inhabitants to fettle in fuch places ; if conjecture can create a town from the earlieft time; I think it merits regard, and fhould be efteemed accordingly. But indeed, were we to reafon from analogy, the faireft of all reafons when prefumptive proofs are wanting, when do we find the ftations of a people in the re-moteft times ever divefted of thefe advantages? And when our notice is attracted to the places they made choice of, we always find them poffeffing every commodious quality which the fituation of a country could poffibly afford them ; an election which is always compatible with human underftanding in its moft un-cultured ftate.

If we obferve the country round Canterbury for feveral miles, we muft immediately decide on its being a fpot of ground moft happily calculated to furnifh a people with comfortable abode. The hills which encircle it are replete with fprings, which add fertility to the valley ; their afcent is gentle, yet commanding ; and their diftance not too near to admit of a fudden furprize : for an enemy coming down upon the city muft be always ex-pofed, and give fufficient time for its inhabitants to prepare its defence. There are alfo woods on the high grounds, which in early ages muft have been impaffable, and which muft have proved a natural defence of themfelves; indeed we have in a fimilar fenfe to feek no further evidence, when we find that,

X x x   in

in the time of king Ethelbert, it was the head city of his dominions ; and his dominions were very powerful, fpreading as
far as the Humber.

A city does not fpring up like a mufhroom ; a concatenation of
events muft concur to render it formidable ; it will take ages
in rifing to fplendor ; the fame of a place, and its convenience
in refpect to opulence and commerce, increafe its power ; but
be it alfo confidered, that a multiplicity of occurrences muft tran-
fpire, before it can poffibly entice the Sovereign to take up his
refidence in it, and in a country fo remote from the refined tranfactions of Greece and Rome ; efpecially when a Potentate, like
Conftantine, has not the power of ranfacking the greateft city in
the world for the fake of tranflating the capital of his empire
into another quarter ; and when we may naturally fuppofe a
multiplicity of circumftances are wanting to confer the neceffary
magnificence on its founder.

We thus find that hiftory and all other confiderations combine
to prove the remote antiquity of Canterbury, as a place of note.

Its importance to a people from commercial advantages, fituated on a navigable river, near the fea, and at the fame time
poffeffing all the advantages of an inland town, by agriculture
and the great fertility of its neighbouring foil ; Romans and
others invited to it, from their zeal of religion, from intereft; and,
to fum up all, ftrangers or troops entering the kingdom, and
inhabitants or troops paffing out of it to any of the three chief
ports on the coaft, muft have added to its fame and its confequence, efpecially as we have before obferved, that the three
chief roads are there concentered.

With thefe united advantages, what place is there to be found,
on the coaft of Kent, that in thofe days could boaft of equal im-

5   portance ?

portance? We have no account of any other city than *Dorovernia*, or one of the *Rutupine* ports. Our beſt of Antiquaries [1] had aſſigned *Richborough* to be this city. All others who have mentioned the ſame take their ideas from him. But be it remembered, had *Richborough* ever conferred upon it, that honour we not only ſhould have heard of ſome remains of more conſequence than coins, potſheards, or ſome other trifling exuviæ, being found there ; but we ſhould have found its ſituation better adapted. A city muſt be well ſupplied with water : *Richborough* is too high for it. When the walls were erected by Theodoſius, partly as a depoſit for military ſtores landed there, or for a *ſpeculatorium* for the *Comes*, the troops that would be ſtationed on the ſpot muſt naturally entice families to ſettle near the walls ; and moſt probably the ground near them was inhabited, as indeed ſeems evident by the blackneſs of the ſoil, and other manifeſt ſigns ; but, had it ever been raiſed to the importance of a city, we ſhould long ere this have diſcovered remains that would put it beyond a doubt, ſuch as *altars*, *inſcriptions*, and which have been frequently found at Canterbury. On this our argument turns : for it is now well known, that this city could be placed on no other ſpot than either *Richborough* or *Canterbury*. *Richborough* could not therefore in this ſenſe be the *Rutuby* of *Bede* but *Canterbury*. The *Rutupian* ports, with Dover and Lymne, were it ſeems the only ports that led out of this iſland to the continent in theſe days, at leaſt the ports of any conſequence. Whether *Dover* or *Lymne* were the ports to which troops, military ſtores, or merchandize, were tranſported, I very much doubt : indeed, I do not find that hiſtory mentions them as ſuch, or of any comparative conſequence to *Richborough* and *Reculver*; I therefore conceive,

[1] See Camden.

ceive,

ccive, that as Bede has confounded the city with the haven, as is
evident from his *miles*, the diftance from the *Rutupine* fhore to the
firft haven town, fo his *Civitas quæ dicitur Rutubi portus* fhould be
tranflated Town, and his miles put out of the queftion ; or the
fentence, according to Ptolomy, changed to *Urbs Rutupiæ*; by
which his miles would agree with the diftance of Canterbury
from the Portus Itius, the fenfe be compleat, and the difpute
finally fettled.

N. B.   I am obliged to Mr. Boys * of Sandwich for the firft
hint, which fuggefted to me the materials of this paper, who,
as a judicious and cautious Antiquary, was led to doubt the affertions of antient and modern writers, on the fituation of the
Urbs Rutupiæ.   J. D.

* From this gentleman the curious may hereafter expect a full and fatisfactory
account of the fubject treated of in this Effay.   Edit.

Leland's account of the *Portus Rutupinus* is very concife in
his Collectanea III. p. **11.**

" Julius cum Britannis fuper Barhondune pugnavit. Julius inchoavit caftel-
" lum de Dovar.

" Arviragus communivit caftellum de Dovar contra Romanos.

" ☞ Obturatus eft Portus Rutupinus, qui modo Dovar dicitur, Anno Domini
" 72°.

" Forfan hoc nomine, quia portus commodiffimus erat Romanis ex Gallia in
" Britanniam trajicientibus."

The firft three fentences fcarcely relate to the *Portus Rutupinus*; but they immediately precede the above extracts in Leland, whofe remark on the name of this port is contained in
the laft paragraph.

M E M O I R S

O F

WILLIAM LAMBARDE, Efq;

AN EMINENT LAWYER AND ANTIQUARY.

Compiled partly from his own Works, and from printed Accounts of him ; partly from private Papers preferved in his Family, and communicated to the Editor by MULTON LAMBARD, Efq; his lineal Defcendant.

DURING the fplendid reign of Queen Elizabeth, befides thofe diftinguifhed perfons who filled the higher and greater ftations of public life, and thereby made themfelves famous in hiftory, there were many others of inferior note and ftation, whofe eminent talents and ufeful labours juftly entitle them to be held forth as an example, and to be honourably remembered by pofterity. It was a period, which was not only great and glorious in the public tranfactions of the nation, but which alfo gave birth to many new kinds of learning, or ufeful improvements of the old. Modern learning of almoft every kind muft go back to thefe times for the date of its very beginning, or of its more fuccefsful progrefs. In fact, the yoke which had overborn both religion and learning was fhaken off, and men began to give free fcope to their exertions. It is ufeful to obferve the confequence, either in general, or in any particular inftance.

Y y y

WILLIAM

WILLIAM LAMBARDE, or LAMBARD, the fubject of thefe memoirs, was one of thofe who diftinguifhed themfelves in a refpectable, though fecondary ftation, fulfilling the duties of it moft faithfully, and was in that very refpect honoured and patronized by the great, and even perfonally by the Queen herfelf.

His difpofition was benevolent, his mind judicious and elegant, his learning folid and deep ; and he devoted himfelf to the fervice of his country, in the profeffion and ftation which he filled, with unremitted zeal and labour. It is juft, it is ufeful, to preferve the remembrance of fuch a man, and to affign to him his due portion of praife.

He was born October the 18th, 1536, being the eldeft fon of John Lambard, alderman of London, and fheriff of the fame in the year 1551, by Juliana his wife, daughter and heir of William Horne, or Herne, of London.

Nothing is recorded concerning the early part of his education till he entered upon the ftudy of the law, and was admitted into the Society of Lincoln's Inn, Auguft 15, 1556. Here he ftudied under Laurence Nowell (brother to Alexander Nowell, dean of St. Paul's), famous for his knowledge of antiquity and of the Saxon language, of whom Camden * fays, " that he was the firft who brought into ufe again and revived " the language of our anceftors the Saxons, which, through " difufe, lay forlorn and buried in oblivion." Wood, quoting this teftimony of Camden to the learning of Nowell, adds, that Lambarde profited fo much by his inftructions, as to be efteemed the fecond beft in thofe ftudies. It was a branch of learning intimately connected with the profeffion to which he had devoted himfelf; and he faw that he fhould lay the foundations of his profeffional knowledge deep, by going back to the cuftoms and jurifprudence of the Saxon times.

* Wood's Athenæ Oxon. Vol. I. p. 186.

I

His

His firſt work, a collection and tranſlation of the Saxon laws, under the title of " Ἀρχαιονομία, ſive de priſcis Anglorum " Legibus libri, 1568," 4to. may be conſidered as the firſt fruits both of his legal and Saxon ſtudies.   The MS. in Saxon, as he ʼells us *, was put into his hands by Nowell, who requeſted him to tranſlate it into Latin, and publiſh it.   He dedicated this work to Sir William Cordell, Knight, maſter of the Rolls.   It was printed by John Day, 1568, 4to; and was afterwards re-publiſhed in folio with Bede's Eccleſiaſtical Hiſtory as a ſupple-mental work to that Hiſtory in 1644, by Abraham Wheelock †, Arabick profeſſor, and publick librarian at Cambridge, who commends highly the elegance of Lambard's interpretation—" Elegantiſſimi harum legum interpretis lucubrationibus clar. " Lambardi vere comptis et politis—ut faveas, humillimè ob-" teſtor," are his words; and he calls him " Legum noſtrarum et " elegantiarum omnium callentiſſimum ‡."

* Preface to Ἀρχαιονομία.

† Wheelock's republication is ſaid to have exceeded Lambarde's original work. The publication of the " Leges Anglo-Saxonicæ," by David Wilkins, in 1721, has taken place of both of them.   Both Wheelock and this Editor complain of Lambarde's having acted in ſome places the part of a paraphraſt, rather than of an interpreter; but his work was the foundation of thoſe which followed.   See the Epiſtle of Nicolſon, biſhop of Derry, prefixed to Wilkins's book: His words are remarkable : " Certè Lambardus in Archaionomiâ ſuâ priora operis egregii " fundamenta poſuit; ſed quod recte a Wheeloco notatum in locis quampluri-" mis paraphraſten potius quam interpretem ſe præbuit.   Hinc viro eleganti et " calamo ejus nimium calenti hallucinatiunculæ quædam exciderunt, quas tu " facili obſervabis negotio," &c.   He afterwards calls Lambarde's work " Irenar-" chæ optimi primitias."

‡ There are ſeveral works in MS. which prove the extraordinary labour and aſſiduity both of Nowell and of Lambarde in the ſtudy of Saxon and Engliſh anti-quities.   In the catalogue of the Cotton library, there is a long liſt of MSS. by each of them, under the name of Collectanea; which are either tranſcripts of antient hiſtorical MSS. or extracts by way of abridgement from them : they were perhaps the gift of Lambarde, who is mentioned in the hiſtory of the library pre-fixed to the catalogue as a contributor to that great repoſitory.   Others are pre-ſerved amongſt the family papers of the Perambulator, of which a catalogue is given in the Appendix, Nº I.

In the year 1570 he married his first wife, Jane Multon, daughter of George Multon, Esq; of St. Clere, in the county of Kent. It is probable that from this time, if not before, he was settled in Kent; Westcombe, near Greenwich, of the manor of which he was possessed, being the place of his residence. For we shall now find, that he devoted a great share of his labours to the service of that county; without giving up at the same time his profession of the law, and his connection with Lincoln's Inn, of which society he was admitted a bencher in 1578 *. He had finished his " Perambulation of Kent" in 1570, in which year he sent it to his friend Thomas Wotton, Esq; (nephew to Wotton dean of Canterbury), a worthy and learned gentleman of Kent. The same was afterwards sent to Parker, archbishop of Canterbury, and by him communicated, in 1573, to the Lord Treasurer Burleigh †. In 1576 it was published, and that;

* There is the following remarkable testimony to his merit, from the Society of Lincoln's Inn, preserved in Dugdale's Orig. Jurid. p. 268. " William Lambard " (a person skilfull in antiquities, publisher of the Saxon Laws), concerning whom " I find this following order, at a council here held 9 Feb. 21 Eliz. Forasmuch " as Mr. William Lambard hath deserved universally well of this Commonwealth " and country, and likewise of the fellowship and society of this house, and is like " hereafter to win greater credit to himself and the society of this house; it is " therefore agreed, that he shall have room to sit amongst the Society of the Fel- " lowship of the Bench, as other assistants use to do, without any thing paying for " the same : Provided always, that this be no precedent to any other that shall " be called to the like place hereafter; but that they shall pay for the said room " such sums of money as shall be assessed by the Bench."

† Strype's Life of Parker, B. 4. C. 23. 20.—Annals, Vol. II. B. 1. C. 3. The following is an extract from a letter of Archbishop Parker's to Lord Burleigh, in which he recommends this work and the author to him.

" I have joined thereunto (which I am sure ye have not seen) a description of " the county of Kent, written and laboured by an honest and well-learned observer " of times and histories; which he sent to me to peruse, to correct, and amend, and " so to be under the reformation of some whom he judgeth to be conversant in " histories; not meaning to put it abroad till it had suffered the hammer of some " of his friends' judgements, and then, at further deliberation, peradventure to set " it forth. Which book, although I have no commission to communicate it, I re- " ferre

that, as it fhould feem, by the order and direction of Mr. Wotton, who himfelf prefixed to it a letter recommending it to the gentlemen of the county. From Lambarde's own letter to Mr. Wotton, accompanying the book, it appears that his defign and refearches reached much farther, and that he had already collected materials for a general account of Great Britain, of which this was but the fpecimen *. The difcovery that the learned Camden was engaged in the fame work, prevented him from proceeding farther †. Mr. Camden himfelf bears the ampleft teftimony to this fpecimen

"-ferre it either to fhew you, as I think ye be not unwilling in fuch knowledge to be " partaker; and thus prefent it to your correction and amendment, when your "·leifure can ferve you. In the mean-time I pray your Lordfhip to keep it to " yourfelf. As I have made this author a judge of fome of my fmall travels, "·whereof I fend you this one bound by my man. I am not minded to fuffer them " abroad in this quarrelous and envious world. I think the rather we both ufed "·this forefight to fupprefs our labours *in ronum annum*, as Horace counfayleth, " rather than to fuffer an undigefted and tumultuous collection to-be gazed on by " many folkes." Strype's Appendix to Parker's Life, B. 4. N° 89.

* This collection of materials, " being digefted into titles by way of alphabet," he called a *Topographical Dictionary*. See his Epiftle to Mr. Wotton, prefixed to the Perambulation. It was publifhed from the original MS. in 1730, 4to, under the title of " *Dictionarium Angliæ Topographicum et Hiftoricum*."

† This may be affirmed with confidence on the ground of his letter to Camden, publifhed in Camdeni Epiftolæ, p. 28. The letter was written to Camden in confequence of his having communicated to him fome parts, or the whole, of his Britannia in MS.—He fpeaks of the pleafure he received from Camden's work; and adds, that it was alfo a caufe of forrowing to him, becaufe he could no longer dwell in meditation on his favourite ftudies. The whole letter breathes a fpirit of candour and modefty which does the writer great honour. It is dated from Halling, July 29, 1585, the year before the firft publication of Camden's Britannia. The letter itfelf, as deferving the reader's notice, is fubjoined in the Appendix, N° II.

For a further explanation of his intention, fee the conclufion of his Perambulation, where he fpeaks of this work as a fpecimen, in order to " prove himfelf, " provoke fome, and pleafure and profit others;" and fhortly after adds, " As " touching the defcription of the refidue of this realm, finding by this one, how " hard it will be for any one (and much more for myfelfe) to accomplifh it for "-all, I can but wifh, in like fort, that fome one in each fhire would make the " enter-

specimen of his great defign. He fays, " that he had defcribed " the county of Kent fo much to the life, as to have left little " for thofe that come after him ;" and readily acknowledges the Perambulation to be " the foundation and fountain" of that part of his Britannia * which treats of Kent, and calls the author eminent for learning and piety.

In fpeaking of his piety, 1 fuppofe he refers to a work which he took in hand foon after his publifhing the Perambulation ; his founding an hofpital for the poor at Eaft Greenwich in Kent. This is faid to have been the firft hofpital founded by a Proteftant. The Queen granted her letters patent for the foundation of this hofpital in 1574. The building was begun in 1575, and finifhed in little more than a year, the poor being

" enterprize for his owne countrie, to the end that, by joyning our pens, and con-
" ferring our labours as it were *(ex fymbolo),* we might at the laft, by the union
" of many parts and papers, compact one whole and perfect bodie and booke of
" our Englifh Topographie."
    In the fecond edition he exprefsly mentions Camden's Britannia, in thefe words annexed :
    " Here left I (good Reader), when I firft fet forth this worke ; fince which
" time I find my defire not a little ferved by Mafter Camden's Britannia : wherein
" as he hath not only farre exceeded whatfoever hath been formerly attempted in
" that kynd, but alfo paffed the expectation of other men, and even of his own
" hope : fo do I acknowledge it written to the great honour of the realm with
" men abroad, and to the fingular delight of us all at home, having for mine
" own particular found myfelf thereby to have learned much, even in that fhyre
" where I had endeavoured to know moft. Neverthelefse, being affured that the
" inwardes of each place may beft be known by fuch as refide therein, I cannot
" but ftill encourage fome one able man in each fhyre to undertake his own,
" whereby both many good particularities will come to difcoverie every where,
" and Mafter Camden himfelf may yet have greater choice wherewith to amplifie
" and enlarge the whole."
    * His words are—" Ad Cantium nunc perveni, quam regionem licet Gul. Lambardus, vir infigni eruditione et moribus fanctiffimis ornatiffimus, adeo graphice jufto volumine defcripferit, ut curiofa ejus felicitas paucula aliis reliquerit, pro fufcepti tamen operis ratione, eam quoque percurram, et ne fubleftâ, ut inquit Comicus, fide me agere quis exiftimet, eum mihi fundum et fontem fuiffe libens merito hic agnofco."

admitted

admitted into it October 1, 1576. He called his hofpital " The College of the Poor of Queen Elizabeth," and endowed it with certain eftates, referving to himfelf a beneficial leafe of the fame, and requefting the prefident and governors to- continue the fame to his heirs at a certain rent. The whole charge of the building, together with the purchafe of eftates, amounted to fomething more than £2,700. The number of poor, during his own life, was to be ten penfioners; the whole number received into the hofpital, with their families, to be about fixteen perfons; each of thefe to enjoy a dwelling-room and garden, and to receive five fhillings monthly, and yearly two loads of faggots. After his death, the number to be increafed to twenty*; then to receive fix fhillings monthly, and one load of faggots yearly, with a dwelling and garden as before. Thus was his charitable defign quickly accomplifhed, and the foundation munificently endowed, not only during his life-time, but whilft he was not yet far advanced in years. He provided alfo for the government and good order of his college; and even drew up a form of prayer, to be approved of by the Bifhop of Rochefter, the diocefan, and to be continually in ufe amongft the penfioners. It is remarkable, that he ordains, that if at any time it fhall not be lawful for the poor of his college to ufe the form of prayer drawn up for them, in fuch cafe the whole grant fhall be void †.

In 1579 he was appointed a juftice of the peace for the county of Kent, by the fpecial order of Lord Chancellor Bromley ‡; to the faithful execution of which office he dedicated his time and labours with the fame zeal as he had done in other in-

---

* The letters patent fay, a warden, fub-warden, and eighteen poor; by the fame, the mafter of the Rolls, and two fenior wardens of the Drapers' Company, are made a body corporate, for the government of the college.

† See the Appendix, N° III. IV. V.

‡ Strype's Annals, Vol. III. B. 2. Ch. 13.

ftances.

ſtances. It was alſo a time which required able and active magiſtrates, and which did not abound in them, ſo many being diſaffected either to the civil or ecclefiaſtical government, or too indolent to oppoſe the diſaffected with activity and courage. His affiduity in the execution of his office appears by ſeveral MS. Charges, which he left behind him, compoſed with care, and ſuited to the circumſtances of the times. It appears from the ſame, that he took the lead amongſt the juſtices of the weſtern diviſion of the county from this time, or ſoon after, to the time of his death. There is a continued ſeries of Charges from 1581 to 1600. He applied alſo his knowledge of the law to the explaining the nature and duties of the office which he bore in common with ſo many others for the public benefit. I allude to his " Eirenarcha, or, of the Office of the Juſtices of Peace, in " Four Books," publiſhed in 1581 *, and dedicated to the Lord Chancellor Bromley. He himſelf, in his preface, explains this work to be " a body of diſcourſe made out by conferring the " writings of Marrow and Fitzherbert with the book caſes and " ſtatutes, and adapted for gentlemen not bred up to the law." It is then the work of a lawyer making uſe of his profeſſional knowledge to explore his ſubject to the bottom, and ſeeking to lay it open to others in a clear method and language; the talent of performing which he poſſeſſed in an eminent degree. In 1583 he publiſhed another work on the " Duties of " Conſtables, Borſholders, Tythingmen, and ſuch other low and " lay Miniſters of the Peace;" which may be conſidered as a ſupplement to the former †.—They are printed together in the edition of 1619.

* This book was republiſhed in 1602 and 1619. In the laſt edition are ſome additions by an author of the time of James I.

† This ſmall tract went through five editions ſeparately, being republiſhed in 1594, 1602, 1631, and 1677.

His

His character and his writings had now recommended him to the notice of fome of the greateft and moft powerful people of the realm. In 1589* he had a deputation from the Lord

" After my moft humble and bounden duty, my Right Honourable good Lord, " your Lordfhip's letters of the 30th of September were even now delivered to " my hand, having (by whofe default I wot not) fuffered that great delay in the " coming towards me.—Which, howfoever it may fall out to my detriment in " the matter that they purport, yet came they not unfeafonably to glad my poor " heart, in that they were the infallible meffengers, not only of the continuance, " but of the increafe (if any may be) of your moft honourable favour and difpo- " fition to work my good—who, as I never demerited any thing at your hands, fo " neverthelefs have I drawn more from the fountain of your mere bounty, than " from all the good wills and wyles of all the perfons that be alive.—Thus tyed, " I may not ceafe to pray to God for your Honour; praying withal, that he will " make my prayer effectual for you.

" As touching the matter contained in your Lordfhip's letter, albeit I know mine " own infufficiency (now alfo increafed by decay of fight and difcontinuance from " ftudy) to ferve in any place where wifdom or learning muft be fet on work; yet, " acknowledging that I do reap fome benefit by her Majefty (which I received from " the free hand of your Honour), I hold myfelf double bounden to ferve her High- " nefs with all the powers that I have. And the rather alfo, for that it hath " pleafed you, my moft honourable Lord, to give my name and your report of me.

" Therefore only I do moft humbly befeech your Lordfhip, to add this unto " the reft of your great favours vouchfafed, that I may not be invefted in the fer- " vice but upon probation, and for this next term only; to the end that after fuch " an experiment, and conference made of my fmall abilities with the office itfelf, I " may faithfully (and in that duty which I bear to God, her Majefty, and your " Honour), affure your good Lordfhip, whether I fhall find myfelf fit to difcharge " the truft that belongeth to the place.

" Thus much I moft humbly pray your good Lordfhip to accept at this time; " and until that I may, as duty bindeth, perfonally attend your good Lordfhip, " which alfo, by the favour of God, I will not fail with all good fpeed to perform. " And fo I moft humbly take my leave of you, my Right Honourable Lord; and " do in my heartieft prayer recommend you to the gracious protection of the Al- " mighty. From Halling, this 4th of October, 1589. Your Lordfhip's moft hum- " ble and bounden, WILLIAM LAMBARDE."
Appendix to Strype's Annals, Vol. III. Book II. N° 42.

Treafurer Burleigh for the compofition for alienations for fines[*].
In 1592 he was appointed a mafter in Chancery by Sir John
Puckering, lord keeper; and in 1597 was appointed keeper of the
rolls and houfe of the rolls, in Chancery-Lane, by Sir Thomas
Egerton, lord keeper.   At length, in 1600, he was perfonally
taken notice of by the Queen herfelf, who fent for him, received
him moft gracioufly, and appointed him keeper of the records in
the Tower.   In confequence of this appointment, he had another
interview with her Majefty on the 4th of Auguft, 1601, and
prefented her with an account of thofe records, which he called
his " Pandecta Rotulorum."   In 'the mean time he had written,
though not publifhed, another work, intituled " Archeion, or a
" Difcourfe upon the High Courts of Juftice in England."   This
was finifhed and prefented to Sir Robert Cecil, with a dedication,
in 1591.   It was not publifhed till 1635, fome years after his
death, by his grandfon Thomas Lambarde.

The courfe of his life, as thus defcribed, has led me to the
mention of feveral of his friends and patrons.   Another was
Lord Cobham, who placed fo much confidence in him, as to
appoint him his executor, with Sir John Levefon and Thomas
Fane, Efq; and a truftee for eftablifhing his college for the
poor at Cobham, in Kent, which he left unfinifhed at his death.
The three perfons above-mentioned procured an act of parlia-

---

[*] This office was erected in the 18th year of Queen Elizabeth, for the purpofe
of ordering and receiving in a new manner the fines due for licences of alienation
of lands holden in chief of her Majefty, or pardons in cafe of alienation of fuch
lands without licence firft had ; together with fines due for original writs, and writs
of covenant.   The office was intrufted to two or three deputies, who had clerks
and officers under them.   There is a MS. work of Lambarde's, in which he treats
of the moderation and juftice of the fines in queftion, of the advantage, both in profit to her Majefty and eafe to the fubject, of this new mode of collecting them, and
of the duty of the deputies and their officers ; and propofes, in the end, fome
farther regulations in the office.   At the end of the fame MS. is an account of the
receipts for feveral years, from the 18th to the 37th of Elizabeth.

ment,

ment, 39 Elizabeth, for the foundation, or rather reftoration of the college, and for making the wardens for Rochefter-bridge prefidents of the fame. Lambarde was afterwards concerned in drawing up rules for the poor, their election, maintenance *, &c. Thus was it his fortune, after having himfelf been the founder of fuch a charitable eftablifhment, to concur with others in the foundation and government of a fecond. Lambarde himfelf mentions this Lord Cobham, in a letter to Lord Burleigh, as his friend and affiftant in a time of diftrefs †.

To return to the more private anecdotes of his life. In 1583, he married Silvefter Dallifon, widow of William Dallifon, Efq; and daughter of Robert Deane, gent. of Halling, in the county of Kent; which was the place of his refidence for fome time after. He had by her three fons and one daughter, of whom the eldeft fon Multon was afterwards knighted; the daughter Margaret was married to Thomas Godfrey, Efq. The other two fons, Gore and Fane, alfo furvived him. In 1592 he married his third wife, Margaret Reader, widow, by whom he had no iffue. He died himfelf Auguft 19, 1601, at his houfe of Weftcombe, and was buried in the parifh church of Greenwich, Kent. A monument was placed over him; which, upon the rebuilding of the church, being with other monuments taken down, was removed, and placed in the parifh church of Sevenoak, Kent, where is now the feat and burying-place of the family ‡.

His

* For an account of the feveral particulars relating to this college, the above-mentioned act of parliament, and ftatutes, fee Thorpe's Regiftrum Roffenfe. In Strype's Annals, Vol. IV. N° 201. there is an original letter from Lambarde himfelf to Lord Burleigh, relating to the death and will of Lord Cobham.

† See his letter in Strype's Annals, Vol. III. B. 2. Ch. 3.

‡ The following epitaph is tranfcribed from a monument which formerly ftood againft the fouth-wall of the old church at Greenwich.

" William

His laſt will contains another well-judged act of charity, viz. the bequeathing to the Drapers' company a moiety of certain rents and profits to be paid into their hands in truſt, for the purpoſe of lending it by way of loan in ſums of fifty pounds, from time to time, without intereſt, *to the poorer occupiers of the ſaid company,* the company taking bond for repayment.

"William Lambard, of Lincoln's Inn, ſome time maſter in Chancery, keeper of "the rolls and records within the Tower, of the office of alienations to Queen Eli- "zabeth, founded the college of the poor of Greenwich, and endowed it.

"Obiit 1601, Aug. 19, at Weſtcomb, in Eaſt Greenwich."

"Sir Moulton Lambard, of Weſtcomb, in Eaſt Greenwich, knight, ſon and heir "of the aforeſaid William Lambard, 1634.—Thomas Lambard, Eſq; his only ſon "and heir, erected this monument to Sir Moulton Lambard, his aged and dear father."

On pulling down the church, in order to rebuild the preſent, this monument was removed at the charge of the late Thomas Lambard, Eſq; and fixed in the church of Sevenoak; where, at the weſt end, on the north ſide, is a mural monument of white marble, and on a tablet of black marble is the following inſcription, in gilt letters:

"Hic ſitus eſt Gulielmus Lambarde, Londinenſis, in hoſpitio jureconſultorum "Lincolnienſi paredrus; in alma cancellaria magiſter; ad tempus cuſtos rotulorum "et recordorum infra turrim London. ab alienationibus (quas vocant) auguſtiſſimæ "Anglorum reginæ Elizabethæ, cujus ſacræ memoriæ et nomini conſecratum ſuo- "ſumptu ſolus, et fundavit et annuo reditu dotavit collegium pauperum Greenovici "in Cantio. Obiit anno Domini 1601, Auguſti 19° die, apud Weſtcombe, in Eaſt "Greenwiche.

"Archaionomia   —   1568.   Juſtice of the Peace 1581.
"Perambulation of Kent 1570.   Pandecta rotulorum 1600.
        "Archeion   —   1591.

"Hic etiam ſitus eſt Moultonus Lambarde de Weſtcombe in Eaſt Greenwiche, in "comitatu Cantiæ, eques auratus, filius et hæres prædicti Gulielmi Lambardi. "Obiit anno Domini 1634, Auguſti 7° die, apud Weſtcombe. Hoc M. S."

Underneath, on a ſmall tablet of black marble, is this:

"Parenti grandævo colendiſſimo, et patri chariſſimo, officii et amoris ergo poſuit "Tho. Lambarde, Armiger, filius unicus et hæres prædicti Moultoni Lambardi, "equitis aurati."

And beneath, on a tablet of white, is the following:

"Inſtaurata funditus vetuſtâ Greenovicenſi eccleſia, et exulantibus, quæ inibi "erant, monumentis: Marmor hoc, abavi proavique memoria ſacrum, huc, veluti "in portum, e communi naufragio evaſit, et cognati cineris libenter ſe in tutelam "tradidit, curante Thoma Lambard, armigero, Gulielmi filio, Thomæ nepote, anno "Domini M.DCC.XXXIII."

From

From the above review of his life it is eafy to collect his character. We find him deeply read in the ftudies belonging to his profeffion, and in the Saxon language properly fubfidiary to them. His turn of mind alfo led him beyond the ftudy of Britifh law to that of Britifh cuftoms, and all manner of local hiftory. Thefe branches of learning are predominant in moft of his works; yet are there here and there manifeft traces of an intimate acquaintance with Latin and Greek literature, and efpecially of that accuracy of diftinction and divifion of which the Greek writers are the beft models, and the beft teachers. As he was affiduous and diligent in fulfilling the duties of every ftation to which he was called, fo did every fucceffive incident of his life, that might be worthy to give a bias to his ftudies, produce from him fome learned and ufeful work. His profeffion of the law gave rife to his " Archaionomia," as the firft fruits of his inftruction under a learned mafter, and afterwards at a later time of life to his " Archeion." His refidence in Kent, his property and connections there, induced him to draw up his " Perambulation." He had not long been in the commiffion for the peace before his " Eirenarcha" fhewed how much he had given up his thoughts to the duties and nature of that office. Queen Elizabeth appointed him keeper of her records in 1600; in the following year he had his " Pandecta Rotulorum" to offer to her, as a proof that he had applied himfelf to her Majefty's fervice in his new office. There are other inedited works * which confirm ftill more this excellent part of his character. It is happy for the ftate, when each man, having firft laid in a ftock of general knowledge, will thus be content to devote himfelf with his whole mind to his duty, without over-ftepping his proper line, or invading the province of another.

* See infra, p. 507 & 508.

In

In his "Perambulation" we may confider him as opening a new fource of learning, as an original author. It was the firft book of county antiquities *; and we have feen that his plan extended farther than one county, though he relinquifhed it in deference to another perfon. Let me add, that what he executed has not often, if ever, been exceeded in its kind. The Perambulation of Lambarde may juftly challenge a comparifon with any other county hiftory, for clearnefs of method, variety and accuracy of information, and for comprehenfive brevity. At the fame time it has its defects. The Roman antiquities of the county he gives up almoft entirely as too remote and obfcure, concerning which there certainly are not wanting many ufeful data; nor has he touched upon the natural hiftory; and he might eafily have en-larged to the advantage and fatisfaction of his reader on the geographical defcription of the county, as the courfe of the hills, rivers, &c. He is moft full on the Saxon and Englifh an-tiquities and hiftorical anecdotes relating to each place. Of the above omiffions he was himfelf fenfible, and has given his rea-fons for them in the conclufion of his work. I cannot but wifh that this example, fet in the firft inftance by Lambarde, Camden, and others, had been more followed, and that the voluminous county hiftories, which it has been the fafhion to compile of late, had not fuperfeded the plan of putting together briefly and clearly the more general fubjects of information; fuch as the Topography, Cuftoms, and Natural Hiftory of the County. This latter plan is much more capable of elegance, and may be read with much more pleafure, and it would be more inftruc-tive, becaufe the contents would be retained by the memory with

---

* Hence Philipot fays of him (Villare Cant. p. 163.) " that he gave us a de-
" fcription of this county (Kent) in his Perambulation, and made this work the
" more eafy to any that fhould endeavour farther progrefs therein. Facile eft in-
" ventis addere, difficile invenire."

much

much more eafe. I fpeak not this to the difparagement of the
larger works; the minute particulars which they contain are
highly valuable for the fake of reference in many cafes, and we
are much indebted to the laborious collectors of them : but it
might be ufeful to feparate them from the topicks of more general information, which are capable of being moulded into fo
inftructive and elegant a form.

Lambarde's common-place-book, mentioned in the preface to
his Perambulation, as containing materials for a general hiftory
of Englifh antiquities, was publifhed long after his death, in
1730, under the title of " *Dictionarium Angliæ Topographicum &*
" *Hiftoricum.*"

Other writings of his, now extant in MS. are feveral Charges
to Juries, and a Treatife of the Service, called the Office of
Compofitions for Alienations *, 1590; to which I referred before,

---

* Tanner, in his Bibliotheca Britannico-Hibernica, mentions this work with
other MS. works, as,

1. Commentarium de nominibus modernis et fincere Saxonicis, Latinis, et Bri-
tannicis Civitatum, Montium, &c. olim penes D. H. Saville. This was nothing
more than the Topographical Dictionary.

2. Caufes in Chancery, gathered by Sir George Cary out of the labours of Mr.
William Lambert, 1601. In MS. Norwicenf. More. 562.

3. A Calendar of the Bible.

What this laft work was, or where to be found, does not now appear. Tanner
himfelf feems to have had no other authority for mentioning it, than a paffage in
Strype's Life of Archbifhop Parker, p. 533. where mention is made of a Saxon
MS. given by the Archbifhop to Ben'et College library, having inferted in it an
Hexaftick in Latin verfe, figned W. L. and a letter to the Archbifhop in praife of
the fame man, once owner of the book. Whoever he was, his knowledge of the
Saxon language and of antiquities is highly commended. His *Calendar of the Bible*
is fpoken of as known to the Archbifhop, and his labours in the Armenian tongue.
The former part of the encomium agrees well with Lambarde; but there are no
traces of his knowledge of the Armenian language in any of his writings publifhed
or MS. Tanner feems haftily to have concluded, after Strype, that he was the
perfon meant.

Strype mentions a defcription of the city of Lincoln, and town of Stamford,
                                                     I   drawn

fore, as additional proofs of his devotion to fervices in which he was engaged.

At this diftance of time it is not eafy to fay much of his private character.   His hofpital at Greenwich is a remarkable proof of his liberality and charity.   His rules for that hofpital, as well as for Cobham college, fhew his prudence and wifdom in ordering fuch matters; and we may difcern in the fame marks of fincere piety *.   Nor ought it to be omitted, that the efteem which many great and noble perfonages, as Archbifhop Parker, Lord Burleigh, Lord Cobham, Lord Bromley, &c. had for him, may juftly be confidered as a teftimony, both to his public and private character.

As the reader may perhaps confider all memorials of fuch times and perfonages worth his attention, we have annexed to this article an account of his interview with Queen Elizabeth †, and a letter to Lord Burleigh ‡, both printed now for the firft time from originals preferved amongft the family papers of the Perambulator.

We might finifh this article with numerous teftimonies to the character and writings of Lambarde; but it may be fufficient to fay, that, befides thofe mentioned before occafionally, others are to be found in Archbifhop Parker's Preface to Afferius. Strype's Annals, Kilburn's Topography of Kent, Tanner's Bibliotheca Britannico-Hibernica, &c.   The following are felected as fignal teftimonies to his merits in three different ways.

drawn up by Lambarde, and fent to the Lord Treafurer Burleigh, and quotes a letter of his in proof of it, dated Halling, Dec. 2, 1584.   Annals, Vol. III. B. 1. Ch. 23.

* It appears alfo, that his common performance of the duties of his profeffion and ftation was ftrongly governed by a fenfe of religion, in proof of which may be alledged a MS. paper here fubjoined, intituled " A Charge by order of the De-" calogue."   Appendix N° VI.

† Appendix, N° VII.   ‡ Ibid. N° VIII.

Kennet

Kennet fays of him (Parochial Antiquities, p. 443.) " that
" he was one who recovered all our ancient, and underftood all
" our modern laws." Archbifhop Parker's teftimony of him, in
his Preface to Afferius, relates to his Saxon learning: " Quibus
" de rebus fi qua forte quis deguftare concupiverit, Gul. Lam-
" bardi (viri fane eruditi et in Hofpitio Lincolnienfi inter legum
" confultos domeftici Juris peritiffimi) præfationem perlegat &
" expendat, quam libro de veteribus Saxonûm legibus præfixit,
" quas nuper Latinis literis eleganter expreffit.   Ibi etenim non-
" nulla de inftituti fui ratione atque confilio prudenter præfatus,
" demum (ut eft in iftiufmodi rebus perfcrutandis fagaci certe in-
" genio et peracri) quorundam verborum vim et naturas fubtiliter
" perfecutus eft : quo in libro fi fe ftudiofius exercuerint ii, qui aut
" hujus linguæ notitiam, aut vetuftarum legum (quas Reges
" antiqui fanxerunt) fcientiam habere defiderant, fapienter meo
" judicio facient, et inde non mediocre fibi ad eas quoque res
" percipiendas inftrumentum facultatemque comparabunt."

Philipot (himfelf an excellent county hiftorian), and Camden
(in the paffages quoted above), bear an equal teftimony to his
knowledge of county antiquities.

4 A   APPEN-

A P P E N D I X.

Nº I.

COLLECTANEA of Lawrence Nowell and William Lambarde, in the possession of Multon Lambard, Esq;

Nº I. 1. Fragmentum Historiæ de serie Regum Occiduorum Saxonum.
    2. Ecclesiastica Venerabilis Bedæ Historia. Anglo-Saxonicè.
    3. Chronica conservata in Monasterio Sancti Martini.
    4. Athelstani Regis Leges.
The above are all in Saxon.
Towards the end of the book is the following note :
Hæc scripsi Laurentius Noellus propriâ manu in Ædibus Cæcillianis, 1562.
Nº II. 1. Topographia Walliæ Magistri Giraldi Cambrensis. Lat.
    2. Ejusdem Itinerarium Walliæ. Lat. Laurentii Noelli. 1562.
These works of Giraldus were published by David Powell, 1585.
Nº III. 1. Excerpta ex Historiis Henrici Huntingdoniensis. Lat.
    Nº IX. is a transcript of the same by Lambarde; who says, in a note prefixed, that he has discovered the same to be (as he had before conjectured) an abridgement of the History of Henry of Huntingdon.
    2. Decreta Will. Bastardi et Emendationes quas posuit in Angliâ.
    3. Chronica Monasterii Sancti Albani. Lat. Laurentii Noelli, 1565.
Nº IV. Chronica Peterburgensis. A transcript by L. Noell, 1565.
Nº V. 1. Excerpta ex Historiâ Abbatum Monasterii Glasconiæ a Gulielmo Malmsburiensi conscriptâ. Lat.
There was another copy of this in the Cotton Library.
William of Malmsbury's work was published by Hearne, 1727.
    2. Vita et Mors Edwardi secundi Gallicè conscripta a generosissimo Milite Thoma de la More, qui sequentium pars nonnulla fuit, et in Latinum traducta ab alio quodam ejus Synchrono.
At the end is the following note :
Libri exemplar est penes Gulielmum Bowierum Chartophylacem Regium, prout mihi retulit Laurentius Noelus, qui hæc transcripsit manu propriâ, 1566. Gulielmus Lambardus.
This work is published in Camdeni Anglia, &c.
    3. Appendix Historiæ Hibernicæ. Vide Nº VIII. Laurentii Noelli, 1556.
Nº VI.

N° VI. Rerum a Ducibus Normanniæ geſtarum Hiſtoria a Gulielmo Gemeticenſi conſcripta. Lat.

At the end is the following note :

Laurentius Noelus tranſcripſit, 1568, in Galliâ naſtus vetuſtiſſimum exemplar. This work is publiſhed in Camdeni Anglia.

N° VII. Excerpta ex Aſſerio Menevenſi vel Simeone Dunelmenſi aliiſque antiquis Hiſtoricis ab anno 743 ad 1100.

Lambarde, after offering conjectures on the original author of part of theſe Excerpta, adds, Exemplar penes adminiſtratores rerum Doctoris Wottoni eſt; hæc autem per L. Noellum tranſcripta ſunt.

N° VIII. Hyberniæ Deſcriptio (opus imperfectum) Laurentio Noello Authore, 1564.

At the end,

Deſiderantur multa quæ Author annotiſſe propoſuerat. W. La.

Tanner was ignorant of this work, for he ſays of Nowell's Collectanea, Omnia tranſcripſit ; nihil de ſuo addidit.

N° IX. Gervaſii Tilberienſis de neceſſariis Scaccarii obſervantiis Dialogus. Lat. A tranſcript by Lambarde, 1574.

The work is publiſhed in Madox's Hiſtory of the Exchequer.

N° X. Copy of the Excerpta from Henry of Huntingdon, by Lambarde, 1565. See N° III.

N° XI. Chronica Monaſterii Sancti Albani a Matthæo Pariſienſi conſcripta. Lat. At the end, W. Lambard ſcripſit propriâ manu, 1565.

N° XII. Rhapſodia ; containing various ſhort Excerpta, written by Lambarde in 1568, of which the following is his own liſt.

    1. Collectanea ex Chronicis Croylandiæ conſcriptis pro parte majori per Abbatem Ingulſum.

    2. Ex Chronicis Cœnobii Wynchelcumbenſis.

    3. Ex Joanne Majore Scoto.

    4. Ex Pontico Virunnio.

    5. Ex Gulielmo Malmſburienſi de ſummis Pontificibus nonnulla.

    6. Ex libro Bibliothecæ Londinenſis, cui titulus eſt Cuſtomes.

    7. Beaumont de Academiâ Cantabrigienſi.

    8. Temporalia Eccleſiaſticorum.

    9. Joannes Reſeus.

    10. Diplomata Regum.

    11. Ex Eulogio nonnulla.

    12. Ex libro Henrici Huntingdonienſis de Miraculis Angliæ et de Viris illuſtribus nonnulla.

    13. Ex Annalibus Gregorii de Caerwent Collectanea.

    14. Ex Chronicis Thomæ Spotte et Willi de Spinâ Collectanea.

    15. Pariſhes of London.

    16. Excerpta quædam de ponte Roffenſi.

    17. Eſtimate

17. Eſtimate of Ireland.
18. Ex textu Roffenſi.
19. Ex anonymo Coventrenſi nonnulla.
20. Ex Alphabeto Willi Poſtelli nonnulla.
21. Fragmenta.

N° XIII. XIV. The Peregrination of Andrew Boarde; two copies—one written by Nowell; the other by Lambarde.

From the former Hearne publiſhed this work, 1735.

N° XV. Copy of a book printed 1581, under the title of " A Brief Conceipte of Ingliſhe Policie, by W. S." being truly written either by Sir Thomas Smythe, or John Yates, in the reign of Henry VIII. or Edward.

This copy was written out by order of Lambarde, 1565.

N° XVI. Liſt of Pariſhes in England, by L. Nowell, 1562.

N° XVII. Chronica Bathoniæ & Welles; Lat. Laurentii Noelli, 1566.

N° II.   Gul. Lambardus Gul. Camdeno.

" Pardon, I pray you, Mr. Camden, this breach of my promiſe, in that I have
" holden your books ſome few days above the time in which I promiſed to re-
" turn them; the which I have done of no other mind but that I might ſend
" them ſafely unto you, as now I doubt not but I ſhall, by the benefit of this an
" aſſured meſſenger. In the reading of theſe your painful topographies, I have
" been contrarily affected; one way taking ſingular delight and pleaſure in the
" peruſing of them; another way by ſorrowing that I may not now, as I wonted,
" dwell in the meditation of the ſame things that you are occupied withal.—And
" yet I muſt confeſs, that the delectation which I reaped by your labours re-
" compenſed the grief that I conceived of mine own bereaving from the like:
" notwithſtanding that in times paſſed I have preferred the reading of antiquities
" before any ſort of ſtudy that ever I frequented. I thank you, therefore, moſt
" heartily, good Mr. Camden, for the uſe of theſe books of yours, ſince they de-
" liver many things that are not (ſo far as I do know) elſewhere to be had, and
" the ſame no leſs learnedly picked out, than delicately uttered and written.—
" What praiſe you deſerve in all, I can beſt tell by Kent, wherein (however I
" have laboured myſelf) I learn many things by you, that I knew not before.
" Your conjecture at the etymon of the word _Cantium_ is ſo probable, that
" you make me now doubt of mine own, which before I took to be moſt aſſured:
" you have ſo truly, as I think, traced out Leneham, Chilham, and Newendene,
" by the old _Durolenum_, _Jul-laber_, and _Anderida_, as I ſhall for ever hereafter reſt
" in your opinion of them. To be plain, I ſeem to myſelf not to have known
" Kent, till I knew Camden. If you have in purpoſe to perform the reſt, go on
" boldly, good Mr. Camden; wherein if you ſhall uſe the ſame dexterity that
" hitherto you have done (as I fear not but you will) _Acefii et Heliconis opera_
" _dixerim._
" Howſoever you ſhall be minded to do, more or leſs, defraud not your coun--
" trymen of ſo great a pleaſure, nor the country itſelf of ſo great an honour, by

7   " forbearing

" forbearing to imprint the fame. If I had any thing that might further your
" ftudy, I would moft willingly impart it : and whether I have or no, I will make
" yourfelf the judge, if it fhall like you to come down into Kent, and look
" amongft my papers. You may not think that I flatter you, good Mr. Camden,.
" in that which I have fpoken in commendation of your labour; for I am far
" from fuch clawing of any man : and in token of my fincere heart towards you,
" and to the end that nothing which I can efpy may efcape you by overfight, I
" will note unto you a trifle or twain that I have obferved in your Kent, affuring
" myfelf, that I fhall not offend you thereby.

" P. 2. *Darentum fluvium obvium babet qui è Suffexiâ*, &c —l think that no head
" of Dareht arifeth in Suffex, but at the furtheft in Surrey, about Titfey or Tan-
" ridge; uhlefs you mean, under the name Suffex, to comprehend Surrey, as in
" the Heptarchy we do.

" *Warbamus, &c. ut cum Hen. VIII. commutare neceffe babuerit*—The exchange
" was not made with Warham, but with Cranmer that fucceeded him.

" P. 3. and 7. The fhire has two gaols, whereof the principal is that of Can-
" terbury Caftle.

" P. 5. *Stowre fluvius, qui duobus, &c.*—The heads of Stowre are not in that
" part which is at this day called the Wealde; although the Wealde of old time
" was thirty miles broad, and then reached over the whole breadth of the fhire.

" This is all that I can quarrel at; and yet have I pried fo far as I could; for
" I reckon not of thofe things that have efcaped him that copied your book,
" knowing that you will revife that before it pafs from you.—Thus much I
" thought to write, as well for teftification of my own thankfulnefs, as for your
" own encouragement; praying you to bear with this hafty letter of mine, written
" in the midft of our preparation for the country mufters, and other fervices, that
" withdraw my mind; the which alfo have made me forget one thing, that of all
" the reft I miflike, I mean the firft five lines of your Kent, the which you muft
" moderate or omit, if you will have me think that you deal fo plainly with me,
" as I mean to do with you.

" And fo praying God to blefs your good ftudies, and eftfoons wifhing that you
" would fpend a week at Halling with me, I heartily bid you well to fare.—
" 29th July, 1585, from Halling. Yours in the Lord, WILLIAM LAMBARD."

N° III. A Form of Morning and Evening Prayer, to be daily faid by them of
the College of the Poor of Queen Elizabeth in Eaft Greenwiche.

For Morning and Evening.

Prepare our hearts, O Lord ! and open our mouths to prayer.

We pray thee (moft Gracious God and tender loving Father) to turn thy face
away from the infinite multitude of our grievous offences, wherewith we continually provoke thy heavy wrath and indignation againft us : and forafmuch as,
thou art a moft righteous God, hating fin, (for which no propitiation can be had
without blood,) and we be miferable finners, too, too vile, and unworthy to ftand
before thy Divine Majefty, it may like thee to behold us in the wounds and blood-

fhedding

ſhedding of thy dear Son Jeſus Chriſt our Saviour, accepting the only defence of that his death and paſſion, as a full ſacrifice and ſatisfaction for all our ſins and iniquities. Vouchſafe, O Lord! to enlighten us with thy Holy Spirite: engraft in us that fear and love which make true obedience; and grant that we, remembring from henceforth that we be waſhed from the filth of our ſins by the blood of thy Son, return not again to the mire of our former miſdeeds. But that (in our vocations) we frame our lives after thy heavenly will; and make our ſteps in the path of thy holy law, which thou haſt expreſſed in theſe ten commandments following:

Thou ſhalt have none other Gods but me, &c. &c. to the end.

Grant us furthermore, we beſeech thee, O Heavenly Father, ſtedfaſt continuance and increaſe in thy holy faith, whereof we make this our unfeigned profeſſion.

I believe in God the Father Almighty, &c. to the end.

For Morning.

Finally, O Almighty God, which haſt ſafely brought us to the beginning of this daye, defend us in the ſame by thy mighty power, and grant that this daie we fall into no ſin, neither run into any kind of danger, but that all our doings may be ordered by thy governance, to do always that which is righteous in thy ſight, thorough Jeſus Chriſt our Lord. Amen.

For the Evening.

Finally, lighten our darkneſs, we beſeech thee, O Lord, and by thy great mercie defend us from all perils and dangers of this night, for the love of thy only Son our Saviour Jeſus Chriſt. Amen.

For Morning and Evening.

Theſe things, O Lord, and all others which thy fatherly wiſdom knoweth to be fit for us, and we for our infirmities cannot aſk, we crave of Thee in that prayer which thy well-beloved Son our heavenly ſchool-maſter hath taught us, ſaying,

Our Father which art in heaven, &c.

God ſave his church univerſal, our gracious Queen Elizabeth, her nobility and counſellors, the maſter of the Rolls, the company of the Drapers, and the whole clergy and commonalty of this realm. Amen.

The grace of God the Father, the peace of our Lord Jeſus Chriſt, and the fellowſhip of the Holy Ghoſt be with us all now and ever. Amen.

Nº IV.

Nᵒ IV. Condition of the Conveyances of Lands to the College.

Provided always, that, if at any time hereafter it fhall happen, either the office of the mafter of the Rolls aforefaid, or the offices of the faid elder (or upper) wardens of the Drapers' aforefaid, or any of them, to be utterly altered, diffolved, or taken away : or if they the faid prefident and governors, or their fucceffors, fhall by the fpace of one whole year together, at any time from and after the death of the faid William Lambarde, willingly forbeare, wafte, and neglect to mainteine, the houfe of the faid college, in fuch convenient eftate or reparation, that poore people may commodioufly bee harboured therein ; or otherwife fhall at any time, from and after the death of him the faid William Lambarde, by the like fpace of time, willingly forbeare, wafte, and neglect to fufteine, mainteine, and finde twentie poore and neadie perfons thearein, with the monthlie ftipend of fix fhillings of lawfull money of England, to eache of them the faid twentie poore and neadie perfons, if fo bee that the cleare yearlie value, for the time being, of all the manors, lands, tenements, and hereditaments, now alreadie (by thefe prefents or otherwife) affured and conveyed, or hereafter in the life of him the faid William Lambarde, to bee affured and conveyed, to them the faid prefident and governours, and their fucceffors for ever, fhall and will fufficientlie and convenientlie fufteine, beare, and afoard fo muche, without any fraude or guile (the charges of neceffarie reparations, the competent fees of needful officers, and other due reprifes, being deducted and allowed) : And if it fhall hereafter happen, that the faid cleare yearelie value of all and fingular the manors, lands, tenements, and hereditaments, fo affured, or to be affured, as is laft before faid, will not fufficientlie and convenientlie fufteine and beare the faid monethlie proportion of fixe fhillings to everie of the faid poore perfons, as is before limited and appointed : Then, if the faid prefident and governours, or their fucceffors, fhall, at any time, from and after the deathe of him the faid William Lambarde, by the fpace of one whole yeare, willingly forbeare, wafte, and neglect to fufteine, mainteine, and finde twentie poore and neadie perfons within the houfe of the faid college, with fuche monthlie ftipend to every of them to be paid, as the cleare yearlie value of all and fingular the manors, lands, tenements, and hereditaments, fo already conveyed, or to be hereafter conveyed, as is aforefaid, fhall and will ratablie, and after the proportion, extend unto, and without any fraud or guile, yield, beare, and fuffer (deducting as is laft before deducted) : Or finally, if at any time hereafter it fhall not be lawful by the lawes and ftatutes of this realme (which God defend) to and for the poore people of the faid college, for the tyme being, to ufe, faye, and frequent, within the houfe of the faid college there, fuche fourme of prayer and fervice unto God in the Inglifhe tongue, as by the faid William Lambarde (with the confent in writing of the Bifhop of Rochefter for the time being) fhall be in writing devifed and appointed, to be theare by them ufed, fayde, and frequented : that then, and from thenceforth, this publick bargaine and fale of all and fingular the premiffes fhall be utterlie voide, and of none effect, any thing before in thefe prefents to the contrarie thearcof in any wife notwithftanding.

Nᵒ V

Nº V. Extracts from the Statutes of the College of the Poor of Queen Elizabeth at Greenwich.

In the election of the poor, a certain order and degrees of preference are established. In the first degree, are the aged past their work—In the second are the lame or maimed by sickness, by service of the prince, or any other misfortune, not their own fault—In the third, the blind,—In the fourth those who have been impoverished by any casualty—In the fifth, those afflicted by any continual sickness, not contagious.—In the sixth, those who are burthened with a numerous family—It is required of all, that they be honest and godly, having been resident in their several parishes three years before at the least, and relieved at the charge of their parish; —no person of a bad or irreligious life to be elected—if a married person be elected, the wife or husband to be received into the college, and the two to receive the pay and privileges of one, the survivor being liable to be turned out on the death of a wife, or husband, elected, if not a proper object. In case of competition between persons of equal degrees, the man to be preferred before the woman, the married before the unmarried, the person who has been longer of the houshold of faith before him that hath longer dwelt in popish idolatry and superstition—The person of unblemished character before him who hath formerly been reputed evil—The person who hath dwelt longer in the parish before him who hath dwelt a less time in it—The person who hath no friends or kindred to relieve him before him that hath. On admission to be examined, whether they can say the Lord's Prayer, the Apostle's Creed, and the Ten Commandments.

It is ordained, that the poor, who are able, go to labour daily; and if offered, by any within the Hundred of Blackheath, such work as they are able to do, at the ordinary price of such labour within a penny a day, on refusal they be punished, by a forfeiture of one shilling and fixpence for the first offence; for the second, a whole month's pay; for the third, by expulsion.—For the farther encouragement of labour, especially of the women and children, a plot of ground behind the house of an acre and an half, to be tilled for them, and planted with hemp:—the produce to be distributed amongst them by equal portions—none allowed to sell his parcel out of the college, nor put it out to be dressed abroad, if any within the college will dress it, taking only one half for their labour.

Nº VI.

Nº VI. A Charge for the Peace, by order of the Decalogue, or Ten Commandments of Almighty God, by William Lambarde, Esq;

The Articles inquirable before the Justices of the Peace, at their Quarter Sessions, drawn through the Ten Commandments of Almighty God.

Τῷ Θεῷ.

FIRST TABLE.

1. *Non habebis Deos alienos,* &c.

If any person have used invocation or conjuration of evil spirits for any cause, *Conjuration.* or have used witchcraft, inchantment, charming or sorcerie, whereby any person is *Felon.* killed or destroyed. 5 Eliz. cap. 16. for that is to make other Gods, and it is also to take the name of God in vain.

If any person have advisedly set forth any fantastical or false prophecy upon *Prophecying* armes, beastes, time, name, &c. to the intent to make rebellion, loss of life, or *Felon.* disturbance, 5 Eliz. cap. 16. or have by calculation, casting of nativity, or other unlawfull means, sought to know, and hath set forth how long her Majesty shall reign, or who shall reign after her, 23 Eliz. cap. 2. for, *solius est Dei futura noscere.*

2. *Non facies tibi sculptile,* &c.

Condemneth the Pope and his religion and ministers, who teach the worshiping of images and of bread, &c. and teach to worship God otherwise than he willeth.

If any person have advisedly defended any jurisdiction ecclesiastical heretofore *Treas.* 3 0 usurped here, 1 Eliz. cap. 1. or have advisedly defended the power of the bishop of Rome, or of his see, heretofore usurped within this realme, 5 Eliz. cap. 1.; or *Præmunire.* if any person have preached to withdraw or absolve any person from his natural *Traitor.* obedience to the Romish religion, or to promise obedience to the see of Rome ; or if any person have been so withdrawn, or hath so promised, 23 Eliz. cap. 1. *Misprison.*

If any person have put in use any bull, or instrument of absolution, gotten from *Treason.* the bishop of Rome, or by colour of any such hath taken upon him to absolve ; or if any person, to whom the same hath been persuaded, hath not signified it to *Misprison.* some of the privy council within six weeks after; or if any person hath brought from the see of Rome, or from any authorized there, any Agnus Dei, crosses, pic- *Præmunire.* tures, beads, grains, or other superstitious things, to be used by any of the Queen's subjects, or if any have not apprehended the offerer thereof, nor disclosed him, nor delivered the things to the ordinary, or some justice of the peace, 13 Eliz. cap. 2. Add the statute of provisions, 13 Rich. II. &c.

If any person have, after 40 days next ensuing the end of the last session of parliament, wittingly and willingly received or maintained any Jesuit, seminaric *Felony.* priest, deacon, or other ecclesiastical person (ordained out of her Majesty's dominions by any authority pretended from the see of Rome, since Midsummer-day

in

in the firſt year of her reign), being out of hold, knowing him to be ſuch a perſon ecclefiaſtical. 27 Eliz. cap. 2.

Fine. If any perſon have ſaid or ſung maſs, or have willingly heard maſs. 23 Eliz.
cap. 1.

3. *Non accipies nomen Dei tui in vanum,* &c.

If any perſon have wilfully committed perjury in any cauſe depending in ſuit
in any of the Queen's courts of Record, or Leet, Court Baron, Hundred, or
Court of Antient Demeſne; or if any perſon have unlawfully procured any thereunto. 5 Eliz. cap. 9. And this may be referred to the Ninth Commandment,
Non dices falſum teſtimonium, &c.

4. *Memento quod diem Sabbati,* &c.

Commandeth the order of all the outward ſervice of God, and condemneth the
contrary. If any perſon (above 16 years of age, and not letted by reaſonable ex-
cuſe) have not reſorted every Sunday, and other holy-day, to his or her accuſtomed
pariſh-church or chapple, or upon let thereof to ſome uſual place where common-
prayer is to be uſed; and hath not there ſoberly abidden during the time of the
ſervice or preaching. 1 Eliz. cap. 2.

If any have maintained any ſchoolmaſter, that reſorteth not to the church, or is
not allowed by the biſhop. 23 Eliz. cap. 1.

If any perſon have (within three months laſt) in any wiſe depraved or reviled
the bleſſed ſacrament of the body and blood of Chriſt. 1 Edw. VI. cap. 1.

If any perſon, vicar, or miniſter, have, ſince the laſt Aſſizes, refuſed to uſe the
order of the book of Common Prayer, or (wilfully ſtanding in the ſame) hath
uſed any other form of open prayer; or hath ſpoken in derogation thereof; or
if any perſon have (ſince that time) ſpoken in derogation of that book, or of any
part thereof; or have cauſed any perſon, vicar, or miniſter, to ſay common-prayer,
or to adminiſter any ſacrament, in other manner than after that book; or have
interrupted any ſuch to ſay or miniſter open prayer, or ſacrament, according to
that book. 1 Eliz. cap. 2.

If any perſon have feloniouſly taken goods out of any church or chapple.

If any perſon have maliciouſly ſtricken any other with any weapon in church,
or church-yard; or drawn any weapon there to that intent. 5 Edw. VI. cap. 4.

If any perſon have kept fair, or market, in the church-yard. Statut. Winton.
13 Edw. 1.

SECOND TABLE.

5. *Honora patrem et matrem.*

Commandeth obedience to the Prince or under officers.

Oath. If any perſon (compellable to take the oath of recognition of the Queen's Majeſtie to be ſupreme governor in all cauſes within her dominions) have refuſed to
take the ſame, after lawful tender thereof to him made. 1 Eliz. cap. 1.

Treaſon. If any perſon have counterfeited the Queen's money. 25 Edw. III. cap. 2. et
3, 4, 5. cap. 7.

If any perſon hath of his own imagination, or of the report of another, adviſedly,

edly, and with a malicious intent againſt the Queen, ſpoken any falſe, ſeditious, and ſlanderous news or ſayings of the Queen. 23 Eliz. cap. 2.

If any perſon hath adviſedly, and with a malicious intent againſt the Queen's Felonie. Majeſtie, deviſed, written, piinted, or ſet forth any book or writing, containing any falſe, ſeditious, and ſlanderous matter to the defamation of her Majeſtie, or to the incouraging or moving of any rebellion; or hath procured any ſuch to be written, printed, or ſeth forth ; or hath, by any words, writing, or printing, deſired or wiſhed her Majeſtie's death or deprivation, or any thing directly to the effect; or have aided or procured any ſuch offender. 23 Eliz. cap. 2.

If any perſon (of or above the number of 12) have aſſembled and gone about Felonie. with force of arms unlawfully to change any laws of the realme, or have continued to herd together after proclamation againſt them made, or have, after proclamation, forcibly attempted to do any ſuch thing ; or if any perſons (to the number of 40 or more) have ſo aſſembled for any of the ſaid intents, or for any other felonious or rebellious act, and have continued together 3 hours, after notice of any proclamation made, at or nigh the place of their aſſembly, or in ſome market-town next adjoining. 1 Mar. Parl. 1. cap. 12.

If any have deviſed maliciouſly to take or keep from the Queen, or to raſe or Felonie. deſtroy any of her caſtles, towns, or holds (the ſame having munition or ſouldiers therein of hers), and have uttered the ſame deviſe. 14 Eliz. cap. 2.

If any have deviſed maliciouſly and unlawfully to ſet at liberty any priſoner Felonie. (indited of treaſon concerning the Queen's perſon), and have expreſsly uttered the ſame deviſe. 14 Eliz. cap. 2.

If any perſon (impriſoned for felonie) have broke a priſon, 1 Eliz. 2.; or if any Felonie. other perſon have broken the priſon to make ſuch a priſoner eſcape ; or if any gaoler have ſuffered ſuch a priſoner to eſcape ; or if any have reſcued any other arreſted for felonie.

If any ſoldier (entered a ſoldier of record, and having taken any part of the Felonie. Queen's wages), or any mariner or gunner (having taken preſt wages to ſerve the Queen on the ſea), have not gone to his captain accordingly (unleſs he were letted by notorious ſickneſs, or other impediment from God), or have departed from his captain without his licence under ſeal. 18. 4. 6.

If any ſervant have killed his or her maſter or miſtreſs ; or any wife her huſ- Petite Tres band, or any child his or her parent, or any eccleſiaſtical perſon his prelate. 25 Eliz. cap. 2.

If any ſervant (being 18 years old, and no apprentice) hath gone away with, or Felonie. converted to his own uſe, any money, jewels, goods, or chattels, of his maſter or miſtreſs, and of his or her deliverie to keep, of the value of xis. to the intent to ſteal the ſame. 21. c. 8. cap. 7.

6. *Non occides.*

Forbiddeth all unlawful force and violence; and commandeth the contrary, as fortitude, for defence of the country, with all the parts thereof.

Murder. If any perfon have of prepenfed malice, or by wilful poyfoning, or by chance-medley, killed another, 1 Eliz. cap. 12.

Felonie. If any perfon have of malice prepenfed cut out the tongue, or put out the eyes, of any of the Queen's fubjects. 5 Eliz. 4. cap. 5.

If any perfon have maimed another of any member of his body; or have committed unlawful affault, beating, or wounding, upon the perfon of another.

Burglarie. If any perfon have by night broken any houfe, tower, walls, or gates, with an intent to do any murder, or felony there; or have burned any dwelling-houfe, or by night burnt any barn near to a dwelling-houfe.

Felonie. If any gaoler, keeper, or under-keeper of any prifon, have by dureffe and paine compelled any his prifoner to become an appeacher of any other againft his will. 4 Eliz. 3. cap. 10.

If any perfon have gone or ridden armed, 25 Eliz. 3. cap. 2. except the Queen's fervants and officers doing her fervice, and their company aiding them in that behalf; or if any have brought force in affray of the people before the Queen's juftices, or otherwife. Stat. Northan. 2 Eliz. 3. cap. 3.

If any be a common quarreller, or barretter, that moveth affrayes between others.

If any perfons, to the number of three or above, have been riotoufly affembled, to beat any man, or to enter upon any poffeffion; or have been affembled in riots for any common quarrel; or, being under the number of 12, have affembled, and intended unlawfully with force to murder any the Queen's fubjects; or to caft down inclofures, &c. 1 Mar.

If any perfon hath lyen in wait to maim or kill any other.

If any have entered into lands or poffeffions with force; or, entering peaceably, have holden the fame with force; 8 H. VI. cap. 9.

If any perfon have unlawfully raifed hue and crye; or if any have not been ready at the hue and cry of the country lawfully raifed, to purfue and arreft felons; and if the fheriffe or any bayliffes have not followed the hue and cry with horfe and armour. 3 Eliz. 1. cap. 9. &c.

If watche by night have been kept in towers between Afcenfion-day and Michaelmas-day, to arreft ftrangers that pafs by. 13 Eliz. 1.

If the Lordes of the foile have not enlarged the highways from market to market, fo that no impediment be there (except great trees) within two hundreth foot of each fide thereof. 13 Eliz. 1.

If any bridges in the highways (out of the Five Ports) be broke or decayed, and who ought to repair the fame. 22 Eliz. 8. cap. 5.

If the conftables and church-wardens of any parifh have not appointed overfeers, and fix days for the highways; and if any perfon have not fet their carriages and men thereto, and wrought upon the fame; or if the owners of the
lands

lands adjoining have not kept the hedges, ditches, trees, and bushes, scoured and cut down. 2 and 3 Phil. et Mar. cap. 8.

If any perfon have ufed or kept any handgun, not being 3 quarters of a yard long; or if any perfon (not having . . . . by the year) have carried crofs-bowe . . . . or gun charged. 33 Eliz. 8. cap. 10.

If any companie of men (other than of fraternities or artifts in cities and bo-rowes) have made any general fort or fuit of apparel to be known by. 7 Eliz. 4. cap. 14.

It any perfon have given any liverie of fign of company, or badge; or retained any man, other than his houfhold fervant, officer, or learned man in the lawe. 1 Eliz. 4. cap. 7.

If watches have not been made upon the fea coafts in fuch places, with fuch a number of people, and in fuch manner as it wonted to be. 5 Eliz. 4. cap. 3.

If any man, being within the age of 60 years (except . . . . . .) have not ready, or ufe not a long bowe and arrowes; or have not for every man-child in his houfe (being above 7 years old) a bowe and arrowe; or have not brought them up in fhooting.

If the inhabitants of any town have not made and . . . . their buttes, as they ought to do.

If any merchant ftranger, of any country from whence bow-ftaves have been fent into this land, have not (for every ton of his burden) brought hither four bow ftaves, and for every butt of Malmfey ten. 12 Eliz. 4. cap. 33.

If any bowier have not (for every ewe-bow) made 4 other of apt-wood for fhooting; or have not made bowes for all ages and at due prices; or if any ftranger born (not being a denizen) have fhot in a long bowe, or have conveyed hence any bowes or arrowes, without the Queen's licenfe 33 Eliz. 8. cap. 9.

If any temporal perfon have not in a readinefs fuch horfe and armour, or furniture for the warrs, as by the proportion of his lands or goods, or by the ap-parel of his wife, he ought to have. 4 & 5 Phil. et Mar. cap. 2.

If the inhabitants of any parifh, town, or borowe, have not fuch common armour and furniture for the wars, as they are appointed to have by the com-miffioners of the mufters. 4 et 5 Phil. et Mar. cap. 2.

If any perfon, generally or fpecially fummoned to the mufters, have, without true and reafonable caufe, abfented himfelf; or have not brought ready his beft furniture of armour for his owne perfon; or if any perfon, being auctorized to mufter or levy men for the Queen's fervice in warre, have taken any reward for the difcharging or fparing of any other; or if any capitaine have not payed to his foldiers their whole wages, conduicte and coat money, or have for gain licenfed any of them, to depart out of the fervice. 4 et 5 Phil. et Mar. cap. 3.

If any foldier, ferving the Queen in her wars, have purloined, or wilfully made away, any horfe, gelding, mare, or harnefs wherewith he was fet forth.. 2 et 3 Eliz. 6. cap. 2.

If any perfon have fold, given, or conveyed beyond the fea out of the Queen's dominions, or to any Scottifhman to be conveyed into Scotland, any horfe, geld-

7   ing

ing (or mare above ten fhillings price), without the Queen's licenfe, unlefs it be to ferve in her wars. 1 Eliz. 6. cap. 5.

If any perfon have put into any foreft, chace, more, heath, waft, or common, where any mares are to be kept, any ftoned horfe above two years old, and not being above 14 handfulles high from the loweft of the hoofe to the top of the withers; and if fuch grounds have not yearly been driven within 15 days after Michaelmas. 32 Eliz. 8. cap. 13.

7. *Non mœchaberis.*

Condemneth all wantonnefs, vain pleafures, &c. and commandeth fobriety, temperance, &c.

Felonie.   If any perfon have committed the deteftable vice of fodomy with man or beaft. 25 Henry VIII. cap. 6.

Felonie.   If any man have ravifhed any maid, widow, or wife, above ten years of age, againft her will, although fhe afterwards confented. Will. II. cap. 34.

Felonie.   If any man have carnally known or abufed any woman under ten years of age, although fhe confented before. 18 Eliz. cap. 7.

Felonie.   If any perfon have taken any maid, widow, or wife (having lands or goods, or being heir-apparent to any) againft her will unlawfully, other than his ward or bondwoman. 3 Hen. VII. cap. 2.

If any perfon, not being the fon of a peer or baron of the realme, nor having c marcs by yeare, nor goods to 1000 marcs, have kept in his houfe any beffet of Gafcoine, Guyon, French, or Rochelle wine, above 10 gallons, to be fpent in his houfe. 7 Edw. VI. cap. 5.

If any perfon (other than by reafon of age, ficknefs, childing, or licence) have, within this year, eaten any flefh in Lent, or upon any fifh-day obferved by the cuftom of this realm. 2 Edw. VI. cap. 19.

If any perfon (above 6 years of age) except maydens, ladies, gentlewomen, nobles, knights, gentlemen of 20 marcs by the year, and their heirs, and fuch as have born office of worfhip, have not worn upon Sundays and holydays on their heads a woollen cap of England, dreffed and finifhed by fome capper. 13 Eliz. cap. 20.

If any man, born within her Majefty's dominions (except the fon and heir of a knight, or of one of higher degree, or fuch as may difpend 20l. yearly, or be worth 200l. or have been head-officer in any city, borough, or corporate town, or be the Queen's ordinary fervant wearing her livery) have worn any manner of filk in or upon his hat, bonnet, night-cap, girdle, fcabbard, hofe, fhoes, or fpur-leathers; or if any perfon, knowing his fervant to offend herein, have not put him away within 14 days after (except apprentice and hired fervant), or have taken him again. 1 & 2 Phil. & Mar. cap. 2. And fee 24 Hen. VIII. cap. 13. a long ftatute.

If any perfon have for lucre maintained any common place for the ufing of unlawfull games, as bowls, coits, ... dice, tables, cards, fhove-groat, or other new-invented and unlawfull game; or if any artificer, hufbandman, apprentice, labourer, fervant at hufbandry, journeyman, or any fervant of artificer,

or

or any mariner, fisherman, waterman, or serving-man (other than of a nobleman, or of one that may dispend 100l. by year, playing within the precincts of his master's house), have played at any of the said games out of the time of Christmas, or than out of his master's presence. 33 Hen. VIII. cap. 9.

If any artificer, labourer, or other layman (not having 40s. by year), or any spiritual person (not advanced to xl. by year), have kept any dog to hunt, or have used any nets, ferrets, or other engines, to take deer, hares, coneys, or other gentleman's game 13 Rich. II. cap. 13.

If any person have traced, killed, and destroyed, any hare in the snow. 14 Hen. VIII. cap. 10.

If any person have taken any where the eggs of any falcon, goshawk, &c. or have purposely driven them out of their covers, &c. 11 Hen. VII. cap. 17.

If any person have willingly (between the first of March and last of June, in any year), taken away or destroyed the eggs of any wild-fowl used to be eaten, from the place where they did lay them. 25 Henry VIII. cap. 11.

8. *Non facies furtum.*

Condemneth all fraudulent and unlawfull getting of goods, and all idleness; and commandeth honest labour, plainness in contracting, alms to the poor.

Felonies before God and by the law.

If any person have robbed another going or riding by the highway, or have robbed any house by day or night, any person being there, and put in fear thereby, or have robbed any person in any part of his dwelling, his wife, children, or servants being within the precincts of the same, or hath robbed any person (being within a tent or booth), in any fair or market, the owner, his wife, children, or any servant being then within the same. 5 Edw. VI. cap. 9. *Felonie.*

If any person have feloniously taken the goods of any other, and whether the same be above the value of xiid. or under. *Felonie.*

If any person hath found a falcon, lanner, lanneret, or other falcon, that was lost, and hath not forthwith brought it to the sheriff to proclaim it, but did steal and carry away the same. 34 Edw. III. cap. 22. *Felonie.*

If any person have unlawfully hunted in the night, in any forest, park, or warren, or with painted faces, or other disguises to be unknown, and have, upon examination before a justice of the peace, wilfully concealed such hunters, or hunting, or disobeyed or made rescue upon the arrest therefore, so as the warrant was not executed. 1 Hen. VII. cap. 7. *Felonie.*

If any person have practised the art of multiplication of gold or silver. 5 Hen. IV. cap. 4. *Felonie.*

If any person have the second time brought, sent, or received into any ship or bottom, any live lambs, sheep, or fawns, to be conveyed out of the Queen's dominions. 8 Eliz. cap. 3. *Felonie.*

If any person have sold, exchanged, or delivered into Scotland, or the batable ground (to the use of any Scot), without the Queen's licence, any horse, gelding, *Felonie.*

or

or mare, and if any have fo bought any of the fame. 23 Hen. VIII. cap. 16.

Felonie. If any calling themfelves Egyptians have remained in the realm one month, or if any (being 14 years of age, hath been in their company, or difguifed himfelf like them, by that fpace at one time together, or at feveral times. 1 & 2 Phil. & Mar. cap. 4.

Felonie. If any rogue have (after 60 days after his judgement to be burnt) fallen again to roguifh life, being then 18 years old; or have. upon his fecond conviction, departed out of his two years fervice; or hath been the third time convicted. 14 Eliz. cap. 5.

Felonie. If any purveyor for the Queen's houfe, or his deputy or fervant, have made any purveyance without warrant, and have carried away any thing againft the will of the owner (being above xiid.) 28 Edw. . cap. 2.; or have taken any carriage otherwife than is contained in his commiffion. 36 Edw. III. cap. 2.; or have made any purveyance without the teftimony and apprifement of the conftable and 4 men of the town, or without delivering rules or indentures, the goods being above xiid. 5 Edw. III. cap. 2.; 25 Edw. III. cap. 15.

Felonie. If any have been acceffary (before or after) to any of thefe felonies.

Felonies before God, but not by the Law.

If any ordinary, archdeacon, official, fheriff, under-fheriff, efcheator, bailiff, gaoler, or other officer, have (by colour of his office, or for doing his office) taken a greater reward or fee than belongeth to him, or have taken any reward for expedition in doing his office, or have unlawfully exacted any oath, or other undue thing. As if any ordinary, or his fcribe, or regifter, have taken above five-pence commiffion for the fcribe for writing the probate of a teftament brought written in parchment, or above five-pence for the adminiftration, where the goods be not above 5l.; or above 2s. and 6d. for the ordinary, and xiid. for the fcribe, if the goods be above 5l. and under 40l.; or above 2s. and 6d. for the ordinary, and likewife for the fcribe, if the goods exceed 40l.; or above one penny for every line at 10 inches length (at the election of the fcribe). And fo alfo for every copy of a teftament or inventory. 21 Hen. VIII. cap. 5.

[The reft of the extortions, the deceits of all artificers, ufury, foreftalling, &c. muft be added.]

9. Non dices falfum teftimonium, &c.

If any perfon have procured, fuborned, or committed perjury in any fuit. 5 Eliz. cap. 9. and 14 Eliz. cap. 11.

Note, That all the ftatutes 27 Eliz. be not comprehended here.

[Remainder miffing.]

N° VII.

N° VII.

"That which paffed from the Excellent Majeftie of Queen ELIZABETH, in her Privie Chamber at Eaft Greenwich, 4° Augufti 1601, 43° reg. fui, towards WILLIAM LAMBARDE.

He prefented her Majeftie with his Pandecta of all her rolls, bundells, membranes, and parcells, that be repofed in her Majefties Tower at London; whereof fhe had given to him the charge 21ft Jan. laft paft.

Her Majeftie chearfullie received the fame into her hands, faying, "You intended to prefent this book unto me by the Counteffe of Warwicke; but I will none of that; for if any fubject of mine do me a fervice, I will thankfully accept it from his own hands:" then opening the book, faid, "You fhall fee that I can read;" and fo, with an audible voice, read over the epiftle, and the title, fo readily, and diftinctly pointed, that it might perfectly appear, that fhe well underftood, and conceived the fame. Then fhe defcended from the beginning of King John, till the end of Richard III. that is 64 pages, ferving XI kings, containing 286 years: in the 1ft page fhe demanded the meaning of *oblata, cartæ, litteræ claufæ, et litteræ patentes.*

W. L. He feverally expounded the right meaning, and laid out the true differences of every of them; her Majeftie feeming well fatisfied, and faid, "that fhe would be a fcholar in her age, and thought it no fcorn to learn during her life, being of the mind of that philofopher, who in his laft years began with the Greek alphabet." Then fhe proceeded to further pages, and afked, where fhe found caufe of ftay, as what *ordinationes, parliamenta, rotulus cambii, redifeifnes.*

W. L. He likewife expounded thefe all according to their original diverfities, which fhe took in gracious and full fatisfaction; fo her Majeftie fell upon the reign of King Richard II. faying, "I am Richard II. know ye not that?"

W. L. "Such a wicked imagination was determined and attempted by a moft unkind gent. the moft adorned creature that ever your Majeftie made."

Her Majeftie. "He that will forget God, will alfo forget his benefactors; this tragedy was played 40ue times in open ftreets and houfes."

Her Majeftie demanded "what was *præftita?*"

W. L. He expounded it to be "monies lent by her progenitors to her fubjects for their good, but with affurance of good bond for repayment."

Her Majeftie. "So did my good grandfather King Henry VII. fparing to diffipate his treafure or lands." Then returning to Richard II. fhe demanded, "Whether I had feen any true picture, or lively reprefentation of his countenance and perfon?"

W. L. "None but fuch as be in common hands."

Elen-

Her Majeſtie. " The Lord Lumley, a lover of antiquities, diſcovered it faſtened on the backſide of a door of a baſe room ; which he preſented unto me, praying, with my good leave, that I might put it in order with the anceſtors and ſucceſſors ; I will command Tho. Kneavet, keeper of my houſe and gallery at Weſtminſter, to ſhew it unto thee."

Then ſhe proceeded to the Rolls,

Romæ, Vaſ.on. Aquitaniæ, Franciæ, Scotiæ, Walliæ, et Hiberniæ.

W. L. He expounded theſe to be records of eſtate, and negotiations with foreign princes or counteries.

Her Majeſtie demanded again, " if *rediſeiſnes* were unlawful and forcible throwing of men out of their lawful poſſeſſions ?"

W. L. " Yea, and therefore theſe be the rolls of fines aſſeſſed and levied upon ſuch wrong doers, as well for the great and wilful contempt of the crown and royal dignity, as diſturbance of common juſtice."

Her Majeſtie. " In thoſe days force and arms did prevail ; but now the wit of the fox is every where on foot, ſo as hardly a faithful and vertuouſe man may be found." Then came ſhe to the whole total of all the membranes and parcels aforeſaid, amounting to . . . . . ; commending the work ; " not only for the pains therein taken, but alſo for that ſhe had not received ſince her firſt coming to the crown any one thing that brought therewith ſo great delectation unto her ;" and ſo being called away to prayer, ſhe put the book in her boſom, having forbidden me from the firſt to the laſt to fall upon my knee before her ; concluding, " Farewell, good and honeſt Lambarde !"

N° VIII. The following is an original letter (from this excellent TOPOGRAPHER,
as fuppofed) to the Lord High Treafurer BURGHLEY.

W. LAMBARDE to the Lord Treafurer, contayning reafons why her Majeftie fhould
with fpeed embrace the action of the defence of the Lowe Countries, 1585.

MY RIGHT HONOURABLE GOOD LORD,

SEGURIS was with me to take his leave, difcontented, but confeffing that you
alone had dealt moft honourablie for his king; which he would not only publifh
here, but affure his king that you were the fole perfonage to whom affairs ought
to be addreffed. He affirmed * . . . .
But I humblie affirme, that if her Majeftie undertake not throughly and royallye
the matter of the Lowe Countries, fhe confumes her treafure to no purpofe; fhe
wafteth her men; undoeth that poore people that muft needs have a faithful fove-
reigne head (the lack whereof is their deftruction, *par enim in parem non habet
imperium*); fhe bringeth the war even to her own doors; and yet can fhe not provoke Spain more than fhe alreadie hath; fhe provokes all princes (as well proteftants as others) againft her; fhe maketh herfelf naked of all aide, and convert-
eth the aides now prefented to be turned againft herfelf; fhe ftaineth her credit
everlaftingly, having importuned the poore people over unto her, and then to
fend them away fruitlefs (for fo it is, if her Majeftie become not their head to
beat down the tyrannie of Spain); fhe abandonneth the church of God in dif-
treffe (her beft bulwarke); and enterteignes the calamities of her neighbours, not
preferves them which are both in her help and near her help; fhe excludes all
traffique at home, by defpifing all friends abroad; fhe diffolveth merchandize,
breaketh the draperly of the realm, and ftirreth up all poore folkes that live of
the fame to a neceffitie that will fhake the frame of the whole ftate, joining the in-
conveniencies that will therewith concur.
The gentleman fhall not fell his woole, the plowman his corne, the grazier his
ware, nor the artificer fhall be employed; all things will be difordered, and we
fhall be fuffocated in our owne fatte, tho' we feele not the force of any foreigne
invafion. Her Majeftie's cuftomes will be nothing; fhe muft live of her own
rentes, and how they will be anfwered it is doubtful: that which fhe moft feareth
will follow, the contempt of her own perfon, the reputation whereof partly hath
been kept in tune thefe 27 years by one policie; but the date is out, and the laft
enterteignement had like to have proved tragical. Her Majeftie fhall neither have
nor fee any thing about her but fadnefs of her fubjects, open difcontent and mur-
muring of all forts; drooping in the nobilitie; in the reft, whifpering, confpiring,
and exclaiming againft the Government, as Queen Marie had a little before her
end, which haftened her end, from the which God of his mercy preferve her Majeftie! This only fequel is able to diffolve a greater kingdome than ours haftily,
which falleth not by pufhing at, but by his own weight, wanting means to refolve:

* A line and an half here blotted fo as not to be legible.

4 C 2
and

and to execute pregnantly, and to know and ufe his own forces : *Sic peribit (ni Deus avertat) regnum florentiſſimum summo tripudio.*

On the other fide, her Majeſtie undertaking the caufe roundly, the prince of Parma fhall myffe of Antwerp, and muſt then lack fome of the cities (capitulated withal) to fatisfie his foldiers, which will breed a general revolt of all the provinces named *difcontentea :* and yet the nobility will be eafily without this drawn to her Majeſtie, if fhe fhew herfelf openly, not mafked ; a ground inconvenient for princes to ſtand upon, which otherwife (to fpeak plainly and reverently withal) argueth fear and no policie, howfoever it may be covered or pretended.

The fubjects of England, with the contribution of the Low Countries, will abundantly defray the charges, without touching her Majeſty's coffers. The matter roundly (not flowly) followed, will make a fhort war and a long peace, without danger to the enterprifor. For againft whome hath her Majeſtie to deal ? With a king augmented by tyrannie and ufurpation, by the fufferings of neighbour kings—a beggar indeed ! hateful to God, without people of his own—living of bankers, his dominions fcattered and chargably maintained by the fword, having nothing but opinion of greatnefs : but now fo overtaken by his overwearing to embery, but to fpoil rather indeed all natio s his meaning was, whereby he is nearer ruin if it be followed. Her Majeſtie was miraculoufly advertifed of his intention by his own warrant, fent in pofte by God's goodneffe. His forces (if he have any) be farre from us, and the fame nothing if they be looked into ; his country like to be ſtarved within this year, and his purfe will be empty tyll the beginning of September. A great Coloffus outwardly, but inwardly ſtuffed with clouts. A man fubject to melancholie, and meeting in thefe years with difgraces, deadly and mortal paffions follow : one that keeps all his owne reckonings to cover his bare eſtate from others. And this is the fcare-crow of the world that her Majeſtie has to contend withal ; of whome, not kings, but mean perfons have fmall caufe to dread : his lieutenant Parma in defpair, and without pay and victuals, wherein our reſtraint hath done great good ; his foldiers few, and worne with neceffities, and he not able to bring many together for want of provifion to feed them. Thefe being the enemies and their eſtate, there wanteth nothing on our fide but the fpirit of God to incline her Majeſtie to that which is juſt and neceffarie. For it feemeth that God hath delivered them into her hands already, which her faithful counfellors (as ye be all) fhould purfue, till fhe hath yielded to the thing that concerneth her fafetie and high honour. Wife counfellors ferve (under correction) as well experienced phyficians, to cure the difeafes of the mind by diverfitie of remedies till they have expelled the griefe. This (with favour) is their office ; and thofe that be under their charge do look for difcharge thereof (with all reverence) at their hands.

In this action her Majeſtie fhall be effectually affiſted by the King of Denmark. The princes of Germany (who never favoured the French nor the Prince of Orange's courfe) will back her Majeſtie, and join to reſtore Truxes to the fee of Colleine ; a matter of high importance. Her Majeſtie fhall be Lady of 10,000 fayle of fhips in Holland and Zealand, and fhall have the ſtaple of the world in her hand, de-

fenfible

fenfible againſt all the world, having only a head that will oppoſe. This will ſtay
and divert the French King's braynſicke projects, who is both a coward and a
beggar: all the provinces (named Malecontents) ſhall be united hereby; her Majeſtie ſhall have infinite obedience; and they ſhall be delivered from extreme cala-
mitie. The glory is God's, the enterprize ſafe and eaſy, and her Majeſtie ſhall
have immortal honour, wealth, and ſecurity.

For her Majeſtie's reaſon, that ſhe would not enter into a war for diſpleaſing of
her people, that have ſo long lived in peace, is (with her Highneſs's favor) no
reaſon at all. Her people generally deſireth this war, as juſt and neceſſarie, taken
in ripe ſeaſon, and will have thoſe that do impugne it as enemies of their countrey,
condemning them of dotage, or malice, or of both. The conſent (ſaith Comineus)
firſt had of the people of England to allow of war, is a marvellous ſtrength to their
kings, and is undertaken with alacrity, and ſupplied with abundance. The King
were then feigne to ſue for the people's favor; but this is offered _ultrò_ with a general conſent and voice of all, the gentry, nobility, and counſellors concurring
therein, which were moſt dangerous to be diſappointed. The realme will diſcharge her Majeſtie of the charge of this war, for the vehement deſire it hath to
the preſervation thereof. I dare (in the fear of God) aſſure her Majeſtie, that if
ſhe deal openly in this action, ſhe ſhall with facility rid the country of Parma and
Spain before Chriſtmas day, and ſo quit herſelf of this war, more fearful in conceit, than dangerous in effect.

I have told her Majeſtie of late ſundry things of good conſequence, proving
true; but I have had Caſſandra's luck. I pray God to open her gracious eyes, and
ſtrengthen her royal heart in true valour, that all weak reſpects be chaced thence:
Une bonne Guerre faiet une bonne paix.

Touching defenſive playſters to be made to help and heal our ſore, is a matter
(in the judgement of men of gravitie) impoſſible by man's brain, but moſt dangerous to him that ſhall take upon him to perſuade that courſe, and to be the author of a new counſell. Without all ſtop, this iſſue by impoſthumation breaks
inwardly, to our preſent and manifeſt deſtruction.

For this my tedious diſcourſe, I crave humble pardon of your Lordſhip that I
am entered ſo far, being tranſported into it ere I was aware: but it is the humble
harmleſs opinion conceived of me, her Majeſtie's poor, loyal, and careful ſervant,
uttered in all humble duty to you alone, and referred to your honourable cenſure,
having my blood ready to ſeal it for her Majeſtie's ſervice, and the preſervation of
my ſweet natural country: and to you, my Lord, my aſſured duty and devotion to
the end of my life: wherewith (weak and ſick) I humbly take my leave. The
16th, and kept till the 18th of July, 1585 *.

Your Lordſhip's ever moſt bounden.

* It may be obſerved, that in this very year 1585, Queen Elizabeth entered into articles with
the Dutch, obliging herſelf to very great ſupplies of men and money, lent upon the ſecurity of
the Briel, Fluſhing, and Ramekins; which ſhe performed. Sir William Temple's Obſervations on
the United Provinces, p. 66.   6

APPENDIX.

Nº IX. PEDIGREE of LAMBARDE.

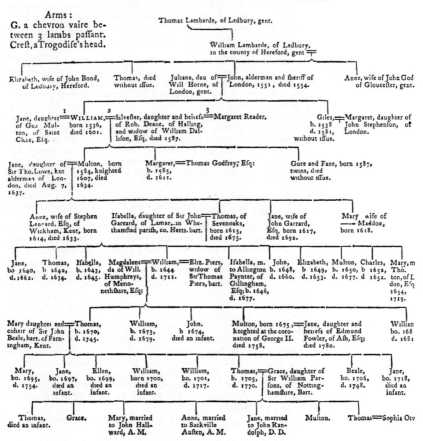

Arms:
G. a chevron vaire be-
tween 3 lambs paſſant.
Creſt, a Trogodiſe's head.

Thomas Lambarde, of Ledbury, gent.

William Lambarde, of Ledbury,
in the county of Hereford, gent.

Elizabeth, wife of John Bond, of Ledbury, Hereford.

Thomas, died without iſſue.

Juliana, dau of Will Horne, of London, gent.

John, alderman and ſheriff of London, 1551, died 1554.

Anne, wife of John God of Gloucester, gent.

Jane, daughter of Geo Mul-ton, of Saint Clere, Eſq.

WILLIAM, born 1536, died 1601.

Silveſter, daughter and heireſs of Rob. Deane, of Halling, and widow of William Dal-liſon, Eſq, died 1587.

Margaret Reader.

Giles, b. 1538 d. 1581, without iſſue.

Margaret, daughter of John Stephenſon, of London.

Jane, daughter of Sir Tho. Lowe, knt alderman of London, died Aug. 7, 1637.

Multon, born 1584, knighted 1607, died 1634.

Margaret, b. 1585, d. 1611.

Thomas Godfrey, Eſq:

Gore and Fane, born 1587, twins, died without iſſue.

Anne, wife of Stephen Lennard, Eſq, of Wickham, Kent, born 1614, died 1633.

Iſabella, daughter of Sir John Garrard, of Lamar, in Whe-thamſted pariſh, co. Herts. bart.

Thomas, of Sevenoaks, born 1615, died 1675.

Jane, wife of John Garrard, Eſq, born 1617, died 1692.

Mary wife of —— Maddox, born 1618.

Jane, bo 1640, d. 1662.

Thomas, b 1642, d. 1674.

Iſabella, b. 1643, d. 1645.

Magdalene, da of Will. Humphreys, of Merio-nethſhire, Eſq:

William, b. 1644 d. 1711.

Eliz. Piers, widow of Sir Thomas Piers, bart.

Iſabella, m. John, to Allington Paynter, of Gillingham, Eſq; b. 1646, d. 1677.

John, b. 1648, d. 1660.

Elizabeth, b 1649, d. 1653.

Multon, b. 1650, d. 1677.

Charles, b 1652, d 1652.

Mary, m Tho. ton, of L don, Eſq 1654, 1719.

Mary daughter and coheir of Sir John Beale, bart. of Farn-ingham, Kent.

Thomas, b. 1670, d. 1745.

William, b. 1673, d. 1679.

John, b 1674, died an infant.

Multon, born 1675, knighted at the coro-nation of George II. died 1758.

Jane, daughter and heireſs of Edmund Fowler, of Aſh, Eſq; died 1780.

William bo. 168 d. 1681

Mary, bo. 1695, d. 1754.

Jane, bo. 1697, died an infant.

Ellen, bo. 1699, died an infant.

William, born 1700, died an infant.

William, bo. 1701, d. 1717.

Thomas, b. 1705, d. 1770.

Grace, daughter of Sir William Par-ſons, of Notting-hamſhire, Bart.

Beale, bo. 1706, d. 1748.

Jane, bo. 1718, died an infant.

Thomas, died an infant.

Grace.

Mary, married to John Hall-ward, A. M.

Anne, married to Sackville Auſten, A. M.

Jane, married to John Ran-dolph, D. D.

Multon.

Thomas

Sophia Otw

The LETTER on SAINT RADIGUND's having been printed off without the final revifal of Mr. LYON; the EDITOR has fince been favoured by that Gentleman with the following Remarks and Corrections.

Page	Line	
454	23	For " this abbey," it may be proper to add, " the church, or the altar of it, belonging to this abbey ;" for, notwithftanding what is faid, p. 462, line 10, it is plain from the date of the Charters, Thomas de Ponyngs, knight, could not be the founder of the abbey : therefore what he fays in his will of the foundation, muft mean either the church, or the altar, or the choir of the church.
455	8	For " Potton-wood," *read* " Polton-wood."
456	11	My MS. has " Walter," not " William."
Ib.	21	For " Hautam," *r.* " Hougham."
Ib.	25	Heaggh Knoll, I rather think fhould be Fleggs Knoll; as *Fleggs Court* belonged to Saint Radigund's.
Ib.		I imagine the lands mentioned by the name of *del Teghe* in the Charter of Thomas Earl of Perche, line 26, are the fame as the lands called *Deltegee* in Henry the Third's Charter, page 459, line 3 ; and that the difference in writing it has been owing to the inattention of the tranfcriber in joining the prepofition *De* and the article to the name of the land.
457	4	For " Pultone," *r.* " Polton."
Ib.	6	*Brichtine* and *Molote*, in my MS. copy of the Charters, are fpelled *Birchtine* and *Molote* ; and are evidently the names of the women called in Henry the Third's Charter *Brittuna* and *Molota*."
458	16	Query whether " Blan-Corbel" fhould not be read " Alanus Corbel ?" I find it fo in my MS. copy of the Charters.
459	9	For " Sibertfwand," *r.* " Sibertfwould."
460	6	For " Haveking," *r.* " Hawking."
461	6	For " Survenden," *r.* " Surenden."
464	22	For " Portiers," *r.* " Poitiers."

A re-

A re-perufal of the Memoirs of Mr. LAMBARDE has produced the following Corrections.

P. 425. l. 24. for *priora* read *prima.*
P. 499. l. 10. for *thefe* read *the Penfioners.*
P. 503. The Letter to Lord Cobham, mentioned in the firft note, is printed at large in the Bibl. Brit. Topog N° VI. p. 8.
P. 506. l. 1. for *to fervices* read *to the fervices.*
P. 510. l. 11. for *Cæcillianis* read *Cecillianis.*
——— l. 16. for N° *IX.* read *X.*
——— l. penult. and p. 511. l. 5. for *Anglia* read *Anglica.*
——— l. 14. for *annotiffe* read *annotâffe.*
P. 512. l. 11. to *Edward* add *VI.*

Speedily will be publifhed,

THE FORTY-FIFTH NUMBER of this WORK; containing an APPENDIX to the HISTORY of RECUI VER and HERNE; a Variety of KENTISH NOTITIA; and a Differtation on the Archiepifcopal Palace of MAYFIELD in SUSSEX, &c.

BIBLIOTHECA
TOPOGRAPHICA
BRITANNICA
N° XXXIII.

CONTAINING

Mr. DOUGLAS's Two DISSERTATIONS

on the Brafs Inftruments called C E L T S,

and other ARMS of the ANTIENTS found in this ISLAND.

Illuftrated with Two fine ENGRAVINGS in the *Aqua Tinta* Style.

[Price Three Shillings and Six Pence.]

AMONG the various Labours of Literary Men, there have always been certain Fragments whose Size could not secure them a general Exemption from the Wreck of Time, which their intrinsic Merit entitled them to survive; but, having been gathered up by the Curious, or thrown into Miscellaneous Collections by Booksellers, they have been recalled into Existence, and by uniting together have defended themselves from Oblivion. Original Pieces have been called in to their Aid, and formed a Phalanx that might withstand every Attack from the Critic to the Cheesemonger, and contributed to the Ornament as well as Value of Libraries.

With a similar view it is here intended to present the Publick with some valuable Articles of BRITISH TOPOGRAPHY, from printed Books and MSS. One Part of this Collection will consist of Re-publications of scarce and various Tracts; another of such MS. Papers as the Editors are already possessed of, or may receive from their Friends.

It is therefore proposed to publish a Number occasionally, not confined to the same Price or Quantity of Sheets, nor always adorned with Cuts; but paged in such a Manner, that the general Articles, or those belonging to the respective Counties, may form a separate Succession, if there should be enough published, to bind in suitable Classes; and each Tract will be completed in a single Number.

Into this Collection all Communications consistent with the Plan will be received with Thanks. And as no Correspondent will be denied the Privilege of controverting the Opinions of another, so none will be denied Admittance without a fair and impartial Reason.

———————

PLATE I. to face p. 9.
PLATE II. to face p. 17.

TWO DISSERTATIONS

ON THE

BRASS INSTRUUMENTS

CALLED

CELTS,

And other ARMS of the ANTIENTS,

Found in this ISLAND.

Quidquid fub terrâ eft, in apricum proferet ætas.　Hor.

By the Reverend JAMES DOUGLAS, F. A. S.

———————

LONDON,

PRINTED BY AND FOR J. NICHOLS,

PRINTER TO THE SOCIETY OF ANTIQUARIES.

MDCCLXXXV.

[5]

LIEUTENANT GENERAL M E L V I L L E, F.R.S. F.A.S. &c.

S I R,

HAVING had fome converfation with you on the fubject of the BRASS ARMS of the Antients, the fubject of thefe fheets, which are frequently digged up in feveral parts of this Ifland; it will be an addition to the pleafure which refults from my Antiquarian ftudies, if, in the moments when you digrefs from more ferious bufinefs, the following paper can afford you any amufement.

I have the honour to be,

S I R,

Your moft obedient humble Servant,

Cniddingfold,
Nov. 3, 1785.

JAMES DOUGLAS.

P R E F A C E.

THE following paper having been read at the Society of Antiquaries, 17 June, 1784, it was, by the opinion of the Council, in compliment to a work which I am writing on the Sepulchres of the Antients difcovered in this ifland, thought to be invading on the materials. Their kind intentions are here ac-knowledged; but it is alfo neceffary to remark in this place, that, in the courfe of my reading, I have had occafion to difcard many obfervations which might poffibly be of fome ufe to literature, and which do not come immediately into the clafs of thofe particlulars which have a more pertinent relation to the above ftudy. Such was the motive for fending the former part of this paper to the learned Society, which, when in their poffeffion, was fubmitted to their decifion, from a confideration that the inftrument called a *Celt* has been by moft Antiquaries thought meriting a more clear explanation than what has been hitherto given; and more par-ticularly from a confideration that the Celts, which were the fubject of this tract, were judged by feveral of our beft-informed Antiquaries of fome importance towards the illuftration of their ufe, and one in particular undefcribed in any work. It is to the candour of the Society of Antiquaries, I now fubmit this apology for printing the difcourfe myfelf—that the little light, if light it may be called, which may arife from the defire I have to publifh fuch cafual difcoveries, may tend, if not to inftruct, perhaps to ftimulate others towards a final decifion on the ufe of thefe inftruments.

A 4   The

The second part of this difcourfe was written for the amufement of the Society ; and which I fhould have had the honour
to have tranfmitted, had it not been fo materially connected with
the former. The many learned and regular correfpondents who-
furnifh them with a continual fupply of curious papers, will
in every refpect put it far from my thoughts, that the fame can
in the leaft degree be acceffary to its repute, or information : I
have therefore taken advantage of the publication of this tract
to fubjoin the fame. On all other occafions, when matter occurs
which may be poffibly of any curious import and worthy of
their regard, I fhall ever hold it my duty, however feeble the
endeavor, as a member, defirous of fupporting a body of learned
men, by fuch a teftimony of my zeal for their welfare, moft
cordially to communicate the fame.

J. DOUGLAS.

Pl. 1

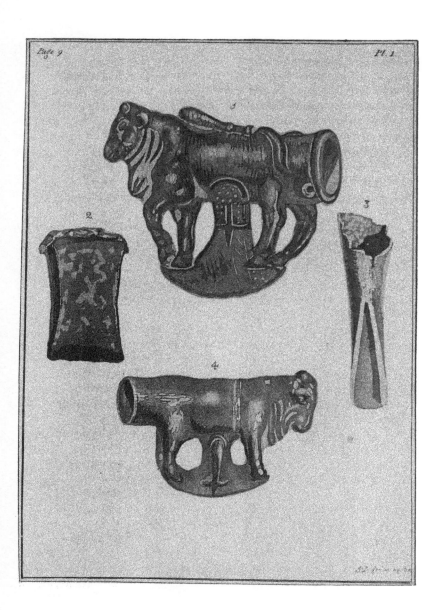

TO THE

PRESIDENT AND SOCIETY OF ANTIQUARIES.

HAVING two fingular *Celts* in my poffeffion, unpublifhed in any work, I thought the drawings of them, with fome remarks, might not be unacceptable to the learned Society, of which I have the honour to be a member. I was more particularly inclined to fend this paper, as thefe inftruments have long occafioned much fpeculation concerning their intended ufe among the antients.

It would be intruding on the patience of the Society to comment on the papers which I have examined on the fubject: I fhall therefore only enter on a fhort detail concerning the peculiarities of thefe inftruments, which may poffibly throw new lights on the fubject, and perhaps tend to diffipate in fome degree the various conjectures which have been publifhed refpecting them.

In PLATE I. is an inftrument compofed of a mixed metal in PLATE I the form of a bull: the workmanfhip is elegant, and not much inferior to the fine ftyle of the Auguftan age. It was found near Canterbury, but in what place, or at what precife time, I am not able to learn. I believe it was firft in the poffeffion of the late Mr. Scott, of Chigwell, in Effex, a man of learning and tafte, who efteemed it as a valuable and rare curiofity: fince

B   which

which it fell into the hands of Mr. John White, of Newgate-ftreet, who fent it to Mr. Jacob, of Faverfham, from whom I received it [1].

On the back of the animal is a lacrnrymatory, or club; the feet reft on the executive part of the inftrument, which in fhape is precifely that which, according to Begerus, we call a *Celt.* The tail of the bull is turned on the back, and which, with much tafte, defines the proportion of the body from the vent that is contrived for the fhaft of the inftrument, fufficiently capacious to admit of a very fubftantial one adapted to the weight of the metal, and which was fecured by a hole for a rivet; under the belly are fome religious, magical, or ornamental marks; the horns are fhort, and, like the bull ordained for facrifice, feem pruned for the purpofe. It muft ftrike every judgement, that if the inftrument fhould be a *lachrymatory* on the back of the bull, it will import the inftrument to be ufed in funereal rites.

The ancients were accuftomed to facrifice bulls and other animals to Pluto, to pacify the *manes* of thofe who were deprived of the rites of burial, and who were fuppofed to be troubled by fpectres or other nocturnal terrors :

> *Parcite pallentes umbras quicumque tenetis*
> *Duraque fortiti tertia regna Dei* [2].

Here we find tears to have been fhed over thefe facrifices.

Again ;

> *Ululantem—fcalpere terram unguibus*
> *Cœperunt cruor in foſſam confufus : ut inde*
> *Manes elicient* [3].

---

[1] The drawing is the exact fize.
[2] Tibullus, 3 Eleg. v.
[3] Hor. 1 Sat. viii. 25.

This

This paffage more properly relates to the invocation of the manes: but tears were fhed as much to appeafe as to invoke them.

In the beautiful prophecy of the Cumæan Sibyl to Æneas, on the death of Mifenus, he is commanded, firft to commit his body to the ground, and then to facrifice black cattle to Pluto, as tutelar deity of the *manes :*

> *Quatuor hic primum nigrantes terga juvencos*
> *Conftituit* [1]———

And in a following paffage,

> *Tum Stygio regi nocturnas inchoat aras,*
> *Et folida imponit taurorum vifcera flammis,* &c.

Hence the infernal deity was called *fummanus* [2] *qua fummus manium* [3].

In St. Paul's Epiftle to the Hebrews [4], there is a paffage which feems to relate to a cuftom which the Romans or Jews had of facrificing to the *manes* which were polluted, by their being deprived the honours of fepulture, or by any other kind of difgrace. *For if the blood of bulls, and of goats, and the afhes of an heifer fprinkling the unclean, fanctifieth to the purifying of the flefh,* &c. Whether this paffage relates to the antient law of the Jews or the Romans, is of no great importance to our enquiry; it is well known that a fimilitude of cuftoms is obfervable between the Jews and Romans in refpect to facrifices.

From thefe apparent and applicable reafons, this *Celt* may be fuppofed to have been the *fecuris*, or fmall hatchet, appropri-

---

[1] Virg. Æn. vi. 243.
[2] Varro, lib. iv.
[3] Cic. de Divin.
[4] Chap. ix. 13.

ated

ated to the facrifices of the minor animals. Before we proceed,
it will be proper to confider it as fuch. At the funeral of
Mifenus, a black fheep was facrificed to night [1]:

—————— *Ipfe atri velleris agnam*
Æneas matri Eumenidum magnæque forori
Enfe ferit ——————

Horace [2] fpeaking of the enchantrefs Canidia, fays,

—————— *et pullam divellere mordicus agnam*
Cœperunt ——————

As the Poet here fpeaks in derifion of thefe rites, I fhould
not think it improbable, that black fheep were alfo flain in
facrifices to the *manes*; efpecially as it is exprefsly defined in this
Satire that the enchantrefs was invoking them: it is not to be
fuppofed that thefe rites were confined only to the larger kind
of animals; few families or individuals could have afforded the
expence, and we all know the antients, in matters of fuperftition, to have been extremely fertile and ingenious in accom-
modating their religion to their exigences. Pliny mentions black
cattle, implying various kinds to have been facrificed in magical
rites [3]. I have no doubt as the paffage in Horace of the enchantrefs, facrificing a black fheep, relates to the *manes*; fo
does this paffage of Pliny.

If from its fize, or little appearance of its executive power
in this refpect, objections are made to its being thus ufed; be it
then faid to have been a funeral enfign for the fervice of the
dead; that it was carried in the proceffion, or that it obviated [4]

the

---

[1] Virg. Æn. vi. 249.
[2] 1 Sat. viii. 28.
[3] Speaking of the power of Nero in procuring every effential for the rites of
magic, *Pecudes vero, quibus non nifi ater color effet facile.* Lib. XXX. c. 2.
[4] I obferve that thefe kind of Celts might have obviated the facrifices of large
animals, and have been depofited near their fepulchres, to appeafe the manes of the
dead;

the actual facrifice of animals, by its being depofited fimply with the afhes.

In the developing of truth, the moft trifling remarks are of confequence. I am therefore inclined to mention the marks under the belly of the bull; which, there is reafon to fuppofe, are magical: as the inftrument feems dedicated to the myfteries of facrifice to Pluto.[1], who was by the ancients fuppofed to be the inventor of magical cyphers, I fhould think the marks in queftion had fome relation to this type of the deity. I have, in the courfe of reading, obferved no fmall analogy between the ceremony of ancient magic practifed by the Romans, and their funeral rites; and it may not be foreign to our purpofe to mention the difcovery of bracelets, which I found in a Roman Britifh barrow, having very fimilar marks on them to thofe which are upon this Celt: Divination by bracelets feems to have likewife been appropriated to magic:

> *Canidiæ dentes, altum Saganæ caliendrum*
> *Excidere, atque herbas, atque incantata lacertis*
> *Vincula ——*[2]

dead; which inference I have made from the apparent lachrymatory on the back of the bull; and from fome relative paffages in the claffics.

This remark I have fince found to be ftrengthened by the following paffage in Horace, 3 Od. xxiii. 14.

> —— Te nihil attinet
> Tentare multâ cæde bidentium.

And a paffage of Cato fets forth, that thefe facrifices to the Lares fhould be made in proportion to the perfon's abilities. *Per eofdem dies Lari familiari pro copiâ fupplicet.* They were made on the *new moon*, to which this Ode refers: but whether the crefcent under the belly of the bull bears any relation to this cuftom, I fhall not pretend to determine; poffibly there might arife fome difference between the facrifices for their vintage and thofe for the manes of their friends. However, I think it right to mention this particular, as having fome foundation for argument.

[1] Pluto was alfo faid to be the firft who invented funeral ceremonies.
[2] Hor. 1 Sat. viii.

I do

I do not mean to infer from this, that the Celt was appropriated to magical operations, but only to obferve from thefe
apparent magical cyphers, that the inftrument might be dedicated
to Pluto, or adapted to fome ufes which were fepulchral and
facred to this Deity. The above obfervations are penned with
an eye to the inftrument's being appropriated to Roman ufes ;
let us confider it with an eye to Britifh, Gaulifh, or Celtic.

There is a paffage in Plutarch, which favours a fuppofition
that the Celtic nation ufed the *bull* as a principal enfign,
like the *eagle* of the Romans. Plutarch fays, that on an affault
of the Barbarians, meaning the Cimbri, who had invaded Italy
in aftonifhing multitudes, like fwarms of locufts, and had taken
a fortrefs on the other fide of the Athefis, finding the garrifon
had behaved in a manner fuitable to the glory and known bra-
very of Romans, they difmiffed them on certain conditions,
having firft made them fwear to them upon a *brazen bull*. In
the battle that followed, this *bull* was taken among the fpoils,
and is faid to have been carried to Catulus's houfe as the firft
fruits of victory. The Cimbri were a people who inhabited the
Cimbrica Cherfonefus, now Jutland ; they are generally mentioned with the Teutons and the other Celtic nations : hiftory fays,
they are defcended from the antient Gomerians, or Celtes, and are
the fame people as the Cimmerians, who inhabited the countries
about the Palus Mæotis, and hence they received their name :
this indeed is highly probable from the fimilitude of name, and
from the defcendants of Gomer having fpread themfelves over
that northern tract [1]. As this paffage occured in the original
paper, I have fuffered it to remain in its place ; otherwife it more
properly relates to the fecond Differtation, p. 18 ; which will

---

[1] See the Life of Marius, p. 18.

more

more clearly explain the ſenſe of this paſſage as relating to the Celt.

Fig. II. Plate I. is a *Celt* in the form of a wedge, and which bears evident marks of a hammer upon it; this inſtrument, I apprehend, will admit of no doubt as to its uſe: the drawing is the exact ſize.

Fig. III. is a *Celt* in the form of a gouge, and which was alſo found near Canterbury; the metal is mixed, uncommonly hard, and capable of being worked to any tolerable edge; it has a ſocket proportionable to an handle for mechanical works: if this inſtrument had been intended for a miſſile weapon of offence, it would have been pointed for execution; it muſt not therefore fail to ſtrike almoſt any capacity, which has reflected on the nature of the *Celts*, that when they have been found in ſhapes ſo apparently fitted for mechanical works, and with weapons of warlike ſhape [1], ſuch as ſpears and ſwords, that they have been uſed for ſuch purpoſes. It has been thought a difficult matter [2] to illuſtrate the uſe of the loop that is fixed to thoſe Celts which are in the form of a chizel: as theſe have been found with military inſtruments, it is natural to ſuppoſe they were uſed by the ſoldier, in works of art; and in ſuch caſes the inſtrument would be ſecured to his perſon as an appendage, while the defenſive or offenſive weapon would be diſengaged, and ready for immediate execution. I have ſeen thoſe that have been found in caſes, and doubtleſs they were ſo made to preſerve their edges from injury. Were ſpears or ſwords ever found in caſes? They needed no ſuch caution: a ſtone under foot would procure edges or points to them ſufficient for execution; but a chizel or an inſtrument for a mechanical work requires a more curious proceſs to procure it an edge, and particularly a fine edge to a braſs inſtrument that would be ſo liable to injury.

[1] Leland, Vol. I. p. 17.　　　[2] See Borlaſe's Hiſtory of Cornwall, p. 269.

The

The Romans had an art of discharging their javelins with a thong which they called *amentum*; it has therefore been conceived that the loop of the Celt was adapted to this art [1]; but as they are in shape so opposite to a military weapon, they must have been unwieldy, aukward, and defective in execution. If, like the instrument of the ancient Franks, called *franciscus*, or the *mataræ* of the Gauls, which were darted at some distance, and recovered again, they would on their offending parts have been differently shaped: with propriety I think we may therefore conclude with this observation, that these instruments, which we call *Celts*, were fabricated, according to their different qualifications, for warlike, mechanical, and sepulchral offices.

As they have been found with Roman coins of Antoninus Augustus, Divo. Constantio Pio, and Severus Alexander [2], we may conclude that they have been the produce either of the Romans or the Britons in this island, perhaps to the final departure of the Roman legionary establishment: that they may possibly have been fabricated for Britain, from a novelty of some military institute, or at a period when the Romans had not an opportunity of sending a reinforcement of arms; the fabrication of which might be difficult, and the convenience not suited to such a remote conquest; and as brass was more easy to work, it was therefore used in preference to iron. It may be alledged, that the Romans, in consequence of their refinement of the Britons, had taught them the art of working iron to any uses; this is granted; but surely the expedition of casting brass arms is far greater; it is very possible, both brass and iron arms were variously blended together for use; and I make no doubt but a time will come when iron arms will be discovered with brass, or the metal arms, which are the subject of this paper.

[1] Borlase's Cornwall.   [2] Ibid.

6

From all the paffages which I have been enabled to felect from the writings of the learned to throw light on the nature of thefe inftruments, I have not the leaft authority for fuppofing that they were ufed before the invention of iron, or that they can be configned to any remote period in hiftory. The Arundelian marbles, ftating that the ufe of iron was not difcovered till 188 years before the wars of Troy, have no relation to our *Celts* ; nor are the quotations of learned men from Homer, Hefiod, or Lucretius, of any advantage to us [1]. They have been found with coins of the Lower Empire ; and iron in thofe times was univerfally ufed in war throughout the ifland of Britain.

In a former paper (on a Roman Hypogeum found on Chatham Lines) I promifed the Society a Differtation on a *Coin of Anthemius,* which, with other relics, I difcovered in a barrow. On a furvey of my materials, I have fince found they would not by any means come within the compafs of a paper ; and I have therefore referved them for a work with which they are more intimately blended.

I have the honour to be,

Gentlemen,

Your devoted and faithful Member,

Feb. 23, 1784.   JAMES DOUGLAS.

[1] See Borlafe's Cornwall.

C   DIS-

DISSERTATION II.

FIG. 4. PLATE I. is in the poffeffion of Mr. Rawle in the Strand: It was a companion to the one which I have in the extenfive collection of the late Mr. Scot; and I am forry to fay, that he has left no hiftory attached to it. The above antiquary has been honoured with the name of a man of great tafte and learning, and I have no right to offer any infinuation to the contrary; yet I fhall not forbear to affert an opinion in this place, that when gentlemen hoard up antique relics as children collect gewgaws, they often expofe the more reflecting antiquary, whofe only view in collecting them is to throw light on hiftory, or place fome doubtful cuftom of an antient people in a more accurate point of light, to the pleafantry of his friends, and the ridicule of the unlettered part of the world.

Mr. D'Hankerville, in his late publication, entitled, *Recherches fur l'Origine, l'Efprit, et les Progrés des Arts de la Grece*, p. 225. mentions the Bull Celt of my former paper, which he faw in my cabinet; he conceives it to be the God *Tho* of the Britons; which people, after the cuftom of the Cimbri, venerated the bull as the *Deus conductor* of their marches and armies; and he adds, *that this fymbol among the Scythians was a fword, a fpear among the Sabins, and alfo an axe among the Britons*; the form of which weapon is

C 2   reprefented

reprefented under the feet of the bull.   This was alfo the God
of the Ifraelites, when they demanded of Aaron the Calf or
heifer as their God, to precede them on their military expedi‐
tions.   If the weapon may be fuppofed to be a *club* on the back
of the bull, Plate I. (fee Fig. 1.) we fhall have no difficulty in
afcribing it to the fymbol of Hercules the God of Might, alfo
the natural fymbol of an army ; Hercules being worfhiped by
the northern nations under the name of *Herculis Magufanus* [1], as
well as by the Romans under the names of *Herculis Erymantini,
Herculis comitis Augufti, Jovis, Victoris, Statoris, Herculis immor‐
talis, Cretenfis, Libyci et Argivi*; and indeed by all the nations of
the then known world.

The focket of the weapon, its fize, as well as that of the
fmaller hatchet, fhew them to be well adapted for the head of
ftaffs, and may have been ufed, from the general obfervance
and confidence repofed in the worfhip of the bull, by in‐
dividuals on their expeditions, as by an army on its march.   See
Plate I. Fig. 1. and Fig. 4.   Nor fhould it feem contrary to my
former argument, that thefe inftruments fhould be alone appro‐
priated for thefe military religious purpofes; but they may, as was
the cuftom of the antients in matters of fuperftition, be adapted
to the ceremonies of interment; as a fepulchral honour to the de‐
ceafed ; and hence we fhall account for their being found in the
earth, and thus handed down to us.   Whether the inftrument on
the back of the animal be the club of Hercules, or a lachrymatory,
we may ftill afcribe it with propriety to the above purpofes [2].

---

[1] See Keyffer's Antiq. Sept. et Celt.

[2] If this inftrument fhould be afcribed to the Britons, we muft difcard the pof‐
fibility of the inftrument on the back of the bull being a lachrymatory ; as we are
given to underftand this was a funeral veffel of the Romans, and not of the Britons.
In literary difcuffions, every thing for and againft the argument fhould be publifhed.
Pedantry and obftinate conceit muft always give way to the moft candid and liberal
expofition ; truth will otherwife for ever remain concealed from us.

Fig.

Fig. 1. Pl. II. Is an Egyptian piece of fculpture in a large Plate II entablature hewn out of a block of bafalt, fent over by M. Wortley Montague, and depofited in the Britifh Mufeum. Like the moft part of Egyptian workmanfhip of this nature, it is both in Cameo and Intaglio; the defign is funk into the ftone, and then worked into relief. That the drawing might be more perfect, I took it from an imbofs off the ftone. It reprefents Ofiris and Ifis, which, under the fymbol of the ox and cow, rife out of an human fhape : here is united the veneration of the Egyptians to Bacchus, the great indigenous leader and deity. The known power of thefe deities fhew them in this inftance to be but one being, imitating both fexes, and fo fymbolized by the Egyptians, Indians, and Grecians. This figure is of equal fignificancy with the Python, which may be feen on another entablature of the fame kind in the veftibule of the Mufeum, before which, as before the Ofiris and Ifis, is a kneeling prieft, prefenting the obilifcal ftone, the emblem of fire ; which feems to be in imitation of the Belemnites [1], which the Greeks copied from the Scythians, and with which they reprefented the rays of the Sun [2].

The kneeling prieft, with the nature of the offering, fhews the power of this deity to be pre-eminent; and hence it was called Apis, which in the Egyptian tongue fignifies Father ; and by the Greeks, the fymbol being the fame as Bacchus (fee Fig. 3. Pl. II.) it was called *Father of the* Gods *and* Men. The Scythians, in the time of Herodotus, gave the earth the name of Apia; Γῆ δὲ, Ἀπια, lib. iv. p. 243. According to this ancient writer, this was the wife of the God Papæus or Father, hence Papæus and Abia imply Father and Mother, male and female. (ἄῤῥηνα ϗ Θῆλυν· Orph. Hymn, xli. ver. 4.) which created all

[1] See Recherches fur l'Origine, l'Efprit, &c. des Arts de la Grece, p. 473.
[2] See Plutarch in *Lyfandro*. The word is derived from *belos*, and fignifies a dart; Belemnites, ftone-darts.

things,

things, and which engendered, or brought the earth out of Chaos.
Papæus and Apia were the fame as Liber and Libera. This
worfhip was tranfported into Peloponefus, and there it was called
by Orpheus Apia, which among the Scythians fignifies the female
Bacchus. The name implies the earth confecrated to that
Deity, and worfhiped under the fymbol of a Cow [1]. This
form is tranfmitted to us on the coins of Corcyre and Dyrra-
chium, the former a colony coin of Corinth. Plutarch fays,
that the moft part of the *Egyptian priefts regarded Ofiris and
Apis as the fame deity.* See alfo Diod. Sic. lib. I. p. 10. *He
was created in the city of Nyfus, in Arabia, near to Egypt.* It is
now neceffary to remark, that as this ox is the fame as Ofiris,
according to the greater part of the Egyptian priefts, who
acknowledged it as the produce of Nyfus, and alfo to be
the fame as the Bacchus of the Greeks; fo it is alfo evident that
the worfhip of the Egyptians, as alfo of the Indians and the
Greeks, arofe from Scythia.

The origin of this emblem on the Celts, Fig. 1. and 4.
Pl. I. is fo curious and interefting, that I cannot difmifs the fubject before I have enlarged a little more on the fubject: Phylarch
in Plutarch fays, *that Bacchus was the firft who carried* from India
into Egypt two oxen, one of which was called Apis, and the
other Ofiris; according to M. D'Hankarville, it is likely that
fomething in this relation was true, for the name of Bacchus
was given to the Scythian conqueft, which extended from India
to Egypt [2]. The Cimbri, who gave the name to the Cimbri
Cherfonefus, now Jutland, were of Scythian origin, an early

---

[1] See Rech. fur l'Origine et le Progrés des Arts, vol. I. p. 139.

[2] According to Phylarch, on the Conqueft of Bacchus, living animals were worfhiped; this may be the reafon why at this day fo much refpect is paid to live oxen
and cows by the Indian nations. See Rech. fur l'Orig. et les Prog. des Arts de la
Grece, p. 141.

colony from the Palus Mæotis [1]; they have a fimilar fymbol
among their idols ; the feet and tail of the bull, with the head
on the thighs ; and this was their enfign which they tranfported
into Italy againft Marius [2].   We fhall now want but little proof
on our fide, to eftablifh the real ufe of the Celts, Fig. I. and
Fig. II. which feem to have been the Celtic enfigns : the great
northern deity, or Nifhen, which prevailed, as it does to this day
in many kingdoms of the world.

Fig. 2. Pl. II. is a Greek coin, with the bull in the act of but-
ting; which difcovers the force of this deity referring to the power
of Bacchus; the animal treads on the fpear, the emblem of Mars
the God of war of the Greeks, conducted by the fupreme Deity,
the mighty father of Gods and men; which fymbol I have before
obferved, was of Scythian origin. Fig. 3. is alfo a Greek coin, the
Minotaur ; and to thofe who are in the leaft converfant with the
true mythic of the antients, they will foon difcover the God
Bacchus of the Greeks; a warlike and powerful king, who at
an early period, as far as human record can carry us, made a
conqueft of almoft all the then known habitable earth [3].   On
comparing therefore the Ofiris and Ifis of the Egyptians, or the
Mnèvis and Apis, Fig. 1. Pl. II. with Fig. 2. and Fig. 3. to
Fig. 1. and Fig. 4. of Plate I. [4] we can have no doubt as to
their ftrict and intimate relation with each other.

Thefe obfervations alfo concur to prove that the antient
theology admitted of one *fupreme Being*, whom they adored, as the

[1] See M. Pezron.
[2] See the firft Differtation, p. 14.
[3] See Diod. Sic.
[4] The crefcent under the belly of Fig. 1. and Fig. 4. may reprefent the horns
of Ifis, typical of the crefcent of the moon; this united in Fig. 1. Pl. II. with
Ofiris, fhews him to be the fun of night.   There is a fceptre apparently under the
crefcents in both of the *Bull Celts*, which may imply *power* or foyereign authority,
equally confonant to the nature of this mythology.

invifible.

invifible *Father of all things,* and reprefented under the emblem of the bull [1]. The word Tho, or Theo, implying this animal, exprefs the word Theos ; hence Deus, God the Father of all.

After having run over a brief defcription of the typical marks of this inftrument, let us digrefs to thofe that have been found in Ireland, in Britain, and indeed all over Europe.

That thefe brafs weapons called Celts, whether in the form of a bull, of a gouge, chizel, fword, fpear, or hatchet, have belonged either to an early people, or a people remote from the feat of refined arts, will need little debate ; we fhall alfo find that they have been ufed perhaps from a very early period down to the loweft of the Roman empire [2].

Herodotus fays [3], " That, between the river Borifthenes and " Hypanis, there is a place called Exampus, in which place there " is a copper veffel, fix times larger than a fimilar veffel at " the mouth of the Euxine fea ; and that Paufanias fon of Cle- " ombrotus confecrated it; it contains about fix thoufand four " hundred gallons, and fix inches in thicknefs. The inha- " bitants of thofe parts fay, that it was made from the heads " of arrows or spears of the Scythians ; that Ariantus king " of Scythia, being defirous of knowing the number of his fub- " jects, demanded that every Scythian fhould, on pain of death, " bring him the point of an arrow, or spear."

---

[1] See this very learnedly treated in Bochart, Hierozoic. p. 973. Alfo Rech. fur l'Orig. et les Prog. des Arts de la Grece, p. 145. 163.

[2] In a work, entitled, *Die gottefdienftlichen Alterthümer der Obotriten, aus dem Tempel zu Rhetra, am Tollenzer-See von* Daniel Wogen, is the defcription of feveral brafs fpear heads, but which in the work are called Messers, or knives : in fhape and fize they anfwer to thofe that are found in Britain and Ireland. They were found with a variety of other Runic relics in the temple of Rhetra, and feem all to have paffed the fire. Moft of the idols have Runic characters on them, as alfo the fpear heads, which bear the names of *Radegart, Vodlia, Padaga, Siba, Pya.* See p. 136, 137, 138.

[3] Lib. IV.

It

It is eaſy, from this relation, to obſerve the hiſtory of the fabrication of this copper veſſel to be fabulous; but it is alſo
obvious that copper or braſs muſt have been very plentiful in
thoſe days; and that the arms of the Scythians appear to have
been made of that metal. If therefore we may think, with
colonel Vallancey [1], that Phænius, the Scythian leader, who
taught their anceſtors letters, might alſo have taught them
the fabrication of their braſs weapons, which are found to this
day in ſuch numbers in that iſland; or if we may adopt a very
probable conjecture, on this ingenious writer's declaration, that
the Iriſh are the deſcendants of the Phœnicians, who were
Scythians or Scythopolans, as we find in the Firſt book of
Maccabees, being one and the ſame people; we may therefore
find no difficulty in aſcertaining the cauſe why theſe arms
are found in that country, the ſtructure and quality of which
ſo much correſpond with the braſs weapons found in moſt
places in Europe where the Scythian nation over-ran.

In a converſation with Sir William Hamilton previous to his
laſt departure for Naples, I took occaſion to enquire the hiſtory
of the numerous Celts and ſome braſs ſwords, which he has
depoſited in the Britiſh Muſeum. He informed me that moſt of
them were collected in Italy, and he believes that many were
found in ſepulchres; but he could not diſcriminate them. This
circumſtance, abſtracted from many others relating that they
have been found in France and Portugal [2], muſt convince the
learned that theſe inſtruments are not peculiar to this iſland.

It has been frequently ſtarted, but I believe from mere conjecture, that the braſs weapons, ſpeaking of the ſwords, were

[1] See his learned preface to his Coll. de Reb. Hib. Numb. XII.
[2] See a paper read this year, 1785, at the Society of Antiquaries.

peculiar

peculiar to the Romans, and that they were not made of *iron*;
whereas the reverfe fhould feem to be the truth; for in all their
fepulchres we do not hear of any brafs weapons being found,
only one of *iron* [1]. It has alfo been argued, that iron will not
preferve itfelf in the earth to this period; but here, I muft take
the liberty, with much fubmiffion, to contradict fuch a report,
having upwards of an hundred iron weapons taken out of the
lower Britifh fepulchres, that, with coins, will evince their having
lain in the earth thirteen hundred years; moft of them are reduced to a calx, and fome few preferve the metal with very
little alteration. This depends very much on the quality of the
foil; but I believe no foil, excepting a foil which is much im-
pregnated with the vitriolic acid, can decompofe iron to that
degree, fo as to leave no trace of the fubftance; this reafon has
alfo been given why iron weapons have feldom been found in
Roman fepulchres, to ftrengthen an idea that the Romans ufed
thefe brafs arms in their armies. That the impropriety of this
remark may be more clearly demonftrated, I fhall beg leave to
advert to the diffimilarity of Roman interment, and other nations
in the neighbourhood of their conquefts; this will alfo produce fome reafon why arms are found in the *Tumuli fepulchrales*
of the northern nations, and not in the graves of the Romans.
For this purpofe it is neceffary to give an example of a tomb
which was opened by Sir William Hamilton, in the year 1757,
in the neighbourhood of Capua, a place famous for the indolent retreat of Hannibal, and which loft him the victory over
the Romans. Near the fide of the fkeleton were found two
fwords of iron, with feveral utenfils of bronze, and a brafs
fimpulum, or ladle ufed in facrifices, and perhaps alfo in the domeftic ufes of the kitchen [2]. Thefe veffels, with fome of the

---

[1] See the iron Gladius at Portici.

[2] Two eggs were found in this grave, the fhells in a perfect ftate of prefervation.

Etrufcan

Etrufcan earth, and the other relics, excepting the inftruments of iron, are preferved in the *Britifh Mufeum.*

It muft occur to any antiquary of reading, that this tomb was the tomb of an ancient Etrufcan, confequently the form of interment the fame as that adopted by all northern nations, the defcendants of the Scythians, as were the Etrufcans; hence we find this cuftom of depofiting the fword, fpear head, and fhield, with the body inhumed, more frequently than burnt, among all the inhabitants of the Pelafgian race, the Canaanites and Egyptians, all united under the general name of Scythians or Phœnicians. Thus in Ezekiel we are told, the warriors were buried with their fwords and other weapons [1]; and when with fome few exceptions we find the northern people preferred burning to burial, we fhall ftill find that weapons of war were thrown into their urns [2]. This cuftom being apparently derived from the Greeks, according to the laws of Solon, from which the Romans feem to have framed the laws of their twelve tables, which enjoin the burning of their dead without the walls. This cuftom of burning has by fome been thought to have originated more from a cleanly than from a pious motive, and which has been adopted in moft warm climates, where putrefaction and contagion are more prevalent than in temperate regions. If we therefore compare the brafs arms found in *Tumuli,* which by their ftructure and fituation belong to a diftinct people from the Romans, and the numberlefs fepulchres of the Romans

---

[1] See chap. xxxii ver. 27. which aludes to the mode of interment of the Pagans, and not of the Jews. *And they fhall not lie with the mighty, that are fallen of the uncircumcifed, which are gone down to hell with their weapons of war: and they have laid their fwords under their heads.*

[2] See a brafs fpear head exhibited by Mr. Brand, Secretary to the Society of Antiquaries, found in the courfe of the fummer, 1784, in one of the barrows on Ridge-way Hill, in Dorfetfhire, and various other fpecimens of this nature, which occur in Englifh Antiquities.

found

found without arms, we muft afcribe this circumftance to a *funereal cuftom*, and not to an accidental one of the quality of the
earth, which has by length of time confumed the metal.

A peculiar cuftom prevailed among the antients, of rendering
those things facred to their funeral rites which were efteemed
facred to their religious inftitutes ; hence we find conftantly in
the tombs of the women [1], many relics which relate to their religious ceremonies; the former ceremony, from a natural
affinity, conftantly arifing from the latter.

The Scythians, from an obfervation made at the beginning of
this Differtation, worfhiped the fword as the tutelar deity prefiding
over their armies, but not under the name of Mars ; the deity of
the Greeks under the like fymbol. *Ferreus acinaces eft Martis
fimulacrum.* Herodot. lib. iv. fect. 62. As this deity was the fame
as the Sabaoth of the Jews, and the God of the Perfians, we fhall
have no difficulty to afcertain a reafon why the fword, fpear-head,
and other weapons, are conftantly found in the tombs of the defcendants of thefe people. *Mars omnium Scytharum Deus* ; *ei
pro fimulacris enfes et tutoria dedicant.* Pomp. Mela, lib. ii. cap. 1.
And thus Solinus, *Pro fimulacris enfes colunt.* This deity, the
Mars of the Greeks, was called Mamers by the Sabines, and reprefented by the latter under the enfign of a fpear, and by the
Amazons under the enfign of a battle-axe, which agrees with
the axe and fword of the Scythians; thefe women, being of
Scythian origin, are always on the antient fculptures reprefented
with the arms of a fhield and battle-axe. From thefe relative
paffages we are to infer, that every nation appears to have
adopted for the fymbol of the god of their armies, that kind

[1] The graves of the Pagan women contain thefe kind of relics more than thofe of
the men : this circumftance may be evinced by thofe who have had opportunities
of feeing the cabinets in Italy, and indeed in our own country : Mr. Townley's
cabinet contains many proofs of this nature among the Romans ; and my own will
exemplify this cuftom, in many inftances, among the Lower Britifh.

of

of weapon which they more particularly ufed, and to have worfhiped it as their general deity : confequently from this motive,
as well as a military one, they may have inftituted it in their
funeral obfequies. When the king of the Sabines fhared the
government with Romulus the founder of Rome, the Sabines
thus fymbolized Mamers their God of war. *Ex Varrone difcimus,*
Romá antiquitas Martis fimulacrum haftam fuiffe. Clem. Alex.
Cohort. ad Gent.

I have now only to remark, that thefe brafs weapons appear
to have been ufed by a people who had not the convenience of
forging iron, and who perhaps were ignorant of the art of rendering it malleable; that nations remote from the difcovery of the
art were obliged to make ufe of that metal which appears to
have been known from the earlieft period of antiquity. Iion
muft be acknowledged to have been a precious metal among the
early Greeks, when *Homer* affigns an iron wedge as a prize in
one of the gymnaftic exercifes, and which, to render it a reward
worthy the victor, he afferts that it would laft him all his life
for the fabrication of his weapons. And at a much more fubfequent period we find, according to the elder Pliny, that this
metal was efteemed of equal value to gold and gems, feeing
that it was worn as rings by the antient fenators and even prætors.
lib. xxxiii. cap. 1. *Ne tum quidem omnes fenatores habuerunt : Ut.*
pote cum memoria avorum multi prætura quoque funkti, in ferro
confenuerint. I fhould not apprehend that Pliny has much reafon
to refer this to primitive œconomy, fince we are well perfuaded
that gold was in general ufe in thofe days ; be this as it may, I
am inclined to think it arofe from the fcarcity of the metal only.
At a period, when the ufe of iron was well known among moft
warlike nations, we read in Tacitus, that the barbarian arms
were pointed with flint or bone ; and I fhould therefore naturally
infer, from a parity of argument, that the brafs weapons would
be

be fabricated as low down as the very lowest æra of the Roman empire; and perhaps even ufed by the Romans themfelves on certain occafions when the legionary appointment was not at hand [1].

I fhall now difmifs this paper with an obfervation of the late Dr. Borlace, who conjectures, becaufe the inftruments called the Celts, in form of a chizel, are not difcovered on the Trajan or Antonine pillars, or have been found among the other numerous utenfils taken from Herculaneum; and that as they do not occur in the Mufeum Rómanum, or in the Mufeum Kercherianum, they muft have been peculiar to the Britons. Thefe kind of Celts are not military inftruments; confequently are not likely to be found on the Antonine or Trajan pillar. In fhort, they appear to have been fabricated in all ages, and to have been more particularly the weapons and mechanical inftruments of a people, who had not the art or convenience of rendering iron malleable for their domeftic and military ufes: this will be the means of affigning a fatisfactory reafon why they have not been found in that unhappy city; which flourifhed at a period when the ufe of iron was generally known among the Romans; confequently the reafon why they do not occur in the works of the afore cited authors, who appear only to have recorded the fineft relics of Roman ingenuity and magnificency.

[1] Thofe who will take the pains to confider thefe brafs inftruments, called Celts, fwords, fpear-heads, or thofe in the form of chizels, will find they are all caft in a mould, a procefs of making arms certainly much more expéditious than forging of tempered iron for warlike ufes. The metal feems to have been rendered extremely hard with an addition of *Lapis Calaminaris,* or fome other ingredient, and will fharpen to a very keen edge. Were it neceffary for that fubduing people the Romans to arm a barbarian people with expedition, what procefs could have been better contrived for all ufes, military as well as mechanical, than that of cafting implements with a fuitable temper, which we know thefe inftruments to have? All nations would certainly give the preference to iron arms, when time, convenience, and fkill unite, for the accomplifhment of fuch an operofe undertaking.

O N

ON THE 1ſt OF M A R C H, 1786,

Will be publiſhed the FIRST NUMBER, in Demy Folio,

O F

N E N I A   B R I T A N N I C A:

OR, AN ACCOUNT OF

S O M E   H U N D R E D   S E P U L C H R E S

Of the Ancient Inhabitants of *B R I T A I N.*

Opened under a careful Inſpection of the AUTHOR ;

THE BARROWS CONTAINING

URNS, SWORDS, SPEAR-HEADS, DAGGERS, KNIVES, BATTLE-AXES, SHIELDS, and
ARMILLÆ :—Decorations of Women; conſiſting of GEMS, PENSILE ORNAMENTS,
BRACELETS, BEADS, GOLD and SILVER BUCKLES, BROACHES ornamented with
Precious Stones; ſeveral MAGICAL IMPLEMENTS, CULINARY UTENSILS; ſome
very ſcarce and unpubliſhed COINS; and a Variety of other curious Relics depoſited
with the Dead.

TENDING PARTIALLY TO ILLUSTRATE

The HISTORY of *B R I T A I N* in the FIFTH CENTURY;

and to fix on a more unqueſtionable CRITERION for the STUDY of ANTIQUITY:

To which are added,

OBSERVATIONS on the *C E L T I C, B R I T I S H, R O M A N,* and *D A N I S H*

B A R R O W S, diſcovered in *B R I T A I N.*

ALSO

Some R E M A R K S ſubmitted to A N T I Q U A R I E S who would wiſh to
engage in this PURSUIT; by which, it is preſumed, they may be enabled to
aſcertain the truth of many Local Diſcoveries, which, for Want of previous Caution, are for ever loſt in Error or Uncertainty.

By the Rev. J A M E S   D O U G L A S, F. A. S.

Quis autem eſt, quem non moveat clariſſimis monumentis teſtata conſignataque Antiquitas ? CIC. de Div. lib. i,

Printed by J. NICHOLS, Printer to the SOCIETY of ANTIQUARIES of LONDON;
and Sold by G. NICOL, in the Strand, Bookſeller to HIS MAJESTY.

C O N D I T I O N S.

THE Work will be comprized in *Twelve* Numbers, with a Frontifpiece ; each Number, excepting the laft, will contain a *Sheet and an Half* of Letter-prefs ; and THREE COPPER PLATES, the Size of the Letter Prefs; at FIVE SHILLINGS each Number.

The laft Number will contain the Bulk of the Letter-prefs, at EIGHT SHILLINGS; which, with the former Numbers, will ftrictly fulfill the original Propofals of the Author to his Subfcribers.

P L A T E S.

The Engravings are finifhed in *Aqua Tinta*. This Style of Engraving is happily adapted to the Nature of Antique Relics, as it conveys a correct Idea of the Originals.

To avoid Repetitions, and to eftablifh the Nature of the Facts, fome Plates will contain felect Specimens of diftinct Sepulchres. Topographical Plans, Elevations, and Sections of *Tumuli*, will occafionally be added ; and a fyftematical Arrangement of the Relics, claffed under different Heads : by which means, Antiquaries will be enabled to compare their Difcoveries in this Country, with the Facts here eftablifhed ; and thus, by Analogy, to affign a fatisfactory Hiftory of them.

Some Copies on Royal Paper at Eight Shillings and Six Pence each Number; excepting the laft, at Eleven Shillings and Six Pence. The Plates will be coloured from the original Drawings.

N. B. The Author is happy to take this Opportunity of returning Thanks to many of his learned and liberal Correfpondents, who have communicated to him feveral curious Difcoveries, which relate to the Nature of his Work.

⁎ The Subfcribers are requefted to fend for their Numbers when publifhed : for which Purpofe, a Lift of them will be delivered to the Publifher.

BIBLIOTHECA
TOPOGRAPHICA
BRITANNICA.

N° XXV.

CONTAINING

Mr. PEGGE's Hiftorical Account of the TEXTUS ROFFENSIS; and of Mr. ELSTOB and his SISTER.

WITH

MEMOIRS of Mr. J O H N S O N, of CRANBROOKE.

[Price One Shilling and Six Pence.]

AMONG the various Labours of Literary Men, there have always been certain Fragments whose Size could not secure them a general Exemption from the Wreck of Time, which their intrinsic Merit entitled them to survive; but, having been gathered up by the Curious, or thrown into Miscellaneous Collections by Bookfellers, they have been recalled into Existence, and by uniting together have defended themselves from Oblivion. Original Pieces have been called in to their Aid, and formed a Phalanx that might withstand every Attack from the Critic to the Cheesemonger, and contributed to the Ornament as well as Value of Libraries.

With a similar view it is here intended to present the Publick with some valuable Articles of BRITISH TOPOGRAPHY, from printed Books and MSS. One Part of this Collection will consist of Re-publications of scarce and various Tracts; another of such MS. Papers as the Editors are already possessed of, or may receive from their Friends.

It is therefore proposed to publish a Number occasionally, not confined to the same Price or Quantity of Sheets, nor always adorned with Cuts; but paged in such a Manner, that the general Articles, or those belonging to the respective Counties, may form a separate Succession, if there should be enough published, to bind in suitable Classes; and each Tract will be completed in a single Number.

Into this Collection all Communications consistent with the Plan will be received with Thanks. And as no Correspondent will be denied the Privilege of controverting the Opinions of another, so none will be denied Admittance without a fair and impartial Reason.

A N

HISTORICAL ACCOUNT

OF THAT VENERABLE

MONUMENT OF ANTIQUITY

THE TEXTUS ROFFENSIS;

INCLUDING

MEMOIRS of the learned SAXONISTS
Mr. WILLIAM ELSTOB and his SISTER.

By SAMUEL PEGGE, M.A.

To which are added,

Biographical Anecdotes of Mr. JOHNSON, Vicar of Cranbrooke;
and EXTRACTS from the REGISTERS of that PARISH.

———————————

LONDON,
PRINTED BY AND FOR J. NICHOLS,
PRINTER TO THE SOCIETY OF ANTIQUARIES;
AND SOLD BY ALL THE BOOKSELLERS IN GREAT BRITAIN AND IRELAND.
MDCCLXXXIV.

An Hiſtorical Account of that venerable Monument of Antiquity the TEXTUS ROFF·ENSIS.

[Read at the SOCIETY of ANTIQUARIΞS, London, June 18, 1767.]

THOUGH the hiſtory of a ſingle book may ſeem at firſt ſight to be both uncommon and trivial, yet when one conſiders the antiquity, and the great importance of the monument, commonly known by the name of TEXTUS ROFFENSIS [1]; the practice of our editors who are ſo careful and induſtrious, as to give us an exact account of every ſingle edition of the author they publiſh; and, laſtly, what has been lately done by Mr. Webb in his pamphlet concerning the record of Domeſday, the following narrative of the compilement, the contents, the fate, hiſtory, tranſcripts, and publications of this auguſt and moſt valuable remain, may not be altogether inſignificant or diſpleaſing; eſpecially as ſome things will ariſe that are very remarkable and intereſting.

I ſuppoſe we may ſafely depend upon Mr. Wharton, who, by the favour of the then dean and chapter of Rocheſter, had the book in his cuſtody for ſome time, for the author of it. He obſerves, that Ernulf [2], biſhop of Rocheſter, ſat in that ſee from A. D. 1114, to A. D. 1124, in the reign of king Henry I. and compiled the book, which is written in a very elegant hand. The biſhop was very old at the time, not leſs than 80, or 82; for

---

[1] In Dugdale's Monaſticon it is called *Chronicon Clauſtri· Roffenſis*; and biſhop Godwin, in his Life of Ernulfus, ſpeaks of an Hiſtory of the Church of Rocheſter, left by Ernulfus, which I ſuppoſe is nothing but the Textus.
[2] He is otherwiſe written *Arnulf, Arnulph, Earnulph.*

B   he

he was 84 when he died, A. D. 1124 [1], and yet the collection. seems to have been made about 1120, according to Dr. Harris, in his Hiftory of Kent [2], or 1122 according to Mr. Hearne [3], and this latter I take to be the truer account; but as to Ernulf's being the author, an infcription in a very antient hand, in the front of the book, fuppofed by Mr. Wanley [4] to be no lefs than 400 years old, attefts the fame, *Textus de ecciefia Roffenfi per Ernulfum epifcopum* [5]; and it is obfervable, that there is nothing in the book of a later date than the time of the prelate here mentioned; for as to the 13 later archbifhops of Canterbury, and the 15 later bifhops of Rochefter, thefe have all been added by a more modern hand, as appears from the form of the letter, and the difference of the ink; one perfon added the 6 bifhops that followed Ernulf in fucceffion, and another, more recent, has added the 9 following them. To thefe may be added, fays Mr. Wharton, fome matters relative to the time of the bifhops, John and Afcelin, inferted after the leaf 203; but all the reft of the book is written in a hand coeval with bifhop Ernulph [6].

In refpect of the contents of this famous MS. the book confifts of two parts; the firft containing the laws and conftitutions of the Anglo-Saxon kings, in Latin and Saxon, tranfcribed from ancient copies; and the fecond giving us a regifter or chartulary of the church of Rochefter, from the autographs, with fome other matters relating to that cathedral, written in the times of Ernulf and his fucceffors; but thefe laft in a later hand. Bifhop

---

[1] Hearne in his *Præfatio*, Wharton, and Gul. Malmfb. p. 234.

[2] Pag. 32. Dr. Harris though varies from himfelf in this refpect, for in a note inferted by him in the original at Rochefter, on the reverfe of the fecond leaf, he conjectures the *text* might be compiled A. D. 1115, which is not fo credible.

[3] See his *Præfatio*, p. xxxv.

[4] Dr. Hickes's Thef. tom. III. p. 273.

[5] Text⁹ de ecce Roffn per Ernulfū Epm̄. Mr. Wanley, l. c.

[6] Mr. Wharton's Angl. Sacr. tom. I. p. xxx. feq.

Ernulf

Ernulf was a Norman [1]; and, in regard to the firſt part of the work, Mr. Hearne applauds him extremely for his great diligence and application, in making himſelf maſter of the Saxon language then growing into difuſe, and his commendable care in preſerving and perpetuating this momentous code. The above ſhort account of the contents is taken from Mr. Wanley, in whom may be ſeen, by thoſe who are deſirous of it, a very exact liſt of all the articles that compoſe the firſt part, with a general repreſentation ſuperadded of what is to be found in the ſecond. I ſhall content myſelf with giving the following abbreviation from Mr. Wharton; ‘ The laws of Ethelbert, Ælfred, ‘ Guthrun, Edward the Elder, Edmund, and Ethelred, in Saxon [2]. ‘ The exorciſm of the Ordeal, the laws of K. Cnut, the con- ‘ ſtitutions of William I. Extracts from the decrees of the Popes; ‘ the inſtitutions of K. Henry I. A. D. 1101, the ſucceſſion of ‘ the Popes and Emperors, of the Patriarchs of Jeruſalem, and ‘ the other four patriarchal ſees [3], the names of the archbiſhops ‘ and biſhops of England, from the time of Auguſtin the monk, ‘ diſtributed according to their ſees, in Latin. *Judicia civitatis* ‘ *London* [4], the genealogy of K. Edward the Confeſſor from ‘ Adam, the genealogies of all the kings of the Heptarchy from ‘ Adam [5], in Saxon. The privileges, charters, and ordinances ‘ of the church of Rocheſter, in Latin and Saxon.’ Biſhop

[1] Whoever deſires a further account of him may conſult Malmſbury, Mr. Hearne's Preface, p. xiv. and Appendix, N° I. II. III. IV. Wharton, A S. tom. I. p. 33. Biſhop Tanner's Biblioth. Gunton's Hiſtory of Peterborough, Cave's Hiſt. Lit. &c.

[2] Theſe are far from being all.

[3] Rather *the other three*, for there were but 5 in all, and thoſe of Rome and Jeruſalem are mentioned before. However, there are only two in the original, Alexandria and Antioch.

[4] Theſe are laws of K. Athelſtan; they are extant in Brompton inter X Script. col. 852. and in Wilkins; ſee alſo biſhop Nicolfon's Hiſt. Libr. p. 134.

[5] i. e. they are carried up to Woden, who in the former is carried up to Adam.

Nicolſon's

Nicolfon's account of this matter is ftill fhorter; but, as he mentions fome things neverthelefs, omitted by Wharton, I fhall infert it. ' It furnifhes us,' fays he, ' with the laws of four ' Kentifh kings (Ethelbert, Hlothere, Eadred [1], and Withred) ' omitted by Lambard '> together with the Saxon form of oaths ' of fealty, and wager of law; the old form of curfing by bell, ' book, and candle ; of Ordale, &c.' [3]

I enter now upon the fate, hiftory, tranfcripts, and imprefsions of this book, and its parts.

The firft perfon that made any ufe of our MS. fince the reftoration of learning, was that great reviver of Saxon literature, Lawrence Nowell archdeacon of Derby,. and dean of Lichfield. The famous Kentifh antiquary William Lambarde was a difciple of his in the Saxon tongue, of which he is reckoned the fecond reftorer [4]; and the dean having made certain tranfcripts from the Textus, imparted them to him, giving him withal other affiftance, and the ufe of his notes, towards the completing his Archæonomia [5]; he alfo gave him his Vocabularium Saxonicum [6], and died A. D. 1577 [7].

The abovementioned Mr. Lambarde publifhed his Archæonomia, A. D. 1568, in quarto, wherein are various tranfcripts from this MS. But thefe, as Dr. Hickes has clearly fhewn [8], were not copied by him from the original book, which he did not fee till the year 1573, when his name occurs in the margin of it, as

---

[1] *Eadrie,* as I fuppofe.
[2] Meaning in the Archæonomia.
[3] Nicolfon, Hift. Libr. p. 134.
[4] Wood, Hift. & Antiq. Lib. II. p. 216.
[5] Wood, Ath. I col. 186.
[6] Tanner, Bibl. p. 554.
[7] Bifhop Tanner fays, 1576; but fee Dr. Br. Willis's Cath. tom. I. p. 400. Mr. Wood is doubtful where he is buried, unlefs at Lichfield ; but Dr. Willis rather thinks it was at Wefton in Derbyfhire.
[8] Hickes, Epift. to Sir Barth. Shower in 2d tome of his Thef. p. 88.

it does in various places, but they were put into his hands by his preceptor the dean of Lichfield, and he publifhed them in this volume with his own Englifh tranflation.

Archbifhop Matthew Parker, and his Affiftant John Jofceline [1], appear next to have ufed our MS. for the Antiq. Brit. Ecclef. being printed A. 1572. *Lib. Roff.* is often cited in the margin.

Afterwards, A. D. 1576, Mr. Lambarde's firft edition of the Perambulation of Kent appeared; and there we have an extract printed from our MS. concerning the maintenance and fupport of Rochefter Bridge, in Saxon and Latin; the Saxon being alfo tranflated by him into modern Englifh [2]. It occurs alfo in Elftob's tranfcript to be mentioned below, and in Mr. Hearne's Appendix, p. 379. Archdeacon Denne has alfo tranfcribed the Latin part into his copy of Hearne's edition; and you have the Latin, Saxon, and Englifh, in Dr. Harris's Hiftory of Kent, p. 260. Mr. Lambarde cites the MS. again, p. 271. 317. and 343. of this firft edition. He has alfo there printed Brihtric's will, p. 357, from it, though he has not noted that, and has given us an Englifh tranflation of it. This curious monument has likewife appeared in Dr. Hickes's Thefaurus [3], both in Saxon and Latin; in Hearne's Textus Roffenfis, p. 110, you have the Saxon part, and in the preface, p. xxv. the Saxon with Mr. Lambarde's Englifh verfion; as likewife in Dr. Harris's Hiftory of Kent, p. 201.

A. D. 1623, Mr. Selden publifhed the Monkifh Hiftorian Eadmer; and in the Spicilegium, 197, has printed from this MS. the famous pleading at Pinnenden Heath, near Maidftone in Kent (now called Pickenden Heath), between archbifhop Lanfranc and Odo bifhop of Baieux, in Latin. This hath been many times reprinted fince, as by Sir William Dugdale in his

[1] Of whom, fee the Hiftory of Lambeth Palace.
[2] Perambul. p. 3 7, feq edit. 576. The Author's 2d Edition of this book was publifhed A. 154'. which is an enlarged, and the beft edition.
[3] Tom. II. in Epift. ad Barth. Shower, p. 51. See alfo tom. III. p. 241.

Origines

Origines Jurid. Mr. Wharton, in Anglia Sacra, tom. I. p. 334;
and laftly, by Dr. Harris, in his Hiftory of Kent, p. 50.

A. D. 1626, came out the firft part of Sir Henry Spelman's
Gloffary; and therein he inferted from this MS. the old form of
excommunication, or curfing by bell, book, and candle [1]. This·
appears alfo in Mr. Hearne's edition of the Textus, p. 55.

The book, after this, was in the utmoft danger of being
fecreted, and finally eftranged from the church, before half of
it had been either printed or tranfcribed; one Leonard, a doctor
of phyfick, had got it into his hands, and kept it two years;
but the dean, Walter Balcanqual, and the chapter, getting fcent
of the purloiner, beftirred themfelves, and at laft recovered
their MS. but not without a bill in chancery. Concerning this
tranfaction, the following note is now entered on the 2d leaf:
' Venerandum hoc antiquitatis monumentum per integrum bien-
' nium defideratum, furreptore tandem detecto, ac reftitutionem
' ftrenue negante, decreto fupremæ curiæ, quam cancellariam
' vocant, non exiguis hujus ecclefiæ fumptibus, recuperavit, red-
' dique priftinis dominis curavit Gualterus Balcanqual hujus
' ecclefiæ decanus anno poft natum incarnatum 1633.' This
memorandum, which is alfo copied by Mr. Wanley in Dr.
Hickes's Thef. tom. III. p. 273. is now pafted on the 2d folio,
and is probably the hand-writing of dean Balcanqual; it is alfo
anew tranfcribed with the following note, *This is written on the
wooden cover of this book, and thence copied by J. H. D. D. P. R.*
that is, John Harris, D. D. Prebendary of Rochefter. It appears
clearly from Hearne's Preface, p. vi. that Dr. Leonard was the
pilferer, for he had the book in his keeping, A. D. 1632.

---

[1] We read there, *In dentibus mordacibus, in labris, fi e molibus*; and fo Mr. Hearne
gives it alfo, p. 58. but certainly we ought to read, *in glebr e five moloribus.* It is
the fault of the original fcribe, for Dr. Denne has not corrected it in his book to
be mentioned below.

Whilft

Whilft the book was in Dr. Leonard's cuftody [1], Sir Edward Dering, the firft baronet of the family, a gentleman of great parts and learning, and of immenfe application, made a tranfcript with his own hand [2] of the whole of this book, that had not been already printed, or was not expected to be printed [3], which will be again mentioned below; and this he did with a public-fpirited defign of having it pafs the prefs. Sir Edward's hand is feen often in the margin of the original book; and from one place it appears, that he had recourfe to the book, A. D. 1644, the very year he died, and after the MS. had been recovered into the hands of the dean and chapter.

The firft volume of Sir Henry Spelman's Councils came out A. D. 1639; wherein he has inferted feveral tranfcripts from this MS. but it is a queftion whether he ever faw the original; for hear what Mr. Johnfon fays, ' By this infpection (of the MS. ' in relation to K. Wihtred's laws) I further learned, that Sir H. ' Spelman did moft probably never view the MS. itfelf. For there ' are fome miftakes fo very grofs, that none ufed to the reading ' of Saxon monuments could poffibly be guilty of them. The ' tranfcript from which he publifhed them feems to have been ' made by fome one that was a ftranger to the Saxonic letters [4].'

A D. 1640, John de Laet, a celebrated fcholar of Antwerp, tranflated the laws of Ethelbert, Hlothere and Eadrie, into Latin. He never faw the original, but had a tranfcript fent him by Sir Henry Spelman; and the original Saxon, with its verfion, may be feen in Dr. Hickes's Thefaurus [5].

---

[1] Hearne's Præfat. p. v.

[2] So I underftand Mr. Hearne.

[3] However, there were many things in this tranfcript that had been already publifhed, as appears from Hearne's edition of it.

[4] Johnfon's Pref. to Collection of Laws, &c. p. iii.

[5] Tom. II. in the Diffent. Epift. p. 88. feq.

Abraham

Abraham Whelock, Arabic Profeſſor and public Librarian at Cambridge, reprinted Mr. Lambarde's Archæonomia, A. 1644, in folio. He had the uſe of a copy of Mr. Lambarde's edition, amended in various places by the editor [1], and moreover made ſeveral additions to the work.

I ſuppoſe it might be about the time that Mr. Somner collated Sir Henry Spelman's firſt volume of Councils, in the articles taken from the *Textus*, with the original; for that he compared the printed book therewith, we learn from Mr. Johnſon [2] and biſhop Kennet's Life of Mr. Somner [3]. The volume ſo emended by him is now in the library of the church of Canterbury, and has been made uſe of by Dr. Wilkins.

During the time of the grand rebellion, biſhop Nicolſon ſuppoſes, this book was wiſely committed to the care of Sir Roger Twyſden, one of the learned editors of the X Scriptores; for in his cuſtody, he ſays, he found it often referred to by Sir William Dugdale, in a work which he compoſed during theſe troubles [4].

A. D. 1655, the firſt volume of Sir William Dugdale's Monaſticon came out, wherein Mr. Dodſworth and he have made good uſe of our MS.

A. D. 1664, the ſecond edition of Sir H. Spelman's Gloſſary was publiſhed; this contained the entire work, of which the former part had been corrected and enlarged by the author; and in the new, or ſecond part, are inſerted the forms of the ordeal trials, from our MS. which were alſo in Sir Edward Dering's tranſcript, and have ſince appeared both in Mr. Hearne's edition of that tranſcript, and in Mr. Browne's Faſciculus to be mentioned below. It ought to be here noted, that though this ſecond part of

[1] Hickes's Theſ. ibid. p 87.
[2] Johnſon's Pref. to Collection of Laws, &c. p. iii.
[3] Biſhop Kennet's Life of Mr. Somner, prefixed to Somner's Roman ports and forts, p. 89.
[4] He means Sir William's Orig. Jurid. See Nic. Hiſt. Libr. p. 134.

the

the Gloſſary did not appear till anno 1664, yet it was compiled at the time the firſt part was, as we are informed in the preface to the laſt and beſt edition, printed A. D. 1687.

A. D. 1666, Sir William Dugdale's *Origines Juridiciales* appeared, into which he copied from our MS. as mentioned above, the famous pleading at Pinnenden Heath, having made uſe of the MS. whilſt it was lodged in the hand of Sir Roger Twyſden.

Mr. Edward Browne, the worthy and learned rector of Sundrich in Kent, reprinted the *Faſciculus rerum expetendarum et fugiendarum*, anno 1689, in folio; and in the Appendix, or vol. II. p. 903, the *Officium Ordalii* is printed, as tranſcribed by him from the original MS. [1]

A. D. 1691, Mr. Wharton publiſhed his *Anglia Sacra* in two tomes, folio. The dean and chapter of Rocheſter intruſted him with their MS. to Lambeth, where Mr. Wharton then reſided as chaplain to archbiſhop Sancroft, and from thence he has tranſmitted into his firſt volume, p. 329, ſeq. whatever was ſuitable to his preſent deſign; and this was the firſt publication of this part of the MS.

In the ſame year, came out Dr. Gale's *Hiſt. Brit. Sax. Anglo-Daniæ Scriptores* XV. and p. 792. he has inſerted from our own MS. *Genealogias per partes in Britannia regum regnari*, which he ſtyles a rare monument, *formerly* tranſcribed by him from this very ancient book. Charles Bertram, of Copenhagen, has ſince reprinted theſe Genealogies from Dr. Gale's edition, in his *Brit. Gent. Hiſt. antiq. Scriptores Tres*, printed at Copenhagen, anno 1757 [2]. A part of theſe genealogies appear alſo in Hearne's edition of Sir Edward Dering's Tranſcript, p. 60, and the whole of them in that Tranſcript which was made by the Elſtobs. See below.

[1] See above, A. D. 1664.
[2] See the Preface prefixed there to Nennius.

C

Dr.

Dr. Hickes, in the fecond tome of his Thefaurus publifhed anno 1703, obliged the world with his famous *Diſſertatio Epiſto-laris ad Bartholomæum Showere*. The doctor was a perfon of great accuracy, and had recourfe to the original MS. not only for the pieces already mentioned, but likewife for feveral others, which he has given us in that excellent epiftle.

In 1705, Mr. Humphrey Wanley's large Catalogue of the northern books, both printed and MS. came out, making the third volume to Dr. Hickes's Thefaurus; and here, p. 273. f q. we have a lift of all the articles contained in our MS. as mentioned above, from his own ocular infpection.

A. D. 1712. the MS. was at London, and, I imagine, for the ufe of Dr. Harris, who was prebendary of Rochefter, and was then upon his Hiftory of Kent; for though this work did not appear till anno 1719, yet he had begun it, as he tells us, eight years before. Mr. Johnfon was defirous of collating Sir H. Spelman's edition of K. Wihtred's laws, with the original, but in a complaining ftrain tells us; 'That noble MS. was not at ' home in its proper repofitory, during the whole time that I was ' compofing this work [1].' The work came out A. D. 1720, being his Collection of Laws, &c. However, the MS. was now in London : for the rev. Mr. William Elftob, and his fifter Mrs. Elizabeth Elftob, employed one James Smith, a boy of ten years old, to make a tranfcript for them, in folio, of fuch parts of the MS. as had not been before publifhed [2]. This tranfcript the brother and fifter collated and examined together, and it was finifhed x kal. June, or 23 May, 1712, being very fairly written in three months time; and a very extraordinary performance it is for fuch a boy. Every page of it anfwers to the

---

[1] Mr. Johnfon's general preface to his Collection of Laws, &c.
[2] There are fome things neverthelefs in this tranfcript that had been printed before, as is noted above in feveral places.

pages

pages of the original book : and as what it contains more than the Dering tranfcript printed by Mr. Hearne will be noted hereafter ; I fhall only obferve here, that this tranfcript, on the death of Mr. Elftob, came into the hands of his uncle, Dr. Charles Elftob, prebendary of Canterbury ; and when he died, it was purchafed with the reft of Mr. William Elftob's Saxon tranfcripts by Mr. Jofeph Ames, fecretary to the Society of Antiquaries at London ; and I bought it at his auction, anno 1760.

But this Mr. William Elftob, and his learned fifter, being perfons not generally known, though both of them exceedingly eminent in their way, I fhall here infert a fhort account of them, from the papers of the fifter, who, about the year 1738, compiled a brief Narrative of her own and her brother's Life, and gave it in her own hand-writing to Mr. George Ballard, whom we fhall often have occafion to mention hereafter, and at whofe requeft fhe drew it up. Dr. Nathanael Wetherell, the worthy mafter of Univerfity College, was fo fortunate as to find the narrative among Mr. Ballard's MSS. in the Bodleian Library, and fent a tranfcript of it to the honourable and right reverend the Lord Bifhop of Carlifle, who was pleafed to communicate it to me, in order to enable me to give the following authentic, though contracted, account.

William Elftob was born January the firft, fixteen hundred and feventy-three, at Newcaftle upon Tyne. He was the fon of Ralph Elftob [1], merchant in that place, who was defcended from a very ancient family in the bifhoprick of Durham [2] ; as appears not only from their pedigree in the Heralds Office, but from feveral writings now in the family, one of which is a grant from William de la More, mafter of the Knights Templars, to Adam

---

[1] By Jane his wife ; Mrs. Elftob's own Life. S. P.
[2] See the notes on the Homily on St. Gregory's Day, p. 17. The name is alfo there accounted for, p. 16. S. P.

de

d Elneftob, in the year thirteen hundred and four, on condition
of their [1] paying twenty-four fhillings to their houfe at Shotton,
et faciendo duos conventus ad curiam fuam de Foxdene.

William had the earlieft part of his education at Newcaftle [2],
from thence at about eleven years of age he removed to Eaton,
where he continued five years. From Eaton, by the advice of
an uncle, who was his guardian [3], he was placed at Catherine
Hall in Cambridge, in a ftation below his birth and fortune.
This, and the air not agreeing with his conftitution, which was
confumptive, was the occafion of his removal to Queen's College,
Oxford, under the tuition of Dr. Maugh, where he was a commoner, and continued till he was elected fellow of Univerfity.
College, by the friendfhip of Dr. Charlett, mafter of that
college, Dr. Hudfon, &c. [4].

In feventeen hundred and two, he was by the dean and chapter
of Canterbury prefented to the united parifhes of St. Swithin and
St. Mary Bothaw, in London [5], where, after he had difcharged
the duty of a faithful and orthodox paftor, with great patience
and refignation, after a long and lingering illnefs, he exchanged
this life for a better, on Saturday, March the third, feventeen
hundred and fourteen-fifteen [6].

[1] I fhould fuppofe from hence that the grant ran to Adam de Elneftob and his
heirs. S. P.

[2] Where his father was fheriff, anno 1685. Bourne's Hiftory of Newcaftle,
p. 242. S. P.

[3] Charles Elftob, D. D. who was inftalled prebendary of Canterbury, anno 1685,
and there died, anno 1721. S. P.

[4] He removed to Univerfity College, 23 July, 1696, and was elected Fellow the
fame year, being then Bachelor of Arts. June 8, 1697, he took the degree of Mafter.
Catalogue of Graduates at Oxford, 1727, 8vo. S. P.

[5] By the procurement, no doubt, of his uncle the prebendary. St. Mary Bothaw,
after the fire of London, was united to St. Swithin; and as the dean and chapter
of Canterbury were patrons of the former, and the Salters Company of the latter,
the two incorporations have an alternate patronage, and the turn at this time was
in the dean and chapter; the livings together are reputed at 140 l. per annum. S. P.

[6] And was buried in the chancel of St. Swithin's Church, London, under the
communion table. S. P.

I   Mrs.

Mrs. Elſtob informed Mr. Ballard by letter, that her brother was chaplain to William Nicolſon, biſhop of Carliſle[1]. Nicolſon was conſecrated 14 June, 1702, and it was probably ſoon after that, that he was appointed chaplain, but I imagine he was only titularly, and not domeſtically ſo. However, in February 1713, upon a proſpect of a vacancy at Lincoln's Inn, on the promotion of Dr. Francis Gaſtrel to the ſee of Cheſter, he ſolicited lord chief juſtice Parker for his intereſt, that he might be appointed preacher there. He intimates in his letter[2] that he had not met with ſucceſs in the world anſwerable to his merits; and it is certain he had not, nor was he more fortunate in the preſent application. The character which the lady gives of her brother, and which the reader would probably like beſt to receive in her own words, runs thus:

' To his parents, while they lived, he was a moſt dutiful ſon,
' affectionate to his relations, a moſt ſincere friend, very chari-
' table to the poor, a kind maſter to his ſervants, and generous
' to all, which was his greateſt fault. He was of ſo ſweet a
' temper, that hardly any thing could make him ſhew his reſent-
' ment, but when any thing was ſaid or done to the prejudice of
' religion, or diſadvantage of his country.

' He had what might juſtly be called an univerſal genius, no
' arts or ſciences being deſpiſed by him; he had a particular
' genius for languages, and was a maſter of the Greek and
' Latin; of the latter he was eſteemed a good judge, and to
' write it with great purity; nor was he ignorant of the Oriental
' languages, as well as the Septentrional. He was a great lover

---

[1] Ballard's addition to Mrs. Elſtob's account of her brother.
[2] In the letter he wrote to the lord chief juſtice on the occaſion, which is now in the hands of my moſt obliging friend Thomas Aſtle, eſq; he obſerves, ' he had been ' a preacher in the city eleven years, and diligent in his profeſſion, as well as la- ' borious in other matters, without ſeeking or finding ſuch aſſiſtances as are both ' uſeful and neceſſary to ſuch as converſe with books.'

' of

' of the antiquities of other countries, but more efpecially thofe
' of our own, having been at the pains and expences of vifiting
' moft of the places in this nation that are remarkable either for
' natural or antient curiofities, architecture, paintings, fculp-
' ture, &c.

' What time he could fpare from the ftudy of divinity, was
' fpent chiefly in the Saxon learning, in which he was a great
' proficient.'

Mrs. Elftob, after this, proceeds to give a detail of her
brother's Works; but as fhe is very fhort upon this fubject, and
indeed has not mentioned them all, I fhall here exhibit an enlarged defcription of them, partly from my own obfervations,
and the information of Dr. Wetherell, but principally from Mr.
Ballard's MS. Preface to his own tranfcript of king Ælfred's
Anglo-Saxon verfion of Orofius, communicated to me by the
moft benevolent and public-fpirited bifhop of Carlifle.

Mr. Elftob was a perfon extremely well verfed in the Saxon
tongue [1], and being then refident in college, the very learned
Dr. Hickes folicited him to give a Latin tranflation of the Saxon
Homily of Lupus, and prevailed. The original, with the Latin
verfion, is inferted by the doctor in his Epiftolary Differtation
abovementioned, p. 99. feq. The Epiftle Dedicatory to Doctor
Hickes, thereunto prefixed, is dated Univerfity College, v Id.
or 9 Auguft, 1701; Mr. Elftob being then joint tutor in the
College with Dr. Clavering, late bifhop of Peterborough, and in
poffeffion of a tranfcript of the original Saxon made by Junius,
to which he hath not only added the Latin verfion beforementioned, but alfo many excellent notes. He ftyles it " the firft fruits
" of his labours in the Saxon tongue."

[1] In Literatura et Antiquitate Septentrionali praeclare eruditus Willielmus Eftob
Collegii Univerfitatis apud Oxonienfes focius digniffimus. Hickefius, in Differt.
Epift. p. 98.

                                                        Mr.

Mr. Elftob was author of ' An Effay on the great affinity and
' mutual agreement of the two profeffions of Divinity and Law,
' and on the joint intereft of Church and State, in vindication of
' the Clergy's concerning themfelves in Political Matters.' Lond.
92 pages 8vo. To this, his friend Dr. Hickes wrote a Preface
of two pages ', on which occafion I may be allowed to obferve, that he maintained an intimacy and correfpondence alfo
with the learned Mr. Humphrey Wanley ², was well known to
Dr. John Batteley, archdeacon of Canterbury, and to Sir Andrew
Fountaine, who, reciting the names of thofe that had furnifhed
him with Saxon coins for his tables, fpeaks of Mr. Elftob in the
following terms : ' Nec non reverendus magifter Elftob, qui pro
' eximia fua humanitate mihi communicavit Iconas nummorum,
' quos ipfe habet Saxonicorum et quidem rariffimorum; atque
' etiam copiam mihi fecit nummorum, quos poffidet reverendus
' C. (lege J.) *Batteley* archidiaconus Cantuarienfis ; fed dolendum
' eft, hofce omnes ad me haud prius delatos effe, quam exculptæ
' fuerint tabulæ ; nec interim licere eofdem commodè tabulis in-
' ferere ; cum fuerint omnes nummi regis Ethelredi, modo unum
' excipias qui erat Ethelftani, et quatuor qui erant Edmundi ³.'
To the above learned authors and antiquaries, I may add the
great lawyers, John Fortefcue Aland, Efq; and lord chief juftice
Parker ⁴. As to Mr. Strype, Mr. Elftob feems to have cultivated
an

' Thorefby, Ducat Leod. p. 129. and the MS. Life by Mrs. Eftob. Hence he
fays to lord chief juftice Parker in the-letter above-mentioned : ' Your lordfhip's
' kind opinion of the refpect I have for the Englifh laws will, I hope, make this
' addrefs at leaft not impertinent.' Indeed his fentiments on this head are moft
evident from his defign hereafter to be mentioned, of publifhing a new edition of
the Saxon Laws.
² He calls Mr. Wanley in the MS. Orofius mentioned below, *Amicus nofter per-*
bumanus doctiffimufque. This is extremely natural, as Wanley had been a ftudent in
Univerfity College. See Hickes Thef. III. p. 90.
³ Sir Andrew Fountaine, in Differt. epiftol. præmiff. tabulis numm. Sax. p. 166.
⁴ He begins the letter to lord chief juftice Parker thus : ' Your lordfhip was
' pleafed to do me a great deal of honour when I was permitted to wait upon you
' with

an early acquaintance with him.: He communicated to Mr. Elftob a copy of an inedited epiftle of Roger Afcham's [1], and Elftob in return tranflated for him the mutilated Difcourfe of Sir John Cheke on Superftition [2], printed with Mr. Elftob's letter to Mr. Strype, prefixed to Strype's Life of Cheke.

Before Mr. Elftob left Oxford, he printed a neat edition of the celebrated Roger Afcham's Epiftles ; to which he fubjoined the letters of John Sturmius, Hieron. Oforius, and others, to Afcham and other Englifh gentlemen, Oxford, 1703, 8vo. He dedicates it to Robert Heath, Efq; his familiar friend, to whom he had been affiftant in his ftudies [3].

Soon after he was fettled in his benefice at London, he pub-lifhed ' A Sermon upon the Thankfgiving for the Victory ob-' tained by her Majefty's forces, and thofe of her allies, over ' the French and Bavarians near Hochftet, under the conduct ' of his Grace the Duke of Marlborough. London, 1704.' The text was Pf. CIII. 10. Alfo,

' A Sermon on the Anniverfary Thankfgiving for her Majefty's ' happy Acceffion to the Throne. London, 1704.' The text 1 Tim. ii. 1, 2.

Sir John Cheke tranflated Plutarch's book on Superftition into Latin, and premifed a Difcourfe of his own upon that fubject in the Latin tongue. A caftrated copy of this Difcourfe, after it had lain long in obfcurity, was difcovered by Mr. Elftob in the Library of Univerfity College ; and he, as Mr. Strype tells us, not only courteoufly tranfcribed it for his ufe, but alfo volun-tarily took the pains of tranflating it into Englifh [4]. The verfion

---

' with Mr. Fortefcue ; the learned converfation, and kind treatment, and generous
' promifes of favour, by which you then made me your lordfhip's debtor, call for
' my largeft acknowledgments, &c.'
  [1] Elftob's edition of Afcham's Epiftles, p. 379.
  [2] See below.   [3] See the Dedication.
  [4] Advertifement prefixed to Strype's Life of Sir John Cheke.

is accordingly printed at the end of Strype's Life of Sir John Cheke, London, 1705, 8vo. There is a particular concerning this piece of Cheke's, which is well worth noting ; several pages, believed to contain the arguments of the author againſt the various fuperſtitions of the Church of Rome, are wanting in the original ; and Mr. Elſtob, who always entertained a thorough deteſtation of the Popiſh innovations in religion, ſuppoſes, with reaſon, that thoſe ſheets were ſurreptitiouſly taken out of the work by the famous Obadiah Walker, when he was maſter of Univerſity College, and had power over the MS. in the reign of king James II. The Papiſts, as he obſerves, being remarkable for their clean conveyances that way [1].

In 1709, his Latin verſion of the Saxon Homily on St. Gregory's Day, which he preſented to his learned ſiſter in a ſhort Latin epiſtle, was printed at the end of her fine edition of the Saxon original.

' Mr. Elſtob has publiſhed [2],' they are the words of Mr. Ballard, ' the larger devotions which the Saxons made uſe of at
' that time in their own language, which from probable con-
' jectures he fancies was the performance either of Ælfric arch-
' biſhop of Canterbury, or of Wolfſtan archbiſhop of York [3].
' And to ſhew the world that they did not contain any thing but
' what is pure and orthodox, he has obliged the public with a
' faithful tranſlation of them [4].'

We are informed by his accompliſhed ſiſter, that Mr. Elſtob had made a collection of materials towards a hiſtory of his native place ; that he had collected a vaſt number of proper

---

[1] Elſtob's Letter to Strype, in Strype's Life of Cheke, where by *Ob.* is meant *Obadiah Walker*, as is evident from p. 275.
[2] At the end of the firſt volume of Dr. Hickes's Letters which paſſed between him and a Popiſh prieſt. London, 1715, 8vo.
[3] See Mr. Elſtob's Letter to Dr. Hickes, prefixed to the Devotions.
[4] Mr. Ballard's MS. Preface to Oroſius, mentioned above.

D   names

names of men and women formerly ufed in northern countries ; and that he likewife wrote an Effay concerning the Latin tongue, with a fhort account of its hiftory and ufe, for the encouragement of fuch adult perfons to fet upon the learning of it, who have either neglected, or been frightened from receiving the benefit of that kind of education in their infancy ; to which is added, fome advice for the moft eafy and fpeedy attainment of it. What is become of the two collections above-mentioned, is uncertain, and not very material ; but as Mr. Elftob was a moft excellent Latinift, his obfervations on that language muft have been highly acceptable to the public, and one has reafon to regret the lofs of them.

But the moft confiderable of Mr. Elftob's defigns, was an edition of the Saxon Laws, of which Mr. Ballard writes thus : ' Mr. ' Elftob had fpent much time and pains in preparing for the ' prefs a very valuable edition of all the Saxon Laws, both in ' print and manufcripts, of which learned performance, there is ' a great character given both by Dr. Hickes in his dedication ' prefixed to his firft volume of Sermons, and by John Fortefcue ' Aland, efq; in his preface to the book of *abfolute and unlimited* [1] ' *Monarchy.* But as the propo als for that work are fallen into ' my hands; and as they will give a more perfect idea of the ' performance, I will here add a tranfcript of them.

' Propofals in order to a new edition of the Saxon Laws.

' I. That thefe Laws which Mr. Lambarde and Mr. Whelock ' publifhed, be publifhed again more correctly.

' II. That the Laws of king Etheberht, with thofe of Edric ' and Hlotharius, and whatever elfe of that kind is to be met ' with, either in the *Textus Roffenfis*, or in any other ancient MSS. ' judged proper to be inferted, be alfo added.

[1] Read *limited.*

' III. That

' III. That that of J. Brompton, and the moſt ancient Tranſ-
' lations, be conſidered and compared, and, if thought conve-
' nient, be likewiſe printed.

' IV. That an entire new Latin tranſlation be added of Mr.
' Somner's.

' V. That ſuch various readings, references, and annotations
' of learned men, viz. Spelman, Selden, Junius, D'Ewes, Laet,
' Hickes, &c. be adjoined, as ſhall ſerve to illuſtrate the work;
' with what other obſervations occur to the editor, untouched by
' theſe learned men.

' VI. A general preface, giving an account of the original
' and progreſs of the Engliſh Laws to the Norman Conqueſt,
' and thence to Magna Charta.

' VII. That there be particular prefaces, giving ſo far an
' account of the ſeveral kings, as concerned their making Laws. |

' VIII. An addition of proper gloſſaries and indexes '.'

The death of Mr. Elſtob prevented, as Mr. Ballard ſays, the
publication of this uſeful performance, concerning which, ſee
Mr. Thoreſby's *Ducatus Leod.* p. 129. and Dr. Wilkins's *Præf.
ad Leges Sax.* But this is the leſs to be lamented, as the learned
Dr. David Wilkins, prebendary of Canterbury, has ſince obliged
the world with a work of the ſame kind, as will be mentioned
hereafter; and yet I think Mr. Elſtob's deſign promiſed to be
more copious and large than the Doctor's, eſpecially in reſpect
of annotation and elucidation.

He was prevented alſo by death in another project, which was
to give us king Ælfred's paraphraſtical Saxon verſion of the
Latin Hiſtorian Oroſius. Notice of this intention we have from
Dr. Hickes, who, ſpeaking of Mr. Elſtob, ſays, ' Ælfredi R.
' qui collegium fundarit, verſionem Oroſii libri hiſtoriarum, qui

' Mr. Ballard's MS. Preface cited above.

' et

' et Ormefta ' dicitur, Deo fofpitante, literario orbi aliquando
' etiam daturus '.'   Our author had proceeded fo far in this work
as to make a fair copy of it with his own hand in the Bodleian
Library, anno 1698, when he was very young, from a tranfcript of Junius's taken from a MS. in the Cotton Library, Tiberius B. 1. Dr. Marfhal afterwards collated Junius's tranfcript
with the MS. in the Lauderdale Library, which had formerly
belonged to Dr. Dee; and Mr. Elftob's copy is collated with the
MS. in the Cotton Library, and there is alfo mention in the faid
copy of the Hatton MS.   But this work, though it had been fo
long and fo well prepared ³, was never put to the prefs, but
came into the hands of Mr. Jofeph Ames, at whofe auction I
bought it.   Here it may be pertinent to note, that Mr. George
Ballard, of Campden, in Gloucefterfhire, made another copy
from Junius's MS. A. D. 1751, in 4to. and prefixed a large
preface, fhewing the ufe and advantages of the Anglo-Saxon
literature.   This volume, which is very fairly written.   Mr.
Ballard bequeathed by will to Dr. Charles Lyttelton, Bifhop of
Carlifle, then Dean of Exeter, to whom the copy is addreffed,
and his lordfhip was fo condefcending as to favour me with
the perufal of it, and I have drawn confiderable helps from the

---

¹ This word is thought to be a corruption of *de miferia mundi*. See Profeffor *Haver-
camp's* Preface to his edition; but rather perhaps of *orbis miferia*, written abbreviately
in the old exemplar, whence the MSS. in being were taken. Or. *mifia*, and mifread
by the copyers *Ormefta*.

² Hickefii Differt. Epift. ad Barth. Shower; p. 98.

³ Mr. Elftob, fpeaking of the method he had ufed in tranflating the Saxon
Homily abovementioned, fays, he had done it, ' iifdem fere verbis repofitis quæ in
' Saxonica olim transfufa, vel ex Turonenfi Gregorio, vel tuo, vel ex Beda noftrate
' vel utroque Diacono, et Johanne et Paulo. *Eadem plane ratione, qua jam pridem
' OROSIUM a nobis elucubratum fuis.' Epift. ad fororem, præmiff. Lat. verf. Homiliæ
Saxonicæ, whence it fhould feem he had added a body of notes upon Orofius in a
volume feparate from the copy he had made of the Saxon verfion, for nothing of
this kind appears in the copy.   Perhaps they were intended to be tranfcribed into
the blank leaves at the end of the copy, which are numerous.

3   preface

preface relative to Mr. Elftob and his learned fifter, as appears above, and will be further evident in the fequel.   Both Dr. Marſhal and Mr. Ballard [1] feem to have had it in their intention to publiſh the Saxon verſion of Orofius [2]; but, however that was, the cafe is clear in regard to Mr. Elftob, concerning whom Mr. Ballard writes, ' It is very certain that the reverend and learned ' Mr. Elftob tranſcribed it with that view, and accordingly ' printed a fpecimen of it, which I have feen ; it bore the fol- ' lowing title.   HORMESTA PAULI OROSII *quam olim patrio fer-* ' *mone donavit* ÆLFREDUS MAGNUS, ANGLO SAXONUM *Rex* ' *doctiſſimus, ad exemplar* JUNIANUM *defcriptam edidit* WILLI- ' ELMUS ELSTOB, *A. M. et Coll. Univ. Socius. Oxoniæ, e Theatro* ' *Sheldoniano A. D.* MDCIC.'

Mr. Elftob was particularly ufeful to his fifter, in the great advances ſhe made in literature, as likewife in her publications. This ſhe teftifies, both in her preface to the edition of the Saxon Homily, and in the MS. Life of her brother. But concerning her, I muſt now fubjoin fome few Memoirs, and the rather, be- caufe, as ſhe was living when Mr. Ballard publiſhed his *Memoirs. of the learned Ladies of Great Britain*, anno 1752, there is no account of her in that work. Mr. Ballard otherwife was well acquainted with her, correfponded with her, and had the higheſt efteem for her on account of her uncommon learning and ac- complifhments, and doubtlefs would have done all proper honour to her memory on that occafion.

She was born in the pariſh of St. Nicholas, in Newcaftle upon Tyne, September 29, 1683, fo that ſhe was ten years younger than her brother. Her mother, who was a great admirer of learning, efpecially in her own fex, obferved the particular fond-

----

[1] See Mr. Ballard's Pref. p. 47.

[2] With which the learned world were favoured in 1773, by the Hon. Daines Bar- rington.   See Ballard's Preface, and alfo Wanley's Catalogue of Saxon MSS. p. 85, and Mrs. Elftob's Preface to Homily on St. Gregory's Day, p. 6.

nefs

nefs which her daughter had for books, and omitted nothing that might tend to her improvement fo long as fhe lived ; but alas ! fhe was fo unfortunate as to lofe her mother when fhe was about eight years of age, and had but juft gone through her Accidence and Grammar.   A ftop was now put to her progrefs for a time, through a vulgar miftaken notion of her guardian, *that one Tongue was enough for a woman.* However, the force of natural inclination ftill carried her to improve her mind in the beft manner fhe could, and as her propenfity was ftrong towards languages, fhe with much difficulty obtained leave to learn the French tongue.   But her fituation in this refpect was happily much altered when fhe went to live with her brother, who, being impreffed with more liberal fentiments concerning the education of women, very joyfully affifted and encouraged her in her ftudies for the whole time he lived.   Under his eye, fhe tranflated and publifhed an *Effay on Glory*, written in French by the celebrated Mademoifelle de Scudery.   But what characterizes Mrs. Elftob moft, fhe, as fhe intimates in her Dedication to the Saxon Homily, was the firft Englifh woman that had ever attempted that ancient and obfolete language, and I fuppofe is alfo the laft. But fhe was an excellent linguift in other refpects, being not only miftrefs of her own and the Latin tongue [1], but alfo of feven other languages.   And fhe owed all her fkill in the learned tongues, except what may be afcribed to her own diligence and application, to her brother.   She was withal a good antiquary and divine, as appears evidently from her works, which I muft now recite.

    She publifhed an Englifh-Saxon Homily on the Birth-day, that is, the Death-day, of St. Gregory, anciently ufed in the Englifh-Saxon church, giving an account of the converfion of the Englifh

[1] Epift. Fratris ad eam citat. fuprà.

from

from Paganifm to Chriftianity, tranflated into modern Englifh, with notes, &c. London, 1709. It is a pompous book, in large octavo, with a fine frontifpiece, headpieces, tailpieces, and blooming letters. She dedicates her work, which was printed by fubfcription, to queen Anne. Mr. Thorefby, in the Ducatus Leod. p. 129, gives notice of this intended publication [1], and there ftyles her the *juftly celebrated Saxon Nymph.* Her preface, which is indeed an excellent and learned performance, was particularly ferviceable to Mr. Ballard, who has made good ufe of it, in evincing the advantages of the Anglo-Saxon literature, and ingenuoufly acknowledges it [2].

A. D. 1715, fhe printed ' The Rudiments of Grammar for ' the Englifh Saxon tongue, firft given in Englifh [3]; with an ' Apology for the Study of Northern Antiquities,' 4to. It was intended to be prefented to the princefs Sophia; but as fhe died before it made its appearance, it is dedicated to the late queen Caroline, then princefs of Wales. The Apology is addreffed to the moft learned Dr. Hickes.

The Life of her brother and of herfelf, written at the requeft of Mr. Ballard, have been noticed above; wherefore I omit them here, only remarking, that it appears from a note of Mr. Ballard's, on the former piece, that fhe had drawn up the pedigree of her family, very curioufly, upon vellum; fhewing, that, by the maternal fide, the *Elftobs* were defcended from the old kings or princes of Wales; in the middle there was a column, on the top of which ftood king Brockmail, on one fide the paternal, and on the other maternal defcents. It was in the earl of Oxford's

---

[1] Her work was publifhed before Mr. Thorefby's, his Dedication bearing date 1714; but, I prefume, he had written this paffage, before her book, to which he was a fubfcriber, was publifhed.

[2] See his MS. Preface to Orofius.

[3] Dr. Hickes's labours on the fubject being in Latin.

library.

library. Moreover, she tells us in her own life, that she had
taken an exact copy of the *Textus Roffensis* upon vellum, ' now
' in the library of that great and generous encourager of learn-
' ing, the late right honourable the earl of Oxford.' My friend
Mr. Astle has now a MS. volume in his collection, chiefly in her
hand-writing, but partly in that of her brother, intituled, *Collectanea quædam Anglo-Saxonica, e Codd. MSS. hinc inde congesta.*
And in this original *Textus Roffensis* there is the Saxon alphabet
on the reverse of the second folio signed *E. E.* which I presume
must be her name.

It appears also from a word of her brother's, that she had
joined with him in preparing and adorning an edition of Gregory's
Pastoral [1] ; a work which, I imagine, was intended to include
both the original, and the Saxon version of it.   And she informs us herself, in her Life, that ' she had transcribed all the
' Hymns from an ancient MS. belonging to the church of
' Sarum.'

In the Preface to the Anglo-Saxon Grammar, p. 11. she speaks
of a work of a larger extent, in which she was engaged, and
which had *amply experienced Dr.* HICKES's *encouragement.*   This
was a Saxon Homilarium, or a collection of the English Saxon
Homilies of Ælfric, archbishop of Canterbury.   It was a noble
though unsuccesful enterprize, and indeed her most capital undertaking.   Mr. Ballard gives the following account of it.   ' Dr.
' Hickes, well knowing the great use which those Homilies had
' been of, and still might be, to the church of England, designed
' to publish, among other Saxon tracts, a volume of Saxon
' Homilies.   But then he tells us [2], that though for want of
' further encouragement he could not carry on any one of those

---

[1] Epist. Fratris ad eam suprà laudata.
[2] Hickes's Dedication to the first volume of his Sermons.

' designs,

' defigns, yet it was no fmall pleafure to him, to fee one of the
' moſt confiderable of them attempted, with fo much fuccefs,
' by Mrs. Elizabeth Elſtob, " who," adds he, " with incredible
" induſtry hath furniſhed a Saxon HOMILARIUM, or a Collection
" of the Engliſh-Saxon Homilies of Alfric, archbiſhop of. Can-
" terbury, which ſhe hath tranſlated, and adorned with learned
" and uſeful notes ', and for the printing of which ſhe hath
" publiſhed propofals; and I cannot but wiſh that for her own
" fake, as well as for the advancement of the Septentrional learn-
" ing, and for the honour of our Engliſh-Saxon anceſtors, the
" ſervice of the Church of England, the credit of our country,
" and the honour of her fex, that learned and moſt ſtudious
" gentlewoman may find fuch encouragement as ſhe and her
" great undertaking deſerve." This work was begun printing
' in a very pompous folio at the theatre in Oxon (and five or
' more of the Homilies were wrought off in a very beautiful
' manner), and was to have born the following title. *The Engliſh*
' *Saxon Homilies of ÆLFRIC, archbiſhop of* CANTERBURY, *who*
' *flouriſhed in the latter end of the tenth century, and the beginning*
' *of the eleventh. Being a Courſe of Sermons collected out of the*
' *Writings of the ancient* LATIN *Fathers, containing the Doctrines,*
' *&c. of the Church of* ENGLAND *before the* NORMAN *Conqueſt,*
' *and ſhewing its purity from many of thoſe Popiſh innovations and*
' *corruptions which were afterwards introduced into the Church.*
' *Now firſt printed and tranſlated into the language of the preſent*
' *times, by* ELIRABETH ELSTOB [2].'

This elogium of Mrs. Elſtob, and her undertaking, by fo great
a man, and a perfon fo well verſed in the ſubject as Dr. Hickes,
redounds infinitely to the lady's honour; the defign, however,
though fo profperouſly begun, and even fo far advanced, proved

---

[1] And, as ſhe mentions in her own Life, had added the various readings.
[2] Ballard's MS. Preface to Oroſius, penes Epiſc. Carleol.

E   abortive,

abortive, for the work was never publifhed, for want, I imagine
of encouragement; what is become of the MS. I have not at
prefent learned.

But this excellent woman, her profound learning, and maf-
culine abilities notwithftanding, was very unfortunate in life.
After the death of her brother, and the ill fuccefs of her ftudies,
fhe was obliged to depend upon her friends for fubfiftence, byt
did not meet with that generofity fhe might reafonably expect,
bifhop Smalridge being the only perfon from whom fhe received
any relief; After being fupported by his friendly hand for a
while, fhe at laft could not bear the thoughts of continuing a
burthen to one who was not very opulent himfelf; and being
fhocked with the cold refpect of fome, and the haughty fcorn
of others, fhe determined to retire to a place unknown, and to
try to get her bread by teaching children to read and work, and
fhe fettled for that purpofe at Evefham in Worcefterfhire.

At Evefham fhe led at firft but an uncomfortable and penurious
life; but growing acquainted afterwards with the gentry of the
town, her affairs mended, but ftill fhe fcarce had time to eat,
much lefs for ftudy [1]. She became known after this to Mr.
Ballard [2] whom I have fo often mentioned; and about the year
1733,

---

[1] Her own account of her fituation at Evefham goes thus: ' I had feveral other
' defigns, but was unhappily hindered by a neceffity of getting my bread, which,
' with much difficulty, labour, and ill health, I have endeavoured to do for many
' years, with very indifferent fuccefs. If it had not been that Almighty God was
' gracioufly pleafed to raife me up lately fome gracious and good friends, I could
' not have fubfifted; to whom I always was, and will, by the grace of God, be
' moft grateful.' MS. Life.

[2] Ballard's Memoirs, p. 249. This Mr. Ballard was a moft extraordinary perfon:
he was bred in low life, a woman's taylor, at Campden, in Gloucefterfhire, but
having a turn for letters, and in particular towards the Saxon learning, he became
acquainted, from a fimilarity of ftudy with Mrs. Elftob, after fhe was fettled at
Evefham. By the affiftance of the Rev. Mr. Talbot, vicar of Keinton, in Warwickfhire, and a recommendation to the Prefident of Magdalen College, Oxon, he
removed

1733, one Mrs. Capon, the wife of a clergyman of French ex-
traction, who kept a private boarding fchool at Stanton, in Glou-
ceftershire, and was herfelf a perfon of literature, enquired of
him after her, and being informed of the place of her abode,
made her a vifit. Mrs. Capon, not being in circumftances to
affift her herfelf, wrote a circular letter to her friends, in order
to promote a fubfcription in her behalf. This letter, which was
extremely well written, defcribing her merit, her extenfive learning, her printed works, her eafe and affluence till her brother's
death, her multiplied diftreffes afterwards, and the meeknefs and
patience with which fhe bore them, had the defired effect, and
an annuity of twenty guineas was raifed for her. This enabled
her to keep an affiftant, by which means fhe could again tafte
of that food of the mind, from which fhe had been fo long
obliged to faft. A lady, foon after, fhewed Mrs. Capon's letter
to queen Caroline, who, recollecting her name [1], and delighted
with the opportunity of taking fuch eminent merit into her
protection, faid, fhe would allow her twenty pounds *per annum*;
but, adds fhe, as fhe is fo proper to be miftrefs of a boarding
fchool for young ladies of a higher rank, I will, inftead of an
annual allowance, fend her one hundred pounds now, and repeat
the fame at the end of every five years. On the death of queen
Caroline, anno 1737, a moft unlucky event in appearance for
poor Mrs. Elftob, fhe was feafonably recommended to the prefent
dutchefs dowager of Portland; and her grace, to whofe father,
the earl of Oxford, fhe had been well known, was pleafed of
her goodnefs to appoint her governefs to her children; this was

removed to that Univerfity. The Prefident appointed him one of the eight clerks
of his college, which furnifhed him with chambers and commons; and thus being
a *Gremial*, he was afterwards elected, by the procurement of the Prefident, one of
the Beadles of the Univerfity. See more of him in the Anecdotes of Bowyer, pp.
10. 500.
[1] On account of the Dedication beforementioned.

in the year 1739; and from this period, the letters she wrote to
Mr. Ballard, which are now in the Bodleian Library, are obferved to have a more fprightly turn, and fhe feems to have been
exceedingly happy in her fituation.   To be fhort, fhe died in
an advanced age, in her Grace's fervice, May 30, 1756, and
was buried at St. Margaret's, Weftminfter.   I am obliged to my
much efteemed friend, Mr. Thomas Seward, refidentiary of
Lichfield, for the above very particular account of the latter part
of Mrs. Elftob's life; and as this gentleman knew both her and
Mrs. Capon perfonally, and was one of the fubfcribers above-
mentioned, the narrative may be depended upon [1].

I proceed now to fpeak of the remaining publications of the
Textus Roffenfis:

Dr. Harris's Hiftory of Kent was publifhed, anno 1719, as
was mentioned.   He has printed feveral extracts from the *Textus*,
as has been already noted, but always gives the Saxon in the
common type ; I think nothing appears here, but what had been
already publifhed, except that p. 32. he gives us the Arabick numeral characters from it, as they appear on the top of each leaf,
or each other page, which he fuppofes to be of the fame age
with the book itfelf, which might be finifhed, as he conjectures,
about anno 1120 [2].   This I think to be a point very doubtful,
fince the numerals that appear in the book, where they are often
applied, are always Roman, a ftrong prefumption, that thefe
characters on the top of the leaves have been added fince.   However, the Doctor has added thefe numeral characters to Mrs.
Elftob's alphabet on the reverfe of the fecond folio in the original,
in his own hand-writing, with this note : *This fhews thefe Arabic
characters to have been ufed here about the year* 1115, *when Ernulfus was confecrated* [3].

---

[1] Some farther particulars both of Mrs. Elftob and her brother may be feen in
the Anecdotes of Bowyer, pp. 11. 48. 110. 316. 498. 502. 528.
[2] See what has been faid above on this fubject.
[3] See what has been faid upon this.

6

I have

I have heard that a bad accident happened to our MS. at this time, which endangered the entire lofs of it.   Being carried by water from Rochefter to London, and back again, the book by fome means or other fell in its return into the water, but was happily recovered, and without much damage [1]; for when I faw it, about the year 1742, by the favour of the late archbifhop Herring, who was then bifhop of Bangor and dean of Rochefter, it was in a very good condition, being a fmall quarto on vellum, bound in red [2].   The book has been in perils both by land and water, and I prefume this laft efcape will prove a fufficient warning to the dean and chapter, not to fuffer it to go any more out of their cuftody.

Upon the return of the book to its abode at Rochefter, the learned Mr. John Johnfon [3], rector of Cranbrook, in Kent, had recourfe to it; thefe are his words: ' Since my tranflation of ' thofe Laws (of Wihfred king of Kent), was printed off, I was ' informed that this *Textus* was reftored to its place of refidence, ' and I had the favour of perufing it; but I found no variation ' of moment, but what Mr. Somner had taken notice of in his ' written notes; yet, by infpecting the original, I was able to ' diftinguifh between Mr. Somner's conjectural emendations, and ' thofe which he made from the text itfelf [4].'   Mr. Johnfon's Collection of Laws, &c. came out, anno 1720, in 2 vols. 8vo.

A. D. 1720, Mr. Hearne, the famous Oxford Antiquary, publifhed Sir Edward Dering's tranfcript in 8vo. by fubfcription, at 5s. for the fmall, and 10s. for the large paper.   The tranfcript had lain in the library at Surenden-Dering, from A. D. 1632,

[1] ' The MS. itfelf,' fays Mr. Johnfon, who faw it after this difafter, ' is in a very ' fair hand, and well preferved, fave where it is *tarnifhed by the falt-water* it took ' in its late travels.'   Pref. to Collection of Laws, &c. p. iv.

[2] It has been new bound fince Dr. Harris ufed it, probably after its recovery from the deep.

[3] Of whom a particular account will be annexed to this Differtation.

[4] Johnfon's Preface to his Collection of Laws, &c. p. iii.

and

and from thence the late John Anftis, Efq. Garter King at Arms, my very worthy friend, borrowed it for Mr. Hearne of the late Sir Edward Dering, a gentleman for whom I fhall always profefs the higheft efteem. The MS. does not now appear in the library, having never been returned by thefe gentlemen ; this, however, is not a thing of much confequence.; fince the firft Baronet always intended his MS. for publication, and as it is now printed, and we can perfectly rely upon this editor for the accuracy of his performance ¹. Mr. Hearne had both Sir Edward Dering's leave for the publication, and that of the late Bifhop Atterbury, which laft was procured for him by Mr. Anftis. The editor has not printed the whole of Sir Edward Dering's tranfcript, for he has omitted fome things, either already publifhed, or that might be publifhed by others, confining himfelf chiefly to fuch matters as might relate *ad rem diplomaticam* ². Thus, for example, he has omitted the *Judicia Civitatis Lundoniæ*, becaufe they are almoft all extant in Brompton, and were intended to be inferted by Dr. Wilkins in his edition of the *Legg. Anglo-Saxon*. It is a miftake, therefore, in Bifhop Tanner, to fay, that the *whole Textus Roffenfis* was printed by Mr. Hearne ³. There were fome additions made by Sir Edward in the margin of his tranfcript; concerning thefe, the editor tells us, left they fhould be thought an objection to the authority of the copy, ' Exfcrip- ' torem fuiffe virum eruditiffimum, ipfique nulla privati emo- ' lumenti fpe fuiffe decretum annotationes paullo prolixiores ac ' uberiores in regiftrum hoc fcribere ⁴.' But we do not find that Sir Edward made any great advances in the defign of a commentary; Mr. Hearne goes on, ' Adeo ut notulæ marginales

---

¹ The inftrument which the accurate Sir William Blackftone has given us, p. iv. of his Introduction to his fuperb edition of Magna Charta, &c. is copied from Hearne's edition.
² Hearne's Præf. p. vii.
³ Tanner's Biblioth. p. 265.
⁴ Hearne's Præf. p. xiii.

' (e quarum

‘ (e quarum fane numero funt clypei cum crucibus decuffatis),
‘ lineæque fub aliquibus vocibus in textu ductæ, funt exfcriptoris;
‘ quas omnes ideo adjungendas cenfuimus, ne eruditorum quif-
‘ quam fidem noftram fufpectam haberet, &c.’ As to thefe
fhields *cum crucibus decuffatis*, they are the arms of Sir Edward
Dering, which Mr. Hearne feems not to be aware of; for the
coat of this family is O. a faltire S. and the fhields are always
put againft thofe places where mention is made of the name of
Dering, or of perfons that might probably belong to his family;
and in order to infinuate the fame: fee pp. 184, 185. 192. 200.
218. 235.

I would further note, that the tranfcript, procured by the
Elftobs, contains fomething more than this of Sir Edward. There
you have the genealogies printed by Dr. Gale; the names of the
popes and emperors, the bifhops of Jerufalem, the bifhops of
Alexandria, the bifhops of Antioch, the archbifhops of Canterbury, the bifhops of Rochefter, printed by Mr. Wharton, and
the bifhops of the feveral fees in England. That chafm in
Hearne, p. 127, is fupplied, as likewife are all the other chafms;
a large Saxon inftrument beginning paða ʒe bɩʃcop ʒaðpɩne, &c.
occurs alfo in Elftob’s tranfcript; and the catalogue of books,
which is fo fhort in Hearne, p. 234, extends here to many
pages.

My late good friend the very worthy and learned Dr. John
Denne, archdeacon of Rochefter, has been at the pains of collating his copy of Mr. Hearne’s edition with the original MS.
throughout. He has noted where every leaf of the original
begins, the true readings of the MS. in feveral places, an omiffion
here and there, and has tranfcribed the marginal additions that
appear in the original by feveral later hands, as Mr. Lambard,
Sir Edward Dering, &c. The Doctor has moreover noted with
the utmoft care and diligence in what other MSS. the feveral
inftruments treafured up in this chartulary are alfo to be found,

as

as in the *Regiſtrum Temp. Roff.* and the Çotton Library, which makes his book of greatly more value than the naked edition of Mr. Hearne. The Doctor was afterwards pleaſed to give me leave to tranſcribe into my copy all the annotations here mentioned, together with the references as above, which I got done by a very careful hand, the Rev. Mr. Richard Huſband, minor canon of Rocheſter, my reſpectable friend.

A. D. 1721, Dr. Wilkins's edition of the *Anglo-Saxon* Laws came out in folio. He has compared the Laws of Ethelbert, Hlothere, and Eadric, with our MS. and ſupplied the defects and chaſms in De Laet's verſion ; what other uſe he has made of the original, may be ſeen in his Preface.

A. D, 1737. This gentleman publiſhed *Concilia Magnæ Britanniæ,* &c. in 4 volumes, folio; and in the firſt volume are many articles from Spelman's former edition, compared with the *Textus*, and chiefly, as I think, by Mr. Somner, as may be collected from the Doctor's Preface, p. iii. compared with Biſhop Kennet's Life of Somner, p. 89.

COROLLARY.

The *Textus Roffenſis* is doubtleſs in very ſafe and good hands ; but if, by any accident, an unexpected misfortune ſhould now happen to it, ſufficient care has been taken to perpetuate it, by the ſeveral publications above-mentioned; the tranſcripts [1] made by the Elſtobs, and the collation made by Dr. Denne, of which laſt there are at preſent two copies. However, whereas Dr. Wilkins ſays, ' Maxime venerandum hoc monumentum antiquitatis ' in ſummum reipublicæ literariæ commodum typis expreſſum ' extat [2];' this is not ſtrictly true, ſome parts of the MS. having not been yet *printed*; but they are nevertheleſs ſecured by the tranſcripts.   SAMUEL PEGGE.

---

[1] I expreſs it plurally, on account of Mrs. Elſtob's own tranſcript on vellum, mentioned above.

[2] Dr. Wilkins, Præf. ad Tanner's Biblioth. p. xliv.

Bio-

Biographical Anecdotes of Mr. J O H N S O N.

JOHN JOHNSON, the celebrated author of a fingular doctrine concerning the Euchariſt, was the ſon of Mr. Thomas Johnſon, vicar of Frindſbury, in Kent, by Mary his wife, daughter of the rev. Mr. Francis Drayton, rector of Little Chart, in the ſame county. He was born December 30, 1662 ; and his father dying when he was ſcarcely four years old, and his mother retiring to the country, he was put to the king's ſchool there, under Mr. Lovejoy, and at little more than 15 years old admitted of Magdalen College, Cambridge, 167⅞. He proceeded B. A. 168½ ; and was ſoon after nominated, by the dean and chapter of Canterbury, to one of archbiſhop Parker's ſcholarſhips in Corpus Chriſti or Bene't College in the ſame univerſity, where he took the degree of M. A. 1685. Soon after, he entered into deacon's orders, and became curate to Mr. Thomas Hondras, at Hardres near Canterbury, and was ordained prieſt by biſhop Sprat, in Henry VII's chapel, 1686. Archbiſhop Sancroft collated him to the vicarage of Boughton under Blean, and allowed him to hold by ſequeſtration the adjoining vicarage of Hernhill, both which churches he ſupplied himſelf every Sunday. In 1689 he married Margaret daughter of Thomas Jenkin, gent. of the Iſle of Thanet, and ſiſter to the rev. Dr. Robert Jenkin, Maſter of St. John's College, Cambridge, and to the rev. Mr. Henry Jenkin, rector of Tilney in Norfolk. About this time, one Sale, who had forged letters of orders, and taking advan-

F   tage

tage of the interval between the fufpenfion of archbifhop Sancroft, and confecration of archbifhop Tillotfon, to find out the
livings held by fequeftration only, had got the broad feal for
one for himfelf and another for his father; Mr. Jenkin took
inftitution to Hernhill, and the archbifhop, being then only fufpended *ab officio* and not *a beneficio*, prefented him to it, to
which he was inftituted, 1689, by Dr. Oxenden, vicar-general
to the archbifhop, but then to the dean and chapter of Canterbury, guardians of the fpiritualities during the fufpenfions; but
as the living had been held by fequeftration fo long as to be lapfed
to the crown, he found it neceffary to take out the broad feal,
1690. In 1697 archbifhop Tenifon prefented him to the vicarage of St. John's Margate, and of Appledore, on the edge of
Romney Marfh, but he chofe to hold the firft by fequeftration
only. Here, for the benefit of educating his two fons, he took
in two or three boarders, the fons of particular friends; but,
finding he could not attend his little fchool and his great curacy,
and his ftudies, in a manner fatisfactory to himfelf, he refigned
Margate, and fettled at Appledore, 1703. When his eldeft fon
went before the age of 15 to the Univerfity, 1705, he difmiffed
his boarders, fending his other fon to fchool to qualify him for
bufinefs. But the marfhy air brought on a fevere illnefs on
himfelf and family. He obtained the vicarage of Cranbrook
of the archb fhop, 1707, and there he continued to his death,
keeping a curate both there and at Appledore. In the years 1710
and 1713, he was chofen proctor in convocation for the diocefe
of Canterbury, which introduced him to the acquaintance of the
moft eminent clergy of the province. A little before he left
Appledore, he printed feveral Tracts, to which he declined putting his name till they came to a fecond edition. The firft was
a Paraphrafe, with notes, on the Pfalms, according to the tranflation in the Common Prayer Book, intituled, " Holy David and
                                                            " his

" his old Englifh Tranflation cleared, 1706 ;" he next printed " The
" Clergyman's Vade Mecum, 1708," which went through a 5th
edition, 1727 ; the fecond part, 1709, had a third edition. In 1710
he wrote and publifhed " Propitiatory Oblations in the holy Eu-
" charift truly ftated and defended from fcripture, and antiquity,
" and the common fervice of the Church of England." He was
quickly known to be the author of this book, which being attackt
by Dr. Wife of Canterbury, put the author quite out of favour
at Lambeth during the reft of archbifhop. Tenifon's time. But this
ferved but to induce him to handle the argument more at large,
and prove the Eucharift to be a true and proper facrifice from
the authority of fcripture and the teftimony of the antient
fathers and liturgies of the firft, fourth, or fifth centuries after
Chrift. This he did in " The unbloody facrifice and altar un-
" veiled and fupported. In which the nature of the Eucharift
" is explained according to the fentiments of the Chriftian
" church in the four firft centuries, proving that the Eucharift
" is a proper material facrifice ; that it is both euchariftic and
" propitiatory; that it is to be offered by proper officers; that the
" oblation is to be made on a proper altar ; that it is to be con-
" fumed by manducation : to which is added, a proof that what
" our Saviour fpeaks concerning eating his flefh, and drinking
" his blood, in the fixth chapter of St. John's Gofpel, is prin-
" cipally meant of the Eucharift. With a prefatory epiftle to
" the Lord Bifhop of Norwich, animadverting on Dr. Wife's book,
" which he calls the Chriftian Eucharift ftated, and fome
" Reflections on a ftitched book, intituled, an Anfwer to the
" Exceptions made againft the Lord Bifhop of Oxford's Charge.
" Part I." To this he fet his name. The fecond part was publifhed 1717, with anfwers to a frefh reply of Dr. Wife ;
another by Mr. Lewis, his fucceffor at Margate ; and a third by
Mr. Pfatty, a Lutheran Divine, tutor to the prince of Wertemberg,

who

who took upon him to be moderator in this controverfy. His next publication was " A Collection of Ecclefiaftical Laws, Canons," &c. in two volumes, 8vo. In 1724, the firft volume of his " Unbloody Sacrifice" was re-printed, with a Reply to Dr. Rymer's " General Reprefentation of Revealed Religion, 1723," and " The Doctrine of the Euchariſt ſtated, 1720;" as alſo to the 12th of Dr. Clarke's XVII Sermons. His " Primitive Communicant," " Explanation of Daniel's LXX Weeks, a Sermon at Canterbury " ſchool-feaſt, with a Preface, ſhewing, that no letters were " before Moſes," were publiſhed after his deceaſe, with his Life, by his friend Mr. Thomas Brett, 1748, as were alſo ſome other poſthumous pieces.

Mr. Johnſon had two ſons and three daughters. His eldeſt daughter died in her infancy : his youngeſt ſon ſoon after he had bound him apprentice to Mr. Knaplock, his bookſeller ; and a few years after, his youngeſt daughter died in the prime of life. His eldeſt ſon was fellow of St. John's College, Cambridge, where he took the degree of Batchelor of Divinity, and was preſented by the Univerſity to the living of Standiſh, in the county of Lancaſter, worth 500 *l. per annum*; but before he had enjoyed it one whole year, he had the misfortune to break his leg, which threw him into a fever, of which he died in a few days, about Chriſtmas, 1723. Mr. Johnſon could not overcome this ſevere ſtroke, though he intermitted not his ſtudies, nor the duties of his office : yet from this time his ſtrength viſibly decayed, and he was afflicted with a ſhortneſs of breath, which increaſed on him till he died, about two years after his ſon, Dec. 15, 1725, having juſt reached the 63d year of his age. He was buried in the church-yard of Cranbrook, cloſe to the veſtry-wall. Over his grave is erected a handſome altar monument of grey marble, with this inſcription : *John Johnſon, Vicar* ; but on the other side fide of the wall within the veftry is the following infcription on a mural monument of white marble.

Extra hunc parietem
fub tumulo lapideo requiefcit
JOANNES JOHNSON, A. M.
per annos octodecim hujus ecclefiæ paftor,
morum caftitate, ingenii acumine,
interioribus & reconditis literis ornatiffimus,
filius reverendi Thomæ Johnfon
de Frindfbury in diocæfi Roffenf. vicariæ,
et Mariæ filiæ reverendi Francifci Drayton
Chart Parvæ hujus diocæfeos rectoris.
Uxorem habuit Margaretam,
filiam Thomæ Jenkin,
in infula de Thanet generofi,
de qua quinque fufcepit liberos,
quorum quatuor fuperftitit,
viz. Margaretæ incunabulis mortuæ,
Thomæ Londini fepulto,
Alteri Margaretæ finiftra patris dormienti
Joanni S. T. B. de Standifh
in comitatu Lancaftrienfi rectori,
Paternæ virtutis, ingenii & eruditionis
exemplari,
cujus poft mortem cum fere per biennium
ægre fufpiria duxiffet
animam fpei beatæ immortalitatis plenam
Deo reftituit 15° die Decembris,
A. D. 1725, ætatis 63.
Ecclefiæ Anglicanæ pugil, fchifmatis debellator
Occidit — fi plura quæris fcripta mortui verfato.
Pientiffima filia Maria Johnfon pofuit.

The following is the character drawn of him by his friend and biographer Dr. Brett.

" As no prieft was more careful and diligent to inftruct thofe committed to his care in the knowledge of their duty by his fermons, fo was he no lefs careful to inftruct them by his
example

example in a regular Chriſtian life. None was better beloved by his pariſhioners, and all who had the happineſs of his acquaintance; and when we conſider his learning, and his critical ſkill in the languages proper, not to ſay neceſſary, for a divine, his great and extenſive knowledge of the canons and conſtitutions of the Chriſtian Church, and the cuſtoms and diſcipline in the ſeveral ages, from the firſt planting of the goſpel downward to our own times, and his capacity to teach them, and alſo his exemplary life and converſation, we may as juſtly ſay of him what was ſaid of the learned Mr. Bingham, in Miſt's Journal, January 4, 172¾. *Qui patriarchatum in ecclefia meruit parochus obiit.* His converſation was eaſy and chearful, and very improving. If any one departed out of his company without learning ſomething from him, it was his own fault. He was very diligent in the performing of all parochial duties: he read prayers every morning in his pariſh church; when he was at home, he preached twice every Sunday; frequently inſtructed children in the Catechiſm; adminiſtered the Holy Euchariſt every month; was diligent in viſiting the ſick, or any other that needed his ghoſtly advice or prayers; and, in a word, uſed that faithful diligence which he promiſed when he was admitted into the order of prieſthood. He was a dutiful ſon, a loving huſband, a tender and careful father, an obliging kind friend, and conſcientiouſly careful to diſcharge his duty in every relation."

The following anecdote the late Mr. Jones of Welwyn had from ſome of his pariſhioners; which is confirmed by the large baptiſtery ſtill ſubſiſting in Cranbrook church. "Mr. Johnſon, when he came to reſide at Cranbrook, finding that many of the inhabitants were Anabaptiſts, or rather *Baptiſts*, as they affected to ſtyle themſelves; uſed many arguments to perſuade them to con-

3   " form

form to the church. They made a great objection to the practice of *sprinkling* in baptifm; and faid, that the church in a manner excluded them from her communion in refufing to baptize by immerfion. Mr. Johnfon readily allowed the propriety of that practice, according to the original inftitution; and, to remove this difficulty, caufed a large baptiftery to be erected in the church. Upon this, moft of the Anabaptifts in his parifh were *dipped,* &c. and were received into the church, to which they owned they had no farther objection. And Mr. Johnfon, on his part, affured them he had no objection to the practice of *dipping*; and from that time they lived in perfect harmony together. R. W."

He was fenfible that the Church of England allowed Immerfion, at the fame time that it allowed alfo Afperfion; and he well knew that he was at liberty to admit adult perfons into the fellowfhip of this church by the ceremony of dipping, &c.

The women had a grave matron (called a Deaconefs), to attend their baptifm. And all was conducted with great decency.

They had afked him where they fhould find room? He readily anfwered, There is a large chancel at liberty.

Thofe that came over to the eftablifhed communion, upon his fhewing them this civility and condefcenfion, affembled by his direction in the chancel to attend divine fervice; for feveral of them were unfupplied with feats in the body of the church.

This anecdote entirely removes the uncharitable fuppofition of Mr. Johnfon's Biographer Dr. Brett, who, after faying that he was much loved and highly efteemed by all his parifhioners at Cranbrook who were friends to the Church of England as by law eftablifhed, adds, " But as there were many diffenters of all ' denominations in that place, and fome who, though they fre-
" quented the church, yet feemed to like Diffenters better than
" Church–

" Churchmen, I cannot say how they loved or esteemed him.
" However, his life and conversation was such that even they
" could find nothing in him to displease them, except his known
" affection to the Church of England.   Some of these favourers
" of the Dissenters endeavoured to make him uneasy, and to spirit
" up a party in the church against him ; but failed in their de-
" signs : his friends were too many for them."

The successor in that vicarage was not of so obliging a temper
as Mr. Johnson ; and the Baptistery is suffered to run to ruin, or
is considerably impaired.

A N E C-

ANECDOTES *inferted in the Regifter of* CRANBROOK, *by the Reverend* JOHN JOHNSON, *Vicar.*

"MEMORANDUM.

HIS grace William archbifhop of Canterbury did, at the requeft of John Johnfon, Vicar of Cranbrook, adminifter confirmation at this place to above thirteen hundred perfons; of which one third at leaft were of this parifh, on Sunday, June 24th, being St. John Baptift's Feaft, anno Domini 1716. There had been no confirmation here in 28 years before, that is, fince the fatal year 1688, when the moft reverend archbifhop Sancroft, of pious memory, being difcharged from his cuftody in the Tower, upon a trial in the King's Bench, fent bifhop Levinz (of Man Inf.) to perform the office of Confirmation throughout the diocefe, as he did bifhop Lloyd, of Norwich, fome years before. The fame archbifhop, of his own free motion, again adminiftered confirmation here on Sunday, June 21, 1724, to about thirteen hundred perfons, as his chaplain who attended him in the office told me; yet one of his grace's liverymen, who faid he numbered them, affirmed to me, that they were but twelve hundred."

G.   Some

Some account of the Vicars of Cranbrook :

1503. The firſt vicar of whom I can get any information, was Richard Wilſon ; I have nothing of him but his name, and that from ſome pannels of glaſs in the vicarage-houſe in yellow paint, bearing date 1503.

1534. Sir Hugh ap Rice returned a certificate into the Exchequer, giving an account of the value of this vicarage ; upon which certificate this vicarage was taxed according to the rate at which it now ſtands in the king's books.

The copy of the certificate here follows :

" Cranbrook, the certificate of Sir Hugh ap Rice, vicar, theſe.

Firſt, a houſe with III roods of meadow, XIIIs. IIIId.

Item, III manſions worth yearly XIIIs. IIIId.

Item, one other manſion worth yearly xxd.

Item, Privy tithes, certain mills, with other caſual profits, worth yearly xIxl.

Item, IIII offering days VIIl. VIs.

Item, other caſual profits LIIIs. IIIId.

Sum , xxxl. VIIs. IIIId. whereof to be deducted for the pariſh prieſt x l.

Item, for the proxies to the archdeacon, VIIs.

Item, in quyt rents paid yearly XIIIId.

Sum deducted x l. VIIIs. (4d. ſhould have been added) and ſo remained de claro xIxl. xIxs. VId."

This was drawn, A. D. 1534, and ſo it ſtandeth to this day.

This I took from a tranſcript of Mr. John Eaſon's, who is an officer of the firſt fruits and tenths.

1556. The pariſh is charged with a debt of 3l. due to Mr. Dr. Hues for books. I ſuppoſe this doctor being vicar, had procured a new ſet of books for the Popiſh ſervice. That this debt was ever paid does not appear.

1558.

1558. Richard Fletcher was made vicar here, the firft Proteftant predeceffor that I meet with. He continued vicar 27 years, and lies buried on the north fide of the chuich towards the upper end. He let a leafe of the tenements belonging to this vicarage for 99 years to come, viz. from 1562 to 1661, and had it confirmed by the archbifhop, and the dean and chapter of Canterbury. During all this time the vicar received but 13s. 4d. per annum for them. His fon Richard was dean of Peterburgh, when the Queen of Scots was executed at Fotheringay Caftle, and fo difplayed his loyalty on that occafion, that he foon became bifhop of Briftol; but not till his father was firft dead, viz. 1589; therefore the monument in our chancel fays not true, when it tells us, the father faw this fon bifhop of Briftol. He was afterterwards advanced to the fee of Worcefter, and from thence to London. There he fell under the queen's difpleafure, and was fufpended; that he was reftored before his death is not certain. Both he and his brother Gibs, the famous embaffador to the Czar of Mufcovy, made Cranbrook vicarage their nurfery. Here their wives lay in, as appears by the regifter. And even after the father's death, fome of his fon Gibs's children are buried here. Venner, the famous Puritan, preached here, whether as curate, or (as I rather fuppofe) lecturer, I know not. This was during the decline of Father Fletcher's life, and the difgrace of archbifhop Grindal. One would wonder, that Richard, afterwards bifhop, did not ufe his intereft with his father (if he brought him hither) or with the Vicar-general, to remove a man of fuch forry notions and fantaftic principles. Mr. Fletcher died 1585.

1585, Robert Roads, formerly prefident of St. John's College, Cambridge (where he was written) and continued here till 1589. His wife and he were buried in the fame year.

1589,

1589, William Eddy fucceeded, and continued here in low circumftances till he died, 1616. I find no memorial of him, but that he was paid by the church-wardens for tranfcribing the regifter fairly from 1558 into the large old parchment book; and that he had the clerk's wages given him for calling the Pfalm, &c. Mr. Fletcher and he continued Vicars 58 years; and I am perfuaded, that, by thefe two long incumbances, the modus for Vicar's tithe was eftablifhed.

1616, Robert Abbot fucceeded. What relation he bore to the archbifhop of that name, I find not. But he was a man of eminent zeal and piety; and few, I am perfuaded, out-did him in learning and all commendable qualities. He defended the Church againft the Brownifts. I do not know that any could do it better. I have read his book, and cannot but wonder to find fuch a man here at that time of day. His Sermons, dedicated to the four principal families of the parifh; viz. Roberts, Baker's, Henly's, and Courthop's, fhew clearly, that he was a much greater man in polemical than in pulpit divinity. His "Young Man's Warning-piece" hath been more read than either of the other. It was publifhed 1635. The reafon of it was, one Rogers, a practifing Apothecary, who, from a very pious youth, became a very de-bauched man, and could not be prevailed upon to receive the facrament at Eafter, though he was to be excommunicated for that omiffion; and died foon after in great horrours and terrours. Abbot weathered out here in the worft of times till 1648 [1]. Then he was by the Rump Committee for Sequeftrations fent to another benefice, which he had long enjoyed together with this. At Smarden there was an Abbot; but, on comparing circumftances, and confidering Smarden books and ours, I remember fome years fince, I concluded that he of Smarden could not be the fame with this of Cranbrook.

[1] 1642-3, Walker's Sufferings of the Clergy, 183.

.6   1648.

1648. John Williamſon, a ſtrict Preſbyterian, was intruded here. The pariſhioners engaged to make the vicarage 100l. *per annum* to him. To this end the churchwardens gathered the tithes and offerings, and the pariſhioners made up the deficiencies; but this could not laſt long.

1652. William Goodrick ſucceeded him. He made himſelf remarkable by walking in the Market-place with his tithing-book in his hand, and his inkhorn hanging on his buttons, every Saturday, and dunning his pariſhioners as he met them.

1662. John Cowper came in upon the Bartholomew Act, and ſo diſmiſſed Goodrick, who yet for ſome time kept a conventicle here. Cowper was a man of great wit and fine parts, but no œconomiſt: he left 4 or 5 children to ſo many families in this country of the beſt quality; who all accepted their ſeveral legacies.

1668. Mr. Charles Buck ſucceeded; a gentleman of good fortune, and who lived here with great hoſpitality; and was remarkable for his long ſermons, till about 1694 it was thought neceſſary that he ſhould retire to London, for the cure of his head. From this time forward, Mr. Crowther the ſchool-maſter ſerved this cure till Mr. Buck died; viz. February 1706; though Mr. Buck returned to the vicarage two or three years before his death."

––––––––––

Mr. Johnſon has noticed he could never find out what relation his predeceſſor Robert Abbot bore to the archbiſhop of that name. His grace had an elder brother John, who was biſhop of Saliſbury: is it likely that Robert was his ſon [1]? Cranbrooke was a vicarage of ſmall value to be ſo long held by an archbiſhop's nephew; it is plain, however, that he alſo long

[1] Not from Wood, who only ſays that he left one ſon or more. Ath. Ox. I. 431. The writer of his life in the Biographia Britannica follows Wood.

enjoyed

enjoyed another benefice with this living. It is mentioned in the Biographical Dictionary that bishop Abbot of Salisbury, who died the latter end of the year 1617, left one son and one daughter; and that he offended the archbishop by a second marriage. Robert was in 1648 removed from Cranbrooke by the committee for sequestrations; the reason assigned for it was, that he had taken another living, which by his own confession was inconsistent. So says Walker [1], adding, the reader will enquire further whether that be true or not. Having been, as Wood says, a frequent writer, we shall subjoin his account of him.

" Robert Abbot was of Cambridge, incorporated of Oxford, July 14, 1607. He was afterwards vicar of Cranbrooke, in Kent, a sider with the Presbyterians in the rebellion which began in 1642, was minister of Southwicke in Hampshire, and at length of St. Austin's church in Watling-street near St. Paul's cathedral in London, where, after he had been tumbled and tossed to and fro, he enjoyed himself quietly for some years in his old age. He hath written and published several things, among which are,

1. Four Sermons, &c. London, 1639, 8vo. dedicated to Walter Curle, bishop of Winchester, to whom he had been servant, and who then exhibited to his two sons, one at Oxford, and the other at Cambridge.

2. Tryal of the Church Forsakers, &c. on Heb. x. 23. London, 1639.

3. Milk for Babes, or a Mother's Catechism for her Children. London, 1646.

4. Three Sermons, printed in the former book.

5. A Christian Family builded by God, or Directions for Governors of Families. London, 1635, at which time the author was two years above the great climacterical year.

[1] Sufferings of the Clergy, p. 183.

Other

Other things he hath alſo publiſhed (among which is, " Be Thankful, London, and her Siſters," a Sermon on Pſalm xxxi. 21. London, 1626), which for brevity ſake I now omit '."

It appears from Le Neve's Faſti that a John Abbot was collated in 1712 to the 6th prebendal ſtall in Canterbury cathedral, and that he was buried Sept. 1, 1615.

Strype, in his Life of Archbiſhop Cranmer, p. 441. has obſerved, that Cranbrooke was one of the large towns in the dioceſe of Canterbury in which that prelate had noticed a learned man ought to be placed with a ſufficient ſtipend. At p. 274 of Strype's Life of Archbiſhop Parker is a table of the rate of arms pro- poſed to be found by the clergy of the dioceſe of Canterbury; and in this table Cranbrooke is one of the places mentioned.

' Athen. Oxon. I. 431. Faſti I. 177.

END OF NUMBER XXV.

Lightning Source UK Ltd.
Milton Keynes UK
UKHW021004031218
333381UK00015B/2270/P

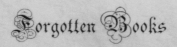